GREAT BOOKS OF THE W

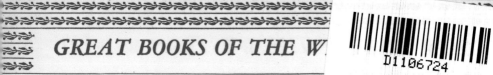

28. GILBERT
    GALILEO
    HARVEY
29. CERVANTES
30. FRANCIS BACON
31. DESCARTES
    SPINOZA
32. MILTON
33. PASCAL
34. NEWTON
    HUYGENS
35. LOCKE
    BERKELEY
    HUME
36. SWIFT
    STERNE
37. FIELDING
38. MONTESQUIEU
    ROUSSEAU
39. ADAM SMITH
40. GIBBON I
41. GIBBON II
42. KANT
43. AMERICAN STATE PAPERS
    THE FEDERALIST
    J. S. MILL
44. BOSWELL
45. LAVOISIER
    FOURIER
    FARADAY
46. HEGEL
47. GOETHE
48. MELVILLE
49. DARWIN
50. MARX
    ENGELS
51. TOLSTOY
52. DOSTOEVSKY
53. WILLIAM JAMES
54. FREUD

GREAT BOOKS OF THE WESTERN WORLD

ROBERT MAYNARD HUTCHINS, *EDITOR IN CHIEF*

5.

AESCHYLUS

SOPHOCLES

EURIPIDES

ARISTOPHANES

· AESCHYLUS ·

· SOPHOCLES · EURIPIDES ·

· ARISTOPHANES ·

WILLIAM BENTON, *Publisher*

ENCYCLOPÆDIA BRITANNICA, INC.

CHICAGO · LONDON · TORONTO

The Plays of Aeschylus are reprinted by arrangement
with the translator, G. M. Cookson

The Plays of Sophocles, translated by Sir Richard C. Jebb, are reprinted
by arrangement with CAMBRIDGE UNIVERSITY PRESS

The Plays of Euripides, translated by Edward P. Coleridge,
and *The Plays of Aristophanes*, translated by Benjamin Bickley Rogers,
are reprinted by arrangement with G. BELL & SONS, LTD., London

GENERAL CONTENTS

THE PLAYS OF
AESCHYLUS

BIOGRAPHICAL NOTE

AESCHYLUS, *c.* 525–456 B.C.

AESCHYLUS the poet was born at Eleusis around the year 525 B.C. His father, Euphorion, belonged to the "Eupatridae," or old nobility, of Athens. Whether Aeschylus was actually initiated into the Eleusinian Mysteries is not known. The accusation that he divulged the secrets of Demeter has been interpreted both as supporting and as refuting the view that he was an initiate.

Aeschylus fought against the Persian invader at Marathon in 490, and he may also have been with the Athenians seven years later at Salamis, and even at Artemisium and Plataea. Some scholars have found in the poet's knowledge of Thracian geography and customs an indication that he took part in one or more of the northern expeditions in the years following the Persian War.

The first of Aeschylus' plays was exhibited in 499, only thirty years after the establishment by Peisistratus of the annual contest in tragedy at the festival of the City Dionysia. Thespis, who won the prize at that competition, was called by the ancients the earliest tragic poet. But Aeschylus himself would seem to be the true founder of tragedy, since, according to Aristotle, he first introduced a second actor, diminished the importance of the chorus, and assigned the leading part to the dialogue.

Aeschylus' first recorded victory was in 484, when he had been competing for fifteen years. Between that date and the performance of his last work, the Oresteian trilogy and the satyr play *Proteus*, in 458, he won the prize at least twelve times. He wrote more than ninety plays, of which seven survive. The oldest of these, the *Suppliant Maidens*, cannot be much later than 490. The *Persians*, which is the only extant Greek tragedy on an historical subject, was exhibited in 472, the *Seven against Thebes* in 467, the *Prometheus* probably not long before 458, the date of the trilogy made up of the *Agamemnon*, the *Choephoroe*, and the *Eumenides*. The plays were exhibited in groups of four—three tragedies and a satyr play. Sometimes, as in the case of the surviving trilogy, but not always, the tragedies formed a dramatic cycle, integrated in fable and in theme. The poet acted in his own plays.

According to Aristotle, Aeschylus was charged with impiety for revealing certain parts of the Eleusinian ritual, and defended himself by saying that he was not aware the matter was a secret. But the ancients knew neither the name of the offending play nor the precise nature of what was revealed. A later tradition adds to the fact of the accusation, the doubtful details that Aeschylus escaped the fury of the audience by clasping the altar of Dionysus in the theater, and that he was later acquitted by the Court of the Areopagus because he had fought bravely at Marathon.

The first of Aeschylus' several trips to Sicily appears to have been made some time between 476 and 473. Like Pindar and Simonides he was invited to visit the court of King Hiero of Syracuse. After the eruption of Etna, Hiero had re-established the town of the same name at the base of the mountain. To celebrate the new city and to honor his patron, Aeschylus wrote and produced the *Women of Etna*. On a second visit to Sicily around 472 the poet is said to have repeated for Hiero the *Persians*, which had just been crowned with the first prize at Athens. Sometime after 458 he was yet a third time in Sicily.

There is little reason to believe the various explanations offered in antiquity for Aeschylus' leaving Athens. Most of them are based upon his supposed envy of the popularity of Sophocles and Simonides, and are made improbable, if not impossible, by known facts and dates. The fable that he met his death from an eagle letting fall a tortoise upon his bald head, presumably mistaking it for a stone upon which to break the animal's shell, may have had its origin in an attempt to interpret the allegorical representation of an apotheosis.

Aeschylus died and was buried at Gela in 456. The epitaph inscribed on his tomb is attributed by some to Aeschylus himself: *This memorial stone covers Aeschylus the Athenian, Euphorion's son, who died in wheat-bearing Gela. His famed valor the precinct of Marathon could tell and the long-haired Mede, who knows it well.*

Shortly after the death of Aeschylus the Athenians passed a decree that his plays should be exhibited at public expense, and that whoever desired to produce one of his plays should "receive a chorus." His tomb became a place of pilgrimage, and in the middle of the fourth century, at the proposal of the orator Lycurgus, his statue was set up in the Theatre of Dionysus at Athens.

CONTENTS

THE SUPPLIANT MAIDENS

DRAMATIS PERSONAE

DANAUS
PELASGUS, *King of Argos*
AN EGYPTIAN HERALD
CHORUS OF THE DANAIDES
ATTENDANTS

Argos. A hill rises in the foreground, and on the summit of it stand altars and statues of many gods. Enter the fifty DANAIDES, *with their slave girls, and* DANAUS.

Chorus

Zeus, the Suppliant's God, be gracious to us,
Pitifully behold us, for fugitives are we;
Where the blown sand-dunes silt the mouths of Nilus,
There we took the highway of the blue, salt sea;
There looked our last at the land of Zeus, her borders
Lapsed and lost in the Syrian marches wild,
Fleeing, not as outlaws banned for blood-guilt
Lest a people perish, but self-exiled.
No way but this to escape abhorred embraces,
Marriage rites unholy that true love shuns;
Better far lands and unfamiliar faces
Than wedded and bedded with King Ægyptus'sons.
As when hard pressed on the board a cautious player
This piece or that from a threatened square withdraws,
One move seemed best unto Danaus our father,
Counsel-in-chief and leader of our cause;
One woe to suffer—and that the noblest sorrow,
Seeing we were compassed in on every hand—
Tarrying not, with the fleeting ocean billow
To fly till our keel touched the Argive strand,
Whence we boast ourselves sprung, from the breath of Zeus' nostrils,
And the touch of his procreant finger laid,
For a dynasty's founding, on a king's daughter,
Even the gnat-tormented heifer-maid.
What land but this would offer us a haven,
Where else the world o'er should we welcome find,
Having no arms but the suppliant's feeble weapons,
Boughs from the woodland plucked with white wool twined?
Realm, broad realm, brown land and sparkling water,
Gods of the sky and holy ones of earth,
Denizens of darkness that visit men with vengeance,
And in that Triad last named but chief in worth,
Zeus, the Protector of travel-weary pilgrims,
Keeper of the threshold never crossed by crime,
Send soft airs to greet our maiden meinie,
Winds of welcome blowing from a sweet, calm clime.
But the ungodly sons of King Ægyptus,
Bulls of the herd, ere they trample this fair ground—
Loamy levels, tilth and fallow land and pasture—
Far over ocean with their swift ship hound!
There let them meet with thunder-blast and lightning,
Wrath of leaping seas and spite of storm-swept rain;
There let destruction find them when rough winter
Looses the lash of the loud hurricane;
Ere they climb loth beds to make of us their minions,
Minions of their pleasure and playthings of their pride;
So kindred blood shall not serve to cool brute passion
Not by sweet exchange of hearts sanctified.

Youngling divine, I hail thee now,
From beyond the sea thine aid I invoke;
Son flower-fed of the Mother Cow,
Quick with Zeus' breath and his handstroke.
So of the dam with hoof and horn
And enchanted body a babe was born,
Man-child made for mortal lot,
Epaphus, the touch-begot.

The naming of thee where long ago
Our Mother roamed this pastoral earth,
And the calling to mind of a vanished woe
Shall bear witness in trials of later birth;
And more sorrow yet may come into ken,
Though we know not how and we guess not when,
Like ours of to-day and hers of old;
And these at long last shall Time unfold.

To one that watcheth the wild birds winging,
Here at ease in his native bower,
The suppliant song of an alien race
Chance-heard, shall seem as the sweet, sad singing
Of Tereus' Daulian paramour,
The nightingale hidden, the hawk in chase.

Spring and summer for sorrow she grieveth
Under the green leaves weeping her pain
And the life that was passed in homelessness:

Spring and summer the story she weaveth
  Of the child she bore by her own hand slain,
  And the wrath of a mother pitiless.

I as the nightingale passioning for sorrow
  To Ionian music tune my pipe,
And these soft cheeks feel the rain-worn furrow
  That on Nilus' bank grew round and ripe:
For my heart hath learnt the meaning of tears,
  And I fill my lap with blossoms pale
  Gathered with grief in the wood of wail,
The better to hush these brooding fears
  That are fain to know to what end I fare
  From the land that lies dim in dust-veiled air,
If there be any who hearkens or hears.

Nay, but ye Gods of the bride-bed and begetting,
  Hear me! Ye should be jealous for the Right!
Grudge lawless youth, with the hot blood fretting,
  Lore that perfects passion's neophyte!
Set the brand of your scorn on lust that profanes,
  And mingle love's rite with austerities sweet!
  What is fiercer than war? Yet for war-weary feet
There standeth an altar, no sacrilege stains:
  To what-so wight would from battle-carnage flee,
  A refuge awe owns and a court of deity,
Where red-handed Havoc halts and refrains.

  Saith the wise saw of old,
  "The purpose Zeus doth hold
Next to his heart no hunter brings to bay."
  All Being in his sight
  Flows in the main of light,
The mirrored glory of his perfect day,
  Where man the babbler with vain lips
Sees but the secular dark of unrelieved eclipse.

  The thing that he hath wrought
  With brow-nod of calm thought
Fallen, stands fast, and, grappled, is not thrown.
  His counsels tread the maze
  Of labyrinthine ways
Through quicks, through glooms with umbrage
    overgrown;
  And in that covert dark and shy
Bold riders check the rein, foiled is the keenest
    cry.

  From towered bastions
  Of Hope he plucks Time's sons
And tosses them to ruin. If one brace
  The mettle weariless
  Of Gods for his duress,
Pride pays with penal pangs, though throned in the
    holy place.

  So let him mark afresh
  How froward is this flesh,
How the polled trunk for lust of me doth grow
  With many a stubborn shoot;
  How pricks to mad pursuit
The unremitting goad, a curse, a cheat, a woe.

So to music impassioned,
  Sung high, sung low,
With tears I have fashioned
  Untuneable woe.
    Alack! 'tis like mourner's grieving.
So sadly my quick spirit graces
  With groanings of death griefs that live,
And I cry unto Apia's high places
  My broken speech to forgive,
And falling down on my linen veil
I mar with rents its fabric frail,
  Tissue of Sidon's weaving.

With amplest oblation
  To high heaven we come,
For hope's consummation,
  When death's wind is dumb;
    But alack! for the woes dark-heaving,
The billow whose path none traces,
  Nor what strand on its crest I shall reach!
I cry unto Apia's high places
  To forgive my broken speech,
And falling oft on my linen veil
I rend and mar its fabric frail,
  Tissue of Sidon's weaving.

Thus far the oar right well hath sped;
And the bark flax-sewn to fend salt seas,
With never a flaw in the following breeze
  Nor winter storm to dread,
Hath constant been as my prayers and vows:
And I pray the Father that all doth scan,
Here on firm earth, that he may send
To well-begun a happy end;
So I, that seed am of his spouse
August, may flee the embrace of man
And live unlorded and unwed.
Zeus' daughter, vowed to maidenhead,
Look with a loving eye on me,
That would keep chaste and pure as she,
Whose virgin arm the arrow sped
And slew the Hunter in his lust
Whom Opis tremblingly outran!
O maid unwon, a maiden grace
With all they power in this sore chase,
That I, the seed of Zeus' spouse august,
May flee the violence of man
And live unlorded and unwed.

But, if these will not, then I will essay
  The sun-loathed courts of Death,
Where never a sick soul is turned away
  That wearies of this breath;
And, since Olympian Gods no help afford,
My corpse shall access find to Zeus, Earth's Lord,
When suppliant boughs shall be decked with the
    knotted cord.

Ah! Mother Io, thee wroth Gods amerce:
  And of the courts celestial I know
That there dwell jealous wives who hate and curse;
  For waves run high when breezes stiffly blow.

Then Right and Wrong shall be unreconciled;
  And Justice shall upbraid
Zeus, that he honoured not the heifer's child,
  Whom once of old he made,
If that at this late hour of time his eye
Be turnéd back when his own offspring cry:
Yet, when we call, he hears—he hears though
    throned on high.

Ah! Mother Io, thee wroth Gods amerce:
  And of the courts celestial I know
That there dwell jealous wives who hate and curse!
  For waves run high when breezes stiffly blow.

During the preceding chorus DANAUS *has climbed to the top of the hill.*

Danaus. Children, ye must be wise and
    circumspect:
Remember, a wise judgment holp ye hither,
With eld for pilot, safe and fatherly,
Across unruly seas. And here on land
I will take thought for you and keep you safe,
If ye set down my words in your heart's tables.
Far off I can discern a cloud of dust,
Ever the voiceless courier of hosts,
Before the noise of wheels reacheth the ear,
When axles pipe unheard. I can distinguish
An armed mass, with shields and tossing spears,
Horses and chariots of war recurved.
'Tis likely that the Princes of this land
Have heard of us from messengers and come
To be their own intelligencers. Whether
They mean no harm, or sharp resentment speeds
This stern array, all things concur herein;
That ye, fair daughters, make this hill your seat;
Dear is it to the gods of festival,
Pastime and sport and peaceful rivalries.
More strong that castle tower an altar stands,
A buckler inexpugnably secure.
Then with all speed ascend; and with you take
In solemn ceremonial your wands
Wound with white favours that appeal to Zeus,
The God of Mercy. To these foreign lords
Answering in such wise as shall move their mercy,
With lamentations and all forms of speech
Proper to your necessity, and fit
For strangers in a strange land, plainly tell
The story of your flight, and how from blood
'Tis wholly free. Let nought of boldness wait
On your discourse: nothing of light or vain
Be seen, but downward looks, untroubled eyes:
Not forward in the telling of your tale,
Nor hanging back: 'tis easy to offend
The race that dwelleth here. Never forget
Your cue is to submit: ye come as poor
And needy suitors, aliens and exiles.
Bold speech consorts not with the weaker side.

Ch. Father, thy cautions find us well disposed
To prudent counsels, and thy wise precepts
I shall with all solicitude obey.
Zeus, our progenitor, watch over us.

Da. Stay not: lay hold upon the means at hand.

Ch. I will be with you instantly. O Zeus,
Pity us, or we perish. *They ascend the hill.*

Da. May he look
Graciously on us: if it pleases him,
All will be well. Call now upon this child
Of Zeus.

Ch. I call upon the radiant Sun,
The saving source of health, to heal our woes,
And pure Apollo once exiled from heaven;
God though he is, he knows this earthly lot,
And feels perhaps for frail mortality.

Da. May he in very deed commiserate
And stand a ready helper by our side.

Ch. Which of these Gods shall I next invoke?

Da. I see
The trident of the Isthmian King.

Ch. He gave
Fair passage to our vessel: welcome fair
May he accord on land.

Da. And here is Hermes,
After the way the Hellenes fashion him.

Ch. Well met indeed: I pray that he may prove
A herald of glad tidings.

Da. Bend in awe
And adoration at the common altar
Of all these sovereignties. On holy ground
Crouch like a flock of doves that fear the hawk
For all his cousinship of wings. Even so
Fearful are ye of foes of your own blood
That would pollute your race. And if one fowl
Prey on another, how can it be pure?
And he who weds a bride against her will,
Her father not consenting, where shall he
Find purity? I trow, that when he's dead
The doer of this deed at Hades' bar
Shall stand arraigned not idly: even there,
So we believe, another Zeus holds court
Among the souls whose earthly race is run,
And passes final sentence on their crimes.
Look to yourselves, and to this lord return
Such answer, that ye fail not in your cause.

Enter PELASGUS.

Pelasgus. What little band is this that I salute?
Whence come ye, not, as Hellenes are, attired,
But with barbaric bravery of robes,
And fine veils finished with the weaver's spathe?
These woman's weeds are not of Argolis
Nor any part of Hellas. Herald ye
Have none; nor minister to be your friend;
Nor guide in a strange land. And how ye dared
Adventure here, thus utterly forlorn,
Is matter for amazement. By your side
Before these Gods of Festival are laid
Branches that well accord with suppliant's law.
In Hellas that surmise confirms itself:
Fair dealing must conjecture all the rest,
Were there no living voice to clear the doubt.

Ch. Touching our garb thy words are words of
    truth:
But how shall I address thee? Art thou one
Of the commonalty? Com'st with formal wand
Equipped for parle? Or as of this fair realm

Foremost and chief?
Pe. Let not that vex thy heart:
Thou may'st with full assurance answer me.
I am the son of Palaechthon earth-born,
Pelasgus, of this soil the supreme lord.
And they who reap its fruits from me their king
Are called, with reason good, Pelasgians.
Over all ground towards the setting sun,
Wherethrough the Haliacmon flows, I reign.
Within my borders I include the land
Of the Perrhaebi, and the parts beyond
Pindus, adjoining the Chaonians,
With the high mountains of Dodona; west
I touch the salt, wet frontiers of the sea.
Thence all that stretches hitherward is mine,
The spot whereon we stand being Apia,
So called of old from one in medicine wise,
Apis, Apollo's son, prophet and healer,
Who from Naupactus crossed, beyond the gulf,
And purged this land of man-devouring beasts,
Which Earth, by bloody deeds done long ago,
Polluted and estranged, in mood most like
A step-dame, gendered, to dispute her soil
With man, his fanged and serpent brood-fellow.
For these did Apis on this Argive ground,
To its no small relief, with shredded herbs
And wholesome charms effect a perfect cure,
His fee, to be remembered in our prayers.
But, now that I have answered you, 'twere well
If one of ye declared what birth ye boast,
With brevity and clearness: this my realm
Hath little liking for long-drawn discourse.
Ch. Briefly and clearly then: Of Argive blood
We boast to be: the mother of our race
A cow made happy in the son she bare.
And I will fix upon this frame of truth
Its proper parts until the whole cohere.
Pe. Women—strange women, ye compose a tale
Not credible. How can ye be of Argive blood,
More like to Libyans than our womankind?
Yea, such a plant might grow on Nilus' bank;
Methinks, these forms were coined in Cyprian
mint
Struck to the life by your progenitors.
Stay: I have heard that nomads of your sex,
Horsed upon camels ride in cushioned selles
Along the coasts of Æthiopia:
They should resemble ye; or, on my life,
Had ye but bows I could have ta'en an oath
That ye were the unlorded Amazons
That fare on flesh. Ye must instruct me further;
I am to know more of this history
And how ye are a seed of Argive strain.
Ch. Runs not the story that on Argos' earth
Io once kept the keys of Hera's house?
Pe. 'Tis very sure she did: the fame thereof
Lives yet throughout the land.
Ch. And more by token;
The heart of Zeus was stung with love of her?
Pe. Troth, 'twas no secret: Hera wrought amain
To foil his fancy.
Ch. And this royal quarrel
How doth it end in the story?
Pe. The Argive goddess
Transformed the maid into a cow.
Ch. And Zeus
Is fain to have the comely beast fair-horned?
Pe. Indeed the tale is told so: to that end
He wore the likeness of a lustful bull.
Ch. What counter-stroke to this dealt Zeus'
haught Queen?
Pe. Why, then she found a keeper for the cow,
Him that hath eyes which look all ways at once.
Ch. And what was he, this all-beholding one,
Sole neatherd of a solitary cow?
Pe. Argus, earth's child, the same that Hermes
slew.
Ch. And the device that followed? What thing
else
Prepared she for the heifer heaven-accursed?
Pe. She did afflict her with the gnat that stings,
A drover's goad-prick to stampeding kine.
Ch. They call him "Gad-fly" on the banks of
Nile.
Pe. What? Did he drive her forth from her own
land
As far as Nile?
Ch. He did so: and thy tale
Tallies in each particular with mine.
Pe. And is it true then that she reached Canopus
And Memphis far inland?
Ch. Surely; and Zeus
By laying-on of hands raised up a son.
Pe. Who then is he that boasts himself the calf
Zeus gendered on this cow?
Ch. Even Epaphus,
True title given from that divine caress.
Pe. And Epaphus—had he issue?
Ch. He begat
Libya, the reaper of a third of earth,
Her amplest fields.
Pe. What scion sprang from her?
Ch. My father's father, Bel, who had two sons.
Pe. Tell me, I pray, thy sire's all-sapient name.
Ch. Danaus: he hath a brother who begot
Two score and ten sons.
Pe. Prithee, indulge me further;
And let me hear by what name he is called.
Ch. Ægyptus. Now thou know'st my ancient
line,
Stretch forth the hand of succour to raise up
Argives, that here have taken sanctuary.
Pe. Anciently, I do verily believe,
A common tie unites ye to this land.
But how had ye the courage to forsake
The house of your fathers? What so sore mischance
Hath fallen on ye?
Ch. King of the Pelasgians!
Calamity is as a ruffling breeze
That glances through a thousand shifting forms;
Nor is there anywhere on earth a place
Where thou could'st point and say, "Here
sorrow's wing
Keeps darkly constant to its native hue."

For which of us in fancy ever dreamed
Of this unlooked for flight; or that a ship
Whereon we sailed should touch this Argive strand
Wherewith we had affinity of old;
Or that in distant Egypt wedlock scorned,
Unhappied by the hymenaeal choir,
Should be the cause of consequence so strange?

Pe. What is the boon thou sayest thou dost crave
Here in the name of these Gods of festival,
Your branches fresh-plucked all with white enwound?

Ch. That I may ne'er become bondslave and thrall
Unto Ægyptus' race.

Pe. And is it hate
That prompts thy plea, or reverence of law?

Ch. Nay, who amongst their own blood kin would buy
Their lords and masters?

Pe. Yet it is a match
That makes for power.

Ch. And if misfortune come
Who cares if wife so wed be put away?

Pe. What shall I do then that I may be found
To-you-ward a respecter of the Right?

Ch. Refuse to yield us up to Ægyptus' sons
When they demand us of thee.

Pe. There thou broachest
Grave matters, that envisage dangerous war.

Ch. Yet Justice champions those that fight for her.

Pe. If I had had my share in these events
From the beginning—

Ch. O! Assume it now!
And, as 'twere, this high deck and laurelled poop
Of a most stately vessel honour duly.

Pe. Indeed, when I look round me and behold
This haunt of Gods all branched and shaded o'er,
I shudder.

Ch. Where is he who would not pause?
The wrath of Zeus the Suppliant's God is heavy.

Stop not thine ears, O son of Palaechthon,
Nor hold thy heart aloof, thou royal man,
But hearken when I cry to thee, whose throne
Is over this wide realm Pelasgian.
Behold, in me a suppliant sues for grace,
A hunted thing still forced to shift her ground,
Like to a heifer with the wolves in chase
That to the herd doth lowingly complain
Upon some rocky precipice crag-bound,
Trusting his strength and telling him her pain.

Pe. Methinks I see this gathering of the Gods
Of festival, with branches freshly plucked
All shaded o'er, nodding in grave assent.
Oh, may your cause who claim to be our kin
Work us no mischief, nor on any hand
Strife grow from what we neither could foresee
Nor have provided for. That to this realm
Were an unwanted, a superfluous care.

Ch. Law that doth vindicate the suppliant's right,
Daughter of Zeus who deals the destiny,
Look to it that I bring not in my flight
Mischief and wrong that wreck felicity.
And, thou with eld's too sober wisdom wise,
From younger hearts 'tis not too late to learn,
The noblest offering, purest sacrifice
On altars of oblation ever laid,
Sweeter than sweetest essence faith can burn,
Is mercy to the weak that ask for aid.

Pe. It is not at my private hearth ye sit;
And if some public mischief be afoot
Then must the commons of this realm work out
Such expiation as shall cleanse them all.
Myself might tender no effectual pledge
But with the privity of all free men.

Ch. Thou art both liberty and law
And commonalty; thine
An absolute prerogative
No captious rights confine;
Thou rul'st the hearth-place of thy land,
The Godhead's central shrine,
By an indisputable nod.
Sole-sceptred on thy throne
All business that concerns the state
Thou dost despatch alone.
Beware lest unregarded wrong
Let in contagion.

Pe. Contagion fall upon mine enemies.
Howbeit, to help thee and take myself
No hurt I scarce know how. Yet 'twere scant kindness
To set thy prayers at nought. Perplexity
And fears possess my heart, whether to act,
Or not to act and let fate have her way.

Ch. Look up unto the Watcher set on high,
The Guardian of necessitous souls who sue,
Crouched on a neighbour's hearth, for sanctuary,
Craving in vain the right which is their due.
For grace denied and suppliants' slighted pleas
Endures the wrath of Zeus no pangs of guilt appease.

Pe. If by the law of the land Ægyptus' sons
Are your rightful lords, to wit, upon the plea
Of next-kin, who would choose resist their claim?
Your answer must be founded on the law
Domestic; and ye must maintain and prove
That over ye they have no power at all.

Ch. Into the hands of tyrant man
God grant that I fall never:
I'll know no bounds but the starry span
That bends o'er earth for ever:
Fled to that virgin liberty
I'll live from forceful marriage free.
Be thou the ally of Justice and not Law;
Judge thou as judge the Gods and stand of them in awe.

Pe. No easy judgment: choose not me for judge.
Have I not said without the people's voice
I will not and I cannot, King though I be,
Do as thou'lt have me do? I will not hear—
If it should chance that aught untoward fall—

Reproachful commons cast it in my teeth
"To honour strangers thou didst wreck thy land!"
Ch. Ancestral Zeus, of both blood-kin,
Eyes suppliant and pursuer:
The ponderable stuff of sin
Is charged to the wrong doer;
Quick is the tell-tale hand to mount
And reckon to the just's account
The fair record of righteousness.
Since equal is the poise why shrink from fair redress?

Pe. This asks deep thought: an eye within the mind,
Keen as a diver salving sunken freight,
To sink into the depths, yet, searching there,
Not lose itself in roving phantasies;
That all end well and mischief follow not
First for the State, which is our chief concern,
Then for ourselves; and neither war lay hold
On loot to pay your loss, nor by our act,
If from this seat of Gods that ye have made
Your seat, we yield you up, the land be crushed
By haunting visitations of the God
Whose business is destruction, Alastor,
The unforgetting instrument of wrath,
Who even in the house of Hades suffers not
The dead man to go free. And asks not this
Heart-searchings, fathom-deep, of saving thought?

Chorus

Search deep and then rise up more strong
For justice: be the minister
That reverentially protects from wrong
The stranger and the sojourner,
Resolved never to yield while thou stand'st by
An exile driven so far in godless outlawry.

O look not on till rapine come
And from these haunts of Powers divine
Hale me for spoil: all masterdom,
All judicature here are thine.
Then in this cause let thy decree go forth:
"Man's lusts here sue for judgment," and beware of wrath.

Submit not to the sight
Of divine Justice set at naught by might,
And the rejected suppliant led away
From statues holy, as by bands of gold
A horse is led, while rough men lay
Rude hands upon my raiment's damask fold.

Thy seed and thy household
As thou art cruel or in mercy bold,
The exact measure of thy "yea" or "nay"
Eternal Law shall utterly requite.
O ponder well these things, and sway
The event as Zeus commands, who judgeth right.

Pe. Nay, I have pondered and my bark of thought
Strikes on this point of peril. There's no choice
But of two sides I must take arms 'gainst one,
And either were a war of magnitude.
Here then you have the naked shell: stark hull,
Triced on the stocks, all rivets driven home,
And all her timbers strained and drawn together,
As 'twere, with shipwright's winches. Once at sea
She's bound for loss before she comes to land.
When there is jettison of merchandize,
By the good grace of Zeus the Garnisher
More may be gotten, a full load to freight
A ship of deeper draught. And, if the tongue
Shoot wildly, for the wound that words inflict
Words will apply the remedy, a balm
For angry humours, spell and counterspell:
But, that there be no letting of the blood
Of kin, compels to earnest sacrifice,
And many victims unto many gods,
Where'er men ask of oracles, must fall,
Preservatives against calamity.
My entrance to this quarrel comes unsought
And every way 'tis to my own undoing.
I'd rather be a seer of little skill
Than deeply learned in prophesying ill:
So, though my judgment goes not with the prayer,
Out of these troubles Heaven send issue fair.

Ch. Hear the conclusion, then, of my much speech
That meant to move your pity.
Pe. I have heard:
But speak: I mark thee closely.
Ch. I have scarves
And girdles that hold up my raiment—
Pe. Why,
All women have them.
Ch. Out of these I'll fashion
An ornament and excellent device
To keep mine honour safe.
Pe. Give thy words meaning:
What is it thou would'st say?
Ch. Give us a pledge,
Plant on some ground of faith these feeble feet;
If not—
Pe. These gatherings, girdlings up of robes,
How shall they stead thee?
Ch. They shall serve to deck
These shapes with votive tablets never yet
Hanged up on hallowed images.
Pe. A riddle!
The manner of this: expound.
Ch. Incontinent
We'll hang ourselves upon these holy Gods.
Pe. Thy menace lays the lash across my heart.
Ch. I see thou understand'st me: now have I
Opened thine eyes to clearer vision.
Pe. Yea,
Turn where I may, griefs ineluctable
Confront my sight: a multitude of ills
Comes on like a river: on this sea of ruin
I am embarked: the bottomless abyss
Below; around unnavigable waves;
And nowhere any harbour from distress.
If I shall fail towards you and not exact
This debt which is your right, ye threaten me
With such pollution, strain words how ye will,

Hyperbole cannot o'ershoot the mark.
And if I stand before the city wall
And try conclusions with Ægyptus' sons,
Your own blood kin, upon the field of battle,
For sake of women men must stain this earth
With blood: and were not that bitter expense
To charge myself withal? Yet there's no help
But I must hold in awe the wrath of Zeus
Who helpeth suppliants: the fear of him
Is for all flesh the highest fear. Now, therefore,
Thou venerable father of these maids,
Take in thy hands branches like these and lay them
On other altars of my country's Gods,
That of your coming all the citizens
May see a visible token: let not fall
One word of me: the commonalty loves
To cast reproach upon their rulers. But,
Looking thereon, pity may move some soul
With hatred for the wickedness of men
Banded against you; and the public heart
Be for your boughs more tender. 'Tis a trait
Common with men to entertain kind thoughts
Towards the weaker side.

Da. That we have found a friend
Pitiful and God-fearing we account
Worth many favours. Wilt thou grant one more
And with me send some native to this land
For escort and as guides, that we may find
The altars of the city deities
That stand before the temples, and the shrines
Of those more warlike that defend your keep?
The form that nature gave us is not yours,
Nor are we habited as ye are. Nile
Nourisheth other folk than Inachus.
Beware lest an unheedful confidence
Hereafter breed dismay. Men have ere now
Slain those that were their friends, not knowing it.

Pe. Go with this stranger, men: for he says well.
Show him the way to the town altars and
The seats of Gods. And look ye bruit it not
At cross-roads, that ye bring this seafarer
To sit upon the hearths of the Holy Ones.

Exit DANAUS *with bodyguard.*

Ch. For him the word is spoken: let him go
Since thou commandest it. But what of me?
What shall I do, and where dost thou assign
For me a place of safety?

Pe. Leave thy branches
Where thou art now as a token of distress.

Ch. I lay them where thy hand and tongue direct.

Pe. Now thou art free to walk about this smooth
And level lawn.

Ch. This lawn where all may tread?
And how shall that protect me?

Pe. Be content:
'Tis not our purpose to expose thee here
A prey for birds.

Ch. For birds? And what of foes
More dangerous than serpents?

Pe. Fair and softly!
Thou see'st I speak thee fair.

Ch. It is not strange
That fear betray uneasiness.

Pe. Methinks
The awe of Kings exceedeth evermore
All fears beside.

Ch. O cheer me with kind words!
And hearten me no less with gracious deeds.

Pe. Nay, but 'tis not for long that thy good sire
Hath left thee. I too leave thee for a while,
But 'tis to call our folk together, make
The commons thy good friends; and teach thy father
How he should speak to them. Tarry meantime,
Therefore, and with thy prayers prevail upon
The gods of the land to grant thy heart's desire.
I will depart hence and make good my words.
Persuasion and fair fortune follow us!

Exit PELASGUS. *The* DANAIDES *descend on to the open lawn below the hill.*

Chorus

King of Kings, among the Blest
In thy bliss the blessedest,
In thy power of all that are
Mighty, mightiest by far,
Happy Zeus, that prayer receive,
And the event our wish achieve.
Drive aloof the lusts of men;
With thy loathing visit them;
Plunge 'neath an empurpled sea
That embodied infamy
Pitched without and black within
With havoc and the purposed sin.
But the woman's cause espouse:
Think upon our storied house,
Tenderly the tale renewing
Of old love and eager wooing:
And our ancestress to be,
Woman, yet once dear to thee.
Ah, remember Long Ago,
Thou Comforter of Io's woe!
For we boast that we can trace
High as Zeus our ancient race:
Sojourners were we at birth;
This is home, this parent earth.

In the print flower-sweet
Of my mother's feet,
Behold, I have planted mine:
Where she stooped to feed
Knee-deep in the mead
That fattens the Argive kine:
And with her alway
To haunt and betray
The eye of the earthborn herd.
Far hence lies her road,
By the gadfly goad,
As a skiff with the oar-blade, spurred:
She must know the pain
Of a maddened brain
And wander through many races,
Till 'twixt either strand
Of the sundered land
A path through the billows she traces.

To the Asian shore
She must pass o'er,
And ever her onward leap
Of her coming tells
To the Phrygian fells
And the fleecy moorland sheep.
By street and tower
That Teuthras' power
Founded for Mysian men
In olden time,
She speeds; she must climb
Through Lydian gorge and glen;
And she must o'erleap
The Cilician steep,
And the wild Pamphylian mountains
No barrier
Shall be to her;
Till fed by eternal fountains,
Broad rivers glide
And her footsteps guide
Through a pleasant land and a mighty,
With all wealth crowned,
The fair, the renowned
Wheatland of Aphrodite.

And still she flew, a hunted thing,
Of Heaven's grace unpitied;
And in and out with darting sting
In dizzy reel and dazzling ring
The wingéd herdsman flitted.

She has reached at last Zeus' own demesne
That is to all Nature boon,
Green with the glow of the melting snow
And scorched by the Typhoon.

She has come to the tide that is deep and wide,
Untouched by the hand of disease;
Yea, to Nile's water King Inachus' daughter,
Hera's crazed Thyiad, flees.

Paled then all dwellers in that lea
With quaking fear a-cold:
Such hybrid shape they ne'er did see:
Half woman and half cow was she,
A monster to behold.

A freakish, eerie, elfin form,
Whose kind 'twere hard to tell;
If human, out of human shape
Tortured by some dread spell.

Ah, then to charm away her grief,
Who at long last relented,
And rested the far-wandered feet
Of Io, the gnat-tormented?

Even Zeus, Lord Paramount, whose reign
Expects no earthly tyrant's bloody doom;
He eased her of her pain
With sweet constraint from all enforcement free
And breathings of his love divinely mild.
Tears as of one half-reconciled
She shed—warm tears of bitter memory;
But, with that heavenly burthen in her womb,
Became the mother of a perfect child.

A happy, long-lived man was he;
Wherefore a voice went through that fertile earth,
"Behold in verity
This is the son of Zeus: this is the seed
He sowed: who else among the Gods had stayed
The crafty plots that Hera laid?
If thou should'st say, 'Here is Zeus' very deed,
This is a child of heavenly birth,'
Clean to the centre shall thine arrow speed."

What God to thee should I prefer
And by a title holier
Ask Justice? Thou, O King,
Our Father art; and thy right hand
Hath planted us in a strange land;
We are thine own offspring.

Thou great unmatched artificer,
In thy calm heart let memory stir
The pulse of vanished days,
O Zeus that art in all things blest,
And whatso'er thou purposest
None hinders nor gainsays!

Thou art no vassal on a throne;
No power that doth transcend thine own
To thee dictates the law;
Nor is there one in higher place
To whom thou turn'st a humble face,
Holding his seat in awe.

Art thou in labour with the pang
Of deeds whereon great issues hang,
Behold, the accomplished fact!
Or if in words goes forth thy breath,
The mind that with them travaileth
Converteth speech to act.

Enter DANAUS.

Da. Take courage, children: the people of the land
With sovran voice have cast their votes right well.

Ch. Dear envoy! Best beloved of tiding-bearers,
All hail! But hide not one thing from us. What
Have they determined? The full master-hand
Of the assembled commons, to what deed
Points it?

Da. Unwaveringly, and in such wise
As made my old heart young—for the free air,
While all freemen made this decision law,
Rustled with multitudes of lifted hands—
The Argives have decreed that we shall hold
This soil with them, immune from all reprisals,
Havoc and harrying of the lustful male;
And of those native here or alien
No man may drive us hence; withal, if force
Be offered, what-so denizen withholds

His aid, shall suffer loss of civil rights
And, furthermore, be banished by the State.
This was the manner of the speech, whereby
The King of the Pelasgians in our cause
Wrought on his auditors; with warning voice
He spake of the hereafter, lest the realm
Feed fat the wrath of Zeus, the Suppliant's God;
We came as fugitives and foreigners,
As citizens we were received; two claims
Conjoinéd in our persons, which, denied,
Would work two-fold contagion, and raise up
Before the city-gates a monster, fed
On sorrow, yet whose craw grief cannot cram.
Then they stayed not to hear the marshal's cry
But on a show of hands would have it so.
It was the voice of the Pelasgians' King
That moved them, suppling the persuasive word,
But Zeus determined what the end should be.
He ascends the hill.

Chorus

Oh come! Let us render
Recompense fair!
A token and tender
Of thanks, and a prayer
That good things be showered upon Argos.
Benediction and laud and honour
In hymns to her praises sung
Shall surely be doubled upon her;
For dear is an alien tongue
To Zeus who cares for the stranger
And governs the counsels of Kings;
To an end free from harm and danger
May he lead our thanksgivings,
With good gifts shed upon Argos.

In your heavenly habitation,
While I pour my heart's libation
With the wine of prayer o'erflowing,
Hear my voice, ye gods! Hereafter
Never roar of ruddy fire
Strike and slay Pelasgia's city,
Nor the song be heard, where laughter
Is not, nor the dance nor lyre,
Lustful Ares' joyless strain,
Who in fields not of his sowing
Reaps the harvest of the slain.
Forasmuch as they had pity;
For that love their voice inspireth,
Honouring suppliants Zeus befriendeth,
Little flock that sorrow tendeth
And whose portion none desireth.

Neither did they give their voices
For proud men, to do them pleasure;
They have dealt us noble measure
Woman's weaker cause befriending:
For their loftier vision saw
The inexorable Awe,
Angry Zeus, whose wrath requiteth,
Whose sure aim the end achieves;
And with him is no contending.
Where's the dwelling that rejoices
'Neath his heavy visitation—
Like a carrion-bird that lighteth,
Dropping down abomination,
Gorged and bloated, on man's eaves?
Heavily the monster squatteth,
An unlifted, leaden burden.
But these kin have not rejected
Claim of kin: they have respected
Suppliants at Zeus' holy seat.
Therefore they shall have their guerdon,
Altars no pollution spotteth,
To the Gods of Heaven sweet.

Forth, thou bird of plume more fair;
From the mouth's dark covert break,
Emulous and eager prayer;
All prayers else do thou o'ertake.

Never pestilence nor dearth
Empty Argos of her men:
Nor civil tumult stain this earth
With blood of fallen brethren.

Youth be here an unplucked flower;
And Ares, who makes men to mourn,
Though lord of Aphrodite's bower,
That comely blossom leave unshorn.

And, where ancient men convene,
Let there not want within these walls
Bearded benchers of grave mien
Throned in old Cyclopian stalls.

So may wise laws and well-obeyed
Order all things in the land,
Long as reverence is paid
To Zeus, and chiefly Him whose hand

Is over strangers. He alone
Maintains the right 'gainst wrong and crime,
And confirms to each his own
By law and precept gray with time.

Everything that fruitful is
Spring anew from fecund earth,
And may arrowy Artemis
Bring the struggling babe to birth.

Havoc, come not to rive this land;
Nor bring no arms for Ares' hand,
Who loveth neither dance nor lyre;
Children he hath at his desire
But they are tears: nor the drawn knife
Whet for the dagger-hand of strife
And civil uproar: keep far hence,
Ye croaking flocks of pestilence;
And all young things in this fair ground
Be with thy love, Lycean, crowned.

Zeus make the earth to teem, and bless
With seasonable toll and cess

Of gathered fruit and corn in shocks:
And may the forward-feeding flocks
In her rich pastures multiply:
And all things have prosperity
By the Gods' favour flourishing:
Let minstrels round her altars sing
Sweet lauds; and while the lute leads on
Pure lips send up their orison.

A power obnoxious to no term
Be here: not novel and infirm;
Soon blown and soon decayed,
But on old honour stayed;
Prescient in counsel, and withal,
Of such foreknowledge liberal;
Not jealous to exclude
The sovran multitude,
But rather guide them. And abroad
Let them be slow to draw the sword,
Much readier to maintain
By processes humane
Their legal right, than prompt to act:
If bounden, faithful to their pact,
Their arbiter the Court,
And war their last resort.
Let them keep fasts and festivals,
Bring wreaths of bay and slaughter bulls,
As did their sires of old,
To the Lord Gods who hold
Their land. For reverence and awe
From son to sire is the third law
Justice hath writ for men
With monumental pen.

Da. Dear children, I commend these temperate prayers.
Tremble not if I break to you bad news.
From this our sanctuary and my watch-tower
I see the ship. No: I am not mistaken
All too discernible is the sail—so bent—
The awnings—and the prow with painted eyes
That look before on the untravelled road—
And the quick sense, too quick for those she loves not,
To hearken to the guiding of the helm.
The men on board, their black limbs clothed in white,
Are plain to see. And now the other craft,
Store-ships and all, are in full view. The admiral
Is shortening sail, and, all oars out, rows hard
Under the lee of the land. This must be faced
With a fixed constancy: let not dismay
Divert your thoughts from these still watchful Gods.
I will return anon when I have gotten
Defence and counsel. Like enough a herald—
Or delegates that mean to force you hence—
Graspers at harsh reprisals—nay, but that
Can never be and ye've no cause to fear it.
Nevertheless, if human aid be slow,
Remember, here ye have a present help.
Be of good cheer then; where is he who scorns
The Gods and shall not in Time's great assize
Upon the day appointed, answer it?

He descends from the hill.

Chorus

Father, I am afraid: the ships have come
So quickly, with scant interval between.

I am possessed with dread,
Doubts and fears importune me,
Lest that my flight far-sped
No way should fortune me.

Oh, when the goal is won,
The struggle nought availeth me;
Father, I am fordone;
For fear my strength faileth me.

Da. Child, pluck up courage. The recorded vote
Of Argos is a sovran people's voice:
Certain I am that they will fight for thee.

Chorus

Ægyptus' sons are wild, abandoned men;
Their lust of battle hard to be appeased:
And if I say so thy heart knows 'tis true.

They have gotten them stalwart ships,
The stout oak braces:
They have gotten them shining ships
With cruel steely faces.

They set a course o'er unknown waves;
They struck an unseen quarry:
And multitudes of tawny slaves
Summoned to their foray.

Da. Ay, but they'll meet their match; a multitude
Whose arms by oft exposure to the blaze
Of burning noon are firm as marble filed.
Ch. I pray you, leave me not alone, my father.
Left to herself a woman is but nought:
She hath no stomach for brave deeds of war.
But they are men in mind and heart deranged;
Possessed, yea, mad with godless lust and pride:
The human soul in them so much estranged
From holy thoughts, mercy and truth and awe,
They reck them less than crows, with beak and claw,
That rob the altars of things sanctified.
Da. My children, this shall nothing profit them:
That which provokes in you resentful thoughts
Shall work the wrath of the immortal Gods.
Ch. Father, they fear no tridents: neither can
Arrow or thunderbolt restrain their hands.
They are too much swollen with their own conceit
For awe to sway them; and in violent pride
Have run too far to stay their reckless feet
For aught that preacheth from these holy bounds:
But like a pack of disobedient hounds
They would not hear, though all the Gods should chide.
Da. Ay, but three dogs are not a match for one

Gray wolf: nor can the byblus-fruit compare
With wheaten corn.

Ch. They are as savage beasts,
All fury and all lust and all uncleanness;
We must defend ourselves against their attack
As quickly, as we may.

Da. Nay, there is time:
Fleets neither set sail nor are brought to anchor
All in a moment: nor, when anchors hold,
Are they who shepherd ships so quick to moor
And trust their safety to a cable's stretch.
And least of all when they have come to a land
That hath no haven, and night draweth on.
For when the sun departeth, night breeds care
For a good seaman; troops cannot be landed
With safety till a ship be snugly berthed.
Then with a quiet mind be vigilant
And ever mindful of the Gods, that so
Ye make their succour certain. For the state,
They shall not need to chide your messenger
Because he's old. For with the spirit of youth
Here in my heart it needs must prompt my tongue.
Exit.

Chorus

Ho! Land of hills—
Protectress, held in awe
Of old—now by new bonds of treaty-law
Knit to our hearts—what ills
Must we yet suffer at the hands of men?
Where shall we find a refuge, holy one?
In all this Apian earth is there no glen,
No haunt of darkness hollowed from the sun,
Where we may hide?
I would I were black smoke; a vapour dun
Drawn upwards to the clouds of Zeus' bright day.
Or might I vanish quite away,
Soaring where none should see me; none
Follow: lost in the wide
Of heaven, like dust that needs no wing
To waft it in aerial vanishing.
No refuge left:
No shelter from the slow
Insistent on-fall of unshunnable woe.
As waters in a cleft
My heart's blood eddies turbulent and black.
And this last touch of bitterest irony
Things in themselves untoward do not lack,
That all my father's lookings forth to sea
My feet enmesh;
'Tis I for fear have well nigh ceased to be.
I would about my neck a noose were bound;
I would that there the fated shaft were found
Winged with the wished-for liberty;
Ere flesh from amorous flesh
Recoiling feel the touch abhorred,
I would that I were dead and Hades had for lord.

Oh for a throne in stainless air
Where the moist and dripping cloud
Touches and is turned to snow.
Oh for a smooth and slippery rock
Where the wild goat fears to climb
And no intruding son of Time
Points a finger. Lone and bare
And wrapped in contemplation proud
It o'erhangs the gulf below;
There lean vultures flap and flock;
And, as if indeed it were
A living spirit, its blind wall
Shall bear record of my fall
Headlong—all my sorrows ending
And heartless love which is heart's rending.

Then, I grudge not dogs their prey;
Then, this body of mine shall feast.
Birds that haunt the valley grounds.
There's no anguish in such wounds:
They can never bleed afresh.
Dying is to be released
From all ills our living flesh
Would with wailing wish away.
Come with swift forestalling stride,
Death, ere darker deed be done
In the chamber of the bride.
For of all the paths that run
O'er the broad earth 'neath the sun
That which leads to the unwinding
Of my sorrow is past finding.

Cry to Heaven; prayer's full oblation
Moves the Gods and sets me free.
Father, from thy habitation
Watch the battle soon to be.

Turn away from guilt the splendour
Of those eyes whose light is law;
Strong, be thou the weak's defender,
Zeus, who hold'st the world in awe.

For the male hath sought and found me.
Fleeing, whither shall I fly?
Egypt's sons will soon have bound me
Wildered with their battle-cry.

Thine the mighty beam suspended;
All things tremble in thy scale.
What can be begun or ended
Without thee for bliss or bale?

Oh me! I am undone!
What evil errand bringeth thee ashore,
Pirate? A rescue! Ho!
This is the entering in of woe,
But more will follow—more!
To our divine protectors run!
Pelasgus—Lord
Wring their hard hearts with pangs they cannot bear!

The CHORUS *ascend the hill. Enter an* EGYPTIAN HERALD *with* SAILORS.

Herald. Aboard! Aboard!
Get to the dhow as fast as feet can carry ye!
Else, I'll pluck out your hair,

Drive ye before me with the slaver's goad,
Hack heads off till blood spouts like rain.
Back to the ship again,
And may the red plague harry ye!

Ch. I would that somewhere on the weltering road
Of multitudinous ocean ye had sunk,
That of its bitter waters ye had drunk
Enough to drown your bark and quench your pride.
Then were we happy sitting side by side,
Even as now we were,
Free from trouble, free from care,
Hid in this leafy bower.
Once and for all hear my commands; lay by
Violence and wrong and mad impiety.
Hence from this holy spot,
And anger not
The Argive power.
Ah, may I never see again the flood
That fatteneth the flesh of Egypt's kine,
And breeds a procreant humour in man's blood
Even as sap clothes the bare bough with green.
Argive I am of long descended line,
Queen, and the daughter of a Queen.

He. Rant—rail your fill,
But whether ye will not or ye will
Ye must aboard!

Ch. Alack! Why tarry they?
Make speed, or we are lost!

He. If ye delay,
From where ye sit I'll drag ye with these hands.

Ch. O'er ocean-lawns sheeted with salt sea-spume
May ye be dragged and driven to and fro,
With helpless tossings of these cruel hands,
Where from the Syrian coast the wild winds blow
With wailing heard along the mounded sands
Beneath Sarpedon's tomb.

He. Shriek, wail and howl and call upon the Gods.
'Tis not so light a thing to overleap
A ship of Egypt. Wherefore tune thy voice
To sadder music, a more bitter curse.

Ch. The dark wave whelm thee rounding ness on ness
Where Cyprus' forests clothe her capes of wrath,
And Nile, that mighty Nile which sent thee forth,
Strike out thy name—one insolent the less.

He. Aboard! Aboard! The ship has put about
Ready to go to sea. Get thee aboard,
Or I will lug thee by the forelock.

He rushes at the DANAIDES, *followed by his men.*

Ch. Father, a thing in human shape and yet
A lurker in the net
That Evil spins for mortal woe,
Like an industrious spider to and fro
Weaves link by link and thread by thread
Its latticed snare.
Earth, Mother Earth, the spectre dread,
The black nightmare
Drive far away,
O Mother Earth! O Father Zeus, I pray!

He. I am not fearful of your Argive Gods:
They suckled not my youth nor fed my age.

Ch. What shall I call thee? A two-footed snake,
A viper creeping from the brake
With venomed fang to bruise
My heel. O Mother Earth,
Drive hence the beast of monstrous birth!
Hear, Mother Earth! Hearken, O Father Zeus!

He. Get thee aboard and with a better grace;
Else shall thy gauzes, muslins and thy veils
Cry out for ruth and rending reck them not.

Ch. They overpower me! Chiefs, lords, princes, save!

He. Anon, anon! Courage! Thou soon shalt have
Princes enow: Ægyptus' fifty sons!
Be of good cheer; thou shalt not lack for lords!

Ch. Lost, lost—O King—O sacrilegious slave!

He. I have thee now; heave her aboard by the hair:
She's a slack one and slow of hearing.

Enter PELASGUS *with armed* ATTENDANTS.

Pe. Hold!
Ruffian, what's this? How darest thou insult
Pelasgian soil, ay, and Pelasgia's sons?
Or dost thou think thou'rt come to a land where none
But women dwell? Barbarian to Greek
Is used to be more humble. Thou wilt find
That thy wild shooting misses the just scope
And aim of action, reckoning up thy wrong.

He. I take thee at thy word and ask thee, where
I reach beyond what law and justice warrant?

Pe. First thou'rt an alien; yet most ignorant
Of what becomes thee in that quality.

He. Who? I? I found what had been lost: no more.

Pe. Have not you aliens your officers?
And which of these didst thou bespeak?

He. Hermes,
The Lord of trover.

Pe. O! are Gods thy patrons,
And dost thou serve them with dishonour?

He. I
Pay worship to the Gods of mighty Nile.

Pe. And ours are nought, if I hear thee aright.

He. Look you, these women are mine and in my power:
Let me see him who dares to take them from me.

Pe. Lay hands upon them at thy peril.

He. This
To a stranger! 'Tis not hospitable.

Pe. Tush!
I waste no courtesy on aliens
Who violate the sanctuary of the Gods.

He. Ægyptus' sons shall hear of this.

Pe. I care not.

He. Good: but that I may make a clear report—
As heralds should—what shall I say? By whom
Am I dismissed, sent empty-handed back,
These women—cousins, close in blood withal—
Taken from me? Not that weight of evidence
Will here determine in what sense the doom
That Ares must pronounce shall be decreed,
Nor are the damages assessed in coin

And there an end. No: long ere that can be
Many a tall fellow first must bite the dust
And lives be gasped away with writhing of limbs.

Pe. Why should I tell thee who I am? In time
Thou'lt learn my name; thou and thy fellows too.
As for these women, went they willingly,
Were they content, thou might'st lead them away,
Could'st thou show cause that piety allows.
But now the sovran people of this realm
Have with one voice established their decree
Never to yield their virtue up to force.
And through and through that act the nail is driven
So that it standeth fast. Thou hast my answer;
Not writ in folded tablets, nor yet sealed
In any secret scroll: but overt, the plain speech
Of an unfettered tongue. Now—quit my sight.

He. May victory and power that victory gives
Be with the men.

Pe. Oh, ye will find men here,
Trust me, no bousers of thin barley-brew.

Exit HERALD *and his followers.*

And now with your handmaidens all of you
Walk boldly to the city. 'Tis well fenced
And locked with deep device of wards and towers.
Many fair dwellings are maintainéd there
At the public charge. With no illiberal hand
Myself am lodged. Here ye may share a house
With others, or, if it likes ye, live alone.
The best is at your service: take your choice
And let it be the fairest ye can find:
'Twill cost ye nothing. Look upon myself
And the whole body of the citizens,
Whose mandate this effects, as your protectors.
More powerful patrons ye've no need to ask.

Ch. Sire, may your great courtesy
Plenteously rewarded be.
Please you now to send to us
Our brave father, Danaus;
His wise forethought points our way;
Where he counsels we obey.
He will choose us our abode
In some kindly neighbourhood.
For so it is, strange speech, strange ways
Are a mark for men's dispraise.
Happier be our lot: may we
Dwell with honour in your land
Free from hatred, censure-free. *Exit* KING.
Captives of the bow and spear,
Yet not uncherished, not less dear,
Each in order take your stand
By your mistresses, for you
Are our maiden retinue
That Danaus in his day of power
Gave us for a queenly dower.

Enter DANAUS *with armed guard.*

Da. Children, unto the Argives offer prayers,
Blood-offerings and libations, as to Gods
Olympian! for our saviours they are
Past question. When I told their magistrates
How ye were used, their friendly hearts received
My tidings in such wise as to our kin
Shall prove a draught of bitter wine. Myself
This body-guard of spearmen they assigned,
Both that I might be honourably attended,
And lest by sudden sword-stroke I should fall
Ere they could rescue me, unto their land
A burden and a curse for ever. Wherefore
Let gratitude to them hold in your hearts
The highest place and set your course. Moreover
To much already graven there add this
Paternal precept. Time assays the worth
Of things unknown; and every tongue is busy
With a new-comer's reputation, not
Oftenest for good: a word and 'tis bespattered.
Shame me not in your youth when all men's eyes
Will look your way. 'Tis difficult to guard
The tender fruit. It is desired of men
With patient watchings—for desire is human—
Of feathered fowls and beasts that walk the earth.
So with the body: when 'tis melting ripe,
Trust Cypris but the world will hear of it
If once she find the orchard-gate unlatched.
Then at the loveliness of virgin bloom
An arrow winged with dangerous charm is shot
From every roving eye, vanquished at sight
By irresistible desire. Let not
Our wills succumb to that the which to escape
We bore much toil, ploughed many perilous seas
On shipboard: neither let us work ourselves
Shame and confusion, to mine enemies
Triumph and very bliss. A double choice
Is ours. Pelasgus and the State at large
Each offer us a home; and both are free.
You see Fate throws us sixes. It remains
That ye your father's precepts strictly keep,
Counting your virtue dearer than your lives.

Chorus

In all things else may the Olympian Gods
Prosper us. For my youth fear not, my father,
In this ripe season of my beauty. If
The Gods have not appointed some new thing
I mean to walk where heretofore I trod.

Set forward to the city then
And to her Gods give thanks,
Lords of their bliss within her walls
Or dwellers by the banks

Of Erasinus old. And you,
Dear maids, our music sweet
Accompany with clapping hands
And dance of rhythmic feet!

Our song is of Pelasgia's town,
And we will hymn no more
The fullness of the fluctuant Nile,
But placid streams that pour

Deep draughts for thirsty lips, and cheer
The land with childish mirth,
Turning stiff tracts of stubborn ground
To soft and fertile earth.

Chaste Artemis, watch over us,
And love come in tender guise,
Not forced by Cytherea's might;
We wish our foes that prize.

Semi-Chorus. But we forget not Cypris. Let none deem
Our harmless song is meant in her dispraise.
For she with Hera sways
The heart of Zeus, and he is Lord Supreme.
The subtle Goddess hath her rites; with young
Desire playing at his mother's side;
Nor less Persuasion to whose charming tongue
No boon that heart can give or worth approves
May be denied.
Yea, music hath her share
In Aphrodite's Empire fair,
Music with all the train of whispering Loves.

Semi-Ch. All is fulfilled as Destiny decrees,
And Zeus is great: it is not given to men
To thwart his purposes
Or reach beyond the bounds that he hath set.
Pray rather, then,
That once the rite be said,
This marriage that we so much dread
May bring more bliss than ever wife knew yet.

Semi-Ch. May the great Zeus grant that I ne'er
Wed with a son of King Ægyptus.

Semi-Ch. Yea,
That boon were best of all; and yet thy prayer
Would move a will that none can sway.

Semi-Ch. And thou can'st not discern futurity.

Semi-Ch. Can I behold the mind of Zeus? Can I
Look into that unfathomable deep?
Due measure when thou prayest thou should'st keep.

Semi-Ch. Where lies the mark that may not be o'ertrod?

Semi-Ch. Search not too far the purposes of God.

Chorus

Zeus is King: may he decree
I be bounden to no lord
Loathed for lust and cruelty!
Mighty and most gentle, he
With remedial touch restored
Io in her misery
To calm of mind from sorrow free.

And may he this woman's war
Crown with victory. Life and Fate
Demand that we exact no more
Than that good preponderate.
It contents me then, whate'er
The judgment which the Gods approve
If there be embodied there
Justice which my prayers could move.

Exeunt.

THE PERSIANS

DRAMATIS PERSONAE

ATOSSA, *Queen of Persia, widow of Darius and mother of Xerxes*
A MESSENGER
THE GHOST OF DARIUS
XERXES
CHORUS OF PERSIAN ELDERS, *the Ministers of State*

An open place before the Tomb of DARIUS.

Chorus

We are the faithful ministers
Of Persia's absent sons,
That marched away to Hellas;
Their golden mansions,
Rich with all wealth and splendour,
Are in our trust and care,
For the great king, King Xerxes,
Darius' son and heir,
Chose us as wise men well in years
The realm for him to hold;
But for his homeward progress
His host a-gleam with gold,
The boding heart is harried
With auguries of ill:
Asia is stripped of manhood;
A young king hath his will:
But to this metropolitan
Proud siege of Persia's kings
No runner comes, no rider
Good news or bad news brings.
To Susa and Ecbatana
They bade a long farewell;
They saw behind them sink from sight
Old Kissia's citadel;
And some rode out on horseback,
And some in long ships sailed;
Stout plodders closing up their ranks
The footmen strode all-mailed.
Amistres hasteth with them,
And great Artaphrenes,
Astaspes, Megabates,
Lords of rich satrapies,
Kings on whose throne a greater
Its majesty uprears,
Marshals of an uncounted host,
Bowmen and cavaliers,
They sweep forever onward;
Their daunting looks dismay,
And jubilant are their high hearts
For joy of coming fray.
Lord of the bow, Imaeus,
Sosthenes, charioteer,
Artembares, the rider bold
Whom charging squadrons cheer,
Masistres and Pharandaces;
With many a doughty fere
Whom Nile, great nourisher of men,
Sent forth; Pegastogon,
Egyptian born; Susiskanes,
And Artames, whose wone
Is sacred Memphis; there he rules;
And Ariomardus, lord
Or Thebes, that ancient child of Time;
Marsh-folk to pull aboard
The galleys, fearsome combatants
Past count; and in their train
The langour-loving Lydians,
Lords of the Asian main.
Two royal men command them,
Arcteus of fair renown,
And the great lord Metrogathes;
And their all-golden town,
Sardis, hath sent forth men that ride
On cars of aspect dread,
With double yoke of horses,
And triple harnessèd:
And Tharubis and Mardon,
Of Tmolus' holy hill
Near neighbours both, have ta'en an oath
(The which may heaven fulfil),
To cast the yoke on Hellas
That holdeth freedom dear;
They are the stuff of iron tough,
Hard anvils to the spear.
Then come the Mysian slingers;
And golden Babylon
Hath sent a mingled, motley host,
Endlessly winding on;
And some are sailors of the fleet,
And others draw the bow;
All Asia pours her falchion-men;
The great king bids them go.
Ay, they are gone! The bloom, the rose,
The pride of Persian earth:
And with a mighty longing

The land that gave them birth,
Asia, their nursing mother, mourns;
And day succeeds to day,
And wives and little ones lose heart,
Sighing the time away.

I grant you that our royal host,
The wallèd city's scourge,
Hath long since reached the neighbour coast
That frowns across the surge;
Hath roped with moorèd rafts the strait,
Their path the heaving deck,
At Athamantid Helle's Gate
Upon the sea's proud neck
Bolting a yoke from strand to strand:
And Asia's hordes, I grant,
Outnumber the uncounted sand:
Our king is valiant:
He shepherdeth a mighty flock,
God's benison therewith,
Till iron arms all Hellas lock,
Port, isle and pass and frith.
And at his word leap captains bold
Ready to do or die,
Being himself of the race of gold,
Equal with God most high.
The dragon-light of his black eyes
Darts awe, as to express
The lord of mighty argosies
And minions numberless.
So, seated in his Syrian car,
He leads 'gainst spear and pike
His sagittaries: death from far
Their wounding arrows strike.
Meseemeth none of mortal birth
That tide of men dare brave,
A sea that delugeth the earth,
A vast resistless wave.
No! Persia's matchless millions
No human power can quell,
Such native valour arms her sons,
Such might incomparable!
For Fate from immemorial age
Chose out her sons for power:
Bade them victorious war to wage
And breach the bastioned tower:
In chivalry to take delight
Where clashing squadrons close:
Kingdoms and polities the might
Of their strong arm o'erthrows.
They gaze on ocean lawns that leap
With bickering billows gray
Swept by fierce winds; their myriads sweep
Ocean's immense highway,
Where, leashed with cables fibre-fine,
Their buoyant galleys bridge
The rough waves of the sundering brine
From ridge to crested ridge.
And yet what man, of woman born,
Outwits the guile of God?
The pit He digs what foot may scorn,
Though with all lightness shod?
For ruin first with laughing face
Lures man into the net,
Whence never wight of mortal race
Leapt free and scatheless yet.

These are the thoughts that fret and fray
The sable garment of my soul.
Shall Persia's host sing "Wellaway,"
With universal shout of dole:
Shall Susa hear, of manhood shorn?
Shall this imperial city mourn?

Yea, and shall Kissia's castle-keep
With answering note of grief reply?
Shall huddled women wail and weep
Bearing the burthen to that cry,
While torn in rents their raiment falls
And tattered hang their costly shawls?

Not one is left: all they that drive
Or ride proud steeds, all footmen stout,
Like swarming bees that quit the hive,
With him that leads the dance, went out;
Shackling two shores across the sea
They thrust a floating promontory.

But beds are wet with many a tear
Where late the longed-for love lay warm;
New luxury of grief is dear
To our fair Persians: some mailed form
She kissed "Goodbye," her love, her own,
Each misses, left in wedlock lone.

Men of Persia, here in council, seated round this ancient roof,
Sounding deep, for sore the need is, let us put it to the proof,
How it fareth with King Xerxes, great Darius' golden heir,
Lord of lieges, mighty dynast, who made Persia rich and fair;
Whether conquest wingeth onward with the drawing of the bow
Or the ashen-hafted spear-head crowns with victory the foe.
But, behold, a light that shineth with august and godlike rays,
Royal Mother of King Xerxes, regnant Queen of my young days;
Rapidly her chariot rolleth; in the dust I lay me prone;
Homage, love and loyal duty proffer we in unison.

Enter the ATOSSA.

Queen-Dowager of Persian dames deep-veiled,
Mother of Xerxes and Darius' wife,
Spouse of a god, and not less justly hailed
As to one godlike authoress of life
Unless the power that prospered us of yore
Now with our armies goeth out no more!

Atossa. Therefore am I come forth into the day
From golden courts and that one chamber fair

Where in my arms the great Darius lay.
My heart too feels the canker-fret of care;
Good friends, I have a story for your ears
That wakes within a train of haunting fears.

What if great wealth should scatter in his stride
The prosperous glory that Darius reared,
God being with him? Doubts new-felt divide
My mind. Possessions must not be revered
Save as men use them; yet they that have none
How poor! To them what lustre hath the sun?

For in themselves great riches are not wrong:
That's not my fear: but when the master's eye
Through absence fails, the thought in me is strong,
A house is blind except its lord be by.
Herein, grave sirs, interpret and advise;
In your sage counsel all my wisdom lies.

Ch. Be sure of this, Queen of this land of ours,
There never was nor ever can be need
To ask us twice for help by word or deed,
So far as ripe experience empowers
Leal hearts to proffer guidance: in our breast
There is no thought save how to serve thee best.

At. I am much conversant with dreams at night
Since with his army my dear son is gone
To ravage and lay waste Ionia,
But nothing yet so startlingly distinct
As yesternight, as you shall forthwith hear.
For there appeared to me in bright apparel
Two women; one with Persian robes adorned,
The other in the Dorian garb; and each
Taller in stature than are women now,
Faultlessly fair, both sisters of one house.
The first in Hellas dwelt, by sortilege
Assigned; the other lived in Barbary.
And so it was, that in my dream methought
There was some kind of quarrel 'twixt the twain,
Which, when my dear son was apprised of it,
He would compose and make them live as friends.
And so he harnessed them to a chariot
Lashing their necks to the yoke. And the tall form
Clad in our raiment answered to the rein;
But the other struggled; tore the tackle up
And without bit or bridle breaking loose
Snapped the strong yoke asunder. My son fell;
And suddenly his father stood beside him,
Even Darius, sorry for his fall.
This is the vision I beheld last night.
But when I rose and in fair-flowing stream
Had washed my hands, so cleansed for sacrifice
I stood before an altar, purposing
To make my offering of the elements
To the Divine Forfenders, whose indeed
The office is. And, lo, an eagle fled
To Phoebus' burning brazier! Good my friends,
When I saw that I was struck dumb with fear.
And presently a falcon flew at him,
Beat him about the body with its wings,
And with its claws his proud crest-feathers plucked.
And strange—and passing strange—the eagle quailed
Nor dared at all retaliate. What I saw
Filled me with dread and will affright your ears.
Well do ye know that if our son succeed
He will become the wonder of the world;
And even if he fail, there is no law
Can call him to account; but unimpaired,
Life granted him, his throne is o'er this land.

Ch. Mother, we would not by aught we might say
Alarm unduly or raise hopes too high.
Better approach the gods, better go pray,
If shapes of ugly seeming haunt thine eye.
Beseech them to deliver thee from ill,
And for thyself, thy children and the State
And all thou lovest good things to fulfil.
This done, with drink-offerings propitiate
Earth and the dead; and then entreat thy spouse,
Darius, whom thou say'st that yesternight
Thou did'st behold, for thee and for thy house
Up from the underworld into the light
To send good luck, and adverse things blindfold
Muffle in nether darkness. Not untaught
By my prophetic soul have I made bold
To speak, convinced so best may good be sought.

At. Well, come what may, my dream hath found in thee
A first expounder loyal to our son
And all our house. May fair as fair can be
Befall. I'll get me home. All shall be done
In honour of the gods and the dear dead
That dwell beneath the earth, as thou hast said.
But, good my friends, tell me where Athens lies?

Ch. Far, far away, westwards—beyond these skies—
Where kingly Helios pales his golden fires.

At. Is that the land that our dear son desires,
Gone on so long a chase, to make his prey?

Ch. Assuredly: if Athens own his sway
All Hellas must before his footstool bend.

At. Is't a great people? Can this Athens send
'Gainst him a numerous armament?

Ch. We Medes
Have cause to know their army by its deeds.

At. Are they great archers then?

Ch. Princess, not so:
'Tis not the arrow's point, the sinewy bow,
That makes them to be feared: stand they or charge
They are close fighters with the spear and targe.

At. What more of mark? Have they much wealth laid by?

Ch. A vein of silver is their treasury.

At. Who is the ruler of this people? Who
Lord of their levies and their revenue?

Ch. Subject they are not unto any man:
They say "slave" sorts not with "Athenian."

At. Have they no master? The less likely they
To stand their ground against invaders.

Ch. Nay,
Darius' armament this kingless folk
For all its spendour and its numbers broke

And utterly destroyed.
At. There's matter here
For anxious questionings, not without fear,
For all whose sons went up 'gainst Athens.
Ch. Thou,
O Queen, if that I err not, shalt even now
Hear the authentic story. Here is a man
Able to tell us how the Persians ran
In this momentous race; and, whether good
Or ill his tidings, he brings certitude.

Enter a MESSENGER.

Messenger. Ye habitations of broad Asia,
And thou, O land of Persia, receipt
Of affluent wealth, how much and how great glory
Hath perished at a blow! Of Persian men
The flower is fall'n and vaded! Woe is me!
Ill is it to be the bearer of bad tidings,
And yet, for hard necessity constrains,
I am to cloak up nothing, Persians—tell
The woeful tale to the end! All's lost; the power
Of Barbary is utterly destroyed.
Ch. O unimagined ruin, dark and drear
And fathomlessly deep!
Weep, men of Persia, while ye hear
And harken while ye weep!
Me. Yea, we have fought it to a finish—I
Thought not to see the day of my return.
Ch. O life! too tedious pilgrimage
To the last span outdrawn!
On fading eyes waxed dim with weary age
Was this dark day to dawn?
Me. Persians, the story that I have to tell
Is not a thing caught up from others' lips;
All ills prepared for our discomfiture
Myself was witness of; yea, had my share.
Ch. Vain, vain the arrow-blast,
The tumult of loud war!
Vain all the missiles Asia idly cast
On Hellas' fatal shore!
Me. The bodies of men miserably slain
Lie heaped upon the shore of Salamis
And glut full many a creek and cove thereby.
Ch. The bodies of the men that died
The breakers buffet, the billows beat!
Tinct with the azure of the sea-salt tide,
Rolled with the wreckage of a shattered fleet!
Me. There was no help in arrow or in bow!
Our whole fleet foundered when their warships rammed.
Ch. Howl! Cry aloud! Call down upon the foe
Ages of anguish and inexorable woe!
All evil that their hearts devised they wrought!
Mourn for the mighty host that they have brought to nought!
Me. O Salamis! thou execrable name!
Athens! My spirit mourns remembering thee!
Ch. Athens! for ever hateful to thy foes!
Written in memory's book for thee the record glows,
The long, long roll, past count, of them that mourn
In every Persian home husbandless and forlorn!
At. I have kept silence long; calamity
Hath struck me dumb: for this surpassing grief
May not be told and stops the mouth of question.
But men must bear the troubles Heaven sends.
Compose thyself then; and this dire disaster,
Much as thou mournest it, fully unfold.
Who hath not fallen? And whom must we lament
Among the leaders of the people? Who
Of titled and of sceptred rank hath left
A gap among our noblest by his death?
Me. Xerxes himself is among the living; he
Beholds the light of day.
At. A light indeed
To me and all my house! A glad day-break
After black mirk of night.
Me. But Artembares
Chief of ten thousand horse, is brayed and beat
All up and down the sharp Silenian shore.
And Dadakas, the Chiliarch, struck by a spear
Dropped like an airy diver in the sea.
And Tenagon, most noble Tenagon,
True Bactrian to the core, is a wanderer now
Round Ajax' wave-washed, ocean-echoing isle.
Lilaeus, Arsames and Argétes
Fell fighting, and are ground against the rocks
That gird the steep holm where the ring-doves breed:
And Arcteus, neighbour once of inland streams,
Founts of Egyptian, Nilus, and Adeues,
Yea, and Pharnuchus, weighted with the load
Of ponderous armour—three from out one ship—
Plunged overboard. The Chrysian Matallus,
Lord of ten thousand fighting men, went down.
And he who marshalled thirty thousand horse,
All black, his dark, flame-coloured, bushy beard
Dyed gules in his own gore. The Arabian
Magus, and Artames the Bactrian,
Far from the rough, stern land he chose for home,
Perished in those disastrous seas. There sank
Amistris; and Amphistreus cast away
His spear. And Ariomardus, good as brave,
To the great grief of Sardis met his death.
And Seisames the Mysian is slain:
And Tharubis, of five times fifty ships
Grand Admiral—he was Lernæan-born
And beautiful withal—is lost. Alack!
He gave his life in an unlucky cause.
The bravest of the brave, Syennesis,
Generalissimo of the Cilicians,
A man whose splendid valour cost more blood
To the enemy than any single foe,
Died gloriously. Thus much have I told
Touching the captains of the host. And now
Some few disasters, where they came in crowds,
I will relate.
At. This is the very crown
And summit of all sorrow. For proud Persia
Direst humiliation: shriek on shriek
Shall follow on thy news. But retrace thy steps;
Tell me how many sail the Hellenes had
That they dared close upon the Persian power
And ram us ship for ship.
Me. Ah, had it lain

With numbers to decide, be well assured
Victory had crowned the fleet of Barbary!
The whole Hellenic navy was no more
Than ten divisions of thirty sail apiece,
And but a tithe of them in the fighting-line!
Xerxes, it is a point within my knowledge,
Went into action with a thousand sail:
Two hundred ships and seven of high speed
Is the reputed reckoning. Accuse us not
That in this fight we failed to play the man:
A God it was who broke our power, weighed down
The judgment scale with no impartial hand.
There are divinities that keep the realm
Of divine Pallas safe.
At. Is Athens safe?
Is not the city sacked?
Me. Ay, but her men!
They live, and therefore her defence is sure.
At. Tell me how first the fleets encountered; who
Began the attack, the Hellenes or my son
Exulting in the number of his ships?
Me. Princess, the first beginner of all the woes
That afterwards ensued, though whence he came
None knoweth, was some genius of wrath,
Some wicked spirit such as lures men on
To their destruction. There came a man,
A Hellene, from the Athenian host, and he
On this wise spake unto Xerxes, thy son—
"If there shall come a dusk and darksome night
The Hellenes will not tarry; leaping down
Upon their rowers' benches they will pull
For safety, hither, thither scattering
In secret flight." And when thy son heard that
He instantly—perceiving not the guile
Of the Hellene nor the spite of jealous Gods—
Made known to all the captains of his ships
That when the burning sun should cease to beam
Across the world, and glimmering twilight took
The court and curtilage of serene air,
The main armada must disperse and form
Three squadrons line abreast, blocking the exits
And narrow channels where the salt waves churn;
The residue to compass Ajax' Isle.
Then, if the Hellenes turned to flee from doom
By privily withdrawing in the dark,
Not one could get away, but their whole fleet
Must fall into our hands. So spake the king
In sanguine mood, with not the least surmise
Of the divine purpose, presently fulfilled.
And not at all in any disarray
But with a disciplined obedience,
They made their dinner ready, every seaman
Lashing his oar-shank to the well-turned thole;
And when the sun waxed dim and night came on,
Each master oarsman went aboard his ship
And every captain of the fighting crews,
And down the long lines of those ships of war
Squadron to squadron spake right cheerily,
Hailing each other; not a ship of them
Lost her allotted station; and all night
The captains kept them cruising to and fro.
And night passed, and the Hellenic armament
Made no attempt to steal away unseen.
But when with her white horses day shone fair
And overspread the broad and ample earth,
There rose and rang from the Hellenic host
A roar of voices musical with psalms;
And loudly from the island precipices
Echo gave back an answering cheer. Thereat
Seeing their judgment grievously at fault,
Fear fell on the barbarians. Not for flight
Did the Hellenes then chant that inspiring hymn,
But resolutely going into battle,
Whereto the trumpet set all hearts on fire.
The word was given, and, instantaneously,
Oars smote the roaring waves in unison
And churned the foam up. Soon their whole fleet appeared;
The port division thrown out like a horn
In precise order; then the main of them
Put out against us. We could plainly hear
The thunder of their shouting as they came.
"Forth, sons of Hellas! free your land, and free
Your children and your wives, the native seats
Of Gods your fathers worshipped and their graves.
This is a bout that hazards all ye have."
And verily from us in the Persian tongue
There rose an answering roar; the long suspense
Was ended. In an instant, ship smote ship,
With thrust of armoured prow. The first to ram
Was a Greek; that impact carried clean away
A tall Phoenician's poop. Then all came on,
Each steering forthright for a ship of ours.
At first the encountering tide of Persians held;
But caught in the narrows, crowded without sea-room,
None could help other; nay, they fell aboard
Their own ships, crashing in with beak of bronze,
Till all their oars were smashed. But the Hellenes
Rowed round and round, and with sure seamanship
Struck where they chose. Many of ours capsized,
Until the very sea was hid from sight
Choked up with drifting wreckage and drowning men.
The beaches and low rocks were stacked with corpses:
The few barbarian vessels still afloat,
Fouling each other, fled in headlong rout.
But they with broken oars and splintered spars
Beat us like tunnies or a draught of fish,
Yea, smote men's backs asunder; and all the while
Shrieking and wailing hushed the ocean surge,
Till night looked down and they were rapt away.
But, truly, if I should discourse the length
Of ten long days I could not sum our woes.
There never yet 'twixt sunrise and sunset
Perished so vast a multitude of men.
At. Woe! woe! An ocean of calamity
Hath broke on Persia and all Barbary.
Me. But this is not the half. A grief ensued
So heavy, its forerunner kicks the beam.
At. Oh, can misfortune come in hatefuller shape?
What spite of malice adverse to our host
Sweeps through some more immeasurable arc

The moving finger that metes out our woes?
Me. The prime of Persian manhood, men who had
True greatness in their souls, illustrious born,
And ever among the first in the king's trust,
Died miserably a most inglorious death.
At. Good friends, was ever woman so accursed
With evil fortune? Tell me how they died.
Me. There is an island opposite the shores
Of Salamis, a little, wretched isle,
With never a safe cove where ships may ride,
But Pan, who loves the choric dance, haunts there,
Footing it lightly on the wave-washed strand.
Thither the king despatched them, with intent
That when the enemy, forced to abandon ship,
Sought safety on that isle, they might with ease
Put all the host of Hellas to the sword,
And rescue their own comrades from the salt
Sea-friths. But he judged ill the event. For when
The Gods the glory of the sea-fight gave
Unto the Hellenes, armed to the teeth they sprang
Ashore and compassed the whole island round,
So that they knew not where to turn. And many
They battered to death with stones: some they shot
dead
With arrows: finally, to make an end,
Rushed in and finished off their butcher's work
Hacking their helpless victims limb from limb,
Until not one of them was left alive.
And Xerxes, when he saw that depth beyond
All depths of sorrow, wailed aloud. For he sat
Upon a throne conspicuous to the host,
On a high hill beside the open sea.
There with rent robes and a heart-piercing cry
Straightway he gave the signal to his troops
Drawn up upon the shore and let them go
In wild, disordered flight. This further stroke
Of fortune's malice fell for thee to mourn.
At. O wicked spirit! How did'st thou beguile
Our Persians' hearts! How bitter a revenge
Upon illustrious Athens was vouchsafed
To our dear son! Not all that Barbary lost
Beforetime on the field of Marathon
Sufficed! But, thinking to repay in kind
All that we suffered there, he hath drawn on
A deluge of immeasurable woe!
But tell me of the ships that 'scaped destruction,
Where didst thou leave these? Hast sure news of
them?
Me. The captains of the remnant hoisted sail
And ran before the wind, a rabble rout.
But the remainder of our army perished
In the Boeotian country, some of thirst
For lack of solace of refreshing springs.
We that were left, taking no time to breathe,
Crossed into Phocis and the Locrian land
And the Maliac gulf where the Spercheius flows
Watering a broad plain with his gracious stream.
Achaia and the Thessalian cities then
Opened to us their gates, but we were sore
Straitened for lack of meat. And there the most
Perished of thirst and hunger, for, God wot,
We must contend with both. Anon we came
To the Magnesian country and the coasts
Of Macedonia by the Axian frith
And Bolbe's reedy marshes and the range
Pangaean—country of Edonia.
And on that very night God caused a frost
Out of due season: Strymon's holy stream
Was frozen over. And many, that heretofore
Denied the Gods, thanked heaven upon their
knees,
Yea, bowed themselves to earth and sky. And when
They had made an end of calling on the Gods
The host began to cross on the firm ice.
And whoso crossed before the beams of God
Were scattered wide, reached safety. But anon
The round, bright sun with blazing rays of fire
Made right across the stream a waterway,
Thawing the midst thereof with glowing heat.
And then they fell in heaps: he happiest
Who soonest gasped away the breath of life.
All that were left, all that had won to safety,
Crossed Thrace and in the teeth of fearful hardships,
That desperate retreat accomplished, came—
But they were few indeed—to their own home.
Behold these things are merest truth: but much
I leave unsaid; many and grievous woes
The wrath of God hurled down upon our host.
Exit MESSENGER.

Ch. Spirit whose dispensation is too hard,
Thou hast set a heavy foot upon our necks,
Ground Persia in the dust!
At. My heart is sick;
I mourn a vanished host! Visions of the night
How plainly ye portended woe! And you,
How fondly ye interpreted my dream!
Natheless, since here at least your oracle
Fails not, I will go pray, first to the Gods;
Then I will take the sacred elements—
Offerings to earth, oblations to the dead—
And come to you again. Things past I know;
But I would fain inquire if what's to come
Promises better fortune. Lend your aid:
With men of trust true counsel take, I charge ye;
And, if our son return in the meantime,
Console him and escort him to our house,
Lest that on woe there follow further woe.
Exit ATOSSA.

Chorus

O Zeus, thou art king! There is none thee beside!
Thou hast shattered our host and humbled our pride!
Thou hast darkened with grief the light of thy day
O'er Susa and Ecbatana!
They have rent their thin veils, their kerchiefs
thread-drawn,
Our delicate mourners; their wimples of lawn
They have drenched with salt tears; the young wife
newly-wed
Looks out for her lord, but he comes not; her bed,
Laid soft with fair linen, where love had his bliss,
Standeth vacant; cold sorrow their banqueter is;
But they rise up an-hungered, though they sit long;
And I too o'er the fallen would utter my song.

This earth, this Asia, wide as east from west,
Mourns—empty, of her manhood dispossessed.
Xerxes the King led forth his war-array!
Xerxes the King hath cast his host away!
Xerxes the King (Oh King unwise!)
Steered in the wake of doom his orient argosies!
How fell it that Darius, lord of the bow,
In Susa long ago,
Fair fortune had? That then
He who ruled Persia won the hearts of men?

The ships, the swarthy ships, with brow of gloom
And wide wings woven on the weary loom,
Landsmen and mariners haled to that far shore!
The ships, the black ships whelmed them evermore!
They struck, they split, they filled,
They sank: and, oh, death's throes Ionian
vengeance stilled.
And now by plain and pass, rude, wild and bare,
In the frore Thracian air,
After long wandering,
Scarce 'scaped with life, comes home our lord
the King.

But they on that wild water,
Firstlings of death and slaughter,
Roam, where the long waves lash Kychrean sands;
Roam, but no wave shall lift them,
Nor ebb nor flood-tide drift them
To this dear earth beloved above all lands.
Wide as the sky, and deep
As those dark waters sweep,
Wail! let grief gnaw your heart, and wring your
hands!

Combed with no tender combing,
Where angry waves break foaming,
Children of Ocean's unpolluted tide
Flesh their dumb mouths, and tear
The dead men once so fair:
Old eyes are wet whose tears Time long since dried;
The sire weeps his lost son,
The home its goodman gone,
And all the woeful tale is bruited far and wide.

They pay no more tribute; they bow them no more!
The word of power is not spoken
By the princes of Persia; their day is o'er,
And the laws of the Medes are broken
Through Asia's myriad-peopled land;
For the staff is snapped in the King's right hand.

And a watch is not set on the free, frank tongue,
Yea, liberty's voice speaks loud;
And the yoke is loosed from the neck that was wrung
And the back to dominion bowed:
For the earth of Ajax isle is red
With the blood of Persia's noble dead!

Enter ATOSSA.

At. Good friends, the heart that hath found
trouble knows
That when calamity is at the flood
We shake at shadows; but, if once the tide
Flow fair, and fortune send a prospering wind,
We cannot think that it will change. To me
All prayers I offer now are full of dread,
And voices loud, but not with victory,
Sound in mine ears; so fell a stroke of fortune
Dismays my soul. Therefore am I returned,
Not as of late with chariots and with pomp;
I bring libations due from son to sire,
Meet for propitiation; gifts that please
Dead bodies in their graves. Milk, white and pure,
And crystal honey cropped from bee-searched
flowers,
And cool cups drawn from virgin founts; and here,
Pressed from wild nature's bosom, is strong wine,
The jocund youngling of an ancient stem;
And I have oil of olive, amber-clear,
Sweet essence of a never-fading tree,
And wreathéd blossoms—children all of earth
That yieldeth every fruit. Then, dear my friends,
Accompany with song acceptable
These luscious draughts that soothe the silent dead,
And forth from his sepulchral monument
Call up Darius' spirit. The cup earth drinks
I will pour out to the Gods of the underworld.

Chorus

Queen of Persia, chief in worth,
'Neath the chambers of the earth,
Send thy rich libations streaming;
We with prayers of holy seeming
Will beseech the dead that there
They may find acceptance fair.
Gods infernal, pure and holy,
Earth and Hermes, melancholy
Lord of death and gloom and night,
Send his soul up to the light.
He will heal—point undismayed
Where grief's far horizons fade.

Peer of the Gods, whose kingly state
Is evermore felicity!
Shifting as the shocks of fate
Sinks and soars our endless cry
Uttered in an ancient tongue:
Hearest thou the shades among?

All ye gods of souls earth-bound,
Hearken! Earth, break up thy sod!
Grant us sight from thy dark ground
Of Susa's son and Persia's god!
To such an ample spirit ne'er
Persian earth gave sepulchre.

Dear was the man; dear is his burial-mound!
A power sleeps here, whose influence shall not fade!
Oh, where he sits sole King 'mong Kings discrowned,
Aidoneus, dim Aidoneus, speed Darius' shade!

In wantonness of heart he ne'er made war,
Nor lost a world wasting the lives of men;

They hailed him their God-given counsellor;
God-given he was, and great was Persia's glory then.

Old majesty! Great Padishah!
Come forth, and from thy barrow high,
Show the white plume of thy tiar,
Thy buskin dipped in crocus-dye!
Unclouded spirit, morning-clear,
King—Sire—Darius! reappear!

Griefs thy glory never knew,
Lord of our Lord, thy coming stay.
A mist hath fallen of Stygian hue;
Persia's youth is cast away!
Unclouded spirit, morning-clear,
King—Sire—Darius! reappear!

Thou, whose passing nations wept,
Wherefore hath ambition swept
Worlds that thou didst hold in fee,
Empire, awe and admiralty,
In one headlong ruin borne?
Ships perfidious, ships foresworn,
Crewless, oarless, scallop-scaled,
Ye your pride to Hellas vailed,
Hidden from the sight of suns
That gild her golden galleons!

The Ghost of DARIUS *ascends from his tomb.*

Darius. Trusty and well-beloved! Comrades of mine
When we were young together; now most grave
Signors of Persia, what afflicts the realm?
Earth groans and jars and frets with fevered pulse;
I see my consort standing by my tomb,
And verily I am afraid. Withal,
The cup of kind remembrance, poured in prayer,
I have received. And ye make lamentation
Beside my sepulchre in such shrill key
As calls up spirits: yea, with piteous cries
Summon me from my grave; and wayleave thence
Is hard to come by; for the infernal Gods
Love better to hold fast than to let go.
Nevertheless, with them have I prevailed,
And ye behold me! Haste! my time is short
And I would not offend. What aileth Persia?
What strange, what heavy stroke hath smitten her?

Ch. I dare not meet thy gaze: I fear
To speak what must offend thine ear;
With veiléd eyes, I bow me prone,
As at the footstool of thy throne!

Da. Know that by strong persuasion of thy grief
I am ascended from the shades. Be brief;
Put awe and forms of courtly speech away,
And utter boldly all thou hast to say.

Ch. Thou askest speech of me, and I
Fear to do that courtesy;
At thy bidding to impart
Tidings which must grieve thy heart.

Da. Since thine old awe is not to be enforced,
Good Queen, dear partner death alone divorced
From spousal joys, though thee the touch of age
Hath changed to outward view, this grief assuage,
These sobs and tears give o'er: take courage then
To speak but one clear word to me; for men
Cast in the mould of frail humanity
Are heirs to all its ills: by land and sea
Evils a-many are reserved for man,
If that Time lengthen out his little span.

At. O of mankind the happiest by far,
While thou didst yet behold the day's bright star,
How enviable in thy life wast thou!
How like a god thy days were passed! And now
I envy thee in death: yea, count it bliss
Not to have lived to search the black abyss,
The bottomless pit of sorrow. Dear my lord,
Darius, to sum all in one brief word;
Persia lies waste—a kingdom desolate!

Da. Speak'st thou of plague and famine! Or is the state
By rancour of domestic faction rent?

At. Nothing of this; her mighty armament
Hath suffered ruin round the Athenian coast.

Da. Tell me; what son of mine led forth our host?

At. Impetuous Xerxes: and to fill his train
Emptied of manhood Asia's vasty plain.

Da. And on this rash attempt, of folly born,
Went he by land or sea?

At. With either horn,
Broadening the thrust of his battle-front, he planned
A double enterprise by sea and land.

Da. How found he means o'er all the realms that lie
'Twixt us and Hellas, plains and mountains high,
To launch on foot an armament so vast?

At. A yoke on Helle's stormy frith he cast
And made a causeway through the unruly sea.

Da. A giant's toil to shut with lock and key
The wrathful Bosphorus!

At. The thing was done!
Methinks, an unseen power helped our son,

Da. A power of might indeed to send him mad!

At. Ay, since the achievement evil issue had!

Da. What fate hath foiled our arms that ye make moan
For fallen men?

At. The fleet is overthrown
And in its ruin whelmed the host on shore.

Da. Then hath my people perished? Hath grim war
Ta'en toll of all?

At. Yea, Susa lieth bare,
And mourns her perished youth, her manhood fair.

Da. Oh, the lost levies! Oh, the bright array
Of proud confederate peoples!

At. Bactria
Through all her clans and Egypt's commonalty
For children lost lift up a bitter cry.

Da. Calamitous adventurer! thine emprise
Hath drained the very sap of thine allies!

At. Xerxes, a lonely man, that few attend,
They say——

Da. What say they? Draws he to an end
Of his long march? And hath he haply found
Some place of safety?

At. Yea, the stormy sound

And the long bridge that spans the sundering sea,
Which when he hailed a happy man was he!
Da. So, he hath crossed the strait and touched the strand
And journeys delicately through the land
Of Asia—or thou hast heard things false and smooth?
At. None challengeth these tidings; they are clear truth
And beyond cavil.
Da. Ah, with how swift stride
Hath come fulfilment of things prophesied!
How on my son hath Zeus in anger sent
The end foretold, which my fears did prevent!
For long ago I knew the Gods would speed
The final consummation of that rede,
And when man, shod with haste and girt with pride,
Beckons his own doom, God is on his side.
And now, methinks, to all men of good will
The fount lies bare whence flowed this broadening ill;
But the event my son too rashly wrought
In the blind arrogance of childish thought.
He dreamed that he could chain, as men chain slaves,
The holy haste of Hellespontine waves,
God's flowing Bosphorus; another measure
Presumed to teach its billows, at his pleasure
Bound them in linkéd fetters hammered fast,
Yea, made a high way, where his army passed.
A mortal man on all the Gods that be
He ventured war; the lordship of the sea,
Poseidon's realm (he judged so much amiss),
Challenged and thought to quell. And was not this
The very madness of a mind diseased?
Prosperity and power and wealth, which eased
The lives of men, my long reign's rich reward,
Is plunder now for some freebooter's sword!
At. All this impetuous Xerxes, over-ruled
By evil men, in their rash counsel schooled,
Learned; for they taught him that thy valour won
Great opulence and wide dominion
For thy succeeding heirs; and 'twas a taunt
Of theirs that he at home was valiant,
But with new wealth no wise increased thy store:
And so detraction oft-repeated bore
Ill fruit: to doom the readiest way he went
And against Hellas launched his armament.
Da. And in all truth the thing that he hath done
Is great in consequence, in memory
Never to be forgotten: such a fall
From power and glory, such a grievous loss
Ne'er yet made Susa empty, since the day
When first King Zeus assigned her pride of place,
Centreing in one man dominion
Over all Asia rich in fleece and flock,
The staff of Empire steady in his hand.
It was a Mede that mastered first her hosts;
His son completed that which he began,
For wisdom laid her hand upon the helm
And caution tempered daring. Third from him
Reigned Cyrus, blest in all he undertook.
He with all friendly powers established peace
On firm foundations. His arm was stretched
Over the land of Lydia, and he
Made Phrygia vassal; all Ionia
He drave before him with the reins of power;
Neither provoked he God to jealous wrath,
So amiable and gracious were his ways.
And Cyrus' fourth son set the host in order;
But the fifth, Mardus, reigning in his stead,
Brought upon fatherland and monarchy
Shame and reproach. And him by subtle craft
Artaphrenes, an honourable man,
Slew in the palace, powerfully helped
By friends resolved upon the deed. And chance
Placed on my head the crown I coveted.
And with great armies I waged many wars,
But ne'er in such calamity involved
The realm: and now Xerxes, my son, because
His thoughts are a young man's thoughts, remembers not
My precepts: for I call ye all to witness,
Friends and coevals, not a man of us
Had ever by misuse of so much power
Made it the instrument of so great a woe.
Ch. O King Darius, whither tends the scope
Of thy discourse? What may we thence conclude?
How may this land of Persia best emerge
From these sore trials and yet see good days?
Da. Wage no more wars 'gainst Hellas, wage no more!
Not though the Medic power were mightier yet;
For verily her soil is her ally.
Ch. How sayst thou "her ally"? How can her soil
Take arms for her and fight upon her side?
Da. The power of numbers, be they ne'er so vast,
She wears away by famine.
Ch. Few and choice
Shall be the muster, with all manner store
Plentifully provided.
Da. They that are left
In Hellas even now shall not escape
Nor see their homes again.
Ch. What hast thou said!
Doth not the armament of Barbary
March out of Europe over Helle's sound?
Da. Few out of many, if the oracles
Of Heaven, by warrant of these late events,
Gain credence: they are individable;
They do not fail in part, nor yet in part
Are they fulfilled. And even were they flawed
With false predictions, Xerxes, in false hopes
Confiding, hath abandoned to their fate
A vast array, the chosen of his host.
Where the Asopus watereth the plain
And maketh fat the deep Boeotian earth
They are cut off; and there is reserved for them
The culmination of their sufferings,
A just reward of pride and godless thoughts,
Because in Hellas they thought it no shame
To strip the ancient statues of the Gods
And burn their temples: yea, cast down the altars,
And from their firm foundations overthrew,
So that they lie in heaps, the builded fanes

Of unseen powers. The evil that they did
Is in like measure meted unto them,
Yea, and more shall be meted; deeper still
Lies the hid vein of suffering; yet a little
And it shall gush forth. So great shall be the carnage
A veritable offering of blood,
Congealed with slaughter, on Plataea's plain,
The dark oblation of the Dorian spear.
High as are heaped the sands their carcases
Shall be hereafter, even to sons' sons,
A silent witness for whoso hath eyes,
That proud thoughts are not for the worm called man;
For pride in blossom, like an ear of corn,
Swells and grows ripe with ruin reaped in tears.
Ye, when ye see these things and think thereon,
Remember Athens and remember Hellas!
Let none of you, that fortune, which is yours
And which God gave, disdaining, set your hearts
On what ye have not, neither in getting more
Pour out like water vast prosperity.
Zeus is a chastener of froward wills
And he correcteth with a heavy hand.
Wherefore be ye instructors of your lord,
And with well-reasoned admonitions teach him
To have a humbler heart and cast away
The sin of pride, for it offendeth God.
And, Xerxes' dear and venerable Mother,
Return to the palace; bring forth fitting raiment
And go therewith to meet thy son: for all
About him, torn by grief, in tatters hangs
The ravelment of his rich-embroidered robe.
Moreover comfort him with gentle words;
Thee only will he hearken. I go hence
Descending through the darkness of the earth.
Farewell, grave elders; in adversity
Find out the soul's true solace day by day;
Where dead men lie wealth nothing profiteth.

The SHADE *of* DARIUS *descends into the tomb.*

Ch. Griefs many, woes that Barbary now endures
And shall endure hereafter wring my heart.

At. O Fate, how endless is the train of sorrow
That entereth my soul! But there's no pang
That gnaws with keener tooth than picturing
My son, his royal person clothed with shame
And trappings of dishonour. I will hence
And take me handsome robes and make essay
To meet him. In the hour of evil fortune
We'll not be false to all we hold most dear.

Exit ATOSSA.

Chorus

All of earth's fullness was ours, all the spacious
Amplitude life yields or law can uphold,
When the unvanquished, the griefless, all-gracious,
Godlike Darius ruled Persia of old.

Glory of conquest and gift of good order
His statutes bestowed and our armies achieved;
Joyous and fresh they came back to our border,
In strength unexhausted, with triumph received.

What commonwealths he captive took
And never once his home forsook
Nor Halys' river passed;
Daughters of Acheloan race,
Where thunder on the shores of Thrace
Strymonian billows vast.

Beyond the marshes stretched his power,
The shadow of a fenced tower
Flung wide o'er Helle's path;
It fell on cities fair that line
Propontis' inlet lacustrine
And stormy Pontus' strath.

His were the surf-beaten islands hard by us,
Where the thrust of the land lifts the wave-flung spray;
Lesbos and Paros and Naxos and Chios
And Samos, with oil of her olive-groves gray;
Myconus's earth paid toll to Darius;
Tenos-by-Andros acknowledged his sway.

Far from both shores, where the waters divide us,
Clasped in the mid-sea's ambient kiss,
Lemnos and Icarus' isle and Cnidus,
Paphos, Rhodes, Soloe were minions of his;
And thy namesake—thy parent—O thou, whose waves hide us,
Mother of mourning, Salamis!

The portion of Javan a wise moderation
Bound to his throne by her people's decrees;
Weariless then was the might of our nation;
Countless the swarm of her mercenaries;
But now in the day of God's sore visitation
We are tamed and chastised with the stripes of strong seas.

Enter XERXES.

Xerxes. My fate is upon me;
My star hath declined;
A grief hath undone me;
A doom none divined
Hath broken the sceptre of Persia as a reed that is snapped in the wind.

Age, thine eyes chide me;
They bow down my head;
My strength is denied me;
My limbs are as lead.
Would God I lay fallen in battle, covered up out of sight with the dead!

Ch. Lord of our splendour,
Our goodly array;
Despoiler and spender
And caster-away
Of thy host; God hath cut off thy lieges and darkened the light of thy day.

And Persia, their mother,
Mourns them that fell:

She, she, and none other,
Acclaimeth thee well,
King Xerxes, that gorged with her children the maw and the belly of Hell!

The pride and the power of her
Thou hast brought low:
Count the fallen flower of her,
Lords of the bow,
Reckon a myriad-muster, 'twere ten times ten thousand, I trow.

Sad lord of lost legions,
Sorrow on thee!
Through Asia's wide regions
Thy welcome shall be
Lamentation and mourning and weeping: she stoopeth; she boweth the knee.

Xe. Wail loud! Be not dumb!
On me be your moan!
For I am become
To kingdom and throne
A plague and a curse; yea, a burden, a weariness unto my own.

Ch. O crowned desolation,
Whose stripes thy land bears;
A sore salutation
She sounds in thy ears;
Mariandyne's death-lament hails thee: the cup of thy feasting is tears.

Xe. Pour forth thy sorrow!
Long, long shall it flow!
Nor to-day nor to-morrow
Sufficeth thy woe.
I have felt the fierce changes of fortune; the blast of God's vengeance I know.

Ch. Fraught with awe for thy fate
My weeping shall be;
Whelmed 'neath the weight
Of the weltering sea
I am fain to wail forth my lament for thy realm and thy house and for thee!

Xe. Ionia's embattled might,
Ionia's men-of-war,
In Ares' fatal armour dight,
Spurred by the foaming oar,
Swept men, ships, honour, all, away:
And there was left the wild waves' play
Heard in the lone of loveless night
On that disastrous shore.

Ch. Woe! Woe! thrice woe!

Xe. Inquire of me and ask all ye are fain to know.

Ch. Where, where is that great multitude,
Leal vassals of thy throne,
Pharandaces, Agabatas,
Susas and Pelagon?
Oh, tell me where is Psammis?
Where is Susiskanes,
Who from Ecbatana rode forth,
And Dotamas?

Xe. All these
Aboard a ship of Tyre
Perished. Where cold waves close
Above the wreck of lost empire
I left them with their foes:
The beaded bubbles hush and hiss,
The strong tide ebbs and flows,
Bruised on the beach at Salamis,
The waves that break on Salamis
Scourge them with bitter blows.

Ch. Woe! Woe! thrice woe! But tell me,
Pharnuchus, where is he?
Ariomardus and Seualkes
Whose fief was a king's fee?
And hast thou lost Lilæus,
Sprung from a noble strain?
And Tharubis and Memphis,
Are they among the slain?
Artembares, Hystaechmas,
For them my heart is fain.

Xe. Woe! Woe! thrice woe!
These many found one overthrow!
Their eyes all dim with coming death
They fixed on Athens, old, diluvial birth
Of Hate; inland on her detested earth
They gasped away their breath.

Ch. A Persian of the Persians,
The very eye of thee,
Who mustered men by thousands ten
Alpistus, where is he?
The son of Batanochus,
The son of Sesamas,
The son of Megabates;
Parthas and Oibaras,
Art thou returned without them?
And will they come no more?
And lie they there forsaken
On that disastrous shore?
Alas! what need of language?
The trouble of thy face
Proclaims this woe beyond all woes
To Persia's sceptred race!

Xe. Wring not my heart! Rouse not again
That insupportable refrain
For friends cut off and comrades slain.
Though sharp your pang and shrill your cry of dole
There is a louder voice that wails within my soul.

Ch. But many, many more I miss!
Xanthes of Mardian clans
Chieftain; and Anchares, who led
The valiant Arians;
And Arsames and Diaexis,
Lords of the lordly steed,
And Dadacas and Lythimnas,
And Tolmus good at need,
A greedy fighter fell to fill
With the red meat of war;

I marvel that they follow not
Thy crimson-curtained car.
Xe. All, all have gone the darkling way
With that great host they led!
Ch. All, all are gone the darkling way
Down to the unmemoried dead!
Xe. Forbear! This stabs me to the heart!
Ch. O unseen power, whoe'er thou art,
Thou hast hurled down a gleaming woe,
Bright ruin's ghastly meteor-glow!
Xe. A stroke hath fallen resonant
To the last beat of time.
Ch. A stroke hath fallen resonant
To earth's remotest clime.
Xe. O strange, new pang! Sharp agony!
Ch. Ionia, mistress of the sea
We struck under an evil star;
Yea, Persia hath ill-hap in war!
Xe. So great a host, and all are gone!
And I am left, a thing men look upon
And weep and wail!
Ch. O royal Persian!
What has thou not lost?
Xe. Nay, behold and see
Of sumptuous superfluity
The poor remains: the remnant left to me!
Ch. Yea, yea; thou hast lost ships, men, gear—
Xe. But worse remains: all Persia's power is here,
Clapped in the compass of an arrow-case!
Ch. Ye gods, into how little space
Is crept thy treasure still unspent!
Xe. Yet in this quiver there is room enough
To hold the relics of my armament.
Ch. Of bag and baggage, store and stuff,
Artillery and equipage, O King,
Hast thou brought back safe home this despicable thing?
Xe. All weapons else wherewith we went arrayed,
All power, and every necessary aid
That armies fight with, have been stripped away!
Ch. Alack! the sons of Javan fly not from a fray!
Xe. They take too much delight in war!
These eyes beheld a grief they looked not for.
Ch. Thy great armada, thy long battle-line
Broken——
Xe. When I saw that such grief was mine
From hem to hem my robe I rent.
Ch. O God!
Xe. Cry loud with all lament!
Yea, the whole almonry of sorrow drain!
No amplest "O" can this large ill contain.
Ch. I feel a twofold, yea, a threefold chain,
And every link a fiery pain,
Constrict my heart.
Xe. Yea, we must weep.
And we must put on sackcloth; but the foe
On this dark anniversary shall keep
Pastime and sport, highday and holiday.
Ch. And all thy strength and all thy bright array—
Xe. Lo! I fled naked: none escorts me home—
Ch. And all thy friends and comrades cast away!
The waters of calamity flow deep;
They break in death and ruin; and they sweep
Wrecks of the wrath of God in their tumultuous foam.
Xe. Weep blood! Yea, with sharp nail
The lank and hollow cheek of dotage tear,
Then each man to his house.
Ch. Weep! Wail!
Xe. Anon with me the burthen bear!
Ch. Shriek for shriek and groan for groan,
In miserable antiphone!
Xe. Shrill forth your loud lament in unison.
Xe. and Ch. Woe! Woe! Woe! Woe!
Ch. O grief the heaviest of all
To hear my lord the King's voice wailing his downfall!
Xe. Weep on, weep on for the King's sake;
Thy woeful service neither stint nor spare!
Ch. Eyes must be wet or hearts will break.
Xe. Anon with me the burthen bear.
Ch. Lord, I am ready to obey.
Xe. Wail and weep with wellaway!
Ch. Wellaway! And wellaway!
Xe. and Ch. Woe! Woe! Woe!
Ch. This mingled cup is mine and thine,
Foamed with the ferment of a black and bitter wine.
Xe. Beat thy breast and wail
The Mysian wail!
Ch. Oh, wail!
Xe. Spare not thy silvery hairs;
Pluck out the reverend beard upon thy chin!
Ch. I spare them not whom no grief spares.
Xe. Renew, renew thy cry! Begin
With mine your voices blending,
Let sorrow have no ending!
Ch. Sorrow, sorrow hath no ending.
Xe. Rend thine ample train!
Ch. Behold! 'tis rent in twain!
Xe. Touch the hair-strung lute
And teach it sorrow for my power laid low!
Ch. All mournful music else be dumb and mute,
That shrill lament shall ever flow!
Xe. To-day and every morrow
Let fall the rain of sorrow.
Ch. To-day shall have a rainy morrow.
Xe. Now with me the burthen bear!
Ch. Woe! Woe! Woe!
Xe. And whence ye came with footstep slow
And cry of wail and weeping go.
Ch. Woe! Woe! Woe!
Xe. Through all the city let your voice be sent!
Ch. Through all the city one lament.
Xe. Groan, ye who did so delicately tread!
Ch. O Persian earth, I stumble on your dead!
Xe. Yea, yea, yea!
In the oared galleys they were cast away!
Ch. My groanings shall thine escort be!
I'll play thee home with such sad minstrelsy!

Exeunt

THE SEVEN AGAINST THEBES

DRAMATIS PERSONAE

Eteocles, *King of Thebes, son of Oedipus*
Chorus of Theban Women
A Messenger
Antigone | Ismene — *Sisters of Eteocles*
A Herald

Before the Citadel which rises in the background, crowded with altars and statues.

Eteocles. Burghers of Cadmus! Seasonable speech,
And apt withal, the world expects from him
Whose business is a kingdom's governance—
High on the hinder-bulwark of the State
At lonely watch—his hand upon the helm
And never a lull from care to latch his lids.
For, if we prosper, God shall have the thanks;
But—if the sorry thing, I wish away,
Calamity befall—one man, and he
My sole self Eteocles, shall hear his name
Sung to loud preludes—universal note
Of wail,—which I pray Zeus, whom we acclaim
Averter, to keep far from Cadmus Town.
And now the hour is ripe when all of you—
Whether your prime's to come or hath gone by—
Must put on strength like buds thick-burgeoning,
Each in such measure as his age allows,
Both for the safety of the realm, her Gods—
Lest their accounted glories be wiped out,
And for your children and this earth—the Mother
And most dear nurse of your young innocence.
For she it was, who, when as yet we sought,
Weak travellers, her hospitable door,
The kindly soil, to us large welcome gave;
The careful nurture of our nonage bare,
And bred us to be denizens-at-arms
And trusty targeteers in this her need.
And, to this day, in God's just equipoise,
To us-ward shifts the moving balance-hand;
For, long time shut within these bastioned walls,
Fair issue (under Heaven) in the main
Our warfare hath. And now, thus saith the Seer,
Who shepherds wingéd flocks; not by things burnt
Divineth he; but inly cogitates,
With deep unerring art his auguries,
By prophecy, which is the voice of God,
Divinely taught: A fresh attack, more strong
Than all that went before, the Achæan host,
Gathering by night, intend against the town.
Therefore make speed unto the battlements
And towered gateways every man of you,
Girded with all the panoply of war!
Man the breast-works! On turret- scaffoldings
Take post! And where forth from the City-gates
The roadways run, hold on with a good heart,
Nor at this rout of runagates be ye
Too sore dismayed; for God shall end all well.
Moreover, I have despatched scouts and spies
To watch the movements of their host; the which
I am persuaded went not out in vain.
And, having their report, there is no fear
I shall be caught in any ticklish snare.

Enter MESSENGER.

Messenger. Eteocles! right valiant Sovereign
Of the Cadmeans! I bring tidings sure
Of happenings yonder with the armament;
Yea, and these eyes have seen what I report.
Know then, Seven Men—mettlesome Captains all—
Spilling bulls' blood in shield with black hide bound—
Their unctuous hands dipped in that gory chrism—
Have taken a great oath—unutterable—
By Enyo and Phobos that drinketh blood,
To raze these walls from battlement to base
And sack the town of Cadmus, or else die,
And leave to us our fair land soaked with carnage.
For a memorial to their folk at home
They hanged up garlands on Adrastus' car,
Weeping the while; but on their savage lips
Ruth was their none: rather the iron soul
Of stern resolve and red-hot hardihood
Panted in them, and in their lion eyes
Glanced Ares. These are no belated news;
For when I left them they were set about
Casting of lots for places at the Gates,
Against which each should march his company.
Therefore, the nation's chosen and her best
At every port assemble with all speed.
By now an Argive power of all arms
Approaches nigh at hand; the dust is stirred
With trampling feet; and their deep-chested steeds
Make the plain white with drops of creaming foam.
Now show thy seamanship, and make all snug
And weather-tight within, or e'er the blast
Of Ares strike; for on the dry land roars
A wave of men, a moving armament.
These are their dispositions: 'tis for thee
To grapple with them quickly; for the rest

My eye shall watch with sure reconnaissance
The progress of the day, and thou, well served
With sure intelligence of all without,
Shalt take no hurt nor harm. *Exit* MESSENGER.

Et. Harken, O Zeus!
Earth and all tutelary Godheads, hear!
And shall I name thee, thou paternal Curse,
With dark Erinys' strong resentment armed?
O pluck not out this city by the roots,
Nor utterly destroy it, rendered up,
The prize of war! with all its settled homes
Sweet with suave fluctuance of Hellenic speech!
Grant that this free earth and King Cadmus' Town
May never pass beneath the yoke of slaves!
Help us! Our common cause methinks, I plead,
For when a happy City sees good days
Laud and great honour have the gods she worships!
Exit.

The CHORUS *enter and rush up to the citadel.*

Chorus

I cry with great pangs of dread! For the foe quit their camp! Yea, their forces
Are loosed as a flood is loosed! and a multitude riding on horses
Runneth before, and mine ear no audible tidings seeks:
An airy signal flies! The dust, dumb messenger, speaks!
Loudly the low-lying plain to their thunderous hoofbeat rings!
The sound draweth nigh! And its speed is the speed of a bird that hath wings!
It roars as waters roar down mountainous channels leaping!
Oh, raise for us your battle-cry! This evil onward sweeping
Turn back, dear Gods! Kind Goddesses, a rescue for our wall!
How the white shields of Argos gleam! How fierce this swift onfall
Of footmen doubling at the charge, in glamorous armour girt!
Oh, of all worshipped deities, who will this woe avert?
I will make haste to cast me down before your holy feet,
Ye shining shapes of old! Hail, Happy Ones, whose seat
Bideth the shock of times! This, the ripe hour to cling,
Cleaving close to your forms, why waste we waymenting?
Hear ye, or hear ye not, the bucklers clang full loud?
Proffer we now our prayers for the garlands erstwhile vowed,
For the robes we wrought on the loom, with worship and delight!
I see—I hear—the brandished spear—and many there be that smite!
Wilt thou aid us, Ares long-in-the-land, or wilt thou thine own betray?
Dear to thee once, God golden-helmed, look down on thy city this day!

Hail, Godheads all that guard this realm and keep her fortress free!
Draw nigh! Behold! 'Gainst bondage pleads a virgin company!
For loud with hissing surges, by blasts of Ares sped,
A wave of men with combing crest our home hath compasséd!
Nevertheless, O Father, Zeus, who o'er-rulest all,
Into the toils of foemen let not their quarry fall!
Round the strong place of Cadmus the Argive beaters close!
Men harry men! The hunt is up for blood of human foes!
These bridles bind no flute-boys' cheeks, filled with soft music's breath!
They buckle bits in war-steeds' mouths! These pipes shrill woundy death!

As fell the lots helm-shaken, the pride of their great host,
Seven Champions clad in spearman's mail at the Seven Ports take post!
Hail, Power Zeus-born, that lovest battle! The city save,
Dread Pallas! Hail, Poseidon, Lord of the horse, the wave!
Smite them, as men smite fishes, even with thy forkéd spear!
Be for our trembling, trembling souls a strong deliverer!
O Ares! of all pity to thine own kin be kind!
Be warder of the town that calls King Cadmus' fame to mind!
Cypris, ancestress of our race! Blood of thy blood are we!
Yet none the less, as men sue Gods, we turn in prayer to thee!
Be Wolf to them, Wolf-Slayer! With gnashing of the teeth
Requite them! Leto's Daughter, thy silver bow unsheathe!
Cry, cry aloud with wailing! Hera, Mistress Supreme!
The chariots rattle round our walls! The grinding axles scream!
Oh, gracious Artemis! Shrill, shrill the note—the song of keening care!
Shook with the rush of volleying spears raves the affrighted air!

How fares it with the city? And what shall be our fate?
And whither doth God lead us? What end doth consummate?
Cry, cry aloud with wailing! Thick, thick, in soaring flight
Bursts on our walls a hail of stones! The parapet they smite!
Benign Apollo! In our gates the bronze-bound bucklers chide!

Queen—Power by Zeus appointed war's issue to
  decide—
Who stand'st above our city—Onka Invincible!
Deliver the seven-gated seat where thou art
  pleased to dwell!

Hearken, O Gods and Goddesses, perfect in might
  and power!
Wardens of march and mountain, watchmen on
  wall and tower!
Yield not by treachery the town that toileth with
  the spear,
But faithfully receive our prayer, who with
  stretched hands draw near!
Loved Spirits, who, of strength to save, move
  striding to and fro
Before our leaguered city, your love for her
  forthshow!
Think of the rich oblations upon your altars laid,
And mindful of our sacrifice and zealous service—
  aid!

Enter ETEOCLES.

Eteocles. Oh, you intolerable pack! You hags!
Will't help the city, think ye?—Will't inspire
A bold assurance in the beleaguered troops,
To cast you down before these antique shapes
—Our Holy Guardians!—there to rave and howl—
Abjects, disgusted decency abhors!
Good times, or bad times, may I never house
With womankind! The courage of a woman
Is insubmissive, rash, not counsellable,
And, when she's timid, she's an added plague
To home and fatherland! So is it now!
Thanks to this hither, thither, to and fro
Coursing of scared feet, the faint-hearted fear,
Like to a chill tide, sounding as it goes,
Runs through all orders of the Commonweal!
And—while the foe without are mightily
Advantaged—we ourselves within the gates
Work for our own destruction! Whoso shares
With womankind his fortunes, let him look
For the like issue! Whatsoe'er he be,
Man, woman—or some despicable thing
Halfway betwixt them both—that from henceforth
Fails in most strict obedience to my will,
The damning pebble shall his lot decide,
And he shall publicly be stoned to death!
It longeth to a man—let womankind
Keep their own counsel and not mell with ours—
To manage matters in the world outside.
Keep within doors and thwart not our designs!
Now—hast thou heard? Or hast thou failed to hear?
Or speak I to the deaf—a girl at that?

Ch. Dear Son of Oedipus! Fear smote
My heart, by reason of the din
Of chariots! For the axle's spin,
The whirring wheel's flute-note!
Because of the bit by fire begot,
That pipeth harsh with breathings hot
Of war-steeds, by the long rein swayed,
  I was afraid!

Et. Think ye that when she labours by the head
With panic rush from high-pooped stern to prow
The seaman goes about to save his ship?

Ch. I hasted to this ancient seat
Because in the Gods I put my trust,
When at the gates with roaring gust
Rattled a hail of deadly sleet.
Then was I moved by fear to pray
Unto the Blessed Gods, that they
Might stretch to shield the town from harm
  A mighty arm.

Et. Pray rather that the battlemented walls
Stand proof against the thrust of foeman's spear.
For were not that behoveful to the Gods?
'Tis a true saying: "When a city falls
The Gods forsake their ancient habitations."

Ch. Not in my time, thou honourable Court
Of Gods, forsake the city: ere that day
When battle riots where her sons resort,
And flames devour her, take my life away!

Et. Let me not hear thee call on the good Gods
When thy base heart deviseth cowardice!
The mother of Good-Hap is Loyalty,
The proverb saith; Helpmeet of Him that Saves!

Ch. Save it he may; yet him God's power
  transcends;
And often out of rough adversity,
Cloud-wrack above us, where the visual ends,
Man's helplessness God stablisheth on high.

Et. These be men's matters—blood of sacrifice,
Offerings to oracles, when deedy war
Puts all things to the test; your business
Is submiss silence, and to bide within.

Ch. It is the Gods who keep yet unsubdued
The land wherein we dwell; our wallèd town
Unravaged of this armèd multitude:
Shall what we do then call their vengeance down?

Et. I grudge not that to the high heavenly race
Ye pay all honour: but, lest ye corrupt,
As cravens can, the manhood of the realm
Calm your wild transports; this is fear's excess.

Ch. The sudden girding on of warlike gear
Confused upon my startled senses came,
Confounding them the more; surprised by fear
I sought this castled crag of ancient fame.

Et. I charge ye, if they tell of wounds and death
Fasten not on the tale with frantic cries,
For human carnage is God Ares' meat.

Ch. I hear the neighing steeds!

Et. Hear if thou must!
Yet seem not so discernibly to hear!

Ch. The builded city groans, as if a voice
Spake from the ground! Oh, we are compassed in
On every side!

Et. Is't not enough that I
With all resources wisdom can command
Confront these perils?

Ch. Loud and louder yet!
The knocking at the gate!

Et. Stifle thy cries!
Must the whole city hear thee?

Ch. O ye Gods,

Keep troth! Betray not to the enemy
The City ye have promised to defend!
Et. Curse thee! Wilt hold thy peace—possess thy soul
In patience?
Ch. O divine co-denizens,
Free while ourselves are free, save me from bondage!
Et. Ye do enslave yourselves; country and king,
Ye make both thrall!
Ch. O Zeus Omnipotent!
Strike the foe dead—dead—with thy bolt!
Et. O Zeus!
What stuff is woman made of, whom thou gav'st
To man for helpmeet!
Ch. Blithesome are we not;
And are men merrier when kingdoms fall?
Et. Thy hand upon the holy images
Speak'st thou untowardly with thy tongue?
Ch. My fears
Are masters and my tongue a run-away.
Et. If I cannot command let me entreat.
Come! With a good grace grant me my request,
And let this quarrel have a gentle close.
Ch. Speak with all speed then: haply thou shalt have
As speedy answer.
Et. Hush, poor weeping wretch,
Or thou wilt scare thy friends.
Ch. Nay, I am dumb:
The fate that they must suffer I can endure.
Et. I more approve that utterance of thine
Than all that went before: but stop not there!
Away from these sequestered images,
And pray to nobler purpose! Say, "Ye Gods,
Make war upon our side!" When ye have heard
The prayer I have to offer, second it
With songs triumphant, lusty, of good cheer—
The sacrificial shout that Hellas knows—
A salutation to embolden friends
And from their souls the battle-fright cast loose!
Hear, then, my prayer. First, I vow to the Gods,
Custodians of polity and soil,
Wardens of field and meeting-place and mart;
Next unto Dirce's river-springs—nor less
Ismenus, do I mean to honour thee—
If fair befall us and the State be saved,
There shall be slaughtering of bulls; the blood
Of sheep shall redden the hearth-place of the Gods.
Thus I confirm by pledge of solemn speech
Mine oath, to them trophies and raiment vowing:
"I will bedeck your shrines inviolate,
Yea, hang the forecourts of your sanctuaries
With spoils spear-rent, the garments of our foes."
On this wise pray ye! Thus acceptably
Approach the Gods with vows; not to vain groans
Addict, beast noises not articulate,
Untutored transports, ineffectual;
For by such flights ye shall no whit the more
Flee the appointed portion. I meanwhile
Will get me forth: and post at the Seven Gates
To match the foe six men of might and mettle,
Myself the seventh, furnished in the style
Greatness approves; ere rumour improvised
Inform them, or with speedier argument
Extremity of need inflame their souls.

The CHORUS *comes down from the Citadel on to the stage.*

Chorus

Fain would I hearken, fain obey,
But my heart's calm slumber-beat dismay
And dread have troubled sore:
And care (ill neighbour I wish away)
Looks in at the open door;
And the trembling flame of fear is fed
Because of the walls encompasséd,
As trembles the dove for her nestling's sake,
For her cradled brood, when the cruel snake
Creeps to their twilight bed.

Hither in complete armour dight
Moveth against these towers
A multiple host; and yonder light
The jagged sling-stone showers.
And our people are smitten from far and near,
And I know not my fate, but I tremble and fear,
And I pray the Gods of race divine
To save the men of Cadmus' line
And the city to Cadmus dear.

Where to redeem your loss shall be found
In earth's wide fields more fertile ground,
If ye yield this land to the foe,
Where, through the deep, rich soil enwound,
The waters of Dirce flow?
Nourisher she of man and mead,
Quencher of thirst and quickener of seed;
No rill more excellent in worth
Of all Poseidon Lord of Earth
Poureth or Tethys' children speed.
Therefore, ye Gods, that are our stay,
Yonder without the wall
Send havoc; with slaughter and casting away
Of shields, when slain men fall:
But dismiss not our prayers unheard, disowned,
Our lamentable cry entoned:
Save us and win for our land renown;
Then reign within the walléd town
Unshakeably enthroned!

Sorrow it were thus to send down to hell a city coeval with grandeurs of old
Captive and spoil of an enemy spear, 'mid the crumbling of ashes; her store and her gold
Sacked by the Achaean as things of no worth, unregarded of Heaven; sore sorrow it were
Should mother and matron and maiden and bride as a horse by the forelock be haled by the hair
With rending of raiment. Loud, loud is the voice of a city made empty: her children's farewells—
As they go to their ruin—confused with exultings; and heavy the doom that my fear foretells.

Woe for the lawless reaping of unripe corn; for the rape of the bride unwed,
For the far strange home and the long, long way to it, travelled with hate, she must tread!
Nay, of a truth, where dead men dwell, there is more of bliss; for with multiple ills
When a city is taken man visiteth man; he leads away captive, he spills
Blood, he thrusts in fire; he anoints with defilement of smoke man's home;
The soul of all reverence a mad breath pollutes when Ares hath masterdom!

Tumult and roaring in all streets and wynds;
The fencéd bulwark fails; and man to man each finds
His foe; and, having found
Lets drive his spear and bears him to the ground.
And blood-bedabbled mothers of babes new-born
For their dead sucklings like the ewe-flock bleat;
By harrying bands
Kindred from kin are torn;
And two shall meet
Each with his load; or one with empty hands
Shall call upon his fellow in like case,
Neither with less nor equal satisfied,
Saying "Since all men for themselves provide,
How shall we fare if backward in the race?"

All manner store the housewife's eyes distress,
Chance-lying where it fell: all earth's largesse
Foamed recklessly to waste.
And, new to sorrow, with worse bonds disgraced,
The young girl-slave looks for a conqueror's bed;
A rich lord, yet in love most destitute,
Whose only mark
Of greatness is the slaver's attribute,
When fierce embraces in the lustful dark
Exact with nightly ravishment his pay;
And her bewailéd griefs find this redress
That tears let fall in day-long loneliness,
Night's all-abhorred endearments wipe away!

Semi-Ch.

Look where our spy comes! Dear ones, he brings tidings
Be certain, of some happening with the host!
With smoothest expedition at high speed
He runneth thither, as the hubbed wheel spins!
And see! With juncture apt to meet his news,
The king himself, the Son of Oedipus!
He, too, all haste, metes out no measured stride!

Enter MESSENGER *and* ETEOCLES.

Me. I bring news—certain—of the enemy,
How the lots fell and at which port each stands.
Fell Tydeus—foremost—fronts the Proetid Gate,
Roaring; but may not pass Ismenus Ford:
The seer forbids: the omens are not good.
There greedy Tydeus, famishing for fight,
Sends forth his voice, like to a venomous snake
Hissing at noon; and lasheth with vile words
The prophet, Oecles' son: damning his lore
For cringing cowardice that shrinks from death
And jeopardy of battle: while he vents
Such blasphemy, he tosses his dwarf-head
All overshadowed with a triple crest,
His bright helm's bristling mane. Beneath his shield,
From its dished rondure dangling, bells of bronze
A yelling menace peal: the broad convex,
Bulging, displays this arrogant device:
The sky in metal wrought, ablaze with stars:
And in the middle of his shield the moon—
Lustrous, full-orbed, leader and paramount
Of all their constellations—looketh forth,
The very eye of night. And like one wood,
Thus in prodigious pride caparisoned,
He holloas up and down the river-bank,
Rampant with lust of battle; as a horse
All fire and fierceness pants upon the bit,
What time, hard-held, he paweth in his place
Mad for the sound of trumpet. Whom wilt thou
To him oppose? What champion safe and sure
Shall stand at Proetid Port, the barriers down?

Et. I am not one to tremble at a plume:
'Tis not the brave device that deals the scar,
And crests and bells without the spear bite not.
As for this night that's blazoned on his shield,
This heaven of shining stars—the folly of it
Will likely prove a night of prophecy.
For if Death's bloody darkness veil his eyes,
Then, for the bearer of that scutcheon proud,
By herald's law these arms are his by right,
And his presumptuous scutcheon damns himself!
'Gainst Tydeus I will post the valiant son
Of Astacus for champion of the Gate.
Right nobly born is he, and one who pays
Due honour to the throne of Modesty,
Abhorrer of the bombast rhetoric;
Backward in baseness he holds honour dear.
Sprung from that seed of men which Ares spared,
A goodly plant, most native to this soil,
Is Melanippus. Ares may decide
With hazard helm-cast how the event shall speed;
But Justice by sure warranty of blood
Commits to him in trust the life of her
Who gave him birth, to shield from thrust of foes.

Ch. Just is his cause who fights for his land! Him may the just Gods prosper and speed!
Yet I see the pale forms of our loved ones lie bleeding, and tremble; for us, their belovéd, they bleed!

Me. May the Gods grant your prayer—and prosper him!
Electrae Portals fell to Capaneus.
Another Earth-born he—in height surpassing
The last—and his proud boast too proud for man.
He monstrously inveighs against these walls
With threats, which may the event forbear to crown!
On this wise boasteth he: "With or without
God's will, by me the City shall be sacked!
Though Zeus dispute my passage, casting down

His lightning for a stumbling-block of fire,
It lets me not!" He scorns your thunderbolt!
Your forkéd lightning he dubs "noonday heat!"
And, for device, carries a firebearer—
An unarmed man—for weapon in his hands
A blazing torch; and, issuing from his mouth,
This golden challenge, "I will fire the town."
Do thou despatch 'gainst such a champion—
But who will stand against him? Who will bide
The man with all his vaunts and never blench?
Et. Gain upon gain, and interest to boot!
The hearts of frenzied men are in their mouths:
The tongue's the true accuser of false thoughts.
When Capaneus threatens he's prepared to act
His blasphemies; and when he dareth all
That tongue may dare, with insane zest the man
Challenges heaven and storms the ear of Zeus
With swelling words. But he shall have, y-wis,
Fit answer, when that firebearer comes
Which is the burning bolt, fashioned no wise
In likeness to the warmth of noonday sun.
'Gainst him a man, exceeding slow of speech,
In spirit very fire, we have set;
The might of Polyphontes; a strong tower
By favour of protecting Artemis
And other Gods withal. Pray you proceed:
Another and the gate that he hath drawn.
Ch. Death to the braggart! Fall, thunder, and stay him! ere with leaping he come and with lifting of spear
To despoil my fair home, my virginal bower—robber and wrecker and ravisher!
Me. Now for the next gate and the man that drew it:
The third cast fell upon Eteoclus;
Third from the upturned helm, goodly with bronze,
For him leapt forth the lot to hurl his troop
Against Neistae Portals. Round and round
He reins his mares, and they toss high their heads
With gleam of glancing harness—all on fire
To fall upon the Gate. Their nozzles pipe
After the mode of barbarous music, filled
With the breath of their proud snortings. On his targe
Is no mean blazon. One armed cap-à-pie
Climbs up a ladder planted 'gainst a tower,
Held by the foe, and means to lay all waste.
In syllables forth-gushing from his lips
He roars "Not Ares' Self shall hurl me down."
'Gainst him too send a trusty one, to save
This land of freemen from the servile yoke.
Et. Here is the man to send, and with him go
Such happy fortune as the Gods vouchsafe!
Not in his mouth his boast, but in his arm.
Megareus, Creon's seed, of the race earth-sown.
The savage, greedy noise of neighing steeds
Shall not affright nor drive him from the Gates;
But either he will fall and with his life
This land for her dear nurture recompense,
Or deck his father's house with two-fold glory:
Two captives taken and that shield-borne tower,
So proudly counterfeited, carried home.
Another boaster: stint me not your tale!
Ch. Good luck, good luck have thou who go'st forth,
Champion of home to me! Foul them befall!
Mouthing in madness beneath our wall,
Zeus the Requiter behold them with wrath.
Me. Next—fourth in order—to the Gate hard by
Athena Onca comes Hippomedon
Shouting his war-shout: a resplendent shape,
Cast in a mould of ample magnitude.
His shield might almost serve for a threshing-floor;
And while its round he threateningly revolved
I own a shudder ran through all my frame.
No despicable artist was the man
Who wrought its blazon. On the disk embossed
A Typhon, shooting forth his burning breath,
A luminous darkness, half smoke and half fire;
The casing of its hollow-bellied orb
Securely hammered on with knots of snakes.
I heard his great voice thunder, saw his eyes
Glare horribly: a frenzied votarist
He leaped, God Ares' reeling reveller,
By him possessed, mad-drunk for deeds of blood!
'Gainst his assault there needeth wary watch.
Even now before the Gates his vaunt is loud,
And swelling with the note that strikes dismay.
Et. Suburban Pallas—Onka-Without-the-Walls—
Hard by the Gate, wroth with his insolence,
Shall keep him off—a serpent, mailed and fanged,
Death in its coils, barred from a brood of birds.
But Oenops' trusty son, Hyperbius,
For mortal succour—matching man with man—
Shall face him. All he asked was choice for service;
Time and the hour should teach him where to serve.
Faultless in form; of fearless courage, perfect
In martial trim, never did Hermes cast
A luckier throw than when with happy choice
He brought the pair together: for betwixt
Him and the man he meets is enmity,
And in the smiting of their shields shall clash
Opposing deities. For the one presents
Typhon that breathes forth fire; but Father Zeus
Sits on the other, moveless on his throne,
And centred in his hand the bolt that burns!
And who hath yet seen Zeus discomfited?
These are the powers whose favour they invoke,
We with the winners, with the losers they,
If Zeus be more than Typhon's match in battle!
Yea, by his blazon each shall stand or fall;
And Zeus displayed upon his shield shall prove
Zeus the strong Saviour to Hyperbius!
Ch. He whose arm Zeus' enemy sustains—
Monster unfriended, Earth whilome bore,
Whom demons and Gods and mortals abhor—
Right at the Gate he shall dash out his brains!
Me. Amen to that. Next in the list and fifth
In order, at the Gates of Boreas,
Hard by Amphion's Tomb, the son of Zeus,
This champion takes ground. A spear he hath
Whereby he sweareth—honouring it more
Than any God—yea, holding it more dear

Than eyesight: "I will ravage Cadmus Town,
Ay, maugre Zeus!" Thus he—a cub, whose dam
Littered among the mountains, a green chit,
Yet of a comely countenance withal,
Man-boy, or boy-man—call him what you will,
The down upon his cheeks buds thick and fast,
For 'tis with him the spring-time of his growth—
But of a savage temper—in no wise
Maidenly, as befits his name—he strode,
His eyeballs rolling, not without his boast
Advancing to the Gates. Our infamy
On his bronze shield, orbed to protect his bulk,
He flashed: the ogrish Sphinx, so riveted
That its embossed and staring ugliness
His arm convulsed to hideous counterfeit
Of life and motion. Underneath he sports
The figure of a man—a wight Cadmean—
As if on him to centre all our bolts!
He'll prove no petty trafficker in war—
Nor for a bagman's profit lose his travel—
Parthenopaeus, waif of Arcady!
Oh, that a rogue like this, an outlander
In Argos, one who pays his reckoning,
A handsome sum for being handsome-bred,
Should hurl against these walls his boyish spite
And spleenful threats, I pray God bring to naught!
Et. If the same measure that they mete the Gods
Be meted out to them, then their bad vows
Shall hurl them far in hopeless overthrow!
But for him too, your churl Arcadian,
A knight is found: no braggart, but his hand
Soon finds the thing to do! Actor his name,
Brother of him just chosen. No foul flood
Of deedless words will he let flow within
To water pale, rank weeds of cowardice;
Nor will he suffer to overpass these walls
The man who comes in guise of foe, escutcheoned
With that abhorréd beast! She shall be wroth
With him that carries her, when, at our gates,
The too industrious hammerstroke of war
Her bulging blazon dints with rude reverse!
Nevertheless, I leave it to the Gods!
And may they prove that I speak verity!
Ch. This rives my heart! Ruffles my braided locks
Until each hair with horror stands up stiff!
Blasphemy of unholy men that mocks
Things holy! O ye Gods—if—if
Ye be indeed Gods that requite,
Smite them! with ruin smite!
Me. I am near ended. Sixth there came a man
In temper most majestical, in might
Excelling all—the prophet, Amphiaraus.
Before the Homoloean Gates he stood
Chiding great Tydeus with much eloquence.
"Assassin! Troubler of the public peace!
In Argos arch-preceptor of all wrong!
Erinys' call-boy! Slaughter's acolyte!
Organ of evil counsel to the soul
Of old Adrastus!" Then he called aloud
The name of Polyneices—thy blood-brother—
And lifting up his eyes to Heaven, paused—
An awful pause—on that last syllable
That speaks of strife. And thus his thoughts break loose:
"Doubtless, this is a deed to please the Gods—
A noble gest, which they who come hereafter
Will much delight to tell or harken to—
To wreck thy father's kingdom and thy Gods,
Hurling upon them an invading host!
Is it in Justice' name thou would'st drain dry
The fount that flowed for thee with mothers milk?
And if thou master with thy jealous sword
Thy fatherland, how will it profit thee?
I shall make fat this earth! Yea, prophesy
Here in my grave, in hostile ground interred.
On then to battle! And for me—to death
Not all unhonoured!" So the prophet spake,
His shield of bronze at rest. It bore no blazon:
For his affections hang not on the show
Of seeming to be best, but being so!
And he reaps only where the soil hath depth
The golden wisdom of well-pondered thought!
My counsel is that thou despatch against him
Antagonists as wise as they are brave;
He's to be feared who reverences the Gods!
Et. This moves me much! 'Tis the unhappy chance
That couples oft the just with many wicked!
In the affairs of men no ill compares
With bad associates! There springeth thence
A crop no man would harvest. The field of Sin
Brings forth the fruits of Death. For, peradventure,
One righteous man who reverences the Gods
Shall shipmate be with a ruffianly crew,
And, furthering some scheme of villainy,
Perish with the whole tribe by God accursed!
Or, in a state where cynic policy
Goes the broad way of international crime,
And men forget the Gods, there shall be found
One just man, who, though he hath done no wrong,
Caught in the snare of his compatriot's guilt,
Falls, smitten with the chastisement of Heaven
That visiteth them all! So is it now
With the seer, Œcles' son! A man most staid,
Just, valiant, God-fearing, greatly endowed
With prophecy, but 'gainst his better mind
Consorting with blasphemers, when they take
The road which to retrace is hard and long—
He, if it be the will of Zeus, shall fall
With all his bad confederates dragged down!
I do not think he will so much as move
Against the Gates; not that he lacks the courage
Or is at heart attaint with cowardice,
But having certain knowledge of the way
The fight must end for him; if the oracle
Of Loxias bear fruit; and he is wont
To speak to purpose if he speak at all.
Nevertheless, I make choice of a man
To send against him, valiant Lasthenes:
He keepeth on the stranger at the Gate
A jealous ward: in wisdom of ripe years
But of a youthful brawn yet immature.
A man so quick of eye, so sure of hand,
That instant through the undefended flesh

Crashes his spear, if aught that's vulnerable
Be left uncovered at the buckler's edge.
Howbeit, howsoe'er we thrust or fend
Victory is a gift men owe to Heaven.
Ch. May the Gods hear our prayers, for they
are just;
And grant them for the safety of our land;
And be the invader's weapon backward thrust,
Yea, in his own breast with a mighty hand!
On them may Zeus his bolt let fall
Yonder without the wall!
Me. Last name of all—seventh at the seventh
Gate—
Thy brother! Hear what woes his prayers invoke
On thee and on this realm! He'll plant his foot
Upon our walls: our land shall hear his name
Heralded; the loud paean he will uplift.
Yea, he will seek thee out and slay thee first,
Then die beside thee! Or "If he fall not,
But live; exile for exile, wrong for wrong,
Measure for measure! As he drove me out,
So shall he wander forth a fugitive."
And for the fair fulfilment of these hopes
He invocates the Gods that knit in love
Each to his kin and all men to their home.
Well named is he "the Mighty One in Quarrel"!
A new-wrought shield he bears—the Argive buckler,
Round, with two-fold device artificered.
Hammered in gold a man completely armed
Led by a woman-form of sober mien.
Justice he calls her; suiting to that name
Her legend, "I will bring home the banished man:
He shall possess his land, and come and go,
Free of his father's house." Here ends the tale
Of all their proud inventions: make thy choice
Whom thou wilt send against him. And as I
Will be the faithful herald of thy word,
Prove thou true Captain of the Ship of State!
Exit MESSENGER.
Et. O house of Œdipus! *Our* house! O race
God-maddened—God-abominate—all tears!
Oh me! here ends,—here ends my father's curse!
And yet this is no time to weep and wail,
Lest sorrow's debt with usury of sorrow
Gender increase of groans! "Mighty in Quarrel"!
Well-named! Well-named! Ay, we shall know anon
Where it will end, that blazon—we shall know
Whether the gilded rant, writ on his shield
And fraught with frenzy, will fetch the bearer
home!
If the maid Justice, Zeus' own child, had been
The inspiration of his thoughts, had lent
Her countenance to his deeds, this might have been!
But neither when from antenatal gloom
He fled—at nurse, in adolescence, nor
When's beard grew thick, did Justice ever own him
Or speak him fair! Nor is it credible
That in this hour when perils thicken fast
To whelm his fatherland, she stands beside him!
No! Justice is Justice! She were falsely named
Succouring such a miscreant! In this faith
I go to meet him! Who hath better right?
Ay, king to king, and brother unto brother,
Foe matched with foe! My greaves! Fetch me my
greaves!
Good gear 'gainst javelin-thrust or cast of stone!
Ch. Be not, belovéd—child of Œdipus—
Like unto him out of whose mouth proceeds
All wickedness! Alas! It is enough
If our Cadmeans with these Argives fight:
There's water for that blood; but brother-murder
Is like the tettered slough that will not off:
'Tis spotted with the guilt that ne'er grows old!
If evil come, so it be free from shame,
Why let it come. All titles else save honour
Die when we die and sleep with us in the grave:
But if to evil thou add infamy
How shall men speak it fair and call it honest?

Child, what crav'st thou? Let not the battle-lust
Bloody with dripping spears thy ruin be!
Forth from thy soul the evil passion thrust
Or e'er it mount apace and master thee!
Et. Since in this power that speeds the event
I feel
The insupportable blast of God's own breath,
Blow, wind! Fill, sails! And where Cocytus' tide
Heaves dark, with gleams of Phoebus' fiery hate,
Down-wind let drift the last of Laius' line!
Ch. This is some fierce unnatural appetite
That hungers after flesh unseethed and raw!
Famished for human victims! The loathed rite
Whose fruit is sour, whose blood sins 'gainst the law!
Et. It is my father's curse! I feel the glare
Of those hard eyes not moist with human tears!
To do things horrible they importune me!
There is a voice which cries "Swift death were
sweet!"
Ch. Hear it not, child! No man shall call thee base
If on thy life there dawn a better day!
Hereafter, if the Gods thy offerings grace,
Will not black-stoled Erinys steal away?
Et. What are the Gods to me! Methinks the hour
When we regarded them is long gone by!
No offering in their eyes is of such worth
As our perdition! Why then pay them court?
Why cringe for respite from the final doom?
Ch. Yield now, while yet thou hast the chance!
The wind
May change with time, that blows so contrary,
And thy bad Genius at last be kind!
But now thou battlest with a boiling sea!
Et. Ay! with the yeasty waves of Œdipus
His curse! There was too much of solid sooth
In the slight, fleeting visions of my dreams:
They make division of my father's substance!
Ch. Thou art no friend to woman: yet, wilt hear
me?
Et. If thou hast ought to say a man may do,
Speak on; and in few words withal!
Ch. Go not
Where thou art going—to the Seventh Gate!
Et. Content thee! Therefore have I filed my
mind;

And words are not the stuff to dull its edge.
Ch. To win is all: get glory he who can:
The victory won wins God's acknowledgment.
Et. He who girds on his armour owes no love
To that wise saw.
Ch. And yet the greater fault—
To lay rash hands upon thy brother's life
And with those crimson juices stain thy soul—
Mislikes thee not!
Et. Sin may be thrust upon us:
Evil when Heaven sends it, who shall shun? *Exit.*

Chorus

By this cold shuddering fit of fear
My heart divines a presence here,
Goddess or Ghost yclept;
Wrecker of homes, and dark adept
Of prophecy, whose vastitude of ill
This hour and all hours shall at last fulfil.
Thou Curse that from the gloom
Of nether Hell
A Sire invoked; implacable
Erinys, whom in fierce excess of wrath
Grief-maddened Œdipus did summon forth,
Thou'rt in this strife to work his children's doom.

Ah, stranger from the far-off land—
Scyth—Chalyb—in thine iron hand
The lots are shaken; thine award
Is dealt with the devouring sword,
Whose biting edge doth make partition cold
Of all the goodly gear men get and hold.
With them so shall it be,
These, next of kin
In blood and guilt and sin,
Of all their father's famous fields widespread
They shall at last be disinherited,
Lords of so much earth as dead men have in fee.

When children, by one sire begot,
To whom one woeful womb gave birth,
In mortal combat meet and die,
And that bright pool wherein they lie
Drunk by the dust of thirsty earth
Is curdled to a darker clot,
What power of prayer shall purify,
What water wash away the stain?
But, ah, what drops incarnadine
The new, the old, the mingled wine,
That Laius' house must drain!

From springs of old transgression flow
The guilt, the sorrow swift to follow.
Not yet, not yet is vengeance spent,
Son's sons abide the chastisement
Of him who hearkened not Apollo—
Laius, first-parent of this woe.
Three sacred embassies he sent,
And thrice where Delphic rocks are piled,
Of earth's vast wheel the massy nave,
The priestess cried "If thou would'st save
Thy kingdom, get no child."

But Love was master; he begot
Death for himself and shame,
The son that slew him, witting not—
King Œdipus his name.
Who eared the womb where he lay hid,
Seed of a curse unborn,
Sowing the sacred field forbid
To reap in blood the corn.
Their bridal torch Erinys fed,
And madness strewed their nuptial bed.

And now, as 'twere a sea of woe
That may not come to rest,
Wave follows after wave; and, lo,
A third with triple crest
That breaks with moaning thunder stored
About the ship of State;
Scarce wall-wide is the weather-board
Stretched betwixt us and Fate;
And I have fears lest Cadmus Town,
Whelmed with its royal house, go down!

Like an old debt unpaid is an ancient curse:
And in the soul's commerce
It comes to audit, hath its settling day:
A heavy reckoning for man to pay
When not one damning entry is passed by.
From deck to keelson there is rummage then
And jettison of wealth of moiling men,
Waxed fat with overmuch prosperity.

This was well seen in Œdipus ill-starred.
High in the Gods' regard
He stood; by the fireside of him was laud;
In streets and squares where'er men walk abroad
Or great assemblies gather in debate,
Was never wight so praised, what time he smote
The she-fiend, gobbling down her gory throat
Comers and goers at the City Gate.

But on his noonday broke a ghastly light;
And, sounding all the sorrow of his wooing,
One final grief he wrought to his undoing
With that same hand that laid his father low;
And put away the eyes that gave him sight
Of his loathed offspring, gotten to his woe.

And then he cursed them
(for they grudged him bread);
With bitter words of grief and anger chiding:
"A day shall come, a day of sharp dividing,
And he that carves shall carve with steel," he cried.
Now the curse falls upon his children's head,
And my hushed heart awaits Erinys' stride.

Enter MESSENGER.

Me. Take courage, weak ones! Mother's children all!
This free land hath escaped the yoke of slaves.
The boastings of the mighty are brought low:
The ship is in still waters: wave on wave
Smote her, but her stout seams have sprung no leak;

Sound are her bulwarks; her ports weather-tight;
Her champions have well-discharged their trust.
Count gate by gate and six have prospered well;
And for the seventh—Apollo, Lord of Seven,
Took that by right of his prerogative:
And there he fitly stayed the Laian rage.
Ch. Is not the measure of her mourning full?
And must this stricken realm find room for more?
Me. The realm is safe: but, for her princely seed—
Ch. I dread so much the thing thou hast to say
I scarce attend thee; what dost thou mean? Speak on!
Me. If thou hast power to listen, mark my words.
The Sons of Œdipus—
Ch. Oh, Misery!
They say prophets of evil utter truth,
And I am of them!
Me. Indistinguishably
They have gone down into the dust.
Ch. So far
Fallen! Thy tale is heaviness; nevertheless
Tell it to the end!
Me. I tell thee they are dead:
They slew each other!
Ch. Ah, fraternal hands!
Too near were ye in birth, too near in blood.
Me. Yea! And their undivided destiny
Twinned them in death: their evil Genius slew
them,
And blotted from the world an ill-starred race.
Such cause we have for thankfulness and tears;
The land is well at ease; that twin-born pair,
Lords and disposers of the Commonwealth,
Have made partition with the hammered steel,
Tough Scyth, of all their substance, scot and lot,
And they shall hold it indefeasibly,
Quieted in possession by the grave!
There, to that final resting place borne down
By the dark current of a father's curse.
The realm is safe: dark earth hath drunk their blood,
The royal blood that like twin fountains rose;
One hour of birth—one hour of combat—one
Of death—dealt mutually by fraternal hands.
Exit MESSENGER.

Chorus

O Sovran Zeus, Protecting Powers,
Who have indeed kept safe these well-beloved
towers,
Whether shall I rejoice
For that the city stand inviolate
Or shall I rather with a lamentable voice
Weep and bewail her leader's fate?
Ah, cruel doom! Ah, children dead!
Mighty in Quarrel ye have ended
Even as the name portended,
Yea in your wickedness ye are perishéd.

O curse of Œdipus! O malison
Dark—unrelenting—damning all his line!
Over this heart of mine
Comes creeping on,
Cold Misery, your chilly breath,
Because, when like a Thyiad in her madness
I seemed to hear
The blood that drips
Where men lie slain,
Then with the voice of mourning and with
rueful lips
I sang the song of death!
O ill refrain,
Glee chanted without mirth or gladness,
That keeps a sorry burden to the spear.

Rather the word, the never wearying
Once uttered malediction of their sire,
Wrought to this issue dire.
Nay, Laius King
Hath here his wish; the course he chose
Begun in blindness and in disobeying
Toucheth its bourne.
Ambitions high
And cares of State
Blunt not the edge of heavenly prophecy.
O, wailed for many woes,
Past belief in hate
And past belief in fratricidal slaying,
Is this a tale or is it sooth we mourn?
The bodies of ETEOCLES *and* POLYNEICES *are borne on to the Stage.*

Behold! self-manifest they come;
They need no harbinger;
A double woe, a mutual doom,
Care that hath slaughtered care.
New sorrows from old sorrows spring,
And both have here their home-bringing.

Ah! pilgrim-ship, your lofty poop
No festal garlands wreathe:
The drowsy sails half idly droop,
And they are dark as death:
Bound where no sunny Cyclads shine,
And bright Apollo hath no shrine.

Waft, waft her down the wind of sighs,
With speed of plangent hand
Row her beyond these happy skies
Unto the sunless land,
Where across Acheron voices call,
And region darkness welcomes all.
Enter ANTIGONE *and* ISMENE.
But dearer lips must chant their threnody;
And that unhappy cause
Here to their brethren draws
A sister pair, the maid Antigone,
Ismene by her side. Tears may be sold,
And raiment rent for mercenary gold
And money purchaseth the hireling's cries:
These warm, white breasts shall heave with
heartfelt sighs;
But ere the dirge begin, let us prolong
With well accordant breath
Erinys' loud, harsh, unmelodious song,
The dismal paean of the Lord of Death.

Unhappy sisters, most unblest
Of all that e'er held brother dear,
Or bound beneath a tender breast
The cincture noble women wear;
From feignéd grief no forced lament I borrow;
The heart's voice speaks when I shrill forth my
sorrow.

O ye perverse, to counsel blind
Ye weariless in woe!
Must courage turn its hand 'gainst kind,
Power its own house lay low?
And sought ye death or sought ye doom
And ruin for your house and home?

Her princely walls ye tumbled flat;
In rivalry for her
A bitter monarchy ye gat—
The sword your peacemaker.
Sceptred Erinys keeps your house,
Wreaking the wrath of Œdipus.

Oh, ill encounter! Fellowship
Of hands that hatred joins!
The drops that from these gashes drip
Flow from the self-same loins!
Woe for the curse with Heaven allied,
Red with the blood of fratricide!

Oh gaping wound, still bleeding fresh:
O rent that ruined all,
And thrusting through fraternal flesh
Struck home at house and hall.
One bitter curse for both; yea, none
Hath less or more of malison!

Realm-wide the sound of mourning runs:
The bastioned walls make moan;
This earth that loveth her strong sons
Sends up a hollow groan;
And all they perished to possess
Waiting new heirs lies ownerless.

Too keen their cause to prosecute,
Too jealous for just share;
And he who solved their bitter suit
Think ye that he judged fair?
Ares that judgeth by the sword,
Small thanks hath he for his reward!

To battle they had made appeal,
And battle heard their cause;
That iron judge, the trenchant steel,
Hath brought them to this pause,
In undisturbéd tenure cold
Their father's grave to have and hold!

Loud is my wail! My heart is rent
With grief's authentic cry!
No gladness lurks in this lament,
Feigned grief false thoughts belie!
The fountains of my being flow
For royal men in death laid low!

How shall we praise them? Shall we say
Their own should love them well,
Seeing they wrought much in their day,
Were wondrous hospitable?
When host met host, the pledge was graced;
They lavished all—in laying waste!

O crown of women, woe-begone!
Of mothers, most unblest!
Who took to husband her own son,
And suckled at her breast
Babes, that in mutual slaughter bleed:
Here ends that sowing—and the seed!

Yea, in their seed-time they were twinned,
And clove in twain by hate
They are clean gone—a stormy wind
Hath swept them to their fate:
Such peace-making these brawlers have,
And their conclusion is the grave.

There they forget to hate: their strife
Springs to no fierce rebirth:
The sundered rivers of their life
Mingle in peaceful earth;
And in that dark, distempered clay
Too near, too near in blood are they.

Alack! The alien of the sea,
Keen iron, fire's own child,
With bitter blows, unlovingly
Their quarrel reconciled;
Ares hath sharp division made;
He heard the prayer their father prayed.

They have their portion! poor, poor souls!
A little fathom-span
Of ground, illiberal fortune doles;
No more the gods give man;
And 'neath them lying stark and cold
Earth's wealth unplumbed, her gems and gold.

Wail for the wreath of victory
That crowns their race with woe!
Wail for the Curse's triumph-cry,
Shrieked for their overthrow!
Wail for the line that broke and fled—
And found a refuge with the dead!

There stands a trophy at the gate,
Where breast to breast they fell;
The votive offering of Hate
And Havoc hot from hell;
There their ill star its strength essayed,
Nor till both sank its fury stayed!

Antigone. Smiter smitten!
Ismene. Slayer slain!
An. Blood on thy spear!
Is. On thy breast that stain!

An. Weep the wrong!
Is. Wail the woe!
An. Make grief thy song!
Is. Let thy tears flow!
An. and Is. Misery! Ah, misery!
An. Oh, maddened breast!
Is. Oh, moaning heart!
An. Wept with all tears thou art!
Is. And thou of all unhappy things unhappiest!
An. Slain by thine own thou liest dead!
Is. Yea, and this hand its own blood shed!
An. So is a tale of grief twice told!
Is. A double horror to behold!
An. Two woes in dreadful neighbourhood!
Is. They lie together mingled in their blood!
Ch. O Fate! How heavy is thy hand!
How grievous are the gifts that thou dost bring!
Great shade of Œdipus who banned
His own offspring—
Offended ghost—Erinys black as hell,
Surely thou art of might unconquerable!

An. and Is. Misery! ah, misery!
An. Sorrow's gifts are ill to see!
Is. These back from exile thou didst bring to me!
An. He fought and slew; yet home is far away!
Is. He won the cause, but perished in the fray!
An. Ill he sped—for he is fled!
Is. And this poor soul is numbered with the dead!
An. Bad brotherhood was this!
Is. Yea, and they had but little bliss!
An. One sorrow! One death-song!
Is. Bewept with tears that weep a threefold wrong!
Ch. O Fate! How heavy is thy hand!
How grievous are the gifts that thou dost bring!
Great shade of Œdipus who banned
His own offspring—
Offended ghost— Erinys black as hell,
Surely thou art of might unconquerable!

An. Now thou know'st thou didst transgress!
Is. Now thou own'st thy wickedness!
An. Back returned with murderous stride!
Is. Fugitive and fratricide!
An. Oh, the woeful victory!
Is. Oh, the sorry sight to see!
An. Wail the grief!
Is. Weep the wrong!
An. To home and country both belong!
Is. Mine the woe!
An. This long anguish ends even so!
Is. Wretchedest of mortal kind!
An. and Is. Sinning with a frenzied mind!
An. Where to lay them—in what grave?
Is. Where most honour they may have!
An. and Is. Yea, these children of his woe
Shall be their father's bedfellow!

Enter a HERALD.

Herald. Hold! Let me first discharge a duty. I
Am come with mandate from the Governors
Appointed by the people of this realm
Cadmean. Their high will and pleasure is
That, forasmuch as good Eteocles
Was loyally affected to this land,
Ye do inter him in its tender soil;
Thereby acknowledging he gave his life
For love of her and hatred of her foes;
And, being perfect and without reproach
God-ward and to the temples of his fathers,
Died, as became his youth, in guiltlessness.
Touching the said deceased Eteocles
So much I am commanded to convey.
But for his brother—Polyneices—ye
Are to cast forth unburied his remains
For dogs to gnaw; as a conspirator
Against the integrity of Cadmus' realm,
Who would have turned this kingdom upside down,
Had not a God from heaven braced yonder arm.
Outlawed in death is he, with the same ban
Wherewith the Gods attached him, when he led
An army hither to possess the land.
Therefore it seemeth good that birds of the air
Shall give him burial; and, in dishonour,
He shall have all the honour he hath earned—
No following of slaves to build his tomb;
No keening note of ceremonial woe;
His own kin shall deny him obsequies.
This touching him is formally resolved
By the good lords that govern Cadmus Town.
An. Tell your good lords that I will bury him
If none will help me. If it be dangerous
To bury mine own brother, I am ready!
Shame have I none for this rebellion!
A mighty yearning draws me; that great bond
Which binds us, sprung from the same parent's loins,
And makes us joint-heirs of their misery.
Therefore, my soul, make thou his griefs thine own,
Though he can neither hear nor answer thee,
And be a sister to the slumbering dead!
This body never hollow-bellied wolf
Shall tear and rend! So let no man "resolve it"!
For I will scoop for him a shallow grave,
Ay, with these woman's hands! I'll fold my robe
And carry him in my lap, and cover him!
Let no "good lords" "resolve it" otherwise!
Courage! For what I will I'll find a way!
He. 'Tis my most strict command that thou forbear!
Flout not authority!
An. And it is mine
That thou refine not on thy herald's office.
He. Let me say this: a people long oppressed
When they win free, turn savage.
An. Let them be
As savage as you please—he shall have his grave.
He. And wilt thou pay the honours of the grave
To one whom the supreme authority
Holdeth accurst?
An. Alas! The Gods, methinks,
Have meted out to him his meed of honour.

He. For grievous outrage on the commonweal!
He did most wickedly imperil her!
An. Gave back what he received! Evil for evil!
He. To be revenged upon one man, his foe,
He struck at all!
An. So might we wrangle on!
And so should wrangling still have the last word!
He. Then I have done; reck thine own rede and
rue it!

Exit HERALD.

Chorus

What sorrow like thine is!
And ye angry ghosts,
Blood-boltered Erinys,
Loud, loud are your boasts!
Race-wreckers, your feet have not tarried!
The tree, root and branch, lies shattered!
The ruins of Œdipus' line
With the dust of its dead shall be scattered!
And how shall my heart incline?
On thy poor corse shall I shed no tear?
Shall I not walk before thy bier
When thou to the grave art carried?

Ah! maugre all pity,
I am afraid!
From the wrath of the city
My soul shrinks dismayed!
New sorrow is here for my grieving!
Yea! for there shall not fail thee
The meed of a multitude's tears!
Thou shalt have many to wail thee,
Lost in the wreck of the years!
And must this poor soul go without his moan
Save the death-song his sister singeth alone?
O bitter past believing!

Semi-Ch. What the city declareth
Be done or forborne!
Littl e my heart careth—
Too deeply I mourn—
Yea, my sorrow their anger despiseth!
Lead on! Though his people disown him
And no proud funeral pomp he shall have,
Together our hearts shall bemoan him,
Together our hands build his grave!
For to-day goeth by as a tale that is told,
And Time metes new censure, revoking the old,
And Justice her dooms reviseth!

Semi-Ch. Go thy ways! Where my trust is
My mourning shall be!
When the stern soul of Justice
And man's censure agree,
Shall I question or shall I upbraid her?
Nay, rather my dirge shall be chanted
For him who wrought most for his land,
And the city that Cadmus planted,
Under Heaven and Zeus' mighty hand,
When she was like to be cast away,
Foundered far from the light of day
'Neath the wave of the strong invader.

Exeunt; one half following ANTIGONE *with the body of* POLYNEICES, *and the other half* ISMENE *with the body of* ETEOCLES.

PROMETHEUS BOUND

DRAMATIS PERSONAE

Kratos	Chorus of the Oceanides
Bia	Oceanus
Hephaestus	Io
Prometheus	Hermes

Mountainous country, and in the middle of a deep gorge a Rock, towards which KRATOS *and* BIA *carry the gigantic form of* PROMETHEUS. HEPHAESTUS *follows dejectedly with hammer, nails, chains, etc.*

Kratos. Now have we journeyed to a spot of earth
Remote—the Scythian wild, a waste untrod.
And now, Hephaestus, thou must execute
The task our father laid on thee, and fetter
This malefactor to the jagged rocks
In adamantine bonds infrangible;
For thine own blossom of all forging fire
He stole and gave to mortals; trespass grave
For which the Gods have called him to account,
That he may learn to bear Zeus' tyranny
And cease to play the lover of mankind.
Hephaestus. Kratos and Bia, for ye twain the hest
Of Zeus is done with; nothing lets you further.
But forcibly to bind a brother God,
In chains, in this deep chasm raked by all storms
I have not courage; yet needs must I pluck
Courage from manifest necessity,
For woe worth him that slights the Father's word.
O high-souled son of Themis sage in counsel,
With heavy heart I must make thy heart heavy,
In bonds of brass not easy to be loosed,
Nailing thee to this crag where no wight dwells,
Nor sound of human voice nor shape of man
Shall visit thee; but the sun-blaze shall roast
Thy flesh; thy hue, flower-fair, shall suffer change;
Welcome will Night be when with spangled robe
She hides the light of day; welcome the sun
Returning to disperse the frosts of dawn.
And every hour shall bring its weight of woe
To wear thy heart away; for yet unborn
Is he who shall release thee from thy pain.
This is thy wage for loving humankind.
For, being a God, thou dared'st the Gods' ill will,
Preferring, to exceeding honour, Man.
Wherefore thy long watch shall be comfortless,
Stretched on this rock, never to close an eye
Or bend a knee; and vainly shalt thou lift,
With groanings deep and lamentable cries,
Thy voice; for Zeus is hard to be entreated,
As new-born power is ever pitiless.
Kr. Enough! Why palter? Why wast idle pity?
Is not the God Gods loathe hateful to thee?
Traitor to man of thy prerogative?
Hep. Kindred and fellowhip are dreaded names.
Kr. Questionless; but to slight the Father's word—
How sayest thou? Is not this fraught with more dread?
Hep. Thy heart was ever hard and overbold.
Kr. But wailing will not ease him! Waste no pains
Where thy endeavour nothing profiteth.
Hep. Oh execrable work! loathed handicraft!
Kr. Why curse thy trade? For what thou hast to do,
Troth, smithcraft is in no wise answerable.
Hep. Would that it were another's craft, not mine!
Kr. Why, all things are a burden save to rule
Over the Gods; for none is free but Zeus.
Hep. To that I answer not, knowing it true.
Kr. Why, then, make haste to cast the chains about him,
Lest glancing down on thee the Father's eye
Behold a laggard and a loiterer.
Hep. Here are the iron bracelets for his arms.
Kr. Fasten them round his arms with all thy strength!
Strike with thy hammer! Nail him to the rocks!
Hep. 'Tis done! and would that it were done less well!
Kr. Harder—I say— strike harder—screw all tight
And be not in the least particular
Remiss, for unto one of his resource
Bars are but instruments of liberty.
Hep. This forearm's fast: a shackle hard to shift.
Kr. Now buckle this! and handsomely! Let him learn
Sharp though he be, he's a dull blade to Zeus.
Hep. None can find fault with this :—save him it tortures.
Kr. Now take thine iron spike and drive it in,
Until it gnaw clean through the rebel's breast.
Hep. Woe's me, Prometheus, for thy weight of woe!
Kr. Still shirking? still a-groaning for the foes
Of Zeus? Anon thou'lt wail thine own mishap.
Hep. Thou seest what eyes scarce bear to look upon!
Kr. I see this fellow getting his deserts!
But strap him with a belt about his ribs.
Hep. I do what I must do: for thee—less words!

Kr. "Words," quotha? Aye, and shout 'em if need be.
Come down and cast a ring-bolt round his legs.
Hep. The thing is featly done; and 'twas quick work.
Kr. Now with a sound rap knock the bolt-pins home!
For heavy-handed is thy task-master.
Hep. So villainous a form vile tongue befits.
Kr. Be thou the heart of wax, but chide not me
That I am gruffish, stubborn and stiff-willed.
Hep. Oh, come away! The tackle holds him fast.
Kr. Now, where thou hang'st insult! Plunder the Gods
For creatures of a day! To thee what gift
Will mortals tender to requite thy pains?
The destinies were out miscalling thee
Designer: a designer thou wilt need
From trap so well contrived to twist thee free.
Exeunt.
Prometheus. O divine air! Breezes on swift bird-wings,
Ye river fountains, and of ocean-waves
The multitudinous laughter! Mother Earth!
And thou all-seeing circle of the sun,
Behold what I, a God, from Gods endure!
Look down upon my shame,
The cruel wrong that racks my frame,
The grinding anguish that shall waste my strength,
Till time's ten thousand years have measured out their length!
He hath devised these chains,
The new throned potentate who reigns,
Chief of the chieftains of the Blest. Ah me!
The woe which is and that which yet shall be
I wail; and question make of these wide skies
When shall the star of my deliverance rise.
And yet—and yet— exactly I foresee
All that shall come to pass; no sharp surprise
Of pain shall overtake me; what's determined
Bear, as I can, I must, knowing the might
Of strong Necessity is unconquerable.
But touching my fate silence and speech alike
Are unsupportable. For boons bestowed
On mortal men I am straitened in these bonds.
I sought the fount of fire in hollow reed
Hid privily, a measureless resource
For man, and mighty teacher of all arts.
This is the crime that I must expiate
Hung here in chains, nailed 'neath the open sky.
Ha! Ha!
What echo, what odour floats by with no sound?
God-wafted or mortal or mingled its strain?
Comes there one to this world's end, this mountain-girt ground,
To have sight of my torment? Or of what is he fain?
A God ye behold in bondage and pain,
The foe of Zeus and one at feud with all
The deities that find
Submissive entry to the tyrant's hall;
His fault, too great a love of humankind.
Ah me! Ah me! what wafture nigh at hand,
As of great birds of prey, is this I hear?
The bright air fanned
Whistles and shrills with rapid beat of wings.
There cometh nought but to my spirit brings
Horror and fear.

The DAUGHTERS OF OCEANUS *draw near in mid-air in their winged chariot.*

Chorus. Put thou all fear away!
In kindness cometh this array
On wings of speed to mountain lone,
Our sire's consent not lightly won.
But a fresh breeze our convoy brought,
For loud the din of iron raught
Even to our sea-cave's cold recess,
And scared away the meek-eyed bashfulness.
I tarried not to tie my sandal shoe
But haste, post haste, through air my wingéd chariot flew.
Pr. Ah me! Ah me!
Fair progeny
That many-childed Tethys brought to birth,
Fathered of Ocean old
Whose sleepless stream is rolled
Round the vast shores of earth!
Look on me! Look upon these chains
Wherein I hang fast held
On rocks high-pinnacled,
My dungeon and my tower of dole,
Where o'er the abyss my soul,
Sad warder, her unwearied watch sustains!
Ch. Prometheus, I am gazing on thee now!
With the cold breath of fear upon my brow,
Not without mist of dimming tears,
While to my sight thy giant stature rears
Its bulk forpined upon these savage rocks
In shameful bonds the linkéd adamant locks.
For now new steersmen take the helm
Olympian; now with little thought
Of right, on strange, new laws Zeus stablisheth his realm,
Bringing the mighty ones of old to naught.
Pr. Oh that he had conveyed me
'Neath earth, 'neath hell that swalloweth up the dead;
In Tartarus, illimitably vast
With adamantine fetters bound me fast—
There his fierce anger on me visited,
Where never mocking laughter could upbraid me
Of God or aught beside!
But now a wretch enskied,
A far-seen vane,
All they that hate me triumph in my pain.
Ch. Who of the Gods is there so pitiless
That he can triumph in thy sore distress?
Who doth not inly groan
With every pang of thine save Zeus alone?
But he is ever wroth, not to be bent
From his resolved intent
The sons of heaven to subjugate;
Nor shall he cease until his heart be satiate,

Or one a way devise
To hurl him from the throne where he doth monarchize.
Pr. Yea, of a surety—though he do me wrong,
Loading my limbs with fetters strong—
The president
Of heaven's high parliament
Shall need me yet to show
What new conspiracy with privy blow
Attempts his sceptre and his kingly seat.
Neither shall words with all persuasion sweet,
Not though his tongue drop honey, cheat
Nor charm my knowledge from me; nor duress
Of menace dire, fear of more grievous pains,
Unseal my lips, till he have loosed these chains,
And granted for these injuries redress.
Ch. High is the heart of thee,
Thy will no whit by bitter woes unstrung,
And all too free
The licence of thy bold, unshackled tongue.
But fear hath roused my soul with piercing cry!
And for thy fate my heart misgives me! I
Tremble to know when through the breakers' roar
Thy keel shall touch again the friendly shore;
For not by prayer to Zeus is access won;
An unpersuadable heart hath Cronos' son.
Pr. I know the heart of Zeus is hard, that he hath tied
Justice to his side;
But he shall be full gentle thus assuaged;
And, the implacable wrath wherewith he raged
Smoothed quite away, nor he nor I
Be loth to seal a bond of peace and amity.
Ch. All that thou hast to tell I pray unfold,
That we may hear at large upon what count
Zeus took thee and with bitter wrong affronts:
Instruct us, if the telling hurt thee not.
Pr. These things are sorrowful for me to speak,
Yet silence too is sorrow: all ways woe!
When first the Blessed Ones were filled with wrath
And there arose division in their midst,
These instant to hurl Cronos from his throne
That Zeus might be their king, and these, adverse,
Contending that he ne'er should rule the Gods,
Then I, wise counsel urging to persuade
The Titans, sons of Ouranos and Chthon,
Prevailed not: but, all indirect essays
Despising, they by the strong hand, effortless,
Yet by main force—supposed that they might seize
Supremacy. But me my mother Themis
And Gaia, one form called by many names,
Not once alone with voice oracular
Had prophesied how power should be disposed—
That not by strength neither by violence
The mighty should be mastered, but by guile.
Which things by me set forth at large, they scorned,
Nor graced my motion with the least regard.
Then, of all ways that offered, I judged best,
Taking my mother with me, to support,
No backward friend, the not less cordial Zeus.
And by my politic counsel Tartarus,
The bottomless and black, old Cronos hides
With his confederates. So helped by me,
The tyrant of the Gods, such service rendered
With ignominious chastisement requites.
But 'tis a common malady of power
Tyrannical never to trust a friend.
And now, what ye inquired, for what arraigned
He shamefully entreats me, ye shall know.
When first upon his high, paternal throne
He took his seat, forthwith to divers Gods
Divers good gifts he gave, and parcelled out
His empire, but of miserable men
Recked not at all; rather it was his wish
To wipe out man and rear another race:
And these designs none contravened but me.
I risked the bold attempt, and saved mankind
From stark destruction and the road to hell.
Therefore with this sore penance am I bowed,
Grievous to suffer, pitiful to see.
But, for compassion shown to man, such fate
I no wise earned; rather in wrath's despite
Am I to be reformed, and made a show
Of infamy to Zeus.
Ch. He hath a heart
Of iron, hewn out of unfeeling rock
Is he, Prometheus, whom thy sufferings
Rouse not to wrath. Would I had ne'er beheld them,
For verily the sight hath wrung my heart.
Pr. Yea, to my friends a woeful sight am I.
Ch. Hast not more boldly in aught else transgressed?
Pr. I took from man expectancy of death.
Ch. What medicine found'st thou for this malady?
Pr. I planted blind hope in the heart of him.
Ch. A mighty boon thou gavest there to man.
Pr. Moreover, I conferred the gift of fire.
Ch. And have frail mortals now the flame-bright fire?
Pr. Yea, and shall master many arts thereby.
Ch. And Zeus with such misfeasance charging thee—
Pr. Torments me with extremity of woe.
Ch. And is no end in prospect of thy pains?
Pr. None; save when he shall choose to make an end.
Ch. How should he choose? What hope is thine? Dost thou
Not see that thou hast erred? But how thou erredst
Small pleasure were to me to tell; to thee
Exceeding sorrow. Let it go then: rather
Seek thou for some deliverance from thy woes.
Pr. He who stands free with an untrammelled foot
Is quick to counsel and exhort a friend
In trouble. But all these things I know well.
Of my free will, my own free will, I erred,
And freely do I here acknowledge it.
Freeing mankind myself have durance found.
Natheless, I looked not for sentence so dread,
High on this precipice to droop and pine,
Having no neighbour but the desolate crags.

And now lament no more the ills I suffer,
But come to earth and an attentive ear
Lend to the things that shall befall hereafter.
Harken, oh harken, suffer as I suffer!
Who knows, who knows, but on some scatheless head,
Another's yet for the like woes reserved,
The wandering doom will presently alight?

Ch. Prometheus, we have heard thy call:
Not on deaf ears these awful accents fall.
Lo! lightly leaving at thy words
My flying car
And holy air, the pathway of great birds,
I long to tread this land of peak and scar,
And certify myself by tidings sure
Of all thou hast endured and must endure.

While the winged chariot of the OCEANIDES *comes to ground their father* OCEANUS *enters, riding on a monster.*

Oceanus. Now have I traversed the unending plain
And unto thee, Prometheus, am I come,
Guiding this wingèd monster with no rein,
Nor any bit, but mind's firm masterdom.
And know that for thy grief my heart is sore;
The bond of kind, methinks, constraineth me;
Nor is there any I would honour more,
Apart from kinship, than I reverence thee.
And thou shalt learn that I speak verity:
Mine is no smooth, false tongue; for do but show
How I can serve thee, grieved and outraged thus,
Thou ne'er shalt say thou hast, come weal, come woe,
A friend more faithful than Oceanus.

Pr. How now? Who greets me? What! Art thou too come
To gaze upon my woes? How could'st thou leave
The stream that bears thy name, thine antres arched
With native rock, to visit earth that breeds
The massy iron in her womb? Com'st thou
To be spectator of my evil lot
And fellow sympathizer with my woes?
Behold, a thing indeed to gaze upon!
The friend of Zeus, co-stablisher of his rule,
See, by this sentence with what pains I am bowed!

Oc. Prometheus, all too plainly I behold:
And for the best would counsel thee: albeit
Thy brain is subtle. Learn to know thy heart,
And, as the times, so let thy manners change,
For by the law of change a new God rules.
But, if these bitter, savage, sharp-set words
Thou ventest, it may be, though he sit throned
Far off and high above thee, Zeus will hear;
And then thy present multitude of ills
Will seem the mild correction of a babe.
Rather, O thou much chastened one, refrain
Thine anger, and from suffering seek release.
Stale, peradventure, seem these words of mine:
Nevertheless, of a too haughty tongue
Such punishment, Prometheus, is the wage.
But thou, not yet brought low by suffering,
To what thou hast of ill would'st add far worse.
Therefore, while thou hast me for schoolmaster,
Thou shalt not kick against the pricks; the more
That an arch-despot who no audit dreads
Rules by his own rough will. And now I leave thee,
To strive with what success I may command
For thy deliv'rance. Keep a quiet mind
And use not over-vehemence of speech—
Knowest thou not, being exceeding wise,
A wanton, idle tongue brings chastisement?

Pr. I marvel that thou art not in my case,
Seeing with me thou did'st adventure all.
And now, I do entreat thee, spare thyself.
Thou wilt not move him: he's not easy moved.
Take heed lest thou find trouble by the way.

Oc. Thou are a better counsellor to others
Than to thyself: I judge by deeds not words.
Pluck me not back when I would fain set forth.
My oath upon it, Zeus will grant my prayer
And free thee from these pangs.

Pr. I tender thee
For this my thanks and ever-during praise.
Certes, no backward friend art thou; and yet
Trouble not thyself; for at the best thy labour
Will nothing serve me, if thou mean'st to serve.
Being thyself untrammelled stand thou fast.
For, not to mitigate my own mischance,
Would I see others hap on evil days.
The thought be far from me. I feel the weight
Of Atlas' woes, my brother, in the west
Shouldering the pillar that props heaven and earth,
No wieldy fardel for his arms to fold.
The giant dweller in Cilician dens
I saw and pitied—a terrific shape,
A hundred-headed monster—when he fell,
Resistless Typhon who withstood the Gods,
With fearsome hiss of beak-mouth horrible,
While lightning from his eyes with Gorgon-glare
Flashed for the ravage of the realm of Zeus.
But on him came the bolt that never sleeps,
Down-crashing thunder, with emitted fire,
Which shattered him and all his towering hopes
Dashed into ruin; smitten through the breast,
His strength as smoking cinder, lightning-charred.
And now a heap, a helpless, sprawling hulk,
He lies stretched out beside the narrow seas,
Pounded and crushed deep under Etna's roots.
But on the mountain-top Hephaestus sits
Forging the molten iron, whence shall burst
Rivers of fire, with red and ravening jaws
To waste fair-fruited, smooth, Sicilian fields.
Such bilious up-boiling of his ire
Shall Typho vent, with slingstone-showers red-hot,
And unapproachable surge of fiery spray,
Although combusted by the bolt of Zeus.
But thou art not unlearned, nor needest me
To be thy teacher: save thyself the way
Thou knowest and I will fortify my heart
Until the wrathfulness of Zeus abate.

Oc. Nay then, Prometheus, art thou ignorant
Words are physicians to a wrath-sick soul?

Pr. Yes, if with skill one soften the ripe core,
Not by rough measures make it obdurate.

Oc. Seest thou in warm affection detriment
Or aught untoward in adventuring?
Pr. A load of toil and a light mind withal.
Oc. Then give me leave to call that sickness mine.
Wise men accounted fools attain their ends.
Pr. But how if I am galled by thine offence?
Oc. There very palpably thou thrustest home.
Pr. Beware lest thou through pity come to broils.
Oc. With one established in Omnipotence?
Pr. Of him take heed lest thou find heaviness.
Oc. I am schooled by thy calamity, Prometheus!
Pr. Pack then! And, prithee, do not change thy mind!
Oc. Thou criest "On" to one in haste to go.
For look, my dragon with impatient wings
Flaps at the broad, smooth road of level air.
Fain would he kneel him down in his own stall.
Exit OCEANUS.
Ch. (*after alighting*) I mourn for thee, Prometheus, minished and brought low,
Watering my virgin cheeks with these sad drops, that flow
From sorrow's rainy fount, to fill soft-lidded eyes
With pure libations for thy fortune's obsequies.
An evil portion that none coveteth hath Zeus
Prepared for thee; by self-made laws established for his use
Disposing all, the elder Gods he purposeth to show
How strong is that right arm wherewith he smites a foe.
There hath gone up a cry from earth, a groaning for the fall
Of things of old renown and shapes majestical,
And for thy passing an exceeding bitter groan;
For thee and for thy brother Gods whose honour was thine own:
These things all they who dwell in Asia's holy seat,
Time's minions, mourn and with their groans thy groans repeat.
Yea, and they mourn who dwell beside the Colchian shore,
The hero maids unwedded that delight in war,
And Scythia's swarming myriads who their dwelling make
Around the borders of the world, the salt Mæotian lake.
Mourns Ares' stock, that flowers in desert Araby,
And the strong city mourns, the hill-fort planted high,
Near neighbour to huge Caucasus, dread mountaineers
That love the clash of arms, the counter of sharp spears.
Beforetime of all Gods one have I seen in pain,
One only Titan bound with adamantine chain,
Atlas in strength supreme, who groaning stoops, downbent
Under the burthen of the earth and heaven's broad firmament.
Bellows the main of waters, surge with foam-seethed surge
Clashing tumultuous; for thee the deep seas chant their dirge;
And Hell's dark under-world a hollow moaning fills;
Thee mourn the sacred streams with all their fountain-rills.
Pr. Think not that I for pride and stubbornness
Am silent: rather is my heart the prey
Of gnawing thoughts, both for the past, and now
Seeing myself by vengeance buffeted.
For to these younger Gods their precedence
Who severally determined if not I?
No more of that: I should but weary you
With things ye know; but listen to the tale
Of human sufferings, and how at first
Senseless as beasts I gave men sense, possessed them
Of mind. I speak not in contempt of man;
I do but tell of good gifts I conferred.
In the beginning, seeing they saw amiss,
And hearing heard not, but, like phantoms huddled
In dreams, the perplexed story of their days
Confounded; knowing neither timber-work
Nor brick-built dwellings basking in the light,
But dug for themselves holes, wherein like ants,
That hardly may contend against a breath,
They dwelt in burrows of their unsunned caves.
Neither of winter's cold had they fixed sign,
Nor of the spring when she comes decked with flowers,
Nor yet of summer's heat with melting fruits
Sure token: but utterly without knowledge
Moiled, until I the rising of the stars
Showed them, and when they set, though much obscure.
Moreover, number, the most excellent
Of all inventions, I for them devised,
And gave them writing that retaineth all,
The serviceable mother of the Muse.
I was the first that yoked unmanaged beasts,
To serve as slaves with collar and with pack,
And take upon themselves, to man's relief,
The heaviest labour of his hands: and I
Tamed to the rein and drove in wheelèd cars
The horse, of sumptuous pride the ornament.
And those sea-wanderers with the wings of cloth,
The shipman's waggons, none but I contrived.
These manifold inventions for mankind
I perfected, who, out upon't, have none—
No, not one shift—to rid me of this shame.
Ch. Thy sufferings have been shameful, and thy mind
Strays at a loss: like to a bad physician
Fallen sick, thou'rt out of heart: nor cans't prescribe
For thine own case the draught to make thee sound.
Pr. But hear the sequel and the more admire
What arts, what aids I cleverly evolved.
The chiefest that, if any man fell sick,
There was no help for him, comestible,
Lotion or potion; but for lack of drugs
They dwindled quite away; until I taught them
To compound draughts and mixtures sanative,
Wherewith they now are armed against disease.

I staked the winding path of divination
And was the first distinguisher of dreams,
The true from false; and voices ominous
Of meaning dark interpreted; and tokens
Seen when men take the road; and augury
By flight of all the greater crook-clawed birds
With nice discrimination I defined;
These by their nature fair and favourable,
Those, flattered with fair name. And of each sort
The habits I described; their mutual feuds
And friendships and the assemblages they hold.
And of the plumpness of the inward parts
What colour is acceptable to the Gods,
The well-streaked liver-lobe and gall-bladder.
Also by roasting limbs well wrapped in fat
And the long chine, I led men on the road
Of dark and riddling knowledge; and I purged
The glancing eye of fire, dim before,
And made its meaning plain. These are my works.
Then, things beneath the earth, aids hid from man,
Brass, iron, silver, gold, who dares to say
He was before me in discovering?
None, I wot well, unless he loves to babble.
And in a single word to sum the whole—
All manner of arts men from Prometheus learned.

Ch. Shoot not beyond the mark in succouring man
While thou thyself art comfortless: for I
Am of good hope that from these bonds escaped
Thou shalt one day be mightier than Zeus.

Pr. Fate, that brings all things to an end, not thus
Apportioneth my lot: ten thousand pangs
Must bow, ten thousand miseries afflict me
Ere from these bonds I freedom find, for Art
Is by much weaker than Necessity.

Ch. Who is the pilot of Necessity?

Pr. The Fates triform, and the unforgetting Furies.

Ch. So then Zeus is of lesser might than these?

Pr. Surely he shall not shun the lot apportioned.

Ch. What lot for Zeus save world-without-end reign?

Pr. Tax me no further with importunate questions.

Ch. O deep the mystery thou shroudest there!

Pr. Of aught but this freely thou may'st discourse;
But touching this I charge thee speak no word;
Nay, veil it utterly: for strictly kept
The secret from these bonds shall set me free.

Chorus

May Zeus who all things swayeth
Ne'er wreak the might none stayeth
On wayward will of mine;
May I stint not nor waver
With offerings of sweet savour
And feasts of slaughtered kine;
The holy to the holy,
With frequent feet and lowly
At altar, fane and shrine,
Over the Ocean marches,
The deep that no drought parches,
Draw near to the divine.
My tongue the Gods estrange not;
My firm set purpose change not,
As wax melts in fire-shine.
Sweet is the life that lengthens,
While joyous hope still strengthens,
And glad, bright thoughts sustain;
But shuddering I behold thee,
The sorrows that enfold thee
And all thine endless pain.
For Zeus thou hast despisèd;
Thy fearless heart misprizèd
All that his vengeance can,
Thy wayward will obeying,
Excess of honour paying,
Prometheus, unto man.

And, oh, belovèd, for this graceless grace
What thanks? What prowess for thy bold essay
Shall champion thee from men of mortal race,
The petty insects of a passing day?
Saw'st not how puny is the strength they spend?
With few, faint steps walking as dreams and blind,
Nor can the utmost of their lore transcend
The harmony of the Eternal Mind.
These things I learned seeing thy glory dimmed,
Prometheus. Ah, not thus on me was shed
The rapture of sweet music, when I hymned
The marriage-song round bath and bridal bed
At thine espousals, and of thy blood-kin,
A bride thou chosest, wooing her to thee
With all good gifts that may a Goddess win,
Thy father's child, divine Hesione.

Enter IO, *crazed and horned.*

Io. What land is this? What people here abide?
And who is he,
The prisoner of this windswept mountain-side?
Speak, speak to me;
Tell me, poor caitiff, how did'st thou transgress,
Thus buffeted?
Whither am I, half-dead with weariness,
For-wanderèd?
Ha! Ha!
Again the prick, the stab of gadfly-sting!
O earth, earth, hide,
The hollow shape—Argus—that evil thing—
The hundred-eyed-
Earth-born-herdsman! I see him yet; he stalks
With stealthy pace
And crafty watch not all my poor wit baulks!
From the deep place
Of earth that hath his bones he breaketh bound,
And from the pale
Of Death, the Underworld, a hell-sent hound
On the blood-trail,
Fasting and faint he drives me on before,
With spectral hand,
Along the windings of the wasteful shore,
The salt sea-sand!
List! List! the pipe! how drowzily it shrills!
A cricket-cry!

See! See! the wax-webbed reeds! Oh, to these ills
Ye Gods on high,
Ye blessed Gods, what bourne? O wandering feet
When will ye rest?
O Cronian child, wherein by aught unmeet
Have I transgressed
To be yoke-fellow with Calamity?
My mind unstrung,
A crack-brained lack-wit, frantic mad am I,
By gad-fly stung,
Thy scourge, that tarres me on with buzzing wing!
Plunge me in fire,
Hide me in earth, to deep-sea monsters fling,
But my desire—
Kneeling I pray—grudge not to grant, O King!
Too long a race
Stripped for the course have I run to and fro;
And still I chase
The vanishing goal, the end of all my woe;
Enough have I mourned!
Hear'st thou the lowing of the maid cow-horned?

Pr. How should I hear thee not? Thou art the child
Of Inachus, dazed with the dizzying fly.
The heart of Zeus thou hast made hot with love
And Hera's curse even as a runner stripped
Pursues thee ever on thine endless round.

Io. How dost thou know my father's name? Impart
To one like thee
A poor, distressful creature, who thou art.
Sorrow with me,
Sorrowful one! Tell me, whose voice proclaims
Things true and sad,
Naming by all their old, unhappy names,
What drove me mad—
Sick! Sick! ye Gods, with suffering ye have sent,
That clings and clings;
Wasting my lamp of life till it be spent!
Crazed with your stings!
Famished I come with trampling and with leaping,
Torment and shame,
To Hera's cruel wrath, her craft unsleeping,
Captive and tame!
Of all wights woe-begone and fortune-crossed,
Oh, in the storm
Of the world's sorrow is there one so lost?
Speak, godlike form,
And be in this dark world my oracle!
Can'st thou not sift
The things to come? Hast thou no art to tell
What subtle shift,
Or sound of charming song shall make me well?
Hide naught of ill!
But—if indeed thou knowest—prophesy—
In words that thrill
Clear-toned through air—what such a wretch as I
Must yet abide—
The lost, lost maid that roams earth's kingdoms wide?

Pr. What thou wouldst learn I will make clear to thee,
Not weaving subtleties, but simple sooth
Unfolding as the mouth should speak to friends.
I am Prometheus, giver of fire to mortals.

Io. Oh universal succour of mankind,
Sorrowful Prometheus, why art thou punished thus?

Pr. I have but now ceased mourning for my griefs.

Io. Wilt thou not grant me then so small a boon?

Pr. What is it thou dost ask? Thou shalt know all.

Io. Declare to me who chained thee in this gorge.

Pr. The hest of Zeus, but 'twas Hephæstus' hand.

Io. But what transgression dost thou expiate?

Pr. Let this suffice thee: thou shalt know no more.

Io. Nay, but the end of my long wandering
When shall it be? This too thou must declare.

Pr. That it is better for thee not to know.

Io. Oh hide not from me what I have to suffer!

Pr. Poor child! Poor child! I do not grudge the gift.

Io. Why then, art thou so slow to tell me all?

Pr. It is not from unkindness; but I fear
'Twill break thy heart.

Io. Take thou no thought for me
Where thinking thwarteth heart's desire!

Pr. So keen
To know thy sorrows! List! and thou shalt learn.

Ch. Not till thou hast indulged a wish of mine.
First let us hear the story of her grief
And she herself shall tell the woeful tale.
After, thy wisdom shall impart to her
The conflict yet to come.

Pr. So be it, then.
And, Io, thus much courtesy thou owest
These maidens being thine own father's kin.
For with a moving story of our woes
To win a tear from weeping auditors
In nought demeans the teller.

Io. I know not
How fitly to refuse; and at your wish
All ye desire to know I will in plain,
Round terms set forth. And yet the telling of it
Harrows my soul; this winter's tale of wrong,
Of angry Gods and brute deformity,
And how and why on me these horrors swooped.
Always there were dreams visiting by night
The woman's chambers where I slept; and they
With flattering words admonished and cajoled me,
Saying, "O lucky one, so long a maid?
And what a match for thee if thou would'st wed!
Why, pretty, here is Zeus as hot as hot—
Love-sick—to have thee! Such a bolt as thou
Hast shot clean through his heart! And he won't rest
Till Cypris help him win thee! Lift not then,
My daughter, a proud foot to spurn the bed
Of Zeus: but get thee gone to meadow deep
By Lerna's marsh, where are thy father's flocks
And cattle-folds, that on the eye of Zeus
May fall the balm that shall assuage desire."
Such dreams oppressed me, troubling all my nights,

Woe's me! till I plucked courage up to tell
My father of these fears that walked in darkness.
And many times to Pytho and Dodona
He sent his sacred missioners, to inquire
How, or by deed or word, he might conform
To the high will and pleasure of the Gods.
And they returned with slippery oracles,
Nought plain, but all to baffle and perplex—
And then at last to Inachus there raught
A saying that flashed clear; the drift, that I
Must be put out from home and country, forced
To be a wanderer at the ends of the earth,
A thing devote and dedicate; and if
I would not, there should fall a thunderbolt
From Zeus, with blinding flash, and utterly
Destroy my race. So spake the oracle
Of Loxias. In sorrow he obeyed,
And from beneath his roof drove forth his child
Grieving as he grieved, and from house and home
Bolted and barred me out. But the high hand
Of Zeus bear hardly on the rein of fate.
And, instantly—even in a moment—mind
And body suffered strange distortion. Horned
Even as ye see me now, and with sharp bite
Of gadfly pricked, with high-flung skip, stark-mad,
I bounded, galloping headlong on, until
I came to the sweet waters of the stream
Kerchneian, hard by Lerna's spring. And thither
Argus, the giant herdsman, fierce and fell
As a strong wine unmixed, with hateful cast
Of all his cunning eyes upon the trail,
Gave chase and tracked me down. And there he perished
By violent and sudden doom surprised.
But I with darting sting—the scorpion whip
Of angry Gods—am lashed from land to land.
Thou hast my story, and, if thou can'st tell
What I have still to suffer, speak; but do not,
Moved by compassion, with a lying tale
Warm my cold heart; no sickness of the soul
Is half so shameful as composèd falsehoods.

Ch. Off! lost one! off! Horror, I cry!
Horror and misery!
Was this the traveller's tale I craved to hear?
Oh, that mine eyes should see
A sight so ill to look upon! Ah me!
Sorrow, defilement, haunting fear,
Fan my blood cold,
Stabbed with a two-edged sting!
O Fate, Fate, Fate, tremblingly I behold
The plight of Io, thine apportioning!

Pr. Thou dost lament too soon, and art as one
All fear. Refrain thyself till thou hast heard
What's yet to be.
Ch. Speak and be our instructor:
There is a kind of balm to the sick soul
In certain knowledge of the grief to come.
Pr. Your former wish I lightly granted ye:
And ye have heard, even as ye desired,
From this maid's lips the story of her sorrow.
Now hear the sequel, the ensuing woes
The damsel must endure from Hera's hate.
And thou, O seed of Inachæan loins,
Weigh well my words, that thou may'st understand
Thy journey's end. First towards the rising sun
Turn hence, and traverse fields that ne'er felt plough
Until thou reach the country of the Scyths,
A race of wanderers handling the long-bow
That shoots afar, and having their habitations
Under the open sky in wattled cotes
That move on wheels. Go not thou nigh to them,
But ever within sound of the breaking waves
Pass through their land. And on the left of thee
The Chalybes, workers in iron, dwell.
Beware of them, for they are savages,
Who suffer not a stranger to come near.
And thou shalt reach the river Hybristes,
Well named. Cross not, for it is ill to cross,
Until thou come even unto Caucasus,
Highest of mountains, where the foaming river
Blows all its volume from the summit ridge
That o'ertops all. And that star-neighboured ridge
Thy feet must climb; and, following the road
That runneth south, thou presently shalt reach
The Amazonian hosts that loathe the male,
And shall one day remove from thence and found
Themiscyra hard by Thermodon's stream,
Where on the craggy Salmadessian coast
Waves gnash their teeth, the maw of mariners
And step-mother of ships. And they shall lead thee
Upon thy way, and with a right good will.
Then shalt thou come to the Cimmerian Isthmus,
Even at the pass and portals of the sea,
And leaving it behind thee, stout of heart,
Cross o'er the channel of Mæotis' Lake.
For ever famous among men shall be
The story of thy crossing, and the strait
Be called by a new name, the Bosporus,
In memory of thee. Then having left
Europa's soil behind thee thou shalt come
To the main land of Asia. What think ye?
Is not the only ruler of the Gods
A complete tyrant, violent to all,
Respecting none? First, being himself a God,
He burneth to enjoy a mortal maid,
And then torments her with these wanderings.
A sorry suitor for thy love, poor girl,
A bitter wooing. Yet having heard so much
Thou art not even in the overture
And prelude of the song.
Io. Alas! Oh! Oh!
Pr. Thou dost cry out, fetching again deep groans:
What wilt thou do when thou hast heard in full
The evils yet to come?
Ch. And wilt thou tell
The maiden something further: some fresh sorrow?
Pr. A stormy sea of wrong and ruining.
Io. What does it profit me to live! Oh, why
Do I not throw myself from this rough crag
And in one leap rid me of all my pain?

Better to die at once than live, and all
My days be evil.
Pr. Thou would'st find it hard
To bear what I must bear: for unto me
It is not given to die,—a dear release
From pain; but now of suffering there is
No end in sight till Zeus shall fall.
Io. And shall
Zeus fall? His power be taken from him?
No matter when if true—
Pr. 'Twould make thee happy
Methinks, if thou could'st see calamity
Whelm him.
Io. How should it not when all my woes
Are of his sending?
Pr. Well, then, thou may'st learn how
These things shall be.
Io. Oh, who will snatch away
The tyrant's rod?
Pr. Himself by his own vain
And fond imaginings.
Io. But how? Oh, speak,
If the declaring draw no evil down!
Pr. A marriage he shall make shall vex him sore.
Io. A marriage? Whether of gods or mortals? Speak!
If this be utterable!
Pr. Why dost thou ask
What I may not declare?
Io. And shall he quit
The throne of all the worlds, by a new spouse
Supplanted?
Pr. She will bear to him a child,
And he shall be in might more excellent
Than his progenitor.
Io. And he will find
No way to parry this strong stroke of fate?
Pr. None save my own self—when these bonds are loosed.
Io. And who shall loose them if Zeus wills not?
Pr. One
Of thine own seed.
Io. How say'st thou? Shall a child
Of mine release thee?
Pr. Son of thine, but son
The thirteenth generation shall beget.
Io. A prophecy oracularly dark.
Pr. Then seek not thou to know thine own fate.
Io. Nay,
Tender me not a boon to snatch it from me.
Pr. Of two gifts thou hast asked one shall be thine.
Io. What gifts? Pronounce and leave to me the choice.
Pr. Nay, thou are free to choose. Say, therefore, whether
I shall declare to thee thy future woes
Or him who shall be my deliverer.
Ch. Nay, but let both be granted! Unto her
That which she chooseth, unto me my choice,
That I, too, may have honour from thy lips.
First unto her declare her wanderings,
And unto me him who shall set thee free;
'Tis that I long to know.
Pr. I will resist
No further, but to your importunacy
All things which ye desire to learn reveal.
And, Io, first to thee I will declare
Thy far-driven wanderings; write thou my words
In the retentive tablets of thy heart.
When thou hast crossed the flood that flows between
And is the boundary of two continents,
Turn to the sun's uprising, where he treads
Printing with fiery steps the eastern sky,
And from the roaring of the Pontic surge
Do thou pass on, until before thee lies
The Gorgonean plain, Kisthene called,
Where dwell the gray-haired three, the Phorcides,
Old, mumbling maids, swan-shaped, having one eye
Betwixt the three, and but a single tooth.
On them the sun with his bright beams ne'er glanceth
Nor moon that lamps the night. Not far from them
The sisters three, the Gorgons, have their haunt;
Winged forms, with snaky locks, hateful to man,
Whom nothing mortal looking on can live.
Thus much that thou may'st have a care of these.
Now of another portent thou shalt hear.
Beware the dogs of Zeus that ne'er give tongue,
The sharp-beaked gryphons, and the one-eyed horde
Of Arimaspians, riding upon horses,
Who dwell around the river rolling gold,
The ferry and the frith of Pluto's port.
Go not thou nigh them. After thou shalt come
To a far land, a dark-skinned race, that dwell
Beside the fountains of the sun, whence flows
The river Æthiops: follow its banks
Until thou comest to the steep-down slope
Where from the Bibline mountains Nilus old
Pours the sweet waters of his holy stream.
And thou, the river guiding thee, shalt come
To the three-sided, wedge-shaped land of Nile,
Where for thyself, Io, and for thy children
Long sojourn is appointed. If in aught
My story seems to stammer and to err
From indirectness, ask and ask again
Till all be manifest. I do not lack
For leisure, having more than well contents me!
Ch. If there be aught that she must suffer yet,
Or aught omitted in the narrative
Of her long wanderings, I pray thee speak.
But if thou hast told all, then grant the boon
We asked and doubtless thou wilt call to mind.
Pr. Nay, she has heard the last of her long journey.
But, as some warrant for her patient hearing
I will relate her former sufferings
Ere she came hither. Much I will omit
That had detained us else with long discourse
And touch at once her journey's thus far goal.

When thou wast come to the Molossian plain
That lies about the high top of Dodona,
Where is an oracle and shrine of Zeus
Thesprotian, and—portent past belief—
The talking oaks, the same from whom the word
Flashed clear and nothing questionably hailed thee
The destined spouse—ah! do I touch old wounds?—
Of Zeus, honoured above thy sex; stung thence
In torment, where the road runs by the sea,
Thou cam'st to the broad gulf of Rhea, whence
Beat back by a strong wind, thou didst retrace
Most painfully thy course; and it shall be
That times to come in memory of thy passage
Shall call that inlet the Ionian Sea.
Thus much for thee in witness that my mind
Beholdeth more than that which leaps to light.
Now for the things to come; what I shall say
Concerns ye both alike. Return we then
And follow our old track. There is a city
Yclept Canobus, built at the land's end,
Even at the mouth and mounded silt of Nile,
And there shall Zeus restore to thee thy mind
With touch benign and laying on of hands.
And from that touch thou shalt conceive and bear
Swarth Epaphus, touch-born; and he shall reap
As much of earth as Nilus watereth
With his broad-flowing river. In descent
The fifth from him there shall come back to Argos,
Thine ancient home, but driven by hard hap,
Two score and ten maids, daughters of one house,
Fleeing pollution of unlawful marriage
With their next kin, who winged with wild desire,
As hawks that follow hard on cushat-doves,
Shall harry prey which they should not pursue
And hunt forbidden brides. But God shall be
Exceeding jealous for their chastity;
And old Pelasgia, for the mortal thrust
Of woman's hands and midnight murder done
Upon their new-wed lords, shall shelter them;
For every wife shall strike her husband down
Dipping a two-edged broadsword in his blood.
Oh, that mine enemies might wed such wives!
But of the fifty, one alone desire
Shall tame, as with the stroke of charming-wand,
So that she shall not lift her hands to slay
The partner of her bed; yea, melting love
Shall blunt her sharp-set will, and she shall choose
Rather to be called weak and womanly
Than the dark stain of blood; and she shall be
Mother of kings in Argos. 'Tis a tale
Were't told in full, would occupy us long.
For, of her sowing, there shall spring to fame
The lion's whelp, the archer bold, whose bow
Shall set me free. This is the oracle
Themis, my ancient Mother, Titan-born,
Disclosed to me; but how and in what wise
Were long to tell, nor would it profit thee.

Io.
Again they come, again
The fury and the pain!
The gangrened wound! The ache of pulses dinned
With raging throes!
It beats upon my brain—the burning wind
That madness blows!
It pricks—the barb, the hook not forged with heat,
The gadfly dart!
Against my ribs with thud of trampling feet
Hammers my heart!
And like a bowling wheel mine eyeballs spin,
And I am flung
By fierce winds from my course, nor can rein in
My frantic tongue
That raves I know not what!—a random tide
Of words—a froth
Of muddied waters buffeting the wide,
High-crested, hateful wave of ruin and God's
wrath!

Exit raving.

Ch. I hold him wise who first in his own mind
This canon fixed and taught it to mankind:
True marriage is the union that mates
Equal with equal; not where wealth emasculates,
Or mighty lineage is magnified,
Should he who earns his bread look for a bride.
Therefore, grave mistresses of fate, I pray
That I may never live to see the day
When Zeus takes me for his bedfellow; or I
Draw near in love to husband from on high.
For I am full of fear when I behold
Io, the maid no human love may fold,
And her virginity disconsolate,
Homeless and husbandless by Hera's hate.
For me, when love is level, fear is far.
May none of all the Gods that greater are
Eye me with his unshunnable regard;
For in that warfare victory is hard,
And of that plenty cometh emptiness.
What should befall me then I dare not guess;
Nor whither I should flee that I might shun
The craft and subtlety of Cronos' Son.

Pr. I tell thee that the self-willed pride of Zeus
Shall surely be abased; that even now
He plots a marriage that shall hurl him forth
Far out of sight of his imperial throne
And kingly dignity. Then, in that hour,
Shall be fulfilled, nor in one tittle fail,
The curse wherewith his father Cronos cursed him,
What time he fell from his majestic place
Established from of old. And such a stroke
None of the Gods save me could turn aside.
I know these things shall be and on what wise.
Therefore let him secure him in his seat,
And put his trust in airy noise, and swing
His bright, two-handed, blazing thunderbolt,
For these shall nothing stead him, nor avert
Fall insupportable and glory humbled.
A wrestler of such might he maketh ready
For his own ruin; yea, a wonder, strong
In strength unmatchable; and he shall find
Fire that shall set at naught the burning bolt
And blasts more dreadful that o'er-crow the thunder.
The pestilence that scourgeth the deep seas
And shaketh solid earth, the three-pronged mace,
Poseidon's spear, a mightier shall scatter;

And when he stumbleth striking there his foot,
Fallen on evil days, the tyrant's pride
Shall measure all the miserable length
That parts rule absolute from servitude.
Ch. Methinks the wish is father to the thought
And whets thy railing tongue.
Pr. Not so: the wish
And the accomplishment go hand in hand.
Ch. Then must we look for one who shall supplant
And reign instead of Zeus?
Pr. Calamity
Far, far more grievous shall bow down his neck.
Ch. Hast thou no fear venting such blasphemy?
Pr. What should I fear who have no part nor lot
In doom of dying?
Ch. But he might afflict thee
With agony more dreadful, pain beyond
These pains.
Pr. Why let him if he will!
All evils I foreknow.
Ch. Ah, they are wise
Who do obeisance, prostrate in the dust,
To the implacable, eternal Will.
Pr. Go thou and worship; fold thy hands in prayer,
And be the dog that licks the foot of power!
Nothing care I for Zeus; yea, less than naught!
Let him do what he will, and sway the world
His little hour; he has not long to lord it
Among the Gods.
Oh! here his runner comes!
The upstart tyrant's lacquey! He'll bring news,
A message, never doubt it, from his master.
Enter HERMES.
Hermes. You, the sophistical rogue, the heart of gall,
The renegade of heaven, to short-lived men
Purveyor of prerogatives and titles,
Fire-thief! Dost hear me? I've a word for thee.
Thou'rt to declare— this is the Father's pleasure
These marriage-feasts of thine, whereof thy tongue
Rattles a-pace, and by the which his greatness
Shall take a fall. And look you rede no riddles,
But tell the truth, in each particular
Exact. I am not to sweat for thee, Prometheus,
Upon a double journey. And thou seest
Zeus by thy dark defiance is not moved.
Pr. A very solemn piece of insolence
Spoken like an underling of the Gods! Ye are young!
Ye are young! New come to power! And ye suppose
Your towered citadel Calamity
Can never enter! Ah, and have not I
Seen from those pinnacles a two-fold fall
Of tyrants? And the third, who his brief "now"
Of lordship arrogates, I shall see yet
By lapse most swift, most ignominious,
Sink to perdition. And dost thou suppose
I crouch and cower in reverence and awe
To Gods of yesterday? I fail of that
So much, the total all of space and time
Bulks in between. Take thyself hence and count
Thy toiling steps back by the way thou camest,
In nothing wiser for thy questionings.
Her. This is that former stubborness of thine
That brought thee hither to foul anchorage.
Pr. Mistake me not; I would not, if I might,
Change my misfortunes for thy vassalage.
Her. Oh! better be the vassal of this rock
Than born the trusty messenger of Zeus!
Pr. I answer insolence, as it deserves,
With insolence. How else should it be answered?
Her. Surely; and, being in trouble, it is plain
You revel in your plight.
Pr. Revel, forsooth!
I would my enemies might hold such revels
And thou amongst the first.
Her. Dost thou blame me
For thy misfortunes?
Pr. I hate all the Gods,
Because, having received good at my hands,
They have rewarded me with evil.
Her. This
Proves thee stark mad!
Pr. Mad as you please, if hating
Your enemies is madness.
Her. Were all well
With thee, thou'dst be insufferable!
Pr. Alas!
Her. Alas, that Zeus knows not that word, Alas!
Pr. But ageing Time teacheth all knowledge.
Her. Time
Hath not yet taught thy rash, imperious will
Over wild impulse to win mastery.
Pr. Nay: had Time taught me that, I had not stooped
To bandy words with such a slave as thou.
Her. This, then, is all thine answer: thou'lt not speak
One syllable of what our Father asks.
Pr. Oh, that I were a debtor to his kindness!
I would requite him to the uttermost!
Her. A cutting speech! You take me for a boy
Whom you may taunt and tease.
Pr. Why art thou not
A boy—a very booby—to suppose
Thou wilt get aught from me? There is no wrong
However shameful, nor no shift of malice
Whereby Zeus shall persuade me to unlock
My lips until these shackles be cast loose.
Therefore let lightning leap with smoke and flame,
And all that is be beat and tossed together,
With whirl of feathery snowflakes and loud crack
Of subterranean thunder; none of these
Shall bend my will or force me to disclose
By whom 'tis fated he shall fall from power.
Her. What good can come of this? Think yet again!
Pr. I long ago have thought and long ago
Determined.
Her. Patience! patience! thou rash fool!
Have so much patience as to school thy mind
To a right judgment in thy present troubles.
Pr. Lo, I am rockfast, and thy words are wave
That weary me in vain. Let not the thought

Enter thy mind, that I in awe of Zeus
Shall change my nature for a girl's, or beg
The Loathed beyond all loathing—with my hands
Spread out in woman's fashion— to cast loose
These bonds; from that I am utterly removed.
Her. I have talked much, yet further not my purpose;
For thou art in no whit melted or moved
By my prolonged entreaties: like a colt
New to the harness thou dost back and plunge,
Snap at thy bit and fight against the rein.
And yet thy confidence is in a straw;
For stubborness, if one be in the wrong,
Is in itself weaker than naught at all.
See now, if thou wilt not obey my words,
What storm, what triple-crested wave of woe
Unshunnable shall come upon thee. First,
This rocky chasm shall the Father split
With earthquake thunder and his burning bolt,
And he shall hide thy form, and thou shalt hang
Bolt upright, dandled in the rock's rude arms.
Nor till thou hast completed thy long term
Shalt thou come back into the light; and then
The wingéd hound of Zeus, the tawny eagle,
Shall violently fall upon thy flesh
And rend it as 'twere rags; and every day
And all day long shall thine unbidden guest
Sit at thy table, feasting on thy liver
Till he hath gnawn it black. Look for no term
To such an agony till there stand forth
Among the Gods one who shall take upon him
Thy sufferings and consent to enter hell
Far from the light of Sun, yea, the deep pit
And mirk of Tartarus, for thee. Be advised;
This is not stuffed speech framed to frighten thee
But woeful truth. For Zeus knows not to lie
And every word of his shall be fulfilled.
Look sharply to thyself then: weigh my words
And do not in thy folly think self-will
Better than prudent counsel.
Ch. To our mind
The words of Hermes fail not of the mark.
For he enjoins thee to let self-will go
And follow after prudent counsels. Him
Harken; for error in the wise is shame.
Pr. These are stale tidings I foreknew;
Therefore, since suffering is the due
A foe must pay his foes,
Let curléd lightnings clasp and clash
And close upon my limbs: loud crash
The thunder, and fierce throes
Of savage winds convulse calm air:
The embowelled blast earth's roots uptear
And toss beyond its bars,
The rough surge, till the roaring deep
In one devouring deluge sweep
The pathway of the stars!
Finally, let him fling my form
Down whirling gulfs, the central storm
Of being; let me lie
Plunged in the black Tartarean gloom;
Yet—yet—his sentence shall not doom
This deathless self to die!
Her. These are the workings of a brain
More than a little touched; the vein
Of voluble ecstasy!
Surely he wandereth from the way,
His reason lost, who thus can pray!
A mouthing madman he!
Therefore, O ye who court his fate,
Rash mourners—ere it be too late
And ye indeed are sad
For vengeance spurring hither fast—
Hence! lest the bellowing thunderblast
Like him should strike you mad!
Ch. Words which might work persuasion speak
If thou must counsel me; nor seek
Thus, like a stream in spate,
To uproot mine honour. Dost thou dare
Urge me to baseness! I will bear
With him all blows of fate;
For false forsakers I despise;
At treachery my gorge doth rise:
I spew it forth with hate!
Her. Only— with ruin on your track—
Rail not at fortune; but look back
And these my words recall;
Neither blame Zeus that he hath sent
Sorrow no warning word forewent!
Ye labour for your fall
With your own hands! Not by surprise
Nor yet by stealth, but with clear eyes,
Knowing the thing ye do,
Ye walk into the yawning net
That for the feet of fools is set
And Ruin spreads for you. *Exit.*
Pr. The time is past for words; earth quakes
Sensibly: hark! pent thunder rakes
The depths, with bellowing din
Of echoes rolling ever nigher:
Lightnings shake out their locks of fire;
The dust cones dance and spin;
The skipping winds, as if possessed
By faction—north, south, east and west,
Puff at each other; sea
And sky are shook together: Lo!
The swing and fury of the blow
Wherewith Zeus smiteth me
Sweepeth apace, and, visibly,
To strike my heart with fear. See, see,
Earth, awful Mother! Air,
That shedd'st from the revolving sky
On all the light they see thee by,
What bitter wrongs I bear!

The scene closes with earthquake and thunder, in the midst of which PROMETHEUS *and the* DAUGHTERS OF OCEANUS *sink into the abyss.*

AGAMEMNON

DRAMATIS PERSONAE

WATCHMAN
CHORUS OF ARGIVE ELDERS
CLYTAEMNESTRA, *wife of Agamemnon*
A HERALD
AGAMEMNON, *King of Argos*
CASSANDRA, *daughter of Priam and slave of Agamemnon*
AEGISTHUS, *son of Thyestes, cousin of Agamemnon*
ATTENDANTS

Argos: The Atreidæ's Palace

Watchman

I have made suit to Heaven for release
A twelvemonth long from this hard service, here
At watch on the Atreidæ's roof to lie
As if these arms were paws and I a dog.
I know the nightly concourse of the stars
And which of the sky's bright regents bring us storm,
Which summer; when they set, and their uprisings.
Once more on guard I look for the signal brand,
The flash of fire that shall bring news from Troy
And bruit her fall: so absolute for hope
Is woman's heart strong with a man's resolve.
And, now the dewy, vast and vagrant night
Is all my lodging, never visited
By dreams; for Fear, not Slumber, stands fast by,
So that sound sleep may never latch my lids;
And would I sing or whistle, physicking
The drowsy sense with music's counter-charm,
Tears in my voice, my song soon sinks to sighs
For the changed fortunes of this house, no more,
As whilome, ruled and wrought with excellence.
Oh, that the hour were come for my release!
Oh, for the gloom's glad glow of herald-fire!
(*The Beacon shines out on Mt. Arachne.*)
Brave lantern! Out of darkness bringing bright
Day! Jolly dance and jocund revelry
To all broad Argos for this fair windfall!
Oho! Below there! Ho!
Mount, Agamemnon's wife, starlike from sleep,
Ascend, and wake the palace with thy rouse!
For by this fiery courier Ilium
Is taken! Heigh! but I will trip it first!
This is king's luck, but it shall vantage me!
This bully brand hath thrown me sixes three!
Oh, good to cherish my King's hand in mine
When he comes home and the household hath a head!
But not a whisper more; the thresher-ox
Hath trampled on my tongue. And yet these walls
Could tell a plain tale. Give me a man that knows,
And I'll discourse with him; else am I mute
And all my memory oblivion.

Exit. Enter CHORUS.

Chorus

Nine years have fled on Time's eternal wings
And now the tenth is well nigh flown,
Since the Atreidæ, of this two-fold throne,
By grace of God, the double-sceptred kings—
Prince Menelaus, Priam's adversary,
And Agamemnon—from our coast
Weighed anchor with a thousand ships,
Mustering the valour of the Argive host.
Their hearts were hot within them, from their lips
Thundered the battle-cry,
Like eagles' scream, when round and round they row,
High o'er their nest in solitary woe,
Because their eyasses are ta'en,
And all their watch was vain,
And all their labour lost.
But One above, Apollo, Pan or Zeus
Shall, at the voice of their despair,
Pitying his co-mates of the cloudless air,
Send the Destroying Angel, that pursues
With penal pangs the feet that have transgressed.
And so One mightier, Zeus of Host and Guest,
The sons of Atreus 'gainst false Paris sent;
And, for a wife of many husbands wooed
Ordains War's tourney in long-drawn prelude,
Knapping of spears, knees in the dust down-bent,
For Greek and Trojan, ere His wrath be spent.
Now, as it may, the quarrel goes;
Fate shapes the close;
None shall appease with cups or fire to faggot laid
For sacrifice unburnt the stubborn wrath unstayed.

We, with old limbs outworn,
Were left behind, unworthy of the fray;
A staff our stay,
Our strength a babe's newborn.
For pith of young bones potent over all
Is eld's compeer, a puny chief;
There is no room for Ares, stark and tall:
And with the yellowing leaf
Life's last must tread the three-foot way;
A babe, a dream stolen forth into the day.
But thou, Tyndareus' daughter, Queen
Clytaemnestra, what's this stir?
What news? What harbinger
Hath thine intelligencer been,
That thou hast passed the word for sacrifice?

No altar, none, in all the City's liberties,
Whether to God of Sky or Earth or Street
Or Entry vowed,
But is ablaze with gifts.
And, from all quarters, even to the abysm
Of night, the dazzling cresset lifts
An odorous cloud,
Exceeding pure and comforting and sweet,
With holy chrism
Of nard and frankincense anointed o'er;
The richest unguents of the royal store.
If there is aught
Thou canst or may'st declare,
Speak on, and be physician to my thought,
Which oft is sick, and oft
When Hope from these brave altars leaps aloft,
Biddeth good-bye to Cark and Care.

Now am I minstrel and master
Of music to chant the Lay
Of the Token, the Mighty Wonder,
That met them on their way,

These two kings ripe in manhood.
I am old, but in me bloweth strong
The wind of God, the rapture
That girds me with valiance for song.

Tell then, my tongue, of the omen
That sped 'gainst the Teucrian land
The Achæans' twit-hroned chieftains,
With spear and vengeful hand.

Lords of the Youth of Hellas,
Right well did they agree,
And the king of the birds these sea-kings
Bade launch and put to sea.

Lo, a black eagle sheen; and, lo,
With him an eagle pied,
By the King's tents, in royal show
Lit on the spear-hand side.

A hare their meat, all quick with young,
Ta'en, her last doublings o'er.
Be Sorrow, Sorrow's burden sung,
But crown Joy conqueror!

Thereat the wise war-prophet
Right well applied his art;
Knowing the sons of Atreus
Were men of diverse heart,

In the pair that devoured the trembler
He read by his deep lore
A symbol of the royal twain
That led the host to war.

And thus he spake: "Long leaguer,
But Priam's city shall fall
At last, her cattle and commons
Butchered without her wall;

Come there from Heaven no wrath-cloud's lower
To dull with dark alloy
The mighty bit that's forged with power,
The host that bridles Troy.

For wrung with ruth is Artemis,
White flower of maidenhood,
Wroth with her Father's wingèd hounds,
That shed the trembler's blood,

Poor doe, that limped with wombèd young:
That meat she doth abhor.
Be Sorrow, Sorrow's burden sung,
But crown Joy conqueror!

Fair One, as thy love can bless
Little whelps as weak as dew
Of the ravening lioness;
And at breast all beastlings small
Shield through forests virginal;
Wingèd weird that fair doth show,
And yet darkly worketh woe,
To some happy end ensue!
And, O Healer, hear my prayer,
Lest in wrath the Goddess rouse
Baffling winds that will not change,
All the Danaan fleet laid by;
Speeding that unlawful, strange,
Unfestal feast, that rite accursed,
Of a quarrel inly nursed,
To a true man perilous,
The abhorred artificer.
For, behold, within the house
Coiled and fanged Conspiracy
Turns to strike with forkèd tongue,
Mindful of her murdered young."

So thundered the voice of Calchas,
From birds with doom in their wings,
Encountered by the marching host,
Telling the Fate of Kings.

Tuned to the prophet's bodeful tongue,
Let your song sink and soar.
Be Sorrow, Sorrow's burden sung,
But crown Joy conqueror!

Zeus—whosoe'er He be, Whose state excels
All language syllables,
Knowing not so much
As whether He love that name or love it not;
Zeus—while I put all knowledge to the touch,
And all experience patiently assay,
I find no other name to heave away
The burden of unmanageable thought.

The sometime greatest wrangler of them all
Hath wrestled to his fall;
His day is done,
He hath no name, his glory's lustreless.
He that doth all outwrestle, all outrun,
Hath whelmed the next that rose up huge and strong.

But if Zeus' triumph be thy victory-song,
Thou shalt be founded in all Soothfastness.

He maketh men to walk in Wisdom's ways;
In Suffering He lays
Foundations deep
Of Knowledge. At the heart remembered Pain,
As of a wound that bleeds, waketh in sleep.
Though we reject her, Wisdom finds a road.
Then 'tis a gift untenderly bestowed
By Thronèd Spirits that austerely reign.

So with the Elder Captain of the power
Achæan in that hour;
No blame he cast
On prophet or seer, but bowed him to the blow;
What time they had no meat to stay their fast,
And all their ships lay idle, straitened sore,
Where betwixt Chalcis and the hither shore
The tides of Aulis battle to and fro.

Strong winds from Strymon ill inaction brought,
Lean fast and layings-up of little ease,
With waste of ships and tackle; yea, there wrought
In men's minds wilderment of weltering seas;
Day like to day, and hour on changeless hour
Fretted of Argive chivalry the flower.

But when was mooted to the Chiefs a way
To work a calm more dread than tempest is,
And clarion-voiced the Prophet in that day
Thundered, unpityingly—"Artemis"—
The Atreidæ with their sceptres smote the earth,
Nor could keep back their tears; and thus in birth

The Elder spake, and gave their sorrow vent:
"It were a heavy doom to disobey;
And heavy, if my Child, the ornament
And glory of my house, I needs must slay,
A Father's slaughterous hands foully imbrued,
Hard by the altar, with her maiden blood."

"What choice is here, where all is ill?" he cried;
"Am I to leave the vessels to their fate?
Am I to lose the friends with me allied?
Lo, now a sacrifice which shall abate
Storm-winds with blood of victim virginal
Law sanctions; they press hard; then God mend
all!"

But, once he let Necessity make fast
Her yoke, no longer chafing to be galled,
His altered spirit, leaning to the blast,
Swept on, unblest, unholy, unappalled.
For a false wisdom first,
Being indeed a madness of the mind,
Tempts with a thought accursed,
And then enures to wrong the wretch of human
kind.
Not backward now, but desperately bold,
The slayer of his Child behold,
That armèd Vengeance woman's rape chastise,
And storm-stayed ships sail free for that rich
sacrifice.

To those stern judges, absolute for war,
Her prayers were nothing, nor her piteous cry,
"Father, father," pleading evermore,
Nor womanhood nor young virginity:
But after uttered prayer
He bade who served the sacrifice be bold;
In her long robe that flowed so fair
Seize her amain, and high above the altar hold
All laxed and drooping, as men hold a kid;
And, that she might not curse his house, he bid
Lock up her lovely lips and mew the sound
Of her sweet voice with curb of dumbing bridle
bound.

Her saffron robe let fall,
She smote her slayers all
With eye-glance piteous, arrowily keen;
And, still and fair as form in picture seen,
Would speak. Oh, in her father's hall,
His guests among,
When the rich board
Was laden with good cheer,
How often had she sung;
And when the third thank-offering was poured,
With girl's voice virginal and clear
Her father's pæan, hymned with holy glee,
Had graced how often and how lovingly!

Thereafter what befell
I saw not, neither tell;
Only, the craft of Calchas cannot fail;
For Justice, casting Suffering in the scale,
Her balance-poise imponderable
With Knowledge trims.
What's far away
Thou'lt know when it is nigh;
But greet not Sorrow, till she swims
Full into ken, nor make fool's haste to sigh;
She comes, clear-seen with morning-ray.
And yet I look to see a happier hour,
As doth the wishful Queen, our Apia's lone watch-
tower.

Enter CLYTAEMNESTRA.

My duty, Clytæmnestra, brings me here,
And that just awe which is his consort's right
When the king's throne stands empty of its lord.
'Twould ease my old heart much might I but know
The meaning of these sacrificial fires.
Are they for good news had, or hope of good?
I ask, but, if thou art not free to speak,
I am no malcontent, I cavil not.

Clytæmnestra. You know the saw, "Good Night
bring forth Good Morrow";
Well, here is happiness surpassing hope:
The Argive power hath taken Priam's city.

Ch. Have taken—troth, thy words have taken
wing;
I think my unfaith scared them.

Cl. Troy is taken;
Troy—do you mark me?—in the Achæans' hands.
Ch. Oh, joy! too sweet, too sudden! It draws tears
From these old eyes.
Cl. Indeed, they speak for thee;
They vouch a loyal heart.
Ch. But is it true?
And hast thou any proof?
Cl. Oh, proof enough—
Or we are gulled by God.
Ch. Whether art thou
In credulous mood under the power of dreams?
Cl. 'Tis not my way to noise abroad a nothing
That nods to me in sleep.
Ch. Then has a tale
Wing-swift made fat your hope?
Cl. You rate me low,
You reckon me a giddy girl.
Ch. How long
Is't since the town was taken?
Cl. This same night
That's now in travail with the birth of day.
Ch. Who was the nimble courier that could bring
The news so quickly?
Cl. Hephæstus; his light
Shone out of Ida; onwards then it streamed,
Beacon to beacon, like a fiery mail,
Posting the news. Ida to Hermes' Ridge
In Lemnos; thence steep Athos, Zeus' own hill,
Caught from the isle the mighty brand. Uplift
It decked the broad deep with a robe of light,
Journeying in strength, journeying in joy. It smote,
All golden-glancing, like the sun in Heaven,
Makistos' warder-towers. Whereat the watch,
Nothing unready, nothing dazed with sleep,
Over Euripus' race its coming told
To far Messapion's sentinels. And they
Sent up from crackling heather old and dry
Answering glare, that flashed the tidings on.
In speed unspent, in power undimmed, it sailed
Across Asopus' plain, like bright moon-beam;
Then on Cithæron's precipice woke fresh
Response of missive fire. The men on guard
Hailed that far traveller and denied him not,
Kindling the mightiest flare of all. It leaped
Gorgopis' Lake; swept Aegiplanctus; bade
No dallying with its rescript, writ in fire.
Instant shook out a great, curled beard of flame,
Luxuriant, that flung a glow beyond
The cape that looks on the Saronic Gulf.
Then down it dropped; on near Arachne's crag
Its long flight stayed; till on this palace-roof
Of Atreus' line yon ray of glory fell,
Of Ida's parent beacon not unsired.
This is my torch-race and the ordering of it;
Rally on rally plenished with new fire.
And he's the winner who ran first, and last.
Here's proof for you, here is your warranty,
The which my husband sent me out of Troy.
Ch. Lady, I'll to my prayers; but satisfy
My wonder first; then I will thank the Gods:
Tell me, as thou know'st how, the tale again,
Again and more at large.
Cl. The Achæans hold
Troy Town to-day; and there is heard within
Her walls, methinks, sounds that are ill to mix.
Pour oil and eisel in the selfsame crock
And they will part unkindly. Even so,
Two voices are there, each distinguishable,
Both vocal of diversities of fate.
Here there are fallings-down about the dead,
Dead husbands and dead brothers; here are sires
Unchilded now, old, sad, and free no more,
Lifting the voice of grief for their best-beloved.
And there night-straggling Rapine sits him down
In after-battle weariness, and breaks
His fast on what the town affords; not now
Quartered by rote, but as fortune of war
Deals each; in the homes of Troy, the captive-homes,
They lie at ease: not under frosty stars,
In dew-drenched bivouacs, how blest shall be
Their sleep, no guard to mount, all the night long!
Now, if they order them with reverence
To the Gods of the fallen city and her shrines,
They shall not spoil to be again despoiled.
Let them not lust after forbidden prey;
For it imported much they come safe home,
Now that their course bends hither. If they come
Free from offence to Heaven, the wound yet green
For those that we have lost shall dress itself
In smiles to welcome them; except for Fate;
Except there fall some sudden stroke of Fate.
Well, now I have possessed you of my thoughts;
A woman's thoughts, but one who would have good
Mount to her triumph, without let or stay.
Much hath matured right well, and 'twere to me
A delicate joy to gather in the fruit.
Ch. Lady, thou surely hast a woman's heart
But a man's sense withal. I doubt no more,
Nor longer will defer my thanks to Heaven;
For all the toil and the long strain of war
There hath been dealt right noble recompense.

Exit CLYTAEMNESTRA.

King Zeus, and Night, the friendly Night,
Our Lady of the Stars, that dropped,
With slow evanishing of light,
A veil that Troy's tall towers o'ertopped,

Till, tangled in the fatal fold,
The strong were as the weak and small,
When Thraldom her deep drag-net trolled
And Ruin at one draught took all.

Because these mighty works He wrought
'Gainst Paris, who so sore transgressed,
I bend, I bow in solemn thought
To Zeus, the God of Host and Guest.

Long time he bent his bow, nor sped
A random shot that deals no scars,
Of feeble length, or overhead
Ranging among the untroubled stars.

Now may men say
"*Zeus smote them*"; from the deed
On to the doom so plain God's footprints lead,
Thou canst not miss thy way.
Now shines the event,
His rescript graven in its accomplishment.

There is a place
Inviolably fair;
There is a Shrine thou shalt not enter; there
Thrones the Immaculate Grace.
"'Tush! Enter, tread it down," quoth one unwise,
"What list the Gods your lovely Sanctities?"

Blasphemer! Shall not Death,
Death by the Sword of God,
Still the bold heart and stop the violent breath?
Have not the bloody feet of Havoc trod
Those marble mansions in the dust
Where Glory swelled and overflowed
Beyond the comely Mean and just?
Oh, give me Wisdom, with such Wealth in store
As I may safely hold, I will not ask for more.

He hath no ramp where he may turn
That, drunkenly, in mere despite
And wanton pride the seat of Justice stern,
Even to the grunsel-edge eterne,
Dings down and tramples out of sight.

To force the plot
That her dam, Death, hath hatched,
Temptation cometh, that foul witch unmatched;
Whoso resisteth not
Her dangerous lure,
There is no herb of grace can work his cure,
Nor any shift
To hide the gleaming woe;
When that pale spot, that did so faintly show,
With ever widening rift
Of ruinous light,
Glares to the gazing world, malignly bright.

Then, as your pinchbeck brass
The ring of gold assays,
The rub of doom, with many a fateful pass,
The black that specks his soul bewrays.
Then is he judged; and God is none
Will hear his prayer; yea, heaven lays
On all his friends the evil done,
When in his hey-day chase, a madcap boy,
He hunts the gaudy bird that shall his realm
destroy.

Such was Childe Paris when he came,
Upon a day with Sorrow rife,
To the Atreidae's house and smutched their fame;
Yea, for fair welcome left foul shame,
And stole away the wedded wife.

She left her land in evil hour
On shore and ship grim war's deep hum,
And desolation was the dower
She took with her to Ilium,
When she went lightly through the gate
And broke the bond inviolate.
And voices in the palace cried,
"Woe's thee, high house! My princes, woe!
Thou deep-sunk bed, whose down doth show
Where love-locked limbs lay side by side!"
And there were twain that nothing spake,
But sat aloof, in mute heart-break,
Of all their honour disarrayed,
Mourning too deeply to upbraid.
A phantom court, a phantom king,
The loveless ghost of Love-longing:
She beckons him yet, she bids him come
Over the sea to Ilium.
The fair, the large-limbed marbles to her lord
Are loveliness abhorred;
This penury, sans eyes love's soul made bright,
The end of all delight.

And then the dream-bliss comes, the lure
That bids us to her with a lie:
Ah, when we think our heaven secure
We are the fools of phantasy.
The fleeting vision will not stay;
Even in his arms it steals away
Featly, on brisk, obedient wings
That wait upon the paths of Sleep.
These sorrows in the courts of kings,
And worse, like shadows cower and leap
Where the household altar burns.
But there's a general sorrow; yea,
In every home all Hellas mourns
The mustering of the war-array;
Her time of heaviness is come
For them that sailed to Ilium.
And there is much in the tragic years
To melt her heart and move her tears.
Him whom they loved and bade go forth men
know—
A living soul; but, oh,
There cometh back to home and Hellas shore
His dust, the arms he bore.

Ares on foughten field sets up his scales;
Bodies of slain men, stark and cold,
These are this merchant-moneyer's bales,
The which in faggot-fires at Ilium turned
To finer dust than is the sifted gold
And worth more tears, he sends
Back to the dead men's friends;
For them that fell too light a freight,
For them that mourn a grievous weight,
All in a clay-cold jar so civilly inurned.

And they mourn them, and praise them; and sadly
one saith,
"Ah, what a soldier was this!
And he died nobly, dealing death";
And ever a mutter of surly breath—
"For a woman that was not his."

And so, with public sorrow blent,
Is heard the voice of discontent,
That loved ones perish and sad hearts pine
To right the wrongs of Atreus' line.

And some there be of shapely limbs and tall
That come no more, but lie beneath the wall,
There they possess the land for which they fought,
Coffined in Ilium's earth that loved them not!

A people's voice on the deep note of wrong
Grates harshly, it becomes a curse;
Nor shall Destruction tarry long,
It falls, as with loud thunder leaps the levin.
Something remains behind of dark, adverse
And night-involved, and I
Listen forbodingly;
And in this black, unquiet mood
I call to mind, men deep in blood
Shall not live out their days, hid from the sight of
Heaven.

Yea, for a season man's thoughts wax bold,
And he draweth lawless breath;
But anon the dark Furies from Hell's hold
Chafe and change his tinsel gold
To the huelessness of death.

And there's no help where dead men lie;
Great glory hath such jeopardy;
Zeus' eye-glance scathes, his lightning scars
The soaring peaks that touch the stars.

Give me the ease of an unenvied lot;
To be hailed "Conqueror" delights me not;
But let me ne'er so far from Fortune's favour fall
As live life's abject and my master's thrall.

1. Rumour runs fast through every street,
As fire the tidings bloweth;
If true—or a divine deceit—
Where is the man that knoweth?

2. Oh, who so fond, in wit so lame,
That kindling through him flashes
News, that one gust can fan to flame,
Another turns to ashes?

3. All's fair that takes a woman's eye;
A breath—a spark—she blazes;
But swift, and passing swift, to die
The glory Woman praises.

Chorus Leader. Soon shall we know this torch-race, these relays
Of bickering brands and rallies of red fire,
If they be true; or like the stuff of dreams
Delight comes dazzling to delude our sense.
A herald hastens hither from the shore
All branched about with olive-boughs. The dry
And droughty dust, mire's twin-born sister, tells
He hath a voice; his message he'll not vent
In flame, with smoke of fire from hill-top pines;
But either cry aloud our joy's increase,
Or else—but I am out of love with words
That contradict our hopes. May this fair show
Find fair addition; and, who wills not so,
But for his country's ruin maketh suit,
Of his misprision reap the bitter fruit.

Enter a HERALD.

Herald. O parent earth! Sweet Argos! Past are the years,
Ten weary years—dawn breaks—and I am home.
Some hopes have parted since, but this hope holds.
I never thought to have in this Argive earth
A fathom of ground to be my wished-for grave.
A blessing on thee, earth; on thee, bright sun,
And Zeus, our High Lord, and the Pythian King
No more to loose on us his arrow-blasts.
Wast wroth enough along Scamander's bank;
Now be our Saviour, our Physician be,
Kingly Apollo! Greetings to the Twelve
Great Gathering-Gods! To Hermes, my Defence,
Herald of Heaven whom earthly heralds worship.
Heroes, whose blessing holp our setting forth,
Receive these remnant ranks, the spear hath spared!
And you, high house of kings, halls ever dear,
Majestic thrones, Godheads the sun salutes,
If in old time returning majesty
Your bright looks graced, beam now on a royal man
After long years restored. Day after night
To you, to us and all in presence here,
Comes Agamemnon King. Oh, greet him well—
For it becomes you well—that hewed down Troy
With the great cross-axe of Justice-dealing Zeus;
Broke up her soil and wasted all her seed.
Such grievous bondage fastened on Troy's neck
Cometh the King, old Atreus' son first-born;
A happy man! Of all men now alive
Most worthy to be had in honour. Not
Lord Paris, nor the guilty city, dare
Boast they dealt us measure more bountiful
Than we requited unto them with tears.
Judged guilty both of rape and larceny,
His spoil is forfeit; he hath harvested
The total ruin of his father's house.
So Priam's sons pay twofold for his crimes.

Ch. Joy to thee, herald of the Achæan host!

He. My joy is at the full; now let me die;
I'll not complain to the Gods, death comes too soon.

Ch. I see how 'tis with thee: love of thy land
Proved a sore exerciser of thy heart.

He. So sore, that now mine eyes are wet with tears
In joy's revulsion.

Ch. Then 'twas a sweet distemper.

He. Was it so sweet? You must expound me that
Or I shall never master it.

Ch. 'Twas love
For love, longing for longing.

He. You would say
That all your heart went with the army, all
Our thoughts were turned towards home.

Ch. Ay, oftentimes
I groaned aloud for dim disquietude.

He. But why so ill at ease? Why such black thoughts
About the war?
Ch. Pardon me; I have found
Long since silence lays balm to a bruised heart.
He. Why, the princes gone, were there ill-doers here
Ye stood in dread of?
Ch. In so much that now—
Said ye not so?—'twere joy to die.
He. In truth
We have done well; but take it all in all,
A man may say that, as the years went by,
We had our good times and our bad times. Who,
Except the Gods, lives griefless all his days?
Our sorry lodging and our seldom rest—
And we lay hard—with all our miseries,
Would furnish forth a tale—why, is there aught
Costs men a groan we knew not every day?
These were sea hardships; but 'twas worse ashore.
There we must lie down under enemy walls.
The sky dropped rain, the earth did ceaselessly
Distil from the low-lying fields her damps
And rotting mildews, drenching our coats of hair,
Which soon grew verminous. Or what of winter
That froze the birds, so perishingly cold
It came from Ida blanketed in snow?
Or the hot months, when on his noon-day bed
Windless and waveless, sank the swooning sea?
Why moan all this? 'Tis past; and for the dead
Is past the need ever to rise again.
Or, why tell o'er the count of those cut off,
Or call to mind that to survive is still
To live obnoxious to calamity?
Farewell, a long farewell, to all misfortune!
For us, the remnant of the Argive power,
Gain conquers, and no grief that good outweighs.
Therefore, in this bright sun, over broad seas
And the wide earth flying on wings of Fame,
Well may we make our boast, "Takers of Troy,
Hard won, but won at last, the Argive power
To the Gods of Hellas nailed these trophies up
To be the glory of their temples old."
Then shall men hear, and sing our country's laud
And her great captains', and extol the grace
Of Zeus that wrought these things. Sir, I have done.
Ch. This wins me; I deny no more; for age
Still leaves us youth enough to learn.
Enter CLYTAEMNESTRA.
But this
Touches the house and Clytæmnestra most,
Though its largesse withal enriches me.
Cl. Oh, ages since I raised my jubilant shout,
When the first fiery messenger of night
Told Ilium was taken, and her stones
Rased, ruined and removed. And one of you
Did gird me then, saying, "Dost think Troy sacked
Because men set a match to wood?—By God,
A woman's heart is lightly lifted up."
So they supposed me crazed; and still I made
Oblation; and a general cry of joy—
Most womanly!—rent the air; and in the shrines
They fed sweet spices to the hungry flame.
And now I will not hear thee more at large;
I shall know all from the king's lips. There's much
Asks swift despatch, that my most sacred lord
May have noblest of welcomes. Sweet the day,
Sweetest of all days in a woman's life,
When for her husband she flings wide the gates
And he comes back from service, saved by God!
Take back this message; that he come with speed,
For his land loves him; tell him he will find
A true wife waiting when he comes, as true
As her he left; the watch-dog of his house,
Loyal to him, but savage to his foes;
In nothing changed; one that has broke no seal,
Nor known delight in other's arms, nor felt
The breath of censure more than she has dipped
Cold steel in blood. *Exit.*
He. Strange how she boasts! Is't not
Though charged with truth, and something over-charged,
Scarce decent in a high-born lady's mouth?
Ch. Well, she has done; you heard her, and I think
You understood her; noble rhetoric
For wise interpreters. But, tell me, herald,
Comes Menelaus with you? Is he safe,
Our realm's dear majesty?
He. What's fair and false
Is soon enjoyed; 'tis fruit that will not keep.
Ch. I would give much, couldst thou speak fair and true;
For true and fair dissevered and at strife,
The secret is soon out.
He. Why, not to glose
And lie to thee, we have no trace at all
Of the man or the ship whereon he sailed.
Ch. Alack
And did he put to sea from Ilium
In sight of all? Or, caught in the track of storm
That jeopardied the fleet, part company?
He. Dextrously thou aimst; indeed you sum great grief
In little space.
Ch. And other mariners—
Do they report him dead or living?
He. None
Knows, nor can certainly resolve our doubts,
Save Helios, the nurturer of all life
Through the vast world.
Ch. Tell me, how rose the storm
And how it ended, with the wrath of Heaven?
He. So fair a day we must not with foul news
Distain; we owe the Gods far other service.
No; when with looks abhorred a herald brings
Calamitous news, of armies overthrown;
When the general heart aches with one wound, and each
Bleeds for his own, by thousands made accursed,
Scourged from their homes by Ares' double lash,
Two-handed havoc, couplings of bloody death,
Well may he sing Erinys' Song, poor man,
Bowed down to earth 'neath that sore load. But when

All's well, and he comes bringing joyful news
To a land that maketh merry, well at ease,
How mix things good and ill, speak of this storm
That, not without Heaven's wrath, smote the
Achæans?
Water and Fire forgat their ancient quarrel
And sware a league together; and, to prove
How well they kept it, brake the Argive power.
Upon a night there rose a naughty sea;
And presently the roaring Thracian gale
Drave ship on ship. Tossed by the horned typhoon,
With spray of salt-sea sleet and drumming rain
In that wild piping they were lost to view.
And, when the bright sun rose, the Aegean wave
Was lilied o'er with drowned men and wreck of
ships.
But our taut hull a Power privily
Conveyed away, or interceded for us.
A God it was, no man, that took the helm.
Fortune, our Saviour, stationed her aboard
Of grace, so that at anchor in the swell
We shipped no seas nor swung upon the rocks.
And from the watery abyss of Death
Preserved, incredulous of our good hap,
In the white dawn, sad food for thought we found,
So sudden was the blow, our men so spent,
Our fleet so shattered. And, if any of them
Is alive to-day, certes, they give us up
For lost, as we think them.
Hope for the best.
And yet of Menelaus your first thought
Must be that he is sore distressed. Howbeit,
If any ray of the sun bring note of him,
His leaf unwithered and his eye unclosed,
There is a hope, that by some artifice
Of Zeus, not minded yet to destroy his house,
He may come home again. Now you have heard
My story, and may warrant all is true. *Exit.*

Chorus

Tell me who it was could frame
So unerringly her name?
Was't not one we cannot see,
Prophet of Futurity?
Did not Fate his tongue inspire,
Calling on her naming day
Her, world's strife, and world's desire,
Bride of Battle, "Helena"?
Helen! Ay, Hell was in her kiss
For ships and men and polities,
When, from behind her amorous veil,
She sallied forth with proud, full sail,
And Love's dallying wind blew fair,
That Iris to earth-born Zephyr bare.
Then followed after, in full cry,
As hounds and huntsmen take the field,
Of gallants a fair company,
That pressed their suit with lance and shield.
Over the blue, undimpled wave,
That told not of her oar-blade's track,
Hard upon Simoeis' strand they drave,
All overhung with leafy wood;
And she whose hands are red with blood,
Eris, was master of the pack.

Wrath, that can nor will remit
Nothing of its purpose, knit
Bonds that Ilium shall find
More than kin and less than kind.
And, for an example, lest
Men in ages yet unborn
Break the bread and foully scorn
Sanctities 'twixt host and guest,
Zeus, who guardeth hearth and bed,
Hath in anger visited
Them that led the merry din,
Over-bold to welcome in
With revel high and Hymen's strain,
Sung of all the marriage-kin,
Bride and groom and bridal train.
But the tide of Fate had turned
'Gainst Priam's city, ere she learned
A new song of sadder measure,
Marrying her complaining breath
To the dirge of dismal death,
Where is neither love nor pleasure
Then was Paris "evil-wed,"
When long years she mourned her dead,
And their blood was on his head.

Once on a time there lived a man, a herd;
And he took home, finding it motherless,
To be his foster-child, all fanged and furred,
A lion-cub, a little lioness.

Still wishful of the warm and milky dug,
It was a gentle beast while tender yet;
Made friends with children, they would kiss and hug
The baby limbs, and 'twas the old folks' pet.

Many a time and oft the wean, bright-eyed,
Like to a child-in-arms they carried;
And, when for meat the lion-belly cried,
'Twould cringe and fawn and coax them to be fed.

Then it grew up; and from what race was sprung
Proved, when as recompense for care and keep
(Ravage let loose the folded flocks among)
It made a supper of the silly sheep.

Then was the homestead soaked in blood, and they
That dwelt there, mastered by this unmatched ill,
Knew they had bred a Mischief born to slay,
A priest of Havoc sent them by God's will.

When first she came to Ilium Town
The windless water's witchery
Was hers; a jewel in the Crown
Of Wealth that sparkles soft was she;
An eye to wound with melting fire,
The rose of ravishing desire.

But wearing now an altered grace
Love's sweet solemnities she soured;

In Priam's house a hated face,
A curse with settled sorrow dowered;
On Zeus the Guest-God's word swift-borne
Erinys that makes brides to mourn.

I know how well the saying wears,
Stricken in years, but still held wise,
That boundless Wealth is blest with heirs
And Grandeur not unchilded dies;
Boon Fortune's bud and branch is she,
The hungry-hearted Misery.

False doctrine; though I stand alone,
I hold that from one wicked deed
A countless family is sown,
And, as the parent, so the seed.
But Justice hands fair Fortune on
And godly sire hath goodly son.

Yea, that old beldame, Pride
Who to her lustful side
Draws evil men, anon, or else anon,
When Fate with hand of power
Beckons the destined hour
Brings forth young Pride, her Mother's minion;
Daughter of Darkness, sabled-hued
As the Tartarean pit, for vengeance armed and thewed.

A Power no stroke can fell,
Nor stubborn warfare quell,
A hag, a goblin, an unholy form,
The Soul of hardihood,
Swift to shed guiltless blood,
Dark Angel of Destruction's whirling storm,
She dances on the roofs of kings,
And by her shape men know from what foul loins she springs.

Oh, in the smoky air
Of poor men's homes, how fair,
How like a star the lamp of Justice shines!
Justice, that most approves
The faithful life, that moves
In the fixed path her Providence assigns;
And constant to that strict control,
Forceful as Fate, pursues the orbit of his soul.

But, where in Splendour's halls,
Gold glitters on the walls,
And on men's hands is filth and foul offence,
With looks averse and cold
She quits the gates of gold,
And hails the hut of humble Innocence.
Wealth's coin of spurious die,
Usurping Sovereignty,
No image bears whereto she bends;
She guides and governs all, and all begun she ends.

Enter AGAMEMNON, *with* CASSANDRA *and his train, seated in chariots.*

Hail to thee, monarch! Conqueror of Troy!
Offspring of Atreus! How shall I content
Thy spirit in thy triumph and thy joy?
Rise to the height of honour's argument,

And yet a chastened gratulation give?
There are of rogues enough, ay, and to spare,
Who in the shows of things are pleased to live,
And thrive on falsehood as their native air.

There's little faith in man; scarce one that breathes
But with misfortune will heave up a sigh;
And yet the cruel sting sorrow unsheathes,
'Fore God, his tender parts it comes not nigh.

And other some, be sure of this, O king,
Can simulate a joy they do not feel;
Come with forced smiles and fulsome welcoming;
And crafty faces cruel thoughts conceal.

But him whose business is with droves and herds
The gipsy's arts can captivate no whit;
Not easy duped with warrantable words
And protestations fair in water writ.

Sir, in all honesty, when thou didst arm
In Helen's cause, to save her launch thy ships,
My portrait of thee lacked the Muses' charm,
And "Wisdom's helm," I said, "a madman grips."

"She doth consent thrice o'er, the wanton! Why
For her make sacrifice of heroes' blood?"
Now from the bottom of my heart I cry,
"Grief, thou wast welcome, since the end is good."

Howbeit, Time hath something yet to say
(Though now he clap a finger to his lip),
Touching this land, when you were far away;
Who well, who ill, discharged his stewardship.

Agamemnon. To Argos and her Gods let me speak first,
Joint authors with me of our safe return
And of that justice I did execute
On Priam's city. Not by the tongues of men,
But by their deaths have the Gods judged our cause,
Nor haltingly, 'twixt two opinions, cast,
For Ilium's overthrow, their suffrages
Into the urn of blood: the other Hope
Drew nigh, but not a pebble dropped. And now
Her smoke discovereth her; death's whirlblasts live;
Her ashes dying with her gasp her wealth
In unctuous evanishings away.
Long should our memory be and large our thanks
To Heaven, for humbled pride and rape revenged;
A kingdom for a wench ground up sand-small;
Whenas the broody horse hatched out her young,
Our basilisk, our Argive bucklermen,
Vaulting to earth, what time the Pleiads sank;
And Argos' Lion, ravening for meat,

Leapt tower and wall, and lapped a bellyful
Of tyrant blood.
So have I opened me
Unto the Gods. And yet I call your words
To mind; your counsel squares with my own
thoughts.
How rare it is in nature, when a man
Can spare his friend, if he stands well with Fortune,
Ungrudging honour! Nay, himself grown sick
In his estate, jealousy lays to his heart
A poison that can make his burden double;
He hath his own griefs, yet must heave more sighs
To see a neighbour happy! Ah, I know
That which I speak; I am too well acquaint
With friendship's glass, the reflex of a shadow;
I mean my professed friends. There was not one
Except Odysseus, the most loth to sail,
That like a horse of mettle pulled his weight,
And whether he be dead or alive, God knows.
Enough of this. We purpose presently
To call a Council touching the state of the realm
And the service of the Gods. What's sound, we shall
Take measures to perpetuate, but where
There's need of physic, we shall in all kindness
Use cautery or the knife, till we have rid
The land of mischief.
Now let me pass within;
And in my high house, mine own hearth, stretch
out
My right hand to the Gods, that sent me forth
And brought me safely home. So victory
That followed in my train attend me still.

CLYTÆMNESTRA *comes to meet him.*

Cl. Good citizens, our Argive seigniory,
I think no shame to speak of the dear love
I bear my lord. Our blushes wear not well;
They pale with time, and I need little schooling
To tell you life to me was weariness
Those years when he beleaguered Ilium.
Merely to sit at home without her lord
Is for a woman to know fearful sorrow.
Scarce hath one crack-voiced kill-joy cried his news
Than comes his fellow, clamouring far worse.
An if this mould of manhood, where he stands,
Had gotten wounds as many as Rumour digged
Channels to be the conduits of his blood
And help it home, he were as full of holes
As, with your leave, a net. Had he but died
As often as men's tongues reported him,
Another triple-bodied Geryon,
Three cloaks of earth's clay—not to pry too deep
And talk of under-strewments—three fair cloaks
Of clay for coverlid—thrice over dead
And buried handsomely as many times—
Conceive his boast—three corpses, a grave apiece!
Well, but these crabbed rumours made me mad;
And many times the noose was round my neck,
Had not my people, much against my will,
Untied the knot. And this will tell you why,
When looked for most, Orestes is not here,
Lord of our plighted loves to him impawned.
You must not think it strange. Your sworn ally,
Strophius the Phocian, hath charged him with
The nurture of the child, foreshadowing
A double jeopardy; yours before Ilium,
And here, lest many-throated Anarchy
Should patch a plot; since 'tis a vice in nature
To trample down the fallen underfoot.
This was his argument, and I believe
Honestly urged. For me the fount of weeping
Hath long run dry, and there's no drop left. Oh!
These eyes, late watchers by the lamp that burned
For thee, but thou kept'st not thy tryst, are sore
With all the tears they shed, thinking of thee.
How often from my sleep did the thin hum
And thresh of buzzing gnat rouse me! I dreamed
More sorrows for thy sake than Time, that played
The wanton with me, reckoned minutes while
I slept. All this have I gone through; and now,
Care-free I hail our mastiff of the fold,
Our ship's great mainstay, pillar pedestalled
To bear a soaring roof up, only son,
Landfall to sailors out of hope of land!
These are the great additions of his worth!
And, I pray God 'tis no offence to Heaven
To make them heard. We have had many sorrows,
And would provoke no more.
Dear Heart, come down;
Step from thy car, but not on the bare ground;
Thy foot that desolated Ilium,
Thou royal man, must never stoop so low!
Spread your rich stuffs before him, girls; make
haste!
That he may walk the purple-pavèd way
Where Justice leads him to his undreamed home.
My sleepless care shall manage all the rest
As Justice and the Heavenly Will approve.

Ag. Offspring of Leda, keeper of my house,
You match your much speech to my absence, both
Are something long; the rather that fine words
Come best from others' lips. Woman me not,
Nor like an eastern slave grovel before me
With your wide-mouthed, extravagant exclaim.
Away with all these strewments! Pave for me
No highway of offence! What can we more
When we would deify the deathless Gods!
But Man to walk these sacramental splendours,
It likes me not, and I do fear it. No,
Honour me as the mortal thing I am,
Not as a God! A foot-cloth, that will pass;
But think how ill will sound on the tongues of
men
These veilings of the precincts! God's best gift
Is to live free from wicked thoughts; call no man
Happy, till his contented clay is cold.
Now I have told thee how I mean to act,
And keep my conscience easy.
Cl. Tell me this,
And speak thy mind to me.
Ag. My mind's made up;
I'll not rase out mine own decree.
Cl. Would'st thou,
Faced with some fearful jeopardy, have made

A vow to Heaven to do what now I ask thee?
Ag. If some wise doctor had prescribed the rite,
I would have vowed to do it.
Cl. What dost thou think
Priam had done, if Priam had achieved
The victory that's thine?
Ag. Oh, he had trod
Your sacrilegious purples.
Cl. Then fear not thou
Man's censure.
Ag. In the general voice resides
A power not to be contemned.
Cl. Good lack!
Unenvied never yet was fortunate!
Ag. This is a war of words, a woman's war;
And yet a woman should not take delight
In battle.
Cl. 'Tis a virtue that becomes
Glory, in his triumphant hour to yield.
Ag. While we stand here at odds, wilt thou pretend
Thou carest for a victory so won?
Cl. Nay, but thou shalt indulge me; thy consent
Leaves thee my master still.
Ag. Have thine own way,
Since nothing else contents thee. One of you
Undo these latchets. Hark ye; loose me quick
These leathern underlings: and when I set
My foot on yon sea-purples, let no eye
Throw me a dart of jealousy from far!
I am heartily ashamed to waste my stuff,
Walking on wealth and woof good money buys.
But I'll waste no more words. Lead in the lady;
Be tender with her, for the Gods above
Look gently down when earthly power is kind.
None loves the bondman's yoke; and she's the flower
Of all our spoils, the army's gift, a part
Of my great train. Now, I'll contend no longer;
Let me pass on under my palace-roof,
Treading your purples.

He descends from his chariot.

Cl. There's the wide sea, and who
Shall drain it dry? Purple! There's more of it
In Mediterranean waves; for ever fresh,
Worth silver ounces, the right juice to wring
Your royal robes withal. And, God be thanked,
We've plenty of them within; we do not know
What 'tis to lack. I would have vowed to tread
Raiment in heaps, if oracles had bid me,
When I was at my wits' end to contrive
How to win back the half of mine own heart!

Now springs the root to life; the climbing leaf,
Tile-high, against Dog Sirius spreads a shade!
And, in thy home-coming, our weather-wise
Winter reads signs of warm days fully come.
Yet, in God's wine-press, when the unripe grape
Is trampled out into the blood-red wine,
Then for the perfect man about the house
There comes a wintry coolness to his cheek.
Zeus, Zeus, Perfecter, perfect now my prayer,
And of Thine own high will be Perfecter!

AGAMEMNON *and* CLYTÆMNESTRA *enter the Palace.*

Chorus

Spirit of Fear, and all Unrest,
Will thy wings never tire?
Song that waitest no man's hest,
Nor askest any hire,

Why this prophetic burden keep?
What Ghost no power can lay,
Not like the cloudy shapes of Sleep,
Heaved with a breath away,

Haunts me with evermore despair,—
Sad phantom still unflown;
And Courage high no more speaks fair,
Lord of my bosom's throne?

The laggard years have told their sum,
The cables are outworn,
Since, to beleaguer Ilium,
Went up the host, sea-borne.

And now I see that host's return,
By witness of these eyes;
Yet in my hand is no cithern;
My soul accompanies

The song that Angry Spirits sing,
The dirge of Vengeance dread:
My confidence hath taken wing,
And my dear hope is dead.

But still 'gainst hope my prayer I press,
The event may yet belie
My fears, and bring to nothingness
My soul's dark prophecy.

Goodman Health for his great train
Findeth his bounds too small,
For the lazar-house of Neighbour Pain
Leaneth against his wall.

Though calm the winds and smooth the wake
And Fortune's ship sail free,
There are Rocks she shall strike where no seas break,
There are shoals of Misery.

Sailor, be yare! Be wise!
Out of her deep hold heave
Of her rich merchandise
With rope and block and sheave.

So you shall save your craft,
Your ship shall founder not,
Though she be of great draught
And perilously fraught.

For the bounty of Zeus shall repair
The ravage of yesterday,

And a season's tilth with the furrowing share
  Chase Famine and Want away.

But the blood of life once shed
  Shall come to no man's call.
He that could raise the dead
  And the flocking Shadows all,

Did not Zeus stop his breath
  And bring him to his pause,
Lest who would heal the wound of death
  Strike at Eternal Laws?

Oh, we are straitened sore;
  If by strict rule dispensed,
Jealous of less or more,
  Heaven's liberties be fenced,

What wish dare mortal frame?
  Else had my hot heart flung
All out, and put to shame
  This inexpressive tongue.

Now I've no hope to unwind
  The clew of Heart's desire;
To think is pain when thought is blind,
  The smoke of a soul on fire.

Enter CLYTÆMNESTRA.

Cl. How now, Cassandra? I must have thee too;
Get in, since Zeus—oh, surely not in wrath!
Hath made thee one of us, asperged with all
Our lustral sprinklings, at our household altar
Stood in thy place with other bondwomen.
Step from thy waggon then and be not proud.
Alcmena's son, thou know'st, was sold for a price
And did endure to eat slave's barley-bread.
He that must call Wealth lord may bless his stars
When 'tis of honourable antiquity.
Who look for nothing and reap affluence
Are cruel masters, stand upon no law;
But here thou shalt be used as use prescribes.

Ch. She waits thine answer; being caught and caged
Yield, if thou mean'st to yield; but, it may be,
Thou'lt not.

Cl. Speaks she some barbarous babblement,
Some chittering swallow-talk, that she's so slow
To take my meaning?

Ch. Lady, 'twere best submit;
She offers all that thy extremity
Gives room to hope for: leave thy waggon-throne,
And follow her, poor princess.

Cl. While she sticks
Fast at my door, I waste my precious time;
The dumb beasts stand about the central hearth
Waiting the knife, and there's to be great slaughter,
Meet for a boon vouchsafed beyond our hope.
Make no more halt, an thou wilt bear a part.
Come, mistress, if you cannot murder Greek,
Make your hand talk and do your jargoning.

Ch. One should interpret for her, she looks wild;
A hunted deer new-taken in the toils.

Cl. Mad, sirrah, mad, and listening to her own
Contrarious heart; a captive newly caught,
Champing the bit, until her puny strength
She foam away in blood. Enough of this:
I'll waste no more words to be so disdained.
Exit.

Ch. My heart's too full of pity to be wroth.
Sad lady, leave thy car; there is no way
But this, come down and take thy yoke upon thee.

Cassandra. Woe! Woe! Woe!
Apollo! Apollo!

Ch. Why dost thou mourn for Loxias? Is he
Natured like us to ask a threnody?

Ca. Woe! Woe! Woe!
Apollo! Apollo!

Ch. Again! She doth affront the God; not so
Must we draw nigh him, wailing, wailing woe.

Ca. Apollo! Apollo! God of the great
Wide ways of the world, my path is made strait!
Not twice shall I shun thee, my Foe and my Fate!

Ch. Ha! Her own grief's her theme; the God-given Mind
Bondage can break not, no, nor fetters bind!

Ca. Apollo! Apollo! God of the Ways,
What road is this, thou darkener of my days?
What house that bends on me so stern a gaze?

Ch. Oh, this is the Atreidæ's royal home;
Ay, truly to their high house thou art come.

Ca. Horrible dungeon! House of Sin!
These stones have secrets, drenched in blood of kin!
Out, human shambles, stifling halls,
The red rain trickling down your walls!

Ch. A huntress-hound! Yea, and by all that's ill,
I fear this find will follow to a kill!

Ca. I know it, by this wailing cry,
These shrieks of slaughtered infancy,
Ta'en from their dam and roast with fire,
Set in a dish, served up for their sire!

Ch. We know thou art a soothsayer; natheless,
It skills not now; we seek no prophetess.

Ca. God, what's conspiring here? What new
And nameless horror cometh into view,
To overtop and pale with bolder hue
Ghosts of old crime that walk this bloody stage,
Making Love weep and wring her anguished hands?
There is no physic can this ache assuage,
And from this woe far off all succour stands.

Ch. Oh, they are published sorrows, griefs that have been;
But I know not what these dark sayings mean.

Ca. Miscreant, what make you there? Why dost thou brim
Yon cauldron for thy lord? On breast and limb
The cool stream glitters. Ah, mine eyes grow dim;
The dreadful consummation, the swift close,
Makes my lips dumb, and stops my breath;
With such a ceaseless hail of savage blows
A white arm flashes, doubling death on death.

Ch. This thick-occulted darkness grows more dense;
Riddles and runes, confounding sound and sense!
Ca. Oh, horrible!
What's this? A net as bottomless as hell?
A net—a snare—ha! And what else is she
That wound him in her arms in love's embrace
And now conspires to murder him! Dogs of the chase,
Devils, still hungry for the blood of Atreus' race,
Over the hideous rite shout, shout with jubilee!
Ch. What's this Avenger thou bidd'st shriek
Within the house? Night sinks
Upon my soul to hear thee; faint and weak,
Drop by drop, the slow blood shrinks
Back to my heart, to sickly pallor blenched;
So pales some fallen warrior, his life's ray
Low down the sky in sallow sunset quenched;
Then with swift stride comes Death with the dying day.
Ca. (*With a piercing shriek*) Ah-h-h-h! look! look! Keep
The Bull from the Cow! Hell-dark and deep
As death her horn: she strikes; and he is caught,
Caught in his long robe—falling—falling—dead
In the warm bath with murder brimming red!
Oh, what a tale is here! A damnèd plot
With bloody treason bubbling in the pot!
Ch. I have small skill in oracles,
But something evil I divine;
And troth, who ever heard that he who mells
With them learnt aught of good at grot or shrine?
No; all the answers prophet ever framed,
All his high-sounding syllables, when the seer
Speaks with the Voice of God, are evil, aimed
To exercise us in a holy fear.
Ca. O death! O doom! Mine own
In the cursed cauldron thrown!
Wherefore hast brought me here! Ah, well I know
I am to follow whither he must go.
Ch. Thou art crazed, on gusts of God-sent madness borne!
Thyself the theme of thy sad ecstasy!
There is nor law nor measure in thy strain;
Like the brown nightingale that still doth mourn,
As if song sought but could not find relief;
'Itys—Itys'—a never-ending cry,
Her life of sorrow telling o'er again
In her undying bower of fadeless grief.
Ca. Ah, happy nightingale!
Sweet singer; little, frail
Form God gave wings to—sweet to live—sans tears!
For me the edge of doom! How fast it nears!
Ch. Whence come these Heaven-sent transports, whence come they?
The meaning of thine anguish none of us knows.
Wherefore dost body forth in melody
These terrors that thou can'st not put away?
These notes, they pierce, they are exceeding shrill,
And bodingly thy passionate utterance flows;
Who made so strait thy path of prophecy
And taught thy tongue to utter only ill?

Ca. Wooing of Paris, thou hast won us woe!
Wedding of Paris, thou hast made us weep!
Native Scamander, where thy waters flow,
I waxed to womanhood;
Now by Acherontian gorges deep,
Or where Cocytus pours his wailing flood,
My boding heart foretells
I presently shall chant my oracles.
Ch. Oh, what is this dark meaning leaps to light?
A child could understand thee, thy keen pangs
Stab through and through me, like the venomous bite
Of serpent's tooth, when he fleshes his fangs;
And I am broken by the wailing cry,
So passing piteous is thine agony.
Ca. Oh, lost, lost labour! Low the city lies,
A wreck, a ruin; rased are tower and wall;
Vainly my father lavished sacrifice
With holocausts of kine,
Poor, pastoral beasts, that nothing stayed her fall!
Oh, heart of flame, Oh, fiery heart of mine,
Go, burn among the dead!
I come—I come—for me the net is spread.
Ch. Still harping on that chord of coming fate!
An Evil Spirit, bidding thee despair,
Sweeps through thy soul with insupportable weight,
And calls from thee this wild and wailful air,
Sorrow and Death making one melody;
And, oh, I know not what the end shall be!
Ca. Now shall mine oracle no more look forth
Out of a dim veil like new-wedded bride,
But put on brightness as a wind that blows
Towards the sun's uprising, 'gainst the light
Hurl, like a hissing wave, a horror far
Huger than this. I'll riddle you no more.
Ye shall take up the chase and bear me out
Whilst I hark back upon the scent of crime.
Oh, there are music-makers in this house
That quit it never; a symphonious Quire,
Yet ill to hear; for evil is their theme.
Being in drink, the more to make them bold,
They will not budge, these Revellers of the race
Of Furies; they sit late, their drunken rouse
The original sin; ay, that incestuous beast,
Mounted on lust, that trampled his brother's bed.
Went that shaft wide, or have I struck the deer?
Or am I but a lying prophetess
That raps at street doors, gabbling as she goes?
Now give me the assurance of your oaths
I know the iniquity of this ancient house.
Ch. What's in an oath, though in all honour sworn,
To help or heal? But I do marvel much
That, bred beyond the seas, thou can'st discourse
Of foreign horrors, alien to thy blood,
As if thou hadst stood by.
Ca. Prophet Appollo
Ordained me to this office.
Ch. Is't not true
He loved thee, though a God?
Ca. There was a time
When I had blushed to own it.

Ch. We are nice
When Fortune's kind, 'tis nothing singular.
Ca. He was a stormy wooer and wrought hard
To win me.
Ch. Was't e'en so? And came ye then,
As is the way of love, to getting children?
Ca. I did consent with Loxias and broke
My promise.
Ch. Had'st thou then the divine gift
Of prophecy?
Ca. Even then I told my people
All that they had to suffer.
Ch. How could'st 'scape
The wrath of Loxias?
Ca. This was my doom;
That none to whom I spake believed on me.
Ch. But we have heard thee speak, and we believe
Thy words are truth.
Ca. Ah-h,—God! Again
The pang—the rocking blast—the reeling brain,
And the clear vision through the pain!
Look there! They sit—they have come home to
roost
These babes, the sorry semblance of sick dreams!
Dead children, dead—butchered by their own kin!
Their hands are full of meat; their mess; their own
Bowels and inward parts; out on the sight!
The lamentable dish—their father supped!
For this, I tell you, one hath planned revenge;
The craven lion tumbling in his bed
To keep it warm, woe's me, till he should come
Who is my master—oh, a slave am I!
The Sea-king, Ravisher of Ilium,
Knows not her false and slavering tongue, thrust
out,
Lewd bitch, to lick and fawn and smile and be
The secret soul of unforgiving hell!
Dare it, She-devil! Unsex thyself, and be
His murderess! O monster, bloody monster,
Thou hast no name! Thou aspic, Amphisbœna,
Scylla of the Rocks, that is the seaman's grave!
Hell's Mother-Bacchant, vowing truceless war
Against thine own! Deep in all guilt how loud
She shouted (as when the tide of battle turns),
Seeming to joy for her lord's home-coming!
Believe me or believe not, 'tis all one,
What is to be will come; a little while
And you shall see it. Then you'll pity me,
And say that I was a true prophetess.
Ch. The babes' flesh served for the Thyestean feast
I know, and shudder at the dreadful tale
In undisguised and naked horror told.
But as for all the rest my thoughts run wild
Clean from the course.
Ca. I tell thee thou shalt see
The death of Agamemnon.
Ch. Peace! Oh, peace!
Fair words, unhappy lady!
Ca. There's no art
Can mend my speech.
Ch. Not, if the thing must be;
But God forbid.
Ca. Thou makest prayer to God,
But they make ready to kill.
Ch. Name me the man!
Ca. Thou dost not understand me.
Ch. Troth, I know
No way at all to compass the king's death.
Ca. And yet I speak good Greek, your tongue I
know
Too well.
Ch. So doth the Pythian oracle,
Yet are his divinations wondrous dark.
Ca. Oh, misery!
I burn! I burn! I am on fire with thee,
Apollo! Wolf-Slayer! Woe is me!
The lioness that wantoned with the wolf,
The kingly lion being from her side,
Shall take away my life; for she hath sworn
To add my wages to the hell-broth she
Brews; while she whets a dagger for her lord
Means in my blood to pay my coming here.
Why do I wear this motley? Why these wands?
These wreaths about my neck for prophecy?
Your death for mine, vile gauds! To Hell with you,
And I will follow after! Go, make rich
Another with damnation! Look, 'tis Apollo
Strips off my godly robes! I am to him
A spectacle, grinned on by friends and foes.
They called me stroller, beggar, mountebank,
Poor drab, poor half-dead starveling; evil names
And ill to bear! But that was not enough;
The prophet who made me a prophetess
Has brought me here to die a violent death!
And, for my father's altar, waits for me
The block warm-reeking with the blood of him
That's butchered first! But we'll not die for nought
We too shall have our champion, the child
For mother's murder born and sire's revenge.
A fugitive, a wandering outlaw, he,
To crown this fatal pyramid of woe,
Shall surely come! The Gods have sworn an oath
His father's curse shall bring him back again!
Why do I shrink? Why do I wail? Since I
Have seen what hath befallen Ilium,
And Ilium's captors come to this bad end,
By the judgement of the Gods, I will go in
And meet my death. Ye Gates of Hell, I greet ye!
Pray God that I may get a mortal stroke,
Without a struggle, dying easily;
A spurt of blood, and then these eyes fast-closed.
Ch. Lady of many sorrows, and in much
Most wise, thou hast discoursed at length; but if
Thou hast indeed foreknowledge of thy death,
How canst thou walk as boldly to the grave
As goes to the altar the God-driven ox?
Ca. Sirs, I must die; delay can stead me not.
Ch. Yet death deferred is best.
Ca. My hour is come:
To fly would nothing profit me.
Ch. Thou hast
A patient and a valiant spirit.
Ca. You praise
Not as men praise the happy.

Ch. Yet to die
Nobly is to have honour among men.
Ca. Oh, father, father, I am woe for thee
And all thy noble children.
She moves to the door of the palace, but recoils.
Ch. Ha!
Why dost thou start? What terror waves thee back?
Ca. Foh! Foh!
Ch. What's this offends thy nostrils? Or is't the mind
That's sick with fear?
Ca. Pah! The house smells of blood.
Ch. Nay, nay, it is the smell of sacrifice.
Ca. It reeks like an open grave.
Ch. No Syrian nard,
God wot!
Ca. Hush! I'll go in; and there too I'll
Wail for my death and Agamemnon's; what
I had of life must be sufficient for me.
O Sirs! Alack!
I am no bird that shrills a wild alarm
Scared at a bush. Bear witness what I am
Hereafter, when, for this my death shall die
Another of my sex, another man,
For one most woefully ill-mated, fall.
And this I ask you on the edge of death.
Ch. Oh! for thy doom foretold I am struck to the heart!
Ca. But one word more, or, rather, my last word,
The dirge of mine own death. I pray the sun,
Now in this last of light, that my avengers
Pay home upon mine enemies the death
I die—a slave despatched with one swift blow!
She enters the palace.
Ch. Oh, state of man! Thy happiness is but
The pencilling of a shadow,—Misery
With a wet sponge wipes out the picture! Ay,
And this is the more pitiable by far.

Oh, maw and ravin of Prosperity!
Hunger, that lives of men can never appease!
There's none stands guard o'er gorgeous palaces,
Bidding thee enter not, neither draw nigh!

Here is a man, the Gods in bliss alway
Gave Priam's Town for spoil, and he hath come,
With divine honours, back to his own home.
But if, for blood he shed not, he must pay,

If, for old crimes, he presently must die,
That of death's glory not a beam be shorn,
Who that hath ears to hear can boast him born
Under a star of scatheless destiny?
Ag. (*Within the palace*) Oh, I am wounded with a mortal wound!
Ch. Hush! Who is he that crieth out? Who shrieks
Wounded unto the death?
Ag. Again! O God!
Ch. Now by the crying of the king I know
The deed is done; but what shall we do?
1. Oh,
Summon the citizens!
2. Break in! Break in!
And put to proof this corrigible sin
At the sword's point!
3. There thou and I are one,
What is to do, let it be quickly done.
4. It leaps to light; now is their signal flown;
This flourish sets oppression on its throne.
5. Yes, for, while we are trifling with the time,
Procrastination the armed heel of Crime
Treads under; neither doth their sword-hand sleep!
6. My wit is out: who dares the dangerous leap
Let him advise.
7. Ay, truly; that's well said;
I have no art with words to raise the dead.
8. Are we, for the sake of a few sorry years,
To crook the knee before these murderers?
Are they that shame the house to lead us?
9. No!
Better lie down in death than stoop so low!
Death is not half so curst as tyranny.
10. Here's too much haste; because we heard a cry
Are we to argue that the king is slain?
11. You're in the right on't! Give not wrath the rein
Until thou hast assurance of the deed.
Hasard surmise and certitude are twain.
12. Why, then as most would have it let's proceed;
And, first, ere fears to acted folly run,
We'll know what hath befallen Atreus' son.
The scene opens and discloses CLYTÆMNESTRA *standing over the bodies of* AGAMEMNON *and* CASSANDRA.
Cl. If I spoke much in terms of policy,
Why should I scruple to recant them now?
If Love be a close traitor, shall not Hate
Dissemble too, environing her prey
In toils too high for Desperation's leap?
This is the finish of an ancient quarrel,
Long brooded, and late come, but come at last.
I stand upon mine act—yea, where I struck.
And, I confess it, I did use such craft,
He could nor fly nor fend him against death.
I caught him in a net as men catch fish;
No room, no rat-hole in his loopless robe.
I struck him twice; and once and twice he groaned;
He doubled up his limbs; and, where he dropped,
I struck him the third time; and with that stroke
Committed him to Zeus, that keeps the dead!
Then he lay still and gasped away his life,
And belching forth a stinging blast of blood
Spattered me with a shower of gory dew;
And I was blithe as with the balm of Heaven
The young corn in the birth-time of the ear.
Wherefore, my very worshipful, good masters,
Be merry, an it like you—I exult!
Would you a decent draught to drench his corpse,
'Tis ready for him, and we'll stint no drop.
The bowl he filled with sorrow in his house,
Now he's come home, he shall suck out to the dregs.
Ch. Inhuman monster! Oh thou wicked tongue
Wilt thou insult over thy murdered lord!
Cl. I am no fool; you cannot touch me there;
This shakes me not; I do but tell you that

You know already. Whether you praise or blame
Matters no jot. Look! This is Agamemnon;
My sometime husband. Here's the hand that
hewed him;
Was't not well done? Is't not a masterpiece
Of Justice? Ay, admire it how you will,
This is the fashion of it.
Ch. Woman, hast eaten some evil root,
Or brewed thee drink of the bubbling sea,
That thou hast nerved thee for this rite?
A thousand voices shall hiss and hoot,
A thousand curses thy soul shall blight,
For the deed thou hast done this day!
Thou hast cut off, cast down, and thou shalt be
Thyself a castaway,
A thing exorcised, excommunicate,
A monster, loaded with thy people's hate.
Cl. Now, in the name of Justice thou hurl'st down
Damnation and abhorrence on my dead;
But when need was, durst cast no stone at him,
Who, with no more concern than for a beast
Taken and slaughtered from a thousand flocks,
Slew his own child, the darling of my womb,
For witchery against the Thracian blow.
Ought'st not thou rather for his wicked deed
To have thrust him forth? You hear what I have
done,
And scowl, the truculent justicer! I'll tell you
This; I am ready for your threats; 'tis odds
But we'll cry quits; or, if you better me,
Do you bear rule; but, if that's not God's way,
Late learner though thou art, I'll teach thee wisdom.
Ch. Thou boastest much and art great to devise;
But when I see thee in thy fury, yea,
When thy heart is a plashing fount of blood,
I think what a foil to thy blazing eyes
Will be that crimson flush at flood
Sealing thy sockets in their own gore,
In the day of God, in that great day,
When thy scarlet sins run o'er;
How comely then these gules will show,
When thy lovers forsake thee, and blow quits blow!
Cl. Now hear the unswerving tenour of mine
oath:
By Justice, that did fully venge my child,
By Ate and Erinys, whose he is,
Theirs by this sword, my onward-treading hope
Shall never stumble through the courts of Fear,
So long as there is fire on my hearth
Aegisthus lights; so long as he's my friend,
My ample buckler, my strong heart's true shield.
He's dead that had his lust of her; the dear
Of every Chryseid under Ilium;
And so's this baggage of his, his fortune-teller,
He hugged abed with him, sooth prophetess,
And trustiest strumpet, she that with him rubbed
The rowers' bench smooth. They have their wage;
thou seest
How 'tis with *him*; and she, that like the swan
Has dirged her last, lies with him, where he lies;
And this poor chewet, nibbled in my bed,
Sets on my board rich diet's sanspareil.

Ch. Come, some quick death, but rack me not
with pain,
Nor keep me long abed;
Let me thy opiate drain
That brings the eternal sleep! My lord is dead,
And I care not for other company;
My keeper graced with kingliest courtesy,
Who for a woman warred on a far strand
And now lies fallen by a woman's hand.
Oh, Helen, Helen, conscienceless and cursed!
How many souls of men under Troy's wall
Didst thou cut off from life and light!
Now thou hast done thy worst,
And in this blood, no water can wash white,
With the most perfect, memorablest of all
The last rose in thy garland twined,
Thou corner-stone of strife; thou woe of human
kind!
Cl. Call not on Death, cast down by what ye see,
Neither on Helen turn your wrath aside,
As if none else were deep in blood but she;
Nor think, because for her our Danaans died,
There is no other hurt past surgery.
Ch. Spirit that on these battlements, plumb-
down,
Dost drop on iron wings,
To pluck away the two-fold crown
And double sceptre of the Tantalid kings,
Thou didst raise up two Queens, and give the twain
Twin Souls, to deal my heart a deadly wound;
Now, like a carrion-bird perched on the slain,
Thou sing'st thy song, to an ill descant crooned.
Cl. Now is thy judgment just, when thou dost
cry
To that cursed Spirit, that thrice-fatted Doom,
A Lust Incarnate, Death that cannot die,
That makes all Tantalids murderers in the womb,
Athirst for fresh blood ere the old be dry.
Ch. 'Tis a Destroying Angel, angered sore
Against this house; a Spirit, great and strong
And evil and insatiable, woe's me!
That stands at Zeus' right hand, to Whom belong
Power and Dominion, now and evermore.
What do we, or what suffer, of good or ill,
But, doing, suffering, we enact His Will?
Ay, without God, none of these things could be.
King, my king, how shall I weep for thee?
What shall my fond heart say?
Thou liest in spider's web-work; gaspingly
In hideous death the fleet life ebbs away.
Woe, woe, that thou should'st bow thy head
On this unkingly bed,
By dagger-hand despatched and treason's felony!
Cl. Nay, sink thy proud boast;
Call not this my deed;
Never suppose me Agamemnon's Spouse;
A spectre in my likeness drew the knife;
The old, the unforgiving Ghost,
Not I that was this piece of carrion's wife.
And his assassination feed
Black Atreus of the Bloody Rouse,
The Revel Grim.

She hath the altar dressed
With brawn of manhood for the tender limb
Of weanling infants taken from the breast.
Ch. Go to: that thou art innocent of this blood
What witness will avouch? Though, it may be,
That Old Destroyer wove with thee the mesh.
This bloody deluge, like an on-coming sea
That may not halt until it makes the flood,
Rolls its rough waves, with kindred-murder red,
Till Justice lave the rank corruption bred
Of that foul, cannibal roast of childish flesh.

King, my king, how shall I weep for thee?
What shall my fond heart say?
Thou liest in spider's web-work; gaspingly
In hideous death, the fleet life ebbs away!
Woe, woe, that thou shouldst bow thy head
On this unkingly bed!
By dagger-hand despatched and treason's felony!

Cl. Is he guile-free?
Hath he not slain
His own, even my branch, raised up from him,
Iphigeneia, wept with all my tears?
Ah, to the traitor, treachery!
He hath discharged in blood his long arrears;
The measure he dealt is meted him again.
Then, let his big voice, in the dim
Darkness of Hell,
Sink low and sadly breathed;
He hath his just quietus; this great quell
Ripostes his stroke, who first the sword
unsheathed.

Ch. Now like a weary wrestler
My fainting heart contends;
Now that the house if falling,
Where shall I find me friends?

But, oh, I fear, to whelm it
Red Ruin roars amain;
For the first shower is over,
The early, morning rain.

Yea, Fate that forgeth Sorrow
Now a new grindstone sets;
There, for fresh hurt, her dagger
The Armourer, Justice, whets.

Oh, Earth, Earth, Earth! Would God I had lain
dead,
Deep in thy mould,
Ere on his silver-sided pallet-bed
I saw my lord lie cold!
Oh, who will bury him, dirge him to his rest?
Wilt thou sing his death-song,
Murderess of thine own man; wail and beat breast
For thy most grievous wrong?
Mock his great spirit with such comfort cold?
Oh, for a voice to sound
The hero's praise, with passionate weeping knolled
Over his low grave-mound!

Cl. Let that alone; it matters not to thee:
For by our hand he fell, he dropped down dead,
And we will dig him deep in earth. Let be;
We'll have no wailers here; but, in their stead,
His child, Iphigeneia, with soft beck,
Where the rapid waves of the Ford of Sorrows hiss,
Shall come; and fling her arms about his neck,
And greet her loving father with a kiss.

Ch. So taunt meets taunt; but Judgment
Is bitter hard to gain.
Now spoiled is the despoiler,
Now is the slayer slain.

For Zeus abides upon His Throne,
And, through all time, all tides,
The Law that quits the Doer,
The changeless Law abides.

Who will cast out the accursed stuff,
Bone of thee, breath of thy breath?
Thy very stones, thou bloody house,
Are bonded in with Death!

Cl. Now is thine oracle come to the fountainhead
Of bitter Truth. As God lives, I would swear
Great oaths to that cursed Spirit, Whose ghostly
tread
Haunteth the House of Pleisthenes, to bear
What's past endurance, and take heart of grace
To pluck these rooted sorrows from my mind,
Would he avaunt, and harry some other race
With the Soul of Murder that seeks out his kind.
Then, with that Horror from this house cast forth
Which mads their blood with mutual butchery,
Oh, what were all its golden treasure worth?
A poor man's portion were enough for me.

Enter AEGISTHUS, *with his guards.*

Aegisthus. Oh, day of grace, meridian of Justice!
Now may I say the Gods are our Avengers
And from on high behold the crimes of earth;
For now I have my wish; I see yon man,
Wound up in raiment of Erinys' woof;
The shroud that shrives his father's handiwork.
Atreus, his sire, who here bear rule, because
His power was challenged, did his father's son
Thyestes, my dear father—dost thou mark me?—
Outlaw and ban from home and kingdom both.
Himself, poor man, a suitor for his life,
Recalled from exile, found fair terms enough;
No death for him, no staining with his blood
This parent soil. But, for his entertainment,
Atreus, this man's cursed father, with more heat
Than heart towards mine, with a pretended stir
Of welcome—oh, a high-day of hot joints!
Dished up for him a mess of his own babes.
The hands and feet he chopped and put aside;
The rest, minced small and indistinguishable,
Served at a special table. So he ate
Knowing not what he ate; but, purge thine eyes,
And own 'twas sauced with sorrow for his seed.
And, when he saw what wickedness was done,

He groaned; fell back, and spewed the gobbets up,
Clamouring damnation down on Pelops' line.
Yea, kicking over board and banquet, cried,
"So perish all the house of Pleisthenes!"
And with that push great Agamemnon fell.
My grudge in this employed some stitchery;
I was my poor sire's third son and sole hope;
And he thrust me out with him; in cradle-clothes;
But I grew up and Justice called me home.
Outside these walls I grappled with yon man,
Yea, had a privy part in the whole plot.
And for all this I am content to die
Now that in Vengeance' toils I see him snared.
Ch. Aegisthus, I hold him a caitiff who
Insults o'er sorrow. You do stand confessed
A murderer; you say you sole conspired
This sorry deed. I say to thee, thou too
Shalt not escape damnation; they shall cast
Stones at thee; ay, heap curses on thy grave!
Ae. You drudge, you Jack that paddles in the bilge,
Say you e'en so, your betters on the bench
Of guidance and command? Your study is
Humility, old man, and you will find
'Tis hard for dullard age to mind his book:
But even for eld prison and hunger-pinch
Are rare physicians. Hast no eyes for that?
Kick not against the pricks lest thou go lame.
Ch. You woman that brings infamy on men
Fresh from the field; ay, bolted safe indoors
Cuckolds a king and plots to strike him down.
Ae. This shall be father to a world of woe!
Oh, Orpheus had a voice, but not like thine:
For, where he carolled, jocund Nature danced!
Plague on thy howlings! Thou shalt dance to them
Whither thou wouldst not, and, by God, once caught
We'll put some tameness in thee.
Ch. You, "my lord,"
You to be king in Argos! Plotting murder,
But not the man to do it!
Ae. Was not the wife
The readiest way to gull him? Was not I
Smoked and suspect, his ancient enemy?
It shall go ill with me, but this man's gold
Shall make me master. He that fights the rein
Shall feel the bit, and I will make it heavy!
No corn-fed colt for me! Hunger that keeps
House with the hateful dark shall humble him.
Ch. Why was thy craven soul not man enough
To slay him in fair fight? Why did a woman,
Wherewith the land reeks and her Gods are sick,
Kill him? Orestes yet beholds the light,
And he shall come in happy hour, and be
The master and destroyer of you both.
Ae. Wilt rave, wilt rant, wilt fall to deeds? Why, then,
Blockhead, thou shalt learn wisdom! Forward, men!
Come, stir, good fellows! Faith, you need not trudge
Far for this fray.
Ch. Out swords!
Ae. As God's my judge,
My sword to yours, I fear not death, not I.
Ch. Not? Then we take the omen, thou shalt die!
Cl. Sweetheart! I charge thee, do no villainy!
Nay, do no more! What's sown is yet to reap;
It is a harvest where the corn stands deep,
And we must carry home full loads of care.
Without our blood, here's trouble and to spare!
Good gentlemen, I pray you, to your homes!
Bend to the hour, when fraught with Fate it comes,
Lest worse befall ye. That which we have done
'Twas fated we should do. Therefore, begone!
Ah, might this prove the end-all of our woe;
How happy should we be to have it so!
So heavy on us is the bloody spur
Of a dread Spirit, Destiny's minister
Here is a woman's counsel, will ye heed
Ae. And shall these crop all rankness tongue can breed;
Drive their own fortune to the hazard; brook
No rein; call no man master?
Ch. When I crook
The knee to evil you may call me hound;
I am no son of this free Argive ground.
Ae. I'll be revenged upon ye yet.
Ch. Not so
If Fate bring back Orestes.
Ae. Tush! I know
The exile's wallet is with hope well-lined.
Ch. Enjoy thy fortune do! Is not Fate kind?
Go on in sin; wax fat; make the strong power
Of Justice reek to heaven; this is thine hour.
Ae. Wild words, but they are reckoned to thy score.
Ch. Ay, strut and crow, a cock his dame before!
Cl. Nay, never heed their howlings! Masterdom
And kingly state are ours, come what may come.
So in the palace thou and I will dwell
And order all things excellently well. *Exeunt.*

CHOEPHOROE

DRAMATIS PERSONAE

ORESTES, *son of Agamemnon and Clytaemnestra*
PYLADES, *friend of Orestes*
CHORUS OF SLAVE WOMEN
ELECTRA, *sister of Orestes*
THE DOORKEEPER
CLYTAEMNESTRA
A NURSE
AEGISTHUS

Argos. the Tomb of Agamemnon. ORESTES *and* PYLADES.

Orestes. O Chthonian Hermes, Steward of thy Sire,
Receive my prayer, save me, and fight for my cause;
For I am journeyed back from banishment,
And on this mounded sepulchre I call
On my dead sire to listen and give ear.

* * *

This lock to Inachus for nurture; this
For mourning.

* * *

Father, I was not by to wail thy death
Or with stretched hand despatch thine exsequies.

* * *

What's this? Look you; what company of women
With such ostent of sable stoles attired
Moves on its way? What trouble's in the wind?
Hath some fresh sorrow fallen on the house?
Or bring they these libations for my father,
As my heart tells me, to appease the Shades?
It cannot be aught else; there is my sister,
Electra, walking with them, and she wears
A woeful look. O Zeus, give me to venge
My father's murder, fight upon my side.
Pylades, let's withdraw; I would fain know
What may this woman's supplication mean.

They withdraw, and the CHORUS *enter, with* ELECTRA.

Chorus

Forth from the house they bid me speed
With graveyard-cups to pour and these ill-tuned
Ungentle hands quick-throbbing drum-beat sent:
These cheeks in tender witness bleed,
A fresh-turned fallow with a gleaming wound;
And my heart's bread is evermore lament.

I tore my robe of fair tissue
And the poor rags, methought, with anguish cried,
Being too linen-soft and delicate
To be so wronged; or as they knew
They wrapped a breast where laughter long had died,
Or wailed a new malignancy of Fate.

For terror wild with lifted hair
Wrung from the soul of sleep, dark dream-adept,
In the dead hour of night a cry aghast:
A shriek it was, a shrill nightmare
That broke from the bower, and where we women slept
In heaviness and sullen anger passed.

And they whose judgment can expound
The meaning of such dreams let a great cry,
The word of power that doth God's word engage:
"Underneath the earth's dark ground
Are grieving spirits wroth exceedingly;
And 'tis against their murderers they rage."

And now with gifts wherein is no remede
I come these woes to ward;
For, oh, Earth-Mother, thus in her sore need
Woos pardon and peace a woman God-abhorred.
How dare I breathe that word? Where shall be found
Ransom for blood that's drenched the ground?
O hearth Calamity enwraps;
O royal siege swift Ruin saps;
What sunless glooms of Night inhearsed,
By human horror held accursed,
Darkeneth thee, thou house of pride,
For the deaths thy masters died?

The sovran awe uncombated, unquelled,
That through the general ear
Smote on the common heart, hath now rebelled;
And yet, God wot, there are who fear.
Our infirm flesh boon Fortune deifies;
The man, grown God, high God outvies.
But Judgment swings through her swift arc
And censuring all doth poise and weigh:
And she can set a soul in light,
Or on the confine of the dark
The lingering agony delay;
Or whelm with elemental night.

Blood, and more blood; 'tis drunk of the dark ground;
This earth, that bred it, kneads it in her clay,
Till it become, indissolubly bound,
A Power, that shall itself arise and slay!

Até with no hot haste to Vengeance spurs,
Though tireless in pursuit, once entered in;
Still she adjourns; the Day of Doom defers,
Till there be full sufficiency of Sin.

Who hath unlatched the door of chastity,
  Enforcing there the bridal bliss embowered,
Shall never turn again the golden key;
  And ravished once is evermore deflowered.

So, though all streams be affluent to one end,
  Lucid and sweet to wash away the stain
Of blood from guilty hands, they do but spend
  Their onward-flowing clarity in vain.

  But I—the hard constraint of heaven
  Environing my city; driven
  From home, my portion slavery—
  If good or evil they debate,
  Must smother up my bitter hate
  And be the mute of sovreignty.
  And yet behind my veil I weep
  My rightful master's wasted days,
  And this hush sorrow on me lays
  The ache of winter's frozen sleep.

Electra. Bondmaids, the household's rule and regimen,
Since in this office ye are postulants
With me, I pray you counsel me herein.
What shall I say when these kind cups I pour?
How find fair words to vow them to my sire?
"Love's gift to love"—Shall I commend them so?
"Husband from wedded wife"? Oh, not from her,
Not from my mother; I should want for that
A tongue of brass; I have no form of prayer
To pour these offerings on my father's grave
Or shall I come with customary terms
And ask a blessing on their heads that sent
These garlands; for fair deeds fair recompense?
Or, in dishonouring silence, as my father
Perished, drain out the drench for Earth to drink,
And get me hence; like one that casts out filth
Fling the crock from me with averted looks?
Resolve me, friends, that you may share my blame;
We live in a community of hate;
Hide not your heart's deep thoughts for any fear;
The thing determined waiteth for the free
And him that's at another's beck and nod.
Know you a better way acquaint me with it.
Ch. Awful as altar is thy father's tomb;
And at thy bidding I will speak my mind.
El. Speak by that awe thou ow'st his sepulchre.
Ch. Pour on; but ask good things for all leal souls.
El. Which of my friends be they? how shall I name them?
Ch. Thyself, and, after, all that hate Aegisthus.
El. Then shall I offer prayer for thee and me?
Ch. I see thy heart instructs thee how to pray.
El. And add no name beside?
Ch. Remember yet
Absent Orestes in thine orisons.
El. Oh, well admonished! Excellently said!
Ch. Mindful of them that did the deed of blood—
El. What then? pray on and I'll pray after thee.
Ch. Ask that on them, carnal or ghostly, come—
El. Doomster or doom's executant?
Ch. A stern
Avenger; 'twill suffice; ask nothing more.
El. Is that a holy thing to ask the Gods?
Ch. Nay, how should it not be a holy thing
With evil to reward an enemy?
El. Great Herald of the Heights and Deeps, be thou
My helper, Chthonian Hermes; cry for me,
And bid the Spirits of the Depths give ear,
That are the Stewards of my father's house.
Cry to the Earth that brings forth life and then
Of all she nursed receives again the seed.
I will pour these libations to the Shades,
Saying, "O Father, have compassion on me
And on Orestes; how shall we bring him home?
We are sold for a price; yea, she that gave us birth
Hath dispossessed us, taken to her bed
Aegisthus, with her guilty of thy blood.
I'm but a slave; banished Orestes hath
No portion of thy substance; with thy labours
They go apparelled in their insolence.
I pray, not knowing how it shall befall,
Orestes may come home: hear me, my father!
And for myself I as a purer heart
Than hath my mother and more innocent hands.
This for ourselves; but on our enemies
I pray Avenging Justice may rise up
And hew them down, even as they hewed thee.
And so, betwixt my prayers that ask good things
Stands this, that imprecates evil on their heads.
For us send benedictions, by the help
Of Heaven and Earth and Justice Triumphing."
Now I pour out these cups, which you must wreathe
With customary crownets of your cries,
Chanting the dismal paean of the dead.
Ch. Fall, perishable tears, with plashing sound;
Fall for our fallen lord;
And, while the abominable cup is poured,
The rite confound;
The good avert,
And, to the miscreant's hurt,
The evil bring to pass,
And, though death dull thy soul and deaf thine ear,
Hearken, O, King; majestic shadow, hear!
  Alas! Alas! Alas!
Oh, for the armed deliverer;
The wielder of a mighty spear;
The archer that shall bend against the foe,
Till horn meet horn, the Scythic bow,
Or, foot to foot and face to face,
Beat caitiffs to the earth with huge, self-hafted mace!
El. Dark Earth hath drunk her potion; in his grave
My father hath it now. But hear what's strange
And passing strange.
Ch. Speak, I implore thee! Speak!
For, oh, my fearful heart is wildly stirred!
El. Here is a lock of hair; laid on the tomb.
Ch. Whose? What tall youth's? Or what deep-girdled girl's?
El. Why, only look; it is not hard to guess.

Ch. I'm an old woman, and shall youth teach me?
El. There's none would shed a hair for him but I.
Ch. Yea, foes are they should mourn with shaven head.
El. 'Tis like; a feather of the self-same wing—
Ch. Whose hair is't like? I am on thorns to know.
El. 'Tis very like the hair of mine own head.
Ch. Not young Orestes' gift in secret brought?
El. It is a tendril of that vine, I swear.
Ch. It is? But how dared he adventure hither?
El. 'Twas sent, this shearling of his filial love.
Ch. That's no less worth my tears to think that he
Will never again set foot in his own land.
El. To me it is the surging of a sea
Bitter as gall; an arrow through my heart.
These tears are but the thirsty thunder-drops
Escaped from unwept deluges; the flood
Is yet to come. Who else that's native here
Could show the fellow to this goodly tress?
Nor was it clipped by her that murdered him;
'Tis not my mother's: what a name is that
For her that hates her own and denies God!
But howsoe'er by this and that I vow
This shining jewel is my best beloved
Orestes' own, I am beguiled by hope.
Oh me!
Would it had sense; a voice to make report
That I be shook no longer to and fro,
But roundly bid to curse and spew it from me,
If 'tis indeed shorn from a murderer's head;
Or that 'twould prove its kin and with me mourn,
This grave's bright ornament, my father's pride.
But when we call upon the Gods, they know
By what great storms, like mariners at sea,
We are tossed and whirled. And, if they mean to save,
Then from small seed a mighty stem may grow.
Ha! Here are footprints! here is double proof!
Look! They are like! They tally with mine own!
Nay, there's a pair—each in outline distinct!
He hath been here with some companion!
Heel, length of tendon, all agrees with mine.
The hope within me struggles to be born,
And I am crazed until it come to birth.
Or. (*disclosing himself*) Henceforth pay fruitful vows to the good Gods
For answered prayer.
El. Wherefore stand I now
So high in heaven's favour?
Or. Thou hast sight
Of that which thou didst pray so long to see.
El. Know'st thou whom my soul craves of all the world?
Or. I know thy heart is woe for Orestes.
El. How have my prayers prospered?
Or. Here am I;
No further seek; for I am all thou lov'st.
El. Sir, art thou come to take me in a snare?
Or. An if I do, I plot against myself.
El. I fear you mean to mock my misery.
Or. I jest at mine, if yours can make me merry.
El. Art thou indeed Orestes?
Or. You are slow
To know me when you see me face to face;
And yet this snip of hair could give you wings;
And when you looked upon it you saw me;
A footprint of your make was proof but now.
Come, put the shorn tress to the shaven head;
Look at this stuff; 'tis of your loom; your spathe
Smoothed it; you broidered this brave brede of beasts.
Refrain thy heart, lest joy unhinge thy wits:
For our dear kin are our most mortal foes.
Ch. Thou darling of thy father's house; sole hope
Of saving seed, watered with many tears!
Now show thy mettle; win back thine own home.
El. Thou eye that centres all sweet thoughts; four selves
Composed in one; for there is none but thee
Left to call father, and the tender love
That was my mother's ere she earned my hate,
Yearns all to thee; and all I felt for her
Twin-sown with me and pitilessly slain;
And ever my true brother; my one name
Of awe; may Power and Justice be with thee
And Zeus, the greatest of the trinity.
Or. Zeus, Zeus, be perfect witness of these woes.
Lo, the young eagles desolate; their sire
Dead in the tight-drawn knot, the twisted coils
Of a fell viperess. Orphans are we
And faint, unfed; unable for the prey
Our father took and to our eyrie bear—
So stand I in thy sight; so she stands,
The sad Electra; fatherless children both;
And either's home is outcast homelessness.
The young of him, Thy sacrificial priest,
A mighty honourer of Thine, if Thou
Cut off, what hand will such rich guerdon give?
And if the eaglets Thou destroy, there's none
To send and show Thy tokens among men;
This royal stem if it be quite consumed
Steads not Thy altars when fat bulls are slain.
Tend it; and out of nothingness exalt
A house that seemeth rased even with the ground.
Ch. Oh, you salvation of your father's house,
Hush; or some rogue, sweethearts, will hear of this
And with his pick-thank tongue carry the tale
To our cursed masters, whom I pray to God
I may see fry in bubbling pinewood blaze!
Or. Great Loxias' word shall never play me false,
That bade me hold upon my perilous way,
Entoning high, and horrors freezing clod,
To make hot livers lumps of ice, forth-telling,
If I tracked not my father's murderers
As they tracked him, nor took my full revenge
With brute, bull-fury gold cannot allay:
My life must answer for it, charged with all
Afflictions that can rob us of our joy.
Of death in life, earth's sop to malice old,
He with dread voice in our frail hearing told;
As foul serpigoes cankering the flesh,
Gnawing the native wholesomeness away,
Till all be furred with the white leprosy.
Next, of the Haunting Furies, conjured up

To take full vengeance for a father's blood,
Seen in the dark, with horrible amaze
Of eyes at stretch and twitch of tortured brows;
And that black arrow winged by pining ghosts
Of murdered kindred, madness and wild fear
Shaped on the night to harry and hound him forth,
Raw with the excommunicating scourge.
He tastes not of the living cup; none spills
With him the red wine in the banquet-hall;
The sightless spirits of his father's wrath
Forbid him every altar; none will house
Nor lodge with him; all sweet civilities
Denied, and no man he may call his friend,
He dies at last, death in each part of him,
A mummied wretch, embalmed in rottenness.
Well—should I hearken to these oracles?
If I do not, the deed is yet to do.
All impulses concur to one great end;
A God's commands, grief for my father, loss
Of all that I am heir to, shame and scorn
That that most famous breed in all the world,
High hearts that humbled Troy, my noble Argives,
Should knee it, like knaves, to a pair of women;
For he is not a man; or if he be
The man he is he passing soon shall see.

Ch. Ye Mighty Destinies, march on,
God with you, till the goal be won
Where Justice' face is set.
"To tongue of gall the bitter word,"
Loud is the voice of Vengeance heard,
When she exacts the debt.
"To dagger-hand the dagger-law,"
"The doer quit"—'tis an old saw
Whose salt hath savour yet.

Or. O father, father of our woe!
How can I serve thee now by word or deed?
From this far world what homing wind shall blow
Where the Eternal Anchors hold thee fast?
There thy long day is night:
And at this gate of death where thou hast passed,
Our grief that are of Atreus' royal seed
Is all thou hast of glory and delight.

Ch. Child, the proud spirit of the dead
Succumbs not to the ravening tooth of fire.
Their passions work, when life is fled:
The mourner's wail
Discovers him that did the wrong.
And lamentation for a murdered sire
A hunter is, that rallies to the trail
All dogs that e'er gave tongue.

Or. Harken then, father, our lament,
While at thy mounded tomb our salt tears flow;
An alternating song, of sad concent,
Dirged by thy children; suppliants that crave
Access to thee; banned, both, from thy high hall,
Met at the common refuge of thy grave.
What's here of good? Where's aught that is not woe?
And is not Doom the master of us all?

Ch. But God can touch the broken strings
To melody divine;
And for this unrejoicing round,
The burden of sepulchral ground,
In the high banquet-hall of kings
Blithe song bring in new wine.

Or. Oh, if 'neath Ilium's wall,
Gashed by some Lycian spear,
Father, thou hadst fall'n in fight,
Then hadst thou left thy house great praise,
And to thy children in the public ways
Honour in the eyes of all.
Then thine had been a sepulchre
Builded of many hands beyond the sea,
And easy would our burden be,
And all its weight of earth how light!

Ch. And in the Kingdom of the Dark,
Welcome wert thou to souls that nobly died;
A lord of majesty and mark,
The cupbearer
Of Hell's vast Thrones; for while thou yet hadst breath
Thou wast a King; and, in that Kingdom wide,
Next them that the huge orb of Fate upbear,
Their rod and sceptre Death!

El. No, not on Troy's far plain
Would I have thee lie, interred,
Where Scamander's waters flow,
With meaner men that fell to the spear,
But none, oh, none, that was thy peer.
Death should have first thy murderers slain;
And, haply, we had heard
Some far-off rumour of their dying,
And never ate the bread of sighing
Nor tasted of this cup of Woe.

Ch. Thy tongue, child, tells of things more worth
Than any weight of gold,
Or aught of fabled bliss that's told
Of that far bourne beyond the bright North Star.
So may'st thou range in fancy uncontrolled;
But our hard hands scourge this unfeeling earth,
And at the massy gate fast shut of old
The summons knocks where our sole helpers are.
They lift not white hands at heaven's judgment bar
Who triumph now, under God's malison;
Yea, and by this the children's cause is won.

Or. Oh, 'twas fledged, that word, it clave
The dull ear that sleeps in the grave.
Zeus, O Zeus, if Thy command
Conjures from the Deeps below
Ghostly Vengeance, footing slow,
Stretching forth an arm to gripe
Sinful soul and felon hand,
Evil lendings, fully ripe,
Loan and interest shall have.

Ch. Oh, to rend the air with a shout
When in their blood they lie,
The woman and her mate!
What wing of Deity
Hovers about me and about?
I cannot hide this huge unrest;
My spirit passionate
Doth like a straining vessel breast
The bitter blast of hate!

El. And when will Zeus, the strong Godhead,

Grasp the bolt with grapplings dread
To cleave their climbing crests amain?
May firm affiance keep our land;
I sue for nothing at God's hand
But that after oppression long
Justice walk the world again.
Hear, Earth; and all the Chthonian throng
Throned in the darkness of the dead!
Ch. It is the Law; when man's blood falls
Man's blood shall pay full cess:
With "Haro! Haro!" Murder calls
God's fell Erinyes,
And in some late succeeding age
For souls slain long ago
Fresh horrors mount the bloody stage
For blacker deeds of woe.
Or. Oho! O heigh! Ye dim Dominions!
Princedoms of Death! Ye potent malisons
Of murdered men! Behold and see
Of Atreus' noble tree
The poor, the pitiful, the last
Scantling, from home and kingly state outcast!
Hear us, O Zeus, for we have none but Thee!
Ch. I listen and tremble; thy cry of dole
Fevers my heart; anon
Faint for wanhope am I;
It thicks my blood, it clouds my soul,
Thy passing piteous cry!
But when the fit is gone,
And my fixed heart is firm to dare,
Pain stands far off; and calm and fair
And cool the brightening sky.
El. How move the dead? How prosper in our plea?
Oh, what can wring them like our misery!
This cloud that overhangs
Our house, these parent-pangs?
Traitress! She could fawn and glose,
But she can never cheat us of our woes;
We are her children and have wolfish fangs.
Ch. I beat to the sound of the Arian dirging,
Yea, to the Kissian wailer's cry;
With wild hands lifted high and high,
Clashing and clutching and tossing and surging;
Faster, faster, never ending;
A tempest of blows on my head descending;
And the noise, like a hammer, dinned through my brain;
A passion of Sorrow, a tumult of Pain!
El. Oh, mother, deep in all
Damnation! Oh, remorseless enemy!
A king borne out to unkind burial,
No liegeman by!
A husband thrust in his grave, and none
To wail or weep or chant an orison!
Or. Ha! Did she use him so despitefully?
She shall aby full dearly her despite!
With Heaven to help and hands to smite,
I'll slay her in her blood and die!
Ch. Hacked like a thief, by her that felon-wise
Graved him; in her cold malice, that his doom
Might insupportably thy days consume;
These were thy father's last death-agonies.
El. They would have none of me; humbled and chidden,
Like a pestilent hound, a cur unwhipped,
Closeted up in the castle-crypt;
There in the kennelled darkness hidden
Freelier flowed my secret weeping
Than ever careless laughter leaping
When the world was gay and my heart was light.
Brother, my wrongs in the memory write!
Ch. Let that thy courage brace,
Like steel-drilled marble, mortised and made one
With thy calm heart's unshaken base.
What's done is done:
But stick not till Expectancy behold
The sequel: on; be firm as thou art bold.
Or. Father, be with us! Father, thee I call!
El. And I with heavy heart and streaming eyes!
Ch. And all our many voices sound as one!
Rise, oh, rise,
And feel the sun:
Be with us 'gainst the common enemy of all!
Or. Plea shall encounter Plea, Power grapple Power!
El. The righteous cause, ye Gods, judge righteously!
Ch. I listen, and I shudder while ye pray:
Destiny
Abides alway,
But prayer can hasten on the inveitable hour!
Or. Oh, heritage of Grief! Incarnate Woe!
Oh, Bloody Hand of Doom that jars the strings!
Now is the voice of melody brought low!
El. Oh, how they grate, these harsh chords Sorrow wrings!
All. Pang on pang, and throe on throe!
Or. Within there is no styptic for this wound,
And the wide world is powerless to aid;
By our own hands our safety must be found,
El. Fury with fury, blood in blood be stayed.
All. This is our hymn to the Gods Earth-bound.
Ch. Hear ,ye Earth dwellers all, that have
Power and bliss beyond the grave!
The seed of Childhood succour and save!
Or. Father, by thy unkingly death, grant me
In thy high house lordship and mastery!
El. Take away my rebuke, let not men say, "Behold,
Aegisthus' chattel, marketed and sold!"
Or. Then, as our fathers used, feasts shall be spread
For thee; else at the banquets of the Dead
Among the steaming bakemeats thou shalt pine.
El. And of my rich dower, plenished from thy store,
To thee refreshing draughts my cup shall pour;
First of all sepulchres I will honour thine.
Or. Earth, grant our sire our combat sore to see!
El. Give, Persephassa, beauteous victory!
Or. Think, father, of the bath, thy life-blood dyed.
El. Think of the cunning-net, the deep and wide!
Or. In gyves, no smith e'er hammered, caught and bound!

El. Veilings of Shame about thee, treason-wound!
Or. Doth not that sting thee, rouse thee from thy Bed?
El. Wilt not lift up thy well-belovéd head?
Or. Bid Justice rise and battle for thine own;
Or let us close with them, as thou wast thrown,
If thou wouldst quell their might that dealt thee doom!
El. Hear this last cry, my father, hear and save!
Lo, the young eagles gather at thy grave;
Pity the man-child and the woman's womb!
Or. Let not this seed of Pelops be destroyed!
For then, in spite of Death, thou art not dead.
El. Children are voices that shake off the lethe
Of drowsy Death; yea, floats, whereby the thread
And thin-wove line of Being is up-buoyed
Above the swallowing gulfs that yawn beneath.
Or. Hear for thy sake the voice of our despair;
Thou sav'st thyself if thou receive our prayer.
Ch. Right well have ye discoursed your argument,
Fit homage to an evil fate unmourned.
And now, since thou hast nerved thee for the act,
Dare it, and put thy Fortune to the touch.
Or. So shall it be; 'tis nothing from my course
To ask the meaning of these cups, and why
Her after-scruple tends a cureless sorrow.
Is Death a simpleton that she dares make
Such poor amends? What shall I think of these
Sorry bestowals for her huge offence?
Why, if a man should lavish all he has
For one least drop of blood, 'twere labour lost.
I prithee, if thou can'st, enlighten me.
Ch. Son, I was there; she was so shook with dreams
And terrors of the night, her wicked heart
So scared, she tremblingly despatched these cups.
Or. Told she her dream?
Ch. She did; "Methought" she cried
"I was delivered of a viper!"
Or. Well,
Finish thy story.
Ch. Then, as 'twere a child,
She hushed and wrapped it up in cradle-clothes.
Or. And what meat craved the dragon-worm new hatched?
Ch. She gave it her own breast, ay, in her dream.
Or. Did she so? Then I warrant her paps are sore.
Ch. It milked her, and sucked out the curded blood.
Or. There was a meaning in this vision.
Ch. She cried in her sleep and started broad awake.
And all the palace-lamps, that hung blind-eyed
In darkness, blazed up for the mistress' sake.
And, presently, she sends these loving-cups;
She thinks them surgery for distempered thoughts.
Or. O parent earth, sepulchre of my father,
Answer my prayer and make this dream come true!
In my interpretation all coheres.
For, look you, if the asp came whence I came,
If it was wound in swaddling clothes, and gaped
With mumbling mouth about the breast that nursed me,
And mingled mother-milk with curded blood,
By this, and by her shriek that saw the dream,
Then, as she gave suck to a devilish thing,
She dies in her blood; and I am dragon-fanged
To kill her as the dream would have me do.
Ch. Oh, good; your reading of it contents me well;
And Heaven fulfil it; but give us first some clew:
Which shall be actors here and who look on.
Or. In sooth, a simple story: she must within,
And it shall be your charge to cloak my plot.
So, as their treason slew a royal man,
They may be tricked and the same noose they rove
Strangle themselves, even as Loxias spake,
Apollo, Prince and Prophet ne'er found false.
My guise a traveller, all my traps complete,
With Pylades here I'll to the palace-gates,
As a friend of the house—trusty—oh, true as steel!
And he and I will talk Parnassian,
Mimic the parle of Phocis for the nonce.
'Tis like enough their varlets will not smile
A welcome, there's such devilment within.
No matter; we will wait; and passers-by
Will say "How comes it Ægisthus denies
A stranger, if he be not gone abroad?"
But once across the threshold of the court,
And if I find him on my father's throne,
Or he come anon and look me in the face,
Hell gapes for him, down drop his dastard eyes,
Ere he can quaver "What's your country?" I
Will spit him on my sword a carcase for crows.
And then Erinys, that stints not her cups,
Shall quaff full healths of slaughter unallayed.
Go, sister; have an eye to all within,
That nothing in our business go agley.
(*To the* CHORUS)
And see that ye offend not with your tongue;
Speak, or say nothing, as occasion serves.
(*To* PYLADES)
Hither to me: second me with thine eye;
Put mettle in my heart and point my sword.
Exeunt ORESTES *and* PYLADES.

Chorus

The tribes of earth are fierce and strong;
And in the arms of ocean throng
The monster enemies of man;
From highest heaven's noonday throne
Flashes and falls the thunderstone
On four-foot beast and feathered clan;
Yea, and remember the hurricane
With his cloak of wrath outblown.

But the pride of man's spirit what tongue can tell,
Or woman's unruly desires, that fell
And hungry flock that feed on death?
These lawless yearnings of the blood
That master wanton womanhood
Corrupt sworn troth with venal breath
And break the bond that comforteth
Man and beast in field and flood,

Is that a fetch of thought beyond thy wing?
Learn of the plot that ill-starred Thestias fired,
And her own child's untimely death conspired,
Casting into the flame
The rusty brand, of his nativity
Prime comrade and coeval, numbering
His minutes, from that hour when with a cry
Forth from her womb he came
To the last day appointed him to die.

Or wist ye not of the girl-murderess
Whose infamy yet lives in legend old?
That for a carcanet of Cretan gold,
King Minos' gift, by foes
Suborned, delivered up a well-loved head?
Stealing from Nisus the immortal tress,
What time—Oh, heart of dog!—in his noon-bed
Breathing he lay in deep repose;
And Hermes drew him down among the dead.

But since old sorrows I recall
That suck no balm from honeyed shower,
Pour out to brim the cup of gall
The sanguine wine of wedlock sour.
Oh, bid them from thy hall
And bid them from thy bower
These dark imaginings of woman's wit
Against her warrior,
Whose mien the foe with darkness smit,
The majesty of war.
Bright shines the hearth were no fierce passions throng
And woman's valour when she shrinks from wrong.

So in the roll of antique time
Her primacy black Lemnos bears;
Her shame is cried in every clime;
And all that horror dreads or dares
Of that cursed Lemnian crime
The sable likeness wears.
She feels the ache of God's most grievous ban:
And her despiséd race
Under the general scorn of man
Is gone to their own place.
That which displeases God none holds in awe;
What cite I here that contradicts His law?

There is a sword, whose biting thrust
God's Law drives home; plunged to the hilt
Clean through the naked heart; for guilt
Lies not down-trodden in the dust
That men may trample as of right
On all that's holy in God's sight.

Now Justice' anvil standeth fast;
The Armourer, Doom, beats out her blade;
Within is privily conveyed
A Child that quits the bloody past;
That true-born Child Erinys brings;
Dark are her deep imaginings.

Before the Palace ORESTES *and* PYLADES. CHORUS.

Or. Boy! Boy! Do you hear me knock? What, boy, I say!
Whos's there? Open, if in Aegisthus' halls
Be welcome for a stranger.

Doorkeeper. Ay, have done!
I hear ye. What's your country, and whence come you?

Or. Announce me to your masters; I bring news
Meant for their ear. And set about it quickly;
For now the chariot of night comes on
Darkling; it is the hour when travel casts
Anchor in hostelries and roadside inns.
Let one of charge and consequence come forth—
Some worthy dame, or, stay, a man were best;
For then nice manners need not overcast
Frank speech; a man is to his brother man
Open in converse, free without offence.

CLYTAEMNESTRA *appears at the Palace-door with* ELECTRA.

Cl. Sirs, what's your will? Here is such entertainment
As fits my house; warm baths, an easy couch
For tired limbs, and looks of honest welcome.
But if there's graver business to despatch,
That's men's concern and they must hear of it.

Or. I come from Phocis; I am a Daulian;
And on the road with mine own merchandise
To Argos here, which is my journey's end,
A man to me unknown, as I to him,
Met me, enquired my way and told me his;
Strophius the Phocian, as appeared anon.
"Sir" quoth he, "since you are travelling to Argos,
Do me the service to inform his parents
Their son Orestes is no more; forget not;
And whether they decide to have him home,
Or leave him ours for ever, bury him
In his adopted land, bring word again.
Meantime, his urn clips in its brazen round
The ashes of a man right nobly mourned."
That was his message; whether chance-delivered
To whom it concerns, who may herein command,
I cannot tell; but they whose son he is
Must surely be apprised of it.

Cl. Oh me!
How are we stormed upon, broke, breached, despoiled!
Unmastered curse of our unhappy house
How wide thy range! Things out of reach thy bolt
Brings down from far, and thou dost pluck from me
To the last hair all, all, that I hold dear!
And now Orestes; he that thought to plant
His foot out of the mire of muddy death,
The hope that physicked this debauch of blood,
Pricked in thy roster answers to his name.

Or. Would I had better news to recommend me
To my so honourable entertainers
And grace their proffered welcome. What can warm
The heart like kindness betwixt host and guest?
And yet it had been wicked to my thinking
Not to discharge an office laid on me
Both by my pledged word and your courtesy.

Cl. Oh, not for that will we scant your deserts
Or make you the less welcome to our house.
Another had brought these tidings, if not thou.
But it is time that day-long travellers
Find full suppliance for the weary road.
(*To* ELECTRA)
Do you bestow him in the men's guest-chambers,
His company and all his retinue.
Let them be treated as becomes our house;
And be it done as you shall answer it.

ELECTRA, ORESTES *and* PYLADES *enter the Palace.*

These news we will impart unto our lord;
And he and I, with help of our good friends,
Take counsel touching this calamity.

CLYTAEMNESTRA *follows.*

Ch. Content! Content! Oh, when shall we,
Dear'st handmaidens, full lustily
Orestes' triumph-song resound?
Majestic earth! Thou cliff high-shored,
Whose shadow sleeps on the longships' lord,
Give ear and send us present aid!
Now is the hour of combat knolled,
And Parley, with the tongue of gold,
In guile unguessed moves darkly dight,
And Nether Hermes cloaked in Night
Shall watch this grim and bloody round
Fought to the death with naked blade.

The NURSE *is seen passing within.*

The mischief works! His hand is in, our guest!
Orestes' nurse, all tear-bedabbled; Hist!
Where steps Kilissa at the dark entry,
Unsalaried Sorrow all her company?

The NURSE *comes to the door.*

Nurse. Why, I am bidden by my lady run
And fetch Aegisthus; she'll have this confirmed;
And man to man before it has time to cool
They are to piece it out. Among her slaves
She wears a knitted brow, but in her eyes
Lurks laughter for this finish and fair close
Of her much care; though 'tis of care compact
For us, this traveller's tale that cleft my heart.
Ah, God, when he has heard it, probed and proved,
How will his spirit dance for joy. Heigh-ho!
Sorrows bygone, ill with worse ill confounding,
The long, sick agonies of Atreus' line,
Did, in the coming of them, wring my heart.
But none of them were half so grievous-heavy,
And I found patience to bear them all.
But my dear Orestes, spendings of my soul,
Whom I took from his mother's womb, nursed in my lap,
And at his peevish piping broke my rest,
And was so patient with him, trudge and drudge,
And get no thanks. 'Tis but a witless thing,
We have to nurse, no whelp more whimsical.
It can't speak plain, a weanling in long clothes;
Woo't drink? woo't eat? make water, woo't? God made
The little belly a law unto itself.
I would divine his wants, and oft as not
Go wrong; and fall to washing dirty napkins,
Laundress and nurse too, all for my sweet babe.
Oh, turn and turn about, I plied both trades
When I took Orestes from his father's arms.
Alack, and now they tell me he is dead;
And I must get me to this dunghill dog
Will take my tidings with a greedy ear.

Ch. How did she bid him come—in what array?
Nu. How? Say't again: I do not understand thee.
Ch. Or with his bodyguard or unattended?
Nu. She bade him bring his Yeomen of the Guard
Ch. Never deliver to the brute her message!
Tell him to come alone, that he may hear
From lips unawed; say, "quickly, cheerly come!"
A tale that's warped oft straightens in the telling!
Nu. Dost mean that these are welcome news to thee?
Ch. 'Tis an ill wind Zeus cannot turn to good.
Nu. Good? And our hope, our dear Orestes dead?
Ch. 'Twere no mean prophet could expound my text.
Nu. What mean'st? Hast aught that squares not with the tale?
Ch. Run! Take thy message, do as thou art bid:
Safe in Heaven's Hands is all that touches Heaven.
Nu. Well, I will suffer ye to have it so;
And by the bounty of God may all end well.

Exit NURSE

Chorus

Father of Heaven, hear me in this hour;
Raise up a fallen house; vouchsafe to bless
Hearts that thirst and eyes that ache
To see the Face of Soothfastness.
Justice is all the plea I make;
Uphold it with the Hand of Power.

Oh, Zeus! Him in yon house of kings
Prefer above his enemies,
And he shall bring Thee free-will offerings,
With triple lauds and threefold sacrifice.

'Tis but a Colt, bethink Thee, sired of One
Beloved, that's linked to the Iron Car of Woe!
Collect those fiery paces! Mete
The measure of his stride, that so
With steady rhythm of galloping feet
He break not till the course be run!

Ye Dwellers of the inmost shrine, adorned
With vessels of fine gold,
Hearken! Ye Gods, that with us wept and mourned!
Cancel with fresh Doom the blood of old
Shed guiltily, till all's undone!
Nevermore, come Time, come Tide,
In the House where Ye abide
Grizzled Murder get a Son!

God of the Grot, the vaulted Fane,
Give these blind walls back their sight!
Make them Man's fair home again!
Give them Freedom! Give them Light!

Through this dark Veil, of Thy Grace,
Make them show a shining face!

Meet is it Maia's child with subtlest craft
Our dubious venture speed:
Is none so deft, so nimble-light, to waft
To port the hazard of a dextrous deed!
He opens or shuts with "Yea" and "Nay"
The gold of His hid Treasury;
His Word is night to the seeing eye,
And darkness in the broad noonday.

Then, for deliverance from Despair,
For a steady breeze and strong,
We'll harp and sing to a merry air
The mumping witch-wives' song:

"The ship rides free; come, fill my lap;
Put money in my purse;
Largesse, fair Sirs, for your good hap
And the boon of a broken Curse."

Thou to the deed march boldly on;
And, when thou hear'st her cry, "My Son"
Answer—"Not thine!"—and with one blow
In blameless blood-guilt blot this Woe!

On! Lest a word should win thee,
A look break down thy guard;
Harden the heart within thee
As Perseus' heart was hard!

Make stern amends; relent not;
Doth the wronged ghost forgive?
Relax not—pause, repent not!
They ask it that yet live!

Strike, strike for Hate's allaying,
The House of Hate within,
And with one sinless Slaying
Slaughter the Seed of Sin!

Enter AEGISTHUS.

Aegisthus. I come not here unasked; a message reached me;
I'm told there's a strange rumour, certain men,
Our guests, have brought, little to pleasure me;
Orestes' death. That were with a fresh load
To chafe a sore that runs with fears unstaunched,
And open bygone Murder's aching scars.
Shall I concede it true? Looks't forth clear-eyed?
Or null and void as woman's vain alarms;
A flight of sparks that presently come to nought?
What canst thou tell me that shall clear my doubt?

Ch. Only that we have heard it; go within:
Question the strangers, man to man; there lies
The marrow and pith of all the news e'er brought.

Ae. I'll see this messenger and question him
Again, if he was present at the death;
Or vents a tale that hath no substance in it.
They that would steal my wits first steal my eyes.

Exit.

Ch. Open my lips, order my prayers aright,
O God above!
Give them the strength, the breadth, the depth, the height,
Of my exceeding love!
Now on the soilure of one slaughterous sword
Hangs Doom and Death
For all the race of Agamemnon Lord;
Or light and breath
Of liberty on its keen edge shall glance;
And, by those brandished fires,
He shall possess a Kingdom's governance
And the glory of his sires.
And, in this gest, a solitary knight,
Two crafty foes grips he,
Even Orestes, girt with a hero's might;
God give him Victory!

A shriek is heard within the Palace.

Hark!—Hush!—which way
Went the battle? What is Heaven's will,
O House, for thee this day?
Let's go aside that in this dark event
It may be thought that we are innocent:
What's done is done; or be it good or ill.

The Inner Court.

Doorkeeper. Alas, my master! Oh, my lord, Aegisthus!
A bloody, bloody end! Open! Be quick!
Unbar the women's gates! Muscle and brawn,
Mettle of manly youth, we need you now,
But not—God help us—for the helpless dead!
Ho there, within! Oho!
'Tis shouting to the deaf; they are asleep;
They heed me not! Where's Clytaemnestra? What
Doth she? Fore God, her neck is for the knife;
Yea, by the hand of Judgement she must fall!

Enter CLYTAEMNESTRA.

Cl. What's this? Why do you keep this bawling here?

Doorkeeper. The dead have come to life and slain the quick.

Cl. Ah, God! Ah, God! I read your riddle; we
Are to perish even as we slaughtered him,
Tricked and betrayed! Bring me a battle-axe!
We'll know if we mount high or fall full low;
I touch the bound and bourn of all my woe.

Enter ORESTES, PYLADES *with him.*

Or. I am come to fetch thee; thy fellow hath his fill.

Cl. Oh—my dear'st love—Aegisthus—dead—dead—dead!

Or. Thou lov'st him? Good! Then thou shalt lie with him
In 's grave; there thy false heart can never betray him.

Cl. Oh, hold thy hand! My child—my babe—look here!
My breast; be tender to it; thy soft gums
Did in thy drowze so often drink its milk.

Or. Pylades, what now? Shall I be tender to her?

Pylades. What then were Loxias' prophesyings worth,

His holy oracles? What oaths deep-sworn?
Better the world thine enemy than Heaven!

Or. Thou art my better mind; thou counsellest well.
Come here; I mean to slay thee where he lies,
Whom thou didst count a better than my father.
Sleep with him in death since thou lov'st him, and hat'st
Him whom thou oughtest truly to have loved.

Cl. I nursed thee; I would fain grow old with thee!

Or. What? Kill my father and make thy home with me!

Cl. Destiny, dear child, was partner in my guilt.

Or. And Destiny accomplished thy doom.

Cl. Child, fear'st thou not a mother's malison?

Or. Mother! You cast me out to misery!

Cl. Not cast thee out. They were our trusty friends!

Or. You basely sold me, born a free man's son.

Cl. Where is the price that I received for thee?

Or. I am ashamed to tell thee openly.

Cl. Nay, do; but leave not out thy father's sins!

Or. He wrought for thee while thou sat'st safe at home.

Cl. 'Tis nature, child; unmanned we ache and pine.

Or. They win ye bread that ye may eat at ease.

Cl. Is it even so? Child, wilt thou slay thy mother?

Or. Thou slay'st thyself, it is not I that kill thee.

Cl. Beware the ban-dogs of a mother's fury!

Or. Except I do this how shall I 'scape my father's?

Cl. I am like one that cries to the deaf grave!

Or. My father's fate strikes thee with airs of death.

Cl. Thou art the aspic I brought forth and nursed!

Or. Thy fearful dream was prophet of thy woe,
And thy foul sin pays forfeit in thy sorrow.

ORESTES *drags in* CLYTAEMNESTRA, *followed by* PYLADES.

Chorus

Oh, my heart's heavy even for their fall.
But since the gory edifice of woe
Orestes copes and crowns; 'tis better so
Than he be quenched who was the eye of all.

There came on Priam's sons at last
Judgement and Retribution sore:
There came two Lions wrapped in one tawny hide
To Agamemnon's house, yea, two-fold War.
But, warned at Pytho, furious and fast,
The banished man drove on amain, with God for Guide.

Shout! Shout, Ho! with a jubilant rouse!
Shout for my lord and my lord's house
Delivered from evil; from the twain that defiled
His hearth and his substance squandered!
Farewell, the lone, the trackless wild,
The waste of Woe we wandered!

Came He that loves the dark surprise
Deep Retribution subtly planned;
And Zeus' own Daughter in this combat dire
Her finger laid on the avenger's hand;
Men call her Justice—on her enemies
She vents the blast of her consuming ire.

The Voice of Loxias,
In great Parnassus' rocky cavern heard,
The word of guile where no guile was,
Though long deferred,
Hath come to pass.
The power of God can never pass away
Because no evil thing is holp thereby;
Meet is it, then, we worship and obey
His governance Whose Hand sustains the starry sky.

The dawn breaks fair; the night is spent;
The bit is loosed and bridle unbound;
Rise, walls! Rise, tower and battlement,
Ye shall no more lie levelled to the ground.

And it shall not be long
Ere pardoning Time, the world's great Hierarch,
Shall pass with sound of charming song
These portals dark,
Absolve the wrong,
And break the spell that bound them, utterly.
Fortune shall throw a main and sweep the board;
And we shall see her face and hear her cry;
"Here will I make my home, to your fair house restored."

The scene discovers ORESTES *and* PYLADES *standing over the dead bodies of* CLYTAEMNESTRA *and* AEGISTHUS.

Or. Behold the tyrants that oppressed your land,
Slayers of fathers, plunderers of kings' houses.
But now they kept great state, seated on thrones;
Yea, and, methinks, they yet lie lovingly
In death, true honourers of their oath and bond.
They sware that they would kill my father, sware
To die together, and were not forsworn.
Behold, ye judges of their heinous crimes,
The thing they wrought, the links that bound my father,
Gyves for his wrists and fetters for his feet.
Shake it abroad, stand round me in a ring,
Hang out these trappings, that a father's eye
Not mine, but he that watcheth all the world,
Helios, may view my mother's handiwork;
Ay, and hereafter testify for me
That justly I pursued even to the death
My mother; I reck not Aegisthus' end;
For by the law the adulterer shall die.
But she that hatched this horror for her lord,
By whom she went with child, carried the load
Of sometime love—but this tells you 'twas hate!

What? Had she conger's teeth or adder's fangs,
She had corrupted where her tooth not bit,
So absolute was she in iniquity.
How shall I name this right and use fair words?
Trap for a beast? Clout for a dead man's feet?
A towel is't? Fore God, a trapper's toil;
A noose; a gown that trips the wearer up;
Some rascal publican might get one like it,
That robs his guests for a living; ay, with this,
Put scores away and feel no cold fit after.
I pray God one like her may never house
With me—I'd liefer go childless to my grave.
Ch. Aiai! the woeful work! This hideous death
Ends thee; thy pride and all thy passions cold;
For him that yet must draw this lethal breath
The flower of suffering begins to unfold.
Or. Was this her work or not? This proves it, this
Robe, sullied with Aegisthus' dagger-plunge.
The tinct of murder, not the touch of Time
Alone, hath—here and here—spoiled its rich brede.
I'll praise and mourn him now, I was not by
To mourn and praise, with his death-robe before me.
Sad act, sad end, thrice-wretched race, triumph
No man need envy, soilure of my soul.
Ch. Time grants not our so perishable clay
Bliss that endures or glory that shall last;
Heaviness wears the instant hour away,
Or it will come before the next be passed.
Or. Mark this: for I know not where it will end,
Dragged like a driver of hot, headlong horses
Quite from the track; beaten and borne afar
By break-neck thoughts; fear at my heart, at stretch
To strike up the grim tune, whereto 'twill dance.
While I am in my senses, I protest
I slew not, friends, my mother save with cause,
My father's blood upon her, and Heaven's hate.
I lay it on the charm that made me bold;
On Pytho's prophet, Loxias, that charged
Me do the deed, and sware to hold me guiltless
If done; if not, I sink the consequence:
No bolt ere shot can hit that height of suffering.
And now behold and see how I am furnished
With branch and wreath, and, thus apparelled, go
To earth's great nombril-precincts, Loxias' ground,
And that famed fount of indestructible fire,
Kin-murder's outlaw; at no hearth but His
Did Loxias bid me look for sanctuary.
Hereafter let all Argives bear me out
Not without strong compunction did I deal
So ruefully with her that gave me life.
I am a wanderer now, I have no friends,
But live or die, this shall be told of me.
Ch. Thou hast done well; let words of evil note
Be far from thy lips: give not ill fancies speech.
Thou hast delivered all the land of Argos;
Sawn off with one sword-sweep two dragon-heads.
Or. Ha! Ha!
Women, they come about me—Gorgon shapes,
Sheeted in grey—clasped round with scaly folds
Of intertwisted snakes,—away! away!
Ch. True son to thy father, what fantastic thoughts
Are these? Stand fast! thou hast triumphed: fear for nought.
Or. These fearful torments are no phantasies;
These are the leashed sleuth-hounds my mother slips!
Ch. Because the blood is fresh upon thy hands,
Therefore this sudden frenzy rocks thy soul.
Or. Apollo! Prince! Look, look!—They come in crowds,
And from their eyeballs blood drips horribly!
Ch. Haste thee where cleansing is! To Loxias!
Hold fast to him and find deliverance!
Or. Ye see them not, but I see them; they turn
Upon me! Hunt me forth! Away! Away!
He rushes out.
Ch. Fair Fortune go with him; God be his Guide;
God keep him ceaselessly, and send him peace!

There rose Three Winds and shook thee, sad palace where Power sat throned,
And now the third bloweth over, the last that the first atoned.
The First Wind came with crying of children slain long ago;
Long, long was it a-dying, the Thyestean Woe!
The next Wind swept with slaughter, but not by the foeman's sword;
All bloody was the water that laved Achaia's lord.
Now the Third Storm hath struck thee from the vast of an infinite gloom;
Shall I hail thee Wind of Deliverance, or art thou a blast of doom?
Oh, when will thy course be finished, when wilt thou change and cease,
And the stormy heart of Havoc be lulled into lasting peace? *Exeunt.*

EUMENIDES

DRAMATIS PERSONAE

The Prophetess
Apollo
Orestes
The Ghost of Clytaemnestra
Chorus of Furies
Athena
The Judges
Escort

Delphi. Before the Temple of Apollo.

Prophetess

Before all Gods my punctual prayer prefers
Gaia, first Prophetess; Themis next her,
Who did succeed her Mother in this seat
Oracular, as some have told us; third
In order, by her free, unforced consent,
Sat here another Titaness, Chthon's child,
Phoebe; and she gave it a birthday-gift,
To Phoebus, who took on him Phoebe's name.
From his still mere, his craggy Delian Isle,
On Pallas' shore, the port of ships, debarked,
Hither he came, to this Parnassian grot;
With fair conduct and worship and great laud
From Hephaestus' sons, that hewed his path, and made
The unreclaimed and savage region tame.
Rich honours had he here from the simple folk
And from Delphos, their prince and governor.
And Zeus possessed him of his mystery,
And planted him fourth seer upon this throne;
Prophet of Zeus is Loxias, Son of Sire.
These are the gods of prefatory prayer.
But Pronaan Pallas hath prime mention, too;
Their lauds the Nymphs of the Corycian Rock,
Hollow birds love, repair of Deities;
The wild is Bromius' chace, never forgot,
Since His Divinity captained the Bacchanals
And toiled King Pentheus like a mountain hare.
On Pleistus' Fountain and Poseidon's Force
I call, and highest Zeus, All-Perfecter,
Ere I go in and take my prophet-throne.
And now good hap all heretofore excelling
Wait on my going in, and every Greek,
By lot admitted and old custom-law.
I deal mine answers as the God me guides.

She enters the Shrine but returns almost immediately.

Horrors past speech, horrors I durst not look on,
Have driven me forth again from Loxias' House!
My limbs failed me; I could not stand upright;
On hands and knees I scrambled along the ground!
Fear makes us old wives naught, helpless as babes.
As I was passing toward the wreath-hung shrine
I saw a man right at the Nombril-Stone,
He did pollute, sit like a suppliant; blood
Dripped from his hands; he held a naked sword
And a high-branched and leafy olive bough,
With a great flock of wool all meekly tied;
A silvery fleece; of that I am very sure.
And over against the man a company
Of awesome women sound asleep on thrones;
And yet not women; rather Gorgon-shapes;
And yet not Gorgons neither by their mien.
I have seen pictures of She-things that snatched
At Phineus' feast; but these, methought, were all
Wingless and black and made my blood run cold.
They snored with blasts I dared not draw anigh,
And from their eyes let ooze an evil rheum;
Their garb no vestment for the marble Gods
Nor fit to carry to the homes of men.
I never saw the kindred or the tribe
Of this strange fellowship, nor know the land
Could breed them and not sorrow for their birth.
Let this be looked to by great Loxias.
Prophet and leech and portent-reader, He;
In homes not His the Purgatorial Power. *Exit.*

The Temple-doors open, disclosing all that the Prophetess has described. APOLLO *stands over* ORESTES.

Apollo. My word is passed: I never will forsake thee,
Thy guardian to the end, close at thy side,
And far away not tender to thy foes.
These ogreish maws are muzzled now, thou seest;
These cursèd carlines cast into a sleep;
Old barreners, the early get of Time,
Ne'er clasped in love by God or man or brute.
For Evil's sake brought forth, since Evil came,
The Dark their pale, and Tartarus 'neath the world;
Fiends loathed of flesh and of Olympian Gods.
Natheless, fly thou and never faint thy heart;
For they will drive thee over continents,
Treading for evermore the travelled earth,
And over the sea and cities far enisled.
Weary not ere thy warfare come; chew not
The cud of fearful phantasy: Get thee
To Pallas' Town; there clasp her statua,
And we will find thee Judges of thy cause,
And frame sooth speeches that shall work like charms
For evermore deliverance from thy sorrow.
I speak, that bade thee strike thy mother down.

Orestes. O Prince Apollo, Thou know'st to do right;

Let not thy lore, oblivious, lapse from use
Thy puissance to effect is my sure bond.
Ap. I charge thee, think on that: fail not from
fear.

He turns to the statue of Hermes.

And thou, My blood-brother, My Father's Son,
Hermes, be Thou his Keeper; prove Thy Name,
Great Guide: be Pastor of my sheep that cries
To me; Zeus careth for the castaway,
With Thy fair escort sent among mankind.

Exit ORESTES. APOLLO *retires into the Sanctuary.*
Enter the Ghost of CLYTAEMNESTRA.

Ghost of Clytaemnestra

Sleep then: Sleep on! And whereto serve your
slumbers?
I only must endure your contumely
In death: the rebuke of my assassination
Clings to me yet among unbodied ghosts;
A vagabond, an outcast! Let me tell ye
They lay a sore indictment to my charge.
And for these fearful wrongs, mine own dealt me,
Not one of all the Invisible Powers is wroth,
Though mine own child lifted his hand against me!
Look at these wounds! Behold them with thy
heart!
When the soul sleeps the inward eye is bright:
No glance of Fate is glimpsed in the waking day.
Times without number at my hand ye lapped
Your draughts not mixed with wine, abstemious
cups;
Your solemn midnight suppers I have roast
At mine own hearth, when no God else is served.
And yet all this is trampled in the dust;
And he is fled, gone like a fleet-foot fawn,
As lightsome leapt the toils, and laughs full loud.
Give ear! For I have pled for soul, for life,
For being! Wake, Goddesses of the Deep!
A dream that once was Clytaemnestra calls.

A noise of whining

Whimper and whine, but you have lost your man.
He hath his friends, and they are not like mine.

Whining

Thou sleepst too sound; thou car'st not for my
wrong;
Orestes that spilled his mother's blood flits free.

Growling

Thou snarling slug-a-bed! Wilt not get up?
What hast thou done but evil since time was?

Growling

Weariness and Sleep, the arch-conspirators,
Have stolen the fell Dragon's strength away!

Two sharp howls

A Fury (*still asleep*). There, there, there, there!
Ware, hound!
Ghost. Thou hunt'st the hart in dream, and like
a dog
That ne'er hath done, criest on the trail in sleep.
What would'st be at? Up, lest sloth master thee
And with its dull balm numb the nerve of pain.
Ache with that inward anguish thou dost owe,
The rankle of remorse, stern virtue's barb!
Let loose on him thy breath, that reeks hot blood!
Dry him up with smoke! Blast him with fire of thy
belly!
Make this fault good and follow to his fall!

She rushes out.

Chorus Leader. Rouse all! Rouse her—and her!
And I'll rouse thee!
Sleep'st? Get thee up! Shake off the shackling
sleep!
Let's see if we have jeopardied our chase!
1. Undone! Undone!
Oho! Oho!
We are shamed! We are shent!
2. I have hunted my woe!
3. Ah, sister, and I,
And all of our cry!
Balked, baffled and foiled;
We panted and toiled,
As hounds on the trail,
While the thicket he kept,
But the deer leaped the pale—
4. While I slumbered and slept!
1. A thief and a knave
Art thou, Zeus' Son!
2. Our ancientry
Thy youth hath o'er-run!
3. The suitor finds grace
At thy hands this day!
The wicked one,
The matricide,
That Heaven defied,
Thou of Heaven's high race
Hast stolen away—
4. And was this well done?

Chorus

It is a knotless cord that cuts me most,
A phantom smart,
A charioteer of Dream, a chiding Ghost,
Hath wrung my heart!
I have been whipped; I stiffen at the stake,
A public show;
The hangman's knout hath stung me with dull
ache,
Blow upon blow!

'Tis the new fashion, their just heritage
They count too small.
They must engross, these godlings come of age,
They will have all!
And we must see the world's great Nombril-Stone
Spout blood, aghast!
Polluting purples desecrate a throne,
Whose gules shall last!

Blind Seer! Himself infects His Holy Seat;
With obscene unction mires
His inmost Altar, whose hearth-embers heat
Prophetic fires.
Self-bidden, self-impelled,
Against Heaven's Law He hath rebelled,
A dying cause He honoureth
And immemorial Rights consigns to death!

He hath become abominable to me!
Nor shall to the end of Time
Cast loose whom He hath bound to Him, go free,
The Patron God of Crime!
Where one takes soil, a thousand cursed
Miscreants shall follow on the first,
Set their unholy feet upon his head,
Trampling His sanctuary with unquiet tread!

Enter APOLLO, *with his bow and quiver of arrows.*

Ap. Out! I command you! Fast and faster yet!
Avoid My precincts! Quit Mine oracle!
Or take with ye a wingèd adder sheen,
Shot from My bow that's strung with golden wire,
And with the pang puke up black froth of men,
The retchy gobbets thou hast sucked from slaughter!
Ye do presume when ye come near My house;
Ye should be with chopped heads and gouged-out eyes,
Dooms, executions, maimed virilities,
Boy-eunuchs, mutilations, whittled trunks,
Stonings, deep groans and agonizing shrieks,
Spines spiked on iron pales! Now have ye heard
Your horrible regale, that makes Gods hate ye,
Your dainty dish? Ay everything about ye
Betokens it. In some blood-bolting den
Of lions hutch and house; but rub not off
Your foul, infectious hides in my rich fane;
Go griesly goats! Get hence, unshepherded!
No son of Heaven would deign to pasture ye!

Ch. Now listen to our answer, King Apollo!
Thou art—I say not the abettor of this—
But the sole Doer; Thou and only Thou.

Ap. How, I beseech thee? So far thou may'st speak.

Ch. Thou bad'st the guestling feigned do matricide.

Ap. I bade him venge his father; what of that?

Ch. Red-handed Thou receivedst the murderer.

Ap. I charged him haste for cleansing to My house.

Ch. And dost Thou rail at them that holp him hither?

Ap. Ye are not fit to enter where I dwell.

Ch. It is our bounden duty and our charge.

Ap. What dignity is this? Cry me your worth!

Ch. We harry mother-murderers from men's homes.

Ap. What do ye to a wife that kills her husband?

Ch. 'Tis not so black as spilling kindred blood.

Ap. Injurious hags, ye make of no account
High Hera's nuptial bond and Zeus' troth-plight:
Cypris the tenour of your pleading scoffs,
That gives to men the dearest joys flesh knows.
The marriage-bed a parcel is of Fate,
Hedged by a holier law than all oaths else.
If there be murder there, and thou relax,
Not punish, nor bend thither an angry brow,
I say, in law thou canst not ban Orestes.
For I perceive ye burn with zeal 'gainst him,
And show towards them a marvellous unconcern.
Not so the Goddess when she tries the cause.

Ch. Not while Time lasts will I relinquish him.

Ap. Pursue him then and multiply thy travail.

Ch. Breathe no abridgement of my majesty.

Ap. Nay, were it tendered me I'd none of it.

Ch. Great art thou, ranked no lower than Zeus' chair.
Ha! I smell mother-blood! It leads me on
To vengeance: I will hunt the miscreant down!

The CHORUS *rush out.*

Ap. I will protect him, and draw him out of harm.
Dreaded of men and feared in Heaven is the wrath
Of him that sues for grace, if I forsake him.

A year or perhaps longer passes: the scene changes to Athens and the Shrine of Pallas, whose image stands in front of the stage.
Enter ORESTES, *weary, with bleeding feet.*

Or. Athena, Queen, by Loxias' command
I am here; be kind; receive a runagate,
But not a recreant with uncleansed hands.
My guilt grows dull, the edge of it worn down
On hearths not mine and the highways of the world.
Across wide continents, over the sea,
To Loxias' oracular command
Obedient, I am come unto Thy house,
Yea, to Thy holy Statua, Goddess,
Here will I harbour and abide Thy Doom.

He crouches down and clasps the image.
Enter the CHORUS.

Chorus

Aha, a palpable trace; we have him now!
Follow this close informer's mute record!
We are the hound and he is the hit fawn;
The blood's the trail, and we mark every drop.
Ha! I breathe hard, this helter-skelter heaves
My hollow flanks; we have quartered the whole earth,
Across the ocean warped our wingless way
Still close abeam, and never lost his sail.
Or here, or not far off he quaketh sore.
The smell of man's blood is laughter to my soul—
A winsome reek!
Go seek, go seek, go seek!
Search and sound
All this ground
Lest the vagabond we chase
Slip into safe hiding-place,
And for mother-murder done
Guilty son
Out of Law's reach scape scot-free.
There—there—there.
Yonder he sits!
See how he knits
His arms about Her image old
That breathes ambrosial air!
And doth Her succour make thee bold?
And do those hands implore
Her sentence? That shall never be!
Sorrow on thee!

The mother-blood those murderous hands have shed
Is irrecoverably fled!

The swallowing earth shall yield it nevermore!
Thy life for hers; thou shalt fill me a cup
 Drawn from those veins of thine;
Deep draughts of jellied blood I will sip and sup,
 Though bitter be the wine.
And then, when I have sucked thy life-blood dry,
 I'll drag thee down below!
There mother's son shall mother's agony
 Expiate, throe for throe!
And thou shalt see all damnèd souls, whilome
 Sinners 'gainst God or guest
Or parent; and of each the righteous doom
 Shall be by thee witnessed!
For Hades is a jealous Judge of Men,
 And in His Black Assize
The record writ with ghostly pen
 Cons with remorseless eyes.

Or. I am made perfect in the rule of Sorrow,
By oft occasions schooled know when to speak
And when refrain. But on this theme I am bid
By a most wise Preceptor ope my lips.
The blood from off this hand fades, fallen on sleep;
The spot of mother-murder is washed white;
That, when 'twas fresh, on Divine Phoebus' hearth
Was purged away with blood of slaughtered swine.
'Twere long to tell from that first hour all those
I have consorted with and harmed no man.
Now with pure lips that can no more offend
I ask Athena, Sovreign of this realm,
To be my helper. Hers are we then, not won
In war, myself, my Argos and her people,
By pact well-kept her fedaries for ever.
If she about the parts of Libya
Round Triton's rapid river, her natal stream,
Her foot advance, or veil with flowing train,
True friend of them she loves; or Phlegra's flats,
Like a bold cateran, lord of his clan, surveys,
Thence let her come—a God can hear from far—
And from this sore distress redeem my soul.

Chorus

Maugre Apollo and Athena's might
Thou goest to perdition, derelict
And damned; no place for joy in thy lost soul;
A calf bled white for fiends to munch, a shadow.
Answerest thou nothing? Art too sick with scorn,
My fatling, for my table sanctified;
My dish, not altar-slain but eaten alive?
Hear then the bitter spell that binds thee fast.

Come, dance and song, in linkèd round!
 More deep than blithe Muse can
We'll make these groaning chanters sound
 Our governance over Man!
No parley! Give us judgement swift!
We vex not in our wrath who spread
White hands to Heaven uplift.
Not unto such; he journeyeth
Unharmed, a happy traveller
Through life to the last pause of Death:
But to the froward soul, that seeks,
Like *him*, to cloak up, if he could,
Plague-spotted hands, with murder red,
To such our apparition speaks,
The faithful witness for the dead,
Plenipotentiary of Blood
And Slaughter's sovran minister.

Hear me, my Mother! Hark,
 Night, in whose womb I lay,
Born to punish dead souls in the dark
 And the living souls in the day!
Lo, Leto's Lion-cub
 My right denies;
He would take my slinking beast of the field,
Mine, mine by mother-murder sealed,
 My lawful sacrifice.

But this is the song for the victim slain,
To blight his heart and blast his brain,
Wilder and wilder and whirl him along;
This is the song, the Furies' song,
 Not sung to harp or lyre,
To bind men's souls in links of brass
And over their bodies to mutter and pass
 A withering fire!

Long the thread Fate spun
 And gave us to have and hold
For ever, through all Time's texture run,
 Our portion from of old.
Who walks with murder wood,
 With him walk we
On to the grave, the deep-dug pit;
And when he's dead, he shall have no whit
 Too large a liberty!

Oh! this is the song for the victim slain,
To blight his heart and blast his brain,
Wilder and wilder and whirl him along!
This is the song, the Furies' song,
 Not sung to harp or lyre,
To bind men's souls in links of brass
And over their bodies to mutter and pass
 A withering fire!

When as yet we were quick in the womb,
 This for our jointure was meted;
And the Gods that know not Death's doom
 Are not at our table seated;

With us they break no bread,
 And of all their raiment shining,
I wear nor thrum nor thread;
 I will have no fane for my shrining!

But when Quarrel comes in at the gate
For the crashing of homes, when Hate
Draweth his sword against kind,
Ho! who shall our fleet feet bind?
Though he putteth his trust in his strength,
The blood that is on him shall blind,
And our arm overtake him at length!

Grave cares of public trust claim we
With sudden, swift appearing;
Let hell's contention set heaven free,
Discharged without a hearing.

For all the Tribe that come
Dropping blood of kin, curse-ridden,
Zeus stoppeth their mouths; they are dumb,
To his high parle unbidden.

But when Quarrel comes in at the gate
For the crashing of homes, when Hate
Draweth his sword against kind,
Ho! who shall our fleet feet bind?
Though he putteth his trust in his strength,
The blood that is on him shall blind,
And our arm overtake him at length!

Glory of Man, to the azure day
Lifted in pomp, shall pass away,
Crumbled to ashes, a glory discrowned,
When we come, black Spirits sable-gowned,
Demon dancers, dour and dun,
That step to the tune of Malison!

A lusty leaper am I
And the feet of me shod with steel
Dint earth with doom from on high,
And the strong limbs quake and reel,
And the stride of the runner slackens full slow
When I trample him down to the night of woe!

He falleth and wotteth no whit of his fall,
Wildered and lost; so sick a pall
Like pestilence hangs o'er the soul that hath sinned;
And rumours wist, like a sobbing wind,
Loud in the land of his blindness tell
And the stately house whereon Darkness fell.

A lusty leaper am I,
And the feet of me shod with steel
Dint earth with doom from on high,
And the strong limbs quake and reel,
And the stride of the runner slackens full slow
When I trample him down to the night of woe!

Ay, Judgement may be stayed,
But it will come!
Skiled craftsmen are we at our trade,
Perfect in masterdom!
Yea, and therewith our memory is good
For all the evil under the sun;
To Man implacable, much wooed,
But hardly won!
Jealous of honours indefeasible,
Though by the Gods held in despite and scorn,
Sundered from them by the great sink of Hell
And sunless gulfs forlorn,
Where who hath eyes, and who hath none
Grope in one twilight over scraes and scars,
And evil are the ways and dusky set the stars.

What man that holds life dear
But bows the knee
In worship, yea, and shuddering fear,
Knowing that this must be?
By mine own lips admonished and advised
Of Power on Law's foundations laid,
To me by olden Destiny demised,
By Gods conveyed
An absolute gift? I am the inheritress
Of Time, and hold my fief since Time has been
By very ancientry; not honoured less,
Nor abject held and mean,
Though deep in ever-during shade
Under the sunny earth my mansion is,
And the thick Dark of the unlamped Abyss.

Enter ATHENA.

Athena. I heard a voice calling me when I chanced
On far Scamander's side, to enfeoff me there
In my new land, the which the kings and captains
Achæan quartered me from their war-spoils,
Mine in eternal seisin absolute,
But set apart, a gift to Theseus' sons
Thence come I speeding not with way-worn foot,
Or wing, but rapt on ægis rustling wide
My harnessed colts high-couraged and my car.
And now this visitation, though I own
No touch of fear, presents a wonder to me.
In wonder's name who are ye? I say to all,
And to yon alien seated at mine image,
Your like I know not among things create,
Whether they be sights gazed on by the Gods
Or aught in the similitude of man.
But to revile deformity offends
Good neighbourhood and much revolts from justice.

Ch. Daughter of Zeus, I will in brief inform thee.
We are Night's children grey and grim and old;
In Hell, our home, called maledictions dire.

At. This tells your title and your lineage.

Ch. Thou art yet to know our state and our high charge.

At. Clearly expound and I shall quickly learn.

Ch. Man-slayers we drive forth from the homes of men.

At. Where is the bound set for the slayer's feet?

Ch. Where gladness is clean fallen out of fashion.

At. Is it in such wise ye beset yon man?

Ch. Yea; he 'sdeigned not to shed his mother's blood.

At. Under some strong constraint of menaced wrath?

Ch. Where is the goad compels to mother-murder?

At. There be twain here, and I have heard but one.

Ch. He is not to be bound, he will not take an oath.

At. Ye would seem just, yet work iniquity,

Ch. How? Tell me that! Thou art not poor in wisdom.

At. Wrong shall not triumph here by force of oaths.

Ch. Question him then and give a righteous judgment.

At. What? Would ye leave the issue in my hands?
Ch. Yea, for Thine own worth and Thy worshipful Sire.
At. Sir, what hast thou to answer touching this?
Tell me thy land, thy lineage and all
Thy griefs; and then speak in thine own defence,
If that thou look'st for judgement; for that cause
Harbourest at my hearth; all rites performed,
A grave appellant, like Ixion old.
Come, to all this make me your clear reply.

Or. Sovran Athena, thou hast kept till last
A grave misgiving I shall first dispel.
I am no suppliant under ban; I come not
To clasp Thine image with polluted hands.
Proof mighty will I offer thereanent.
By law the blood-stained murderer must be mute
Till one with power to cleanse strike over him
The sacrificial blood of sucking swine.
Long since in homes not ours have we been purged
With all due rites, dumb beast and running stream.
Thus I resolve Thy doubt. By birth I am
Argive; my sire—'tis well thou askest me—
Was Agamemnon, Admiral of the sea,
With whom thou didst dispeople Ilium,
Yea, unstate Troy. Returned to his own house
Foully he fell, by my black-hearted mother
Cut down, ta'en, netted in the trammelling toils
That bare grim witness of his bloody bath.
I, then an exile, presently returned
And killed my mother—I deny it not—
In murderous revenge for my dear father.
And Loxias with me is answerable,
Who spake of torments dire to goad my heart,
Except I dealt with them after their guilt.
Judge Thou if I have justly done or no:
Whate'er Thy doom, in Thee I rest content.
At. If any man think he can judge herein,
'Tis much too weighty; neither were it lawful
That I try murder, wreaked in bitter wrath.
And, namely, when thou com'st a sacrosanct
Suitor, aneled and hurtless to my house:
Preferred withal as guiltless to my realm;
While these hold powers not easily dismissed,
And if they triumph not in the event,
Poison of hurt pride will fall presently
And the land ail with age-long pestilence.
So stands it; whether they stay or I bid them hence
I shall find trouble and perplexity.
But, since so jump the business comes this way,
I will appoint a court for murder sworn
And make it a perpetual ordinance.
Call up your witnesses, bring in your proofs,
Justice' sworn helpers and oath-bounden aids.
The prime in worth I'll choose from out my sons
And come, and well and truly try the cause
By the unswerving tenour of their troth. ***Exit.***

Chorus

Now comes the crack of doom, by strong
Subversive stroke of rebel laws,
If he have room to plead his wrong,
And justice vindicate his cause,
Whose hands are stained with his mother's blood.
This knits all in one brotherhood,
The easy fellowship of crime.
And from this instance loom in long array
Blood-boltered parents whom their sons shall slay
Down the dark glimpses of disordered Time.
And we that wont to watch mankind,
That thirst for cups incarnadined,
No more our anger shall unleash:
I'll give Death leave to slay all flesh.
And each shall prophesy his own
Doom from his neighbour's fate foreknown;
All comers then from the world's ends
They shall accost in search of some relief;
And learn from ashy lips and looks of grief
Such feeble physic as despair commends.

Who reeleth then go the fatal blow
Let him look not for redress,
Nor bootless clamour "Justice, Ho!
Ho, the Throned Erinyes!"

Fathers, mothers, let your loud
Death-wound shriek shrill through your halls;
For a mightier frame is bowed;
Yea, the House of Justice falls.

There is a place for Fear; she tries
The reins, a warder weariless;
And it is well with tears and sighs
To follow after Soothfastness.

What man, what power through the wide earth,
Whose soul is not with child of Fear
Nor tends her as a blessed birth,
Can be of Law true worshipper?

Let not thy heart commend
Life without Law, nor lend
Thy fulsome breath to fan a tyrant's lust;
God doth to power advance,
Though His wise governance
Change with the shifting forms of things, the comely
Mean and just.

Hark, how my graver rhyme
To that just Mean keeps time:
From Godlessness springs Pride, the Prodigal;
But he that doth possess
Soul's health hath Happiness,
The child of many prayers, the best beloved of all.

Lay to thy heart this law,
O Man; stand thou in awe
Of Justice' Altar; not for any lure
Or glitter of false gain
Plant there thy foot profane
To tread it in the dust, for chastisement is sure.

The deed is done, but thence
Ensues the consequence,
That crowns, completes, the master-stroke of all;
Honour, ye sons of men,
Your parents first, and then
The guest that goeth in and out, the stranger in your hall.

So virtuous as I would have thee be,
Self-taught, by no compulsion overborne,
Thou canst not wholly miss Felicity,
Nor ever founder, utterly forlorn.
But this I say: who venturously puts forth
And every law of Righteousness outbraves,
His trash, his traffic, got 'neath evil stars,
In the dread Day of Wrath,
He shall commit to the devouring waves,
When splits the sail and splintered are the spars.

Then at deaf ears his cry unheard shall knock,
Swooning in gulfs where none to land may win;
Unearthly laughter shall his summons mock
Whose soul is fuel for the fires of Sin.
He boasted he would never see that day,
But now his Angel sees him weak and spent,
Powerless to top those seas; and, all his teen
And travail cast away,
On the uncharted reef of Justice rent,
He sinks with none to wail him and is no more seen.

The Areopagus.

At. Make proclamation, herald; keep the press back,
And let the braying trump Tyrrhenian
That's heard in Heaven, filled with thy man's breath,
Sound in the public ear a mighty parle.
For while the synod fills my Judgement Hall
There must be silence; so shall the whole realm
Learn my commandments everlastingly,
And these, my chosen, that thy judge aright.

Enter APOLLO.

Ch. Apollo! King! O'er what is Thine bear rule!
Say, wherefore art Thou come to meddle here?
Ap. First I am come to testify; for ye
Have here a suitor and a suppliant
Of mine; his blood-guilt I did purge and cleanse.
Next, I am in the bill, myself arraigned
For this man's mother's murder.
(*To* ATHENA) Call the case;
And, as thou knowest how, maintain the Right.
At. (*To the* FURIES) The word's with you; the trial may proceed;
And 'tis sound law and justice both, that he
Who doth prefer the charge shall first begin.
Ch. Though we be many, we shall use few words.
Do thou make answer as I question thee.
And tell us first if thou didst slay thy mother.
Or. Yea, I make no denial; I killed her.
Ch. So, in this thrice encounter one round ends.
Or. Ye have not thrown your man, ye crow too soon.
Ch. No matter; how was't thou didst take her life?
Or. I answer—with my sword; I cut her throat.
Ch. By whom seduced? Whose ill admonishment?
Or. At His behest: Himself is witness for me.
Ch. The Prophet bade thee murder thine own mother?
Or. Even so; and to this hour I rue it not.
Ch. Not? But a pebble-cast may change thy tune.
Or. I have my faith; my sire sends help from his grave.
Ch. What! Kill thy mother and put trust in ghosts!
Or. She was aspersed with two-fold villainy.
Ch. How can that be? I charge thee, tell the court.
Or. She slew her husband and struck down my father.
Ch. Thou liv'st; but she is quit by her bloody death.
Or. Why did ye not hunt her while yet she lived?
Ch. She was not of one blood with him she slew.
Or. Am I accounted of my mother's blood?
Ch. Thou gory villain, was not thy body framed,
Fed in her womb? Wilt thou deny thy mother?
Or. Do Thou bear witness for me now; pronounce
Apollo, if I slew her with just cause;
For that 'twas done I have and do confess;
But whether justly done or no, do Thou
Give sentence, that the court may hear me plead.
Ap. To you, Athena's great Consistory,
Justly I'll speak, and, withal, truthfully,
For that I am a prophet and lie not.
My throne of Divination never yet
To man nor woman, no, nor polity,
Delivered aught, but I was bidden speak
By Zeus, the Father of the Olympian Gods.
Weigh well the force of that, ye Councillors,
And then ensue the thing my Father wills:
For Zeus is of more might than all oaths else.
Ch. Zeus, then, thou say'st, delivered the oracle
That bade Orestes venge his father's death
And reckon not the cost of a mother's life?
Ap. Far other was the murder of a man
Noble, by God-given sceptre high exalt,
At the hands of a woman, not with valiant
Arrows far sped by archer Amazon,
But in such wise as thou shalt hear, Pallas,
And you, upon whose vote the verdict hangs.
When from war's business prosperous in the main
He was returned, she gave him loving welcome.
He took his bath, and, when his bath was done,
She wrapped him in a cloak, a sleeveless robe,
And in its shackling mazes hewed him down.
This was the manner of his taking off,
The majesty of the world, the lord of ships;
And such was she; oh, lay it to your hearts,
Ye judges, that are set to try the cause.
Ch. Zeus, thou pretendest, holds a father's life
Precious exceedingly; and yet Himself
Cast his own Father Cronos into chains!
Why, is not this confounding contraries?
Mark well his argument, I conjure you!

Ap. You worse than beasts! You hag-seed
God abhorred!
Bonds He may loose, for durance find a balm,
And work, howso He please, deliverance.
But when the dust hath drunk the blood of man
And he's once dead, there's no uprising; spell
For that my Father hath created not;
Though saving only this the frame of things
Is as a wheel He can revolve at will
And, nothing scant of breath, turn upside-down.
Ch. A sorry plea, look you, to save your man!
Shall he that spilt his mother's, his own, blood
Live here in Argos, in his father's house?
What public altars, think you, will he use?
Who will admit him to the Holy Stoup?
Ap. Listen, and thou shalt own my deeper lore.
To be called mother is no wise to be
Parent, but rather nurse of seed new-sown.
The male begets: she's host to her small guest;
Preserves the plant, except it please God blight it.
I'll furnish reasons for my argument.
There hath been and there can be fatherhood
Though there should be no mother; witness here
Olympian Zeus' own self-created child,
That grew not in the womb's dark coverture;
A branch so goodly never Goddess bore.
Pallas, as it hath ever been my care
To make thy city great, famous thine arms,
I have sent thee this sitter on thy hearth,
That he may be Thy true man evermore,
And Thou, Goddess, may'st count him Thine ally
And all his seed; and to remotest age
These men's sons' may keep Thy covenant.
At. Shall I direct them now to cast their votes,
As conscience dictates? Hath enough been said?
Ch. We have shot every arrow from our bow;
Nothing remains but to abide the event.
At. Surely. (*To* APOLLO *and* ORESTES) And how
shall I do right by you?
Ap. Ye have heard what ye have heard: think
on your oaths;
Carry to the urn the verdict of your hearts.
At. Ye men of Athens, hear my law; ye judges
That try this cause, the first for man's blood shed.
Henceforth to Aegeus' congregated host
This Court shall be an ordinance for ever;
This Hill of Ares, once a place of arms
Where leaguering Amazons pitched their tents,
what time
They warred with Theseus and their jealous towers
New-raised against our sovran citadel;
And sacrificed to Ares, whence the Rock
Is called the Rock Areian. There shall Awe,
With civil Fear, her kinsman, night and day
Perpetual sessions hold to punish wrong,
If that my sons depart not from my law.
For, an thou foul the spring with flood or mire
The fresh and sparkling cup thou'lt find no more.
Nor anarchy nor arbitrary power
Would I have Athens worship or uphold,
Nor utterly banish Fear from civic life.
For who is virtuous except he fear?
This seat of Awe kept ever formidable
Shall be a wall, a bulwark of salvation,
Wide as your land, as your imperial state;
None mightier in the habitable world
From Scythia to the parts of the Peloponnese.
A Place of Judgement incorruptible,
Compassionate, yet quick in wrath, to wake
And watch while Athens sleeps I stablish here.
My large discourse these precepts would commend
To my sons yet unborn. Rise from your seats;
Take up your counters and upon your oaths
Return a righteous verdict. I have done.

The Judges cast their votes during the ensuing dialogue.

Ch. Take heed, we are ungentle visitors;
Learn of our wisdom and misprise us not.
Ap. My words that are God's Voice hold ye in awe;
Make them not as blind plants that bear no fruit.
Ch. Thou hallowest deeds of blood that are not
Thine,
And shalt no more prophesy holy things.
Ap. Faileth the Father's Wisdom, for that He
Sheltered Ixion, the first murderer?
Ch. Thou sayest; but, if I am baulked of justice
I'll vex this land and visit it in wrath.
Ap. The younger Gods regard thee not; the old
Pay thee no honour; victory is mine.
Ch. So didst thou sometime deal in Pheres' house;
Tempting the Fates to make mankind immortal.
Ap. Is it not just to help a worshipper,
And doubly, trebly just in the day of need?
Ch. Thou didst break down earth's parcelled
governance,
With new wine practise on the Goddesses old.
Ap. Nay, when the cause is lost, thy venom void;
It hath no power to hurt thine adversaries.
Ch. Since Thy hot youth o'er-rides our ancientry
I wait on judgement; doubtful yet to launch
My indignation 'gainst the State of Athens.
At. It shall be mine, if judgement hang in poise,
To cast this counter that Orestes live.
Mother is none that gave my Godhead life;
I am the male's; saving my never-wed
Virginity, my Father's child thrice o'er.
Therefore I rate not high a woman's death
That slew her lord, the master of her house.
Orestes wins, yea, though the votes be paired.
Come, Sirs, despatch; ye whose the office is
To make an end, empty me out the urns.
Or. Phoebus Apollo, how will judgement go?
Ch. Swarth Night, my Mother, watchest Thou
unseen?
Or. I near mine end, the halter or the day!
Ch. We fall, or have great glory evermore!
Ap. Sirs, count the votes; make strictest scrutiny,
With holy fear, lest Judgement go awry.
A vote o'er-looked may work most grievous wrong:
A single pebble save a tottering house.

A pause.

At. The accused is found "not guilty" of the
charge;
The tellers certify an equal count.

Or. O Pallas! O Preserver of my race!
To my lost realm my father once possessed
Thou hast restored me! Now shall all Greece say,
"True Son of Argos, lord of his father's substance,
He dwelleth with his own." Pallas wrought this
And Loxias and the Almighty Third,
The Saviour. Moved by my sire's fate, He saw,
And saved from them that pled my mother's cause.
Now e'er I go to mine own house I swear
Unto Thy land and all Thy host an oath
Succeeding ages shall fulfil: no prince
Of earth shall carry here the barbèd spear.
When we are in our graves we will confound
Who break this oath with sorry misadventure;
Their ways be weariness, their paths forbid,
And for their rapine they shall reap but ruth.
But if they shall keep faith, gird them with might
For Pallas' city, we will show them grace.
Goddess, farewell; be matchless still in arms,
Find still a valiant people strong to throw
All who rise up against Thee; keep Thee safe
And with their sword win for Thee victory!
Exit.

Ch. Oh, ye young Gods! Ye have ridden the old laws down, ye have reft
My prey, and I am left
Dishonoured and undone!
But for these pangs
Athens shall have my malison!
Ay, on these lips there hangs
(Ho, Vengeance, soon to shed)
A venomed drop of my heart's agony!
And it shall multiply and spread,
Bitter and barren! It shall be
A mildew and a leprosy,
A canker to the leafless tree,
A curse to the childless bed;
On everything that hath breath
Corrosion, purulence and death!
Wail—and wail—and wail?
Or witch them? Shadowing their land with bale?
Transmute to unimaginable woe
Grief insupportable? Oho,
Ye Virgin Daughters to black Midnight born,
How sharp your sorrow! How is your honour shorn!

At. Nay, take it not with such a heavy heart;
Ye are not vanquished; equal are the votes
In simple truth, not thy disparagement.
Oh, here were proofs radiant with God's own light!
And He that gave the oracle bare witness
Orestes should not suffer for his deed.
Let not your heavy wrath light on this ground;
Consider, be not angry, shed no drops
To blast the fruitful earth with barrenness
And with keen tooth devour the pregnant seed.
I will provide you, pledge hereto my oath,
A hold, a hollow in this righteous land,
Altars and shining thrones where ye shall sit,
And worship and great honour from her sons.

Ch. Oh, ye young Gods! Ye have ridden the old laws down, ye have reft
My prey, and I am left
Dishonoured and undone!
But for these pangs
Athens shall have my malison!
Ay, on these lips there hangs,
(Ho, Vengeance, soon to shed)
A venomed drop of my heart's agony!
And it shall multiply and spread
Bitter and barren; it shall be
A mildew and a leprosy,
A canker to the leafless tree,
A curse to the childless bed;
On everything that hath breath
Corrosion, purulence and death!
Wail—and wail—and wail?
Or witch them? Shadowing their land with bale?
Transmute to unimaginable woe
Grief insupportable? Oho,
Ye Virgin Daughters to black Midnight born,
How sharp your sorrow! How is your honour shorn!

At. Your honour is safe; are ye not Goddesses?
Curse not this soil that giveth life to man.
I too have faith in Zeus; but why waste words?
I only know the keys of the arsenal
Of Heaven, stored with the sealed thunderbolt.
But we shall need no thunder. Listen to me;
Vent no wild words in sour despite, to make
All that yields increase utterly miscarry.
This dark wave's bitter fury put to sleep.
Be what ye are, majestic, denizens
With me in this fair land; prime offerings
Shall then be yours through all her borders wide
For children and the sacred marriage rite
For evermore, and ye shall bless my words.

Ch. Oho! Am I to take these buffets, I
To have my elder wisdom scoffed at, be
Bid to my place, to house with infamy
Here on this plot, this patch, this ell of earth?
Blast it, my fury! Pain, pain, pain,
Here at my heart—whence comes it? Why
Am I to suffer? Darkness, Death and Dearth!
Night, Mother Night, shall my wroth heart be hot
And wilt thou hearken not?
Strong craft of subtle Gods hath reft my ancient majesty!

At. I will be patient with thy passioning;
Thou art mine elder, wiser then than I.
Yet Zeus hath not denied me understanding.
Find out a new race, other soil; yet here
Your heart will be; I speak this for your warning.
The tide of Time shall for my people roll
With ever-mantling glory: thou shalt have
Thy mansion here hard by Erectheus' house,
And men and women come with frequent pomp
And greater laud than the wide world can give.
But in my borders bring no grindery
To whet sharp daggers, in the breast of Youth
Bloody and dangerous; with more madness edged
Than works with wicked ferment in new wine.
Nor take, as 'twere, the gamecock's heart, to plant
Domestic Havoc here that fights with kind.
Without their gates let my sons go to war,
And who loves honour shall have all he craves.

Your bantam-bully, ruffler of the yard,
Arrides me not, and I will none of him.
Take thou thy choice and take it from my hand;
Fair service, fair content, fair recompense,
A portion in this realm the Gods love most.
Ch. Oho! am I to take these buffets, I
To have mine elder wisdom scoffed at, be
Bid to my place, to house with Infamy
Here on this plot, this patch, this ell of earth!
Blast it, my fury! Pain, pain, pain,
Here at my heart! Whence comes it? Why
Am I to suffer? Darkness, Death and Dearth!
Night, Mother Night, shall my wroth heart be hot
And wilt thou hearken not?
Strong craft of subtle gods hath reft my ancient majesty.
At. Still will I bless, thou shalt not weary me,
Nor say my nonage set thy years at nought,
Nor churlish men scorned thy Divinity
And drave thee from their gates discomfited.
If thou hold sacred the sweet Soul of Reason,
If there be any virtue, any balm,
Upon these lips, thou wilt remain. If not,
Though thou should'st cast all anger in the scale
To sink the land, all malice, all despite,
It is not justly done. Justice gives thee
A realm to share, a rich inheritance,
And nothing of thine honour takes away.
Ch. Athena Queen, what mansion wilt Thou give me?
At. One where Grief cometh not; accept it thou.
Ch. An if I do, what honour shall I have?
At. This that no home shall prosper without thee.
Ch. But hast Thou power to make thy promise good?
At. We will establish him that worships thee.
Ch. Wilt Thou assure me this for evermore?
At. I promise not except I can perform.
Ch. Methinks, Thy magic works; I am no more wroth.
At. Possess the land and thou shalt win its love.
Ch. What shall I sing that hath a blessing in it?
At. A song to celebrate a cause well won.
From the sweet earth, from the sea-dews and damps,
From skies and winds ask inspirations, airs
That travel on over a sunlit land;
Fruit from the ground, and increase of strong cattle
For all my sons, that Time can never tire;
And saving Health for seed of human kind.
Natheless, on Virtue chiefly shed thy balm;
Like a wise gardener of the Soul, I hold
There is no graft nor bud blooms half so fair;
And this is thine; but thou shalt leave to me
Glory of battle, where the cause is just,
Death, but death garlanded with victory;
And grudge if I be found herein remiss.
Ch. Pallas' home contenteth me;
Honour to the strong citie
Zeus Almighty made His own
And Ares' armèd strength sustains;
A fortress for the Gods of Greece,
A jewel flashing forth anew,
When ravished were her costly fanes
And her high altars overthrown.
Breathe on her blessings, breathe the dew
Of prayer; Earth yield her thine increase;
Shine, thou rejoicing Sun, and speed
All nature sends and mortals need!
At. Not that I cherish Athens less,
But that I love her well, have I
Throned in her midst Great Goddesses,
Spirits hard to pacify.
All that makes up Man's moving story
Is theirs to govern and dispense;
He whom their hard hand ne'er made sorry,
Who hath not met them on his way,
Walking in blindness knows not whence
The shock that beats him to his knees.
The sin of some forgotten day
Delivers up his soul to these.
Destruction, like a voiceless ghost,
Silenceth all his empty boast
And minisheth his glory.
Ch. I will have nor storm nor flood
Scathe her vines and olive-bowers;
No scorching wind shall blind the bud
In the waking-time of flowers.
By my grace all airs that blow
Their appointed bounds shall know.
No distemper blast her clime
With perpetual barrenness;
Flocks and herds in yeaning time
Pan shall with twin offspring bless;
And Earth's wombèd wealth, God-sealed,
All its lucky ingots yield.
At. Warders of Athens, have ye heard
Her voice? Know ye what these things mean?
Wist ye how mighty is the word
Erinys spake, the Queen?
Mighty 'mid deathless Gods her crying
'Mid Powers that Hell's hid glooms invest,
And in this world of living, dying
Mighty and manifest!
She biddeth one make melody,
And one down dark ways leadeth She,
Blinded with tears undrying.
Ch. Untoward and untimely Doom
Bring not strong Youth to his death-bed:
Ye maidens, in your beauty bloom,
Live not unloved, nor die unwed.
You Heavenly Pair, this good gift grant.
Grant it, ye Elder Destinies,
Our Sisters, whom one Mother bare,
Spirits whose governance is law,
Of every home participant,
And at all seasons, foul or fair,
Just Inmates, Righteous Presences,
Shadows of an Unseen Awe;
Over the wide earth and the deep seas
Honoured above all Deities.
At. Oh, bounty dealt with loving hand!
It needs must fill my heart with glee,
Such largesse lavished on my land.
Wise Spirit, thanks to thee,

Spirit of Counsel, suave and holy,
Whose sober eye could lead me on
Till, though the stubborn will yield slowly,
Yet their wild hearts were won!
But Zeus, the Lord of Civic Life,
Gave victory; in this noble strife
He made Good triumph solely.
Ch. Tiger-throated Faction fed
On the meat of human woe,
Filled but never surfeited,
Come not hither growling low,
Nor wake Athens with thy roar.
Never be this thirsty ground
Drunk with fratricidal blood,
Nor lust of Power insatiate
Snatch at vengeance evermore.
In one fellowship of Good
Each be to his neighbour bound,
One in love and one in hate;
For such grace, where'er 'tis found,
Lays the balm to many a wound.
At. Are they not wise? Speaks she not fair?
Her tongue of gold makes counsel sweet
And points the happy highway where
Soft words and Wisdom meet.
Mine eyes see visions; fair foundations
Rise round these forms with fury fraught!
Serve them! Bring them your rich oblations,
And ye serve not for nought.
Bless them, and they will surely bless;
At home the reign of Righteousness,
Renown throughout all nations.
Ch. Joy to you, joy and all good things!
Joy to the fortunate city that lies
With Zeus about her and above;
Vowed to the Unmarried Maiden's love
And in the dawn of Time made wise,
Whom Pallas covers with her wings
And the Father sanctifies!
At. Joy to you too in amplest store!
But it is time; I go before;
I lead you on your road;
And by your escort's holy light
Conduct you through the Shades of Night
Down to your dark Abode.
Set forward then your priestly train;
Speed them with blood of victims slain
Under this holy ground;
Bind whatsoever bringeth death,
And whatsoever profiteth
Be by your spell unbound.
As ye help Athens by your charms
She shall be great in arts and arms,
Still, still with victory crowned!
Lead on, ye sons of Cranaus;
For those that make their home with us
A path and passage find;
And by their good gifts freely given,
By these sweet charities of Heaven
Be all men of one mind!
Ch. Joy, joy to Athens! Oh, twice blest
Be all that in her borders dwell,
Or be they men of mortal mould
Or deathless Deities that hold
Pallas' rock-built citadel!
Love me that am your Sacred Guest
And bid to Grief a long farewell!
At. Take all my thanks; my heart goes with your prayers.
Myself will lead you by the torches' blaze
Down to your habitation 'neath the earth
With these my ministrants round my Statua
On duteous watch; the apple of the eye
Of Theseus' land, a famous company
Of little ones and wives and beldames old.
We'll mantle them in cloaks of scarlet fine.
And all about them shake the bright fireshine,
Give these New Dwellers noble welcoming
That goodly men from their goodwill may spring.
Escort. Pass on your way, ye mighty,
Ye Jealous in honour pass on,
Children of Night unbegotten,
Seed of her womb unsown,
With pomp and triumph and holy mirth,
(Hush! Good words, all ye people!)
And prayer and sacrifice descend
Down to the dark, diluvial earth.
(Hush! Good words all ye people!)
Come, ye Majestic Spirits, come,
Bring good luck to your new-found home
By the glad bright light of the burning brand!
(Cry, cry aloud with jubilee!)
Peace to thee and peace to thee
And peace for ever in Pallas' land!
Partnered with happy Destiny
All-seeing Zeus hath wrought to this end!
(Cry, cry aloud with jubilee!)

Exeunt.

THE PLAYS OF
SOPHOCLES

BIOGRAPHICAL NOTE

Sophocles, *c.* 495–406 B.C.

Sophocles was born at Colonus in Attica around 495 B.C. His father, Sophillus, was a maker of munitions. That Sophillus himself worked as a smith or carpenter, as has sometimes been said, seems unlikely, in view of his son's social position and civic offices. According to Pliny, Sophocles was born in the highest station. This tradition gains support from the story that at the age of fifteen or sixteen he led the Boys' Chorus, which celebrated with song and the music of the lyre the victory of Salamis.

As a schoolboy Sophocles was already famous for his beauty and won prizes in athletics and in literature. He was taught music by Lamprus, whom Plutarch praised for sobriety and preferred to the more impassioned and "realistic" Timotheus, who influenced Euripides in his later choruses.

From the ancient *Life*, which is probably of Alexandrian origin, and from references in other authors it is evident that Sophocles both as poet and as citizen played a prominent and varied role in the life of Athens. His own life was co-extensive with the rise and fall of the city. Between his birth a few years before Marathon and his death on the eve of the defeat of Athens in the Peloponnesian War, the greatest events of Athenian history took place. During that time Sophocles wrote and produced over one hundred and twenty plays. In 443, as president of the imperial treasury, he was in charge of collecting the tribute of the allies. In 440 he was elected general and served with Pericles in the Samian War. He went on embassies, and he was probably the Sophocles referred to by Aristotle in the *Rhetoric* as one of the ten elders chosen to manage the affairs of the city after the Sicilian disaster. He was a friend of Cimon and a member of his social circle, which included such distinguished foreigners as Ion of Chios, the tragic poet, and the painter, Polygnotus. Among other friends of Sophocles were Archelaus and Herodotus, to whom he wrote elegiac poems.

Plutarch, in his *Life of Cimon*, says that Sophocles won his first victory with the first play he produced. His first victory came in 468 when he defeated Aeschylus with the *Triptolemus*, which is now lost. He was thus twenty-seven when he began his public dramatic career. In the remaining sixty-two years of his life he wrote on an average two plays a year and competed for the tragic prize thirty-one times. He won at least eighteen victories and was never placed third.

Of the seven plays that survive, the *Ajax* is probably the earliest. The *Antigone* belongs to 443 or 441. The chronological order of the *Trachiniae* and the *Oedipus the King* is uncertain, the *Electra* is later, and all three are assigned to the years between 435 and 410. The *Philoctetes* is known to have been produced in 408 when Sophocles was eighty-seven years old. The *Oedipus at Colonus*, according to the story made famous by the *De Senectute* of Cicero, was Sophocles' last play. Sophocles is supposed to have been accused by his son of being unable to manage his property, and to have convinced his judges of his competence by reciting a chorus from this play, which he had just completed.

Aristotle says in the *Poetics* that Sophocles raised the number of actors to three and added scene-painting. Sophocles is also said to have written his plays with certain actors in mind and not to have acted in them himself because of the weakness of his voice. That he was interested in the theory as well as the practice of dramatic art is evident from his having written a book "on the chorus," and having formed a "company of the educated" in honor of the Muses. "Chorus" was the official name for tragedy, and a book on the chorus would have dealt, presumably, with all aspects of the tragic poet's art. The "company of the educated" was probably a society of cultivated Athenians who met to discuss poetry and music, though it has also been suggested that its members were actors who had been trained by Sophocles.

Sophocles died in 406 B.C., as we know from the *Frogs* of Aristophanes, brought out in the following year. His epitaph, attributed to Simmias, the friend of Socrates, honors his learning and wisdom and calls him "the favorite of the Graces and the Muses." While Aeschylus and Euripides visited the courts of foreign kings and died abroad, Sophocles never left home, except in the service of the city, and died where he had lived, in Athens.

CONTENTS

OEDIPUS THE KING

DRAMATIS PERSONAE

Oedipus, *King of Thebes*
Priest of Zeus
Creon, *brother of Iocasta*
Teiresias, *the blind prophet*
Iocasta
First Messenger, *a shepherd from Corinth*
A Shepherd, *formerly in the service of Laius*
A Second Messenger, *from the house*
Chorus of Theban Elders

Mute: *A train of suppliants* (*old men, youths, and children*) *The children* Antigone *and* Ismene, *daughters of Oedipus and Iocasta*

Before the Royal Palace at Thebes. The priest of zeus *stands facing the central doors. These are thrown open.* oedipus *enters.*

Oedipus. My children, latest-born to Cadmus who was of old, why are ye set before me thus with wreathed branches of suppliants, while the city reeks with incense, rings with prayers for health and cries of woe? I deemed it unmeet, my children, to hear these things at the mouth of others, and have come hither myself, I, Oedipus renowned of all.

Tell me, then, thou venerable man—since it is thy natural part to speak for these—in what mood are ye placed here, with what dread or what desire? Be sure that I would gladly give all aid; hard of heart were I, did I not pity such suppliants as these.

Priest of Zeus. Nay, Oedipus, ruler of my land, thou seest of what years we are who beset thy altars—some, nestlings still too tender for far flights, some, bowed with age, priests, as I of Zeus—and these, the chosen youth; while the rest of the folk sit with wreathed branches in the market-places, and before the two shrines of Pallas, and where Ismenus gives answer by fire.

For the city, as thou thyself seest, is now too sorely vexed, and can no more lift her head from beneath the angry waves of death; a blight is on her in the fruitful blossoms of the land, in the herds among the pastures, in the barren pangs of women; and withal the flaming god, the malign plague, hath swooped on us, and ravages the town; by whom the house of Cadmus is made waste, but dark Hades rich in groans and tears.

It is not as deeming thee ranked with gods that I and these children are suppliants at thy hearth, but as deeming thee first of men, both in life's common chances, and when mortals have to do with more than man: seeing that thou camest to the town of Cadmus, and didst quit us of the tax that we rendered to the hard songstress; and this, though thou knewest nothing from us that could avail thee, nor hadst been schooled; no, by a god's aid, 'tis said and believed, didst thou uplift our life.

And now, Oedipus, king glorious in all eyes, we beseech thee, all we suppliants, to find for us some succour, whether by the whisper of a god thou knowest it, or haply as in the power of man; for I see that, when men have been proved in deeds past, the issues of their counsels, too, most often have effect.

On, best of mortals, again uplift our State! On, guard thy fame, since now this land calls thee saviour for thy former zeal; and never be it our memory of thy reign that we were first restored and afterward cast down: nay, lift up this State in such wise that it fall no more!

With good omen didst thou give us that past happiness; now also show thyself the same. For if thou art to rule this land, even as thou art now its lord, 'tis better to be lord of men than of a waste: since neither walled town nor ship is anything, if it is void and no men dwell with thee therein.

Oed. Oh my piteous children, known, well known to me are the desires wherewith ye have come: well wot I that ye suffer all; yet, sufferers as ye are, there is not one of you whose suffering is as mine. Your pain comes on each one of you for himself alone, and for no other; but my soul mourns at once for the city, and for myself, and for thee.

So that ye rouse me not, truly, as one sunk in sleep: no, be sure that I have wept full many tears, gone many ways in wanderings of thought. And the sole remedy which, well pondering, I could find, this I have put into act. I have sent the son of Menoeceus, Creon, mine own wife's brother, to the Pythian house of Phoebus, to learn by what deed or word I might deliver this town. And already, when the lapse of days is reckoned, it troubles me what he doth; for he tarries strangely, beyond the fitting space. But when he comes, then shall I be no true man if I do not all that the god shows.

Pr. Nay, in season hast thou spoken; at this moment these sign to me that Creon draws near.

Oed. O king Apollo, may he come to us in the brightness of saving fortune, even as his face is bright!

Pr. Nay, to all seeming, he brings comfort; else would he not be coming crowned thus thickly with berry-laden bay.

Oed. We shall know soon: he is at range to hear.

Enter CREON.

Prince, my kinsman, son of Menoeceus, what news hast thou brought us from the god?

Creon. Good news: I tell thee that even troubles hard to bear—if haply they find the right issue—will end in perfect peace.

Oed. But what is the oracle? So far, thy words make me neither bold nor yet afraid.

Cr. If thou wouldest hear while these are nigh, I am ready to speak; or else to go within.

Oed. Speak before all: the sorrow which I bear is for these more than for mine own life.

Cr. With thy leave, I will tell what I heard from the god. Phoebus our lord bids us plainly to drive out a defiling thing, which (he saith) hath been harboured in this land, and not to harbour it, so that it cannot be healed.

Oed. By what rite shall we cleanse us? What is the manner of the misfortune?

Cr. By banishing a man, or by bloodshed in quittance of bloodshed, since it is that blood which brings the tempest on our city.

Oed. And who is the man whose fate he thus reveals?

Cr. Laïus, king, was lord of our land before thou wast pilot of this State.

Oed. I know it well—by hearsay, for I saw him never.

Cr. He was slain; and the god now bids us plainly to wreak vengeance on his murderers—whosoever they be.

Oed. And where are they upon the earth? Where shall the dim track of this old crime be found?

Cr. In this land—said the god. What is sought for can be caught; only that which is not watched escapes.

Oed. And was it in the house, or in the field, or on strange soil that Laïus met this bloody end?

Cr. 'Twas on a visit to Delphi, as he said, that he had left our land; and he came home no more, after he had once set forth.

Oed. And was there none to tell? Was there no comrade of his journey who saw the deed, from whom tidings might have been gained, and used?

Cr. All perished, save one who fled in fear, and could tell for certain but one thing of all that he saw.

Oed. And what was that? One thing might show the clue to many, could we get but a small beginning for hope.

Cr. He said that robbers met and fell on them, not in one man's might, but with full many hands.

Oed. How, then, unless there was some trafficking in bribes from here, should the robber have dared thus far?

Cr. Such things were surmised; but, Laïus once slain, amid our troubles no avenger arose.

Oed. But, when royalty had fallen thus, what trouble in your path can have hindered a full search?

Cr. The riddling Sphinx had made us let dark things go, and was inviting us to think of what lay at our doors.

Oed. Nay, I will start afresh, and once more make dark things plain. Right worthily hath Phoebus, and worthily hast thou, bestowed this care on the cause of the dead; and so, as is meet, ye shall find me too leagued with you in seeking vengeance for this land, and for the god besides. On behalf of no far-off friend, no, but in mine own cause, shall I dispel this taint. For whoever was the slayer of Laïus might wish to take vengeance on me also with a hand as fierce. Therefore, in doing right to Laïus, I serve myself.

Come, haste ye, my children, rise from the altar-steps, and lift these suppliant boughs; and let some other summon hither the folk of Cadmus, warned that I mean to leave nought untried; for our health (with the god's help) shall be made certain—or our ruin.

Pr. My children, let us rise; we came at first to seek what this man promises of himself. And may Phoebus, who sent these oracles, come to us therewith, our saviour and deliverer from the pest.

Exeunt OEDIPUS *and* PRIEST. ENTER CHORUS OF THEBAN ELDERS.

Chorus

O sweetly-speaking message of Zeus, in what spirit hast thou come from golden Pytho unto glorious Thebes? I am on the rack, terror shakes my soul, O thou Delian healer to whom wild cries rise, in holy fear of thee, what thing thou wilt work for me, perchance unknown before, perchance renewed with the revolving years: tell me, thou immortal Voice, born of Golden Hope!

First call I on thee, daughter of Zeus, divine Athena, and on thy sister, guardian of our land, Artemis, who sits on her throne of fame, above the circle of our Agora, and on Phoebus the far-darter: O shine forth on me, my three-fold help against death! If ever aforetime, in arrest of ruin hurrying on the city, ye drove a fiery pest beyond our borders, come now also!

Woe is me, countless are the sorrows that I bear; a plague is on all our host, and thought can find no weapon for defence. The fruits of the glorious earth grow not; by no birth of children do women surmount the pangs in which they shriek; and life on life mayest thou see sped, like bird on nimble wing, aye, swifter than resistless fire, to the shore of the western god.

By such deaths, past numbering, the city perishes: unpitied, her children lie on the ground, spreading pestilence, with none to mourn: and meanwhile young wives, and gray-haired mothers with them, uplift a wail at the steps of the altars, some here, some there, entreating for their weary woes. The prayer to the Healer rings clear, and, blent therewith, the voice of lamentation: for these things, golden daughter of Zeus, send us the bright face of comfort.

And grant that the fierce god of death, who now with no brazen shields, yet amid cries as of battle, wraps me in the flame on his onset, may turn his back in speedy flight from our land, borne by a fair wind to the great deep of Amphitritè, or to those waters in which none find haven, even to the Thracian wave; for if night leave aught undone, day follows to accomplish this. O thou who wieldest the powers of the fire-fraught lightning, O Zeus our father, slay him beneath thy thunderbolt!

Lycean King, fain were I that thy shafts also, from thy bent bow's string of woven gold, should go abroad in their might, our champions in the face of the foe; yea, and the flashing fires of Artemis wherewith she glances through the Lycian hills. And I call him whose locks are bound with gold, who is named with the name of this land, ruddy Bacchus to whom Bacchants cry, the comrade of the Maenads, to draw near with the blaze of his blithe torch, our ally against the god unhonoured among gods.

Enter OEDIPUS.

Oed. Thou prayest: and in answer to thy prayer—if thou wilt give a loyal welcome to my words and minister to thine own disease—thou mayest hope to find succour and relief from woes. These words will I speak publicly, as one who has been a stranger to this report, a stranger to the deed; for I should not be far on the track, if I were tracing it alone, without a clue. But as it is—since it was only after the time of the deed that I was numbered a Theban among Thebans—to you, the Cadmeans all, I do thus proclaim.

Whosoever of you knows by whom Laïus son of Labdacus was slain, I bid him to declare all to me. And if he is afraid, I tell him to remove the danger of the charge from his path by denouncing himself; for he shall suffer nothing else unlovely, but only leave the land, unhurt. Or if any one knows an alien, from another land, as the assassin, let him not keep silence; for I will pay his guerdon, and my thanks shall rest with him besides.

But if ye keep silence—if any one, through fear, shall seek to screen friend or self from my behest—hear ye what I then shall do. I charge you that no one of this land, whereof I hold the empire and the throne, give shelter or speak word unto that murderer, whosoever he be, make him partner of his prayer or sacrifice, or serve him with the lustral rite; but that all ban him their homes, knowing that *this* is our defiling thing, as the oracle of the Pythian god hath newly shown me. I then am on this wise the ally of the god and of the slain. And I pray solemnly that the slayer, whoso he be, whether his hidden guilt is lonely or hath partners, evilly, as he is evil, may wear out his unblest life. And for myself I pray that if, with my privity, he should become an inmate of my house, I may suffer the same things which even now I called down upon others. And on you I lay it to make all these words good, for my sake, and for the sake of the god, and for our land's, thus blasted with barrenness by angry heaven.

For even if the matter had not been urged on us by a god, it was not meet that ye should leave the guilt thus unpurged, when one so noble, and he your king, had perished; rather were ye bound to search it out. And now, since 'tis I who hold the powers which once he held, who possess his bed and the wife who bare seed to him; and since, had his hope of issue not been frustrate, children born of one mother would have made ties betwixt him and me—but, as it was, fate swooped upon his head; by reason of these things will I uphold this cause, even as the cause of mine own sire, and will leave nought untried in seeking to find him whose hand shed that blood, for the honour of the son of Labdacus and of Polydorus and elder Cadmus and Agenor who was of old.

And for those who obey me not, I pray that the gods send them neither harvest of the earth nor fruit of the womb, but that they be wasted by their lot that now is, or by one yet more dire. But for all you, the loyal folk of Cadmus to whom these things seem good, may Justice, our ally, and all the gods be with you graciously for ever.

Ch. As thou hast put me on my oath, on my oath, O king, I will speak. I am not the slayer, nor can I point to him who slew. As for the question, it was for Phoebus, who sent it, to tell us this thing—who can have wrought the deed.

Oed. Justly said; but no man on the earth can force the gods to what they will not.

Ch. I would fain say what seems to me next best after this.

Oed. If there is yet a third course, spare not to show it.

Ch. I know that our lord Teiresias is the seer most like to our lord Phoebus; from whom, O king, a searcher of these things might learn them most clearly.

Oed. Not even this have I left out of my cares. On the hint of Creon, I have twice sent a man to bring him; and this long while I marvel why he is not here.

Ch. Indeed (his skill apart) the rumours are but faint and old.

Oed. What rumours are they? I look to every story.

Ch. Certain wayfarers were said to have killed him.

Oed. I, too, have heard it, but none sees him who saw it.

Ch. Nay, if he knows what fear is, he will not stay when he hears thy curses, so dire as they are.

Oed. When a man shrinks not from a deed, neither is he scared by a word.

Ch. But there is one to convict him. For here they bring at last the godlike prophet, in whom alone of men doth live the truth.

Enter TEIRESIAS, *led by a Boy.*

Oed. Teiresias, whose soul grasps all things, the lore that may be told and the unspeakable, the secrets of heaven and the low things of earth, thou feelest, though thou canst not see, what a plague doth haunt our State, from which, great prophet, we find in thee our protector and only saviour. Now, Phoebus—if indeed thou knowest it not from the messengers—sent answer to our question that the only riddance from this pest which could come was if we should learn aright the slayers of Laïus, and slay them, or send them into exile from our land. Do thou, then, grudge neither voice of birds nor any other way of seer-lore that thou hast, but rescue thyself and the State, rescue me, rescue all that is defiled by the dead. For we are in thy hand; and man's noblest task is to help others by his best means and powers.

Teiresias. Alas, how dreadful to have wisdom where it profits not the wise! Aye, I knew this well, but let it slip out of mind; else would I never have come here.

Oed. What now? How sad thou hast come in!

Te. Let me go home; most easily wilt thou bear thine own burden to the end, and I mine, if thou wilt consent.

Oed. Thy words are strange, nor kindly to this State which nurtured thee, when thou withholdest this response.

Te. Nay, I see that thou, on thy part, openest not thy lips in season: therefore I speak not, that neither may I have thy mishap.

Oed. For the love of the gods, turn not away, if thou hast knowledge: all we suppliants implore thee on our knees.

Te. Aye, for ye are all without knowledge; but never will I reveal my griefs—that I say not thine.

Oed. How sayest thou? Thou knowest the secret, and wilt not tell it, but art minded to betray us and to destroy the State?

Te. I will pain neither myself nor thee. Why vainly ask these things? Thou wilt not learn them from me.

Oed. What, basest of the base—for thou wouldest anger a very stone—wilt thou never speak out? Can nothing touch thee? Wilt thou never make an end?

Te. Thou blamest my temper, but seest not that to which thou thyself art wedded: no, thou findest fault with me.

Oed. And who would not be angry to hear the words with which thou now dost slight this city?

Te. The future will come of itself, though I shroud it in silence.

Oed. Then, seeing that it must come, thou on thy part shouldst tell me thereof.

Te. I will speak no further; rage, then, if thou wilt, with the fiercest wrath thy heart doth know.

Oed. Aye, verily, I will not spare—so wroth I am—to speak all my thought. Know that thou seemest to me e'en to have helped in plotting the deed, and to have done it, short of slaying with thy hands. Hadst thou eyesight, I would have said that the doing, also, of this thing was thine alone.

Te. In sooth? I charge thee that thou abide by the decree of thine own mouth, and from this day speak neither to these nor to me: *thou* art the accursed defiler of this land.

Oed. So brazen with thy blustering taunt? And wherein dost thou trust to escape thy due?

Te. I have escaped: in my truth is my strength.

Oed. Who taught thee this? It was not, at least, thine art.

Te. Thou: for thou didst spur me into speech against my will.

Oed. What speech? Speak again that I may learn it better.

Te. Didst thou not take my sense before? Or art thou tempting me in talk?

Oed. No, I took it not so that I can call it known:—speak again.

Te. I say that thou art the slayer of the man whose slayer thou seekest.

Oed. Now thou shalt rue that thou hast twice said words so dire.

Te. Wouldst thou have me say more, that thou mayest be more wroth?

Oed. What thou wilt; it will be said in vain.

Te. I say that thou hast been living in unguessed shame with thy nearest kin, and seest not to what woe thou hast come.

Oed. Dost thou indeed think that thou shalt always speak thus without smarting?

Te. Yes, if there is any strength in truth.

Oed. Nay, there is, for all save thee; for thee that strength is not, since thou art maimed in ear, and in wit, and in eye.

Te. Aye, and thou art a poor wretch to utter taunts which every man here will soon hurl at thee.

Oed. Night, endless night hath thee in her keeping, so that thou canst never hurt me, or any man who sees the sun.

Te. No, thy doom is not to fall by *me:* Apollo is enough, whose care it is to work that out.

Oed. Are these Creon's devices, or thine?

Te. Nay, Creon is no plague to thee; thou art thine own.

Oed. O wealth, and empire, and skill surpassing skill in life's keen rivalries, how great is the envy that cleaves to you, if for the sake, yea, of this power which the city hath put into my hands, a gift unsought, Creon the trusty, Creon mine old friend, hath crept on me by stealth, yearning to thrust me out of it, and hath suborned such a scheming juggler as this, a tricky quack, who hath eyes only for his gains, but in his art is blind!

Come, now, tell me, where hast thou proved thyself a seer? Why, when the Watcher was here who wove dark song, didst thou say nothing that could free this folk? Yet the riddle, at least, was not for the first comer to read; there was need of a seer's skill; and none such thou wast found to have, either by help of birds, or as known from any god: no, I came, I, Oedipus the ignorant, and made her mute, when I had seized the answer by my wit, untaught of birds. And it is I whom thou art trying to oust, thinking to stand close to Creon's throne. Methinks thou and the plotter of these things will rue your zeal to purge the land. Nay, didst thou not seem to be an old man, thou shouldst have learned to thy cost how bold thou art.

Ch. To our thinking, both this man's words and thine, Oedipus, have been said in anger. Not for such words is our need, but to seek how we shall best discharge the mandates of the god.

Te. King though thou art, the right of reply, at least, must be deemed the same for both; of that I too am lord. Not to thee do I live servant, but to Loxias; and so I shall not stand enrolled under Creon for my patron. And I tell thee—since thou hast taunted me even with blindness—that thou hast sight, yet seest not in what misery thou art, nor where thou dwellest, nor with whom. Dost thou know of what stock thou art? And thou hast been an unwitting foe to thine own kin, in the shades, and on the earth above; and the double lash of thy mother's and thy father's curse shall one day drive thee from this land in dreadful haste, with darkness then on the eyes that now see true.

And what place shall not be harbour to thy shriek, what of all Cithaeron shall not ring with it soon, when thou hast learnt the meaning of the nuptials in which, within that house, thou didst find a fatal haven, after a voyage so fair? And a throng of other ills thou guessest not, which shall make thee level with thy true self and with thine own brood.

Therefore heap thy scorns on Creon and on my message: for no one among men shall ever be crushed more miserably than thou.

Oed. Are these taunts to be indeed borne from *him?*—Hence, ruin take thee! Hence, this instant! Back!—away!—avaunt thee from these doors!

Te. I had never come, not I, hadst thou not called me.

Oed. I knew not that thou wast about to speak folly, or it had been long ere I had sent for thee to my house.

Te. Such am I—as thou thinkest, a fool; but for the parents who begat thee, sane.

Oed. What parents? Stay...and who of men is my sire?

Te. This day shall show thy birth and shall bring thy ruin.

Oed. What riddles, what dark words thou always speakest!

Te. Nay, art not thou most skilled to unravel dark speech?

Oed. Make that my reproach in which thou shalt find me great.

Te. Yet 'twas just that fortune that undid thee.

Oed. Nay, if I delivered this town, I care not.

Te. Then I will go: so do thou, boy, take me hence.

Oed. Aye, let him take thee: while here, thou art a hindrance, thou, a trouble: when thou hast vanished, thou wilt not vex me more.

Te. I will go when I have done mine errand, fearless of thy frown: for thou canst never destroy me. And I tell thee—the man of whom thou hast this long while been in quest, uttering threats, and proclaiming a search into the murder of Laïus—that man is here, in seeming, an alien sojourner, but anon he shall be found a native Theban, and shall not be glad of his fortune. A blind man, he who now hath sight, a beggar, who now is rich, he shall make his way to a strange land, feeling the ground before him with his staff. And he shall be found at once brother and father of the children with whom he consorts; son and husband of the woman who bore him; heir to his father's bed, shedder of his father's blood.

So go thou in and think on that; and if thou find that I have been at fault, say thenceforth that I have no wit in prophecy.

TEIRESIAS *is led out by the Boy.* OEDIPUS *enters the palace.*

Chorus

Who is he of whom the divine voice from the Delphian rock hath spoken, as having wrought with red hands horrors that no tongue can tell?

It is time that he ply in flight a foot stronger than the feet of storm-swift steeds: for the son of Zeus is springing on him, all armed with fiery lightnings, and with him come the dread, unerring Fates.

Yea, newly given from snowy Parnassus, the message hath flashed forth to make all search for the unknown man. Into the wild wood's covert, among caves and rocks he is roaming, fierce as a bull, wretched and forlorn on his joyless path, still seeking to put from him the doom spoken at Earth's central shrine: but that doom ever lives, ever flits around him.

Dreadly, in sooth, dreadly doth the wise augur move me, who approve not, nor am able to deny. How to speak, I know not; I am fluttered with forebodings; neither in the present have I clear vision, nor of the future. Never in past days, nor in these, have I heard how the house of Labdacus or the son of Polybus had, either against other, any grief that I could bring as proof in assailing the public fame of Oedipus, and seeking to avenge the line of Labdacus for the undiscovered murder.

Nay, Zeus indeed and Apollo are keen of thought, and know the things of earth; but that mortal seer wins knowledge above mine, of this there can be no sure test; though man may surpass man in lore. Yet, until I see the word made good, never will I assent when men blame Oedipus. Before all eyes, the winged maiden came against him of old, and he was seen to be wise; he bore the test, in welcome service to our State; never, therefore, by the verdict of my heart shall he be adjudged guilty of crime.

Enter CREON.

Cr. Fellow-citizens, having learned that Oedipus the king lays dire charges against me, I am here, indignant. If, in the present troubles, he thinks that he has suffered from *me*, by word or deed, aught that tends to harm, in truth I crave not my full term of years, when I must bear such blame as this. The wrong of this rumour touches me not in one point alone, but has the largest scope, if I am to be called a traitor in the city, a traitor too by thee and by my friends.

Ch. Nay, but this taunt came under stress, perchance, of anger, rather than from the purpose of the heart.

Cr. And the saying was uttered, that *my* counsels won the seer to utter his falsehoods?

Ch. Such things were said—I know not with what meaning.

Cr. And was this charge laid against me with steady eyes and steady mind?

Ch. I know not; I see not what my masters do: but here comes our lord forth from the house.

Enter OEDIPUS.

Oed. Sirrah, how camest thou here? Hast thou a front so bold that thou hast come to my house, who art the proved assassin of its master, the palpable robber of my crown? Come, tell me, in the name of the gods, was it cowardice or folly that thou sawest in me, that thou didst plot to do this thing? Didst thou think that I would not note this deed of thine creeping on me by stealth, or, aware, would not ward it off? Now is not thine attempt foolish, to seek, without followers or friends, a throne, a prize which followers and wealth must win?

Cr. Mark me now—in answer to thy words, hear a fair reply, and then judge for thyself on knowledge.

Oed. Thou art apt in speech, but I have a poor wit for thy lessons, since I have found thee my malignant foe.

Cr. Now first hear how I will explain this very thing—

Oed. Explain me not one thing—that thou art not false.

Cr. If thou deemest that stubbornness without sense is a good gift, thou art not wise.

Oed. If thou deemest that thou canst wrong a kinsman and escape the penalty, thou art not sane.

Cr. Justly said, I grant thee: but tell me what is the wrong that thou sayest thou hast suffered from me.

Oed. Didst thou advise, or didst thou not, that I should send for that reverend seer?

Cr. And now I am still of the same mind.

Oed. How long is it, then, since Laïus—

Cr. Since Laïus... ? I take not thy drift...

Oed. —was swept from men's sight by a deadly violence?

Cr. The count of years would run far into the past.

Oed. Was this seer, then, of the craft in those days?

Cr. Yea, skilled as now, and in equal honour.

Oed. Made he, then, any mention of me at that time?

Cr. Never, certainly, when I was within hearing.

Oed. But held ye not a search touching the murder?

Cr. Due search we held, of course—and learned nothing.

Oed. And how was it that this sage did not tell his story *then*?

Cr. I know not; where I lack light, 'tis my wont to be silent.

Oed. Thus much, at least, thou knowest, and couldst declare with light enough.

Cr. What is that? If I know it, I will not deny.

Oed. That, if he had not conferred with thee, he would never have named *my* slaying of Laïus.

Cr. If so he speaks, thou best knowest; but I claim to learn from thee as much as thou hast now from me.

Oed. Learn thy fill: I shall never be found guilty of the blood.

Cr. Say, then—thou hast married my sister?

Oed. The question allows not of denial.

Cr. And thou rulest the land as she doth, with like sway?

Oed. She obtains from me all her desire.

Cr. And rank not I as a third peer of you twain?

Oed. Aye, 'tis just therein that thou art seen a false friend.

Cr. Not so, if thou wouldst reason with thine own heart as I with mine. And first weigh this—whether thou thinkest that any one would choose to rule amid terrors rather than in unruffled peace, granting that he is to have the same powers. Now I, for one, have no yearning in my nature to be a king rather than to do kingly deeds, no, nor hath any man who knows how to keep a sober mind. For now I win all boons from thee without fear; but, were I ruler myself, I should be doing much e'en against mine own pleasure.

How, then, could royalty be sweeter for me to have than painless rule and influence? Not yet am I so misguided as to desire other honours than those which profit. Now, all wish me joy; now, every man has a greeting for me; now, those who have a suit to thee crave speech with me, since therein is all their hope of success. Then why should I resign these things, and take those? No mind will become false, while it is wise. Nay, I am no lover of such policy, and, if another put it into deed, never could I bear to act with him.

And, in proof of this, first, go to Pytho, and ask if I brought thee true word of the oracle; then next, if thou find that I have planned aught in concert with the soothsayer, take and slay me, by the sentence not of one mouth, but of twain—by mine own, no less than thine. But make me not guilty in a corner, on unproved surmise. It is not right to adjudge bad men good at random, or good men bad. I count it a like thing for a man to cast off a true friend as to cast away the life in his own bosom, which most he loves. Nay, thou wilt learn these things with sureness in time, for time alone shows a just man; but thou couldst discern a knave even in one day.

Ch. Well hath he spoken, O king, for one who giveth heed not to fall: the quick in counsel are not sure.

Oed. When the stealthy plotter is moving on me in quick sort, I, too, must be quick with my counterplot. If I await him in repose, his ends will have been gained, and mine missed.

Cr. What wouldst thou, then? Cast me out of the land?

Oed. Not so: I desire thy death—not thy banishment—that thou mayest show forth what manner of thing is envy.

Cr. Thou speakest as resolved not to yield or to believe?

[*Oed.* No; for thou persuadest me not that thou art worthy of belief.]

Cr. No, for I find thee not sane.

Oed. Sane, at least, in mine own interest.

Cr. Nay, thou shouldst be so in mine also.

Oed. Nay, thou art false.

Cr. But if thou understandest nought?

Oed. Yet must I rule.

Cr. Not if thou rule ill.

Oed. Hear him, O Thebes!

Cr. Thebes is for me also—not for thee alone.

Enter IOCASTA.

Ch. Cease, princes; and in good time for you I see Iocasta coming yonder from the house, with whose help ye should compose your present feud.

Iocasta. Misguided men, why have ye raised such foolish strife of tongues? Are ye not ashamed, while the land is thus sick, to stir up troubles of your own? Come, go thou into the house—and thou, Creon, to thy home—and forbear to make much of a petty grief.

Cr. Kinswoman, Oedipus thy lord claims to do dread things unto me, even one or other of two ills—to thrust me from the land of my fathers, or to slay me amain.

Oed. Yea; for I have caught him, lady, working evil, by ill arts, against my person.

Cr. Now may I see no good, but perish accursed, if I have done aught to thee of that wherewith thou chargest me!

Io. O, for the gods' love, believe it, Oedipus—first, for the awful sake of this oath unto the gods, then for my sake and for theirs who stand before thee?

(*The following lines between the* CHORUS *and* OEDIPUS *and between the* CHORUS, IOCASTA, *and* OEDIPUS *are chanted responsively*.)

Ch. Consent, reflect, hearken, O my king, I pray thee!

Oed. What grace, then, wouldest thou have me grant thee?

Ch. Respect him who aforetime was not foolish, and who now is strong in his oath.

Oed. Now dost thou know what thou cravest?

Ch. Yea.

Oed. Declare, then, what thou meanest.

Ch. That thou shouldest never use an unproved rumour to cast a dishonouring charge on the friend who has bound himself with a curse.

Oed. Then be very sure that, when thou seekest this, for me thou art seeking destruction, or exile from this land.

Ch. No, by him who stands in the front of all the heavenly host, no, by the Sun! Unblest, unfriended, may I die by the uttermost doom, if I have that thought! But my unhappy soul is worn by the withering of the land, and again by the thought that our old sorrows should be crowned by sorrows springing from you twain.

Oed. Then let him go, though I am surely doomed to death, or to be thrust dishonoured from the land. Thy lips, not his, move my compassion by their plaint; but he, where'er he be, shall be hated.

Cr. Sullen in yielding art thou seen, even as vehement in the excesses of thy wrath; but such natures are justly sorest for themselves to bear.

Oed. Then wilt thou not leave me in peace, and get thee gone?

Cr. I will go my way; I have found thee undiscerning, but in the sight of these I am just. *Exit.*

Ch. Lady, why dost thou delay to take yon man into the house?

Io. I will do so, when I have learned what hath chanced.

Ch. Blind suspicion, bred of talk, arose; and, on the other part, injustice wounds.

Io. It was on both sides?

Ch. Aye.

Io. And what was the story?

Ch. Enough, methinks, enough—when our land is already vexed—that the matter should rest where it ceased.

Oed. Seest thou to what thou hast come, for all thy honest purpose, in seeking to slack and blunt my zeal?

Ch. King, I have said it not once alone—be sure that I should have been shown a madman, bankrupt in sane counsel, if I put thee away—thee, who gavest a true course to my beloved country when distraught by troubles—thee, who now also art like to prove our prospering guide.

Io. In the name of the gods, tell me also, O king, on what account thou hast conceived this steadfast wrath.

Oed. That will I; for I honour thee, lady, above yonder men: the cause is Creon, and the plots that he hath laid against me.

Io. Speak on—if thou canst tell clearly how the feud began.

Oed. He says that I stand guilty of the blood of Laïus.

Io. As on his own knowledge? Or on hearsay from another?

Oed. Nay, he hath made a rascal seer his mouthpiece; as for himself, he keeps his lips wholly pure.

Io. Then absolve thyself of the things whereof thou speakest; hearken to me, and learn for thy comfort that nought of mortal birth is a sharer in the science of the seer. I will give thee pithy proof of that.

An oracle came to Laïus once—I will not say from Phoebus himself, but from his ministers—that the doom should overtake him to die by the hand of his child, who should spring from him and me.

Now Laïus—as, at least, the rumour saith—was murdered one day by foreign robbers at a place where three highways meet. And the child's birth was not three days past, when Laïus pinned its ankles together, and had it thrown, by others' hands, on a trackless mountain.

So, in that case, Apollo brought it not to pass that the babe should become the slayer of his sire, or that Laïus should die—the dread thing which he feared—by his child's hand. Thus did the messages of seer-craft map out the future. Regard them, thou, not at all. Whatsoever needful things the god seeks, he himself will easily bring to light.

Oed. What restlessness of soul, lady, what tumult of the mind hath just come upon me since I heard thee speak!

Io. What anxiety hath startled thee, that thou sayest this?

Oed. Methought I heard this from thee—that Laïus was slain where three highways meet.

Io. Yea, that was the story; nor hath it ceased yet.

Oed. And where is the place where this befell?

Io. The land is called Phocis; and branching roads lead to the same spot from Delphi and from Daulia.

Oed. And what is the time that hath passed since these things were?

Io. The news was published to the town shortly before thou wast first seen in power over this land.

Oed. O Zeus, what hast thou decreed to do unto me?

Io. And wherefore, Oedipus, doth this thing weigh upon thy soul?

Oed. Ask me not yet; but say what was the stature of Laïus, and how ripe his manhood.

Io. He was tall, the silver just lightly strewn among his hair; and his form was not greatly unlike to thine.

Oed. Unhappy that I am! Methinks I have been laying myself even now under a dread curse, and knew it not.

Io. How sayest thou? I tremble when I look on thee, my king.

Oed. Dread misgivings have I that the seer can see. But thou wilt show better if thou wilt tell me one thing more.

Io. Indeed—though I tremble—I will answer all thou askest, when I hear it.

Oed. Went he in small force, or with many armed followers, like a chieftain?

Io. Five they were in all—a herald one of them; and there was one carriage, which bore Laïus.

Oed. Alas! 'Tis now clear indeed.—Who was he who gave you these tidings, lady?

Io. A servant—the sole survivor who came home.

Oed. Is he haply at hand in the house now?

Io. No, truly; so soon as he came thence, and found thee reigning in the stead of Laïus, he supplicated me, with hand laid on mine, that I would send him to the fields, to the pastures of the flocks, that he might be far from the sight of this town. And I sent him; he was worthy, for a slave, to win e'en a larger boon than that.

Oed. Would, then, that he could return to us without delay!

Io. It is easy: but wherefore dost thou enjoin this?

Oed. I fear, lady, that mine own lips have been unguarded; and therefore am I fain to behold him.

Io. Nay, he shall come. But I too, methinks, have a claim to learn what lies heavy on thy heart, my king.

Oed. Yea, and it shall not be kept from thee, now that my forebodings have advanced so far. Who, indeed, is more to me than thou, to whom I should speak in passing through such a fortune as this?

My father was Polybus of Corinth, my mother, the Dorian Merope; and I was held the first of all the folk in that town, until a chance befell me, worthy, indeed, of wonder, though not worthy of mine own heat concerning it. At a banquet, a man full of wine cast it at me in his cups that I was not the true son of my sire. And I, vexed, restrained myself for that day as best I might; but on the next I went to my mother and father, and questioned them; and they were wroth for the taunt with him who had let that word fly. So on their part I had comfort; yet was this thing ever rankling in my heart; for it still crept abroad with strong rumour. And, unknown to mother or father, I went to Delphi; and Phoebus sent me forth disappointed of that knowledge for which I came, but in his response set forth other things, full of sorrow and terror and woe; even that I was fated to defile my mother's bed; and that I should show unto men a brood which they could not endure to behold; and that I should be the slayer of the sire who begat me.

And I, when I had listened to this, turned to flight from the land of Corinth, thenceforth wotting of its region by the stars alone, to some spot where I should never see fulfilment of the infamies foretold in mine evil doom. And on my way I came to the regions in which thou sayest that this prince perished. Now, lady, I will tell thee the truth. When in my journey I was near to those three roads, there met me a herald, and a man seated in a carriage drawn by colts, as thou hast described; and he who was in front, and the old man himself, were for thrusting me rudely from the path. Then, in anger, I struck him who pushed me aside—the driver; and the old man, seeing it, watched the moment when I was passing, and, from the carriage, brought his goad with two teeth down full upon my head. Yet was he paid with interest; by one swift blow from the staff in this hand he was rolled right out of the carriage, on his back; and I slew every man of them.

But if this stranger had any tie of kinship with Laïus, who is now more wretched than the man before thee? What mortal could prove more hated of heaven? Whom no stranger, no citizen, is allowed to receive in his house; whom it is unlawful that any one accost; whom all must repel from their homes! And this—this curse—was laid on me by no mouth but mine own! And I pollute the bed of the slain man with the hands by which he perished. Say, am I vile? Oh, am I not utterly unclean?—seeing that I must be banished, and in banishment see not mine own people, nor set foot in mine own land, or else be joined in wedlock to my mother, and slay my sire, even Polybus, who begat and reared me.

Then would not he speak aright of Oedipus, who judged these things sent by some cruel power above man? Forbid, forbid, ye pure and awful gods, that I should see that day! No, may I be swept from among men, ere I behold myself visited with the brand of such a doom!

Ch. To us, indeed, these things, O king, are fraught with fear; yet have hope, until at least thou hast gained full knowledge from him who saw the deed.

Oed. Hope, in truth, rests with me thus far alone; I can await the man summoned from the pastures.

Io. And when he has appeared—what wouldst thou have of him?

Oed. I will tell thee. If his story be found to tally with thine, I, at least, shall stand clear of disaster.

Io. And what of special note didst thou hear from me?

Oed. Thou wast saying that he spoke of Laïus as slain by robbers. If, then, he still speaks, as before, of several, I was not the slayer: a solitary man could not be held the same with that band. But if he names one lonely wayfarer, then beyond doubt this guilt leans to me.

Io. Nay, be assured that thus, at least, the tale was first told; he cannot revoke that, for the city heard it, not I alone. But even if he should diverge somewhat from his former story, never, king, can he show that the murder of Laïus, at least, is truly square to prophecy; of whom Loxias plainly said that he must die by the hand of my child. Howbeit that poor innocent never slew him, but perished first itself. So henceforth, for what touches divination, I would not look to my right hand or my left.

Oed. Thou judgest well. But nevertheless send some one to fetch the peasant, and neglect not this matter.

Io. I will send without delay. But let us come into the house: nothing will I do save at thy good pleasure. OEDIPUS *and* IOCASTA *go into the palace.*

Chorus

May destiny still find me winning the praise of reverent purity in all words and deeds sanctioned by those laws of range sublime, called into life throughout the high clear heaven, whose father is Olympus alone; their parent was no race of mortal men, no, nor shall oblivion ever lay them to sleep; the god is mighty in them, and he grows not old.

Insolence breeds the tyrant; Insolence, once vainly surfeited on wealth that is not meet nor good for it, when it hath scaled the topmost ramparts, is hurled to a dire doom, wherein no service of the feet can serve. But I pray that the god never quell such rivalry as benefits the State; the god will I ever hold for our protector.

But if any man walks haughtily in deed or word, with no fear of Justice, no reverence for the images of gods, may an evil doom seize him for his ill-starred pride, if he will not win his vantage fairly, nor keep him from unholy deeds, but must lay profaning hands on sanctities.

Where such things are, what mortal shall boast any more that he can ward the arrows of the gods from his life? Nay, if such deeds are in honour, wherefore should we join in the sacred dance?

No more will I go reverently to earth's central and inviolate shrine, no more to Abae's temple or Olympia, if these oracles fit not the issue, so that all men shall point at them with the finger. Nay, king—if thou art rightly called—Zeus all-ruling, may if not escape thee and thine ever-deathless power!

The old prophecies concerning Laïus are fading; already men are setting them at nought, and nowhere is Apollo glorified with honours; the worship of the gods is perishing.

IOCASTA *comes forth, bearing a branch, wreathed with festoons of wool, which, as a suppliant, she is about to lay on the altar of the household god, Lycean Apollo, in front of the palace.*

Io. Princes of the land, the thought has come to me to visit the shrines of the gods, with this wreathed branch in my hands, and these gifts of incense. For Oedipus excites his soul overmuch with all manner of alarms, nor, like a man of sense, judges the new things by the old, but is at the will of the speaker, if he speak terrors.

Since, then, by counsel I can do no good, to thee, Lycean Apollo, for thou are nearest, I have come, a suppliant with these symbols of prayer, that thou mayest find us some riddance from uncleanness. For now we are all afraid, seeing *him* affrighted, even as they who see fear in the helmsman of their ship.

While IOCASTA *is offering her prayers to the god, a* MESSENGER *enters and addresses The* CHORUS.

Messenger. Might I learn from you, strangers, where is the house of the King Oedipus? Or, better still, tell me where he himself is—if ye know.

Ch. This is his dwelling, and he himself, stranger, is within; and this lady is the mother of his children.

Me. Then may she be ever happy in a happy home, since she is his heaven-blest queen.

Io. Happiness to thee also, stranger! 'tis the due of thy fair greeting. But say what thou hast come to seek or to tell.

Me. Good tidings, lady, for thy house and for thy husband.

Io. What are they? And from whom hast thou come?

Me. From Corinth: and at the message which I will speak anon thou wilt rejoice—doubtless; yet haply grieve.

Io. And what is it? How hath it thus a double potency?

Me. The people will make him king of the Isthmian land, as 'twas said there.

Io. How then? Is the aged Polybus no more in power?

Me. No, verily: for death holds him in the tomb.

Io. How sayest thou? Is Polybus dead, old man?

Me. If I speak not the truth, I am content to die.

Io. O handmaid, away with all speed, and tell this to thy master! O ye oracles of the gods, where stand ye now! This is the man whom Oedipus long feared and shunned, lest he should slay him; and now this man hath died in the course of destiny, not by his hand.

Enter OEDIPUS.

Oed. Iocasta, dearest wife, why hast thou summoned me forth from these doors?

Io. Hear this man, and judge, as thou listenest, to what the awful oracles of the gods have come.

Oed. And he—who may he be, and what news hath he for me?

Io. He is from Corinth, to tell that thy father Polybus lives no longer, but hath perished.

Oed. How, stranger? Let me have it from thine own mouth.

Me. If I must first make these tidings plain, know indeed that he is dead and gone.

Oed. By treachery, or by visit of disease?

Me. A light thing in the scale brings the aged to their rest.

Oed. Ah, he died, it seems, of sickness?

Me. Yea, and of the long years that he had told.

Oed. Alas, alas! Why, indeed, my wife, should one look to the hearth of the Pythian seer, or to the birds that scream above our heads, on whose showing I was doomed to slay my sire? But he is dead, and hid already beneath the earth; and here am I, who have not put hand to spear. Unless, perchance, he was killed by longing for me: thus, indeed, I should be the cause of his death. But the oracles as they stand, at least, Polybus hath swept with him to his rest in Hades: they are worth nought.

Io. Nay, did I not so foretell to thee long since?

Oed. Thou didst: but I was misled by my fear.

Io. Now no more lay aught of those things to heart.

Oed. But surely I must needs fear my mother's bed?

Io. Nay, what should mortal fear, for whom the decrees of fortune are supreme, and who hath clear foresight of nothing? 'Tis best to live at random, as one may. But fear not thou touching wedlock with thy mother. Many men ere now have so fared in dreams also: but he to whom these things are as nought bears his life most easily.

Oed. All these bold words of thine would have been well, were not my mother living; but as it is, since she lives, I must needs fear—though thou sayest well.

Io. Howbeit thy father's death is a great sign to cheer us.

Oed. Great, I know; but my fear is of her who lives.

Me. And who is the woman about whom ye fear?

Oed. Meropé, old man, the consort of Polybus.

Me. And what is it in her that moves your fear?

Oed. A heaven-sent oracle of dread import, stranger.

Me. Lawful, or unlawful, for another to know?

Oed. Lawful, surely. Loxias once said that I was doomed to espouse mine own mother, and to shed with mine own hands my father's blood. Wherefore my home in Corinth was long kept by me afar; with happy event, indeed—yet still 'tis sweet to see the face of parents.

Me. Was it indeed for fear of this that thou wast an exile from the city?

Oed. And because I wished not, old man, to be the slayer of my sire.

Me. Then why have I not freed thee, king, from this fear, seeing that I came with friendly purpose?

Oed. Indeed thou shouldst have guerdon due from me.

Me. Indeed 'twas chiefly for this that I came—that, on thy return home, I might reap some good.

Oed. Nay, I will never go near my parents.

Me. Ah my son, 'tis plain enough that thou knowest not what thou doest.

Oed. How, old man? For the gods' love, tell me.

Me. If for these reasons thou shrinkest from going home.

Oed. Aye, I dread lest Phoebus prove himself true for me.

Me. Thou dreadest to be stained with guilt through thy parents?

Oed. Even so, old man—this it is that ever affrights me.

Me. Dost thou know, then, that thy fears are wholly vain?

Oed. How so, if I was born of those parents?

Me. Because Polybus was nothing to thee in blood.

Oed. What sayest thou? Was Polybus not my sire?

Me. No more than he who speaks to thee, but just so much.

Oed. And how can my sire be level with him who is as nought to me?

Me. Nay, he begat thee not, any more than I.

Oed. Nay, wherefore, then, called he me his son?

Me. Know that he had received thee as a gift from my hands of yore.

Oed. And yet he loved me so dearly, who came from another's hand?

Me. Yea, his former childlessness won him thereto.

Oed. And thou—hadst thou bought me or found me by chance, when thou gavest me to him?

Me. Found thee in Cithaeron's winding glens.

Oed. And wherefore wast thou roaming in those regions?

Me. I was there in charge of mountain flocks.

Oed. What, thou wast a shepherd—a vagrant hireling?

Me. But thy preserver, my son, in that hour.

Oed. And what pain was mine when thou didst take me in thine arms?

Me. The ankles of thy feet might witness.

Oed. Ah me, why dost thou speak of that old trouble?

Me. I freed thee when thou hadst thine ankles pinned together.

Oed. Aye, 'twas a dread brand of shame that I took from my cradle.

Me. Such, that from that fortune thou wast called by the name which still is thine.

Oed. Oh, for the gods' love—was the deed my mother's or father's? Speak!

Me. I know not; he who gave thee to me wots better of that than I.

Oed. What, thou hadst me from another? Thou didst not light on me thyself?

Me. No: another shepherd gave thee up to me.

Oed. Who was he? Art thou in case to tell clearly?

Me. I think he was called one of the household of Laïus.

Oed. The king who ruled this country long ago?

Me. The same: 'twas in his service that the man was a herd.

Oed. Is he still alive, that I might see him?

Me. Nay, ye folk of the country should know best.

Oed. Is there any of you here present that knows the herd of whom he speaks—that hath seen him in the pastures or the town? Answer! The hour hath come that these things should be finally revealed.

Ch. Methinks he speaks of no other than the peasant whom thou wast already fain to see; but our lady Iocasta might best tell that.

Oed. Lady, wottest thou of him whom we lately summoned? Is it of him that this man speaks?

Io. Why ask of whom he spoke? Regard it not... waste not a thought on what he said...'twere idle.

Oed. It must not be that, with such clues in my grasp, I should fail to bring my birth to light.

Io. For the gods' sake, if thou hast any care for thine own life, forbear this search! My anguish is enough.

Oed. Be of good courage; though I be found the son of servile mother—aye, a slave by three descents—*thou* wilt not be proved base-born.

Io. Yet hear me, I implore thee: do not thus.

Oed. I must not hear of not discovering the whole truth.

Io. Yet I wish thee well—I counsel thee for the best.

Oed. These best counsels, then, vex my patience.

Io. Ill-fated one! Mayest thou never come to know who thou art!

Oed. Go, some one, fetch me the herdsman hither, and leave yon woman to glory in her princely stock.

Io. Alas, alas, miserable!—that word alone can I say unto thee, and no other word henceforth for ever.

She rushes into the palace.

Ch. Why hath the lady gone, Oedipus, in a transport of wild grief? I misdoubt, a storm of sorrow will break forth from this silence.

Oed. Break forth what will! Be my race never so lowly, I must crave to learn it. Yon woman, perchance—for she is proud with more than a woman's pride—thinks shame of my base source. But I, who hold myself son of Fortune that gives good, will not be dishonoured. She is the mother from whom I spring; and the months, my kinsmen, have marked me sometimes lowly, sometimes great. Such being my lineage, never more can I prove false to it, or spare to search out the secret of my birth.

Ch. If I am a seer or wise of heart, O Cithaeron, thou shalt not fail—by yon heaven, thou shalt not!—to know at tomorrow's full moon that Oedipus honours thee as native to him, as his nurse, and his mother, and that thou art celebrated in our dance and song, because thou art well-pleasing to our prince. O Phoebus to whom we cry, may these things find favour in thy sight!

Who was it, my son, who of the race whose years are many that bore thee in wedlock with Pan, the mountain-roaming father? Or was it a bride of Loxias that bore thee? For dear to him are all the upland pastures. Or perchance 'twas Cyllene's lord, or the Bacchants' god, dweller on the hill-tops, that received thee, a new-born joy, from one of the Nymphs of Helicon, with whom he most doth sport.

Oed. Elders, if 'tis for me to guess, who have never met with him, I think I see the herdsman of whom we have long been in quest; for in his venerable age he tallies with yon stranger's years, and withal I know those who bring him, methinks, as servants of mine own. But perchance thou mayest have the advantage of me in knowledge, if thou hast seen the herdsman before.

Ch. Aye, I know him, be sure; he was in the service of Laïus—trusty as any man, in his shepherd's place.

The HERDSMAN *is brought in.*

Oed. I ask thee first, Corinthian stranger, is this he whom thou meanest?

Me. This man whom thou beholdest.

Oed. Ho thou, old man—I would have thee look this way, and answer all that I ask thee. Thou wast once in the service of Laïus?

Herdsman. I was—a slave not bought, but reared in his house.

Oed. Employed in what labour, or what way of life?

He. For the best part of my life I tended flocks.

Oed. And what the regions that thou didst chiefly haunt?

He. Sometimes it was Cithaeron, sometimes the neighbouring ground.

Oed. Then wottest thou of having noted yon man in these parts—

He. Doing what?...What man dost thou mean?...

Oed. This man here—or of having ever met him before?

He. Not so that I could speak at once from memory.

Me. And no wonder, master. But I will bring clear recollection to his ignorance. I am sure that he well wots of the time when we abode in the region of Cithaeron—he with two flocks, I, his comrade, with one—three full half-years, from spring to Arcturus; and then for the winter I used to drive my flock to mine own fold, and he took his to the fold of Laïus. Did aught of this happen as I tell, or did it not?

He. Thou speakest the truth—though 'tis long ago.

Me. Come, tell me now—wottest thou of having given me a boy in those days, to be reared as mine own foster-son?

He. What now? Why dost thou ask the question?

Me. Yonder man, my friend, is he who then was young.

He. Plague seize thee—be silent once for all!

Oed. Ha! chide him not, old man—thy words need chiding more than his.

He. And wherein, most noble master, do I offend?

Oed. In not telling of the boy concerning whom he asks.

He. He speaks without knowledge—he is busy to no purpose.

Oed. Thou wilt not speak with a good grace, but thou shalt on pain.

He. Nay, for the gods' love, misuse not an old man!

Oed. Ho, some one—pinion him this instant!

He. Alas, wherefore? what more wouldst thou learn?

Oed. Didst thou give this man the child of whom he asks?

He. I did—and would I had perished that day!

Oed. Well, thou wilt come to that, unless thou tell the honest truth.

He. Nay, much more am I lost, if I speak.

Oed. The fellow is bent, methinks on more delays...

He. No, no! I said before that I gave it to him.

Oed. Whence hadst thou got it? In thine own house, or from another?

He. Mine own it was not—I had received it from a man.

Oed. From whom of the citizens here? from what home?

He. Forbear, for the gods' love, master, forbear to ask more!

Oed. Thou art lost if I have to question thee again.

He. It was a child, then, of the house of Laïus.

Oed. A slave? or one born of his own race?

He. Ah me—I am on the dreaded brink of speech.

Oed. And I of hearing; yet must I hear.

He. Thou must know, then, that 'twas said to be his own child—but thy lady within could best say how these things are.

Oed. How? She gave it to thee?

He. Yea, O king.

Oed. For what end?

He. That I should make away with it.

Oed. Her own child, the wretch?

He. Aye, from fear of evil prophecies.

Oed. What were they?

He. The tale ran that he must slay his sire.

Oed. Why, then, didst thou give him up to this old man?

He. Through pity, master, as deeming that he would bear him away to another land, whence he himself came; but he saved him for the direst woe. For if thou art what this man saith, know that thou wast born to misery.

Oed. Oh, oh! All brought to pass—all true! Thou light, may I now look my last on thee—I who have been found accursed in birth, accursed in wedlock, accursed in the shedding of blood!

He rushes into the palace.

Chorus

Alas, ye generations of men, how mere a shadow do I count your life! Where, where is the mortal who wins more of happiness than just the seeming, and, after the semblance, a falling away? Thine is a fate that warns me—thine, thine, unhappy Oedipus—to call no earthly creature blest.

For he, O Zeus, sped his shaft with peerless skill, and won the prize of an all-prosperous fortune; he slew the maiden with crooked talons who sang darkly; he arose for our land as a tower against death. And from that time, Oedipus, thou hast been called our king, and hast been honoured supremely, bearing sway in great Thebes.

But now whose story is more grievous in men's ears? Who is a more wretched captive to fierce plagues and troubles, with all his life reversed?

Alas, renowned Oedipus! The same bounteous place of rest sufficed thee, as child and as sire also, that thou shouldst make thereon thy nuptial couch. Oh, how can the soil wherein thy father sowed, unhappy one, have suffered thee in silence so long?

Time the all-seeing hath found thee out in thy despite: he judgeth the monstrous marriage wherein begetter and begotten have long been one.

Alas, thou child of Laïus, would, would that I had never seen thee! I wail as one who pours a dirge from his lips; sooth to speak, 'twas thou that gavest me new life, and through thee darkness hath fallen upon mine eyes.

Enter SECOND MESSENGER *from the house.*

Second Messenger. Ye who are ever most honoured in this land, what deeds shall ye hear, what deeds behold, what burden of sorrow shall be yours, if, true to your race, ye still care for the house of Labdacus! For I ween that not Ister nor Phasis could wash this house clean, so many are the ills that it shrouds, or will soon bring to light—ills wrought not unwittingly, but of purpose. And those griefs smart most which are seen to be of our own choice.

Ch. Indeed those which we knew before fall not short of claiming sore lamentation: besides them, what dost thou announce?

2 *Me.* This is the shortest tale to tell and to hear: our royal lady Iocasta is dead.

Ch. Alas, hapless one! From what cause?

2 *Me.* By her own hand. The worst pain in what hath chanced is not for you, for yours it is not to behold. Nevertheless, so far as mine own memory serves, ye shall learn that unhappy woman's fate.

When, frantic, she had passed within the vestibule, she rushed straight towards her nuptial couch, clutching her hair with the fingers of both hands; once within the chamber, she dashed the doors together at her back; then called on the name of Laïus, long since a corpse, mindful of that son, begotten long ago, by whom the sire was slain, leaving the mother to breed accursed offspring with his own.

And she bewailed the wedlock wherein, wretched, she had borne a twofold brood, husband by husband, children by her child. And how thereafter she perished, is more than I know. For with a shriek Oedipus burst in, and suffered us not to watch her woe unto the end; on him, as he rushed around, our eyes were set. To and fro he went, asking us to give him a sword, asking where he should find the wife who was no wife, but a mother whose womb had borne alike himself and his children. And, in his frenzy, a power above man was his guide; for 'twas none of us mortals who were nigh. And with a dread shriek, as though someone beckoned him on, he sprang at the double doors, and from their sockets forced the bending bolts, and rushed into the room.

There beheld we the woman hanging by the neck in a twisted noose of swinging cords. But he, when he saw her, with a dread, deep cry of misery, loosed the halter whereby she hung. And when the hapless woman was stretched upon the ground, then was the sequel dread to see. For he tore from her raiment the golden brooches wherewith she was decked, and lifted them, and smote full on his own eye-balls, uttering words like these: "No more shall ye behold such horrors as I was suffering and working! long enough have ye looked on those whom ye ought never to have seen, failed in knowledge of those whom I yearned to know—henceforth ye shall be dark!"

To such dire refrain, not once alone but oft struck he his eyes with lifted hand; and at each blow the ensanguined eye-balls bedewed his beard, nor sent forth sluggish drops of gore, but all at once a dark shower of blood came down like hail.

From the deeds of twain such ills have broken forth, not on one alone, but with mingled woe for man and wife. The old happiness of their ancestral fortune was aforetime happiness indeed; but to-day —lamentation, ruin, death, shame, all earthly ills that can be named—all, all are theirs.

Ch. And hath the sufferer now any respite from pain?

2 *Me.* He cries for some one to unbar the gates and show to all the Cadmeans his father's slayer, his mother's—the unholy word must not pass my lips—as purposing to cast himself out of the land, and abide no more, to make the house accursed under his own curse. Howbeit he lacks strength, and one to guide his steps; for the anguish is more than man may bear. And he will show this to thee also; for lo, the bars of the gates are withdrawn, and soon thou shalt behold a sight which even he who abhors it must pity.

Enter OEDIPUS.

Ch. O dread fate for men to see, O most dreadful of all that have met mine eyes! Unhappy one, what madness hath come on thee? Who is the unearthly foe that, with a bound of more than mortal range, hath made thine ill-starred life his prey?

Alas, alas, thou hapless one! Nay, I cannot e'en look on thee, though there is much that I would fain ask, fain learn, much that draws my wistful gaze —with such a shuddering dost thou fill me!

Oed. Woe is me! Alas, alas, wretched that I am! Whither, whither am I borne in my misery? How is my voice swept abroad on the wings of the air? Oh my Fate, how far hast thou sprung!

Ch. To a dread place, dire in men's ears, dire in their sight.

Oed. O thou horror of darkness that enfoldest me, visitant unspeakable, resistless, sped by a wind too fair!

Ay me! and once again, ay me!

How is my soul pierced by the stab of these goads, and withal by the memory of sorrows!

Ch. Yea, amid woes so many a twofold pain may well be thine to mourn and to bear.

Oed. Ah, friend, thou still art steadfast in thy tendance of me, thou still hast patience to care for the blind man! Ah me! Thy presence is not hid from me—no, dark though I am, yet know I thy voice full well.

Ch. Man of dread deeds, how couldst thou in such wise quench thy vision? What more than human power urged thee?

Oed. Apollo, friends, Apollo was he that brought these my woes to pass, these my sore, sore woes: but the hand that struck the eyes was none save mine, wretched that I am! Why was I to see, when sight could show me nothing sweet?

Ch. These things were even as thou sayest.

Oed. Say, friends, what can I more behold, what can I love, what greeting can touch mine ear with joy? Haste, lead me from the land, friends, lead me hence, the utterly lost, the thrice accursed, yea, the mortal most abhorred of heaven!

Ch. Wretched alike for thy fortune and for thy sense thereof, would that I had never so much as known thee!

Oed. Perish the man, whoe'er he was, that freed me in the pastures from the cruel shackle on my feet, and saved me from death, and gave me back to life—a thankless deed! Had I died then, to my friends and to mine own soul I had not been so sore a grief.

Ch. I also would have had it thus.

Oed. So had I not come to shed my father's blood, nor been called among men the spouse of her from whom I sprang: but now am I forsaken of the gods, son of a defiled mother, successor to his bed who gave me mine own wretched being: and if there be yet a woe surpassing woes, it hath become the portion of Oedipus.

Ch. I know not how I can say that thou hast counselled well: for thou wert better dead than living and blind.

Oed. Show me not at large that these things are not best done thus: give me counsel no more. For, had I sight, I know not with what eyes I could e'en have looked on my father, when I came to the place of the dead, aye, or on my miserable mother, since against both I have sinned such sins as strangling could not punish. But deem ye that the sight of children, born as mine were born, was lovely for me to look upon? No, no, not lovely to mine eyes for ever! No, nor was this town with its towered walls, nor the sacred statues of the gods, since I, thrice wretched that I am—I, noblest of the sons of Thebes —have doomed myself to know these no more, by mine own command that all should thrust away the impious one—even him whom gods have shown to be unholy—and of the race of Laïus!

After bearing such a stain upon me, was I to look with steady eyes on this folk? No, verily: no, were there yet a way to choke the fount of hearing, I had not spared to make a fast prison of this wretched frame, that so I should have known nor sight nor sound; for 'tis sweet that our thought should dwell beyond the sphere of griefs.

Alas, Cithaeron, why hadst thou a shelter for me? When I was given to thee, why didst thou not slay me straightway, that so I might never have revealed my source to men? Ah, Polybus, ah, Corinth, and thou that wast called the ancient house of my fathers, how seeming-fair was I your nurseling, and what ills were festering beneath! For now I am found evil, and of evil birth. O ye three roads, and thou secret glen—thou coppice, and narrow way where three paths met—ye who drank from my hands that father's blood which was mine own—remember ye, perchance, what deeds I wrought for you to see—and then, when I came hither, what fresh deeds I went on to do?

O marriage-rites, ye gave me birth, and when ye had brought me forth, again ye bore children to your child, ye created an incestuous kinship of fathers, brothers, sons—brides, wives, mothers—yea, all the foulest shame that is wrought among men! Nay, but 'tis unmeet to name what 'tis unmeet to do:—haste ye, for the gods' love, hide me somewhere beyond the land, or slay me, or cast me into the sea, where ye shall never behold me more! Approach, deign to lay your hands on a wretched man; hearken, fear not,—my plague can rest on no mortal beside.

Enter CREON.

Ch. Nay, here is Creon, in meet season for thy requests, crave they act or counsel; for he alone is left to guard the land in thy stead.

Oed. Ah me, how indeed shall I accost him? What claim to credence can be shown on my part? For in the past I have been found wholly false to him.

Cr. I have not come in mockery, Oedipus, nor to reproach thee with any bygone fault. (*To the attendants*) But ye, if ye respect the children of men no more, revere at least the all-nurturing flame of our lord the Sun, spare to show thus nakedly a pollution such as this—one which neither earth can welcome, nor the holy rain, nor the light. Nay, take him into the house as quickly as ye may; for it best accords with piety that kinsfolk alone should see and hear a kinsman's woes.

Oed. For the gods' love—since thou hast done a gentle violence to my presage, who hast come in a spirit so noble to me, a man most vile—grant me a boon: for thy good I will speak, not for mine own.

Cr. And what wish art thou so fain to have of me?

Oed. Cast me out of this land with all speed, to a place where no mortal shall be found to greet me more.

Cr. This would I have done, be thou sure, but that I craved first to learn all my duty from the god.

Oed. Nay, his behest hath been set forth in full—to let me perish, the parricide, the unholy one, that I am.

Cr. Such was the purport; yet, seeing to what a pass we have come, 'tis better to learn clearly what should be done.

Oed. Will ye, then, seek a response on behalf of such a wretch as I am?

Cr. Aye, for thou thyself wilt now surely put faith in the god.

Oed. Yea; and on thee lay I this charge, to thee will I make this entreaty: give to her who is within such burial as thou thyself wouldest; for thou wilt meetly render the last rites to thine own. But for me—never let this city of my sire be condemned to have me dwelling therein, while I live: no, suffer me to abide on the hills, where yonder is Cithaeron, famed as mine—which my mother and sire, while they lived, set for my appointed tomb—that so I may die by their decree who sought to slay me. Howbeit of thus much am I sure—that neither sickness nor aught else can destroy me; for never had I been snatched from death, but in reserve for some strange doom.

Nay, let *my* fate go whither it will: but as touching my children, I pray thee, Creon, take no care on thee for my sons; they are men, so that, be they where they may, they can never lack the means to live. But my two girls, poor hapless ones—who never knew my table spread apart, or lacked their father's presence, but ever in all things shared my daily bread—I pray thee, care for *them;* and—if thou canst—suffer me to touch them with my hands, and to indulge my grief. Grant it, prince, grant it, thou noble heart! Ah, could I but once touch them with my hands, I should think that they were with me, even as when I had sight...

Creon's attendants lead in the children, ANTIGONE *and* ISMENE.

Ha? O ye gods, can it be my loved ones that I hear sobbing, can Creon have taken pity on me and sent me my children—my darlings? Am I right?

Cr. Yea: 'tis of my contriving, for I knew thy joy in them of old, the joy that now is thine.

Oed. Then blessed be thou, and, for guerdon of this errand, may heaven prove to thee a kinder guardian than it hath to me! My children, where are ye? Come hither, hither to the hands of him whose mother was your own, the hands whose offices have wrought that your sire's once bright eyes should be such orbs as these—his, who seeing nought, knowing nought, became your father by her from whom he sprang! For you also do I weep—behold you I cannot—when I think of the bitter life in days to come which men will make you live. To what company of the citizens will ye go, to what festival, from which ye shall not return home in tears, instead of sharing in the holiday? But when ye are now come to years ripe for marriage, who shall he be, who shall be the man, my daughters, that will hazard taking unto him such reproaches as must be baneful alike to my offspring and to yours? For what misery is wanting? Your sire slew his sire, he had seed of her who bare him, and begat you at the sources of his own being! Such are the taunts that will be cast at you; and who then will wed? The man lives not, no, it cannot be, my children, but ye must wither in barren maidenhood.

Ah, son of Menoeceus, hear me—since thou art the only father left to them, for we, their parents, are lost, both of us—allow them not to wander poor and unwed, who are thy kinswomen, nor abase them to the level of my woes. Nay, pity them, when thou seest them at this tender age so utterly forlorn, save for thee. Signify thy promise, generous man, by the touch of thy hand! To you, my children, I would have given much counsel, were your minds mature; but now I would have this to be your prayer—that ye live where occasion suffers, and that the life which is your portion may be happier than your sire's.

Cr. Thy grief hath had large scope enough: nay, pass into the house.

Oed. I must obey, though 'tis in no wise sweet.

Cr. Yea: for it is in season that all things are good.

Oed. Knowest thou, then, on what conditions I will go?

Cr. Thou shalt name them; so shall I know them when I hear.

Oed. See that thou send me to dwell beyond this land.

Cr. Thou askest me for what the god must give.

Oed. Nay, to the gods I have become most hateful.

Cr. Then shalt thou have thy wish anon.

Oed. So thou consentest?

Cr. 'Tis not my wont to speak idly what I do not mean.

Oed. Then 'tis time to lead me hence.

Cr. Come, then—but let thy children go.

Oed. Nay, take not these from me!

Cr. Crave not to be master in all things: for the mastery which thou didst win hath not followed thee through life.

Ch. Dwellers in our native Thebes, behold, this is Oedipus, who knew the famed riddle, and was a man most mighty; on whose fortunes what citizen did not gaze with envy? Behold into what a stormy sea of dread trouble he hath come!

Therefore, while our eyes wait to see the destined final day, we must call no one happy who is of mortal race, until he hath crossed life's border, free from pain.

OEDIPUS AT COLONUS

DRAMATIS PERSONAE

OEDIPUS	CREON, *of Thebes*
ANTIGONE } *his daughters*	POLYNEICES, *the elder son of Oedipus*
ISMENE } *his daughters*	A MESSENGER
STRANGER, *a man of Colonus*	CHORUS OF ELDERS OF COLONUS
THESEUS, *King of Athens*	

At Colonus, about a mile and a quarter N.W. of Athens, in front of a grove sacred to the Erinyes or Furies—there worshipped under the propitiatory name of the Eumenides, or Kindly Powers. Enter OEDIPUS, *blind, led by* ANTIGONE.

Oedipus. Daughter of the blind old man, to what region have we come, Antigone, or what city of men? Who will entertain the wandering Oedipus to-day with scanty gifts? Little crave I, and win yet less than that little, and therewith am content; for patience is the lesson of suffering, and of the years in our long fellowship, and lastly of a noble mind. My child, if thou seest any resting-place, whether on profane ground or by groves of the gods, stay me and set me down, that we may inquire where we are: for we stand in need to learn as strangers of denizens, and to perform their bidding.

Antigone. Father, toil-worn Oedipus, the towers that guard the city, to judge by sight, are far off; and this place is sacred, to all seeming—thick-set with laurel, olive, vine; and in its heart a feathered choir of nightingales makes music. So sit thee here on this unhewn stone; thou hast travelled a long way for an old man.

Oed. Seat me, then, and watch over the blind.

An. If time can teach, I need not to learn that.

Oed. Canst thou tell me, now, where we have arrived?

An. Athens I know, but not this place.

Oed. Aye, so much every wayfarer told us.

An. Well shall I go and learn how the spot is called?

Oed. Yes, child—if indeed 'tis habitable.

An. Nay, inhabited it surely is; but I think there is no need; yonder I see a man near us.

Oed. Hitherward moving and setting forth?

An. Nay, he is at our side already. Speak as the moment prompts thee, for the man is here.

Enter STRANGER, *a man of Colonus.*

Oed. Stranger, hearing from this maiden, who hath sight for herself and for me, that thou hast drawn nigh with timely quest for the solving of our doubts—

Stranger. Now, ere thou question me at large, quit this seat; for thou art on ground which 'tis not lawful to tread.

Oed. And what is this ground? To what deity sacred?

St. Ground inviolable, whereon none may dwell: for the dread goddesses hold it, the daughters of Earth and Darkness.

Oed. Who may they be, whose awful name I am to hear and invoke?

St. The all-seeing Eumenides the folk here would call them: but other names please otherwhere.

Oed. Then graciously may they receive their suppliant! for nevermore will I depart from my rest in this land.

St. What means this?

Oed. 'Tis the watchword of my fate.

St. Nay, for my part, I dare not remove thee without warrant from the city, ere I report what I am doing.

Oed. Now for the gods' love, stranger, refuse me not, hapless wanderer that I am, the knowledge for which I sue to thee.

St. Speak, and from me thou shalt find no refusal.

Oed. What, then, is the place that we have entered?

St. All that *I* know, thou shalt learn from my mouth. This whole place is sacred; awful Poseidon holds it, and therein is the fire-fraught god, the Titan Prometheus; but as for the spot whereon thou treadest, 'tis called the "Brazen Threshold" of this land, the stay of Athens; and the neighbouring fields claim yon knight Colonus for their primal lord, and all the people bear his name in common for their own. Such, thou mayest know, stranger, are these haunts, not honoured in story, but rather in the life that loves them.

Oed. Are there indeed dwellers in this region?

St. Yea, surely, the namesakes of yonder god.

Oed. Have they a king? Or doth speech rest with the folk?

St. These parts are ruled by the king in the city.

Oed. And who is thus sovereign in counsel and in might?

St. Theseus he is called, son of Aegeus who was before him.

Oed. Could a messenger go for him from among you?

St. With what aim to speak, or to prepare his coming?

Oed. That by small service he may find a great gain.

St. And what help can be from one who sees not?

Oed. In all that I speak there shall be sight.

St. Mark me now, friend—I would not have thee come to harm, for thou art noble, if one may judge by thy looks, leaving thy fortune aside; stay here, e'en where I found thee, till I go and tell these things to the folk on this spot, not in the town: they will decide for thee whether thou shalt abide or retire. *Exit.*

Oed. My child, say, is the stranger gone?

An. He is gone, and so thou canst utter what thou wilt, father, in quietness, as knowing that I alone am near.

Oed. Queens of dread aspect, since your seat is the first in this land whereat I have bent the knee, show not yourselves ungracious to Phoebus or to myself; who, when he proclaimed that doom of many woes, spake of *this* as a rest for me after long years—on reaching my goal in a land where I should find a seat of the Awful Goddesses, and a hospitable shelter—even that there I should close my weary life, with benefits, through my having dwelt therein, for mine hosts, but ruin for those who sent me forth—who drove me away. And he went on to warn me that signs of these things should come, in earthquake, or in thunder, haply, or in the lightning of Zeus.

Now I perceive that in this journey some faithful omen from you hath surely led me home to this grove: never else could I have met with you, first of all, in my wanderings—I, the austere, with you who delight not in wine—or taken this solemn seat not shaped by man.

Then, goddesses, according to the word of Apollo, give me at last some way to accomplish and close my course—unless, perchance, I seem beneath your grace, thrall that I am evermore to woes the sorest on the earth. Hear, sweet daughters of primeval Darkness! Hear, thou that art called the city of great Pallas—Athens, of all cities most honoured! Pity this poor wraith of Oedipus—for verily 'tis the man of old no more.

An. Hush! Here come some aged men, I wot, to spy out thy resting-place.

Oed. I will be mute—and do thou hide me in the grove, apart from the road, till I learn how these men will speak; for in knowledge is the safeguard of our course. *Exeunt.*

The CHORUS OF ELDERS OF COLONUS *enter the orchestra, from the right of the spectators, as if in eager search.*

Chorus. Give heed—who was he, then? Where lodges he?—whither hath he rushed from this place, insolent, he, above all who live? Scan the ground, look well, urge the quest in every part.

A wanderer that old man must have been—a wanderer, not a dweller in the land; else never would he have advanced into this untrodden grove of the maidens with whom none may strive, whose name we tremble to speak, by whom we pass with eyes turned away, moving our lips, without sound or word, in still devotion.

But now 'tis rumoured that one hath come who in no wise reveres them; and him I cannot yet discern, though I look round all the holy place, nor wot I where to find his lodging.

Oed. (*stepping forward, with* ANTIGONE, *from his place of concealment in the grove*). Behold the man whom ye seek! for in sound is my sight, as the saying hath it.

Ch. O! O!

Dread to see, and dread to hear!

Oed. Regard me not, I entreat you, as a lawless one.

Ch. Zeus defend us! who may the old man be?

Oed. Not wholly of the best fortune, that ye should envy him, O guardians of this land! 'Tis plain: else would I not be walking thus by the eyes of others, and buoying my strength upon weakness.

Ch. Alas! wast thou sightless e'en from thy birth? Evil have been thy days, and many, to all seeming; but at least, if I can help, thou shalt not add this curse to thy doom. Too far thou goest—too far! But, lest thy rash steps intrude on the sward of yonder voiceless glade, where the bowl of water blends its stream with the flow of honied offerings (be thou well ware of such trespass, unhappy stranger)—retire, withdraw! A wide space parts us: hearest thou, toil-worn wanderer? If thou hast aught to say in converse with us, leave forbidden ground, and speak where 'tis lawful for all; but, till then, refrain.

Oed. Daughter, to what counsel shall we incline?

An. My father, we must conform us to the customs of the land, yielding, where 'tis meet, and hearkening.

Oed. Then give me thy hand.

An. 'Tis laid in thine.

Oed. Strangers, oh let me not suffer wrong when I have trusted in you, and have passed from my refuge!

Ch. Never, old man, never shall any one remove thee from this place of rest against thy will.

OEDIPUS *now begins to move forward.*

Oed. (*pausing in his gradual advance*). Further, then?

Ch. Come still further.

Oed. (*having advanced another step*). Further?

Ch. Lead him onward, maiden, for thou understandest.

[A verse for ANTIGONE, a verse for OEDIPUS, and then another verse for ANTIGONE, seem to have been lost here.]

An. * * * Come, follow me this way with thy dark steps, father, as I lead thee.

[Here has been lost a verse for OEDIPUS.]

Ch. A stranger in a strange land, ah, hapless one, incline thy heart to abhor that which the city holds in settled hate, and to reverence what she loves!

Oed. Lead me thou, then, child, to a spot where I may speak and listen within piety's domain, and let us not wage war with necessity.

Moving forward, he now sets foot on a platform of rock at the verge of the grove.

Ch. There!—bend not thy steps beyond that floor of native rock.

Oed. Thus far?

Ch. Enough, I tell thee.

Oed. Shall I sit down?

Ch. Yea, move sideways and crouch low on the edge of the rock.

An. Father, this is my task: to quiet step (*Oed.* Ah me! ah me!) knit step, and lean thy aged frame upon my loving arm.

Oed. Woe for the doom of a dark soul!

ANTIGONE *seats him on the rock.*

Ch. Ah, hapless one, since now thou hast ease, speak,—whence art thou sprung? In what name art thou led on thy weary way? What is the fatherland whereof thou hast to tell us?

Oed. Strangers, I am an exile—but forbear......

Ch. What is this that thou forbiddest, old man?

Oed. —forbear, forbear to ask me who I am; seek—probe—no further!

Ch. What means this?

Oed. Dread the birth...

Ch. Speak!

Oed. (*to* ANTIGONE). My child—alas!—what shall I say?

Ch. What is thy lineage, stranger—speak!—and who thy sire?

Oed. Woe is me!—What will become of me, my child?

An. Speak, for thou art driven to the verge.

Oed. Then speak I will—I have no way to hide it.

Ch. Ye twain make a long delay—come, haste thee!

Oed. Know ye a son of Laïus...O!...(*The* CHORUS *utter a cry*)...and the race of the Labdacidae?...

Ch. O Zeus!

Oed. The hapless Oedipus? . . .

Ch. THOU art he?

Oed. Have no fear of any words that I speak—

The CHORUS *drown his voice with a great shout of execration, half turning away, and holding their mantles before their eyes.*

Oed. Unhappy that I am! . . . (*The clamour of the* CHORUS *continues*). . . Daughter, what is about to befall?

Ch. Out with you! forth from the land!

Oed. And thy promise—to what fulfilment wilt thou bring it?

Ch. No man is visited by fate if he requites deeds which were first done to himself; deceit on the one part matches deceits on the other, and gives pain, instead of benefit, for reward. And thou—back with thee! out from these seats! avaunt! away from my land with all speed, lest thou fasten some heavier burden on my city!

An. Strangers of reverent soul, since ye have not borne with mine aged father—knowing, as ye do, the rumour of his unpurposed deeds—pity, at least, my hapless self, I implore you, who supplicate you for my sire alone, supplicate you with eyes that can still look on your own, even as though I were sprung from your own blood, that the sufferer may find compassion.

On you, as on a god, we depend in our misery. Nay, hear us! grant the boon for which we scarce dare hope! By everything sprung from you that ye hold dear, I implore you, yea, by child—by wife, or treasure, or god! Look well and thou wilt not find the mortal who if a god should lead him on, could escape.

Ch. Nay, be thou sure, daughter of Oedipus, we pity thee and him alike for your fortune; but, dreading the judgment of the gods, we could not say aught beyond what hath now been said to thee.

Oed. What good comes, then, of repute or fair fame, if it ends in idle breath; seeing that Athens, as men say, has the perfect fear of Heaven, and the power, above all cities, to shelter the vexed stranger, and the power, above all, to succour him?

And where find I these things, when, after making me rise up from these rocky seats, ye then drive me from the land, afraid of my name alone? Not, surely, afraid of my person or of mine acts; since mine acts, at least, have been in suffering rather than doing—were it seemly that I should tell you the story of my mother or my sire, by reason whereof ye dread me—that know I full well.

And yet in *nature* how was I evil? I, who was but requiting a wrong, so that, had I been acting with knowledge, even then I could not be accounted wicked; but, as it was, all unknowing went I—whither I went—while they who wronged me knowingly sought my ruin.

Wherefore, strangers, I beseech you by the gods, even as ye made me leave my seat, so protect me, and do not, while ye honour the gods, refuse to give those gods their due; but rather deem that they look on the god-fearing among men, and on the godless, and that never yet hath escape been found for an impious mortal on the earth.

With the help of those gods, spare to cloud the bright fame of Athens by ministering to unholy deeds; but, as ye have received the suppliant under your pledge, rescue me and guard me to the end; nor scorn me when ye look on this face unlovely to behold: for I have come to you as one sacred, and pious, and fraught with comfort for this people. But when the master is come, whosoever he be that is your chief, then shall ye hear and know all; meanwhile in no wise show yourself false.

Ch. The thoughts urged on thy part, old man, must needs move awe; they have been set forth in words not light; but I am content that the rulers of our country should judge in this cause.

Oed. And where, strangers, is the lord of this realm?

Ch. He is at the city of his father in our land; and the messenger who sent us hither hath gone to fetch him.

Oed. Think ye that he will have any regard or care for the blind man, so as to come hither himself?

Ch. Yea, surely, so soon as he learns thy name.

Oed. Who is there to bring him that message?

Ch. The way is long, and many rumours from wayfarers are wont to go abroad; when he hears them, he will soon be with us, fear not. For thy name, old man, hath been mightily noised through all lands; so that, even if he is taking his ease, and slow to move, when he hears of *thee* he will arrive with speed.

Oed. Well, may he come with a blessing to his own city, as to me!—What good man is not his own friend?

An. O Zeus! what shall I say, what shall I think, my father?

Oed. What is it, Antigone, my child?

An. I see a woman coming towards us, mounted on a colt of Etna; she wears a Thessalian bonnet to screen her face from the sun. What shall I say? Is it she, or is it not? Doth fancy cheat me? Yes—no—I cannot tell—ah me! It is no other—yes!—she greets me with bright glances as she draws nigh, and shows that Ismene, and no other, is before me.

Oed. What sayest thou, my child?

An. That I see thy daughter and my sister; thou canst know her straightway by her voice.

Enter ISMENE.

Ismene. Father and sister, names most sweet to me! How hardly have I found you! and now I scarce can see you for my tears.

Oed. My child, thou hast come?

Is. Ah, father, sad is thy fate to see!

Oed. Thou art with us, my child!

Is. And it hath cost me toil.

Oed. Touch me, my daughter!

Is. I give a hand to each.

Oed. Ah, children—ah, ye sisters!

Is. Alas, twice-wretched life!

Oed. Her life and mine?

Is. And mine, hapless, with you twain.

Oed. Child, and why hast thou come?

Is. Through care, father, for thee.

Oed. Through longing to see me?

Is. Yes, and to bring thee tidings by mine own mouth,—with the only faithful servant that I had.

Oed. And where are the young men thy brothers at our need?

Is. They are—where they are: 'tis their dark hour.

Oed. O, true image of the ways of Egypt that they show in their spirit and their life! For there the men sit weaving in the house, but the wives go forth to win the daily bread. And in your case, my daughters, those to whom these toils belonged keep the house at home like girls, while ye, in their stead, bear your hapless father's burdens.

One, from the time when her tender age was past and she came to a woman's strength, hath ever been the old man's guide in weary wanderings, oft roaming, hungry and bare-foot, through the wild wood, oft sore-vexed by rains and scorching heat—but regarding not the comforts of home, if so her father should have tendance.

And thou, my child, in former days camest forth, bringing thy father, unknown of the Cadmeans, all the oracles that had been given touching Oedipus; and thou didst take on thee the office of a faithful watcher in my behalf, when I was being driven from the land. And now what new tidings hast thou brought thy father, Ismene? On what mission hast thou set forth from home? For thou comest not empty-handed, well I wot, or without some word of fear for me.

Is. The sufferings that I bore, father, in seeking where thou wast living, I will pass by; I would not renew the pain in the recital. But the ills that now beset thine ill-fated sons—'tis of these that I have come to tell thee.

At first it was their desire that the throne should be left to Creon, and the city spared pollution, when they thought calmly on the blight of the race from of old, and how it hath clung to thine ill-starred house. But now, moved by some god and by a sinful mind, an evil rivalry hath seized them, thrice infatuate!—to grasp at rule and kingly power.

And the hot-brained youth, the younger born, hath deprived the elder, Polyneices, of the throne, and hath driven him from his father-land. But he, as the general rumour saith among us, hath gone, an exile, to the hill-girt Argos, and is taking unto him a new kinship, and warriors for his friends—as deeming that Argos shall soon possess the Cadmean land in honour, or lift that land's praise to the stars.

These are no vain words, my father, but deeds terrible; and where the gods will have pity on thy griefs, I cannot tell.

Oed. What, hadst thou come to hope that the gods would ever look on me for my deliverance?

Is. Yea, mine is that hope, father, from the present oracles.

Oed. What are they? What hath been prophesied, my child?

Is. That thou shalt yet be desired, alive and dead, by the men of that land, for their welfare's sake.

Oed. And who could have good of such an one as I?

Is. Their power, 'tis said, comes to be in *thy* hand.

Oed. When I am nought, in that hour, then, I am a man?

Is. Yea, for the gods lift thee now, but before they were working thy ruin.

Oed. 'Tis little to lift age, when youth was ruined.

Is. Well, know, at least, that Creon will come to thee in this cause—and rather soon than late.

Oed. With what purpose, daughter? expound to me.

Is. To plant thee near the Cadmean land, so that they may have thee in their grasp, but thou mayest not set foot on their borders.

Oed. And how can I advantage them while I rest beyond their gates?

Is. Thy tomb hath a curse for them, if all be not well with it.

Oed. It needs no god to help our wit so far.

Is. Well, therefore they would fain acquire thee as a neighbour, in a place where thou shalt not be thine own master.

Oed. Will they also shroud me in Theban dust?

Is. Nay, the guilt of a kinsman's blood debars thee, father.

Oed. Then never shall they become my masters.

Is. Some day, then, this shall be a grief for the Cadmeans.

Oed. In what conjuncture of events, my child?

Is. By force of thy wrath, when they take their stand at thy tomb.

Oed. And who hath told thee what thou tellest, my child?

Is. Sacred envoys, from the Delphian hearth.

Oed. And Phoebus hath indeed spoken thus concerning me?

Is. So say the men who have come back to Thebes.

Oed. Hath either of my sons, then, heard this?

Is. Yea, both have heard, and know it well.

Oed. And then those base ones, aware of this, held the kingship dearer than the wish to recall me?

Is. It grieves me to hear that, but I must bear it.

Oed. Then may the gods quench not their fated strife, and may it become mine to decide this warfare whereto they are now setting their hands, spear against spear! For then neither should he abide who now holds the sceptre and the throne, nor should the banished one ever return; seeing that when I, their sire, was being thrust so shamefully from my country, they hindered not, nor defended me; no, they saw me sent forth homeless, they heard my doom of exile cried aloud.

Thou wilt say that it was mine own wish then, and that the city meetly granted me that boon. No, verily: for in that first day, when my soul was seething, and my darling wish was for death, aye, death by stoning, no one was found to help me in that desire: but after a time, when all my anguish was now assuaged, and when I began to feel that my wrath had run too far in punishing those past errors, then it was that the city, on her part, went about to drive me perforce from the land—after all that time; and my sons, when they might have brought help—the sons to the sire—would not do it: no—for lack of one little word from them, I was left to wander, an outcast and a beggar evermore.

'Tis to these sisters, girls as they are, that, so far as nature enables them, I owe my daily food, and a shelter in the land, and the offices of kinship; the brothers have bartered their sire for a throne, and sceptred sway, and rule of the realm. Nay, never shall they win Oedipus for an ally, nor shall good ever come to them from this reign at Thebes; that know I, when I hear this maiden's oracles, and meditate the old prophecies stored in mine own mind, which Phoebus hath fulfilled for me at last.

Therefore let them send Creon to seek me, and whoso beside is mighty in Thebes. For if ye, strangers,—with the championship of the dread goddesses who dwell among your folk—are willing to succour, ye shall procure a great deliverer for this State, and troubles for my foes.

Ch. Right worthy art thou of compassion, Oedipus, thou, and these maidens; and since to this plea thou addest thy power to save our land, I fain would advise thee for thy weal.

Oed. Kind sir, be sure, then, that I will obey in all —stand thou my friend.

Ch. Now make atonement to these deities, to whom thou hast first come, and on whose ground thou hast trespassed.

Oed. With what rites? instruct me, strangers.

Ch. First, from a perennial spring fetch holy drink-offerings, borne in clean hands.

Oed. And when I have gotten this pure draught?

Ch. Bowls there are, the work of a cunning craftsman: crown their edges and the handles at either brim.

Oed. With branches, or woollen cloths, or in what wise?

Ch. Take the freshly-shorn wool of an ewe-lamb.

Oed. Good; and then—to what last rite shall I proceed?

Ch. Pour thy drink-offerings, with thy face to the dawn.

Oed. With these vessels whereof thou speakest shall I pour them?

Ch. Yea, in three streams; but empty the last vessel wholly.

Oed. Wherewith shall I fill this, ere I set it? Tell me this also.

Ch. With water and honey; but bring no wine thereto.

Oed. And when the ground under the dark shade hath drunk of these?

Ch. Lay on it thrice nine sprays of olive with both thine hands, and make this prayer the while.

Oed. The prayer I fain would hear—'tis of chief moment.

Ch. That, as we call them "Benign Powers," with hearts benign they may receive the suppliant for saving, be this the prayer—thine own, or his who prays for thee; speak inaudibly, and lift not up thy voice; then retire, without looking behind. Thus do, and I would be bold to stand by thee; but otherwise, stranger, I would fear for thee.

Oed. Daughters, hear ye these strangers, who dwell near?

An. We have listened; and do thou bid us what to do.

Oed. I cannot go; for I am disabled by lack of strength and lack of sight, evils twain. But let one of you two go and do these things. For I think that one soul suffices to pay this debt for ten thousand, if it come with good will to the shrine. Act, then, with speed; yet leave me not solitary; for the strength would fail me to move without help or guiding hand.

Is. Then I will go to perform the rite; but where I am to find the spot—this I fain would learn.

Ch. On the further side of this grove, maiden. And if thou hast need of aught, there is a guardian of the place, who will direct thee.

Is. So to my task: but thou, Antigone, watch our father here. In parents' cause, if toil there be, we must not reck of toil.

Exit.

Ch. Dread is it, stranger, to arouse the old grief that hath so long been laid to rest: and yet I yearn to hear......

Oed. What now?......

Ch. —of that grievous anguish, found cureless, wherewith thou hast wrestled.

Oed. By thy kindness for a guest, bare not the shame that I have suffered!

Ch. Seeing, in sooth, that the tale is wide-spread, and in no wise wanes, I am fain, friend, to hear it aright.

Oed. Woe is me!

Ch. Be content, I pray thee!

Oed. Alas, alas!

Ch. Grant my wish, as I have granted thine in its fulness.

Oed. I have suffered misery, strangers, suffered it through unwitting deeds, and of those acts—be Heaven my witness!—no part was of mine own choice.

Ch. But in what regard?

Oed. By an evil wedlock, Thebes bound me, all unknowing, to the bride that was my curse......

Ch. Can it be, as I hear, that thou madest thy mother the partner of thy bed, for its infamy?

Oed. Woe is me! Cruel as death, strangers, are these words in mine ears;—but those maidens, begotten of me—

Ch. What wilt thou say?—

Oed. —two daughters—two curses—

Ch. O Zeus!

Oed. —sprang from the travail of the womb that bore me.

Ch. These, then, are at once thine offspring, and...

Oed. —yea, very sisters of their sire.

Ch. Oh, horror!

Oed. Horror indeed—yea, horrors untold sweep back upon my soul!

Ch. Thou hast suffered—

Oed. Suffered woes dread to bear—

Ch. Thou hast sinned—

Oed. No wilful sin—

Ch. How?—

Oed. A gift was given to me—O, broken-hearted that I am, would I had never won from Thebes that meed for having served her!

Ch. Wretch! How then?...thine hand shed blood?...

Oed. Wherefore this? What wouldst thou learn?

Ch. A father's blood?

Oed. Oh! oh! a second stab—wound on wound!

Ch. Slayer!

Oed. Aye, slayer—yet have I a plea—

Ch. What canst thou plead?—

Oed. —a plea in justice....

Ch. What?...

Oed. Ye shall hear it; they whom I slew would have taken mine own life: stainless before the law, void of malice, have I come unto this pass!

Ch. Lo, yonder cometh our prince, Theseus son of Aegeus, at thy voice, to do the part whereunto he was summoned.

Enter THESEUS, *on spectators' right.*

Theseus. Hearing from many in time past concerning the cruel marring of thy sight, I have recognised thee, son of Laïus; and now, through hearsay in this my coming, I have the fuller certainty. For thy garb, and that hapless face, alike assure me of thy name; and in all compassion would I ask thee, ill-fated Oedipus, what is thy suit to Athens or to me that thou hast taken thy place here, thou and the hapless maiden at thy side. Declare it; dire indeed must be the fortune told by thee, from which I should stand aloof; who know that I myself also was reared in exile, like to thine, and in strange lands wrestled with perils to my life, as no man beside. Never, then, would I turn aside from a stranger, such as thou art now, or refuse to aid in his deliverance; for well know I that I am a man, and that in the morrow my portion is no greater than thine.

Oed. Theseus, thy nobleness hath in brief words shown such grace that for me there is need to say but little. Thou hast rightly said who I am, from what sire I spring, from what land I have come; and so nought else remains for me but to speak my desire,—and the tale is told.

Th. Even so—speak that—I fain would hear.

Oed. I come to offer thee my woe-worn body as a gift—not goodly to look upon; but the gains from it are better than beauty.

Th. And what gain dost thou claim to have brought?

Oed. Hereafter thou shalt learn; not yet, I think.

Th. At what time, then, will thy benefit be shown?

Oed. When I am dead, and thou hast given me burial.

Th. Thou cravest life's boon; for all between thou hast no memory—or no care.

Oed. Yea, for by that boon I reap all the rest.

Th. Nay, then, this grace which thou cravest from me hath small compass.

Oed. Yet give heed; this issue is no light one—no, verily.

Th. Meanest thou, as between thy sons and me?

Oed. King, they would fain convey me to Thebes.

Th. But if to thy content, then for thee exile is not seemly.

Oed. Nay, when *I* was willing, *they* refused.

Th. But, foolish man, temper in misfortune is not meet.

Oed. When thou hast heard my story, chide; till then, forbear.

Th. Say on: I must not pronounce without knowledge.

Oed. I have suffered, Theseus, cruel wrong on wrong.

Th. Wilt thou speak of the ancient trouble of thy race?

Oed. No, verily: *that* is noised throughout Hellas.

Th. What, then, is thy grief that passeth the griefs of man?

Oed. Thus it is with me. From my country I have been driven by mine own offspring; and my doom is to return no more, as guilty of a father's blood.

Th. How, then, should they fetch thee to them, if ye must dwell apart?

Oed. The mouth of the god will constrain them.

Th. In fear of what woe foreshown?

Oed. That they must be smitten in this land.

Th. And how should bitterness come between them and me?

Oed. Kind son of Aegeus, to the gods alone comes never old age or death, but all else is confounded by all-mastering time. Earth's strength decays, and the strength of the body; faith dies, distrust is born; and the same spirit is never steadfast among friends, or betwixt city and city; for, be it soon or be it late, men find sweet turn to bitter, and then once more to love.

And if now all is sunshine between Thebes and thee, yet time, in his untold course, gives birth to days and nights untold, wherein for a small cause they shall sunder with the spear that plighted concord of to-day; when my slumbering and buried corpse, cold in death, shall one day drink their warm blood, if Zeus is still Zeus, and Phoebus, the son of Zeus, speaks true.

But, since I would not break silence touching mysteries, suffer me to cease where I began; only make thine own word good, and never shalt thou say that in vain didst thou welcome Oedipus to dwell in this realm—unless the gods cheat my hope.

Ch. King, from the first yon man hath shown the mind to perform these promises, or the like, for our land.

Th. Who, then, would reject the friendship of such an one?—to whom, first, the hearth of an ally is ever open, by mutual right, among us; and then he hath come as a suppliant to our gods, fraught with no light recompense for this land and for me. In reverence for these claims, I will never spurn his grace, but will establish him as a citizen in the land. And if it is the stranger's pleasure to abide here, I will charge you to guard him; or if to come with me be more pleasing,—this choice, or that, Oedipus, thou canst take; thy will shall be mine.

Oed. O Zeus, mayest thou be good unto such men!

Th. What wouldst thou, then? wouldst thou come to my house?

Oed. Yea, were it lawful; but *this* is the place—

Th. What art thou to do here? I will not thwart thee...

Oed. —where I shall vanquish those who cast me forth.

Th. Great were this promised boon from thy presence.

Oed. It shall be—if thy pledge is kept with me indeed.

Th. Fear not touching me; never will I fail thee.

Oed. I will not bind thee with an oath, as one untrue.

Th. Well, thou wouldst win nought more than by my word.

Oed. How wilt thou act, then?

Th. What may be thy fear?

Oed. Men will come—

Th. Nay, these will look to that.

Oed. Beware lest, if thou leave me—

Th. Teach me not my part.

Oed. Fear constrains—

Th. My heart feels not fear.

Oed. Thou knowest not the threats—

Th. I know that none shall take thee hence in my despite. Oft have threats blustered, in men's wrath, with threatenings loud and vain; but when the mind is lord of himself once more, the threats are gone. And for yon men, haply—aye, though they have waxed bold to speak dread things of bringing thee back—the sundering waters will prove wide, and hard to sail. Now I would have thee be of a good courage, apart from any resolve of mine, if indeed Phoebus hath sent thee on thy way; still, though I be not here, my name, I wot, will shield thee from harm.

Exit THESEUS.

Ch. Stranger, in this land of goodly steeds thou hast come to earth's fairest home, even to our white Colonus; where the nightingale, a constant guest, trills her clear note in the covert of green glades, dwelling amid the wine-dark ivy and the god's inviolate bowers, rich in berries and fruit, unvisited by sun, unvexed by wind of any storm; where the reveller Dionysus ever walks the ground, companion of the nymphs that nursed him.

And, fed of heavenly dew, the narcissus blooms morn by morn with fair clusters, crown of the Great Goddesses from of yore; and the crocus blooms with golden beam. Nor fail the sleepless founts whence the waters of Cephisus wander, but each day with stainless tide he moveth over the plains of the land's swelling bosom, for the giving of quick increase; nor hath the Muses' quire abhorred this place, nor Aphrodite of the golden rein.

And a thing there is such as I know not by fame on Asian ground, or as ever born in the great Dorian isle of Pelops—a growth unconquered, self-renewing, a terror to the spears of the foemen, a growth which mightily flourishes in this land—the gray-leafed olive, nurturer of children. Youth shall not mar it by the ravage of his hand, nor any who dwells with old age; for the sleepless eye of the Morian Zeus beholds it, and the gray-eyed Athena.

And another praise have I to tell for this the city our mother, the gift of a great god, a glory of the land most high; the might of horses, the might of young horses, the might of the sea.

For thou, son of Cronus, our lord Poseidon, hast throned her in this pride, since in these roads first thou didst show forth the curb that cures the rage of steeds. And the shapely oar, apt to men's hands, hath a wondrous speed on the brine, following the hundred-footed Nereids.

An. O land that art praised above all lands, now is it for thee to make those bright praises seen in deeds!

Oed. What new thing hath chanced, my daughter?

An. Yonder Creon draws near us—not without followers, father.

Oed. Ah, kind elders, now give me, I pray you, the final proof of my safety!

Ch. Fear not—it shall be thine. If *I* am aged, this country's strength hath not grown old.

Enter CREON, *with attendants.*

Creon. Sirs, noble dwellers in this land, I see that a sudden fear hath troubled your eyes at my coming; but shrink not from me, and let no ungentle word escape you.

I am here with no thought of force; I am old, and I know that the city whereunto I have come is mighty, if any in Hellas hath might; no, I have been sent, in these my years, to plead with yonder man that he return with me to the land of Cadmus; not one man's envoy am I, but with charge from our people all; since 'twas mine, by kinship, to mourn his woes as no Theban beside.

Nay, unhappy Oedipus, hear us, and come home! Rightfully art thou called by all the Cadmean folk, and in chief by me, even as I—unless I am the basest of all men born—chiefly sorrow for thine ills, old man, when I see thee, hapless one, a stranger and a wanderer evermore, roaming in beggary, with one handmaid for thy stay. Alas, I had not thought that she could fall to such a depth of misery as that whereunto she hath fallen—yon hapless girl!—while she ever tends thy dark life amid penury—in ripe youth, but unwed—a prize for the first rude hand.

Is it not a cruel reproach—alas!—that I have cast at thee, and me, and all our race? But indeed an open shame cannot be hid; then—in the name of thy fathers' gods, hearken to me, Oedipus!—hide it *thou*, by consenting to return to the city and the house of thy fathers, after a kindly farewell to this State—for she is worthy: yet thine own hath the first claim on thy piety, since 'twas she that nurtured thee of old.

Oed. All-daring, who from any plea of right wouldst draw a crafty device, why dost thou attempt me thus, and seek once more to take me in the toils where capture would be sorest? In the old days—when, distempered by my self-wrought woes, I yearned to be cast out of the land—thy will went not with mine to grant the boon. But when my fierce grief had spent its force, and the seclusion of the house was sweet, *then* wast thou for thrusting me from the house and from the land—nor had this kinship any dearness for thee then: and now, again—when thou seest that I have kindly welcome from this city and from all her sons, thou seekest to pluck me away, wrapping hard thoughts in soft words. And yet what joy is there here, in kindness shown to us against our will? As if a man should give thee no gift, bring thee no aid, when thou wast fain of the boon; but after thy soul's desire was sated, should grant it then, when the grace could be gracious no more: wouldst thou not find that pleasure vain? Yet such are thine own offers unto me,—good in name, but in their substance evil.

And I will declare it to these also, that I may show thee false. Thou hast come to fetch me, not that thou mayest take me home, but that thou mayest plant me near thy borders, and so thy city may escape unscathed by troubles from this land. *That* portion is not for thee, but *this*—my curse upon the country, ever abiding therein; and for my sons, this heritage—room enough in my realm wherein—to die.

Am I not wiser than thou in the fortunes of Thebes? Yea, wiser far, as truer are the sources of my knowledge, even Phoebus, and his father, Zeus most high. But thou hast come hither with fraud on thy lips, yea, with a tongue keener than the edge of the sword; yet by thy pleading thou art like to reap more woe than weal. Howbeit, I know that I persuade thee not of this—go!—and suffer us to live here; for even in this plight our life would not be evil, so were we content therewith.

Cr. Which, thinkest thou, most suffers in this parley—I by thy course, or thou by thine own?

Oed. For me,' tis enough if thy pleading fails, as with me, so with yon men are nigh.

Cr. Unhappy man, shall it be seen that not even thy years have brought thee wit? Must thou live to be the reproach of age?

Oed. Thou hast a ready tongue, but I know not the honest man who hath fair words for every cause.

Cr. Words may be many, and yet may miss their aim.

Oed. As if thine, forsooth, were few, but aimed aright.

Cr. No, truly, for one whose wit is such as thine.

Oed. Depart—for I will say it in the name of yon men also!—and beset me not with jealous watch in the place where I am destined to abide.

Cr. These men—not thee—call I to witness: but, as for the strain of thine answer to thy kindred, if ever I take thee—

Oed. And who could take me in despite of these allies?

Cr. I promise thee, thou soon shalt smart without that.

Oed. Where is the deed which warrants that blustering word?

Cr. One of thy two daughters hath just been seized by me, and sent hence—the other I will remove forthwith.

Oed. Woe is me!

Cr. More woeful thou wilt find it soon.

Oed. Thou hast my child?

Cr. And will have this one ere long.

Oed. Alas! friends, what will ye do? Will ye forsake me? will ye not drive the godless man from this land?

Ch. Hence, stranger, hence—begone! Unrighteous is thy present deed—unrighteous the deed which thou hast done.

Cr. (*to his attendants*). 'Twere time for you to lead off yon girl perforce, if she will not go of her free will.

An. Wretched that I am! whither shall I fly?—where find help from gods or men?

Ch. (*threateningly, to* CREON). What wouldst thou, stranger?

Cr. I will not touch yon man, but her who is mine.

Oed. O, elders of the land!

Ch. Stranger—thy deed is not just.

Cr. 'Tis just.

Ch. How just?

Cr. I take mine own.

(*He lays his hand on* ANTIGONE.)

Oed. Hear, O Athens!

Ch. What wouldst thou, stranger? Release her! Thy strength, and ours, will soon be proved.

(*They approach him with threatening gestures.*)

Cr. Stand back!

Ch. Not from thee, while this is thy purpose.

Cr. Nay, 'twill be war with Thebes for thee, if thou harm me.

Oed. Said I not so?

Ch. Unhand the maid at once!

Cr. Command not where thou art not master.

Ch. Leave hold, I tell thee!

Cr. (*to one of his guards, who at a signal seizes* ANTIGONE). And I tell thee—begone!

Ch. To the rescue, men of Colonus—to the rescue! Athens—yea, Athens—is outraged with the strong hand! Hither, hither to our help!

An. They drag me hence—ah me!—friends, friends!

Oed. Where art thou, my child? (*blindly seeking for her*).

An. I am taken by force—

Oed. Thy hands, my child!—

An. Nay, I am helpless.

Cr. (*to his guards*). Away with you!

Oed. Ah me, ah me!

Exeunt guards with ANTIGONE.

Cr. So *those* two crutches shall never more prop thy steps. But since 'tis thy will to worst thy country and thy friends—whose mandate, though a prince, I here discharge—then be that victory thine. For hereafter, I wot, thou wilt come to know all this—that now, as in time past, thou hast done thyself no good, when, in despite of friends, thou hast indulged anger, which is ever thy bane.

(*He turns to follow his guards.*)

Ch. Hold, stranger!

Cr. Hands off, I say!

Ch. I will not let thee go, unless thou give back the maidens.

Cr. Then wilt thou soon give Thebes a still dearer prize: I will seize more than those two girls.

Ch. What—whither wilt thou turn?

Cr. Yon man shall be my captive.

Ch. A valiant threat!

Cr. 'Twill forthwith be a deed.

Ch. Aye, unless the ruler of this realm hinder thee.

Oed. Shameless voice! Wilt thou indeed touch me?

Cr. Be silent!

Oed. Nay, may the powers of this place suffer me to utter yet this curse! Wretch, who, when these eyes were dark, hast reft from me by force the helpless one who was mine eyesight! Therefore to thee and to thy race may the Sun-god, the god who sees all things, yet grant an old age such as mine!

Cr. See ye this, people of the land?

Oed. They see both me and thee; they know that my wrongs are deeds, and my revenge—but breath.

Cr. I will not curb my wrath—nay, alone though I am, and slow with age, I'll take yon man by force.

(*He approaches* OEDIPUS *as if to seize him.*)

Oed. Woe is me!

Ch. 'Tis a bold spirit that thou hast brought with thee, stranger, if thou thinkest to achieve this.

Cr. I do.

Ch. Then will I deem Athens a city no more.

Cr. In a just cause the weak vanquishes the strong.

Oed. Hear ye his words?

Ch. Yea, words which he shall not turn to deeds, Zeus knows!

Cr. Zeus haply knows—thou dost not.

Ch. Insolence!

Cr. Insolence which thou must bear.

Ch. What ho, people, rulers of the land, ho, hither with all speed, hither! These men are on their way to cross our borders!

Enter THESEUS.

Th. What means this shout? What is the trouble? What fear can have moved you to stay my sacrifice at the altar unto the sea-god, the lord of your Colonus? Speak, that I may know all, since therefore have I sped hither with more than easeful speed of foot.

Oed. Ah, friend—I know thy voice—yon man, but now, hath done me foul wrong.

Th. What is that wrong? And who hath wrought it? Speak!

Oed. Creon, whom thou seest there, hath torn away from me my two children—mine all.

Th. What dost thou tell me?

Oed. Thou hast heard my wrong.

Th. (*to his attendants*). Haste, one of you, to the altars yonder—constrain the folk to leave the sacrifice, and to speed—footmen, horsemen all, with slack rein, to the region where the two highways meet, lest the maidens pass, and I become a mockery to this stranger, as one spoiled by force. Away, I tell thee—quick! (*Turning towards* CREON.) As for yon man—if my wrath went as far as he deserves—I would not have suffered him to go scatheless from my hand. But now such law as he himself hath brought, and no other, shall be the rule for his correction.—(*Addressing* CREON.) Thou shalt not quit this land until thou bring those maidens, and produce them in my sight; for thy deed is a disgrace to me, and to thine own race, and to thy country. Thou hast come unto a city that observes justice, and sanctions nothing without law—yet thou hast put her lawful powers aside, thou hast made this rude inroad, thou art taking captives at thy pleasure, and snatching prizes by violence, as in the belief that my city was void of men, or manned by slaves, and I a thing of nought.

Yet 'tis not by Theban training that thou art base; Thebes is not wont to rear unrighteous sons;

nor would she praise thee, if she learned that thou art spoiling me—yea, spoiling the gods, when by force thou leadest off their hapless suppliants. Now, were my foot upon thy soil, never would I wrest or plunder, without licence from the ruler of the land, whoso he might be—no, though my claim were of all claims most just: I should know how an alien ought to live among citizens. But thou art shaming a city that deserves it not, even thine own; and the fulness of thy years brings thee an old age bereft of wit.

I have said, then, and I say it once again—let the maidens be brought hither with all speed, unless thou wouldst sojourn in this land by no free choice; and this I tell thee from my soul, as with my lips.

Ch. Seest thou thy plight, O stranger? Thou art deemed to come of a just race; but thy deeds are found evil.

Cr. Not counting this city void of manhood, son of Aegeus, nor of counsel—as thou sayest—have I wrought this deed; but because I judged that its folk could never be so enamoured of my kinsfolk as to foster them against my will. And I knew that this people would not receive a parricide, a polluted man, a man with whom had been found the unholy bride of her son. Such the wisdom, I knew, that dwells on the Mount of Ares in their land; which suffers not such wanderers to dwell within this realm. In that faith, I sought to take this prize. Nor had I done so, but that he was calling down bitter curses on me, and on my race; when, being so wronged, I deemed that I had warrant for this requital. For anger knows no old age, till death come; the dead alone feel no smart.

Therefore thou shalt act as seems to thee good; for, though my cause is just, the lack of aid makes me weak: yet, old though I am, I will endeavour to meet deed with deed.

Oed. O shameless soul, where, thinkest thou, falls this thy taunt—on my age, or on thine own? Bloodshed—incest—misery—all this thy lips have launched against me—all this that I have borne, woe is me! by no choice of mine: for such was the pleasure of the gods, wroth, haply, with the race from of old. Take me alone, and thou couldst find no sin to upbraid me withal, in quittance whereof I was driven to sin thus against myself and against my kin. Tell me, now—if, by voice of oracle, some divine doom was coming on my sire, that he should die by a son's hand, how couldst thou justly reproach me therewith, who was then unborn, whom no sire had yet begotten, no mother's womb conceived? And if, when born to woe—as I was born—I met my sire in strife, and slew him, all ignorant what I was doing, and to whom—how couldst thou justly blame the unknowing deed?

And my mother—wretch, hast thou no shame in forcing me to speak of her nuptials, when she was thy sister, and they such as I will now tell—for verily I will not be silent, when thou hast gone so far in impious speech. Yea, she was my mother—oh, misery!—my mother—I knew it not, nor she—and, for her shame, bare children to the son whom she had borne. But one thing, at least, I know—that thy will consents thus to revile her and me; but not of my free will did I wed her, and not of free will do I speak now.

Nay, not in this marriage shall I be called guilty, nor in that slaying of my sire which thou ever urgest against me with bitter reviling. Answer me but one thing that I ask thee. If, here and now, one should come up and seek to slay thee—thee, the righteous—wouldst thou ask if the murderer was thy father, or wouldst thou reckon with him straightway? I think, as thou lovest thy life, thou wouldst requite the culprit, nor look around thee for thy warrant. But such the plight into which *I* came, led by gods; and in this, could my sire come back to life, methinks he would not gainsay me.

Yet *thou*—for thou art not a just man, but one who holds all things meet to utter, knowing no barrier betwixt speech and silence—*thou* tauntest me in such wise, before yon men. And thou findest it timely to flatter the renowned Theseus, and Athens, saying how well her state hath been ordered: yet, while giving such large praise, thou forgettest this—that if any land knows how to worship the gods with due rites, this land excels therein; whence thou hadst planned to steal me, the suppliant, the old man, and didst seek to seize me, and hast already carried off my daughters. Wherefore I now call on yon goddesses, I supplicate them, I adjure them with prayers, to bring me help and to fight in my cause, that thou mayest learn well by what manner of men this realm is guarded.

Ch. The stranger is a good man, O king; his fate hath been accurst; but 'tis worthy of our succour.

Th. Enough of words: the doers of the deed are in flight, while we, the sufferers, stand still.

Cr. What, then, wouldst thou have a helpless man to do?

Th. Show the way in their track—while I escort thee—that, if in these regions thou hast the maidens of our quest, thou thyself mayest discover them to me; but if thy men are fleeing with the spoil in their grasp, we may spare our trouble; the chase is for others, from whom they will never escape out of this land, to thank their gods.

Come—forward! The spoiler hath been spoiled, I tell thee—Fate hath taken the hunter in the toils; gains got by wrongful arts are soon lost. And thou shalt have no ally in thine aim, for well wot I that not without accomplice or resource hast thou gone to such a length of violence in the daring mood which hath inspired thee here: no—there was some one in whom thou wast trusting when thou didst essay these deeds. And to this I must look, nor make this city weaker than one man. Dost thou take my drift? Or seem these words as vain as seemed the warnings when thy deed was still a-planning?

Cr. Say what thou wilt while thou art here—I will not cavil: but at home I, too, will know how to act.

Th. For the present, threaten, but go forward. Do thou, Oedipus, stay here in peace, I pray thee—with my pledge that, unless I die before, I will not cease till I put thee in possession of thy children.

Oed. Heaven reward thee, Theseus, for thy nobleness, and thy loyal care in my behalf!

Exeunt THESEUS *and attendants, with* CREON, *on spectators' left.*

Chorus

Oh to be where the foeman, turned to bay, will soon join in the brazen clangour of battle, haply by the shores loved of Apollo, haply by that torch-lit strand where the Great Goddesses cherish dread rites for mortals, on whose lips the ministrant Eumolpidae have laid the precious seal of silence; where, methinks, the war-waking Theseus and the captives twain, the sister maids, will soon meet within our borders, amid a war-cry of men strong to save!

Or perchance they will soon draw nigh to the pastures on the west of Oea's snowy rock, borne on horses in their flight, or in chariots racing at speed.

Creon will be worsted! Terrible are the warriors of Colonus, and the followers of Theseus are terrible in their might. Yea, the steel of every bridle flashes,—with slack bridle-rein all the knighthood rides apace that worships our Queen of Chivalry, Athena, and the earth-girdling Sea-god, the son of Rhea's love.

Is the battle now, or yet to be? For somehow my soul woos me to the hope that soon I shall be face to face with the maidens thus sorely tried, thus sorely visited by the hand of a kinsman.

To-day, to-day, Zeus will work some great thing: I have presage of victory in the strife. O to be a dove with swift strength as of the storm, that I might reach an airy cloud, with gaze lifted above the fray!

Hear, all-ruling lord of heaven, all-seeing Zeus! Enable the guardians of this land, in might triumphant, to achieve the capture that gives the prize to their hands! So grant thy daughter also, our dread Lady, Pallas Athena! And Apollo, the hunter, and his sister, who follows the dappled, swift-footed deer—fain am I that they should come, a twofold strength, to this land and to her people.

Ah, wanderer friend, thou wilt not have to tax thy watcher with false augury—for yonder I see the maidens drawing near with an escort.

Oed. Where—where? How? What sayest thou?

Enter ANTIGONE *and* ISMENE, *with* THESEUS *and his attendants, on the spectators' left.*

An. O father, father, that some god would suffer thine eyes to see this noble man, who hath brought us here to thee!

Oed. My child!—ye are here indeed?

An. Yea, for these strong arms have saved us—Theseus, and his trusty followers.

Oed. Come ye hither, my child, let me embrace you—restored beyond all hope!

An. Thy wish shall be granted—we crave what we bestow.

Oed. Where, then, where are ye?

An. Here approaching thee together.

Oed. My darlings!

An. A father loves his own.

Oed. Props of mine age!

An. And sharers of thy sorrow.

Oed. I hold my dear ones; and now, should I die, I were not wholly wretched, since ye have come to me. Press close to me on either side, children, cleave to your sire, and repose from this late roaming, so forlorn, so grievous! And tell me what hath passed as shortly as ye may; brief speech sufficeth for young maidens.

An. Here is our deliverer: from him thou shouldst hear the story, father, since his is the deed; so shall my part be brief.

Oed. Sir, marvel not, if with such yearning I prolong my words unto my children, found again beyond my hope. For well I wot that this joy in respect of them hath come to me from thee, and thee alone: thou hast rescued them, and no man beside. And may the gods deal with thee after my wish, with thee and with this land; for among you, above all human kind, have I found the fear of heaven, and the spirit of fairness, and the lips that lie not. I know these things, which with these words I requite; for what I have, I have through thee, and no man else.

Stretch forth thy right hand, O king, I pray thee, that I may touch it, and, if 'tis lawful, kiss thy cheek. But what am I saying? Unhappy as I have become, how could I wish thee to touch one with whom all stain of sin hath made its dwelling? No, not I—nor allow thee, if thou wouldst. They alone can share this burden, to whom it hath come home. Receive my greeting where thou standest; and in the future still give me thy loyal care, as thou hast given it to this hour.

Th. No marvel is it to me, if thou hast shown some mind to large discourse, for joy in these thy children, and if thy first care hath been for their words, rather than for me; indeed, there is nought to vex me in that. Not in words so much as deeds would I make the lustre of my life. Thou hast the proof; I have failed in nothing of my sworn faith to thee, old man; here am I, with the maidens living—yea, scatheless of those threats. And how the fight was won, what need that I should idly boast, when thou wilt learn it from these maidens in converse?

But there is a matter that hath newly chanced to me, as I came hither; lend me thy counsel thereon, for, small though it be, 'tis food for wonder; and mortal man should deem nothing beneath his care.

Oed. What is it, son of Aegeus? Tell me; I myself know nought of that whereof thou askest.

Th. A man, they say—not thy countryman, yet thy kinsman—hath somehow cast himself, a suppliant, at our altar of Poseidon, where I was sacrificing when I first set out hither.

Oed. Of what land is he? What craves he by the supplication?

Th. I know one thing only, they say, he asks brief speech with thee, which shall not irk thee much.

Oed. On what theme? That suppliant posture is not trivial.

Th. He asks, they say, no more than that he may confer with thee, and return unharmed from his journey hither.

Oed. Who can he be who thus implores the god?

Th. Look if ye have any kinsman at Argos, who might crave this boon of thee.

Oed. O friend! Say no word more!

Th. What ails thee?

Oed. Ask it not of me—

Th. Ask what?—Speak!

Oed. By those words I know who is the suppliant.

Th. And who can he be, against whom I should have a grief?

Oed. My son, O king—the hated son whose words would vex mine ear as the words of no man beside.

Th. What? Canst thou not listen, without doing what thou wouldst not? Why should it pain thee to hear him?

Oed. Most hateful, king, hath that voice become to his sire: lay me not under constraint to yield in this.

Th. But think whether his suppliant state constrains thee: what if thou hast a duty of respect for the god?

An. Father, hearken to me, though I be young who counsel. Allow the king to gratify his own heart, and to gratify the god as he wishes; and, for thy daughter's sake, allow our brother to come. For he will not pluck thee perforce from thy resolve—never fear—by such words as shall not be spoken for thy good. But to hear him speak—what harm can be in that? Ill-devised deeds, thou knowest, are bewrayed by speech. Thou art his sire; so that, e'en if he were to wrong thee with the most impious of foul wrongs, my father, it is not lawful for thee to wrong him again.

Oh, let him come: other men, also, have evil offspring, and are swift to wrath; but they hear advice, and are charmed from their mood by the gentle spells of friends.

Look thou to the past, not to the present—think on all that thou hast borne through sire and mother; and if thou considerest those things, well I wot, thou wilt discern how evil is the end that waits on evil wrath; not slight are thy reasons to think thereon, bereft, as thou art, of the sight that returns no more.

Nay, yield to us! It is not seemly for just suitors to sue long; it is not seemly that a man should receive good, and thereafter lack the mind to requite it.

Oed. My child, 'tis sore for me, this pleasure that ye win from me by your pleading; but be it as ye will. Only, if that man is to come hither—friend, let no one ever become master of my life!

Th. I need not to hear such words more than once, old man: I would not boast; but be sure that thy life is safe, while any god saves mine.

Exit THESEUS, *to the right of the spectators.*

Chorus.

Whoso craves the ampler length of life, not content to desire a modest span, him will I judge with no uncertain voice; he cleaves to folly.

For the long days lay up full many things nearer unto grief than joy; but as for thy delights, their place shall know them no more, when a man's life hath lapsed beyond the fitting term; and the Deliverer comes at the last to all alike—when the doom of Hades is suddenly revealed, without marriage-song, or lyre, or dance—even Death at the last.

Not to be born is, past all prizing, best; but, when a man hath seen the light, this is next best by far, that with all speed he should go thither, whence he hath come.

For when he hath seen youth go by, with its light follies, what troublous affliction is strange to his lot, what suffering is not therein?—envy, factions, strife, battles and slaughters; and, last of all, age claims him for her own—age, dispraised, infirm, unsociable, unfriended, with whom all woe of woe abides.

In such years is yon hapless one, not I alone: and as some cape that fronts the North is lashed on every side by the waves of winter, so he also is fiercely lashed evermore by the dread troubles that break on him like billows, some from the setting of the sun, some from the rising, some in the region of the noon-tide beam, some from the gloom-wrapped hills of the North.

An. Lo, yonder, methinks, I see the stranger coming hither—yea, without attendants, my father—the tears streaming from his eyes.

Oed. Who is he?

An. The same who was in our thoughts from the first; Polyneices hath come to us.

Enter POLYNEICES, *on the spectators' left.*

Polyneices. Ah me, what shall I do? Whether shall I weep first for mine own sorrows, sisters, or for mine aged sire's, as I see them yonder? Whom I have found in a strange land, an exile here with you twain, clad in such raiment, whereof the foul squalor hath dwelt with that aged form so long, a very blight upon his flesh—while above the sightless eyes the unkempt hair flutters in the breeze; and matching with these things, meseems, is the food that he carries, hapless one, against hunger's pinch.

Wretch that I am! I learn all this too late: and I bear witness that I am proved the vilest of men in all that touches care for thee: from mine own lips hear what I am. But, seeing that Zeus himself, in all that he doeth, hath Mercy for the sharer of his throne, may she come to thy side also, my father; for the faults can be healed, but can never more be made worse.

(*A pause.*)

Why art thou silent? . . . . Speak, father—turn not away from me. Hast thou not even an answer for me? Wilt thou dismiss me in mute scorn, without telling wherefore thou art wroth?

O ye, his daughters, sisters mine, strive ye, at least, to move our sire's implacable, inexorable silence, that he send me not away dishonoured—who am the suppliant of the god—in such wise as this, with no word of response.

An. Tell him thyself, unhappy one, what thou hast come to seek. As words flow, perchance they touch to joy, perchance they glow with anger, or with tenderness, and so they somehow give a voice to the dumb.

Po. Then will I speak boldly—for thou dost admonish me well—first claiming the help of the god himself, from whose altar the king of this land raised me, that I might come hither, with warranty to speak and hear, and go my way unharmed. And I will crave, strangers, that these pledges be kept with me by you, and by my sisters here, and by my sire. But now I would fain tell thee, father, why I came.

I have been driven, an exile, from my fatherland, because, as eldest-born, I claimed to sit in thy sovereign seat. Wherefore Eteocles, though the younger, thrust me from the land, when he had neither worsted me in argument, nor come to trial of might and deed—no, but won the city over. And of this I deem it most likely that the curse on thy house is the cause; then from soothsayers also I so hear. For when I came to Dorian Argos, I took the daughter of Adrastus to wife; and I bound to me by oath all of the Apian land who are foremost in renown of war, that with them I might levy the sevenfold host of spearmen against Thebes, and die in my just cause, or cast the doers of this wrong from the realm.

Well, and wherefore have I come hither now? With suppliant prayers, my father, unto thee—mine own, and the prayers of mine allies, who now, with seven hosts behind their seven spears, have set their leaguer round the plain of Thebes; of whom is swift-speared Amphiaraus, matchless warrior, matchless augur; then the son of Oeneus, Aetolian Tydeus; Eteoclus third, of Argive birth; the fourth, Hippomedon, sent by Talaos, his sire; while Capaneus, the fifth, vaunts that he will burn Thebes with fire, unto the ground; and sixth, Arcadian Parthenopaeus rushes to the war, named from that virgin of other days whose marriage in after-time gave him birth, trusty son of Atalanta. Last, I, thy son—or if not thine, but offspring of an evil fate, yet thine at least in name—lead the fearless host of Argos unto Thebes.

And we, by these thy children and by thy life, my father, implore thee all, praying thee to remit thy stern wrath against me, as I go forth to chastise my brother, who hath thrust me out and robbed me of my fatherland. For if aught of truth is told by oracles, they said that victory should be with those whom thou shouldst join.

Then, by our fountains and by the gods of our race, I ask thee to hearken and to yield; a beggar and an exile am I, an exile thou; by court to others we have a home, both thou and I, sharers of one doom; while *he*, king in the house—woe is me!—mocks in his pride at thee and me alike. But, if thou assist my purpose, small toil or time, and I will scatter his strength to the winds: and so will I bring thee and stablish thee in thine own house, and stablish myself, when I have cast him out by force. Be thy will with me, and that boast may be mine: without thee, I cannot e'en return alive.

Ch. For his sake who hath sent him, Oedipus, speak, as seems thee good, ere thou send the man away.

Oed. Nay, then, my friends, guardians of this land, were not Theseus he who had sent him hither to me, desiring that he should have my response, never should he have heard this voice. But now he shall be graced with it, ere he go—yea, and hear from me such words as shall never gladden his life: villain, who when thou hadst the sceptre and the throne, which now thy brother hath in Thebes, dravest me, thine own father, into exile, and madest me citiless, and madest me to wear this garb which now thou weepest to behold, when thou hast come unto the same stress of misery as I. The time for tears is past: no, *I* must bear this burden while I live, ever thinking of thee as of a murderer; for 'tis thou that hast brought my days to this anguish, 'tis thou that hast thrust me out; to thee I owe it that I wander, begging my daily bread from strangers. And, had these daughters not been born to be my comfort, verily I had been dead, for aught of help from thee. Now, these girls preserve me, these my nurses, these who are men, not women, in true service: but ye are aliens, and no sons of mine.

Therefore the eyes of Fate look upon thee—not yet as they will look anon, if indeed those hosts are moving against Thebes. Never canst thou overthrow that city; no, first shalt thou fall stained with bloodshed, and thy brother likewise. Such the curses that my soul sent forth before against you twain, and such do I now invoke to fight for me, that ye may deem it meet to revere parents, nor scorn your father utterly, because he is sightless who begat such sons; for these maidens did not thus. So my curses have control of thy "supplication" and thy "throne," if indeed Justice, revealed from of old, sits with Zeus in the might of the eternal laws.

And thou—begone, abhorred of me, and unfathered!—begone, thou vilest of the vile, and with thee take these my curses which I call down on thee—never to vanquish the land of thy race, no, nor ever return to hill-girt Argos, but by a kindred hand to die, and slay him by whom thou hast been driven out. Such is my prayer; and I call the paternal darkness of dread Tartarus to take thee unto another home—I call the spirits of this place—I call the Destroying God, who hath set that dreadful hatred in you twain. Go, with these words in thine ears—go, and publish it to the Cadmeans all, yea, and to thine own staunch allies, that Oedipus hath divided such honours to his sons.

Ch. Polyneices, in thy past goings I take no joy; and now go thy way with speed.

Po. Alas, for my journey and my baffled hope: alas, for my comrades! What an end was that march to have, whereon we sallied forth from Argos: woe is me!—aye, such an end, that I may not even utter it to any of my companions, or turn them back, but must go in silence to meet this doom.

Ah ye, his daughters and my sisters—since ye hear these hard prayers of your sire—if this father's curses be fulfilled, and some way of return to Thebes be found for you, oh, as ye fear the gods, do not, for your part, dishonour me—nay, give me burial, and due funeral rites. And so the praise which ye now win from yonder man, for your service, shall be increased by another praise not less, by reason of the office wrought for me.

An. Polyneices, I entreat thee, hear me in one thing!

Po. What is it, dearest Antigone? Speak!

An. Turn thy host back to Argos—aye, with all speed—and destroy not thyself and Thebes.

Po. Nay, it cannot be: for how again could I lead the same host, when once I had blenched?

An. But why, my brother, should thine anger rise again? What gain is promised thee in destroying thy native city?

Po. 'Tis shame to be an exile, and, eldest born as I am, to be thus mocked on my brother's part.

An. Seest thou, then, to what sure fulfilment thou art bringing his prophecies, who bodes mutual slaying for you twain?

Po. Aye, for he wishes it: but I must not yield.

An. Ah me unhappy! But who will dare to follow thee, hearing what prophecies yon man hath uttered?

Po. I will not e'en report ill tidings: 'tis a good leader's part to tell the better news, and not the worse.

An. Brother! Thy resolve, then, is thus fixed?

Po. Yea—and detain me not. For mine it now shall be to tread yon path, with evil doom and omen from this my sire and from his Furies; but for you twain, may Zeus make your path bright, if ye do my wishes when I am dead—since in my life ye can do them no more. (*He gently disengages himself from their embrace.*) Now, release me, and farewell; for nevermore shall ye behold me living.

An. Woe is me!

Po. Mourn not for me.

An. And who would not bewail thee, brother, who thus art hurrying to death foreseen?

Po. If 'tis fate, I must die.

An. Nay, nay—hear my pleading!

Po. Plead not amiss.

An. Then woe is me, indeed, if I must lose thee!

Po. Nay, that rests with Fortune—that end or another. For you twain, at least, I pray the gods that ye never meet with ill; for in all men's eyes ye are unworthy to suffer.

Exit, on spectators' left.

Ch. Behold, new ills have newly come, in our hearing, from the sightless stranger—ills fraught with a heavy doom; unless, perchance, Fate is finding its goal. For 'tis not mine to say that a decree of Heaven is ever vain: watchful, aye watchful of those decrees is Time, overthrowing some fortunes, and on the morrow lifting others, again, to honour. Hark that sound in the sky! Zeus defend us!

(*Thunder is heard.*)

Oed. My children, my children! If there be any man to send, would that some one would fetch hither the peerless Theseus!

An. And what, father, is the aim of thy summons?

Oed. This winged thunder of Zeus will lead me anon to Hades: nay, send, and tarry not.

(*A second peal is heard.*)

Ch. Hark! With louder noise it crashes down, unutterable, hurled by Zeus! The hair of my head stands up for fear, my soul is sore dismayed; for again the lightning flashes in the sky. Oh, to what event will it give birth? I am afraid, for never in vain doth it rush forth, or without grave issue. O thou dread sky! O Zeus!

Oed. Daughters, his destined end hath come upon your sire; he can turn his face from it no more.

An. How knowest thou? What sign hath told thee this?

Oed. I know it well. But let some one go, I pray you, with all speed, and bring hither the lord of this realm.

(*Another peal.*)

Ch. Ha! Listen! Once again that piercing thunder-voice is around us! Be merciful, O thou god, be merciful, if thou art bringing aught of gloom for the land our mother! Gracious may I find thee, nor, because I have looked on a man accurst, have some meed, not of blessing for my portion! O Zeus our lord, to thee I cry!

Oed. Is the man near? Will he find me still alive, children, and master of my mind?

An. And what is the pledge which thou wouldst have fixed in thy mind?

Oed. In return for his benefits, I would duly give him the requital promised when I received them.

Ch. What ho, my son, hither, come hither! Or if in the glade's inmost recess, for the honour of the sea-god Poseidon, thou art hallowing his altar with sacrifice—come thence! Worthy art thou in the stranger's sight, worthy are thy city and thy folk, that he should render a just recompense for benefits. Haste, come quickly, O king!

Enter THESEUS, *on the spectators' right.*

Th. Wherefore once more rings forth a summons from you all—from my people as clearly as from our guest? Can a thunderbolt from Zeus be the cause, or rushing hail in its fierce onset? All forebodings may find place, when the god sends such a storm.

Oed. King, welcome is thy presence; and 'tis some god that hath made for thee the good fortune of this coming.

Th. And what new thing hath now befallen, son of Laïus?

Oed. My life hangs in the scale: and I fain would die guiltless of bad faith to thee and to this city, in respect of my pledges.

Th. And what sign of thy fate holds thee in suspense?

Oed. The gods, their own heralds, bring me the tidings, with no failure in the signs appointed of old.

Th. What sayest thou are the signs of these things, old man?

Oed. The thunder, peal on peal, the lightning, flash on flash, hurled from the unconquered hand.

Th. Thou winnest my belief, for in much I find thee a prophet whose voice is not false; then speak what must be done.

Oed. Son of Aegeus, I will unfold that which shall be a treasure for this thy city, such as age can never mar. Anon, unaided, and with no hand to guide me, I will show the way to the place where I must die. But that place reveal thou never unto mortal man—tell not where it is hidden, nor in what region it lies; that so it may ever make for thee a defence, better than many shields, better than the succouring spear of neighbours.

But, for mysteries which speech may not profane, thou shalt mark them for thyself, when thou comest to that place alone: since neither to any of this people can I utter them, nor to mine own children, dear though they are. No, guard them thou alone; and when thou art coming to the end of life, disclose them to thy heir alone; let him teach his heir; and so thenceforth.

And thus shalt thou hold this city unscathed from the side of the Dragon's brood; full many States lightly enter on offence, e'en though their neighbour lives aright. For the gods are slow, though they are sure, in visitation, when men scorn godliness, and turn to frenzy. Not such be thy fate, son of Aegeus. Nay, thou knowest such things, without my precepts.

But to that place—for the divine summons urges me—let us now set forth, and hesitate no more. (*As if suddenly inspired, he moves with slow but firm steps towards the left of the scene, beckoning the others onward.*) My children, follow me—thus—for I now have in strange wise been made your guide, as ye were your sire's. On—touch me not—nay, suffer me unaided to find out that sacred tomb where 'tis my portion to be buried in this land.

This way—hither, this way!—for this way doth Guiding Hermes lead me, and the goddess of the dead!

O light—no light to me—mine once thou wast, I ween, but now my body feels thee for the last time! For now go I to hide the close of my life with Hades. Truest of friends! blessed be thou, and this land, and thy lieges; and, when your days are blest, think on me the dead, for your welfare evermore.

He passes from the stage on the spectators' left, followed by his daughters, THESEUS, *and attendants.*

Ch. If with prayer I may adore the Unseen Goddess, and thee, lord of the children of night, O hear me, Aïdoneus, Aïdoneus! Not in pain, not by a doom that wakes sore lament, may the stranger pass to the fields of the dead below, the all-enshrouding, and to the Stygian house. Many were the sorrows that came to him without cause; but in requital a just god will lift him up.

Goddesses Infernal! And thou, dread form of the unconquered hound, thou who hast thy lair in those gates of many guests, thou untameable Watcher of Hell, gnarling from the cavern's jaws, as rumour from the beginning tells of thee!

Hear me, O Death, son of Earth and Tartarus! May that Watcher leave a clear path for the stranger on his way to the nether fields of the dead! To thee I call, giver of the eternal sleep.

Enter a MESSENGER, *from the left.*

Messenger. Countrymen, my tidings might most shortly be summed thus: Oedipus is gone. But the story of the hap may not be told in brief words, as the deeds yonder were not briefly done.

Ch. He is gone, hapless one?

Me. Be sure that he hath passed from life.

Ch. Ah, how? by a god-sent doom, and painless?

Me. There thou touchest on what is indeed worthy of wonder. How he moved hence, thou thyself must know, since thou wast here—with no friend to show the way, but guide himself unto us all.

Now, when he had come to the sheer Threshold, bound by brazen steps to earth's deep roots, he paused in one of many branching paths, near the basin in the rock, where the inviolate covenant of Theseus and Peirithous hath its memorial. He stood midway between that basin and the Thorician stone—the hollow pear-tree and the marble tomb; then sate him down, and loosed his sordid raiment.

And then he called his daughters, and bade them fetch water from some fount, that he should wash, and make a drink-offering. And they went to the hill which was in view, Demeter's hill who guards the tender plants, and in short space brought that which their father had enjoined; then they ministered to him with washing, and dressed him, as use ordains.

But when he had content of doing all, and no part of his desire was now unheeded, then was thunder from the Zeus of the Shades: and the maidens shuddered as they heard; they fell at their father's knees, and wept, nor ceased from beating the breast, and wailing very sore.

And when he heard their sudden bitter cry, he put his arms around them, and said: "My children, this day ends your father's life. For now all hath perished that was mine, and no more shall ye bear the burden of tending me, no light one, well I know, my children; yet one little word makes all those toils as nought; *love* had ye from me, as from none beside; and now ye shall have me with you no more, through all your days to come."

On such wise, close-clinging to each other, sire and daughters sobbed and wept. But when they had made an end of wailing, and the sound went up no more, there was a stillness; and suddenly a voice of one who cried aloud to him, so that the hair of all stood up on their heads for sudden fear, and they were afraid. For the god called him with many callings and manifold: "*Oedipus, Oedipus, why delay we to go? Thou tarriest too long.*"

But when he perceived that he was called of the god, he craved that the king Theseus should draw near; and when he came near, said: "O my friend, give, I pray thee, the solemn pledge of thy right hand to my children, and ye, daughters, to him; and promise thou never to forsake them of thy free will, but to do all things for their good, as thy friendship and the time may prompt." And he, like a man of noble spirit, without making lament, sware to keep that promise to his friend.

But when Theseus had so promised, straightway Oedipus felt for his children with blind hands, and said: "O my children, ye must be nobly brave of heart, and depart from this place, nor ask to behold unlawful sights, or to hear such speech as may not be heard. Nay, go with all haste; only let Theseus be present, as is his right, a witness of those things which are to be."

So spake he, and we all heard; and with streaming tears and with lamentation we followed the maidens away. But when we had gone apart, after no long time we looked back, and Oedipus we saw nowhere any more, but the king alone, holding his hand before his face to screen his eyes, as if some dread sight had been seen, and such as none might endure to behold. And then, after a short space, we saw him salute the earth and the home of the gods above, both at once, in one prayer.

But by what doom Oedipus perished, no man can tell, save Theseus alone. No fiery thunderbolt of the god removed him in that hour, nor any rising of storm from the sea; but either a messenger from the gods, or the world of the dead, the nether adamant, riven for him in love, without pain; for the passing of the man was not with lamentation, or in sickness and suffering, but, above mortal's, wonderful. And if to any I seem to speak folly, I would not woo their belief, who count me foolish.

Ch. And where are the maidens, and their escort?

Me. Not far hence; for the sounds of mourning tell plainly that they approach.

ANTIGONE *and* ISMENE *enter*.

An. Woe, woe! Now, indeed, is it for us, unhappy sisters, in all fulness to bewail the curse on the blood that is ours from our sire! For him, while he lived, we bore that long pain without pause; and at the last a sight and a loss that baffle thought are ours to tell.

Ch. And how is it with you?

An. We can but conjecture, friends.

Ch. He is gone?

An. Even as thou mightest wish: yea, surely, when death met him not in war, or on the deep, but he was snatched to the viewless fields by some swift, strange doom. Ah me! and a night as of death hath come on the eyes of us twain: for how shall we find our bitter livelihood, roaming to some far land, or on the waves of the sea?

Is. I know not. Oh that deadly Hades would join me in death unto mine aged sire! Woe is me! I cannot live the life that must be mine.

Ch. Best of daughters, sisters twain, Heaven's doom must be borne: be no more fired with too much grief: ye have so fared that ye should not repine.

An. Ah, so care past can seem lost joy! For that which was no way sweet had sweetness, while therewith I held *him* in mine embrace. Ah, father, dear one, ah thou who hast put on the darkness of the under-world for ever, not even there shalt thou ever lack our love—her love and mine.

Ch. He hath fared—

An. He hath fared as he would.

Ch. In what wise?

An. On foreign ground, the ground of his choice, he hath died; in the shadow of the grave he hath his bed for ever; and he hath left mourning behind him, not barren of tears. For with these streaming eyes, father, I bewail thee; nor know I, ah me, how to quell my sorrow for thee, my sorrow that is so great. Ah me! 'twas thy wish to die in a strange land; but now thou hast died without gifts at my hand.

Is. Woe is me! What new fate, think'st thou, awaits thee and me, my sister, thus orphaned of our sire?

Ch. Nay, since he hath found a blessed end, my children, cease from this lament; no mortal is hard for evil fortune to capture.

An. Sister, let us hasten back.

Is. Unto what deed?

An. A longing fills my soul.

Is. Whereof?

An. To see the dark home—

Is. Of whom?

An. Ah me! of our sire.

Is. And how can this thing be lawful? Hast thou no understanding?

An. Why this reproof?

Is. And knowest thou not this also—

An. What wouldst thou tell me more?

Is. That he was perishing without tomb, apart from all?

An. Lead me thither, and then slay me also.

Is. Ah me unhappy! Friendless and helpless, where am I now to live my hapless life?

Ch. My children, fear not.

An. But whither am I to flee?

Ch. Already a refuge hath been found—

An. How meanest thou?

Ch. —for your fortunes, that no harm should touch them.

An. I know it well.

Ch. What, then, is thy thought?

An. How we are to go home, I cannot tell.

Ch. And do not seek to go.

An. Trouble besets us.

Ch. And erstwhile bore hardly on you.

An. Desperate then, and now more cruel than despair.

Ch. Great, verily, is the sea of your troubles.

An. Alas, alas! O Zeus, whither shall we turn? To what last hope doth fate now urge us?

Enter THESEUS, *on the spectators' right*.

Th. Weep no more, maidens; for where the kindness of the Dark Powers is an abiding grace to the quick and to the dead, there is no room for mourning; divine anger would follow.

An. Son of Aegeus, we supplicate thee!

Th. For the obtaining of what desire, my children?

An. We fain would look with our own eyes upon our father's tomb.

Th. Nay, it is not lawful.

An. How sayest thou, king, lord of Athens?

Th. My children, he gave me charge that no one should draw nigh unto that place, or greet with voice the sacred tomb wherein he sleeps. And he said that, while I duly kept that word, I should always hold the land unharmed. These pledges, therefore, were heard from my lips by the god, and by the all-seeing Watcher of oaths, the servant of Zeus.

An. Nay, then, if this is pleasing to the dead, with this we must content us. But send us to Thebes the ancient, if haply we may hinder the bloodshed that is threatened to our brothers.

Th. So will I do; and if in aught beside I can profit you, and pleasure the dead who hath lately gone from us, I am bound to spare no pains.

Ch. Come, cease lamentation, lift it up no more; for verily these things stand fast.

ANTIGONE

DRAMATIS PERSONAE

ANTIGONE | ISMENE — *daughters of Oedipus*

CREON, *King of Thebes*

EURYDICE, *his wife*

HAEMON, *his son*

TEIRESIAS, *the blind prophet*

GUARD, *set to watch the corpse of Polyneices*

FIRST MESSENGER

SECOND MESSENGER, *from the house*

CHORUS OF THEBAN ELDERS

Before the Royal Palace at Thebes. ANTIGONE *calls* ISMENE *forth from the palace in order to speak to her alone.*

Antigone. Ismene, sister, mine own dear sister, knowest thou what ill there is, of all bequeathed by Oedipus, that Zeus fulfils not for us twain while we live? Nothing painful is there, nothing fraught with ruin, no shame, no dishonour, that I have not seen in thy woes and mine.

And now what new edict is this of which they tell, that our Captain hath just published to all Thebes? Knowest thou aught? Hast thou heard? Or is it hidden from thee that our friends are threatened with the doom of our foes?

Ismene. No word of friends, Antigone, gladsome or painful, hath come to me, since we two sisters were bereft of brothers twain, killed in one day by a twofold blow; and since in this last night the Argive host hath fled, I know no more, whether my fortune be brighter, or more grievous.

An. I knew it well, and therefore sought to bring thee beyond the gates of the court, that thou mightest hear alone.

Is. What is it? 'Tis plain that thou art brooding on some dark tidings.

An. What, hath not Creon destined our brothers, the one to honoured burial, the other to unburied shame? Eteocles, they say, with due observance of right and custom, he hath laid in the earth, for his honour among the dead below. But the hapless corpse of Polyneices—as rumour saith, it hath been published to the town that none shall entomb him or mourn, but leave unwept, unsepulchred, a welcome store for the birds, as they espy him, to feast on at will.

Such, 'tis said, is the edict that the good Creon hath set forth for thee and for me—yes, for *me*—and is coming hither to proclaim it clearly to those who know it not; nor counts the matter light, but, whoso disobeys in aught, his doom is death by stoning before all the folk. Thou knowest it now; and thou wilt soon show whether thou art nobly bred, or the base daughter of a noble line.

Is. Poor sister—and if things stand thus, what could I help to do or undo?

An. Consider if thou wilt share the toil and the deed.

Is. In what venture? What can be thy meaning?

An. Wilt thou aid this hand to lift the dead?

Is. Thou wouldst bury him—when 'tis forbidden to Thebes?

An. I will do my part—and thine, if thou wilt not—to a brother. False to him will I never be found.

Is. Ah, over-bold! when Creon hath forbidden?

An. Nay, he hath no right to keep me from mine own.

Is. Ah me! think, sister, how our father perished, amid hate and scorn, when sins bared by his own search had moved him to strike both eyes with self-blinding hand; then the mother wife, two names in one, with twisted noose did despite unto her life; and last, our two brothers in one day—each shedding, hapless one, a kinsman's blood—wrought out with mutual hands their common doom. And now *we* in turn—we two left all alone—think how we shall perish, more miserably than all the rest, if, in defiance of the law, we brave a king's decree or his powers. Nay, we must remember, first, that we were born women, as who should not strive with men; next, that we are ruled of the stronger, so that we must obey in these things, and in things yet sorer. I, therefore, asking the Spirits Infernal to pardon, seeing that force is put on me herein, will hearken to our rulers; for 'tis witless to be over busy.

An. I will not urge thee—no, nor, if thou yet shouldst have the mind, wouldst thou be welcome as a worker with *me*. Nay, be what thou wilt; but I will bury him: well for me to die in doing that. I shall rest, a loved one with him whom I have loved, sinless in my crime; for I owe a longer allegiance to the dead than to the living: in that world I shall abide for ever. But if *thou* wilt, be guilty of dishonouring laws which the gods have stablished in honour.

Is. I do them no dishonour; but to defy the State—I have no strength for that.

An. Such be thy plea: I, then, will go to heap the earth above the brother whom I love.

Is. Alas, unhappy one! How I fear for thee!

An. Fear not for me: guide thine own fate aright.

Is. At least, then, disclose this plan to none, but hide it closely—and so, too, will I.

An. Oh, denounce it! Thou wilt be far more hateful for thy silence, if thou proclaim not these things to all.

Is. Thou hast a hot heart for chilling deeds.

An. I know that I please where I am most bound to please.

Is. Aye, if thou canst; but thou wouldst what thou canst not.

An. Why, then, when my strength fails, I shall have done.

Is. A hopeless quest should not be made at all.

An. If thus thou speakest, thou wilt have hatred from me, and will justly be subject to the lasting hatred of the dead. But leave me, and the folly that is mine alone, to suffer this dread thing; for I shall not suffer aught so dreadful as an ignoble death.

Is. Go, then, if thou must; and of this be sure—that, though thine errand is foolish, to thy dear ones thou art truly dear.

Exit ANTIGONE *on the spectators' left.* ISMENE *retires into the palace by one of the two side doors. When they have departed, the* CHORUS OF THEBAN ELDERS *enters.*

Chorus

Beam of the sun, fairest light that ever dawned on Thebè of the seven gates, thou hast shone forth at last, eye of golden day, arisen above Dircè's streams! The warrior of the white shield, who came from Argos in his panoply, hath been stirred by thee to headlong flight, in swifter career;

who set forth against our land by reason of the vexed claims of Polyneices; and, like shrill-screaming eagle, he flew over into our land, in snow-white pinion sheathed, with an armed throng, and with plumage of helms.

He paused above our dwellings; he ravened around our sevenfold portals with spears athirst for blood; but he went hence, or ever his jaws were glutted with our gore, or the Fire-god's pine-fed flame had seized our crown of towers. So fierce was the noise of battle raised behind him, a thing too hard for him to conquer, as he wrestled with his dragon foe.

For Zeus utterly abhors the boasts of a proud tongue; and when he beheld them coming on in a great stream, in the haughty pride of clanging gold, he smote with brandished fire one who was now hasting to shout victory at his goal upon our ramparts.

Swung down, he fell on the earth with a crash, torch in hand, he who so lately, in the frenzy of the mad onset, was raging against us with the blasts of his tempestuous hate. But those threats fared not as he hoped; and to other foes the mighty War-god dispensed their several dooms, dealing havoc around, a mighty helper at our need.

For seven captains at seven gates matched against seven, left the tribute of their panoplies to Zeus who turns the battle; save those two of cruel fate, who, born of one sire and one mother, set against each other their twain conquering spears, and are sharers in a common death.

But since Victory of glorious name hath come to us, with joy responsive to the joy of Thebè whose chariots are many, let us enjoy forgetfulness after the late wars, and visit all the temples of the gods with night-long dance and song; and may Bacchus be our leader, whose dancing shakes the land of Thebè.

But lo, the king of the land comes yonder, Creon, son of Menoeceus, our new ruler by the new fortunes that the gods have given; what counsel is he pondering, that he hath proposed this special conference of elders, summoned by his general mandate?

Enter CREON, *from the central doors of the palace, in the garb of king; with two attendants.*

Creon. Sirs, the vessel of our State, after being tossed on wild waves, hath once more been safely steadied by the gods: and ye, out of all the folk, have been called apart by my summons, because I knew, first of all, how true and constant was your reverance for the royal power of Laïus; how, again, when Oedipus was ruler of our land, and when he had perished, your steadfast loyalty still upheld their children. Since, then, his sons have fallen in one day by a twofold doom—each smitten by the other, each stained with a brother's blood—I now possess the throne and all its powers, by nearness of kinship to the dead.

No man can be fully known, in soul and spirit and mind, until he hath been seen versed in rule and lawgiving. For if any, being supreme guide of the State, cleaves not to the best counsels, but, through some fear, keeps his lips locked, I hold, and have ever held, him most base; and if any makes a friend of more account than his fatherland, that man hath no place in my regard. For I—be Zeus my witness, who sees all things always—would not be silent if I saw ruin, instead of safety, coming to the citizens; nor would I ever deem the country's foes a friend to myself; remembering this, that our country is the ship that bears us safe, and that only while she prospers in our voyage can we make true friends.

Such are the rules by which I guard this city's greatness. And in accord with them is the edict which I have now published to the folk touching the sons of Oedipus; that Eteocles, who hath fallen fighting for our city, in all renown of arms, shall be entombed, and crowned with every rite that follows the noblest dead to their rest. But for his brother, Polyneices—who came back from exile, and sought to consume utterly with fire the city of his fathers and the shrines of his fathers' gods—sought to taste of kindred blood, and to lead the remnant into slavery; touching this man, it hath been proclaimed to our people that none shall grace him with sepulture or lament, but leave him unburied, a corpse for birds and dogs to eat, a ghastly sight of shame.

Such the spirit of my dealing; and never, by deed of mine, shall the wicked stand in honour before the just; but whoso hath good will to Thebes, he shall be honoured of me, in his life and in his death.

Ch. Such is thy pleasure, Creon, son of Menoeceus, touching this city's foe, and its friend; and thou hast power, I ween, to take what order thou wilt, both for the dead, and for all us who live.

Cr. See, then, that ye be guardians of the mandate.

Ch. Lay the burden of this task on some younger man.

Cr. Nay, watchers of the corpse have been found.

Ch. What, then, is this further charge that thou wouldst give?

Cr. That ye side not with the breakers of these commands.

Ch. No man is so foolish that he is enamoured of death.

Cr. In sooth, that is the meed; yet lucre hath oft ruined men through their hopes.

Enter GUARD.

Guard. My liege, I will not say that I come breathless from speed, or that I have plied a nimble foot; for often did my thoughts make me pause, and wheel round in my path, to return. My mind was holding large discourse with me; "Fool, why goest thou to thy certain doom?" "Wretch, tarrying again? And if Creon hears this from another, must not thou smart for it?" So debating, I went on my way with lagging steps, and thus a short road was made long. At last, however, it carried the day that I should come hither—to thee; and, though my tale be nought, yet will I tell it; for I come with a good grip on one hope—that I can suffer nothing but what is my fate.

Cr. And what is it that disquiets thee thus?

Gu. I wish to tell thee first about myself—I did not do the deed—I did not see the doer—it were not right that I should come to any harm.

Cr. Thou hast a shrewd eye for thy mark; well dost thou fence thyself round against the blame: clearly thou hast some strange thing to tell.

Gu. Aye, truly; dread news makes one pause long.

Cr. Then tell it, wilt thou, and so get thee gone?

Gu. Well, this is it. The corpse—some one hath just given it burial, and gone away, after sprinkling thirsty dust on the flesh, with such other rites as piety enjoins.

Cr. What sayest thou? What living man hath dared this deed?

Gu. I know not; no stroke of pickaxe was seen there, no earth thrown up by mattock; the ground was hard and dry, unbroken, without track of wheels; the doer was one who had left no trace. And when the first day-watchman showed it to us, sore wonder fell on all. The dead man was veiled from us; not shut within a tomb, but lightly strewn with dust, as by the hand of one who shunned a curse. And no sign met the eye as though any beast of prey or any dog had come nigh to him, or torn him.

Then evil words flew fast and loud among us, guard accusing guard; and it would e'en have come to blows at last, nor was there any to hinder. Every man was the culprit, and no one was convicted, but all disclaimed knowledge of the deed. And we were ready to take red-hot iron in our hands—to walk through fire; to make oath by the gods that we had not done the deed—that we were not privy to the planning or the doing.

At last, when all our searching was fruitless, one spake, who made us all bend our faces on the earth in fear; for we saw not how we could gainsay him, or escape mischance if we obeyed. His counsel was that this deed must be reported to thee, and not hidden. And this seemed best; and the lot doomed my hapless self to win this prize. So here I stand, as unwelcome as unwilling, well I wot; for no man delights in the bearer of bad news.

Ch. O king, my thoughts have long been whispering, can this deed, perchance, be e'en the work of gods?

Cr. Cease, ere thy words fill me utterly with wrath, lest thou be found at once an old man and foolish. For thou sayest what is not to be borne, in saying that the gods have care for this corpse. Was it for high reward of trusty service that they sought to hide his nakedness, who came to burn their pillared shrines and sacred treasures, to burn their land, and scatter its laws to the winds? Or dost thou behold the gods honouring the wicked? It cannot be. No! From the first there were certain in the town that muttered against me, chafing at this edict, wagging their heads in secret; and kept not their necks duly under the yoke, like men contented with my sway. 'Tis by them, well I know, that these have been beguiled and bribed to do this deed. Nothing so evil as money ever grew to be current among men. This lays cities low, this drives men from their homes, this trains and warps honest souls till they set themselves to works of shame; this still teaches folk to practice villanies, and to know every godless deed.

But all the men who wrought this thing for hire have made it sure that, soon or late, they shall pay the price. Now, as Zeus still hath my reverence, know this—I tell it thee on my oath: If ye find not the very author of this burial, and produce him before mine eyes, death alone shall not be enough for you, till first, hung up alive, ye have revealed this outrage—that henceforth ye may thieve with better knowledge whence lucre should be won, and learn that it is not well to love gain from every source. For thou wilt find that ill-gotten pelf brings more men to ruin than to weal.

Gu. May I speak? Or shall I just turn and go?

Cr. Knowest thou not that even now thy voice offends?

Gu. Is thy smart in the ears, or in the soul?

Cr. And why wouldst thou define the seat of my pain?

Gu. The doer vexes thy mind, but I, thine ears.

Cr. Ah, thou art a born babbler, 'tis well seen.

Gu. May be, but never the doer of this deed.

Cr. Yea, and more—the seller of thy life for silver.

Gu. Alas! 'Tis sad, truly, that he who judges should misjudge.

Cr. Let thy fancy play with "judgment" as it will; but, if ye show me not the doers of these things, ye shall avow that dastardly gains work sorrows. *Exit.*

Gu. Well, may he be found! so 'twere best. But, be he caught or be he not—fortune must settle that—truly thou wilt not see me here again. Saved, even now, beyond hope and thought, I owe the gods great thanks. *Exit.*

Chorus

Wonders are many, and none is more wonderful than man; the power that crosses the white sea, driven by the stormy south-wind, making a path under surges that threaten to engulf him; and Earth, the eldest of the gods, the immortal, the unwearied, doth he wear, turning the soil with the offspring of horses, as the ploughs go to and fro from year to year.

And the light-hearted race of birds, and the tribes of savage beasts, and the sea-brood of the deep, he snares in the meshes of his woven toils, he leads captive, man excellent in wit. And he masters by his arts the beast whose lair is in the wilds, who roams the hills; he tames the horse of shaggy mane, he puts the yoke upon its neck, he tames the tireless mountain bull.

And speech, and wind-swift thought, and all the moods that mould a state, hath he taught himself; and how to flee the arrows of the frost, when 'tis hard lodging under the clear sky, and the arrows of the rushing rain; yea, he hath resource for all; without resource he meets nothing that must come: only against Death shall he call for aid in vain; but from baffling maladies he hath devised escapes.

Cunning beyond fancy's dream is the fertile skill which brings him, now to evil, now to good. When he honours the laws of the land, and that justice which he hath sworn by the gods to uphold, proudly stands his city: no city hath he who, for his rashness, dwells with sin. Never may he share my hearth, never think my thoughts, who doth these things!

Enter the GUARD *on the spectators' left, leading in* ANTIGONE.

What portent from the gods is this?—my soul is amazed. I know her—how can I deny that yon maiden is Antigone?

O hapless, and child of hapless sire—of Oedipus! What means this? Thou brought a prisoner?—thou, disloyal to the king's laws, and taken in folly?

Gu. Here she is, the doer of the deed—we caught this girl burying him—but where is Creon?

Ch. Lo, he comes forth again from the house, at our need.

Enter CREON.

Cr. What is it? What hath chanced, that makes my coming timely?

Gu. O king, against nothing should men pledge their word; for the after-thought belies the first intent. I could have vowed that I should not soon be here again, scared by thy threats, with which I had just been lashed: but—since the joy that surprises and transcends our hopes is like in fulness to no other pleasure—I have come, though 'tis in breach of my sworn oath, bringing this maid; who was taken showing grace to the dead. This time there was no casting of lots; no, this luck hath fallen to me, and to none else. And now, sire, take her thyself, question her, examine her, as thou wilt; but I have a right to free and final quittance of this trouble.

Cr. And thy prisoner here—how and whence hast thou taken her?

Gu. She was burying the man; thou knowest all.

Cr. Dost thou mean what thou sayest? Dost thou speak aright?

Gu. I saw her burying the corpse that thou hadst forbidden to bury. Is that plain and clear?

Cr. And how was she seen? how taken in the act?

Gu. It befell on this wise. When we had come to the place—with those dread menaces of thine upon us—we swept away all the dust that covered the corpse, and bared the dank body well; and then sat us down on the brow of the hill, to windward, heedful that the smell from him should not strike us; every man was wide awake, and kept his neighbour alert with torrents of threats, if any one should be careless of this task.

So went it, until the sun's bright orb stood in mid-heaven, and the heat began to burn: and then suddenly a whirlwind lifted from the earth a storm of dust, a trouble in the sky, and filled the plain, marring all the leafage of its woods; and the wide air was choked therewith: we closed our eyes, and bore the plague from the gods.

And when, after a long while, this storm had passed, the maid was seen; and she cried aloud with the sharp cry of a bird in its bitterness—even as when, within the empty nest, it sees the bed stripped of its nestlings. So she also, when she saw the corpse bare, lifted up a voice of wailing, and called down curses on the doers of that deed. And straightway she brought thirsty dust in her hands; and from a shapely ewer of bronze, held high, with thrice-poured drink-offering she crowned the dead.

We rushed forward when we saw it, and at once closed upon our quarry, who was in no wise dismayed. Then we taxed her with her past and present doings; and she stood not on denial of aught—at once to my joy and to my pain. To have escaped from ills one's self is a great joy; but 'tis painful to bring friends to ill. Howbeit, all such things are of less account to me than mine own safety.

Cr. Thou—thou whose face is bent to earth—dost thou avow, or disavow, this deed?

An. I avow it; I make no denial.

Cr. (*To* GUARD.) Thou canst betake thee whither thou wilt, free and clear of a grave charge.

Exit GUARD.

(*To* ANTIGONE.) Now, tell me thou—not in many words, but briefly—knewest thou that an edict had forbidden this?

An. I knew it: could I help it? It was public.

Cr. And thou didst indeed dare to transgress that law?

An. Yes; for it was not Zeus that had published me that edict; not such are the laws set among men by the Justice who dwells with the gods below; nor deemed I that thy decrees were of such force, that a mortal could override the unwritten and unfailing statutes of heaven. For their life is not of to-day or yesterday, but from all time, and no man knows when they were first put forth.

Not through dread of any human pride could I answer to the gods for breaking *these*. Die I must—I knew that well (how should I not?)—even without thy edicts. But if I am to die before my time, I count that a gain: for when any one lives, as I do, compassed about with evils, can such an one find aught but gain in death?

So for me to meet this doom is trifling grief; but if I had suffered my mother's son to lie in death an unburied corpse, that would have grieved me; for this, I am not grieved. And if my present deeds are foolish in thy sight, it may be that a foolish judge arraigns my folly.

Ch. The maid shows herself passionate child of passionate sire, and knows not how to bend before troubles.

Cr. Yet I would have thee know that o'er-stubborn spirits are most often humbled; 'tis the stiffest iron, baked to hardness in the fire, that thou shalt oftenest see snapped and shivered; and I have known horses that show temper brought to order by a little curb; there is no room for pride, when thou art thy neighbour's slave. This girl was already versed in insolence when she transgressed the laws that had been set forth; and, that done, lo, a second insult—to vaunt of this, and exult in her deed.

Now verily I am no man, she is the man, if this victory shall rest with her, and bring no penalty. No! be she sister's child, or nearer to me in blood than any that worships Zeus at the altar of our house—she and her kinsfolk shall not avoid a doom most dire; for indeed I charge that other with a like share in the plotting of this burial.

And summon her—for I saw her e'en now within, raving, and not mistress of her wits. So oft, before the deed, the mind stands self-convicted in its treason, when folks are plotting mischief in the dark. But verily this, too, is hateful—when one who hath been caught in wickedness then seeks to make the crime a glory.

An. Wouldst thou do more than take and slay me?

Cr. No more, indeed; having that, I have all.

An. Why then dost thou delay? In thy discourse there is nought that pleases me—never may there be—and so my words must needs be unpleasing to thee. And yet, for glory—whence could I have won a nobler, than by giving burial to mine own brother? All here would own that they thought it well, were not their lips sealed by fear. But royalty, blest in so much besides, hath the power to do and say what it will.

Cr. Thou differest from all these Thebans in that view.

An. These also share it; but they curb their tongues for thee.

Cr. And art thou not ashamed to act apart from them?

An. No; there is nothing shameful in piety to a brother.

Cr. Was it not a brother, too, that died in the opposite cause?

An. Brother by the same mother and the same sire.

Cr. Why, then, dost thou render a grace that is impious in his sight?

An. The dead man will not say that he so deems it.

Cr. Yea, if thou makest him but equal in honour with the wicked.

An. It was his brother, not his slave, that perished.

Cr. Wasting this land; while *he* fell as its champion.

An. Nevertheless, Hades desires these rites.

Cr. But the good desires not a like portion with the evil.

An. Who knows but this seems blameless in the world below?

Cr. A foe is never a friend—not even in death.

An. 'Tis not my nature to join in hating, but in loving.

Cr. Pass, then, to the world of the dead, and, if thou must needs love, love them. While I live, no woman shall rule me.

Enter ISMENE *from the house, led in by two attendants.*

Ch. Lo, yonder Ismene comes forth, shedding such tears as fond sisters weep; a cloud upon her brow casts its shadow over her darkly-flushing face, and breaks in rain on her fair cheek.

Cr. And thou, who, lurking like a viper in my house, wast secretly draining my life-blood, while I knew not that I was nurturing two pests, to rise against my throne—come, tell me now, wilt thou also confess thy part in this burial, or wilt thou forswear all knowledge of it?

Is. I have done the deed—if she allows my claim—and share the burden of the charge.

An. Nay, justice will not suffer thee to do that: thou didst not consent to the deed, nor did I give thee part in it.

Is. But, now that ills beset thee, I am not ashamed to sail the sea of trouble at thy side.

An. Whose was the deed, Hades and the dead are witnesses: a friend in words is not the friend that I love.

Is. Nay, sister, reject me not, but let me die with thee, and duly honour the dead.

An. Share not thou my death, nor claim deeds to which thou hast not put thy hand: my death will suffice.

Is. And what life is dear to me, bereft of thee?

An. Ask Creon; all thy care is for him.

Is. Why vex me thus, when it avails thee nought?

An. Indeed, if I mock, 'tis with pain that I mock thee.

Is. Tell me—how can I serve thee, even now?

An. Save thyself: I grudge not thy escape.

Is. Ah, woe is me! And shall I have no share in thy fate?

An. Thy choice was to live; mine, to die.

Is. At least thy choice was not made without my protest.

An. One world approved thy wisdom; another, mine.

Is. Howbeit, the offence is the same for both of us.

An. Be of good cheer; thou livest; but my life hath long been given to death, that so I might serve the dead.

Cr. Lo, one of these maidens hath newly shown herself foolish, as the other hath been since her life began.

Is. Yea, O king, such reason as nature may have given abides not with the unfortunate, but goes astray.

Cr. Thine did, when thou chosest vile deeds with the vile.

Is. What life could I endure, without her presence?

Cr. Nay, speak not of her "presence"; she lives no more.

Is. But wilt thou slay the betrothed of thine own son?

Cr. Nay, there are other fields for him to plough.

Is. But there can never be such love as bound him to her.

Cr. I like not an evil wife for my son.

An. Haemon, beloved! How thy father wrongs thee!

Cr. Enough, enough of thee and of thy marriage!

Ch. Wilt thou indeed rob thy son of this maiden?

Cr. 'Tis Death that shall stay these bridals for me.

Ch. 'Tis determined, it seems, that she shall die.

Cr. Determined, yes, for thee and for me. (*To the two attendants.*) No more delay—servants, take them within! Henceforth they must be women, and not range at large; for verily even the bold seek to fly, when they see Death now closing on their life.

Exeunt attendants, guarding ANTIGONE *and* ISMENE. CREON *remains.*

Chorus

Blest are they whose days have not tasted of evil. For when a house hath once been shaken from heaven, there the curse fails nevermore, passing from life to life of the race; even as, when the surge is driven over the darkness of the deep by the fierce breath of Thracian sea-winds, it rolls up the black sand from the depths, and there is a sullen roar from wind-vexed headlands that front the blows of the storm.

I see that from olden time the sorrows in the house of the Labdacidae are heaped upon the sorrows of the dead; and generation is not freed by generation, but some god strikes them down, and the race hath no deliverance.

For now that hope of which the light had been spread above the last root of the house of Oedipus—that hope, in turn, is brought low—by the blood-stained dust due to the gods infernal, and by folly in speech, and frenzy at the heart.

Thy power, O Zeus, what human trespass can limit? That power which neither Sleep, the all-ensnaring, nor the untiring months of the gods can master; but thou, a ruler to whom time brings not old age, dwellest in the dazzling splendour of Olympus.

And through the future, near and far, as through the past, shall this law hold good: Nothing that is vast enters into the life of mortals without a curse.

For that hope whose wanderings are so wide is to many men a comfort, but to many a false lure of giddy desires; and the disappointment comes on one who knoweth nought till he burn his foot against the hot fire.

For with wisdom hath some one given forth the famous saying, that evil seems good, soon or late, to him whose mind the god draws to mischief; and but for the briefest space doth he fare free of woe.

But lo, Haemon, the last of thy sons; comes he grieving for the doom, of his promised bride, Antigone, and bitter for the baffled hope of his marriage?

Enter HAEMON.

Cr. We shall know soon, better than seers could tell us. My son, hearing the fixed doom of thy betrothed, art thou come in rage against thy father? Or have I thy good will, act how I may?

Haemon. Father, I am thine; and thou, in thy wisdom, tracest for me rules which I shall follow. No marriage shall be deemed by me a greater gain than thy good guidance.

Cr. Yea, this, my son, should be thy heart's fixed law—in all things to obey thy father's will. 'Tis for this that men pray to see dutiful children grow up around them in their homes—that such may requite their father's foe with evil, and honour, as their father doth, his friend. But he who begets unprofitable children—what shall we say that he hath sown, but troubles for himself, and much triumph for his foes? Then do not thou, my son, at pleasure's beck, dethrone thy reason for a woman's sake; knowing that this is a joy that soon grows cold in clasping arms—an evil woman to share thy bed and thy home. For what wound could strike deeper than a false friend? Nay, with loathing, and as if she were thine enemy, let this girl go to find a husband in the house of Hades. For since I have taken her, alone of all the city, in open disobedience, I will not make myself a liar to my people—I will slay her.

So let her appeal as she will to the majesty of kindred blood. If I am to nurture mine own kindred in naughtiness, needs must I bear with it in aliens. He who does his duty in his own household will be found righteous in the State also. But if any one transgresses, and does violence to the laws, or thinks to dictate to his rulers, such an one can win no praise from me. No, whomsoever the city may appoint, that man must be obeyed, in little things and great, in just things and unjust; and I should feel sure that one who thus obeys would be a good ruler no less than a good subject, and in the storm of spears would stand his ground where he was set, loyal and dauntless at his comrade's side.

But disobedience is the worst of evils. This it is that ruins cities; this makes homes desolate; by this, the ranks of allies are broken into headlong rout; but, of the lives whose course is fair, the greater part owes safety to obedience. Therefore we must support the cause of order, and in no wise suffer a woman to worst us. Better to fall from power, if we must, by a man's hand; then we should not be called weaker than a woman.

Ch. To us, unless our years have stolen our wit, thou seemest to say wisely what thou sayest.

Hae. Father, the gods implant reason in men, the highest of all things that we call our own. Not mine the skill—far from me be the quest!—to say wherein thou speakest not aright; and yet another man, too, might have some useful thought. At least, it is my natural office to watch, on thy behalf, all that men say, or do, or find to blame. For the dread of thy frown forbids the citizen to speak such words as would offend thine ear; but I can hear these murmurs in the dark, these moanings of the city for this maiden; "no woman," they say, "ever merited her doom less—none ever, was to die so shamefully for deeds so glorious as hers; who, when her own brother had fallen in bloody strife, would not leave him unburied, to be devoured by carrion dogs, or by any bird: deserves not *she* the meed of golden honour?"

Such is the darkling rumour that spreads in secret. For me, my father, no treasure is so precious as thy welfare. What, indeed, is a nobler ornament for children than a prospering sire's fair fame, or for sire than son's? Wear not, then, one mood only in thyself; think not that thy word, and thine alone, must be right. For if any man thinks that he alone is wise—that in speech, or in mind, he hath no peer—such a soul, when laid open, is ever found empty.

No, though a man be wise, 'tis no shame for him to learn many things, and to bend in season. Seest thou, beside the wintry torrent's course, how the trees that yield to it save every twig, while the stiff-necked perish root and branch? And even thus he who keeps the sheet of his sail taut, and never slackens it, upsets his boat, and finishes his voyage with keel uppermost.

Nay, forego thy wrath; permit thyself to change. For if I, a younger man, may offer my thought, it were far best, I ween, that men should be all-wise by nature; but, otherwise—and oft the scale inclines not so—'tis good also to learn from those who speak aright.

Ch. Sire, 'tis meet that thou shouldest profit by his words, if he speaks aught in season, and thou, Haemon, by thy father's; for on both parts there hath been wise speech.

Cr. Men of my age—are we indeed to be schooled, then, by men of his?

Hae. In nothing that is not right; but if I am young, thou shouldest look to my merits, not to my years.

Cr. Is it a merit to honour the unruly?

Hae. I could wish no one to show respect for evil-doers.

Cr. Then is not she tainted with that malady?

Hae. Our Theban folk, with one voice, denies it.

Cr. Shall Thebes prescribe to me how I must rule?

Hae. See, there thou hast spoken like a youth indeed.

Cr. Am I to rule this land by other judgment than mine own?

Hae. That is no city, which belongs to one man.

Cr. Is not the city held to be the ruler's?

Hae. Thou wouldst make a good monarch of a desert.

Cr. This boy, it seems, is the woman's champion.

Hae. If thou art a woman; indeed, my care is for thee.

Cr. Shameless, at open feud with thy father!

Hae. Nay, I see thee offending against justice.

Cr. Do I offend, when I respect mine own prerogatives?

Hae. Thou dost not respect them, when thou tramplest on the gods' honours.

Cr. O dastard nature, yielding place to woman!

Hae. Thou wilt never find me yield to baseness.

Cr. All thy words, at least, plead for that girl.

Hae. And for thee, and for me, and for the gods below.

Cr. Thou canst never marry her, on this side the grave.

Hae. Then she must die, and in death destroy another.

Cr. How! doth thy boldness run to open threats?

Hae. What threat is it, to combat vain resolves?

Cr. Thou shalt rue thy witless teaching of wisdom.

Hae. Wert thou not my father, I would have called thee unwise.

Cr. Thou woman's slave, use not wheedling speech with me.

Hae. Thou wouldest speak, and then hear no reply?

Cr. Sayest thou so? Now, by the heaven above us—be sure of it—thou shalt smart for taunting me in this opprobrious strain. Bring forth that hated thing, that she may die forthwith in his presence—before his eyes—at her bridegroom's side!

Hae. No, not at my side—never think it—shall she perish; nor shalt thou ever set eyes more upon my face:—rave, then, with such friends as can endure thee. *Exit* HAEMON.

Ch. The man is gone, O king, in angry haste; a youthful mind, when stung, is fierce.

Cr. Let him do, or dream, more than man—good speed to him! But he shall not save these two girls from their doom.

Ch. Dost thou indeed purpose to slay both?

Cr. Not her whose hands are pure: thou sayest well.

Ch. And by what doom mean'st thou to slay the other?

Cr. I will take her where the path is loneliest, and hide her, living, in a rocky vault, with so much food set forth as piety prescribes, that the city may avoid a public stain. And there, praying to Hades, the only god whom she worships, perchance she will obtain release from death; or else will learn, at last, though late, that it is lost labour to revere the dead.

Exit CREON.

Chorus

Love, unconquered in the fight, Love, who makest havoc of wealth, who keepest thy vigil on the soft cheek of a maiden; thou roamest over the sea, and among the homes of dwellers in the wilds; no immortal can escape thee, nor any among men whose life is for a day; and he to whom thou hast come is mad.

The just themselves have their minds warped by thee to wrong, for their ruin: 'tis thou that hast stirred up this present strife of kinsmen; victorious is the love-kindling light from the eyes of the fair bride; it is a power enthroned in sway beside the eternal laws; for there the goddess Aphrodite is working her unconquerable will.

ANTIGONE *is led out of the palace by two of* CREON'S *attendants who are about to conduct her to her doom.*

But now I also am carried beyond the bounds of loyalty, and can no more keep back the streaming tears, when I see Antigone thus passing to the bridal chamber where all are laid to rest.

An. See me, citizens of my fatherland, setting forth on my last way, looking my last on the sunlight that is for me no more; no, Hades who gives sleep to all leads me living to Acheron's shore; who have had no portion in the chant that brings the bride, nor hath any song been mine for the crowning of bridals; whom the lord of the Dark Lake shall wed.

Ch. Glorious, therefore, and with praise, thou departest to that deep place of the dead: wasting sickness hath not smitten thee; thou hast not found the wages of the sword; no, mistress of thine own fate, and still alive, thou shalt pass to Hades, as no other of mortal kind hath passed.

An. I have heard in other days how dread a doom befell our Phrygian guest, the daughter of Tantalus, on the Sipylian heights; how, like clinging ivy, the growth of stone subdued her; and the rains fail not, as men tell, from her wasting form, nor fails the snow, while beneath her weeping lids the tears bedew her bosom; and most like to hers is the fate that brings me to my rest.

Ch. Yet she was a goddess, thou knowest, and born of gods; we are mortals, and of mortal race. But 'tis great renown for a woman who hath perished that she should have shared the doom of the godlike, in her life, and afterward in death.

An. Ah, I am mocked! In the name of our fathers' gods, can ye not wait till I am gone—must ye taunt me to my face, O my city, and ye, her wealthy sons? Ah, fount of Dircè, and thou holy ground of Thebè whose chariots are many; ye, at least, will bear me witness, in what sort, unwept of friends, and by what laws I pass to the rock-closed prison of my strange tomb, ah me unhappy! who have no home on the earth or in the shades, no home with the living or with the dead.

Ch. Thou hast rushed forward to the utmost verge of daring; and against that throne where Justice sits on high thou hast fallen, my daughter, with a grievous fall. But in this ordeal thou art paying, haply, for thy father's sin.

An. Thou hast touched on my bitterest thought, awaking the ever-new lament for my sire and for all the doom given to us, the famed house of Labdacus. Alas for the horrors of the mother's bed! alas for the wretched mother's slumber at the side of her own son—and my sire! From what manner of parents did I take my miserable being! And to them I go thus, accursed, unwed, to share their home. Alas, my brother, ill-starred in thy marriage, in thy death thou hast undone my life!

Ch. Reverent action claims a certain praise for reverence; but an offence against power cannot be brooked by him who hath power in his keeping. Thy self-willed temper hath wrought thy ruin.

An. Unwept, unfriended, without marriage-song, I am led forth in my sorrow on this journey that can be delayed no more. No longer, hapless one, may I behold yon day-star's sacred eye; but for my fate no tear is shed, no friend makes moan.

CREON *enters from the palace.*

Cr. Know ye not that songs and wailings before death would never cease, if it profited to utter them? Away with her—away! And when ye have enclosed her, according to my word, in her vaulted grave, leave her alone, forlorn—whether she wishes to die, or to live a buried life in such a home. Our hands are clean as touching this maiden. But this is certain—she shall be deprived of her sojourn in the light.

An. Tomb, bridal-chamber, eternal prison in the caverned rock, whither I go to find mine own, those many who have perished, and whom Persephone hath received among the dead! Last of all shall I pass thither, and far most miserably of all, before the term of my life is spent. But I cherish good hope that my coming will be welcome to my father, and pleasant to thee, my mother, and welcome, brother, to thee; for, when ye died, with mine own hands I washed and dressed you, and poured drink-offerings at your graves; and now, Polyneices, 'tis for tending thy corpse that I win such recompense as this.

And yet I honoured thee, as the wise will deem, rightly. Never, had I been a mother of children, or if a husband had been mouldering in death, would I have taken this task upon me in the city's despite. What law, ye ask, is my warrant for that word? The husband lost, another might have been found, and child from another, to replace the first-born; but, father and mother hidden with Hades, no brother's life could ever bloom for me again. Such was the law whereby I held thee first in honour; but Creon deemed me guilty of error therein, and of outrage, ah brother mine! And now he leads me thus, a captive in his hands; no bridal bed, no bridal song hath been mine, no joy of marriage, no portion in the nurture of children; but thus, forlorn of friends, unhappy one, I go living to the vaults of death.

And what law of heaven have I transgressed? Why, hapless one, should I look to the gods any more—what ally should I invoke—when by piety I have earned the name of impious? Nay, then, if these things are pleasing to the gods, when I have suffered my doom, I shall come to know my sin; but if the sin is with my judges, I could wish them no fuller measure of evil than they, on their part, mete wrongfully to me.

Ch. Still the same tempest of the soul vexes this maiden with the same fierce gusts.

Cr. Then for this shall her guards have cause to rue their slowness.

An. Ah me! that word hath come very near to death.

Cr. I can cheer thee with no hope that this doom is not thus to be fulfilled.

An. O city of my fathers in the land of Thebè! O ye gods, eldest of our race!—they lead me hence—now, now—they tarry not! Behold me, princes of Thebes, the last daughter of the house of your kings—see what I suffer, and from whom, because I feared to cast away the fear of Heaven!

ANTIGONE *is led away by the guards.*

Chorus

Even thus endured Danaë in her beauty to change the light of day for brass-bound walls; and in that chamber, secret as the grave, she was held close prisoner; yet was she of a proud lineage, O my daughter, and charged with the keeping of the seed of Zeus, that fell in the golden rain.

But dreadful is the mysterious power of fate; there is no deliverance from it by wealth or by war, by fenced city, or dark, sea-beaten ships.

And bonds tamed the son of Dryas, swift to wrath, that king of the Edonians; so paid he for his frenzied taunts, when, by the will of Dionysus, he was pent in a rocky prison. There the fierce exuberance of his madness slowly passed away. That man learned to know the god, whom in his frenzy he had provoked with mockeries; for he had sought to quell the god-possessed women, and the Bacchanalian fire; and he angered the Muses that love the flute.

And by the waters of the Dark Rocks, the waters of the twofold sea, are the shores of Bosporus, and Thracian Salmydessus; where Ares, neighbour to the city, saw the accurst, blinding wound dealt to the two sons of Phineus by his fierce wife—the wound that brought darkness to those vengeance-craving orbs, smitten with her bloody hands, smitten with her shuttle for a dagger.

Pining in their misery, they bewailed their cruel doom, those sons of a mother hapless in her marriage; but she traced her descent from the ancient line of the Erechtheidae; and in far-distant caves she was nursed amid her father's storms, that child of Boreas, swift as a steed over the steep hills, a daughter of gods; yet upon her also the gray Fates bore hard, my daughter.

Enter TEIRESIAS, *led by a Boy, on the spectators' right.*

Teiresias. Princes of Thebes, we have come with linked steps, both served by the eyes of one; for thus, by a guide's help, the blind must walk.

Cr. And what, aged Teiresias, are thy tidings?

Te. I will tell thee; and do thou hearken to the seer.

Cr. Indeed, it has not been my wont to slight thy counsel.

Te. Therefore didst thou steer our city's course aright.

Cr. I have felt, and can attest, thy benefits.

Te. Mark that now, once more, thou standest on fate's fine edge.

Cr. What means this? How I shudder at thy message!

Te. Thou wilt learn, when thou hearest the warnings of mine art. As I took my place on mine old seat of augury, where all birds have been wont to gather within my ken, I heard a strange voice among them; they were screaming with dire, feverish rage, that drowned their language in a jargon; and I knew that they were rending each other with their talons, murderously; the whirr of wings told no doubtful tale.

Forthwith, in fear, I essayed burnt-sacrifice on a duly kindled altar: but from my offerings the Fire-god showed no flame; a dank moisture, oozing from the thigh-flesh, trickled forth upon the embers, and smoked, and sputtered; the gall was scattered to the air; and the streaming thighs lay bared of the fat that had been wrapped round them.

Such was the failure of the rites by which I vainly asked a sign, as from this boy I learned; for he is my guide, as I am guide to others. And 'tis thy counsel that hath brought this sickness on our State. For the altars of our city and of our hearths have been tainted, one and all, by birds and dogs, with carrion from the hapless corpse, the son of Oedipus: and therefore the gods no more accept prayer and sacrifice at our hands, or the flame of meat-offering; nor doth any bird give a clear sign by its shrill cry, for they have tasted the fatness of a slain man's blood.

Think, then, on these things, my son. All men are liable to err; but when an error hath been made, that man is no longer witless or unblest who heals the ill into which he hath fallen, and remains not stubborn.

Self-will, we know, incurs the charge of folly. Nay, allow the claim of the dead; stab not the fallen; what prowess is it to slay the slain anew? I have sought thy good, and for thy good I speak: and never is it sweeter to learn from a good counsellor than when he counsels for thine own gain.

Cr. Old man, ye all shoot your shafts at me, as archers at the butts; ye must needs practise on me with seer-craft also; aye, the seer-tribe hath long trafficked in me, and made me their merchandise. Gain your gains, drive your trade, if ye list, in the silver-gold of Sardis and the gold of India; but ye shall not hide that man in the grave—no, though the eagles of Zeus should bear the carrion morsels to their Master's throne—no, not for dread of that defilement will I suffer his burial: for well I know that no mortal can defile the gods. But, aged Teiresias, the wisest fall with a shameful fall, when they clothe shameful thoughts in fair words, for lucre's sake.

Te. Alas! Doth any man know, doth any consider...

Cr. Whereof? What general truth dost thou announce?

Te. How precious, above all wealth, is good counsel.

Cr. As folly, I think, is the worst mischief.

Te. Yet thou art tainted with that distemper.

Cr. I would not answer the seer with a taunt.

Te. But thou dost, in saying that I prophesy falsely.

Cr. Well, the prophet-tribe was ever fond of money.

Te. And the race bred of tyrants loves base gain.

Cr. Knowest thou that thy speech is spoken of thy king?

Te. I know it; for through me thou hast saved Thebes.

Cr. Thou art a wise seer; but thou lovest evil deeds.

Te. Thou wilt rouse me to utter the dread secret in my soul.

Cr. Out with it! Only speak it not for gain.

Te. Indeed, methinks, I shall not—as touching thee.

Cr. Know that thou shalt not trade on my resolve.

Te. Then know thou—aye, know it well—that thou shalt not live through many more courses of the sun's swift chariot, ere one begotten of thine own loins shall have been given by thee, a corpse for corpses; because thou hast thrust children of the sunlight to the shades, and ruthlessly lodged a living soul in the grave; but keepest in this world one who belongs to the gods infernal, a corpse unburied, unhonoured, all unhallowed. In such thou hast no part, nor have the gods above, but this is a violence done to them by thee. Therefore the avenging destroyers lie in wait for thee, the Furies of Hades and of the gods, that thou mayest be taken in these same ills.

And mark well if I speak these things as a hireling. A time not long to be delayed shall awaken the wailing of men and of women in thy house. And a tumult of hatred against thee stirs all the cities whose mangled sons had the burial-rite from dogs, or from wild beasts, or from some winged bird that bore a polluting breath to each city that contains the hearths of the dead.

Such arrows for thy heart—since thou provokest me—have I launched at thee, archer-like, in my anger, sure arrows, of which thou shalt not escape the smart. Boy, lead me home, that he may spend his rage on younger men, and learn to keep a tongue more temperate, and to bear within his breast a better mind than now he bears. *Exit* TEIRESIAS.

Ch. The man hath gone, O king, with dread prophecies. And, since the hair on this head, once dark, hath been white, I know that he hath never been a false prophet to our city.

Cr. I, too, know it well, and am troubled in soul. 'Tis dire to yield; but, by resistance, to smite my pride with ruin—this, too, is a dire choice.

Ch. Son of Menoeceus, it behoves thee to take wise counsel.

Cr. What should I do, then? Speak, and I will obey.

Ch. Go thou, and free the maiden from her rocky chamber, and make a tomb for the unburied dead.

Cr. And this is thy counsel? Thou wouldst have me yield?

Ch. Yea, King, and with all speed; for swift harms from the gods cut short the folly of men.

Cr. Ah me, 'tis hard, but I resign my cherished resolve—I obey. We must not wage a vain war with destiny.

Ch. Go, thou, and do these things; leave them not to others.

Cr. Even as I am I'll go: on, on, my servants, each and all of you, take axes in your hands, and hasten to the ground that ye see yonder! Since our judgment hath taken this turn, I will be present to unloose her, as I myself bound her. My heart misgives me, 'tis best to keep the established laws, even to life's end.

Chorus

O thou of many names, glory of the Cadmeian bride, offspring of loud-thundering Zeus! thou who watchest over famed Italia, and reignest, where all guests are welcomed, in the sheltered plain of Eleusinian Deô! O Bacchus, dweller in Thebè, mother-city of Bacchants, by the softly-gliding stream of Ismenus, on the soil where the fierce dragon's teeth were sown!

Thou hast been seen where torch-flames glare through smoke, above the crests of the twin peaks, where move the Corycian nymphs, thy votaries, hard by Castalia's stream.

Thou comest from the ivy-mantled slopes of Nysa's hills, and from the shore green with many-clustered vines, while thy name is lifted up on strains of more than mortal power, as thou visitest the ways of Thebè:

Thebè, of all cities, thou holdest first in honour, thou, and thy mother whom the lightning smote; and now, when all our people is captive to a violent plague, come thou with healing feet over the Parnassian height, or over the moaning strait!

O thou with whom the stars rejoice as they move, the stars whose breath is fire; O master of the voices of the night; son begotten of Zeus; appear, O king, with thine attendant Thyiads, who in night-long frenzy dance before thee, the giver of good gifts, Iacchus!

Enter MESSENGER, *on the spectators' left hand.*

Messenger. Dwellers by the house of Cadmus and of Amphion, there is no estate of mortal life that I would ever praise or blame as settled. Fortune raises and Fortune humbles the lucky or unlucky from day to day, and no one can prophesy to men concerning those things which are established. For Creon was blest once, as I count bliss; he had saved this land of Cadmus from its foes; he was clothed with sole dominion in the land; he reigned, the glorious sire of princely children. And now all hath been lost. For when a man hath forfeited his pleasures, I count him not as living—I hold him but a breathing corpse. Heap up riches in thy house, if thou wilt; live in kingly state; yet, if there be no gladness therewith, I would not give the shadow of a vapour for all the rest, compared with joy.

Ch. And what is this new grief that thou hast to tell for our princes?

Me. Death; and the living are guilty for the dead.

Ch. And who is the slayer? Who the stricken? Speak.

Me. Haemon hath perished; his blood hath been shed by no stranger.

Ch. By his father's hand, or by his own?

Me. By his own, in wrath with his sire for the murder.

Ch. O prophet, how true, then, hast thou proved thy word!

Me. These things stand thus; ye must consider of the rest.

Ch. Lo, I see the hapless Eurydicè, Creon's wife, approaching; she comes from the house by chance, haply, or because she knows the tidings of her son.

Enter EURYDICE.

Eurydice. People of Thebes, I heard your words as I was going forth, to salute the goddess Pallas with my prayers. Even as I was loosing the fastenings of the gate, to open it, the message of a household woe smote on mine ear: I sank back, terror-stricken, into the arms of my handmaids, and my senses fled. But say again what the tidings were; I shall hear them as one who is no stranger to sorrow.

Me. Dear lady, I will witness of what I saw, and will leave no word of the truth untold. Why, indeed, should I soothe thee with words in which I must presently be found false? Truth is ever best. I attended thy lord as his guide to the furthest part of the plain, where the body of Polyneices, torn by dogs, still lay unpitied. We prayed the goddess of the roads, and Pluto, in mercy to restrain their wrath; we washed the dead with holy washing; and with freshly-plucked boughs we solemnly burned such relics as there were. We raised a high mound of his native earth; and then we turned away to enter the maiden's nuptial chamber with rocky couch, the caverned mansion of the bride of Death. And, from afar off, one of us heard a voice of loud wailing at that bride's unhallowed bower; and came to tell our master Creon.

And as the king drew nearer, doubtful sounds of a bitter cry floated around him; he groaned, and said in accents of anguish, "Wretched that I am, can my foreboding be true? Am I going on the wofullest way that ever I went? My son's voice greets me. Go, my servants, haste ye nearer, and when ye have reached the tomb, pass through the gap, where the stones have been wrenched away, to the cell's very mouth, and look, and see if 'tis Haemon's voice that I know, or if mine ear is cheated by the gods."

This search, at our despairing master's word, we went to make; and in the furthest part of the tomb we descried *her* hanging by the neck, slung by a thread-wrought halter of fine linen; while *he* was embracing her with arms thrown around her waist, bewailing the loss of his bride who is with the dead, and his father's deeds, and his own ill-starred love.

But his father, when he saw him, cried aloud with a dread cry and went in, and called to him with a voice of wailing: "Unhappy, what a deed hast thou done! What thought hath come to thee? What manner of mischance hath marred thy reason? Come forth, my child! I pray thee—I implore!" But the boy glared at him with fierce eyes, spat in his face, and, without a word of answer, drew his cross-hilted sword: as his father rushed forth in flight, he missed his aim; then, hapless one, wroth with himself, he straightway leaned with all his weight against his sword, and drove it, half its length, into his side; and, while sense lingered, he clasped the maiden to his faint embrace, and, as he gasped, sent forth on her pale cheek the swift stream of the oozing blood.

Corpse enfolding corpse he lies; he hath won his nuptial rites, poor youth, not here, yet in the halls of Death; and he hath witnessed to mankind that, of all curses which cleave to man, ill counsel is the sovereign curse.

EURYDICE *retires into the house.*

Ch. What wouldst thou augur from this? The lady hath turned back, and is gone, without a word, good or evil.

Me. I, too, am startled; yet I nourish the hope that, at these sore tidings of her son, she cannot deign to give her sorrow public vent, but in the privacy of the house will set her handmaids to mourn the household grief. For she is not untaught of discretion, that she should err.

Ch. I know not; but to me, at least, a strained silence seems to portend peril, no less than vain abundance of lament.

Me. Well, I will enter the house, and learn whether indeed she is not hiding some repressed purpose in the depths of a passionate heart. Yea, thou sayest well: excess of silence, too, may have a perilous meaning.

Exit MESSENGER.

Enter CREON, *on the spectators' left, with attendants, carrying the shrouded body of* HAEMON *on a bier.*

Ch. Lo, yonder the king himself draws near, bearing that which tells too clear a tale—the work of no stranger's madness—if we may say it—but of his own misdeeds.

Cr. Woe for the sins of a darkened soul, stubborn sins, fraught with death! Ah, ye behold us, the sire who hath slain, the son who hath perished! Woe is me, for the wretched blindness of my counsels!

Alas, my son, thou hast died in thy youth, by a timeless doom, woe is me! thy spirit hath fled, not by thy folly, but by mine own!

Ch. Ah me, how all too late thou seemest to see the right!

Cr. Ah me, I have learned the bitter lesson! But then, methinks, oh then, some god smote me from above with crushing weight, and hurled me into ways of cruelty, woe is me, overthrowing and trampling on my joy! Woe, woe, for the troublous toils of men!

Enter MESSENGER *from the house.*

Me. Sire, thou hast come, methinks, as one whose hands are not empty, but who hath store laid up besides; thou bearest yonder burden with thee; and thou art soon to look upon the woes within thy house.

Cr. And what worse ill is yet to follow upon ills?

Me. Thy queen hath died, true mother of yon corpse—ah, hapless lady!—by blows newly dealt.

Cr. Oh Hades, all-receiving, whom no sacrifice can appease! Hast thou, then, no mercy for me? O thou herald of evil, bitter tidings, what word dost thou utter? Alas, I was already as dead, and thou hast smitten me anew! What sayest thou, my son? What is this new message that thou bringest—woe, woe is me!—of a wife's doom, of slaughter heaped on slaughter?

Ch. Thou canst behold: 'tis no longer hidden within.

The doors of the palace are opened, and the corpse of EURYDICE *is disclosed.*

Cr. Ah me, yonder I behold a new, a second woe! What destiny, ah what, can yet await me? I have but now raised my son in my arms, and there, again, I see a corpse before me! Alas, alas, unhappy mother! Alas, my child!

Me. There, at the altar, self-stabbed with a keen knife, she suffered her darkening eyes to close, when she had wailed for the noble fate of Megareus who died before, and then for his fate who lies there, and when, with her last breath, she had invoked evil fortunes upon thee, the slayer of thy sons.

Cr. Woe, woe! I thrill with dread. Is there none to strike me to the heart with two-edged sword? O miserable that I am, and steeped in miserable anguish!

Me. Yea, both this son's doom, and that other's, were laid to thy charge by her whose corpse thou seest.

Cr. And what was the manner of the violent deed by which she passed away?

Me. Her own hand struck her to the heart, when she had learned her son's sorely lamented fate.

Cr. Ah me, this guilt can never be fixed on any other of mortal kind, for my acquittal! I, even I, was thy slayer, wretched that I am—I own the truth. Lead me away, O my servants, lead me hence with all speed, whose life is but as death!

Ch. Thy counsels are good, if there can be good with ills; briefest is best, when trouble is in our path.

Cr. Oh, let it come, let it appear, that fairest of fates for me, that brings my last day—aye, best fate of all! Oh, let it come, that I may never look upon to-morrow's light.

Ch. These things are in the future; present tasks claim our care: the ordering of the future rests where it should rest.

Cr. All my desires, at least, were summed in that prayer.

Ch. Pray thou no more; for mortals have no escape from destined woe.

Cr. Lead me away, I pray you; a rash, foolish man; who have slain thee, ah my son, unwittingly, and thee, too, my wife—unhappy that I am! I know not which way I should bend my gaze, or where I should seek support; for all is amiss with that which is in my hands,—and yonder, again, a crushing fate hath leapt upon my head.

As CREON *is being conducted into the house, the* CORYPHAEUS *speaks the closing verses.*

Ch. Wisdom is the supreme part of happiness; and reverence towards the gods must be inviolate. Great words of prideful men are ever punished with great blows, and, in old age, teach the chastened to be wise.

AJAX

DRAMATIS PERSONAE

ATHENA	TEUCER
AJAX	MENELAUS
ODYSSEUS	AGAMEMNON
TECMESSA	CHORUS OF SALAMINIAN SAILORS

MUTE: *The child* EURYSACES *and his attendant; Two heralds accompanying Menelaus (v.* 1047*); Two bodyguards in attendance on Agamemnon; Attendants of Teucer (v.* 977*)*

Before the tent of Ajax, at the eastern end of the Greek camp, near Cape Rhoeteum on the northern coast of the Troad. ODYSSEUS *is closely examining footprints in the sandy ground.* ATHENA *is seen in the air.*

Athena. Ever have I seen thee, son of Lartius, seeking to snatch some occasion against thy foes; and now at the tent of Ajax by the ships, where he hath his station at the camp's utmost verge, I see thee long while pausing on his trail and scanning his fresh tracks, to find whether he is within or abroad. Well doth it lead thee to thy goal, thy course keen-scenting as a Laconian hound's. For the man is even now gone within, sweat streaming from his face and from hands that have slain with the sword. And there is no further need for thee to peer within these doors; but say what is thine aim in this eager quest, that thou mayest learn from her who can give thee light.

Odysseus. Voice of Athena, dearest to me of the Immortals, how clearly, though thou be unseen, do I hear thy call and seize it in my soul, as when a Tyrrhenian clarion speaks from mouth of bronze! And now thou hast discerned aright that I am hunting to and fro on the trail of a foeman, even Ajax of the mighty shield. 'Tis he, and no other, that I have been tracking so long.

This night he hath done to us a thing which passes thought—if he is indeed the doer; for we know nothing certain, but drift in doubt; and I took upon me the burden of this search. We have lately found the cattle, our spoil, dead—yea, slaughtered by human hand—and dead, beside them, the guardians of the flock.

Now, all men lay this crime to him. And a scout who had descried him bounding alone over the plain with reeking sword brought me tidings, and declared the matter. Then straightway I rushed upon his track; and sometimes I recognise the footprints as his, but sometimes I am bewildered, and cannot read whose they are. Thy succour is timely; thine is the hand that ever guides my course—as in the past, so for the days to come.

Ath. I know it, Odysseus, and came early on the path, a watcher friendly to thy chase.

Od. Dear mistress, do I toil to purpose?

Ath. Know that yon man is the doer of these deeds.

Od. And why was his insensate hand put forth so fiercely?

Ath. In bitter wrath touching the arms of Achilles.

Od. Why, then, this furious onslaught upon the flocks?

Ath. 'Twas in your blood, as he deemed, that he was dyeing his hand.

Od. What? Was this design aimed against the Greeks?

Ath. He would have accomplished it, too, had I been careless.

Od. And how had he laid these bold plans? What could inspire such hardihood?

Ath. In the night he went forth against you, by stealth, and alone.

Od. And did he come near us? Did he reach his goal?

Ath. He was already at the doors of the two chiefs.

Od. What cause, then, stayed his eager hand from murder?

Ath. I, even I, withheld him, for I cast upon his eyes the tyrannous fancies of his baneful joy; and I turned his fury aside on the flocks of sheep, and the confused droves guarded of herdsmen, the spoil which ye had not yet divided. Then he fell on, and dealt death among the horny throng, as he hewed them to the earth around him; and now he deemed that the two Atreidae were the prisoners whom he slew with his hand, now 'twas this chief, now 'twas that, at each new onset. And while the man raved in the throes of frenzy, I still urged him, hurled him into the toils of doom. Anon, when he rested from this work, he bound together the living oxen, with all the sheep, and brought them home, as though his captives were men, not goodly kine. And now he torments them, bound together, in the house.

But to thee also will I show this madness openly, that when thou hast seen it thou mayest proclaim it to all the Greeks. And be thou steadfast and of a good courage, nor look for evil from the man; for I will turn away the vision of his eyes, and keep them from beholding thy face.

Ho, thou who art binding with cords the back-bent arms of thy captives, I call thee, come hither! Ajax, what ho! come forth from the house!

Od. What dost thou, Athena? Never call him forth.

Ath. Hold thy peace! Do not earn the name of coward!

Od. Forbear, I pray thee; be content that he stay within.

Ath. What is the danger? Was he not a man before?

Od. Yea, a foeman to thy servant, and still is.

Ath. And to mock at foes—is not that the sweetest mockery?

Od. Enough for me that he abide within his doors.

Ath. Thou fearest to see a madman in full view?

Od. No fear had made me shun him, if he were sane.

Ath. Nay, even now, he shall not see thee, though thou art near.

Od. How so, if he still sees with the same eyes?

Ath. I will darken them, though they are open.

Od. Well, all is possible when a god contrives.

Ath. Stand silent, then, and stay where thou art.

Od. I must stay. Would that I were far from here!

Ath. What ho, Ajax, once again I call thee! is this thy scanty regard for thine ally?

Enter AJAX, *holding a blood-stained scourge in his hand.*

Ajax. Hail, Athena! Hail, Zeus-born maid! How well hast thou stood by me! Yea, I will crown thy shrine with trophies of pure gold for this prize!

Ath. 'Tis fairly spoken. But tell me this—hast thou dyed thy sword well in the Greek camp?

Aj. That vaunt is mine; I disclaim it not.

Ath. And perchance turned thine armed hand on the Atreidae?

Aj. So that nevermore will they dishonour Ajax.

Ath. The men are dead, as I take thy meaning:

Aj. Dead: now let them rob me of my arms!

Ath. Good: and then the son of Laertius—in what plight hast thou left him? Hath he escaped thee?

Aj. What, thou askest me of that accursed fox?

Ath. Yea, in sooth—of Odysseus, thine adversary.

Aj. No guest so welcome, Lady: he is sitting in the house—in bonds: I do not mean him to die just yet.

Ath. What wouldst thou do first? What larger advantage wouldst thou win?

Aj. First, he shall be bound to a pillar beneath my roof—

Ath. The hapless man—what despite wilt thou do unto him?

Aj. —and have his back crimsoned with the scourge, ere he die.

Ath. Nay, do not torture the wretch so cruelly.

Aj. In all else, Athena, I say, have thy will; but *his* doom shall be none but this.

Ath. Nay, then, since it delights thee to do thus, hold not thy hand, abate no jot of thine intent.

Aj. I go to my work: but thou, I charge thee, stand ever at my side as thou hast stood to-day!

Exit AJAX.

Ath. Seest thou, Odysseus, how great is the strength of the gods? Whom couldest thou have found more prudent than this man, or more valiant for the service of the time?

Od. I know none; and I pity him in his misery, for all that he is my foe, because he is bound fast to a dread doom: I think of mine own lot no less than his. For I see that we are but phantoms, all we who live, or fleeting shadows.

Ath. Therefore, beholding such things, look that thine own lips never speak a haughty word against the gods, and assume no swelling port, if thou prevailest above another in prowess or by store of ample wealth. For a day can humble all human things, and a day can lift them up; but the wise of heart are loved of the gods, and the evil are abhorred.

Enter the CHORUS OF SALAMINIAN SAILORS, *followers of* AJAX.

Chorus

Son of Telamon, thou whose wave-girt Salamis is firmly throned upon the sea, when thy fortunes are fair, I rejoice: but when the stroke of Zeus comes on thee, or the angry rumour of the Danai with noise of evil tongues, then I quake exceedingly and am sore afraid, like a winged dove with troubled eye.

And so, telling of the night now spent, loud murmurs beset us for our shame; telling how thou didst visit the meadow wild with steeds, and didst destroy the cattle of the Greeks, their spoil—prizes of the spear which had not yet been shared—slaying them with flashing sword.

Such are the whispered slanders that Odysseus breathes into all ears; and he wins large belief. For now the tale that he tells of thee is specious; and each hearer rejoices more than he who told, despitefully exulting in thy woes.

Yea, point thine arrow at a noble spirit, and thou shalt not miss; but should a man speak such things against me, he would win no faith. 'Tis on the powerful that envy creeps. Yet the small without the great can ill be trusted to guard the walls; lowly leagued with great will prosper best, great served by less.

But foolish men cannot be led to learn these truths. Even such are the men who rail against thee, and we are helpless to repel these charges, without thee, O king. Verily, when they have escaped thine eye, they chatter like flocking birds: but, terrified by the mighty vulture, suddenly, perchance—if thou shouldst appear— they will cower still and dumb.

Was it the Tauric Artemis, child of Zeus, that drave thee—O dread rumour, parent of my shame! —against the herds of all our host—in revenge, I ween, for a victory that had paid no tribute, whether it was that she had been disappointed of glorious spoil, or because a stag had been slain without a thank-offering? Or can it have been the mail-clad Lord of War that was wroth for dishonour to his aiding spear, and took vengeance by nightly wiles?

Never of thine own heart, son of Telamon, wouldst thou have gone so far astray as to fall upon the flocks. Yea, when the gods send madness, it must come; but may Zeus and Phoebus avert the evil rumour of the Greeks!

And if the great chiefs charge thee falsely in the furtive rumours which they spread, or sons of the wicked line of Sisyphus, forbear, O my king, forbear to win me an evil name, by still keeping thy face thus hidden in the tent by the sea.

Nay, up from thy seat, wheresoever thou art brooding in this pause of many days from battle, making the flame of mischief blaze up to heaven! But the insolence of thy foes goes abroad without fear in the breezy glens, while all men mock with taunts most grievous; and my sorrow passes not away.

Enter TECMESSA.

Tecmessa. Mariners of Ajax, of the race that springs from the Erechtheidae, sons of the soil—mourning is our portion who care for the house of Telamon afar. Ajax, our dread lord of rugged might, now lies stricken with a storm that darkens the soul.

Ch. And what is the heavy change from the fortune of yesterday which this night hath brought forth? Daughter of the Phrygian Teleutas, speak: for to thee, his spear-won bride, bold Ajax hath borne a constant love; therefore mightest thou hint the answer with knowledge.

Te. Oh, how shall I tell a tale too dire for words? Terrible as death is the hap which thou must hear. Seized with madness in the night, our glorious Ajax hath been utterly undone. For token, thou mayest see within his dwelling the butchered victims weltering in their blood, sacrifices of no hand but his.

Ch. What tidings of the fiery warrior hast thou told, not to be borne, nor yet escaped—tidings which the mighty Danai noise abroad, which their strong rumour spreads! Woe is me, I dread the doom to come: shamed before all eyes, the man will die, if his frenzied hand hath slain with dark sword the herds and the horse-guiding herdsmen.

Te. Alas! 'twas thence, then—from those pastures—that he came to me with his captive flock! Of part, he cut the throats on the floor within; some, hewing their sides, he rent asunder. Then he caught up two white-footed rams; he sheared off the head of one, and the tongue-tip, and flung them away; the other he bound upright to a pillar, and seized a heavy thong of horse-gear, and flogged with shrill, doubled lash, while he uttered revilings which a god, and no mortal, had taught.

Ch. The time hath come for each of us to veil his head and betake him to stealthy speed of foot, or to sit on the bench at the quick oar, and give her way to the sea-faring ship. Such angry threats are hurled against us by the brother-kings, the sons of Atreus: I fear to share a bitter death by stoning, smitten at this man's side, who is swayed by a fate to which none may draw nigh.

Te. It sways him no longer: the lightnings flash no more; like a southern gale, fierce in its first onset, his rage abates; and now, in his right mind, he hath new pain. To look on self-wrought woes, when no other hath had a hand therein—this lays sharp pangs to the soul.

Ch. Nay, if his frenzy hath ceased, I have good hope that all may yet be well: the trouble is of less account when once 'tis past.

Te. And which, were the choice given thee, wouldst thou choose—to pain thy friends, and have delights thyself, or to share the grief of friends who grieve?

Ch. The twofold sorrow, lady, is the greater ill.

Te. Then are we losers now, although the plague is past.

Ch. What is thy meaning? I know not how thou meanest.

Te. Yon man, while frenzied, found his own joy in the dire fantasies that held him, though his presence was grievous to us who were sane; but now, since he hath had pause and respite from the plague, *he* is utterly afflicted with sore grief, and we likewise, no less than before. Have we not here two sorrows, instead of one?

Ch. Yea verily: and I fear lest the stroke of a god hath fallen. How else, if his spirit is no lighter, now that the malady is overpast, than when it vexed him?

Te. Thus stands the matter, be well assured.

Ch. And in what wise did the plague first swoop upon him? Declare to us, who share thy pain, how it befell.

Te. Thou shalt hear all that chanced, as one who hath part therein. At dead of night, when the evening lamps no longer burned, he seized a two-edged sword, and was fain to go forth on an aimless path. Then I chid him, and said; "What dost thou, Ajax? why wouldst thou make this sally unsummoned—not called by messenger, not warned by trumpet? Nay, at present the whole army sleeps."

But he answered me in curt phrase and trite: "Woman, silence graces women." And I, thus taught, desisted; but he rushed forth alone. What happened abroad, I cannot tell: but he came in with his captives bound together—bulls, shepherd dogs, and fleecy prisoners. Some he beheaded; of some, he cut the back-bent throat, or cleft the chine; others, in their bonds, he tormented as though they were men, with onslaughts on the cattle.

At last, he darted forward through the door, and began ranting to some creature of his brain—now against the Atreidae, now about Odysseus—with many a mocking vaunt of all the despite that he had wreaked on them in his raid. Anon, he rushed back once more into the house; and then, by slow, painful steps, regained his reason.

And as his gaze ranged over the room full of his wild work, he struck his head, and uttered a great cry: he fell down, a wreck amid the wrecks of the slaughtered sheep, and there he sat, with clenched nails tightly clutching his hair. At first, and for a long while, he sat dumb: then he threatened me with those dreadful threats, if I declared not all the chance that had befallen; and asked in what strange plight he stood. And I, friends, in my fear, told all that had been done, so far as I surely knew it. But he straightway broke into bitter lamentations, such as never had I heard from him before. For he had ever taught that such wailing was for craven and low-hearted men; no cry of shrill complaint would pass his lips; only a deep sound, as of a moaning bull.

But now, prostrate in his utter woe, tasting not of food or drink, the man sits quiet where he has fallen, amidst the sword-slain cattle. And plainly he yearns to do some dread deed: there is some such meaning in his words and his laments. Ah, my friends —indeed, this was my errand—come in and help, if in any wise ye can. Men in his case can be won by the words of friends.

Ch. Tecmessa, daughter of Teleutas, dread are thy tidings, that our lord hath been frenzied by his sorrows.

Aj. (*within*) Woe, woe is me!

Te. Soon there will be worse, belike. Heard ye not Ajax—heard ye not that resounding cry?

Aj. Woe, woe is me!

Ch. The man seems to be distempered, or else to be grieving for the distempers which lately vexed him, when he sees their work.

Aj. O my son, my son!

Te. Ah me! Eurysaces, 'tis for thee he calls! What can be his purpose? Where art thou? Unhappy that I am!

Aj. Ho, Teucer! Where is Teucer? Will his foray last for ever? And I perish!

Ch. He seems to be sane. Come, open there! open —perchance e'en at the sight of me he may come to a more sober mood.

Te. Behold, I open: thou canst look on yon man's deeds, and his own plight.

AJAX *is discovered sitting amidst the slaughtered cattle.*

Aj. Alas, good sailors, alone of my friends, alone still constant to your loyalty, behold what a wave hath but now surged around me and hemmed me in, under stress of a deadly storm!

Ch. Ah, lady, how sadly true seems thy report! The fact proves that no sane mind is here.

Aj. Alas, ye mates staunch in sea-craft, ye who manned the ship and made the oar-blade flash upon the brine—in you, in you alone I see a defence against misery: come, slay me also!

Ch. Hush thy wild lips: cure not ill by ill, nor increase the anguish of the doom.

Aj. Seest thou the bold, the strong of heart, the dauntless in battles with the foe—seest thou how I have shown my prowess on creatures that feared no harm? Alas, the mockery! How then have I been shamed!

Te. Ajax, my lord, I implore thee, speak not thus!

Aj. Hence! out with thee! avaunt—begone!—Woe is me! woe is me!

Ch. For the gods' love, yield to counsel, and learn wisdom!

Aj. Wretch that I am, who suffered the accursed men to slip through my hands, but fell on horned kine and goodly flocks, and made their dark blood flow!

Ch. Why grieve when the deed is past recall These things can never be but as they are.

Aj. Ah, thou who watchest all things, thou ready tool of every crime, ah, son of Lartius, thou foulest knave in all the host, I warrant thou laughest loud and long for joy!

Ch. As the god gives, so every man laughs or mourns.

Aj. Yet would that I could see him, shattered though I am! Ah me, ah me!

Ch. Speak no proud word: seest thou not to what a plight thou hast come?

Aj. O Zeus, father of my sires, would that I might slay that deep dissembler, that hateful knave, and the two brother-chiefs, and lastly die myself also!

Te. When thou makest that prayer, pray therewith for me also that I die: wherefore should I live when thou art dead?

Aj. Alas, thou darkness, my sole light! O thou nether gloom, fairer for me than any sunshine! take me to dwell with you—yea, take me; for I am no longer worthy to look for help to the race of the gods, or for any good from men, the children of a day.

No, the daughter of Zeus, the strong goddess, torments me to the death. Whither then shall a man flee? Whither shall I go to find rest? If my past fame is destroyed, my friends, along with such victims as these near me—if I have set myself to win a madman's triumphs, and all the host, with sword uplifted in both hands, would strike me dead!

Te. Ah me unhappy, that a good man and true should utter such words—words that, till now, he ne'er would have deigned to speak!

Aj. Alas, ye paths of the sounding wave, ye seacaves and wooded pastures by the shore, long time, long time and very weary have ye known me tarrying at Troy; but no more shall ye know me—no more with the breath of life: of so much let sane men be sure.

Ah, streams of Scamander near us, kindly to the Greeks, never shall ye look on Ajax more; whose peer in the host—for I will utter a proud word— never hath Troy seen come from the land of Hellas: but now, behold, he hath been humbled to the dust!

Ch. In sooth I know not how to restrain thee, or how suffer thee to speak, whom woes so grievous have befallen.

Aj. Ay me! Who could e'er have thought that my name would chime so meetly with my doom? For well may I now mourn—yea, twice and three times mourn—in those sad syllables that shape my name; such heavy griefs are mine, whose sire by his prowess won the fairest prize of all the host, and brought all glory home from this land of Ida; but I his son, who came after him in might not less to this same ground of Troy, and proved the service of mine hand in no meaner deeds, thus perish, dishonoured of the Greeks. Yet, methinks, of thus much am I sure; if

Achilles lived, and had been called to decree the first place in valour to any claimant of his arms, no one would have grasped them before me. But now the Atreidae have conveyed them to a villain, and thrust away the high deeds of Ajax.

And if these eyes, if this warped mind had not swerved from the purpose that was mine, never would they have procured such a judgment against another man. As it was, the daughter of Zeus, the fierce-eyed, unconquerable goddess, foiled me at the instant when I was making ready my hand against them, struck me with a plague of frenzy, made me imbrue my hands in the blood of these poor cattle. And yon men exult to have escaped me—by no good-will of mine; but if a god send harm, verily e'en the base man can elude the worthier.

And now what shall I do; who plainly am hateful to the gods, abhorred by the Greek host, hated by all Troy and all these plains? Shall I forsake the station of the ships, and leave the Atreidae forlorn, and go homeward across the Aegean? And what face shall I show to my father when I come—to Telamon? How will he find heart to look on me, when I stand before him ungraced—without that meed of valour whereby *he* won a great crown of fame? 'Tis not to be endured.

But then shall I go to the stronghold of the Trojans—attack alone, where all are foes—and, in doing some good service, lastly die? Nay, thus I might haply gladden the Atreidae. It must not be. Some emprise must be sought whereby I may prove to mine aged sire that in heart, at least, his son is not a dastard.

'Tis base for a man to crave the full term of life, who finds no varying in his woes. What joy is there in day following day—now pushing us forward, now drawing us back, on the verge—of death? I rate that man as nothing worth, who feels the glow of idle hopes. Nay, one of generous strain should nobly live, or forthwith nobly die: thou hast heard all.

Ch. No man shall say that thou hast spoken a bastard word, Ajax, or one not bred of thy true soul. Yet forbear: dismiss these thoughts, and suffer friends to overrule thy purpose.

Te. Ajax, my lord, the doom given by fate is the hardest of evils among men. I was the daughter of a free-born sire, wealthy and mighty, if any Phrygian was; and now I am a slave: for so the gods ordained, I ween, and chiefly thy strong hand. Therefore, since wedlock hath made me thine, I wish thee well; and I do entreat thee, by the Zeus of our hearth, by the marriage that hath made us one, doom me not to the cruel rumour of thy foes, abandon me not to the hand of a stranger! On what day soever thou die and leave me lonely by thy death, on that same day, be sure, I also shall be seized forcibly by the Greeks, and, with thy son, shall have the portion of a slave. Then shall some one of my masters name me in bitter phrase, with keen taunts: "See the concubine of Ajax, his, who was the mightiest of the host; see what menial tasks are hers, who had such bliss!" Thus shall men speak; and destiny will afflict me; but these words will be shameful for thee and for thy race.

Nay, have thought for thy father, whom thou forsakest in a drear old age; for thy mother—and hers are many years—who oft prays to the gods that thou come home alive; and pity, O king, thy son, if, bereft of fostering care, he must spend his days forlorn of thee, the ward of unloving guardians; think how great is this sorrow, which at thy death thou wilt bequeath to him and me.

I have nothing left whereunto I can look, save thee. Thou didst ravage my country with the spear, and another doom hath laid low my mother and my sire, that they should dwell with Hades in their death. What home, then, could I find, if I lost thee? What wealth? On thee hangs all my welfare. Nay, have thought for me also: a true man should cherish remembrance, if anywhere he reap a joy. Tis kindness that still begets kindness. But whosoever suffers the memory of benefits to slip from him, that man can no more rank as noble.

Ch. Ajax, I would that pity touched thy soul as it doth mine: so wouldst thou approve her words.

Aj. Verily she shall have approval on my part, if only she take heart to do my bidding well.

Te. Nay, dear Ajax, I will obey in all things.

Aj. Then bring me my son, that I may see him.

Te. Oh, but in those fears I released him from my keeping.

Aj. During these troubles of mine? Or what meanest thou?

Te. Yea, lest haply the poor child should meet thee, and die.

Aj. Aye truly, that would have been worthy of my fortune.

Te. Well, at least I was watchful to avert *that* woe.

Aj. I praise thy deed, and the foresight which thou hast shown.

Te. How, then, can I serve thee, as the case stands now?

Aj. Let me speak to him, and see him face to face.

Te. Oh yes—he is close by, in charge of attendants.

Aj. Then wherefore is his coming delayed?

Te. My child, thy father calls thee. Bring him hither, servant, whosoever of you is guiding his steps.

Aj. Comes the man at thy call? Or hath he failed to hear thy words?

Te. Even now one of the servants there draws near with him.

Enter Attendant with EURYSACES.

Aj. Lift him, lift him to mine arms. He will feel no dread, I ween, in looking on this newly shed blood, if he is indeed my true-born son. But he must at once be broken into his father's rugged ways, and moulded to the likeness of his nature. Ah, boy, mayest thou prove happier than thy sire, but in all else like him; and thou wilt prove not base. Yet even now I may well envy thee for this, that thou hast no sense of these ills. Yea, life is sweetest before the feelings are awake, [for lack of feeling is a painless ill]—until one learns to know joy or pain. But when thou shalt come unto that knowledge, then must thou see to prove among thy father's foes of what mettle and what sire thou art.

Meanwhile feed on light breezes, and nurse thy tender life, for this thy mother's joy. No fear, I wot, lest any of the Greeks assail thee with cruel outrage, even when thou hast me no more. So trusty is the warder whom I will leave to guard thee, even Teucer; who will not falter in his care for thee, albeit now he is following a far path, busied with chase of foes.

O my warriors, seafaring comrades! On you, as on him, I lay this task of love; and give ye my behest to Teucer, that he take this child to mine own home, and set him before the face of Telamon, and of my mother, Eribeoa, that so he may prove the comfort of their age evermore [until they come unto the deep places of the nether god]. And charge him that no stewards of games, nor he who worked my ruin, make mine arms a prize for the Greeks. No, *this* take thou, my son—the broad shield from which thou hast thy name—hold and wield it by the well-wrought thong, that sevenfold, spear-proof targe! But the rest of my armour shall be buried in my grave.

(*To* TECMESSA) Come, tarry not; take the child straightway, make fast the doors, and utter no laments before the house: in sooth a woman is a plaintive thing. Quick, close the house! It is not for a skilful leech to whine charms over a sore that craves the knife.

Ch. I am afraid when I mark this eager haste: I like not the keen edge of thy speech.

Te. Ajax, my lord, on what deed can thy mind be set?

Aj. Ask not, inquire not; 'tis good to be discreet.

Te. Ah, my heavy heart! Now, by thy child,—by the gods—I implore thee, be not guilty of forsaking us!

Aj. Nay, thou vexest me over much: knowest thou not that I no longer owe aught of service to the gods?

Te. Hush, hush!

Aj. Speak to those who hear.

Te. And wilt *thou* not hearken?

Aj. Already thy words have been too many.

Te. I am afraid, O prince!

Aj. (*To the Attendants*). Close the doors, I say, this instant!

Te. For the gods' love, be softened!

Aj. 'Tis a foolish hope, methinks, if thou wouldst begin now to school my temper.

AJAX *is shut into the tent. Exit* TECMESSA *with* EURYSACES.

Chorus

O famous Salamis, thou, I ween, hast thy happy seat among the waves that lash thy shore, the joy of all men's eyes for ever; but I, hapless, have long been tarrying here, still making my couch, through countless months, in the camp on the fields of Ida, worn by time, and darkly looking for the day when I shall pass to Hades, the abhorred, the unseen.

And now I must wrestle with a new grief, woe is me!—the incurable malady of Ajax, visited by a heaven-sent frenzy; whom in a bygone day thou sentest forth from thee, mighty in bold war; but now, a changed man who nurses lonely thoughts, he hath been found a heavy sorrow to his friends. And the former deeds of his hands, deeds of prowess supreme, have fallen dead, nor won aught of love from the loveless, the miserable Atreidae.

Surely his mother, full of years and white with eld, will uplift a voice of wailing when she hears that he hath been stricken with the spirit's ruin: not in the nightingale's plaintive note will she utter her anguish: in shrill-toned strains the dirge will rise, with sound of hands that smite the breast, and with rending of hoary hair.

Yes, better hid with Hades is he whom vain fancies vex; he who by the lineage whence he springs is noblest of the war-tried Achaeans, yet now is true no more to the promptings of his inbred nature, but dwells with alien thoughts.

Ah, hapless sire, how heavy a curse upon thy son doth it rest for thee to hear, a curse which never yet hath clung to any life of the Aeacidae save his!

Enter AJAX, *with a sword in his hand.*

Aj. All things the long and countless years first draw from darkness, then bury from light; and there is nothing for which man may not look; the dread oath is vanquished, and the stubborn will. For even I, erst so wondrous firm—yea, as iron hardened in the dipping—felt the keen edge of my temper softened by yon woman's words; and I feel the pity of leaving her a widow with my foes, and the boy an orphan.

But I will go to the bathing-place and the meadows by the shore, that in purging of my stains I may flee the heavy anger of the goddess. Then I will seek out some untrodden spot, and bury this sword, hatefullest of weapons, in a hole dug where none shall see; no, let Night and Hades keep it underground! For since my hand took this gift from Hector, my worst foe, to this hour I have had no good from the Greeks. Yes, men's proverb is true: "*The gifts of enemies are no gifts, and bring no good.*"

Therefore henceforth I shall know how to yield to the gods, and learn to revere the Atreidae. They are rulers, so we must submit. How else? Dread things and things most potent bow to office; thus it is that snow-strewn winter gives place to fruitful summer; and thus night's weary round makes room for day with her white steeds to kindle light; and the breath of dreadful winds can allow the groaning sea to slumber; and, like the rest, almighty Sleep looses whom he has bound, nor holds with a perpetual grasp.

And we—must we not learn discretion? I, at least, will learn it; for I am newly aware that our enemy is to be hated but as one who will hereafter be a friend; and towards a friend I would wish but thus far to show aid and service, as knowing that he will not always abide. For to most men the haven of friendship is false.

But concerning these things it will be well. Woman, go thou within, and pray to the gods that in all fulness the desires of my heart may be fulfilled. And ye, my friends—honour ye these my wishes even as she doth; and bid Teucer, when he comes, have care for me, and good-will towards you withal. For I will go whither I must pass; but do ye what I bid; and ere long, perchance, though now I suffer, ye will hear that I have found peace. *Exit* AJAX.

Ch. I thrill with rapture, I soar on the wings of sudden joy! O Pan, O Pan, appear to us, O Pan, roving o'er the sea, from the craggy ridge of snow-beaten Cyllené, king who makest dances for the gods, that with me thou mayest move blithely in the measures that none hath taught thee, the measures of Nysa and of Cnosus! For now am I fain to dance. And may Apollo, lord of Delos, come over the Icarian waters to be with me, in presence manifest and spirit ever kind!

The destroying god hath lifted the cloud of dread trouble from our eyes. Joy, joy! Now, once again, now, O Zeus, can the pure brightness of good days come to the swift sea-cleaving ships; since Ajax again forgets his trouble, and hath turned to perform the law of the gods with all due rites, in perfectness of loyal worship.

The strong years make all things fade; nor would I say that aught was too strange for belief, when thus, beyond our hopes, Ajax hath been led to repent of his wrath against the Atreidae, and his dread feuds.

Enter MESSENGER *from the Greek camp.*

Messenger. Friends, I would first tell you this—Teucer is but now returned from the Mysian heights; he hath come to the generals' quarters in mid camp, and is being reviled by all the Greeks at once. They knew him from afar as he drew near, gathered around him, and then assailed him with taunts from this side and from that, every man of them, calling him "that kinsman of the maniac, of the plotter against the host," saying that he should not save himself from being mangled to death by stoning. And so they had come to this, that swords plucked from sheaths were drawn in men's hands; then the strife, when it had run well-nigh to the furthest, was allayed by the soothing words of elders. But where shall I find Ajax, to tell him this? He whom most it touches must hear all the tale.

Ch. He is not within; he hath gone forth but now; for he hath yoked a new purpose to his new mood.

Me. Alas! Alas! Too late, then, was he who sent me on this errand—or I have proved a laggard.

Ch. And what urgent business hath been scanted here?

Me. Teucer enjoined that the man should not go forth from the house, until he himself should come.

Ch. Well, he is gone, I tell thee—intent on the purpose that is best for him—to make his peace with the gods.

Me. These are the words of wild folly, if there is wisdom in the prophecy of Calchas.

Ch. What doth he prophesy? And what knowledge of this matter dost thou bring?

Me. Thus much I know—for I was present. Leaving the circle of chiefs who sat in council, Calchas drew apart from the Atreidae: then he put his right hand with all kindness in the hand of Teucer, and straitly charged him that, by all means in his power, he should keep Ajax within the house for this day that now is shining on us, and suffer him not to go abroad—if he wished ever to behold him alive. This day alone will the wrath of divine Athena vex him—so ran the warning.

"Yea," said the seer, "lives that have waxed too proud, and avail for good no more, are struck down by heavy misfortunes from the gods, as often as one born to man's estate forgets it in thoughts too high for man. But Ajax, even at his first going forth from home, was found foolish, when his sire spake well. His father said unto him: 'My son, seek victory in arms, but seek it ever with the help of heaven.' Then haughtily and foolishly he answered: 'Father, with the help of gods e'en a man of nought might win the mastery; but I, even without their aid, trust to bring that glory within my grasp.' So proud was his vaunt. Then once again, in answer to divine Athena—when she was urging him onward and bidding him turn a deadly hand upon his foes—in that hour he uttered a speech too dread for mortal lips: 'Queen, stand thou beside the other Greeks; where Ajax stands, battle will never break our line.' By such words it was that he brought upon him the appalling anger of the goddess, since his thoughts were too great for man. But if he lives this day, perchance with the god's help we may find means to save him."

Thus far the seer: and Teucer had no sooner risen from where they sat than he sent me with these mandates for thy guidance. But if we have been foiled, that man lives not, or Calchas is no prophet.

Ch. Hapless Tecmessa, born to misery, come forth and see what tidings yon man tells; this peril touches us too closely for our peace.

Enter TECMESSA.

Te. Why do ye break my rest again, ah me, when I had but just found peace from relentless woes?

Ch. Hearken to yon man, and the tidings of Ajax that he hath brought us, to my grief.

Te. Alas, what sayest thou, man? Are we undone?

Me. I know not of thy fortune, but only that, if Ajax is abroad, my mind is ill at ease for him.

Te. He is abroad indeed, so that I am in anguish to know thy meaning.

Me. Teucer straitly commands that ye keep Ajax under shelter of the roof, and suffer him not to go forth alone.

Te. And where is Teucer, and wherefore speaks he thus?

Me. He hath but now returned; and forbodes that this going forth is fraught with death to Ajax.

Te. Unhappy me! from whom can he have learned this?

Me. From Thestor's son, the seer, this day—when the issue is one of life or death for Ajax.

Te. Ah me, my friends, protect me from the doom threatened by fate! Speed, some of you, to hasten Teucer's coming; let others go to the westward bays, and others to the eastward, and seek the man's ill-omened steps. I see now that I have been deceived by my lord, and cast out of the favour that once I found with him. Ah me, my child, what shall I do? We must not sit idle: nay, I too will go as far as I have strength. Away—let us be quick—'tis no time to rest, if we would save a man who is in haste to die.

Ch. I am ready, and will show it in more than word; speed of act and foot shall go therewith.

(*The scene changes to a lonely place on the shore of the Hellespont, with underwood or bushes.*)

Enter AJAX.

Aj. The slayer stands so that he shall do his work most surely—if leisure serves for so much thought—the gift of Hector, that foeman-friend who was most hateful to my soul and to my sight; 'tis fixed in hostile soil, the land of Troy, with a new edge from the iron-biting whet; and I have planted it with heedful care, so that it should prove most kindly to me in a speedy death.

Thus on my part all is ready; and next be thou, O Zeus—as is meet—the first to aid me: 'tis no large boon that I will crave. Send, I pray thee, some messenger with the ill news to Teucer, that he may be the first to raise me where I have fallen on this reeking sword, lest I be first espied by some enemy, and cast forth a prey to dogs and birds. For thus much, O Zeus, I entreat thee; and I call also on Hermes, guide to the nether world, that he lay me softly asleep, without a struggle, at one quick bound, when I have driven this sword into my side.

And I call for help to the maidens who live for ever, and ever look on all the woes of men, the dread, far-striding Furies; let them mark how my miserable life is blasted by the Atreidae. And may they overtake those evil men with doom most evil and with utter blight [even as they behold me fall self-slain, so, slain by kinsfolk, may those men perish at the hand of their best-loved offspring]. Come, ye swift and vengeful Furies, glut your wrath on all the host, and spare not!

And thou whose chariot-wheels climb the heights of heaven, thou Sun-god, when thou lookest on the land of my sires, draw in thy rein o'erspread with gold, and tell my disasters and my death to mine aged father and to the hapless woman who reared me. Poor mother! I think, when she hears those tidings, her loud wail will ring through all the city. But it avails not to make idle moan: now for the deed, as quickly as I may.

O Death, Death, come now and look upon me! Nay, to thee will I speak in that other world also, when I am with thee. But thee, thou present beam of the bright day, and the Sun in his chariot, I accost for the last, last time—as never more hereafter. O sunlight! O sacred soil of mine own Salamis, firm seat of my father's hearth! O famous Athens, and thy race kindred to mine! And ye, springs and rivers of this land—and ye plains of Troy, I greet you also—farewell, ye who have cherished my life! This is the last word that Ajax speaks to you: henceforth he will speak in Hades with the dead.

AJAX *falls upon his sword.*

The CHORUS *re-enters, in two bands.*

First Semi-Chorus. Toil follows toil, and brings but toil! Where, where have my steps not been? And still no place is conscious of a secret that I share. Hark—a sudden noise!

Second Semi-Chorus. 'Tis we, the shipmates of your voyage.

Semi-Ch I. How goes it?

Semi-Ch. II. All the westward side of the ships hath been paced.

Semi-Ch. I. Well, hast thou found aught?

Semi-Ch. II. Only much toil, and nothing more to see.

Semi-Ch. I. And clearly the man hath not been seen either along the path that fronts the morning ray.

Ch. O for tidings from some toiling fisher, busy about his sleepless quest, or from some nymph of the Olympian heights, or of the streams that flow toward Bosporus—if anywhere such hath seen the man of fierce spirit roaming! 'Tis hard that I, the wanderer who have toiled so long, cannot come near him with prospered course, but fail to descry where the sick man is.

Enter TECMESSA.

Te. Ah me, ah me!

Ch. Whose cry broke from the covert of the wood near us?

Te. Ah, miserable!

Ch. I see the spear-won bride, hapless Tecmessa: her soul is steeped in the anguish of that wail.

Te. I am lost, undone, left desolate, my friends!

Ch. What ails thee?

Te. Here lies our Ajax, newly slain—a sword buried and sheathed in his corpse.

Ch. Alas for my hopes of return! Ah, prince, thou hast slain me, the comrade of thy voyage! Hapless man—broken-hearted woman!

Te. Even thus is it with him: 'tis ours to wail.

Ch. By whose hand, then, can the wretched man have done the deed?

Te. By his own; 'tis well seen: this sword, which he planted in the ground, and on which he fell, convicts him.

Ch. Alas for my blind folly, all alone, then, thou hast fallen in blood, unwatched of friends! And I took no heed, so dull was I, so witless! Where, where lies Ajax, that wayward one, of ill-boding name?

Te. No eye shall look on him: nay, in this enfolding robe I will shroud him wholly; for no man who loved him could bear to see him, as up to nostril and forth from red gash he spirts the darkened blood from the self-dealt wound. Ah me, what shall I do? What friend shall lift thee in his arms? Where is Teucer? How timely would be his arrival, might he but come, to compose the corpse of this his brother!

Ah, hapless Ajax, from what height fallen how low! How worthy, even in the sight of foes, to be mourned!

Ch. Thou wast fated, hapless one, thou wast fated, then, with that unbending soul, at last to work out an evil doom of woes untold! Such was the omen of those complainings which by night and by day I heard thee utter in thy fierce mood, bitter against the Atreidae with a deadly passion. Aye, that time was a potent source of sorrows, when the golden arms were made the prize in a contest of prowess!

Te. Woe, woe is me!

Ch. The anguish pierces, I know, to thy true heart.

Te. Woe, woe is me!

Ch. I marvel not, lady, that thou shouldst wail, and wail again, who hast lately been bereft of one so loved.

Te. 'Tis for thee to conjecture of these things—for me, to feel them but too sorely.

Ch. Yea, even so.

Te. Alas, my child, to what a yoke of bondage are we coming, seeing what task-masters are set over thee and me!

Ch. Oh, the two Atreidae would be ruthless—those deeds of theirs would be unspeakable, which thou namest in hinting at such a woe! But may the gods avert it!

Te. Never had these things stood thus, save by the will of the gods.

Ch. Yea, they have laid on us a burden too heavy to be borne.

Te. Yet such the woe that the daughter of Zeus, the dread goddess, engenders for Odysseus' sake.

Ch. Doubtless, the patient hero exults in his dark soul, and mocks with keen mockery at these sorrows born of frenzy. Alas! And with him, when they hear the tidings, laugh the royal brothers, the Atreidae.

Te. Then let them mock, and exult in this man's woes. Perchance, though they missed him not while he lived, they will bewail him dead, in the straits of warfare. Ill-judging men know not the good that was in their hands, till they have lost it. To my pain hath he died more than for their joy, and to his own content. All that he yearned to win hath he made his own—the death for which he longed. Over this man, then, wherefore should they triumph? His death concerns the gods, not them—no, verily. Then let Odysseus revel in empty taunts. Ajax is for them no more: to me he hath left anguish and mourning—and is gone.

Teucer, (*approaching*) Woe, woe is me!

Ch. Hush—methinks I hear the voice of Teucer, raised in a strain that hath regard to this dire woe.

Enter TEUCER.

Teu. Beloved Ajax, brother whose face was so dear to me—hast thou indeed fared as rumour holds?

Ch. He hath perished, Teucer: of that be sure.

Teu. Woe is me, then, for my heavy fate!

Ch. Know that thus it stands—

Teu. Hapless, hapless that I am!

Ch. And thou hast cause to mourn.

Teu. O fierce and sudden blow!

Ch. Thou sayest but too truly, Teucer.

Teu. Ay me!—But tell me of yon man's child—where shall I find him in the land of Troy?

Ch. Alone, by the tent.

Teu. (*To* TECMESSA.) Then bring him hither with all speed, lest some foeman snatch him up, as a whelp from a lioness forlorn! Away—haste—bear help! 'Tis all men's wont to triumph o'er the dead, when they lie low. *Exit* TECMESSA.

Ch. Yea, while he yet lived, Teucer, yon man charged thee to have care for the child, even as thou hast care indeed.

Teu. O sight most grievous to me of all that ever mine eyes have beheld! O bitter to my heart above all paths that I have trod, the path that now hath led me hither, when I learned thy fate, ah best-loved Ajax, as I was pursuing and tracking out thy footsteps! For a swift rumour about thee, as from some god, passed through the Greek host, telling that thou wast dead and gone. I heard it, ah me, while yet far off, and groaned low; but now the sight breaks my heart!

Come—lift the covering, and let me see the worst. (*The corpse of* AJAX *is uncovered.*)

O thou form dread to look on, wherein dwelt such cruel courage, what sorrows hast thou sown for me in thy death!

Whither can I betake me, to what people, after bringing thee no succour in thy troubles? Telamon, methinks thy sire and mine, is like to greet me with sunny face and gracious mien, when I come without thee. Aye, surely—he who, even when good fortune befalls him, is not wont to smile more brightly than before.

What will such an one keep back? What taunt will he not utter against the bastard begotten from the war-prize of his spear, against him who betrayed thee, beloved Ajax, like a coward and a craven—or by guile, that, when thou wast dead, he might enjoy thy lordship and thy house? So will he speak—a passionate man, peevish in old age, whose wrath makes strife even without a cause. And in the end I shall be thrust from the realm, and cast off—branded by his taunts as no more a freeman but a slave.

Such is my prospect at home; while at Troy I have many foes, and few things to help me. All this have I reaped by thy death! Ah me, what shall I do? how draw thee, hapless one, from the cruel point of this gleaming sword, the slayer, it seems, to whom thou hast yielded up thy breath? Now seest thou how Hector, though dead, was to destroy thee at the last?

Consider, I pray you, the fortune of these two men. With the very girdle that had been given to him by Ajax, Hector was gripped to the chariot-rail, and mangled till he gave up the ghost. 'Twas from Hector that Ajax had this gift, and by this hath he perished in his deadly fall. Was it not the Fury who forged this blade, was not that girdle wrought by Hades, grim artificer? I, at least, would deem that these things, and all things ever, are planned by gods for men; but if there be any in whose mind this wins no favour, let him hold to his own thoughts, as I hold to mine.

Ch. Speak not at length, but think how thou shalt lay the man in the tomb, and what thou wilt say anon: for I see a foe, and perchance he will come with mocking of our sorrows, as evil-doers use.

Teu. And what man of the host dost thou behold?

Ch. Menelaüs, for whom we made this voyage.

Teu. I see him; he is not hard to know, when near.

Enter MENELAÜS.

Menelaüs. Sirrah, I tell thee to bear no hand in raising yon corpse, but to leave it where it lies.

Teu. Wherefore hast thou spent thy breath in such proud words?

Me. 'Tis my pleasure, and his who rules the host.

Teu. And might we hear what reason thou pretendest?

Me. This—that, when we had hoped we were bringing him from home to be an ally and a friend for the Greeks, we found him, on trial, a worse than Phrygian foe; who plotted death for all the host, and sallied by night against us, to slay with the spear; and, if some god had not quenched this attempt, ours would have been the lot which he hath found, to lie slain by an ignoble doom, while he would have been living. But now a god hath turned his outrage aside, to fall on sheep and cattle.

Wherefore there is no man so powerful that he shall entomb the corpse of Ajax; no, he shall be cast forth somewhere on the yellow sand, and become food for the birds by the sea. Then raise no storm of angry threats. If we were not able to control him while he lived, at least we shall rule him in death, whether thou wilt or not, and control him with our hands; since, while he lived, there never was a time when he would hearken to my words.

Yet 'tis the sign of an unworthy nature when a subject deigns not to obey those who are set over him. Never can the laws have prosperous course in a city where dread hath no place; nor can a camp be ruled discreetly any more, if it lack the guarding force of fear and reverence. Nay, though a man's frame have waxed mighty, he should look to fall, perchance, by a light blow. Whoso hath fear, and shame therewith, be sure that he is safe; but where there is licence to insult and act at will, doubt not that such a State, though favouring gales have sped her, some day, at last, sinks into the depths.

No, let me see fear, too, where fear is meet, established; let us not dream that we can do after our desires, without paying the price in our pains. These things come by turns. This man was once hot and insolent; now 'tis my hour to be haughty. And I warn thee not to bury him, lest through that deed thou thyself shouldst come to need a grave.

Ch. Menelaüs, after laying down wise precepts, do not thyself be guilty of outrage on the dead.

Teu. Never, friends, shall I wonder more if a low-born man offends after his kind, when they who are accounted of noble blood allow such scandalous words to pass their lips.

Come, tell me from the first once more—Sayest thou that *thou* broughtest the man hither to the Greeks, as an ally found by *thee*? Sailed he not forth of his own act—as his own master? What claim hast thou to be his chief? On what ground hast thou a right to kingship of the lieges whom he brought from home? As Sparta's king thou camest, not as master over us. Nowhere was it laid down among thy lawful powers that thou shouldst dictate to him, any more than he to thee. Under the command of others didst thou sail hither, not as chief of all, so that thou shouldst ever be captain over Ajax.

No, lord it over them whose lord thou art, lash *them* with thy proud words: but this man will I lay duly in the grave, though thou forbid it—aye, or thy brother-chief—nor shall I tremble at thy word. 'Twas not for thy wife's sake that Ajax came unto the war, like yon toil-worn drudges—no, but for the oath's sake that bound him—no whit for thine; he was not wont to reck of nobodies. So, when thou comest again, bring more heralds, and the Captain of the host; at *thy* noise I would not turn my head, while thou art the man that thou art now.

Ch. Such speech again, in the midst of ills, I love not; for harsh words, how just soever, sting.

Me. The bowman, methinks, hath no little pride.

Teu. Even so; 'tis no sordid craft that I profess.

Me. How thou wouldst boast, wert thou given a shield!

Teu. Without a shield, I were a match for thee full-armed.

Me. How dreadful the courage that inspires thy tongue!

Teu. When right is with him, a man's spirit may be high.

Me. Is it right that this my murderer should have honour?

Teu. Murderer? A marvel truly, if, though slain, thou livest.

Me. A god rescued me: in yon man's purpose, I am dead.

Teu. The gods have saved thee: then dishonour not the gods.

Me. What, would *I* disparage the laws of Heaven?

Teu. If thou art here to forbid the burying of the dead.

Me. Yea, of my country's foes: for it is not meet.

Teu. Did Ajax e'er confront thee as public foe?

Me. There was hate betwixt us; thou, too, knewest this.

Teu. Yea, 'twas found that thou hadst suborned votes, to rob him.

Me. At the hands of the judges, not at mine, he had that fall.

Teu. Thou couldst put a fair face on many a furtive villainy.

Me. That saying tends to pain—I know, for whom.

Teu. Not greater pain, methinks, than we shall inflict.

Me. Hear my last word—that man must not be buried.

Teu. And hear my answer—he shall be buried forthwith.

Me. Once did I see a man bold of tongue, who had urged sailors to a voyage in time of storm, in whom thou wouldst have found no voice when the stress of the tempest was upon him, but, hidden beneath his cloak, he would suffer the crew to trample on him at will. And so with thee and thy fierce speech—perchance a great tempest, though its breath come from a little cloud, shall quench thy blustering.

Teu. Yea, and I have seen a man full of folly, who triumphed in his neighbour's woes; and it came to pass that a man like unto me, and of like mood, beheld him, and spake such words as these: "Man, do not evil to the dead; for, if thou dost, be sure that thou wilt come to harm." So warned he the misguided one before him; and know that I see that man, and methinks he is none else but thou: have I spoken in riddles?

Me. I will go: it were a disgrace to have it known that I was chiding when I have the power to compel.

Teu. Begone then! For me 'tis the worse disgrace that I should listen to a fool's idle prate.

Exit MENELAÜS.

Ch. A dread strife will be brought to the trial. But thou, Teucer, with what speed thou mayest, haste to seek a hollow grave for yon man, where he shall rest in his dark, dank tomb, that men shall ever hold in fame.

Enter TECMESSA *and Child.*

Teu. Lo, just in time our lord's child and his wife draw nigh, to tend the burial of the hapless corpse.

My child, come hither: take thy place near him, and lay thy hand, as a suppliant, upon thy sire. And kneel as one who implores help, with locks of hair in thy hand—mine, hers, and thirdly thine—the suppliant's store. But if any man of the host should tear thee by violence from this dead, then, for evil doom on evil deed, may he perish out of the land and find no grave, and with him be his race cut off, root and branch, even as I sever this lock. Take it, boy, and keep; and let no one move thee, but kneel there, and cling unto the dead.

And ye, be not as women at his side, but bear you like men for his defence, till I return, when I have prepared a grave for this man, though all the world forbid.

Exit TUECER.

Chorus

When, ah when, will the number of the restless years be full, at what term will they cease, that bring on me the unending woe of a warrior's toils throughout the wide land of Troy, for the sorrow and the shame of Greece?

Would that the man had passed into the depths of the sky, or to all-receiving Hades, who taught Greeks how to league themselves for war in hateful arms! Ah, those toils of his, from which so many toils have sprung! Yea, he it was who wrought the ruin of men.

No delight of garlands or bounteous wine-cups did that man give me for my portion, no sweet music of flutes, the wretch, or soothing rest in the night; and from love, alas, from love he hath divorced my days.

And here I have my couch, uncared for, while heavy dews ever wet my hair, lest I should forget that I am in the cheerless land of Troy.

Erewhile, bold Ajax was alway my defence against nightly terror and the darts of the foe; but now he hath become the sacrifice of a malignant fate. What joy, then, what joy shall crown me more?

O to be wafted where the wooded sea-cape stands upon the laving sea, O to pass beneath Sunium's level summit, that so we might greet sacred Athens!

Enter TEUCER, *followed by* AGAMEMNON.

Teu. Lo, I am come in haste, for I saw the Captain of the host, Agamemnon, moving hither apace; and I wot he will not bridle perverse lips.

Agamemnon. So 'tis thou, they tell me, who hast dared to open thy mouth with such blustering against us—and hast yet to smart for it? Yea, I mean thee—thee, the captive woman's son. Belike, hadst thou been bred of well-born mother, lofty had been thy vaunt and proud thy strut, when, nought as thou art, thou hast stood up for him who is as nought, and hast vowed that we came out with no title on sea or land to rule the Greeks or thee; no, as chief in his own right, thou sayest, sailed Ajax forth.

Are not these presumptuous taunts for us to hear from slaves? What was the man whom thou vauntest with such loud arrogance? Whither went he, or where stood he, where I was not? Have the Greeks, then, no other men but him? Methinks we shall rue that day when we called the Greeks to contest the arms of Achilles, if, whatever the issue, we are to be denounced as false by Teucer, and if ye never will consent, though defeated, to accept that doom for which most judges gave their voice, but must ever assail us somewhere with revilings, or stab us in the dark—ye, the losers in the race.

Now, where such ways prevail, no law could ever be firmly stablished, if we are to thrust the rightful winners aside, and bring the rearmost to the front. Nay, this must be checked. 'Tis not the burly, broad-shouldered men that are surest at need; no, 'tis the wise who prevail in every field. A large-ribbed ox is yet kept straight on the road by a small whip. And this remedy, methinks, will visit thee ere long, if thou fail to gain some measure of wisdom; thou who, when the man lives no more, but is now a shade, art so boldly insolent, and givest such licence to thy tongue. Sober thyself, I say; recall thy birth; bring hither some one else—a freeborn man—who shall plead thy cause for thee before us. When thou speakest, I can take the sense no more; I understand not thy barbarian speech.

Ch. Would that ye both could learn the wisdom of a temperate mind! No better counsel could I give you twain.

Teu. Ah, gratitude to the dead—in what quick sort it falls away from men and is found a traitor, if this man hath no longer the slightest tribute of remembrance for thee, Ajax—he for whom thou didst toil so often, putting thine own life to the peril of the spear! No—'tis all forgotten, all flung aside!

Man, who but now hast spoken many words and vain, hast thou no more memory of the time when ye were shut within your lines—when ye were as lost in the turning back of your battle—and he came alone and saved you—when the flames were already wrapping the decks at your ships' stern, and Hector was bounding high over the trench towards the vessels? Who averted that? Were these deeds not his, who, thou sayest, nowhere set foot where thou wast not?

Would ye allow that he did his duty there? Or when, another time, all alone, he confronted Hector in single fight—not at any man's bidding, but by right of ballot, for the lot which he cast in was not one to skulk behind, no lump of moist earth, but such as would be the first to leap lightly from the crested helm! His were these deeds, and at his side was I—the slave, the son of the barbarian mother.

Wretch, how canst thou be so blind as to rail thus? Knowst thou not that thy sire's sire was Pelops of old—a barbarian, a Phrygian? That Atreus, who begat thee, set before his brother a most impious feast—the flesh of that brother's children? And thou thyself wert born of a Cretan mother, with whom her sire found a paramour, and doomed her to be food for the dumb fishes? Being such, makest thou his origin a reproach to such as I am? The father from whom I sprang is Telamon, who, as prize for valour peerless in the host, won my mother for his bride, by birth a princess, daughter of Laomedon; and as the flower of the spoil was she given to Telamon by Alcmena's son.

Thus nobly born from two noble parents, could I disgrace my kinsman, whom, now that such sore ills have laid him low, thou wouldst thrust forth without burial—yea, and art not ashamed to say it? Now be thou sure of this—wheresoever ye cast this man, with him ye will cast forth our three corpses also. It beseems me to die in his cause, before all men's eyes, rather than for thy wife—or thy brother's, should I say? Be prudent, therefore, not for my sake, but for thine own also; for, if thou harm me, thou wilt wish anon that thou hadst been a very coward, ere thy rashness had been wreaked on me.

Enter ODYSSEUS.

Ch. King Odysseus, know that thou hast come in season, if thou art here, not to embroil, but to mediate.

Od. What ails you, friends? Far off I heard loud speech of the Atreidae over this brave man's corpse.

Ag. Nay, King Odysseus, have we not been hearing but now most shameful taunts from yonder man?

Od. How was that? I can pardon a man who is reviled if he engage in wordy war.

Ag. I *had* reviled him; for his deeds toward me were vile.

Od. And what did he unto thee, that thou hast a wrong?

Ag. He says that he will not leave yon corpse ungraced by sepulture, but will bury it in my despite.

Od. Now may a friend speak out the truth, and still, as ever, ply his oar in time with thine?

Ag. Speak: else were I less than sane; for I count thee my greatest friend of all the Greeks.

Od. Listen, then. For the love of the gods, take not the heart to cast forth this man unburied so ruthlessly; and in no wise let violence prevail with thee to hate so utterly that thou shouldest trample justice under foot.

To me also this man was once the worst foe in the army, from the day that I became master of the arms of Achilles; yet, for all that he was such toward me, never would I requite him with indignity, or refuse to avow that, in all our Greek host which came to Troy, I have seen none who was his peer, save Achilles. It were not just, then, that he should suffer dishonour at thy hand; 'tis not he, 'tis the law of Heaven that thou wouldst hurt. When a brave man is dead, 'tis not right to do him scathe—no, not even if thou hate him.

Ag. *Thou*, Odysseus, thus his champion against me?

Od. I am; yet hated him, when I could honourably hate.

Ag. And shouldst thou not also set thy heel on him in death?

Od. Delight not, son of Atreus, in gains which sully honour.

Ag. 'Tis not easy for a king to observe piety.

Od. But he can show respect to his friends, when they counsel well.

Ag. A loyal man should hearken to the rulers.

Od. Enough: the victory is thine, when thou yieldest to thy friends.

Ag. Remember to what a man thou showest the grace

Od. Yon man was erst my foe, yet noble.

Ag. What canst thou mean? Such reverence for a dead foe?

Od. His worth weighs with me far more than his enmity.

Ag. Nay, such as thou are the unstable among men.

Od. Full many are friends at one time, and foes anon.

Ag. Dost thou approve, then, of our making such friends?

Od. 'Tis not my wont to approve a stubborn soul.

Ag. Thou wilt make us appear cowards this day.

Od. Not so, but just men in the sight of all the Greeks.

Ag. So thou wouldst have me allow the burying of the dead?

Od. Yea: for I too shall come to that need.

Ag. Truly in all things alike each man works for himself!

Od. And for whom should I work rather than for myself!

Ag. It must be called thy doing, then, not mine.

Od. Call it whose thou wilt, in any case thou wilt be kind.

Ag. Nay, be well assured that I would grant *thee* a larger boon than this; yon man, however, as on earth, so in the shades, shall have my hatred. But thou canst do what thou wilt.

Exit AGAMEMNON.

Ch. Whoso saith, Odysseus, that thou hast not inborn wisdom, being such as thou art, that man is foolish.

Od. Yea, and I tell Teucer now that henceforth I am ready to be his friend—as staunch as I was once a foe. And I would join in the burying of your dead, and partake your cares, and omit no service which mortals should render to the noblest among men.

Teu. Noble Odysseus, I have only praise to give thee for thy words; and greatly hast thou belied my fears. Thou wast his deadliest foe of all the Greeks, yet thou alone hast stood by him with active aid; thou hast found no heart, in this presence, to heap the insults of the living on the dead—like yon crazed chief that came, he and his brother, and would have cast forth the outraged corpse without burial. Therefore may the Father supreme in the heaven above us, and the remembering Fury, and Justice that brings the end, destroy those evil men with evil doom, even as they sought to cast forth this man with unmerited despite.

But, son of aged Laertes, I scruple to admit thy helping hand in these funeral rites, lest so I do displeasure to the dead; in all else be thou indeed our fellow-worker; and if thou wouldst bring any man of the host, we shall make thee welcome. For the rest, I will make all things ready; and know that to us thou hast been a generous friend.

Od. It was my wish; but if it is not pleasing to thee that I should assist here, I accept thy decision, and depart.

Exit ODYSSEUS.

Teu. Enough: already the delay hath been long drawn out. Come, haste some of you to dig the hollow grave; place, some, the high-set caldron girt with fire, in readiness for holy ablution; and let another band bring the body-armour from the tent.

And thou, too, child, with such strength as thou hast, lay a loving hand upon thy sire, and help me to uplift this prostrate form; for still the warm channels are spouting upward their dark tide.

Come, each one here who owns the name of friend, haste, away, in service to this man of perfect prowess; and never yet was service rendered to a nobler among men.

Ch. Many things shall mortals learn by seeing; but, before he sees, no man may read the future, or his fate.

ELECTRA

DRAMATIS PERSONAE

Orestes, *son of Agamemnon and Clytaemnestra*
Electra | Chrysothemis — *sisters of Orestes*
Paedagogus, *an old man, formerly the attendant of Orestes*
Clytaemnestra
Aegisthus
Chorus of Women of Mycenae

Mute: Pylades, *son of Strophius, king of Crisa, the friend of Orestes; A handmaid of Clytaemnestra* (*v.* 634): *Two attendants of Orestes* (*v.* 1123)

At Mycenae, before the Palace of the Pelopidae. The paedagogus *enters, on the left of the spectators, accompanied by the two youths,* orestes *and* pylades.

Paedagogus. Son of him who led our hosts at Troy of old, son of Agamemnon—now thou mayest behold with thine eyes all that thy soul hath desired so long. There is the ancient Argos of thy yearning—that hallowed scene whence the gad-fly drove the daughter of Inachus; and there, Orestes, is the Lycean Agora, named from the wolf-slaying god; there, on the left, Hera's famous temple; and in this place to which we have come, deem that thou seest Mycenae rich in gold, with the house of the Pelopidae there, so often stained with bloodshed; whence I carried thee of yore, from the slaying of thy father, as thy kinswoman, thy sister, charged me; and saved thee, and reared thee up to manhood, to be the avenger of thy murdered sire.

Now, therefore, Orestes, and thou, best of friends, Pylades, our plans must be laid quickly; for lo, already the sun's bright ray is waking the songs of the birds into clearness, and the dark night of stars is spent. Before, then, anyone comes forth from the house, take counsel; seeing that the time allows not of delay, but is full ripe for deeds.

Orestes. True friend and follower, how well dost thou prove thy loyalty to our house! As a steed of generous race, though old, loses not courage in danger, but pricks his ear, even so thou urgest us forward, and art foremost in our support. I will tell thee, then, what I have determined; listen closely to my words, and correct me, if I miss the mark in aught.

When I went to the Pythian oracle, to learn how I might avenge my father on his murderers, Phoebus gave me the response which thou art now to hear: that alone, and by stealth, without aid of arms or numbers, I should snatch the righteous vengeance of my hand. Since, then, the god spake to us on this wise, thou must go into yonder house, when opportunity gives thee entrance, and learn all that is passing there, so that thou mayest report to us from sure knowledge. Thine age, and the lapse of time, will prevent them from recognising thee; they will never suspect who thou art, with that silvered hair. Let thy tale be that thou art a Phocian stranger, sent by Phanoteus; for he is the greatest of their allies. Tell them, and confirm it with thine oath, that Orestes hath perished by a fatal chance, hurled, at the Pythian games, from his rapid chariot; be that the substance of thy story.

We, meanwhile, will first crown my father's tomb, as the god enjoined, with drink-offerings and the luxuriant tribute of severed hair; then come back, bearing in our hands an urn of shapely bronze—now hidden in the brushwood, as I think thou knowest—so to gladden them with the false tidings that this my body is no more, but has been consumed with fire and turned to ashes. Why should the omen trouble me, when by a feigned death I find life indeed, and win renown? I trow, no word is ill-omened, if fraught with gain. Often ere now have I seen wise men die in vain report; then, when they return home, they are held in more abiding honour: as I trust that from this rumour I also shall emerge in radiant life, and yet shine like a star upon my foes.

O my fatherland, and ye gods of the land, receive me with good fortune in this journey—and ye also, halls of my fathers, for I come with a divine mandate to cleanse you righteously; send me not dishonoured from the land, but grant that I may rule over my possessions, and restore my house!

Enough; be it now thy care, old man, to go and heed thy task; and we twain will go forth; for so occasion bids, chief ruler of every enterprise for men.

Electra (*within*). Ah me, ah me!

Pae. Hark, my son—from the doors, methought, came the sound of some handmaid moaning within.

Or. Can it be the hapless Electra? Shall we stay here, and listen to her laments?

Pae. No, no: before all else, let us seek to obey the

command of Loxias, and thence make a fair beginning, by pouring libations to thy sire; that brings victory within our grasp, and gives us the mastery in all that we do.

Exeunt PAEDAGOGUS *on the spectator's left,* ORESTES *and* PYLADES *on the right.—Enter* ELECTRA, *from the house.*

El. O thou pure sunlight, and thou air, earth's canopy, how often have ye heard the strains of my lament, the wild blows dealt against this bleeding breast, when dark night fails! And my wretched couch in yonder house of woe knows well, ere now, how I keep the watches of the night, how often I bewail my hapless sire; to whom deadly Ares gave not of his gifts in a strange land, but my mother, and her mate Aegisthus, cleft his head with murderous axe, as woodmen fell an oak. And for this no plaint bursts from any lip save mine, when thou, my father, hath died a death so cruel and so piteous!

But never will I cease from dirge and sore lament, while I look on the trembling rays of the bright stars, or on this light of day; but like the nightingale, slayer of her offspring, I will wail without ceasing, and cry aloud to all, here, at the doors of my father.

O home of Hades and Persephone! O Hermes of the shades! O potent Curse, and ye, dread daughters of the gods, Erinyes—ye who behold when a life is reft by violence, when a bed is dishonoured by stealth—come, help me, avenge the murder of my sire, and send to me my brother; for I have no more the strength to bear up alone against the load of grief that weighs me down.

Enter CHORUS OF WOMEN OF MYCENAE. *The following lines between* ELECTRA *and the* CHORUS *are chanted responsively.*

Chorus. Ah, Electra, child of a wretched mother, why art thou ever pining thus in ceaseless lament for Agamemnon, who long ago was wickedly ensnared by thy false mother's wiles, and betrayed to death by a dastardly hand? Perish the author of that deed, if I may utter such a prayer!

El. Ah, noble-hearted maidens, ye have come to soothe my woes. I know and feel it, it escapes me not; but I cannot leave this task undone, or cease from mourning for my hapless sire. Ah, friends whose love responds to mine in every mood, leave me to rave thus—oh leave me, I entreat you!

Ch. But never by laments or prayers shalt thou recall thy sire from that lake of Hades to which all must pass. Nay, thine is a fatal course of grief, passing ever from due bounds into a cureless sorrow; wherein there is no deliverance from evils. Say, wherefore art thou enamoured of misery?

El. Foolish is the child who forgets a parent's piteous death. No, dearer to my soul is the mourner that laments for Itys, Itys, evermore, that bird distraught with grief, the messenger of Zeus. Ah, queen of sorrow, Niobe, thee I deem divine—thee, who evermore weepest in thy rocky tomb!

Ch. Not to thee alone of mortals, my daughter, hath come any sorrow which thou bearest less calmly than those within, thy kinswomen and sisters, Chrysothemis and Iphianassa, who still live, as he, too, lives, sorrowing in a secluded youth, yet happy in that this famous realm of Mycenae shall one day welcome him to his heritage, when the kindly guidance of Zeus shall have brought him to this land—Orestes.

El. Yes, I wait for him with unwearied longing, as I move on my sad path from day to day, unwed and childless, bathed in tears, bearing that endless doom of woe; but he forgets all that he has suffered and heard. What message comes to me, that is not belied? He is ever yearning to be with us, but, though he yearns, he never resolves.

Ch. Courage, my daughter, courage; great still in heaven is Zeus, who sees and governs all: leave thy bitter quarrel to him; forget not thy foes, but refrain from excess of wrath against them; for Time is a god who makes rough ways smooth. Not heedless is the son of Agamemnon, who dwells by Crisa's pastoral shore; not heedless is the god who reigns by Acheron.

El. Nay, the best part of life hath passed away from me in hopelessness, and I have no strength left; I, who am pining away without children, whom no loving champion shields, but, like some despised alien, I serve in the halls of my father, clad in this mean garb, and standing at a meagre board.

Ch. Piteous was the voice heard at his return, and piteous, as thy sire lay on the festal couch, when the straight, swift blow was dealt him with the blade of bronze. Guile was the plotter, Lust the slayer, dread parents of a dreadful shape; whether it was mortal that wrought therein, or god.

El. O that bitter day, bitter beyond all that have come to me; O that night, O the horrors of that unutterable feast, the ruthless death-strokes that my father saw from the hands of twain, who took my life captive by treachery, who doomed me to woe! May the great god of Olympus give them sufferings in requital, and never may their splendour bring them joy, who have done such deeds!

Ch. Be advised to say no more; canst thou not see what conduct it is which already plunges thee so cruelly in self-made miseries? Thou hast greatly aggravated thy troubles, ever breeding wars with thy sullen soul; but such strife should not be pushed to a conflict with the strong.

El. I have been forced to it, forced by dread causes; I know my own passion, it escapes me not; but, seeing that the causes are so dire, I will never curb these frenzied plaints, while life is in me. Who indeed, ye kindly sisterhood, who that thinks aright, would deem that any word of solace could avail me? Forbear, forbear, my comforters! Such ills must be numbered with those which have no cure; I can never know a respite from my sorrows, or a limit to this wailing.

Ch. At least it is in love, like a true-hearted mother, that I dissuade thee from adding misery to miseries.

El. But what measure is there in my wretchedness? Say, how can it be right to neglect the dead? Was that impiety ever born in mortal? Never may

I have praise of such; never, when my lot is cast in pleasant places, may I cling to selfish ease, or dishonour my sire by restraining the wings of shrill lamentation!

For if the hapless dead is to lie in dust and nothingness, while the slayers pay not with blood for blood, all regard for man, all fear of heaven, will vanish from the earth.

Ch. I came, my child, in zeal for thy welfare no less than for mine own; but if I speak not well, then be it as thou wilt; for we will follow thee.

El. I am ashamed, my friends, if ye deem me too mpatient for my oft complaining; but, since a hard constraint forces me to this, bear with me. How indeed could any woman of noble nature refrain, who saw the calamities of a father's house, as I see them by day and night continually, not fading, but in the summer of their strength? I, who, first, from the mother that bore me have found bitter enmity; next, in mine own home I dwell with my father's murderers; they rule over me, and with them it rests to give or to withhold what I need.

And then think what manner of days I pass, when I see Aegisthus sitting on my father's throne, wearing the robes which he wore, and pouring libations at the hearth where he slew my sire; and when I see the outrage that crowns all, the murderer in our father's bed at our wretched mother's side, if mother she should be called, who is his wife; but so hardened is she that she lives with that accursed one, fearing no Erinys; nay, as if exulting in her deeds, having found the day on which she treacherously slew my father of old, she keeps it with dance and song, and month by month sacrifices sheep to the gods who have wrought her deliverance.

But I, hapless one, beholding it, weep and pine in the house, and bewail the unholy feast named after my sire, weep to myself alone; since I may not even indulge my grief to the full measure of my yearning. For this woman, in professions so noble, loudly upbraids me with such taunts as these: "Impious and hateful girl, hast thou alone lost a father, and is there no other mourner in the world? An evil doom be thine, and may the gods infernal give thee no riddance from thy present laments."

Thus she insults; save when any one brings her word that Orestes is coming: then, infuriated, she comes up to me, and cries: "Hast not *thou* brought this upon me? Is not this deed thine, who didst steal Orestes from my hands, and privily convey him forth? Yet be sure that thou shalt have thy due reward." So she shrieks; and, aiding her, the renowned spouse at her side is vehement in the same strain—that abject dastard, that utter pest, who fights his battles with the help of women. But I, looking ever for Orestes to come and end these woes, languish in my misery. Always intending to strike a blow, he has worn out every hope that I could conceive. In such a case, then, friends, there is no room for moderation or for reverence; in sooth, the stress of ills leaves no choice but to follow evil ways.

Ch. Say, is Aegisthus near while thou speakest thus, or absent from home?

El. Absent, certainly; do not think that I should have come to the doors, if he had been near; but just now he is a-field.

Ch. Might I converse with thee more freely, if this is so?

El. He is not here, so put thy question; what wouldst thou?

Ch. I ask thee, then, what sayest thou of thy brother? Will he come soon, or is he delaying? I fain would know.

El. He promises to come; but he never fulfils the promise.

Ch. Yea, a man will pause on the verge of a great work.

El. And yet I saved *him* without pausing.

Ch. Courage; he is too noble to fail his friends.

El. I believe it; or I should not have lived so long.

Ch. Say no more now; for I see thy sister coming from the house, Chrysothemis, daughter of the same sire and mother, with sepulchral gifts in her hands, such as are given to those in the world below.

Enter CHRYSOTHEMIS.

Chrysothemis. Why, sister, hast thou come forth once more to declaim thus at the public doors? Why wilt thou not learn with any lapse of time to desist from vain indulgence of idle wrath? Yet this I know—that I myself am grieved at our plight; indeed, could I find the strength, I would show what love I bear them. But now, in these troubled waters, 'tis best, methinks, to shorten sail; I care not to seem active, without the power to hurt. And would that thine own conduct were the same! Nevertheless, right is on the side of thy choice, not of that which I advise; but if I am to live in freedom, our rulers must be obeyed in all things.

El. Strange indeed, that thou, the daughter of such a sire as thine, shouldst forget him, and think only of thy mother! All thy admonitions to me have been taught by her; no word is thine own. Then take thy choice—to be imprudent; or prudent, but forgetful of thy friends: thou, who hast just said that, couldst thou find the strength, thou wouldst show thy hatred of them; yet, when I am doing my utmost to avenge my sire, thou givest no aid, but seekest to turn thy sister from her deed.

Does not this crown our miseries with cowardice? For tell me—or let me tell thee—what I should gain by ceasing from these laments? Do I not live?—miserably, I know, yet well enough for me. And I vex *them*, thus rendering honour to the dead, if pleasure can be felt in that world. But thou, who tellest me of thy hatred, hatest in word alone, while in deeds thou art with the slayers of thy sire. I, then, would never yield to them, though I were promised the gifts which now make thee proud; thine be the richly-spread table and the life of luxury. For me, be it food enough that I do not wound mine own conscience; I covet not such privilege as thine—nor wouldst thou, wert thou wise. But now, when thou mightest be called daughter of the noblest father among men, be called the child of thy mother; so shall thy baseness be most widely seen, in betrayal of thy dead sire and of thy kindred.

Ch. No angry word, I entreat! For both of you there is good in what is urged—if thou, Electra, wouldst learn to profit by her counsel, and she, again, by thine.

Chr. For my part, friends, I am not wholly unused to her discourse; nor should I have touched upon this theme, had I not heard that she was threatened with a dread doom, which shall restrain her from her long-drawn laments.

El. Come, declare it then, this terror! If thou canst tell me of aught worse than my present lot, I will resist no more.

Chr. Indeed, I will tell thee all that I know. They purpose, if thou wilt not cease from these laments, to send thee where thou shalt never look upon the sunlight, but pass thy days in a dungeon beyond the borders of this land, there to chant thy dreary strain. Bethink thee, then, and do not blame me hereafter, when the blow hath fallen; now is the time to be wise.

El. Have they indeed resolved to treat me thus?

Chr. Assuredly, whenever Aegisthus comes home.

El. If that be all, then may he arrive with speed!

Chr. Misguided one! what dire prayer is this?

El. That he may come, if he hath any such intent.

Chr. That thou mayst suffer—what? Where are thy wits?

El. That I may fly as far as may be from you all.

Chr. But hast thou no care for thy present life?

El. Aye, my life is marvellously fair.

Chr. It might be, couldst thou only learn prudence.

El. Do not teach me to betray my friends.

Chr. I do not—but to bend before the strong.

El. Thine be such flattery: those are not my ways.

Chr. 'Tis well, however, not to fall by folly.

El. I will fall, if need be, in the cause of my sire.

Chr. But our father, I know, pardons me for this.

El. It is for cowards to find peace in such maxims.

Chr. So thou wilt not hearken, and take my counsel?

El. No, verily; long may be it before I am so foolish.

Chr. Then I will go forth upon mine errand.

El. And whither goest thou? To whom bearest thou these offerings?

Chr. Our mother sends me with funeral libations for our sire.

El. How sayest thou? For her deadliest foe?

Chr. Slain by her own hand—so thou wouldest say.

El. What friend hath persuaded her? Whose wish was this?

Chr. The cause, I think, was some dread vision of the night.

El. Gods of our house! be ye with me—now at last!

Chr. Dost thou find any encouragement in this terror?

El. If thou wouldst tell me the vision, then I could answer.

Chr. Nay, I can tell but little of the story.

El. Tell what thou canst; a little word hath often marred, or made, men's fortunes.

Chr. 'Tis said that she beheld our sire, restored to the sunlight, at her side once more; then he took the sceptre—once his own, but now borne by Aegisthus—and planted it at the hearth; and thence a fruitful bough sprang upward, wherewith the whole land of Mycenae was overshadowed. Such was the tale that I heard told by one who was present when she declared her dream to the Sun-god. More than this I know not, save that she sent me by reason of that fear. So by the gods of our house I beseech thee, hearken to me, and be not ruined by folly! For if thou repel me now, thou wilt come back to seek me in thy trouble.

El. Nay, dear sister, let none of these things in thy hands touch the tomb; for neither custom nor piety allows thee to dedicate gifts or bring libations to our sire from a hateful wife. No—to the winds with them! or bury them deep in the earth, where none of them shall ever come near his place of rest; but, when she dies, let her find these treasures laid up for her below.

And were she not the most hardened of all women, she would never have sought to pour these offerings of enmity on the grave of him whom she slew. Think now if it is likely that the dead in the tomb should take these honours kindly at her hand, who ruthlessly slew him, like a foeman, and mangled him, and, for ablution, wiped off the blood-stains on his head? Canst thou believe that these things which thou bringest will absolve her of the murder?

It is not possible. No, cast these things aside; give him rather a lock cut from thine own tresses, and on my part, hapless that I am—scant gifts these, but my best—this hair, not glossy with unguents, and this girdle, decked with no rich ornament. Then fall down and pray that he himself may come in kindness from the world below, to aid us against our foes; and that the young Orestes may live to set his foot upon his foes in victorious might, that henceforth we may crown our father's tomb with wealthier hands than those which grace it now.

I think, indeed, I think that he also had some part in sending her these appalling dreams; still, sister, do this service, to help thyself, and me, and him, that most beloved of all men, who rests in the realm of Hades, thy sire and mine.

Ch. The maiden counsels piously; and thou, friend, wilt do her bidding, if thou art wise.

Chr. I will. When a duty is clear, reason forbids that two voices should contend, and claims the hastening of the deed. Only, when I attempt this task, aid me with your silence, I entreat you, my friends; for, should my mother hear of it, methinks I shall yet have cause to rue my venture. *Exit.*

Ch. If I am not an erring seer and one who fails in wisdom, Justice, that hath sent the presage, will come, triumphant in her righteous strength, will come ere long, my child, to avenge. There is courage in my heart, through those new tidings of the dream that breathes comfort. Not forgetful is thy sire, the lord of Hellas; not forgetful is the two-edged axe of bronze that struck the blow of old, and slew him with foul cruelty.

The Erinys of untiring feet, who is lurking in her dread ambush, will come, as with the march and with the might of a great host. For wicked ones have been fired with passion that hurried them to a forbidden bed, to accursed bridals, to a marriage stained with guilt of blood. Therefore am I sure that the portent will not fail to bring woe upon the partners in crime. Verily mortals cannot read the future in fearful dreams or oracles, if this vision of the night find not due fulfilment.

O chariot-race of Pelops long ago, source of many a sorrow, what weary troubles hast thou brought upon this land! For since Myrtilus sank to rest beneath the waves, when a fatal and cruel hand hurled him to destruction out of the golden car, this house was never yet free from misery and violence.

Enter CLYTAEMNESTRA.

Clytaemnestra. At large once more, it seems, thou rangest, for Aegisthus is not here, who always kept thee at least from passing the gates, to shame thy friends. But now, since he is absent, thou takest no heed of me; though thou hast said of me oft-times, and to many, that I am a bold and lawless tyrant, who insults thee and thine. I am guilty of no insolence; I do but return the taunts that I often hear from thee.

Thy father—this is thy constant pretext—was slain by me. Yes, by me—I know it well; it admits of no denial; for Justice slew him, and not I alone—Justice, whom it became thee to support, hadst thou been right-minded; seeing that this father of thine, whom thou art ever lamenting, was the one man of the Greeks who had the heart to sacrifice thy sister to the gods—he, the father, who had not shared the mother's pangs.

Come, tell me now, wherefore, or to please whom, did he sacrifice her? To please the Argives, thou wilt say? Nay, they had no right to slay my daughter. Or if, forsooth, it was to screen his brother Menelaüs that he slew my child, was he not to pay me the penalty for that? Had not Menelaüs two children, who should in fairness have been taken before my daughter, as sprung from the sire and mother who had caused that voyage? Or had Hades some strange desire to feast on my offspring, rather than on hers? Or had that accursèd father lost all tenderness for the children of my womb, while he was tender to the children of Menelaüs? Was not that the part of a callous and perverse parent? I think so, though I differ from thy judgment; and so would say the dead, if she could speak. For myself, then, I view the past without dismay; but if thou deemest me perverse, see that thine own judgment is just, before thou blame thy neighbour.

El. This time thou canst not say that I have done anything to provoke such words from thee. But, if thou wilt give me leave, I fain would declare the truth, in the cause alike of my dead sire and of my sister.

Cl. Indeed, thou hast my leave; and didst thou always address me in such a tone, thou wouldst be heard without pain.

El. Then I will speak. Thou sayest that thou hast slain my father. What word could bring thee deeper shame than that, whether the deed was just or not? But I must tell thee that thy deed was not just; no, thou wert drawn on to it by the wooing of the base man who is now thy spouse.

Ask the huntress Artemis what sin she punished when she stayed the frequent winds at Aulis; or I will tell thee; for we may not learn from her. My father—so I have heard—was once disporting himself in the grove of the goddess, when his footfall startled a dappled and antlered stag; he shot it, and chanced to utter a certain boast concerning its slaughter. Wroth thereat, the daughter of Leto detained the Greeks, that, in quittance for the wild creature's life, my father should yield up the life of his own child. Thus it befell that she was sacrificed; since the fleet had no other release, homeward or to Troy; and for that cause, under sore constraint and with sore reluctance, at last he slew her—not for the sake of Menelaüs.

But grant—for I will take thine own plea—grant that the motive of his deed was to benefit his brother; was that a reason for his dying by thy hand? Under what law? See that, in making such a law for men, thou make not trouble and remorse for thyself; for, if we are to take blood for blood, thou wouldst be the first to die, didst thou meet with thy desert.

But look if thy pretext is not false. For tell me, if thou wilt, wherefore thou art now doing the most shameless deeds of all—dwelling as wife with that blood-guilty one, who first helped thee to slay my sire, and bearing children to him, while thou hast cast out the earlier-born, the stainless offspring of a stainless marriage. How can I praise these things? Or wilt thou say that this, too, is thy vengeance for thy daughter? Nay, a shameful plea, if so thou plead; 'tis not well to wed an enemy for a daughter's sake.

But indeed I may not even counsel thee—who shriekest that I revile my mother; and truly I think that to me thou art less a mother than a mistress; so wretched is the life that I live, ever beset with miseries by thee and by thy partner. And that other, who scarce escaped thy hand, the hapless Orestes, is wearing out his ill-starred days in exile. Often hast thou charged me with rearing him to punish thy crime; and I would have done so, if I could, thou mayst be sure: for that matter, denounce me to all, as disloyal, if thou wilt, or petulant, or impudent; for if I am accomplished in such ways, methinks I am no unworthy child of thee.

Ch. I see that she breathes forth anger; but whether justice be with her, for this she seems to care no longer.

Cl. And what manner of care do I need to use against her, who hath thus insulted a mother, and this at her ripe age? Thinkest thou not that she would go forward to any deed, without shame?

El. Now be assured that I do feel shame for this, though thou believe it not; I know that my behaviour is unseemly, and becomes me ill. But then the enmity on thy part, and thy treatment, compel me in mine own despite to do thus; for base deeds are taught by base.

Cl. Thou brazen one! Truly I and my sayings and my deeds give thee too much matter for words.

El. The words are thine, not mine; for thine is the action; and the acts find the utterance.

Cl. Now by our lady Artemis, thou shalt not fail to pay for this boldness, so soon as Aegisthus returns.

El. Lo, thou art transported by anger, after granting me free speech, and hast no patience to listen.

Cl. Now wilt thou not hush thy clamour, or even suffer me to sacrifice, when I have permitted *thee* to speak unchecked?

El. I hinder not—begin thy rites, I pray thee; and blame not my voice, for I shall say no more.

Cl. Raise then, my handmaid, the offerings of many fruits, that I may uplift my prayers to this our king, for deliverance from my present fears. Lend now a gracious ear, O Phoebus our defender, to my words, though they be dark; for I speak not among friends, nor is it meet to unfold my whole thought to the light, while *she* stands near me, lest with her malice and her garrulous cry she spread some rash rumour throughout the town: but hear me thus, since on this wise I must speak.

That vision which I saw last night in doubtful dreams—if it hath come for my good, grant, Lycean king, that it be fulfilled; but if for harm, then let it recoil upon my foes. And if any are plotting to hurl me by treachery from the high estate which now is mine, permit them not; rather vouchsafe that, still living thus unscathed, I may bear sway over the house of the Atreidae and this realm, sharing prosperous days with the friends who share them now, and with those of my children from whom no enmity or bitterness pursues me.

O Lycean Apollo, graciously hear these prayers, and grant them to us all, even as we ask! For the rest, though I be silent, I deem that thou, a god, must know it; all things, surely, are seen by the sons of Zeus.

Enter the PAEDAGOGUS.

Pae. Ladies, might a stranger crave to know if this be the palace of the king Aegisthus?

Ch. It is, sir; thou thyself hast guessed aright.

Pae. And am I right in surmising that this lady is his consort? She is of queenly aspect.

Ch. Assuredly; thou art in the presence of the queen.

Pae. Hail, royal lady! I bring glad tidings to thee and to Aegisthus, from a friend.

Cl. I welcome the omen; but I would fain know from thee, first, who may have sent thee.

Pae. Phanoteus the Phocian, on a weighty mission.

Cl. What is it, sir? Tell me: coming from a friend, thou wilt bring, I know, a kindly message.

Pae. Orestes is dead; that is the sum.

El. Oh, miserable that I am! I am lost this day!

Cl. What sayest thou, friend, what sayest thou?—listen not to her!

Pae. I said, and say again—Orestes is dead.

El. I am lost, hapless one, I am undone!

Cl. (*to* ELECTRA). See thou to thine own concerns. But do thou, sir, tell me exactly—how did he perish?

Pae. I was sent for that purpose, and will tell thee all. Having gone to the renowned festival, the pride of Greece, for the Delphian games, when he heard the loud summons to the foot-race which was first to be decided, he entered the lists, a brilliant form, a wonder in the eyes of all there; and, having finished his course at the point where it began, he went out with the glorious meed of victory. To speak briefly, where there is much to tell, I know not the man whose deeds and triumphs have matched his; but one thing thou must know; in all the contests that the judges announced, he bore away the prize; and men deemed him happy, as oft as the herald proclaimed him an Argive, by name Orestes, son of Agamemnon, who once gathered the famous armament of Greece.

Thus far, 'twas well; but, when a god sends harm, not even the strong man can escape. For, on another day, when chariots were to try their speed at sunrise, he entered, with many charioteers. One was an Achaean, one from Sparta, two masters of yoked cars were Libyans; Orestes, driving Thessalian mares, came fifth among them; the sixth from Aetolia, with chestnut colts; a Magnesian was the seventh; the eighth, with white horses, was of Aenian stock; the ninth, from Athens, built of gods; there was a Boeotian too, making the tenth chariot.

They took their stations where the appointed umpires placed them by lot and ranged the cars; then, at the sound of the brazen trump, they started. All shouted to their horses, and shook the reins in their hands; the whole course was filled with the noise of rattling chariots; the dust flew upward; and all, in a confused throng, plied their goads unsparingly, each of them striving to pass the wheels and the snorting steeds of his rivals; for alike at their backs and at their rolling wheels the breath of the horses foamed and smote.

Orestes, driving close to the pillar at either end of the course, almost grazed it with his wheel each time, and, giving rein to the trace-horse on the right, checked the horse on the inner side. Hitherto, all the chariots had escaped overthrow; but presently the Aenian's hard-mouthed colts ran away, and, swerving, as they passed from the sixth into the seventh round, dashed their foreheads against the team of the Barcaean. Other mishaps followed the first, shock on shock and crash on crash, till the whole race-ground of Crisa was strewn with the wreck of the chariots.

Seeing this, the wary charioteer from Athens drew aside and paused, allowing the billow of chariots, surging in mid course, to go by. Orestes was driving last, keeping his horses behind, for his trust was in the end; but when he saw that the Athenian was alone left in, he sent a shrill cry ringing through the ears of his swift colts, and gave chase. Team was brought level with team, and so they raced—first one man, then the other, showing his head in front of the chariots.

Hitherto the ill-fated Orestes had passed safely through every round, steadfast in his steadfast car; at last, slackening his left rein while the horse was turning, unawares he struck the edge of the pillar; he broke the axle-box in twain; he was thrown over the chariot-rail; he was caught in the shapely reins; and, as he fell on the ground, his colts were scattered into the middle of the course.

But when the people saw him fallen from the car, a cry of pity went up for the youth, who had done such deeds and was meeting such a doom—now dashed to earth, now tossed feet uppermost to the sky—till the charioteers, with difficulty checking the career of his horses, loosed him, so covered with blood that no friend who saw it would have known the hapless corpse. Straightway they burned it on a pyre; and chosen men of Phocis are bringing in a small urn of bronze the sad dust of that mighty form, to find due burial in his fatherland.

Such is my story—grievous to hear, if words can grieve; but for us, who beheld, the greatest of sorrows that these eyes have seen.

Ch. Alas, alas! Now, methinks, the stock of our ancient masters hath utterly perished, root and branch.

Cl. O Zeus, what shall I call these tidings—glad tidings? Or dire, but gainful? 'Tis a bitter lot, when mine own calamities make the safety of my life.

Pae. Why art thou so downcast, lady, at this news?

Cl. There is a strange power in motherhood; a mother may be wronged, but she never learns to hate her child.

Pae. Then it seems that we have come in vain.

Cl. Nay, not in vain; how canst thou say "in vain," when thou hast brought me sure proofs of his death? His, who sprang from mine own life, yet, forsaking me who had suckled and reared him, became an exile and an alien; and, after he went out of this land, he saw me no more; but, charging me with the murder of his sire, he uttered dread threats against me; so that neither by night nor by day could sweet sleep cover mine eyes, but from moment to moment I lived in fear of death. Now, however—since this day I am rid of terror from him, and from this girl, that worse plague who shared my home, while still she drained my very life-blood—now, methinks, for aught that she can threaten, I shall pass my days in peace.

El. Ah, woe is me! Now, indeed, Orestes, thy fortune may be lamented, when it is thus with thee, and thou art mocked by this thy mother! Is it not well?

Cl. Not with thee; but his state is well.

El. Hear, Nemesis of him who hath lately died!

Cl. She hath heard who should be heard, and hath ordained well.

El. Insult us, for this is the time of thy triumph.

Cl. Then will not Orestes and thou silence me?

El. We are silenced; much less should we silence thee.

Cl. Thy coming, sir, would deserve large recompense, if thou hast hushed her clamorous tongue.

Pae. Then I may take my leave, if all is well.

Cl. Not so; thy welcome would then be unworthy of me, and of the ally who sent thee. Nay, come thou in; and leave her without, to make loud lament for herself and for her friends.

CLYTAEMNESTRA *and the* PAEDAGOGUS *enter the house.*

El. How think ye? Was there not grief and anguish there, wondrous weeping and wailing of that miserable mother, for the son who perished by such a fate? Nay, she left us with a laugh! Ah, woe is me! Dearest Orestes, how is my life quenched by thy death! Thou hast torn away with thee from my heart the only hopes which still were mine—that thou wouldst live to return some day, an avenger of thy sire, and of me unhappy. But now—whither shall I turn? I am alone, bereft of thee, as of my father.

Henceforth I must be a slave again among those whom most I hate, my father's murderers. Is it not well with me? But never, at least, henceforward, will I enter the house to dwell with them; nay, at these gates I will lay me down, and here, without a friend, my days shall wither. Therefore, if any in the house be wroth, let them slay me; for 'tis a grace, if I die, but if I live, a pain; I desire life no more.

Ch. Where are the thunderbolts of Zeus, or where is the bright Sun, if they look upon these things, and brand them not, but rest?

El. Woe, woe, ah me, ah me!

Ch. O daughter, why weepest thou?

El. (*with hands outstretched to heaven*). Alas!

Ch. Utter no rash cry!

El. Thou wilt break my heart!

Ch. How meanest thou?

El. If thou suggest a hope concerning those who have surely passed to the realm below, thou wilt trample yet more upon my misery.

Ch. Nay, I know how, ensnared by a woman for a chain of gold, the prince Amphiaraüs found a grave; and now beneath the earth—

El. Ah me, ah me!

Ch. —he reigns in fulness of force.

El. Alas!

Ch. Alas indeed! for the murderess—

El. Was slain.

Ch. Yea.

El. I know it, I know it; for a champion arose to avenge the mourning dead; but to me no champion remains; for he who yet was left hath been snatched away.

Ch. Hapless art thou, and hapless is thy lot!

El. Well know I that, too well, I, whose life is a torrent of woes dread and dark, a torrent that surges through all the months!

Ch. We have seen the course of thy sorrow.

El. Cease, then, to divert me from it, when no more—

Ch. How sayest thou?

El. —when no more can I have the comfort of hope from a brother, the seed of the same noble sire.

Ch. For all men it is appointed to die.

El. What, to die as that ill-starred one died, amid the tramp of racing steeds, entangled in the reins that dragged him?

Ch. Cruel was his doom, beyond thought!

El. Yea, surely; when in foreign soil, without ministry of my hands—

Ch. Alas!

El. —he is buried, ungraced by me with sepulture or with tears.

Enter CHRYSOTHEMIS.

Chr. Joy wings my feet, dear sister, not careful of seemliness, if I come with speed; for I bring joyful news, to relieve thy long sufferings and sorrows.

El. And whence couldst *thou* find help for my woes, whereof no cure can be imagined?

Chr. Orestes is with us—know this from my lips—in living presence, as surely as thou seest me here.

El. What, art thou mad, poor girl? Art thou laughing at my sorrows, and thine own?

Chr. Nay, by our father's hearth, I speak not in mockery; I tell thee that he is with us indeed.

El. Ah, woe is me! And from whom hast thou heard this tale, which thou believest so lightly?

Chr. I believe it on mine own knowledge, not on hearsay; I have seen clear proofs.

El. What hast thou seen, poor girl, to warrant thy belief? Whither, I wonder hast thou turned thine eyes, that thou art fevered with this baneful fire?

Chr. Then, for the gods' love, listen, that thou mayest know my story, before deciding whether I am sane or foolish.

El. Speak on, then, if thou findest pleasure in speaking.

Chr. Well, thou shalt hear all that I have seen. When I came to our father's ancient tomb, I saw that streams of milk had lately flowed from the top of the mound, and that his sepulchre was encircled with garlands of all flowers that blow. I was astonished at the sight, and peered about, lest haply some one should be close to my side. But when I perceived that all the place was in stillness, I crept nearer to the tomb; and on the mound's edge I saw a lock of hair, freshly severed.

And the moment that I saw it, ah me, a familiar image rushed upon my soul, telling me that there I beheld a token of him whom most I love, Orestes. Then I took it in my hands, and uttered no ill-omened word, but the tears of joy straightway filled mine eyes. And I know well, as I knew then, that this fair tribute has come from none but him. Whose part else was that, save mine and thine? And I did it not, I know, nor thou; how shouldst thou?—when thou canst not leave this house, even to worship the gods, but at thy peril. Nor, again, does our mother's heart incline to do such deeds, nor could she have so done without our knowledge.

No, these offerings are from Orestes! Come, dear sister, courage! No mortal life is attended by a changeless fortune. Ours was once gloomy; but this day, perchance, will seal the promise of much good.

El. Alas for thy folly! How I have been pitying thee!

Chr. What, are not my tidings welcome?

El. Thou knowest not whither or into what dreams thou wanderest.

Chr. Should I not know what mine own eyes have seen?

El. He is dead, poor girl; and thy hopes in that deliverer are gone: look not to him.

Chr. Woe, woe is me! From whom hast thou heard this?

El. From the man who was present when he perished.

Chr. And where is he? Wonder steals over my mind.

El. He is within, a guest not unpleasing to our mother.

Chr. Ah, woe is me! Whose, then, can have been those ample offerings to our father's tomb?

El. Most likely, I think, some one brought those gifts in memory of the dead Orestes.

Chr. Oh, hapless that I am! And I was bringing such news in joyous haste, ignorant, it seems, how dire was our plight; but now that I have come, I find fresh sorrows added to the old!

El. So stands thy case; yet, if thou wilt hearken to me, thou wilt lighten the load of our present trouble.

Chr. Can I ever raise the dead to life?

El. I meant not that; I am not so foolish.

Chr. What biddest thou, then, for which my strength avails?

El. That thou be brave in doing what I enjoin.

Chr. Nay, if any good can be done, I will not refuse.

El. Remember, nothing succeeds without toil.

Chr. I know it, and will share thy burden with all my power.

El. Hear, then, how I am resolved to act. As for the support of friends, thou thyself must know that we have none; Hades hath taken our friends away, and we two are left alone. I, so long as I heard that my brother still lived and prospered, had hopes that he would yet come to avenge the murder of our sire. But now that he is no more, I look next to thee, not to flinch from aiding me thy sister to slay our father's murderer, Aegisthus: I must have no secret from thee more.

How long art thou to wait inactive? What hope is left standing, to which thine eyes can turn? Thou hast to complain that thou art robbed of thy father's heritage; thou hast to mourn that thus far thy life is fading without nuptial song or wedded love. Nay, and do not hope that such joys will ever be thine; Aegisthus is not so ill-advised as ever to permit that children should spring from thee or me for his own sure destruction. But if thou wilt follow my counsels, first thou wilt win praise of piety from our dead sire, below, and from our brother too; next, thou shalt be called free henceforth, as thou wert born, and shalt find worthy bridals; for noble natures draw the gaze of all.

Then seest thou not what fair fame thou wilt win for thyself and for me, by hearkening to my word? What citizen or stranger, when he sees us, will not greet us with praises such as these?—"Behold these two sisters, my friends, who saved their father's house; who, when their foes were firmly planted of yore, took their lives in their hands and stood forth as avengers of blood! Worthy of love are these twain, worthy of reverence from all; at festivals, and wherever the folk are assembled, let these be honoured of all men for their prowess." Thus will every one speak of us, so that in life and in death our glory shall not fail.

Come, dear sister, hearken! Work with thy sire, share the burden of thy brother, win rest from woes for me and for thyself—mindful of this, that an ignoble life brings shame upon the noble.

Ch. In such case as this, forethought is helpful for those who speak and those who hear.

Chr. Yea, and before she spake, my friends were she blest with a sound mind, she would have remembered caution, as she doth not remember it.

Now whither canst thou have turned thine eyes, that thou art arming thyself with such rashness, and calling me to aid thee? Seest thou not, thou art a woman, not a man, and no match for thine adversaries in strength? And their fortune prospers day by day, while ours is ebbing and coming to nought. Who, then, plotting to vanquish a foe so strong, shall escape without suffering deadly scathe? See that we change not our evil plight to worse, if any one hears these words. It brings us no relief or benefit, if, after winning fair fame, we die an ignominious death; for mere death is not the bitterest, but rather when one who craves to die cannot obtain even that boon.

Nay, I beseech thee, before we are utterly destroyed, and leave our house desolate, restrain thy rage! I will take care that thy words remain secret and harmless; and learn thou the prudence, at last though late, of yielding, when so helpless, to thy rulers.

Ch. Hearken; there is no better gain for mortals to win than foresight and a prudent mind.

El. Thou hast said nothing unlooked-for; I well knew that thou wouldst reject what I proffered. Well! I must do this deed with mine own hand, and alone; for assuredly I will not leave it void.

Chr. Alas! Would thou hadst been so purposed on the day of our father's death! What mightst thou not have wrought?

El. My nature was the same then, but my mind less ripe.

Chr. Strive to keep such a mind through all thy life.

El. These counsels mean that thou wilt not share my deed.

Chr. No; for the venture is likely to bring disaster.

El. I admire thy prudence; thy cowardice I hate.

Chr. I will listen not less calmly when thou praise me.

El. Never fear to suffer that from me.

Chr. Time enough in the future to decide that.

El. Begone; there is no power to help in thee.

Chr. Not so; but in thee, no mind to learn.

El. Go, declare all this to thy mother!

Chr. But, again, I do not hate thee with such a hate.

El. Yet know at least to what dishonour thou bringest me.

Chr. Dishonour, no! I am only thinking of thy good.

El. Am I bound, then, to follow thy rule of right?

Chr. When thou art wise, then thou shalt be our guide.

El. Sad, that one who speaks so well should speak amiss!

Chr. Thou hast well described the fault to which thou cleavest.

El. How? Dost thou not think that I speak with justice?

Chr. But sometimes justice itself is fraught with harm.

El. I care not to live by such a law.

Chr. Well, if thou must do this, thou wilt praise me yet.

El. And do it I will, no whit dismayed by thee.

Chr. Is this so indeed? Wilt thou not change thy counsels?

El. No, for nothing is more hateful than bad counsel.

Chr. Thou seemest to agree with nothing that I urge.

El. My resolve is not new, but long since fixed.

Chr. Then I will go; thou canst not be brought to approve my words, nor I to commend thy conduct.

El. Nay, go within; never will I follow thee, however much thou mayst desire it; it were great folly even to attempt an idle quest.

Chr. Nay, if thou art wise in thine own eyes, be such wisdom thine; by and by, when thou standest in evil plight, thou wilt praise my words. *Exit.*

Chorus

When we see the birds of the air, with sure instinct, careful to nourish those who give them life and nurture, why do not we pay these debts in like measure? Nay, by the lightning-flash of Zeus, by Themis throned in heaven, it is not long till sin brings sorrow.

Voice that comest to the dead beneath the earth, send a piteous cry, I pray thee, to the son of Atreus in that world, a joyless message of dishonour;

tell him that the fortunes of his house are now distempered; while, among his children, strife of sister with sister hath broken the harmony of loving days. Electra, forsaken, braves the storm alone; she bewails alway, hapless one, her father's fate, like the nightingale unwearied in lament; she recks not of death, but is ready to leave the sunlight, could she but quell the two Furies of her house. Who shall match such noble child of noble sire?

No generous soul deigns, by a base life, to cloud a fair repute, and leave a name inglorious; as thou, too, O my daughter, hast chosen to mourn all thy days with those that mourn, and hast spurned dishonour, that thou mightest win at once a twofold praise, as wise, and as the best of daughters.

May I yet see thy life raised in might and wealth above thy foes, even as now it is humbled beneath their hand! For I have found thee in no prosperous estate; and yet, for observance of nature's highest laws, winning the noblest renown, by thy piety towards Zeus.

Enter ORESTES, *with* PYLADES *and two attendants.*

Or. Ladies, have we been directed aright, and are we on the right path to our goal?

Ch. And what seekest thou? With what desire hast thou come?

Or. I have been searching for the home of Aegisthus.

Ch. Well, thou hast found it; and thy guide is blameless.

Or. Which of you, then, will tell those within that our company, long desired, hath arrived?

Ch. This maiden—if the nearest should announce it.

Or. I pray thee, mistress, make it known in the house that certain men of Phocis seek Aegisthus.

El. Ah, woe is me! Surely ye are not bringing the visible proofs of that rumour which we heard?

Or. I know nothing of thy "rumour"; but the aged Strophius charged me with tidings of Orestes.

El. What are they, sir? Ah, how I thrill with fear!

Or. He is dead; and in a small urn, as thou seest, we bring the scanty relics home.

El. Ah me unhappy! There, at last, before mine eyes, I see that woful burden in your hands!

Or. If thy tears are for aught which Orestes hath suffered, know that yonder vessel holds his dust.

El. Ah, sir, allow me, then, I implore thee, if this urn indeed contains him, to take it in my hands—that I may weep and wail, not for these ashes alone, but for myself and for all our house therewith!

Or. (*to the attendants*). Bring it and give it her, whoe'er she be; for she who begs this boon must be one who wished him no evil, but a friend, or haply a kinswoman in blood.

(*The urn is placed in* ELECTRA'S *hands.*)

El. Ah, memorial of him whom I loved best on earth! Ah, Orestes, whose life hath no relic left save this—how far from the hopes with which I sent thee forth is the manner in which I receive thee back! Now I carry thy poor dust in my hands; but thou wert radiant, my child, when I sped thee forth from home! Would that I had yielded up my breath, ere, with these hands, I stole thee away, and sent thee to a strange land, and rescued thee from death; that so thou mightest have been stricken down on that self-same day, and had thy portion in the tomb of thy sire!

But now, an exile from home and fatherland, thou hast perished miserably, far from thy sister; woe is me, these loving hands have not washed or decked thy corpse, nor taken up, as was meet, their sad burden from the flaming pyre. No! at the hands of strangers, hapless one, thou hast had those rites, and so art come to us, a little dust in a narrow urn.

Ah, woe is me for my nursing long ago, so vain, that I oft bestowed on thee with loving toil! For thou wast never thy mother's darling so much as mine; nor was any in the house thy nurse but I; and by thee I was ever called "sister." But now all this hath vanished in a day, with thy death; like a whirlwind, thou hast swept all away with thee. Our father is gone; I am dead in regard to thee; thou thyself hast perished: our foes exult; that mother, who is none, is mad with joy—she of whom thou didst oft send me secret messages, thy heralds, saying that thou thyself wouldst appear as an avenger. But our evil fortune, thine and mine, hath reft all that away, and hath sent thee forth unto me thus—no more the form that I loved so well, but ashes and an idle shade.

Ah me, ah me! O piteous dust! Alas, thou dear one, sent on a dire journey, how hast undone me—undone me indeed, O brother mine!

Therefore take me to this thy home, me who am as nothing, to thy nothingness, that I may dwell with thee henceforth below; for when thou wert on earth, we shared alike; and now I fain would die, that I may not be parted from thee in the grave. For I see that the dead have rest from pain.

Ch. Bethink thee, Electra, thou art the child of mortal sire, and mortal was Orestes; therefore grieve not too much. This is a debt which all of us must pay.

Or. Alas, what shall I say? What words can serve me at this pass? I can restrain my lips no longer!

El. What hath troubled thee? Why didst thou say that?

Or. Is this the form of the illustrious Electra that I behold?

El. It is; and very grievous is her plight.

Or. Alas, then, for this miserable fortune!

El. Surely, sir, thy lament is not for *me*?

Or. O form cruelly, godlessly misused!

El. Those ill-omened words, sir, fit no one better than me.

Or. Alas for thy life, unwedded and all unblest!

El. Why this steadfast gaze, stranger, and these laments?

Or. How ignorant was I, then, of mine own sorrows!

El. By what that hath been said hast thou perceived this?

Or. By seeing thy sufferings, so many and so great.

El. And yet thou seest but a few of my woes.

Or. Could any be more painful to behold?

El. This, that I share the dwelling of the murderers.

Or. Whose murderers? Where lies the guilt at which thou hintest?

El. My father's; and then I am their slave perforce.

Or. Who is it that subjects thee to this constraint?

El. A mother—in name, but no mother in her deeds.

Or. How doth she oppress thee? With violence or with hardship?

El. With violence, and hardships, and all manner of ill.

Or. And is there none to succour, or to hinder?

El. None. I *had* one; and thou hast shown me his ashes.

Or. Hapless girl, how this sight hath stirred my pity!

El. Know, then, that thou art the first who ever pitied me.

Or. No other visitor hath ever shared thy pain.

El. Surely thou art not some unknown kinsman?

Or. I would answer, if these were friends who hear us.

El. Oh, they are friends; thou canst speak without mistrust.

Or. Give up this urn, then, and thou shalt be told all.

El. Nay, I beseech thee be not so cruel to me, sir!

Or. Do as I say, and never fear to do amiss.

El. I conjure thee, rob me not of my chief treasure!

Or. Thou must not keep it.

El. Ah woe is me for thee, Orestes, if I am not to give thee burial!

Or. Hush! no such word! Thou hast no right to lament.

El. No right to lament for my dead brother?

Or. It is not meet for thee to speak of him thus.

El. Am I so dishonoured of the dead?

Or. Dishonoured of none: but this is not thy part.

El. Yes, if these are the ashes of Orestes that I hold.

Or. They are not; a fiction clothed them with his name.

(*He gently takes the urn from her.*)

El. And where is that unhappy one's tomb?

Or. There is none; the living have no tomb.

El. What sayest thou, boy?

Or. Nothing that is not true.

El. The man is alive?

Or. If there be life in me.

El. What? Art thou he?

Or. Look at this signet, once our father's, and judge if I speak truth.

El. O blissful day!

Or. Blissful, in very deed!

El. Is this thy voice?

Or. Let no other voice reply.

El. Do I hold thee in my arms?

Or. As mayest thou hold me always!

El. Ah, dear friends and fellow-citizens, behold Orestes here, who was feigned dead, and now, by that feigning hath come safely home!

Ch. We see him, daughter; and for this happy fortune a tear of joy trickles from our eyes.

El. Offspring of him whom I loved best, thou hast come even now, thou hast come, and found and seen her whom thy heart desired!

Or. I am with thee; but keep silence for a while.

El. What meanest thou?

Or. 'Tis better to be silent, lest some one within should hear.

El. Nay, by ever-virgin Artemis, I will never stoop to fear women, stay-at-homes, vain burdens of the ground!

Or. Yet remember that in women, too, dwells the spirit of battle; thou hast had good proof of that I ween.

El. Alas! ah me! Thou hast reminded me of my sorrow, one which, from its nature, cannot be veiled, cannot be done away with, cannot forget!

Or. I know this also; but when occasion prompts, then will be the moment to recall those deeds.

El. Each moment of all time, as it comes, would be meet occasion for these my just complaints; scarcely now have I had my lips set free.

Or. I grant it; therefore guard thy freedom.

El. What must I do?

Or. When the season serves not, do not wish to speak too much.

El. Nay, who could fitly exchange speech for such silence, when thou hast appeared? For now I have seen thy face, beyond all thought and hope!

Or. Thou sawest it, when the gods moved me to come....

* * *

El. Thou hast told me of a grace above the first, if a god hath indeed brought thee to our house; I acknowledge therein the work of heaven.

Or. I am loth, indeed, to curb thy gladness, but yet this excess of joy moves my fear.

El. O thou who, after many a year, hast deigned thus to gladden mine eyes by thy return, do not, now that thou hast seen me in all my woe—

Or. What is thy prayer?

El. —do not rob me of the comfort of thy face; do not force me to forego it!

Or. I should be wroth, indeed, if I saw another attempt it.

El. My prayer is granted?

Or. Canst thou doubt?

El. Ah, friends, I heard a voice that I could never have hoped to hear; nor could I have restrained my emotion in silence, and without a cry, when I heard it.

Ah me! But now I have thee; thou art come to me with the light of that dear countenance, which never, even in sorrow, could I forget.

Or. Spare all superfluous words; tell me not of our mother's wickedness, or how Aegisthus drains the wealth of our father's house by lavish luxury or aimless waste; for the story would not suffer thee to keep due limit. Tell me rather that which will serve our present need—where we must show ourselves, or wait in ambush, that this our coming may confound the triumph of our foes.

And look that our mother read not thy secret in thy radiant face, when we twain have advanced into the house, but make lament, as for the feigned disaster; for when we have prospered, then there will be leisure to rejoice and exult in freedom.

El. Nay, brother, as it pleases thee, so shall be my conduct also; for all my joy is a gift from thee, and not mine own. Nor would I consent to win a great good for myself at the cost of the least pain to thee; for so should I ill serve the divine power that befriends us now.

But thou knowest how matters stand here, I doubt not: thou must have heard that Aegisthus is from home, but our mother within; and fear not that she will ever see my face lit up with smiles; for mine old hatred of her hath sunk into my heart; and, since I have beheld thee, for very joy I shall never cease to weep. How indeed should I cease, who have seen thee come home this day, first as dead, and then in life? Strangely hast thou wrought on me; so that, if my father should return alive, I should no longer doubt my senses, but should believe that I saw him. Now, therefore, that thou hast come to me so wondrously, command me as thou wilt; for, had I been alone, I should have achieved one of two things—a noble deliverance, or a noble death.

Or. Thou hadst best be silent; for I hear some one within preparing to go forth.

El. (*to* ORESTES *and* PYLADES). Enter, sirs; especially as ye bring that which no one could repulse from these doors, though he receive it without joy.

Enter the PAEDAGOGUS.

Pae. Foolish and senseless children! Are ye weary of your lives, or was there no wit born in you, that ye see not how ye stand, not on the brink, but in the very midst of deadly perils? Nay, had I not kept watch this long while at these doors, your plans would have been in the house before yourselves; but, as it is, my care shielded you from that. Now have done with this long discourse, these insatiate cries of joy, and pass within; for in such deeds delay is evil, and 'tis well to make an end.

Or. What, then, will be my prospects when I enter?

Pae. Good; for thou art secured from recognition.

Or. Thou hast reported me, I presume, as dead?

Pae. Know that here thou art numbered with the shades.

Or. Do they rejoice, then, at these tidings? Or what say they?

Pae. I will tell thee at the end; meanwhile, all is well for us on their part—even that which is not well.

El. Who is this, brother? I pray thee, tell me.

Or. Dost thou not perceive?

El. I cannot guess.

Or. Knowest thou not the man to whose hands thou gavest me once?

El. What man? How sayest thou?

Or. By whose hands, through thy forethought, I was secretly conveyed forth to Phocian soil.

El. Is this he in whom, alone of many, I found a true ally of old, when our sire was slain?

Or. 'Tis he; question me no further.

El. O joyous day! O sole preserver of Agamemnon's house, how hast thou come? Art thou he indeed, who didst save my brother and myself from many sorrows? O dearest hands; O messenger whose feet were kindly servants! How couldst thou be with me so long, and remain unknown, nor give a ray of light, but afflict me by fables, while possessed of truths most sweet? Hail, father—for 'tis a father that I seem to behold! All hail—and know that I have hated thee, and loved thee, in one day, as never man before!

Pae. Enough, methinks; as for the story of the past, many are the circling nights, and days as many, which shall show it thee, Electra, in its fulness.

(*To* ORESTES *and* PYLADES.) But this is my counsel to you twain, who stand there—now is the time to act; now Clytaemnestra is alone—no man is now within: but, if ye pause, consider that ye will have to fight, not with the inmates alone, but with other foes more numerous and better skilled.

Or. Pylades, this our task seems no longer to crave many words, but rather that we should enter the house forthwith—first adoring the shrines of my father's gods, who keep these gates.

ORESTES *and* PYLADES *enter the house, followed by the* PAEDAGOGUS. ELECTRA *remains outside.*

El. O King Apollo! graciously hear them, and hear me besides, who so oft have come before thine altar with such gifts as my devout hand could bring! And now, O Lycean Apollo, with such vows as I can make, I pray thee, I supplicate, I implore, grant us thy benignant aid in these designs, and show men how impiety is rewarded by the gods!

ELECTRA *enters the house.*

Chorus

Behold how Ares moves onward, breathing deadly vengeance, against which none may strive!

Even now the pursuers of dark guilt have passed beneath yon roof, the hounds which none may flee. Therefore the vision of my soul shall not long tarry in suspense.

The champion of the spirits infernal is ushered with stealthy feet into the house, the ancestral palace of his sire, bearing keen-edged death in his hands; and Hermes, son of Maia, who hath shrouded the guile in darkness, leads him forward, even to the end, and delays no more.

Enter ELECTRA *from the house.*

El. Ah, dearest friends, in a moment the men will do the deed; but wait in silence.

Ch. How is it? what do they now?

El. She is decking the urn for burial, and those two stand close to her.

Ch. And why hast thou sped forth?

El. To guard against Aegisthus entering before we are aware.

Cl. (*within*). Alas! Woe for the house forsaken of friends and filled with murderers!

El. A cry goes up within: hear ye not, friends?

Ch. I heard, ah me, sounds dire to hear, and shuddered!

Cl. (*within*). O hapless that I am! Aegisthus, where, where art thou?

El. Hark, once more a voice resounds!

Cl. (*within*). My son, my son, have pity on thy mother!

El. Thou hadst none for him, nor for the father that begat him.

Ch. Ill-fated realm and race, now the fate that hath pursued thee day by day is dying—is dying!

Cl. (*within*). Oh, I am smitten!

El. Smite, if thou canst, once more!

Cl. (*within*). Ah, woe is me again!

El. Would that the woe were for Aegisthus too!

Ch. The curses are at work; the buried live; blood flows for blood, drained from the slayers by those who died of yore.

Enter ORESTES *and* PYLADES *from the house.*

Behold, they come! That red hand reeks with sacrifice to Ares; nor can I blame the deed.

El. Orestes, how fare ye?

Or. All is well within the house, if Apollo's oracle spake well.

El. The guilty one is dead?

Or. Fear no more that thy proud mother will ever put thee to dishonour.

* * *

Ch. Cease; for I see Aegisthus full in view.

El. Rash boys, back, back!

Or. Where see ye the man?

El. Yonder, at our mercy, he advances from the suburb, full of joy.

Ch. Make with all speed for the vestibule; that, as your first task prospered, so this again may prosper now.

Or. Fear not—we will perform it.

El. Haste, then, wither thou wouldst.

Or. See, I am gone.

El. I will look to matters here.

Exeunt ORESTES *and* PYLADES.

Ch. 'Twere well to soothe his ear with some few words of seeming gentleness, that he may rush blindly upon the struggle with his doom.

Enter AEGISTHUS.

Aegisthus. Which of you can tell me, where are those Phocian strangers, who, 'tis said, have brought us tidings of Orestes slain in the wreck of his chariot? Thee, thee I ask, yes, thee, in former days so bold—for methinks it touches thee most nearly; thou best must know, and best canst tell.

El. I know assuredly; else were I a stranger to the fortune of my nearest kinsfolk.

Aeg. Where then may be the strangers? Tell me.

El. Within; they have found a way to the heart of their hostess.

Aeg. Have they in truth reported him dead?

El. Nay, not reported only; they have shown him.

Aeg. Can I, then, see the corpse with mine own eyes?

El. Thou canst, indeed; and 'tis no enviable sight.

Aeg. Indeed, thou hast given me a joyful greeting, beyond thy wont.

El. Joy be thine, if in these things thou findest joy.

Aeg. Silence, I say, and throw wide the gates, for all Mycenaeans and Argives to behold; that, if any of them were once buoyed on empty hopes from this man, now, seeing him dead, they may receive my curb, instead of waiting till my chastisement make them wise perforce!

El. No loyalty is lacking on my part; time hath taught me the prudence of concord with the stronger.

(*A shrouded corpse is disclosed.* ORESTES *and* PYLADES *stand near it.*)

Aeg. O Zeus, I behold that which hath not fallen save by the doom of jealous Heaven; but, if Nemesis attend that word, be it unsaid!

Take all the covering from the face, that kinship, at least, may receive the tribute of lament from me also.

Or. Lift the veil thyself; not my part this, but thine, to look upon these relics, and to greet them kindly.

Aeg. 'Tis good counsel, and I will follow it. (*To* ELECTRA) But thou—call me Clytaemnestra, if she is within.

Or. Lo, she is near thee: turn not thine eyes elsewhere.

(AEGISTHUS *removes the face-cloth from the corpse.*)

Aeg. O, what sight is this!

Or. Why so scared? Is the face so strange?

Aeg. Who are the men into whose mid toils I have fallen, hapless that I am?

Or. Nay, hast thou not discovered ere now that the dead, as thou miscallest them, are living?

Aeg. Alas, I read the riddle: this can be none but Orestes who speaks to me!

Or. And, though so good a prophet, thou wast deceived so long?

Aeg. Oh lost, undone! Yet suffer me to say one word...

El. In heaven's name, my brother, suffer him not to speak further, or to plead at length! When mortals are in the meshes of fate, how can such respite avail one who is to die? No—slay him forthwith, and cast his corpse to the creatures from whom such as he should have burial, far from our sight! To me, nothing but this can make amends for the woes of the past.

Or. (*to* AEGISTHUS) Go in, and quickly; the issue here is not of words, but of thy life.

Aeg. Why take me into the house? If this deed be fair, what need of darkness? Why is thy hand not prompt to strike?

Or. Dictate not, but go where thou didst slay my father, that in the same place thou mayest die.

Aeg. Is this dwelling doomed to see all woes of Pelops' line, now, and in time to come?

Or. Thine, at least; trust my prophetic skill so far.

Aeg. The skill thou vauntest belonged not to thy sire.

Or. Thou bandiest words, and our going is delayed. Move forward!

Aeg. Lead thou.

Or. Thou must go first.

Aeg. Lest I escape thee?

Or. No, but that thou mayest not choose how to die; I must not spare thee any bitterness of death. And well it were if this judgment came straightway upon all who dealt in lawless deeds, even the judgment of the sword: so should not wickedness abound.

ORESTES *and* PYLADES *drive* AEGISTHUS *into the palace*.

Ch. O house of Atreus, through how many sufferings hast thou come forth at last in freedom, crowned with good by this day's enterprise!

TRACHINIAE

DRAMATIS PERSONAE

Deianeira
Nurse
Hyllus, *son of Heracles and Deianeira*
Messenger
Lichas, *the herald of Heracles*
Heracles
An Old Man
Chorus of Trachinian Maidens

At Trachis, before the house of Heracles. Enter DEIANEIRA *from the house, accompanied by the* NURSE.

Deianeira. There is a saying among men, put forth of old, that thou canst not rightly judge whether a mortal's lot is good or evil, ere he die. But I, even before I have passed to the world of death, know well that my life is sorrowful and bitter; I, who in the house of my father Oeneus, while yet I dwelt at Pleuron, had such fear of bridals as never vexed any maiden of Aetolia. For my wooer was a river-god, Acheloüs, who in three shapes was ever asking me from my sire—coming now as a bull in bodily form, now as a serpent with sheeny coils, now with trunk of man and front of ox, while from a shaggy beard the streams of fountain-water flowed abroad. With the fear of such a suitor before mine eyes, I was always praying in my wretchedness that I might die, or ever I should come near to such a bed.

But at last, to my joy, came the glorious son of Zeus and Alcmena; who closed with him in combat, and delivered me. How the fight was waged, I cannot clearly tell, I know not; if there be any one who watched that sight without terror, such might speak: I, as I sat there, was distraught with dread, lest beauty should bring me sorrow at the last. But finally the Zeus of battles ordained well—if well indeed it be: for since I have been joined to Heracles as his chosen bride, fear after fear hath haunted me on his account; one night brings a trouble, and the next night, in turn, drives it out. And then children were born to us; whom he has seen only as the husbandman sees his distant field, which he visits at seed-time, and once again at harvest. Such was the life that kept him journeying to and fro, in the service of a certain master.

But now, when he hath risen above those trials, now it is that my anguish is sorest. Ever since he slew the valiant Iphitus, we have been dwelling here in Trachis, exiles from our home, and the guests of a stranger; but where he is, no one knows; I only know that he is gone, and hath pierced my heart with cruel pangs for him. I am almost sure that some evil hath befallen him; it is no short space that hath passed, but ten long months, and then five more—and still no message from him. Yes, there has been some dread mischance; witness that tablet which he left with me ere he went forth: oft do I pray to the gods that I may not have received it for my sorrow.

Nurse. Deianeira, my mistress, many a time have I marked thy bitter tears and lamentations, as thou bewailedst the going forth of Heracles; but now—if it be meet to school the free-born with the counsels of a slave, and if I must say what behoves thee—why, when thou art so rich in sons, dost thou send no one of them to seek thy lord; Hyllus, before all, who might well go on that errand, if he cared that there should be tidings of his father's welfare? Lo! there he comes, speeding towards the house with timely step; if, then, thou deemest that I speak in season, thou canst use at once my counsel, and the man.

Enter HYLLUS.

De. My child, my son, wise words may fall, it seems, from humble lips; this woman is a slave, but hath spoken in the spirit of the free.

Hyllus. How, mother? Tell me, if it may be told.

De. It brings thee shame, she saith, that, when thy father hath been so long a stranger, thou hast not sought to learn where he is.

Hy. Nay, I know—if rumour can be trusted.

De. And in what region, my child, doth rumour place him?

Hy. Last year, they say, through all the months, he toiled as bondman to a Lydian woman.

De. If he bore that, then no tidings can surprise.

Hy. Well, he has been delivered from that, as I hear.

De. Where, then, is he reported to be now—alive, or dead?

Hy. He is waging or planning a war, they say, upon Euboea, the realm of Eurytus.

De. Knowest thou, my son, that he hath left with me sure oracles touching that land?

Hy. What are they, mother? I know not whereof thou speakest.

De. That either he shall meet his death, or, having achieved this task, shall have rest thenceforth, for all his days to come.

So, my child, when his fate is thus trembling in the scale, wilt thou not go to succour him? For we are saved, if he find safety, or we perish with him.

Hy. Ay, I will go, my mother; and, had I known the import of these prophecies, I had been there long since; but, as it was, my father's wonted fortune suffered me not to feel fear for him, or to be anxious overmuch. Now that I have the knowledge,

I will spare no pains to learn the whole truth in this matter.

De. Go, then, my son; be the seeker ne'er so late, he is rewarded if he learn tidings of joy.

HYLLUS *departs as the* CHORUS OF TRACHINIAN MAIDENS *enters. They are the friends and confidantes of* DEIANEIRA.

Chorus

Thou whom Night brings forth at the moment when she is despoiled of her starry crown, and lays to rest in thy splendour, tell me, I pray thee, O Sun-god, tell me where abides Alcmena's son? Thou glorious lord of flashing light, say, is he threading the straits of the sea, or hath he found an abode on either continent? Speak, thou who seest as none else can see!

For Deianeira, as I hear, hath ever an aching heart; she, the battle-prize of old, is now like some bird lorn of its mate; she can never lull her yearning, nor stay her tears; haunted by a sleepless fear for her absent lord, she pines on her anxious, widowed couch, miserable in her foreboding of mischance.

As one may see billow after billow driven over the wide deep by the tireless southwind or the north, so the trouble of his life, stormy as the Cretan sea, now whirls back the son of Cadmus, now lifts him to honour. But some god ever saves him from the house of death, and suffers him not to fail.

Lady, I praise not this thy mood; with all reverence will I speak, yet in reproof. Thou dost not well, I say, to kill fair hope by fretting; remember that the son of Cronus himself, the all-disposing king, hath not appointed a painless lot for mortals. Sorrow and joy come round to all, as the Bear moves in his circling paths.

Yea, starry night abides not with men, nor tribulation, nor wealth; in a moment it is gone from us, and another hath his turn of gladness, and of bereavement. So would I wish thee also, the Queen, to keep that prospect ever in thy thoughts; for when hath Zeus been found so careless of his children?

De. Ye have heard of my trouble, I think, and that hath brought you here; but the anguish which consumes my heart—ye are strangers to that; and never may ye learn it by suffering! Yes, the tender plant grows in those sheltered regions of its own; and the Sun-god's heat vexes it not, nor rain, nor any wind; but it rejoices in its sweet, untroubled being, till such time as the maiden is called a wife, and finds her portion of anxious thoughts in the night, brooding on danger to husband or to children. Such an one could understand the burden of my cares; she could judge them by her own.

Well, I have had many a sorrow to weep for ere now; but I am going to speak of one more grievous than them all.

When Heracles my lord was going from home on his last journey, he left in the house an ancient tablet, inscribed with tokens which he had never brought himself to explain to me before, many as were the ordeals to which he had gone forth. He had always departed as if to conquer, not to die. But now, as if he were a doomed man, he told me what portion of his substance I was to take for my dower, and how he would have his sons share their father's land amongst them. And he fixed the time; saying that, when a year and three months should have passed since he had left the country, then he was fated to die; or, if he should have survived that term, to live thenceforth an untroubled life.

Such, he said, was the doom ordained by the gods to be accomplished in the toils of Heracles; as the ancient oak at Dodona had spoken of yore, by the mouth of the two Peleiades. And this is the precise moment when the fulfilment of that word becomes due; so that I start up from sweet slumber, my friends, stricken with terror at the thought that I must remain widowed of the noblest among men.

Ch. Hush—no more ill-omened words; I see a man approaching, who wears a wreath, as if for joyous tidings.

Enter MESSENGER.

Messenger. Queen Deianeira, I shall be the first of messengers to free thee from fear. Know that Alcmena's son lives and triumphs, and from battle brings the first-fruits to the gods of this land.

De. What news is this, old man, that thou hast told me?

Me. That thy lord, admired of all, will soon come to thy house, restored to thee in his victorious might.

De. What citizen or stranger hath told thee this?

Me. In the meadow, summer haunt of oxen, Lichas the herald is proclaiming it to many: from him I heard it, and flew hither, that I might be the first to give thee these tidings, and so might reap some guerdon from thee, and win thy grace.

De. And why is *he* not here, if he brings good news?

Me. His task, lady, is no easy one; all the Malian folk have thronged around him with questions, and he cannot move forward: each and all are bent on learning what they desire, and will not release him until they are satisfied. Thus their eagerness detains him against his will; but thou shalt presently see him face to face.

De. O Zeus, who rulest the meads of Oeta, sacred from the scythe, at last, though late, thou hast given us joy! Uplift your voices, ye women within the house and ye beyond our gates, since now we are gladdened by the light of this message, that hath risen on us beyond my hope!

Ch. Let the maidens raise a joyous strain for the house, with songs of triumph at the hearth; and, amidst them, let the shout of the men go up with one accord for Apollo of the bright quiver, our Defender! And at the same time, ye maidens, lift up a paean, cry aloud to his sister, the Ortygian Artemis, smiter of deer, goddess of the twofold torch, and to the Nymphs her neighbours!

My spirit soars; I will not reject the wooing of the flute. O thou sovereign of my soul! Lo, the ivy's spell begins to work upon me! Euoe! even now it moves me to whirl in the swift dance of Bacchanals!

Praise, praise unto the Healer! See, dear lady, see! Behold, these tidings are taking shape before thy gaze.

De. I see it, dear maidens; my watching eyes had not failed to note yon company. (*Enter* LICHAS, *followed by Captive Maidens.*) All hail to the herald, whose coming hath been so long delayed! if indeed thou bringest aught than can give joy.

Lichas. We are happy in our return, and happy in thy greeting, lady, which befits the deed achieved; for when a man hath fair fortune, he needs must win good welcome.

De. O best of friends, tell me first what first I would know—shall I receive Heracles alive?

Li. I, certainly, left him alive and well—in vigorous health, unburdened by disease.

De. Where, tell me—at home, or on foreign soil?

Li. There is a headland of Euboea, where to Cenaean Zeus he consecrates altars, and the tribute of fruitful ground.

De. In payment of a vow, or at the bidding of an oracle?

Li. For a vow, made when he was seeking to conquer and despoil the country of these women who are before thee.

De. And these—who are they, I pray thee, and whose daughters? They deserve pity, unless their plight deceives me.

Li. These are captives whom he chose out for himself and for the gods, when he sacked the city of Eurytus.

De. Was it the war against that city which kept him away so long, beyond all forecast, past all count of days?

Li. Not so: the greater part of the time he was detained in Lydia—no free man, as he declares, but sold into bondage. No offence should attend on the word, lady, when the deed is found to be of Zeus. So he passed a whole year, as he himself avows, in thraldom to Omphalè the barbarian. And so stung was he by that reproach, he bound himself by a solemn oath that he would one day enslave, with wife and child, the man who had brought that calamity upon him. Nor did he speak the word in vain; but, when he had been purged, gathered an alien host, and went against the city of Eurytus. That man, he said, alone of mortals, had a share in causing his misfortune. For when Heracles, an old friend, came to his house and hearth, Eurytus heaped on him the taunts of a bitter tongue and spiteful soul, saying, "Thou hast unerring arrows in thy hands, and yet my sons surpass thee in the trial of archery", "Thou art a slave," he cried, "a free man's broken thrall": and at a banquet, when his guest was full of wine, he thrust him from his doors.

Wroth thereat, when afterward Iphitus came to the hill of Tiryns, in search for horses that had strayed, Heracles seized a moment when the man's wandering thoughts went not with his wandering gaze, and hurled him from a tower-like summit. But in anger at that deed, Zeus our lord, Olympian sire of all, sent him forth into bondage, and spared not, because, this once, he had taken a life by guile. Had he wreaked his vengeance openly, Zeus would surely have pardoned him the righteous triumph; for the gods, too, love not insolence.

So those men, who waxed so proud with bitter speech, are themselves in the mansions of the dead, all of them, and their city is enslaved; while the women whom thou beholdest, fallen from happiness to misery, come here to thee; for such was thy lord's command, which I, his faithful servant, perform. He himself, thou mayest be sure—so soon as he shall have offered holy sacrifice for his victory to Zeus from whom he sprang—will be with thee. After all the fair tidings that have been told, this, indeed, is the sweetest word to hear.

Ch. Now, O Queen, thy joy is assured; part is with thee, and thou hast promise of the rest.

De. Yea, have I not the fullest reason to rejoice at these tidings of my lord's happy fortune? To such fortune, such joy must needs respond. And yet a prudent mind can see room for misgiving lest he who prospers should one day suffer reverse. A strange pity hath come over me, friends, at the sight of these ill-fated exiles, homeless and fatherless in a foreign land; once the daughters, perchance, of freeborn sires, but now doomed to the life of slaves. O Zeus, who turnest the tide of battle, never may I see child of mine thus visited by thy hand; nay, if such visitation is to be, may it not fall while Deianeira lives! Such dread do I feel, beholding these.

(*To* IOLÈ) Ah, hapless girl, say, who art thou? A maiden, or a mother? To judge by thine aspect, an innocent maiden, and of a noble race. Lichas, whose daughter is this stranger? Who is her mother, who her sire? Speak, I pity her more than all the rest, when I behold her; as she alone shows a due feeling for her plight.

Li. How should I know? Why should'st thou ask me? Perchance the offspring of not the meanest in yonder land.

De. Can she be of royal race? Had Eurytus a daughter?

Li. I know not; indeed, I asked not many questions.

De. And thou hast not heard her name from any of her companions?

Li. No, indeed, I went through my task in silence.

De. Unhappy girl, let me, at least, hear it from thine own mouth. It is indeed distressing not to know *thy* name.

Li. It will be unlike her former behaviour, then, I can tell thee, if she opens her lips: for she hath not uttered one word, but hath ever been travailing with the burden of her sorrow, and weeping bitterly, poor girl, since she left her wind-swept home,

Such a state is grievous for herself, but claims our forbearance.

De. Then let her be left in peace, and pass under our roof as she wishes; her present woes must not be crowned with fresh pains at my hands; she hath enough already. Now let us all go in, that thou mayest start speedily on thy journey, while I make all things ready in the house.

(LICHAS, *followed by the Captives, moves into the house.*)

Me. (*coming nearer to* DEIANEIRA) Ay, but first tarry here a brief space, that thou mayest learn, apart from yonder folk, whom thou art taking to thy hearth, and mayest gain the needful knowledge of things which have not been told to thee. Of these I am in full possession.

De. What means this? Why wouldest thou stay my departure?

Me. Pause and listen. My former story was worth thy hearing, and so will this one be, methinks.

De. Shall I call those others back? Or wilt thou speak before me and these maidens?

Me. To thee and these I can speak freely; never mind the others.

De. Well, they are gone; so thy story can proceed.

Me. Yonder man was not speaking the straightforward truth in aught that he has just told. He has given false tidings now, or else his former report was dishonest.

De. How sayest thou? Explain thy whole drift clearly; thus far, thy words are riddles to me.

Me. I heard this man declare, before many witnesses, that for this maiden's sake Heracles overthrew Eurytus and the proud towers of Oechalia; Love, alone of the gods, wrought on him to do those deeds of arms—not the toilsome servitude to Omphalè in Lydia, nor the death to which Iphitus was hurled. But now the herald has thrust Love out of sight, and tells a different tale.

Well, when he could not persuade her sire to give him the maiden for his paramour, he devised some petty complaint as a pretext, and made war upon her land—that in which, as he said, this Eurytus bore sway—and slew the prince her father, and sacked her city. And now, as thou seest, he comes sending her to this house not in careless fashion, lady, nor like a slave; no, dream not of that—it is not likely, if his heart is kindled with desire.

I resolved, therefore, O Queen, to tell thee all that I had heard from yonder man. Many others were listening to it, as I was, in the public place where the Trachinians were assembled; and they can convict him. If my words are unwelcome, I am grieved; but nevertheless I have spoken out the truth.

De. Ah me unhappy! In what plight do I stand? What secret bane have I received beneath my roof? Hapless that I am! Is she nameless, then, as her convoy sware?

Me. Nay, illustrious by name as by birth; she is the daughter of Eurytus, and was once called Iolè; she of whose parentage Lichas could say nothing, because, forsooth, he asked no questions.

Ch. Accursed, above other evil-doers, be the man whom deeds of treachery dishonour!

De. Ah, maidens, what am I to do? These latest tidings have bewildered me!

Ch. Go and inquire from Lichas; perchance he will tell the truth, if thou constrain him to answer.

De. Well, I will go; thy counsel is not amiss.

Me. And I, shall I wait here? Or what is thy pleasure?

De. Remain; here he comes from the house of his own accord, without summons from me.

Enter LICHAS.

Li. Lady, what message shall I bear to Heracles? Give me thy commands, for, as thou seest, I am going.

De. How hastily thou art rushing away, when thy visit had been so long delayed—before we have had time for further talk.

Li. Nay, if there be aught that thou would'st ask, I am at thy service.

De. Wilt thou indeed give me the honest truth?

Li. Yes, be great Zeus my witness, in anything that I know.

De. Who is the woman, then, whom thou hast brought?

Li. She is Euboean; but of what birth, I cannot say.

Me. Sirrah, look at me: to whom art thou speaking, think'st thou?

Li. And thou—what dost thou mean by such a question?

Me. Deign to answer me, if thou comprehendest.

Li. To the royal Deianeira, unless mine eyes deceive me—daughter of Oeneus, wife of Heracles, and my queen.

Me. The very word that I wished to hear from thee: thou sayest that she is thy queen?

Li. Yes, as in duty bound.

Me. Well, then, what art thou prepared to suffer, if found guilty of failing in that duty?

Li. Failing in duty? What dark saying is this?

Me. 'Tis none; the darkest words are thine own.

Li. I will go—I was foolish to hear thee so long.

Me. No, not till thou hast answered a brief question.

Li. Ask what thou wilt; thou art not taciturn.

Me. That captive, whom thou hast brought home—thou knowest whom I mean?

Li. Yes; but why dost thou ask?

Me. Well, saidst thou not that thy prisoner—she, on whom thy gaze now turns so vacantly—was Iolè, daughter of Eurytus?

Li. Said it to whom? Who and where is the man that will be thy witness to hearing this from me?

Me. To many of our own folk thou saidst it: in the public gathering of Trachinians, a great crowd heard thus much from thee.

Li. Ay—said they heard; but 'tis one thing to report a fancy, and another to make the story good.

Me. A fancy! Didst thou not say on thine oath that thou wast bringing her as a bride for Heracles?

Li. I? bringing a bride? In the name of the gods, dear mistress, tell me who this stranger may be?

Me. One who heard from thine own lips that the conquest of the whole city was due to love for this girl: the Lydian woman was not its destroyer, but the passion which this maid has kindled.

Li. Lady, let this fellow withdraw: to prate with the brainsick befits not a sane man.

De. Nay, I implore thee by Zeus whose lightnings go forth over the high glens of Oeta, do not cheat me of the truth! For she to whom thou wilt speak is not ungenerous, nor hath she yet to learn that the human heart is inconstant to its joys. They are not wise, then, who stand forth to buffet against Love; for Love rules the gods as he will, and me; and why not another woman, such as I am? So I am mad indeed, if I blame my husband, because that distemper hath seized him; or this woman, his partner in a thing which is no shame to them, and no wrong to me. Impossible! No; if he taught thee to speak falsely, 'tis not a noble lesson that thou art learning; or if thou art thine own teacher in this, thou wilt be found cruel when it is thy wish to prove kind. Nay, tell me the whole truth. To a free-born man, the name of liar cleaves as a deadly brand. If thy hope is to escape detection, that, too, is vain; there are many to whom thou hast spoken, who will tell me.

And if thou art afraid, thy fear is mistaken. *Not* to learn the truth, that, indeed, would pain me; but to know it—what is there terrible in that? Hath not Heracles wedded others erenow,—ay, more than living man,—and no one of them hath had harsh word or taunt from me; nor shall this girl, though her whole being should be absorbed in her passion; for indeed I felt a profound pity when I beheld her, because her beauty hath wrecked her life, and she, hapless one, all innocent, hath brought her fatherland to ruin and to bondage.

Well, those things must go with wind and stream. To thee I say—deceive whom thou wilt, but ever speak the truth to me.

Ch. Hearken to her good counsel, and hereafter thou shalt have no cause to complain of this lady; our thanks, too, will be thine.

Li. Nay, then, dear mistress—since I see that thou thinkest as mortals should think, and canst allow for weakness—I will tell thee the whole truth, and hide it not. Yes, it is even as yon man saith. This girl inspired that overmastering love which long ago smote through the soul of Heracles; for this girl's sake the desolate Oechalia, her home, was made the prey of his spear. And he—it is just to him to say so—never denied this, never told me to conceal it. But I, lady, fearing to wound thy heart by such tidings, have sinned, if thou count this in any sort a sin.

Now, however, that thou knowest the whole story, for both your sakes—for his, and not less for thine own—bear with the woman, and be content that the words which thou hast spoken regarding her should bind thee still. For he, whose strength is victorious in all else, hath been utterly vanquished by his passion for this girl.

De. Indeed, mine own thoughts move me to act thus. Trust me, I will not add a new affliction to my burdens by waging a fruitless fight against the gods.

But let us go into the house, that thou mayest receive my messages; and, since gifts should be meetly recompensed with gifts, that thou mayest take these also. It is not right that thou shouldest go back with empty hands, after coming with such a goodly train.

Exit MESSENGER, *as* LICHAS *and* DEIANEIRA *go into the house.*

Ch. Great and mighty is the victory which the Cyprian queen ever bears away. I stay not now to speak of the gods; I spare to tell how she beguiled the son of Cronus, and Hades, the lord of darkness, or Poseidon, shaker of the earth.

But, when this bride was to be won, who were the valiant rivals that entered the contest for her hand? Who went forth to the ordeal of battle, to the fierce blows and the blinding dust?

One was a mighty river-god, the dread form of a horned and four-legged bull, Acheloüs, from Oeniadae: the other came from Thebè, dear to Bacchus, with curved bow, and spears, and brandished club, the son of Zeus: who then met in combat, fain to win a bride: and the Cyprian goddess of nuptial joy was there with them, sole umpire of their strife.

Then was there clatter of fists and clang of bow, and the noise of a bull's horns therewith; then were there close-locked grapplings, and deadly blows from the forehead, and loud deep cries from both.

Meanwhile, she, in her delicate beauty, sat on the side of a hill that could be seen afar, awaiting the husband that should be hers.

[So the battle rages] as I have told; but the fair bride who is the prize of the strife abides the end in piteous anguish. And suddenly she is parted from her mother, as when a heifer is taken from its dam.

DEIANEIRA *enters from the house alone, carrying in her arms a casket containing a robe.*

De. Dear friends, while our visitor is saying his farewell to the captive girls in the house, I have stolen forth to you—partly to tell you what these hands have devised, and partly to crave your sympathy with my sorrow.

A maiden—or, methinks, no longer a maiden, but a mistress—hath found her way into my house, as a freight comes to a mariner, a merchandise to make shipwreck of my peace. And now we twain are to share the same marriage-bed, the same embrace. Such is the reward that Heracles hath sent me—he whom I called true and loyal—for guarding his home through all that weary time. I have no thought of anger against him, often as he is vexed with this distemper. But then to live with her, sharing the same union—what woman could endure it? For I see that the flower of her age is blossoming, while mine is fading; and the eyes of men love to cull the bloom of youth, but they turn aside from the old. This, then, is my fear—lest Heracles, in name my spouse, should be the younger's mate.

But, as I said, anger ill beseems a woman of understanding. I will tell you, friends, the way by which I hope to find deliverance and relief. I had a gift, given to me long ago by a monster of olden time, and stored in an urn of bronze; a gift which, while yet a girl, I took up from the shaggy-breasted Nessus—from his life-blood, as he lay dying; Nessus, who used to carry men in his arms for hire across the deep waters of the Evenus, using no oar to waft them, nor sail of ship.

I, too, was carried on his shoulders—when, by my father's sending, I first went forth with Heracles as his wife; and when I was in mid-stream, he touched me with wanton hands. I shrieked; the son of Zeus turned quickly round, and shot a feathered arrow; it whizzed through his breast to the lungs; and, in his mortal faintness, thus much the Centaur spake:

"Child of aged Oeneus, thou shalt have at least this profit of my ferrying—if thou wilt hearken—because thou wast the last whom I conveyed. If thou gatherest with thy hands the blood clotted round my wound, at the place where the Hydra, Lerna's monstrous growth, hath tinged the arrow with black gall, this shall be to thee a charm for the soul of Heracles, so that he shall never look upon any woman to love her more than thee."

I bethought me of this, my friends—for, after his death, I had kept it carefully locked up in a secret place; and I have anointed this robe, doing everything to it as he enjoined while he lived. The work is finished. May deeds of wicked daring be ever far from my thoughts, and from my knowledge—as I abhor the women who attempt them! But if in any wise I may prevail against this girl by love-spells and charms used on Heracles, the means to that end are ready; unless, indeed, I seem to be acting rashly: if so, I will desist forthwith.

Ch. Nay, if these measures give any ground of confidence, we think that thy design is not amiss.

De. Well, the ground stands thus—there is a fair promise; but I have not yet essayed the proof.

Ch. Nay, knowledge must come through action; thou canst have no test which is not fanciful, save by trial.

De. Well, we shall know presently: for there I see the man already at the doors; and he will soon be going. Only may my secret be well kept by you! While thy deeds are hidden, even though they be not seemly, thou wilt never be brought to shame.

Enter LICHAS.

Li. What are thy commands? Give me my charge, daughter of Oeneus; for already I have tarried over long.

De. Indeed, I have just been seeing to this for thee, Lichas, while thou wast speaking to the stranger maidens in the house; that thou shouldest take for me this long robe, woven by mine own hand, a gift to mine absent lord.

And when thou givest it, charge him that he, and no other, shall be the first to wear it; that it shall not be seen by the light of the sun, nor by the sacred precinct, nor by the fire at the hearth, until he stand forth, conspicuous before all eyes, and show it to the gods on a day when bulls are slain.

For thus had I vowed, that if I should ever see or hear that he had come safely home, I would duly clothe him in this robe, and so present him to the gods, newly radiant at their altar in new garb.

As proof, thou shalt carry a token, which he will quickly recognise within the circle of this seal.

Now go thy way; and, first, remember the rule that messengers should not be meddlers; next, so bear thee that my thanks may be joined to his, doubling the grace which thou shalt win.

Li. Nay, if I ply this herald-craft of Hermes with any sureness, I will never trip in doing thine errand: I will not fail to deliver this casket as it is, and to add thy words in attestation of thy gift.

De. Thou mayest be going now; for thou knowest well how things are with us in the house.

Li. I know, and will report, that all hath prospered.

De. And then thou hast seen the greeting given to the stranger maiden—thou knowest how I welcomed her?

Li. So that my heart was filled with wondering joy.

De. What more, then, is there for thee to tell? I am afraid that it would be too soon to speak of the longing on my part, before we know if I am longed for there.

LICHAS *departs with the casket.* DEIANEIRA *retires into the house.*

Chorus

O ye who dwell by the warm springs between haven and crag, and by Oeta's heights; O dwellers by the land-locked waters of the Malian sea, on the shore sacred to the virgin-goddess of the golden shafts, where the Greeks meet in famous council at the Gates;

Soon shall the glorious voice of the flute go up for you again, resounding with no harsh strain of grief, but with such music as the lyre maketh to the gods! For the son whom Alcmena bore to Zeus is hastening homeward, with the trophies of all prowess.

He was lost utterly to our land, a wanderer over sea, while we waited through twelve long months, and knew nothing; and his loving wife, sad dweller with sad thoughts, was ever pining amid her tears. But now the War-god, roused to fury, hath delivered her from the days of her mourning.

May he come, may he come! Pause not the many-oared ship that carries him, till he shall have reached this town, leaving the island altar where, as rumour saith, he is sacrificing! Thence may he come, full of desire, steeped in love by the specious device of the robe, on which Persuasion hath spread her sovereign charm!

DEIANEIRA *comes out of the house in agitation.*

De. Friends, how I fear that I may have gone too far in all that I have been doing just now!

Ch. What hath happened, Deianeira, daughter of Oeneus?

De. I know not; but feel a misgiving that I shall presently be found to have wrought a great mischief, the issue of a fair hope.

Ch. It is nothing, surely, that concerns thy gift to Heracles?

De. Yea, even so. And henceforth I would say to all, act not with zeal, if ye act without light.

Ch. Tell us the cause of thy fear, if it may be told.

De. A thing hath come to pass, my friends, such that, if I declare it, ye will hear a marvel whereof none could have dreamed.

That with which I was lately anointing the festal robe—a white tuft of fleecy sheep's wool—hath disappeared,—not consumed by anything in the house, but self-devoured and self-destroyed, as it crumbled down from the surface of a stone. But I must tell the story more at length, that thou mayest know exactly how this thing befell.

I neglected no part of the precepts which the savage Centaur gave me, when the bitter barb was rankling in his side: they were in my memory, like the graven words which no hand may wash from a tablet of bronze. Now these were his orders, and I obeyed them: to keep this unguent in a secret place, always remote from fire and from the sun's warm ray, until I should apply it, newly spread, where I wished. So had I done. And now, when the moment for action had come, I performed the anointing privily in the house, with a tuft of soft wool which I had plucked from a sheep of our homeflock; then I folded up my gift, and laid it, unvisited by sunlight, within its casket, as ye saw.

But as I was going back into the house, I beheld a thing too wondrous for words, and passing the wit of man to understand. I happened to have thrown the shred of wool, with which I had been preparing the robe, into the full blaze of the sunshine. As it grew warm, it shrivelled all away, and quickly crumbled to powder on the ground, like nothing so much as the dust shed from a saw's teeth where men work timber. In such a state it lies as it fell. And from the earth, where it was strewn, clots of foam seethed up, as when the rich juice of the blue fruit from the vine of Bacchus is poured upon the ground.

So I know not, hapless one, whither to turn my thoughts; I only see that I have done a fearful deed. Why or wherefore should the monster, in his death-throes, have shown good will to me, on whose account he was dying? Impossible! No, he was cajoling me, in order to slay the man who had smitten him: and I gain the knowledge of this too late, when it avails no more. Yes, I alone—unless my foreboding prove false—I, wretched one, must destroy him! For I know that the arrow which made the wound did scathe even to the god Cheiron; and it kills all beasts that it touches. And since 'tis this same black venom in the blood that hath passed out through the wound of Nessus, must it not kill my lord also? I ween it must.

Howbeit, I am resolved that, if he is to fall, at the same time I also shall be swept from life; for no woman could bear to live with an evil name, if she rejoices that her nature is not evil.

Ch. Mischief must needs be feared; but it is not well to doom our hope before the event.

De. Unwise counsels leave no room even for a hope which can lend courage.

Ch. Yet towards those who have erred unwittingly, men's anger is softened; and so it should be towards thee.

De. Nay, such words are not for one who has borne a part in the ill deed, but only for him who has no trouble at his own door.

Ch. 'Twere well to refrain from further speech, unless thou would'st tell aught to thine own son; for he is at hand, who went erewhile to seek his sire.

Enter HYLLUS.

Hy. O mother, would that one of three things had befallen thee! Would that thou wert dead—or, if living, no mother of mine, or that some new and better spirit had passed into thy bosom.

De. Ah, my son, what cause have I given thee to abhor me?

Hy. I tell thee that thy husband—yea, my sire—hath been done to death by thee this day!

De. Oh, what word hath passed thy lips, my child!

Hy. A word that shall not fail of fulfilment; for who may undo that which hath come to pass?

De. What saidst thou, my son? Who is thy warranty for charging me with a deed so terrible?

Hy. I have seen my father's grievous fate with mine own eyes; I speak not from hearsay.

De. And where didst thou find him—where didst thou stand at his side?

Hy. If thou art to hear it, then must all be told.

After sacking the famous town of Eurytus, he went his way with the trophies and first-fruits of victory. There is a sea-washed headland of Euboea, Cape Cenaeum, where he dedicated altars and a sacred grove to the Zeus of his fathers; and there I first beheld him, with the joy of yearning love.

He was about to celebrate a great sacrifice, when his own herald, Lichas, came to him from home, bearing thy gift, the deadly robe; which he put on, according to thy precept; and then began his offering with twelve bulls, free from blemish, the firstlings of the spoil; but altogether he brought a hundred victims, great or small, to the altar.

At first, hapless one, he prayed with serene soul, rejoicing in his comely garb. But when the blood-fed flame began to blaze from the holy offerings and from the resinous pine, a sweat broke forth upon his flesh, and the tunic clung to his sides, at every joint, close-glued, as if by a craftsman's hand; there came a biting pain that racked his bones; and then the venom, as of some deadly, cruel viper, began to devour him.

Thereupon he shouted for the unhappy Lichas—in no wise to blame for thy crime—asking what treason had moved him to bring that robe; but he, all-unknowing, hapless one, said that he had brought the gift from thee alone, as it had been sent. When his master heard it, as a piercing spasm clutched his lungs, he caught him by the foot, where the ankle turns in the socket, and hurled him at a surf-beaten rock in the sea; and he made the white brain to ooze from the hair, as the skull was dashed to splinters, and blood scattered therewith.

But all the people lifted up a cry of awe-struck grief, seeing that one was frenzied, and the other slain; and no one dared to come before the man. For the pain dragged him to earth, or made him leap into the air, with yells and shrieks, till the cliffs rang around, steep headlands of Locris, and Euboean capes.

But when he was spent with oft throwing himself on the ground in his anguish, and oft making loud lament—cursing his fatal marriage with thee, the vile one, and his alliance with Oeneus, saying how he had found in it the ruin of his life—then, from out of the shrouding altar-smoke, he lifted up his wildly-rolling eyes, and saw me in the great crowd, weeping. He turned his gaze on me, and called me: "O son, draw near; do not fly from my trouble, even though thou must share my death. Come, bear me forth, and set me, if thou canst, in a place where no man shall see me; or, if thy pity forbids that, at least convey me with all speed out of this land, and let me not die where I am."

That command sufficed; we laid him in mid-ship, and brought him—but hardly brought him—to this shore, moaning in his torments. And ye shall presently behold him, alive, or lately dead.

Such, mother, are the designs and deeds against my sire whereof thou hast been found guilty. May avenging Justice and the Erinys visit thee for them! Yes, if it be right, that is my prayer: and right it is—for I have seen thee trample on the right, by slaying the noblest man in all the world, whose like thou shalt see nevermore!

DEIANEIRA *moves towards the house.*

Ch. (*to* DEIANEIRA). Why dost thou depart in silence? Knowest thou not that such silence pleads for thine accuser?

DEIANEIRA *goes into the house.*

Hy. Let her depart. A fair wind speed her far from my sight! Why should the name of mother bring her a semblance of respect, when she is all unlike a mother in her deeds? No, let her go—farewell to her; and may such joy as she gives my sire become her own!

Chorus

See, maidens, how suddenly the divene word of the old prophecy hath come upon us, which said that, when the twelfth year should have run through its full tale of months, it should end the series of toils for the true-born son of Zeus! And that promise is wafted surely to its fulfilment. For how shall he who beholds not the light have toilsome servitude any more beyond the grave?

If a cloud of death is around him, and the doom wrought by the Centaur's craft is stinging his sides, where cleaves the venom which Thanatos begat and the gleaming serpent nourished, how can he look upon to-morrow's sun,—when that appalling Hydra-shape holds him in its grip, and those murderous goads, prepared by the wily words of black-haired Nessus, have started into fury, vexing him with tumultuous pain?

Of such things this hapless lady had no foreboding; but she saw a great mischief swiftly coming on her home from the new marriage. Her own hand applied the remedy; but for the issues of a stranger's counsel, given at a fatal meeting,—for these, I ween, she makes despairing lament, shedding the tender dew of plenteous tears. And the coming fate foreshadows a great misfortune, contrived by guile.

Our streaming tears break forth: alas, a plague is upon him more piteous than any suffering that foemen ever brought upon that glorious hero.

Ah, thou dark steel of the spear foremost in battle, by whose might yonder bride was lately borne so swiftly from Oechalia's heights! But the Cyprian goddess, ministering in silence, hath been plainly proved the doer of these deeds.

First Semi-Chorus. Is it fancy, or do I hear some cry of grief just passing through the house? What is this?

Second Semi-Ch. No uncertain sound, but a wail of anguish from within: the house hath some new trouble.

Ch. And mark how sadly, with what a cloud upon her brow, that aged woman approaches, to give us tidings.

Enter NURSE, *from the house.*

Nurse. Ah, my daughters, great, indeed, were the sorrows that we were to reap from the gift sent to Heracles!

Ch. Aged woman, what new mischance hast thou to tell?

Nu. Deianeira hath departed on the last of all her journeys, departed without stirring foot.

Ch. Thou speakest not of death?

Nu. My tale is told.

Ch. Dead, hapless one?

Nu. Again thou hearest it.

Ch. Hapless, lost one! Say, what was the manner of her death?

Nu. Oh, a cruel deed was there!

Ch. Speak, woman, how hath she met her doom?

Nu. By her own hand hath she died.

Ch. What fury, what pangs of frenzy have cut her off by the edge of a dire weapon? How contrived she this death, following death—all wrought by her alone?

Nu. By the stroke of the sword that makes sorrow.

Ch. Sawest thou that violent deed, poor helpless one?

Nu. I saw it; yea, I was standing near.

Ch. Whence came it? How was it done? Oh, speak!

Nu. 'Twas the work of her own mind and her own hand.

Ch. What dost thou tell us?

Nu. The sure truth.

Ch. The first-born, the first-born of that new bride is a dread Erinys for this house!

Nu. Too true; and, hadst thou been an eye-witness of the action, verily thy pity would have been yet deeper.

Ch. And could a woman's hand dare to do such deeds?

Nu. Yea, with dread daring; thou shalt hear, and then thou wilt bear me witness.

When she came alone into the house, and saw her son preparing a deep litter in the court, that he might go back with it to meet his sire, then she hid herself where none might see; and, falling before the altars, she wailed aloud that they were left desolate; and, when she touched any household thing that she had been wont to use, poor lady, in the past, her tears would flow; or when, roaming hither and thither through the house, she beheld the form of any well-loved servant, she wept, hapless one, at that sight, crying aloud upon her own fate, and that of the household which would thenceforth be in the power of others.

But when she ceased from this, suddenly I beheld her rush into the chamber of Heracles. From a secret place of espial, I watched her; and saw her spreading coverings on the couch of her lord. When she had done this, she sprang thereon, and sat in the middle of the bed; her tears burst forth in burning streams, and thus she spake: "Ah, bridal bed and bridal chamber mine, farewell now and for ever; never more shall ye receive me to rest upon this couch." She said no more, but with a vehement hand loosed her robe, where the gold-wrought brooch lay above her breast, baring all her left side and arm. Then I ran with all my strength, and warned her son of her intent. But lo, in the space between my going and our return, she had driven a two-edged sword through her side to the heart.

At that sight, her son uttered a great cry; for he knew, alas, that in his anger he had driven her to that deed; and he had learned, too late, from the servants in the house that she had acted without knowledge, by the prompting of the Centaur. And now the youth, in his misery, bewailed her with all passionate lament; he knelt, and showered kisses on her lips; he threw himself at her side upon the ground, bitterly crying that he had rashly smitten her with a slander, weeping, that he must now live bereaved of both alike—of mother and of sire.

Such are the fortunes of this house. Rash indeed, is he who reckons on the morrow, or haply on days beyond it; for to-morrow is not, until to-day is safely past.

Ch. Which woe shall I bewail first, which misery is the greater? Alas, 'tis hard for me to tell.

One sorrow may be seen in the house; for one we wait with foreboding: and suspense hath a kinship with pain.

Oh that some strong breeze might come with wafting power unto our hearth, to bear me far from this land, lest I die of terror, when I look but once upon the mighty son of Zeus!

For they say that he is approaching the house in torments from which there is no deliverance, a wonder of unutterable woe.

Ah, it was not far off, but close to us, that woe of which my lament gave warning, like the nightingale's piercing note!

Men of an alien race are coming yonder. And how, then, are they bringing him? In sorrow, as for some loved one, they move on their mournful, noiseless march.

Alas, he is brought in silence! What are we to think; that he is dead, or sleeping?

Enter HYLLUS *and an* OLD MAN, *with attendants, bearing* HERACLES *upon a litter.*

Hy. Woe is me for thee, my father, woe is me for thee, wretched that I am! Whither shall I turn? What can I do? Ah me!

Old Man (*whispering*). Hush, my son! Rouse not the cruel pain that infuriates thy sire! He lives, though prostrated. Oh, put a stern restraint upon thy lips!

Hy. How sayest thou, old man—is he alive?

O.M. (*whispering*). Thou must not awake the slumberer! Thou must not rouse and revive the dread frenzy that visits him, my son!

Hy. Nay, I am crushed with this weight of misery—there is madness in my heart!

Heracles (*awaking*). O Zeus, to what land have I come? Who are these among whom I lie, tortured with unending agonies? Wretched, wretched that I am! Oh, that dire pest is gnawing me once more!

O.M. (*to* HYLLUS). Knew I not how much better it was that thou shouldest keep silence, instead of scaring slumber from his brain and eyes?

Hy. Nay, I cannot be patient when I behold this misery.

He. O thou Cenaean rock whereon mine altars rose, what a cruel reward hast thou won me for those fair offerings—be Zeus my witness! Ah, to what ruin hast thou brought me, to what ruin! Would that I had never beheld thee for thy sorrow! Then had I never come face to face with this fiery madness, which no spell can soothe! Where is the charmer, where is the cunning healer, save Zeus alone, that shall lull this plague to rest? I should marvel, if he ever came within my ken!

Ah!

Leave me, hapless one, to my rest—leave me to my last rest!

Where art thou touching me? Whither wouldst thou turn me? Thou wilt kill me, thou wilt kill me! If there be any pang that slumbers, thou hast aroused it!

It hath seized me, oh, the pest comes again! Whence are ye, most ungrateful of all the Greeks? I wore out my troublous days in ridding Greece of pests, on the deep and in all forests; and now, when I am stricken, will no man succour me with merciful fire or sword?

Oh, will no one come and sever the head, at one fierce stroke, from this wretched body? Woe, woe is me!

O.M. Son of Heracles, this task exceeds my strength —help thou—for strength is at thy command, too largely to need my aid in his relief.

Hy. My hands are helping; but no resource, in myself or from another, avails me to make his life forget its anguish: such is the doom appointed by Zeus!

He. O my son, where art thou? Raise me,—take hold of me,—thus, thus! Alas, my destiny!

Again, again the cruel pest leaps forth to rend me, the fierce plague with which none may cope!

O Pallas, Pallas, it tortures me again! Alas, my son, pity thy sire,—draw a blameless sword, and smite beneath my collar-bone, and heal this pain wherewith thy godless mother hath made me wild! So may I see her fall,—thus, even thus, as she hath destroyed me! Sweet Hades, brother of Zeus, give me rest, give me rest, end my woe by a swiftly-sped doom!

Ch. I shudder, friends, to hear these sorrows of our lord; what a man is here, and what torments afflict him!

He. Ah, fierce full oft, and grievous not in name alone, have been the labours of these hands, the burdens borne upon these shoulders! But no toil ever laid on me by the wife of Zeus or by the hateful Eurystheus was like unto this thing which the daughter of Oeneus, fair and false, hath fastened upon my back—this woven net of the Furies, in which I perish! Glued to my sides, it hath eaten my flesh to the inmost parts; it is ever with me, sucking the channels of my breath; already it hath drained my fresh life-blood, and my whole body is wasted, a captive to these unutterable bonds.

Not the warrior on the battle-field, not the Giants' earth-born host, nor the might of savage beasts, hath ever done unto me thus—not Hellas, nor the land of the alien, nor any land to which I have come as a deliverer: no, a woman, a weak woman, born not to the strength of man, all alone hath vanquished me, without stroke of sword!

Son, show thyself my son indeed, and do not honour a mother's name above a sire's: bring forth the woman that bare thee, and give her with thine own hands into my hand, that I may know of a truth which sight grieves thee most—my tortured frame, or hers, when she suffers her righteous doom!

Go, my son, shrink not—and show thy pity for me, whom many might deem pitiful, for me, moaning and weeping like a girl; and the man lives not who can say that he ever saw me do thus before; no, without complaining I still went whither mine evil fortune led. But now, alas, the strong man hath been found a woman.

Approach, stand near thy sire, and see what a fate it is that hath brought me to this pass; for I will lift the veil. Behold! Look, all of you, on this miserable body; see how wretched, how piteous is my plight!

Ah, woe is me!

The burning throe of torment is there anew, it darts through my sides—I must wrestle once more with that cruel, devouring plague!

O thou lord of the dark realm, receive me! Smite me, O fire of Zeus! Hurl down thy thunderbolt, O King, send it, O father, upon my head! For again the pest is consuming me; it hath blazed forth, it hath started into fury! O hands, my hands, O shoulders and breast and trusty arms, ye, now in this plight, are the same whose force of old subdued the dweller in Nemea, the scourge of herdsmen, the lion, a creature that no man might approach or confront; ye tamed the Lernaean Hydra, and that monstrous host of double form, man joined to steed, a race with whom none may commune, violent, lawless, of surpassing might; ye tamed the Erymanthian beast, and the three-headed whelp of Hades underground, a resistless terror, offspring of the dread Echidna; ye tamed the dragon that guarded the golden fruit in the utmost places of the earth.

These toils and countless others have I proved, nor hath any man vaunted a triumph over my prowess. But now, with joints unhinged and with flesh torn to shreds, I have become the miserable prey of an unseen destroyer—I, who am called the son of noblest mother, I, whose reputed sire is Zeus, lord of the starry sky.

But ye may be sure of one thing: though I am as nought, though I cannot move a step, yet she who hath done this deed shall feel my heavy hand even now: let her but come, and she shall learn to proclaim this message unto all, that in my death, as in my life, I chastised the wicked!

Ch. Ah, hapless Greece, what mourning do I foresee for her, if she must lose this man!

Hy. Father, since thy pause permits an answer, hear me, afflicted though thou art. I will ask thee for no more than is my due. Accept my counsels, in a calmer mood than that to which this anger stings thee: else thou canst not learn how vain is thy desire for vengeance, and how causeless thy resentment.

He. Say what thou wilt, and cease; in this my pain I understand nought of all thy riddling words.

Hy. I come to tell thee of my mother—how it is now with her, and how she sinned unwittingly.

He. Villain! What—hast thou dared to breathe her name again in my hearing, the name of the mother who hath slain thy sire?

Hy. Yea, such is her state that silence is unmeet.

He. Unmeet, truly, in view of her past crimes.

Hy. And also of her deeds this day—as thou wilt own.

He. Speak—but give heed that thou be not found a traitor.

Hy. These are my tidings. She is dead, lately slain.

He. By whose hand? A wondrous message, from a prophet of ill-omened voice!

Hy. By her own hand, and no stranger's.

He. Alas, ere she died by mine, as she deserved!

Hy. Even thy wrath would be turned, couldst thou hear all.

He. A strange preamble; but unfold thy meaning.

Hy. The sum is this; she erred, with a good intent.

He. Is it a good deed, thou wretch, to have slain thy sire?

Hy. Nay, she thought to use a love-charm for thy heart, when she saw the new bride in the house; but missed her aim.

He. And what Trachinian deals in spells so potent?

Hy. Nessus the Centaur persuaded her of old to inflame thy desire with such a charm.

He. Alas, alas, miserable that I am! Woe is me, I am lost—undone, undone! No more for me the light of day! Alas, now I see in what a plight I stand! Go, my son—for thy father's end hath come—summon, I pray thee, all thy brethren; summon, too, the hapless Alcmena, in vain the bride of Zeus, that ye may learn from my dying lips what oracles I know.

Hy. Nay, thy mother is not here; as it chances, she hath her abode at Tiryns by the sea. Some of thy children she hath taken to live with her there, and others, thou wilt find, are dwelling in Thebè's town. But we who are with thee, my father, will render all service that is needed, at thy bidding.

He. Hear, then, thy task: now is the time to show what stuff is in thee, who art called my son.

It was foreshown to me by my Sire of old that I should perish by no creature that had the breath of life, but by one that had passed to dwell with Hades. So I have been slain by this savage Centaur, the living by the dead, even as the divine will had been foretold.

And I will show thee how later oracles tally therewith, confirming the old prophecy. I wrote them down in the grove of the Selli, dwellers on the hills, whose couch is on the ground; they were given by my Father's oak of many tongues; which said that, at the time which liveth and now is, my release from the toils laid upon me should be accomplished. And I looked for prosperous days; but the meaning, it seems, was only that I should die; for toil comes no more to the dead.

Since, then, my son, those words are clearly finding their fulfilment, thou, on thy part, must lend me thine aid. Thou must not delay, and so provoke me to bitter speech: thou must consent and help with a good grace, as one who hath learned that best of laws, obedience to a sire.

Hy. Yea, father—though I fear the issue to which our talk hath brought me—I will do thy good pleasure.

He. First of all, lay thy right hand in mine.

Hy. For what purpose dost thou insist upon this pledge?

He. Give thy hand at once—disobey me not!

Hy. Lo, there it is: thou shalt not be gainsaid.

He. Now, swear by the head of Zeus my sire!

Hy. To do what deed? May this also be told?

He. To perform for me the task that I shall enjoin.

Hy. I swear it, with Zeus for witness of the oath.

He. And pray that, if thou break this oath, thou mayest suffer.

Hy. I shall not suffer, for I shall keep it: yet so I pray.

He. Well, thou knowest the summit of Oeta, sacred to Zeus?

Hy. Ay; I have often stood at his altar on that height.

He. Thither, then, thou must carry me up with thine own hands, aided by what friends thou wilt; thou shalt lop many a branch from the deep-rooted oak, and hew many a faggot also from the sturdy stock of the wild-olive; thou shalt lay my body thereupon, and kindle it with flaming pine-torch.

And let no tear of mourning be seen there; no, do this without lament and without weeping, if thou art indeed my son. But if thou do it not, even from the world below my curse and my wrath shall wait on thee for ever.

Hy. Alas; my father, what hast thou spoken? How hast thou dealt with me!

He. I have spoken that which thou must perform; if thou wilt not, then get thee some other sire, and be called my son no more!

Hy. Woe, woe is me! What a deed dost thou require of me, my father,—that I should become thy murderer, guilty of thy blood!

He. Not so, in truth, but healer of my sufferings, sole physician of my pain!

Hy. And how, by enkindling thy body, shall I heal it?

He. Nay, if that thought dismay thee, at least perform the rest.

Hy. The service of carrying thee shall not be refused.

He. And the heaping of the pyre, as I have bidden?

Hy. Yea, save that I will not touch it with mine own hand. All else will I do, and thou shalt have no hindrance on my part.

He. Well, so much shall be enough. But add one small boon to thy large benefits.

Hy. Be the boon never so large, it shall be granted.

He. Knowest thou, then, the girl whose sire was Eurytus?

Hy. It is of Iolè that thou speakest, if I mistake not.

He. Even so. This, in brief, is the charge that I give thee, my son. When I am dead, if thou wouldest show a pious remembrance of thine oath unto thy father, disobey me not, but take this woman to be thy wife. Let no other espouse her who hath lain at my side, but do thou, O my son, make that marriage-bond thine own. Consent: after loyalty in great matters, to rebel in less is to cancel the grace that had been won.

Hy. Ah me, it is not well to be angry with a sick man: but who could bear to seè him in such a mind?

He. Thy words show no desire to do my bidding.

Hy. What! When she alone is to blame for my mother's death, and for thy present plight besides? Lives there the man who would make such a choice, unless he were maddened by avenging fiends?

Better were it, father, that I too should die, rather than live united to the worst of our foes!

He. He will render no reverence, it seems, to my dying prayer. Nay, be sure that the curse of the gods will attend thee for disobedience to my voice.

Hy. Ah, thou wilt soon show, methinks, how distempered thou art!

He. Yea, for thou art breaking the slumber of my plague.

Hy. Hapless that I am! What perplexities surround me!

He. Yea, since thou deignest not to hear thy sire.

Hy. But must I learn, then, to be impious, my father?

He. 'Tis not impiety, if thou shalt gladden my heart.

Hy. Dost thou command me, then, to do this deed, as a clear duty?

He. I command thee—the gods bear me witness!

Hy. Then will I do it, and refuse not—calling upon the gods to witness thy deed. I can never be condemned for loyalty to thee, my father.

He. Thou endest well; and to these words, my son, quickly add the gracious deed, that thou mayest lay me on the pyre before any pain returns to rend or sting me.

Come, make haste and lift me! This, in truth, is rest from troubles; this is the end, and the last end, of Heracles!

Hy. Nothing, indeed, hinders the fulfilment of thy wish, since thy command constrains us, my father.

He. Come, then, ere thou arouse this plague, O my stubborn soul, give me a curb as of steel on lips set like stone to stone, and let no cry escape them; seeing that the deed which thou art to do, though done perforce, is yet worthy of thy joy!

Hy. Lift him, followers! And grant me full forgiveness for this; but mark the great cruelty of the gods in the deeds that are being done. They beget children, they are hailed as fathers, and yet they can look upon such sufferings.

The attendants raise HERACLES *on the litter and move slowly off, as* HYLLUS *chants to the Chorus in the closing lines.*

No man foresees the future; but the present is fraught with mourning for us, and with shame for the powers above, and verily with anguish beyond compare for him who endures this doom.

Maidens, come ye also, nor linger at the house; ye who have lately seen a dread death, with sorrows manifold and strange: and in all this there is nought but Zeus.

PHILOCTETES

DRAMATIS PERSONAE

ODYSSEUS
NEOPTOLEMUS
PHILOCTETES
MERCHANT, *a follower of Neoptolemus in disguise*
HERACLES
CHORUS OF SAILORS, *belonging to the ship of Neoptolemus*

On the north-east coast of Lemnos, near the promontory of Mount Hermaeum. A rocky cliff rises steeply from the sea-shore: in it is seen the cave of Philoctetes. ODYSSEUS, NEOPTOLEMUS *and an attendant enter.*

Odysseus. This is the shore of the sea-girt land of Lemnos, untrodden of men and desolate. O thou whose sire was the noblest of the Greeks, true-bred son of Achilles, Neoptolemus, here, long ago, I put ashore the Malian, the son of Poeas (having charge from my chiefs so to do), his foot all ulcerous with a gnawing sore, when neither drink-offering nor sacrifice could be attempted by us in peace, but with his fierce, ill-omened cries he filled the whole camp continually, shrieking, moaning. But what need to speak of that? 'Tis no time for many words, lest he learn that I am here, and I waste the whole plan whereby I think to take him anon.

Come, to work! 'tis for thee to help in what remains, and to seek where in this region is a cave with twofold mouth, such that in cold weather either front offers a sunny seat, but in summer a breeze wafts sleep through the tunnelled grot. And a little below, on the left hand, perchance thou wilt see a spring, if it hath not failed.

Move thither silently, and signify to me whether he still dwells in this same place, or is to be sought elsewhere—that so our further course may be explained by me, and heard by thee, and sped by the joint work of both.

Neoptolemus. King Odysseus, the task that thou settest lies not far off; methinks I see such a cave as thou hast described.

Od. Above thee, or below? I perceive it not.

Ne. Here, high up; and of footsteps not a sound.

Od. Look that he be not lodged there, asleep.

Ne. I see an empty chamber—no man therein.

Od. And no provision in it for man's abode?

Ne. Aye, a mattress of leaves, as if for some one who makes his lodging here.

Od. And all else is bare? Nought else beneath the roof?

Ne. Just a rude cup of wood, the work of a sorry craftsman; and this tinder-stuff therewith.

Od. His is the household store whereof thou tellest.

Ne. Ha! Yes, and here are some rags withal, drying in the sun—stained with matter from some grievous sore.

Od. The man dwells in these regions, clearly, and is somewhere not far off; how could one go far afield, with foot maimed by that inveterate plague? No, he hath gone forth in quest of food, or of some soothing herb, haply, that he hath noted somewhere. Send thine attendant, therefore, to keep watch, lest the foe come on me unawares; for he would rather take me than all the Greeks beside.

Ne. Enough, the man is going, and the path shall be watched. And now, if thou wouldst say more, proceed. *Exit Attendant, on the spectators' left.*

Od. Son of Achilles, thou must be loyal to thy mission—and not with thy body alone. Shouldst thou hear some new thing, some plan unknown to thee till now, thou must help it; for to help is thy part here.

Ne. What is thy bidding?

Od. Thou must beguile the mind of Philoctetes by a story told in thy converse with him. When he asks thee who and whence thou art, say, the son of Achilles—there must be no deception touching that; but thou art homeward bound—thou hast left the fleet of the Achaean warriors, and hast conceived a deadly hatred for them; who, when they had moved thee by their prayers to come from home (since this was their only hope of taking Ilium), deemed thee not worthy of the arms of Achilles, deigned not to give them to thee when thou camest and didst claim them by right, but made them over to Odysseus. Of me, say what thou wilt, the vilest of vile reproaches; thou wilt cost me no pang by that; but if thou fail to do this deed, thou wilt bring sorrow on all our host. For if yon man's bow is not to be taken, never canst thou sack the realm of Dardanus.

And mark why thine intercourse with him may be free from mistrust or danger, while mine cannot. *Thou* hast come to Troy under no oath to any man, and by no constraint; nor hadst thou part in the earlier voyage: but none of these things can I deny. And so, if he shall perceive me while he is still master of his bow, I am lost, and thou, as my comrade, wilt share my doom. No; the thing that must be plotted is just this—how thou mayest win the resistless arms by stealth. I well know, my son, that by nature thou art not apt to utter or contrive such guile; yet, seeing that victory is a sweet prize to gain, bend thy will thereto; our honesty shall be shown forth another time. But now lend thyself to me for one little knavish day, and then, through all thy days to come, be called the most righteous of mankind.

Ne. When counsels pain my ear, son of Laertes, then I abhor to aid them with my hand. It is not in my nature to compass aught by evil arts, nor was it, as men say, in my sire's. But I am ready to take the man by force, not by fraud; for, having the use of one foot only, he cannot prevail in fight against us who are so many. And yet, having been sent to act with thee, I am loth to be called traitor. But my wish, O King, is to do right and miss my aim, rather than succeed by evil ways.

Od. Son of brave sire, time was when I too, in my youth, had a slow tongue and a ready hand: but now, when I come forth to the proof, I see that words, not deeds, are ever the masters among men.

Ne. What, then, is thy command? What, but that I should lie?

Od. I say that thou art to take Philoctetes by guile.

Ne. And why by guile rather than by persuasion?

Od. He will never listen; and by force thou canst not take him.

Ne. Hath he such dread strength to make him bold?

Od. Shafts inevitable, and winged with death.

Ne. None may dare, then, e'en to approach that foe?

Od. No, unless thou take him by guile, as I say.

Ne. Thou thinkest it no shame, then, to speak falsehoods?

Od. No, if the falsehood brings deliverance.

Ne. And how shall one have the face to speak those words?

Od. When thy deed promises gain, 'tis unmeet to shrink.

Ne. And what gain is it for me, that he should come to Troy?

Od. With these shafts, alone can Troy be taken.

Ne. Then *I* am not to be the conqueror, as ye said?

Od. Neither thou apart from these, nor these from thee.

Ne. 'Twould seem that we must try to win them, if it stands thus.

Od. Know that, if thou dost this thing, two prizes are thine.

Ne. What are they? Tell me, and I will not refuse the deed.

Od. Thou wilt be called at once wise and valiant.

Ne. Come what may, I'll do it, and cast off all shame.

Od. Art thou mindful, then, of the counsels that I gave?

Ne. Be sure of it—now that once I have consented.

Od. Do thou, then, stay here, in wait for him; but I will go away, lest I be espied with thee, and will send our watcher back to the ship. And, if ye seem to be tarrying at all beyond the due time, I will send that same man hither again, disguised as the captain of a merchant-ship, that secrecy may aid us; and then, my son, as he tells his artful story, take such hints as may help thee from the tenor of his words.

Now I will go to the ship, having left this charge with thee; and may speeding Hermes, the lord of stratagem, lead us on, and Victory, even Athena Polias, who saves me ever!

Exit ODYSSEUS, *on the spectators' left.*

The CHORUS *enters and chants the following lines with* NEOPTOLEMUS *responsively.*

Chorus. A stranger in a strange land, what am I to hide, what am I to speak, O Master, before a man who will be swift to think evil? Be thou my guide: his skill excels all other skill, his counsel hath no peer, with whom is the sway of the godlike sceptre given by Zeus. And to thee, my son, that sovereign power hath descended from of old; tell me, therefore, wherein I am to serve thee.

Ne. For the present—as haply thou wouldst behold the place where he abides on ocean's verge—survey it fearlessly: but when the dread wayfarer, who hath left this dwelling, shall return, come forward at my beck from time to time, and try to help as the moment may require.

Ch. Long have I been careful of that care, my prince, that mine eye should be watchful for thy good, before all else. And now tell me, in what manner of shelter hath he made his abode? In what region is he? 'Twere not unseasonable for me to learn, lest he surprise me from some quarter. What is the place of his wandering, or of his rest? Where planteth he his steps, within his dwelling, or abroad?

Ne. Here thou seest his home, with its two portals—his rocky cell.

Ch. And its hapless inmate—whither is he gone?

Ne. I doubt not but he is trailing his painful steps somewhere near this spot, in quest of food. For rumour saith that in this fashion he lives, seeking prey with his winged shafts, all-wretched that he is; and no healer of his woe draws nigh unto him.

Ch. I pity him, to think how, with no man to care for him, and seeing no companion's face, suffering, lonely evermore, he is vexed by fierce disease, and bewildered by each want as it arises. How, how doth he endure in his misery? Alas, the dark dealings of the gods! Alas, hapless races of men, whose destiny exceeds due measure!

This man—noble, perchance, as any scion of the noblest house—reft of all life's gifts, lies lonely, apart from his fellows, with the dappled or shaggy beasts of the field, piteous alike in his torments and his hunger, bearing anguish that finds no cure; while the mountain nymph, babbling Echo, appearing afar, makes answer to his bitter cries.

Ne. Nought of this is a marvel to me. By heavenly ordinance, if such as I may judge, those first sufferings came on him from relentless Chrysè; and the woes that now he bears, with none to tend him, surely he bears by the providence of some god, that so he should not bend against Troy the resistless shafts divine, till the time be fulfilled when, as men say, Troy is fated by those shafts to fall.

Ch. Hush, peace, my son!

Ne. What now?

Ch. A sound rose on the air, such as might haunt the lips of a man in weary pain. From this point it came, I think—or this. It smites, it smites indeed upon my ear—the voice of one who creeps painfully on his way; I cannot mistake that grievous cry of human anguish from afar—its accents are too clear.

Then turn thee, O my son—

Ne. Say, whither?

Ch. —to new counsels: for the man is not far off, but near; not with music of the reed he cometh, like shepherd in the pastures—no, but with far-sounding moan, as he stumbles, perchance, from stress of pain, or as he gazes on the haven that hath no ship for guest: loud is his cry, and dread.

Enter PHILOCTETES, *on the spectators' right.*

Philoctetes. O strangers!

Who may ye be, and from what country have ye put into this land, that is harbourless and desolate? What should I deem to be your city or your race?

The fashion of your garb is Greek—most welcome to my sight—but I fain would hear your speech: and do not shrink from me in fear, or be scared by my wild looks; nay, in pity for one so wretched and so lonely, for a sufferer so desolate and so friendless, speak to me, if indeed ye have come as friends. Oh, answer! 'Tis not meet that I should fail of this, at least, from you, or ye from me.

Ne. Then know this first, good Sir, that we are Greeks—since thou art fain to learn that.

Ph. O well-loved sound! Ah, that I should indeed be greeted by such a man, after so long a time! What quest, my son, hath drawn thee towards these shores, and to this spot? What enterprise? What kindliest of winds? Speak, tell me all, that I may know who thou art.

Ne. My birthplace is the sea-girt Scyros; I am sailing homeward; Achilles was my sire; my name is Neoptolemus: thou know'st all.

Ph. O son of well-loved father and dear land, foster-child of aged Lycomedes, on what errand hast thou touched this coast? Whence art thou sailing?

Ne. Well, it is from Ilium that I hold my present course.

Ph. What? Thou wast not, certainly, our shipmate at the beginning of the voyage to Ilium.

Ne. Hadst thou, indeed, a part in that emprise?

Ph. O my son, then thou know'st not who is before thee?

Ne. How should I know one whom I have never seen before?

Ph. Then thou hast not even heard my name, or any rumour of those miseries by which I was perishing?

Ne. Be assured that I know nothing of what thou askest.

Ph. O wretched indeed that I am, O abhorred of heaven, that no word of this my plight should have won its way to my home, or to any home of Greeks! No, the men who wickedly cast me out keep their secret and laugh, while my plague still rejoices in its strength, and grows to more!

O my son, O boy whose father was Achilles, behold, I am he of whom haply thou hast heard as lord of the bow of Heracles—I am the son of Poeas, Philoctetes, whom the two chieftains and the Cephallenian king foully cast upon this solitude, when I was wasting with a fierce disease, stricken down by the furious bite of the destroying serpent; with that plague for sole companion, O my son, those men put me out here, and were gone, when from sea-girt Chrysè they touched at this coast with their fleet. Glad, then, when they saw me asleep—after much tossing on the waves—in the shelter of a cave upon the shore, they abandoned me—first putting out a few rags, good enough for such a wretch, and a scanty dole of food withal: may Heaven give them the like!

Think now, my son, think what a waking was mine, when they had gone, and I rose from sleep that day! What bitter tears started from mine eyes, what miseries were those that I bewailed when I saw that the ships with which I had sailed were all gone, and that there was no man in the place, not one to help, not one to ease the burden of the sickness that vexed me, when, looking all around, I could find no provision, save for anguish—but of that a plenteous store, my son!

So time went on for me, season by season; and, alone in this narrow house, I was fain to meet each want by mine own service. For hunger's needs this bow provided, bringing down the winged doves; and, whatever my string-sped shaft might strike, I, hapless one, would crawl to it myself, trailing my wretched foot just so far; or if, again, water had to be fetched—or if (when the frost was out, perchance, as oft in winter) a bit of fire-wood had to be broken, I would creep forth, poor wretch, and manage it. Then fire would be lacking; but by rubbing stone on stone I would at last draw forth the hidden spark; and this it is that keeps life in me from day to day. Indeed, a roof over my head, and fire therewith, gives all that I want—save release from my disease.

Come now, my son, thou must learn what manner of isle this is. No mariner approaches it by choice; there is no anchorage; there is no sea-port where he can find a gainful market or a kindly welcome. This is not a place to which prudent men make voyages. Well, suppose that some one has put in against his will; such things may oft happen in the long course of a man's life. These visitors, when they come, have compassionate words for me; and perchance, moved by pity, they give me a little food, or some raiment: but there is one thing that no one will do, when I speak of it—take me safe home; no, this is now the tenth year that I am wearing out my wretched days, in hunger and in misery, feeding the plague that is never sated with my flesh.

Thus have the Atreidae and the proud Odysseus dealt with me, my son: may the Olympian gods some day give them the like sufferings, in requital for mine!

Ch. Methinks I too pity thee, son of Poeas, in like measure with thy former visitors.

Ne. And I am myself a witness to thy words—I know that they are true; for I have felt the villainy of the Atreidae and the proud Odysseus.

Ph. What, hast thou, too, a grief against the accursed sons of Atreus—a cause to resent ill-usage?

Ne. Oh that it might be mine one day to wreak my hatred with my hand, that so Mycenae might learn, and Sparta, that Scyros also is a mother of brave men!

Ph. Well said, my son! Now wherefore hast thou come in this fierce wrath which thou denouncest against them?

Ne. Son of Poeas, I will speak out—and yet 'tis hard to speak—concerning the outrage that I suffered from them at my coming. When fate decreed that Achilles should die—

Ph. Ah me! Tell me no more, until I first know this—say'st thou that the son of Peleus is dead?

Ne. Dead—by no mortal hand, but by a god's; laid low, as men say, by the arrow of Phoebus.

Ph. Well, noble alike are the slayer and the slain! I scarce know, my son, which I should do first—inquire into thy wrong, or mourn the dead.

Ne. Methinks thine own sorrows, unhappy man are enough for thee, without mourning for the woes of thy neighbour.

Ph. Thou sayest truly. Resume thy story, then, and tell me wherein they did thee a despite.

Ne. They came for me in a ship with gaily decked prow—princely Odysseus, and he who watched over my father's youth—saying, (whether truly or falsely, I know not,) that since my father had perished, fate now forbad that the towers of Troy should be taken by any hand but mine.

Saying that these things stood thus, my friend, they made me pause not long ere I set forth in haste, chiefly through my yearning towards the dead, that I might see him before burial—for I had never seen him; then, besides, there was a charm in their promise, if, when I went, I should sack the towers of Troy.

It was now the second day of my voyage, when, sped by breeze and oar, I drew nigh to cruel Sigeum. And when I landed, straightway all the host thronged around me with greetings, vowing that they saw their lost Achilles once more alive.

He, then, lay dead; and I, hapless one, when I had wept for him, presently went to the Atreidae—to friends, as I well might deem—and claimed my father's arms, with all else that had been his. O, 'twas a shameless answer that they made! "Seed of Achilles, thou canst take all else that was thy sire's; but of those arms another man now is lord,—the son of Laertes." The tears came into my eyes, I sprang up in passionate anger, and said in my bitterness, "Wretch! What, have ye dared to give my arms to another man, without my leave?" Then said Odysseus, for he chanced to be near, "Yea, boy, this award of theirs is just; I saved the arms and their master at his need." Then straightway, in my fury, I began to hurl all manner of taunts at him, and spared not one, if I was indeed to be robbed of my arms by *him*. At this point—stung by the abuse, though not prone to wrath—he answered, "Thou wast not here with us, but absent from thy duty. And since thou must talk so saucily, thou shalt never carry those arms back to Scyros."

Thus upbraided, thus insulted, I sail for home, despoiled of mine own by that worst offspring of an evil breed, Odysseus. And yet he, I think, is less to blame than the rulers. For an army, like a city, hangs wholly on its leaders: and when men do lawless deeds, 'tis the counsel of their teachers that corrupts them. My tale is told; and may the foe of the Atreidae have the favour of Heaven, as he hath mine!

Ch. Goddess of the hills, all-fostering Earth mother of Zeus most high, thou through whose realm the great Pactolus rolls golden sands—there also, dread Mother, I called upon thy name, when all the insults of the Atreidae were being heaped upon this man—when they were giving his sire's armour, that peerless marvel, to the son of Lartius —hear it, thou immortal one, who ridest on bull-slaughtering lions!

Ph. It seems that ye have come to me, friends, well commended by a common grief; and your story is of a like strain with mine, so that I can recognise the work of the Atreidae and of Odysseus. For well I know that he would lend his tongue to any base pretext, to any villainy, if thereby he could hope to compass some dishonest end. No, 'tis not at this that I wonder, but rather that the elder Ajax, if he was there, could endure to see it.

Ne. Ah, friend, he was no more; I should never have been thus plundered while he lived.

Ph. How sayest thou? What, is he, too, dead and gone?

Ne. Think of him as of one who sees the light no more.

Ph. Woe is me! But the son of Tydeus, and the offspring of Sisyphus that was bought by Laertes—they will not die; for they ought not to live.

Ne. Not they, be sure of it; no, they are now prospering full greatly in the Argive host.

Ph. And what of my brave old friend, Nestor of Pylos—is he not alive? *Their* mischiefs were often baffled by his wise counsels.

Ne. Aye, he has trouble now; death has taken Antilochus, the son that was at his side.

Ph. Ah me! These two, again, whom thou hast named, are men of whose death I had least wished to hear. Alas! What are we to look for, when these have died, and, here again, Odysseus lives—when he, in their place, should have been numbered with the dead?

Ne. A clever wrestler he; but even clever schemes, Philoctetes, are often tripped up.

Ph. Now tell me, I pray thee, where was Patroclus in this thy need—he whom thy father loved so well?

Ne. He, too, was dead. And to be brief, I would tell thee this—war takes no evil man by choice, but good men always.

Ph. I bear thee witness; and for that same reason I will ask thee how fares a man of little worth, but shrewd of tongue and clever—

Ne. Surely this will be no one but Odysseus?

Ph. I meant not him: but there was one Thersites, who could never be content with brief speech, though all men chafed: know'st thou if he is alive?

Ne. I saw him not, but heard that he still lives.

Ph. It was his due. No evil thing has been known to perish; no, the gods take tender care of such, and have a strange joy in turning back from Hades all things villainous and knavish, while they are ever sending the just and the good out of life. How am I to deem of these things, or wherein shall I praise them, when, praising the ways of the gods, I find that the gods are evil?

Ne. Son of Oetean sire, I, at least, shall be on my guard henceforth against Ilium and the Atreidae, nor look on them save from afar; and where the worse man is stronger than the good—where honesty fails and the dastard bears sway—among such men will I never make my friends. No, rocky Scyros shall suffice for me henceforth, nor shall I ask a better home.

Now to my ship! And thou, son of Poeas, farewell—heartily farewell; and the gods deliver thee from thy sickness, even as thou wouldst! But we must be going, so that we may set forth whenever the god permits our voyage.

Ph. Do ye start now, my son?

Ne. Aye, prudence bids us watch the weather near our ship, rather than from afar.

Ph. Now by thy father and by thy mother, my son—by all that is dear to thee in thy home—solemnly I implore thee, leave me not thus forlorn, helpless amid these miseries in which I live, such as thou seest, and many as thou hast heard! Nay, spare a passing thought to me. Great is the discomfort, I well know, of such a freight; yet bear with it: to noble minds baseness is hateful, and a good deed is glorious. Forsake this task, and thy fair name is sullied; perform it, my son, and a rich meed of glory will be thine, if I return alive to Oeta's land. Come, the trouble lasts not one whole day: make the effort—take and thrust me where thou wilt, in hold, in prow, in stern, wherever I shall least annoy my shipmates.

O consent, by the great Zeus of suppliants, my son—be persuaded! I supplicate thee on my knees, infirm as I am, poor wretch, and maimed! Nay, leave me not thus desolate, far from the steps of men! Nay, bring me safely to thine own home, or to Euboea, Chalcodon's seat; and thence it will be no long journey for me to Oeta, and the Trachinian heights, and the fair-flowing Spercheius, that thou mayest show me to my beloved sire; of whom I have long feared that he may have gone from me. For often did I summon him by those who came, with imploring prayers that he would himself send a ship, and fetch me home. But either he is dead, or else, methinks, my messengers—as was likely—made small account of my concerns, and hastened on their homeward voyage.

Now, however—since in thee I have found one who can carry at once my message and myself—do thou save me, do thou show me mercy, seeing how all human destiny is full of the fear and the peril that good fortune may be followed by evil. He who stands clear of trouble should beware of dangers; and when a man lives at ease, then it is that he should look most closely to his life, lest ruin come on it by stealth.

Ch. Have pity, O king; he hath told of a struggle with sufferings manifold and grievous; may the like befall no friend of mine! And if, my prince, thou hatest the hateful Atreidae, then, turning their misdeed to this man's gain, I would waft him in thy good swift ship to the home for which he yearns, that so thou flee the just wrath of Heaven.

Ne. Beware lest, though now, as a spectator, thou art pliant, yet, when wearied of his malady by consorting with it, thou be found no longer constant to these words.

Ch. No, verily: never shalt thou have cause to utter that reproach against me!

Ne. Nay, then, it were shame that the stranger should find me less prompt than thou art to serve him at his need. Come, if it please you, let us sail: let the man set forth at once; our ship, for her part, will carry him, and will not refuse. Only may the gods convey us safely out of this land, and hence to our haven, wheresoever it be!

Ph. O most joyful day! O kindest friend—and ye, good sailors—would that I could prove to you in deeds what love ye have won from me! Let us be going, my son, when thou and I have made a solemn farewell to the homeless home within,—that thou mayest e'en learn by what means I sustained life, and how stout a heart hath been mine. For I believe that the bare sight would have deterred any other man from enduring such a lot; but I have been slowly schooled by necessity to patience.

(NEOPTOLEMUS *is about to follow* PHILOCTETES *into the cave.*)

Ch. Stay, let us give heed: two men are coming, one a seaman of thy ship, the other a stranger: ye should hear their tidings before ye go in.

Enter MERCHANT, *on the spectators' left, accompanied by a Sailor.*

Merchant. Son of Achilles, I asked my companion here—who, with two others, was guarding thy ship—to tell me where thou mightest be, since I have fallen in with thee, when I did not expect it, by the chance of coming to anchor off the same coast. Sailing, in trader's wise, with no great company, homeward bound from Ilium to Peparethus with its cluster-laden vines, when I heard that the sailors were all of thy crew, I resolved not to go on my voyage in silence, without first giving thee my news, and reaping guerdon due. Thou knowest nothing, I suspect, of thine own affairs—the new designs that the Greeks have regarding thee, nay, not designs merely, but deeds in progress, and no longer tarrying.

Ne. Truly, Sir, the grace shown me by thy forethought, if I be not unworthy, shall live in my grateful thoughts. But tell me just what it is whereof thou hast spoken—that I may learn what strange design on the part of the Greeks thou announcest to me.

Me. Pursuers have started in quest of thee with ships—the aged Phoenix and the sons of Theseus.

Ne. To bring me back by force, or by fair words?

Me. I know not; but I have come to tell thee what I have heard.

Ne. Can Phoenix and his comrades be showing such zeal on such an errand, to please the Atreidae?

Me. The errand is being done, I can assure thee, and without delay.

Ne. Why, then, was not Odysseus ready to sail for this purpose, and to bring the message himself? Or did some fear restrain him?

Me. Oh, he and the son of Tydeus were setting forth in pursuit of another man, as I was leaving port.

Ne. Who was this other in quest of whom Odysseus himself was sailing?

Me. There was a man... But tell me first who that is yonder—and whatever thou sayest, speak not loud.

Ne. Sir, thou seest the renowned Philoctetes.

Me. Ask me no more, then, but convey thyself with all speed out of this land.

Ph. What is he saying, my son? Why is the sailor trafficking with thee about me in these dark whispers?

Ne. I know not his meaning yet; but whatever he would say he must say openly to thee and me and these.

Me. Seed of Achilles, do not accuse me to the army of saying what I should not; I receive many benefits from them for my services—as a poor man may.

Ne. I am the foe of the Atreidae, and this man is my best friend, because he hates them. Since, then, thou hast come with a kindly purpose towards me thou must not keep from us any part of the tidings that thou hast heard.

Me. See what thou doest, my son.

Ne. I am well aware.

Me. I will hold thee accountable.

Ne. Do so, but speak.

Me. I obey. 'Tis in quest of this man that those two are sailing whom I named to thee—the son of Tydeus and mighty Odysseus—sworn to bring him, either by winning words or by constraining force. And all the Achaeans heard this plainly from Odysseus, for his confidence of success was higher than his comrade's.

Ne. And wherefore, after so long a time, did the Atreidae turn their thoughts towards this man, whom long since they had cast forth? What was the yearning that came to them—what compulsion, or what vengeance, from gods who requite evil deeds?

Me. I can expound all that to thee—since it seems that thou hast not heard it. There was a seer of noble birth, a son of Priam, by name Helenus, whom this man, going forth by night—this guileful Odysseus, of whom all shameful and dishonouring words are spoken—made his prisoner; and, leading him in bonds, showed him publicly to the Achaeans, a goodly prize: who then prophesied to them whatso else they asked, and that they should never sack the towers of Troy, unless by winning words they should bring this man from the island whereon he now dwells.

And the son of Laertes, when he heard the seer speak thus, straightway promised that he would bring this man and show him to the Achaeans—most likely, he thought, as a willing captive, but, if reluctant, then by force; adding that, should he fail in this, whoso wished might have his head. Thou hast heard all, my son, and I commend speed to thee, and to any man for whom thou carest.

Ph. Hapless that I am! Hath he, that utter pest, sworn to bring me by persuasion to the Achaeans? As soon shall I be persuaded, when I am dead, to come up from Hades to the light, as his father came!

Me. I know nothing about that: but I must go to ship, and may Heaven be with you both for all good. *Exit* MERCHANT.

Ph. Now is not this wondrous, my son, that the offspring of Laertes should have hoped, by means of soft words, to lead me forth from his ship and show me amidst the Greeks? No! sooner would I hearken to that deadliest of my foes, the viper which made me the cripple that I am! But there is nothing that *he* would not say, or dare; and now I know that he will be here. Come, my son, let us be moving, that a wide sea may part us from the ship of Odysseus. Let us go: good speed in good season brings sleep and rest, when toil is o'er.

Ne. We will sail, then, as soon as the head wind falls; at present it is adverse.

Ph. 'Tis ever fair sailing, when thou fleest from evil.

Ne. Nay, but this weather is against them also.

Ph. No wind comes amiss to pirates, when there is a chance to steal, or to rob by force.

Ne. Well, let us be going, if thou wilt—when thou hast taken from within whatever thou needest or desirest most.

Ph. Aye, there are some things that I need—though the choice is not large.

Ne. What is there that will not be found on board my ship?

Ph. I keep by me a certain herb, wherewith I can always best assuage this wound, till it is wholly soothed.

Ne. Fetch it, then, Now, what else wouldst thou take?

Ph. Any of these arrows that may have been forgotten, and may have slipped away from me—lest I leave it to be another's prize.

Ne. Is that indeed the famous bow which thou art holding?

Ph. This, and no other, that I carry in my hand.

Ne. Is it lawful for me to have a nearer view of it—to handle it and to salute it as a god?

Ph. To thee, my son, this shall be granted, and anything else in my power that is for thy good.

Ne. I certainly long to touch it, but my longing is on this wise; if it be lawful, I should be glad; if not, think no more of it.

Ph. Thy words are reverent, and thy wish, my son, is lawful; for thou alone hast given to mine eyes the light of life—the hope to see the Oetean land, to see mine aged father and my friends—thou who, when I lay beneath the feet of my foes, hast lifted me beyond their reach. Be of good cheer; the bow shall be thine, to handle, and to return to the hand that gave it; thou shalt be able to vaunt that, in reward of thy kindness, thou, alone of mortals, hast touched it; for 'twas by a good deed that I myself won it.

Ne. I rejoice to have found thee, and to have gained thy friendship; for whosoever knows how to render benefit for benefit must prove a friend above price. Go in, I pray thee.

Ph. Yes, and I will lead thee in; for my sick estate craves the comfort of thy presence.

They enter the cave.

Chorus

I have heard in story, but seen not with mine eyes, how he who once came near the bed of Zeus was bound upon a swift wheel by the almighty son of Cronus; but of no other mortal know I, by hearsay or by sight, that hath encountered a doom so dreadful as this man's; who, though he had wronged none by force or fraud, but lived at peace with his fellow-men, was left to perish thus cruelly.

Verily I marvel how, as he listened in his solitude to the surges that beat around him, he kept his hold upon a life so full of woe;

where he was neighbour to himself alone—powerless to walk—with no one in the land to be near him while he suffered, in whose ear he could pour forth the lament, awaking response, for the plague that gnawed his flesh and drained his blood; no one to assuage the burning flux, oozing from the ulcers of his envenomed foot, with healing herbs gathered from the bounteous earth, so often as the torment came upon him.

Then would he creep this way or that, with painful steps, like a child without kindly nurse, to any place whence his need might be supplied, whenever the devouring anguish abated;

gathering not for food the fruit of holy Earth, nor aught else that we mortals gain by toil; save when haply he found wherewith to stay his hunger by winged shafts from his swift-smiting bow. Ah, joyless was his life, who for ten years never knew the gladness of the wine-cup, but still bent his way towards any stagnant pool that he could descry as he gazed around him.

But now, after those troubles, he shall be happy and mighty at the last; for he hath met with the son of a noble race, who in the fulness of many months bears him on sea-cleaving ship to his home, haunt of Malian nymphs, and to the banks of the Spercheius; where, above Oeta's heights, the lord of the brazen shield drew near to the gods, amid the splendour of the lightnings of his sire.

NEOPTOLEMUS *and* PHILOCTETES *enter from the cave.*

Ne. I pray thee, come on. Why art thou so silent? Why dost thou halt, as if dismayed, without a cause?

Ph. Alas, alas!

Ne. What is the matter?

Ph. Nothing serious:—go on, my son.

Ne. Art thou in pain from the disease that vexes thee?

Ph. No indeed—no, I think I am better just now. Ye gods!

Ne. Why groanest thou thus, and callest on the gods?

Ph. That they may come to us with power to save and soothe. Ah me! ah me!

Ne. What ails thee? Speak—persist not in this silence: 'tis plain that something is amiss with thee.

Ph. I am lost, my son—I can never hide my trouble from you: ah, it pierces me, it pierces! O misery, O wretched that I am! I am undone, my son—it devours me. Oh, for the gods' love, if thou hast a sword ready to thy hand, strike at my heel, shear it off straightway—heed not my life! Quick, quick, my son!

Ne. And what new thing hath come on thee so suddenly, that thou bewailest thyself with such loud laments?

Ph. Thou knowest, my son.

Ne. What is it?

Ph. Thou knowest, boy.

Ne. What is the matter with thee? I know not.

Ph. How canst thou help knowing? Oh, oh!

Ne. Dread, indeed, is the burden of the malady.

Ph. Aye, dread beyond telling. Oh, pity me!

Ne. What shall I do?

Ph. Forsake me not in fear. This visitant comes but now and then—when she hath been sated, haply, with her roamings.

Ne. Ah, hapless one! Hapless, indeed, art thou found in all manner of woe! Shall I take hold of thee, or lend thee a helping hand?

Ph. No, no: but take this bow of mine, I pray thee—as thou didst ask of me just now—and keep it safe till this present access of my disease is past. For indeed sleep falls on me when this plague is passing away, nor can the pain cease sooner; but ye must allow me to slumber in peace. And if meanwhile those men come, I charge thee by Heaven that in no wise, willingly or unwillingly, thou give up this bow to them—lest thou bring destruction at once on thyself and on me, who am thy suppliant.

Ne. Have no fears as to my caution. The bow shall pass into no hands but thine and mine. Give it to me, and may good luck come with it!

Ph. There it is, my son: and pray the jealous gods that it may not bring thee troubles, such as it brought to me and to him who was its lord before me.

Ne. Ye gods, grant this to us twain! Grant us a voyage prosperous and swift, whithersoever the god approves and our purpose tends!

Ph. Nay, my son, I fear that thy prayers are vain; for lo, once more the dark blood oozes drop by drop from the depths, and I look for worse to come. Ah me, oh, oh! Thou hapless foot, what torment wilt thou work for me! It creeps on me, it is drawing near! Woe, woe is me! Ye know it now: flee not, I pray you!

O Cephallenian friend, would that this anguish might cleave to thee, and transfix thy breast! Ah me! Ah me! O ye chieftains twain, Agamemnon, Menelaus, would that ye, instead of me, might have this malady upon you, and for as long! Ah me, ah me! O Death, Death, when I am thus ever calling thee, day by day, why canst thou never come? O my son, generous youth, come, seize me, burn me up, true-hearted friend, in yonder fire, famed as Lemnian: I, too, once deemed it lawful to do the same unto the son of Zeus, for the meed of these same arms, which are now in thy keeping. What sayest thou, boy, what sayest thou? Why art thou silent? Where are thy thoughts, my son?

Ne. I have long been grieving in my heart for thy load of pain.

Ph. Nay, my son, have good hope withal; this visitor comes sharply, but goes quickly. Only, I beseech thee, leave me not alone.

Ne. Fear not, we will remain.

Ph. Thou wilt remain?

Ne. Be sure of it.

Ph. Well, I do not ask to put thee on thine oath, my son.

Ne. Rest satisfied: 'tis not lawful for me to go without thee.

Ph. Thy hand for pledge!

Ne. I give it—to stay.

Ph. Now take me yonder, yonder—

Ne. Whither meanest thou?

Ph. Up yonder—

Ne. What is this new frenzy? Why gazest thou on the vault above us?

Ph. Let me to, let me go!

Ne. Whither?

Ph. Let me go, I say!

Ne. I will not.

Ph. Thou wilt kill me, if thou touch me.

Ne. There, then—I release thee, since thou art calmer.

Ph. O Earth, receive me as I die, here and now! This pain no longer suffers me to stand upright.

Ne. Methinks sleep will come to him ere long: see, his head sinks backward; yes, a sweat is bathing his whole body, and a thin stream of dark blood hath broken forth from his heel.

Come, friends, let us leave him in quietness, that he may fall on slumber.

Ch. Sleep, stranger to anguish, painless Sleep, come, at our prayer, with gentle breath, come with benison, O king, and keep before his eyes such light as is spread before them now; come, I pray thee, come with power to heal!

O son, bethink thee where thou wilt stand, and to what counsels thou wilt next turn our course. Thou seest how 'tis now! Why should we delay to act? Opportunity, arbiter of all action, oft wins a great victory by one swift stroke.

Ne. Nay, though he hears nothing, I see that in vain have we made this bow our prize, if we sail without him. His must be the crown; 'tis he that the god bade us bring. 'Twere a foul shame for us to boast of deeds in which failure hath waited on fraud.

Ch. Nay, my son, the god will look to that. But when thou answerest me again, softly, softly whisper thy words, my son: for sick men's restless sleep is ever quick of vision.

But, I pray thee, use thine utmost care to win that prize, that great prize, by stealth. For if thou maintain thy present purpose towards this man—thou knowest of what purpose I speak—a prudent mind can foresee troubles most grievous.

Now, my son, now the wind is fair for thee: sightless and helpless, the man lies stretched in darkness—sleep in the heat is sound—with no command of hand or foot, but reft of all his powers, like unto one who rests with Hades.

Take heed, look if thy counsels be seasonable: so far as my thoughts can seize the truth, my son, the best strategy is that which gives no alarm.

Ne. Hush, I say, and let not your wits forsake you: yon man opens his eyes, and lifts his head.

Ph. Ah, sunlight following on sleep, ah, ye friendly watchers, undreamed of by my hopes! Never, my son, could I have dared to look for this—that thou shouldest have patience to wait so tenderly upon my sufferings, staying beside me, and helping to relieve me. The Atreidae, certainly, those valiant chieftains, had no heart to bear this burden so lightly. But thy nature, my son, is noble, and of noble breed; and so thou hast made little of all this, though loud cries and noisome odours vexed thy senses.

And now, since the plague seems to allow me a space of forgetfulness and peace at last, raise me thyself, my son, set me on my feet, so that, when the faintness shall at length release me, we may set forth to the ship, and delay not to sail.

Ne. Right glad am I to see thee, beyond my hope, living and breathing, free from pain; for, judged by the sufferings that afflict thee, thy symptoms seemed to speak of death. But now lift thyself; or, if thou prefer it, these men will carry thee; the trouble would not be grudged, since thou and I are of one mind.

Ph. Thanks, my son—and help me to rise, as thou sayest: but do not trouble these men, that they may not suffer from the noisome smell before the time. It will be trial enough for them to live on board with me.

Ne. So be it. Now stand up, and take hold of me thyself.

Ph. Fear not, the old habit will help me to my feet.

Ne. Alack! What am I to do next!

Ph. What is the matter, my son? Whither strays thy speech?

Ne. I know not how I should turn my faltering words.

Ph. Faltering? Wherefore? Say not so, my son.

Ne. Indeed, perplexity has now brought me to that pass.

Ph. It cannot be that the offence of my disease hath changed thy purpose of receiving me in thy ship?

Ne. All is offence when a man hath forsaken his true nature, and is doing what doth not befit him.

Ph. Nay, thou, at least, art not departing from thy sire's example in word or deed, by helping one who deserves it.

Ne. I shall be found base; this is the thought that torments me.

Ph. Not in thy present deeds; but the presage of thy words disquiets me.

Ne. O Zeus, what shall I do? Must I be found twice a villain—by disloyal silence, as well as by shameful speech?

Ph. If my judgment errs not, yon man means to betray me, and forsake me, and go his way!

Ne. Forsake thee—no; but take thee, perchance, on a bitter voyage—that is the pain that haunts me.

Ph. What meanest thou, my son? I understand not.

Ne. I will tell thee all. Thou must sail to Troy, to the Achaeans and the host of the Atreidae.

Ph. Oh, what hast thou said?

Ne. Lament not, till thou learn—

Ph. Learn what? What would'st thou do to me?

Ne. Save thee, first, from this misery—then go and ravage Troy's plains with thee.

Ph. And this is indeed thy purpose?

Ne. A stern necessity ordains it; be not wroth to hear it.

Ph. I am lost, hapless one—betrayed! What hast thou done unto me, stranger? Restore my bow at once!

Ne. Nay, I cannot: duty and policy alike constrain me to obey my chiefs.

Ph. Thou fire, thou utter monster, thou hateful masterpiece of subtle villainy—how hast thou dealt with me, how hast thou deceived me! And thou art not ashamed to look upon me, thou wretch—the suppliant who turned to thee for pity? In taking my bow, thou hast despoiled me of my life. Restore it, I beseech thee—restore it, I implore thee, my son! By the gods of thy fathers, do not rob me of my life! Ah me! No—he speaks to me no more; he looks away—he will not give it up!

O ye creeks and headlands, O ye wild creatures of the hills with whom I dwell, O ye steep cliffs! to you—for to whom else can I speak?—to you, my wonted listeners, I bewail my treatment by the son of Achilles: he swore to convey me home—to Troy he carries me: he clinched his word with the pledge of his right hand,—yet hath he taken my bow—the sacred bow, once borne by Heracles son of Zeus—and keeps it, and would fain show it to the Argives as his own.

He drags me away, as if he had captured a strong man, and sees not that he is slaying a corpse, the shadow of a vapour, a mere phantom. In my strength he would not have taken me—no, nor as I am, save by guile. But now I have been tricked, unhappy that I am. What shall I do? Nay, give it back—return, even now, to thy true self! What sayest thou? Silent? Woe is me, I am lost!

Ah, thou cave with twofold entrance, familiar to mine eyes, once more must I return to thee—but disarmed, and without the means to live. Yes, in yon chamber my lonely life shall fade away; no winged bird, no beast that roams the hills shall I slay with yonder bow; rather I myself, wretched one, shall make a feast for those who fed me, and become a prey to those on whom I preyed; alas, I shall render my life-blood for the blood which I have shed—the victim of a man who seemed innocent of evil! Perish! no, not yet, till I see if thou wilt still change thy purpose; if thou wilt not, mayest thou die accurs'd!

Ch. What shall we do? It now rests with thee, O prince, whether we sail, or hearken to yon man's prayer.

Ne. A strange pity for him hath smitten my heart —and not now for the first time, but long ago.

Ph. Show mercy, my son, for the love of the gods, and do not give men cause to reproach thee for having ensnared me.

Ne. Ah me, what shall I do? Would I had never left Scyros! so grievous is my plight.

Ph. Thou art no villain; but thou seemest to have come hither as one schooled by villains to a base part. Now leave that part to others, whom it befits, and sail hence,—when thou hast given me back mine arms.

Ne. What shall we do, friends?

ODYSSEUS *appears suddenly from behind the cave.*

Od. Wretch, what art thou doing? Back with thee —and give up this bow to me!

Ph. Ah, who is this? Do I hear Odysseus?

Od. Odysseus, be sure of it—me, whom thou beholdest.

Ph. Ah me, I am betrayed—lost! He it was, then, that entrapped me and robbed me of mine arms.

Od. I, surely, and no other: I avow it.

Ph. Give back my bow—give it up, my son.

Od. That shall he never do, even if he would. And moreover thou must come along with it, or they will bring thee by force.

Ph. What, thou basest and boldest of villains—are these men to take *me* by force?

Od. Unless thou come of thy free will.

Ph. O Lemnian land, and thou all-conquering flame whose kindler is Hephaestus—is this indeed to be borne, that yonder man should take me from thy realm by force?

Od. 'Tis Zeus, let me tell thee, Zeus, who rules this land—Zeus, whose pleasure this is; and I am his servant.

Ph. Hateful wretch, what pleas thou canst invent! Sheltering thyself behind gods, thou makest those gods liars.

Od. Nay, true prophets. Our march must begin.

Ph. Never!

Od. But I say, Yes. There is no help for it.

Ph. Woe is me! Plainly, then, my father begat me to be a slave and no free man.

Od. Nay, but to be the peer of the bravest, with whom thou art destined to take Troy by storm, and raze it to the dust.

Ph. No, never—though I must suffer the worst—while I have this isle's steep crags beneath me!

Od. What would'st thou do?

Ph. Throw myself straightway from the rock and shatter this head upon the rock below!

Od. Seize him, both of you! Put it out of his power!

Ph. Ah, hands, how ill ye fare, for lack of the bow! that ye loved to draw—yon man's close prisoners! O thou who canst not think one honest or one generous thought, how hast thou once more stolen upon me, how hast thou snared me—taking this boy for thy screen, a stranger to me, too good for thy company, but meet for mine, who had no thought but to perform thy bidding, and who already shows remorse for his own errors and for my wrongs. But thy base soul, ever peering from some ambush, had well trained him—all unapt and unwilling as he was—to be cunning in evil.

And now, wretch, thou purposest to bind me hand and foot, and take me from this shore where thou didst fling me forth, friendless, helpless, homeless—dead among the living!

Alas!

Perdition seize thee! So have I often prayed for thee. But, since the gods grant nothing sweet to me, thou livest and art glad, while life itself is pain to me, steeped in misery as I am—mocked by thee and by the sons of Atreus, the two chieftains, for whom thou doest this errand. Yet thou sailedst with them only when brought under their yoke by stratagem and constraint; but I—thrice-wretched that I am—joined the fleet of mine own accord, with seven ships, and then was spurned and cast out—by *them*, as thou sayest, or, as they say, by thee.

And now, why would ye take me? why carry me with you? for what purpose? I am nought; for you, I have long been dead. Wretch abhorred of heaven, how is it that thou no longer findest me lame and noisome? How, if I sail with you, can ye burn sacrifices to the gods, or make drink-offerings any more? That was thy pretext for casting me forth.

Miserably may ye perish! and perish ye shall, for the wrong that ye have wrought against me, if the gods regard justice. But I know that they regard it; for ye would never have come on this voyage in quest of one so wretched, unless some heaven-sent yearning for me had goaded you on.

O, my fatherland, and ye watchful gods, bring your vengeance, bring your vengeance on them all,—at last though late—if in my lot ye see aught to pity! Yes, a piteous life is mine; but, if I saw those men overthrown, I could dream that I was delivered from my plague.

Ch. Bitter with his soul's bitterness are the stranger's words, Odysseus; he bends not before his woes.

Od. I could answer him at length, if leisure served; but now I can say one thing only. Such as the time needs, such am I. Where the question is of just men and good, thou wilt find no man more scrupulous. Victory, however, is my aim in every field—save with regard to thee—to thee, in this case, I will gladly give way.

Yes, release him, lay no finger upon him more—let him stay here. Indeed we have no further need of thee, now that these arms are ours; for Teucer is there to serve us, well-skilled in this craft, and I, who deem that I can wield this bow no whit worse than thou, and point it with as true a hand. What need, then, of thee? Pace thy Lemnos, and joy be with thee! We must be going. And perchance thy treasure will bring to me the honour which ought to have been thine own.

Ph. Ah, unhappy that I am, what shall I do? Shalt *thou* be seen among the Argives graced with the arms that are mine?

Od. Bandy no more speech with me—I am going.

Ph. Son of Achilles, wilt thou, too, speak no more to me, but depart without a word?

Od. (*to* NEOPTOLEMUS) Come on! Do not look at him, generous though thou art, lest thou mar our fortune.

Ph. (*to* CHORUS) Will ye also, friends, indeed leave me thus desolate, and show no pity?

Ch. This youth is our commander; whatsoever he saith to thee, that answer is ours also.

Ne. (*to* CHORUS) I shall be told by my chief that I am too soft-hearted; yet tarry ye here, if yon man will have it so, until the sailors have made all ready on board, and we have offered our prayers to the gods. Meanwhile, perhaps, he may come to a better mind concerning us. So we two will be going: and ye, when we call you, are to set forth with speed.

Exeunt ODYSSEUS *and* NEOPTOLEMUS.

Ph. Thou hollow of the caverned rock, now hot, now icy cold—so, then, it was my hapless destiny never to leave thee! No, thou art to witness my death also. Woe, woe is me! Ah, thou sad dwelling, so long haunted by the pain of my presence, what shall be my daily portion henceforth? Where and whence, wretched that I am, shall I find a hope of sustenance? Above my head, the timorous doves will go on their way through the shrill breeze; for I can arrest their flight no more.

Ch. 'Tis thou, 'tis thou thyself, ill-fated man, that hast so decreed; this fortune to which thou art captive comes not from without, or from a stronger hand: for, when it was in thy power to show wisdom, thy choice was to reject the better fate, and to accept the worse.

Ph. Ah, hapless, hapless then that I am, and broken by suffering; who henceforth must dwell here in my misery, with no man for companion in the days to come, and waste away—woe, woe, is me—no longer bringing food to my home, no longer gaining it with the winged weapons held in my strong hands.

But the unsuspected deceits of a treacherous soul beguiled me. Would that I might see him, the contriver of this plot, doomed to my pangs, and for as long a time!

Ch. Fate, heaven-appointed fate hath come upon thee in this,—not any treachery to which my hand was lent. Point not at me thy dread and baneful curse! Fain indeed am I that thou shouldest not reject my friendship.

Ph. Ah me, ah me! And sitting, I ween, on the marge of the white waves, he mocks me, brandishing the weapon that sustained my hapless life, the weapon which no other living man had borne! Ah, thou well-loved bow, ah, thou that hast been torn from loving hands, surely, if thou canst feel, thou seest with pity that the comrade of Heracles is now to use thee nevermore! Thou hast found a new and wily master; by him art thou wielded; foul deceits thou seest, and the face of that abhorred foe by whom countless mischiefs, springing from vile arts, have been contrived against me—be thou, O Zeus, my witness!

Ch. It is the part of a man ever to assert the right; but, when he hath done so, to refrain from stinging with rancorous taunts. Odysseus was but the envoy of the host, and, at their mandate, achieved a public benefit for his friends.

Ph. Ah, my winged prey, and ye tribes of bright-eyed beasts that this place holds in its upland pastures, start no more in flight from your lairs; for I bear not in my hands those shafts which were my strength of old—ah, wretched that I now am! Nay, roam at large—the place hath now no more terrors for you, no more! Now is the moment to take blood for blood, to glut yourselves at will on my discoloured flesh! Soon shall I pass out of life; for whence shall I find the means to live? Who can feed thus on the winds, when he no longer commands aught that life-giving earth supplies?

Ch. For the love of the gods, if thou hast any regard for a friend who draws near to thee in all kindness, approach him! Nay, consider, consider well—it is in thine own power to escape from this plague. Cruel is it to him on whom it feeds; and time cannot teach patience under the countless woes that dwell with it.

Ph. Again, again, thou hast recalled the old pain to my thoughts—kindest though thou art of all who have visited this shore! Why hast thou afflicted me? What hast thou done unto me!

Ch. How meanest thou?

Ph. If it was thy hope to take me to that Trojan land which I abhor.

Ch. Nay, so I deem it best.

Ph. Leave me, then—begone!

Ch. Welcome is thy word, right welcome. I am not loth to obey. Come, let us be going, each to his place in the ship! *They begin to move away.*

Ph. By the Zeus who hears men's curses, depart not, I implore you!

Ch. Be calm.

Ph. Friends, in the gods' name, stay!

Ch. Why dost thou call?

Ph. Alas, alas! My doom, my doom! Hapless, I am undone! O foot, foot, what shall I do with thee, wretched that I am, in the days to come? O friends, return!

Ch. What would'st thou have us do, different from the purport of thy former bidding?

Ph. 'Tis no just cause for anger if one who is distraught with stormy pain speaks frantic words.

Ch. Come, then, unhappy man, as we exhort thee.

Ph. Never, never—of that be assured—no, though the lord of the fiery lightning threaten to wrap me in the blaze of his thunderbolts! Perish Ilium, and the men before its walls, who had the heart to spurn me from them, thus crippled! But oh, my friends, grant me one boon!

Ch. What would'st thou ask?

Ph. A sword, if ye can find one, or an axe, or any weapon—oh, bring it to me!

Ch. What rash deed would'st thou do?

Ph. Mangle this body utterly, hew limb from limb with mine own hand! Death, death is my thought now—

Ch. What means this?

Ph. I would seek my sire—

Ch. In what land?

Ph. In the realm of the dead; he is in the sunlight no more. Ah, my home, city of my fathers! Would I might behold thee—misguided, indeed, that I was who left thy sacred stream, and went forth to help the Danai, mine enemies! Undone—undone!

Ch. Long since should I have left thee, and should now have been near my ship, had I not seen Odysseus approaching, and the son of Achilles, too, coming hither to us.

Enter NEOPTOLEMUS, *followed by* ODYSSEUS.

Od. Wilt thou not tell me on what errand thou art returning in such hot haste?

Ne. To undo the fault that I committed before.

Od. A strange saying; and what was the fault?

Ne. When, obeying thee and all the host—

Od. What deed didst thou, that became thee not?

Ne. When I ensnared a man with base fraud and guile.

Od. Whom? Alas!—canst thou be planning some rash act?

Ne. Rash—no: but to the son of Poeas—

Od. What wilt thou do? A strange fear comes over me...

Ne. —from whom I took this bow, to him again—

Od. Zeus! what would'st thou say? Thou wilt not give it back?

Ne. Yea, I have gotten it basely and without right.

Od. In the name of the gods, sayest thou this to mock me?

Ne. If it be mockery to speak the truth.

Od. What meanest thou, son of Achilles? What hast thou said?

Ne. Must I repeat the same words twice and thrice?

Od. I should have wished not to hear them at all.

Ne. Rest assured that I have nothing more to say.

Od. There is a power, I tell thee, that shall prevent thy deed.

Ne. What meanest thou? Who is to hinder me in this?

Od. The whole host of the Achaeans—and I for one.

Ne. Wise though thou be, thy words are void of wisdom.

Od. Thy speech is not wise, nor yet thy purpose.

Ne. But if just, that is better than wise.

Od. And how is it just, to give up what thou hast won by my counsels?

Ne. My fault hath been shameful, and I must seek to retrieve it.

Od. Hast thou no fear of the Achaean host, in doing this?

Ne. With justice on my side, I do not fear thy terrors.

Od. But I will compel thee.

Ne. Nay, not even to thy force do I yield obedience.

Od. Then we shall fight, not with the Trojans, but with thee.

Ne. Come, then, what must.

Od. Seest thou my right hand on my sword-hilt?

Ne. Nay, thou shalt see me doing the same, and that promptly.

Od. Well, I will take no more heed of thee; but I will go and tell this to all the host, and by them thou shalt be punished.

Ne. Thou hast come to thy senses; and if thou art thus prudent henceforth, perchance thou mayest keep clear of trouble. *Exit* ODYSSEUS.

But thou, O son of Poeas, Philoctetes, come forth, leave the shelter of thy rocky home!

Ph. (*within*). What means this noise of voices once more rising beside my cave?

Why do you call me forth? What would ye have of me, sirs? (*He appears at the mouth of the cave, and sees* NEOPTOLEMUS.) Ah me! this bodes no good. Can ye have come as heralds of new woes for me, to crown the old?

Ne. Fear not, but hearken to the words that I bring.

Ph. I am afraid. Fair words brought me evil fortune once before, when I believed thy promises.

Ne. Is there no room, then, for repentance?

Ph. Even such wast thou in speech, when seeking to steal my bow—a trusty friend, with treason in his heart.

Ne. But not so now; and I fain would learn whether thy resolve is to abide here and endure, or to sail with us.

Ph. Stop, speak no more! All that thou canst say will be said in vain.

Ne. Thou art resolved?

Ph. More firmly, believe me, than speech can tell.

Ne. Well, I could have wished that thou hadst listened to my words; but if I speak not in season, I have done.

Ph. Aye, thou wilt say all in vain.

Never canst thou win the amity of my soul, thou who hast taken the stay of my life by fraud, and robbed me of it—and then hast come here to give me counsel—thou most hateful offspring of a noble sire! Perdition seize you all, the Atreidae first, and next the son of Laertes, and thee!

Ne. Utter no more curses; but receive these weapons from my hand.

Ph. What sayest thou? Am I being tricked a second time?

Ne. No, I swear it by the pure majesty of Zeus most high!

Ph. O welcome words—if thy words be true!

Ne. The deed shall soon prove the word: come, stretch forth thy right hand, and be master of thy bow!

As he hands the bow and arrows to PHILOCTETES, ODYSSEUS *suddenly appears.*

Od. But I forbid it—be the gods my witnesses—in the name of the Atreidae and all the host!

Ph. My son, whose voice was that? Did I hear Odysseus?

Od. Be sure of it—and thou seest him at thy side, who will carry thee to the plains of Troy perforce, whether the son of Achilles will or no.

Ph. But to thy cost, if this arrow fly straight. (*Bends his bow.*)

Ne. (*seizing his arm*). Ah, for the gods' love, forbear—launch not thy shaft!

Ph. Unhand me, in Heaven's name, dear youth!

Ne. I will not.

Ph. Alas! why hast thou disappointed me of slaying my hated enemy with my bow!

Ne. Nay, it suits not with my honour, nor with thine. *Exit* ODYSSEUS.

Ph. Well, thou mayest be sure of one thing—that the chiefs of the host, the lying heralds of the Greeks, though brave with words, are cowards in fight.

Ne. Good; the bow is thine; and thou hast no cause of anger or complaint against me.

Ph. I grant it; and thou hast shown the race, my son, from which thou springest—no child, thou, of Sisyphus, but of Achilles, whose fame was fairest when he was with the living, as it is now among the dead.

Ne. Sweet to me is thy praise of my sire, and of myself; but hear the boon that I am fain to win from thee. Men must needs bear the fortunes given by the gods; but when they cling to self-inflicted miseries, as thou dost, no one can justly excuse or pity them. Thou hast become intractable; thou canst tolerate no counsellor; and if one advise thee, speaking with good will, thou hatest him, deeming him a foe who wishes thee ill. Yet I will speak, calling Zeus to witness, who hears men's oaths; and do thou mark these words, and write them in thy heart.

Thou sufferest this sore plague by a heaven-sent doom, because thou didst draw near to Chrysè's watcher, the serpent, secret warder of her home, that guards her roofless sanctuary. And know that relief from this grievous sickness can never be thy portion, so long as the sun still rises in the east and sets in the west, until thou come, of thine own free will, to the plains of Troy, where thou shalt meet with the sons of Asclepius, our comrades, and shalt be eased of this malady; and, with this bow's aid and mine, shalt achieve the capture of the Ilian towers.

I will tell thee how I know that these things are so ordained. We have a Trojan prisoner, Helenus, foremost among seers; who saith plainly that all this must come to pass; and further, that this present summer must see the utter overthrow of Troy: or else he is willing that his life be forfeit, if this his word prove false.

Now, therefore, that thou knowest this, yield with a good grace; 'tis a glorious heightening of thy gain, to be singled out as bravest of the Greeks—first, to come into healing hands, then to take the Troy of many tears, and so to win a matchless renown.

Ph. O hateful life, why, why dost thou keep me in the light of day, instead of suffering me to seek the world of the dead? Ah me, what shall I do? How can I be deaf to this man's words, who hath counselled me with kindly purpose? But shall I yield, then? How, after doing that, shall I come into men's sight, wretched that I am? Who will speak to me? Ye eyes that have beheld all my wrongs, how could ye endure to see me consorting with the sons of Atreus, who wrought my ruin, or with the accursed son of Lærtes?

It is not the resentment for the past that stings me—I seem to foresee what I am doomed to suffer from these men in the future; for, when the mind hath once become a parent of evil, it teaches men to be evil thenceforth. And in thee, too, this conduct moves my wonder. It behoved thee never to revisit Troy thyself, and to hinder me from going thither; seeing that those men have done thee outrage, by wresting from thee the honours of thy sire; they, who in their award of thy father's arms, adjudged the hapless Ajax inferior to Odysseus: after that, wilt thou go to fight at their side,—and wouldest thou constrain me to do likewise?

Nay, do not so, my son; but rather, as thou hast sworn to me, convey me home; and, abiding in Scyros thyself, leave those evil men to their evil doom. So shalt thou win double thanks from me, as from my sire, and shalt not seem, through helping bad men, to be like them in thy nature.

Ne. There is reason in what thou sayest; nevertheless, I would have thee put thy trust in the gods and in my words, and sail forth from this land with me, thy friend.

Ph. What! to the plains of Troy, and to the abhorred son of Atreus—with this wretched foot?

Ne. Nay, but to those who will free thee and thine ulcered limb from pain, and will heal thy sickness.

Ph. Thou giver of dire counsel, what canst thou mean?

Ne. What I see is fraught with the best issue for us both.

Ph. Hast thou no shame that the gods should hear those words?

Ne. Why should a man be ashamed of benefiting his friends?

Ph. Is this benefit to the Atreidae, or for me?

Ne. For thee, I ween; I am thy friend, and speak in friendship.

Ph. How so, when thou would'st give me up to my foes?

Ne. Prithee, learn to be less defiant in misfortune.

Ph. Thou wilt ruin me, I know thou wilt, with these words.

Ne. *I* will not; but I say that thou dost not understand.

Ph. Do I not know that the Atreidae cast me out?

Ne. They cast thee out, but look if they will not restore thee to welfare.

Ph. Never—if I must first consent to visit Troy.

Ne. What am I to do, then, if my pleading cannot win thee to aught that I urge? The easiest course for me is that I should cease from speech, and that thou shouldest live, even as now, without deliverance.

Ph. Let me bear the sufferings that are my portion; but the promise which thou madest to me, with hand laid in mine—to bring me home—that promise do thou fulfil, my son; and tarry not, nor speak any more of Troy; for the measure of my lamentation is full.

Ne. If thou wilt, let us be going.

Ph. O generous word!

Ne. Now plant thy steps firmly.

Ph. To the utmost of my strength.

Ne. But how shall I escape blame from the Achaeans?

Ph. Heed it not.

Ne. What if they ravage my country?

Ph. I will be there—

Ne. And what help wilt thou render?

Ph. With the shafts of Heracles—

Ne. What is thy meaning?

Ph. I will keep them afar.

Ne. Take thy farewell of this land, and set forth.

HERACLES *appears above them.*

Heracles. Nay, not yet, till thou hast hearkened unto my words, son of Poeas: know that the voice of Heracles soundeth in thine ears, and thou lookest upon his face.

For thy sake have I come from the heavenly seats, to show thee the purposes of Zeus, and to stay the journey whereon thou art departing; give thou heed unto my counsel.

First I would tell thee of mine own fortunes—how, after enduring many labours to the end, I have won deathless glory, as thou beholdest. And for thee, be sure, the destiny is ordained that through these thy sufferings thou shouldest glorify thy life.

Thou shalt go with yon man to the Trojan city, where, first, thou shalt be healed of thy sore malady; then, chosen out as foremost in prowess of the host, with my bow shalt thou slay Paris, the author of these ills; thou shalt sack Troy; the prize of valour shall be given to thee by our warriors; and thou shalt carry the spoils to thy home, for the joy of Poeas thy sire, even to thine own Oetaean heights. And whatsoever spoils thou receivest from that host, thence take a thank-offering for my bow unto my pyre.

(And these my counsels are for thee also, son of Achilles; for thou canst not subdue the Trojan realm without his help, nor he without thine: ye are as lions twain that roam together; each of you guards the other's life.)

For the healing of thy sickness, I will send Asclepius to Troy; since it is doomed to fall a second time before mine arrows. But of this be mindful, when ye lay waste the land—that ye show reverence towards the gods. All things else are of less account in the sight of our father Zeus; for piety dies not with men; in their life and in their death, it is immortal.

Ph. Ah, thou whose accents I had yearned to hear, thou whose form is seen after many days, I will not disobey thy words!

Ne. I, too, consent.

He. Tarry not long, then, ere ye act; for occasion urges, and the fair wind yonder at the stern. *Exit.*

Ph. Come, then, let me greet this land, as I depart. Farewell, thou chamber that hast shared my watches, farewell, ye nymphs of stream and meadow, and thou, deep voice of the sea-lashed cape—where, in the cavern's inmost recess, my head was often wetted by the south-wind's blasts, and where oft the Hermaean mount sent an echo to my mournful cries, in the tempest of my sorrow!

But now, O ye springs, and thou Lycian fount, I am leaving you—leaving you at last—I, who had never attained to such a hope!

Farewell, thou sea-girt Lemnos; and speed me with fair course, for my contentment, to that haven whither I am borne by mighty fate, and by the counsel of friends, and by the all-subduing god who hath brought these things to fulfilment.

Ch. Now let us all set forth together, when we have made our prayer to the Nymphs of the sea, that they come to us for the prospering of our return.

THE PLAYS OF
EURIPIDES

BIOGRAPHICAL NOTE

Euripides, *c.* 480–406 b.c.

Euripides, "the philosopher of the stage," as he was already called by the ancients, was born of Athenian parents on the island of Salamis. The year of his birth seems to have been a matter of conjecture. One tradition groups the three tragedians round the battle of Salamis in 480 b.c.: Aeschylus fought in the ranks, Sophocles danced in the Boys' Chorus, Euripides was born. Another source associates his birth with Aeschylus' first victory in 484.

Euripides' father, Mnesarchus, was a merchant; his mother, Cleito, is known to have been "of very high family." Yet for some reason it was a recognized joke to say she was a greengrocer and sold inferior greens. Despite the gibes of the comedians, he was probably neither poor nor of humble origin. As a boy he poured wine for the dancers and carried a torch in religious festivals, which he could not have done had he not enjoyed a certain social position. Since he was called upon for costly public duties, such as equipping, in whole or in part, a warship and acting as consul for Magnesia, he must have had independent means. He also possessed a large library, which was a rare thing in Greece for a private citizen.

In accordance with a prophecy that the boy would win victories, the poet's father is said to have had him trained as a professional athlete. He may have thought at one time of turning from boxing to painting as a career, for paintings attributed to him were shown at Megara in later times. He is also known to have been friendly with the philosophers. He is said to have been a pupil of Anaxagoras and a close friend of Protagoras, and we are told that Socrates never went to the theater unless there was a play by Euripides, when he would walk as far as the Peiraeus to see it.

Euripides early discovered his dramatic gift. He began to write at the age of eighteen, and in 455 b.c. he was "granted a chorus," that is, he was permitted to compete for the tragic prize. In the fifty years of his dramatic career he wrote between eighty and ninety plays, but he did not win a victory until 442, thirteen years after his first appearance before the public. His fifth and last victory was for plays exhibited after his death, in 405, by his son, the younger Euripides. He was incessantly assailed by the comedians, especially by Aristophanes, and was frequently defeated by lesser poets, but long before his death he had acquired a great reputation throughout the Greek world. Plutarch, in his *Life of Nicias*, says that Athenian prisoners in Syracuse escaped death and even received their freedom if they could recite passages from the works of Euripides, and that some of them, upon returning home, expressed their gratitude directly to the poet. Aristotle, in spite of specific strictures, calls Euripides "the most tragic" of the poets, and Euripides is more often quoted by him and by Plato than are Aeschylus and Sophocles.

Of the nineteen plays that survive under the name of Euripides, one, the *Cyclops*, is a satyr play, and the *Rhesus* is frequently, though not always, considered spurious. The oldest of the extant plays is the *Alcestis*, which appeared in 438. The *Bacchantes* and the *Iphigenia at Aulis* were posthumously presented. The other plays that can be approximately dated are the *Medea*, 431, the *Hippolytus*, 428, the *Trojan Women*, 415, the *Helen*, 412, the *Orestes*, 408.

Unlike Aeschylus and Sophocles, Euripides seems to have taken little part in politics and war, although there is an allusion to him in Aristotle which seems to imply that he had on one occasion a diplomatic post. The ancients thought of Euripides as a gloomy recluse who never laughed. According to these stories, he wore a long beard, lived much alone and hated society; he had crowds of books and did not like women; he lived in Salamis, in a cave with two openings and a beautiful sea view, and there he could be seen "all day long, thinking to himself and writing, for he despised anything that was not great and high."

Towards the end of his life Euripides received honors and distinctions in Macedonia, where, like other men of letters, he went at the invitation of King Archelaus. He spent his last years at the Macedonian court, high in the favor and confidence of the king, and when he died, the king cut off his hair as an expression of his grief.

Euripides died in 406 b.c., a few months before Sophocles, who wore mourning for him in the tragic competition of that year. The Athenians sent an embassy to Macedonia to bring back his body, but King Archelaus refused to give it up. A cenotaph to the memory of Euripides was then erected on the road between Athens and the Peiraeus. The poet's lyre, stylus, and tablets were bought for a talent of gold by Dionysius of Syracuse, who enshrined them in the temple of the Muses.

CONTENTS

RHESUS

DRAMATIS PERSONAE

Chorus of Trojan Sentinels
Hector
Æneas
Dolon
Messenger, *a shepherd*
Rhesus
Odysseus
Diomedes
Paris
Athena
The Muse
The Charioteer of Rhesus

Before Hector's tent at the gates of Troy. Enter chorus.

Chorus. To Hector's couch away, one of you wakeful squires that tend the prince, to see if he have any fresh tidings from the warriors who were set to guard the assembled host during the fourth watch of the night. (*Calls to* hector *in the tent*) Lift up thy head! Prop thine arm beneath it! Unseal that louring eye from its repose; thy lowly couch of scattered leaves, O Hector, quit! 'Tis time to hearken. *Enter* hector.

Hector. Who goes there? Is it a friend who calls? Who art thou? Thy watchword? Speak! Who in the dark hours comes nigh my couch, must tell me who he is.

Ch. Sentinels we of the army.

He. Why this tumultuous haste?

Ch. Be of good courage.

He. Is there some midnight ambuscade?

Ch. Nay.

He. Then why dost thou desert thy post and rouse the army, save thou have some tidings of the night? Art not aware how near the Argive host we take our night's repose in all our harness clad?

Ch. To arms! O Hector, seek thine allies' sleeping camp! Bid them wield the spear! Awake them! To thine own company despatch a friend. Saddle and bridle the steeds. Who will to the son of Panthus? who to Europa's son, captain of the Lycian band? Where are they who should inspect the victims? Where be the leaders of the light-armed troops? Ye Phrygian archers, string your horn-tipped bows.

He. Now fear, now confidence thy tidings inspire; nothing is plainly set forth. Can it be that thou art smitten with wild affright by Pan, the son of Cronion, and leaving thy watch therefore dost rouse the host? What means thy noisy summons? What tidings can I say thou bringest? Thy words are many, but no plain statement hast thou made.

Ch. The long night through, O Hector, the Argive host hath kindled fires, and bright with torches shines the anchored fleet. To Agamemnon's tent the whole army moves clamorously by night, eager for fresh orders maybe, for never before have I seen such commotion among yon sea-faring folk. Wherefore I was suspicious of what might happen and came to tell thee, that thou mayest have no cause to blame me hereafter.

He. In good season com'st thou, albeit thy tidings are fraught with terror; for those cowards are bent on giving me the slip and stealing away from this land in their ships by night; their midnight signalling convinces me of this. Ah! Fortune, to rob me in my hour of triumph, a lion of his prey, or ever this spear of mine with one fell swoop had made an end for aye of yonder Argive host! Yea, had not the sun's bright lamp withheld his light, I had not stayed my victor's spear, ere I had fired their ships and made my way from tent to tent, drenching this hand in Achæan gore. Right eager was I to make a night attack and take advantage of the stroke of luck by heaven sent, but those wise seers of mine, who have heaven's will so pat, persuaded me to wait the dawn, and then leave not one Achæan in the land. But those others await not the counsels of my soothsayers; darkness turns runaways to heroes. Needs must we now without delay pass this word along the line "Arm, arm! from slumber cease!" for many a man of them, e'en as he leaps aboard his ship, shall be smitten through the back and sprinkle the ladders with blood, and others shall be fast bound with cords and learn to till our Phrygian glebe.

Ch. Thou hastest, Hector, before thou knowest clearly what is happening; for we do not know for certain whether our foes are flying.

He. What reason else had the Argive host to kindle fires?

Ch. I cannot say; my soul doth much misgive me.

He. If this thou fearest, be sure there's nought thou wouldst not fear.

Ch. Never aforetime did the enemy kindle such a blaze.

He. No, nor ever before did they suffer such shameful defeat and rout.

Ch. This thou didst achieve; look now to what remains to do.

He. I have but one word to say, "Arm, arm against the foe!"

Ch. Lo! where Æneas comes, in hot haste too, as though he hath news to tell his friends.

Enter æneas.

Æneas. Why, Hector, have the sentinels in terror

made their way through the host to thy couch to hold a midnight conclave and disturb the army?

He. Case thee in thy coat of mail, Æneas.

Æn. How now? are tidings come of some secret stratagem set on foot during the night by the foe?

He. They are flying, these foes of ours, and going aboard their ships.

Æn. What sure proof canst thou give of this?

He. The livelong night they are kindling blazing torches; methinks they will not wait for the morrow, but after lighting brands upon their ships' decks will leave this land and fly to their homes.

Æn. And thou, wherefore dost thou gird thee with thy sword?

He. With my spear will I stop them even as they fly and leap aboard their ships, and my hand shall be heavy upon them; for shameful it were in us, aye, and cowardly as well as shameful, when God gives them into our hands, to let our foes escape without a blow after all the injuries they have done us.

Æn. Would thou wert as sage as thou art bold! But lo! among mortals the same man is not dowered by nature with universal knowledge; each hath his special gift appointed him, thine is arms, another's is sage counsel. Thou hearest their torches are blazing, and art fired with the hope that the Achæans are flying, and wouldst lead on our troops across the trenches in the calm still night. Now after crossing the deep yawning trench, supposing thou shouldst find the enemy are not flying from the land, but are awaiting thy onset, beware lest thou suffer defeat and so never reach this city again; for how wilt thou pass the palisades in a rout? And how shall thy charioteers cross the bridges without dashing the axles of their cars to pieces? And, if victorious, thou hast next the son of Peleus to engage; he will ne'er suffer thee to cast the firebrand on the fleet, no, nor to harry the Achæans as thou dost fondly fancy. Nay, for yon man is fierce as fire, a very tower of valiancy. Let us rather then leave our men to sleep calmly under arms after the weariness of battle, while we send, as I advise, whoe'er will volunteer, to spy upon the enemy; and if they really are preparing to fly, let us arise and fall upon the Argive host, but if this signalling is a trap to catch us, we shall discover from the spy the enemy's designs and take our measures; such is my advice, O King.

Ch. It likes me well; so change thy mind and adopt this counsel. I love not hazardous commands in generals. What better scheme could be than for a fleet spy to approach the ships and learn why our foes are lighting fires in front of their naval station?

He. Since this finds favour with you all, prevail. (*To* ÆNEAS.) Go thou and marshal our allies; mayhap the host hearing of our midnight council is disturbed. Mine shall it be to send one forth to spy upon the foe. And if I discover any plot amongst them, thou shalt fully hear thereof, and at the council-board shalt learn our will; but in case they be starting off in flight, with eager ear await the trumpet's call, for then I will not stay, but will this very night engage the Argive host there where their ships are hauled up.

Æn. Send out the spy forthwith; there's safety in thy counsels now. And thou shalt find me steadfast at thy side, whene'er occasion call. *Exit* ÆNEAS.

He. What Trojan now af all our company doth volunteer to go and spy the Argive fleet? Who will be that patriot? Who saith "I will"? Myself cannot at every point serve my country and my friends in arms.

Dolon (*Comes from the rear*). I for my country will gladly run this risk and go to spy the Argive fleet, and when I have learnt fully all that the Achæans plot I will return. Hear the conditions on which I undertake this toil.

He. True to his name in sooth, his country's friend is Dolon. Thy father's house was famed of yore, but thou hast made it doubly so.

Do. So must I toil, but for my pains a meet reward should I receive. For set a price on any deed, and then and there it gives to it a double grace.

He. Yea, that is but fair; I cannot gainsay it. Name any prize for thyself save the sway I bear.

Do. I covet not thy toilsome sovereignty.

He. Well then, marry a daughter of Priam and become my good brother.

Do. Nay, I care not to wed amongst those beyond my station.

He. There's gold, if this thou'lt claim as thy guerdon.

Do. Gold have I in my home; no sustenance lack I.

He. What then is thy desire of all that Ilium stores within her?

Do. Promise me my gift when thou dost conquer the Achæans.

He. I will give it thee; do thou ask anything except the captains of the fleet.

Do. Slay them; I do not ask thee to keep thy hand off Menelaus.

He. Is it the son of Oileus thou wouldst ask me for?

Do. Ill hands to dig and delve are those mid luxury nursed.

He. Whom then of the Achæans wilt thou have alive to hold to ransom?

Do. I told thee before, my house is stored with gold.

He. Why then, thou shalt come and with thine own hands choose out some spoil.

Do. Nail up the spoils for the gods on their temple walls.

He. Prithee, what higher prize than these wilt ask me for?

Do. Achilles' coursers. Needs must the prize be worth the toil when one stakes one's life on Fortune's die.

He. Ah! but thy wishes clash with mine anent those steeds; for of immortal stock, they and their sires before them, are those horses that bear the son of Peleus on his headlong course. Them did king Poseidon, ocean's god, break and give to Peleus, so runs the legend—yet, for I did urge thee on, I will not break my word; to thee will I give Achilles' team, to add a splendour to thy house.

Do. I thank thee; in receiving them I avow I am taking a fairer gift than any other Phrygian for my bravery. Yet thee it needs not to be envious; countless joys besides this will glad thy heart in thy kingship o'er this land. *Exit* HECTOR.

Ch. Great the enterprise, and great the boon thou designest to receive. Happy, ay, happy wilt thou be, if thou succeed; fair the fame thy toil shall win. Yet to wed with a prince's sister were a distinction high. On Heaven's decrees let Justice keep her eye! what man can give thou hast, it seems, in full.

Do. Now will I set forth, and going within my house will don such garb as suits, and then will hasten to the Argive fleet.

Ch. Why, what dress in place of this wilt thou assume?

Do. Such as suits my task and furtive steps.

Ch. One should ever learn wisdom from the wise; tell me wherewith thou wilt drape thy body.

Do. I will fasten a wolf skin about my back, and o'er my head put the brute's gaping jaws; then fitting its fore-feet to my hands and its hind-feet to my legs I will go on all-fours in imitation of its gait to puzzle the enemy when I approach their trenches and barriers round the ships. But whenever I come to a deserted spot, on two feet will I walk; such is the ruse I have decided on.

Ch. May Hermes, Maia's child, escort thee safely there and back, prince of tricksters as he is! Thou knowest what thou hast to do; good luck is all thou needest now.

Do. I shall return in safety, and bring to thee the head of Odysseus when I have slain him, or maybe the son of Tydeus, and with this clear proof before thee thou shalt avow that Dolon went unto the Argive fleet; for, ere the dawn appear, I will win back home with bloodstained hand. *Exit* DOLON.

Ch. O Apollo, blest godhead, lord of Thymbra and of Delos, who hauntest thy fane in Lycia, come with all thy archery, appear this night, and by thy guidance save our friend now setting forth, and aid the Dardans' scheme, almighty god whose hands in days of yore upreared Troy's walls! Good luck attend his mission to the ships! may he reach the host of Hellas and spy it out, then turn again and reach the altars of his father's home in Ilium!

Grant him to mount the chariot drawn by Phthia's steeds, when Hector, our master, hath sacked Achæ's camp, those steeds that the sea-god gave to Peleus, son of Æacus; for he and he alone had heart enough for home and country to go and spy the naval station; his spirit I admire; how few stout hearts there be, when on the sea the sunlight dies and the city labours in the surge; Phrygia yet hath left a valiant few, and bold hearts in the battle's press; 'tis only Mysia's sons who scorn us as allies.

Which of the Achæans will their four-footed murderous foe slay in their beds, as he crosses the ground, feigning to be a beast? May he lay Menelaus low or slay Agamemnon and bring his head to Helen's hands, causing her to lament her evil kinsman, who hath come against my city, against the land of Troy with his countless host of ships.

DOLON *reappears disguised and departs for the Greek camp. Enter* MESSENGER.

Messenger (*a Shepherd*). Great king, ever in days to come be it mine to bring my masters such news as I am bearing now unto thine ears.

Enter HECTOR.

He. Full oft the rustic mind is afflicted with dulness; so thou, as like as not, art come to this ill-suited place to tell thy master that his flocks are bearing well. Knowest thou not my palace or my father's throne? Thither thou shouldst carry thy tale when thou hast prospered with thy flocks.

Me. Dull we herdsmen are; I do not gainsay thee. But none the less I bring thee joyful news.

He. A truce to thy tale of how the sheep-fold fares; I have battles to fight and spears to wield.

Me. The very things of which I, too, came to tell thee; for a chieftain of a countless host is on his way to join thee as thy friend and to champion this land.

He. His country? and the home that he hath left?

Me. His country, Thrace: men call his father Strymon.

He. Didst say that Rhesus was setting foot in Troy?

Me. Thou hast it; and savest me half my speech.

He. How is it that he comes to Ida's meadows, wandering from the broad waggon track across the plain?

Me. I cannot say for certain, though I might guess. To make his entry by night is no idle scheme, when he hears that the plains are packed with foemen's troops. But he frightened us rustic hinds who dwell along the slopes of Ida,[1] the earliest settlement in the land, as he came by night through yon wood where wild beasts couch. On surged the tide of Thracian warriors with loud shouts; whereat in wild amaze we drove our flocks unto the heights, for fear that some Argives were coming to plunder and harry thy steading, till that we caught the sound of voices other than Greek and ceased from our alarm. Then went I and questioned in the Thracian tongue those who were reconnoitring the road, who it was that lead them, and whose he avowed him to be, that came to the city to help the sons of Priam. And when I had heard all I wished to learn, I stood still awhile; and lo! I see Rhesus mounted like a god upon his Thracian chariot. Of gold was the yoke that linked the necks of his steeds whiter than the snow; and on his shoulders flashed his targe with figures welded in gold; while a gorgon of bronze like that which gleams from the ægis of the goddess was bound upon the frontlet of his horses, ringing out its note of fear with many a bell. The number of his host thou couldst not reckon to a sum exact, for it was beyond one's comprehension; many a knight was there, and serried ranks of targeteers, and archers

[1]Cf. Homer, *Iliad*, xx. 216.

not a few, with countless swarms of light-armed troops, in Thracian garb arrayed, to bear them company. Such the ally who comes to Troy's assistance; him the son of Peleus will ne'er escape or if he fly or meet him spear to spear.

Ch. Whenso the gods stand by the burghers staunch and true, the tide of fortune glides with easy flow to a successful goal.

He. I shall find a host of friends now that fortune smiles upon my warring and Zeus is on my side. But no need have we of those who shared not our toils of erst, what time the War-god, driving all before him, was rending the sails of our ship of state with his tempestuous blast. Rhesus hath shewn the friendship he then bore to Troy; for he cometh to the feast, albeit he was not with the hunters when they took the prey, nor joined his spear with theirs.

Ch. Thou art right to scorn and blame such friends; yet welcome those who fain would help the state.

He. Sufficient we who long have kept Ilium safe.

Ch. Art so sure thou hast already caught the foe?

He. Quite sure I am; to-morrow's light will make that plain.

Ch. Beware of what may chance; full oft doth fortune veer.

He. I loathe the friend who brings his help too late.

Me. O prince, to turn away allies earns hatred. His mere appearing would cause a panic amongst the foe.

Ch. Let him, at least, since he *is* come, approach thy genial board as guest, if not ally, for the gratitude of Priam's sons is forfeit in his case.

He. Thou counsellest aright; thou too dost take the proper view. Let Rhesus in his gilded mail join the allies of this land, thanks to the messenger's report. *Exeunt the* MESSENGER *and* HECTOR.

Ch. May Nemesis, daughter of Zeus, check the word that may offend; for lo! I will utter all that my soul fain would say. Thou art come, O son of the river god, art come, thrice welcome in thy advent, to the halls of Phrygia; late in time thy Pierian mother and Strymon thy sire, that stream with bridges fair, are sending thee to us—Strymon who begat thee his strong young son, that day his swirling waters found a refuge in the tuneful Muse's virgin bosom. Thou art my Zeus, my god of light, as thou comest driving thy dappled steeds. Now, O Phrygia, O my country, now mayst thou by God's grace address thy saviour Zeus! Shall old Troy once more at last spend the live-long day in drinking toasts and singing love's praise, while the wildering wine-cup sends a friendly challenge round, as o'er the sea for Sparta bound, the sons of Atreus quit the Ilian strand? Ah! best of friends, with thy strong arm and spear mayst thou this service do me, then safe return. Come, appear, brandish that shield of gold full in Achilles' face; raise it aslant along the chariot's branching rail, urging on thy steeds the while, and shaking thy lance with double point. For none after facing thee will ever join the dance on the lawns of Argive Hera; no, but he shall die by Thracians slain, and this land shall bear the burden of his corpse and be glad.

Enter RHESUS.

Hail, all hail! O mighty prince! fair the scion thou hast bred, O Thrace, a ruler in his every look. Mark his stalwart frame cased in golden corslet! Hark to the ringing bells that peal so proudly from his targe-handle hung. A god, O Troy, a god, a very Ares, a scion of Strymon's stream and of the tuneful Muse, breathes courage into thee.

Re-enter HECTOR.

Rhesus. Brave son of sire as brave, Hector, prince of this land, all hail! After many a long day I greet thee. Right glad am I of thy success, to see thee camped hard on the foemen's towers; I come to help thee raze their walls and fire their fleet of ships.

He. Son of that tuneful mother, one of the Muses nine, and of Thracian Strymon's stream, I ever love to speak plain truth; nature gave me not a double tongue. Long, long ago shouldst thou have come and shared the labours of this land nor suffered Troy for any help of thine to fall o'er thrown by hostile Argive spears. Thou canst not say 'twas any want of invitation that kept thee from coming with thy help to visit us. How oft came heralds and embassies from Phrygia urgently requiring thine aid for our city? What sumptuous presents did we not send to thee? But thou, brother barbarian though thou wert, didst pledge away to Hellenes us thy barbarian brethren, for all the help thou gavest. Yet 'twas I with this strong arm that raised thee from thy paltry princedom to high lordship over Thrace, that day I fell upon the Thracian chieftains face to face around Pangæus in Pæonia's land and broke their serried ranks, and gave their people up to thee with the yoke upon their necks; but thou hast trampled on this great favour done thee, and comest with laggard step to give thine aid when friends are in distress. While they, whom no natural tie of kin constrains, have long been here, and some are dead and in their graves beneath the heaped-up cairn, no mean proof of loyalty to the city, and others in harness clad and mounted on their cars, with steadfast soul endure the icy blast and parching heat of the sun, not pledging one another, as thou art wont, in long deep draughts on couches soft. This is the charge I bring against thee and utter to thy face, that thou mayst know how frank is Hector's tongue.

Rh. I too am such another as thyself; straight to the point I cut my way; no shuffling nature mine. My heart was wrung with sorer anguish than ever thine was at my absence from this land; I fumed and chafed, but Scythian folk, whose borders march with mine, made war on me on the very eve of my departure for Ilium; already had I reached the strand of the Euxine sea, there to transport my Thracian army. Then did my spear pour out o'er Scythia's soil great drops of bloody rain, and Thrace too shared in the mingled slaughter. This then was what did chance to keep me from coming to the land of Troy and joining thy standard. But soon as I had conquered these and taken their children as hostages and appointed the yearly tribute they should pay my house, I crossed the firth, and lo! am here; on foot I traversed all thy borders that remained to pass, not as thou in thy jeers at those carousals of my countrymen hintest, nor sleeping soft in gilded palaces, but amid the frozen hurricanes that vex the Thracian main and the Pæonian shores, learning as I lay awake what suffering is, this soldier's cloak my only wrap. True my coming hath tarried, but yet am I in time; ten long years already hast thou been at the fray, and naught accomplished yet; day in, day out, thou riskest all in this game of war with Argives. While I will be content once to see the sun-god rise, and sack yon towers and fall upon their anchored fleet and slay the Achæans; and on the morrow home from Ilium will I go, at one stroke ending all thy toil. Let none of you lay hand to spear to lift it, for I, for all my late arrival, will with my lance make utter havoc of those vaunting Achæans.

Ch. Joy, joy! sweet champion sent by Zeus! Only may Zeus, throned on high, keep jealousy, resistless foe, from thee for thy presumptuous words! Yon fleet of ships from Argos sent, never brought, nor formerly nor now, among all its warriors a braver than thee; how I wonder will Achilles, how will Aias stand the onset of thy spear? Oh! to live to see that happy day, my prince, that thou mayest wreak vengeance on them, gripping thy lance in thy death-dealing hand!

Rh. Such exploits am I ready to achieve to atone for my long absence; (with due submission to Nemesis I say this;) then when we have cleared this city of its foes and thou hast chosen out firstfruits for the gods, I fain would march with thee against the Argives' country and coming thither, lay Hellas waste with war, that they in turn may know the taste of ill.

He. If thou couldst rid the city of this present curse and restore it to its old security, sure I should feel deep gratitude towards heaven. But as for sacking Argos and the pasture-lands of Hellas, as thou sayest, 'tis no easy task.

Rh. Avow they not that hither came the choicest chiefs of Hellas?

He. Aye, and I scorn them not; enough have I to do in driving them away.

Rh. Well, if we slay these, our task is fully done.

He. Leave not the present need, nor look to distant schemes.

Rh. Thou art, it seems, content to suffer tamely and make no return.

He. I rule an empire wide enough, e'en though I here abide. But on the left wing or the right or in the centre of the allies thou mayst plant thy shield and marshal thy troops.

Rh. Alone will I face the foe, Hector. But if thou art ashamed, after all thy previous toil, to have no share in firing their ships' prows, place me face to face at least with Achilles and his host.

He. 'Gainst him thou canst not range thy eager spear.

Rh. Why, 'twas surely said he sailed to Ilium.

He. He sailed and is come hither; but he is wroth and takes no part with the other chieftains in the fray.

Rh. Who next to him hath won a name in their host?

He. Aias and the son of Tydeus are, I take it, no whit his inferiors; there is Odysseus too, a noisy knave to talk, but bold enough withal, of all men he hath wrought most outrage on this country. For he came by night to Athena's shrine and stole her image and took it to the Argive ships; next he made his way inside our battlements, clad as a vagrant in a beggar's garb, and loudly did he curse the Argives, sent as a spy to Ilium; and then sneaked out again, when he had slain the sentinels and warders at the gate. He is ever to be found lurking in ambush about the altar of Thymbræan Apollo nigh the city. In him we have a troublous pest to wrestle with.

Rh. No brave man deigns to smite his foe in secret, but to meet him face to face. If I can catch this knave alive, who, as thou sayest, skulks in stealthy ambuscade and plots his mischief, I will impale him at the outlet of the gates and set him up for vultures of the air to make their meal upon. This is the death he ought to die, pirate and temple-robber that he is.

He. To your quarters now, for night draws on. For thee I will myself point out a spot where thy host can watch this night apart from our array. Our watchword is Phœbus, if haply there be need thereof; hear and mark it well and tell it to the Thracian army. Ye must advance in front of our ranks and keep a watchful guard, and so receive Dolon who went to spy the ships, for he, if safe he is, is even now approaching the camp of Troy.

Exeunt HECTOR *and* RHESUS.

Ch. Whose watch is it? who relieves me? night's earlier stars are on the wane, and the seven Pleiads mount the sky; athwart the firmament the eagle floats. Rouse ye, why delay? Up from your beds to the watch! See ye not the moon's pale beam? Dawn is near, day is coming, and lo! a star that heralds it.

Semi-Chorus. Who was told off to the first watch?

The son of Mygdon, whom men call Corœbus.

Who after him?

The Pæonian contingent roused the Cilicians;

And the Mysians us.

Is it not then high time we went and roused the Lycians for the fifth watch, as the lot decided?

Ch. Hark! hark! a sound; 'tis the nightingale, that slew her child, singing where she sits upon her blood-stained nest by Simois her piteous plaint, sweet singer of the many trills; already along Ida's slopes they are pasturing the flocks, and o'er the night I catch the shrill pipe's note; sleep on my closing eyelids softly steals, the sweetest sleep that comes at dawn to tired eyes.

Semi-Ch. Why doth not our scout draw near, whom Hector sent to spy the fleet?

He is so long away, I have my fears.

Is it possible he hath plunged into a hidden ambush and been slain?

Soon must we know.

My counsel is we go and rouse the Lycians to the fifth watch, as the lot ordained.

Exit SEMI-CHORUS. *Enter* DIOMEDES *and* ODYSSEUS *cautiously with drawn swords.*

Odysseus. Didst not hear, O Diomedes, the clash of arms? or is it an idle noise that rings in my ears?

Diomedes. Nay, 'tis the rattle of steel harness on the chariot-rails; me, too, did fear assail, till I perceived 'twas but the clang of horses' chains.

Od. Beware thou stumble not upon the guard in the darkness.

Di. I will take good care how I advance even in this gloom.

Od. If however thou shouldst rouse them, dost know their watchword?

Di. Yea, 'tis "Phœbus"; I heard Dolon use it.

They enter the tent, then return.

Od. Ha! the foe I see have left this bivouac.

Di. Yet Dolon surely said that here was Hector's couch, against whom this sword of mine is drawn.

Od. What can it mean? Is his company withdrawn elsewhere?

Di. Perhaps to form some stratagem against us.

Od. Like enough, for Hector now is grown quite bold by reason of his victory.

Di. What then are we to do, Odysseus? we have not found our man asleep; our hopes are dashed.

Od. Let us to the fleet with what speed we may. Some god, whiche'er it be that gives him his good luck, is preserving him; 'gainst fate we must not strive.

Di. Well, we twain must go against Æneas or Paris, most hateful of Phrygians, and with our swords cut off their heads.

Od. How, pray, in the darkness canst thou find them amid a hostile army, and slay them without risk?

Di. Yet 'twere base to go unto the Agrive ships if we have worked the enemy no harm.

Od. What! no harm! Have we not slain Dolon who spied upon the anchored fleet, and have we not his spoils safe here? Dost thou expect to sack the entire camp? Be led by me, let us return; and good luck go with us!

ATHENA *appears.*

Athena. Whither away from the Trojan ranks, with sorrow gnawing at your hearts, because fortune granteth not you twain to slay Hector or Paris? Have ye not heard that Rhesus is come to succour Troy in no mean sort? If he survive this night until to-morrow's dawn, neither Achilles nor Aias, stout spearman, can stay him from utterly destroying the Argive fleet, razing its palisades and carrying the onslaught of his lance far and wide within the gates; slay him, and all is thine; let Hector's sleep alone, nor hope to leave him a weltering trunk, for he shall find death at another hand.

Od. Queen Athena, 'tis the well-known accent of thy voice I hear; for thou art ever at my side to help me in my toil. Tell us where the warrior lies asleep, in what part of the barbarian army he is stationed.

Ath. Here lies he close at hand, not marshalled with the other troops, but outside the ranks hath Hector given him quarters, till night gives place to day. And nigh him are tethered his white steeds to his Thracian chariot, easy to see in the darkness; glossy white are they like to the plumage of a river swan. Slay their master and bear them off, a glorious prize to any home, for nowhere else in all the world is such a splendid team to be found.

Od. Diomedes, either do thou slay the Thracian folk, or leave that to me, while thy care must be the horses.

Di. I will do the killing, and do thou look to the steeds. For thou art well versed in clever tricks, and hast a ready wit. And 'tis right to allot a man to the work he can best perform.

Ath. Lo! yonder I see Paris coming towards us; he hath heard maybe from the guard a rumour vague that foes are near.

Di. Are others with him or cometh he alone?

Ath. Alone; to Hector's couch he seems to wend his way, to announce to him that spies are in the camp.

Di. Ought not he to head the list of slain?

Ath. Thou canst not o'erreach Destiny. And it is not decreed that he should fall by thy hand; but hasten on thy mission of slaughter fore-ordained, (*exeunt* ODYSSEUS *and* DIOMEDES) while I feigning to be Cypris, his ally, and to aid him in his efforts will answer thy foe with cheating words. Thus much I have told you, but the fated victim knoweth not, nor hath he heard one word, for all he is so near.

Enter PARIS.

Paris. To thee I call, general and brother, Hector! Sleep'st thou? shouldst not thou awake? Some foeman draws anigh our host, or thieves maybe, or spies.

Ath. Courage! lo! Cypris watches o'er thee in gracious mood. Thy warfare is my care, for I do not forget the honour thou once didst me, and I thank thee for thy good service. And now, when the host of Troy is triumphant, am I come bringing to thee a powerful friend, the Thracian child of the Muse, the heavenly songstress, whose father's name is Strymon.

Pa. Ever unto this city and to me a kind friend art thou, and I am sure that decision I then made conferred upon this city the highest treasure life affords in thy person. I heard a vague report, and so I came, for there prevailed amongst the guard a rumour that Achæan spies are here. One man, that saw them not, saith so, while another, that saw them come, cannot describe them, and so I am on my way to Hector's tent.

Ath. Fear naught; all is quiet in the host, and Hector is gone to assign a sleeping-place to the Thracian army.

Pa. Thou dost persuade me, and I believe thy words, and will go to guard my post, free of fear.

Ath. Go, for 'tis my pleasure ever to watch thy interests, that so I may see my allies prosperous. Yea, and thou too shalt recognize my zeal. *Exit* PARIS.

Enter ODYSSEUS *and* DIOMEDES.

O son of Laertes, I bid you sheathe your whetted swords, ye warriors all too keen; for dead before you lies the Thracian chief, his steeds are captured, but the foe have wind thereof, and are coming forth against you; fly with all speed to the ships' station. Why delay to save your lives when the foemen's storm is just bursting on you?

Ch. On, on! strike, strike, lay on, lay on! deal death in every blow!

Semi-Ch. Who goes there?

Look you, that man I mean. There are the thieves who in the gloom disturbed this host. Hither, come hither, every man of you! I have them—I have clutched them fast.

What is the watchword? Whence cam'st thou? Thy country?

Od. 'Tis not for thee to know.

Semi-Ch. Speak, or thou diest as a vile traitor this day.

Wilt not the watchword declare, ere my sword finds its way to thy heart?

Od. What! hast thou slain Rhesus?

Semi-Ch. Nay, I am asking thee about him who came to slay us.

Od. Be of good heart, approach.

Semi-Ch. Strike every man of you, strike, strike home!

Od. Stay, every man of you!

Semi-Ch. No, no, lay on!

Od. Ah! slay not a friend.

Semi-Ch. What is the watchword, then?

Od. Phœbus.

Semi-Ch. Right! stay every man his spear! Dost know whither those men are gone?

Od. Somewhere here I caught a sight of them.

Semi-Ch. Close on their track each man of you, or else must we shout for aid.

Od. Nay, 'twere conduct strange to disturb our friends with wild alarms by night.

Exeunt ODYSSEUS *and* DIOMEDES.

Ch. Who was that man who slipped away? Who was he that will loudly boast his daring in escaping me? How shall I catch him now? to whom liken him? the man who came by night with fearless step passing through our ranks and the guard we set. Is he a Thessalian or a dweller in some seacoast town of Locris, or hath he his home amid the scattered islands of the main? Who was he, and whence came he? What is his fatherland? What god doth he avow as lord of all the rest?

Semi-Ch. Whose work is this? is it the deed of Odysseus?

If one may conjecture from his former acts, of course it is.

Dost think so really? Why, of course.

He is a bold foe for us.

Who is? whom art thou praising for valiancy?

Odysseus.

Praise not the crafty weapons that a robber uses.

Ch. Once before he came into this city, with swimming bleary eyes, in rags and tatters clad, his sword hidden in his cloak. And like some vagrant menial he slunk about begging his board, his hair all tousled and matted with filth, and many a bitter curse he uttered against the royal house of the Atreidæ, as though forsooth he were to those chiefs opposed. Would, oh! would he had perished, as was his due, or ever he set foot on Phrygia's soil!

Semi-Ch. Whether it were really Odysseus or not, I am afeard.

Aye surely, for Hector will blame us sentinels.

What can he allege?

He will suspect.

What have we done? why art afeard?

By us did pass—

Well, who?

They who this night came to the Phrygian host.

Enter CHARIOTEER.

Charioteer. O cruel stroke of fate. Woe, woe!

Ch. Hush! be silent all! Crouch low, for maybe there cometh someone into the snare.

Cha. Oh, oh! dire mishap to the Thracian allies.

Ch. Who is he that groans?

Cha. Alack, alack! woe is me and woe is thee, O king of Thrace! How curst the sight of Troy to thee! how sad the blow that closed thy life!

Ch. Who art thou? an ally? which? night's gloom hath dulled these eyes, I cannot clearly recognize thee.

Cha. Where can I find some Trojan chief? Where doth Hector take his rest under arms? Alack and well-a-day! To which of the captains of the host am I to tell my tale? What sufferings ours! What dark deeds someone hath wrought on us and gone his way, when he had wound up a clew of sorrow manifest to every Thracian!

Ch. From what I gather of this man's words, some calamity, it seems, is befalling the Thracian host.

Cha. Lost is all our host, our prince is dead, slain by a treacherous blow. Woe worth the hour! woe worth the day! O the cruel anguish of this bloody wound that inly racks my frame! Would I were dead! Was it to die this inglorious death that Rhesus and I did come to Troy?

Ch. This is plain language; in no riddles he declares the disaster; all too clearly he asserts our friends' destruction.

Cha. A sorry deed it was, and more than that a deed most foul; yea, 'tis an evil doubly bad; to die with glory, if die one must, is bitterness enough I trow to him who dies; assuredly it is; though to the living it add dignity and honour for their house. But we, like fools, have died a death of shame. No sooner had great Hector given us our quarters and told us the watchword than we laid us down to sleep upon the ground, o'ercome by weariness. No guard our army set to watch by night. Our arms we set not in array, nor were the whips hung ready on the horses' yokes, for our prince was told that you were masters now, and had encamped hard on their ships; so carelessly we threw us down to sleep. Now I with thoughtful mind awoke from my slumber, and with ungrudging hand did measure out the horses' feed, expecting to harness them at dawn unto the fray;

when lo! through the thick gloom two men I see roaming around our army. But when I roused myself they fled away, and were gone once more; and I called out to them to keep away from our army, for I thought they might be thieves from our allies. No answer made they, so I too said no more, but came back to my couch and slept again. And lo! as I slept came a strange fancy o'er me: I saw, methought as in a dream, those steeds that I had groomed and used to drive, stationed at Rhesus' side, with wolves mounted on their backs; and these with their tails did lash the horses' flanks and urge them on, while they did snort and breathe fury from their nostrils, striving in terror to unseat their riders. Up I sprang to defend the horses from the brutes, for the horror of the night scared me. Then as I raised my head I heard the groans of dying men, and a warm stream of new-shed blood bespattered me where I lay close to my murdered master as he gave up the ghost. To my feet I start, but all unarmed; and as I peer about and grope to find my sword, a stalwart hand from somewhere nigh dealt me a sword-thrust beneath the ribs. I know the sword that dealt that blow from the deep gaping wound it gave me. Down on my face I fell, while they fled clean away with steeds and chariot. Alack, alack! Tortured with pain, too weak to stand, a piteous object I! I know what happened, for I saw it; but how the victims met their death I cannot say, nor whose the hand that smote them; but I can well surmise we have our friends to thank for this mischance.

Ch. O charioteer of Thrace's hapless king, never suspect that any but foes have had a hand in this. Lo! Hector himself is here, apprized of thy mischance; he sympathizes as he should with thy hard fate. *Enter* HECTOR.

He. Ye villains who have caused this mischief dire, how came the foemen's spies without your knowledge, to your shame, and spread destruction through the host, and you drove them not away as they passed in or out? Who but you shall pay the penalty for this? You, I say, were stationed here to guard the host. But they are gone without a wound, with many a scoff at Phrygian cowardice, and at me their leader. Now mark ye this—by father Zeus I swear—at least the scourge, if not the headsman's axe, awaits such conduct; else count Hector a thing of naught, a mere coward.

Ch. Woe, woe is me! A grievous, grievous woe came on me, I can see, great lord of my city, in the hour that I brought my news to thee that the Argive host was kindling fires about the ships; for by the springs of Simois I vow my eye kept sleepless watch by night, nor did I slumber or sleep. O be not angered with me, my lord; I am guiltless of all; yet if hereafter thou find that I in word or deed have done amiss, bury me alive beneath the earth; I ask no mercy.

Cha. Why threaten these? Why try to undermine my poor barbarian wit by crafty words, barbarian thou thyself? Thou didst this deed; nor they who have suffered all, nor we by wounds disabled will believe it was any other. A long and subtle speech thou'lt need to prove to me thou didst not slay thy friends because thou didst covet the horses, and to gain them didst murder thine own allies, after bidding them come so straitly. They came, and they are dead. Why, Paris found more decent means to shame the rights of hospitality than thou, with thy slaughter of thy allies. Never tell me some Argive came and slaughtered us. Who could have passed the Trojan lines and come against us without detection? Thou and thy Phrygian troops were camped in front of us. Who was wounded, who was slain amongst thy friends, when that foe thou speak'st of came? 'Twas we were wounded, while some have met a sterner fate and said farewell to heaven's light. Briefly, then, no Achæan do I blame. For what enemy could have come and found the lowly bed of Rhesus in the dark, unless some deity were guiding the murderers' steps? They did not so much as know of his arrival. No, 'tis thy plot this!

He. 'Tis many a long year now since I have had to do with allies, aye, ever since Achæa's host settled in this land, and never an ill word have I known them say of me; but with thee I am to make a beginning. Never may such longing for horses seize me that I should slay my friends! This is the work of Odysseus. Who of all the Argives but he would have devised or carried out such a deed? I fear him much; and somewhat my mind misgives me lest he have met and slain Dolon as well; for 'tis long since he set out, nor yet appears.

Cha. I know not this Odysseus of whom thou speakest. 'Twas no foe's hand that smote me.

He. Well, keep that opinion for thyself, if it please thee.

Cha. O land of my fathers, would I might die in thee!

He. Die! No! Enough are those already dead.

Cha. Where am I to turn, I ask thee, reft of my master now?

He. My house shall shelter thee and cure thee of thy hurt.

Cha. How shall murderers' hands care for me?

He. This fellow will never have done repeating the same story.

Cha. Curses on the doer of this deed! On thee my tongue doth fix no charge, as thou complainest; but Justice is over all.

He. Ho! take him hence! Carry him to my palace and tend him carefully, that he may have no fault to find. And you must go to those upon the walls, to Priam and his aged councillors, and tell them to give orders for the burial of the dead at the place where folk turn from the road to rest.

CHARIOTEER *is carried off.*

Ch. Why, with what intent doth fortune change and bring Troy once again to mourning after her famous victory? See, see! O look! What goddess, O king, is hovering o'er our heads, bearing in her hands as on a bier the warrior slain but now? I shudder at this sight of woe. THE MUSE *appears.*

The Muse. Behold me, sons of Troy! Lo! I the

Muse, one of the sisters nine, that have honour among the wise, am here, having seen the piteous death his foes have dealt my darling son. Yet shall the crafty Odysseus, that slew him, one day hereafter pay a fitting penalty. O my son, thy mother's grief, I mourn for thee in self-taught strains of woe! What a journey thou didst make to Troy, a very path of woe and sorrow! starting, spite of all my warnings and thy father's earnest prayers, in defiance of us. Woe is me for thee, my dear, dear son! Ah, woe! my son, my son!

Ch. I, too, bewail and mourn thy son, as far as one can who hath no common tie of kin.

Muse. Curses on the son[1] of Œneus! Curses on Laertes' child! who hath reft me of my fair son and made me childless! and on that woman, too, that left her home in Hellas, and sailed hither with her Phrygian paramour, bringing death to thee, my dearest son, 'neath Ilium's walls, and stripping countless cities of their heroes brave. Deep, deep the wounds, son[2] of Philammon, hast thou inflicted on my heart, in life, nor less in Hades' halls. Yea, for 'twas thy pride, thy own undoing, and thy rivalry with us Muses that made me mother of this poor son of mine. For as I crossed the river's streams I came too nigh to Strymon's fruitful couch, that day we Muses came unto the brow of Mount Pangæus with its soil of gold, with all our music furnished forth for one great trial of minstrel skill with that clever Thracian bard, and him we reft of sight, even Thamyris, the man who oft reviled our craft. Anon, when I gave birth to thee, because I felt shame of my sisters and my maiden years, I sent thee to the swirling stream of thy sire, the water-god; and Strymon did not entrust thy nurture to mortal hands, but to the fountain nymphs. There wert thou reared most fairly by the maiden nymphs, and didst rule o'er Thrace, a leader amongst men, my child. So long as thou didst range thy native land in quest of bloody deeds of prowess I feared not for thy death, but I bade thee ne'er set out for Troy-town, for well I knew thy doom; but Hector's messages and those countless embassies urged thee to go and help thy friends. This was thy doing, Athena; thou alone art to blame for his death (neither Odysseus nor the son of Tydeus had aught to do with it); think not it hath escaped mine eye. And yet we sister Muses do special honour to thy city, thy land we chiefly haunt; yea, and Orpheus, own cousin of the dead whom thou hast slain, did for thee unfold those dark mysteries with their torch processions. Musæus, too, thy holy citizen, of all men most advanced in lore, him did Phœbus with us sisters train. And here is my reward for this; dead in my arms I hold my child and mourn for him. Henceforth no other learned man I'll bring to thee.

Ch. Vainly it seems the Thracian charioteer reviled us with plotting this man's murder, Hector.

He. I knew it; it needed no seer to say that he had perished by the arts of Odysseus. Now I, when I saw the Hellene host camped in my land, of course would not hesitate to send heralds to my friends, bidding them come and help my country; and so I sent, and he as in duty bound came my toils to share. It grieves me sorely to see him dead; and now am I ready to raise a tomb for him and burn at his pyre great store of fine raiment; for he came as a friend and in sorrow is he going hence.

Muse. He shall not descend into earth's darksome soil; so earnest a prayer will I address to the bride of the nether world, the daughter of the goddess Demeter, giver of increase, to release his soul, and debtor, as she is to me, show that she honours the friends of Orpheus. Yet from henceforth will he be to me as one dead that seeth not the light; for never again will he meet me or see his mother's face, but will lurk hidden in a cavern of the land with veins of silver, restored to life, no longer man but god, even as the prophet of Bacchus did dwell in a grotto 'neath Pangæus, a god whom his votaries honoured. Lightly now shall I feel the grief of the sea-goddess, for her son[3] too must die. First then for thee we sisters must chaunt our dirge, and then for Achilles when Thetis mourns some day. Him shall not Pallas, thy slayer, save; so true the shaft Loxias keeps in his quiver for him. Ah me! the sorrows that a mother feels! the troubles of mortals! whoso fairly reckons you up will live and die a childless man and will have no children to bury. THE MUSE *disappears.*

Ch. His mother now must see to this her son's burial; but for thee, Hector, if thou wilt carry out any scheme, now is the time, for day is dawning.

He. Go, bid our comrades arm at once; yoke the horses; torch in hand ye must await the blast of the Etrurian trumpet; for I hope with this day's mounting sun to pass beyond their lines and walls and fire the ships of the Achæans, restoring freedom's light once more to Troy.

Ch. Obedience to our prince! let us array ourselves in mail, and go forth and these orders tell to our allies, and haply the god who is on our side will grant us victory.

[1]Tydeus, father of Diomedes.
[2]Thamyris.
[3]Achilles.

MEDEA

DRAMATIS PERSONAE

Nurse of Medea	Creon
Attendant *of her children*	Jason
Medea	Ægeus
Chorus of Corinthian Women	Messenger

The Two Sons of Jason and Medea

Before the Palace of Creon at Corinth. Enter NURSE.

Nurse. Ah! would to Heaven the good ship Argo ne'er had sped its course to the Colchian land through the misty blue Symplegades, nor ever in the glens of Pelion the pine been felled to furnish with oars the chieftain's hands, who went to fetch the golden fleece for Pelias; for then would my own mistress Medea never have sailed to the turrets of Iolcos, her soul with love for Jason smitten, nor would she have beguiled the daughters of Pelias to slay their father and come to live here in the land of Corinth with her husband and children, where her exile found favour with the citizens to whose land she had come, and in all things of her own accord was she at one with Jason, the greatest safeguard this when wife and husband do agree; but now their love is all turned to hate, and tenderest ties are weak. For Jason hath betrayed his own children and my mistress dear for the love of a royal bride, for he hath wedded the daughter of Creon, lord of this land. While Medea his hapless wife, thus scorned, appeals to the oaths he swore, recalls the strong pledge his right hand gave, and bids heaven be witness what requital she is finding from Jason. And here she lies fasting, yielding her body to her grief, wasting away in tears ever since she learnt that she was wronged by her husband, never lifting her eye nor raising her face from off the ground; and she lends as deaf an ear to her friend's warning as if she were a rock or ocean billow, save when she turns her snow-white neck aside and softly to herself bemoans her father dear, her country and her home, which she gave up to come hither with the man who now holds her in dishonour. She, poor lady, hath by sad experience learnt how good a thing it is never to quit one's native land. And she hates her children now and feels no joy at seeing them; I am afeard she may contrive some untoward scheme; for her mood is dangerous nor will she brook her cruel treatment; full well I know her, and I much do dread that she will plunge the keen sword through their heart, stealing without a word into the chamber where their marriage couch is spread, or else that she will slay the prince and bridegroom too, and so find some calamity still more grievous than the present; for dreadful is her wrath; verily the man that doth incur her hate will have no easy task to raise o'er her a song of triumph. Lo! where her sons come hither from their childish sports; little they reck of their mother's woes, for the soul of the young is no friend to sorrow.

Enter ATTENDANT, *with the Children.*

Attendant. Why dost thou, so long my lady's own handmaid, stand here at the gate alone, loudly lamenting to thyself the piteous tale? how comes it that Medea will have thee leave her to herself?

Nu. Old man, attendant on the sons of Jason, our master's fortunes when they go awry make good slaves grieve and touch their hearts. Oh! I have come to such a pitch of grief that there stole a yearning wish upon me to come forth hither and proclaim to heaven and earth my mistress's hard fate.

At. What! has not the poor lady ceased yet from her lamentation?

Nu. Would I were as thou art! the mischief is but now beginning; it has not reached its climax yet.

At. O foolish one, if I may call my mistress such a name; how little she recks of evils yet more recent!

Nu. What mean'st, old man? grudge not to tell me.

At. 'Tis naught; I do repent me even of the words I have spoken.

Nu. Nay, by thy beard I conjure thee, hide it not from thy fellow-slave; I will be silent, if need be, on that text.

At. I heard one say, pretending not to listen as I approached the place where our greybeards sit playing draughts near Pirene's sacred spring, that Creon, the ruler of this land, is bent on driving these children and their mother from the boundaries of Corinth; but I know not whether the news is to be relied upon, and would fain it were not.

Nu. What! will Jason brook such treatment of his sons, even though he be at variance with their mother?

At. Old ties give way to new; he bears no longer any love to this family.

Nu. Undone, it seems, are we, if to old woes fresh ones we add, ere we have drained the former to the dregs.

At. Hold thou thy peace, say not a word of this; 'tis no time for our mistress to learn hereof.

Nu. O children, do ye hear how your father feels

towards you? Perdition catch him, but no! he is my master still; yet is he proved a very traitor to his nearest and dearest.

At. And who 'mongst men is not? Art learning only now, that every single man cares for himself more than for his neighbour, some from honest motives, others for mere gain's sake? seeing that to indulge his passion their father has ceased to love these children.

Nu. Go, children, within the house; all will be well. Do thou keep them as far away as may be, and bring them not near their mother in her evil hour. For ere this have I seen her eyeing them savagely, as though she were minded to do them some hurt, and well I know she will not cease from her fury till she have pounced on some victim. At least may she turn her hand against her foes, and not against her friends.

Medea (*Within*). Ah, me! a wretched suffering woman I! O would that I could die!

Nu. 'Tis as I said, my dear children; wild fancies stir your mother's heart, wild fury goads her on. Into the house without delay, come not near her eye, approach her not, beware her savage mood, the fell tempest of her reckless heart. In, in with what speed ye may. For 'tis plain she will soon redouble her fury; that cry is but the herald of the gathering storm-cloud whose lightning soon will flash; what will her proud restless soul, in the anguish of despair, be guilty of?

Exit ATTENDANT *with the children.*

Med. (*Within*) Ah, me! the agony I have suffered deep enough to call for these laments! Curse you and your father too, ye children damned, sons of a doomed mother! Ruin seize the whole family!

Nu. Ah me! ah me! the pity of it! Why, pray, do thy children share their father's crime? Why hatest thou them? Woe is you, poor children, how do I grieve for you lest ye suffer some outrage! Strange are the tempers of princes, and maybe because they seldom have to obey, and mostly lord it over others, change they their moods with difficulty. 'Tis better then to have been trained to live on equal terms. Be it mine to reach old age, not in proud pomp, but in security! Moderation wins the day first as a better word for men to use, and likewise it is far the best course for them to pursue; but greatness that doth o'erreach itself, brings no blessing to mortal men; but pays a penalty of greater ruin whenever fortune is wroth with a family.

Enter CHORUS OF CORINTHIAN WOMEN.

Chorus. I heard the voice, uplifted loud, of our poor Colchian lady, nor yet is she quiet; speak, aged dame, for as I stood by the house with double gates I heard a voice of weeping from within, and I do grieve, lady, for the sorrows of this house, for it hath won my love.

Nu. 'Tis a house no more; all that is passed away long since; a royal bride keeps Jason at her side, while our mistress pines away in her bower, finding no comfort for her soul in aught her friends can say.

Med. (*Within*) Oh, oh! Would that Heaven's levin bolt would cleave this head in twain! What gain is life to me? Woe, woe is me! O, to die and win release, quitting this loathed existence!

Ch. Didst hear, O Zeus, thou earth, and thou, O light, the piteous note of woe the hapless wife is uttering? How shall a yearning for that insatiate resting-place ever hasten for thee, poor reckless one, the end that death alone can bring? Never pray for that. And if thy lord prefers a fresh love, be not angered with him for that; Zeus will judge 'twixt thee and him herein. Then mourn not for thy husband's loss too much, nor waste thyself away.

Med. (*Within*) Great Themis, and husband of Themis, behold what I am suffering now, though I did bind that accursed one, my husband, by strong oaths to me? O, to see him and his bride some day brought to utter destruction, they and their house with them, for that they presume to wrong me thus unprovoked. O my father, my country, that I have left to my shame, after slaying my own brother.

Nu. Do ye hear her words, how loudly she adjures Themis, oft invoked, and Zeus, whom men regard as keeper of their oaths? On no mere trifle surely will our mistress spend her rage.

Ch. Would that she would come forth for us to see, and listen to the words of counsel we might give, if haply she might lay aside the fierce fury of her wrath, and her temper stern. Never be my zeal at any rate denied my friends! But go thou and bring her hither outside the house, and tell her this our friendly thought; haste thee ere she do some mischief to those inside the house, for this sorrow of hers is mounting high.

Nu. This will I do; but I have my doubts whether I shall persuade my mistress; still willingly will I undertake this trouble for you; albeit, she glares upon her servants with the look of a lioness with cubs, whenso anyone draws nigh to speak to her. Wert thou to call the men of old time rude uncultured boors thou wouldst not err, seeing that they devised their hymns for festive occasions, for banquets, and to grace the board, a pleasure to catch the ear, shed o'er our life, but no man hath found a way to allay hated grief by music and the minstrel's varied strain, whence arise slaughters and fell strokes of fate to o'erthrow the homes of men. And yet this were surely a gain, to heal men's wounds by music's spell, but why tune they their idle song where rich banquets are spread? for of itself doth the rich banquet, set before them, afford to men delight.

Exit NURSE.

Ch. I heard a bitter cry of lamentation! loudly, bitterly she calls on the traitor of her marriage bed, her perfidious spouse; by grievous wrongs oppressed she invokes Themis, bride of Zeus, witness of oaths, who brought her unto Hellas, the land that fronts the strand of Asia, o'er the sea by night through ocean's boundless gate.

Enter MEDEA.

Med. From the house I have come forth, Corinthian ladies, for fear lest you be blaming me; for well I know that amongst men many by showing pride have gotten them an ill name and a reputation for indifference, both those who shun men's gaze and those who move amid the stranger crowd, and likewise they who choose a quiet walk in life. For there is no just discernment in the eyes of men, for they, or ever they have surely learnt their neighbour's heart, loathe him at first sight, though never wronged by him; and so a stranger most of all should adopt a city's views; nor do I commend that citizen, who, in the stubbornness of his heart, from churlishness resents the city's will.

But on me hath fallen this unforeseen disaster, and sapped my life; ruined I am, and long to resign the boon of existence, kind friends, and die. For he who was all the world to me, as well thou knowest, hath turned out the veriest villain, my own husband. Of all things that have life and sense we women are the most hapless creatures; first must we buy a husband at an exorbitant price, and o'er ourselves a tyrant set which is an evil worse than the first; and herein lies the most important issue, whether our choice be good or bad. For divorce is discreditable to women, nor can we disown our lords. Next must the wife, coming as she does to ways and customs new, since she hath not learnt the lesson in her home, have a diviner's eye to see how best to treat the partner of her life. If haply we perform these tasks with thoroughness and tact, and the husband live with us, without resenting the yoke, our life is a happy one; if not, 'twere best to die. But when a man is vexed with what he finds indoors, he goeth forth and rids his soul of its disgust, betaking him to some friend or comrade of like age; whilst we must needs regard his single self.

And yet they say we live secure at home, while they are at the wars, with their sorry reasoning, for I would gladly take my stand in battle array three times o'er, than once give birth. But enough! this language suits not thee as it does me; thou hast a city here, a father's house, some joy in life, and friends to share thy thoughts, but I am destitute, without a city, and therefore scorned by my husband, a captive I from a foreign shore, with no mother, brother, or kinsman in whom to find a new haven of refuge from this calamity. Wherefore this one boon and only this I wish to win from thee—thy silence, if haply I can some way or means devise to avenge me on my husband for this cruel treatment, and on the man who gave to him his daughter, and on her who is his wife. For though a woman be timorous enough in all else, and as regards courage, a coward at the mere sight of steel, yet in the moment she finds her honour wronged, no heart is filled with deadlier thoughts than hers.

Ch. This will I do; for thou wilt be taking a just vengeance on thy husband, Medea. That thou shouldst mourn thy lot surprises me not. But lo! I see Creon, king of this land coming hither, to announce some new resolve.

Enter CREON.

Creon. Hark thee, Medea, I bid thee take those sullen looks and angry thoughts against thy husband forth from this land in exile, and with thee take both thy children and that without delay, for I am judge in this sentence, and I will not return unto my house till I banish thee beyond the borders of the land.

Med. Ah, me! now is utter destruction come upon me, unhappy that I am! For my enemies are bearing down on me full sail, nor have I any landing-place to come at in my trouble. Yet for all my wretched plight I will ask thee, Creon, wherefore dost thou drive me from the land?

Cr. I fear thee—no longer need I veil my dread 'neath words—lest thou devise against my child some cureless ill. Many things contribute to this fear of mine; thou art a witch by nature, expert in countless sorceries, and thou art chafing for the loss of thy husband's affection. I hear, too, so they tell me, that thou dost threaten the father of the bride, her husband, and herself with some mischief; wherefore I will take precautions ere our troubles come. For 'tis better for me to incur thy hatred now, lady, than to soften my heart and bitterly repent it hereafter.

Med. Alas! this is not now the first time, but oft before, O Creon, hath my reputation injured me and caused sore mischief. Wherefore whoso is wise in his generation ought never to have his children taught to be too clever; for besides the reputation they get for idleness, they purchase bitter odium from the citizens. For if thou shouldst import new learning amongst dullards, thou will be thought a useless trifler, void of knowledge; while if thy fame in the city o'ertops that of the pretenders to cunning knowledge, thou wilt win their dislike. I too myself share in this ill-luck. Some think me clever and hate me, others say I am too reserved, and some the very reverse; others find me hard to please and not so very clever after all. Be that as it may, thou dost fear me lest I bring on thee something to mar thy harmony. Fear me not, Creon, my position scarce is such that I should seek to quarrel with princes. Why should I, for how hast thou injured me? Thou hast betrothed thy daughter where thy fancy prompted thee. No, 'tis my husband I hate, though I doubt not thou hast acted wisely herein. And now I grudge not thy prosperity; betroth thy child, good luck to thee, but let me abide in this land, for though I have been wronged I will be still and yield to my superiors.

Cr. Thy words are soft to hear, but much I dread lest thou art devising some mischief in thy heart, and less than ever do I trust thee now; for a cunning woman, and man likewise, is easier to guard against when quick-tempered than when taciturn. Nay, begone at once! speak me no speeches, for this is decreed, nor hast thou any art whereby thou shalt abide amongst us, since thou hatest me.

Med. O, say not so! by thy knees and by thy daughter newly-wed, I do implore!

Cr. Thou wastest words; thou wilt never persuade me.

Med. What, wilt thou banish me, and to my prayers no pity yield?

Cr. I will, for I love not thee above my own family.

Med. O my country! what fond memories I have of thee in this hour!

Cr. Yea, for I myself love my city best of all things save my children.

Med. Ah me! ah me! to mortal man how dread a scourge is love!

Cr. That, I deem, is according to the turn our fortunes take.

Med. O Zeus! let not the author of these my troubles escape thee.

Cr. Begone, thou silly woman, and free me from my toil.

Med. The toil is mine, no lack of it.

Cr. Soon wilt thou be thrust out forcibly by the hand of servants.

Med. Not that, not that, I do entreat thee, Creon!

Cr. Thou wilt cause disturbance yet, it seems.

Med. I will begone; I ask thee not this boon to grant.

Cr. Why then this violence? why dost thou not depart?

Med. Suffer me to abide this single day and devise some plan for the manner of my exile, and means of living for my children, since their father cares not to provide his babes therewith. Then pity them; thou too hast children of thine own; thou needs must have a kindly heart. For my own lot I care naught, though I an exile am, but for those babes I weep, that they should learn what sorrow means.

Cr. Mine is a nature anything but harsh; full oft by showing pity have I suffered shipwreck; and now albeit I clearly see my error, yet shalt thou gain this request, lady; but I do forewarn thee, if to-morrow's rising sun shall find thee and thy children within the borders of this land, thou diest; my word is spoken and it will not lie. So now, if abide thou must, stay this one day only, for in it thou canst not do any of the fearful deeds I dread. *Exit.*

Ch. Ah! poor lady, woe is thee! Alas, for thy sorrows! Whither wilt thou turn? What protection, what home or country to save thee from thy troubles wilt thou find? O Medea, in what a hopeless sea of misery heaven hath plunged thee!

Med. On all sides sorrow pens me in. Who shall gainsay this? But all is not yet lost! think not so. Still are there troubles in store for the new bride, and for her bridegroom no light toil. Dost think I would ever have fawned on yonder man, unless to gain some end or form some scheme? Nay, I would not so much as have spoken to him or touched him with my hand. But he has in folly so far stepped in that, though he might have checked my plot by banishing me from the land, he hath allowed me to abide this day, in which I will lay low in death three of my enemies—a father and his daughter and my husband too. Now, though I have many ways to compass their deaths, I am not sure, friends, which I am to try first. Shall I set fire to the bridal mansion, or plunge the whetted sword through their hearts, softly stealing into the chamber where their couch is spread? One thing stands in my way. If I am caught making my way into the chamber, intent on my design, I shall be put to death and cause my foes to mock. 'Twere best to take the shortest way—the way we women are most skilled in—by poison to destroy them. Well, well, suppose them dead; what city will receive me? What friendly host will give me a shelter in his land, a home secure, and save my soul alive? None. So I will wait yet a little while in case some tower of defence rise up for me; then will I proceed to this bloody deed in crafty silence; but if some unexpected mischance drive me forth, I will with mine own hand seize the sword, e'en though I die for it, and slay them, and go forth on my bold path of daring. By that dread queen whom I revere before all others and have chosen to share my task, by Hecate who dwells within my inmost chamber, not one of them shall wound my heart and rue it not. Bitter and sad will I make their marriage for them; bitter shall be the wooing of it, bitter my exile from the land. Up, then, Medea, spare not the secrets of thy art in plotting and devising; on to the danger. Now comes a struggle needing courage. Dost see what thou art suffering? 'Tis not for thee to be a laughing-stock to the race of Sisyphus by reason of this wedding of Jason, sprung, as thou art, from a noble sire, and of the Sun-god's race. Thou hast cunning; and, more than this, we women, though by nature little apt for virtuous deeds, are most expert to fashion any mischief.

Ch. Back to their source the holy rivers turn their tide. Order and the universe are being reversed. 'Tis men whose counsels are treacherous, whose oath by heaven is no longer sure. Rumour shall bring a change o'er my life, bringing it into good repute. Honour's dawn is breaking for woman's sex; no more shall the foul tongue of slander fix upon us. The songs of the poets of old shall cease to make our faithlessness their theme. Phœbus, lord of minstrelsy, hath not implanted in our mind the gift of heavenly song, else had I sung an answering strain to the race of males, for time's long chapter affords many a theme on their sex as well as ours. With mind distraught didst thou thy father's house desert on thy voyage betwixt ocean's twin rocks, and on a foreign strand thou dwellest, thy bed left husbandless, poor lady, and thou an exile from the land, dishonoured, persecuted. Gone is the grace that oaths once had. Through all the breadth of Hellas honour is found no more; to heaven hath it sped away. For thee no father's house is open, woe is thee! to be a haven from the troublous storm, while o'er thy home is set another queen, the bride that is preferred to thee.

Enter JASON.

Jason. It is not now I first remark, but oft ere this, how unruly a pest is a harsh temper. For instance, thou, hadst thou but patiently endured the will of thy superiors, mightest have remained here in this land and house, but now for thy idle words wilt thou be banished. Thy words are naught to me. Cease not to call Jason basest of men; but for those words thou has spoken against our rulers, count it all gain that exile is thy only punishment. I ever tried to check the outbursts of the angry monarch, and would have had thee stay, but thou wouldst not forego thy silly rage, always reviling our rulers, and so thou wilt be banished. Yet even after all this I weary not of my goodwill, but am come with thus much forethought, lady, that thou mayst not be destitute nor want for aught, when, with thy sons, thou art cast out. Many an evil doth exile bring in its train with it; for even though thou hatest me, never will I harbour hard thoughts of thee.

Med. Thou craven villain (for that is the only name my tongue can find for thee, a foul reproach on thy unmanliness)! comest thou to me, thou, most hated foe of gods, of me, and of all mankind? 'Tis no proof of courage or hardihood to confront thy friends after injuring them, but that worst of all human diseases—loss of shame. Yet hast thou done well to come; for I shall ease my soul by reviling thee, and thou wilt be vexed at my recital. I will begin at the very beginning. I saved thy life, as every Hellene knows who sailed with thee aboard the good ship Argo, when thou wert sent to tame and yoke fire-breathing bulls, and to sow the deadly tilth. Yea, and I slew the dragon which guarded the golden fleece, keeping sleepless watch o'er it with many a wreathed coil, and I raised for thee a beacon of deliverance. Father and home of my free will I left and came with thee to Iolcos, 'neath Pelion's hills, for my love was stronger than my prudence. Next I caused the death of Pelias by a doom most grievous, even by his own children's hand, beguiling them of all their fear. All this have I done for thee, thou traitor! and thou hast cast me over, taking to thyself another wife, though children have been born to us. Hadst thou been childless still, I could have pardoned thy desire for this new union. Gone is now the trust I put in oaths. I cannot even understand whether thou thinkest that the gods of old no longer rule, or that fresh decrees are now in vogue amongst mankind, for thy conscience must tell thee thou hast not kept faith with me. Ah! poor right hand, which thou didst often grasp. These knees thou didst embrace! All in vain, I suffered a traitor to touch me! How short of my hopes I am fallen! But come, I will deal with thee as though thou wert my friend. Yet what kindness can I expect from one so base as thee? but yet I will do it, for my questioning will show thee yet more base. Whither can I turn me now? to my father's house, to my own country, which I for thee deserted to come hither? to the hapless daughters of Pelias? A glad welcome, I trow, would they give me in their home, whose father's death I compassed! My case stands even thus: I am become the bitter foe to those of mine own home, and those whom I need ne'er have wronged I have made mine enemies to pleasure thee. Wherefore to reward me for this thou hast made me doubly blest in the eyes of many a wife in Hellas; and in thee I own a peerless, trusty lord. O woe is me, if indeed I am to be cast forth an exile from the land, without one friend; one lone woman with her babes forlorn! Yea, a fine reproach to thee in thy bridal hour, that thy children and the wife who saved thy life are beggars and vagabonds! O Zeus! why hast thou granted unto man clear signs to know the sham in gold, while on man's brow no brand is stamped whereby to gauge the villain's heart?

Ch. There is a something terrible and past all cure, when quarrels arise 'twixt those who are near and dear.

Ja. Needs must I now, it seems, turn orator, and, like a good helmsman on a ship with close-reefed sails, weather that wearisome tongue of thine. Now, I believe, since thou wilt exaggerate thy favours, that to Cypris alone of gods or men I owe the safety of my voyage. Thou hast a subtle wit enough; yet were it a hateful thing for me to say that the Love-god constrained thee by his resistless shaft to save my life. However, I will not reckon this too nicely; 'twas kindly done, however thou didst serve me. Yet for my safety hast thou received more than ever thou gavest, as I will show. First, thou dwellest in Hellas, instead of thy barbarian land, and hast learnt what justice means and how to live by law, not by the dictates of brute force; and all the Hellenes recognize thy cleverness, and thou hast gained a name; whereas, if thou hadst dwelt upon the confines of the earth, no tongue had mentioned thee. Give me no gold within my halls, nor skill to sing a fairer strain than ever Orpheus sang, unless therewith my fame be spread abroad! So much I say to thee about my own toils, for 'twas thou didst challenge me to this retort. As for the taunts thou urgest against my marriage with the princess, I will prove to thee, first, that I am prudent herein, next chastened in my love, and last a powerful friend to thee and to thy sons; only hold thy peace. Since I have here withdrawn from Iolcos with many a hopeless trouble at my back, what happier device could I, an exile, frame than marriage with the daughter of the king? 'Tis not because I loathe thee for my wife—the thought that rankles in thy heart; 'tis not because I am smitten with desire for a new bride, nor yet that I am eager to vie with others in begetting many children, for those we have are quite enough, and I do not complain. Nay, 'tis that we—and this is most important—may dwell in comfort, instead of suffering want (for well I know that every whilom friend avoids the poor), and that I might rear my sons as doth befit my house; further, that I might be the father of brothers for the children thou hast borne, and raise these to the same high rank, uniting the family in one—to my lasting bliss. Thou, indeed, hast no need of more children, but me it profits to help my present family by that which is to be. Have I miscarried here? Not even thou wouldest say so unless a rival's charms rankled in thy bosom. No, but you women have such strange ideas, that you think all is well so long as your married life runs smooth; but if some mischance occur to ruffle your love, all that was good and lovely erst you reckon as your foes. Yea, men should have begotten children from some other source, no female race existing; thus would no evil ever have fallen on mankind.

Ch. This speech, O Jason, hast thou with specious art arranged; but yet I think—albeit in saying so I betray indiscretion—that thou hast sinned in casting over thy wife.

Med. No doubt I differ from the mass of men on many points; for, to my mind, whoso hath skill to fence with words in an unjust cause, incurs the heaviest penalty; for such an one, confident that he can cast a decent veil of words o'er his injustice, dares to practise it; and yet he is not so very clever after all. So do not thou put forth thy specious pleas and clever words to me now, for one word of mine will lay thee low. Hadst thou not had a villain's heart, thou shouldst have gained my consent, then made this match, instead of hiding it from those who loved thee.

Ja. Thou wouldst have lent me ready aid, no doubt, in this proposal, if I had told thee of my marriage, seeing that not even now canst thou restrain thy soul's hot fury.

Med. This was not what restrained thee; but thine eye was turned towards old age, and a foreign wife began to appear discreditable to thee.

Ja. Be well assured of this: 'twas not for the woman's sake I wedded the king's daughter, my present wife; but, as I have already told thee, I wished to insure thy safety and to be the father of royal sons bound by blood to my own children—a bulwark to our house.

Med. May that prosperity, whose end is woe, ne'er be mine, nor such wealth as would ever sting my heart!

Ja. Change that prayer as I will teach thee, and thou wilt show more wisdom. Never let happiness appear in sorrow's guise, nor, when thy fortune smiles, pretend she frowns!

Med. Mock on; thou hast a place of refuge; I am alone, an exile soon to be.

Ja. Thy own free choice was this; blame no one else.

Med. What did I do? Marry, then betray thee?

Ja. Against the king thou didst invoke an impious curse.

Med. On thy house too maybe I bring the curse.

Ja. Know this, I will no further dispute this point with thee. But, if thou wilt of my fortune somewhat take for the children or thyself to help thy exile, say on; for I am ready to grant it with ungrudging hand, yea and to send tokens to my friends elsewhere who shall treat thee well. If thou refuse this offer, thou wilt do a foolish deed, but if thou cease from anger the greater will be thy gain.

Med. I will have naught to do with friends of thine, naught will I receive of thee, offer it not to me; a villain's gifts can bring no blessing.

Ja. At least I call the gods to witness, that I am ready in all things to serve thee and thy children, but thou dost scorn my favours and thrustest thy friends stubbornly away; wherefore thy lot will be more bitter still. *Exit.*

Med. Away! By love for thy young bride entrapped, too long thou lingerest outside her chamber; go wed, for, if God will, thou shalt have such a marriage as thou wouldst fain refuse.

Ch. When in excess and past all limits Love doth come, he brings not glory or repute to man; but if the Cyprian queen in moderate might approach, no goddess is so full of charm as she. Never, O never, lady mine, discharge at me from thy golden bow a shaft invincible, in passion's venom dipped. On me may chastity, heaven's fairest gift, look with a favouring eye; never may Cypris, goddess dread, fasten on me a temper to dispute, or restless jealousy, smiting my soul with mad desire for unlawful love, but may she hallow peaceful married life and shrewdly decide whom each of us shall wed. O my country, O my own dear home! God grant I may never be an outcast from my city, leading that cruel helpless life, whose every day is misery. Ere that may I this life complete and yield to death, ay, death; for there is no misery that doth surpass the loss of fatherland. I have seen with mine eyes, nor from the lips of others have I the lesson learnt; no city, not one friend doth pity thee in this thine awful woe. May he perish and find no favour, whoso hath not in him honour for his friends, freely unlocking his heart to them. Never shall he be friend of mine.

Enter ÆGEUS.

Ægeus. All hail, Medea! no man knoweth fairer prelude to the greeting of friends than this.

Med. All hail to thee likewise, Ægeus, son of wise Pandion. Whence comest thou to this land?

Æg. From Phœbus' ancient oracle.

Med. What took thee on thy travels to the prophetic centre of the earth?

Æg. The wish to ask how I might raise up seed unto myself.

Med. Pray tell me, hast thou till now dragged on a childless life?

Æg. I have no child owing to the visitation of some god.

Med. Hast thou a wife, or hast thou never known the married state?

Æg. I have a wife joined to me in wedlock's bond.

Med. What said Phœbus to thee as to children?

Æg. Words too subtle for man to comprehend.

Med. Surely I may learn the god's answer?

Æg. Most assuredly, for it is just thy subtle wit it needs.

Med. What said the god? speak, if I may hear it.

Æg. He bade me "not loose the wineskin's pendent neck."

Med. Till when? what must thou do first, what country visit?

Æg. Till I to my native home return.

Med. What object hast thou in sailing to this land?

Æg. O'er Trœzen's realm is Pittheus king.

Med. Pelops' son, a man devout they say.

Æg. To him I fain would impart the oracle of the god.

Med. The man is shrewd and versed in such-like lore.

Æg. Aye, and to me the dearest of all my warrior friends.

Med. Good luck to thee! success to all thy wishes!

Æg. But why that downcast eye, that wasted cheek?

Med. O Ægeus, my husband has proved a monster of iniquity.

Æg. What meanest thou? explain to me clearly the cause of thy despondency.

Med. Jason is wronging me though I have given him no cause.

Æg. What hath he done? tell me more clearly.

Med. He is taking another wife to succeed me as mistress of his house.

Æg. Can he have brought himself to such a dastard deed?

Med. Be assured thereof; I, whom he loved of yore, am in dishonour now.

Æg. Hath he found a new love? or does he loathe thy bed?

Med. Much in love is he! A traitor to his friend is he become.

Æg. Enough! if he is a villain as thou sayest.

Med. The alliance he is so much enamoured of is with a princess.

Æg. Who gives his daughter to him? go on, I pray.

Med. Creon, who is lord of this land of Corinth.

Æg. Lady, I can well pardon thy grief.

Med. I am undone, and more than that, am banished from the land.

Æg. By whom? fresh woe this word of thine unfolds.

Med. Creon drives me forth in exile from Corinth.

Æg. Doth Jason allow it? This too I blame him for.

Med. Not in words, but he will not stand out against it. O, I implore thee by this beard and by thy knees, in suppliant posture, pity, O pity my sorrows; do not see me cast forth forlorn, but receive me in thy country, to a seat within thy halls. So may thy wish by heaven's grace be crowned with a full harvest of offspring, and may thy life close in happiness! Thou knowest not the rare good luck thou findest here, for I will make thy childlessness to cease and cause thee to beget fair issue; so potent are the spells I know.

Æg. Lady, on many grounds I am most fain to grant thee this thy boon, first for the gods' sake, next for the children whom thou dost promise I shall beget; for in respect of this I am completely lost. 'Tis thus with me; if e'er thou reach my land, I will attempt to champion thee as I am bound to do. Only one warning I do give thee first, lady; I will not from this land bear thee away, yet if of thyself thou reach my halls, there shalt thou bide in safety and I will never yield thee up to any man. But from this land escape without my aid, for I have no wish to incur the blame of my allies as well.

Med. It shall be even so; but wouldst thou pledge thy word to this, I should in all be well content with thee.

Æg. Surely thou dost trust me? or is there aught that troubles thee?

Med. Thee I trust; but Pelias' house and Creon are my foes. Wherefore, if thou art bound by an oath, thou wilt not give me up to them when they come to drag me from the land, but, having entered into a compact and sworn by heaven as well, thou wilt become my friend and disregard their overtures. Weak is any aid of mine, whilst they have wealth and a princely house.

Æg. Lady, thy words show much foresight, so if this is thy will, I do not refuse. For I shall feel secure and safe if I have some pretext to offer to thy foes, and thy case too the firmer stands. Now name thy gods.

Med. Swear by the plain of Earth, by Helios my father's sire, and, in one comprehensive oath, by all the race of gods.

Æg. What shall I swear to do, from what refrain? tell me that.

Med. Swear that thou wilt never of thyself expel me from thy land, nor, whilst life is thine, permit any other, one of my foes maybe, to hale me thence if so he will.

Æg. By earth I swear, by the sun-god's holy beam and by all the host of heaven that I will stand fast to the terms I hear thee make.

Med. 'Tis enough. If thou shouldst break this oath, what curse dost thou invoke upon thyself?

Æg. Whate'er betides the impious.

Med. Go in peace; all is well, and I with what speed I may, will to thy city come, when I have wrought my purpose and obtained my wish.

Exit ÆGEUS.

Ch. May Maia's princely son go with thee on thy way to bring thee to thy home, and mayest thou attain that on which thy soul is set so firmly, for to my mind thou seemest a generous man, O Ægeus.

Med. O Zeus, and Justice, child of Zeus, and sun-god's light, now will I triumph o'er my foes, kind friends; on victory's road have I set forth; good hope have I of wreaking vengeance on those I hate. For where we were in most distress this stranger hath appeared, to be a haven in my counsels; to him will we make fast the cables of our ship when we come to the town and citadel of Pallas. But now will I explain to thee my plans in full; do not expect to hear a pleasant tale. A servant of mine will I to Jason send and crave an interview; then when he comes I will address him with soft words, say, "this pleases me," and, "that is well," even the marriage with the princess, which my treacherous lord is celebrating, and add "it suits us both, 'twas well thought out"; then will I entreat that here my children may abide, not that I mean to leave them in a hostile land for foes to flout, but that I may slay the king's daughter by guile. For I will send them with gifts in their hands, carrying them unto the bride to save them from banishment, a robe of finest woof and a chaplet of gold. And if these ornaments she take and put them on, miserably shall she die, and likewise everyone who touches her; with such fell poisons will I smear my gifts. And here I quit this theme; but I shudder at the deed I must do next; for I will slay the children I have borne; there is none shall take them from my toils; and when I have utterly confounded Jason's house I will leave the land, escaping punishment for my dear children's murder, after my most unholy deed. For I cannot endure the taunts of enemies, kind friends; enough! what gain is life to me? I have no country, home, or refuge left. O, I did wrong, that hour I left my father's home, persuaded by that Hellene's words, who now shall pay the penalty, so help me God. Never shall he see again alive the children I bore to him, nor from his new bride shall he beget issue, for she must die a hideous death, slain by my drugs. Let no one deem me a poor weak woman who sits with folded hands, but of another mould, dangerous to foes and well-disposed to friends; for they win the fairest fame who live their life like me.

Ch. Since thou hast imparted this design to me, I bid thee hold thy hand, both from a wish to serve thee and because I would uphold the laws man make.

Med. It cannot but be so; thy words I pardon since thou art not in the same sorry plight that I am.

Ch. O lady, wilt thou steel thyself to slay thy children twain?

Med. I will, for that will stab my husband to the heart.

Ch. It may, but thou wilt be the saddest wife alive.

Med. No matter; wasted is every word that comes 'twixt now and then. (*Enter* NURSE) Ho! thou, go call me Jason hither, for thee I do employ on every mission of trust. No word divulge of all my purpose, as thou art to thy mistress loyal and likewise of my sex.

Exeunt MEDEA *and* NURSE.

Ch. Sons of Erechtheus, heroes happy from of yore, children of the blessed gods, fed on wisdom's glorious food in a holy land ne'er pillaged by its foes, ye who move with sprightly step through a climate ever bright and clear, where, as legend tells, the Muses nine, Pieria's holy maids, were brought to birth by Harmonia with the golden hair; and poets sing how Cypris drawing water from the streams of fair-flowing Cephissus breathes o'er the land a gentle breeze of balmy winds, and ever as she crowns her tresses with a garland of sweet rose-buds sends forth the Loves to sit by wisdom's side, to take a part in every excellence. (*Re-enter* MEDEA) How then shall the city of sacred streams, the land that welcomes those it loves, receive thee, the murderess of thy children, thee whose presence with others is a pollution? Think on the murder of thy children, consider the bloody deed thou takest on thee. Nay, by thy knees we, one and all, implore thee, slay not thy babes. Where shall hand or heart find hardihood enough in wreaking such a fearsome deed upon thy sons? How wilt thou look upon thy babes, and still without a tear retain thy bloody purpose? Thou canst not, when they fall at thy feet for mercy, steel thy heart and dip in their blood thy hand.

Enter JASON.

Ja. I am come at thy bidding, for e'en though thy hate for me is bitter thou shalt not fail in this small boon, but I will hear what new request thou hast to make of me, lady.

Med. Jason, I crave thy pardon for the words I spoke, and well thou mayest brook my burst of passion, for ere now we twain have shared much love. For I have reasoned with my soul and railed upon me thus, "Ah! poor heart! why am I thus distraught, why so angered 'gainst all good advice, why have I come to hate the rulers of the land, my husband too, who does the best for me he can, in wedding with a princess and rearing for my children noble brothers? Shall I not cease to fret? What possesses me, when heaven its best doth offer? Have I not my children to consider? do I forget that we are fugitives, in need of friends?" When I had thought all this I saw how foolish I had been, how senselessly enraged. So now I do commend thee and think thee most wise in forming this connexion for us; but I was mad, I who should have shared in these designs, helped on thy plans, and lent my aid to bring about the match, only too pleased to wait upon thy bride. But what we are, we are, we women, evil I will not say; wherefore thou shouldst not sink to our sorry level nor with our weapons meet our childishness.

I yield and do confess that I was wrong then, but now have I come to a better mind. Come hither, my children, come, leave the house, step forth, and with me greet and bid farewell to your father, be reconciled from all past bitterness unto your friends, as now your mother is; for we have made a truce and anger is no more.

Enter the Children.

Take his right hand; ah me! my sad fate! when I reflect, as now, upon the hidden future. O my children, since there awaits you even thus a long, long life, stretch forth the hand to take a fond farewell. Ah me! how new to tears am I, how full of fear! For now that I have at last released me from my quarrel with your father, I let the tear-drops stream adown my tender cheek.

Ch. From my eyes too burst forth the copious tear; O, may no greater ill than the present e'er befall!

Ja. Lady, I praise this conduct, not that I blame what is past; for it is but natural to the female sex to vent their spleen against a husband when he trafficks in other marriages besides his own. But thy heart is changed to wiser schemes and thou art determined on the better course, late though it be; this is acting like a woman of sober sense. And for you, my sons, hath your father provided with all good heed a sure refuge, by God's grace; for ye, I trow, shall with your brothers share hereafter the foremost rank in this Corinthian realm. Only grow up, for all the rest your sire and whoso of the gods is kind to us is bringing to pass. May I see you reach man's full estate, high o'er the heads of those I hate! But thou, lady, why with fresh tears dost thou thine eyelids wet, turning away thy wan cheek, with no welcome for these my happy tidings?

Med. 'Tis naught; upon these children my thoughts were turned.

Ja. Then take heart; for I will see that it is well with them.

Med. I will do so; nor will I doubt thy word; woman is a weak creature, ever given to tears.

Ja. Why prithee, unhappy one, dost moan o'er these children?

Med. I gave them birth; and when thou didst pray long life for them, pity entered into my soul to think that these things must be. But the reason of thy coming hither to speak with me is partly told, the rest will I now mention. Since it is the pleasure of the rulers of the land to banish me, and well I know 'twere best for me to stand not in the way of thee or of the rulers by dwelling here, enemy as I am thought unto their house, forth from this land in exile am I going, but these children, that they may know thy fostering hand, beg Creon to remit their banishment.

Ja. I doubt whether I can persuade him, yet must I attempt it.

Med. At least do thou bid thy wife ask her sire this boon, to remit the exile of the children from this land.

Ja. Yea, that will I; and her methinks I shall persuade, since she is a woman like the rest.

Med. I too will aid thee in this task, for by the children's hand I will send to her gifts that far surpass in beauty, I well know, aught that now is seen 'mongst men, a robe of finest tissue and a chaplet of chased gold. But one of my attendants must haste and bring the ornaments hither. (*Maid goes*) Happy shall she be not once alone but ten thousandfold, for in thee she wins the noblest soul to share her love, and gets these gifts as well which on a day my father's sire, the Sun-god, bestowed on his descendants. (*Maid returns with casket*) My children, take in your hands these wedding gifts, and bear them as an offering to the royal maid, the happy bride; for verily the gifts she shall receive are not to be scorned.

Ja. But why so rashly rob thyself of these gifts? Dost think a royal palace wants for robes or gold? Keep them, nor give them to another. For well I know that if my lady hold me in esteem, she will set my price above all wealth.

Med. Say not so; 'tis said that gifts tempt even gods; and o'er men's minds gold holds more potent sway than countless words. Fortune smiles upon thy bride, and heaven now doth swell her triumph; youth is hers and princely power; yet to save my children from exile I would barter life, not dross alone. Children, when ye are come to the rich palace, pray your father's new bride, my mistress, with suppliant voice to save you from exile, offering her these ornaments the while; for it is most needful that she receive the gifts in her own hand. Now go and linger not; may ye succeed and to your mother bring back the glad tidings she fain would hear!

Exeunt JASON *with children.*

Ch. Gone, gone is every hope I had that the children yet might live; forth to their doom they now proceed. The hapless bride will take, ay, take the golden crown that is to be her ruin; with her own hand will she lift and place upon her golden locks the garniture of death. Its grace and sheen divine will tempt her to put on the robe and crown of gold, and in that act will she deck herself to be a bride amid the dead. Such is the snare whereinto she will fall, such is the deadly doom that waits the hapless maid, nor shall she from the curse escape. And thou, poor wretch, who to thy sorrow art wedding a king's daughter, little thinkest of the doom thou art bringing on thy children's life, or of the cruel death that waits thy bride.

Woe is thee! how art thou fallen from thy high estate!

Next do I bewail thy sorrows, O mother hapless in thy children, thou who wilt slay thy babes because thou hast a rival, the babes thy husband hath deserted impiously to join him to another bride.

Enter ATTENDANT *with children.*

At. Thy children, lady, are from exile freed, and gladly did the royal bride accept thy gifts in her own hands, and so thy children made their peace with her.

Med. Ah!

At. Why art so disquieted in thy prosperous hour? Why turnest thou thy cheek away, and hast no welcome for my glad news?

Med. Ah me!

At. These groans but ill accord with the news I bring.

Med. Ah me! once more I say.

At. Have I unwittingly announced some evil tidings? Have I erred in thinking my news was good?

Med. Thy news is as it is; I blame thee not.

At. Then why this downcast eye, these floods of tears?

Med. Old friend, needs must I weep; for the gods and I with fell intent devised these schemes.

At. Be of good cheer; thou too of a surety shalt by thy sons yet be brought home again.

Med. Ere that shall I bring others to their home, ah! woe is me!

At. Thou art not the only mother from thy children reft. Bear patiently thy troubles as a mortal must.

Med. I will obey; go thou within the house and make the day's provision for the children. (*Exit* ATTENDANT) O my babes, my babes, ye have still a city and a home, where far from me and my sad lot you will live your lives, reft of your mother for ever; while I must to another land in banishment, or ever I have had my joy of you, or lived to see you happy, or ever I have graced your marriage couch, your bride, your bridal bower, or lifted high the wedding torch. Ah me! a victim of my own self-will. So it was all in vain I reared you, O my sons; in vain did suffer, racked with anguish, enduring the cruel pangs of childbirth. 'Fore Heaven I once had hope, poor me! high hope of ye that you would nurse me in my age and deck my corpse with loving hands, a boon we mortals covet; but now is my sweet fancy dead and gone; for I must lose you both and in bitterness and sorrow drag through life. And ye shall never with fond eyes see your mother more, for o'er your life there comes a change. Ah me! ah me! why do ye look at me so, my children? why smile that last sweet smile? Ah me! what am I to do? My heart gives way when I behold my children's laughing eyes. O, I cannot; farewell to all my former schemes; I will take the children from the land, the babes I bore. Why should I wound their sire by wounding them, and get me a twofold measure of sorrow? No, no, I will not do it. Farewell my scheming! And yet what am I coming to? Can I consent to let those foes of mine escape from punishment, and incur their mockery? I must face this deed. Out upon my craven heart! to think that I should even have let the soft words escape my soul. Into the house, children! (*Exeunt Children*) And whoso feels he must not be present at my sacrifice, must see to it himself; I will not spoil my handiwork. Ah! ah! do not, my heart, O do not do this deed! Let the children go, unhappy one, spare the babes! For if they live, they will cheer thee in our exile there.[1] Nay, by the fiends of hell's abyss, never, never will I hand my children over to their foes to mock and flout. Die they must in any case, and since 'tis so, why I, the mother who bore them, will give the fatal blow. In any case their doom is fixed and there is no escape. Already the crown is on her head, the robe is round her, and she is dying, the royal bride; that do I know full well. But now since I have a piteous path to tread, and yet more piteous still the path I send my children on, fain would I say farewell to them. (*Re-enter Children*) O my babes, my babes, let your mother kiss your hands. Ah! hands I love so well, O lips most dear to me! O noble form and features of my children, I wish ye joy, but in that other land, for here your father robs you of your home. O the sweet embrace, the soft young cheek, the fragrant breath! my children! Go, leave me; I cannot bear to longer look upon ye; my sorrow wins the day. (*Exeunt Children*) At last I understand the awful deed I am to do; but passion, that cause of direst woes to mortal man, hath triumphed o'er my sober thoughts.

Ch. Oft ere now have I pursued subtler themes and have faced graver issues than woman's sex should seek to probe; but then e'en we aspire to culture, which dwells with us to teach us wisdom; I say not all; for small is the class amongst women—(one maybe shalt thou find 'mid many)—that is not incapable of culture. And amongst mortals I do assert that they who are wholly without experience and have never had children far surpass in happiness those who are parents. The childless, because they have never proved whether children grow up to be a blessing or curse to men are removed from all share in many troubles; whilst those who have a sweet race of children growing up in their houses do wear away, as I perceive, their whole life through; first with the thought how they may train them up in virtue, next how they shall leave their sons the means to live; and after all this 'tis far from clear whether on good or bad children they bestow their toil. But one last crowning woe for every mortal man I now will name; suppose that they have found sufficient means to live, and seen their children grow to man's estate and walk in virtue's path, still if fortune so befall, comes Death and bears the children's bodies off to Hades. Can it be any profit to the gods to heap upon us mortal men beside our other woes this further grief for children lost, a grief surpassing all?

Med. Kind friends, long have I waited expectantly to know how things would at the palace chance. And lo! I see one of Jason's servants coming hither, whose hurried gasps for breath proclaim him the bearer of some fresh tidings. *Enter* MESSENGER.

Messenger. Fly, fly, Medea! who hast wrought an awful deed, transgressing every law; nor leave behind or sea-borne bark or car that scours the plain.

Med. Why, what hath chanced that calls for such a flight of mine?

Mes. The princess is dead, a moment gone, and Creon too, her sire, slain by those drugs of thine.

Med. Tidings most fair are thine! Henceforth shalt thou be ranked amongst my friends and benefactors.

Mes. Ha! What? Art sane? Art not distraught, lady, who hearest with joy the outrage to our royal house done, and art not at the horrid tale afraid?

Med. Somewhat have I, too, to say in answer to thy words. Be not so hasty, friend, but tell the manner of their death, for thou wouldst give me double joy, if so they perished miserably.

Mes. When the children twain whom thou didst bear came with their father and entered the palace of the bride, right glad were we thralls who had shared thy griefs, for instantly from ear to ear a rumour spread that thou and thy lord had made up your former quarrel. One kissed thy children's hands, another their golden hair, while I for very joy went with them in person to the women's chambers. Our mistress, whom now we do revere in thy room, cast a longing glance at Jason, ere she saw thy children twain; but then she veiled her eyes and turned her blanching cheek away, disgusted at their coming; but thy husband tried to check his young bride's angry humour with these words. "O, be not angered 'gainst thy friends; cease from wrath and turn once more thy face this way, counting as friends whomso thy husband counts, and accept these gifts, and for my sake crave thy sire to remit these children's exile." Soon as she saw the ornaments, no longer she held out, but yielded to her lord in all; and ere the father and his sons were far from the palace gone, she took the broidered robe and put it on, and set the golden crown about her tresses, arranging her hair at her bright mirror, with many a happy smile at her breathless counterfeit. Then rising from her seat she passed across the chamber, tripping lightly on her fair white foot, exulting in the gift, with many a glance at her uplifted ankle. When lo! a

[1]At Athens.

scene of awful horror did ensue. In a moment she turned pale, reeled backwards, trembling in every limb, and sinks upon a seat scarce soon enough to save herself from falling to the ground. An aged dame, one of her company, thinking belike it was a fit from Pan or some god sent, raised a cry of prayer, till from her mouth she saw the foam-flakes issue, her eyeballs rolling in their sockets, and all the blood her face desert; then did she raise a loud scream far different from her former cry. Forthwith one handmaid rushed to her father's house, another to her new bridegroom to tell his bride's sad fate, and the whole house echoed with their running to and fro. By this time would a quick walker have made the turn in a course of six plethra and reached the goal, when she with one awful shriek awoke, poor sufferer, from her speechless trance and oped her closed eyes, for against her a twofold anguish was warring. The chaplet of gold about her head was sending forth a wondrous stream of ravening flame, while the fine raiment, thy children's gift, was preying on the hapless maiden's fair white flesh; and she starts from her seat in a blaze and seeks to fly, shaking her hair and head this way and that, to cast the crown therefrom, but the gold held firm to its fastenings, and the flame, as she shook her locks, blazed forth the more with double fury. Then to the earth she sinks, by the cruel blow o'ercome, past all recognition now save to a father's eye; for her eyes had lost their tranquil gaze, her face no more its natural look preserved, and from the crown of her head blood and fire in mingled stream ran down; and from her bones the flesh kept peeling off beneath the gnawing of those secret drugs, e'en as when the pine tree weeps its tears of pitch, a fearsome sight to see. And all were afraid to touch the corpse, for we were warned by what had chanced. Anon came her hapless father unto the house, all unwitting of her doom, and stumbles o'er the dead, and loud he cried, and folding his arms about her kissed her, with words like these the while, "O my poor, poor child, which of the gods hath destroyed thee thus foully? Who is robbing me of thee, old as I am and ripe for death? O my child, alas! would I could die with thee!" He ceased his sad lament, and would have raised his aged frame, but found himself held fast by the finespun robe as ivy that clings to the branches of the bay, and then ensued a fearful struggle. He strove to rise, but she still held him back; and if ever he pulled with all his might, from off his bones his aged flesh he tore. At last he gave it up, and breathed forth his soul in awful suffering; for he could no longer master the pain. So there they lie, daughter and aged sire, dead side by side, a grievous sight that calls for tears. And as for thee, I leave thee out of my consideration, for thyself must discover a means to escape punishment. Not now for the first time I think this human life a shadow; yea, and without shrinking I will say that they amongst men who pretend to wisdom and expend deep thought on words do incur a serious charge of folly; for amongst mortals no man is happy; wealth may pour in and make one luckier than another, but none can happy be. *Exit.*

Ch. This day the deity, it seems, will mass on Jason, as he well deserves, a heavy load of evils. Woe is thee, daughter of Creon! We pity thy sad fate, gone as thou art to Hades' halls as the price of thy marriage with Jason.

Med. My friends, I am resolved upon the deed; at once will I slay my children and then leave this land, without delaying long enough to hand them over to some more savage hand to butcher. Needs must they die in any case; and since they must, I will slay them—I, the mother that bare them. O heart of mine, steel thyself! Why do I hesitate to do the awful deed that must be done? Come, take the sword, thou wretched hand of mine! Take it, and advance to the post whence starts thy life of sorrow! Away with cowardice! Give not one thought to thy babes, how dear they are or how thou art their mother. This one brief day forget thy children dear, and after that lament; for though thou wilt slay them yet they were thy darlings still, and I am a lady of sorrows. *Exit.*

Ch. O earth, O sun whose beam illumines all, look, look upon this lost woman, ere she stretch forth her murderous hand upon her sons for blood; for lo! these are scions of thy own golden seed, and the blood of gods is in danger of being shed by man. O light, from Zeus proceeding, stay her, hold her hand, forth from the house chase this fell bloody fiend by demons led. Vainly wasted were the throes thy children cost thee; vainly hast thou born, it seems, sweet babes, O thou who hast left behind thee that passage through the blue Symplegades, that strangers justly hate. Ah! hapless one, why doth fierce anger thy soul assail? Why in its place is fell murder growing up? For grievous unto mortal men are pollutions that come of kindred blood poured on the earth, woes to suit each crime hurled from heaven on the murderer's house.

1st Son (*Within*) Ah, me; what can I do? Whither fly to escape my mother's blows?

2nd Son (*Within*) I know not, sweet brother mine; we are undone.

Ch. Didst hear, didst hear the children's cry? O lady, born to sorrow, victim of an evil fate! Shall I enter the house? For the children's sake I am resolved to ward off the murder.

1st Son (*Within*) Yea, by heaven I adjure you; help, your aid is needed.

2nd Son (*Within*) Even now the toils of the sword are closing round us.

Ch. O hapless mother, surely thou hast a heart of stone or steel to slay the offspring of thy womb by such a murderous doom. Of all the wives of yore I know but one who laid her hand upon her children dear, even Ino, whom the gods did madden in the day that the wife of Zeus drove her wandering from her home. But she, poor sufferer, flung herself into the sea because of the foul murder of her children, leaping o'er the wave-beat cliff, and in her death was she united to her children twain. Can there be any deed of horror left to follow this? Woe for the wooing of women fraught with disaster! What sorrows hast thou caused for men ere now!

Enter JASON.

Ja. Ladies, stationed near this house, pray tell me is the author of these hideous deeds, Medea, still within, or hath she fled from hence? For she must hide beneath the earth or soar on wings towards heaven's vault, if she would avoid the vengeance of the royal house. Is she so sure she will escape herself unpunished from this house, when she hath slain the rulers of the land? But enough of this! I am forgetting her children. As for her, those whom she hath wronged will do the like by her; but I am come to save the children's life, lest the victim's kin visit their wrath on me, in vengeance for the murder foul, wrought by my children's mother.

Ch. Unhappy man, thou knowest not the full extent of thy misery, else had thou never said those words.

Ja. How now? Can she want to kill me too?

Ch. Thy sons are dead; slain by their own mother's hand.

Ja. O God! what sayest thou? Woman, thou hast sealed my doom.

Ch. Thy children are no more; be sure of this.

Ja. Where slew she them; within the palace or outside?

Ch. Throw wide the doors and see thy children's murdered corpses.

Ja. Haste, ye slaves, loose the bolts, undo the fastenings, that I may see the sight of twofold woe, my murdered sons and her, whose blood in vengeance I will shed.

MEDEA *in mid air, on a chariot drawn by dragons; the children's corpses by her.*

Med. Why shake those doors and attempt to loose their bolts, in quest of the dead and me their murderess? From such toil desist. If thou wouldst aught with me, say on, if so thou wilt; but never shalt thou lay hand on me, so swift the steeds the sun, my father's sire, to me doth give to save me from the hand of my foes.

Ja. Accursed woman! by gods, by me and all mankind abhorred as never woman was, who hadst the heart to stab thy babes, thou their mother, leaving me undone and childless; this hast thou done and still dost gaze upon the sun and earth after this deed most impious. Curses on thee! I now perceive what then I missed in the day I brought thee, fraught with doom, from thy home in a barbarian land to dwell in Hellas, traitress to thy sire and to the land that nurtured thee. On me the gods have hurled the curse that dogged thy steps, for thou didst slay thy brother at his hearth ere thou cam'st aboard our fair ship "Argo." Such was the outset of thy life of crime; then didst thou wed with me, and having borne me sons to glut thy passion's lust, thou now hast slain them. Not one amongst the wives of Hellas e'er had dared this deed; yet before them all I chose thee for my wife, wedding a foe to be my doom, no woman, but a lioness fiercer than Tyrrhene Scylla in nature. But with reproaches heaped a thousandfold I cannot wound thee, so brazen is thy nature. Perish, vile sorceress, murderess of thy babes! Whilst I must mourn my luckless fate, for I shall ne'er enjoy my new-found bride, nor shall I have the children, whom I bred and reared, alive to say the last farewell to me; nay, I have lost them.

Med. To this thy speech I could have made a long retort, but Father Zeus knows well all I have done for thee, and the treatment thou hast given me. Yet thou wert not ordained to scorn my love and lead a life of joy in mockery of me, nor was thy royal bride nor Creon, who gave thee a second wife, to thrust me from this land and rue it not. Wherefore, if thou wilt, call me e'en a lioness, and Scylla, whose home is in the Tyrrhene land; for I in turn have wrung thy heart, as well I might.

Ja. Thou, too, art grieved thyself, and sharest in my sorrow.

Med. Be well assured I am; but it relieves my pain to know thou canst not mock at me.

Ja. O my children, how vile a mother ye have found!

Med. My sons, your father's feeble lust has been your ruin!

Ja. 'Twas not my hand, at any rate, that slew them.

Med. No, but thy foul treatment of me, and thy new marriage.

Ja. Didst think that marriage cause enough to murder them?

Med. Dost think a woman counts this a trifling injury?

Ja. So she be self-restrained; but in thy eyes all is evil.

Med. Thy sons are dead and gone. That will stab thy heart.

Ja. They live, methinks, to bring a curse upon thy head.

Med. The gods know, whoso of them began this troublous coil.

Ja. Indeed, they know that hateful heart of thine.

Med. Thou art as hateful. I am aweary of thy bitter tongue.

Ja. And I likewise of thine. But parting is easy.

Med. Say how; what am I to do? for I am fain as thou to go.

Ja. Give up to me those dead, to bury and lament.

Med. No, never! I will bury them myself, bearing them to Hera's sacred field, who watches o'er the Cape, that none of their foes may insult them by pulling down their tombs; and in this land of Sisyphus I will ordain hereafter a solemn feast and mystic rites to atone for this impious murder. Myself will now to the land of Erechtheus, to dwell with Ægeus, Pandion's son. But thou, as well thou mayest, shalt die a caitiff's death, thy head crushed 'neath a shattered relic of Argo, when thou hast seen the bitter ending of my marriage.

Ja. The curse of our sons' avenging spirit and of Justice, that calls for blood, be on thee!

Med. What god or power divine hears thee, breaker of oaths and every law of hospitality?

Ja. Fie upon thee! cursed witch! child-murderess!

Med. To thy house! go, bury thy wife.

Ja. I go, bereft of both my sons.

Med. Thy grief is yet to come; wait till old age is with thee too.

Ja. O my dear, dear children!

Med. Dear to their mother, not to thee.

Ja. And yet thou didst slay them?

Med. Yea, to vex thy heart.

Ja. One last fond kiss, ah me! I fain would on their lips imprint.

Med. Embraces now, and fond farewells for them; but then a cold repulse!

Ja. By heaven I do adjure thee, let me touch their tender skin.

Med. No, no! in vain this word has sped its flight.

Ja. O Zeus, dost hear how I am driven hence; dost mark the treatment I receive from this she-lion, fell murderess of her young? Yet so far as I may and can, I raise for them a dirge, and do adjure the gods to witness how thou hast slain my sons, and wilt not suffer me to embrace or bury their dead bodies. Would I had never begotten them to see thee slay them after all!

Ch. Many a fate doth Zeus dispense, high on his Olympian throne; oft do the gods bring things to pass beyond man's expectation; that, which we thought would be, is not fulfilled, while for the unlooked-for god finds out a way; and such hath been the issue of this matter.

Exeunt OMNES.

HIPPOLYTUS

DRAMATIS PERSONAE

APHRODITE	PHAEDRA
HIPPOLYTUS	THESEUS
ATTENDANTS OF HIPPOLYTUS	FIRST MESSENGER
CHORUS OF TROEZENIAN WOMEN	SECOND MESSENGER
NURSE OF PHAEDRA	ARTEMIS

Before the palace of Pittheus at Trœzen. Enter APHRODITE.

Aphrodite. Wide o'er man my realm extends, and proud the name that I, the goddess Cypris, bear, both in heaven's courts and 'mongst all those who dwell within the limits of the sea[1] and the bounds of Atlas, beholding the son-god's light; those that respect my power I advance to honour, but bring to ruin all who vaunt themselves at me. For even in the race of gods this feeling finds a home, even pleasure at the honour men pay them. And the truth of this I soon will show; for that son of Theseus, born of the Amazon, Hippolytus, whom holy Pittheus taught, alone of all the dwellers in this land of Trœzen, calls me vilest of the deities. Love he scorns, and, as for marriage, will none of it; but Artemis, daughter of Zeus, sister of Phœbus, he doth honour, counting her the chief of goddesses, and ever through the greenwood, attendant on his virgin goddess, he clears the earth of wild beasts with his fleet hounds, enjoying the comradeship of one too high for mortal ken. 'Tis not this I grudge him, no! why should I? But for his sins against me, I will this very day take vengeance on Hippolytus; for long ago I cleared the ground of many obstacles, so it needs but trifling toil. For as he came one day from the home of Pittheus to witness the solemn mystic rites and be initiated therein in Pandion's land,[2] Phædra, his father's noble wife, caught sight of him, and by my designs she found her heart was seized with wild desire. And ere she came to this Trœzenian realm, a temple did she rear to Cypris hard by the rock of Pallas where it o'erlooks this country, for love of the youth in another land; and to win his love in days to come she called after his name the temple she had founded for the goddess. Now, when Theseus left the land of Cecrops, flying the pollution of the blood of Pallas'[3] sons, and with his wife sailed to this shore, content to suffer exile for a year, then began the wretched wife to pine away in silence, moaning 'neath love's cruel scourge, and none of her servants knows what ails her. But this passion of hers must not fail thus. No, I will discover the matter to Theseus, and all shall be laid bare. Then will the father slay his child, my bitter foe, by curses, for the lord Poseidon granted this boon to Theseus; three wishes of the god to ask, nor ever ask in vain. So Phædra is to die, an honoured death 'tis true, but still to die; for I will not let her suffering outweigh the payment of such forfeit by my foes as shall satisfy my honour. But lo! I see the son of Theseus coming hither—Hippolytus, fresh from the labours of the chase. I will get me hence. At his back follows a long train of retainers, in joyous cries of revelry uniting and hymns of praise to Artemis, his goddess; for little he recks that Death hath oped his gates for him, and that this is his last look upon the light.

Enter HIPPOLYTUS *and* ATTENDANT.

Hippolytus. Come follow, friends, singing to Artemis, daughter of Zeus, throned in the sky, whose votaries we are.

Attendant. Lady goddess, awful queen, daughter of Zeus, all hail! hail! child of Latona and of Zeus, peerless mid the virgin choir, who hast thy dwelling in heaven's wide mansions at thy noble father's court, in the golden house of Zeus.

Hi. All hail! most beauteous Artemis, lovelier far than all the daughters of Olympus! For thee, O mistress mine, I bring this woven wreath, culled from a virgin meadow, where nor shepherd dares to herd his flock nor ever scythe hath mown, but o'er the mead unshorn the bee doth wing its way in spring; and with the dew from rivers drawn purity that garden tends. Such as know no cunning lore, yet in whose nature self-control, made perfect, hath a home, these may pluck the flowers, but not the wicked world. Accept, I pray, dear mistress, mine this chaplet from my holy hand to crown thy locks of gold; for I, and none other of mortals, have this high guerdon, to be with thee, with thee converse, hearing thy voice, though not thy face beholding. So be it mine to end my life as I began.

At. My prince! we needs must call upon the gods, our lords, so wilt thou listen to a friendly word from me?

Hi. Why, that will I! else were I proved a fool.

At. Dost know, then, the way of the world?

Hi. Not I; but wherefore such a question?

At. It hates reserve which careth not for all men's love.

[1] *i.e.* the Euxine.

[2] *i.e.* Attica.

[3] Descendants of Pandion, king of Cecropia, slain by Theseus to obtain the kingdom.

Hi. And rightly too; reserve in man is ever galling.

At. But there's a charm in courteous affability?

Hi. The greatest surely; aye, and profit, too, at trifling cost.

At. Dost think the same law holds in heaven as well?

Hi. I trow it doth, since all our laws we men from heaven draw.

At. Why, then, dost thou neglect to greet an august goddess?

Hi. Whom speak'st thou of? Keep watch upon thy tongue lest it some mischief cause.

At. Cypris I mean, whose image is stationed o'er thy gate.

Hi. I greet her from afar, preserving still my chastity.

At. Yet is she an august goddess, far renowned on earth.

Hi. 'Mongst gods as well as men we have our several preferences.

At. I wish thee luck, and wisdom too, so far as thou dost need it.

Hi. No god, whose worship craves the night, hath charms for me.

At. My son, we should avail us of the gifts that gods confer.

Hi. Go in, my faithful followers, and make ready food within the house; a well-filled board hath charms after the chase is o'er. Rub down my steeds ye must, that when I have had my fill I may yoke them to the chariot and give them proper exercise. As for thy Queen of Love, a long farewell to her.

Exit HIPPOLYTUS.

At. Meantime I with sober mind, for I must not copy my young master, do offer up my prayer to thy image, lady Cypris, in such words as it becomes a slave to use. But thou should'st pardon all, who, in youth's impetuous heat, speak idle words of thee; make as though thou hearest not, for gods must needs be wiser than the sons of men. *Exit.*

Enter CHORUS OF TRŒZENIAN WOMEN.

Chorus. A rock there is, where, as they say, the ocean dew distils, and from its beetling brow it pours a copious stream for pitchers to be dipped therein; 'twas here I had a friend washing robes of purple in the trickling stream, and she was spreading them out on the face of a warm sunny rock; from her I had the tidings, first of all, that my mistress was wasting on the bed of sickness, pent within her house, a thin veil o'ershadowing her head of golden hair. And this is the third day I hear that she hath closed her lovely lips and denied her chaste body all sustenance, eager to hide her suffering and reach death's cheerless bourn. Maiden, thou must be possessed, by Pan made frantic or by Hecate, or by the Corybantes dread, and Cybele the mountain mother. Or maybe thou hast sinned against Dictynna, huntress-queen, and art wasting for thy guilt in sacrifice unoffered. For she doth range o'er lakes' expanse and past the bounds of earth upon the ocean's tossing billows. Or doth some rival in thy house beguile thy lord, the captain of Erechtheus' sons, that hero nobly born, to secret amours hid from thee? Or hath some mariner sailing hither from Crete reached this port that sailors love, with evil tidings for our queen, and she with sorrow for her grievous fate is to her bed confined? Yea, and oft o'er woman's wayward nature settles a feeling of miserable perplexity, arising from labour-pains or passionate desire. I, too, have felt at times this sharp thrill shoot through me, but I would cry to Artemis, queen of archery, who comes from heaven to aid us in our travail, and thanks to heaven's grace she ever comes at my call with welcome help. Look! where the aged nurse is bringing her forth from the house before the door, while on her brow the cloud of gloom is deepening. My soul longs to learn what is her grief, the canker that is wasting our queen's fading charms.

Enter PHAEDRA *and* NURSE.

Nurse. O, the ills of mortal men! the cruel diseases they endure! What can I do for thee? from what refrain? Here is the bright sun-light, here the azure sky; lo! we have brought thee on thy bed of sickness without the palace; for all thy talk was of coming hither, but soon back to thy chamber wilt thou hurry. Disappointment follows fast with thee, thou hast no joy in aught for long; the present has no power to please; on something absent next thy heart is set. Better be sick than tend the sick; the first is but a single ill, the last unites mental grief with manual toil. Man's whole life is full of anguish; no respite from his woes he finds; but if there is aught to love beyond this life, night's dark pall doth wrap it round. And so we show our mad love of this life because its light is shed on earth, and because we know no other, and have naught revealed to us of all our earth may hide; and trusting to fables we drift at random.

Phædra. Lift my body, raise my head! My limbs are all unstrung, kind friends. O handmaids, lift my arms, my shapely arms. The tire on my head is too heavy for me to wear; away with it, and let my tresses o'er my shoulders fall.

Nu. Be of good heart, dear child; toss not so wildly to and fro. Lie still, be brave, so wilt thou find thy sickness easier to bear; suffering for mortals is nature's iron law.

Ph. Ah! would I could draw a draught of water pure from some dew-fed spring, and lay me down to rest in the grassy meadow 'neath the poplar's shade!

Nu. My child, what wild speech is this? O say not such things in public, wild whirling words of frenzy bred!

Ph. Away to the mountain take me! to the wood, to the pine-trees I will go, where hounds pursue the prey, hard on the scent of dappled fawns. Ye gods! what joy to hark them on, to grasp the barbed dart, to poise Thessalian hunting-spears close to my golden hair, then let them fly.

Nu. Why, why, my child, these anxious cares? What hast thou to do with the chase? Why so eager for the flowing spring, when hard by these towers stands a hill well watered, whence thou may'st freely draw?

Ph. O Artemis, who watchest o'er sea-beat Limna[1] and the race-course thundering to the horse's hoofs, would I were upon thy plains curbing Venetian steeds!

Nu. Why betray thy frenzy in these wild whirling words? Now thou wert for hasting hence to the hills away to hunt wild beasts, and now thy yearning is to drive the steed over the waveless sands. This needs a cunning seer to say what god it is that reins thee from the course, distracting thy senses, child.

Ph. Ah me! alas! what have I done? Whither have I strayed, my senses leaving? Mad, mad! stricken by some demon's curse! Woe is me! Cover my head again, nurse. Shame fills me for the words I have spoken. Hide me then; from my eyes the tear-drops stream, and for very shame I turn them away. 'Tis painful coming to one's senses again, and madness, evil though it be, has this advantage, that one has no knowledge of reason's over-throw.

Nu. There then I cover thee; but when will death hide my body in the grave? Many a lesson length of days is teaching me. Yea, mortal men should pledge themselves to moderate friendships only, not to such as reach the very heart's core; affection's ties should be light upon them to let them slip or draw them tight. For one poor heart to grieve for twain, as I do for my mistress, is a burden sore to bear. Men say that too engrossing pursuits in life more oft cause disappointment than pleasure, and too oft are foes to health. Wherefore I do not praise excess so much as moderation, and with me wise men will agree.

Ch. O aged dame, faithful nurse of Phædra, our queen, we see her sorry plight; but what it is that ails her we cannot discern, so fain would learn of thee and hear thy opinion.

Nu. I question her, but am no wiser, for she will not answer.

Ch. Nor tell what source these sorrows have?

Nu. The same answer thou must take, for she is dumb on every point.

Ch. How weak and wasted is her body!

Nu. What marvel? 'tis three days now since she has tasted food.

Ch. Is this infatuation, or an attempt to die?

Nu. 'Tis death she courts; such fasting aims at ending life.

Ch. A strange story! is her husband satisfied?

Nu. She hides from him her sorrow, and vows she is not ill.

Ch. Can he not guess it from her face?

Nu. He is not now in his own country.

Ch. But dost thou insist in thy endeavour to find out her complaint, her crazy mind?

Nu. I have tried every plan, and all in vain; yet not even now will I relax my zeal, that thou too, if thou stayest, mayst witness my devotion to my unhappy mistress. Come, come, my darling child, let us forget, the twain of us, our former words; be thou more mild, smoothing that sullen brow and changing the current of thy thought, and I, if in aught before I failed in humouring thee, will let that be and find some better course. If thou art sick with ills thou canst not name, there be women here to help to set thee right; but if thy trouble can to men's ears be divulged, speak, that physicians may pronounce on it. Come, then, why so dumb? Thou shouldst not so remain, my child, but scold me if I speak amiss, or, if I give good counsel, yield assent. One word, one look this way! Ah me! Friends, we waste our toil to no purpose; we are as far away as ever; she would not relent to my arguments then, nor is she yielding now. Well, grow more stubborn than the sea, yet be assured of this, that if thou diest thou art a traitress to thy children, for they will ne'er inherit their father's halls, nay, by that knightly queen the Amazon who bore a son to lord it over thine, a bastard born but not a bastard bred, whom well thou knowest, e'en Hippolytus.

Ph. Oh! oh!

Nu. Ha! doth that touch the quick?

Ph. Thou hast undone me, nurse; I do adjure by the gods, mention that man no more.

Nu. There now! thou art thyself again, but e'en yet refusest to aid thy children and preserve thy life.

Ph. My babes I love, but there is another storm that buffets me.

Nu. Daughter, are thy hands from bloodshed pure?

Ph. My hands are pure, but on my soul there rests a stain.

Nu. The issue of some enemy's secret witchery?

Ph. A friend is my destroyer, one unwilling as myself.

Nu. Hath Theseus wronged thee in any wise?

Ph. Never may I prove untrue to him!

Nu. Then what strange mystery is there that drives thee on to die?

Ph. O, let my sin and me alone! 'tis not 'gainst thee I sin.

Nu. Never willingly! and, if I fail, 'twill rest at thy door.

Ph. How now? thou usest force in clinging to my hand.

Nu. Yea, and I will never loose my hold upon thy knees.

Ph. Alas for thee! my sorrows, shouldst thou learn them, would recoil on thee.

Nu. What keener grief for me than failing to win thee?

Ph. 'Twill be death to thee; though to me that brings renown.

Nu. And dost thou then conceal this boon despite my prayers?

Ph. I do, for 'tis out of shame I am planning an honourable escape.

Nu. Tell it, and thine honour shall the brighter shine.

Ph. Away, I do conjure thee; loose my hand.

Nu. I will not, for the boon thou shouldst have granted me is denied.

[1] A sea-coast town of Trœzen.

Ph. I will grant it out of reverence for thy holy suppliant touch.

Nu. Henceforth I hold my peace; 'tis thine to speak from now.

Ph. Ah! hapless mother,[1] what a love was thine!

Nu. Her love for the bull? daughter, or what meanest thou?

Ph. And woe to thee! my sister,[2] bride of Dionysus.

Nu. What ails thee, child? speaking ill of kith and kin.

Ph. Myself the third to suffer! how am I undone!

Nu. Thou strik'st me dumb! Where will this history end?

Ph. That "love" has been our curse from time long past.

Nu. I know no more of what I fain would learn.

Ph. Ah! would thou couldst say for me what I have to tell.

Nu. I am no prophetess to unriddle secrets.

Ph. What is it they mean when they talk of people being in "love"?

Nu. At once the sweetest and the bitterest thing, my child.

Ph. I shall only find the latter half.

Nu. Ha! my child, art thou in love?

Ph. The Amazon's son, whoever he may be—

Nu. Mean'st thou Hippolytus?

Ph. 'Twas thou, not I, that spoke his name.

Nu. O heavens! what is this, my child? Thou hast ruined me. Outrageous! friends; I will not live and bear it; hateful is life, hateful to mine eyes the light. This body I resign, will cast it off, and rid me of existence by my death. Farewell, my life is o'er. Yea, for the chaste have wicked passions, 'gainst their will maybe, but still they have. Cypris, it seems, is not a goddess after all, but something greater far, for she hath been the ruin of my lady and of me and our whole family.

Ch. O, too clearly didst thou hear our queen uplift her voice to tell her startling tale of piteous suffering. Come death ere I reach thy state of feeling,[3] loved mistress. O horrible! woe, for these miseries! woe, for the sorrows on which mortals feed! Thou art undone! thou hast disclosed thy sin to heaven's light. What hath each passing day and every hour in store for thee? Some strange event will come to pass in this house. For it is no longer uncertain where the star of thy love is setting, thou hapless daughter of Crete.

Ph. Ladies of Trœzen, who dwell here upon the frontier edge of Pelops' land, oft ere now in heedless mood through the long hours of night have I wondered why man's life is spoiled; and it seems to me their evil case is not due to any natural fault of judgment, for there be many dowered with sense, but we must view the matter in this light; by teaching and experience we learn the right but neglect it in practice, some from sloth, others from preferring pleasure of some kind or other to duty. Now life has many pleasures, protracted talk, and leisure, that seductive evil; likewise there is shame which is of two kinds, one a noble quality, the other a curse to families; but if for each its proper time were clearly known, these twain could not have had the selfsame letters to denote them. So then since I had made up my mind on these points, 'twas not likely any drug would alter it and make me think the contrary. And I will tell thee too the way my judgment went. When love wounded me, I bethought me how I best might bear the smart. So from that day forth I began to hide in silence what I suffered. For I put no faith in counsellors, who know well to lecture others for presumption, yet themselves have countless troubles of their own. Next I did devise noble endurance of these wanton thoughts, striving by continence for victory. And last when I could not succeed in mastering love hereby, methought it best to die; and none can gainsay my purpose. For fain I would my virtue should to all appear, my shame have few to witness it. I knew my sickly passion now; to yield to it I saw how infamous; and more, I learnt to know so well that I was but a woman, a thing the world detests. Curses, hideous curses on that wife, who first did shame her marriage-vow for lovers other than her lord! 'Twas from noble families this curse began to spread among our sex. For when the noble countenance disgrace, poor folk of course will think that it is right. Those too I hate who make profession of purity, though in secret reckless sinners. How can these, queen Cypris, ocean's child, e'er look their husbands in the face? do they never feel one guilty thrill that their accomplice, night, or the chambers of their house will find a voice and speak? This it is that calls on me to die, kind friends, that so I may ne'er be found to have disgraced my lord, or the children I have born; no! may they grow up and dwell in glorious Athens, free to speak and act, heirs to such fair fame as a mother can bequeath. For to know that father or mother have sinned doth turn the stoutest heart to slavishness. This alone, men say, can stand the buffets of life's battle, a just and virtuous soul in whomsoever found. For time unmasks the villain sooner or later, holding up to them a mirror as to some blooming maid. 'Mongst such may I be never seen!

Ch. Now look! how fair is chastity however viewed whose fruit is good repute amongst men.

Nu. My queen, 'tis true thy tale of woe, but lately told, did for the moment strike me with wild alarm, but now I do reflect upon my foolishness; second thoughts are often best even with men. Thy fate is no uncommon one nor past one's calculations; thou art stricken by the passion Cypris sends. Thou art in love; what wonder? so are many more. Wilt thou, because thou lov'st, destroy thyself? 'Tis little gain, I trow, for those who love or yet may love their fellows, if death must be their end; for though the Love-Queen's onset in her might is more than man can bear, yet doth she gently visit yielding hearts,

[1] Pasiphæ, wife of Minos, deceived by Aphrodite into a fatal passion for a bull. Cf. Virgil, *Æneid* vi.

[2] Ariadne.

[3] *Or* "before thou accomplish thy purpose."

and only when she finds a proud unnatural spirit, doth she take and mock it past belief. Her path is in the sky, and mid the ocean's surge she rides; from her all nature springs; she sows the seeds of love, inspires the warm desire to which we sons of earth all owe our being. They who have aught to do with books of ancient scribes, or themselves engage in studious pursuits, know how Zeus of Semele was enamoured, how the bright-eyed goddess of the Dawn once stole Cephalus to dwell in heaven for the love she bore him; yet these in heaven abide nor shun the gods' approach, content, I trow, to yield to their misfortune. Wilt thou refuse to yield? thy sire, it seems, should have begotten thee on special terms or with different gods for masters, if in these laws thou wilt not acquiesce. How many, prithee, men of sterling sense, when they see their wives unfaithful, make as though they saw it not? How many fathers, when their sons have gone astray, assist them in their amours? 'tis part of human wisdom to conceal the deed of shame. Nor should man aim at excessive refinement in his life; for they cannot with exactness finish e'en the roof that covers in a house; and how dost thou, after falling into so deep a pit, think to escape? Nay, if thou hast more of good than bad, thou wilt fare exceeding well, thy human nature considered. O cease, my darling child, from evil thoughts, let wanton pride be gone, for this is naught else, this wish to rival gods in perfectness. Face thy love; 'tis heaven's will thou shouldst. Sick thou art, yet turn thy sickness to some happy issue. For there are charms and spells to soothe the soul; surely some cure for thy disease will be found. Men, no doubt, might seek it long and late if our women's minds no scheme devise.

Ch. Although she gives thee at thy present need the wiser counsel, Phædra, yet do I praise thee. Still my praise may sound more harsh and jar more cruelly on thy ear than her advice.

Ph. 'Tis even this, too plausible a tongue, that overthrows good governments and homes of men. We should not speak to please the ear but point the path that leads to noble fame.

Nu. What means this solemn speech? No need of rounded phrases; but at once must we sound the prince, telling him frankly how it is with thee. Had not thy life to such a crisis come, or wert thou with self-control endowed, ne'er would I to gratify thy passions have urged thee to this course; but now 'tis a struggle fierce to save thy life, and therefore less to blame.

Ph. Accursed proposal! peace, woman! never utter those shameful words again!

Nu. Shameful, maybe, yet for thee better than honour's code. Better this deed, if it shall save thy life, than that name thy pride will kill thee to retain.

Ph. I conjure thee, go no further! for thy words are plausible but infamous; for though as yet love has not undermined my soul, yet, if in specious words thou dress thy foul suggestion, I shall be beguiled into the snare from which I am now escaping.

Nu. If thou art of this mind, 'twere well thou ne'er hadst sinned; but as it is, hear me; for that is the next best course; I in my house have charms to soothe thy love; 'twas but now I thought of them; these shall cure thee of thy sickness on no disgraceful terms, thy mind unhurt, if thou wilt be but brave. But from him thou lovest we must get some token, a word or fragment of his robe, and thereby unite in one love's twofold stream.

Ph. Is thy drug a salve or potion?

Nu. I cannot tell; be content, my child, to profit by it and ask no questions.

Ph. I fear me thou wilt prove too wise for me.

Nu. If thou fear this, confess thyself afraid of all; but why thy terror?

Ph. Lest thou shouldst breathe a word of this to Theseus' son.

Nu. Peace, my child! I will do all things well; only be thou, queen Cypris, ocean's child, my partner in the work! And for the rest of my purpose, it will be enough for me to tell it to our friends within the house. *Exit* NURSE.

Ch. O Love, Love, that from the eyes diffusest soft desire, bringing on the souls of those, whom thou dost camp against, sweet grace, O never in evil mood appear to me, nor out of time and tune approach! Nor fire nor meteor hurls a mightier bolt than Aphrodite's shaft shot by the hands of Love, the child of Zeus. Idly, idly by the streams of Alpheus and in the Pythian shrines of Phœbus, Hellas heaps the slaughtered steers; while Love we worship not, Love, the king of men, who holds the key to Aphrodite's sweetest bower—worship not him who, when he comes, lays waste and marks his path to mortal hearts by wide-spread woe. There was that maiden[1] in Œchalia, a girl unwed, that knew no wooer yet nor married joys; her did the queen of Love snatch from her home across the sea and gave unto Alcmena's son, mid blood and smoke and murderous marriage-hymns, to be to him a frantic fiend of hell; woe! woe for his wooing!

Ah! holy walls of Thebes, ah! fount of Dirce, ye could testify what course the Love-Queen follows. For with the blazing levin-bolt did she cut short the fatal marriage of Semele, mother of Zeus-born Bacchus. All things she doth inspire, dread goddess, winging her flight hither and thither like a bee.

Ph. Peace, ladies, peace! I am undone.

Ch. What, Phædra, is this dread event within thy house?

Ph. Hush! let me hear what those within are saying.

Ch. I am silent; this is surely the prelude to mischief.

Ph. Great gods! how awful are my sufferings!

Ch. What a cry was there! what loud alarm! say what sudden terror, lady, doth thy soul dismay.

Ph. I am undone. Stand here at the door and hear the noise arising in the house.

Ch. Thou art already by the bolted door; 'tis for thee to note the sounds that issue from within. And tell me, O tell me what mischief can be on foot.

[1]Iole, daughter of Eurytus, king of Œchalia.

Ph. 'Tis the son of the horse-loving Amazon who calls, Hippolytus, uttering foul curses on my servant.

Ch. I hear a noise, but cannot clearly tell which way it comes. Ah! 'tis through the door the sound reached thee.

Ph. Yes, yes, he is calling her plainly enough a go-between in vice, traitress to her master's honour.

Ch. Woe, woe is me! thou art betrayed, dear mistress! What counsel shall I give thee? thy secret is out; thou art utterly undone.

Ph. Ah me! ah me!

Ch. Betrayed by friends!

Ph. She hath ruined me by speaking of my misfortune; 'twas kindly meant, but an ill way to cure my malady.

Ch. O what wilt thou do now in thy cruel dilemma?

Ph. I only know one way, one cure for these my woes, and that is instant death.

Enter HIPPOLYTUS *and* NURSE.

Hi. O mother earth! O sun's unclouded orb! What words, unfit for any lips, have reached my ears!

Nu. Peace, my son, lest some one hear thy outcry.

Hi. I cannot hear such awful words and hold my peace.

Nu. I do implore thee by thy fair right hand.

Hi. Let go my hand, touch not my robe.

Nu. O by thy knees I pray, destroy me not utterly.

Hi. Why say this, if, as thou pretendest, thy lips are free from blame?

Nu. My son, this is no story to be noised abroad.

Hi. A virtuous tale grows fairer told to many.

Nu. Never dishonour thy oath, thy son.

Hi. My tongue an oath did take, but not my heart.

Nu. My son, what wilt thou do? destroy thy friends?

Hi. Friends indeed! the wicked are no friends of mine.

Nu. O pardon me; to err is only human, child.

Hi. Great Zeus, why didst thou, to man's sorrow, put woman, evil counterfeit, to dwell where shines the sun? If thou wert minded that the human race should multiply, it was not from women they should have drawn their stock, but in thy temples they should have paid gold or iron or ponderous bronze and bought a family, each man proportioned to his offering, and so in independence dwelt, from women free. But now as soon as ever we would bring this plague into our home we bring its fortune to the ground. 'Tis clear from this how great a curse a woman is; the very father, that begot and nurtured her, to rid him of the mischief, gives her a dower and packs her off; while the husband, who takes the noxious weed into his home, fondly decks his sorry idol in fine raiment and tricks her out in robes, squandering by degrees, unhappy wight! his house's wealth. For he is in this dilemma; say his marriage has brought him good connections, he is glad then to keep the wife he loathes; or, if he gets a good wife but useless relations, he tries to stifle the bad luck with the good. But it is easiest for him who has settled in his house as wife a mere nobody, incapable from simplicity. I hate a clever woman; never may she set foot in *my* house who aims at knowing more than women need; for in these clever women Cypris implants a larger store of villainy, while the artless woman is by her shallow wit from levity debarred. No servant should ever have had access to a wife, but men should put to live with them, beasts, which bite, not talk, in which case they could not speak to any one nor be answered back by them. But, as it is, the wicked in their chambers plot wickedness, and their servants carry it abroad. Even thus, vile wretch, thou cam'st to make me partner in an outrage on my father's honour; wherefore I must wash that stain away in running streams, dashing the water into my ears. How could I commit so foul a crime when by the very mention of it I feel myself polluted? Be well assured, woman, 'tis only my religious scruple saves thee. For had not I unawares been caught by an oath, 'fore heaven! I would not have refrained from telling all unto my father. But now I will from the house away, so long as Theseus is abroad, and will maintain strict silence. But, when my father comes, I will return and see how thou and thy mistress face him, and so shall I learn by experience the extent of thy audacity. Perdition seize you both! (*To the audience*) I can never satisfy my hate for women, no! not even though some say this is ever my theme, for of a truth they always are evil. So either let some one prove them chaste, or let me still trample on them forever. *Exit.*

Ch. O the cruel, unhappy fate of women! What arts, what arguments have we, once we have made a slip, to loose by craft the tight-drawn knot?

Ph. I have met my deserts. O earth, O light of day! How can I escape the stroke of fate? How my pangs conceal, kind friends? What god will appear to help me, what mortal to take my part or help me in unrighteousness? The present calamity of my life admits of no escape. Most hapless I of all my sex!

Ch. Alas, alas! the deed is done, thy servant's schemes have gone awry, my queen, and all is lost.

Ph. Accursed woman! traitress to thy friends! How hast thou ruined me! May Zeus, my ancestor, smite thee with his fiery bolt and uproot thee from thy place. Did I not foresee thy purpose, did I not bid thee keep silence on the very matter which is now my shame? But thou wouldst not be still; wherefore my fair name will not go with me to the tomb. But now I must another scheme devise. Yon youth, in the keenness of his fury, will tell his father of my sin, and the aged Pittheus of my state, and fill the world with stories to my shame. Perdition seize thee and every meddling fool who by dishonest means would serve unwilling friends!

Nu. Mistress, thou may'st condemn the mischief I have done, for sorrow's sting o'ermasters thy judgment; yet can I answer thee in face of this, if thou wilt hear. 'Twas I who nurtured thee; I love thee still; but in my search for medicine to cure thy sickness I found what least I sought. Had I but succeeded, I had been counted wise, for the credit we get for wisdom is measured by our success.

Ph. Is it just, is it any satisfaction to me, that thou shouldst wound me first, then bandy words with me?

Nu. We dwell on this too long; I was not wise, I own; but there are yet ways of escape from the trouble, my child.

Ph. Be dumb henceforth; evil was thy first advice to me, evil too thy attempted scheme. Begone and leave me, look to thyself; I will my own fortunes for the best arrange. (*Exit* NURSE) Ye noble daughters of Trœzen, grant me the only boon I crave; in silence bury what ye here have heard.

Ch. By majestic Artemis, child of Zeus, I swear I will never divulge aught of thy sorrows.

Ph. 'Tis well. But I, with all my thought, can but one way discover out of this calamity, that so I may secure my children's honour, and find myself some help as matters stand. For never, never will I bring shame upon my Cretan home, nor will I, to save one poor life, face Theseus after my disgrace.

Ch. Art thou bent then on some cureless woe?

Ph. On death; the means thereto must I devise myself.

Ch. Hush!

Ph. Do thou at least advise me well. For this very day shall I gladden Cypris, my destroyer, by yielding up my life, and shall own myself vanquished by cruel love. Yet shall my dying be another's curse, that he may learn not to exult at my misfortunes; but when he comes to share the self-same plague with me, he will take a lesson in wisdom.

Exit PHÆDRA.

Ch. O to be nestling 'neath some pathless cavern, there by god's creating hand to grow into a bird amid the wingèd tribes! Away would I soar to Adria's wave-beat shore and to the waters of Eridanus; where a father's hapless daughters in their grief for Phäethon distil into the glooming flood the amber brilliance of their tears. And to the apple-bearing strand of those minstrels in the west I then would come, where ocean's lord no more to sailors grants a passage o'er the deep dark main, finding there the heaven's holy bound, upheld by Atlas, where water from ambrosial founts wells up beside the couch of Zeus inside his halls, and holy earth, the bounteous mother, causes joy to spring in heavenly breasts. O white-winged bark, that o'er the booming ocean-wave didst bring my royal mistress from her happy home, to crown her queen 'mongst sorrow's brides! Surely evil omens from either port, at least from Crete, were with that ship, what time to glorious Athens it sped its way, and the crew made fast its twisted cable-ends upon the beach of Munychus, and on the land stept out. Whence comes it that her heart is crushed, cruelly afflicted by Aphrodite with unholy love; so she by bitter grief o'erwhelmed will tie a noose within her bridal bower to fit it to her fair white neck, too modest for this hateful lot in life, prizing o'er all her name and fame, and striving thus to rid her soul of passion's sting.

Enter MESSENGER.

Messenger. Help! ho! To the rescue all who near the palace stand! She hath hung herself, our queen, the wife of Theseus.

Ch. Woe worth the day! the deed is done; our royal mistress is no more, dead she hangs in the dangling noose.

Me. Haste! some one bring a two-edged knife wherewith to cut the knot about her neck!

Semi-Chorus I. Friends, what shall we do? think you we should enter the house, and loose the queen from the tight-drawn noose?

Semi-Chorus II. Why should *we*? Are there not young servants here? To do too much is not a safe course in life.

Me. Lay out the hapless corpse, straighten the limbs. This was a bitter way to sit at home and keep my master's house! *Exit* MESSENGER.

Ch. She is dead, poor lady, so I hear. Already are they laying out the corpse.

Enter THESEUS.

Theseus. Ladies, can ye tell me what the uproar in the palace means? There came the sound of servants weeping bitterly to mine ear. None of my household deign to open wide the gates and give me glad welcome as a traveller from prophetic shrines. Hath aught befallen old Pittheus? No. Though he be well advanced in years, yet should I mourn, were he to quit this house.

Ch. 'Tis not against the old, Theseus, that fate, to strike thee, aims this blow; prepare thy sorrow for a younger corpse.

Th. Woe is me! is it a child's life death robs me of?

Ch. They live; but, cruellest news of all for thee, their mother is no more.

Th. What! my wife dead? By what cruel mischance?

Ch. About her neck she tied the hangman's knot.

Th. Had grief so chilled her blood? or what had befallen her?

Ch. I know but this, for I am myself but now arrived at the house to mourn thy sorrows, O Theseus.

Th. Woe is me! why have I crowned my head with woven garlands, when misfortune greets my embassage? Unbolt the doors, servants, loose their fastenings, that I may see the piteous sight, my wife, whose death is death to me.

The palace opens, disclosing the corpse.

Ch. Woe! woe is thee for thy piteous lot! thou hast done thyself a hurt deep enough to overthrow this family. Ah! ah! the daring of it! done to death by violence and unnatural means, the desperate effort of thy own poor hand! Who cast the shadow o'er thy life, poor lady?

Th. Ah me, my cruel lot! sorrow hath done her worst on me. O fortune, how heavily hast thou set thy foot on me and on my house, by fiendish hands inflicting an unexpected stain? Nay, 'tis complete effacement of my life, making it impossible; for I see, alas! so wide an ocean of grief that I can never swim to shore again, nor breast the tide of this calamity. How shall I speak of thee, my poor wife, what tale of direst suffering tell? Thou art vanished like a bird from the covert of my hand, taking one headlong leap from me to Hades' halls. Alas, and woe! this is a bitter, bitter sight! This must be a judgment sent by God for the sins of an ancestor, which from some far source I am bringing on myself.

Ch. My prince, 'tis not to thee alone such sorrows come; thou hast lost a noble wife, but so have many others.

Th. Fain would I go hide me 'neath earth's blackest depth, to dwell in darkness with the dead in misery, now that I am reft of thy dear presence! for thou hast slain me than thyself e'en more. Who can tell me what caused the fatal stroke that reached thy heart, dear wife? Will no one tell me what befell? doth my palace all in vain give shelter to a herd of menials? Woe, woe for thee, my wife! sorrows past speech, past bearing, I behold within my house; myself a ruined man, my home a solitude, my children orphans!

Ch. Gone and left us hast thou, fondest wife and noblest of all women 'neath the sun's bright eye or night's star-lit radiance. Poor house, what sorrows are thy portion now! My eyes are wet with streams of tears to see thy fate; but the sequel to this tragedy has long with terror filled me.

Th. Ha! what means this letter? clasped in her dear hand it hath some strange tale to tell. Hath she, poor lady, as a last request, written her bidding as to my marriage and her children? Take heart, poor ghost; no wife henceforth shall wed thy Theseus or invade his house. Ah! how yon seal of my dead wife stamped with her golden ring affects my sight! Come, I will unfold the sealed packet and read her letter's message to me.

Ch. Woe unto us! Here is yet another evil in the train by heaven sent. Looking to what has happened, I should count my lot in life no longer worth one's while to gain. My master's house, alas! is ruined, brought to naught, I say. Spare it, O Heaven, if it may be. Hearken to my prayer, for I see, as with prophetic eye, an omen boding mischief.

Th. O horror! woe on woe! and still they come, too deep for words, too heavy to bear. Ah me!

Ch. What is it? speak, if I may share in it.

Th. This letter loudly tells a hideous tale! where can I escape my load of woe? For I am ruined and undone, so awful are the words I find here written clear as if she cried them to me; woe is me!

Ch. Alas! thy words declare themselves the harbingers of woe.

Th. I can no longer keep the cursed tale within the portal of my lips, cruel though its utterance be. Ah me! Hippolytus hath dared by brutal force to violate my honour, recking naught of Zeus, whose awful eye is over all. O father Poseidon, once didst thou promise to fulfil three prayers of mine; answer one of these and slay my son, let him not escape this single day, if the prayers thou gavest me were indeed with issue fraught.

Ch. O king, I do conjure thee, call back that prayer; hereafter thou wilt know thy error. Hear, I pray.

Th. Impossible! Moreover I will banish him from this land, and by one of two fates shall he be struck down; either Poseidon, out of respect to my prayer, will cast his dead body into the house of Hades; or exiled from this land, a wanderer to some foreign shore, shall he eke out a life of misery.

Ch. Lo! where himself doth come, thy son Hippolytus, in good time; dismiss thy hurtful rage, King Theseus, and bethink thee what is best for thy family.

Enter HIPPOLYTUS.

Hi. I heard thy voice, father, and hasted to come hither; yet know I not the cause of thy present sorrow, but would fain learn of thee. Ha! what is this? thy wife a corpse I see; this is passing strange; 'twas but now I left her; a moment since she looked upon the light. How came she thus? the manner of her death? this would I learn of thee, father. Art dumb? silence availeth not in trouble; nay, for the heart that fain would know all must show its curiosity even in sorrow's hour. Be sure it is not right, father, to hide misfortunes from those who love, ay, more than love thee.

Th. O ye sons of men, victims of a thousand idle errors, why teach your countless crafts, why scheme and seek to find a way for everything, while one thing ye know not nor ever yet have made your prize, a way to teach them wisdom whose souls are void of sense?

Hi. A very master in his craft the man, who can force fools to be wise! But these ill-timed subtleties of thine, father, make me fear thy tongue is running riot through trouble.

Th. Fie upon thee! man needs should have some certain test set up to try his friends, some touchstone of their hearts, to know each friend whether he be true or false; all men should have two voices, one the voice of honesty, expediency's the other, so would honesty confute its knavish opposite, and then we could not be deceived.

Hi. Say, hath some friend been slandering me and hath he still thine ear? am I, though guiltless, banned? I am amazed indeed; thy random, frantic words fill me with wild alarm.

Th. O the mind of mortal man! to what lengths will it proceed? What limit will its bold assurance have? for if it goes on growing as man's life advances, and each successor outdo the man before him in villainy, the gods will have to add another sphere unto the world, which shall take in the knaves and villains. Behold this man; he, my own son, hath outraged mine honour, his guilt most clearly proved by my dead wife. Now, since thou hast dared this loathly crime, come, look thy father in the face. Art thou the man who dost with gods consort, as one above the vulgar herd? art thou the chaste and sinless saint? Thy boasts will never persuade me to be guilty of attributing ignorance to gods. Go then, vaunt thyself, and drive thy petty trade in viands formed of lifeless food; take Orpheus for thy chief and go a-revelling, with all honour for the vapourings of many a written scroll, seeing thou now art caught.

Let all beware, I say, of such hypocrites! who hunt their prey with fine words, and all the while are scheming villainy. She is dead; dost think that this will save thee? Why this convicts thee more than all, abandoned wretch! What oaths, what pleas can outweigh this letter, so that thou shouldst 'scape thy doom? Thou wilt assert she hated thee, that 'twixt the bastard and the true-born child nature has herself put war; it seems then by thy showing she made a sorry bargain with her life, if to gratify her hate of thee she lost what most she prized. 'Tis said, no doubt, that frailty finds no place in man but is innate in woman; my experience is, young men are no more secure than women, whenso the Queen of Love excites a youthful breast; although their sex comes in to help them. Yet why do I thus bandy words with thee, when before me lies the corpse, to be the clearest witness? Begone at once, an exile from this land, and ne'er set foot again in god-built Athens nor in the confines of my dominion. For if I am tamely to submit to this treatment from such as thee, no more will Sinis,[1] robber of the Isthmus, bear me witness how I slew him, but say my boasts are idle, nor will those rocks Scironian, that fringe the sea, call me the miscreants' scourge.

Ch. I know not how to call happy any child of man; for that which was first has turned and now is last.

Hi. Father, thy wrath and the tension of thy mind are terrible; yet this charge, specious though its arguments appear, becomes a calumny, if one lay it bare. Small skill have I in speaking to a crowd, but have a readier wit for comrades of mine own age and small companies. Yea, and this is as it should be; for they, whom the wise despise, are better qualified to speak before a mob. Yet am I constrained under the present circumstances to break silence. And at the outset will I take the point which formed the basis of thy stealthy attack on me, designed to put me out of court unheard; dost see yon sun, this earth? These do not contain, for all thou dost deny it, chastity surpassing mine. To reverence God I count the highest knowledge, and to adopt as friends not those who attempt injustice, but such as would blush to propose to their companions aught disgraceful or pleasure them by shameful services; to mock at friends is not my way, father, but I am still the same behind their backs as to their face. The very crime thou thinkest to catch me in, is just the one I am untainted with, for to this day have I kept me pure from women. Nor know I aught thereof, save what I hear or see in pictures, for I have no wish to look even on these, so pure my virgin soul. I grant my claim to chastity may not convince thee; well, 'tis then for thee to show the way I was corrupted. Did this woman exceed in beauty all her sex? Did I aspire to fill the husband's place after thee and succeed to thy house? That surely would have made me out a fool, a creature void of sense. Thou wilt say, "Your chaste man loves to lord it." No, no! say I, sovereignty pleases only those whose hearts are quite corrupt. Now, I would be the first and best at all the games in Hellas, but second in the state, for ever happy thus with the noblest for my friends. For there one may be happy, and the absence of danger gives a charm beyond all princely joys. One thing I have not said, the rest thou hast. Had I a witness to attest my purity, and were I pitted 'gainst her still alive, facts would show thee on enquiry who the culprit was. Now by Zeus, the god of oaths, and by the earth, whereon we stand, I swear to thee I never did lay hand upon thy wife nor would have wished to, or have harboured such a thought. Slay me, ye gods! rob me of name and honour, from home and city cast me forth, a wandering exile o'er the earth! nor sea nor land receive my bones when I am dead, if I am such a miscreant! I cannot say if she through fear destroyed herself, for more than this am I forbid. With her discretion took the place of chastity, while I, though chaste, was not discreet in using this virtue.

Ch. Thy oath by heaven, strong security, sufficiently refutes the charge.

Th. A wizard or magician must the fellow be, to think he can first flout me, his father, then by coolness master my resolve.

Hi. Father, thy part in this doth fill me with amaze; wert thou my son and I thy sire, by heaven! I would have slain, not let thee off with banishment, hadst thou presumed to violate my honour.

Th. A just remark! yet shalt thou not die by the sentence thine own lips pronounce upon thyself; for death, that cometh in a moment, is an easy end for wretchedness. Nay, thou shalt be exiled from thy fatherland, and wandering to a foreign shore drag out a life of misery; for such are the wages of sin.

Hi. Oh! what wilt thou do? Wilt thou banish me, without so much as waiting for Time's evidence on my case?

Th. Ay, beyond the sea, beyond the bounds of Atlas, if I could, so deeply do I hate thee.

Hi. What! banish me untried, without even testing my oath, the pledge I offer, or the voice of seers?

Th. This letter here, though it bears no seers' signs, arraigns thy pledges; as for birds that fly o'er our heads, a long farewell to them.

Hi. (*Aside*) Great gods! why do I not unlock my lips, seeing that I am ruined by you, the objects of my reverence? No, I will not; I should nowise persuade those whom I ought to, and in vain should break the oath I swore.

Th. Fie upon thee! that solemn air of thine is more than I can bear. Begone from thy native land forthwith!

Hi. Whither shall I turn? Ah me! whose friendly house will take me in, an exile on so grave a charge?

Th. Seek one who loves to entertain as guests and partners in his crimes corrupters of men's wives.

Hi. Ah me! this wounds my heart and brings me nigh to tears to think that I should appear so vile, and thou believe me so.

Th. Thy tears and forethought had been more in

[1] Sinis and Sciron were two notorious evil-doers, whom Theseus had slain.

season when thou didst presume to outrage thy father's wife.

Hi. O house, I would thou couldst speak for me and witness if I am so vile!

Th. Dost fly to speechless witnesses? This deed, though it speaketh not, proves thy guilt clearly.

Hi. Alas! Would I could stand and face myself, so should I weep to see the sorrows I endure.

Th. Ay, 'tis thy character to honour thyself far more than reverence thy parents, as thou shouldst.

Hi. Unhappy mother! son of sorrow! Heaven keep all friends of mine from bastard birth!

Th. Ho! servants, drag him hence! You heard my proclamation long ago condemning him to exile.

Hi. Whoso of them doth lay a hand on me shall rue it; thyself expel me, if thy spirit move thee, from the land.

Th. I will, unless my word thou straight obey; no pity for thy exile steals into my heart. *Exit* THESEUS.

Hi. The sentence then, it seems, is passed. Ah, misery! How well I know the truth herein, but know no way to tell it! O daughter of Latona, dearest to me of all deities, partner, comrade in the chase, far from glorious Athens must I fly. Farewell, city and land of Erechtheus; farewell, Trœzen, most joyous home wherein to pass the spring of life; 'tis my last sight of thee, farewell! Come, my comrades in this land, young like me, greet me kindly and escort me forth, for never will ye behold a purer soul, for all my father's doubts. *Exit* HIPPOLYTUS.

Ch. In very deed the thoughts I have about the gods, whenso they come into my mind, do much to soothe its grief, but though I cherish secret hopes of some great guiding will, yet am I at fault when I survey the fate and doings of the sons of men; change succeeds to change, and man's life veers and shifts in endless restlessness. Fortune grant me this, I pray, at heaven's hand—a happy lot in life and a soul from sorrow free; opinions let me hold not too precise nor yet too hollow; but, lightly changing my habits to each morrow as it comes, may I thus attain a life of bliss! For now no more is my mind free from doubts, unlooked-for sights greet my vision; for lo! I see the morning star of Athens, eye of Hellas, driven by his father's fury to another land. Mourn, ye sands of my native shores, ye oak-groves on the hills, where with his fleet hounds he would hunt the quarry to the death, attending on Dictynna, awful queen. No more will he mount his car drawn by Venetian steeds, filling the course round Limna with the prancing of his trained horses. Nevermore in his father's house shall he wake the Muse that never slept beneath his lute-strings; no hand will crown the spots where rests the maiden Latona 'mid the boskage deep; nor evermore shall our virgins vie to win thy love, now thou art banished; while I with tears at thy unhappy fate shall endure a lot all undeserved. Ah! hapless mother, in vain didst thou bring forth, it seems. I am angered with the gods; out upon them! O ye linkèd Graces, why are ye sending from his native land this poor youth, a guiltless sufferer, far from his home?

But lo! I see a servant of Hippolytus hasting with troubled looks towards the palace.

Enter 2nd MESSENGER.

2nd Messenger. Ladies, where may I find Theseus, king of the country? pray, tell me if ye know; is he within the palace here?

Ch. Lo! himself approaches from the palace.

Enter THESEUS.

2nd Me. Theseus, I am the bearer of troublous tidings to thee and all citizens who dwell in Athens or the bounds of Trœzen.

Th. How now? hath some strange calamity o'ertaken these two neighbouring cities?

2nd Me. In one brief word, Hippolytus is dead. 'Tis true one slender thread still links him to the light of life.

Th. Who slew him? Did some husband come to blows with him, one whose wife, like mine, had suffered brutal violence?

2nd Me. He perished through those steeds that drew his chariot, and through the curses thou didst utter, praying to thy sire, the ocean-king, to slay thy son.

Th. Ye gods and king Poseidon, thou hast proved my parentage by hearkening to my prayer! Say how he perished; how fell the uplifted hand of Justice to smite the villain who dishonoured me?

2nd Me. Hard by the wave-beat shore were we combing out his horses' manes, weeping the while, for one had come to say that Hippolytus was harshly exiled by thee and nevermore would return to set foot in this land. Then came he, telling the same doleful tale to us upon the beach, and with him was a countless throng of friends who followed after. At length he stayed his lamentation and spake: "Why weakly rave on this wise? My father's commands must be obeyed. Ho! servants, harness my horses to the chariot; this is no longer now city of mine." Thereupon each one of us bestirred himself, and, ere a man could say 'twas done, we had the horses standing ready at our master's side. Then he caught up the reins from the chariot-rail, first fitting his feet exactly in the hollows made for them. But first with outspread palms he called upon the gods, "O Zeus, now strike me dead, if I have sinned, and let my father learn how he is wronging me, in death at least, if not in life." Therewith he seized the whip and lashed each horse in turn; while we, close by his chariot, near the reins, kept up with him along the road that leads direct to Argos and Epidaurus. And just as we were coming to a desert spot, a strip of sand beyond the borders of this country, sloping right to the Saronic gulf, there issued thence a deep rumbling sound, as it were an earthquake, a fearsome noise, and the horses reared their heads and pricked their ears, while we were filled with wild alarm to know whence came the sound; when, as we gazed toward the wave-beat shore, a wave tremendous we beheld towering to the skies, so that from our view the cliffs of Sciron vanished, for it hid the isthmus and the rock of Asclepius; then swelling and frothing with a crest of foam, the sea discharged it toward the beach where stood the harnessed car, and in the moment that it broke, that mighty wall of waters, there issued from the wave a monstrous bull, whose bellowing filled the land with fearsome echoes, a sight too awful as it seemed to us who witnessed it. A panic seized the horses there and then, but our master, to horses' ways quite used, gripped in both hands his reins, and tying them to his body pulled them backward as the sailor pulls his oar; but the horses gnashed the forged bits between their teeth and bore him wildly on, regardless of their master's guiding hand or rein or jointed car. And oft as he would take the guiding rein and steer for softer ground, showed that bull in front to turn him back again, maddening his team with terror; but if in their frantic career they ran towards the rocks, he would draw nigh the chariot-rail, keeping up with them, until, suddenly dashing the wheel against a stone, he upset and wrecked the car; then was dire confusion, axle-boxes and linch-pins springing into the air. While he, poor youth, entangled in the reins was dragged along, bound by a stubborn knot, his poor head dashed against the rocks, his flesh all torn, the while he cried out piteously, "Stay, stay, my horses whom my own hand hath fed at the manger, destroy me not utterly. O luckless curse of a father! Will no one come and save me for all my virtue?" Now we, though much we longed to help, were left far behind. At last, I know not how, he broke loose from the shapely reins that bound him, a faint breath of life still in him; but the horses disappeared, and that portentous bull, among the rocky ground, I know not where. I am but a slave in thy house, 'tis true, O king, yet will I never believe so monstrous a charge against thy son's character, no! not though the whole race of womankind should hang itself, or one should fill with writing every pine-tree tablet grown on Ida, sure as I am of his uprightness.

Ch. Alas! new troubles come to plague us, nor is there any escape from fate and necessity.

Th. My hatred for him who hath thus suffered made me glad at thy tidings, yet from regard for the gods and him, because he is my son, I feel neither joy nor sorrow at his sufferings.

2nd Me. But say, are we to bring the victim hither, or how are we to fulfil thy wishes? Bethink thee; if by me thou wilt be schooled, thou wilt not harshly treat thy son in his sad plight.

Th. Bring him hither, that when I see him face to face, who hath denied having polluted my wife's honour, I may by words and heaven's visitation convict him. *Exit* SECOND MESSENGER.

Ch. Ah! Cypris, thine the hand that guides the stubborn hearts of gods and men; thine, and that attendant boy's, who, with painted plumage gay, flutters round his victims on lightning wing. O'er the land and booming deep on golden pinion borne flits the God of Love, maddening the heart and beguiling the senses of all whom he attacks, savage whelps on mountains bred, ocean's monsters, creatures of this sun-warmed earth, and man; thine, O Cypris, thine alone the sovereign power to rule them all. *Enter* ARTEMIS.

Artemis. Hearken, I bid thee, noble son of Ægeus: lo! 'tis I, Latona's child, that speak, I, Artemis. Why, Theseus, to thy sorrow dost thou rejoice at these tidings, seeing that thou hast slain thy son most impiously, listening to a charge not clearly proved, but falsely sworn to by thy wife? though clearly has the curse therefrom upon thee fallen. Why dost thou not for very shame hide beneath the dark places of the earth, or change thy human life and soar on wings to escape this tribulation? 'Mongst men of honour thou hast now no share in life. Hearken, Theseus; I will put thy wretched case. Yet will it naught avail thee, if I do, but vex thy heart; still with this intent I came, to show thy son's pure heart —that he may die with honour—as well the frenzy and, in a sense, the nobleness of thy wife; for she was cruelly stung with a passion for thy son by that goddess whom all we, that joy in virgin purity, detest. And though she strove to conquer love by resolution, yet by no fault of hers she fell, thanks to her nurse's strategy, who did reveal her malady unto thy son under oath. But he would none of her counsels, as indeed was right, nor yet, when thou didst revile him, would he break the oath he swore, from piety. She meantime, fearful of being found out, wrote a lying letter, destroying by guile thy son, but yet persuading thee.

Th. Woe is me!

Ar. Doth my story wound thee, Theseus? Be still awhile; hear what follows, so wilt thou have more cause to groan. Dost remember those three prayers thy father granted thee, fraught with certain issue? 'Tis one of these thou hast misused, unnatural wretch, against thy son, instead of aiming it at an enemy. Thy sea-god sire, 'tis true, for all his kind intent, hath granted that boon he was compelled, by reason of his promise, to grant. But thou alike in his eyes and in mine hast shewn thy evil heart, in that thou hast forestalled all proof or voice prophetic, hast made no inquiry, nor taken time for consideration, but with undue haste cursed thy son even to the death.

Th. Perdition seize me! Queen revered!

Ar. An awful deed was thine, but still even for this thou mayest obtain pardon; for it was Cypris that would have it so, sating the fury of her soul. For this is law amongst us gods; none of us will thwart his neighbour's will, but ever we stand aloof. For be well assured, did I not fear Zeus, never would I have incurred the bitter shame of handing over to death a man of all his kind to me most dear. As for thy sin, first thy ignorance absolves thee from its villainy, next thy wife, who is dead, was lavish in her use of convincing arguments to influence thy mind. On thee in chief this storm of woe hath burst, yet is it some grief to me as well; for when the righteous die, there is no joy in heaven, albeit we try to destroy the wicked, house and home.

Ch. Lo! where he comes, this hapless youth, his fair young flesh and auburn locks most shamefully handled. Unhappy house! what twofold sorrow doth o'ertake its halls, through heaven's ordinance!

HIPPOLYTUS *is carried in.*

Hi. Ah! ah! woe is me! foully undone by an impious father's impious imprecation! Undone, undone! woe is me! Through my head shoot fearful pains; my brain throbs convulsively. Stop, let me rest my worn-out frame. Oh, oh! Accursèd steeds, that mine own hand did feed, ye have been my ruin and my death. O by the gods, good sirs, I beseech ye, softly touch my wounded limbs. Who stands there at my right side? Lift me tenderly, with slow and even step conduct a poor wretch cursed by his mistaken sire. Great Zeus, dost thou see this? Me thy reverent worshipper, me who left all men behind in purity, plunged thus into yawning Hades 'neath the earth, reft of life, in vain the toils I have endured through my piety towards mankind. Ah me! ah me! O the thrill of anguish shooting through me! Set me down, poor wretch I am; come Death to set me free! Kill me, end my sufferings. O for a sword two-edged to hack my flesh, and close this mortal life! Ill-fated curse of my father! the crimes of bloody kinsmen,[1] ancestors of old, now pass their boundaries and tarry not, and upon me are they come all guiltless as I am; ah! why? Alas, alas! what can I say? How from my life get rid of this relentless agony? O that the stern Death-god, night's black visitant, would give my sufferings rest!

Ar. Poor sufferer! cruel the fate that links thee to it! Thy noble soul hath been thy ruin.

Hi. Ah! the fragrance from my goddess wafted! Even in my agony I feel thee near and find relief; she is here in this very place, my goddess Artemis.

Ar. She is, poor sufferer! the goddess thou hast loved the best.

Hi. Dost see me, mistress mine? dost see my present suffering?

Ar. I see thee, but mine eyes no tear may weep.

Hi. Thou hast none now to lead the hunt or tend thy fane.

Ar. None now; yet e'en in death I love thee still.

Hi. None to groom thy steeds, or guard thy shrines

Ar. 'Twas Cypris, mistress of iniquity, devised this evil.

Hi. Ah me! now know I the goddess who destroyed me.

Ar. She was jealous of her slighted honour, vexed at thy chaste life.

Hi. Ah! then I see her single hand hath struck down three of us.

Ar. Thy sire and thee, and last thy father's wife.

Hi. My sire's ill-luck as well as mine I mourn.

Ar. He was deceived by a goddess' design.

Hi. Woe is thee, my father, in this sad mischance!

Th. My son, I am a ruined man; life has no joys for me.

Hi. For this mistake I mourn thee rather than myself.

Th. O that I had died for thee, my son!

Hi. Ah! those fatal gifts thy sire Poseidon gave.

Th. Would God these lips had never uttered that prayer!

Hi. Why not? thou wouldst in any case have slain me in thy fury then.

Th. Yes; Heaven had perverted my power to think.

Hi. O that the race of men could bring a curse upon the gods!

Ar. Enough! for though thou pass to gloom beneath the earth, the wrath of Cypris shall not, at her will, fall on thee unrequited, because thou hadst a noble righteous soul. For I with mine own hand will with these unerring shafts avenge me on another,[2] who is her votary, dearest to her of all the sons of men. And to thee, poor sufferer, for thy anguish now will I grant high honours in the city of Trœzen; for thee shall maids unwed before their marriage cut off their hair, thy harvest through the long roll of time of countless bitter tears. Yea, and for ever shall the virgin choir hymn thy sad memory, nor shall Phædra's love for thee fall into oblivion and pass away unnoticed. But thou, O son of old Ægeus, take thy son in thine arms, draw him close to thee, for unwittingly thou slewest him, and men may well commit an error when gods put it in their way. And thee Hippolytus, I admonish; hate not thy sire, for in this death thou dost but meet thy destined fate. And now farewell! 'tis not for me to gaze upon the dead, or pollute my sight with death-scenes, and e'en now I see thee nigh that evil moment. *Exit* ARTEMIS.

Hi. Farewell, blest virgin queen! leave me now! How easily thou resignest our long friendship! I am reconciled with my father at thy desire, yea, for ever before I would obey thy bidding. Ah me! the darkness is settling even now upon my eyes. Take me, father, in thy arms, lift me up.

Th. Woe is me, my son! what art thou doing to me thy hapless sire!

Hi. I am a broken man; yes, I see the gates that close upon the dead.

Th. Canst leave me thus with murder on my soul!

Hi. No, no; I set thee free from this blood-guiltiness.

Th. What sayest thou? dost absolve me from blood-shed?

Hi. Artemis, the archer-queen, is my witness that I do.

Th. My own dear child, how generous dost thou show thyself to thy father!

Hi. Farewell, dear father! a long farewell to thee!

Th. O that holy, noble soul of thine!

Hi. Pray to have children such as me born in lawful wedlock.

Th. O leave me not, my son; endure awhile.

Hi. 'Tis finished, my endurance; I die, father; quickly cover my face with a mantle. *Dies.*

Th. O glorious Athens, realm of Pallas, what a splendid hero ye have lost! Ah me, ah me! How oft shall I remember thy evil work, O Cypris!

Ch. On all our citizens hath come this universal sorrow, unforeseen. Now shall the copious tear gush forth, for sad news about great men takes more than usual hold upon the heart. *Exeunt* OMNES.

[1]Such as Tantalus and Pelops, Atreus and Thyestes.

[2]Adonis.

ALCESTIS

DRAMATIS PERSONAE

Apollo	Alcestis
Death	Attendant
Chorus of Old Men of Pherae	Admetus
Maid	Eumelus
Pheres	Heracles

Before Admetus' palace in Pheræ. Enter APOLLO.

Apollo. Halls of Admetus, wherein I steeled my heart to be content with a servant's board, god though I was. Zeus was to blame; he slew my son Asclepius, piercing his bosom with a thunderbolt; whereat I was enraged and smote his Cyclopes, forgers of the heavenly fire; so my sire in recompense for this forced me to become a slave in a mortal's home. Then came I to this land and kept a stranger's flocks, and to this day have been the saviour of this house. For in Pheres' son I found a man as holy as myself, and him I saved from death by cheating Destiny, for they promised me, those goddesses of fate, that Admetus should escape the impending doom, if he found a substitute for the powers below. So he went through all his list of friends, made trial of each, his father and the aged mother that bare him, but none he found save his wife alone that was willing to die for him and forego the light of life; she now within the house is upheld in his arms, gasping out her life; for to-day is she doomed to die and pass from life to death. (*Enter* DEATH) But I, for fear pollution overtake me in the house, am leaving the shelter of this roof I love so well, for already I see Death hard by, the priest of souls departed, who is on his way to lead her to the halls of Hades; true to time he comes, watching this day that calls her to her doom.

Death. Ha! What dost thou at this house? why is it thou art ranging here, Phœbus? Once again thou wrongest me, circumscribing and limiting the honours of the nether world. Wert thou not content to hinder the death of Admetus, by thy knavish cunning baulking Destiny? but now again hast thou armed thee with thy bow and art keeping guard o'er her, this daughter of Pelias, who undertook, of her free will, to die for her lord and set him free.

Ap. Never fear; I have, be sure, justice and fair pleas to urge.

De. What has that bow to do, if thou hast justice on thy side?

Ap. 'Tis my habit ever to carry it.

De. Ay, and to help this house more than is right.

Ap. The reason is, I cannot bear a friend's distress.

De. Wilt rob me of this second corpse likewise?

Ap. Come! I did not take the other from thee by violence.

De. Then how is it he lives above the earth and not beneath?

Ap. He gave his wife instead, her whom now thou art come to fetch.

De. Yea, and I will bear her hence to the nether world.

Ap. Take her and go, for I do not suppose I can persuade thee.

De. To slay my rightful victim? Why, that is my appointed task.

Ap. Nay, but to lay thy deadly hand on those who soon would die.

De. I see thy drift, thy eager plea.

Ap. Is it then possible that Alcestis should attain old age?

De. It is not possible; I too, methinks, find a pleasure in my rights.

Ap. Thou canst not anyhow take more than one life.

De. When young lives die I reap a higher honour.

Ap. Should she die old, a sumptuous funeral will she have.

De. Phœbus, the law thou layest down is all in favour of the rich.

Ap. What mean'st thou? art so wise, and I never knew it?

De. Those who have wealth would buy the chance of their dying old.

Ap. It seems then thou wilt not grant me this favour.

De. Not I; my customs well thou knowest.

Ap. That I do, customs men detest and gods abhor.

De. Thou canst not realise every lawless wish.

Ap. Mark me, thou shalt have a check for all thy excessive fierceness; such a hero shall there come to Pheres' halls, by Eurystheus sent to fetch a team of steeds from the wintry world of Thrace; he, a guest awhile in these halls of Admetus, will wrest this woman from thee by sheer force. So wilt thou get no thanks from me but yet wilt do this all the same, and earn my hatred too. *Exit*.

De. Thou wilt not gain thy purpose any the more for all thy many words; that woman shall to Hades' halls go down, I tell thee. Lo! I am going for her, that with the sword I may begin my rites, for he whose hair this sword doth hallow is sacred to the gods below. *Exit.*

Enter CHORUS.

Semi-Chorus I. What means this silence in front of the palace? why is the house of Admetus stricken dumb?

Semi-Chorus II. Not one friend near to say if we must mourn our queen as dead, or if she liveth yet and sees the sun, Alcestis, daughter of Pelias, by me and all esteemed the best of wives to her husband.

Semi-Ch. I. Doth any of you hear a groan, or sound of hands that smite together, or the voice of lamentation, telling all is over and done? Yet is there no servant stationed about the gate, no, not one. O come, thou saving god, to smooth the swelling waves of woe!

Semi-Ch. II. Surely, were she dead, they would not be so still.

Semi-Ch. I. Maybe her corpse is not yet from the house borne forth.

Semi-Ch. II. Whence that inference? I am not so sanguine. What gives thee confidence?

Semi-Ch. I. How could Admetus let his noble wife go unattended to the grave?

Semi-Ch. II. Before the gates I see no lustral water from the spring, as custom doth ordain should be at the gates of the dead, no shorn lock lies on the threshold, which, as thou knowest, falls in mourning for the dead, no choir of maidens smites its youthful palms together.

Semi-Ch. I. And yet this is the appointed day.

Semi-Ch. II. What meanest thou by this?

Semi-Ch. I. The day appointed for the journey to the world below.

Semi-Ch. II. Thou hast touched me to the heart, e'en to the soul.

Ch. Whoso from his youth up has been accounted virtuous, needs must weep to see the good suddenly cut off. 'Tis done; no single spot in all the world remains whither one might steer a course, either to Lycia[1] or to the parched abodes[2] of Ammon to release the hapless lady's soul; on comes death with step abrupt, nor know I to whom I should go of all who at the gods' altars offer sacrifice. Only the son of Phœbus,[3] if he yet saw this light of day—Ah! then might she have left the dark abode and gates of Hades and have come again, for he would raise the dead to life, till that the thunderbolt's forked flame, hurled by Zeus, smote him. But now what further hope of life can I welcome to me? Our lords have ere this done all they could; on every altar streams the blood of abundant sacrifice; yet our sorrows find no cure.

Enter MAID.

Lo! from the house cometh a handmaid weeping; what shall I be told hath chanced? Grief may well be pardoned, if aught happeneth to one's master; yet I fain would learn whether our lady still is living or haply is no more.

Maid. Alive, yet dead thou may'st call her.

Ch. Why, how can the same person be alive, yet dead?

Ma. She is sinking even now, and at her last gasp.

Ch. My poor master! how sad thy lot to lose so good a wife!

Ma. He did not know his loss, until the blow fell on him.

Ch. Is there then no more a hope of saving her?

Ma. None; the fated day comes on so fast.

Ch. Are then the fitting rites already taking place o'er her body?

Ma. Death's garniture is ready, wherewith her lord will bury her.

Ch. Well let her know, though die she must, her fame ranks far above any other wife's beneath the sun.

Ma. Far above! of course it does; who will gainsay it? What must the woman be who hath surpassed her? For how could any wife have shown a clearer regard for her lord than by offering in his stead to die? Thus much the whole city knows right well; but thou shalt hear with wonder what she did within the house. For when she knew the fatal day was come, she washed her fair white skin with water from the stream, then from her cedar chests drew forth vesture and ornaments and robed herself becomingly; next, standing before the altar-hearth, she prayed, "Mistress mine, behold! I pass beneath the earth; to thee in suppliant wise will I my latest prayer address; be mother to my orphans, and to my boy unite a loving bride, to my daughter a noble husband. Let them not die, as I, their mother, perish now, untimely in their youth, but let them live their glad lives out, happy in their native land." To every altar in Admetus' halls she went and crowned them and prayed, plucking from myrtle boughs their foliage, with never a tear or groan, nor did her coming trouble change the colour of her comely face. Anon into her bridal bower she burst, and then her tears brake forth and thus she cried, "O couch, whereon I loosed my maiden state for the man in whose cause I die, farewell! no hate I feel for thee; for me alone hast thou undone, dying as I die from fear of betraying thee and my lord. Some other wife will make thee hers, more blest maybe than me, but not more chaste." And she fell upon her knees and kissed it, till with her gushing tears the whole bed was wet. At last, when she had had her fill of weeping, she tore herself from the bed and hurried headlong forth, and oft as she was leaving the chamber turned she back and cast herself once more upon the couch; while her children were weeping as they clung to their mother's robes; but she took them each in turn in her arms and kissed them fondly, as a dying mother might. And all the servants in the house fell a-crying in sorrow for their mistress; but she held out her hand to each, nor was there one so mean but she gave him a word and took his answer back. Such are the sorrows in the halls of Admetus. Dying he had died once for all, but by avoiding

[1]To a shrine of Apollo.

[2]The temple of Zeus Ammon in the deserts of Libya.

[3]Asclepius.

death he hath a legacy of grief that he will ne'er forget.

Ch. Doubtless Admetus sorrows in this calamity, if he must lose so good a wife.

Ma. Ah yes! he weeps, holding in his arms his darling wife, and prays her not to leave him, impossible request! for she is worn and wasted with illness, and lies exhausted, a sad burden in his arms. Still, though her breath comes short and scant, she yearns to gaze yet on the sunshine, for nevermore, but now the last and latest time her eye shall see his radiant orb. But I will go, thy presence to announce, for 'tis not all who have the goodwill to stand by their masters with kindly hearts in adversity. But thou of old hast been my master's friend. *Exit.*

Ch. O Zeus, what way out of these sorrows can be found? how can we loose the bonds of fate that bind our lord?

Comes some one forth? Am I at once to cut my hair, and cast the sable robe about me?

Too plainly, ay too plainly, friends; still let us to heaven pray; for the gods' power is very great.

O king Pæan, devise for Admetus some means of escape from his sorrows.

Yes, yes, contrive it; for thou in days gone by didst find salvation for him, so now be thou a saviour from the toils of death and stay bloodthirsty Hades.

Woe! woe! alas! Thou son of Pheres, woe! Ah, thy fate in losing thy wife!

Is not this enough to make thee slay thyself, ah! more than cause enough to tie the noose aloft and fit it to the neck?

Yea, for to-day wilt thou witness the death of her that was not merely dear, but dearest of the dear.

Look, look! she cometh even now, her husband with her, from the house.

Cry aloud and wail, O land of Pheræ, wail for the best of women, as with sickness worn she passes 'neath the earth to Hades, lord below.

Never, never will I say that marriage brings more joy than grief, as I conjecture by the past and witness these misfortunes of our king, for he when widowed of this noble wife will for the future lead a life that is no life at all.

Enter ALCESTIS, ADMETUS, *and* CHILDREN.

Alcestis. O sun-god, lamp of day! O scudding clouds that dance along the sky!

Admetus. He sees us both with anguish bowed, albeit guiltless of any crime against the gods, for the which thy death is due.

Al. O earth, O sheltering roof, and ye my maiden chambers in my native land Iolcos!

Ad. Lift thyself, unhappy wife, forsake me not; entreat the mighty gods to pity us.

Al. I see the two-oared skiff, I see it; and Charon, death's ferryman, his hand upon the boatman's pole, is calling me e'en now, "Why lingerest thou? Hasten. Thou art keeping me." Thus in his eager haste he hurries me.

Ad. Ah me! bitter to me is this voyage thou speakest of. Unhappy wife, what woes are ours!

Al. One draws me, draws me hence, seest thou not? to the courts of death, winged Hades glaring from beneath his dark brows. What wilt thou with me? Unhand me. On what a journey am I setting out, most wretched woman I!

Ad. Bitter journey to thy friends, yet most of all to me and to thy babes, the partners in this sorrow.

Al. Hands off! hands off at once!

Lay me down, I cannot stand. Hades standeth near; and with its gloom steals night upon my eyes.

O my children, my children, ye have no mother now. Fare ye well, my babes, live on beneath the light!

Ad. Woe is me! this is a message of sorrow to me, worse than aught that death can do. Steel not thy heart to leave me, I implore, by heaven, by thy babes whom thou wilt make orphans; nay, raise thyself, have courage. For if thou die I can no longer live; my life, my death are in thy hands; thy love is what I worship.

Al. Admetus, lo! thou seest how it is with me; to thee I fain would tell my wishes ere I die. Thee I set before myself, and instead of living have ensured thy life, and so I die, though I need not have died for thee, but might have taken for my husband whom I would of the Thessalians, and have had a home blest with royal power; reft of thee, with my children orphans, I cared not to live, nor, though crowned with youth's fair gifts, wherein I used to joy, did I grudge them. Yet the father that begat thee, the mother that bare thee, gave thee up, though they had reached a time of life when to die were well, so saving thee their child, and winning noble death. For thou wert their only son, nor had they any hope, when thou wert dead, of other offspring. And I should have lived and thou the remnant of our days, nor wouldst thou have wept thy wife's loss, nor have had an orphan family. But some god hath caused these things to be even as they are. Enough! Remember thou the gratitude due to me for this; yea, for I shall never ask thee for an adequate return, for naught is prized more highly than our life; but just is my request, as thou thyself must say, since thou no less than I dost love these children, if so be thou think'st aright. Be content to let them rule my house, and do not marry a new wife to be a stepmother to these children, for she from jealousy, if so she be a woman worse than me, will stretch out her hand against the children of our union. Then do not this, I do beseech thee. For the stepmother that succeeds, hateth children of a former match, cruel as the viper's are her tender mercies. A son 'tis true, hath in his sire a tower of strength to whom he speaks and has his answer back; but thou, my daughter, how shall thy maidenhood be passed in honour? What shall thy experience be of thy father's wife? She may fasten on thee some foul report in thy youthful bloom, and frustrate thy marriage. Never shall thy mother lead thee to the bridal bed, nor by her presence in thy travail hearten thee, my child, when a mother's kindness triumphs over all. No, for I must die; and lo! this evil cometh to me not to-morrow nor yet on the third day of the month, but in a moment shall I be counted among the souls that are no more. Fare ye well, be happy; and thou, husband, canst boast thou hadst a peerless wife, and you, children, that you had such an one for mother.

Ch. Take heart; I do not hesitate to answer for him; he will perform all this, unless his mind should go astray.

Ad. It shall be so, fear not, it shall; alive thou wert the only wife I had, and dead shalt thou, none else, be called mine; no Thessalian maid shall ever take thy place and call me lord; not though she spring from lineage high nor though besides she be the fairest of her sex. Of children I have enough; god grant I may in them be blessed! for in thee has it been otherwise. No year-long mourning will I keep for thee, but all my life through, lady: loathing the mother that bare me, and hating my father, for they were friends in word but not in deed. But thou didst give thy dearest for my life and save it. May I not then mourn to lose a wife like thee? And I will put an end to revelry, to social gatherings o'er the wine, forego the festal crown and music which once reigned in my halls. For nevermore will I touch the lyre nor lift my soul in song to the Libyan flute, for thou hast taken with thee all my joy in life. But in my bed thy figure shall be laid full length, by cunning artists fashioned; thereon will I throw myself and, folding my arms about thee, call upon thy name, and think I hold my dear wife in my embrace, although I do not; chill comfort this, no doubt but still I shall relieve my soul of its sad weight; and thou wilt come to me in dreams and gladden me. For sweet it is to see our friends, come they when they will, e'en by night.

Had I the tongue, the tuneful voice of Orpheus to charm Demeter's daughter or her husband by my lay and bring thee back from Hades, I had gone down, nor Pluto's hound, nor Charon, ferryman of souls, whose hand is on the oar, had held me back, till to the light I had restored thee alive. At least do thou await me there, against the hour I die, prepare a home for me to be my true wife still. For in this same cedar coffin I will bid these children lay me with thee and stretch my limbs by thine; for never even in death may I be severed from thee, alone found faithful of them all.

Ch. Lo! I too will share with thee thy mourning for her, friend with friend; for this is but her due.

Al. My children, ye with your own ears have heard your father's promise, that he will never wed another wife to set her over you, nor e'er dishonour me.

Ad. Yea, so I promise now, and accomplish it I will.

Al. On these conditions receive the children from my hand.

Ad. I receive them, dear pledges by a dear hand given.

Al. Take thou my place and be a mother to these babes.

Ad. Sore will be their need when they are reft of thee.

Al. O my children, I am passing to that world below, when my life was needed most.

Ad. Ah me, what can I do bereft of thee?

Al. Thy sorrow Time will soothe; 'tis the dead who are as naught.

Ad. Take me, O take me, I beseech, with thee 'neath the earth.

Al. Enough that I in thy stead am dying.

Ad. O Destiny! of what a wife art thou despoiling me!

Al. Lo! the darkness deepens on my drooping eyes.

Ad. Lost indeed am I, if thou, dear wife, wilt really leave me.

Al. Thou mayst speak of me as naught, as one whose life is o'er.

Ad. Lift up thy face, leave not thy children.

Al. 'Tis not my own free will; O my babes, farewell!

Ad. Look, look on them but once.

Al. My end is come.

Ad. What mean'st thou? art leaving us?

Al. Farewell! *Dies.*

Ad. Lost! lost! woe is me!

Ch. She is gone, the wife of Admetus is no more.

Eumelus. O my hard fate! My mother has passed to the realms below; she lives no more, dear father, 'neath the sun. Alas for her! she leaves us ere her time and to me bequeaths an orphan's life. Behold that staring eye, those nerveless hands! Hear me, mother, hear me, I implore! 'tis I who call thee now, I thy tender chick, printing my kisses on thy lips.

Ad. She cannot hear, she cannot see; a heavy blow hath fortune dealt us, you children and me.

Eu. O father, I am but a child to have my loving mother leave me here alone; O cruel my fate, alas! and thine, my sister, sharer in my cup of woe. Woe to thee, father! in vain, in vain didst thou take a wife and hast not reached the goal of eld with her; for she is gone before, and now that thou art dead, my mother, our house is all undone.

Ch. Admetus, these misfortunes thou must bear. Thou art by no means the first nor yet shalt be the last of men to lose a wife of worth; know this, we all of us are debtors unto death.

Ad. I understand; this is no sudden flight of ill hither; I was ware of it and long have pined. But since I am to carry the dead forth to her burial, stay here with me and to that inexorable god in Hades raise your antiphone. While to all Thessalians in my realm I do proclaim a general mourning for this lady, with hair shorn off and robes of sable hue; all ye who harness steeds for cars, or single horses ride, cut off their manes with the sharp steel. Hush'd be every pipe, silent every lyre throughout the city till twelve full moons are past; for never again shall I bury one whom I love more, no! nor one more loyal to me; honour from me is her due, for she for me hath died, she and she alone.

Exeunt ADMETUS *and* EUMELUS, *with the other children.*

Ch. Daughter of Pelias, be thine a happy life in that sunless home in Hades' halls! Let Hades know, that swarthy god, and that old man who sits to row and steer alike at his death-ferry, that he hath carried o'er the lake of Acheron in his two-oared skiff a woman peerless amidst her sex. Oft of thee the Muses' votaries shall sing on the seven-stringed mountain shell and in hymns that need no harp, glorifying thee, oft as the season in his cycle cometh round at Sparta in that Carnean[1] month when all night long the moon sails high o'erhead, yea, and in splendid Athens, happy town. So glorious a theme has thy death bequeathed to tuneful bards. Would it were in my power and range to bring thee to the light from the chambers of Hades and the streams of Cocytus with the oar that sweeps yon nether flood! For thou, and thou alone, most dear of women, hadst the courage to redeem thy husband from Hades in exchange for thy own life. Light lie the earth above thee, lady! And if ever thy lord take to him a new wife, I vow he will earn my hatred and thy children's too. His mother had no heart to plunge into the darkness of the tomb for her son, no! nor his aged sire. Their own child they had not the courage to rescue, the wretches! albeit they were grey-headed. But thou in thy youth and beauty hast died for thy lord and gone thy way. O be it mine to have for partner such a loving wife! for this lot is rare in life. Surely she should be my helpmeet all my life and never cause one tear.

Enter HERACLES.

Heracles. Mine hosts, dwellers on this Pheræan soil! say, shall I find Admetus in the house?

Ch. The son of Pheres is within, Heracles. Tell me what need is bringing thee to the Thessalian land, to visit this city of the Pheræans?

He. I am performing a labour for Tirynthian Eurystheus.

Ch. And whither art thou journeying? on what wandering art thou forced to go?

He. To fetch the chariot-steeds of Thracian Diomedes.

Ch. How canst thou? art a stranger to the ways of thy host?

He. I am; for never yet have I gone to the land of the Bistones.

Ch. Thou canst not master his horses without fighting.

He. Still I cannot refuse these labours.

Ch. Then shalt thou slay them and return, or thyself be slain and stay there.

He. It will not be the first hard course that I have run.

Ch. And what will be thy gain, suppose thou master their lord?

He. The steeds will I drive away to the Tirynthian king.

Ch. No easy task to bit their jaws.

He. Easy enough, unless their nostrils vomit fire.

Ch. With ravening jaws they rend the limbs of men.

He. Thou speakest of the food of mountain beasts, not of horses.

Ch. Their mangers blood-bedabbled thou shalt see.

He. Whose son doth he who feeds them boast to be?

Ch. Ares' son, king of the golden targe of Thrace.

He. This toil again is but a piece of my ill-luck; hard it ever is and still is growing steeper, if I with Ares' own-begotten sons must fight, first with Lycaon, next with Cycnus, while now I am bound on this third contest to engage the horses and their master. Yet shall no man ever see Alcmena's son trembling at his foemen's prowess.

Ch. See where Admetus, lord of this land, comes in person from the palace forth.

Enter ADMETUS.

Ad. Hail! son of Zeus, from Perseus sprung.

He. Joy to thee also, Admetus, king of Thessaly.

Ad. Would there were! yet thy kindly heart I know full well.

He. Why dost thou appear with head shorn thus in mourning?

Ad. To-day I am to bury one who is dead.

He. Heaven avert calamity from thy children!

Ad. The children I have begotten are alive within my house.

He. Thy father maybe is gone; well, he was ripe to go.

Ad. No, Heracles, he lives; my mother too.

He. It cannot be thy wife is dead, thy Alcestis?

Ad. I can a twofold tale tell about her.

He. Dost mean that she is dead, or living still?

Ad. She lives, yet lives no more; that is my grief.

He. I am no wiser yet; thy words are riddles to me.

Ad. Knowest thou not the doom she must undergo?

He. I know she did submit to die in thy stead.

Ad. How then is she still alive, if so she promised?

He. Ah! weep not thy wife before the day, put that off till then.

Ad. The doomed is dead; the dead no more exists.

He. Men count to be and not to be something apart.

Ad. Thy verdict this, O Heracles, mine another.

He. Why weepest then? which of thy dear ones is the dead?

Ad. 'Tis a woman; I spoke of a woman just now.

He. A stranger, or one of thine own kin?

Ad. A stranger, yet in another sense related to my house.

He. How then came she by her death in house of thine?

Ad. Her father dead, she lived here as an orphan.

He. Ah! would I had found thee free from grief, Admetus!

Ad. With what intent dost thou devise this speech?

He. I will seek some other friendly hearth.

Ad. Never, O prince! Heaven forefend such dire disgrace!

[1] April.

He. A guest is a burden to sorrowing friends, if come he should.

Ad. The dead are dead. Come in.

He. To feast in a friend's house of sorrow is shameful.

Ad. The guest chambers lie apart, whereto we will conduct thee.

He. Let me go; ten thousandfold shall be my thanks to thee.

Ad. Thou must not go to any other hearth. (*To a Servant*) Go before, open the guest-rooms that face not these chambers, and bid my stewards see there is plenty of food; then shut the doors that lead into the courtyard; for 'tis not seemly that guests when at their meat should hear the voice of weeping or be made sad. *Exit* HERACLES.

Ch. What dost thou? With such calamity before thee, hast thou the heart, Admetus, to welcome visitors? What means this folly?

Ad. Well, and if I had driven him from my house and city when he came to be my guest, wouldst thou have praised me more? No indeed! for my calamity would have been no whit less, while I should have been more churlish. And this would have been another woe to add to mine, that my house should be called no friend to guests. Yea, and I find him myself the best of hosts whene'er to Argos' thirsty land I come.

Ch. Why then didst thou conceal thy present misfortune, if, as thy own lips declare, it was a friend that came?

Ad. He would never have entered my house, had he known aught of my distress. Maybe there are those who think me but a fool for acting thus, and these will blame me; but my halls have never learnt to drive away or treat with scorn my guests.

Ch. O home of hospitality, thrown open by thy lord to all now and ever! In thee it was that Pythian Apollo, the sweet harper, deigned to make his home and in thy halls was content to lead a shepherd's life, piping o'er the sloping downs shepherd's madrigals to thy flocks. And spotted lynxes couched amid his sheep in joy to hear his melody, and the lions' tawny troop left the glen of Othrys and came; came too the dappled fawn on nimble foot from beyond the crested pines and frisked about thy lyre, O Phœbus, for very joy at thy gladsome minstrelsy. And so it is thy lord inhabits a home rich in countless flocks by Bœbe's lovely mere, bounding his tilled corn-land and his level pastures with the clime of the Molossi near the sun's dark stable, and holding sway as far as the harbourless strand of the Ægean 'neath Pelion's shadow. Now too hath he opened wide his house and welcomed a guest although his eye is wet with tears in mourning for his wife so dear but lately dead within his halls; yea, for noble birth to noble feeling is inclined. And in the good completest wisdom dwells; and at my heart sits the bold belief that heaven's servant will be blessed.

Ad. Men of Pheræ, kindly gathered here, lo! even now my servants are bearing the corpse with all its trappings shoulder-high to the funeral pyre for burial; do ye, as custom bids, salute the dead on her last journey starting.

Ch. Look! I see thy father advancing with aged step, and servants too bearing in their arms adornment for thy wife, offerings for the dead.

Enter PHERES.

Pheres. My son, I come to share thy sorrow, for thou hast lost a noble, peerless wife; that no man will deny. Yet must thou needs bear this blow, hard though it be. Accept this garniture, and let it go beneath the earth, for rightly is her body honoured, since she died to save thy life, my son, and gave me back my child, suffering me not to lose thee and pine away in an old age of sorrow. Thus by the generous deed she dared, hath she made her life a noble example for all her sex. Farewell to thee, who hast saved this son of mine and raised me up when falling; be thine a happy lot even in Hades' halls! Such marriages I declare are gain to man, else to wed is not worth while.

Ad. Thou hast come uncalled by me to this burial, nor do I count thy presence as a friendly act. Never shall she be clad in any garniture of thine, nor in her burial will she need aught of thine. Thou shouldst have shewn thy sympathy at the time my doom was sealed. But thou didst stand aloof and let another die, though thou wert old, the victim young; shalt thou then mourn the dead? Methinks thou wert no real sire of mine nor was she my true mother who calls herself and is called so, but I was sprung of slave's blood and privily substituted at thy wife's breast. Brought to the test thou hast shewn thy nature; I cannot think I am thy child by birth.

By heaven, thou art the very pattern of cowards, who at thy age, on the borderland of life, wouldst not, nay! couldst not find the heart to die for thy own son; but ye, my parents, left to this stranger, whom I henceforth shall justly hold e'en as mother and as father too, and none but her. And yet 'twas a noble exploit to achieve, to die to save thy son, and in any case the remnant of thy time to live was but short; and I and she would have lived the days that were to be, nor had I lost my wife and mourned my evil fate. Moreover thou hast had all treatment that a happy man should have; in princely pomp thy youth was spent, thou hadst a son, myself, to be the heir of this thy home, so thou hadst no fear of dying childless and leaving thy house desolate, for strangers to pillage. Nor yet canst thou say I did dishonour thy old age and give thee up to die, seeing I have ever been to thee most dutiful, and for this thou, my sire, and she my mother, have made me this return. Go then, get other sons to tend thy closing years, prepare thy body for the grave, and lay out thy corpse. For I will never bury thee with hand of mine; for I am dead for all thou didst for me; but if I found a saviour in another and still live, his son I say I am, and his fond nurse in old age will be. 'Tis vain, I see, the old man's prayer for death, his plaints at age and life's long weariness. For if death do but draw near, not one doth wish to die; old age no more they count so burdensome.

Ch. Peace! enough the present sorrow, O my son; goad not thy father's soul to fury.

Ph. Child, whom think'st thou art reviling? some Lydian or Phrygian bought with thy money? Art not aware I am a freeborn Thessalian, son of a Thessalian sire? Thou art too insolent; yet from hence thou shalt not go as thou camest, after shooting out thy braggart tongue at me. To rule my house I begat and bred thee up; I own no debt of dying in thy stead; this is not the law that I received from my ancestors that fathers should die for children, nor is it a custom in Hellas. For weal or woe, thy life must be thine own; whate'er was due from me to thee, thou hast. Dominion wide is thine, and acres broad I will leave to thee, for from my father did I inherit them. How, pray, have I wronged thee? of what am I robbing thee? Die not thou for me, nor I for thee. Thy joy is in the light, think'st thou thy sire's is not? By Heaven! 'tis a weary while, I trow, that time beneath the earth, and life, though short, is sweet. Thou at least didst struggle hard to 'scape thy death, lost to shame, and by her death dost live beyond thy destined term. Dost thou then speak of cowardice in me, thou craven heart! no match for thy wife, who hath died for thee, her fine young lord? A clever scheme hast thou devised to stave off death for ever, if thou canst persuade each new wife to die instead of thee; and dost thou then taunt thy friends, who will not do the like, coward as thou art thyself? Hold thy peace; reflect, if thou dost love thy life so well, this love by all is shared; yet if thou wilt speak ill of me, thyself shalt hear a full and truthful list of thy own crimes.

Ch. Too long that list both now and heretofore; cease, father, to revile thy son.

Ad. Say on, for I have said my say; but if it vexes thee to hear the truth, thou shouldst not have sinned against me.

Ph. My sin had been the deeper, had I died for thee.

Ad. What! is it all one for young or old to die?

Ph. To live one life, not twain, is all our due.

Ad. Outlive then Zeus himself!

Ph. Dost curse thy parents, though unharmed by them?

Ad. Yea, for I see thy heart is set on length of days.

Ph. Is it not to save thyself thou art carrying to the tomb this corpse?

Ad. A proof of thy cowardice, thou craven heart!

Ph. At any rate her death was not due to me; this thou canst not say.

Ad. Ah! mayst thou some day come to need my aid!

Ph. Woo many wives, that there may be the more to die.

Ad. That is thy reproach, for thou didst refuse to die.

Ph. Dear is the light of the sun-god, dear to all.

Ad. A coward soul is thine, not to be reckoned among men.

Ph. No laughing now for thee at bearing forth my aged corpse.

Ad. Thy death will surely be a death of shame, come when it will.

Ph. Once dead I little reck of foul report.

Ad. Alas! how void of shame the old can be!

Ph. Hers was no want of shame; 'twas want of sense in her that thou didst find.

Ad. Begone! and leave me to bury my dead.

Ph. I go; bury thy victim, thyself her murderer. Her kinsmen yet will call for an account. Else surely has Acastus ceased to be a man, if he avenge not on thee his sister's blood.

Ad. Perdition seize thee and that wife of thine! grow old, as ye deserve, childless, though your son yet lives, for ye shall never enter the same abode with me; nay! were it needful I should disown thy paternal hearth by heralds' voice, I had disowned it. (*Exit* PHERES) Now, since we must bear our present woe, let us go and lay the dead upon the pyre. *Exit* ADMETUS.

Ch. Woe, woe for thee! Alas, for thy hardihood! Noble spirit, good beyond compare, farewell! May Hermes in the nether world, and Hades, too, give thee a kindly welcome! and if even in that other life the good are rewarded, mayst thou have thy share therein and take thy seat by Hades' bride! *Exit* CHORUS.

Enter ATTENDANT.

Attendant. Many the guests ere now from every corner of the world I have seen come to the halls of Admetus, for whom I have spread the board, but never yet have I welcomed to this hearth a guest so shameless as this; a man who, in the first place, though he saw my master's grief, yet entered and presumed to pass the gates, then took what cheer we had in no sober spirit, though he knew our sorrow; no! was there aught we failed to bring? he called for it. Next in his hands he took a goblet of ivy-wood and drank the pure juice of the black grape, till the mounting fumes of wine heated him, and he crowned his head with myrtle-sprays, howling discordantly, while two-fold strains were there to hear, for he would sing without a thought for the troubles in Admetus' halls, while we servants mourned our mistress, though we did not let the stranger see our streaming eyes, for such was the bidding of Admetus. So now here am I entertaining as a guest some miscreant thief maybe, or robber, while she is gone forth from the house, nor did I follow her nor stretch my hand towards her bier, in mourning for my lady, who, to me and all her servants, was a mother, for she would save us from countless trouble, appeasing her husband's angry mood. Have I not good cause then to loathe this guest who cometh in our hour of woe?

Enter HERACLES.

He. Ho! sirrah, why that solemn, thoughtful look? 'Tis not the way for servants to scowl on guests, but with courteous soul to welcome them. But thou, seeing a friend of thy master arrive, receivest him with sullen, lowering brow, though 'tis but a stranger that is the object of thy mourning. Come hither, that thou too mayst learn more wisdom. Dost know the nature of this mortal state? I trow not; how shouldst thou? Well, lend an ear to me. Death is the common debt of man; no mortal really knows if he will live to see the morrow's light; for Fortune's issues are not in our ken, beyond the teacher's rule they lie, no art can master them. Hearken then to this and learn of me, be merry, drink thy cup, and count the present day thine own, the rest to Fortune yield. And to Cypris too, sweetest of the gods by far to man, thy tribute pay, for kindly is her mood. Let be those other cares, and heed my counsel if thou think'st I speak aright; methinks I do. Come, banish this excessive grief, and drink a cup with me when thou hast passed beyond these doors and wreathed thy brow; and I feel sure the plash of wine within the cup will bring thee to a better haven from this crabbed mood, this cabined state of mind. Mortals we are, and mortals' thoughts should have; for all they who frown and scowl do miss—leastways I think so—the true life and get themselves misfortune.

At. I know all that, but our present state has little claim on revelry or laughter.

He. The dead was a stranger woman; grieve not to excess; for the rulers of thy house are living.

At. How, living? Thou knowest not the trouble in the house.

He. I do, unless thy master did in aught deceive me.

At. Too hospitable is he.

He. Was I to miss good cheer because a stranger had died?

At. A stranger surely! quite a stranger she!

He. Is there some trouble that he withheld from me?

At. Farewell, go thy way! my master's troubles are my care.

He. This word of thine heralds not a grief for strangers felt.

At. Had it been, the sight of thy merriment had not grieved me so.

He. Can it be mine host hath strangely wronged me?

At. Thou camest at no proper time for our house to welcome thee, for sorrow is come upon us; lo! thou seest our shorn heads and robes of sable hue.

He. Who is it that is dead? Is it a child or his aged sire that hath passed away?

At. Nay, sir guest, 'tis Admetus' wife that is no more.

He. What sayest thou? and did ye then in spite of that admit me to your cheer?

At. Yes, for his regard would not let him send thee from his door.

He. Unhappy husband, what a wife hast thou lost!

At. We are all undone, not she alone.

He. I knew it when I saw his streaming eye, shorn head and downcast look, yet did he persuade me, saying it was a stranger he was bearing to burial. So I did constrain myself and passed his gates and sat drinking in his hospitable halls, when he was suffering thus. And have I wreathed my head and do I revel still? But—thou to hold thy peace when such a crushing sorrow lay upon the house! Where is he burying her? Whither shall I go to find her?

At. Beside the road that leadeth straight to Larissa, shalt thou see her carved tomb outside the suburb. *Exit.*

He. O heart, O soul, both sufferers oft, now show the mettle of that son Tirynthian Alcmena, daughter of Electryon, bare to Zeus. For I must save this woman, dead but now, setting Alcestis once again within this house, and to Admetus this kind service render. So I will go and watch for Death the black-robed monarch of the dead, and him methinks I shall find as he drinks of the blood-offering near the tomb. And if, from ambush rushing, once I catch and fold him in my arms' embrace, none shall ever wrest him thence with smarting ribs, ere he give up the woman unto me. But should I fail to find my prey and he come not to the clotted blood, I will go to the sunless home of those beneath the earth, to Persephone and her king, and make to them my prayer, sure that I shall bring Alcestis up again, to place her in the hands of him, my host, who welcomed me to his house nor drove me thence, though fortune smote him hard, but this his noble spirit strove to hide out of regard for me. What host more kind than him in Thessaly? or in the homes of Hellas? Wherefore shall he never say his generous deeds were lavished on a worthless wretch. *Exit.*

Enter ADMETUS *and* CHORUS.

Ad. Ah me! I loathe this entering in, and loathe to see my widowed home. Woe, woe is me! Whither shall I go? Where stand? what say? or what suppress? Would God that I were dead! Surely in an evil hour my mother gave me birth. The dead I envy, and would fain be as they, and long to dwell within their courts. No joy to me to see the light, no joy to tread the earth; such a hostage death hath reft me of and handed o'er to Hades.

Ch. Move forward, go within the shelter of thy house.

Ad. Woe is me!

Ch. Thy sufferings claim these cries of woe.

Ad. Ah me!

Ch. Through anguish hast thou gone, full well I know.

Ad. Alas! alas!

Ch. Thou wilt not help the dead one whit.

Ad. O misery!

Ch. Nevermore to see thy dear wife face to face is grief indeed.

Ad. Thy words have probed the sore place in my heart. What greater grief can come to man than the loss of a faithful wife? Would I had never married or shared with her my home! I envy those 'mongst men who have nor wife nor child. Theirs is but one life; to grieve for that is no excessive burden; but to see children fall ill and bridal beds emptied by death's ravages is too much to bear, when one might go through life without wife or child.

Ch. A fate we cannot cope with is come upon us.

Ad. Woe is me!

Ch. But thou to sorrow settest no limit.

Ad. Ah! ah!

Ch. 'Tis hard to bear, but still—

Ad. Woe is me!

Ch. Thou art not the first to lose—

Ad. O! woe is me!

Ch. A wife; misfortune takes a different shape for every man she plagues.

Ad. O the weary sorrow! O the grief for dear ones dead and gone! Why didst thou hinder me from plunging into the gaping grave, there to lay me down and die with her, my peerless bride? Then would Hades for that one have gotten these two faithful souls at once, crossing the nether lake together.

Ch. I had a kinsman once, within whose home died his only son, worthy of a father's tears; yet in spite of that he bore his grief resignedly, childless though he was, his hair already turning grey, himself far on in years, upon life's downward track.

Ad. O house of mine, how can I enter thee? how can I live here, now that fortune turns against me? Ah me! How wide the gulf 'twixt then and now! Then with torches cut from Pelion's pines, with marriage hymns I entered in, holding my dear wife's hand; and at our back a crowd of friends with cheerful cries, singing the happy lot of my dead wife and me, calling us a noble pair made one, children both of highborn lineage; but now the voice of woe instead of wedding hymns, and robes of black instead of snowy white usher me into my house to my deserted couch.

Ch. Hard upon prosperous fortune came this sorrow to thee, a stranger to adversity; yet hast thou saved thy soul alive. Thy wife is dead and gone; her love she leaves with thee. What new thing is here? Death ere now from many a man hath torn a wife.

Ad. My friends, I count my dead wife's lot more blest than mine, for all it seems not so; for nevermore can sorrow touch her for ever; all her toil is over, and glorious is her fame. While I, who had no right to live, have passed the bounds of fate only to live a life of misery; I know it now. For how shall I endure to enter this my house? Whom shall I address, by whom be answered back, to find aught joyful in my entering in? Whither shall I turn? Within the desolation will drive me forth, whensoe'er I see my widowed couch, the seat whereon she sat, the floor all dusty in the house, and my babes falling at my knees with piteous tears for their mother, while my servants mourn the good mistress their house hath lost. These are the sorrows in my home, while abroad the marriages among Thessalians and the thronging crowds of women will drive me mad,[1] for I can never bear to gaze upon the compeers of my wife. And whoso is my foe will taunt me thus, "Behold him living in his shame, a wretch who quailed at death himself, but of his coward heart gave up his wedded wife instead, and escaped from Hades; doth he deem himself a man after that? And he loathes his parents, though himself refused to die." Such ill report shall I to my evils add. What profit, then, my friends, for me to live, in fame and fortune ruined.

Ch. Myself have traced the Muses' path, have soared amid the stars, have laid my hold on many a theme, and yet have found naught stronger than necessity, no spell inscribed on Thracian tablets written there by Orpheus, the sweet singer, no! nor aught among the simples culled by Phœbus for the toiling race of men, and given to Asclepius' sons. The only goddess she, whose altar or whose image man cannot approach; victims she heedeth not. O come not to me, dread goddess, in greater might than heretofore in my career. Even Zeus requires thy aid to bring to pass whatso he wills. Thou too it is that by sheer force dost bend the steel among the Chalybes; nor is there any pity in thy relentless nature.

This is the goddess that hath gripped thee too in chains thou canst not 'scape; yet steel thy heart, for all thy weeping ne'er will bring to light again the dead from the realms below. Even sons of gods perish in darkness in the hour of death. We loved her while she was with us, we love her still though dead; noblest of her sex was she, the wife thou tookest to thy bed. Her tomb let none regard as the graves of those who die and are no more, but let her have honours equal with the gods, revered by every traveller; and many a one will cross the road and read this verse aloud, "This is she that died in days gone by to save her lord; now is she a spirit blest. Hail, lady revered; be kind to us!" Such glad greeting shall she have. But see, Admetus! yonder, I believe, comes Alcmena's son toward thy hearth.

Enter HERACLES *with a veiled woman.*

He. Admetus, to a friend we should speak freely, not hold our peace and harbour in our hearts complaints. I came to thee in thy hour of sorrow and claimed the right to prove myself thy friend, but thou wouldst not tell me that she, thy wife, lay stretched in death; but didst make me a welcome guest in thy halls, as though thy whole concern was centred on a stranger's loss. So I crowned my head and poured drink-offerings to the gods in that thy house of sorrow. Wherefore I do blame thee for this treatment of me, yet would not grieve thee in thy trouble. So now the reason I have turned my steps and come hither again, I will tell. This lady take and keep for me until I come bringing hither the steeds of Thrace, after I have slain the lord of the Bistones. But should I fare as fare I fain would not, I give her to thee to serve within thy halls. With no small toil she came into my hands. 'Twas thus: I found folk just appointing an open contest for athletes, well worth a struggle, and there I won her as a prize and brought her thence; now those who were successful in the lighter contests had horses for their prize, but

[1] *Or,* "drive me away."

those who conquered in severer feats, in boxing and wrestling, won herds of oxen, and this woman was to be added thereto; with such a chance 'twere shame indeed to pass so fair a guerdon by. So thou must take her in thy charge, as I said; for not by theft but honest toil I won the prize I bring; and maybe e'en thou in time wilt thank me.

Ad. 'Twas not because of any slight or unkind thought of thee that I concealed my wife's sad fate; but this were adding grief to grief if thou hadst gone from hence to the halls of some other friend; and it sufficed that I should mourn my sorrow. But I do beseech thee, prince, if 'tis possible, bid some other Thessalian, one who hath not suffered as I have, keep the maiden for thee—and thou hast many friends in Pheræ; remind me not of my misfortune. For I could not see her in my house and stay my tears. Oh! add not new affliction to my stricken heart, for sure by sorrow am I bowed enough. And where within my halls could a tender maiden live? for such she is, as her dress and vesture show. Is she to dwell where men consort? Then how shall she retain her maiden purity, if 'mid our youths she come and go? O Heracles, it is no easy task to check a young man's fancy, and I am anxious for thy sake. Or am I to take her to my dead wife's bower and care for her? How can I bring her there to fill the other's bed? Twofold reproach I fear; first, some fellow-townsman may taunt me with betraying my benefactress in eagerness to wed a new young bride; next, there is my dead wife, whom I should much regard, for she doth merit all my reverence. Thou too, lady, whosoe'er thou art, believe me, art the very counterfeit presentment of Alcestis, the picture of her form, ah me! O take this maiden, I conjure thee, from my sight; slay me not already slain. For in her I seem once more to see my wife; and my heart is darkly troubled, and the fountains of my eyes are loosed. Ah, woe is me! Now do I taste the bitterness of this my grief.

Ch. Indeed I cannot call thy fortune blest, yet heaven's gift must thou endure, whoe'er the god that comes to bring it.

He. Would I had the power to bring thy wife up to the light from the halls of death, and confer this kindness on thee!

Ad. Right well I know thou wouldst. But what of that? The dead can never come to life again.

He. Do not exceed the mark, but bear thy grief with moderation.

Ad. 'Tis easier to advise than to suffer and endure.

He. Yet what thy gain, if thou for aye wilt mourn.

Ad. I too know that myself, but some strange yearning leads me on.

He. Love for the dead compels a tear.

Ad. Her death was mine, more than any words of mine can tell.

He. Thou hast lost a noble wife; who shall gainsay it?

Ad. Life henceforth hath lost all charm for me.

He. Time will soothe the smart; as yet thy grief is young.

Ad. "Time"! Use that word, if death and time are one.

He. A new wife and a longing for a fresh marriage will stay thy sorrow.

Ad. Peace! What words are thine? I ne'er of thee had thought it.

He. What! wilt never wed, but preserve thy widowed state?

Ad. There is no woman living that shall share my couch.

He. Dost think that this will help the dead at all?

Ad. My reverence she deserves, where'er she is.

He. I praise thee, yes; but still thou bringest on thyself the charge of folly.

Ad. So that thou never call'st me bridegroom, praise me if thou wilt.

He. I praise thee for thy loyalty to thy wife.

Ad. Come death! if ever I betray her, dead though she be.

He. Well, take this maiden to the shelter of thy noble house.

Ad. Spare me, I entreat thee by Zeus, thy sire.

He. Be sure, if thou refuse, 'twill be a sad mistake.

Ad. If I comply, remorse will gnaw my heart.

He. Yield; for in god's good time maybe thou wilt give me thanks.

Ad. Ah! would thou hadst never won her in the games!

He. Yet thou too sharest in my victory.

Ad. True; still let this maiden go away.

He. Go she shall, if go she must; but first see if this is needful.

Ad. I needs must, else wilt thou be wroth with me.

He. I have a reason good to press the matter thus.

Ad. Have thy way then. Yet know well thy deed I disapprove.

He. A day will come that thou wilt praise me; only yield.

Ad. (*To his servants*) Take her in, if I needs must give her welcome in my house.

He. To thy servants will I not hand her over.

Ad. Conduct her then thyself within, if so thou thinkest good.

He. Nay, but into thy hands shall mine consign her.

Ad. I will not touch her, though she is free to go within my halls.

He. To thy hand, and thine alone I her entrust.

Ad. Prince, against my will thou dost constrain me to this deed.

He. Boldly stretch out thy hand and touch the stranger maid.

Ad. There, then, I stretch it out as toward the Gorgon's severed head.

He. Hast hold of her?

Ad. I have.

He. (*Removes the veil*) So; keep her safely then, and in days to come thou wilt confess the son of Zeus proved himself a noble guest. Look well at her, if haply to thy gaze she have a semblance of thy wife; and now that thou art blest, cease from sorrowing.

Ad. Great gods, what shall I say? a marvel past all hope is here! My wife, my own true wife I see, or is some mocking rapture sent by heaven to drive me mad?

He. No, no; 'tis thy own wife thou seest here.

Ad. Beware it be not a phantom from that nether world.

He. No necromancer was this guest whom thou didst welcome.

Ad. Do I behold my wife, her whom I buried?

He. Be well assured thereof; still I marvel not thou dost distrust thy luck.

Ad. May I touch her, may I speak to her as my living wife?

He. Speak to her. For thou hast all thy heart's desire.

Ad. O form and features of my well-loved wife! past all hope I hold thee, never expecting to see thee again.

He. So thou dost; may no jealous god rise against thee!

Ad. O noble son of almighty Zeus, good luck to thee! may the father that begat thee hold thee in his keeping; for thou and none else hast raised my fallen fortunes. How didst thou bring her from the world below to this light of day?

He. By encountering the god who had her in his power.

Ad. Where didst thou engage with Death? tell me this.

He. Just by the tomb I from my ambush sprang and caught him in my grip.

Ad. But why thus speechless stands my wife?

He. 'Tis not lawful yet for thee to hear her speak, ere she be purified from the gods below and the third day be come. So lead her in; and hereafter, e'en as now, be just and kind to guests, Admetus. Now farewell! for I must go to perform my appointed task for the lordly son of Sthenelus.

Ad. Abide with us and be our welcome guest.

He. Another time; now must I use all haste.

Ad. Good luck to thee! and mayst thou come again! (*Exit* HERACLES) To the citizens and all my realm I make this proclamation, that they institute dances in honour of the glad event, and make the altars steam with sacrifice, and offer prayers; for now have I moored my bark of life in a happier haven than before, and so will own myself a happy man.

Ch. Many are the shapes that fortune takes, and oft the gods bring things to pass beyond our expectation. That which we deemed so sure is not fulfilled, while for that we never thought would be, God finds out a way. And such hath been the issue in the present case. *Exeunt* OMNES.

HERACLEIDÆ

DRAMATIS PERSONAE

Iolaus	Servant, *of Hyllus*
Copreus	Alcmena
Demophon	Messenger
Macaria	Eurystheus
Chorus of Aged Athenians	

Before the altar of Zeus at Marathon. Enter IOLAUS *with the children of Heracles.*

Iolaus. I hold this true, and long have held: Nature hath made one man upright for his neighbours' good, while another hath a disposition wholly given over to gain, useless alike to the state and difficult to have dealings with, but for himself the best of men; and this I know, not from mere hearsay. I, for instance, from pure regard and reverence for my kith and kin, though I might have lived at peace in Argos, alone of all my race shared with Heracles his labours, while he was yet with us, and now that he dwells in heaven, I keep these his children safe beneath my wing, though myself I need protection. For when their father passed from earth away, Eurystheus would first of all have slain us, but we escaped. And though our home is lost, our life was saved. But in exile we wander from city to city, ever forced to roam. For, added to our former wrongs, Eurystheus thought it fit to put this further outrage upon us: wheresoe'er he heard that we were settling, thither would he send heralds demanding our surrender and driving us from thence, holding out this threat, that Argos is no mean city to make a friend or foe, and furthermore pointing to his own prosperity. So they, seeing how weak my means, and these little ones left without a father, bow to his superior might and drive us from their land. And I share the exile of these children, and help them bear their evil lot by my sympathy, loth to betray them, lest someone say, "Look you! now that the children's sire is dead, Iolaus no more protects them, kinsman though he is." Not one corner left us in the whole of Hellas, we are come to Marathon and its neighbouring land, and here we sit as suppliants at the altars of the gods, and pray their aid; for 'tis said two sons of Theseus dwell upon these plains, the lot of their inheritance, scions of Pandion's stock, related to these children; this the reason we have come on this our way to the borders of glorious Athens. To lead the flight two aged guides are we; my care is centred on these boys, while she, I mean Alcmena, clasps her son's daughter in her arms, and bears her for safety within this shrine, for we shrink from letting tender maidens come anigh the crowd or stand as suppliants at the altar. Now Hyllus and the elder of his brethren are seeking some place for us to find a refuge, if we are driven by force from this land. O children, children, come hither! hold unto my robe; for lo! I see a herald coming towards us from Eurystheus, by whom we are persecuted, wanderers excluded from every land. (*Enter* COPREUS) A curse on thee and him that sent thee, hateful wretch! for that same tongue of thine hath oft announced its master's evil hests to these children's noble sire as well.

Copreus. Doubtless thy folly lets thee think this is a good position to have taken up, and that thou art come to a city that will help thee. No! there is none that will prefer thy feeble arm to the might of Eurystheus. Begone! why take this trouble? Thou must arise and go to Argos, where awaits thee death by stoning.

Io. Not so, for the god's altar will protect me, and this land of freedom, wherein we have set foot.

Co. Wilt give me the trouble of laying hands on thee?

Io. By force at least shalt thou never drag these children hence.

Co. That shalt thou soon learn; it seems thou wert a poor prophet, after all, in this.

COPREUS *here seizes the children.*

Io. This shall never happen whilst I live.

Co. Begone! for I will take them hence, for all thy refusals, for I hold that they belong to Eurystheus, as they do indeed.

Io. Help, ye who long have had your home in Athens! we suppliants at Zeus' altar in your marketplace are being haled by force away, our sacred wreaths defiled, shame to your city, to the gods dishonour.

Enter CHORUS.

Chorus. Hark, hark! What cry is this that rises near the altar? At once explain the nature of the trouble.

Io. See this aged frame hurled in its feebleness upon the ground! Woe is me!

Ch. Who threw thee down thus pitiably?

Io. Behold the man who flouts your gods, kind sirs, and tries by force to drag me from my seat before the altar of Zeus.

Ch. From what land, old stranger, art thou come to this confederate state of four cities? or have ye left Eubœa's cliffs, and, with the oar that sweeps the sea, put in here from across the firth?

Io. Sirs, no island life I lead, but from Mycenæ to thy land I come.

Ch. What do they call thee, aged sir, those folk in Mycenæ?

Io. Maybe ye have heard of Iolaus, the comrade of Heracles, for he was not unknown to fame.

Ch. Yea, I have heard of him in bygone days; but tell me, whose are the tender boys thou bearest in thine arms?

Io. These, sirs, are the sons of Heracles, come as suppliants to you and your city.

Ch. What is their quest? Are they anxious, tell me, to obtain an audience of the state?

Io. That so they may escape surrender, nor be torn with violence from thy altars, and brought to Argos.

Co. Nay, this will nowise satisfy thy masters, who o'er thee have a right, and so have tracked thee hither.

Ch. Stranger, 'tis but right we should reverence the gods' suppliants, suffering none with violent hand to make them leave the altars, for that will dread Justice ne'er permit.

Co. Do thou then drive these subjects of Eurystheus forth, and this hand of mine shall abstain from violence.

Ch. 'Twere impious for the state to neglect the suppliant stranger's prayer.

Co. Yet 'tis well to keep clear of troubles, by adopting that counsel, which is the wiser.

Ch. Thou then shouldst have told the monarch of this land thy errand before being so bold, out of regard to his country's freedom, instead of trying to drag strangers by force from the altars of the gods.

Co. Who is monarch of this land and state?

Ch. Demophon, son of gallant Theseus.

Co. Surely it were most to the purpose to discuss this matter somewhat with him; all else has been said in vain.

Ch. Lo! here he comes in person, in hot haste, and Acamas his brother, to hear what thou hast to say.

Enter DEMOPHON *and* ACAMAS.

Demophon. Since thou for all thy years hast outstripped younger men in coming to the rescue to this altar of Zeus, do thou tell me what hath chanced to bring this crowd together.

Ch. There sit the sons of Heracles as suppliants, having wreathed the altar, as thou seest, O king, and with them is Iolaus, trusty comrade of their sire.

De. Why should this event have called for cries of pain?

Ch. (*Turning to* COPREUS) This fellow caused the uproar by trying to drag them forcibly from this altar, and he tripped up the old man, till my tears for pity flowed.

De. Hellenic dress and fashion in his robes doth he no doubt adopt, but deeds like these betray the barbarian. Thou, sirrah, tell me straight the country whence thou camest hither.

Co. An Argive I; since that thou seek'st to know. Who sent me, and the object of my coming, will I freely tell. Eurystheus, king of Mycenæ, sends me hither to fetch these back; and I have come, sir stranger, with just grounds in plenty, alike for speech or action. An Argive myself, Argives I come to fetch, taking with me these runaways from my native city, on whom the doom of death was passed by our laws there; and we have a right, since we rule our city independently, to ratify its sentences. And though they have come as suppliants to the altars of numerous others, we have taken our stand on these same arguments, and no one has ventured to bring upon himself evils of his own getting. But they have come hither, either because they perceived some folly in thee, or, in their perplexity, staking all on one risky throw to win or lose; for surely they do not suppose that thou, if so thou hast thy senses still, and only thou, in all the breadth of Hellas they have traversed, wilt pity their foolish troubles. Come now, put argument against argument: what will be thy gain, suppose thou admit them to thy land, or let us take them hence? From us these benefits are thine to win: this city can secure as friends Argos, with its far-reaching arm, and Eurystheus' might complete, whilst if thou lend an ear to their piteous pleading and grow soft, the matter must result in trial of arms; for be sure we shall not yield this struggle without appealing to the sword. What pretext wilt thou urge? Of what domains art thou robbed that thou shouldst take and wage war with the Tirynthian Argives? What kind of allies art thou aiding? For whom will they have fallen whom thou buriest? Surely thou wilt get an evil name from the citizens, if for the sake of an old man with one foot in the grave, a mere shadow I may say, and for these children, thou wilt plunge into troublous waters. The best thou canst say is, that thou wilt find in them a hope, and nothing more; and yet this falls far short of the present need; for these would be but a poor match for Argives even when fully armed and in their prime, if haply that raises thy spirits; moreover, the time 'twixt now and then is long, wherein ye may be blotted out. Nay, hearken to me; give me naught, but let me take mine own, and so gain Mycenæ; but forbear to act now, as is your Athenian way, and take the weaker side, when it is in thy power to choose the stronger as thy friends.

Ch. Who can decide a cause or ascertain its merits, till from both sides he clearly learn what they would say?

Io. O king, in thy land I start with this advantage, the right to hear and speak in turn, and none, ere that, will drive me hence as elsewhere they would. 'Twixt us and him is naught in common, for we no longer have aught to do with Argos since that decree was passed, but we are exiles from our native land; how then can he justly drag us back as subjects of Mycenæ, seeing that they have banished us? For we are strangers. Or do ye claim that every exile from Argos is exiled from the bounds of Hellas?

Not from Athens surely; for ne'er will she for fear of Argos drive the children of Heracles from her land. Here is no Trachis, not at all; no! nor that Achæan town, whence thou, defying justice, but boasting of the might of Argos in the very words thou now art using, didst drive the suppliants from their station at the altar. If this shall be, and they thy words approve, why then I trow this is no more Athens, the home of freedom. Nay, but I know the temper and nature of these citizens; they would rather die, for honour ranks before mere life with men of worth. Enough of Athens! for excessive praise is apt to breed disgust; and oft ere now I have myself felt vexed at praise that knows no bounds. But to thee, as ruler of this land, I fain would show the reason why thou art bound to save these children. Pittheus was the son of Pelops; from him sprung Æthra, and from her Theseus thy sire was born. And now will I trace back these children's lineage for thee. Heracles was son of Zeus and Alcmena; Alcmena sprang from Pelops' daughter; therefore thy father and their father would be the sons of first cousins. Thus then art thou to them related, O Demophon, but thy just debt to them beyond the ties of kinship do I now declare to thee; for I assert, in days gone by, I was with Theseus on the ship, as their father's squire, when they went to fetch that girdle fraught with death; yea, and from Hades' murky dungeons did Heracles bring thy father up; as all Hellas doth attest. Wherefore in return they crave this boon of thee, that they be not surrendered up nor torn by force from the altars of thy gods and cast forth from the land. For this were shame on thee, and hurtful likewise in thy state, should suppliants, exiles, kith and kin of thine, be haled away by force. For pity's sake! cast one glance at them. I do entreat thee, laying my suppliant bough upon thee, by thy hands and beard, slight not the sons of Heracles, now that thou hast them in thy power to help. Show thyself their kinsman and their friend; be to them father, brother, lord; for better each and all of these than to fall beneath the Argives' hand.

Ch. O king, I pity them, hearing their sad lot. Now more than ever do I see noble birth o'ercome by fortune; for these, though sprung from a noble sire, are suffering what they ne'er deserved.

De. Three aspects of the case constrain me, Iolaus, not to spurn the guests thou bringest; first and foremost, there is Zeus, at whose altar thou art seated with these tender children gathered round thee; next come ties of kin, and the debt I owe to treat them kindly for their father's sake; and last, mine honour, which before all I must regard; for if I permit this altar to be violently despoiled by stranger hands, men will think the land I inhabit is free no more, and that through fear I have surrendered suppliants to Argives, and this comes nigh to make one hang oneself. Would that thou hadst come under a luckier star! yet, as it is, fear not that any man shall tear thee and these children from the altar by force. Get thee (*to* COPREUS) to Argos and tell Eurystheus so; yea and more, if he have any charge against these strangers, he shall have justice; but never shalt thou drag them hence.

Co. Not even if I have right upon my side and prove my case?

De. How can it be right to drag the suppliant away by force?

Co. Well, mine is the disgrace; no harm will come to thee.

De. 'Tis harm to me, if I let them be haled away by thee.

Co. Banish them thyself, and then will I take them from elsewhere.

De. Nature made thee a fool, to think thou knowest better than the god.

Co. It seems then evildoers are to find a refuge here.

De. A temple of the gods is an asylum open to the world.

Co. Maybe they will not take this view in Mycenæ.

De. What! am I not lord of this domain?

Co. So long as thou injure not the Argives, and if wise, thou wilt not.

De. Be injured for all I care, provided I sin not against the gods.

Co. I would not have thee come to blows with Argos.

De. I am of like mind in this; but I will not dismiss these from my protection.

Co. For all that, I shall take and drag my own away.

De. Why then perhaps thou wilt find a difficulty in returning to Argos.

Co. That shall I soon find out by making the attempt.

De. Touch them and thou shalt rue it, and that without delay.

Ch. I conjure thee, never dare to strike a herald.

De. Strike I will, unless that herald learn discretion.

Ch. Depart; and thou, O king, touch him not.

Co. I go; for 'tis feeble fighting with a single arm. But I will come again, bringing hither a host of Argive troops, spearmen clad in bronze; for countless warriors are awaiting my return, and king Eurystheus in person at their head; anxiously he waits the issue here on the borders of Alcathous' realm.[1] And when he hears thy haughty answer, he will burst upon thee, and thy citizens, on this land and all that grows therein; for all in vain should we possess such hosts of picked young troops in Argos, should we forbear to punish thee.

Exit COPREUS.

De. Perdition seize thee! I am not afraid of thy Argos. Be very sure thou shalt not drag these suppliants hence by force, to my shame; for I hold not this city subject unto Argos, but independently.

Ch. 'Tis time to use our forethought, ere the host of Argos approach our frontier, for exceeding fierce are the warriors of Mycenæ, and in the present case still more than heretofore. For all heralds observe

[1]Megara.

this custom, to exaggerate what happened twofold. Bethink thee what a tale he will tell his master of dreadful treatment, how he came very near losing his life altogether.

Io. Children have no fairer prize than this, the being born of a good and noble sire, and the power to wed from noble families; but whoso is enslaved by passion and makes a lowborn match, I cannot praise for leaving to his children a legacy of shame, to gratify himself. For noble birth offers a stouter resistance to adversity than base parentage; we, for instance, in the last extremity of woe, have found friends and kinsmen here, the only champions of these children through all the length and breadth of this Hellenic world. Give, children, give to them your hand, and they the same to you; draw near to them. Ah! children, we have made trial of our friends, and if ever ye see the path that leads you back to your native land, and possess your home and the honours of your father, count them ever as your friends and saviours, and never lift against their land the foeman's spear, in memory of this, but hold this city first midst those ye love. Yea, they well deserve your warm regard, in that they have shifted from our shoulders to their own the enmity of so mighty a land as Argos and its people, though they saw we were vagabonds and beggars; still they did not give us up nor drive us forth. So while I live, and after death, come when it will, loudly will I sing thy praise, good friend, and will extol thee as I stand at Theseus' side, and cheer his heart, as I tell how thou didst give kind welcome and protection to the sons of Heracles, and how nobly thou dost preserve thy father's fame through the length of Hellas, and hast not fallen from the high estate, to which thy father brought thee, a lot which few others can boast; for 'monsgt the many wilt thou find one maybe, that is not degenerate from his sire.

Ch. This land is ever ready in an honest cause to aid the helpless. Wherefore ere now it hath endured troubles numberless for friends, and now in this I see a struggle nigh at hand.

De. Thou hast spoken well, and I feel confident their conduct will be such; our kindness will they not forget. Now will I muster the citizens and set them in array, that I may receive Mycenæ's host with serried ranks. But first will I send scouts to meet them, lest they fall upon me unawares; for at Argos every man is prompt to answer to the call, and I will assemble prophets and ordain a sacrifice. But do thou leave the altar of Zeus and go with the children into the house; for there are those, who will care for thee, even though I be abroad. Enter then my house, old man.

Io. I will not leave the altar. Let[1] us sit here still, praying for the city's fair success, and when thou hast made a glorious end of this struggle, will we go unto the house; nor are the gods who champion us weaker than the gods of Argos, O king; Hera, wife of Zeus, is their leader; Athena ours. And this I say is an omen of success, that we have the stronger deity, for Pallas will not brook defeat.

Exit DEMOPHON.

Ch. Though loud thy boasts, there be others care no more for thee for that, O stranger from the land of Argos; nor wilt thou scare my soul with swelling words. Not yet be this the fate of mighty Athens, beauteous town! But thou art void of sense, and so is he, who lords it o'er Argos, the son of Sthenelus—thou that comest to another state, in no wise weaker than Argos, and, stranger that thou art, wouldst drag away by force suppliants of the gods, wanderers that cling to my land for help, refusing to yield to our king, nor yet having any honest plea to urge. How can such conduct count as honourable, at least in wise men's judgment? I am for peace myself; yet I tell thee, wicked king, although thou come unto my city, thou shalt not get so easily what thou expectest. Thou art not the only man to wield a sword or targe with plates of brass. Nay, thou eager warrior, I warn thee, bring not war's alarms against our lovely town; restrain thyself.

Re-enter DEMOPHON.

Io. My son, why, prithee, art thou returned with that anxious look? Hast thou news of the enemy? Are they coming, are they here, or what thy tidings? For of a surety yon herald will not play us false. No! sure I am their captain, prosperous heretofore, will come, with thoughts exceeding proud against Athens. But Zeus doth punish overweening pride.

De. The host of Argos is come, and Eurystheus its king; my own eyes saw him, for the man who thinks he knows good generalship must see the foe not by messengers alone. As yet, however, he hath not sent his host into the plain, but camped upon a rocky brow, is watching—I only tell thee what I think this means—to see by which road to lead his army hither without fighting, and how to take up a safe position in this land. However, all my plans are by this time carefully laid; the city is under arms, the victims stand ready to be slain to every god, whose due this is; my seers have filled the town with sacrifices, to turn the foe to flight and keep our country safe. All those who chant prophetic words have I assembled, and have examined ancient oracles, both public and secret, as means to save this city. And though the several answers differ in many points, yet in one is the sentiment of all clearly the same; they bid me sacrifice to Demeter's daughter some maiden from a noble father sprung. Now I, though in your cause I am as zealous as thou seest, yet will not slay my child, nor will I compel any of my subjects to do so against his will; for who of his own will doth harbour such an evil thought as to yield with his own hands the child he loves? And now thou mayest see angry gatherings, where some declare, 'tis right to stand by suppliant strangers, while others charge me with folly; but if I do this deed, a civil war is then and there on foot. Do thou then look to this and help to find a way to save

[1] *Or* "let us keep our suppliant seat, awaiting the city's success."

yourselves and this country without causing me to be slandered by the citizens. For I am no despot like a barbarian monarch; but provided I do what is just, just will my treatment be.

Ch. Can it be that heaven forbids this city to help strangers, when it hath the will and longing so to do?

Io. My children, we are even as those mariners, who have escaped the storm's relentless rage, and have the land almost within their reach, but after all are driven back from shore by tempests to the deep again. Even so we, just as we reach the shore in seeming safety, are being thrust back from this land. Ah me! Why, cruel hope, didst thou then cheer my heart, though thou didst not mean to make the boon complete? The king may well be pardoned, if he will not slay his subjects' children; and with my treatment here I am content; if indeed 'tis heaven's will, I thus should fare, still is my gratitude to thee in no wise lost. Children, I know not what to do for you. Whither shall we turn? for what god's altar have we left uncrowned? to what fenced city have we failed to go? Ruin and surrender are our instant lot, poor children! If I must die, 'tis naught to me, save that thereby I give those foes of mine some cause for joy. But you, children, I lament and pity, and that aged mother of your sire, Alcmena. Ah, woe is thee for thy long span of life! and woe is me for all my idle toil! 'Twas after all our destined doom to fall into the hands of our hated foe, and die a death of shame and misery. But lend me thine aid, thou knowest how; for all hope of these children's safety has not yet left me. Give me up instead of them to the Argives, O king; run no risk, but let me save the children; to love my life becomes me not; let it pass. Me will Eurystheus be most glad to take and treat despitefully, as I was Heracles' companion; for the man is but a boor; wherefore wise men ought to pray to get a wise man for their foe, and not a proud senseless fool; for so, even if by fortune flouted, one would meet with much consideration.

Ch. Old man, blame not this city; for though perhaps a gain to us, yet would it be a foul reproach that we betrayed strangers.

De. A generous scheme is thine, but impossible. 'Tis not in quest of thee yon king comes marching hither; what would Eurystheus gain by the death of one so old? Nay, 'tis these children's blood he wants. For there is danger to a foe in the youthful scions of a noble race, whose memory dwells upon their father's wrongs; all this Eurystheus must foresee. But if thou hast any scheme besides, that better suits the time, be ready with it, for, since I heard that oracle, I am at a loss and full of fear.

Enter MACARIA.

Macaria. Sirs, impute not boldness to me, because I venture forth; this shall be my first request, for a woman's fairest crown is this, to practise silence and discretion, and abide at home in peace. But when I heard thy lamentations, Iolaus, I came forth, albeit I was not appointed to take the lead in my family. Still in some sense am I fit to do so, for these my brothers are my chiefest care, and I fain would ask, as touching myself, whether some new trouble, added to the former woes, is gnawing at thy heart.

Io. My daughter, 'tis nothing new that I should praise thee, as I justly may, above all the children of Heracles. Our house seemed to be prospering, when back it fell again into a hopeless state; for the king declares the prophets signify that he must order the sacrifice, not of bull or heifer, but of some tender maid of noble lineage, if we and this city are to exist. Herein is our perplexity; the king refuses either to sacrifice his own or any other's child. Wherefore, though he use not terms express, yet doth he hint, that, unless we find some way out of this perplexity, we must seek some other land, for he this country fain would save.

Ma. Are these indeed the terms on which our safety depends?

Io. Yea, on these; if, that is, we are successful otherwise.

Ma. No longer then cower before the hated Argive spear; for I, of my own free will, or ever they bid me, am ready to die and offer myself as a victim. For what excuse have we, if, while this city deems it right to incur a great danger on our behalf, we, though we might save ourselves, fly from death, by foisting our trouble on others? No! indeed, 'twere surely most ridiculous to sit and mourn as suppliants of the gods, and show ourselves but cowards, children as we are of that illustrious sire. Where among the brave is such conduct seen? Better, I suppose, this city should be taken and I (which Heaven forefend!) fall into the hands of the enemy, and then, for all I am my noble father's child, meet an awful doom, and face the Death-god none the less. Shall I wander as an exile from this land? Shall I not feel shame then, when someone says, as say they will, "Why are ye come hither with suppliant boughs, loving your lives too well? Begone from our land! for we will not succour cowards." Nay, if these be slain and I alone be saved, I have no hope in any wise of being happy, though many ere now have in this hope betrayed their friends. For who will care to wed a lonely maid or make me mother of his children? 'Tis better I should die than meet such treatment, little as I merit it. This were fitter treatment for some other, one that is not born to fame as I am. Conduct me to the scene of death, crown me with garlands, and begin the rites, if so it please you; then be victorious o'er the foe, for here I offer my life freely and without constraint, and for my brothers and myself I undertake to die. For I, by loving not my life too well, have found a treasure very fair, a glorious means to leave it.

Ch. Ah, what shall I say on hearing the maid's brave words, she that is ready to die for her brothers? Who can speak more noble words or do more noble deeds henceforth for ever?

Io. Daughter, thou art his own true child, no other man's but Heracles', that godlike soul; proud am I of thy words, though I sorrow for thy lot. Yet will I propose a fairer method: 'tis right to summon hither all the sisters of this maiden, and then let her, on whom the lot shall fall, die for her family; for that thou shouldst die without the lot is not just.

Ma. My death shall no chance lot decide; there is no graciousness in that; peace! old friend. But if ye accept and will avail you of my readiness, freely do I offer my life for these, and without constraint.

Io. Ah, this is even nobler than thy former word; that was matchless, but thou dost now surpass thy bravery and noble speech. I cannot bid, will not forbid thy dying, O my daughter! for by thy death thou dost thy brothers serve.

Ma. A cautious bidding thine! Fear not to take a stain of guilt from me; only let me die as one whose death is free. Follow me, old friend, for in thy arms I fain would die; stand by and veil my body with my robe, for I will go even to the dreadful doom of sacrifice, seeing whose daughter I avow myself.

Io. I cannot stand by and see thee bleed.

Ma. At least do thou beg me this boon of the king, that I may breathe out my life in women's arms instead of men's.

De. It shall be so, unhappy maid; for this were shame to me to refuse thee honour due, for many reasons: because thou hast a soul so brave; because 'tis right; and thou hast shown more courage than any of thy sex my eyes have ever seen. Now, if thou hast aught to say to these children or thy aged guide, oh! say the last thou hast to say—then go. *Exit.*

Ma. Farewell, old friend, farewell! and prithee teach these children to be like thyself, wise at every point; let them strive no further, for that will suffice them. And seek to save them from death, even as thou art anxious to do; thy children are we, thy care it was that nurtured us. Thou seest how I yield my bridal bloom to die for them. For you, my brothers gathered here, may you be happy! and may every blessing be yours, for the which my blood shall pay the price! Honour this old friend, and her that is within the house, Alcmena, the aged mother of my sire, and these strangers too. And if ever heaven for you devise release from trouble and a return to your home, remember the burial due to her that saved you, a funeral fair as I deserve; for I have not failed, but stood by you, and died to save my race. This shall be my pearl of price instead of children, and for the maiden life I leave, if there be really aught beyond the grave—God grant there may not be! For if, e'en there, we who are to die shall find a life of care, I know not whither one shall turn; for death is held a sovereign cure for every ill.

Io. Maiden of heroic soul, transcending all thy race, be sure the fame that thou shalt win from us, in life, in death, shall leave the rest of women far behind; farewell to thee! I dare not say harsh words of her to whom thou art devoted, the goddess-daughter of Demeter. (*Exit* MACARIA) Children, I am undone, grief unnerves my limbs; take hold and support me to a seat hard by, when ye have drawn my mantle o'er my face, my sons. For I am grieved at what hath happened, and yet, were it not fulfilled, we could not live; thus were the mischief worse, though this is grief enough.

Ch. Without the will of heaven none is blest, none curst, I do maintain; nor doth the same house for ever tread the path of bliss; for one kind of fortune follows hard upon another; one man it brings to naught from his high estate, another though of no account it crowns with happiness. To shun what fate decrees, is no wise permitted; none by cunning shall thrust it from him; but he, who vainly would do so, shall have unceasing trouble. Then fall not prostrate thou, but bear what heaven sends, and set a limit to thy soul's grief; for she, poor maid! in dying for her brothers and this land, hath won a glorious death, and splendid fame shall be her meed from all mankind; for virtue's path leads through troublous ways. Worthy of her father, worthy of her noble birth is this conduct. And if thou dost honour the virtuous dead, I share with thee that sentiment.

Enter SERVANT.

Servant. All hail, ye children! Where is aged Iolaus? where the mother of your sire, absent from their place at this altar?

Io. Here am I, so far as I can be present at all.

Se. Why dost thou lie there? Why that downcast look?

Io. There is come a sorrow on my house, whereby I am distressed.

Se. Arise, lift up thy head.

Io. I am old, and all my strength is gone.

Se. But I come with tidings of great joy for thee.

Io. Who art thou? Where have I met thee? I have no remembrance.

Se. I am a vassal of Hyllus; dost not recognize me now?

Io. Best of friends, art thou come to save us twain from hurt?

Se. Assuredly; and moreover thou art lucky in the present case.

Io. Alcmena, mother of a noble son, to thee I call! come forth, hear this welcome news. For long has anguish caused thee inwardly to waste, wondering if those, who now are here, would ever come.

Enter ALCMENA.

Alcmena. What means that shout, that echoes throughout the house? Hath there come yet a herald from Argos, O Iolaus, and is he treating thee with violence? Feeble is any strength of mine; yet thus much let me tell thee, stranger, never, whilst I live, shalt thou drag them hence. Shouldst thou succeed, no more let me be thought the mother of that hero. And if thou lay a finger on them, thou wilt struggle to thy shame with two aged foes.

Io. Courage, aged dame, fear not; not from Argos is a herald come, with hostile messages.

Al. Why then didst raise a cry, fear's harbinger?

Io. I called thee to come to me in front of this temple.

Al. I know not what it means; who is this?

Io. A messenger who says thy grandson cometh hither.

Al. All hail to thee for these thy tidings! But why is he not here, where is he? if in this land he hath set foot. What hath happened to keep him from coming hither with thee, to cheer my heart?

Se. He is posting the army he brought with him, and seeing it marshalled.

Al. Then have I no concern herein.

Io. Yes, thou hast; though it is my business to inquire into these matters.

Se. What then wouldst thou learn of these events?

Io. About how many allies has he with him?

Se. A numerous force; I cannot otherwise describe the number.

Io. The leaders of the Athenians know this, I suppose?

Se. They do; already is their left wing set in array.

Io. Is then the host already armed for battle?

Se. Yea, and already are the victims brought near the ranks.

Io. About what distance is the Argive host from us?

Se. Near enough for their general to be plainly seen.

Io. What is he about? marshalling the enemy's line?

Se. So we guessed; we could not hear exactly. But I must go, for I would not that my master should engage the foe without me, if I can help it.

Io. I also will go with thee; for I like thee am minded, so it seems, to be there and help my friends.

Se. It least of all becomes thee thus to utter words of folly.

Io. Far less to shrink from sharing with my friends the stubborn fight.

Se. Mere looks can wound no one, if the arm do naught.

Io. Why, cannot I smite even through their shields?

Se. Smite perhaps, more likely be smitten thyself.

Io. No foe will dare to meet me face to face.

Se. Friend, the strength, that erst was thine, is thine no more.

Io Well, at any rate, I will fight with as many as ever I did.

Se. Small the weight thou canst throw into the balance for thy friends.

Io. Detain me not, when I have girded myself for action.

Se. The power to act is thine no more, the will maybe is there.

Io. Stay here I will not, say what else thou wilt.

Se. How shalt thou show thyself before the troops unarmed?

Io. There be captured arms within this shrine; these will I use, and, if I live, restore; and, if I am slain, the god will not demand them of me back. Go thou within, and from its peg take down a suit of armour and forthwith bring it to me. To linger thus at home is infamous, while some go fight, and others out of cowardice remain behind.

Exit SERVANT.

Ch. Not yet hath time laid low thy spirit, 'tis young as ever; but thy body's strength is gone. Why toil to no purpose? 'Twill do thee hurt and benefit our city little. At thy age thou shouldst confess thy error and let impossibilities alone. Thou canst in no way get thy vigour back again.

Al. What means this mad resolve to leave me with my children undefended here?

Io. Men must fight; and thou must look to them.

Al. And what if thou art slain? what safety shall I find?

Io. Thy son's surviving children will care for thee.

Al. Suppose *they* meet with some reverse? which Heaven forefend!

Io. These strangers will not give thee up, fear not.

Al. They are my last and only hope, I have no other.

Io. Zeus too, I feel sure, cares for thy sufferings.

Al. Ah! of Zeus will I never speak ill, but himself doth know, whether he is just to me.

Exit ALCMENA. *Re-enter* SERVANT.

Se. Lo! here thou seest a full coat of mail; make haste to case thyself therein; for the strife is nigh, and bitterly doth Ares loathe loiterers; but if thou fear the weight of the armour, go for the present without it, and in the ranks do on this gear; meantime will I carry it.

Io. Well said! keep the harness ready to my hand, put a spear within my grasp, and support me on the left side, guiding my steps.

Se. Am I to lead this warrior like a child?

Io. To save the omen, we must go without stumbling.

Se. Would thy power to act were equal to thy zeal!

Io. Hasten; I shall feel it grievously, if I am too late for the battle.

Se. 'Tis thou who art slow, not I, though thou fanciest thou art doing wonders.

Io. Dost not mark how swift my steps are hasting?

Se. I mark more seeming than reality in thy haste.

Io. Thou wilt tell a different tale when thou seest me there.

Se. What shall I see thee do? I wish thee all success, at any rate.

Io. Thou shalt see me smite some foeman through the shield.

Se. Perhaps, if ever we get there. I have my fears of that.

Io. Ah! would to Heaven that thou, mine arm, e'en as I remember thee in thy lusty youth, when with Heracles thou didst sack Sparta, couldst so champion me to-day! how I would put Eurystheus to flight! since he is too craven to wait the onslaught. For prosperity carries with it this error too, a reputation for bravery; for we think the prosperous man a master of all knowledge. *Exeunt.*

Ch. O earth, and moon that shines by night, and dazzling radiance of the god, that giveth light to man, bear the tidings to me, shout aloud to heaven for joy, and beside our ruler's throne, and in the shrine of grey-eyed Athene. For my fatherland and home will I soon decide the issue of the strife with the gleaming sword, because I have taken suppliants under my protection. 'Tis a fearful thing, that a city prosperous as Mycenæ is, one famed for martial prowess, should harbour wrath against my land; still, my countrymen, it were a shameful thing in us to yield up suppliant strangers at the bidding of Argos. Zeus is on my side, I am not afraid; Zeus hath a favour unto me, as is my due; never by me shall gods be thought weaker than mortal men. O dread goddess,[1] thine the soil whereon we stand, thine this city, for thou art its mother, queen, and saviour; wherefore turn some other way the impious king, who leadeth a host from Argos with brandished lance against this land; for, such my worth, I little merit exile from my home. For thy worship[2] is aye performed with many a sacrifice, and never art thou forgotten as each month draweth to its close, when young voices sing and dancers' music is heard abroad, while on our wind-swept hill goes up the cry of joy to the beat of maidens' feet by night.

Enter ALCMENA *and* SERVANT.

Se. Mistress, the message that I bring is very short for thee to hear and fair for me, who stand before thee, to announce. O'er our foes we are victorious, and trophies are being set up, with panoplies upon them, taken from thy enemies.

Al. Best of friends! this day hath wrought thy liberty by reason of these tidings. But there still remains one anxious thought thou dost not free me from, a thought of fear: are those, whose lives I cherish, spared to me?

Se. They are, and high their fame through all the army spreads.

Al. The old man Iolaus—is he yet alive?

Se. Aye, that he is, a hero whom the gods delight to honour.

Al. How so? Did he perform some deed of prowess?

Se. He hath passed from age to youth once more.

Al. Thy tale is passing strange; but first I would that thou shouldst tell me, how our friends won the day.

Se. One speech of mine puts it all clearly before thee. When we had deployed our troops and marshalled them face to face with one another, Hyllus dismounted from his four-horsed chariot and stood midway betwixt the hosts. Then cried he, "Captain, who art come from Argos, why cannot we leave this land alone? No hurt wilt thou do Mycenæ, if of one man thou rob her; come! meet me in single combat, and, if thou slay me, take the children of Heracles away with thee, but, if thou fall, leave me to possess my ancestral honours and my home." The host cried yes! saying the scheme he offered was a fair one, both to rid them of their trouble and satisfy their valour. But that other, feeling no shame before those who heard the challenge or at his own cowardice, quailed, general though he was, to come within reach of the stubborn spear, showing himself an abject coward; yet with such a spirit he came to enslave the children of Heracles. Then did Hyllus withdraw to his own ranks again, and the prophets seeing that no reconciliation would be effected by single combat, began the sacrifice without delay and forthwith let flow from a human throat auspicious streams of blood. And some were mounting chariots, while others couched beneath the shelter of their shields, and the king of the Athenians, as a highborn chieftain should, would exhort his host: "Fellow-citizens, the land, that feeds you and that gave you birth, demands to-day the help of every man." Likewise Eurystheus besought his allies that they should scorn to sully the fame of Argos and Mycenæ. Anon the Etrurian trumpet sounded loud and clear, and hand to hand they rushed; then think how loudly clashed their ringing shields, what din arose of cries and groans confused! At first the onset of the Argive spearmen broke our ranks; then they in turn gave ground; next, foot to foot and man to man, they fought their stubborn fray, many falling the while. And either chief cheered on his men, "Sons of Athens! Ye who till the fields of Argos! ward from your land disgrace." Do all we could, and spite of every effort, scarce could we turn the Argive line in flight. When lo! old Iolaus sees Hyllus starting from the ranks, whereon he lifts his hands to him with a prayer to take him up into his chariot. Thereon he seized the reins and went hard after the horses of Eurystheus. From this point onward must I speak from hearsay, though hitherto as one whose own eyes saw. For as he was crossing Pallene's hill, sacred to the goddess Athene, he caught sight of Eurystheus' chariot, and prayed to Hebe and to Zeus, that for one single day he might grow young again and wreak his vengeance on his foes. Now must thou hear a wondrous tale: two stars settled on the horses' yokes and threw the chariot into dark shadow, which—at least so say our wiser folk—were thy son and Hebe; and from that murky gloom appeared that aged man in the form of a youth with strong young arms; then by the rocks of Sciron the hero Iolaus o'ertakes Eurystheus' chariot. And he bound his hands with gyves, and is bringing that chieftain once so prosperous as a trophy hither, whose fortune now doth preach a lesson, clear as day, to all the sons of men, that none should envy him, who seems to thrive, until they see his death; for fortune's moods last but a day.

Ch. O Zeus, who puttest my foes to flight, now may I behold the day that frees me from cruel fear!

Al. At last, O Zeus, hast thou turned a favouring eye on my affliction; yet do I thank thee for what has happened. And though ere this I did not believe my son was gathered to the gods, now am I convinced thereof. My children, now at last from toil shall ye be free, free from him, whom hideous death awaits, Eurystheus; now shall ye behold your father's city, and set foot in the land of your inheritance, and sacrifice to those ancestral gods, from whom ye have been debarred and forced to lead in strangers' lands a life of wretched vagrancy. But tell me,

[1]Pallas.
[2]The festival of the Panathenæa.

what sage purpose Iolaus nursed in his heart, that he spared the life of Eurystheus, for to my mind this is no wisdom, to catch a foe and wreak no vengeance on him.

Se. 'Twas his regard for thee, that thou might'st see him subject to thy hand, and triumph o'er him. Rest assured, 'twas no willing prisoner he made, but by strong constraint he bound him, for Eurystheus was loth indeed to come alive into thy presence and pay his penalty. Farewell, my aged mistress; I pray thee remember thy first promise when I was beginning my story; set me free; for, at such a time as this, sincerity becometh noble lips. *Exit* SERVANT.

Ch. Sweet is the dance to me, whenso the clear-toned flute and lovely Aphrodite shed grace upon the feast; and a joyful thing too it is, I trow, to witness the good luck of friends, who till then ne'er dreamt of it. For numerous is the offspring of Fate, that bringeth all to pass, and of Time, the son of Cronos. Thine is the path of justice, O my city; this must no man wrest from thee, thy reverence for the gods, and, whoso denieth it of thee, draws nigh to frenzy's goal, with these plain proofs in view. Yea, for the god proclaims it clearly, by cutting short the bad man's pride in every case. In heaven, mother, lives thy son, passed from earth away; that he went down to Hades' halls, his body burnt by the fire's fierce flame, is past belief; in golden halls reclined he has to wife Hebe, lovely nymph. Thou, O Hymen, hast honoured them, children both of Zeus. Things for the most part form a singe chain; for instance, men say Athene used to champion their father, and now the citizens of that goddess have saved his children, and checked the insolence of him, whose heart preferred violence to justice. God save me from such arrogance, such greed of soul!

Enter MESSENGER, *with* EURYSTHEUS, *bound.*

Messenger. Mistress, though thine eyes see him, yet will I announce we have brought Eurystheus hither for thy pleasure, an unexpected sight for him no less a chance he ne'er foresaw; for little he thought of ever falling into thy hands, what time he marched from Mycenæ with his toil-worn warriors, to sack Athens, thinking himself far above fortune. But a power divine hath reversed our destinies, changing their position. Now Hyllus and brave Iolaus I left raising an image to Zeus, who routs the foe, for their triumphant victory, whilst they bid me bring this prisoner to thee, wishing to gladden thy heart; for 'tis the sweetest sight to see a foe fall on evil days after prosperity.

Al. Art come, thou hateful wretch? Hath Justice caught thee then at last? First, turn thy head this way to me, and endure to look thy enemies in the face, for thou art no more the ruler, but the slave. Art thou the man—for this I fain would learn—who didst presume to heap thy insults on my son, who now is where he is, thou miscreant? What outrage didst thou abstain from putting upon him? Thou that didst make him go down alive even to Hades, and wouldst send him with an order to slay hydras and lions? Thy other evil schemes I mention not, for to tell them were a tedious task for me. Nor did it content thee to venture thus far only; no! but from all Hellas wouldst thou drive me and my children, heaven's suppliants though we were, greyheads some of us, and some still tender babes. But here hast thou found men and a free city, that feared not thee. Die in torment must thou, and e'en so wilt thou gain in every way, for one death is not thy due, after all the sorrow thou hast caused.

Me. Thou mayst not slay him.

Al. Then have we taken him captive in vain. But say, what law forbids his death?

Me. It is not the will of the rulers of this land.

Al. Why, what is this? Do they not approve of slaying enemies?

Me. Not such as they have taken alive in battle.

Al. Did Hyllus uphold this decision?

Me. He, I suppose, ought to have disobeyed the law of the land.

Al. The prisoner's life ought not to have been spared a moment.

Me. It was then that he was wronged, by not being slain at first.

Al. Why, then, he is still in time to pay his penalty.

Me. There is no one who will slay him now.

Al. I will; and yet I count myself someone.

Me. Well, thou wilt incur great blame, if thou do this deed.

Al. I love this city well; that cannot be gainsaid. But since this man hath fallen into my power, no mortal hand shall wrest him from me. Wherefore let who will, call me the woman bold, with thoughts too high for her sex; yet shall this deed be brought to pass by me.

Ch. Lady, full well I understand thou hast a dire quarrel with this man, and 'tis pardonable.

Eurystheus. Woman, be sure I will not flatter thee nor say aught to save my life, that can give any occasion for a charge of cowardice. It was not of my own free will I took this quarrel up; I am aware that I was born thy cousin, and kinsman to Heracles, thy son; but whether I would or no, Hera, by her power divine, caused me to be afflicted thus. Still, when I undertook to be his foe, and when I knew I had to enter on this struggle, I set myself to devise trouble in plenty, and oft from time to time my midnight communing bore fruit, scheming how to push aside and slay my foes, and for the future divorce myself from fear; for I knew that son of thine was no mere cipher, but a man indeed; yea, for, though he was my foe, I will speak well of him, because he was a man of worth. Now, after he was taken hence, was I not forced, by reason of these children's hatred, and because I was conscious of an hereditary feud, to leave no stone unturned by slaying, banishing, and plotting against them? So long as I did so, my safety was assured. Suppose thyself hadst had my lot, wouldst not thou have set to harassing the lion's angry whelps, instead of letting them dwell at Argos undisturbed? Thou wilt not persuade us otherwise. Now therefore, since they did not slay me then, when I was prepared to die, by the laws of Hellas my death becomes a curse on him, who slays me now. The city wisely let me go, in that she regarded the gods more than her hatred of me. Thou hast had my answer to thy words; henceforth must I be called avenging spirit and noble hero too.[1] 'Tis even thus with me; to die have I no wish, but, if I leave my life, I shall in no way be grieved.

Ch. Alcmena, fain I would advise thee somewhat; let this man go, for 'tis the city's will.

Al. Suppose he die, and yet I obey the city?

Ch. That would be best of all; but how can this be?

Al. I will teach thee easily. I will slay him and then give up his corpse to those of his friends, who come for it, for, as regards his body, I will not disobey the state; but by his death shall he pay me the penalty.

Eu. Slay me, I do not ask thee for mercy; yet since this city let me go and shrunk from slaying me, I will reward it with an old oracle of Loxias, which in time will benefit them more than doth appear. Bury my body after death in its destined grave in front of the shrine of the virgin goddess[2] at Pallene. And I will be thy friend and guardian of thy city for ever, where I lie buried in a foreign soil, but a bitter foe to these children's descendants, whensoe'er with gathered host they come against this land, traitors to your kindness now; such are the strangers ye have championed. Why then came I hither, if I knew all this, instead of regarding the god's oracle? Because I thought, that Hera was mightier far than any oracle, and would not betray me. Waste no drink-offering on my tomb, nor spill the victim's blood; for I will requite them for my treatment here with a journey they shall rue; and ye shall have double gain for me, for I will help you and harm them by my death.

Al. Why, why delay to kill this man, after hearing this, since this is needed to secure the safety of your city and your children? Himself points out the safest road. Though the man is now our foe, yet after death is he our gain. Away with him, ye servants, and cast him to the dogs when ye have slain him. Think not thou shalt live to cast me forth from my native land again.

Exeunt MESSENGER *with* EURYSTHEUS.

Ch. I agree. Lead on, servants. Our conduct shall bring no stain of guilt upon our rulers.

Exeunt OMNES.

[1] *i.e.* I will meet my doom like a hero, and haunt you after death.

[2] Pallas.

THE SUPPLIANTS

DRAMATIS PERSONAE

ÆTHRA	HERALD
CHORUS OF ARGIVE MOTHERS	MESSENGER
THESEUS	EVADNE
ADRASTUS	IPHIS
	CHILDREN
ATHENA	

The Temple of Demeter at Eleusis. Enter ÆTHRA, ADRASTUS, *and* CHORUS OF ARGIVE MOTHERS.

Æthra. O Demeter, guardian of this Eleusinian land, and ye servants of the goddess who attend her fane, grant happiness to me and my son Theseus, to the city of Athens and the country of Pittheus, wherein my father reared me, Æthra, in a happy home, and gave me in marriage to Ægeus, Pandion's son, according to the oracle of Loxias. This prayer I make, when I behold these aged dames, who, leaving their homes in Argos, now throw themselves with suppliant branches at my knees in their awful trouble; for around the gates of Cadmus have they lost their seven noble sons, whom on a day Adrastus, king of Argos, led thither, eager to secure for exiled Polynices, his son-in-law, a share in the heritage of Œdipus; so now their mothers would bury in the grave the dead, whom the spear hath slain, but the victors prevent them and will not allow them to take up the corpses, spurning Heaven's laws. Here lies Adrastus on the ground with streaming eye, sharing with them the burden of their prayer to me, and bemoaning the havoc of the sword and the sorry fate of the warriors whom he led from their homes. And he doth urge me use entreaty, to persuade my son to take up the dead and help to bury them, either by winning words or force of arms, laying on my son and on Athens this task alone. Now it chanced, that I had left my house and come to offer sacrifice on behalf of the earth's crop at this shrine, where first the fruitful corn showed its bristling shocks above the soil. And here at the holy altars of the twain goddesses, Demeter and her daughter, I wait, holding these sprays of foliage, a bond that bindeth not, in compassion for these childless mothers, hoary with age, and from reverence for the sacred fillets. To call Theseus hither is my herald to the city gone, that he may rid the land of that which grieveth them, or loose these my suppliant bonds, with pious observance of the gods' will; for such as are discreet amongst women should in all cases invoke the aid of men.

Ch. At thy knees I fall, aged dame, and my old lips beseech thee; arise, rescue from the slain my children's bodies, whose limbs, by death relaxed, are left a prey to savage mountain beasts, beholding the bitter tears which spring to my eyes and my old wrinkled skin torn by my hands; for what can I do else? who never laid out my children dead within my halls, nor now behold their tombs heaped up with earth. Thou too, honoured lady, once a son didst bear, crowning thy lord's marriage with fond joy; then share, O share with me thy mother's feelings, in such measure as my sad heart grieves for my own dead sons; and persuade thy son, whose aid we implore, to go unto the river Ismenus, there to place within my hapless arms the bodies of my children, slain in their prime and left without a tomb. Though[1] not as piety enjoins, yet from sheer necessity I have come to the fire-crowned altars of the gods, falling on my knees with instant supplication, for my cause is just, and 'tis in thy power, blest as thou art in thy children, to remove from me my woe; so in my sore distress I do beseech thee of my misery place in my hands my son's dead body, that I may throw my arms about his hapless limbs.

Semi-Chorus. Behold a rivalry in sorrow! woe takes up the tale of woe; hark! thy servants beat their breasts. Come ye who join the mourners' wail, come, O sympathetic band, to join the dance, which Hades honours; let the pearly nail be stained red, as it rends your cheeks, let your skin be streaked with gore; for honours rendered to the dead are a credit to the living. Sorrow's charm doth drive me wild, insatiate, painful, endless, even as the trickling stream that gushes from some steep rock's face; for 'tis woman's way to fall a-weeping o'er the cruel calamity of children dead. Ah me! would I could die and forget my anguish! *Enter* THESEUS.

Theseus. What is this lamentation that I hear, this beating of the breast, these dirges for the dead, with cries that echo from this shrine? How fluttering fear disquiets me, lest haply my mother have gotten some mischance, in quest of whom I come, for she hath been long absent from home. Ha! what now? A strange sight challenges my speech; I see my aged mother sitting at the altar and stranger dames are with her, who in various note proclaim their woe;

[1]Because they had arrived during a festival and their supplication at such a time was a bad omen.

from aged eyes the piteous tear is starting to the ground, their hair is shorn, their robes are not the robes of joy. What means it, mother? 'Tis thine to make it plain to me, mine to listen; yea, for I expect some tidings strange.

Æ. My son, these are the mothers of those chieftains seven, who fell around the gates of Cadmus' town. With suppliant boughs they keep me prisoner, as thou seest, in their midst.

Th. And who is yonder man, that moaneth piteously in the gateway?

Æ. Adrastus, they inform me, king of Argos.

Th. Are those his children, those boys who stand round him?

Æ. Not his, but the sons of the fallen slain.

Th. Why are they come to us, with suppliant hand outstretched?

Æ. I know; but 'tis for them to tell their story, my son.

Th. To thee, in thy mantle muffled, I address my inquiries; unveil thy head, let lamentation be, and speak; for naught can be achieved save through the utterance of thy tongue.

Adrastus. Victorious prince of the Athenian realm, Theseus, to thee and to thy city I, a suppliant, come.

Th. What seekest thou? What need is thine?

Ad. Dost know how I did lead an expedition to its ruin?

Th. Assuredly; thou didst not pass through Hellas, all in silence.

Ad. There I lost the pick of Argos' sons.

Th. These are the results of that unhappy war.

Ad. I went and craved their bodies from Thebes.

Th. Didst thou rely on heralds, Hermes' servants, in order to bury them?

Ad. I did; and even then their slayers said me nay.

Th. Why, what say they to thy just request?

Ad. Say! Success makes them forget how to bear their fortune.

Th. Art come to me then for counsel? or wherefore?

Ad. With the wish that thou, O Theseus, shouldst recover the sons of the Argives.

Th. Where is your Argos now? were its vauntings all in vain?

Ad. Defeat and ruin are our lot. To thee for aid we come.

Th. Is this thy own private resolve, or the wish of all the city?

Ad. The sons of Danaus, one and all, implore thee to bury the dead.

Th. Why didst lead thy seven armies against Thebes?

Ad. To confer that favour on the husbands of my daughters twain.

Th. To which of the Argives didst thou give thy daughters in marriage?

Ad. I made no match for them with kinsmen of my family.

Th. What! didst give Argive maids to foreign lords?

Ad. Yea, to Tydeus, and to Polynices, who was Theban-born.

Th. What induced thee to select this alliance?

Ad. Dark riddles of Phœbus stole away my judgment.

Th. What said Apollo to determine the maidens' marriage?

Ad. That I should give my daughters twain to a wild boar and a lion.

Th. How dost thou explain the message of the god?

Ad. One night came to my door two exiles.

Th. The name of each declare; thou art speaking of both together.

Ad. They fought together, Tydeus with Polynices.

Th. Didst thou give thy daughters to them as to wild beasts?

Ad. Yea, for, as they fought, I likened them to those monsters twain.

Th. Why had they left the borders of their native land and come to thee?

Ad. Tydeus was exiled for the murder of a kinsman.

Th. Wherefore had the son of Œdipus left Thebes?

Ad. By reason of his father's curse, not to spill his brother's blood.

Th. Wise no doubt that voluntary exile.

Ad. But those who stayed at home were for injuring the absent.

Th. What! did brother rob brother of his inheritance?

Ad. To avenge this I set out; hence my ruin.

Th. Didst consult seers, and gaze into the flame of burnt-offerings?

Ad. Ah me! thou pressest on the very point, wherein I most did fail.

Th. It seems thy going was not favoured by heaven.

Ad. Worse; I went in spite even of Amphiaraus.

Th. And so heaven lightly turned its face from thee.

Ad. I was carried away by the clamour of younger men.

Th. Thou didst favour courage instead of discretion.

Ad. True; and many a general owes defeat to that. O king of Athens, bravest of the sons of Hellas, I blush to throw myself upon the ground and clasp thy knees, I a grey-haired king, blest in days gone by; yet needs must I yield to my misfortunes. I pray thee save the dead; have pity on my sorrows and on these, the mothers of the slain, whom hoary eld finds reft of their sons; yet they endured to journey hither and tread a foreign soil with aged tottering steps, bearing no embassy to Demeter's mysteries; only seeking burial for their dead, which lot should have been theirs, e'en burial by the hands of sons still in their prime. And 'tis wise in the rich to see the poor man's poverty, and in the poor man to turn ambitious eyes toward the rich, that so he may himself indulge a longing for property; and they, whom fortune frowns not on, should gaze on misery's presentment; likewise, who maketh songs should take a pleasure in their making; for if it be not so with him, he will in no wise avail to gladden others, if himself have sorrow in his home; nay, 'tis not even right to expect it. Mayhap thou'lt say, "Why pass the land of Pelops o'er, and lay this toil on Athens?" This am I bound to declare. Sparta is cruel, her customs variable; the other states are small and weak. Thy city alone would be able to undertake this labour; for it turns an eye on suffering, and hath in thee a young and gallant king, for want whereof to lead their hosts states ere now have often perished.

Ch. I too, Theseus, urge the same plea to thee; have pity on my hard fate.

Th. Full oft have I argued out this subject with others. For there are who say, there is more bad than good in human nature, to the which I hold a contrary view, that good o'er bad predóminates in man, for if it were not so, we should not exist. He hath my praise, whoe'er of gods brought us to live by rule from chaos and from brutishness, first by implanting reason, and next by giving us a tongue to declare our thoughts, so as to know the meaning of what is said, bestowing fruitful crops, and drops of rain from heaven to make them grow, wherewith to nourish earth's fruits and to water her lap; and more than this, protection from the wintry storm, and means to ward from us the sun-god's scorching heat; the art of sailing o'er the sea, so that we might exchange with one another whatso our countries lack. And where sight fails us and our knowledge is not sure, the seer foretells by gazing on the flame, by reading signs in folds of entrails, or by divination from the flight of birds. Are we not then too proud, when heaven hath made such preparation for our life, not to be content therewith? But our presumption seeks to lord it over heaven, and in the pride of our hearts we think we are wiser than the gods. Methinks thou art even of this number, a son of folly, seeing that thou, though obedient to Apollo's oracle in giving thy daughters to strangers, as if gods really existed, yet hast hurt thy house by mingling the stream of its pure line with muddy waters; no! never should the wise man have joined the stock of just and unjust in one, but should have gotten prosperous friends for his family. For the deity, confusing their destinies, doth oft destroy by the sinner's fate him who never sinned nor committed injustice. Thou didst lead all Argos forth to battle, though seers proclaimed the will of heaven, and then in scorn of them and in violent disregard of the gods hast ruined thy city, led away by younger men, such as court distinction, and add war to war unrighteously, destroying their fellow-citizens; one aspires to lead an army; another fain would seize the reins of power and work his wanton will; a third is bent on gain, careless of any mischief the people thereby suffer. For there are three ranks of citizens; the rich, a useless set, that ever crave for more; the poor and destitute, fearful folk, that cherish envy more than is right, and shoot out grievous stings against the men who have aught, beguiled as they are by the eloquence of vicious leaders; while the class that is midmost of the three preserveth cities, observing such order as the state ordains. Shall I then become thy ally? What fair pretext should I urge before my countrymen? Depart in peace! For why shouldst thou, having been ill-advised thyself, seek to drag our fortune down?

Ch. He erred; but with the young men rests this error, while he may well be pardoned.

Ad. I did not choose thee, king, to judge my affliction, but came to thee to cure it; no! nor if in aught my fortunes prove me wrong, came I to thee to punish or correct them, but to seek thy help. But if thou wilt not, I must be content with thy decision; for how can I help it? Come, aged dames, away! Yet leave behind you here the woven leaves of pale green foliage, calling to witness heaven and earth, Demeter, that fire-bearing goddess, and the sun-god's light, that our prayers to heaven availed us naught.

Ch. . . . .[1] who was Pelops' son, and we are of the land of Pelops and share with thee the blood of ancestors. What art thou doing? wilt thou betray these suppliant symbols, and banish from thy land these aged women without the boon they should obtain? Do not so; e'en the wild beast finds a refuge in the rock, the slave in the altars of the gods, and a state when tempest-tossed cowers to its neighbour's shelter; for naught in this life of man is blest unto its end.

Rise, hapless one, from the sacred floor of Persephone; rise, clasp him by the knees and implore him, "O recover the bodies of our dead sons, the children that I lost—ah, woe is me!—beneath the walls of Cadmus' town." Ah me! ah me! Take me by the hand, poor aged sufferer that I am, support and guide and raise me up. By thy beard, kind friend, glory of Hellas, I do beseech thee, as I clasp thy knees and hands in my misery; O pity me as I entreat for my sons with my tale of wretched woe, like some beggar; nor let my sons lie there unburied in the land of Cadmus, glad prey for beasts, whilst thou art in thy prime, I implore thee. See the teardrop tremble in my eye, as thus I throw me at thy knees to win my children burial.

Th. Mother mine, why weepest thou, drawing o'er thine eyes thy veil? Is it because thou didst hear their piteous lamentations? To my own heart it goes. Raise thy silvered head, weep not where thou sittest at the holy altar of Demeter.

Æ. Ah woe!

Th. 'Tis not for thee their sorrows to lament.

Æ. Ye hapless dames!

Th. Thou art not of their company.

Æ. May I a scheme declare, my son, that shall add to thy glory and the state's?

Th. Yea, for oft even from women's lips issue wise counsels.

[1]Something is lost here, referring to claims of relationship. The sense perhaps is "thou art thyself related to Pittheus, who was," etc.

Æ. Yet the word, that lurks within my heart, makes me hesitate.

Th. Shame! to hide from friends' good counsel.

Æ. Nay then, I will not hold my peace to blame myself hereafter for having now kept silence to my shame, nor will I forego my honourable proposal, from the common fear that it is useless for women to give good advice. First, my son, I exhort thee give good heed to heaven's will, lest from slighting it thou suffer shipwreck; for in this one single point thou failest, though well-advised in all else. Further, I would have patiently endured, had it not been my duty to venture somewhat for injured folk; and this, my son, it is that brings thee now thy honour, and causes me no fear to urge that thou shouldst use thy power to make men of violence, who prevent the dead from receiving their meed of burial and funeral rites, perform this bounden duty, and check those who would confound the customs of all Hellas; for this it is that holds men's states together—strict observance of the laws. And some, no doubt, will say, 'twas cowardice made thee stand aloof in terror, when thou mightest have won for thy city a crown of glory, and, though thou didst encounter a savage swine,[1] labouring for a sorry task, yet when the time came for thee to face the helmet and pointed spear, and do thy best, thou wert found to be a coward. Nay! do not so if thou be son of mine. Dost see how fiercely thy country looks on its revilers when they mock her for want of counsel? Yea, for in her toils she groweth greater. But states, whose policy is dark and cautious, have their sight darkened by their carefulness. My son, wilt thou not go succour the dead and these poor women in their need? I have no fears for thee, starting as thou dost with right upon thy side; and although I see the prosperity of Cadmus' folk, still am I confident they will throw a different die; for the deity reverses all things again.

Ch. Ah! best of friends, right well hast thou pleaded for me and for Adrastus, and hence my joy is doubled.

Th. Mother, the words that I have spoken are his fair deserts, and I have declared my opinion of the counsels that ruined him; yet do I perceive the truth of thy warning to me, that it ill suits my character to shun dangers. For by a long and glorious career have I displayed this my habit among Hellenes, of ever punishing the wicked. Wherefore I cannot refuse toil. For what will spiteful tongues say of me, when thou, my mother, who more than all others fearest for my safety, bidst me undertake this enterprise? Yea, I will go about this business and rescue the dead by words persuasive; or, failing that, the spear forthwith shall decide this issue, nor will heaven grudge me this. But I require the whole city's sanction also, which my mere wish will ensure; still by communicating the proposal to them I shall find the people better disposed. For them I made supreme, when I set this city free, by giving all an equal vote. So I will take Adrastus as a text for what I have to say and go to their assembly, and when I have won them to these views, I will return hither, after collecting a picked band of young Athenians; and then remaining under arms I will send a message to Creon, begging the bodies of the dead. But do ye, aged ladies, remove from my mother your holy wreaths, that I may take her by the hand and conduct her to the house of Ægeus; for a wretched son is he who rewards not his parents by service; for, when he hath conferred on them the best he hath, he in his turn from his own sons receives all such service as he gave to them.

Exeunt THESEUS *and* ÆTHRA.

Ch. O Argos, home of steeds, my native land! ye have heard with your ears these words, the king's pious will toward the gods in the sight of great Pelasgia and throughout Argos. May he reach the goal! yea, and triumph o'er my sorrows, rescuing the gory corpse, the mother's idol, and making the land of Inachus his friend by helping her. For pious toil is a fair ornament to cities, and carries with it a grace that never wastes away. What will the city decide, I wonder? Will it conclude a friendly truce with me, and shall we obtain burial for our sons? Help, O help, city of Pallas, the mother's cause, that so they may not pollute the laws of all mankind. Thou, I know, dost reverence right, and to injustice dealest out defeat, a protection at all times to the afflicted.

Enter THESEUS *with Athenian* HERALD.

Th. (*To* HERALD) Forasmuch as with this thy art thou hast ever served the state and me by carrying my proclamations far and wide, so now cross Asopus and the waters of Ismenus, and declare this message to the haughty king of the Cadmeans: "Theseus, thy neighbour, one who well may win the boon he craves, begs as a favour thy permission to bury the dead, winning to thyself thereby the love of all the Erechthidæ." And if they will acquiesce, come back again, but if they hearken not, thy second message runneth thus, they may expect my warrior host; for at the sacred fount of Callichorus my army camps in readiness and is being reviewed. Moreover, the city gladly of its own accord undertook this enterprise, when it perceived my wish. Ha! who comes hither to interrupt my speech? A Theban herald, so it seems, though I am not sure thereof. Stay; haply he may save thee thy trouble. For by his coming he meets my purpose half-way.

Enter Theban HERALD.

Herald. Who is the despot of this land? To whom must I announce the message of Creon, who rules o'er the land of Cadmus, since Eteocles was slain by the hand of his brother Polynices, at the sevenfold gates of Thebes?

Th. Sir stranger, thou hast made a false beginning to thy speech, in seeking here a despot. For this city is not ruled by one man, but is free. The people rule in succession year by year, allowing no preference to wealth, but the poor man shares equally with the rich.

He. Thou givest me here an advantage, as it might

[1]The monster Phæa, which infested the neighbourhood of Corinth.

be in a game of draughts; for the city, whence I come, is ruled by one man only, not by the mob; none there puffs up the citizens with specious words, and for his own advantage twists them this way or that, one moment dear to them and lavish of his favours, the next a bane to all; and yet by fresh calumnies of others he hides his former failures and escapes punishment. Besides, how shall the people, if it cannot form true judgments, be able rightly to direct the state? Nay, 'tis time, not haste, that affords a better understanding. A poor hind, granted he be not all unschooled, would still be unable from his toil to give his mind to politics. Verily the better sort count it no healthy sign when the worthless man obtains a reputation by beguiling with words the populace, though aforetime he was naught.

Th. This herald is a clever fellow, a dabbler in the art of talk. But since thou hast thus entered the lists with me, listen awhile, for 'twas thou didst challenge a discussion. Naught is more hostile to a city than a despot; where he is, there are in the first place no laws common to all, but one man is tyrant, in whose keeping and in his alone the law resides, and in that case equality is at an end. But when the laws are written down, rich and poor alike have equal justice, and it is open to the weaker to use the same language to the prosperous when he is reviled by him, and the weaker prevails over the stronger if he have justice on his side. Freedom's mark is also seen in this: "Who hath wholesome counsel to declare unto the state?" And he who chooses to do so gains renown, while he, who hath no wish, remains silent. What greater equality can there be in a city? Again, where the people are absolute rulers of the land, they rejoice in having a reserve of youthful citizens, while a king counts this a hostile element, and strives to slay the leading men, all such as he deems discreet, for he feareth for his power. How then can a city remain stable, where one cuts short all enterprise and mows down the young like meadow-flowers in spring-time? What boots it to acquire wealth and livelihood for children, merely to add to the tyrant's substance by one's toil? Why train up virgin daughters virtuously in our homes to gratify a tyrant's whim, whenso he will, and cause tears to those who rear them? May my life end if ever my children are to be wedded by violence! This bolt I launch in answer to thy words. Now say, why art thou come? what needest thou of this land? Had not thy city sent thee, to thy cost hadst thou come with thy outrageous utterances; for it is the herald's duty to tell the message he is bidden and hie him back in haste. Henceforth let Creon send to my city some other messenger less talkative than thee.

Ch. Look you! how insolent the villains are, when Fortune is kind to them, just as if it would be well with them for ever.

He. Now will I speak. On these disputed points hold thou this view, but I the contrary. So I and all the people of Cadmus forbid thee to admit Adrastus to this land, but if he is here, drive him forth in disregard of the holy suppliant bough he bears, ere sinks yon blazing sun, and attempt not violently to take up the dead, seeing thou hast naught to do with the city of Argos. And if thou wilt hearken to me, thou shalt bring thy barque of state into port unharmed by the billows; but if not, fierce shall the surge of battle be, that we and our allies shall raise. Take good thought, nor, angered at my words, because forsooth thou rulest thy city with freedom, return a vaunting answer from thy feebler means. Hope is man's curse; many a state hath it involved in strife, by leading them into excessive rage. For whenso the city has to vote on the question of war, no man ever takes his own death into account, but shifts this misfortune on to his neighbour; but if death had been before their eyes when they were giving their votes, Hellas would ne'er have rushed to her doom in mad desire for battle. And yet each man amongst us knows which of the two to prefer, the good or ill, and how much better peace is for mankind than war—peace, the Muses' chiefest friend, the foe of sorrow, whose joy is in glad throngs of children, and its delight in prosperity. These are the blessings we cast away and wickedly embark on war, man enslaving his weaker brother, and cities following suit. Now thou art helping our foes even after death, trying to rescue and bury those whom their own acts of insolence have ruined. Verily then it would seem Capaneus was unjustly blasted by the thunderbolt and charred upon the ladder he had raised against our gates, swearing he would sack our town, whether the god would or no; nor should the yawning earth have snatched away the seer,[1] opening wide her mouth to take his chariot and its horses in, nor should the other chieftains be stretched at our gates, their skeletons to atoms crushed 'neath boulders. Either boast thy wit transcendeth that of Zeus, or else allow that gods are right to slay the ungodly. The wise should love their children first, next their parents and country, whose fortunes it behoves them to increase rather than break down. Rashness in a leader, as in a pilot, causeth shipwreck; who knoweth when to be quiet is a wise man. Yea and this too is bravery, even forethought.

Ch. The punishment Zeus hath inflicted was surely enough; there was no need to heap this wanton insult on us.

Ad. Abandoned wretch!

Th. Peace, Adrastus! say no more; set not thy words before mine, for 'tis not to thee this fellow is come with his message, but to me, and I must answer him. Thy first assertion will I answer first: I am not aware that Creon is my lord and master, or that his power outweigheth mine, that so he should compel Athens to act on this wise; nay! for then would the tide of time have to flow backward, if we are to be ordered about, as he thinks. 'Tis not I who choose this war, seeing that I did not even join these warriors to go unto the land of Cadmus; but still I claim to bury the fallen dead, not injuring any state nor yet introducing murderous strife, but preserving the

[1]Amphiaraus.

law of all Hellas. What is not well in this? If ye suffered aught from the Argives—lo! they are dead; ye took a splendid vengeance on your foes and covered them with shame, and now your right is at an end. Let the dead now be buried in the earth, and each element return to the place from whence it came to the body, the breath to the air, the body to the ground; for in no wise did we get it for our own, but to live our life in, and after that its mother earth must take it back again. Dost think 'tis Argos thou art injuring in refusing burial to the dead? Nay! all Hellas shares herein, if a man rob the dead of their due and keep them from the tomb; for, if this law be enacted, it will strike dismay into the stoutest hearts. And art thou come to cast dire threats at me, while thy own folk are afraid of giving burial to the dead? What is your fear? Think you they will undermine your land in their graves, or that they will beget children in the womb of earth, from whom shall rise an avenger? A silly waste of words, in truth it was, to show your fear of paltry groundless terrors. Go, triflers, learn the lesson of human misery; our life is made up of struggles; some men there be that find their fortune soon, others have to wait, while some at once are blest. Fortune lives a dainty life; to her the wretched pays his court and homage to win her smile; her likewise doth the prosperous man extol, for fear the favouring gale may leave him. These lessons should we take to heart, to bear with moderation, free from wrath, our wrongs, and do naught to hurt a whole city. What then? Let us, who will the pious deed perform, bury the corpses of the slain. Else is the issue clear; I will go and bury them by force. For never shall it be proclaimed through Hellas that heaven's ancient law was set at naught, when it devolved on me and the city of Pandion.

Ch. Be of good cheer; for if thou preserve the light of justice, thou shalt escape many a charge that men might urge.

He. Wilt thou that I sum up in brief all thou wouldst say?

Th. Say what thou wilt; for thou art not silent as it is.

He. Thou shalt never take the sons of Argos from our land.

Th. Hear, then, my answer too to that, if so thou wilt.

He. I will hear thee; not that I wish it, but I must give thee thy turn.

Th. I will bury the dead, when from Asopus' land I have removed them.

He. First must thou adventure somewhat in the front of war.

Th. Many an enterprise and of a different kind have I ere this endured.

He. Wert thou then begotten of thy sire to cope with every foe?

Th. Ay, with all wanton villains; virtue I punish not.

He. To meddle is aye thy wont and thy city's too.

Th. Hence her enterprise on many a field hath won her frequent success.

He. Come then, that the warriors of the dragon-crop may catch thee in our city.

Th. What furious warrior-host could spring from dragon's seed?

He. Thou shalt learn that to thy cost. As yet thou art young and rash.

Th. Thy boastful speech stirs not my heart at all to rage. Yet get thee gone from my land, taking with thee the idle words thou broughtest; for we are making no advance. (*Exit* HERALD) 'Tis time for all to start, each stout footman, and whoso mounts the car; 'tis time the bit, dripping with foam, should urge the charger on toward the land of Cadmus. For I will march in person to the seven gates thereof with the sharp sword in my hand, and be myself my herald. But thee, Adrastus, I bid stay, nor blend with mine thy fortunes, for I will take my own good star to lead my host, a chieftain famed in famous deeds of arms. One thing alone I need, the favour of all gods that reverence right, for the presence of these things insures victory. For their valour availeth men naught, unless they have the god's goodwill. *Exit* THESEUS.

Semi-Chorus I. Unhappy mothers of those hapless chiefs! How wildly in my heart pale fear stirs up alarm!

Semi-Chorus II. What is this new cry thou utterest?

Semi-Ch. I. I fear the issue of the strife, whereto the hosts of Pallas march.

Semi-Ch. II. Dost speak of issues of the sword, or interchange of words?

Semi-Ch. I. That last were gain indeed; but if the carnage of battle, fighting, and the noise of beaten breasts again be heard in the land, what, alas! will be said of me, who am the cause thereof?

Semi-Ch. II. Yet may fate again bring low the brilliant victor; 'tis this brave thought that twines about my heart.

Semi-Ch. I. Thou speak'st of the gods as if they were just.

Semi-Ch. II. For who but they allot whate'er betides?

Semi-Ch. I. I see many a contradiction in their dealings with men.

Semi-Ch. II. The former fear hath warped thy judgment. Vengeance calls vengeance forth; slaughter calls for slaughter, but the gods give respite from affliction, holding in their own hands each thing's allotted end.

Semi-Ch. I. Would I could reach yon plains with turrets crowned, leaving Callichorus, fountain of the goddess!

Semi-Ch. II. O that some god would give me wings to fly to the city of rivers twain!

Semi-Ch. I. So might'st thou see and know the fortunes of thy friends.

Semi-Ch. II. What fate, what issue there awaits the valiant monarch of this land?

Semi-Ch. I. Once more do we invoke the gods we called upon before; yea, in our fear this is our first and chiefest trust.

Semi-Ch. II. O Zeus, father to the child the heifer-mother bore in days long past, that daughter of Inachus!

Semi-Ch. I. O be gracious, I pray, and champion this city!

Semi-Ch. II. 'Tis thy own darling, thy own settler in the city of Argos that I am striving to rescue for the funeral pyre from outrageous insult.

Enter MESSENGER.

Messenger. Ladies, I bring you tidings of great joy, myself escaped—for I was taken prisoner in the battle which cost those chieftains seven their lives near Dirce's fount—to bear the news of Theseus' victory. But I will save thee tedious questioning; I was the servant of Capaneus, whom Zeus with scorching bolt to ashes burnt.

Ch. Friend of friends, fair thy news of thy own return, nor less the news about Theseus; and if the host of Athens, too, is safe, welcome will all thy message be.

Me. 'Tis safe, and all hath happened as I would it had befallen Adrastus and his Argives, whom from Inachus he led, to march against the city of the Cadmeans.

Ch. How did the son of Ægeus and his fellow-warriors raise their trophy to Zeus? Tell us, for thou wert there and canst gladden us who were not.

Me. Bright shone the sun, one levelled line of light, upon the world, as by Electra's gate I stood to watch, from a turret with a far outlook. And lo! I saw the host in three divisions, deploying its mail-clad warriors on the high ground by the banks of Ismenus; this last I heard; and with them was the king himself, famous son of Ægeus; his own men, natives of old Cecropia, were ranged upon the right; while on the left, hard by the fountain of Ares, were the dwellers by the sea, harnessed spearmen they; on either wing were posted cavalry, in equal numbers, and chariots were stationed in the shelter of Amphion's holy tomb. Meantime, the folk of Cadmus set themselves before the walls, placing in the rear the bodies for which they fought. Horse to horse, and car to car stood ranged. Then did the herald of Theseus cry aloud to all: "Be still, ye folk! hush, ye ranks of Cadmus, hearken! we are come to fetch the bodies of the slain, wishing to bury them in observance of the universal law of Hellas; no wish have we to lengthen out the slaughter." Not a word would Creon let his herald answer back, but there he stood in silence under arms. Then did the drivers of the four-horse cars begin the fray; on, past each other they drave their chariots, bringing the warriors at their sides up into line. Some fought with swords, some wheeled the horses back to the fray again for those they drove. Now when Phorbas, who captained the cavalry of the Erechthidæ, saw the thronging chariots, he and they who had the charge of the Theban horse met hand to hand, and by turns were victors and vanquished. The many horrors happening there I saw, not merely heard about, for I was at the spot where the chariots and their riders met and fought, but which to tell of first I know not—the clouds of dust that mounted to the sky, the warriors tangled in the reins and dragged this way and that, the streams of crimson gore, when men fell dead, or when, from shattered chariot-seats, they tumbled headlong to the ground, and, mid the splinters of their cars, gave up the ghost. But Creon, when he marked our cavalry's success on one wing, caught up a shield and rushed into the fray, ere that despondency should seize his men; but not for that did Theseus recoil in fear; no! snatching up at once his glittering harness he hied him on. And the twain, clashing their shields together as they met in the midst of the assembled host, were dealing death and courting it, shouting loudly each to his fellow the battle-cry: "Slay, and with thy spear strike home against the sons of Erechtheus." Fierce foes to cope with were the warriors whom the dragon's teeth to manhood reared; so fierce, they broke our left wing, albeit theirs was routed by our right and put to flight, so that the struggle was evenly balanced. Here again our chief deserved all praise, for this success was not the only advantage he gained; no! next he sought that part of his army which was wavering; and loud he called to them, that the earth rang again, "My sons, if ye cannot restrain the earth-born warriors' stubborn spear, the cause of Pallas is lost." His word inspired new courage in all the Danaid host. Therewith himself did seize a fearsome mace, weapon of Epidaurian warfare, and swung it to and fro, and with that club, as with a sickle, he shore off necks and heads and helmets thereupon. Scarce even then they turned themselves to fly. For joy cried I, and danced and clapped my hands; while to the gates they ran. Throughout the town echoed the shrieks of young and old, as they crowded the temples in terror. But Theseus, when he might have come inside the walls, held back his men, for he had not come, said he, to sack the town, but to ask for the bodies of the dead. Such the general men should choose, one who shows his bravery in danger, yet hates the pride of those that in their hour of fortune lose the bliss they might have enjoyed, through seeking to scale the ladder's topmost step.

Ch. Now do I believe in the gods after seeing this unexpected day, and I feel my woes are lighter now that these have paid their penalty.

Ad. O Zeus, why do men assert the wisdom of the wretched human race? On thee we all depend, and all we do is only what thou listest. We thought our Argos irresistible, ourselves a young and lusty host, and so when Eteocles was for making terms, in spite of his fair offer we would not accept them, and so we perished. Then in their turn those foolish folk of Cadmus, to fortune raised, like some beggar with his newly-gotten wealth, waxed wanton, and, waxing so, were ruined in their turn. Ye foolish sons of men! who strain your bow like men who shoot beyond their mark, and only by suffering many evils as ye deserve, though deaf to friends, yet yield to circumstances; ye cities likewise, though ye might by parley end your mischief, yet ye choose the sword instead of reason to settle all disputes. But wherefore these reflections? This I fain would learn, the way thou didst escape; and after that I will ask thee of the rest.

Me. During the uproar which prevailed in the city owing to the battle, I passed the gates, just as the host had entered them.

Ad. Are ye bringing the bodies, for the which the strife arose?

Me. Ay, each of the seven chiefs who led their famous hosts.

Ad. What sayest thou? the rest who fell—say, where are they?

Me. They have found burial in the dells of Cithæron.

Ad. On this or that side of the mount? And who did bury them?

Me. Theseus buried them 'neath the shadow of Eleutheræ's cliff.

Ad. Where didst thou leave the dead he hath not buried?

Me. Not far away; earnest haste makes every goal look close.

Ad. No doubt in sorrow slaves would gather them from the carnage.

Me. Slaves! not one of them was set to do this toil.

Ad. . . . .[1]

Me. Thou wouldst say so, hadst thou been there to see his loving tendance of the dead.

Ad. Did he himself wash the bloody wounds of the hapless youths?

Me. Ay, and strewed their biers and wrapped them in their shrouds.

Ad. An awful burden this, involving some disgrace.

Me. Why, what disgrace to men are their fellows' sorrows?

Ad. Ah me! how much rather had I died with them!

Me. 'Tis vain to weep and move to tears these women.

Ad. Methinks 'tis they who give the lesson. Enough of that! My hands I lift at meeting of the dead, and pour forth a tearful dirge to Hades, calling on my friends, whose loss I mourn in wretched solitude; for this one thing, when once 'tis spent, man cannot recover, the breath of life, though he knoweth ways to get his wealth again.

Ch. Joy is here and sorrow too—for the state, fair fame, and for our captains, double meed of honour. Bitter for me it is to see the limbs of my dead sons, and yet a welcome sight withal, because I shall behold the unexpected day after sorrow's cup was full. Would that Father Time had kept me unwed from my youth up e'en till now when I am old! What need had I of children? Methinks I should not have suffered excessively, had I never borne the marriage-yoke; but now I have my sorrow full in view, the loss of children dear.

Lo! I see the bodies of the fallen youths. Woe is me! would I could join these children in their death and descend to Hades with them!

Enter THESEUS.

Ad. Mothers, raise the wail for the dead departed; cry in answer when ye hear my note of woe.

Ch. My sons, my sons! O bitter words for loving mothers to address to you! To thee, my lifeless child, I call.

Ad. Woe! woe!

Ch. Ah me, my sufferings!

Ad. Alas!

Ch. . . .[2]

Ad. We have endured, alas!

Ch. Sorrows most grievous.

Ad. O citizens of Argos! do ye not behold my fate?

Ch. They see thee, and me the hapless mother, reft of her children.

Ad. Bring near the blood-boltered corpses of those hapless chiefs, foully slain by foes unworthy, with whom lay the decision of the contest.

Ch. Let me embrace and hold my children to my bosom in my enfolding arms.

Ad. There, there! thou hast—

Ch. Sorrows heavy enough to bear.

Ad. Ah me!

Ch. Thy groans mingle with those of their parents.

Ad. Hear me.

Ch. O'er both of us thou dost lament.

Ad. Would God the Theban ranks had laid me dead in the dust!

Ch. Oh that I had ne'er been wedded to a husband!

Ad. Ah! hapless mothers, behold this sea of troubles!

Ch. Our nails have ploughed our cheeks in furrows, and o'er our heads have we strewn ashes.

Ad. Ah me! ah me! Oh that earth's floor would swallow me, or the whirlwind snatch me away, or Zeus' flaming bolt descend upon my head!

Ch. Bitter the marriages thou didst witness, bitter the oracle of Phœbus! The curse of Œdipus, fraught with sorrow, after desolating his house, is come on thee.

Th. I meant to question thee when thou wert venting thy lamentations to the host, but I will let it pass; yet, though I dropped the matter then and left it alone, I now do ask Adrastus, "Of what lineage sprang those youths, to shine so bright in chivalry?" Tell it to our younger citizens of thy fuller wisdom, for thou art skilled to know. Myself beheld their daring deeds, too high for words to tell, whereby they thought to capture Thebes. One question will I spare thee, lest I provoke thy laughter; the foe that each of them encountered in the fray, the spear from which each received his death-wound. These be idle tales alike for those who hear or him who speaks, that any man amid the fray, when clouds of darts are hurtling before his eyes, should declare for certain who each champion is. I could not ask such questions, nor yet believe those who dare assert the like; for when a man is face to face with the foe, he scarce can see even that which 'tis his bounden duty to observe.

[1]A line is missing here.

[2]A lacuna in the MS.

Ad. Hearken then. For in giving this task to me thou findest a willing eulogist of friends, whose praise I would declare in all truth and sincerity. Dost see yon corpse by Zeus' bolt transfixed? That is Capaneus; though he had ample wealth, yet was he the last to boast of his prosperity; nor would he ever vaunt himself above a poorer neighbour, but shunned the man whose sumptuous board had puffed him up too high and made him scorn mere competence, for he held that virtue lies not in greedy gluttony, but that moderate means suffice. True friend was he, alike to present or to absent friends the same; of such the number is not great. His was a guileless character, a courteous address, that left no promise unperformed either towards his own household or his fellow-citizens. The next I name is Eteocles; a master he of other kinds of excellence; young, nor richly dowered with store, yet high in honour in the Argive land. And though his friends oft offered gifts of gold, he would not have it in his house, to make his character its slave by taking wealth's yoke upon him. Not his city, but those that sinned against her did he hate, for a city is no wise to be blamed if it get an evil name by reason of an evil governor. Such another was Hippomedon, third of all this band; from his very boyhood he refrained from turning towards the allurements of the Muses, to lead a life of ease; his home was in the fields, and gladly would he school his nature to hardships with a view to manliness, aye hasting to the chase, rejoicing in his steeds or straining of his bow, because he would make himself of use unto his state. Next behold the huntress Atalanta's son, Parthenopæus, a youth of peerless beauty; from Arcady he came even to the streams of Inachus, and in Argos spent his boyhood. There, when he grew to man's estate, first, as is the duty of strangers settled in another land, he showed no pique or jealousy against the state, became no quibbler, chiefest source of annoyance citizen or stranger can give, but took his stand amid the host, and fought for Argos as he were her own son, glad at heart whenso the city prospered, deeply grieved if e'er reverses came; many a lover though he had midst men and maids, yet was he careful to avoid offence. Of Tydeus next the lofty praise I will express in brief; no brilliant spokesman he, but a clever craftsman in the art of war, with many a shrewd device; inferior in judgment to his brother Meleager, yet through his warrior skill lending his name to equal praise, for he had found in arms a perfect science; his was an ambitious nature, a spirit rich in store of deeds, with words less fully dowered. From this account then wonder not, Theseus, that they dared to die before the towers; for noble nurture carries honour with it, and every man, when once he hath practised virtue, scorns the name of villain. Courage may be learnt, for even a babe doth learn to speak and hear things it cannot comprehend; and whatso'er a child hath learnt, this it is his wont to treasure up till he is old. So train up your children in a virtuous way.

Ch. Alas! my son, to sorrow I bare thee and carried thee within my womb, enduring the pangs of travail; but now Hades takes the fruit of all my hapless toil, and I that had a son am left, ah me! with none to nurse my age.

Th. As for the noble son of Œcleus, him, while yet he lived, the gods snatched hence to the bowels of the earth, and his chariot too, manifestly blessing him; while I myself may truthfully tell the praises of the son of Œdipus, that is, Polynices, for he was my guest-friend ere he left the town of Cadmus and crossed to Argos in voluntary exile. But dost thou know what I would have thee do in this matter?

Ad. I know naught save this—to yield obedience to thy hests.

Th. As for yon Capaneus, stricken by the bolt of Zeus—

Ad. Wilt bury him apart as a consecrated corpse?

Th. Even so; but all the rest on one funeral pyre.

Ad. Where wilt thou set the tomb apart for him?

Th. Here near this temple have I builded him a sepulchre.

Ad. Thy thralls forthwith must undertake this toil.

Th. Myself will look to those others; let the biers advance.

Ad. Approach your sons, unhappy mothers.

Th. This thy proposal, Adrastus, is anything but good.

Ad. Must not the mothers touch their sons?

Th. It would kill them to see how they are altered.

Ad. 'Tis bitter, truly, to see the dead even at the moment of death.

Th. Why then wilt thou add fresh grief to them?

Ad. Thou art right. Ye needs must patiently abide, for the words of Theseus are good. But when we have committed them unto the flames, ye shall collect their bones. O wretched sons of men! Why do ye get you weapons and bring slaughter on one another? Cease therefrom, give o'er your toiling, and in mutual peace keep safe your cities. Short is the span of life, so 'twere best to run its course as lightly as we may, from trouble free.

Ch. No more a happy mother I, with children blest; no more I share, among Argive women, who have sons, their happy lot; nor any more will Artemis in the hour of travail kindly greet these childless mothers. Most dreary is my life, and like some wandering cloud I drift before the howling blast. The seven noblest sons in Argos once we had, we seven hapless mothers; but now my sons are dead, I have no child, and on me steals old age in piteous wise, nor 'mongst the dead nor 'mongst the living do I count myself, having as it were a lot apart from these. Tears alone are left me; in my house sad memories of my son are stored; mournful tresses shorn from his head, chaplets that he wore, libations for the dead departed, and songs, but not such as golden-haired Apollo welcometh; and when I wake to weep, my tears will ever drench the folds of my robe upon my bosom. Ah! there I see the sepulchre ready e'en now for Capaneus, his consecrated tomb, and the votive offerings Theseus gives unto the dead outside the shrine, and nigh yon lightning-smitten chief I see his noble bride, Evadne, daughter of King Iphis. Wherefore stands she on the towering rock, which o'ertops this temple, advancing along yon path?

Enter EVADNE *above pyre of Capaneus.*

Evadne. What light, what radiancy did the sun-god's car dart forth, and the moon athwart the firmament, while round her in the gloom swift stars careered, in the day that the city of Argos raised the stately chant of joy at my wedding, in honour of my marriage with mail-clad Capaneus? Now from my home in frantic haste with frenzied mind I rush to join thee, seeking to share with thee the fire's bright flame and the self-same tomb, to rid me of my weary life in Hades' halls, and of the pains of existence; yea, for 'tis the sweetest end to share the death of those we love, if only fate will sanction it.

Ch. Behold yon pyre, which thou art overlooking, nigh thereto, set apart for Zeus! There is thy husband's body, vanquished by the blazing bolt.

Ev. Life's goal I now behold from my station here; may fortune aid me in my headlong leap from this rock in honour's cause, down into the fire below, to mix my ashes in the ruddy blaze with my husband's, to lay me side by side with him, there in the couch of Persephone; for ne'er will I, to save my life, prove untrue to thee where thou liest in thy grave. Away with life and marriage too! Oh! may my children live to see the dawn of a fairer, happier wedding-day in Argos! May loyalty inspire the husband's heart, his nature fusing with his wife's!

Ch. Lo! the aged Iphis, thy father, draweth nigh to hear thy startling scheme, which yet he knows not and will grieve to learn.

Enter IPHIS.

Iphis. Unhappy child! lo! I am come, a poor old man, with twofold sorrow in my house to mourn, that I may carry to his native land the corpse of my son Eteocles, slain by the Theban spear, and further in quest of my daughter who rushed headlong from the house, for she was the wife of Capaneus and longed with him to die. Ere this she was well guarded in my house, but, when I took the watch away in the present troubles, she escaped. But I feel sure that she is here; tell me if ye have seen her.

Ev. Why question them? Lo, here upon the rock, father, o'er the pyre of Capaneus, like some bird I hover lightly, in my wretchedness.

Ip. What wind hath blown thee hither, child? Whither away? Why didst thou pass the threshold of my house and seek this land?

Ev. It would but anger thee to hear what I intend, and so I fain would keep thee ignorant, my father.

Ip. What! hath not thy own father a right to know?

Ev. Thou wouldst not wisely judge my intention.

Ip. Why dost thou deck thyself in that apparel?

Ev. A purport strange this robe conveys, father.

Ip. Thou hast no look of mourning for thy lord.

Ev. No, the reason why I thus am decked is strange, maybe.

Ip. Dost thou in such garb appear before a funeral-pyre?

Ev. Yea, for hither it is I come to take the meed of victory.

Ip. "Victory!" what victory? This would I learn of thee.

Ev. A victory o'er all women on whom the sun looks down.

Ip. In Athena's handiwork or in prudent counsel?

Ev. In bravery; for I will lay me down and die with my lord.

Ip. What dost thou say? What is this silly riddle thou propoundest?

Ev. To yonder pyre where lies dead Capaneus, I will leap down.

Ip. My daughter, speak not thus before the multitude!

Ev. The very thing I wish, that every Argive should learn it.

Ip. Nay, I will ne'er consent to let thee do this deed.

Ev. (*As she is throwing herself*) 'Tis all one; thou shalt never catch me in thy grasp. Lo! I cast me down, no joy to thee, but to myself and to my husband blazing on the pyre with me.

Ch. O lady, what a fearful deed!

Ip. Ah me! I am undone, ye dames of Argos!

Ch. Alack, alack! a cruel blow is this to thee, but thou must yet witness, poor wretch, the full horror of this deed.

Ip. A more unhappy wretch than me ye could not find.

Ch. Woe for thee, unhappy man! Thou, old sir, hast been made partaker in the fortune of Œdipus, thou and my poor city too.

Ip. Ah, why are mortal men denied this boon, to live their youth twice o'er, and twice in turn to reach old age? If aught goes wrong within our homes, we set it right by judgment more maturely formed, but our life we may not so correct. Now if we had a second spell of youth and age, this double term of life would let us then correct each previous slip. I, for instance, seeing others blest with children, longed to have them too, and found my ruin in that wish. Whereas if I had had my present experience, and by a father's light had learnt how cruel a thing it is to be bereft of children, never should I have fallen on such evil days as these—I who did beget a brave young son, proud parent that I was, and after all am now bereft of him. Enough of this. What remains for such a hapless wretch as me? Shall I to my home, there to see its utter desolation and the blank within my life? or shall I to the halls of that dead Capaneus?—halls I smiled to see in days gone by, when yet my daughter was alive. But she is lost and gone, she that would ever draw down my cheek to her lips, and take my head between her hands; for naught is there more sweet unto an aged sire than a daughter's love; our sons are made of sterner stuff, but less winning are their caresses. Oh! take me to my house at once, in darkness hide me there, to waste and fret this aged frame with fasting! What shall it avail me to touch my daughter's bones? Old age, resistless foe, how do I loathe thy presence! Them too I hate, whoso desire to lengthen out the span of life, seeking to turn the tide of death aside by philtres, drugs, and magic spells—folk that death should take away to leave the young their place, when they no more can benefit the world.

Ch. Woe, woe! Behold your dead sons' bones are brought hither; take them, servants of your weak old mistress, for in me is no strength left by reason of my mourning for my sons; time's comrade long have I been, and many a tear for many a sorrow have I shed. For what sharper pang wilt thou ever find for mortals than the sight of children dead?

Enter CHILDREN *of slain chiefs.*

Children. Poor mother mine, behold I bring my father's bones gathered from the fire, a burden grief has rendered heavy, though this tiny urn contains my all.

Ch. Ah me! ah me! Why bear thy tearful load to the fond mother of the dead, a handful of ashes in the stead of those who erst were men of mark in Mycenæ?

Chil. Woe worth the hour! woe worth the day! Reft of my hapless sire, a wretched orphan shall I inherit a desolate house, torn from my father's arms.

Ch. Woe is thee! Where is now the toil I spent upon my sons? what thank have I for nightly watch? Where the mother's nursing care? the sleepless vigils mine eyes have kept? the loving kiss upon my children's brow?

Chil. Thy sons are dead and gone. Poor mother! dead and gone; the boundless air now wraps them round.

Ch. Turned to ashes by the flame, they have winged their flight to Hades.

Chil. Father, thou hearest thy children's lamentation; say, shall I e'er, as warrior dight, avenge thy slaughter?

Ch. God grant it, O my child!

Chil. Some day, if god so will, shall the avenging of my father be my task; not yet this sorrow sleeps.

Ch. Alas! Fortune's sorrows are enough for me, I have troubles and to spare already.

Chil. Shall Asopus' laughing tide ever reflect my brazen arms as I lead on my Argive troops?

Ch. To avenge thy fallen sire.

Chil. Methinks I see thee still before my eyes, my father—

Ch. Printing a loving kiss upon thy cheek.

Chil. But thy words of exhortation are borne on the winds away.

Ch. Two mourners hath he left behind, thy mother and thee, bequeathing to thee an endless legacy of grief for thy father.

Chil. The weight of grief I have to bear hath crushed me utterly.

Ch. Come, let me clasp the ashes of my son to my bosom.

Chil. I weep to hear that piteous word; it stabs me to the heart.

Ch. My child, thou art undone; no more shall I behold thee, thy own fond mother's treasure.

Th. Adrastus, and ye dames from Argos sprung, ye see these children bearing in their hands the bodies of their valiant sires whom I redeemed; to thee I give these gifts, I and Athens. And ye must bear in mind the memory of this favour, marking well the treatment ye have had of me. And to these children I repeat the self-same words, that they may honour this city, to children's children ever handing on the kindness ye received from us. Be Zeus the witness, with the gods in heaven, of the treatment we vouchsafed you ere you left us.

Ad. Theseus, well we know all the kindness thou hast conferred upon the land of Argos in her need, and ours shall be a gratitude that never waxeth old, for your generous treatment makes us debtors for a like return.

Th. What yet remains, wherein I can serve you?

Ad. Fare thee well, for such is thy desert and such thy city's too.

Th. Even so. Mayst thou too have the self-same fortune!

ATHENA *appears above temple.*

Athena. Hearken, Theseus, to the words that I Athena utter, telling thee thy duty, which, if thou perform it, will serve thy city. Give not these bones to the children to carry to the land of Argos, letting them go so lightly; nay, take first an oath of them that they will requite thee and thy city for your efforts. This oath must Adrastus swear, for as their king it is his right to take the oath for the whole realm of Argos. And this shall be the form thereof: "We Argives swear we never will against this land lead on our mail-clad troops to war, and, if others come, we will repel them." But if they violate their oath and come against the city, pray that the land of Argos may be miserably destroyed. Now hearken while I tell thee where thou must slay the victims. Thou hast within thy halls a tripod with brazen feet, which Heracles, in days gone by, after he had o'erthrown the foundations of Ilium and was starting on another enterprise, enjoined thee to set up at the Pythian shrine. O'er it cut the throats of three sheep; then grave within the tripod's hollow belly the oath; this done, deliver it to the god who watches over Delphi to keep, a witness and memorial unto Hellas of the oath. And bury the sharp-edged knife, wherewith thou shalt have laid the victims open and shed their blood, deep in the bowels of the earth, hard by the pyres where the seven chieftains burn; for its appearance shall strike them with dismay, if e'er against thy town they come, and shall cause them to return with sorrow. When thou hast done all this, dismiss the dead from thy land. And to the god resign as sacred land the spot where their bodies were purified by fire, there by the meeting of the triple roads that lead unto the Isthmus. Thus much to thee, Theseus, I address; next to the sons of Argos I speak; when ye are grown to men's estate, the town beside Ismenus shall ye sack, avenging the slaughter of your dead sires; thou too, Ægialeus, shalt take thy father's place and in thy youth command the host, and with thee Tydeus' son marching from Ætolia—him whom his father named Diomedes. Soon as the beards your cheeks o'ershadow must ye lead an armed Danaid host against the battlements of Thebes with sevenfold gates. For to their sorrow shall ye come like lion's whelps in full-grown might to sack their city. No otherwise is it to be; and ye shall be a theme for minstrels' songs in days to come, known through Hellas as "the After-born"; so famous shall your expedition be, thanks to Heaven.

Th. Queen Athena, I will hearken to thy bidding; for thou it is dost set me up, so that I go not astray. And I will bind this monarch by an oath; do thou but guide my steps aright. For if thou art friendly to our state, we shall henceforth live secure.

Ch. Let us go, Adrastus, and take the oath to this monarch and his state; for the service they have already done us claims our warm regard.

Exeunt OMNES.

THE TROJAN WOMEN

DRAMATIS PERSONAE

Poseidon	Talthybius
Athena	Cassandra
Hecuba	Andromache
Chorus of Captive Trojan Women	Menelaus
	Helen

Before Agamemnon's Tent in the Camp near Troy. HECUBA *asleep. Enter* POSEIDON.

Poseidon. Lo! from the depths of salt Ægean floods I, Poseidon, come, where choirs of Nereids trip in the mazes of the graceful dance; for since the day that Phœbus and myself with measurement exact set towers of stone about this land of Troy and ringed it round, never from my heart hath passed away a kindly feeling for my Phrygian town, which now is smouldering and o'erthrown, a prey to Argive prowess. For, from his home beneath Parnassus, Phocian Epeus, aided by the craft of Pallas, framed a horse to bear within its womb an armed host, and sent it within the battlements, fraught with death; whence in days to come men shall tell of "the wooden horse," with its hidden load of warriors. Groves forsaken stand and temples of the gods run down with blood, and at the altar's very base, before the god who watched his home, lies Priam dead. While to Achæan ships great store of gold and Phrygian spoils are being conveyed, and they who came against this town, those sons of Hellas, only wait a favouring breeze to follow in their wake, that after ten long years they may with joy behold their wives and children. Vanquished by Hera, Argive goddess, and by Athena, who helped to ruin Phrygia, I am leaving Ilium, that famous town, and the altars that I love; for when drear desolation seizes on a town, the worship of the gods decays and tends to lose respect. Scamander's banks re-echo long and loud the screams of captive maids, as they by lot receive their masters. Arcadia taketh some, and some the folk of Thessaly; others are assigned to Theseus' sons, the Athenian chiefs. And such of the Trojan dames as are not portioned out, are in these tents, set apart for the leaders of the host; and with them Spartan Helen, daughter of Tyndarus, justly counted among the captives. And wouldst thou see that queen of misery, Hecuba, thou canst; for there she lies before the gates, weeping many a bitter tear for many a tribulation; for at Achilles' tomb—though she knows not this—her daughter Polyxena has died most piteously; likewise is Priam dead, and her children too; Cassandra, whom the king Apollo left to be a virgin, frenzied maid, hath Agamemnon, in contempt of the god's ordinance and of piety, forced to a dishonoured wedlock. Farewell, O city prosperous once! farewell, ye ramparts of hewn stone! had not Pallas, daughter of Zeus, decreed thy ruin, thou wert standing firmly still.

Enter ATHENA.

Athena. May I address the mighty god whom Heaven reveres and who to my own sire is very nigh in blood, laying aside our former enmity?

Po. Thou mayst; for o'er the soul the ties of kin exert no feeble spell, great queen Athena.

At. For thy forgiving mood my thanks! Somewhat have I to impart affecting both thyself and me, O king.

Po. Bringst thou fresh tidings from some god, from Zeus, or from some lesser power?

At. From none of these; but on behalf of Troy, whose soil we tread, am I come to seek thy mighty aid, to make it one with mine.

Po. What! hast thou laid thy former hate aside to take compassion on the town now that it is burnt to ashes?

At. First go back to the former point; wilt thou make common cause with me in the scheme I purpose?

Po. Ay surely; but I would fain learn thy wishes, whether thou art come to help Achæans or Phrygians.

At. I wish to give my former foes, the Trojans, joy, and on the Achæan host impose a return that they will rue.

Po. Why leap'st thou thus from mood to mood? Thy love and hate both go too far, on whomsoever centred.

At. Dost not know the insult done to me and to the shrine I love?

Po. Surely, in the hour that Aias tore Cassandra thence.

At. Yea, and the Achæans did naught, said naught to him.

Po. And yet 'twas by thy mighty aid they sacked Ilium.

At. For which cause I would join with thee to work their bane.

Po. My powers are ready at thy will. What is thy intent?

At. A returning fraught with woe will I impose on them.

Po. While yet they stay on shore, or as they cross the briny deep?

At. When they have set sail from Ilium for their homes. On them will Zeus also send his rain and fearful hail, and inky tempests from the sky; yea, and he promises to grant me his levin-bolts to hurl on the Achæans and fire their ships. And do thou, for thy part, make the Ægean strait to roar with mighty billows and whirlpools, and fill Eubœa's hollow bay with corpses, that Achæans may learn henceforth to reverence my temples and regard all other deities.

Po. So shall it be, for the boon thou cravest needs but few words. I will vex the broad Ægean sea; and the beach of Myconus and the reefs round Delos, Scyros and Lemnos too, and the cliffs of Caphareus shall be strown with many a corpse. Mount thou to Olympus, and taking from thy father's hand his lightning bolts, keep careful watch against the hour when Argos' host lets slip its cables. A fool is he who sacks the towns of men, with shrines and tombs, the dead man's hallowed home, for at the last he makes a desert round himself, and dies. *Exeunt.*

Hecuba (*Awakening*) Lift thy head, unhappy lady, from the ground; thy neck upraise; this is Troy no more, no longer am I queen in Ilium. Though fortune change, endure thy lot; sail with the stream, and follow fortune's tack, steer not thy barque of life against the tide, since chance must guide thy course. Ah me! ah me! What else but tears is now my hapless lot, whose country, children, husband, all are lost? Ah! the high-blown pride of ancestors! how cabined now! how brought to nothing after all! What woe must I suppress, or what declare? What plaintive dirge shall I awake? Ah, woe is me! the anguish I suffer lying here stretched upon this pallet hard! O my head, my temples, my side! Ah! could I but turn over, and lie now on this, now on that, to rest my back and spine, while ceaselessly my tearful wail ascends. For e'en this is music to the wretched, to chant their cheerless dirge of sorrow.

Ye swift-prowed ships, rowed to sacred Ilium o'er the deep dark sea, past the fair havens of Hellas, to the flute's ill-omened music and the dulcet voice of pipes, even to the bays of Troyland (alack the day!), wherein ye tied your hawsers, twisted handiwork from Egypt, in quest of that hateful wife of Menelaus, who brought disgrace on Castor, and on Eurotas foul reproach; murderess she of Priam, sire of fifty children, the cause why I, the hapless Hecuba, have wrecked my life upon this troublous strand. Oh that I should sit here o'er against the tent of Agamemnon! Forth from my home to slavery they hale my aged frame, while from my head in piteous wise the hair is shorn for grief. Ah! hapless wives of those mail-clad sons of Troy! Ah! poor maidens, luckless brides, come weep, for Ilium is now but a smouldering ruin; and I, like some mother-bird that o'er her fledgelings screams, will begin the strain; how different from that song I sang to the gods in days long past, as I leaned on Priam's staff, and beat with my foot in Phrygian time to lead the dance!

Enter CHORUS OF CAPTIVE TROJAN WOMEN.

Semi-Chorus I. O Hecuba! why these cries, these piercing shrieks? What mean thy words? For I heard thy piteous wail echo through the building, and a pang of terror shoots through each captive Trojan's breast, as pent within these walls they mourn their slavish lot.

Hec. My child, e'en now the hands of Argive rowers are busy at their ships.

Semi-Ch. I. Ah, woe is me! what is their intent? Will they really bear me hence in sorrow from my country in their fleet?

Hec. I know not, though I guess our doom.

Semi-Ch. I. O misery! woe to us Trojan dames, soon to hear the order given, "Come forth from the house; the Argives are preparing to return."

Hec. Oh! do not bid the wild Cassandra leave her chamber, the frantic prophetess, for Argives to insult, nor to my griefs add yet another. Woe to thee, ill-fated Troy, thy sun is set; and woe to thy unhappy children, quick and dead alike, who are leaving thee behind!

Semi-Chorus II. With trembling step, alas! I leave this tent of Agamemnon to learn of thee, my royal mistress, whether the Argives have resolved to take my wretched life, whether the sailors at the prow are making ready to ply their oars.

Hec. My child, a fearful dread seized on my wakeful heart and sent me hither.

Semi-Ch. II. Hath a herald from the Danai already come? To whom am I, poor captive, given as a slave?

Hec. Thou art not far from being allotted now.

Semi-Ch. II. Woe worth the day! What Argive or Phthiotian chief will bear me far from Troy, alas! unto his home, or haply to some island fastness?

Hec. Ah me! ah me! Whose slave shall I become in my old age? in what far clime? a poor old drone, the wretched copy of a corpse, set to keep the gate or tend their children, I who once held royal rank in Troy.

Ch. Woe, woe is thee! What piteous dirge wilt thou devise to mourn the outrage done thee? No more through Ida's looms shall I ply the shuttle to and fro. I look my last and latest on my children's bodies; henceforth shall I endure surpassing misery; it may be as the unwilling bride of some Hellene (perish the night and fortune that brings me to this!); it may be as a wretched slave I from Peirene's sacred fount shall draw their store of water.

Oh! be it ours to come to Theseus' famous realm, a land of joy! Never, never let me see Eurotas' swirling tide, hateful home of Helen, there to meet and be the slave of Menelaus, whose hand laid Troyland waste! Yon holy land by Peneus fed, nestling in all its beauty at Olympus' foot, is said, so have I heard, to be a very granary of wealth and teeming fruitage; next to the sacred soil of Theseus, I could wish to reach that land. They tell me too Hephæstus' home, beneath the shadow of Ætna, fronting Phœnicia, the mother of Sicilian hills, is famous for the crowns it gives to worth. Or may I find a home on that shore which lieth very nigh Ionia's sea, a land by Crathis watered, lovely stream, that dyes the hair an auburn tint, feeding with its holy waves and making glad therewith the home of heroes good and true.

But mark! a herald from the host of Danai, with store of fresh proclamations, comes hasting hither. What is his errand? what saith he? List, for we are slaves to Dorian lords henceforth.

Enter TALTHYBIUS.

Talthybius. Hecuba, thou knowest me from my many journeys to and fro as herald 'twixt the Achæan host and Troy; no stranger I to thee, lady, even aforetime, I Talthybius, now sent with a fresh message.

Hec. Ah, kind friends, 'tis come! what I so long have dreaded.

Ta. The lot has decided your fates already, if that was what you feared.

Hec. Ah me! What city didst thou say, Thessalian, Phthian, or Cadmean?

Ta. Each warrior took his prize in turn; ye were not all at once assigned.

Hec. To whom hath the lot assigned us severally? Which of us Trojan dames doth a happy fortune await?

Ta. I know, but ask thy questions separately, not all at once.

Hec. Then tell me, whose prize is my daughter, hapless Cassandra?

Ta. King Agamemnon hath chosen her out for himself.

Hec. To be the slave-girl of his Spartan wife? Ah me!

Ta. Nay, to share with him his stealthy love.

Hec. What! Phœbus' virgin-priestess, to whom the god with golden locks granted the boon of maidenhood?

Ta. The dart of love hath pierced his heart, love for the frenzied maid.

Hec. Daughter, cast from thee the sacred keys, and from thy body tear the holy wreaths that drape thee in their folds.

Ta. Why! is it not an honour high that she should win our monarch's love?

Hec. What have ye done to her whom late ye took from me—my child?

Ta. Dost mean Polyxena, or whom dost thou inquire about?

Hec. To whom hath the lot assigned her?

Ta. To minister at Achilles' tomb hath been appointed her.

Hec. Woe is me! I the mother of a dead man's slave! What custom, what ordinance is this amongst Hellenes, good sir?

Ta. Count thy daughter happy: 'tis well with her.

Hec. What wild words are these? say, is she still alive?

Ta. Her fate is one that sets her free from trouble.

Hec. And what of mail-clad Hector's wife, sad Andromache? declare her fate.

Ta. She too was a chosen prize; Achilles' son did take her.

Hec. As for me whose hair is white with age, who need to hold a staff to be to me a third foot, whose servant am I to be?

Ta. Odysseus, king of Ithaca, hath taken thee to be his slave.

Hec. O God! Now smite the close-shorn head! tear your cheeks with your nails. God help me! I have fallen as a slave to a treacherous foe I hate, a monster of lawlessness, one that by his double tongue hath turned against us all that once was friendly in his camp, changing this for that and that for this again. Oh weep for me, ye Trojan dames! Undone! undone and lost! ah woe! a victim to a most unhappy lot!

Ch. Thy fate, royal mistress, now thou knowest; but for me, what Hellene or Achæan is master of my destiny?

Ta. Ho, servants! haste and bring Cassandra forth to me here, that I may place her in our captain's hands, and then conduct to the rest of the chiefs the captives each hath had assigned. Ha! what is the blaze of torches there within? What do these Trojan dames? Are they firing the chambers, because they must leave this land and be carried away to Argos? Are they setting themselves aflame in their longing for death? Of a truth the free bear their troubles in cases like this with a stiff neck. Ho, there! open! lest their deed, which suits them well but finds small favour with the Achæans, bring blame on me.

Hec. 'Tis not that they are setting aught ablaze, but my child Cassandra, frenzied maid, comes rushing wildly hither.

Enter CASSANDRA *carrying torches.*

Cassandra. Bring the light, uplift and show its flame! I am doing the god's service, see! see! making his shrine to glow with tapers bright. O Hymen, king of marriage! blest is the bridegroom; blest am I also, the maiden soon to wed a princely lord in Argos. Hail Hymen, king of marriage! Since thou, my mother, art ever busied with tears and lamentations in thy mourning for my father's death and for our country dear, I at my own nuptials am making this torch to blaze and show its light, in thy honour, O Hymen, king of marriage! Grant thy light too, Hecate, at the maiden's wedding, as the custom is. Nimbly lift the foot aloft, lead on the dance, with cries of joy, as if to greet my father's happy fate. To dance I hold a sacred duty; come, Phœbus, lead the way, for 'tis in thy temple mid thy bay-trees that I minister. Hail Hymen, god of marriage! Hymen, hail! Come, mother mine, and join the dance, link thy steps with me, and circle in the gladsome measure, now here, now there. Salute the bride on her wedding-day with hymns and cries of joy. Come, ye maids of Phrygia in raiment fair, sing my marriage with the husband fate ordains that I should wed.

Ch. Hold the frantic maiden, royal mistress mine, lest with nimble foot she rush to the Argive army.

Hec. Thou god of fire, 'tis thine to light the bridal

torch for men, but piteous is the flame thou kindlest here, beyond my blackest bodings. Ah, my child! how little did I ever dream that such would be thy marriage, a captive, and of Argos too! Give up the torch to me; thou dost not bear its blaze aright in thy wild frantic course, nor have thy afflictions left thee in thy sober senses, but still art thou as frantic as before. Take in those torches, Trojan friends, and for her wedding madrigals weep your tears instead.

Ca. O mother, crown my head with victor's wreaths; rejoice in my royal match; lead me to my lord; nay, if thou find me loth at all, thrust me there by force; for if Loxias be indeed a prophet, Agamemnon, that famous king of the Achæans, will find in me a bride more fraught with woe to him than Helen. For I will slay him and lay waste his home to avenge my father's and my brethren's death. But of the deed itself I will not speak; nor will I tell of that axe which shall sever my neck and the necks of others, or of the conflict ending in a mother's death, which my marriage shall cause, nor of the overthrow of Atreus' house; but I, for all my frenzy, will so far rise above my frantic fit, that I will prove this city happier far than those Achæans, who for the sake of one woman and one man's love of her have lost a countless host in seeking Helen. Their captain too, whom men call wise, hath lost for what he hated most what most he prized, yielding to his brother for a woman's sake—and she a willing prize whom no man forced—the joy he had of his own children in his home. For from the day that they did land upon Scamander's strand, their doom began, not for loss of stolen frontier nor yet for fatherland with frowning towers; whomso Ares slew, those never saw their babes again, nor were they shrouded for the tomb by hand of wife, but in a foreign land they lie. At home the case was still the same; wives were dying widows, parents were left childless in their homes, having reared their sons for others, and none is left to make libations of blood upon the ground before their tombs. Truly to such praise as this their host can make an ample claim. 'Tis better to pass their shame in silence by, nor be mine the Muse to tell that evil tale. But the Trojans were dying, first for their fatherland, fairest fame to win; whomso the sword laid low, all these found friends to bear their bodies home and were laid to rest in the bosom of their native land, their funeral rites all duly paid by duteous hands. And all such Phrygians as escaped the warrior's death lived ever day by day with wife and children by them—joys the Achæans had left behind. As for Hector and his griefs, prithee hear how stands the case; he is dead and gone, but still his fame remains as bravest of the brave, and this was a result of the Achæans' coming; for had they remained at home, his worth would have gone unnoticed. So too with Paris, he married the daughter of Zeus, whereas, had he never done so, the alliance he made in his family would have been forgotten. Whoso is wise should fly from making war; but if he be brought to this pass, a noble death will crown his city with glory, a coward's end with shame. Wherefore, mother mine, thou shouldst not pity thy country or my spousal, for this my marriage will destroy those whom thou and I most hate.

Ch. How sweetly at thy own sad lot thou smilest, chanting a strain, which, spite of thee, may prove thee wrong!

Ta. Had not Apollo turned thy wits astray, thou shouldst not for nothing have sent my chiefs with such ominous predictions forth on their way. But, after all, these lofty minds, reputed wise, are nothing better than those that are held as naught. For that mighty king of all Hellas, own son of Atreus, has yielded to a passion for this mad maiden of all others; though I am poor enough, yet would I ne'er have chosen such a wife as this. As for thee, since thy senses are not whole, I give thy taunts 'gainst Argos and thy praise of Troy to the winds to carry away. Follow me now to the ships to grace the wedding of our chief. And thou too follow, whensoe'er the son of Laertes demands thy presence, for thou wilt serve a mistress most discreet, as all declare who came to Ilium.

Ca. A clever fellow this menial! Why is it heralds hold the name they do? All men unite in hating with one common hate the servants who attend on kings or governments. Thou sayest my mother shall come to the halls of Odysseus; where then be Apollo's words, so clear to me in their interpretation, which declare that here she shall die? What else remains, I will not taunt her with. Little knows he, the luckless wight, the sufferings that await him; or how these ills I and my Phrygians endure shall one day seem to him precious as gold. For beyond the ten long years spent at Troy he shall drag out other ten and then come to his country all alone, by the route where fell Charybdis lurks in a narrow channel 'twixt the rocks; past Cyclops the savage shepherd, and Ligurian Circe that turneth men to swine; shipwrecked oft upon the salt sea-wave; fain to eat the lotus, and the sacred cattle of the sun, whose flesh shall utter in the days to come a human voice, fraught with misery to Odysseus. But to briefly end this history, he shall descend alive to Hades, and, though he 'scape the waters' flood, yet shall he find a thousand troubles in his home when he arrives. Enough! why do I recount the troubles of Odysseus? Lead on, that I forthwith may wed my husband for his home in Hades' halls. Base thou art, and basely shalt thou be buried, in the dead of night when day is done, thou captain of that host of Danai, who thinkest so proudly of thy fortune! Yea, and my corpse cast forth in nakedness shall the rocky chasm with its flood of wintry waters give to wild beasts to make their meal upon, hard by my husband's tomb, me the handmaid of Apollo. Farewell, ye garlands of that god most dear to me! farewell, ye mystic symbols! I here resign your feasts, my joy in days gone by. Go, I tear ye from my body, that, while yet mine honour is intact, I may give them to the rushing winds to waft to thee, my prince of prophecy! Where is yon general's ship? Whither must I go to take my place thereon? Lose no further time in watching for a favouring breeze to fill thy sails, doomed as thou art to carry from this land one of the three avenging spirits. Fare thee well, mother mine! dry thy tears, O country dear! yet a little while, my brothers sleeping in the tomb and my own father true, and ye shall welcome me; yet shall victory crown my advent 'mongst the dead, when I have overthrown the home of our destroyers, the house of the sons of Atreus.

Exeunt TALTHYBIUS *and* CASSANDRA.

Ch. Ye guardians of the grey-haired Hecuba, see how your mistress is sinking speechless to the ground! Take hold of her! will ye let her fall, ye worthless slaves? lift up again, from where it lies, her silvered head.

Hec. Leave me lying where I fell, my maidens—unwelcome service grows not welcome ever—my sufferings now, my troubles past, afflictions yet to come, all claim this lowly posture. Gods of heaven! small help I find in calling such allies, yet is there something in the form of invoking heaven, whenso we fall on evil days. First will I descant upon my former blessings; so shall I inspire the greater pity for my present woes. Born to royal estate and wedded to a royal lord, I was the mother of a race of gallant sons; no mere ciphers they, but Phrygia's chiefest pride, children such as no Trojan or Hellenic or barbarian mother ever had to boast. All these have I seen slain by the spear of Hellas, and at their tombs have I shorn off my hair; with these my eyes I saw their sire, my Priam, butchered on his own hearth, and my city captured, nor did others bring this bitter news to me. The maidens I brought up to see chosen for some marriage high, for strangers have I reared them, and seen them snatched away. Nevermore can I hope to be seen by them, nor shall my eyes behold them ever in the days to come. And last, to crown my misery, shall I be brought to Hellas, a slave in my old age. And there the tasks that least befit the evening of my life will they impose on me, to watch their gates and keep the keys, me Hector's mother, or bake their bread, and on the ground instead of my royal bed lay down my shrunken limbs, with tattered rags about my wasted frame, a shameful garb for those who once were prosperous. Ah, woe is me! and this is what I bear and am to bear for one weak woman's wooing! O my daughter, O Cassandra! whom gods have summoned to their frenzied train, how cruel the lot that ends thy virgin days! And thou, Polyxena! my child of sorrow, where, oh! where art thou? None of all the many sons and daughters have I born comes to aid a wretched mother. Why then raise me up? What hope is left us? Guide me, who erst trod so daintily the streets of Troy, but now am but a slave, to a bed upon the ground, nigh some rocky ridge, that thence I may cast me down and perish, after I have wasted my body with weeping. Of all the prosperous crowd, count none a happy man before he die.

Ch. Sing me, Muse, a tale of Troy, a funeral dirge in strains unheard as yet, with tears the while; for now will I uplift for Troy a piteous chant, telling how I met my doom and fell a wretched captive to the Argives by reason of a four-footed beast that moved on wheels, in the hour that Achæa's sons left at our gates that horse, loud rumbling on its way, with its trappings of gold and its freight of warriors; and our folk cried out as they stood upon the rocky citadel, "Up now ye whose toil is o'er, and drag this sacred image to the shrine of the Zeus-born maiden, goddess of our Ilium!" Forth from his house came every youth and every grey-head too; and with songs of joy they took the fatal snare within. Then hastened all the race of Phrygia to the gates, to make the goddess a present of an Argive band ambushed in the polished mountain-pine, Dardania's ruin, a welcome gift to be to her, the virgin queen of deathless steeds; and with nooses of cord they dragged it, as it had been a ship's dark hull, to the stone-built fane of the goddess Pallas, and set it on that floor so soon to drink our country's blood. But, as they laboured and made merry, came on the pitchy night; loud the Libyan flute was sounding, and Phrygian songs awoke, while maidens beat the ground with airy foot, uplifting their gladsome song; and in the halls a blaze of torchlight shed its flickering shadows on sleeping eyes. In that hour around the house was I singing as I danced to that maiden of the hills, the child of Zeus; when lo! there rang along the town a cry of death which filled the homes of Troy, and little babes in terror clung about their mothers' skirts, as forth from their ambush came the warrior-band, the handiwork of maiden Pallas. Anon the altars ran with Phrygian blood, and desolation reigned o'er every bed where young men lay beheaded, a glorious crown for Hellas won, ay, for her, the nurse of youth, but for our Phrygian fatherland a bitter grief. Look, Hecuba! dost see Andromache advancing hither on a foreign car? and with her, clasped to her throbbing breast, is her dear Astyanax, Hector's child.

Enter ANDROMACHE.

Hec. Whither art thou borne, unhappy wife, mounted on that car, side by side with Hector's brazen arms and Phrygian spoils of war, with which Achilles' son will deck the shrines of Phthia on his return from Troy?

Andromache. My Achæan masters drag me hence.

Hec. Woe is thee!

An. Why dost thou in note of woe utter the dirge that is mine?

Hec. Ah me!

An. For these sorrows.

Hec. O Zeus!

An. And for this calamity.

Hec. O my children!

An. Our day is past.

Hec. Joy is fled, and Troy o'erthrown.

An. Woe is me!

Hec. Dead too all my gallant sons!

An. Alack and well-a-day!

Hec. Ah me for my—

An. Misery!

Hec. Piteous the fate—

An. Of our city,

Hec. Smouldering in the smoke.

An. Come, my husband, come to me!

Hec. Ah hapless wife! thou callest on my son who lieth in the tomb.

An. Thy wife's defender, come!

Hec. Do thou, who erst didst make the Achæans grieve, eldest of the sons I bare to Priam in the days gone by, take me to thy rest in Hades' halls!

An. Bitter are these regrets, unhappy mother, bitter these woes to bear; our city ruined, and sorrow evermore to sorrow added, through the will of angry heaven, since the day that son[1] of thine escaped his doom, he that for a bride accursed brought destruction on the Trojan citadel. There lie the gory corpses of the slain by the shrine of Pallas for vultures to carry off; and Troy is come to slavery's yoke.

Hec. O my country, O unhappy land, I weep for thee now left behind; now dost thou behold thy piteous end; and thee, my house, I weep, wherein I suffered travail. O my children! reft of her city as your mother is, she now is losing you. Oh, what mourning and what sorrow! oh, what endless streams of tears in our houses! The dead alone forget their griefs and never shed a tear.

Ch. What sweet relief to sufferers 'tis to weep, to mourn, lament, and chant the dirge that tells of grief!

An. Dost thou see this, mother of that Hector, who once laid low in battle many a son of Argos?

Hec. I see that it is heaven's way to exalt what men accounted naught, and ruin what they most esteemed.

An. Hence with my child as booty am I borne; the noble are to slavery brought—a bitter, bitter change.

Hec. This is necessity's grim law; it was but now Cassandra was torn with brutal violence from my arms.

An. Alas, alas! it seems a second Aias hath appeared to wrong thy daughter; but there be other ills for thee.

Hec. Ay, beyond all count or measure are my sorrows; evil vies with evil in the struggle to be first.

An. Thy daughter Polyxena is dead, slain at Achilles' tomb, an offering to his lifeless corpse.

Hec. O woe is me! This is that riddle Talthybius long since told me, a truth obscurely uttered.

An. I saw her with mine eyes; so I alighted from the chariot, and covered her corpse with a mantle, and smote upon my breast.

Hec. Alas! my child, for thy unhallowed sacrifice! and yet again, ah me! for this thy shameful death!

An. Her death was even as it was, and yet that death of hers was after all a happier fate than this my life.

Hec. Death and life are not the same, my child; the one is annihilation, the other keeps a place for hope.

An. Hear, O mother of children! give ear to what I urge so well, that I may cheer my drooping spirit. 'Tis all one, I say, ne'er to have been born and to be dead, and better far is death than life with misery. For the dead feel no sorrow any more and know no grief; but he who has known prosperity and has fallen on evil days feels his spirit straying from the scene of former joys. Now that child of thine is dead as though she ne'er had seen the light, and little she recks of her calamity; whereas I, who aimed at a fair repute, though I won a higher lot than most, yet missed my luck in life. For all that stamps the wife a woman chaste, I strove to do in Hector's home. In the first place, whether there is a slur upon a woman, or whether there is not, the very fact of her not staying at home brings in its train an evil name; therefore I gave up any wish to do so, and abode ever within my house, nor would I admit the clever gossip women love, but conscious of a heart that told an honest tale I was content therewith. And ever would I keep a silent tongue and modest eye before my lord; and well I knew where I might rule my lord, and where 'twas best to yield to him; the fame whereof hath reached the Achæan host, and proved my ruin; for when I was taken captive, Achilles' son would have me as his wife, and I must serve in the house of murderers. And if I set aside my love for Hector, and ope my heart to this new lord, I shall appear a traitress to the dead, while, if I hate him, I shall incur my master's displeasure. And yet they say a single night removes a woman's dislike for her husband; nay, I do hate the woman who, when she hath lost her former lord, transfers her love by marrying another. Not e'en the horse, if from his fellow torn, will cheerfully draw the yoke; and yet the brutes have neither speech nor sense to help them, and are by nature man's inferiors. O Hector mine! in thee I found a husband amply dowered with wisdom, noble birth and fortune, a brave man and a mighty; whilst thou didst take me from my father's house a spotless bride, thyself the first to make this maiden wife. But now death hath claimed thee, and I to Hellas am soon to sail, a captive doomed to wear the yoke of slavery. Hath not then the dead Polyxena, for whom thou wailest, less evil to bear than I? I have not so much as hope, the last resource of every human heart, nor do I beguile myself with dreams of future bliss, the very thought whereof is sweet.

Ch. Thou art in the self-same plight as I; thy lamentations for thyself remind me of my own sad case.

Hec. I never yet have set foot on a ship's deck, though I have seen such things in pictures and know of them from hearsay. Now sailors, if there come a storm of moderate force, are all eagerness to save themselves by toil; one at the tiller stands, another

[1] Paris, who had been exposed to die on account of an oracle foretelling the misery he would cause if he grew to man's estate; but shepherds had found him on the hills and reared him.

sets himself to work the sheets, a third meantime is baling out the ship; but if tempestuous waves arise to overwhelm them, they yield to fortune and commit themselves to the driving billows. Even so I, by reason of my countless troubles, am dumb and forbear to say a word; for Heaven with its surge of misery is too strong for me. Cease, Oh cease, my darling child, to speak of Hector's fate; no tears of thine can save him; honour thy present lord, offering thy sweet nature as the bait to win him. If thou do this, thou wilt cheer thy friends as well as thyself, and thou shalt rear my Hector's child to lend stout aid to Ilium, that so thy children in the after-time may build her up again, and our city yet be stablished. But lo! our talk must take a different turn; who is this Achæan menial I see coming hither, sent to tell us of some new design?

Enter TALTHYBIUS.

Ta. Oh hate me not, thou that erst wert Hector's wife, the bravest of the Phrygians! for my tongue would fain not tell that which the Danai and sons of Pelops both command.

An. What is it? Thy prelude bodeth evil news.

Ta. 'Tis decreed thy son is—how can I tell my news?

An. Surely not to have a different master from me?

Ta. None of all Achæa's chiefs shall ever lord it over him.

An. Is it their will to leave him here, a remnant yet of Phrygia's race?

Ta. I know no words to break the sorrow lightly to thee.

An. I thank thee for thy consideration, unless indeed thou hast good news to tell.

Ta. They mean to slay thy son; there is my hateful message to thee.

An. O God! this is worse tidings than my forced marriage.

Ta. So spake Odysseus to the assembled Hellenes, and his word prevails.

An. Oh once again ah me! there is no measure in the woes I bear.

Ta. He said they should not rear so brave a father's son.

An. May such counsels yet prevail about children of his!

Ta. From Troy's battlements he must be thrown. Let it be even so, and thou wilt show more wisdom; cling not to him, but bear thy sorrows with heroic heart, nor in thy weakness deem that thou art strong. For nowhere hast thou any help; consider this thou must; thy husband and thy city are no more, so thou art in our power, and I alone am match enough for one weak woman; wherefore I would not see thee bent on strife, or any course to bring thee shame or hate, nor would I hear thee rashly curse the Achæans. For if thou say aught whereat the host grow wroth, this child will find no burial nor pity either. But if thou hold thy peace and with composure take thy fate, thou wilt not leave his corpse unburied, and thyself wilt find more favour with the Achæans.

An. My child! my own sweet babe and priceless treasure! thy death the foe demands, and thou must leave thy wretched mother. That which saves the lives of others, proves thy destruction, even thy sire's nobility; to thee thy father's valiancy has proved no boon. O the woful wedding rites, that brought me erst to Hector's home, hoping to be the mother of a son that should rule o'er Asia's fruitful fields instead of serving as a victim to the sons of Danaüs! Dost weep, my babe? dost know thy hapless fate? Why clutch me with thy hands and to my garment cling, nestling like a tender chick beneath my wing? Hector will not rise again and come gripping his famous spear to bring thee salvation; no kinsman of thy sire appears, nor might of Phrygian hosts; one awful headlong leap from the dizzy height and thou wilt dash out thy life with none to pity thee! Oh to clasp thy tender limbs, a mother's fondest joy! Oh to breathe thy fragrant breath! In vain it seems these breasts did suckle thee, wrapped in thy swaddling-clothes; all for naught I used to toil and wore myself away! Kiss thy mother now for the last time, nestle to her that bare thee, twine thy arms about my neck and join thy lips to mine! O ye Hellenes, cunning to devise new forms of cruelty, why slay this child who never wronged any? Thou daughter of Tyndarus, thou art no child of Zeus, but sprung, I trow, of many a sire, first of some evil demon, next of Envy, then of Murder and of Death, and every horror that the earth begets. That Zeus was never sire of thine I boldly do assert, bane as thou hast been to many a Hellene and barbarian too. Destruction catch thee! Those fair eyes of thine have brought a shameful ruin on the fields of glorious Troy. Take the babe and bear him hence, hurl him down if so ye list, then feast upon his flesh! 'Tis heaven's high will we perish, and I cannot ward the deadly stroke from my child. Hide me and my misery; cast me into the ship's hold; for 'tis to a fair wedding I am going, now that I have lost my child!

Ch. Unhappy Troy! thy thousands thou hast lost for one woman's sake and her accursed wooing.

Ta. Come, child, leave fond embracing of thy woful mother, and mount the high coronal of thy ancestral towers, there to draw thy parting breath, as is ordained. Take him hence. His should the duty be to do such herald's work, whose heart knows no pity and who loveth ruthlessness more than my soul doth.

Exeunt ANDROMACHE *and* TALTHYBIUS *with* ASTYANAX.

Hec. O child, son of my hapless boy, an unjust fate robs me and thy mother of thy life. How is it with me? What can I do for thee, my luckless babe? for thee I smite upon my head and beat my breast, my only gift; for that alone is in my power. Woe for my city! woe for thee! Is not our cup full? What is wanting now to our utter and immediate ruin?

Ch. O Telamon, King of Salamis, the feeding-ground of bees, who hast thy home in a sea-girt isle that lieth nigh the holy hills where first Athena made the grey olive-branch to appear, a crown for heavenly heads and a glory unto happy Athens, thou didst come in knightly brotherhood with that great archer, Alcmena's son, to sack our city Ilium, in days gone by, on thy advent from Hellas, what time he led the chosen flower of Hellas, vexed for the steeds denied him, and at the fair stream of Simois he stayed his sea-borne ship and fastened cables to the stern, and forth therefrom he took the bow his hand could deftly shoot, to be the doom of Laomedon; and with the ruddy breath of fire he wasted the masonry squared by Phœbus' line and chisel, and sacked the land of Troy; so twice in two attacks hath the bloodstained spear destroyed Dardania's walls.

In vain, it seems, thou Phrygian boy,[1] pacing with dainty step amid thy golden chalices, dost thou fill high the cup of Zeus, a service passing fair; seeing that the land of thy birth is being consumed by fire. The shore re-echoes to our cries; and, as a bird bewails its young, so we bewail our husbands or our children, or our grey-haired mothers. The dew-fed springs where thou didst bathe, the course where thou didst train, are now no more; but thou beside the throne of Zeus art sitting with a calm, sweet smile upon thy fair young face, while the spear of Hellas lays the land of Priam waste. Ah! Love, Love, who once didst seek these Dardan halls, deep-seated in the hearts of heavenly gods, how high didst thou make Troy to tower in those days, allying her with deities! But I will cease to urge reproaches against Zeus; for white-winged dawn, whose light to man is dear, turned a baleful eye upon our land and watched the ruin of our citadel, though she had within her bridal bower a husband from this land, whom on a day a car of gold and spangled stars caught up and carried thither, great source of hope to his native country; but all the love the gods once had for Troy is passed away.

Enter MENELAUS.

Menelaus. Hail! thou radiant orb by whose fair light I now shall capture her that was my wife, e'en Helen; for I am that Menelaus, who hath toiled so hard, I and Achæa's host. To Troy I came, not so much as men suppose to take this woman, but to punish him who from my house stole my wife, traitor to my hospitality. But he, by heaven's will, hath paid the penalty, ruined, and his country too, by the spear of Hellas. And I am come to bear that Spartan woman hence—wife I have no mind to call her, though she once was mine; for now she is but one among the other Trojan dames who share these tents as captives. For they—the very men who toiled to take her with the spear—have granted her to me to slay, or, if I will, to spare and carry back with me to Argos. Now my purpose is not to put her to death in Troy, but to carry her to Hellas in my sea-borne ship, and then surrender her to death, a recompense to all whose friends were slain in Ilium. Ho! my trusty men, enter the tent, and drag her out to me by her hair with many a murder foul; and when a favouring breeze shall blow, to Hellas will we convey her.

Hec. O thou that dost support the earth and restest thereupon, whosoe'er thou art, a riddle past our ken! be thou Zeus, or natural necessity, or man's intellect, to thee I pray; for, though thou treadest o'er a noiseless path, all thy dealings with mankind are by justice guided.

Me. How now? Strange the prayer thou offerest unto heaven!

Hec. I thank thee, Menelaus, if thou wilt slay that wife of thine. Yet shun the sight of her, lest she smite thee with regret. For she ensnares the eyes of men, o'erthrows their towns, and burns their houses, so potent are her witcheries! Well I know her; so dost thou and those her victims too.

Enter HELEN.

Helen. Menelaus! this prelude well may fill me with alarm; for I am haled with violence by thy servants' hands and brought before these tents. Still, though I am well-nigh sure thou hatest me, yet would I fain inquire what thou and Hellas have decided about my life.

Me. To judge thy case required no great exactness; the host with one consent—that host whom thou didst wrong—handed thee over to me to die.

Hel. May I answer this decision, proving that my death, if to die I am, will be unjust?

Me. I came not to argue, but to slay thee.

Hec. Hear her, Menelaus; let her not die for want of that, and let me answer her again, for thou knowest naught of her villainies in Troy; and the whole case, if thus summed up, will insure her death against all chance of an escape.

Me. This boon needs leisure; still, if she wishes to speak, the leave is given. Yet will I grant her this because of thy words, that she may hear them, and not for her own sake.

Hel. Perhaps thou wilt not answer me, from counting me a foe, whether my words seem good or ill. Yet will I put my charges and thine over against each other, and then reply to the accusations I suppose thou wilt advance against me. First, then, she was the author of these troubles by giving birth to Paris; next, old Priam ruined Troy and me, because he did not slay his babe Alexander, baleful semblance of a fire-brand, long ago. Hear what followed. This Paris was to judge the claims of three rival goddesses; so Pallas offered him command of all the Phrygians, and the destruction of Hellas; Hera promised he should spread his dominion over Asia, and the utmost bounds of Europe, if he would decide for her; but Cypris spoke in rapture of my loveliness, and promised him this boon, if she should have the preference o'er those twain for beauty; now mark the inference I deduce from this; Cypris won the day o'er them, and thus far hath my marriage proved of benefit to Hellas, that ye are not subject to barbarian rule, neither vanquished in the strife, nor yet by tyrants crushed. What Hellas

[1] Ganymede.

gained, was ruin to me, a victim for my beauty sold, and now am I reproached for that which should have set a crown upon my head. But thou wilt say I am silent on the real matter at issue, how it was I started forth and left thy house by stealth. With no mean goddess at his side he came, my evil genius, call him Alexander or Paris, as thou wilt; and him didst thou, thrice guilty wretch, leave behind thee in thy house, and sail away from Sparta to the land of Crete. Enough of this! For all that followed I must question my own heart, not thee; what frantic thought led me to follow the stranger from thy house, traitress to my country and my home? Punish the goddess, show thyself more mighty e'en than Zeus, who, though he lords it o'er the other gods, is yet her slave; wherefore I may well be pardoned. Still, from hence thou mightest draw a specious argument against me; when Paris died, and Earth concealed his corpse, I should have left his house and sought the Argive fleet, since my marriage was no longer in the hands of gods. That was what I fain had done; yea, and the warders on the towers and watchmen on the walls can bear me witness, for oft they found me seeking to let myself down stealthily by cords from the battlements; but there was that new husband, Deiphobus, that carried me off by force to be his wife against the will of Troy. How then, my lord, could I be justly put to death by thee, with any show of right, seeing that he wedded me against my will, and those my other natural gifts have served a bitter slavery, instead of leading on to triumph? If 'tis thy will indeed to master gods, that very wish displays thy folly.

Ch. O my royal mistress, defend thy children's and thy country's cause, bringing to naught her persuasive arguments, for she pleads well in spite of all her villainy; 'tis monstrous this!

Hec. First will I take up the cause of those goddesses, and prove how she perverts the truth. For I can ne'er believe that Hera or the maiden Pallas would have been guilty of such folly, as to sell, the one, her Argos to barbarians, or that Pallas e'er would make her Athens subject to the Phrygians, coming as they did in mere wanton sport to Ida to contest the palm of beauty. For why should goddess Hera set her heart so much on such a prize? Was it to win a nobler lord than Zeus? or was Athena bent on finding 'mongst the gods a husband, she who in her dislike of marriage won from her sire the boon of remaining unwed? Seek not to impute folly to the goddesses, in the attempt to gloze o'er thy own sin; never wilt thou persuade the wise. Next thou hast said—what well may make men jeer—that Cypris came with my son to the house of Menelaus. Could she not have stayed quietly in heaven and brought thee and Amyclæ to boot to Ilium? Nay! my son was passing fair, and when thou sawest him thy fancy straight became thy Cypris; for every sensual act that men commit, they lay upon this goddess, and rightly does her name of Aphrodite begin the word for "senselessness"; so when thou didst catch sight of him in gorgeous foreign garb, ablaze with gold, thy senses utterly forsook thee. Yea, for in Argos thou hadst moved in simple state, but, once free of Sparta, 'twas thy fond hope to deluge by thy lavish outlay Phrygia's town, that flowed with gold; nor was the palace of Menelaus rich enough for thy luxury to riot in. Ha! my son carried thee off by force, so thou sayest; what Spartan saw this? what cry for help didst thou ever raise, though Castor was still alive, a vigorous youth, and his brother also, not yet amid the stars? Then when thou wert come to Troy, and the Argives were on thy track, and the mortal combat was begun, whenever tidings came to thee of Menelaus' prowess, him wouldst thou praise, to grieve my son, because he had so powerful a rival in his love; but if so the Trojans prospered, Menelaus was nothing to thee. Thy eye was fixed on Fortune, and by such practice wert thou careful to follow in her steps, careless of virtue's cause. And then, in spite of all, thou dost assert that thou didst try to let thyself down from the towers by stealth with twisted cords, as if loth to stay? Pray then, wert thou ever found fastening the noose about thy neck, or whetting the knife, as a noble wife would have done in regret for her former husband? And yet full oft I advised thee saying, "Get thee gone, daughter, and let my sons take other brides; I will help thee to steal away, and convey thee to the Achæan fleet; oh end the strife 'twixt us and Hellas!" But this was bitter in thy ears. For thou wert wantoning in Alexander's house, fain to have obeisance done thee by barbarians. Yes, 'twas a proud time for thee; and now after all this thou hast bedizened thyself, and come forth and hast dared to appear under the same sky as thy husband, revolting wretch! Better hadst thou come in tattered raiment, cowering humbly in terror, with hair shorn short, if for thy past sins thy feeling were one of shame rather than effrontery. O Menelaus, hear the conclusion of my argument; crown Hellas by slaying her as she deserves, and establish this law for all others of her sex, e'en death to every traitress to her husband.

Ch. Avenge thee, Menelaus, on thy wife, as is worthy of thy home and ancestors, clear thyself from the reproach of effeminacy at the lips of Hellas, and let thy foes see thy spirit.

Me. Thy thoughts with mine do coincide, that she, without constraint, left my palace, and sought a stranger's love, and now Cypris is introduced for mere bluster. Away to those who shall stone thee, and by thy speedy death requite the weary toils of the Achæans, that thou mayst learn not to bring shame on me!

Hel. Oh, by thy knees, I implore thee, impute not that heaven-sent affliction to me, nor slay me; pardon, I entreat!

Hec. Be not false to thy allies, whose death this woman caused; on their behalf, and for my children's sake, I sue to thee.

Me. Peace, reverend dame; to her I pay no heed. Lo! I bid my servants take her hence, aboard the ship, wherein she is to sail.

Hec. Oh never let her set foot within the same ship as thee.

Me. How now? is she heavier than of yore?

Hec. Who loveth once, must love alway.

Me. Why, that depends how those we love are minded. But thy wish shall be granted; she shall not set foot upon the same ship with me; for thy advice is surely sound; and when she comes to Argos she shall die a shameful death as is her due, and impress the need of chastity on all her sex; no easy task; yet shall her fate strike their foolish hearts with terror, e'en though they be more lost to shame than she.

Exit MENELAUS, *dragging* HELEN *with him.*

Ch. So then thou hast delivered into Achæa's hand, O Zeus, thy shrine in Ilium and thy fragrant altar, the offerings of burnt sacrifice with smoke of myrrh to heaven uprising, and holy Pergamos, and glens of Ida tangled with ivy's growth, where rills of melting snow pour down their flood, a holy sunlit land that bounds the world and takes the god's first rays! Gone are thy sacrifices! gone the dancer's cheerful shout! gone the vigils of the gods as night closed in! Thy images of carven gold are now no more; and Phrygia's holy festivals, twelve times a year, at each full moon, are ended now. 'Tis this that filleth me with anxious thought whether thou, O king, seated on the sky, thy heavenly throne, carest at all that my city is destroyed, a prey to the furious fiery blast. Ah! my husband, fondly loved, thou art a wandering spectre; unwashed, unburied lies thy corpse, while o'er the sea the ship sped by wings will carry me to Argos, land of steeds, where stand Cyclopian walls of stone upreared to heaven. There in the gate the children gather, hanging round their mothers' necks, and weep their piteous lamentation, "O mother, woe is me! torn from thy sight Achæans bear me away from thee to their dark ship to row me o'er the deep to sacred Salamis or to the hill[1] on the Isthmus, that o'erlooks two seas, the key to the gates of Pelops." Oh may the blazing thunderbolt, hurled in might from its holy home, smite the barque of Menelaus full amidships as it is crossing the Ægean main, since he is carrying me away in bitter sorrow from the shores of Ilium to be a slave in Hellas, while the daughter of Zeus still keeps her golden mirrors, delight of maidens' hearts. Never may he reach his home in Laconia or his father's hearth and home, nor come to the town of Pitane[2] or the temple of the goddess[3] with the gates of bronze, having taken as his captive her whose marriage brought disgrace on Hellas through its length and breadth and woful anguish on the streams of Simois! Ah me! ah me! new troubles on my country fall, to take the place of those that still are fresh! Behold, ye hapless wives of Troy, the corpse of Astyanax! whom the Danai have cruelly slain by hurling him from the battlements.

[1]Acrocorinthus.

[2]Part of Sparta was so called.

[3]Athena of "the Brazen House," a temple on the Acropolis.

Enter TALTHYBIUS *and attendants, bearing the corpse of* ASTYANAX *on* HECTOR'S *shield.*

Ta. Hecuba, one ship alone delays its plashing oars, and it is soon to sail to the shores of Phthia freighted with the remnant of the spoils of Achilles' son; for Neoptolemus is already out at sea, having heard that new calamities have befallen Peleus, for Acastus, son of Pelias, hath banished him the realm. Wherefore he is gone, too quick to indulge in any delay, and with him goes Andromache, who drew many a tear from me what time she started hence, wailing her country and crying her farewell to Hector's tomb. And she craved her master leave to bury this poor dead child of Hector who breathed his last when from the turrets hurled, entreating too that he would not carry this shield, the terror of the Achæans—this shield with plates of brass wherewith his father would gird himself—to the home of Peleus or to the same bridal bower whither she, herself the mother of this corpse, would be led, a bitter sight to her, but let her bury the child therein instead of in a coffin of cedar or a tomb of stone, and to thy hands commit the corpse that thou mayst deck it with robes and garlands as best thou canst with thy present means; for she is far away and her master's haste prevented her from burying the child herself. So we, when thou the corpse hast decked, will heap the earth above and set thereon a spear; but do thou with thy best speed perform thy allotted task; one toil however have I already spared thee, for I crossed Scamander's stream and bathed the corpse and cleansed its wounds. But now will I go to dig a grave for him, that our united efforts shortening our task may speed our ship towards home.

Exit TALTHYBIUS.

Hec. Place the shield upon the ground, Hector's shield so deftly rounded, a piteous sight, a bitter grief for me to see. O ye Achæans, more reason have ye to boast of your prowess than your wisdom! Why have ye in terror of this child been guilty of a murder never matched before? Did ye fear that some day he would rear again the fallen walls of Troy? It seems then ye were nothing after all, when, though Hector's fortunes in the war were prosperous and he had ten thousand other arms to back him, we still were daily overmatched; and yet, now that our city is taken and every Phrygian slain, ye fear a tender babe like this! Out upon his fear! say I, who fears, but never yet hath reasoned out the cause. Ah! my beloved, thine is a piteous death indeed! Hadst thou died for thy city, when thou hadst tasted of the sweets of manhood, of marriage, and of godlike power o'er others, then wert thou blest, if aught herein is blest. But now after one glimpse, one dream thereof thou knowest them no more, my child, and hast no joy of them, though heir to all. Ah, poor babe! how sadly have thy own father's walls, those towers that Loxias reared, shorn from thy head the locks thy mother fondled, and so oft caressed, from which through fractured bones the face of murder grins—briefly to dismiss my shocking theme. O hands, how sweet the likeness ye retain of his father, and yet ye lie limp in your sockets before me! Dear mouth, so often full of words of pride, death hath closed thee, and thou hast not kept the promise thou didst make, when nestling in my robe, "Ah, mother mine, many a lock of my hair will I cut off for thee, and to thy tomb will lead my troops of friends, taking a fond farewell of thee." But now 'tis not thy hand that buries me, but I, on whom is come old age with loss of home and children, am burying thee, a tender child untimely slain. Ah me! those kisses numberless, the nurture that I gave to thee, those sleepless nights—they all are lost! What shall the bard inscribe upon thy tomb about thee? "Argives once for fear of him slew this child!" Foul shame should that inscription be to Hellas. O child, though thou hast no part in all thy father's wealth, yet shalt thou have his brazen shield wherein to find a tomb. Ah! shield that didst keep safe the comely arm of Hector, now hast thou lost thy valiant keeper! How fair upon thy handle lies his imprint, and on the rim, that circles round the targe, are marks of sweat, that trickled oft from Hector's brow as he pressed it 'gainst his beard in battle's stress. Come, bring forth, from such store as we have, adornment for the hapless dead, for fortune gives no chance now for offerings fair; yet of such as I possess, shalt thou receive these gifts. Foolish mortal he! who thinks his luck secure and so rejoices; for fortune, like a madman in her moods, springs towards this man, then towards that; and none ever experiences the same unchanging luck.

Ch. Lo! all is ready and they are bringing at thy bidding from the spoils of Troy garniture to put upon the dead.

Hec. Ah! my child, 'tis not as victor o'er thy comrades with horse or bow—customs Troy esteems, without pursuing them to excess—that Hector's mother decks thee now with ornaments from the store that once was thine, though now hath Helen, whom the gods abhor, reft thee of thine own, yea, and robbed thee of thy life and caused thy house to perish root and branch.

Ch. Woe! thrice woe! my heart is touched, and thou the cause, my mighty prince in days now passed!

Hec. About thy body now I swathe this Phrygian robe of honour, which should have clad thee on thy marriage-day, wedded to the noblest of Asia's daughters. Thou too, dear shield of Hector, victorious parent of countless triumphs past, accept thy crown, for though thou share the dead child's tomb, death cannot touch thee; for thou dost merit honours far beyond those arms[1] that the crafty knave Odysseus won.

Ch. Alas! ah me! thee, O child, shall earth take to her breast, a cause for bitter weeping. Mourn, thou mother!

Hec. Ah me!

Ch. Wail for the dead.

Hec. Woe is me!

Ch. Alas! for thy unending sorrow!

[1]The arms of Achilles.

Hec. Thy wounds in part will I bind up with bandages, a wretched leech in name alone, without reality; but for the rest, thy sire must look to that amongst the dead.

Ch. Smite, oh smite upon thy head with frequent blow of hand. Woe is me!

Hec. My kind, good friends!

Ch. Speak out, Hecuba, the word that was on thy lips.

Hec. It seems the only things that heaven concerns itself about are my troubles and Troy hateful in their eyes above all other cities. In vain did we sacrifice to them. Had not the god caught us in his grip and plunged us headlong 'neath the earth, we should have been unheard of, nor ever sung in Muses' songs, furnishing to bards of after-days a subject for their minstrelsy. Go, bury now in his poor tomb the dead, wreathed all duly as befits a corpse. And yet I deem it makes but little difference to the dead, although they get a gorgeous funeral; for this is but a cause of idle pride to the living.

The corpse is carried off to burial.

Ch. Alas! for thy unhappy mother, who o'er thy corpse hath closed the high hopes of her life! Born of a noble stock, counted most happy in thy lot, ah! what a tragic death is thine! Ha! who are those I see on yonder pinnacles darting to and fro with flaming torches in their hands? Some new calamity will soon on Troy alight.

Enter TALTHYBIUS *above. Soldiers are seen on the battlements of Troy, torch in hand.*

Ta. Ye captains, whose allotted task it is to fire this town of Priam, to you I speak. No longer keep the firebrand idle in your hands, but launch the flame, that when we have destroyed the city of Ilium we may set forth in gladness on our homeward voyage from Troy. And you, ye sons of Troy—to let my orders take at once a double form—start for the Achæan ships for your departure hence, soon as ever the leaders of the host blow loud and clear upon the trumpet. And thou, unhappy greyhaired dame, follow; for yonder come servants from Odysseus to fetch thee, for to him thou art assigned by lot to be a slave far from thy country.

Hec. Ah, woe is me! This surely is the last, the utmost limit this, of all my sorrows; forth from my land I go; my city is ablaze with flame. Yet, thou aged foot, make one painful struggle to hasten, that I may say a farewell to this wretched town. O Troy, that erst hadst such a grand career amongst barbarian towns, soon wilt thou be reft of that splendid name. Lo! they are burning thee, and leading us e'en now from our land to slavery. Great gods! Yet why call on the gods? They did not hearken e'en aforetime to our call. Come, let us rush into the flames, for to die with my country in its blazing ruin were a noble death for me.

Ta. Thy sorrows drive thee frantic, poor lady. Go, lead her hence, make no delay, for ye must deliver her into the hand of Odysseus, conveying to him his prize.

Hec. O son of Cronos, prince of Phrygia, father

of our race, dost thou behold our sufferings now, unworthy of the stock of Dardanus?

Ch. He sees them, but our mighty city is a city no more, and Troy's day is done.

Hec. Woe! thrice woe upon me! Ilium is ablaze; the homes of Pergamos and its towering walls are now one sheet of flame.

Ch. As the smoke soars on wings to heaven, so sinks our city to the ground before the spear. With furious haste both fire and foeman's spear devour each house.

Hec. Hearken, my children, hear your mother's voice.

Ch. Thou art calling on the dead with voice of lamentation.

Hec. Yea, as I stretch my aged limbs upon the ground, and beat upon the earth with both my hands.

Ch. I follow thee and kneel, invoking from the nether world my hapless husband.

Hec. I am being dragged and hurried away—

Ch. O the sorrow of that cry!

Hec. From my own dear country, to dwell beneath a master's roof. Woe is me! O Priam, Priam, slain, unburied, left without a friend, naught dost thou know of my cruel fate.

Ch. No, for o'er his eyes black death hath drawn his pall—a holy man by sinners slain!

Hec. Woe for the temples of the gods! Woe for our dear city!

Ch. Woe!

Hec. Murderous flame and foeman's spear are now your lot.

Ch. Soon will ye tumble to your own loved soil, and be forgotten.

Hec. And the dust, mounting to heaven on wings like smoke, will rob me of the sight of my home.

Ch. The name of my country will pass into obscurity; all is scattered far and wide, and hapless Troy has ceased to be.

Hec. Did ye hear that and know its purport?

Ch. Aye, 'twas the crash of the citadel.

Hec. The shock will whelm our city utterly. O woe is me! trembling, quaking limbs, support my footsteps! away! to face the day that begins thy slavery.

Ch. Woe for our unhappy town! And yet to the Achæan fleet advance.

Hec. Woe for thee, O land that nursed my little babes!

Ch. Ah! woe! *Exeunt* OMNES.

ION

DRAMATIS PERSONAE

Hermes
Ion
Chorus of Creusa's Handmaidens
Creusa
Xuthus
Old Man Servant
Servant, *of Creusa*
Pythian Priestess
Athena

Before Apollo's temple at Delphi. Enter HERMES.

Hermes. Atlas, who bears upon his brazen back the pressure of the sky, ancient dwelling of the gods, begat Maia from a daughter of one of those gods, and she bare me Hermes to mighty Zeus, to be the servant of the powers divine. Lo! I am come to this land of Delphi where sits Phœbus on the centre of the world and giveth oracles to men, ever chanting lays prophetic of things that are to be. Now there is a city in Hellas of no small note, called after Pallas, goddess of the golden lance; there did Phœbus force his love on Creusa, daughter of Erechtheus, beneath the rock of Pallas, northward of Athens' steep realm, called Macræ by the kings of Attica. And she without her father's knowledge—for such was the god's good pleasure—bore the burden in her womb unto the end, and when her time came, she brought forth a child in the house and carried him away to the selfsame cave wherein the god declared his love to her, and she cradled him in the hollow of a rounded ark and cast him forth to die, observant of the custom of her ancestors and of earth-born Erichthonius, whom the daughter of Zeus gave into the charge of the daughters[1] of Agraulus, after setting on either side, to keep him safe, a guard of serpents twain. Hence in that land among the Erechthidæ 'tis a custom to protect their babes with charms of golden snakes. But ere she left the babe to die, the young mother tied about him her own broidered robe. And this is the request that Phœbus craves of me, for he is my brother, "Go, brother, to those children of the soil that dwell in glorious Athens, for well thou knowest Athena's city, and take a new-born babe from out the hollow rock, his cradle and his swaddling-clothes as well, and bear him to my prophetic shrine at Delphi, and set him at the entering-in of my temple. What else remains shall be my care, for that child is mine, that thou mayst know it." So I, to do my brother Loxias a service, took up the woven ark and bore it off, and at the threshold of the shrine I have laid the babe, after opening the lid of the wicker cradle that the child might be seen. But just as the sun-god was starting forth to run his course, a priestess chanced to enter the god's shrine; and when her eyes lit upon the tender babe she thought it strange that any Delphian maid should dare to cast her child of shame down at the temple of the god; wherefore her purpose was to remove him beyond the altar, but from pity she renounced her cruel thought, and the god to help his child did second her pity to save the babe from being cast out. So she took and brought him up, but she knew not that Phœbus was his sire nor of the mother that bare him, nor yet did the child know his parents. While yet he was a child, around the altar that fed him he would ramble at his play, but when he came to man's estate, the Delphians made him treasurer of the god and steward of all his store, and found him true, and so until the present day he leads a holy life in the god's temple. Meantime Creusa, mother of this youth, is wedded to Xuthus; and thus it came to pass; a war broke out 'twixt Athens and the folk of Chalcodon[2] who dwell in the land of Eubœa; and Xuthus took part therein and helped to end it, for which he received the hand of Creusa as his guerdon, albeit he was no native, but an Achæan, sprung from Æolus, the son of Zeus; and after many years of wedded life he and Creusa still are childless; wherefore they are come to this oracle of Apollo in their desire for offspring. To this end is Loxias guiding their destiny nor hath it escaped his ken, as some suppose. For when Xuthus enters this shrine, the god will give him his own son and declare that Xuthus is the sire, that so the boy may come to his mother's home and be acknowledged by Creusa, while the marriage of Loxias remains a secret and the child obtains his rights; and he shall cause him to be called Ion, founder of a realm in Asia, through all the breadth of Hellas. But now will I get me to yon grotto 'neath the laurel's shade that I may learn what is decreed about the child. For I see the son of Loxias now coming forth to cleanse the gateway in front of the temple with boughs of laurel. I greet him first of all the gods by his name Ion which he soon shall bear. *Exit.*

Enter ION.

Ion. Lo! the sun-god is e'en now turning towards the earth his chariot-car resplendent; before yon fire

[1]The daughters of Cecrops, a mythical king of Attica.

[2]The Eubœans are so called from Chalcodon, a king of Eubœa.

the stars retire to night's mysterious gloom from forth the firmament; the peaks of Parnassus, where no man may set foot, are all ablaze and hail the car of day for mortal's service. To Phœbus' roof mounts up the smoke of myrrh, offering of the desert; there on the holy tripod sits the Delphian priestess, chanting to the ears of Hellas in numbers loud, whate'er Apollo doth proclaim. Ye Delphians, votaries of Phœbus, away! to Castalia's gushing fount as silver clear, and, when ye have bathed you in its waters pure, enter the shrine; and keep your lips in holy silence that it may be well, careful to utter words of good omen amongst yourselves to those who wish to consult the oracle; while I with laurel-sprays and sacred wreaths and drops of water sprinkled o'er the floor will purify the entrance to the shrine of Phœbus, my task each day from childhood's hour; and with my bow will I put to flight the flocks of feathered fowls that harm his sacred offerings; for here in Phœbus' shrine, which nurtured me, I minister, an orphan, fatherless and motherless.

Come, thou tender laurel-shoot, gathered from gardens divine to wait upon the glorious god, thou that sweepest clean the altar of Phœbus hard by his shrine, where holy founts, that ever gush with ceaseless flow, bedew the myrtle's hallowed spray wherewith I cleanse the temple-floor the livelong day, so soon as the swift sun-god wings his flight on high, in my daily ministration. Hail Pæan, prince of healing! blest, ah! doubly blest be thou, child of Latona! Fair the service that I render to thee, Phœbus, before thy house, honouring thy seat of prophecy; a glorious task I count it, to serve not mortal man but deathless gods; wherefore I never weary of performing holy services. Phœbus is to me as the father that begot me, for as such I praise the god that gives me food. 'Tis Phœbus, who dwelleth in the temple, whom I call by that helpful name of father. Hail Pæan, healing god, good luck to thee and blessing, child of Latona! My task is nearly done of sweeping with the laurel broom, so now from a golden ewer will I sprinkle o'er the ground water from Castalia's gushing spring, scattering the liquid dew with hands from all defilement free. Oh may I never cease thus to serve Phœbus, or, if I do, may fortune smile upon me!

Ha! they come, the feathered tribes, leaving their nests on Parnassus. I forbid ye to settle on the coping or enter the gilded dome. Thou herald of Zeus, that masterest the might of other birds with those talons of thine, once more shall my arrow o'ertake thee.

Lo! another comes sailing towards the altar, a swan this time; take thy bright plumes elsewhere; the lyre that Phœbus tuneth to thy song shall never save thee from the bow; so fly away, and settle at the Delian mere, for if thou wilt not hearken, thy blood shall choke the utterance of thy fair melody.

Ha! what new bird comes now? Does it mean to lodge a nest of dry straw for its brood beneath the gables? Soon shall my twanging bow drive thee away. Dost not hear me? Away and rear thy young amid the streams of swirling Alpheus, or get thee to the woody Isthmian glen, that Phœbus' offerings and his shrine may take no hurt. I am loth to slay ye, ye messengers to mortal man of messages from heaven; still must I serve Phœbus, to whose tasks I am devoted, nor will I cease to minister to those that give me food.

Enter CHORUS OF CREUSA'S HANDMAIDENS.

Chorus. I. It is not in holy Athens only that there are courts of the gods with fine colonnades, and the worship of Apollo, guardian of highways; but here, too, at the shrine of Loxias, son of Latona, shines the lovely eye of day on faces twain.

Ch. II. Just look at this! here is the son of Zeus killing with his scimitar of gold the watersnake of Lerna. Do look at him, my friend!

Ch. I. Yes, I see. And close to him stands another with a blazing torch uplifted; who is he? Can this be the warrior Iolaus whose story is told on my broidery, who shares with the son of Zeus his labours and helps him in the moil?

Ch. III. Oh! but look at this! a man mounted on a winged horse, killing a fire-breathing monster with three bodies.

Ch. I. I am turning my eyes in every direction. Behold the rout of the giants carved on these walls of stone.

Ch. IV. Yes, yes, good friends, I am looking.

Ch. V. Dost see her standing over Enceladus brandishing her shield with the Gorgon's head?

Ch. VI. I see Pallas, my own goddess.

Ch. VII. Again, dost see the massy thunderbolt all aflame in the far-darting hands of Zeus?

Ch. VIII. I do; 'tis blasting with its flame Mimas, that deadly foe.

Ch. IX. Bromius too, the god of revelry, is slaying another of the sons of Earth with his thyrsus of ivy, never meant for battle.

Ch. I. Thou that art stationed by this fane, to thee I do address me, may we pass the threshold of these vaults, with our fair white feet?

Ion. Nay, ye must not, stranger ladies.

Ch. X. May I ask thee about something I have heard?

Ion. What wouldst thou ask?

Ch. XI. Is it really true that the temple of Phœbus stands upon the centre of the world?

Ion. Aye, there it stands with garlands decked and gorgeous all around.

Ch. XII. E'en so the legend saith.

Ion. If ye have offered a sacrificial cake before the shrine and have aught ye wish to ask Phœbus, approach the altar; but enter not the inmost sanctuary, save ye have sacrificed sheep.

Ch. XIII. I understand; but we have no mind to trespass against the god's law; the pictures here without will amuse us.

Ion. Feast your eyes on all ye may.

Ch. XIV. My mistress gave me leave to see these vaulted chambers.

Ion. Whose handmaids do ye avow yourselves?

Ch. XV. The temple, where Pallas dwells, is the

nursing-home of my lords. But lo! here is she of whom thou askest.

Ion. Lady, whosoe'er thou art, I see thou art of noble birth, and thy bearing proves thy gentle breeding. For from his bearing one may mostly judge whether a man is nobly born. Yet am I much amazed to see thee close thine eyes in grief and with tears bedew thy noble face, when thou standest face to face with the holy oracle of Loxias. Why, lady, art thou thus disquieted? Here, where all others show their joy at sight of Phœbus' sanctuary, thine eye is wet with tears.

Enter CREUSA.

Creusa. Most courteously, sir stranger, dost thou express surprise at these my tears; the sight of this temple of Apollo recalled to me a memory of long ago, and somehow my thoughts went wandering home, though I am here myself. Ah, hapless race of women! ah, ye reckless gods! What shall I say? to what standard shall we refer justice if through the injustice of our lords and masters we are brought to ruin?

Ion. Why, lady, art thou thus cast down, past all finding out?

Cr. 'Tis naught; I have shot my bolt; for what remains, I say no more, nor seek thou further to inquire.

Ion. Who art thou and whence? who is the father that begat thee? by what name are we to call thee?

Cr. Creusa is my name, the daughter of Erechtheus I; my native land is Athens.

Ion. A glorious city thine, lady, a noble line of ancestry! with what reverence I behold thee!

Cr. Thus far, no further goes my luck, good sir.

Ion. Pray, is the current legend true—

Cr. What is thy question? I fain would learn.

Ion. Was thy father's grandsire really sprung from Earth?

Cr. Yes, Erichthonius was; but my high birth avails me not.

Ion. Is it true Athena reared him from the ground?

Cr. Aye, and into maidens' hands, though not his mother's—

Ion. Consigned him, did she? as 'tis wont to be set forth in painting.

Cr. Yes, to the daughters of Cecrops, to keep him safe unseen.

Ion. I have heard the maidens opened the ark wherein the goddess laid him.

Cr. And so they died, dabbling with their blood the rocky cliff.

Ion. Even so. But what of this next story? Is it true or groundless?

Cr. What is thy question? Ask on, I have no calls upon my leisure.

Ion. Did thy sire Erechtheus offer thy sisters as a sacrifice?

Cr. For his country's sake he did endure to slay the maids as victims.

Ion. And how didst thou, alone of all thy sisters, escape?

Cr. I was still a tender babe in my mother's arms.

Ion. Did the earth really open its mouth and swallow thy father?

Cr. The sea-god smote and slew him with his trident.

Ion. Is there a spot there called Macræ?

Cr. Why ask that? what memories thou recallest!

Ion. Doth the Pythian god with his flashing fire do honour to the place?

Cr. Honour, yes! Honour, indeed! would I had never seen the spot!

Ion. How now? dost thou abhor that which the god holds dear?

Cr. No, no; but I and that cave are witnesses of a deed of shame.

Ion. Lady, who is the Athenian lord that calls thee wife?

Cr. No citizen of Athens, but a stranger from another land.

Ion. Who is he? he must have been one of noble birth.

Cr. Xuthus, son of Æolus, sprung from Zeus.

Ion. And how did he, a stranger, win thee a native born?

Cr. Hard by Athens lies a neighbouring township, Eubœa.

Ion. With a bounding line of waters in between, so I have heard.

Cr. This did he sack, making common cause with Cecrops' sons.

Ion. Coming as an ally, maybe; he won thy hand for this?

Cr. Yes, this was his dower of battle, the prize of his prowess.

Ion. Art thou come to the oracle alone, or with thy lord?

Cr. With him. But he is now visiting the cavern of Trophonius.

Ion. As a spectator merely, or to consult the oracle?

Cr. 'Tis his wish to hear the self-same answer from Trophonius and Phœbus too.

Ion. Is it to seek earth's produce or fruit of offspring that ye come?

Cr. We are childless, though wedded these many years.

Ion. Hast thou never been a mother? art thou wholly childless?

Cr. Phœbus knows whether I am childless.

Ion. Unhappy wife! how this doth mar thy fortune else so happy!

Cr. But who art thou? how blest I count thy mother!

Ion. Lady, I am called the servant of Apollo, and so I am.

Cr. An offering of thy city, or sold to him by some master?

Ion. Naught know I but this, that I am called the slave of Loxias.

Cr. Then do I in my turn pity thee, sir stranger.

Ion. Because I know not her that bare me, or him that begat me.

Cr. Is thy home here in the temple, or hast thou a house to dwell in?

Ion. The god's whole temple is my house, wherever sleep o'ertakes me.

Cr. Was it as a child or young man that thou camest to the temple?

Ion. Those who seem to know the truth, say I was but a babe.

Cr. What Delphian maid, then, weaned thee?

Ion. I never knew a mother's breast. But she who brought me up—

Cr. Who was she, unhappy youth? I see thy sufferings in my own.

Ion. The priestess of Phœbus; I look on her as my mother.

Cr. Until thou camest unto man's estate, what nurture hadst thou?

Ion. The altar fed me, and the bounty of each casual guest.

Cr. Woe is thy mother, then, whoe'er she was!

Ion. Maybe my birth was some poor woman's wrong.

Cr. Hast thou any store, for thy dress is costly enough?

Ion. The god I serve gives me these robes to wear.

Cr. Wert thou never eager to inquire into thy birth?

Ion. Ah! yes, lady! but I have no clue at all to guide me.

Cr. Alas! I know another woman who hath suffered as thy mother did.

Ion. Who is she? If she would but help me in the task, how happy should I be!

Cr. 'Tis she on whose account I have preceded my husband hither.

Ion. What are thy wishes? be sure I will serve thee, lady.

Cr. I would fain obtain a secret answer from Apollo's oracle.

Ion. Name it, then; the rest will I undertake for thee.

Cr. Hear, then, this story. Yet am I ashamed.

Ion. Thus wilt thou accomplish naught, for shame is a goddess slow to act.

Cr. A friend of mine asserts that Phœbus lay with her.

Ion. Phœbus with a mortal woman? Stranger lady, say not so.

Cr. Yea, and she bare the god a child without her father's knowledge.

Ion. It cannot be; some man did wrong her, and she is ashamed of it.

Cr. This she denies herself; and she hath suffered further woe.

Ion. How so, if she was wedded to a god?

Cr. The babe she bare she did expose.

Ion. Where is the child who was thus cast forth? is he yet alive?

Cr. No man knoweth. That is the very thing I would ask the oracle.

Ion. But if he be no more, how did he perish?

Cr. She supposes that beasts devoured the hapless babe.

Ion. What proof led her to form this opinion?

Cr. She came to the place where she exposed him, but found him no longer there.

Ion. Were any drops of blood upon the path?

Cr. None, she says; and yet she ranged the ground to and fro.

Ion. How long is it since the babe was destroyed?

Cr. Thy age and his would measure out the selfsame span, were he alive.

Ion. Hath she given birth to no other child since then?

Cr. The god doth wrong her, and wretched is she in having no child.

Ion. But what if Phœbus privily removed her child, and is rearing it?

Cr. Then is he acting unfairly in keeping to himself alone a joy he ought to share.

Ion. Ah me! this misfortune sounds so like my own.

Cr. Thee too, fair sir, thy poor mother misses, I am sure.

Ion. Oh! call me not back to piteous thoughts I had forgotten.

Cr. I am dumb; proceed with that which touches my inquiry.

Ion. Dost know the one weak point in this thy story?

Cr. 'Tis all weak in that poor lady's case.

Ion. How should the god declare that which he wishes hidden?

Cr. He must, if here upon the tripod he sits for all Hellas to seek to.

Ion. He is ashamed of the deed; do not question him.

Cr. Aye, but his victim has her sorrows too.

Ion. There is none who will act as thy medium in this. For were Phœbus in his own temple proved a villain, he would justly wreak his vengeance on the man who expounded to thee his oracles; desist then, lady; we must not prophesy against the god's will, for it would be the height of folly in us, were we to try and make the gods against their will declare reluctant truths either by sacrifice of sheep at their altars, or by omens from birds. For those answers we strive to extort from heaven, lady, are goods that bring no blessing on our getting; but what they freely offer, thereby we profit.

Ch. Many are the chances that befall the many tribes of men, and diverse are their forms. But scarce one happy scene canst thou find in all the life of man.

Cr. Ah! Phœbus, here as there, art thou unjust to that absent sufferer, whose cause I now am pleading. Thou didst not preserve thy child, as in duty bound, nor wilt thou, for all thy prophetic skill, answer his mother's questioning, that, if he be no more, a mound may be raised o'er him, or, if he live, he may some day be restored to his mother's eyes. In vain is this the home of oracles if the god prevents me from learning what I wish to ask. But lo! I see my noble lord, Xuthus, nigh at hand, returning from the lair of Trophonius; say nothing, sir, to my husband of what I have told thee, lest I incur reproach for troubling about secrets, and the matter take a different turn to that which I sought to give it. For women stand towards men in a difficult position, and the virtuous from being mingled with the wicked amongst us are hated; such is our unhappy destiny.

Enter XUTHUS.

Xuthus. First to the god all hail! for he must receive the first-fruits of my salutation, and next all hail to thee, my wife! Has my delay in arriving caused thee alarm?

Cr. By no means; but thou art come at an anxious time. Tell me what response thou bringest from Trophonius, touching our future hopes of mutual offspring.

Xu. He deigned not to forestal the prophecies of Phœbus. This only did he say, that neither thou nor I should return unto our house childless from the shrine.

Cr. Majestic mother of Phœbus, to our journey grant success, and may our previous dealings with thy son now find a better issue!

Xu. It will be so; but who acts as the god's spokesman here?

Ion. I serve outside the shrine, others within, who stand near the tripod, even the noblest of the Delphians chosen by lot, sir stranger.

Xu. 'Tis well; I have attained the utmost of my wishes. I will go within; for I am told that a victim has been slain in public before the temple for strangers, and to-day—for it is a lucky day—I would fain receive the god's oracle. Do thou, my wife, take branches of laurel, and seated at the altars pray to the gods that I may carry home from Apollo's shrine an answer that bodeth well for offspring.

Cr. All this shall be. Now, at any rate, if Loxias would retrieve his former sins, e'en though he cannot be my friend entirely, yet will I accept whate'er he deigns to give, because he is a god.

Exeunt XUTHUS *and* CREUSA.

Ion. Why doth this stranger lady hint dark reproaches against the god unceasingly, either out of affection for her on whose behalf she seeks the oracle, or maybe because she is hiding something needing secrecy? Yet what have I to do with the daughter of Erechtheus? She is naught to me. No, I will go to the laver, and from golden ewers sprinkle the holy water. Yet must I warn Phœbus of what is happening to him; he ravishes a maid and proves unfaithful to her, and after secretly begetting a son leaves him to die. O! Phœbus, do not so, but as thou art supreme, follow in virtue's track; for whosoever of mortal men transgresses, him the gods punish. How, then, can it be just that you should enact your laws for men, and yourselves incur the charge of breaking them? Now I will put this case, though it will never happen. Wert thou, wert Poseidon, and Zeus, the lord of heaven, to make atonement to mankind for every act of lawless love, ye would empty your temples in paying the fines for your misdeeds. For when ye pursue pleasure in preference to the claims of prudence, ye act unjustly; no longer is it fair to call men wicked, if we are imitating the evil deeds of gods, but rather those who give us such examples. *Exit* ION.

Ch. On thee I call, Athena mine, at whose birth-throes no kindly goddess lent her aid, delivered as thou wert by Titan Prometheus from the forehead of Zeus. Come, O lady Victory, come to the Pythian shrine, winging thy way from the gilded chambers of Olympus to the city's streets, where Phœbus at his altar on the centre of the world brings his oracles to pass beside the dance-encircled tripod; come, too, thou daughter of Latona, together come, ye virgin goddesses, fair sisters of Phœbus! And be this your prayer, fair maidens, that the ancient house of Erechtheus may obtain by clear oracles the blessing of children, though late it come. For this brings to man a settled source of all-surpassing bliss, even to such as see in their ancestral halls a splendid race of strong young parents blest with offspring, to inherit from their sires their wealth in due succession after other children; yea, for they are a defence in time of trouble, and add a charm to weal, affording to their fatherland a saving help in battle. Give me before the pomp of wealth or royal marriages the careful nurture of noble children. The childless life I do abhor, and him who thinks it good I blame; to a happy life amongst my children, blest with moderate wealth, may I hold fast.

Ye haunts of Pan, and rocks hard by the grots of Macræ, where Agraulos' daughters three trip it lightly o'er the green grass-lawns before the shrine of Pallas, to the music of the piper's varied note, what time thou, Pan, art piping in those caves of thine, where a maiden once that had a child by Phœbus, unhappy mother! exposed her babe, forced issue of her woful wooing, for birds to tear and beasts to rend, a bloody banquet! Never have I seen it told in woven tale or legend that children born to gods by daughters of earth have any share in bliss.

Enter ION.

Ion. Attendant maids, that watch and wait your mistress here at the steps of the temple fragrant with incense, say, hath Xuthus already left the holy tripod and the sanctuary, or doth he still abide within to ask yet further of his childlessness?

Ch. He is still in the temple, sir, nor hath he passed this threshold yet. But hark! I hear a footstep at the outlet of the door, and lo! thou mayst see my master this moment coming out.

Enter XUTHUS.

Xu. All hail! my son; that word suits well as my first greeting to thee.

Ion. 'Tis well with me; do but restrain thyself, and then both of us will be happy.

Xu. Give me thy hand to grasp, thy body to embrace.

Ion. Art thou in thy senses, sir, or hath some spiteful god reft thee of them?

Xu. I am in my senses, for I have found what I hold most dear, and am eager to show my love.

Ion. Cease! touch me not, nor tear these garlands of the god!

Xu. I will embrace thee, for I am not seizing what

is not my own, but only finding my own that I love full well.

Ion. Hands off! or thou shalt feel an arrow pierce thy ribs.

Xu. Why dost thou shun me, now that thou findest in me thy nearest and dearest?

Ion. I am not fond of schooling boors and crazy strangers.

Xu. Kill me, burn me, if thou wilt; for, if thou dost, thou wilt be thy father's murderer.

Ion. Thou my father, indeed! Oh! is not news like this enough to make me laugh?

Xu. Not so; my tale, as it proceeds, will prove to thee what I assert.

Ion. Pray, what hast thou to tell me?

Xu. That I am thy own father, and thou my very child.

Ion. Who says so?

Xu. Loxias, who gave thee nurture, though thou wert my son.

Ion. Thou art thy own witness.

Xu. Nay, I have learnt the answer of the god.

Ion. Thou art mistaken in the dark riddle thou hast heard.

Xu. It seems then I do not hear aright.

Ion. What said Phœbus?

Xu. That the man who met me——

Ion. When and where?

Xu. As I came forth from the god's temple——

Ion. Well! what should happen to him?

Xu. Should be my own true son.

Ion. Thy own true son, or a gift from others?

Xu. A gift, but mine for all that.

Ion. Am I the first that thou didst meet?

Xu. I have met no other, my son.

Ion. Whence came this piece of luck?

Xu. To both of us alike it causes surprise.

Ion. Ah! but who was my mother?

Xu. I cannot tell.

Ion. Did not Phœbus tell thee that?

Xu. I was so pleased with this, I did not ask him that.

Ion. I must have sprung from mother earth.

Xu. The ground brings forth no children.

Ion. How can I be thine?

Xu. I know not; I refer it to the god.

Ion. Come, let us try another theme.

Xu. Better hold to this, my son.

Ion. Didst thou e'er indulge in illicit amours?

Xu. Yes, in the folly of youth.

Ion. Ere thou didst win Erechtheus' daughter?

Xu. Never since.

Ion. Could it be, then, thou didst beget me?

Xu. The time coincides therewith.

Ion. In that case, how came I hither?

Xu. That puzzles me.

Ion. After that long journey too?

Xu. That, too, perplexes me.

Ion. Didst thou in days gone by come to the Pythian rock?

Xu. Yes, to join in the mystic rites of Bacchus.

Ion. Didst thou lodge with one of the public hosts?

Xu. With one who at Delphi—

Ion. Initiated thee? or what is it thou sayest?

Xu. Among the frantic votaries of Bacchus.

Ion. Wert thou sober, or in thy cups?

Xu. I had indulged in the pleasures of the winecup.

Ion. That is just the history of my birth.

Xu. Fate hath discovered thee, my son.

Ion. How came I to the temple?

Xu. Maybe the maid exposed thee.

Ion. I have escaped the shame of slavish birth.

Xu. Acknowledge then thy father, my son.

Ion. It is not right that I should mistrust the god.

Xu. Thou art right there.

Ion. What more can I desire—

Xu. Thine eyes now open to the sights they should.

Ion. Than from a son of Zeus to spring?

Xu. Which is indeed thy lot.

Ion. May I embrace the author of my being?

Xu. Aye, put thy trust in the god.

Ion. Hail to thee, father mine.

Xu. With joy that title I accept.

Ion. This day—

Xu. Hath made me blest.

Ion. Ah, mother dear! shall I ever see thee too? Now more than ever do I long to gaze upon thee, whoe'er thou art. But thou perhaps art dead, and I shall never have the chance.

Ch. We share the good luck of thy house; but still I could have wished my mistress too, and Erechtheus' line, had been blest with children.

Xu. My son, albeit the god hath for thy discovery brought his oracle to a true issue, and united thee to me, while thou, too, hast found what most thou dost desire, till now unconscious of it; still, as touching this anxiety so proper in thee, I feel an equal yearning that thou, my child, mayst find thy mother, and I the wife that bare thee unto me. Maybe we shall discover this, if we leave it to time. But now leave the courts of the god, and this homeless life of thine, and come to Athens, in accordance with thy father's wishes, for there his happy realm and bounteous wealth await thee; nor shalt thou be taunted with base origin and poverty to boot, because in one of these respects thou something lackest, but thou shalt be renowned alike for birth and wealth. Art silent? why dost fix thy eyes upon the ground? Thou art lost in thought, and by this sudden change from thy former cheerfulness, thou strikest thy father with dismay.

Ion. Things assume a different form according as we see them before us, or far off. I am glad at what has happened, since I have found in thee a father; but hear me on some points which I am now deciding. Athens, I am told—that glorious city of a native race—owns no aliens; in which case I shall force my entrance there under a twofold disadvantage, as an alien's son and base-born as I am. Branded with this reproach, while as yet I am unsupported, I shall get the name of a mere nobody, a son of nobodies; and if I win my way to the highest place in the state, and seek to be some one, I shall be hated by those who have no influence, for superiority is galling; while 'mongst men of worth who could show their wisdom, but are silent, and take no interest in politics, I shall incur ridicule and be thought a fool for not keeping quiet in such a fault-finding city. Again, if I win a name amongst the men of mark who are engaged in politics, still more will jealous votes bar my progress; for thus, father, is it ever wont to be; they who have the city's ear, and have already made their mark, are most bitter against all rivals. Again, if I, a stranger, come to a home that knows me not, and to that childless wife who before had thee as partner in her sorrow, but now will feel the bitterness of having to bear her fortune all alone—how, I ask, shall I not fairly earn her hatred, when I take my stand beside thee; while she, still childless, sees thy dear pledge with bitter eyes; and then thou have to choose between deserting me and regarding her, or honouring me and utterly confounding thy home? How many a murder, and death by deadly drugs have wives devised for husbands! Besides, I pity that wife of thine, father, with her childless old age beginning; she little deserves to pine in barrenness, a daughter of a noble race. That princely state we fondly praise is pleasant to the eye; but yet in its mansions sorrow lurks; for who is happy, or by fortune blest, that has to live his life in fear of violence with many a sidelong glance? Rather would I live among the common folk, and taste their bliss, than be a tyrant who delights in making evil men his friends, and hates the good, in terror of his life. Perchance thou wilt tell me, "Gold outweighs all these evils, and wealth is sweet." I have no wish to be abused for holding tightly to my pelf, nor yet to have the trouble of it. Be mine a moderate fortune free from annoyance! Now hear the blessings, father, that here were mine; first, leisure, man's chiefest joy, with but moderate trouble; no villain ever drove me from my path, and that is a grievance hard to bear, to make room and give way to sorry knaves. My duty was to pray unto the gods, or with mortal men converse, a minister to their joys, not to their sorrows. And I was ever dismissing one batch of guests, while another took their place, so that I was always welcome from the charm of novelty. That honesty which men must pray for, even against their will, custom and nature did conspire to plant in me in the sight of Phœbus. Now when I think on this, I deem that I am better here than there, father. So let me live on here, for 'tis an equal charm to joy in high estate, or in a humble fortune find a pleasure.

Ch. Well said! if only those I love find their happiness in thy statement of the case.

Xu. Cease such idle talk, and learn to be happy; for on that spot where I discovered thee, my son, will I begin the rites, since I have chanced on the general banquet, open to all comers, and I will offer thy birth sacrifice which aforetime I left undone. And now will I bring thee to the banquet as my guest and rejoice thy heart, and take thee to the Athenian land as a visitor forsooth, not as my own son. For I will not grieve my wife in her childless sorrow by my good fortune. But in time will I seize a happy moment and prevail on her to let thee wield my sceptre o'er the realm. Thy name shall be Ion, in accordance with what happened, for that thou wert the first to cross my path as I came forth from Apollo's sanctuary. Go, gather every friend thou hast, and with them make merry o'er the flesh of sacrifice, on the eve of thy departure from the town of Delphi. On you, ye handmaids, silence I enjoin, for, if ye say one word to my wife, death awaits you.

Exit XUTHUS.

Ion. Well, I will go; one thing my fortune lacks, for if I find not her that gave me birth, life is no life to me, my father; and, if I may make the prayer, Oh may that mother be a daughter of Athens! that from her I may inherit freedom of speech. For if a stranger settle in a city free from aliens, e'en though in name he be a citizen, yet doth he find himself tongue-tied and debarred from open utterance.

Exit ION.

Ch. Weeping and lamentation and the beginning of mourning I foresee, when my mistress shall see her lord blest with a son, while she is childless and forlorn. What was this oracle thou didst vouchsafe, prophetic son of Latona? Whence came this boy, thy foster-child who lingers in thy temple? who was his mother? I like not thy oracle; I fear there is some treachery. In terror I await the issue of this chance; for strange are these tidings and strange it is that the god declares them to me. There is guile connected with this waif's fortune. All must allow that. Shall we, good friends, throw off disguise and tell our mistress this story about her husband in whom her all was centred and whose hopes, poor lady, she once shared? But now in misery is she plunged, while he enjoys the smiles of fortune; to hoary eld she drifteth fast, while he, her lord, pays no regard to his loved ones—the wretch, who came an alien to her house to share great wealth and failed to guard her fortunes! Perdition catch this traitor to my lady! never may he succeed in offering to the gods upon their blazing altar a hallowed cake with flames that augur well! He shall know to his cost my regard for my mistress. Now are sire and new-found son bent on the approaching feast. Ho! ye peaks of Parnassus that rear your rocky heads to heaven, where Bacchus with uplifted torch of blazing pine bounds nimbly amid his bacchanals, that range by night! Never to my city come this boy! let him die and leave his young life as it dawns! For should our city fall on evil days, this bringing-in of strangers would supply it with a reason. Enough, enough for us Erechtheus' line that erst held sway!

Enter CREUSA *and* OLD SERVANT.

Cr. Aged retainer of my father Erechtheus while yet he lived and saw the light of day, mount to the god's prophetic shrine that thou mayst share my gladness, if haply Loxias, great king, vouchsafe an answer touching my hopes of offspring; for sweet it is to share with friends prosperity, and sweet likewise to see a friendly face if any ill betide—which God forbid! As thou of yore didst tend my sire, so now, thy mistress though I am, I take his place in tending thee.

Old Servant. Daughter, thy manners bear good witness still to thy noble lineage; thou hast never brought shame upon those ancestors of thine, the children of the soil. A hand, I prithee, to the shrine! a hand to lean upon! 'Tis a steep path thither, truly; but lend thy aid to guide my steps and make me young again.

Cr. Come follow then, and look where thou art treading.

O. S. Behold! though my steps loiter, my thoughts take wings.

Cr. Lean on thy staff as thou climbest this winding path.

O. S. Even this staff is a blind guide when I myself can scarcely see.

Cr. True, but do not yield through fatigue.

O. S. Never willingly, but I am not master of that which is mine no more.

Cr. Maidens mine, my trusty servants at the loom and web, declare to me how my lord hath fared as touching the question of offspring which brought us hither: for if ye give me good news, ye will cause joy to a mistress who will not prove faithless to her word.

Ch. O fortune!

O. S. This prelude to your speech is unlucky.

Ch. Woe is me!

O. S. Can it be that the oracles delivered to my master wound me at all?

Ch. Enough! why have aught to do with that which brings down death?

Cr. What means this piteous strain? wherefore this alarm?

Ch. Are we to speak or keep silence? What shall we do?

Cr. Speak; for thou hast somewhat to tell that touches me.

Ch. Then speak I will, though twice to die were mine. O mistress mine! never shalt thou hold a babe within thy arms or clasp him to thy breast.

Cr. Ah me! would I were dead!

O. S. My daughter!

Cr. O woe is me for my calamity! Mine is a heritage of suffering and woe that poisons life, good friends.

O. S. Ah, my child, 'tis death to us!

Cr. Ah me! ah me! grief drives its weapon through this heart of mine.

O. S. Stay thy lamentations.

Cr. Nay, but sorrow lodges here.

O. S. Till we learn—

Cr. Ah, what further news is there for me?

O. S. Whether our master is in the same plight and shares thy misfortune, or thou art alone in thy misery.

Ch. On him, old sir, Loxias hath bestowed a son, and he is enjoying his good fortune apart from her.

Cr. Herein hast thou declared a further evil crowning all, a grief for me to mourn.

O. S. The child of whom thou speakest—is he some woman's destined babe, or did the god declare the fate of one already born?

Ch. A youth already born and grown to man's estate doth Phœbus give to him; for I was there myself.

Cr. What sayest thou? nor tongue nor lip should speak the word thou tellest me.

O. S. And me. But declare more clearly how this oracle is finding its fulfilment, and say who is the child.

Ch. Whomso thy husband first should meet as he issued from the shrine, him the god gave him for his son.

Cr. Ah me! my fate, it seems, has doomed me to a childless life, and all forlorn am I to dwell in my halls, without an heir.

O. S. To whom did the oracle refer? whom did our poor lady's husband meet? how and where did he see him?

Ch. Dear mistress mine, dost know that youth that was sweeping yonder shrine? He is that son.

Cr. Oh! for wings to cleave the liquid air beyond the land of Hellas, away to the western stars, so keen the anguish of my soul, my friends!

O. S. Dost know the name his father gave to him, or is that left as yet unsettled and unsaid?

Ch. He called him Ion, because he was the first to cross his path.

O. S. Who is his mother?

Ch. That I cannot say. But—to tell thee all I know, old sir—her lord is gone, with furtive step, into the hallowed tent, there to offer on this child's behalf such gifts and victims as are offered for a birth, and with his new-found son to celebrate the feast.

O. S. Mistress mine, we are betrayed by thy husband, fellow-sufferers thou and I; 'tis a deep-laid plot to outrage us and drive us from Erechtheus' halls. And this I say not from any hatred of thy lord but because I bear thee more love than him; for he, after coming as a stranger to thy city and thy home, and wedding thee, and of thy heritage taking full possession, has been detected in a secret marriage with another woman, by whom he hath children. His secret will I now disclose; when he found thee barren, he was not content to share with thee thy hard lot, but took to himself a slave to be his stealthy paramour and thus begat a son, whom he sent abroad, giving him to some Delphian maid to nurse; and, to escape detection, the child was dedicated to the god and reared in his temple. But when he heard his boy was grown to manhood, he persuaded thee to come hither to inquire about thy childless state. And after this, 'twas not the god that lied, but thy husband, who long had been rearing the child, and he it was that wove this tissue of falsehood, intending, if he were detected, to refer it to the god, whereas if he escaped exposure, to repel all odium, he meant to vest the sovereignty in this son of his. Likewise he devised anew his name, coined to suit the circumstances, Ion, because, as he asserts, he met him on his way.

Ch. Ah! how I ever hate the wicked who plot unrighteousness and then cunningly trick it out. Far rather would I have a virtuous friend of no great intellect than a knave of subtler wit.

O. S. Of all thy wretched fate this will be the crowning sorrow, the bringing to thy house to be its lord some slave-girl's child, whose mother is unknown, himself of no account. For this evil had been to itself confined, had he persuaded thee, pleading thy childlessness, to let him establish in the house some high-born mother's son; or if this had displeased thee, he ought to have sought a daughter of Æolus in marriage. Wherefore must thou now put thy woman's wit to work; either take the dagger, or by guile or poison slay thy husband and his son, ere they deal out death to thee; since if thou spare him, thou wilt lose thy own life; for when two foes meet beneath one roof, one or the other must rue it. Myself too am ready to share this labour with thee, and to help destroy the child when I have made my way into the chamber where he is furnishing the feast, and so repaying my masters for my maintenance I am willing either to die or still behold the light of life. 'Tis but a single thing that brands the slave with shame—his name; in all else no upright slave is a whit worse than free-born men.

Ch. I too, beloved mistress, am ready to share thy fate, be it death or victory.

Cr. Ah! my suffering soul! how am I to keep silence? Am I to disclose the secrets of my love and lose all claim to modesty? What is there to keep me back any longer? With whom have I to pit myself in virtue's lists? Hath not my husband proved untrue? Home and children, both are torn from me; all hope is dead; I have not realized my wish to set the matter straight, by hushing up my former union and saying naught about my son of sorrow. No! by the starry seat of Zeus, by her whose home is on my rocks, and by the hallowed strand of Triton's mere with brimming flood, I will no more conceal my love; for if I can lift that burden from my breast I shall rest easier. With tears my eyes are streaming and my heart is wrung with anguish for the treacherous counsels both of men and gods—traitors they! as I will show, ungrateful traitors to their loves!

O! thou who dost awake that tuneful lyre with seven strings till to its sweet note of music the lifeless pegs of wild ox-horn resound again, thou child of Latona, to yon bright orb of thine will I publish thy reproach. Yes, I saw thee come, the glint of gold upon thy locks, as I was gathering in my folded robe the saffron blooms that blazed like flowers of gold; and by my lily wrist didst thou catch me and ledst me to the cavern's bed, what time I cried aloud upon my mother's name—thou a god to mate with me in shameless wise to pleasure lady Cypris! Then to my sorrow I bore thee a son, whom, though anguish thrilled my mother's breast, I cast upon that bed of thine, where thou didst join in woful wedlock this unhappy maid. Ah! woe is me! that poor babe I bare thee is now no more; winged fowls have torn and devoured him, but thou art gaily carolling unto thy lyre some song of joy. Hark! thou son of Latona, to thee I call, for that thou dispensest warnings; there at thy golden throne on earth's centre planted will I proclaim a word into thy ear. O! thou wicked bridegroom who art bringing to my husband's house an heir, though from him thou hast received no boon; while that child of thine and mine hath died unrecognized, a prey to carrion birds, his mother's swaddling-clothes all lost. Delos hates thee now, thy bay-tree loves thee not, whose branches sprout beside the tufted palm, where in holy throes Latona, big with child by Zeus, gave birth to thee.

Ch. Ah me! what store of sorrows is here disclosed, enough to draw a tear from every eye!

O. S. Daughter, with pity am I filled as a gaze upon thy face; my reason leaves me; for just as I am striving to lighten my spirit of its sea of troubles, comes another wave astern and catches me by reason of thy words; for no sooner hadst thou uttered this tale of present troubles than thou didst turn aside into a fresh track of other woes. What is it thou sayest? What charge against Apollo dost thou bring? What child is this thou dost assert that thou didst bear? Where was it in the city that thou didst expose him, for beasts to rejoice o'er his burial? Tell me once again.

Cr. Old friend, although to meet thine eye, I am ashamed, yet will I tell thee.

O. S. Full well I know how to lend my friends a generous sympathy.

Cr. Then hearken; dost know a cave toward the north of Cecrops' rock, that we call Macræ?

O. S. I know it; there is the shrine of Pan, and his altar hard by.

Cr. That was the scene of my dire conflict.

O. S. What conflict? see how my tears start forth to meet thy words.

Cr. Phœbus forced me to a woful marriage.

O. S. Was it then this, my daughter, that I noticed myself?

Cr. I know not; but I will tell thee if thou speak the truth.

O. S. At the time thou wert mourning in secret some hidden complaint?

Cr. Yes, 'twas then this trouble happened, which now I am declaring to thee.

O. S. How then didst conceal thy union with Apollo?

Cr. I bore a child; hear me patiently, old friend.

O. S. Where? and who helped thy travail? or didst thou labour all alone?

Cr. All alone, in the cave where I became a wife.

O. S. Where is the child? that thou mayst cease thy childless state.

Cr. Dead, old friend, to beasts exposed.

O. S. Dead? did Apollo, evil god, no help afford?

Cr. None; my boy is in the halls of Hades.

O. S. Who then exposed him? surely not thyself.

Cr. Myself, when 'neath the gloom of night I had wrapped him in my robe.

O. S. Did no one share thy secret of the babe's exposure?

Cr. Ill-fortune and secrecy alone.

O. S. How couldst thou in the cavern leave thy babe?

Cr. Ah! how? but still I did, with many a word of pity uttered o'er him.

O. S. Oh for thy hard heart! Oh for the god's, more hard than thine!

Cr. Hadst thou but seen the babe stretch forth his hands to me!

O. S. To find thy mother's breast, to nestle in thy arms?

Cr. By being kept therefrom he suffered grievous wrong from me.

O. S. How camest thou to think of casting forth thy babe?

Cr. Methought the god would save his own begotten child.

O. S. Ah me! what storms assail thy family's prosperity!

Cr. Why weepest thou, old man, with head close-veiled?

O. S. To see the sorrows of thy sire and thee.

Cr. Such is our mortal life; naught abideth in one stay.

O. S. Daughter, let us cease to dwell on themes of woe.

Cr. What must I do? Misfortune leaves us helpless.

O. S. Avenge thee on the god who first did injure thee.

Cr. How can I, weak mortal as I am, outrun those mightier powers?

O. S. Set fire to Apollo's awful sanctuary.

Cr. I am afraid; my present sorrows are enough for me.

O. S. Then what thou canst, that dare—thy husband's death.

Cr. Nay, I do respect his former love in the days when he was good and true.

O. S. At least, then, slay the boy who hath appeared to supplant thee.

Cr. How can I? would it were possible! how I wish it were!

O. S. Arm thy followers with daggers.

Cr. I will about it; but where is the deed to be done?

O. S. In the sacred tent, where he is feasting his friends.

Cr. The murder will be too public, and slaves are poor support.

O. S. Ah! thou art turning coward. Devise some scheme thyself.

Cr. Well, I too have subtle plans that cannot fail.

O. S. If both conditions they fulfil, I will assist thee.

Cr. Hearken then; knowest thou the battle of the earth-born men?

O. S. Surely; the fight at Phlegra waged by giants against the gods.

Cr. There Earth brought Gorgon forth, dreadful prodigy.

O. S. To aid her sons maybe, and cause the gods hard toil?

Cr. Yea, and Pallas, daughter of Zeus, slew the monster.

O. S. What savage form had it assumed?

Cr. A breast-plate of vipers fenced its body.

O. S. Is this the tale I heard in days of yore?

Cr. That Athena wears its skin upon her corslet.

O. S. Is it this that Pallas wears, called by men her ægis?

Cr. This was the name it received, that day she came to do battle for the gods.

O. S. How, daughter, can this harm thy enemies?

Cr. Hast heard of Erichthonius, or no? of course thou hast.

O. S. Him whom Earth produced, the founder of thy race?

Cr. To him whilst yet a babe did Pallas give—

O. S. Ha! what? thou hast something yet to add.

Cr. Two drops of Gorgon's blood.

O. S. What power could they exert on the nature of a human creature?

Cr. The one with death is fraught, the other cures disease.

O. S. What held them when she tied them to the child's body?

Cr. With links of gold she fastened them; this to my sire did Erichthonius give.

O. S. And at his death it came to thee?

Cr. Yea, and here at my wrist I wear it.

O. S. How works the spell of this double gift of Pallas?

Cr. Each drop of gore which trickled from the hollow vein—

O. S. What purpose does it serve? what virtue does it carry?

Cr. Wards off disease, and nourishes man's life.

O. S. What doth that second drop effect, of which thou madest mention?

Cr. It kills, for it is venom from the Gorgon's snakes.

O. S. Dost thou carry this charm mixed in one phial, or separate?

Cr. Separate; for good is no companion for evil.

O. S. Daughter dear, thou art fully armed with all thou needest.

Cr. By this must the boy die, and thou must do the deadly deed.

O. S. How and where? thine it is to speak, and mine to dare and do.

Cr. In Athens, when to my house he comes.

O. S. That is not wisely said; I may object to thy plan as thou to mine.

Cr. How so? Hast thou the same mistrust that I experience?

O. S. Thou wilt get the credit of his death, although thou slay him not.

Cr. True; men say stepdames are jealous of their husband's children.

O. S. Kill him here then, that so thou mayst deny the murder.

Cr. Well, thus I do anticipate the pleasure.

O. S. Yea, and thou wilt from thy husband keep the very secret he would keep from thee.

Cr. Dost know then what to do? Take from my arm this golden bracelet, Athena's gift, some ancient craftsman's work, and seek the spot where my lord is offering secret sacrifice; then when their feasting is o'er and they are about to pour drink-offering to the gods, take this phial in thy robe and pour it into the young man's goblet; not for all, but for him alone, providing a separate draught, who thinks to lord it o'er my house. And if once it pass his lips, never shall he come to glorious Athens, but here abide, of life bereft.

O. S. Go thou within the house of our public hosts; I the while will set about my appointed task. On! aged foot, grow young again in action, for all that time saith no to thee. Go, aid thy mistress against her enemy, help slay and drag him from her house. 'Tis well to honour piety in the hour of fortune, but when thou wouldst harm thy foe, no law doth block thy path.

Exeunt CREUSA *and* OLD SERVANT.

Ch. Daughter[1] of Demeter, goddess of highways, queen as thou art of haunting powers of darkness, oh! guide as well the hand that fills by day a cup of death, against those to whom my revered mistress is sending a philtre of the gore that dripped from hellish Gorgon's severed head, yea, 'gainst him who would obtrude upon the halls of the Erechthidæ. Never may alien, from alien stock, lord it o'er my city, no! none save noble Erechtheus' sons! For if this deadly deed and my lady's aims pass unfulfilled, and the right moment for her daring go by, and with it the hope which now sustains her, either will she seize the whetted knife or fasten the noose about her neck, and by ending one sorrow by another will go down to other phases of existence. For never will that daughter of a noble line, while life is hers, endure within the sunshine of her eyes the sight of alien rulers in her halls. I blush for that god of song, if this stranger is to witness the torch-dance,[2] that heralds in the twentieth dawn, around Callichorus' fair springs, a sleepless votary in midnight revels, what time the star-lit firmament of Zeus, the moon, and Nereus' fifty daughters, that trip it lightly o'er the sea and the eternal rivers' tides, join the dance in honour of the maiden with the crown of gold and her majestic mother; where this vagabond, by Phœbus favoured, thinks to reign, entering into other men's hard toil. Look to it, all ye bards, who, in malicious strains, expose our amours and unholy bonds of lawless love; see how far our virtue surpasses man's disloyalty. Change the burden of your song and keep your spiteful verse to brand man's faithlessness. For this scion of the stock of Zeus shows himself a heedless wight, denying to the mistress of his halls the lot of mutual offspring, and, paying all his court to some strange love, hath gotten him a bastard son.

Enter SERVANT.

[1]Hecate.

[2]Bacchus was escorted with a solemn torch procession from Athens to Eleusis on the 20th day of the month Boedromion.

Servant. Ladies of another land, where may I find your mistress, daughter of Erechtheus? For I have searched each nook and corner of this town, and cannot find her.

Ch. What news, my fellow-thrall? why that hurried gait? what tidings bringest thou?

Se. I am pursued; the rulers of this land are seeking her to stone her to death.

Ch. Alas, what is thy tale? say not we are detected in our secret plot for murdering the boy?

Se. Thou hast guessed aright; nor wilt thou be the last to share the trouble.

Ch. How was the hidden scheme laid bare?

Se. The god found means to master wrong with right, unwilling to see his shrine polluted.

Ch. How so? I do conjure thee, tell us all. For if to die or yet to live be ours, 'twere sweeter so, when we know all.

Se. Soon as Xuthus, husband of Creusa, had left the god's prophetic shrine, taking with him his new-found son, to hold the feast and sacrifice that he designed to offer to the gods, himself departed to the place where leaps the Bacchic flame, with blood of sacrifice to dew the double peaks of Dionysus for the son now offered to his gaze, and thus he spake, "My son, abide thou here, and raise a spacious tent by craftsmen's toiling skill; and if I remain long time away after I have sacrificed to the gods of thy birth, let the feast be spread for all friends present." Therewith he took the heifers and went his way. Meantime his stripling son in solemn form set up with upright stays the tent, inclosed but not with walls, taking good heed to guard it 'gainst the blazing midday sun, nor less against his westering beams, the limit of his course; an oblong space of five score feet he meted out so that it contained ten thousand feet within that measure's square, as science phrases it, intending to invite all Delphi to the feast. Then from the temple-treasury tapestry he took and therewith made a shelter, wondrous sight to see. First o'er the roof-tree he threw a canopy of robes, an offering Heracles, the son of Zeus, had brought unto the god from his Amazonian spoils. On them was broidered many a pictured scene, to wit, Heaven marshalling his host of stars upon the vaulted sky; there was the sun-god urging on his steeds toward his fiery goal, the bright star of evening at his heels. Night too in sable robes went hurrying by, drawn by a single pair, and the stars did bear her company. Across the zenith a Pleiad sailed, and Orion too with falchion dight was there; above was the bear making his tail to turn upon the golden pole. Up shot the moon's full face, that parts the months in twain; there too the Hyades showed their unerring light to mariners; and Dawn, that brings the morning back, was chasing the stars before her. Next on the sides he hung yet other tapestry; barbarian ships bearing down on the fleet of Hellas; and monsters half-man, half-beast; the capture of the Thracian steeds; the hunting of savage stags and lions fierce; while at the entry Cecrops close to his daughters was wreathing his coils, an offering of some Athenian votary; and in the midst of the banquet-hall he set goblets of gold, while a herald hasted and invited to the feast all citizens who would come. Then, when the tent was full, they decked themselves with garlands and took their fill of the rich viands. Anon after they had put from them the pleasure of eating came an old man and stood in the midst, where his officious zeal provoked loud laughter among the guests; for he would draw from the drinking-pitchers water to wash the hands withal and was wasting as incense the liquid myrrh, and in his charge he took the golden beakers, setting himself unasked to this office. Now when they were come to the time for the flute-players and the general libation, cried out that aged servitor, "Hence with these tiny cups! bring larger goblets, that our guests may find a quicker route to joyousness." Thereon came servants bending 'neath the weight of goblets chased with silver and golden chalices; and that old man, as if to do his youthful lord a special service, chose out and offered to him a brimming bumper, when he had cast into the wine that potent philtre which, men say, his mistress gave to him to end the young man's days on earth; and no man knew of this; but just as he so lately found held in his hand the drink-offering, the others following suit, some servant there uttered a word of evil import; whereat the stripling, as one who had been reared within the shrine amid reputed seers, deemed this an omen and bade them fill a fresh goblet, but that first drink-offering to the god he poured upon the ground and bade all others do the like. And silence stole upon them; while we with water and Phœnician wine were filling high the sacred bowls. While thus we were busied, comes a flight of doves and settles in the tent, for these dwell fearlessly in the courts of Loxias. Soon as the guests had poured away the luscious juice, those thirsty birds did dip their beaks therein, drawing it up into their feathered throats. Now all the rest received no hurt from the god's libation, but one that settled on the spot where the son new-found had poured his wine, no sooner had tasted thereof, than convulsions seized her feathered form and she went mad, and screaming aloud uttered strange unwonted cries; and all the feasters gathered there marvelled to see the bird's cruel agony, for she lay writhing in the toils of death, and her red claws relaxed their hold.

Forthwith the son, vouchsafed by oracles, bared his arm by casting off his cloak and stretched it out across the board crying "Who was it strove to slay me? Proclaim it, old sirrah, for thine was the officious zeal and thine the hand from which I took the cup." With that he caught the grey-beard by the arm and set to searching him that he might take the old man red-handed in the act. So was he detected, and under strong constraint declared Creusa's daring deed and all the trick of the poisoned draught. Forth rushed the young man, whom the oracle of Loxias to his sire assigned, taking with him the banqueters, and standing mid the Delphic nobles made harangue, "O! hallowed soil, a stranger woman, daughter of Erechtheus, seeks to poison me." And the lords of Delphi decreed by general vote that my mistress should be hurled from the rock to die, because she strove to slay the priest and compass his death in the temple. So now is the whole city seeking her, who hath to her sorrow sped a hapless journey; for, coming to crave the boon of offspring from Phœbus, she hath lost her life and children too.

Ch. Ah me! I see no way at all to turn death's hand aside; all, all, ere this, is brought to light owing to that fatal draught of the wine-god's juice mixed for death with drops of viper's gore, quick to slay; detected is our offering to the dead; for me my life must end in woe, while death by stoning waits my mistress. How can I escape? Shall I take wings and fly away, or creep beneath the darksome caverns of the earth, striving to shun the doom of death by stoning? or shall I mount the car drawn by swiftest steeds, or embark upon a ship? No man may hide his guilt, save when some god of his own will steals him away. Ah! my poor mistress! what suffering now awaits thy soul? Must then our wish to work another harm end in our own discomfiture, as justice doth decree?

Enter CREUSA.

Cr. My trusty maids, the men of death are on my track, the vote of Delphi goes against me; they give me up to die.

Ch. Unhappy one! we know thy sad mischance, how thou art placed.

Cr. Oh! whither can I fly? for scarce had I the start of my pursuers from the house in my race for life; 'tis by stealth alone that I have thus far escaped my foes.

Ch. Where shouldst thou fly except to the altar?

Cr. What good is that to me?

Ch. To slay a suppliant is forbidden.

Cr. Aye, but the law has given me over to death.

Ch. Only if thou fall into their hands.

Cr. Look! here they come, cruel champions of vengeance, eagerly brandishing their swords.

Ch. Sit thee down upon the altar of burnt-offering! for if thou art slain there, thou wilt fix upon thy murderers the stain of bloodguiltiness; but we must bear our fortune.

Enter ION.

Ion. O father Cephissus, with the bull-shaped head, what a viper is this thy child, or dragon with fiery eyes that dart a murderous gleam, in whose heart is throned incarnate daring, noxious as those Gorgon drops of venom wherewith she sought to compass my death. Seize her, that the peaks of Parnassus may card the flowing tresses of her hair, for thence shall she be hurled headlong amid the rocks. My lucky star hath kept me from going to Athens, there to fall beneath the power of a step-mother. For I have gauged thy feelings towards me—the full extent of thy bitter hostility—whilst yet amongst my friends; for hadst thou once shut me up within thy house, my road to Hades' halls had led direct from thence. This altar shall not save thee, nor yet Apollo's courts, for that pity thou implorest cries out more loudly for me and my mother, who, though absent in the flesh, is never in name far from me. Behold this cursed woman, see the web of trickery she hath woven! yet comes she cowering to Apollo's altar, thinking to escape the punishment of her misdeeds.

Cr. I warn thee not to slay me, both in my own name and in his at whose altar I am stationed.

Ion. What hast thou to do with Phœbus?

Cr. This body I devote unto that god to keep.

Ion. And yet thou wert for poisoning his minister?

Cr. But thou wert not Apollo's any longer, but thy father's.

Ion. Nay, I was his son, that is, in absence of a real father.

Cr. Thou wert so then; now 'tis I, not thou, who am Apollo's.

Ion. Well, thou art not guiltless now, whereas I was then.

Cr. I sought to slay thee as an enemy to my house.

Ion. And yet I never invaded thy country, sword in hand.

Cr. Thou didst; and thou it was that wert casting a fire-brand into the halls of Erechtheus.

Ion. What sort of brand or flaming fire was it?

Cr. Thou didst design to seize my home against my will, and make it thine.

Ion. What! when my father offered me a kingdom of his getting.

Cr. How had the sons of Æolus any share in the realm of Pallas?

Ion. Arms, not words, he brought to champion it.

Cr. No mere ally could enter into an inheritance in my land.

Ion. And was it then from fear of consequences that thou didst try to slay me?

Cr. Yes, lest I should myself perish if thou wert spared.

Ion. Doth thy childlessness make thee envious that my father found me?

Cr. And thou, wilt thou rob the childless of her home?

Ion. Had I then no share at all in my father's heritage?

Cr. All that his sword and shield had won was thine, and thine alone.

Ion. Quit the altar and sanctuary built for gods.

Cr. Go bid thy own mother, wherever she is, do that.

Ion. Shalt thou escape all punishment, after trying to kill me?

Cr. Not if thou choose to butcher me within this shrine.

Ion. What joy can it give thee to be slain amid the sacred wreaths?

Cr. There is one whom I shall grieve of those who have grieved me.

Ion. Oh! 'tis passing strange how badly the deity hath enacted laws for mortal men, contrary to all sound judgment; for instance, they should ne'er have suffered impious men to sit at their altars, but should have driven them away; for it was nowise right that hands unclean should touch the altars of the gods, though the righteous deserved to find a refuge there from their oppressors, instead of good and bad alike having recourse to the same divine protection with equal success.

Enter PYTHIAN PRIESTESS.

Pythian Priestess. Refrain thyself, my son; for I, the priestess of Phœbus, chosen from all the maids of Delphi in accordance with the tripod's ancient rite, have left that prophetic seat, and am passing o'er this threshold.

Ion. Hail to thee, dear mother mine—mother, though thou didst not give me birth.

P. P. Yes, so have I ever been called, and the title causes me no regret.

Ion. Hast heard how this woman plotted my death?

P. P. I have; thou, too, art wrong because of thy harshness.

Ion. Am I not to pay back murderers in their coin?

P. P. Wives ever hate the children of a former marriage.

Ion. As I hate stepdames for their evil treatment of me.

P. P. Do not so; but leaving, as thou art, the shrine, and setting forth for thy country—

Ion. What then wouldst thou advise me do?

P. P. With clean hands seek Athens, attended by good omens.

Ion. Surely any man hath clean hands who slays his enemies.

P. P. Do not thou do this; but take the counsel that I have for thee.

Ion. Say on; whate'er thou say'st will be prompted by thy good will.

P. P. Dost see this basket that I carry in my arms?

Ion. An ancient ark with chaplets crowned.

P. P. Herein I found thee long ago, a newborn babe.

Ion. What sayest thou? there is novelty in the story thou art introducing.

P. P. Yea, for I was keeping these relics a secret, but now I show them.

Ion. How camest thou to hide them on that day, now long ago, when thou didst find me?

P. P. The god wished to have thee as his servant in his courts.

Ion. Does he no longer wish it? How am I to know this?

P. P. By declaring to thee thy sire, he dismisses thee from this land.

Ion. Is it by his command thou keepest these relics, or why?

P. P. Loxias put in my heart that day—

Ion. What purpose? Oh! speak, finish thy story.

P. P. To preserve what I had found until the present time.

Ion. What weal or woe doth this import to me?

P. P. Herein were laid the swaddling-clothes in which thou wert enwrapped.

Ion. These relics thou art producing may help me to find my mother.

P. P. Yes, for now the deity so wills it, though not before.

Ion. Hail! thou day of visions blest to me!

P. P. Take then the relics and seek thy mother diligently. And when thou hast traversed Asia and the bounds of Europe, thou wilt learn this for thyself; for the god's sake I reared thee, my child, and now to thee do I entrust these relics, which he willed that I should take into my safekeeping, without being bidden; why he willed it I cannot tell thee. For no living soul wist that I had them in my possession, nor yet their hiding-place. And now farewell! as a mother might her child, so I greet thee. The starting-point of thy inquiry for thy mother must be this; first, was it a Delphian maid that gave birth to thee, and exposed thee in this temple; next, was it a daughter of Hellas at all? That is all that I and Phœbus, who shares in thy lot, can do for thee.

Exit PYTHIAN PRIESTESS.

Ion. Ah me! the tears stream from my eyes when I think of the day my mother bore me, as the fruit of her secret love, only to smuggle her babe away privily, without suckling it; nameless I led a servant's life in the courts of the god. His service truly was kindly, yet was my fortune heavy; for just when I ought to have lain softly in a mother's arms, tasting somewhat of the joys of life, was I deprived of a fond mother's fostering care. Nor less is she a prey to sorrow that bare me, seeing she hath suffered the self-same pang in losing all the joy a son might bring. Now will I take and bear this ark unto the god as an offering, that herein I may discover naught that I would rather not. For if haply my mother proves to be some slave-girl, 'twere worse to find her out than let her rest in silence. O! Phœbus, to thy temple do I dedicate this ark. Yet why? this is to war against the god's intention, who saved these tokens of my mother for my sake. I must undo the lid and bear the worst. For that which fate ordains, I may ne'er o'erstep. O! hallowed wreaths and fastenings, that have kept so safe these relics dear to me; why, ah! why were ye hidden from me? Behold the covering of this rounded ark! No signs of age are here, owing to some miracle; decay hath not touched these chaplets; and yet 'tis long enough since these were stored away.

Cr. Ha! what unlooked-for sight is here?

Ion. Peace, woman! now, as erst, thou art my enemy.

Cr. Silence is not for me. Bid me not be still; for lo! I see the ark wherein I did expose thee, my child, in days gone by, whilst yet a tender babe in the cavern of Cecrops, 'neath the rocky roof of Macræ. So now will I leave this altar, though death await me.

Ion. Seize her; she is mad, springing thus from the shelter of the carved altar. Bind her arms.

Cr. Kill! spare not! for I to thee will cleave, and to this ark, and all that is within it.

Ion. Is not this monstrous? here am I laid claim to on a specious pretext.

Cr. Nay, nay, but as a friend art thou by friends now found.

Ion. I a friend of thine! and wouldst thou, then, have slain me privily?

Cr. Thou art my child, if that is what a parent holds most dear.

Ion. An end to thy web of falsehood! Right well will I convict thee.

Cr. My child, that is my aim; God grant I reach it!

Ion. Is this ark empty, or hath it aught within?

Cr. Thy raiment wherein I exposed thee long ago.

Ion. Wilt put a name thereto before thou see it?

Cr. Unless I describe it, I offer to die.

Ion. Say on; there is something strange in this thy confidence.

Cr. Behold the robe my childish fingers wove.

Ion. Describe it; maidens weave many a pattern.

Cr. 'Tis not perfect, but a first lesson, as it were, in weaving.

Ion. Describe its form; thou shalt not catch me thus.

Cr. A Gorgon figures in the centre of the warp.

Ion. Great Zeus! what fate is this that dogs my steps?

Cr. 'Tis fringed with snakes like an ægis.

Ion. Lo! 'tis the very robe; how true we find the voice of God!

Cr. Ah! woven work that erst my virgin shuttle wrought.

Ion. Is there aught beside, or stays thy lucky guessing here?

Cr. There be serpents, too, with jaws of gold, an old-world symbol.

Ion. Is that Athena's gift, bidding her race grow up under their guardianship?

Cr. Yes, to copy our ancestor Erichthonius.

Ion. What is their object? what the use of these golden gauds? pray, tell.

Cr. Necklaces for the newborn babe to wear, my child.

Ion. Lo! here they lie. Yet would I know the third sign.

Cr. About thy brow I bound an olive-wreath that day, plucked from the tree Athena first made grow on her own rock. If haply that is there, it hath not lost its verdure yet, but still is fresh, for it came from the stock that grows not old.

Ion. Mother, dearest mother, with what rapture I behold thee, as on thy cheeks, that share my joy, I press my lips!

Cr. My son, light that in thy mother's eye outshinest yonder sun—I know the god will pardon me—in my arms I hold thee, whom I never hoped to find, for I thought thy home was in that nether world, among the ghosts with Queen Persephone.

Ion. Ah, dear mother mine! within thy arms I rest, the dead now brought to light, and dead no more.

Cr. Hail, thou broad expanse of bright blue sky! What words can I find to utter my joy aloud? Whence comes to me such unexpected rapture? To what do I owe this bliss?

Ion. This is the last thing that ever would have occurred to me, mother, that I was thy child.

Cr. With fear I tremble still.

Ion. Dost thou doubt my reality?

Cr. Far from me had I banished these hopes. Whence, O whence, lady, didst thou take my babe into thy arms? Who carried him to the courts of Loxias?

Ion. 'Tis a miracle! Oh! may we for the rest of our career be happy, as we were hapless heretofore.

Cr. In tears wert thou brought forth, my child, and with sorrow to thy mother didst thou leave her arms; but now I breathe again as I press my lips to thy cheek, in full enjoyment of happiness.

Ion. Thy words express our mutual feelings.

Cr. No more am I of son and heir bereft; my house is stablished and my country hath a prince; Erechtheus groweth young again; no longer is the house of the earth-born race plunged in gloom, but lifts its eyes unto the radiant sun.

Ion. Mother mine, since my father too is here, let him share the joy I have brought to thee.

Cr. My child, my child, what sayst thou? How is my sin finding me out!

Ion. What meanest thou?

Cr. Thou art of a different, far different stock.

Ion. Alas for me! Am I a bastard, then, born in thy maiden days?

Cr. Nor nuptial torch nor dance, my child, ushered in my wedding and thy birth.

Ion. O mother, mother! whence do I draw my base origin?

Cr. Be witness she who slew the Gorgon,

Ion. What meanest thou?

Cr. She that on my native rocks makes the olive-clad hill her seat.

Ion. Thy words to me are but as cunning riddles. I cannot read them.

Cr. Hard by the rock with nightingales melodious, Phœbus.

Ion. Why dost thou mention Phœbus?

Cr. Forced on me his secret love.

Ion. Say on; for thy story will crown me with fame and fortune.

Cr. And as the tenth month came round I bore a child to Phœbus in secret.

Ion. Oh! thy happy tidings, if thy story is true.

Cr. And about thee as swaddling-clothes I fastened this my maiden work, the faulty efforts of my loom. But to my breast I never held thy lips, or suckled or washed thee with a mother's care; but in a desert cave wert thou cast out to die, for taloned kites to rend and feast upon.

Ion. An awful deed! O mother!

Cr. Fear held me captive, and I cast thy life away, my child; I would, though loth, have slain thee too.

Ion. Thou too wert all but slain by me most impiously.

Cr. O the horror of all I suffered then! O the horror of what is to follow now! To and fro from bad to good we toss, though now the gale is shifting round. May it remain steady! the past brought sorrows enough; but now hath a fair breeze sprung up, my son, to waft us out of woe.

Ch. Let no man ever deem a thing past hoping for, when he turns an eye towards what is happening now.

Ion. O Fortune! who ere now hast changed the lot of countless mortals first to grief, and then to joy again, to what a goal my life had come, even to staining my hands with a mother's blood and enduring sufferings ill-deserved! Ah well! may we not learn these truths daily in all that the bright sun embraces? O mother, in thee have I made a happy discovery, and from my point of view there is no fault to find with my birth; but what remains I fain would speak to thee apart. Come hither, for I would say a word in thine ear, and o'er these matters cast the veil of silence. Bethink thee, mother, carefully; didst thou make the fatal slip, that maidens will, as touching secret amours, and then upon the god wouldst foist the blame, in thy anxiety to escape the shame of my birth asserting that Phœbus is my sire, albeit the god was not the parent.

Cr. Nay, by our queen of Victory, Athena, that fought by Zeus, in days gone by, high on his car against the earth-born giants I swear, no mortal is thy father, my son, but King Loxias himself who brought thee up.

Ion. How then is it he gave his own child to another father, declaring that I was begotten of Xuthus?

Cr. "Begotten" he never said, but as a gift he doth bestow thee his own son on him; for friend might give to friend even his own son to rule his house.

Ion. Mother mine, this thought disturbs my breast, as well it may, whether the god speaks truth or gives an idle oracle.

Cr. Hear, then, my son, the thought that hath occurred to me; Loxias out of kindness is establishing thee in a noble family, for hadst thou been called the god's son, thou hadst never inherited a father's home and name. How couldst thou, when I strove to hide my marriage with him and would have slain thee privily? But he for thy interest is handing thee over to another father.

Ion. Not thus lightly do I pursue the inquiry; nay, I will enter Apollo's shrine and question him whether I am the child of a mortal sire or his own son. (ATHENA *appears above the temple*) Ha! who is that hovering o'er the incense-smoking roof, and showing to our gaze a heavenly face, bright as the sun? Let us fly, mother, that we see not sights divine, unless haply it is right we should.

Athena. Fly not! I am no foe ye seek to shun, but alike in Athens and this place your kindly friend. 'Tis I, Pallas, after whom your land is named, that am here, by Apollo sent in headlong haste; for he thought not fit to appear before you twain, lest his coming might provoke reproaches for the past; but me he sends to proclaim to you his words, how that this is thy mother, and Apollo thy sire; while thyself he doth bestow, as seems him good, not indeed on him that begat thee, nay, but that he may bring thee to a house of high repute. For when this matter was brought to light, he devised a way of deliverance, fearing that thou wouldst be slain by thy mother's wiles and she by thine. Now it was King Apollo's wish to keep this matter secret awhile, and then in Athens to acknowledge this lady as thy mother and thyself as the child of her and Phœbus. But to end the business and discharge his oracles for the god, I bid you hearken; for such was my purpose in yoking my chariot-steeds. Do thou, Creusa, take this stripling and to Cecrops' land set forth; and there upon the monarch's throne establish him, for from Erechtheus' stock is he sprung, and therefore hath a right to rule that land of mine. Through Hellas shall his fame extend; for his children—four branches springing from one root—shall give their names to the land and to the tribes of folk therein that dwell upon the rock I love. Teleon shall be the first; and next in order shall come the Hopletes and Argades; and then the Ægicores, called after my ægis, shall form one tribe. And their children again shall in the time appointed found an island home amid the Cyclades and on the sea-coast, thereby strengthening my country; for they shall dwell upon the shores of two continents, of Europe and of Asia, on either side the strait; and in honour of Ion's name shall they be called Ionians and win them high renown. From Xuthus too and thee I see a common stock arise; Dorus, whence the famous Dorian state will spring; and after him Achæus in the land of Pelops; he shall lord it o'er the seaboard nigh to Rhium, and his folk, that bear his name, shall win the proud distinction of their leader's title. Thus in all hath Apollo rightly done; first did he deliver thee of thy babe without sickness, so that thy friends knew naught; and after thou didst bear this child and in swaddling-clothes hadst laid him, he bade Hermes carry him in his arms hither, and did rear him, suffering him not to die. Now therefore hold thy peace as to this thy child's real parentage, that Xuthus may delight in his fond fancy, and thou, lady, continue to enjoy thy blessing. So fare ye well! for to you I bring tidings of a happier fate after this respite from affliction.

Ion. O Pallas, daughter of almighty Zeus, in full assurance will we accept thy words; for I am convinced of my parentage from Loxias and this lady; which even before was not incredible.

Cr. To what I say give ear. My former blame of Phœbus now is turned to praise, because he now restores to me the babe whom erst he slighted. Now are these portals fair unto mine eyes and this oracle of the god, though before I hated them. With joy now I even cling to the knocker on the door and salute the gates.

At. I commend thee for thy sudden change, and thy fair words about the god. 'Tis ever thus; Heaven's justice may tarry awhile, yet comes it at the last in no wise weakened.

Cr. My son, let us set out for home.

At. Go; I will follow.

Ion. A guide we well may prize.

Cr. Aye, and one that holds our city dear.

At. Go, sit thee down upon the throne of thy ancestors.

Ion. 'Tis my heritage and I value it.

Ch. All hail, Apollo, son of Zeus and Latona! 'Tis only right that he, whose house is sore beset with trouble, should reverence God and keep good heart; for at the last the righteous find their just reward, but the wicked, as their nature is, will never prosper. *Exeunt* OMNES.

• • •

HELEN

DRAMATIS PERSONAE

HELEN
TEUCER
CHORUS, *ladies attendant on Helen*
MENELAUS
PORTRESS, *an old woman*
MESSENGER
THEONOE
THEOCLYMENUS
THE DIOSCURI

Tomb of Proteus in the island of Pharos. Enter HELEN.

Helen. Lo! these are the fair virgin streams of Nile, the river that waters Egypt's tilth, fed by pure melting snow instead of rain from heaven. Proteus during his lifetime was king of this land, dwelling in the isle of Pharos, and ruling o'er Egypt; and he took to wife one of the daughters of the sea, Psamathe, after she left the embraces of Æacus. Two children she bare in this his palace, a son Theoclymenus, who hath passed his life in duteous service to the gods, and likewise a noble daughter, her mother's pride, called Eido in her infancy, but when she reached her youthful prime, the age for wedded joys, renamed Theonoe; for well she knew whate'er the gods design, both present and to come, for she had won this guerdon from her grandsire Nereus. Nor is my fatherland unknown to fame, e'en Sparta, or my sire Tyndareus; for a legend tells how Zeus winged his way to my mother Leda's breast, in the semblance of a bird, even a swan, and thus as he fled from an eagle's pursuit, achieved by guile his amorous purpose, if this tale be true. My name is Helen, and I will now recount the sorrows I have suffered. To a hollow vale on Ida came three goddesses to Paris, for beauty's prize contending, Hera and Cypris, and the virgin child of Zeus, eager to secure his verdict on their loveliness. Now Cypris held out my beauty—if aught so wretched deserves that name—as a bribe before the eyes of Paris, saying he should marry me; and so she won the day; wherefore the shepherd of Ida left his steading, and came to Sparta, thinking to win me for his bride. But Hera, indignant at not defeating the goddesses, brought to naught my marriage with Paris, and gave to Priam's princely son not Helen, but a phantom endowed with life, that she made in my image out of the breath of heaven; and Paris thought that I was his, although I never was—an idle fancy! Moreover, the counsels of Zeus added further troubles unto these; for upon the land of Hellas and the hapless Phrygians he brought a war, that he might lighten mother-earth of her myriad hosts of men, and to the bravest of the sons of Hellas bring renown. So I was set up as a prize for all the chivalry of Hellas, to test the might of Phrygia, yet not I, but my name alone; for Hermes caught me up in the embracing air, and veiled me in a cloud; for Zeus was not unmindful of me; and he set me down here in the house of Proteus, judging him to be the most virtuous of all mankind; that so I might preserve my marriage with Menelaus free from taint. Here then I abide, while my hapless lord has gathered an army, and is setting out for the towers of Ilium to track and recover me. And there by Scamander's streams hath many a life breathed out its last, and all for me; and I, that have endured all this, am accursed, and seem to have embroiled all Hellas in a mighty war by proving a traitress to my husband. Why, then, do I prolong my life? Because I heard Hermes declare, that I should yet again make my home on Sparta's glorious soil, with my lord—for Hermes knew I never went to Ilium—that so I might never submit to any other's wooing. Now as long as Proteus gazed upon yon glorious sun, I was safe from marriage; but when o'er him the dark grave closed, the dead man's son was eager for my hand. But I, from regard to my former husband, am throwing myself down in suppliant wise before this tomb of Proteus, praying him to guard my husband's honour, that, though through Hellas I bear a name dishonoured, at least my body here may not incur disgrace.

Enter TEUCER.

Teucer. Who is lord and master of this fenced palace? The house is one I may compare to the halls of Plutus, with its royal bulwarks and towering buildings. Ha! great gods! what sight is here? I see the counterfeit of that fell murderous dame, who ruined me and all the Achæans. May Heaven show its loathing for thee, so much dost thou resemble Helen! Were I not standing on a foreign soil, with this well-aimed shaft had I worked thy death, thy reward for resembling the daughter of Zeus.

He. Oh! why, poor man, whoe'er thou art, dost thou turn from me, loathing me for those troubles Helen caused?

Te. I was wrong; I yielded to my anger more than I ought; my reason was, the hate all Hellas bears to that daughter of Zeus. Pardon me, lady, for the words I uttered.

He. Who art thou? whence comest thou to visit this land?

Te. One of those hapless Achæans am I, lady.

He. No wonder then that thou dost hate Helen. But say, who art thou? Whence comest? By what name am I to call thee?

Te. My name is Teucer; my sire was Telamon, and Salamis is the land that nurtured me.

He. Then why art thou visiting these meadows by the Nile?

Te. A wanderer I, an exile from my native land.

He. Thine must be a piteous lot; who from thy country drives thee out?

Te. My father Telamon. Couldst find a nearer and a dearer?

He. But why? This case is surely fraught with woe.

Te. The death of Aias my brother at Troy, was my ruin.

He. How so? surely 'twas not thy sword that stole his life away?

Te. He threw himself on his own blade and died.

He. Was he mad? for who with sense endowed would bring himself to this?

Te. Dost thou know aught of Achilles, son of Peleus?

He. He came, so I have heard, to woo Helen once.

Te. When he died, he left his arms for his comrades to contest.

He. Well, if he did, what harm herein to Aias?

Te. When another won these arms, to himself he put an end.

He. Art thou then a sufferer by woes that he inflicted?

Te. Yes, because I did not join him in his death.

He. So thou camest, sir stranger, to Ilium's famous town?

Te. Aye, and, after helping to sack it, myself did learn what ruin meant.

He. Is Troy already fired and utterly by flames consumed?

Te. Yea, so that not so much as one vestige of her walls is now to be seen.

He. Woe is thee, poor Helen! thou art the cause of Phrygia's ruin.

Te. And of Achæa's too. Ah! 'tis a tale of grievous misery!

He. How long is it since the city was sacked?

Te. Nigh seven fruitful seasons have come and gone.

He. And how much longer did ye abide in Troy?

Te. Many a weary month, till through ten full years the moon had held her course.

He. And did ye capture that Spartan dame?

Te. Menelaus caught her by the hair, and was for dragging her away.

He. Didst thou thyself behold that unhappy one? or art thou speaking from hearsay?

Te. As plain as I now see thee, I then saw her.

He. Consider whether ye were but indulging an idle fancy sent by heaven.

Te. Bethink thee of some other topic; no more of her!

He. Are you so sure this fancy was reliable?

Te. With these eyes I saw her face to face, if so be I see thee now.

He. Hath Menelaus reached his home by this time with his wife?

Te. No; he is neither in Argos, nor yet by the streams of Eurotas.

He. Ah me! here is evil news for those to whom thou art telling it.

Te. 'Tis said he disappeared with his wife.

He. Did not all the Argives make the passage together?

Te. Yes; but a tempest scattered them in every direction.

He. In what quarter of the broad ocean?

Te. They were crossing the Ægean in mid channel.

He. And after that, doth no man know of Menelaus' arrival?

Te. No, none; but through Hellas is he reported to be dead.

He. Then am I lost. Is the daughter of Thestius alive?

Te. Dost speak of Leda? She is dead; aye, dead and gone.

He. Was it Helen's shame that caused her death?

Te. Aye, 'tis said she tied the noose about her noble neck.

He. Are the sons of Tyndareus still alive or not?

Te. Dead, and yet alive: 'tis a double story.

He. Which is the more credible report? Woe is me for my sorrows!

Te. Men say that they are gods in the likeness of stars.

He. That is happy news; but what is the other rumour?

Te. That they by self-inflicted wounds gave up the ghost because of their sister's shame. But enough of such talk! I have no wish to multiply my griefs. The reason of my coming to this royal palace was a wish to see that famous prophetess Theonoe. Do thou the means afford, that I from her may obtain an oracle how I shall steer a favourable course to the sea-girt shores of Cyprus; for there Apollo hath declared my home shall be, giving to it the name of Salamis, my island home, in honour of that fatherland across the main.

He. That shall the voyage itself explain, sir stranger; but do thou leave these shores and fly, ere the son of Proteus, the ruler of this land, catch sight of thee. Now is he away with his trusty hounds tracking his savage quarry to the death; for every stranger that he catcheth from the land of Hellas doth he slay. His reason never ask to know; my lips are sealed; for what could word of mine avail thee?

Te. Lady, thy words are fair. Heaven grant thee a fair requital for this kindness! For though in form thou dost resemble Helen, thy soul is not like hers, nay, very different. Perdition seize her! May she never reach the streams of Eurotas! But thine be joy for evermore, lady! *Exit* TEUCER.

He. Ah me! what piteous dirge shall I strive to utter, now that I am beginning my strain of bitter lamentation? What Muse shall I approach with tears or songs of death or woe? Ah me! ye Sirens, Earth's virgin daughters, wingèd maids, come, oh! come to aid my mourning, bringing with you the Libyan flute or pipe, to waft to Persephone's ear a tearful plaint, the echo of my sorrow, with grief for grief, and mournful chant for chant, with songs of death and doom to match my lamentation, that in return she may receive from me, besides my tears, dirges for the departed dead beneath her gloomy roof!

Enter CHORUS.

Chorus. Beside the deep-blue water I chanced to be hanging purple robes along the tendrils green and on the sprouting reeds, to dry them in the sun-god's golden blaze, when lo! I heard a sound of woe, a mournful wail, the voice of one crying aloud in her anguish; yea, such a cry of woe as Naiad nymph might send ringing o'er the hills, while to her cry the depths of rocky grots re-echo her screams at the violence of Pan.

He. Woe! woe! ye maids of Hellas, booty of barbarian sailors! one hath come, an Achæan mariner, bringing fresh tears to me, the news of Ilium's overthrow, how that it is left to the mercy of the foeman's flame, and all for me the murderess, or for my name with sorrow fraught. While for anguish at my deed of shame, hath Leda sought her death by hanging; and on the deep, to weary wandering doomed my lord hath met his end; and Castor and his brother, twin glory of their native land, are vanished from men's sight, leaving the plains that shook to their galloping steeds, and the course beside reed-fringed Eurotas, where those youthful athletes strove.

Ch. Ah, misery! Alas! for thy grievous destiny! Woe for thy sad lot, lady! Ah! 'twas a day of sorrow meted out for thee when Zeus came glancing through the sky on snowy pinions like a swan and won thy mother's heart. What evil is not thine? Is there a grief in life that thou hast not endured? Thy mother is dead; the two dear sons of Zeus have perished miserably, and thou art severed from thy country's sight, while through the towns of men a rumour runs, consigning thee, my honoured mistress, to a barbarian's bed; and 'mid the ocean waves thy lord hath lost his life, and never, never more shalt thou fill with glee thy father's halls or Athena's temple of the "Brazen House."

He. Ah! who was that Phrygian, who was he, that felled that pine with sorrow fraught for Ilium, and for those that came from Hellas? Hence it was that Priam's son his cursed barque did build, and sped by barbarian oars sailed unto my home, in quest of beauty, woman's curse, to win me for his bride; and with him sailed the treacherous queen of Love, on slaughter bent, with death alike for Priam's sons, and Danai too. Ah me! for my hard lot! Next, Hera, stately bride of Zeus, seated on her golden throne, sent the son of Maia, swift of foot, who caught me up as I was gathering fresh rose-buds in the folds of my robe, that I might go to the "Brazen House," and bore me through the air to this loveless land, making me an object of unhappy strife 'twixt Hellas and the race of Priam. And my name is but a sound without reality beside the streams of Simois.

Ch. Well I know thou hast a bitter lot to bear; still 'tis best to bear as lightly as we may the ills that life is heir to.

He. Good friends, to what a fate am I united? Did not my mother bear me to be a monster to the world? For no woman, Hellene or barbarian, gives birth to babes in eggs inclosed, as they say Leda bare me to Zeus. My life and all I do is one miracle, partly owing to Hera, and partly is my beauty to blame. Would God I could rub my beauty out like a picture, and assume hereafter in its stead a form less comely, and oh! that Hellas had forgotten the evil fate that now I bear, and were now remembering my career of honour as surely as they do my deeds of shame. Now, if a man doth turn his eyes to a single phase of fortune, and meets ill-usage at heaven's hands, 'tis hard no doubt; but still it can be borne; but I in countless troubles am involved. First, although I never sinned, my good name is gone. And this is a grief beyond the reality, if a man incurs blame for sins that are not his. Next, have the gods removed me from my native land, to dwell with men of barbarous habits, and reft of every friend, I am become a slave though free by birth; for amongst barbarians all are slaves but one. And the last anchor that held my fortunes, the hope that my husband would return one day, and rid me of my woes, is now no more, lost since the day he died. My mother too, is dead, and I am called her murderess, unjustly it is true, but still that injustice is mine to bear; and she that was the glory of my house, my darling child, is growing old and grey, unwedded still; and those twin brethren, called the sons of Zeus, are now no more. But 'tis fortune, not my own doing, that hath crushed me with sorrow and slain me. And this is the last evil of all; if ever I come to my native land, they will shut me up in prison, thinking me that Helen of Ilium, in quest of whom Menelaus came thither. Were my husband still alive, we might have recognized each other, by having recourse to tokens which ourselves alone would know. But now this may not be, nor is there any chance of his escape. Why then do I prolong my life? What fortune have I still in store? Shall I choose marriage as an alternative of evils, and dwell with a barbarian lord, seated at his sumptuous board? No! when a husband she loathes is mated with a woman, even life is loathly to her. Best for her to die; but how shall I die a noble death? The dangling noose is an uncomely end; even slaves consider it a disgrace; to stab oneself hath something fair and noble in it; 'tis a small thing that moment of ridding the flesh of life. Yes, it must be; I am plunged so deep in misery; for that beauty, which to other women is a boon, to me hath been a very bane.

Ch. Helen, never believe that the stranger, whoe'er he was that came, has spoken naught but truth.

He. Yet he said so clearly that my lord was dead.

Ch. There is much that falsehood seems to make quite clear.

He. The word of truth hath a very different sound to falsehood.

Ch. Thou art inclined to misfortune, rather than to luck.

He. Fear girds me with terrors as with a garment, and takes me in her train.

Ch. What friends hast thou within the palace?

He. All are my friends here save him who seeks to wed me.

Ch. Thy action then is clear; leave thy seat at the tomb.

He. To what words or advice art thou leading up?

Ch. Go in and question the daughter of the ocean Nereid, who knoweth all things, even Theonoe, whether thy husband is still alive, or whether he hath left the light of day; and when thou knowest for certain, be glad or sorrowful, as fits thy fortune. But before thou hast any correct information, what shall sorrow avail thee? Nay, hearken to me; leave this tomb and seek the maiden's company, that she may tell thee the truth, for from her shalt thou learn all. If thou abide here in this building, what prospect hast thou? And I will myself go in with thee, and with thee inquire of the maiden's oracles; for 'tis a woman's bounden duty to share a sister's trouble.

He. Kind friends, I welcome your advice. Come in, come in, that ye may learn the result of my struggle within the palace.

Ch. Thy invitation comes to very willing ears.

He. Woe for this heavy day! Ah me! what mournful tidings shall I hear?

Ch. Dear mistress mine, be not a prophetess of sorrow, forestalling lamentation.

He. What is the fate of my poor husband? Doth he still behold the light turning towards the sun-god's chariot and the stars in their courses?

Ch. * * *

He. * * *

Or among the dead, beneath the earth, is he to death consigned?

Ch. Of the future take a brighter view, whatever shall betide.

He. On thee I call, and thee adjure, Eurotas green with river-reeds, to tell me if this rumour of my husband's death be true.

Ch. What boots this meaningless appeal?

He. About my neck will I fasten the deadly noose from above, or drive the murderous knife with self-aimed thrust deep into my throat to sever it, striving to cut my flesh, a sacrifice to those goddesses three and to that son of Priam, who in days gone by would wake the music of his pipe around his steading.

Ch. Oh may sorrow be averted otherwhither, and thou be blest!

He. Woe is thee, unhappy Troy! Thou through deeds not done by thee art ruined, and hast suffered direst woe; for the gift that Cypris gave to me, hath caused a sea of blood to flow, and many an eye to weep, with grief on grief and tear on tear. All this hath Ilium suffered . . . . and mothers have lost their children; and virgin sisters of the slain have cut off their tresses by the swollen tide of Phrygian Scamander. And the land of Hellas hath lifted her voice of woe and broken forth in wailing, smiting on her head, and making tender cheeks to stream with gore beneath the rending nail. Ah blest maid Callisto, who long ago in Arcady didst find favour with Zeus, in the semblance of a beast four-footed, how much happier was thy lot than my mother's, for thou hast changed the burden of thy grief and now with savage eye art weeping o'er thy shaggy monster-shape; aye, and hers was a happier lot, whom on a day Artemis drove from her choir, changed to a hind with horns of gold, the fair Titanian maid, daughter of Merops, because of her beauty; but my fair form hath proved the curse of Dardan Troy and doomed Achæa's sons.

Enter MENELAUS. *Exeunt* HELEN *and* CHORUS.

Menelaus. Ah! Pelops, easy victor long ago o'er thy rival Œnomaus in the chariot-race on Pisa's plain, would thou hadst ended thy career amongst the gods that day thou wert beguiled into making a banquet for them, or ever thou hadst begotten my father Atreus, to whom were born by Ærope his wife, Agamemnon and myself Menelaus, an illustrious pair; and herein I make no idle boast, for 'twas a mighty host, I trow, that I their leader carried o'er the sea to Troy, using no violence to make them follow me, but leading all the chivalry of Hellas by voluntary consent. And some of these must we number 'mid the slain, and some to their joy have 'scaped the sea, bearing to their homes again names long reckoned dead. But I, poor wretch, go wandering o'er grey Ocean's swell a weary space, long as that which saw me sack the towers of Ilium; and for all my longing to reach my country I am not counted worthy of this boon by heaven, but to Libya's desert cheerless roadsteads have I sailed, to each and all of them; and whensoe'er I draw me near my native land, the storm-wind drives me back again, and never yet have favouring breezes filled my sails, to let me reach my fatherland. And now a wretched, shipwrecked mariner, my friends all lost, am I cast up upon this shore; and my ship is shattered in a thousand pieces against the rocks; and its keel was wrested from its cunning fastenings; thereon did I with difficulty escape, most unexpectedly, and Helen also, for her had I rescued from Troy and had with me. But the name of this country and its people I know not; for I blushed to mingle with the crowd to question them, anxious for very shame to hide my misfortunes which reduce me to these sorry rags. For when a man of high degree meets with adversity, he feels the strangeness of his fallen state more keenly than a sufferer of long standing. Dire want is wasting me; for I have neither food, nor raiment to gird myself withal; behold the facts before you to judge from—I am clad in tatters cast up from the ship; while all the robes I once did wear, glorious attire and ornaments, hath the sea swallowed; and in a cavern's deep recesses have I hidden my wife, the cause of all my trouble, and have come hither, after straitly charging the survivors of my friends to watch her. Alone am I come, seeking for those there left some help, if haply I may find it after careful search. So when I saw this palace girt with towering walls and stately gates of some prosperous lord, I drew nigh; for I have hope to obtain somewhat for my sailors from this wealthy house, whereas from houses which have no store, the inmates for all their goodwill could furnish naught. Ho! there, who keeps the gate and will come forth to bear my tale of woe into the house?

Enter PORTRESS.

Portress. Who stands before the door? Begone from the house! stand not at the court-yard gate, annoying my masters! otherwise shalt thou die, for thou art a Hellene born, and with them have we no dealings.

Men. Mother, herein sayest thou rightly on all points. 'Tis well; I will obey; but moderate thy words.

Po. Away! stranger, my orders are to admit no Hellene to this palace.

Men. Ha! do not seek to push me hence, or thrust me away by violence.

Po. Thou dost not heed my words, and therefore hast thyself to blame.

Men. Carry my message to thy master in the palace.

Po. Some one would rue it, methinks, were I to take thy message.

Men. I come as a shipwrecked man and a stranger, whom heaven protects.

Po. Well, get thee to some other house than this.

Men. Nay, but I will pass into the house; so listen to me.

Po. Let me tell thee thou art unwelcome, and soon wilt be forcibly ejected.

Men. Ah me! where are now those famous troops of mine?

Po. Elsewhere maybe thou wert a mighty man; thou art not here.

Men. O fortune! I have not deserved such contumely.

Po. Why are thy eyes with tear-drops wet? Why so sad?

Men. 'Tis the contrast with my fortunes erst so blest.

Po. Hence! then, and give thy friends those tears.

Men. What land is this? whose is the palace?

Po. Proteus lives here. It is the land of Egypt.

Men. Egypt? Woe is me! to think that hither I have sailed!

Po. Pray, what fault hast thou to find with the race of Nile?

Men. 'Twas no fault I found; my own disasters I lament.

Po. There be plenty in evil case; thou art not the only one.

Men. Is the king, of whom thou speakest, here within?

Po. There is his tomb; his son rules in his stead.

Men. And where may he be? abroad, or in the house?

Po. He is not within. To Hellas is he a bitter foe.

Men. His reason, pray, for this enmity? the results whereof I have experienced.

Po. Beneath this roof dwells the daughter of Zeus, Helen.

Men. What mean'st thou? what is it thou hast said? Repeat, I pray, thy words.

Po. The daughter of Tyndareus is here, who erst in Sparta dwelt.

Men. Whence came she? What means this business?

Po. She came from Lacedæmon hither.

Men. When? Surely I have never been robbed of my wife from the cave!

Po. Before the Achæans went to Troy, sir stranger. But get thee hence; for somewhat hath chanced within, whereat the whole palace is in an uproar. Thou comest most unseasonably; and if my master catch thee, death will be thy stranger's gift. This say I, because to Hellas I am well disposed, albeit I gave thee harsh answers for fear of my master.

Exit PORTRESS.

Men. What can I think or say? For after my previous troubles, this is a fresh piece of ill-luck I hear, if, indeed, after recovering my wife from Troy and bringing her hither, and putting her for safety in the cave, I am then to find another woman living here with the same name as my wife. She called her the begotten child of Zeus. Can there be a man that hath the name of Zeus by the banks of Nile? The Zeus of heaven is only one, at any rate. Where is there a Sparta in the world save where Eurotas glides between his reedy banks? The name of Tyndareus is the name of one alone. Is there any land of the same name as Lacedæmon or Troy? I know not what to say; for naturally there are many in the wide world that have the same names, cities and women too; there is nothing, then, to marvel at. Nor yet again will I fly from the alarm a servant raises; for there is none so cruel of heart as to refuse me food when once he hears my name. All have heard of Ilium's burning, and I, that set it ablaze, am famous now throughout the world, I, Menelaus .... I therefore wait the master of this house. There are two issues I must watch; if he prove somewhat stern of heart, I will to my wreck and there conceal myself; but if he show any sign of pity, I will ask for help in this my present strait. This is the crowning woe in all my misery, to beg the means of life from other princes, prince though I be myself; still needs must I. Yea, this is no saying of mine, but a word of wisdom, "Naught in might exceedeth dread necessity."

Enter CHORUS.

Ch. I have heard the voice of the maiden inspired. Clear is the answer she hath vouchsafed within yon palace, declaring that Menelaus is not yet dead and buried, passed to the land of shades, where darkness takes the place of light; but on the stormy main is wearing out his life, nor yet hath reached the haven of his country, a wanderer dragging out a piteous existence, reft of every friend, setting foot in every corner of the world, as he voyageth home from Troy.

Enter HELEN.

He. Lo! once again I seek the shelter of this tomb, with Theonoe's sweet tidings in my ears; she that knoweth all things of a truth; for she saith my lord is yet alive and in the light of day, albeit he is roaming to and fro after many a weary voyage, and hither shall he come whenso he reach the limit of his toils, no novice in the wanderer's life. But one thing did she leave unsaid. Is he to escape when he hath come? And I refrained from asking that question clearly, so glad was I when she told me he was safe. For she said that he was somewhere nigh this shore, cast up by shipwreck with a handful of friends. Ah! when shall I see thee come? How welcome will thy advent be! Ha! who is this? Am I being snared by some trick of Proteus' impious son? Oh! let me, like a courser at its speed, or a votary of Bacchus, approach the tomb! for there is something wild about this fellow's looks, who is eager to o'ertake me.

Men. Ho there! thou that with fearful effort seekest to reach the basement of the tomb and the pillars of burnt sacrifice, stay thee. Wherefore art flying? Ah! with what speechless amaze the sight of thee affects me!

He. O friends! I am being ill-treated. This fellow is keeping me from the tomb, and is eager to take and give me to his master, whose wooing I was seeking to avoid.

Men. No robber I, or minister of evil.

He. At any rate the garb wherein thou art clad, is unsightly.

Men. Stay thy hasty flight; put fear aside.

He. I do so, now that I have reached this spot.

Men. Who art thou? whom do I behold in thee, lady?

He. Nay, who art thou? The self-same reason prompts us both.

Men. I never saw a closer resemblance.

He. Great God! Yea, for to recognize our friends is of God.

Men. Art thou from Hellas, or a native of this land?

He. From Hellas; but I would learn thy story too.

Men. Lady, in thee I see a wondrous likeness to Helen.

He. And I in thee to Menelaus; I know not what to say.

Men. Well ,thou hast recognized aright a man of many sorrows.

He. Hail! to thy wife's arms restored at last!

Men. Wife indeed! Lay not a finger on my robe.

He. The wife that Tyndareus, my father, gave thee.

Men. O Hecate, giver of light, send thy visions favourably!

He. In me thou beholdest no spectre of the night, attendant on the queen of phantoms.

Men. Nor yet am I in my single person the husband of two wives.

He. What other woman calls thee lord?

Men. The inmate of yonder cave, whom I from Troy convey.

He. Thou hast none other wife but me.

Men. Can it be my mind is wandering, my sight failing?

He. Dost not believe thou seest in me thy wife?

Men. Thy form resembles her, but the real truth robs me of this belief.

He. Observe me well; what need hast thou of clearer proof?

Men. Thou art like her; that will I never deny.

He. Who then shall teach thee, unless it be thine own eyes?

Men. Herein is my dilemma; I have another wife.

He. To Troy I never went; that was a phantom.

Men. Pray, who fashions living bodies?

He. The air, whence thou hast a wife of heaven's workmanship.

Men. What god's handiwork? Strange is the tale thou tellest.

He. Hera made it as a substitute, to keep me from Paris.

Men. How then couldst thou have been here, and in Troy, at the same time?

He. The name may be in many a place at once, though not the body.

Men. Unhand me! the sorrows I brought with me suffice.

He. What! wilt leave me, and take that phantom bride away?

Men. For thy likeness unto Helen, fare thee well.

He. Ruined! in thee I found my lord only to lose thee.

Men. The greatness of my troubles at Troy convinces me; thou dost not.

He. Ah, woe is me! who was ever more unfortunate than I? Those whom I love best are leaving me, nor shall I ever reach Hellas, my own dear native land.

Messenger (*Entering hurriedly*) At last I find thee, Menelaus, after an anxious search, not till I have wandered through the length and breadth of this foreign strand; I am sent by thy comrades, whom thou didst leave behind.

Men. What news? surely you are not being spoiled by the barbarians?

Mes. A miracle hath happened; my words are too weak for the reality.

Men. Speak; for judging by this haste, thou hast stirring news.

Mes. My message is: thy countless toils have all been toiled in vain.

Men. That is an old tale of woe to mourn! come, thy news?

Mes. Thy wife hath disappeared, soaring away into the embracing air; in heaven she now is hidden, and as she left the hollowed cave where we were guarding her, she hailed us thus, "Ye hapless Phrygians, and all Achæa's race! for me upon Scamander's strand by Hera's arts ye died from day to day, in the false belief that Helen was in the hands of Paris.

But I, since I have stayed my appointed time, and kept the laws of fate, will now depart unto the sky that gave me birth; but the unhappy daughter of Tyndareus, through no fault of hers, hath borne an evil name without reason." (*Catching sight of* HELEN) Daughter of Leda, hail to thee, so thou art here after all! I was just announcing thy departure to the hidden starry realms, little knowing that thou couldst fly at will. I will not a second time let thee flout us thus, for thou didst cause thy lord and his comrades trouble all for naught in Ilium.

Men. This is even what she said; her words are proved true; O longed-for day, how hath it restored thee to my arms!

He. O Menelaus, dearest husband, the time of sorrow has been long, but joy is now ours at last. Ah, friends, what joy for me to hold my husband in a fond embrace after many a weary cycle of yon blazing lamp of day!

Men. What joy for me to hold my wife! but with all the questions I have to ask about the interval I know not with which to begin now.

He. O rapture! the very hair upon my head starts up for joy! my tears run down! Around thy neck I fling my arms, dear husband, to hug my joy to me.

Men. O happy, happy sight! I have no fault to find; my wife, the daughter of Zeus and Leda, is mine again, she whom her brothers on their snow-white steeds, whilst torches blazed, made my happy bride, but gods removed her from my home. Now is the deity guiding us to a new destiny, happier than of yore.

He. Evil into good transformed hath brought us twain together at last, dear husband; but late though it be, God grant me joy of my good luck!

Men. God grant thee joy! I join thee in the self-same prayer; for of us twain one cannot suffer without the other.

He. No more, my friends, I mourn the past; no longer now I grieve. My own dear husband is restored to me, whose coming from Troy I have waited many a long year.

Men. I to thee, and thou to me. And after these long, long years I have at last discovered the fraud of the goddess. But these tears, in gladness shed, are tears of thankfulness rather than of sorrow.

He. What can I say? What mortal heart could e'er have had such hope? To my bosom I press thee, little as I ever thought to.

Men. And I to mine press thee, who all men thought hadst gone to Ida's town and the hapless towers of Ilium.

He. Ah me! ah me! that is a bitter subject to begin on.

Men. Tell me, I adjure thee, how wert thou from my home conveyed?

He. Alas! alas! 'tis a bitter tale thou askest to hear.

Men. Speak, for I must hear it; all that comes is Heaven's gift.

He. I loathe the story I am now to introduce.

Men. Tell it for all that. 'Tis sweet to hear of trouble past.

He. I ne'er set forth to be the young barbarian's bride, with oars and wings of lawless love to speed me on my way.

Men. What deity or fate tore thee from thy country, then?

He. Ah, my lord! 'twas Hermes, the son of Zeus, that brought and placed me by the banks of Nile.

Men. A miracle! Who sent thee thither? O monstrous story!

He. I wept, and still my eyes are wet with tears. 'Twas the wife of Zeus that ruined me.

Men. Hera? wherefore should she afflict us twain?

He. Woe is me for my awful fate! Woe for those founts and baths where the goddesses made brighter still that beauty, which evoked the fatal verdict!

Men. Why did Hera visit thee with evil regarding this verdict?

He. To wrest the promise of Cypris—

Men. How now? Say on.

He. From Paris, to whom that goddess pledged me.

Men. Woe for thee!

He. And so she brought me hither to Egypt to my sorrow.

Men. Then she gave him a phantom in thy stead, as thou tellest me?

He. And then began those woes of thine, ah mother! woe is me!

Men. What meanest thou?

He. My mother is no more; my shameful marriage made her fix the noose about her neck.

Men. Ah me! is our daughter Hermione yet alive?

He. Still unwed, and childless still, she mourns my fatal marriage.

Men. O Paris, who didst utterly o'erthrow my home, here was thy ruin too and theirs, those countless mail-clad Danai.

He. From my country, city, and from thee heaven cast me forth unhappy and accursed, because I left —and yet not I—home and husband for a union of foul shame.

Ch. If haply ye find happiness in the future, it will suffice when to the past ye look.

Mes. Menelaus, grant me too a portion of that joy which, though mine own eyes see, I scarcely comprehend.

Men. Come then, old friend, and share with us our talk.

Mes. Was it not then in her power to decide all the trouble in Troy?

Men. It was not; I was tricked by the gods into taking to my arms a misty phantom-form, to my sorrow.

Mes. How so? was it then for this we vainly toiled?

Men. 'Twas Hera's handiwork, and the jealousy of three goddesses.

Mes. Is this real woman, then, thy wife?

Men. This is she; trust my word for that.

Mes. Daughter, how changeful and inscrutable is the nature of God! With some good end doth he vary men's fortune—now up, now down; one suffers; another who ne'er knew suffering, is in his turn to awful ruin brought, having no assurance in his lot from day to day. Thou and thy husband have had your share of trouble—thou in what the world has said, he in battle's heat. For all the striving that he strove, he got him naught; while now, without an effort made, every blessing fortune boasts is his. And thou, in spite of all, hast brought no shame upon thy aged sire, or those twin sons of Zeus, nor art thou guilty of those rumoured crimes. Now again do I recall thy wedding rites, remembering the blazing torch I bore beside thee in a four-horsed chariot at full gallop; while thou with this thy lord, a new-made bride, wert driving forth from thy happy home. A sorry servant he, whoso regardeth not his master's interest, sympathizing with his sorrows and his joys. Slave though I was born, yet may I be numbered amongst honest servants; for in heart, though not in name, I am free. For this is better far than in my single person to suffer these two evils, to feel my heart corrupt, and as the slave of others to be at my neighbour's beck and call.

Men. Come, old friend, oft hast thou stood side by side with me and taken thy full share of toil; so now be partner in my happiness. Go, tell my comrades, whom I left behind, the state of matters here, as thou hast found them, and the issue of my fortunes; and bid them wait upon the beach and abide the result of the struggle, which I trow awaits me; and if mayhap we find a way to take this lady from the land by stealth, tell them to keep good watch that we may share the luck and escape, if possible, from the barbarian's clutch.

Mes. It shall be done, O king. Now I see how worthless are the seers' tricks, how full of falsehood; nor is there after all aught trustworthy in the blaze of sacrifice or in the cry of feathered fowls; 'tis folly, the very notion that birds can help mankind. Calchas never by word or sign showed the host the truth, when he saw his friends dying on behalf of a phantom, nor yet did Helenus; but the city was stormed in vain. Perhaps thou wilt say, 'twas not heaven's will that they should do so. Then why do we employ these prophets? Better were it to sacrifice to the gods, and crave a blessing, leaving prophecy alone; for this was but devised as a bait to catch a livelihood, and no man grows rich by divination if he is idle. No! sound judgment and discernment are the best of seers. *Exit* MESSENGER.

Ch. My views about seers coincide exactly with this old man's: whoso hath the gods upon his side will have the best seer in his house.

He. Good! so far all is well. But how camest thou, poor husband, safe from Troy? though 'tis no gain to know, yet friends feel a longing to learn all that their friends have suffered.

Men. That one short sentence of thine contains a host of questions. Why should I tell thee of our losses in the Ægean, or of the beacon Nauplius lighted on Eubœa? or of my visits to Crete and the cities of Libya, or of the peaks of Perseus? For I should never satisfy thee with the tale, and by telling thee should add to my own pain, though I suffered enough at the time; and so would my grief be doubled.

He. Thy answer shows more wisdom than my question. Omit the rest, and tell me only this; how long wert thou a weary wanderer o'er the wide sea's face?

Men. Seven long years did I see come and go, besides those ten in Troy.

He. Alas, poor sufferer! 'twas a weary while. And thou hast thence escaped only to bleed here.

Men. How so? what wilt thou tell? Ah wife, thou hast ruined me.

He. Thou wilt be slain by him whose house this is.

Men. What have I done to merit such a fate?

He. Thou hast arrived unexpectedly to thwart my marriage.

Men. What! is some man bent on wedding my wife?

He. Aye, and on heaping those insults on me, which I have hitherto endured.

Men. Is he some private potentate, or a ruler of this land?

He. The son of Proteus, king of the country.

Men. This was that dark saying I heard the servant tell.

He. At which of the barbarian's gates wert thou standing?

Men. Here, whence like a beggar I was like to be driven.

He. Surely thou wert not begging victuals? Ah, woe is me!

Men. That was what I was doing, though I had not the name of beggar.

He. Of course thou knowest, then, all about my marriage.

Men. I do. But whether thou hast escaped thy lover, I know not.

He. Be well assured I have kept my body chaste.

Men. How wilt thou convince me of this? If true, thy words are sweet.

He. Dost see the wretched station I have kept at this tomb?

Men. I see, alas! a bed of straw; but what hast thou to do with it?

He. There I crave escape from this marriage as a suppliant.

Men. For want of an altar, or because it is the barbarians' way?

He. This was as good a protection to me as the gods' temples.

Men. May I not then even bear thee homeward on my ship?

He. The sword far sooner than thy wife's embrace is waiting thee.

Men. So should I be of all men the most miserable.

He. Put shame aside, and fly from this land.

Men. Leaving thee behind? 'twas for thy sake I sacked Troy.

He. Better so, than that our union should cause thy death.

Men. Oh! these are coward words, unworthy of those days at Troy!

He. Thou canst not slay the prince, thy possible intention.

Men. Hath he, then, a body which steel cannot wound?

He. Thou shalt hear. But to attempt impossibilities is no mark of wisdom.

Men. Am I to let them bind my hands, and say nothing?

He. Thou art in a dilemma; some scheme must be devised.

Men. I had liefer die in action than sitting still.

He. There is one hope, and only one, of our safety.

Men. Will gold, or daring deeds, or winning words procure it?

He. We are safe if the prince learn not of thy coming.

Men. Will any one tell him it is I? He certainly will not know who I am.

He. He hath within his palace an ally equal to the gods.

Men. Some voice divine within the secret chambers of his house?

He. No; his sister; Theonoe men call her.

Men. Her name hath a prophetic sound; tell me what she doth.

He. She knoweth everything, and she will tell her brother thou art come.

Men. Then must we die; for I cannot escape her ken.

He. Perchance we might by suppliant prayers win her over.

Men. To what end? To what vain hope art thou leading me?

He. That she should not tell her brother thou art here.

Men. Suppose we persuade her, can we get away?

He. Easily, if she connive thereat; without her knowledge, no.

Men. Be that thy task; women deal best with women.

He. I will not fail, be sure, to clasp her knees.

Men. Come, then; only, suppose she reject our proposals?

He. Thou wilt be slain, and I, alas! wedded by force.

Men. Thou wilt betray me; that "force" of thine is all an excuse.

He. Nay, by thy life I swear a sacred oath.

Men. What meanest thou? dost swear to die and never to another husband yield?

He. Yes, by the self-same sword; I will fall by thy side.

Men. On these conditions touch my right hand.

He. I do so, swearing I will quit the light of day if thou art slain.

Men. I, too, will end my life if I lose thee.

He. How shall we die so as to insure our reputation for this?

Men. I will slay thee and then myself upon the summit of the tomb. But first will I in doughty fight contest another's claim to thee; and let who will draw nigh! for I will not sully the lustre of my Trojan fame, nor will I, on my return to Hellas, incur a storm of taunts, as one who robbed Thetis of Achilles; saw Aias, son of Telamon, fall a weltering corpse; and the son of Neleus of his child bereft; shall I then flinch myself from death for my own wife? No, no! For if the gods are wise, o'er a brave man by his foes laid low they lightly sprinkle the earth that is his tomb, while cowards they cast forth on barren rocky soil.

Ch. Grant, heaven, that the race of Tantalus may at last be blest, and pass from sorrow unto joy!

He. Ah, woe is me! Yea, all my lot is woe; O Menelaus, we are utterly undone! Behold! from forth the house comes Theonoe, the prophetess. The palace echoes as the bolts are unfastened; fly! yet what use to fly? For whether absent or present she knows of thy arrival here. Ah me! how lost am I! Saved from Troy and from a barbarian land, thou hast come only to fall a prey to barbarian swords.

Enter THEONOE *with handmaids.*

Theonoe. Lead on, bearing before me blazing brands, and, as sacred rites ordain, purge with incense every cranny of the air, that I may breathe heaven's breath free from taint; meanwhile do thou, in case the tread of unclean feet have soiled the path, wave the cleansing flame above it, and brandish the torch in front, that I may pass upon my way. And when to heaven ye have paid the customs I exact, bear back into the house the brand from off the hearth. What of my prophecy, Helen? how stands it now? Thou hast seen thy husband Menelaus arrive without disguise, reft of his ships, and of thy counterfeit. Ah, hapless man! what troubles hast thou escaped, and art come hither, and yet knowest not whether thou art to return or to abide here; for there is strife in heaven, and Zeus this very day will sit in solemn conclave on thee. Hera, who erst was thy bitter foe, is now grown kind, and is willing to bring thee and thy wife safe home, that Hellas may learn that the marriage of Paris was all a sham, assigned to him by Cypris; but Cypris fain would mar thy homeward course, that she may not be convicted, or proved to have bought the palm of beauty at the price of Helen in a futile marriage. Now the decision rests with me, whether to ruin thee, as Cypris wishes, by telling my brother of thy presence here, or to save thy life by taking Hera's side, keeping my brother in the dark, for his orders are that I should tell him, whensoe'er thou shouldst reach these shores. Ho! one of you, go show my brother this man is here, that I may secure my position.

He. Maiden, at thy knees I fall a suppliant, and seat myself in this sad posture on behalf of myself and him, whom I am in danger of seeing slain, after I have so hardly found him. Oh! tell not thy brother that my husband is returned to these loving arms; save us, I beseech thee; never for thy brother's sake sacrifice thy character for uprightness, by evil and unjust means bidding for his favour. For the deity hates violence, and biddeth all men get lawful gains without plundering others. Wealth unjustly gotten, though it bring some power, is to be eschewed. The breath of heaven and the earth are man's common heritage, wherein to store his home, without taking the goods of others, or wresting them away by force. Me did Hermes at a critical time, to my sorrow, intrust to thy father's safe keeping for this my lord, who now is here and wishes to reclaim me. But how can he recover me if he be slain? How could thy sire restore the living to the dead? Oh! consider ere that the will of heaven and thy father's too; would the deity or would thy dead sire restore their neighbour's goods, or would they forbear? restore them, I feel sure. It is not, therefore, right that thou shouldst attach more importance to thy wanton brother than to thy righteous father. Yet if thou, prophetess as thou art and believer in divine providence, shalt pervert the just intention of thy father and gratify thy unrighteous brother, 'tis shameful thou shouldst have full knowledge of the heavenly will, both what is and what is not, and yet be ignorant of justice. Oh! save my wretched life from the troubles which beset it, granting this as an accession to our good fortune; for every living soul loathes Helen, seeing that there is gone a rumour throughout Hellas that I was false unto my lord, and took up my abode in Phrygia's sumptuous halls. Now, if I come to Hellas, and set foot once more in Sparta, they will hear and see how they were ruined by the wiles of goddesses, while I was no traitress to my friends after all; and so will they restore to me my virtuous name again, and I shall give my daughter in marriage, whom no man now will wed; and, leaving this vagrant life in Egypt, shall enjoy the treasures in my home. Had Menelaus met his doom at some funeral pyre,[1] with tears should I be cherishing his memory in a far-off land, but must I lose him now when he is alive and safe? Ah! maiden, I beseech thee, say not so; grant me this boon, I pray, and reflect thy father's justice; for this is the fairest ornament of children, when the child of a virtuous sire resembles its parents in character.

Ch. Piteous thy pleading, and a piteous object thou! But I fain would hear what Menelaus will say to save his life.

Men. I will not deign to throw myself at thy knees, or wet mine eyes with tears; for were I to play the coward, I should most foully blur my Trojan fame. And yet men say it shows a noble soul to let the tear-drop fall in misfortune. But that will not be the honourable course that I will choose in preference to bravery, if what I shall say is honourable. Art thou disposed to save a stranger seeking in mere justice to recover his wife, why then restore her and save us to boot; if not, this will not be the first by many a time that I have suffered, though thou wilt get an evil name. All that I deem worthy of me and honest, all that will touch thy heart most nearly, will I utter at the tomb of thy sire with regret for his loss. Old king beneath this tomb of stone reposing, pay back thy trust! I ask of thee my wife whom Zeus sent hither unto thee to keep for me. I know thou canst never restore her to me thyself, for thou art dead; but this thy daughter will never allow her father once so glorious, whom I invoke in his grave, to bear a tarnished name; for the decision rests with her now. Thee, too, great god of death, I call to my assistance, who hast received full many a corpse, slain by me for Helen, and art keeping thy wage; either restore those dead now to life again, or compel the daughter to show herself a worthy equal of her virtuous sire, and give me back my wife. But if ye will rob me of her, I will tell you that which she omitted in her speech. Know then, maiden, I by an oath am bound, first, to meet thy brother sword to sword, when he or I must die; there is no alternative. But if he refuse to meet me fairly front to front, and seek by famine to chase away us suppliants twain at this tomb, I am resolved to slay Helen, and then to plunge this two-edged sword through my own heart, upon the top of the sepulchre, that our streaming blood may trickle down the tomb; and our two corpses will be lying side by side upon this polished slab, a source of deathless grief to thee, and to thy sire reproach. Never shall thy brother wed Helen, nor shall any other; I will bear her hence myself, if not to my house, at any rate to death. And why this stern resolve? Were I to resort to women's ways and weep, I should be a pitiful creature, not a man of action. Slay me, if it seems thee good; I will not die ingloriously; but better yield to what I say, that thou mayst act with justice, and I recover my wife.

Ch. On thee, maiden, it rests to judge between these arguments. Decide in such a way as to please one and all.

Theon. My nature and my inclination lean towards piety; myself, too, I respect, and I will never sully my father's fair name, or gratify my brother at the cost of bringing myself into open discredit. For justice hath her temple firmly founded in my nature, and since I have this heritage from Nereus I will strive to save Menelaus; wherefore, seeing it is Hera's will to stand thy friend, I will give my vote with her. May Cypris be favourable to me! though in me she hath no part, and I will try to remain a maid alway. As for thy reproaches against my father at this tomb; lo! I have the same words to utter; I should be wronging thee, did I not restore thy wife; for my sire, were he living, would have given her back into thy keeping, and thee to her. Yea, for there is recompense for these things as well amongst the dead as amongst all those who breathe the breath of life. The soul indeed of the dead lives no more, yet hath it a consciousness that lasts for ever, eternal as the ether into which it takes the final plunge. Briefly then to end the matter, I will observe strict silence on all that ye prayed I should, and never with my counsel will I aid my brother's wanton will. For I am doing him good service, though he little thinks it, if I turn him from his godless life to holiness. Wherefore devise yourselves some way of

[1]Slain as a prisoner of war to grace some hero's funeral obsequies.

escape; my lips are sealed; I will not cross your path. First with the goddesses begin, and of the one—and that one Cypris—crave permission to return unto thy country; and of Hera, that her goodwill may abide in the same quarter, even her scheme to save thee and thy husband. And thou, my own dead sire, shalt never, in so far as rests with me, lose thy holy name to rank with evil-doers. *Exit* THEONOE.

Ch. No man ever prospered by unjust practices, but in a righteous cause there is hope of safety.

He. Menelaus, on the maiden's side are we quite safe. Thou must from that point start, and by contributing thy advice, devise with me a scheme to save ourselves.

Men. Hearken then; thou hast been a long while in the palace, and art intimate with the king's attendants.

He. What dost thou mean thereby? for thou art suggesting hopes, as if resolved on some plan for our mutual help.

Men. Couldst thou persuade one of those who have charge of cars and steeds to furnish us with a chariot?

He. I might; but what escape is there for us who know nothing of the country and the barbarian's kingdom?

Men. True; a dilemma. Well, supposing I conceal myself in the palace and slay the king with this two-edged sword?

He. His sister would never refrain from telling her brother that thou wert meditating his death.

Men. We have not so much as a ship to make our escape in; for the sea hath swallowed the one we had.

He. Hear me, if haply even a woman can utter words of wisdom. Dost thou consent to be dead in word, though not really so?

Men. 'Tis a bad omen; still, if by saying so I shall gain aught, I am ready to be dead in word, though not in deed.

He. I, too, will mourn thee with hair cut short and dirges, as is women's way, before this impious wretch.

Men. What saving remedy doth this afford us twain? There is a flavour of deception in thy scheme.

He. I will beg the king of this country leave to bury thee in a cenotaph, as if thou hadst really died at sea.

Men. Suppose he grant it; how, e'en then, are we to escape without a ship, after having committed me to my empty tomb?

He. I will bid him give me a vessel, from which to let drop into the sea's embrace thy funeral offerings.

Men. A clever plan in truth, save in one particular; suppose he bid thee rear the tomb upon the strand, thy pretext comes to naught.

He. But I shall say it is not the custom in Hellas to bury those who die at sea upon the shore.

Men. Thou removest this obstacle too; I then will sail with thee and help stow the funeral garniture in the same ship.

He. Above all, it is necessary that thou and all thy sailors who escaped from the wreck should be at hand.

Men. Be sure if once I find a ship at her moorings, they shall be there man for man, each with his sword.

He. Thou must direct everything; only let there be winds to waft our sails and a good ship to speed before them!

Men. So shall it be; for the deities will cause my troubles to cease. But from whom wilt thou say thou hadst tidings of my death?

He. From thee; declare thyself the one and only survivor, telling how thou wert sailing with the son of Atreus, and didst see him perish.

Men. Of a truth the garments I have thrown about me, will bear out my tale that they were rags collected from the wreckage.

He. They come in most opportunely, but they were near being lost just at the wrong time. Maybe that misfortune will turn to fortune.

Men. Am I to enter the palace with thee, or are we to sit here at the tomb quietly?

He. Abide here; for if the king attempts to do thee any mischief, this tomb and thy good sword will protect thee. But I will go within and cut off my hair, and exchange my white robe for sable weeds, and rend my cheek with this hand's bloodthirsty nail. For 'tis a mighty struggle, and I see two possible issues; either I must die if detected in my plot, or else to my country shall I come and save thy soul alive. O Hera! awful queen, who sharest the couch of Zeus, grant some respite from their toil to two unhappy wretches; to thee I pray, tossing my arms upward to heaven, where thou hast thy home in the star-spangled firmament. Thou, too, that didst win the prize of beauty at the price of my marriage; O Cypris! daughter of Dione, destroy me not utterly. Thou hast injured me enough aforetime, delivering up my name, though not my person, to live amongst barbarians. Oh! suffer me to die, if death is thy desire, in my native land. Why art thou so insatiate in mischief, employing every art of love, of fraud, and guileful schemes, and spells that bring bloodshed on families? Wert thou but moderate, only that!—in all else thou art by nature man's most welcome deity; and I have reason to say so. *Exit* HELEN.

Ch. Thee let me invoke, tearful Philomel, lurking 'neath the leafy covert in thy place of song, most tuneful of all feathered songsters, oh! come to aid me in my dirge, trilling through thy tawny throat, as I sing the piteous woes of Helen, and the tearful fate of Trojan dames made subject to Achæa's spear, on the day that there came to their plains one who sped with foreign oar across the dashing billows, bringing to Priam's race from Lacedæmon thee his hapless bride, O Helen—even Paris, luckless bridegroom, by the guidance of Aphrodite. And many an Achæan hath breathed his last amid the spearmen's thrusts and hurtling hail of stones, and gone to his sad end; for these their wives cut off their hair in sorrow, and their houses are left without a bride; and one of the Achæans, that had but a single ship, did light a blazing beacon on sea-girt Eubœa, and destroy full many of them, wrecking them on the rocks of Caphareus and the shores that front the Ægean main, by the treacherous gleam he kindled; when thou, O Menelaus, from the very day of thy start, didst drift to harbourless hills, far from thy country before the breath of the storm, bearing on thy ship a prize that was no prize, but a phantom made by Hera out of cloud for the Danai to struggle over. What mortal claims, by searching to the utmost limit, to have found out the nature of God, or of his opposite, or of that which comes between, seeing as he doth this world of man tossed to and fro by waves of contradiction and strange vicissitudes? Thou, Helen, art the daughter of Zeus; for thy sire was the bird that nestled in Leda's bosom; and yet for all that art thou become a by-word for wickedness, through the length and breadth of Hellas, as faithless, treacherous wife and godless woman; nor can I tell what certainty is, whatever may pass for it amongst men. That which gods pronounce have I found true. O fools! all ye who try to win the meed of valour through war and serried ranks of chivalry, seeking thus to still this mortal coil, in senselessness; for if bloody contests are to decide, there will never be any lack of strife in the towns of men; the maidens of the land of Priam left their bridal bowers, though arbitration might have put thy quarrel right, O Helen. And now Troy's sons are in Hades' keeping in the world below, and fire hath darted on her walls, as darts the flame of Zeus, and thou art bringing woe on woe to hapless sufferers in their misery.

Enter THEOCLYMENUS.

Theoclymenus. All hail, my father's tomb! I buried thee, Proteus, at the place where men pass out, that I might often greet thee; and so, ever as I go out and in, I, thy son Theoclymenus, call on thee, father. Ho! servants, to the palace take my hounds and hunting nets! How often have I blamed myself for never punishing those miscreants with death! I have just heard that a son of Hellas has come openly to my land, escaping the notice of the guard, a spy maybe or a would-be thief of Helen; death shall be his lot if only I can catch him. Ha! I find all my plans apparently frustrated; the daughter of Tyndareus has deserted her seat at the tomb and sailed away from my shores. Ho! there, undo the bars, loose the horses from their stalls, bring forth my chariot, servants, that the wife, on whom my heart is set, may not get away from these shores unseen, for want of any trouble I can take. (*Enter* HELEN) Yet stay; for I see the object of my pursuit is still in the palace, and has not fled. How now, lady, why hast thou arrayed thee in sable weeds instead of white raiment, and from thy fair head hast shorn thy tresses with the steel, bedewing thy cheeks the while with tears but lately shed? Is it in response to visions of the night that thou art mourning, or, because thou hast heard some warning voice within, art thus distraught with grief?

He. My lord—for already I have learnt to say that name—I am undone; my luck is gone; I cease to be.

Theoc. In what misfortune art thou plunged? What hath happened?

He. Menelaus, ah me! how can I say it? is dead, my husband.

Theoc. I show no exultation in this news, yet am I blest herein.

He. * * * *

Theoc. How knowest thou? Did Theonoe tell thee this?

He. Both she, and one who was there when he perished.

Theoc. What! hath one arrived who actually announces this for certain?

He. One hath; oh may he come e'en as I wish him to!

Theoc. Who and where is he? that I may learn this more surely.

He. There he is, sitting crouched beneath the shelter of this tomb.

Theoc. Great Apollo! what a bundle of unsightly rags!

He. Ah me! methinks my own husband too is in like plight.

Theoc. From what country is this fellow? whence landed he here?

He. From Hellas, one of the Achæans who sailed with my husband.

Theoc. What kind of death doth he declare that Menelaus died?

He. The most piteous of all; amid the watery waves at sea.

Theoc. On what part of the savage ocean was he sailing?

He. Cast up on the harbourless rocks of Libya.

Theoc. How was it this man did not perish if he was with him aboard?

He. There are times when churls have more luck than their betters.

Theoc. Where left he the wreck, on coming hither?

He. There, where perdition catch it, but not Menelaus!

Theoc. He is lost; but on what vessel came this man?

He. According to his story sailors fell in with him and picked him up.

Theoc. Where then is that mischievous thing that was sent to Troy in thy stead?

He. Dost mean the phantom-form of cloud? It hath passed into the air.

Theoc. O Priam, and thou land of Troy, how fruitless thy ruin!

He. I too have shared with Priam's race their misfortunes.

Theoc. Did this fellow leave thy husband unburied, or consign him to the grave?

He. Unburied; woe is me for my sad lot!

Theoc. Wherefore hast thou shorn the tresses of thy golden hair?

He. His memory lingers fondly in this heart, whate'er his fate.

Theoc. Are thy tears in genuine sorrow for this calamity?

He. An easy task no doubt to escape thy sister's detection!

Theoc. No, surely; impossible. Wilt thou still make this tomb thy abode?

He. Why jeer at me? canst thou not let the dead man be?

Theoc. No, thy loyalty to thy husband's memory makes thee fly from me.

He. I will do so no more; prepare at once for my marriage.

Theoc. Thou hast been long in bringing thyself to it; still I do commend thee now.

He. Dost know thy part? Let us forget the past.

Theoc. On what terms? One good turn deserves another.

He. Let us make peace; be reconciled to me.

Theoc. I relinquish my quarrel with thee; let it take wings and fly away.

He. Then by thy knees, since thou art my friend indeed—

Theoc. What art so bent on winning, that to me thou stretchest out a suppliant hand?

He. My dead husband would I fain bury.

Theoc. What tomb can be bestowed on lost bodies? Wilt thou bury a shade?

He. In Hellas we have a custom, whene'er one is drowned at sea—

Theoc. What is your custom? The race of Pelops truly hath some skill in matters such as this.

He. To hold a burial with woven robes that wrap no corpse.

Theoc. Perform the ceremony; rear the tomb where'er thou wilt.

He. 'Tis not thus we give drowned sailors burial.

Theoc. How then? I know nothing of your customs in Hellas.

He. We unmoor, and carry out to sea all that is the dead man's due.

Theoc. What am I to give thee then for thy dead husband?

He. Myself I cannot say; I had no such experience in my previous happy life.

Theoc. Stranger, thou art the bearer of tidings I welcome.

Men. Well, I do not, nor yet doth the dead man.

Theoc. How do ye bury those who have been drowned at sea?

Men. Each according to his means.

Theoc. As far as wealth goes, name thy wishes for this lady's sake.

Men. There must be a blood-offering first to the dead.

Theoc. Blood of what? Do thou show me and I will comply.

Men. Decide that thyself; whate'er thou givest will suffice.

Theoc. Amongst barbarians 'tis customary to sacrifice a horse or bull.

Men. If thou givest at all, let there be nothing mean in thy gift.

Theoc. I have no lack of such in my rich herds.

Men. Next an empty bier is decked and carried in procession.

Theoc. It shall be so; what else is it customary to add?

Men. Bronze arms; for war was his delight.

Theoc. These will be worthy of the race of Pelops, and these will we give.

Men. And with them all the fair increase of productive earth.

Theoc. And next, how do ye pour these offerings into the billows?

Men. There must be a ship ready and rowers.

Theoc. How far from the shore does the ship put out?

Men. So far that the foam in her wake can scarce be seen from the strand.

Theoc. Why so? wherefore doth Hellas observe this custom?

Men. That the billow may not cast up again our expiatory offerings.

Theoc. Phœnician rowers will soon cover the distance.

Men. 'Twill be well done, and gratifying to Menelaus, too.

Theoc. Canst thou not perform these rites well enough without Helen?

Men. This task belongs to mother, wife, or children.

Theoc. 'Tis her task then, according to thee, to bury her husband.

Men. To be sure; piety demands that the dead be not robbed of their due.

Theoc. Well, let her go; 'tis my interest to foster piety in a wife. And thou, enter the house and choose adornment for the dead. Thyself, too, will I not send empty-handed away, since thou hast done her a service. And for the good news thou hast brought me, thou shalt receive raiment instead of going bare, and food, too, that thou mayst reach thy country; for as it is, I see thou art in sorry plight. As for thee, poor lady, waste not thyself in a hopeless case; Menelaus has met his doom, and thy dead husband cannot come to life.

Men. This then is thy duty, fair young wife; be content with thy present husband, and forget him who has no existence; for this is thy best course in face of what is happening. And if ever I come to Hellas and secure my safety, I will clear thee of thy former ill-repute, if thou prove a dutiful wife to thy true husband.

He. I will; never shall my husband have cause to blame me; thou shalt thyself attend us and be witness thereto. Now go within, poor wanderer, and seek the bath, and change thy raiment. I will show my kindness to thee, and that without delay. For thou wilt perform all service due with kindlier feeling for my dear lord Menelaus, if at my hands thou meet with thy deserts.

Exeunt THEOCLYMENUS, HELEN, MENELAUS.

Ch. Through wooded glen, o'er torrent's flood, and ocean's booming waves rushed the mountain-goddess, mother of the gods, in frantic haste, once long ago, yearning for her daughter lost, whose name men dare not utter; loudly rattled the Bacchic castanets in shrill accord, what time those maidens, swift as whirlwinds, sped forth with the goddess on her chariot yoked to wild creatures, in quest of her that was ravished from the circling choir of virgins; here was Artemis with her bow, and there the grim-eyed goddess, sheathed in mail, and spear in hand. . . . But Zeus looked down from his throne in heaven, and turned the issue otherwhither. Soon as the mother ceased from her wild wandering toil, in seeking her daughter stolen so subtly as to baffle all pursuit, she crossed the snow-capped heights of Ida's nymphs; and in anguish cast her down amongst the rocks and brushwood deep in snow; and, denying to man all increase to his tillage from those barren fields, she wasted the human race; nor would she let the leafy tendrils yield luxuriant fodder for the cattle, wherefore many a beast lay dying; no sacrifice was offered to the gods, and on the altars were no cakes to burn; yea, and she made the dew-fed founts of crystal water to cease their flow, in her insatiate sorrow for her child. But when for gods and tribes of men alike she made an end to festal cheer, Zeus spoke out, seeking to sooth the mother's moody soul, "Ye stately Graces, go banish from Demeter's angry heart the grief her wanderings bring upon her for her child, and go, ye Muses too, with tuneful choir." Thereon did Cypris, fairest of the blessed gods, first catch up the crashing cymbals, native to that land, and the drum with tight-stretched skin, and then Demeter smiled, and in her hand did take the deep-toned flute, well pleased with its loud note.

Thou hast wedded as thou never shouldst have done in defiance of all right, and thou hast incurred, my daughter, the wrath of the great mother by disregarding her sacrifices. Oh! mighty is the virtue in a dress of dappled fawn-skin, in ivy green that twineth round a sacred thyrsus, in whirling tambourines struck as they revolve in air, in tresses wildly streaming for the revelry of Bromius, and likewise in the sleepless vigils of the goddess, when the moon looks down and sheds her radiance o'er the scene. Thou wert confident in thy charms alone.

Enter HELEN.

He. My friends, within the palace all goes well for us; for the daughter of Proteus, who is privy to our stealthy scheme, told her brother nothing when questioned as to my husband's coming, but for my sake declared him dead and buried. Most fortunate it is my lord hath had the luck to get these weapons; for he is now himself clad in the harness he was to plunge into the sea, his stalwart arm thrust through the buckler's strap, and in his right hand a spear, on pretence of joining in homage to the dead. He hath girded himself most serviceably for the fray, as if to triumph o'er a host of barbarian foes when once we are aboard yon oarèd ship; instead of his rags from the wreck hath he donned the robes I gave for his attire, and I have bathed his limbs in water from the stream, a bath he long hath wanted. But I must be silent, for from the house comes forth the man who thinks he has me in his power, prepared to be his bride; and thy goodwill I also claim and thy strict silence, if haply, when we save ourselves, we may save thee too some day.

Enter THEOCLYMENUS *and* MENELAUS.

Theoc. Advance in order, servants, as the stranger hath directed, bearing the funeral gifts the sea demands. But thou, Helen, if thou wilt not misconstrue my words, be persuaded and here abide; for thou wilt do thy husband equal service whether thou art present or not. For I am afraid that some sudden shock of fond regret may prompt thee to plunge into the swollen tide, in an ecstasy of gratitude toward thy former husband; for thy grief for him, though he is lost, is running to excess.

He. O my new lord, needs must I honour him with whom I first shared married joys; for I could even die with my husband, so well I loved him; yet how could he thank me, were I to share death's doom with him? Still, let me go and pay his funeral rites unto the dead in person. The gods grant thee the boon I wish and this stranger too, for the assistance he is lending here! And thou shalt find in me a wife fit to share thy house, since thou art rendering kindness to Menelaus and to me; for surely these events are to some good fortune tending. But now appoint someone to give us a ship wherein to convey these gifts, that I may find thy kindness made complete.

Theoc. (*To an attendant*) Go thou, and furnish them with a Sidonian galley of fifty oars and rowers also.

He. Shall not he command the ship who is ordering the funeral?

Theoc. Most certainly; my sailors are to obey him.

He. Repeat the order, that they may clearly understand thee.

Theoc. I repeat it, and will do so yet again if that is thy pleasure.

He. Good luck to thee and to me in my designs!

Theoc. Oh! waste not thy fair complexion with excessive weeping.

He. This day shall show my gratitude to thee.

Theoc. The state of the dead is nothingness; to toil for them is vain.

He. In what I say, this world, as well as that, hath share.

Theoc. Thou shalt not find in me a husband at all inferior to Menelaus.

He. With thee have I no fault to find; good luck is all I need.

Theoc. That rests with thyself, if thou show thyself a loving wife to me.

He. This is not a lesson I shall have to learn now, to love my friends.

Theoc. Is it thy wish that I should escort thee in person with active aid?

He. God forbid! become not thy servant's servant, O king!

Theoc. Up and away! I am not concerned with customs which the race of Pelops holds. My house is pure, for Menelaus did not die here; go some one now and bid my vassal chiefs bring marriage-offerings to my palace; for the whole earth must re-echo in glad accord the hymn of my wedding with Helen, to make men envious. Go, stranger, and pour into the sea's embrace these offerings to Helen's former lord, and then speed back again with my bride, that after sharing with me her marriage-feast thou mayst set out for home, or here abide in happiness.

Exit THEOCLYMENUS.

Men. O Zeus, who art called the father of all and god of wisdom, look down on us and change our woe to joy! Lend us thy ready help, as we seek to drag our fortunes up the rugged hill; if with but thy finger-tip thou touch us, we shall reach our longed-for goal. Sufficient are the troubles we ere this have undergone. Full oft have I invoked you gods to hear my joys and sorrows; I do not deserve to be for ever unhappy, but to advance and prosper. Grant me but this one boon, and so will ye crown my future with blessing. *Exeunt* MENELAUS *and* HELEN.

Ch. Hail! thou swift Phœnician ship of Sidon! dear to the rowers, mother to the foam, leader of fair dolphins' gambols, what time the deep is hushed and still, and Ocean's azure child, the queen of calm, takes up her parable and says: "Away! and spread your canvas to the ocean-breeze. Ho! sailors, ho! come grip your oars of pine, speeding Helen on her way to the sheltered beach where Perseus dwelt of yore."[1] It may be thou wilt find the daughters[2] of Leucippus beside the brimming river[3] or before the temple of Pallas, when at last with dance and revelry thou joinest in the merry midnight festival of Hyacinthus, him whom Phœbus slew in the lists by a quoit hurled o'er the mark; wherefore did the son of Zeus ordain that Laconia's land should set apart that day for sacrifice; there too shalt thou find the tender maid,[4] whom ye left in your house, for as yet no nuptial torch has shed its light for her.

Oh! for wings to cleave the air in the track of Libyan cranes, whose serried ranks leave far behind the wintry storm at the shrill summons of some veteran leader, who raises his exultant cry as he wings his way o'er plains that know no rain and yet bear fruitful increase. Ye feathered birds with necks outstretched, comrades of the racing clouds, on! on! till ye reach the Pleiads in their central station and Orion, lord of the night; and as ye settle on Eurotas' banks proclaim the glad tidings that Menelaus hath sacked the city of Dardanus, and will soon be home. Ye sons of Tyndareus at length appear, speeding in your chariot through the sky, denizens of heaven's courts beneath the radiant whirling stars, guide this lady Helen safely o'er the azure main, across the foam-flecked billows of the deep-blue sea, sending the mariners a favouring gale from Zeus; and from your sister snatch the ill-repute of wedding with a barbarian, even the punishment bequeathed to her from that strife on Ida's mount, albeit she never went to the land of Ilium, to the battlements of Phœbus.

Enter THEOCLYMENUS *and* MESSENGER.

Messenger. O king, at last have I found thee in the palace; for new tidings of woe art thou soon to hear from me.

Theoc. How now?

Mes. Make haste to woo a new wife; for Helen hath escaped.

Theoc. Borne aloft on soaring wings, or treading still the earth?

Mes. Menelaus has succeeded in bearing her hence; 'twas he that brought the news of his own death.

Theoc. O monstrous story! what ship conveyed her from these shores? Thy tale is past belief.

Mes. The very ship thou didst thyself give the stranger; and that thou mayest briefly know all, he is gone, taking thy sailors with him.

Theoc. How was it? I long to know, for I never gave it a thought that a single arm could master all those sailors with whom thou wert despatched.

Mes. Soon as the daughter of Zeus had left this royal mansion and come unto the sea, daintily picking her way, most craftily she set to mourn her husband, though he was not dead but at her side. Now when we reached thy docks well walled, we began to launch the fastest of Sidonian ships, with her full complement of fifty rowers, and each task in due succession followed; some set up the mast, others ranged the oars with their blades ready, and stored the white sails within the hold, and the rudder was let down astern and fastened securely. While we were thus employed, those Hellenes, who had been fellow-voyagers with Menelaus, were watching us, it seems, and they drew nigh the beach, clad in the rags of shipwrecked men—well built enough, but squalid to look upon. And the son of Atreus, directly he saw them approach, bespoke them, craftily introducing the reason for his mourning: "Ye hapless mariners, how have ye come hither? your Achæan ship where wrecked? Are ye here to help bury dead Atreus' son, whose missing body this lady, daughter of Tyndareus, is honouring with a cenotaph?" Then they with feigned tears proceeded to the ship, bearing aboard the offerings to be thrown into the deep for Menelaus. Thereat were we suspicious, and communed amongst ourselves regarding the number of extra passengers; but still we kept silence out of respect for thy orders, for by intrusting the command of the vessel to the stranger thou didst thus spoil all. Now the other victims gave no trouble, and we easily put them aboard; only the bull refused to go forward along the gangway, but rolled his eyes around and kept bellowing, and, arching his back and glaring askance toward his horns, he would not let us touch him. But Helen's lord cried out: "O! ye who laid waste the town of Ilium, come pick up yon bull, the dead man's offering, on your stout shoulders, as is the way in Hellas, and cast him into the

[1] *i.e.* to Mycenæ, said to have been founded by Perseus.

[2] The daughters of Leucippus were priestesses of Athena and Artemis.

[3] *i.e.* the Eurotas in Sparta, and the temple of the "Brazen House."

[4] *i.e.* Hermione.

hold"; and as he spoke he drew his sword in readiness. Then they at his command came and caught up the bull and carried him bodily on to the deck. And Menelaus stroked the horse on neck and brow, coaxing it to go aboard. At length, when the ship was fully freighted, Helen climbed the ladder with graceful step and took her seat midway betwixt the rowers' benches, and he sat by her side, even Menelaus who was called dead; and the rest, equally divided on the right and left side of the ship, sat them down, each beside his man, with swords concealed beneath their cloaks, and the billows soon were echoing to the rowers' song, as we heard the boatswain's note. Now when we were put out a space not very far nor very near, the helmsman asked, "Shall we, sir stranger, sail yet further on our course, or will this serve? For thine it is to command the ship." And he answered: "'Tis far enough for me," while in his right hand he gripped his sword and stepped on to the prow; then standing o'er the bull to slay it, never a word said he of any dead man, but cut its throat and thus made prayer: "Poseidon, lord of the sea, whose home is in the deep, and ye holy daughters of Nereus, bring me and my wife safe and sound to Nauplia's strand from hence!" Anon a gush of blood, fair omen for the stranger, spouted into the tide. One cried, "There is treachery in this voyage; why should we now sail to Nauplia? Give the order, helmsman, turn thy rudder." But the son of Atreus, standing where he slew the bull, called to his comrades, "Why do ye, the pick of Hellas, delay to smite and slay the barbarians and fling them from the ship into the waves?" While to thy crew the boatswain cried the opposite command: "Ho! some of you catch up chance spars, break up the benches, or snatch the oar-blade from the thole, and beat out the brains of these our foreign foes." Forthwith up sprang each man, the one part armed with poles that sailors use, the other with swords. And the ship ran down with blood; while Helen from her seat upon the stern thus cheered them on: "Where is the fame ye won in Troy? show it against these barbarians." Then as they hasted to the fray, some would fall and some rise up again, while others hadst thou seen laid low in death. But Menelaus in full armour, made his way, sword in hand, to any point where his watchful eye perceived his comrades in distress; so we leapt from the ship and swam, and he cleared the benches of thy rowers. Then did the prince set himself to steer, and bade them make a straight course to Hellas. So they set up the mast, and favouring breezes blew; and they are clear away, while I, from death escaped, let myself down by the anchor chain into the sea; and, just as I was spent, one threw me a rope and rescued me, and drew me to land to bring to thee this message. Ah! there is naught more serviceable to mankind than a prudent distrust.

Ch. I would never have believed that Menelaus could have eluded us and thee, O king, in the way he did on his coming.

Theoc. Woe is me! cozened by a woman's tricks! My bride hath escaped me. If the ship could have been pursued and overtaken, I would have used every means forthwith to catch the strangers; as it is, I will avenge myself upon my treacherous sister, in that she saw Menelaus in my palace and did not tell me. Wherefore shall she nevermore deceive another by her prophetic art.

Enter PORTRESS.

Po. Ho, there! whither away so fast, my lord? on what bloody thought intent?

Theoc. Whither Justice calls me. Out of my path!

Po. I will not loose thy robe, for on grievous mischief art thou bent.

Theoc. Shalt thou, a slave, control thy master?

Po. Yea, for I am in my senses.

Theoc. I should not say so, if thou wilt not let me—

Po. Nay, but that I never will.

Theoc. Slay my sister most accursed.

Po. Say rather, most righteous.

Theoc. "Righteous"? she who betrayed me.

Po. There is an honourable treachery, which 'tis right to commit.

Theoc. By giving my bride to another?

Po. Only to those who had a better right.

Theoc. Who hath any rights o'er mine?

Po. He that received her from her father.

Theoc. Nay, but fortune gave her to me.

Po. And destiny took her away.

Theoc. 'Tis not for thee to decide my affairs.

Po. Only supposing mine be the better counsel.

Theoc. So I am thy subject, not thy ruler.

Po. Aye, a subject bound to do the right, and eschew the wrong.

Theoc. It seems thou art eager to be slain.

Po. Slay me; thy sister shalt thou never slay with my consent, but me perchance; for to die for their masters is the fairest death, that noble slaves can find.

THE DIOSCURI *appears above the stage.*

The Dioscuri. Restrain those bursts of rage that hurry thee to undue lengths, O Theoclymenus king of this country. We are the twin sons of Zeus that call to thee by name, whom Leda bore one day, with Helen too who hath fled from thy palace. For thou art wroth for a marriage never destined for thee; nor is thy sister Theonoe, daughter of a Nereid goddess, wronging thee because she honours the word of God and her father's just behests. For it was ordained that Helen should abide within thy halls up till the present time, but since Troy is razed to the ground and she hath lent her name to the goddesses, no longer need she stay, now must she be united in the self-same wedlock as before, and reach her home and share it with her husband. Withhold then thy malignant blade from thy sister, and believe that she herein is acting with discretion. Long, long ago had we our sister saved, seeing that Zeus has made us gods, but we were too weak for destiny as well as the deities, who willed these things to be. This is my bidding to thee; while to my sister I say, "Sail on with thy husband; and ye shall have a prosperous breeze; for we, thy brethren twain, will course along the deep and bring you safely to your fatherland. And when at last thy goal is reached and thy life ended, thou shalt be famous as a goddess, and with thy twin brethren share the drink-offering, and like us receive gifts from men, for such is the will of Zeus. Yea, and that spot[1] where the son of Maia first appointed thee a home when from Sparta he removed thee, after stealing an image of thee from heaven's mansions to prevent thy marriage with Paris, even the isle that lies like a sentinel along the Attic coast, shall henceforth be called by thy name amongst men, for that it welcomed thee when stolen from thy home. Moreover, Heaven ordains that the wanderer Menelaus shall find a home within an island of the blest; for to noble souls hath the deity no dislike, albeit these oft suffer more than those of no account."

Theoc. Ye sons of Leda and of Zeus, I will forego my former quarrel about your sister, nor seek to slay mine own any more. Let Helen to her home repair, if such is Heaven's pleasure. Ye know that ye are sprung of the same stock as your sister, best of women, chastest too; hail then for the true nobility of Helen's soul, a quality too seldom found amongst her sex!

Ch. Many are the forms the heavenly will assumes; and many a thing God brings to pass contrary to expectation: that which was looked for is not accomplished, while Heaven finds out a way for what we never hoped; e'en such has been the issue here. *Exeunt* OMNES.

[1]Cranae, off Sunium, or Macri.

ANDROMACHE

DRAMATIS PERSONAE

ANDROMACHE
MAID
CHORUS OF PHTHIAN WOMEN
HERMIONE
MENELAUS
MOLOSSUS
PELEUS
NURSE OF HERMIONE
ORESTES
MESSENGER
THETIS

Before the temple of Thetis in Thessaly. Enter ANDROMACHE.

Andromache. O city of Thebes,[1] glory of Asia, whence on a day I came to Priam's princely home with many a rich and costly thing in my dower, affianced unto Hector to be the mother of his children, I, Andromache, envied name in days of yore, but now of all women that have been or yet shall be the most unfortunate; for I have lived to see my husband Hector slain by Achilles, and the babe Astyanax, whom I bore my lord, hurled from the towering battlements, when the Hellenes sacked our Trojan home; and I myself am come to Hellas as a slave, though I was esteemed a daughter of a race most free, given to Neoptolemus that island-prince, and set apart for him as his special prize from the spoils of Troy. And here I dwell upon the boundaries of Phthia and Pharsalia's town, where Thetis erst, the goddess of the sea, abode with Peleus apart from the world, avoiding the throng of men; wherefore the folk of Thessaly call it the sacred place of Thetis, in honour of the goddess's marriage. Here dwells the son of Achilles and suffers Peleus still to rule Pharsalia, not wishing to assume the sceptre while the old man lives. Within these halls have I born a boy to the son of Achilles, my master. Now aforetime for all my misery I ever had a hope to lead me on, that, if my child were safe, I might find some help and protection from my woes; but since my lord in scorn of his bondmaid's charms hath wedded that Spartan Hermione, I am tormented by her most cruelly; for she saith that I by secret enchantment am making her barren and distasteful to her husband, and that I design to take her place in this house, ousting her the rightful mistress by force; whereas I at first submitted against my will and now have resigned my place; be almighty Zeus my witness that it was not of my own free will I became her rival!

But I cannot convince her, and she longs to kill me, and her father Menelaus is an accomplice in this. E'en now is he within, arrived from Sparta for this very purpose, while I in terror am come to take up a position here in the shrine of Thetis adjoining the house, if haply it may save me from death; for Peleus and his descendants hold it in honour as a symbol of his marriage with the Nereid. My only son am I secretly conveying to a neighbour's house in fear for his life. For his sire stands not by my side to lend his aid and cannot avail his child at all, being absent in the land of Delphi, where he is offering recompense to Loxias for the madness he committed, when on a day he went to Pytho and demanded of Phœbus satisfaction for his father's death, if haply his prayer might avert those past sins and win for him the god's goodwill hereafter.

Enter MAID.

Maid. Mistress mine, be sure I do not hesitate to call thee by that name, seeing that I thought it thy right in thine own house also, when we dwelt in Troy-land; as I was ever thy friend and thy husband's while yet he was alive, so now have I come with strange tidings, in terror lest any of our masters learn hereof but still out of pity for thee; for Menelaus and his daughter are forming dire plots against thee, whereof thou must beware.

An. Ah! kind companion of my bondage, for such thou art to her, who, erst thy queen, is now sunk in misery; what are they doing? What new schemes are they devising in their eagerness to take away my wretched life?

Ma. Alas! poor lady, they intend to slay thy son, whom thou hast privily conveyed from out the house.

An. Ah me! Has she[2] heard that my babe was put out of her reach? Who told her? Woe is me! how utterly undone!

Ma. I know not, but thus much of their schemes I heard myself; and Menelaus has left the house to fetch him.

An. Then am I lost; ah, my child! those vultures twain will take and slay thee; while he who is called thy father lingers still in Delphi.

Ma. True, for had he been here thou wouldst not have fared so hardly, I am sure; but, as it is, thou art friendless.

An. Have no tidings come of the possible arrival of Peleus?

[1]In Cilicia.

[2]Hermione.

Ma. He is too old to help thee if he came.

An. And yet I sent for him more than once.

Ma. Surely thou dost not suppose that any of thy messengers heed thee?

An. Why should they? Wilt thou then go for me?

Ma. How shall I explain my long absence from the house?

An. Thou art a woman; thou canst invent a hundred ways.

Ma. There is a risk, for Hermione keeps no careless guard.

An. Dost look to that? Thou art disowning thy friends in distress.

Ma. Not so; never taunt me with that. I will go, for of a truth a woman and a slave is not of much account, e'en if aught befall me.

An. Go then, while I will tell to heaven the lengthy tale of lamentation, mourning, and weeping, that has ever been my hard lot; (*Exit* MAID.) for 'tis woman's way to delight in present misfortunes even to keeping them always on her tongue and lips. But I have many reasons, not merely one for tears—my city's fall, my Hector's death, the hardness of the lot to which I am bound, since I fell on slavery's evil days undeservedly. 'Tis never right to call a son of man happy, till thou hast seen his end, to judge from the way he passes it how he will descend to that other world.

'Twas no bride Paris took with him to the towers of Ilium, but a curse to his bed when he brought Helen to her bower. For her sake, O Troy, did eager warriors, sailing from Hellas in a thousand ships, capture and make thee a prey to fire and sword; and the son of sea-born Thetis mounted on his chariot dragged my husband Hector round the walls, ah woe is me! while I was hurried from my chamber to the beach, with slavery's hateful pall upon me. And many a tear I shed as I left my city, my bridal bower, and my husband in the dust. Woe, woe is me! why should I prolong my life, to serve Hermione? Her cruelty it is that drives me hither to the image of the goddess to throw my suppliant arms about it, melting to tears as doth a spring that gushes from the rock.

Enter CHORUS OF PHTHIAN WOMEN.

Chorus. Lady, thus keeping thy weary station without pause upon the floor of Thetis' shrine Phthian though I am, to thee a daughter of Asia I come, to see if I can devise some remedy for these perplexing troubles, which have involved thee and Hermione in fell discord, because to thy sorrow thou sharest with her the love of Achilles' son. Recognize thy position, weigh the present evil into the which thou art come. Thou art a Trojan captive; thy rival is thy mistress, a true-born daughter of Sparta. Leave then this home of sacrifice, the shrine of our sea-goddess. How can it avail thee to waste thy comeliness and disfigure it by weeping by reason of a mistress's harsh usage? Might will prevail against thee; why vainly toil in thy feebleness? Come, quit the bright sanctuary of the Nereid divine. Recognize that thou art in bondage on a foreign soil, in a strange city, where thou seest none of all thy friends, luckless lady, cast on evil days. Yea, I did pity thee most truly, Trojan dame, when thou camest to this house; but from fear of my mistress I hold my peace, albeit I sympathize with thee, lest she, whom Zeus' daughter bore, discover my good will toward thee.

Enter HERMIONE.

Hermione. With a crown of golden workmanship upon my head and about my body this embroidered robe am I come hither; no presents these I wear from the palace of Achilles or Peleus, but gifts my father Menelaus gave me together with a sumptuous dower from Sparta in Laconia, to insure me freedom of speech. Such is my answer to you; but as for thee, slave and captive, thou wouldst fain oust me and secure this palace for thyself, and thanks to thy enchantment I am hated by my husband; thou it is that hast made my womb barren and cheated my hopes; for Asia's daughters have clever heads for such villainy; yet will I check thee therefrom, nor shall this temple of the Nereid avail thee aught, no! neither its altar or shrine, but thou shalt die. But if or god or man should haply wish to save thee, thou must atone for thy proud thoughts of happier days now past by humbling thyself and crouching prostrate at my knees, by sweeping out my halls, and by learning, as thou sprinklest water from a golden ewer, where thou now art. Here is no Hector, no Priam with his gold, but a city of Hellas. Yet thou, miserable woman, hast gone so far in wantonness that thou canst lay thee down with the son of the very man that slew thy husband, and bear children to the murderer. Such is all the race of barbarians; father and daughter, mother and son, sister and brother mate together; the nearest and dearest stain their path with each other's blood, and no law restrains such horrors. Bring not these crimes amongst us, for here we count it shame that one man should have the control of two wives, and men are content to turn their attention to one lawful love, that is, all who care to live an honourable life.

Ch. Women are by nature somewhat jealous, and do ever show the keenest hate to rivals in their love.

An. Ah! well-a-day! Youth is a bane to mortals, in every case, that is, where a man embraces injustice in his early days. Now I am afraid that my being a slave will prevent thee listening to me in spite of many a just plea, or if I win my case, I fear I may be damaged on this very ground, for the high and mighty cannot brook refuting arguments from their inferiors; still I will not be convicted of betraying my own cause. Tell me, proud young wife, what assurance can make me confident of wresting from thee thy lawful lord? Is it that Laconia's capital yields to Phrygia? is it that my fortune outstrips thine? or that in me thou seest a free woman? Am I so elated by my youth, my full healthy figure, the extent of my city, the number of my friends that I wish to supplant thee in thy home? Is my purpose to take thy place and rear myself a race of slaves, mere appendages to my misery? or, supposing thou bear no children, will any one endure that sons of mine should rule o'er Phthia? Ah no! there is the love that Hellas bears me, both for Hector's sake and for my own humble rank forsooth, that never knew a queen's estate in Troy. 'Tis not my sorcery that makes thy husband hate thee, nay, but thy own failure to prove thyself his help-meet. Herein lies love's only charm; 'tis not beauty, lady, but virtuous acts that win our husbands' hearts. And though it gall thee to be told so, albeit thy city in Laconia is no doubt a mighty fact, yet thou findest no place for his Scyros, displaying wealth 'midst poverty and setting Menelaus above Achilles: and that is what alienates thy lord. Take heed; for a woman, though bestowed upon a worthless husband, must be with him content, and ne'er advance presumptuous claims. Suppose thou hadst wedded a prince of Thrace, the land of flood and melting snow, where one lord shares his affections with a host of wives, wouldst thou have slain them? If so, thou wouldst have set a stigma of insatiate lust on all our sex. A shameful charge! And yet herein we suffer more than men, though we make a good stand against it. Ah! my dear lord Hector, for thy sake would I e'en brook a rival, if ever Cypris led thee astray, and oft in days gone by I held thy bastard babes to my own breast, to spare thee any cause for grief. By this course I bound my husband to me by virtue's chains, whereas thou wilt never so much as let the drops of dew from heaven above settle on thy lord, in thy jealous fear. Oh! seek not to surpass thy mother in hankering after men, for 'tis well that all wise children should avoid the habits of such evil mothers.

Ch. Mistress mine, be persuaded to come to terms with her, as far as readily comes within thy power.

He. Why this haughty tone, this bandying of words, as if, forsooth, thou, not I, wert the virtuous wife?

An. Thy present claims at any rate give thee small title thereto.

He. Woman, may my bosom never harbour such ideas as thine!

An. Thou art young to speak on so delicate a subject.

He. As for thee, thou dost not speak thereof, but, as thou canst, dost put it into action against me.

An. Canst thou not conceal thy pangs of jealousy?

He. What! doth not every woman put this first of all?

An. Yes, if her experiences are happy; otherwise, there is no honour in speaking of them.

He. Barbarians' laws are not a standard for our city.

An. Alike in Asia and in Hellas infamy attends base actions.

He. Clever, clever quibbler! yet die thou must and shalt.

An. Dost see the image of Thetis with her eye upon thee?

He. A bitter foe to thy country because of the death of Achilles.

An. 'Twas not I that slew him, but Helen that mother of thine.

He. Pray, is it thy intention to probe my wounds yet deeper?

An. Behold, I am dumb, my lips are closed.

He. Tell me that which was my only reason for coming hither.

An. No! all I tell thee is, thou hast less wisdom than thou needest.

He. Wilt thou leave these hallowed precincts of the sea-goddess?

An. Yes, if I am not to die for it; otherwise, I never will.

He. Since that is thy resolve, I shall not even wait my lord's return.

An. Nor yet will I, at any rate ere that, surrender to thee.

He. I will bring fire to bear on thee, and pay no heed to thy entreaties.

An. Kindle thy blaze then; the gods will witness it.

He. And make thy flesh to writhe by cruel wounds.

An. Begin thy butchery, stain the altar of the goddess with blood, for she will visit thy iniquity.

He. Barbarian creature, hardened in impudence, wilt thou brave death itself? Still will I find speedy means to make thee quit this seat of thy free-will; such a bait have I to lure thee with. But I will hide my meaning, which the event itself shall soon declare. Yes, keep thy seat, for I will make thee rise, though molten lead is holding thee there, before Achilles' son, thy trusted champion, arrive.

Exit HERMIONE.

An. My trusted champion, yes! how strange it is, that, though some god hath devised cures for mortals against the venom of reptiles, no man ever yet hath discovered aught to cure a woman's venom, which is far worse than viper's sting or scorching flame; so terrible a curse are we to mankind.

Ch. Ah! what sorrows did the son of Zeus and Maia herald, in the day he came to Ida's glen, guiding that fair young trio of goddesses, all girded for the fray in bitter rivalry about their beauty, to the shepherd's fold, where dwelt the youthful herdsman all alone by the hearth of his lonely hut. Soon as they reached the wooded glen, in gushing mountain springs they bathed their dazzling skin, then sought the son of Priam, comparing their rival charms in more than rancorous phrase. But Cypris won the day by her deceitful promises, sweet-sounding words, but fraught with ruthless overthrow to Phrygia's hapless town and Ilium's towers. Would God his mother had smitten him a cruel death-blow on the head before he made his home on Ida's slopes, in the hour Cassandra, standing by the holy bay-tree, cried out, "Slay him, for he will bring most grievous bane on Priam's town." To every prince she went, to every elder sued for the babe's destruction. Ah! had they listened, Ilium's daughters ne'er had felt the yoke of slavery, and thou, lady, hadst been established in the royal palace; and Hellas had been freed of all the anguish she suffered during those ten long years her sons went wandering, spear in hand, around the walls of Troy; brides had never been left desolate, nor hoary fathers childless.

Enter MENELAUS, *with* MOLOSSUS.

Menelaus. Behold I bring thy son with me, whom thou didst steal away to a neighbour's house without my daughter's knowledge. Thou wert so sure this image of the goddess would protect thee and those who hid him, but thou hast not proved clever enough for Menelaus. And so if thou refuse to leave thy station here, he shall be slain instead of thee. Wherefore weigh it well: wilt die thyself, or see him slain for the sin whereof thou art guilty against me and my daughter?

An. O fame, fame! full many a man ere now of no account hast thou to high estate exalted. Those, indeed, who truly have a fair repute, I count blest; but those who get it by false pretences, I will never allow have aught but the accidental appearance of wisdom. Thou for instance, caitiff that thou art, didst thou ever wrest Troy from Priam with thy picked troops of Hellenes? thou that hast raised such a storm, at the word of thy daughter, a mere child, and hast entered the lists with a poor captive; unworthy I count thee of Troy's capture, and Troy still more disgraced by thy victory. Those who only in appearance are men of sense make an outward show, but inwardly resemble the common herd save it be in wealth, which is their chiefest strength.

Come now, Menelaus, let us discuss this argument. Suppose I am slain by thy daughter, and she work her will on me, yet can she never escape the pollution of murder, and public opinion will make thee too an accomplice in this deed of blood, for thy share in the business must needs implicate thee. But even supposing I escape death myself, will ye kill my child? Even then, how will his father brook the murder of his child? Troy has no such coward's tale to tell of him; nay, he will follow duty's call; his actions will prove him a worthy scion of Peleus and Achilles. Thy daughter will he thrust forth from his house; and what wilt thou say when seeking to betroth her to another? wilt say her virtue made her leave a worthless lord? Nay, that will be false. Who then will wed her? wilt thou keep her without a husband in thy halls, grown grey in widowhood? Unhappy wretch! dost not see the flood-gates of trouble opening wide for thee? How many a wrong against a wife wouldst thou prefer thy daughter to have found to suffering what I now describe? We ought not on trifling grounds to promote serious mischief; nor should men, if we women are so deadly a curse, bring their nature down to our level. No! if, as thy daughter asserts, I am practising sorcery against her and making her barren, right willingly will I, without any crouching at altars, submit in my own person to the penalty that lies in her husband's hands, seeing that I am no less chargeable with injuring him if I make him childless. This is my case; but for thee, there is one thing I fear in thy disposition; it was a quarrel for a woman that really induced thee to destroy poor Ilium's town.

Ch. Thou hast said too much for a woman speaking to men; *that* discretion hath shot away its last shaft from thy soul's quiver.

Men. Woman, these are petty matters, unworthy, as thou sayest, of my despotic sway, unworthy too of Hellas. Yet mark this well; his special fancy of the hour is of more moment to a man than Troy's capture. I then have set myself to help my daughter because I consider her loss of a wife's rights a grave matter; for whatever else a woman suffers is secondary to this; if she loses her husband's love she loses her life therewith. Now, as it is right Neoptolemus should rule my slaves, so my friends and I should have control of his; for friends, if they be really friends, keep nothing to themselves, but have all in common. So if I wait for the absent instead of making the best arrangement I can at once of my affairs, I show weakness, not wisdom. Arise then, leave the goddess's shrine, for by thy death this child escapeth his, whereas, if thou refuse to die, I will slay him; for one of you twain must perish.

An. Ah me! 'tis a bitter lot thou art offering about my life; whether I take it or not I am equally unfortunate. Attend to me, thou who for a trifling cause art committing an awful crime. Why art thou bent on slaying me? What reason hast thou? What city have I betrayed? Which of thy children was ever slain by me? What house have I fired? I was forced to be my master's concubine; and spite of that wilt thou slay me, not him who is to blame, passing by the cause and hurrying to the inevitable result? Ah me! my sorrows! Woe for my hapless country! How cruel my fate! Why had I to be a mother too and take upon me a double load of suffering? Yet why do I mourn the past, and o'er the present never shed a tear or compute its griefs? I that saw Hector butchered and dragged behind the chariot, and Ilium, piteous sight! one sheet of flame, while I was haled away by the hair of my head to the Argive ships in slavery, and on my arrival in Phthia was assigned to Hector's murderer as his mistress. What pleasure then has life for me? Whither am I to turn my gaze? to the present or the past? My babe alone was left me, the light of my life; and him these ministers of death would slay. No! they shall not, if my poor life can save him; for if he be saved, hope in him lives on, while to me 'twere shame to refuse to die for my son. Lo! here I leave the altar and give myself into your hands, to cut or stab, to bind or hang. Ah! my child, to Hades now thy mother passes to save thy dear life. Yet if thou escape thy doom, remember me, my sufferings and my death, and tell thy father how I fared, with fond caress and streaming eye and arms thrown round his neck. Ah! yes, his children are to every man as his own soul; and whoso sneers at this through inexperience, though he suffers less anguish, yet tastes the bitter in his cup of bliss.

Ch. Thy tale with pity fills me; for every man alike, stranger though he be, feels pity for another's distress. Menelaus, 'tis thy duty to reconcile thy daughter and this captive, giving her a respite from sorrow.

Men. Ho! sirrahs, catch me this woman; hold her fast; for 'tis no welcome story she will have to hear.

It was to make thee leave the holy altar of the goddess that I held thy child's death before thy eyes, and so induced thee to give thyself up to me to die. So stands thy case, be well assured; but as for this child, my daughter shall decide whether she will slay him or no. Get thee hence into the house, and there learn to bridle thy insolence in speaking to the free, slave that thou art.

An. Alas! thou hast by treachery beguiled me; I was deceived.

Men. Proclaim it to the world; I do not deny it.

An. Is this counted cleverness amongst you who dwell by the Eurotas?

Men. Yes, and amongst Trojans too, that those who suffer should retaliate.

An. Thinkest thou God's hand is shortened, and that thou wilt not be punished?

Men. Whene'er that comes, I am ready to bear it. But thy life will I have.

An. Wilt likewise slay this tender chick, whom thou hast snatched from 'neath my wing?

Men. Not I, but I will give him to my daughter to slay if she will.

An. Ah me! why not begin my mourning then for thee, my child?

Men. Of a truth 'tis no very sure hope that he has left.

An. O citizens of Sparta, the bane of all the race of men, schemers of guile, and masters in lying, devisers of evil plots, with crooked minds and tortuous methods and ne'er one honest thought, 'tis wrong that ye should thrive in Hellas. What crime is wanting in your list? How rife is murder with you! How covetous ye are! One word upon your lips, another in your heart, this is what men always find with you. Perdition catch ye! Still death is not so grievous, as thou thinkest, to me. No! for my life ended in the day that hapless Troy was destroyed with my lord, that glorious warrior, whose spear oft made a coward like thee quit the field and seek thy ship. But now against a woman hast thou displayed the terrors of thy panoply, my would-be murderer. Strike then! for this my tongue shall never flatter thee or that daughter of thine. For though thou wert of great account in Sparta, why so was I in Troy. And if I am now in sorry plight, presume not thou on this; thou too mayst be so yet.

Exeunt ANDROMACHE, MENELAUS, *and* MOLOSSUS.

Ch. Never, oh! never will I commend rival wives or sons of different mothers, a cause of strife, of bitterness, and grief in every house. I would have a husband content with one wife whose rights he shareth with no other. Not even in states is dual monarchy better to bear than undivided rule; it only doubles burdens and causes faction amongst the citizens. Often too will the Muse sow strife 'twixt rivals in the art of minstrelsy. Again, when strong winds are drifting mariners, the divided counsel of the wise is not conducive to steering, and their collective wisdom has less weight than the inferior intelligence of the single man who has sole authority; for this is the essence of power alike in house and state, whene'er men care to find the proper moment. This Spartan, the daughter of the great chief Menelaus, proves this; for she hath kindled hot fury against a rival, and is bent on slaying the hapless Trojan maid and her child to further her bitter quarrel. 'Tis a murder gods and laws and kindness all forbid. Ah! lady, retribution for this deed will visit thee yet.

But lo! before the house I see those two united souls, condemned to die. Alas! for thee, poor lady, and for thee, unhappy child, who art dying on account of thy mother's marriage, though thou hast no share therein and canst not be blamed by the royal house.

Enter MENELAUS, *leading* ANDROMACHE *and* MOLOSSUS.

An. Behold me journeying on the downward path, my hands so tightly bound with cords that they bleed.

Molossus. O mother, mother mine! I too share thy downward path, nestling 'neath thy wing.

An. A cruel sacrifice! ye rulers of Phthia!

Mo. Come, father! succour those thou lovest.

An. Rest there, my babe, my darling! on thy mother's bosom, e'en in death and in the grave.

Mo. Ah, woe is me! what will become of me and thee too, mother mine?

Men. Away, to the world below! from hostile towers ye came, the pair of you; two different causes necessitate your deaths; my sentence takes away thy life, and my daughter Hermione's requires his; for it would be the height of folly to leave our foemen's sons, when we might kill them and remove the danger from our house.

An. O husband mine! I would I had thy strong arm and spear to aid me, son of Priam.

Mo. Ah, woe is me! what spell can I now find to turn death's stroke aside?

An. Embrace thy master's knees, my child, and pray to him.

Mo. Spare, O spare my life, kind master!

An. Mine eyes are wet with tears, which trickle down my cheeks, as doth a sunless spring from a smooth rock. Ah me!

Mo. What remedy, alas! can I provide me 'gainst my ills?

Men. Why fall at my knees in supplication? hard as the rock and deaf as the wave am I. My own friends have I helped, but for thee have I no tie of affection; for verily it cost me a great part of my life to capture Troy and thy mother; so thou shalt reap the fruit thereof and into Hades' halls descend.

Ch. Behold! I see Peleus drawing nigh; with aged step he hasteth hither.

Enter PELEUS, *with attendant.*

Peleus (*Calling out as he comes in sight*) What means this? I ask you and your executioner; why is the palace in an uproar? give a reason; what mean your lawless machinations? Menelaus, hold thy hand. Seek not to outrun justice. (*To his attendant*) Forward! faster, faster! for this matter, methinks, admits of no delay; now if ever would I fain resume the vigour of my youth. First however will I breathe new life into this captive, being to her as the breeze that blows a ship before the wind. Tell me, by what right have they pinioned thine arms and are dragging thee and thy child away? like a ewe with her lamb art thou led to the slaughter, while I and thy lord were far away.

An. Behold them that are haling me and my child to death, e'en as thou seest, aged prince. Why should I tell thee? For not by one urgent summons alone but by countless messengers have I sent for thee. No doubt thou knowest by hearsay of the strife in this house with this man's daughter, and the reason of my ruin. So now they have torn and are dragging me from the altar of Thetis, the goddess of thy chiefest adoration and the mother of thy gallant son, without any proper trial, yea, and without waiting for my absent master; because, forsooth, they knew my defencelessness and my child's, whom they mean to slay with me his hapless mother, though he has done no harm. But to thee, O sire, I make my supplication, prostrate at thy knees, though my hand cannot touch thy friendly beard; save me, I adjure thee, reverend sir, or to thy shame and my sorrow shall we be slain.

Pe. Loose her bonds, I say, ere some one rue it; untie her folded hands.

Men. I forbid it, for besides being a match for thee, I have a far better right to her.

Pe. What! art thou come hither to set my house in order? Art not content with ruling thy Spartans?

Men. She is my captive; I took her from Troy.

Pe. Aye, but my son's son received her as his prize.

Men. Is not all I have his, and all his mine?

Pe. For good, but not evil ends; and surely not for murderous violence.

Men. Never shalt thou wrest her from my grasp.

Pe. With this good staff I'll stain thy head with blood!

Men. Just touch me and see! Approach one step!

Pe. What! shalt thou rank with men? chief of cowards, son of cowards! What right hast thou to any place 'mongst men? Thou who didst let a Phrygian rob thee of thy wife, leaving thy home without bolt or guard, as if forsooth the cursed woman thou hadst there was a model of virtue. No! a Spartan maid could not be chaste, e'en if she would, who leaves her home and bares her limbs and lets her robe float free, to share with youths their races and their sports—customs I cannot away with. Is it any wonder then that ye fail to educate your women in virtue? Helen might have asked thee this, seeing that she said goodbye to thy affection and tripped off with her young gallant to a foreign land. And yet for her sake thou didst marshal all the hosts of Hellas and lead them to Ilium, whereas thou shouldst have shown thy loathing for her by refusing to stir a spear, once thou hadst found her false; yea, thou shouldst have let her stay there, and even paid a price to save ever having her back again. But that was not at all the way thy thoughts were turned; wherefore many a brave life hast thou ended, and many an aged mother hast thou left childless in her home, and grey-haired sires of gallant sons hast reft. Of that sad band am I a member, seeing in thee Achilles' murderer like a malignant fiend; for thou and thou alone hast returned from Troy without a scratch, bringing back thy splendid weapons in their splendid cases just as they went. As for me, I ever told that amorous boy to form no alliance with thee nor take unto his home an evil mother's child; for daughters bear the marks of their mothers' ill-repute into their new homes. Wherefore, ye wooers, take heed to this my warning: "Choose the daughter of a good mother." And more than this, with what wanton insult didst thou treat thy brother, bidding him sacrifice his daughter in his simpleness! So fearful wast thou of losing thy worthless wife. Then after capturing Troy—for thither too will I accompany thee—thou didst not slay that woman, when she was in thy power; but as soon as thine eyes caught sight of her breast, thy sword was dropped and thou didst take her kisses, fondling the shameless traitress, too weak to stem thy hot desire, thou caitiff wretch! Yet spite of all thou art the man to come and work havoc in my grandson's halls when he is absent, seeking to slay with all indignity a poor weak woman and her babe; but that babe shall one day make thee and thy daughter in thy home rue it, e'en though his birth be trebly base. Yea, for oft ere now hath seed, sown on barren soil, prevailed o'er rich deep tilth, and many a bastard has proved a better man than children better born. Take thy daughter hence with thee! Far better is it for mortals to have a poor honest man either as married kin or friend than a wealthy knave; but as for thee, thou art a thing of naught.

Ch. The tongue from trifling causes contrives to breed great strife 'mongst men; wherefore are the wise most careful not to bring about a quarrel with their friends.

Men. Why, pray, should one call these old men wise, or those who once had a reputation in Hellas for being so? when thou, the great Peleus, son of a famous father, connected with me by marriage, employest language disgraceful to thyself and abusive of me because of a barbarian woman, though thou shouldst have banished her far beyond the streams of Nile or Phasis, and ever encouraged me; seeing that she comes from Asia's continent where fell so many of the sons of Hellas, victims to the spear; and likewise because she shared in the spilling of thy son's blood; for Paris who slew thy son Achilles, was brother to Hector, whose wife she was. And dost *thou* enter the same abode with her, and deign to let her share thy board, and suffer her to rear her brood of vipers in thy house? But I, after all this foresight for thee, old man, and myself, am to have her torn from my clutches for wishing to slay her. Yet come now, for there is no disgrace in arguing the matter out; suppose my daughter has no child, while this woman's sons grow up, wilt thou set them up to rule the land of Phthia, barbarians born and bred to lord it over Hellenes? Am I then so void of sense because I hate injustice, and thou so full of cleverness? Consider yet another point; say thou hadst given a daughter of thine to some citizen, and hadst then seen her thus treated, wouldst thou have sat looking on in silence? I trow not. Dost thou then for a foreigner rail thus at thy nearest friends? Again, thou mayst say, husband and wife have an equally strong case if she is wronged by him, and similarly if he find her guilty of indiscretion in his house; yet while he has ample powers in his own hands, she depends on parents and friends for her case. Surely then I am right in helping my own kin! Thou art in thy dotage; for thou wilt do me more good by speaking of my generalship than by concealing it. Helen's trouble was not of her own choosing, but sent by heaven, and it proved a great benefit to Hellas; her sons, till then untried in war or arms, turned to deeds of prowess, and it is experience which teaches man all he knows. I showed my wisdom in refraining from slaying my wife, directly I caught sight of her. Would that thou too hadst ne'er slain Phocus! All this I bring before thee in pure goodwill, not from anger. But if thou resent it, thy tongue may wag till it ache, yet shall I gain by prudent forethought.

Ch. Cease now from idle words, 'twere better far, for fear ye both alike go wrong.

Pe. Alas! what evil customs now prevail in Hellas! Whene'er the host sets up a trophy o'er the foe, men no more consider this the work of those who really toiled, but the general gets the credit for it. Now he was but one among ten thousand others to brandish his spear; he only did the work of one; but yet he wins more praise than they. Again, as magistrates in all the grandeur of office they scorn the common folk, though they are naught themselves; whereas those others are ten thousand times more wise than they, if daring combine with judgment. Even so thou and thy brother, exalted by the toilsome efforts of others, now take your seats in all the swollen pride of Trojan fame and Trojan generalship. But I will teach thee henceforth to consider Idaean Paris a foe less terrible than Peleus, unless forthwith thou pack from this roof, thou and thy childless daughter too, whom my own true son will hale through his halls by the hair of her head; for her barrenness will not let her endure fruitfulness in others, because she has no children herself. Still if she is unlucky in the matter of offspring, is that a reason why we should be left childless? Begone! ye varlets, let her go! I will soon see if anyone will hinder me from loosing her hands. (*To* ANDROMACHE) Arise; these trembling hands of mine will untie the twisted thongs that bind thee. Out on thee, coward! is this how thou hast galled her wrists? Didst think thou wert lashing up a lion or bull? or wert afraid she would snatch a sword and defend herself against thee? Come, child, nestle to thy mother's arms; help me loose her bonds; I will yet rear thee in Phthia to be their bitter foe. If your reputation for prowess and the battles ye have fought were taken from you Spartans, in all else, be very sure, you have not your inferiors.

Ch. The race of old men practises no restraint; and their testiness makes it hard to check them.

Men. Thou art only too ready to rush into abuse; while, as for me, I came to Phthia by constraint and have therefore no intention either of doing or suffering anything mean. Now must I return home, for I have no time to waste; for there is a city not so very far from Sparta, which aforetime was friendly but now is hostile; against her will I march with my army and bring her into subjection. And when I have arranged that matter as I wish, I will return; and face to face with my son-in-law I will give my version of the story and hear his. And if he punish her, and for the future she exercise self-control, she shall find me do the like; but if he storm, I'll storm as well; and every act of mine shall be a reflex of his own. As for thy babbling, I can bear it easily; for, like to a shadow as thou art, thy voice is all thou hast, and thou art powerless to do aught but talk.

Exit MENELAUS.

Pe. Lead on, my child, safe beneath my sheltering wing, and thou too, poor lady; for thou art come into a quiet haven after the rude storm.

An. Heaven reward thee and all thy race, old sire, for having saved my child and me his hapless mother! Only beware lest they fall upon us twain in some lonely spot upon the road and force me from thee, when they see thy age, my weakness, and this child's tender years; take heed to this, that we be not a second time made captive, after escaping now.

Pe. Forbear such words, prompted by a woman's cowardice. Go on thy way; who will lay a finger on you? Methinks he will do it to his cost. For by heaven's grace I rule o'er many a knight and spearman bold in my kingdom of Phthia; yea, and myself can still stand straight, no bent old man as thou dost think; such a fellow as that a mere look from me will put to flight in spite of my years. For e'en an old man, be he brave, is worth a host of raw youths; for what avails a fine figure if a man is a coward?

Exeunt PELEUS, ANDROMACHE, *and* MOLOSSUS.

Ch. Oh! to have never been born, or sprung from noble sires, the heir to mansions richly stored; for if aught untoward e'er befall, there is no lack of champions for sons of noble parents, and there is honour and glory for them when they are proclaimed scions of illustrious lines; time detracts not from the legacy these good men leave, but the light of their goodness still burns on when they are dead. Better is it not to win a discreditable victory, than to make justice miscarry by an invidious exercise of power; for such a victory, though men think it sweet for the moment, grows barren in time and comes very near being a family reproach. This is the life I commend, this the life I set before me as my ideal, to exercise no authority beyond what is right either in the marriage-chamber or in the state. O aged son of Æacus! now am I sure that thou wert with the Lapithæ, wielding thy famous spear, when they fought the Centaurs; and on Argo's deck didst pass the cheerless strait beyond the sea-beat Symplegades on her voyage of note; and when in days long gone the son of Zeus spread slaughter round Troy's famous town, thou too didst share his triumphant return to Europe.

Enter NURSE.

Nurse. Alas! good friends, what a succession of troubles is to-day provided us! My mistress Hermione within the house, deserted by her father and in remorse for her monstrous deed in plotting the death of Andromache and her child, is bent on dying; for she is afraid her husband will in requital for this expel her with dishonour from his house or put her to death, because she tried to slay the innocent. And the servants that watch her can scarce restrain her efforts to hang herself, scarce catch the sword and wrest it from her hand. So bitter is her anguish, and she hath recognized the villainy of her former deeds. As for me, friends, I am weary of keeping my mistress from the fatal noose; do ye go in and try to save her life; for if strangers come, they prove more persuasive than the friends of every day.

Ch. Ah yes! I hear an outcry in the house amongst the servants, confirming the news thou hast brought. Poor sufferer! she seems about to show a lively grief for her grave crimes; for she has escaped her servants' hands and is rushing from the house, eager to end her life.

He. (*Rushing wildly on to the stage*) Woe, woe is me! I will tear my hair and scratch cruel furrows in my cheeks.

Nu. My child, what wilt thou do? Wilt thou disfigure thyself?

He. Ah me! ah me! Begone, thou fine-spun veil! float from my head away!

Nu. Daughter, cover up thy bosom, fasten thy robe.

He. Why should I cover it? My crimes against my lord are manifest and clear, they cannot be hidden.

Nu. Art so grieved at having devised thy rival's death?

He. Indeed I am; I deeply mourn my fatal deeds of daring; alas! I am now accursed in all men's eyes!

Nu. Thy husband will pardon thee this error.

He. Oh! why didst thou hunt me to snatch away my sword? Give, oh! give it back, dear nurse, that I may thrust it through my heart. Why dost thou prevent me hanging myself?

Nu. What! was I to let thy madness lead thee on to death?

He. Ah me, my destiny! Where can I find some friendly fire? To what rocky height can I climb above the sea or 'mid some wooded mountain glen, there to die and trouble but the dead?

Nu. Why vex thyself thus? on all of us sooner or later heaven's visitation comes.

He. Thou hast left me, O my father, left me like a stranded bark, all alone, without an oar. My lord will surely slay me; no home is mine henceforth beneath my husband's roof. What god is there to whose statue I can as a suppliant haste? or shall I throw myself in slavish wise at slavish knees? Would I could speed away from Phthia's land on bird's dark pinion, or like that pine-built ship,[1] the first that ever sailed betwixt the rocks Cyanean!

Nu. My child, I can as little praise thy previous sinful excesses, committed against the Trojan captive, as thy present exaggerated terror. Thy husband will never listen to a barbarian's weak pleading and reject his marriage with thee for this. For thou wast no captive from Troy whom he wedded, but the daughter of a gallant sire, with a rich dower, from a city too of no mean prosperity. Nor will thy father forsake thee, as thou dreadest, and allow thee to be cast out from this house. Nay, enter now, nor show thyself before the palace, lest the sight of thee there bring reproach upon thee, my daughter.

Ch. Lo! a stranger of foreign appearance from some other land comes hurrying towards us.

Enter ORESTES.

Orestes. Ladies of this foreign land! is this the home, the palace of Achilles' son?

Ch. Thou hast it; but who art thou to ask such a question?

Or. The son of Agamemnon and Clytaemnestra, by name Orestes, on my way to the oracle of Zeus at Dodona. But now that I am come to Phthia, I am resolved to inquire about my kinswoman, Hermione of Sparta; is she alive and well? for though she dwells in a land far from my own, I love her none the less.

He. Son of Agamemnon, thy appearing is as a haven from the storm to sailors; by thy knees I pray, have pity on me in my distress, on me of whose fortunes thou art inquiring. About thy knees I twine my arms with all the force of sacred fillets.

Or. Ha! what is this? Am I mistaken or do I really see before me the queen of this palace, the daughter of Menelaus?

He. The same, that only child whom Helen, daughter of Tyndareus, bore my father in his halls; never doubt that.

Or. O saviour Phœbus, grant us respite from our woe! But what is the matter? art thou afflicted by gods or men?

He. Partly by myself, partly by the man who wedded me, and partly by some god. On every side I see ruin.

Or. Why, what misfortune could happen to a woman as yet childless, unless her honour is concerned?

He. My very complaint! Thou hast hit my case exactly.

Or. On whom has thy husband set his affections in thy stead?

He. On his captive, Hector's wife.

Or. An evil case indeed, for a man to have two wives.

He. 'Tis even thus. So I resented it.

Or. Didst thou with woman's craft devise a plot against thy rival?

He. Yes, to slay her and her bastard child.

Or. And didst thou slay them, or did something happen to rescue them from thee?

[1]Argo.

He. It was old Peleus, who showed regard to the weaker side.

Or. Hadst thou any accomplice in this attempted murder?

He. My father came from Sparta for this very purpose.

Or. And was he after all defeated by that old man's prowess?

He. Oh no! but by shame; and he hath gone and left me all alone.

Or. I understand; thou art afraid of thy husband for what thou hast done.

He. Thou hast guessed it; for he will have a right to slay me. What can I say for myself? Yet I beseech thee by Zeus the god of our family, send me to a land as far as possible from this, or to my father's house; for these very walls seem to cry out "Begone!" and all the land of Phthia hates me. But if my lord return ere that from the oracle of Phœbus, he will put me to death on a shameful charge, or enslave me to his mistress, whom I ruled before. Maybe some one will say, "How was it thou didst go thus astray?" I was ruined by mischievous women who came to me and puffed me up with words like these: "What! wilt thou suffer that vile captive, a mere bondmaid, to dwell within thy house and share thy wedded rights? By Heaven's queen! if it were my house she should not live to reap my marriage-harvest!" And I listened to the words of these Sirens, the cunning, knavish, subtle praters, and was filled with silly thoughts. What need had I to care about my lord? I had all I wanted, wealth in plenty, a house in which I was mistress, and as for children, mine would be born in wedlock, while hers would be bastards, half-slaves to mine. Oh! never, never—this truth will I repeat—should men of sense, who have wives, allow women-folk to visit them in their homes, for they teach them mischief; one, to gain some private end, helps to corrupt their honour; another, having made a slip herself, wants a companion in misfortune, while many are wantons; and hence it is men's houses are tainted. Wherefore keep strict guard upon the portals of your houses with bolts and bars; for these visits of strange women lead to no good result, but a world of mischief.

Ch. Thou hast given thy tongue too free a rein regarding thy own sex. I can pardon thee in this case, but still women ought to smooth over their sisters' weaknesses.

Or. 'Twas sage counsel he gave who taught men to hear the arguments on both sides. I, for instance, though aware of the confusion in this house, the quarrel between thee and Hector's wife, waited awhile and watched to see whether thou wouldst stay here or from fear of that captive art minded to quit these halls. Now it was not so much regard for thy message that brought me hither, as the intention of carrying thee away from this house, if, as now, thou shouldst grant me a chance of saying so. For thou wert mine formerly, but art now living with thy present husband through thy father's baseness; since he, before invading Troy's domains, betrothed thee to me, and then afterwards promised thee to thy present lord, provided he captured the city of Troy.

So, as soon as Achilles' son returned hither, I forgave thy father, but entreated the bridegroom to forego his marriage with thee, telling him all I had gone through and my present misfortune; I might get a wife, I said, from amongst friends, but outside their circle 'twas no easy task for one exiled like myself from home. Thereat he grew abusive, taunting me with my mother's murder and those blood-boltered fiends. And I was humbled by the fortunes of my house, and though 'tis true, I grieved, yet did I endure my sorrow, and reluctantly departed, robbed of thy promised hand. Now therefore, since thou findest thy fortune so abruptly changed and art fallen thus on evil days and hast no help, I will take thee hence and place thee in thy father's hands. For kinship hath strong claims, and in adversity there is naught better than a kinsman's kindly aid.

He. As for my marriage, my father must look to it; 'tis not for me to decide that. Yes, take me hence as soon as may be, lest my husband come back to his house before I am gone, or Peleus hear that I am deserting his son's abode and pursue me on horseback.

Or. Rest easy about the old man's power; and, as for Achilles' son with all his insolence to me, never fear him; such a crafty net this hand hath woven and set for his death with knots that none can loose; whereof I will not speak before the time, but, when my plot begins to work, Delphi's rock will witness it. If but my allies in the Pythian land abide by their oaths, this same murderer of his mother will show that no one else shall marry thee my rightful bride. To his cost will he demand satisfaction of King Phœbus for his father's blood; nor shall his repentance avail him, though he is now submitting to the god. No! he shall perish miserably by Apollo's hand and my false accusations; so shall he find out my enmity. For the deity upsets the fortune of them that hate him, and suffers them not to be high-minded. *Exeunt* ORESTES *and* HERMIONE.

Ch. O Phœbus! who didst fence the hill of Ilium with a fair coronal of towers, and thou, ocean-god! coursing o'er the main with thy dark steeds, wherefore did ye hand over in dishonour your own handiwork to the war-god, master of the spear, abandoning Troy to wretchedness? Many a well-horsed car ye yoked on the banks of Simois, and many a bloody tournament did ye ordain with never a prize to win; and Ilium's princes are dead and gone; no longer in Troy is seen the blaze of fire on altars of the gods with the smoke of incense. The son of Atreus is no more, slain by the hand of his wife, and she herself hath paid the debt of blood by death, and from her children's hands received her doom. The god's own bidding from his oracle was levelled against her, in the day that Agamemnon's son set forth from Argos and visited his shrine; so he slew her, aye, spilt his own mother's blood. O Phœbus, O thou power divine, how can I believe the story? Anon wherever

Hellenes gather, was heard the voice of lamentation, mothers weeping o'er their children's fate, as they left their homes to mate with strangers. Ah! thou art not the only one, nor thy dear ones either, on whom the cloud of grief hath fallen. Hellas had to bear the visitation, and thence the scourge crossed to Phrygia's fruitful fields, raining the bloody drops the death-god loves.

Enter PELEUS.

Pe. Ye dames of Phthia, answer my questions. I heard a vague rumour that the daughter of Menelaus had left these halls and fled; so now am I come in hot haste to learn if this be true; for it is the duty of those who are at home to labour in the interests of their absent friends.

Ch. Thou hast heard aright, O Peleus; ill would it become me to hide the evil case in which I now find myself; our queen has fled and left these halls.

Pe. What was she afraid of? explain that to me.

*Ch.*She was fearful her lord would cast her out.

*Pe.*In return for plotting his child's death? surely not?

Ch. Yea, and she was afraid of yon captive.

Pe. With whom did she leave the house? with her father?

Ch. The son of Agamemnon came and took her hence.

Pe. What view hath he to further thereby? Will he marry her?

Ch. Yes, and he is plotting thy grandson's death.

Pe. From an ambuscade, or meeting him fairly face to face?

Ch. In the holy place of Loxias, leagued with Delphians.

Pe. God help us! This is an immediate danger. Hasten one of you with all speed to the Pythian altar and tell our friends there what has happened here, ere Achilles' son be slain by his enemies.

Enter a MESSENGER.

Messenger. Woe worth the day! what evil tidings have I brought for thee, old sire, and for all who love my master! woe is me!

Pe. Alas! my prophetic soul hath a presentiment.

Mes. Aged Peleus, hearken! Thy grandson is no more; so grievously is he smitten by the men of Delphi and the stranger[1] from Mycenæ.

Ch. Ah! what wilt thou do, old man? Fall not; uplift thyself.

Pe. I am a thing of naught; death is come upon me. My voice is choked, my limbs droop beneath me.

Mes. Hearken; if thou art eager also to avenge thy friends, lift up thyself and hear what happened.

Pe. Ah, destiny! how tightly hast thou caught me in thy toils, a poor old man at life's extremest verge! But tell me how he was taken from me, my one son's only child; unwelcome as such news is, I fain would hear it.

Mes. As soon as we reached the famous soil of Phœbus, for three whole days were we feasting our eyes with the sight. And this, it seems, caused suspicion; for the folk, who dwell near the god's shrine, began to collect in groups, while Agamemnon's son, going to and fro through the town, would whisper in each man's ear malignant hints: "Do ye see yon fellow, going in and out of the god's treasure-chambers, which are full of the gold stored there by all mankind? He is come hither a second time on the same mission as before, eager to sack the temple of Phœbus." Thereon there ran an angry murmur through the city, and the magistrates flocked to their council-chamber, while those, who have charge of the god's treasures, had a guard privately placed amongst the colonnades. But we, knowing naught as yet of this, took sheep fed in the pastures of Parnassus, and went our way and stationed ourselves at the altars with vouchers and Pythian seers. And one said: "What prayer, young warrior, wouldst thou have us offer to the god? Wherefore art thou come? And he answered: "I wish to make atonement to Phœbus for my past transgression; for once I claimed from him satisfaction for my father's blood." Thereupon the rumour, spread by Orestes, proved to have great weight, suggesting that my master was lying and had come on a shameful errand. But he crosses the threshold of the temple to pray to Phœbus before his oracle, and was busy with his burnt-offering; when a body of men armed with swords set themselves in ambush against him in the cover of the bay-trees, and Clytaemnestra's son, that had contrived the whole plot was one of them. There stood the young man praying to the god in sight of all, when lo! with their sharp swords they stabbed Achilles' unprotected son from behind. But he stepped back, for it was not a mortal wound he had received, and drew his sword, and snatching armour from the pegs where it hung on a pillar, took his stand upon the altar-steps, the picture of a warrior grim; then cried he to the sons of Delphi, and asked them: "Why seek to slay me when I am come on a holy mission? What cause is there why I should die?" But of all that throng of bystanders, no man answered him a word, but they set to hurling stones. Then he, though bruised and battered by the showers of missiles from all sides, covered himself behind his mail and tried to ward off the attack, holding his shield first here, then there, at arm's length, but all of no avail; for a storm of darts, arrows and javelins, hurtling spits with double points, and butchers' knives for slaying steers, came flying at his feet; and terrible was the war-dance thou hadst then seen thy grandson dance to avoid their marksmanship. At last, when they were hemming him in on all sides, allowing him no breathing space, he left the shelter of the altar, the hearth where victims are placed, and with one bound was on them as on the Trojans of yore; and they turned and fled like doves when they see the hawk. Many fell in the confusion; some wounded, and others trodden down by one another along the narrow passages; and in that hushed holy house uprose unholy din and echoed back from the rocks. Calm and still my master stood there in his

[1] *i.e.* Orestes.

gleaming harness like a flash of light, till from the inmost shrine there came a voice of thrilling horror, stirring the crowd to make a stand. Then fell Achilles' son, smitten through the flank by some Delphian's biting blade, some fellow that slew him with a host to help; and as he fell, there was not one that did not stab him, or cast a rock and batter his corpse. So his whole body, once so fair, was marred with savage wounds. At last they cast the lifeless clay, lying near the altar, forth from the fragrant fane. And we gathered up his remains forthwith and are bringing them to thee, old prince, to mourn and weep and honour with a deep-dug tomb.

This is how that prince who vouchsafeth oracles to others, that judge of what is right for all the world, hath revenged himself on Achilles' son, remembering his ancient quarrel as a wicked man would. How then can he be wise?

Exit MESSENGER.

The body of NEOPTOLEMUS *is carried in on a bier.*

Ch. Lo! e'en now our prince is being carried on a bier from Delphi's land unto his home. Woe for him and his sad fate, and woe for thee, old sire! for this is not the welcome thou wouldst give Achilles' son, the lion's whelp; thyself too by this sad mischance dost share his evil lot.

Pe. Ah! woe is me! here is a sad sight for me to see and take unto my halls! Ah me! ah me! I am undone, thou city of Thessaly! My line now ends; I have no children left me in my home. Oh! the sorrows I seem born to endure! What friend can I look to for relief? Ah, dear lips, and cheeks, and hands! Would thy destiny had slain thee 'neath Ilium's walls beside the banks of Simois!

Ch. Had he so died, my aged lord, he had won him honour thereby, and thine had been the happier lot.

Pe. O marriage, marriage, woe to thee! thou bane of my home, thou destroyer of my city! Ah my child, my boy! would that the honour of wedding thee, fraught with evil as it was to my children and house, had not thrown o'er thee, my son, Hermione's deadly net! O that the thunderbolt had slain her sooner! and that thou, rash mortal, hadst never charged the great god Phœbus with aiming that murderous shaft that spilt thy hero-father's blood!

Ch. Woe! woe! alas! With due observance of funeral rites will I begin the mourning for my dead master.

Pe. Alack and well-a-day! I take up the tearful dirge, ah me! old and wretched as I am.

Ch. 'Tis Heaven's decree; God willed this heavy stroke.

Pe. O darling child, thou hast left me all alone in my halls, old and childless by thy loss.

Ch. Thou shouldst have died, old sire, before thy children.

Pe. Shall I not tear my hair, and smite upon my head with grievous blows? O city! of both my children hath Phœbus robbed me.

Ch. What evils thou hast suffered, what sorrows thou hast seen, thou poor old man! what shall be thy life hereafter?

Pe. Childless, desolate, with no limit to my grief, I must drain the cup of woe, until I die.

Ch. 'Twas all in vain the gods wished thee joy on thy wedding day.

Pe. All my hopes have flown away, fallen short of my high boasts.

Ch. A lonely dweller in a lonely home art thou.

Pe. I have no city any longer; there! on the ground my sceptre do I cast; and thou, daughter of Nereus, 'neath thy dim grotto, shalt see me grovelling in the dust, a ruined king.

Ch. Look, look! (*A dim form of divine appearance is seen hovering in mid air*) What is that moving? what influence divine am I conscious of? Look, maidens, mark it well; see, yonder is some deity, wafted through the lustrous air and alighting on the plains of Phthia, home of steeds.

THETIS *descends onto the stage.*

Thetis. O Peleus! because of my wedded days with thee now long agone, I Thetis am come from the halls of Nereus. And first I counsel thee not to grieve to excess in thy present distress, for I too who need ne'er have born children to my sorrow, have lost the child of our love, Achilles swift of foot, foremost of the sons of Hellas. Next will I declare why I am come, and do thou give ear. Carry yonder corpse, Achilles' son, to the Pythian altar and there bury it, a reproach to Delphi, that his tomb may proclaim the violent death he met at the hand of Orestes. And for his captive wife Andromache—she must dwell in the Molossian land, united in honourable wedlock with Helenus, and with her this babe, the sole survivor as he is of all the line of Æacus, for from him a succession of prosperous kings of Molossia is to go on unbroken; for the race that springs from thee and me, my aged lord, must not thus be brought to naught; no! nor Troy's line either; for her fate too is cared for by the gods, albeit her fall was due to the eager wish of Pallas. Thee too, that thou mayst know the saving grace of wedding me, will I, a goddess born and daughter of a god, release from all the ills that flesh is heir to and make a deity to know not death nor decay. From henceforth in the halls of Nereus shalt thou dwell with me, god and goddess together; thence shalt thou rise dry-shod from out the main and see Achilles, our dear son, settled in his island-home by the strand of Leuce, that is girdled by the Euxine sea. But get thee to Delphi's god-built town, carrying this corpse with thee, and, after thou hast buried him, return and settle in the cave which time hath hollowed in the Sepian rock and there abide, till from the sea I come with choir of fifty Nereids to be thy escort thence; for fate's decree thou must fulfil; such is the pleasure of Zeus. Cease then to mourn the dead; this is the lot which heaven assigns to all, and all must pay their debt to death.

Pe. Great queen, my honoured wife, from Nereus sprung, all hail! thou art acting herein as befits thyself and thy children. So I will stay my grief at thy bidding, goddess, and, when I have buried the dead, will seek the glens of Pelion, even the place where I took thy beauteous form to my embrace. (*Exit* THETIS.) Surely after this every prudent man will seek to marry a wife of noble stock and give his daughter to a husband good and true, never setting his heart on a worthless woman, not even though she bring a sumptuous dowry to his house. So would men ne'er suffer ill at heaven's hand.

Ch. Many are the shapes of Heaven's denizens, and many a thing they bring to pass contrary to our expectation; that which we thought would be is not accomplished, while for the unexpected God finds out a way. E'en such hath been the issue of this matter.

Exeunt OMNES.

ELECTRA

DRAMATIS PERSONAE

PEASANT, *of Mycenae*	CLYTAEMNESTRA
ELECTRA	OLD MAN
ORESTES	MESSENGER
CHORUS OF ARGIVE COUNTRY-WOMEN	THE DIOSCURI

Mute: PYLADES

On the borders of Argolis. Enter PEASANT.

Peasant. O Argos, ancient land, and streams of Inachus, whence on a day king Agamemnon sailed to the realm of Troy, carrying his warriors aboard a thousand ships; and after he had slain Priam who was reigning in Ilium and captured the famous city of Dardanus, he came hither to Argos and has set up high on the temple-walls many a trophy, spoil of the barbarians. Though all went well with him in Troy, yet was he slain in his own palace by the guile of his wife Clytaemnestra and the hand of Ægisthus, son of Thyestes. So he died and left behind him the ancient sceptre of Tantalus, and Ægisthus reigns in his stead, with the daughter of Tyndareus, Agamemnon's queen, to wife. Now as for those whom he left in his halls, when he sailed to Troy, his son Orestes and his tender daughter Electra—the boy Orestes, as he was like to be slain by Ægisthus, his sire's old foster-father secretly removed to the land of Phocis and gave to Strophius to bring up, but the maid Electra abode in her father's house, and soon as she had budded into maidenhood, came all the princes of Hellas asking her hand in marriage. But Ægisthus kept her at home for fear she might bear a son to some chieftain who would avenge Agamemnon, nor would he betroth her unto any. But when e'en thus there seemed some room for fear that she might bear some noble lord a child by stealth and Ægisthus was minded to slay her, her mother, though she had a cruel heart, yet rescued the maiden from his hand. For she could find excuses for having slain her husband, but she feared the hatred she would incur for her children's murder. Wherefore Ægisthus devised this scheme; on Agamemnon's son who had escaped his realm by flight he set a price to be paid to any who should slay him, while he gave Electra to me in marriage, whose ancestors were citizens of Mycenæ. It is not *that* I blame myself for; my family was noble enough, though certainly impoverished, and so my good birth suffers. By making for her this weak alliance he thought he would have little to fear. For if some man of high position had married her, he might have revived the vengeance for Agamemnon's murder, which now is sleeping; in which case Ægisthus would have paid the penalty. But Cypris is my witness that I have ever respected her maidenhood; she is still as though unwed. Unworthy as I am, honour forbids that I should so affront the daughter of a better man. Yea, and I am sorry for Orestes, hapless youth, who is called my kinsman, to think that he should ever return to Argos and behold his sister's wretched marriage. And whoso counts me but a fool for leaving a tender maid untouched when I have her in my house, to him I say, he measures purity by the vicious standard of his own soul, a standard like himself.

Enter ELECTRA.

Electra. O sable night, nurse of the golden stars! beneath thy pall I go to fetch water from the brook with my pitcher poised upon my head, not indeed because I am reduced to this necessity, but that to the gods I may display the affronts Ægisthus puts upon me, and to the wide firmament pour out my lamentation for my sire. For my own mother, the baleful daughter of Tyndareus, hath cast me forth from her house to gratify her lord; for since she hath born no other children to Ægisthus she puts me and Orestes on one side at home.

Pe. Oh! why, poor maiden, dost thou toil so hard on my behalf, thou that aforetime wert reared so daintily? why canst thou not forego thy labour, as I bid thee?

El. As a god's I count thy kindness to me, for in my distress thou hast never made a mock at me. 'Tis rare fortune when mortals find such healing balm for their cruel wounds as 'tis my lot to find in thee. Wherefore I ought, though thou forbid me, to lighten thy labours, as far as my strength allows, and share all burdens with thee to ease thy load. Thou hast enough to do abroad; 'tis only right that I should keep thy house in order. For when the toiler cometh to his home from the field, it is pleasant to find all comfortable in the house.

Pe. If such thy pleasure, go thy way; for, after all, the spring is no great distance from my house. And at break of day I will drive my steers to my glebe and sow my crop. For no idler, though he has the gods' names ever on his lips, can gather a livelihood without hard work.

Exeunt PEASANT *and* ELECTRA.

Enter ORESTES *and* PYLADES.

Orestes. Ah! Pylades, I put thee first 'mongst men

for thy love, thy loyalty and friendliness to me; for thou alone of all my friends wouldst still honour poor Orestes, in spite of the grievous plight whereto I am reduced by Ægisthus, who with my accursed mother's aid slew my sire. I am come from Apollo's mystic shrine to the soil of Argos, without the knowledge of any, to avenge my father's death upon his murderers. Last night I went unto his tomb and wept thereon, cutting off my hair as an offering and pouring o'er the grave the blood of a sheep for sacrifice, unmarked by those who lord it o'er this land. And now though I enter not the walled town, yet by coming to the borders of the land I combine two objects; I can escape to another country if any spy me out and recognize me, and at the same time seek my sister, for I am told she is a maid no longer but is married and living here, that I may meet her, and after enlisting her aid in the deed of blood, learn for certain what is happening in the town. Let us now, since dawn is uplifting her radiant eye, step aside from this path. For maybe some labouring man or serving maid will come in sight, of whom we may inquire whether it is here that my sister hath her home. Lo! yonder I see a servant bearing a full pitcher of water on her shaven head; let us sit down and make inquiry of this bondmaid, if haply we may glean some tidings of the matter which brought us hither, Pylades. (*They retire a little*)

Re-enter ELECTRA.

El. Bestir thy lagging feet, 'tis high time; on, on o'er thy path of tears! ah misery! I am Agamemnon's daughter, she whom Clytæmnestra, hateful child of Tyndareus, bare; hapless Electra is the name my countrymen call me. Ah me! for my cruel lot, my hateful existence! O my father Agamemnon! in Hades art thou laid, butchered by thy wife and Ægisthus. Come, raise with me that dirge once more; uplift the woful strain that brings relief. On, on o'er thy path of tears! ah misery! And thou, poor brother, in what city and house art thou a slave, leaving thy suffering sister behind in the halls of our fathers to drain the cup of bitterness? Oh! come, great Zeus, to set me free from this life of sorrow, and to avenge my sire in the blood of his foes, bringing the wanderer home to Argos.

Take this pitcher from my head, put it down, that I may wake betimes, while it is yet night, my lamentation for my sire, my doleful chant, my dirge of death, for thee, my father in thy grave, which day by day I do rehearse, rending my skin with my nails, and smiting on my shaven head in mourning for thy death. Woe, woe! rend the cheek; like a swan with clear loud note beside the brimming river calling to its parent dear that lies a-dying in the meshes of the crafty net, so I bewail thee, my hapless sire, after that fatal bath of thine laid out most piteously in death.

Oh! the horror of that axe which hacked thee so cruelly, my sire! oh! the bitter thought that prompted thy return from Troy! With no garlands or victor's crowns did thy wife welcome thee, but with his two-edged sword she made thee the sad sport of Ægisthus and kept her treacherous paramour.

Enter CHORUS OF ARGIVE COUNTRY-WOMEN.

Chorus. O Electra, daughter of Agamemnon, to thy rustic cot I come, for a messenger hath arrived, a highlander from Mycenæ, one who lives on milk, announcing that the Argives are proclaiming a sacrifice for the third day from now, and all our maidens are to go to Hera's temple.

El. Kind friends, my heart is not set on festivity, nor do necklaces of gold cause any flutter in my sorrowing bosom, nor will I stand up with the maidens of Argos to beat my foot in the mazy dance. Tears have been my meat day and night; ah misery! See my unkempt hair, my tattered dress; are they fit for a princess, a daughter of Agamemnon, or for Troy which once thought of my father as its captor?

Ch. Mighty is the goddess; so come, and borrow of me broidered robes for apparel and jewels of gold that add a further grace to beauty's charms. Dost think to triumph o'er thy foes by tears, if thou honour not the gods? 'Tis not by lamentation but by pious prayers to heaven that thou, my daughter, wilt make fortune smile on thee.

El. No god hearkens to the voice of lost Electra, or heeds the sacrifices offered by my father long ago. Ah woe for the dead! woe for the living wanderer, who dwelleth in some foreign land, an outcast and a vagabond at a menial board, sprung though he is of a famous sire! Myself, too, in a poor man's hut do dwell, wasting my soul with grief, an exile from my father's halls, here by the scarred hill-side; while my mother is wedded to a new husband in a marriage stained by blood.

Ch. Many a woe to Hellas and thy house did Helen, thy mother's sister, cause.

El. Ha! (*Catching sight of* ORESTES *and* PYLADES) Friends, I break off my lament; yonder are strangers just leaving the place of ambush where they were couching, and making for the house. We must seek to escape the villains by flying, thou along the path and I into my cottage.

Or. Stay, poor maid; fear no violence from me.

El. O Phœbus Apollo! I beseech thee spare my life.

Or. Give me the lives of others more my foes than thou!

El. Begone! touch me not! thou hast no right to.

Or. There is none I have better right to touch.

El. How is it then thou waylayest me, sword in hand, near my house?

Or. Wait and hear, and thou wilt soon agree with me.

El. Here I stand; I am in thy power in any case, since thou art the stronger.

Or. I am come to thee with news of thy brother.

El. O best of friends! is he alive or dead?

Or. Alive; I would fain give thee my good news first.

El. God bless thee! in return for thy welcome tidings.

Or. I am prepared to share that blessing between us.

El. In what land is my poor brother spending his dreary exile?

Or. His ruined life does not conform to the customs of any one city.

El. Surely he does not want for daily bread?

Or. Bread he has, but an exile is a helpless man at best.

El. What is this message thou hast brought from him?

Or. He asks, "Art thou alive? and if so, How art thou faring?"

El. Well, first thou seest how haggard I am grown

Or. So wasted with sorrow that I weep for thee.

El. Next mark my head, shorn and shaven like a Scythian's.

Or. Thy brother's fate and father's death no doubt distress thee.

El. Yes, alas! for what have I more dear than these?

Or. Ah! and what dost thou suppose is dearer to thy brother?

El. He is far away, not here to show his love to me.

Or. Wherefore art thou living here far from the city?

El. I am wedded, sir; a fatal match!

Or. Alas! for thy brother; I pity him. Is thy husband of Mycenæ?

El. He is not the man to whom my father ever thought of betrothing me.

Or. Tell me all, that I may report it to thy brother.

El. I live apart from my husband in this house.

Or. The only fit inmate would be a hind or herd.

El. Poor he is, yet he displays a generous consideration for me.

Or. Why, what is this consideration that attaches to thy husband?

El. He has never presumed to claim from me a husband's rights.

Or. Is he under a vow of chastity? or does he disdain thee?

El. He thought he had no right to flout my ancestry.

Or. How was it he was not overjoyed at winning uch a bride?

El. He does not recognize the right of him who disposed of my hand.

Or. I understand; he was afraid of the vengeance of Orestes hereafter.

El. There was that fear, but he was a virtuous man as well.

Or. Ah! a noble nature this! He deserves kind treatment.

El. Yes, if ever the wanderer return.

Or. But did thy own mother give in to this?

El. 'Tis her husband, not her children that a woman loves, sir stranger.

Or. Wherefore did Ægisthus put this affront on thee?

El. His design in giving me to such a husband was to weaken my offspring.

Or. To prevent thee bearing sons, I suppose, who should punish him?

El. That was his plan; God grant I may avenge me on him for it!

Or. Does thy mother's husband know that thou art yet a maid?

El. He does not; our silence robs him of that knowledge.

Or. Are these women friends of thine, who overhear our talk?

El. They are, and they will keep our conversation perfectly secret.

Or. What could Orestes do in this matter, if he *did* return?

El. Canst thou ask? Shame on thee for that! Is not this the time for action?

Or. But suppose he comes, how could he slay his father's murderers?

El. By boldly meting out the same fate that his father had meted out to him by his foes.

Or. Wouldst thou be brave enough to help him slay his mother?

El. Aye, with the self-same axe that drank my father's blood.

Or. Am I to tell him this, and that thy purpose firmly holds?

El. Once I have shed my mother's blood o'er his, then welcome death!

Or. Ah! would Orestes were standing near to hear that!

El. I should not know him, sir, if I saw him.

Or. No wonder; you were both children when you parted.

El. There is only one of my friends would recognize him.

Or. The man maybe who is said to have snatched him away from being murdered?

El. Yes, the old servant who tended my father's childhood long ago.

Or. Did thy father's corpse obtain burial?

El. Such burial as it was, after his body had been flung forth from the palace.

Or. O God! how awful is thy story! Yes, there *is* a feeling, arising even from another's distress, that wrings the human heart. Say on, that when I know the loveless tale, which yet I needs must hear, I may carry it to thy brother. For pity, though it has no place in clownish natures, is inborn in the wise; still it may cause mischief to find excessive cleverness amongst the wise.

Ch. I too am animated by the same desire as the stranger. For dwelling so far from the city I know nothing of the town's scandals, and I should like to hear about them now myself.

El. I will tell you, if I may; and surely I may tell a friend about my own and my father's grievous misfortunes. Now since thou movest me to speak, I entreat thee, sir, tell Orestes of our sorrows; first, describe the dress I wear, the load of squalor that oppresses me, the hovel I inhabit after my royal home; tell him how hard I have to work at weaving clothes myself or else go barely clad and do without; how I carry home on my head water from the brook; no part have I in holy festival, no place amid the dance; a maiden still I turn from married dames and from Castor too, to whom they betrothed me before he joined the heavenly host, for I was his kinswoman. Meantime my mother, 'mid the spoils of Troy, is seated on her throne, and at her footstool slaves from Asia stand and wait, captives of my father's spear, whose Trojan robes are fastened with brooches of gold. And there on the wall my father's blood still leaves a deep dark stain, while his murderer mounts the dead man's car and fareth forth, proudly grasping in his blood-stained hands the sceptre with which Agamemnon would marshal the sons of Hellas. Dishonoured lies his grave; naught as yet hath it received a drink outpoured or myrtle-spray, but bare of ornament his tomb is left. Yea, and 'tis said that noble hero who is wedded to my mother, in his drunken fits, doth leap upon the grave, and pelt with stones my father's monument, boldly gibing at us on this wise, "Where is thy son Orestes? Is he ever coming in his glory to defend thy tomb?" Thus is Orestes flouted behind his back. Oh! tell him this, kind sir, I pray thee. And there be many calling him to come—I am but their mouthpiece—these suppliant hands, this tongue, my broken heart, my shaven head, and his own father too. For 'tis shameful that the sire should have exterminated Troy's race and the son yet prove too weak to pit himself against one foe unto the death, albeit he has youth and better blood to boot.

Ch. Lo! here is thy husband hurrying homeward, his day's work done.

Pe. (*Entering and catching sight of strangers talking to* ELECTRA) Ha! who are these strangers I see at my door? And why are they come hither to my rustic gate? can they want my help? for 'tis unseemly for a woman to stand talking with young men.

El. Dear husband, be not suspicious of me. For thou shalt hear the truth; these strangers have come to bring me news of Orestes. Good sirs, pardon him those words.

Pe. What say they? is that hero yet alive and in the light of day?

El. He is; at least they say so, and I believe them.

Pe. Surely then he hath some memory of his father and thy wrongs?

El. These are things to hope for; a man in exile is helpless.

Pe. What message have they brought from Orestes?

El. He sent them to spy out my evil case.

Pe. Well, they only see a part of it, though maybe thou art telling them the rest.

El. They know all; there is nothing further they need ask.

Pe. Long ere this then shouldst thou have thrown open our doors to them. Enter, sirs; for in return for your good tidings, shall ye find such cheer as my house affords. Ho! servants, take their baggage within; make no excuses, for ye are friends sent by one I love; and poor though I am, yet will I never show meanness in my habits.

Or. 'Fore heaven! is this the man who is helping thee to frustrate thy marriage, because he will not shame Orestes?

El. This is he whom they call my husband, woe is me!

Or. Ah! there is no sure mark to recognize a man's worth; for human nature hath in it an element of confusion. For instance, I have seen ere now the son of a noble sire prove himself a worthless knave, and virtuous children sprung from evil parents; likewise dearth in a rich man's spirit, and in a poor man's frame a mighty soul. By what standard then shall we rightly judge these things? By wealth? An evil test to use. By poverty then? Nay, poverty suffers from this, that it teaches a man to play the villain from necessity. To martial prowess must I turn? But who could pronounce who is the valiant man merely from the look of his spear? Better is it to leave these matters to themselves without troubling. For here is a man of no account in Argos, with no family reputation to boast, one of the common herd, proved a very hero. A truce to your folly! ye self-deceivers, swollen with idle fancies; learn to judge men by their converse, and by their habits decide who are noble. Such are they who rule aright both states and families; while those forms of flesh, devoid of intellect, are but figure-heads in the market-place. The strong arm, again, no more than the weak awaits the battle-shock, for this depends on natural courage. Well! absent or present, Agamemnon's son, whose business brings us here, deserves this of us, so let us accept a lodging in this house. (*Calling to his servants*) Ho! sirrahs, go within. A humble host, who does his best, in preference to a wealthy man for me! And so I thankfully accept this peasant's proffered welcome, though I could have preferred that thy brother were conducting me to share his fortune in his halls. Maybe he yet will come; for the oracles of Loxias are sure, but to man's divining "Farewell" say I.

Exeunt ORESTES *and* PYLADES.

Ch. Electra, I feel a warmer glow of joy suffuse my heart than ever heretofore; perchance our fortune, moving on at last, will find a happy resting-place.

El. O reckless man, why didst thou welcome strangers like these, so far beyond thy station, knowing the poverty of thy house?

Pe. Why? if they are really as noble as they seem, surely they will be equally content with rich or humble fare.

El. Well, since thou hast made this error, poor man as thou art, go to my father's kind old foster-sire; on the bank of the river Tanaus, the boundary 'twixt Argos and the land of Sparta, he tends his flocks, an outcast from the city; bid him come hither to our house and make some provision for the strangers' entertainment. Glad will he be, and will offer thanks to heaven to hear that the child, whom once he saved, is yet alive. I shall get nothing from my mother from my ancestral halls; for we should rue our message, were she to learn, unnatural wretch! that Orestes liveth.

Pe. I will take this message to the old man, if it seem good to thee; but get thee in at once and there make ready. A woman, when she chooses, can find dainties in plenty to garnish a feast. Besides, there is quite enough in the house to satisfy them with victuals for one day at least. 'Tis in such cases, when I come to muse thereon, that I discern the mighty power of wealth, whether to give to strangers, or to expend in curing the body when it falls sick; but our daily food is a small matter; for all of us, rich as well as poor, are in like case, as soon as we are satisfied.

Exeunt ELECTRA *and* PEASANT.

Ch. Ye famous ships, that on a day were brought to land at Troy by those countless oars, what time ye led the Nereid's dance, where the dolphin music-loving rolled and gambolled round your dusky prows, escorting Achilles, nimble son of Thetis, when he went with Agamemnon to the banks of Trojan Simois; when Nereids left Eubœa's strand, bringing from Hephæstus' golden forge the harness he had fashioned for that warrior's use; him long they sought o'er Pelion and Ossa's spurs, ranging the sacred glens and the peaks of Nymphæa, where his knightly sire was training up a light for Hellas, even the sea-born son of Thetis, a warrior swift to help the sons of Atreus.

One that came from Ilium, and set foot in the haven of Nauplia, told me that on the circle of thy far-famed targe, O son of Thetis, was wrought this blazon, a terror to the Phrygians; on the rim of the buckler Perseus with winged sandals, was bearing in his hand across the main the Gorgon's head, just severed by the aid of Hermes, the messenger of Zeus, that rural god whom Maia bore; while in the centre of the shield the sun's bright orb flashed light on the backs of his winged coursers; there too was the heavenly choir of stars, Pleiades and Hyades, to dazzle Hector's eyes and make him flee; and upon his gold-forged helm were sphinxes, bearing in their talons the prey of which the minstrels sing;[1] on his breast-plate was a lioness breathing flame, her eye upon Peirene's steed, in eagerness to rend it. There too in murderous fray four-footed steeds were prancing, while o'er their backs uprose dark clouds of dust. But he who led these warriors stout, was slain by wedding thee, malignant child of Tyndareus! Wherefore shall the gods of heaven one day send thee to thy doom, and I shall yet live to see the sword at thy throat, drinking its crimson tide.

Enter OLD MAN.

Old Man. Where is the young princess, my mistress, Agamemnon's daughter, whom I nursed in days gone by? Oh! how steep is the approach to this house, a hard climb for these old wasted feet of mine! Still, to reach such friends as these, I must drag my bent old back and tottering knees up it. Ah, daughter!—for I see thee now at thy door—lo! I have brought thee this tender lamb from my own flock, having taken it from its dam, with garlands too and cheese straight from the press, and this flask of choice old wine with fragrant bouquet; 'tis small perhaps, but pour a cup thereof into some weaker drink, and it is a luscious draught. Let some one carry these gifts into the house for the guests; for I would fain wipe from my eyes the rising tears on this tattered cloak.

El. Why stands the tear-drop in thine eye, old friend? Is it that my sorrows have been recalled to thee after an interval? or art thou bewailing the sad exile of Orestes, and my father's fate, whom thou didst once fondle in thy arms, in vain, alas! for thee and for thy friends?

O.M. Ah yes! in vain; but still I could not bear to leave him thus; and so I added this to my journey that I sought his grave, and, falling thereupon, wept o'er its desolation; then did I open the wine-skin, my gift to thy guests, and poured a libation, and set myrtle-sprigs round the tomb. And lo! upon the grave itself I saw a black ram had been offered, and there was blood, not long poured forth, and severed locks of auburn hair. Much I wondered, my daughter, who had dared approach the tomb; certainly 'twas no Argive. Nay, thy brother may perchance have come by stealth, and going thither have done honour to his father's wretched grave. Look at the hair, compare it with thy own, to see if the colour of these cut locks is the same; for children in whose veins runs the same father's blood, have usually a close bodily resemblance in most points.

El. Old sir, thy words are unworthy of a wise man, if thou thinkest my own brave brother would have come to this land by stealth for fear of Ægisthus. In the next place how should our hair correspond? His is the hair of a gallant youth trained up in manly sports, mine a woman's curled and combed; nay, that is a hopeless clue. Besides, thou couldst find many, whose hair is of the same colour, albeit not sprung from the same blood. No, maybe 'twas some stranger cut off his hair in pity at his tomb, or one that came to spy this land privily.

O.M. Put thy foot in the print of his shoe and mark whether it correspond with thine, my child.

El. How should the foot make any impression on stony ground? and if it did, the foot of brother and sister would not be the same in size, for a man's is the larger.

O.M. Hast thou no mark, in case thy brother *should* come, whereby to recognize the weaving of thy loom, the robe wherein I snatched him from death that day?

El. Dost thou forget I was still a babe when Orestes left the country? and even if I had woven him a robe, how should he, a mere child then, be wearing the same now, unless our clothes and bodies grow together?

O.M. Where are these guests? I fain would question them face to face about thy brother.

El. There they are, in haste to leave the house.

Enter ORESTES *and* PYLADES.

O.M. Wellborn, it seems, but that may be a

[1] *i.e.* carrying off a man.

sham; for there be plenty such prove knaves. Still I give them greeting.

Or. All hail, father! To which of thy friends, Electra, does this old relic of mortality belong?

El. This is he who nursed my sire, sir stranger.

Or. What! do I behold him who removed thy brother out of harm's way?

El. Behold the man who saved his life; if, that is, he liveth still.

Or. Ha! why does he look so hard at me, as if he were examining the bright device on silver coin? Is he finding in me a likeness to some other?

El. Maybe he is glad to see in thee a companion of Orestes.

Or. A man I love full well. But why is he walking round me?

El. I, too, am watching his movements with amaze, sir stranger.

O.M. My honoured mistress, my daughter Electra, return thanks to heaven—

El. For past or present favours? which?

O.M. That thou hast found a treasured prize, which God is now revealing.

El. Hear me invoke the gods. But what dost thou mean, old man?

O.M. Behold before thee, my child, thy nearest and dearest.

El. I have long feared thou wert not in thy sound senses.

O.M. Not in my sound senses, because I see thy brother?

El. What mean'st thou, aged friend, by these astounding words?

O.M. That I see Orestes, Agamemnon's son, before me.

El. What mark dost see that I can trust?

O.M. A scar along his brow, where he fell and cut himself one day in his father's home when chasing a fawn with thee.

El. Is it possible? True; I see the mark of the fall.

O.M. Dost hesitate then to embrace thy own dear brother?

El. No! not any longer, old friend; for my soul is convinced by the tokens thou showest. O my brother, thou art come at last, and I embrace thee, little as I ever thought to.

Or. And thee to my bosom at last I press.

El. I never thought that it would happen.

Or. All hope in me was also dead.

El. Art thou really he?

Or. Aye, thy one and only champion, if I can but safely draw to shore the cast I mean to throw; and I feel sure I shall; else must we cease to believe in gods, if wrong is to triumph o'er right.

Ch. At last, at last appears thy radiant dawn, O happy day! and as a beacon to the city hast thou revealed the wanderer, who, long ago, poor boy! was exiled from his father's halls. Now, lady, comes our turn for victory, ushered in by some god. Raise hand and voice in prayer, beseech the gods that good fortune may attend thy brother's entry to the city.

Or. Enough! sweet though the rapture of this greeting be, I must wait and return it hereafter. Do thou, old friend so timely met, tell me how I am to avenge me on my father's murderer, and on my mother, the partner in his guilty marriage. Have I still in Argos any band of kindly friends? or am I, like my fortunes, bankrupt altogether? With whom am I to league myself? by night or day shall I advance? point out a road for me to take against these foes of mine.

O.M. My son, thou hast no friend now in thy hour of adversity. No! that is a piece of rare good luck, to find another share thy fortunes alike for better and for worse. Thou art of every friend completely reft, all hope is gone from thee; be sure of what I tell thee; on thy own arm and fortune art thou wholly thrown to win thy father's home and thy city.

Or. What must I do to compass this result?

O.M. Slay Thyestes' son and thy mother.

Or. I came to win that victor's crown, but how can I attain it?

O.M. Thou wouldst never achieve it if thou didst enter the walls.

Or. Are they manned with guards and armed sentinels?

O.M. Aye truly; for he is afraid of thee, and cannot sleep secure.

Or. Well then, do thou next propose a scheme, old friend.

O.M. Hear me a moment; an idea has just occurred to me.

Or. May thy counsel prove good, and my perception keen!

O.M. I saw Ægisthus, as I was slowly pacing hither—

Or. I welcome thy words. Where was he?

O.M. Not far from these fields, at his stables.

Or. What was he doing? I see a gleam of hope after our dilemma.

O.M. I thought he was preparing a feast for the Nymphs.

Or. In return for the bringing up of children or in anticipation of a birth?

O.M. All I know is this, he was preparing to sacrifice oxen.

Or. How many were with him? or was he alone with his servants?

O.M. There was no Argive there; only a band of his own followers.

Or. Is it possible that any of them will recognize me, old man?

O.M. They are only servants, and they have never even seen thee.

Or. Will they support me, if I prevail?

O.M. Yes, that is the way of slaves, luckily for thee.

Or. On what pretext can I approach him?

O.M. Go to some place where he will see thee as he sacrifices.

Or. His estate is close to the road then, I suppose.

O.M. Yes, and when he sees thee there, he will invite thee to the feast.

Or. So help me God! He shall rue his invitation.

O.M. After that, form thy own plan according to circumstances.

Or. Good advice! But my mother, where is she?

O.M. At Argos; but she will yet join her husband for the feast.

Or. Why did she not come forth with him?

O.M. From fear of the citizens' reproach she stayed behind.

Or. I understand; she knows that the city suspects her.

O.M. Just so; her wickedness makes her hated.

Or. How shall I slay her and him together?

El. Mine be the preparation of my mother's slaying!

Or. Well, as for that other matter, fortune will favour us.

El. Our old friend here must help us both.

O.M. Aye, that will I; but what is thy scheme for slaying thy mother?

El. Go, old man, and tell Clytæmnestra from me that I have given birth to a son.

O.M. Some time ago, or quite recently?

El. Ten days ago, which are the days of my purification.

O.M. Suppose it done; but how doth this help towards slaying thy mother?

El. She will come, when she hears of my confinement.

O.M. What! dost think she cares aught for thee, my child?

El. Oh yes! she will weep no doubt over my child's low rank.

O.M. Perhaps she may; but go back again to the point.

El. Her death is certain, if she comes.

O.M. In that case, let her come right up to the door of the house.

El. Why then it were a little thing to turn her steps into the road to Hades' halls.

O.M. Oh! to see this one day, then die!

El. First of all, old friend, act as my brother's guide.

O.M. To the place where Ægisthus is now sacrificing to the gods?

El. Then go, find my mother and give her my message.

O.M. Aye that I will, so that she shall think the very words are thine.

El. (*To* ORESTES) Thy work begins at once; thou hast drawn the first lot in the tragedy.

Or. I will go, if some one will show me the way.

O.M. I will myself conduct thee nothing loth.

Or. O Zeus, god of my fathers, vanquisher of my foes, have pity on us, for a piteous lot has ours been.

El. Oh! have pity on thy own descendants.

Or. O Hera, mistress of Mycenæ's altars, grant us the victory, if we are asking what is right.

El. Yes, grant us vengeance on them for our father's death.

Or. Thou too, my father, sent to the land of shades by wicked hands, and Earth, the queen of all, to whom I spread my suppliant palms, up and champion thy dear children. Come with all the dead to aid, all they who helped thee break the Phrygians' power, and all who hate ungodly crime. Dost hear me, father, victim of my mother's rage?

El. Sure am I he heareth all; but 'tis time to part. For this cause too I bid thee strike Ægisthus down, because, if thou fall in the struggle and perish, I also die; no longer number me amongst the living; for I will stab myself with a two-edged sword. And now will I go indoors and make all ready there, for, if there come good news from thee, my house shall ring with women's cries of joy; but, if thou art slain, a different scene must then ensue. These are my instructions to thee.

Or. I know my lesson well.

El. Then show thyself a man. (*Exeunt* ORESTES, PYLADES, *and* OLD MAN) And you, my friends, signal to me by cries the certain issue of this fray. Myself will keep the sword ready in my grasp, for I will never accept defeat, and yield my body to my enemies to insult. *Exit* ELECTRA.

Ch. Still the story finds a place in time-honoured legends, how on a day Pan, the steward of husbandry, came breathing dulcet music on his jointed pipe, and brought with him from its tender dam on Argive hills, a beauteous lamb with fleece of gold; then stood a herald high upon the rock and cried aloud, "Away to the place of assembly, ye folk of Mycenæ! to behold the strange and awful sight vouchsafed to our blest rulers." Anon the dancers did obeisance to the family of Atreus; the altar-steps of beaten gold were draped; and through that Argive town the altars blazed with fire; sweetly rose the lute's clear note, the handmaid of the Muse's song; and ballads fair were written on the golden lamb, saying that Thyestes had the luck; for he won the guilty love of the wife of Atreus, and carried off to his house the strange creature, and then coming before the assembled folk he declared to them that he had in his house that hornèd beast with fleece of gold. In the self-same hour it was that Zeus changed the radiant courses of the stars, the light of the sun, and the joyous face of dawn, and drave his car athwart the western sky with fervent heat from heaven's fires, while northward fled the rainclouds, and Ammon's strand grew parched and faint and void of dew, when it was robbed of heaven's genial showers. 'Tis said, though I can scarce believe it, the sun turned round his glowing throne of gold, to vex the sons of men by this change because of the quarrel amongst them. Still, tales of horror have their use in making men regard the gods; of whom thou hadst no thought, when thou slewest thy husband, thou mother of this noble pair.

Hark! my friends, did ye hear that noise, like to the rumbling of an earthquake, or am I the dupe of idle fancy? Hark! hark! once more that windborne sound swells loudly on mine ear. Electra! mistress mine! come forth from the house!

Enter ELECTRA.

El. What is it, good friends? how goes the day with us?

Ch. I hear the cries of dying men; no more I know.

El. I heard them too, far off, but still distinct.

Ch. Yes, the sound came stealing from afar, but yet 'twas clear.

El. Was it the groan of an Argive, or of my friends?

Ch. I know not; for the cries are all confused.

El. That word of thine is my death-warrant; why do I delay?

Ch. Stay, till thou learn thy fate for certain.

El. No, no; we are vanquished; where are our messengers?

Ch. They will come in time; to slay a king is no light task.

Enter MESSENGER.

Messenger. All hail! ye victors, maidens of Mycenæ, to all Orestes' friends his triumph I announce; Ægisthus, the murderer of Agamemnon, lies weltering where he fell; return thanks to heaven.

El. Who art thou? What proof dost thou give of this?

Me. Look at me, dost thou not recognize thy brother's servant?

El. O best of friends! 'twas fear that prevented me from recognizing thee; now I know thee well. What sayst thou? Is my father's hateful murderer slain?

Me. He is; I repeat it since it is thy wish.

Ch. Ye gods, and Justice, whose eye is on all, at last art thou come.

El. I fain would learn the way and means my brother took to slay Thyestes' son.

Me. After we had set out from this house, we struck into the broad high-road, and came to the place where was the far-famed King of Mycenæ. Now he was walking in a garden well-watered, culling a wreath of tender myrtle-sprays for his head, and when he saw us, he called out, "All hail! strangers; who are ye? whence come ye? from what country?" To him Orestes answered, "We are from Thessaly, on our way to Alpheus' banks to sacrifice to Olympian Zeus." When Ægisthus heard that, he said, "Ye must be my guests to-day, and share the feast, for I am even now sacrificing to the Nymphs; and by rising with tomorrow's light ye will be just as far upon your journey; now let us go within." Therewith he caught us by the hand and led us by the way; refuse we could not; and when we were come to the house, he gave command: "Bring water for my guests to wash forthwith, that they may stand around the altar near the laver." But Orestes answered, "'Twas but now we purified ourselves and washed us clean in water from the river. So if we strangers are to join your citizens in sacrifice, we are ready, King Ægisthus, and will not refuse." So ended they their private conference. Meantime the servants, that composed their master's bodyguard, laid aside their weapons, and one and all were busied at their tasks. Some brought the bowl to catch the blood, others took up baskets, while others kindled fire and set cauldrons round about the altars, and the whole house rang. Then did thy mother's husband take the barley for sprinkling, and began casting it upon the hearth with these words, "Ye Nymphs, who dwell among the rocks, grant that I may often sacrifice with my wife, the daughter of Tyndareus within my halls, as happily as now, and ruin seize my foes!" (whereby he meant Orestes and thyself.) But my master, lowering his voice, offered a different prayer, that he might regain his father's house. Next Ægisthus took from a basket a long straight knife, and cutting off some of the calf's hair, laid it with his right hand on the sacred fire, and then cut its throat when the servants had lifted it upon their shoulders, and thus addressed thy brother; "Men declare that amongst the Thessalians this is counted honourable, to cut up a bull neatly and to manage steeds. So take the knife, sir stranger, and show us if rumour speaks true about the Thessalians." Thereon Orestes seized the Dorian knife of tempered steel and cast from his shoulders his graceful buckled robe; then choosing Pylades to help him in his task, he made the servants withdraw, and catching the calf by the hoof, proceeded to lay bare its white flesh, with arm outstretched, and he flayed the hide quicker than a runner ever finishes the two laps of the horses' race-course; next he laid the belly open, and Ægisthus took the entrails in his hands and carefully examined them. Now the liver had no lobe, while the portal vein leading to the gall-bladder, portended a dangerous attack on him who was observing it. Dark grows Ægisthus' brow, but my master asks, "Why so despondent, good sir?" Said he, "I fear treachery from a stranger. Agamemnon's son of all men most I hate, and he hates my house." But Orestes cried, "What! fear treachery from an exile! thou the ruler of the city? Ho! take this Dorian knife away and bring me a Thessalian cleaver, that we by sacrificial feast may learn the will of heaven; let me cleave the breastbone." And he took the axe and cut it through. Now Ægisthus was examining the entrails, separating them in his hands, and as he was bending down, thy brother rose on tiptoe and smote him on the spine, severing the vertebræ of his back; and his body gave one convulsive shudder from head to foot and writhed in the death-agony. No sooner did his servants see it, than they rushed to arms, a host to fight with two; yet did Pylades and Orestes of their valiancy meet them with brandished spears. Then cried Orestes, "I am no foe that come against this city and my own servants, but I have avenged me on the murderer of my sire, I, ill-starred Orestes. Slay me not, my father's former thralls!" They, when they heard him speak, restrained their spears, and an old man, who had been in the family many a long year, recognized him. Forthwith they crown thy brother with a wreath, and utter shouts of joy. And lo! he is coming to show thee the head, not the Gorgon's, but the head of thy hated foe Ægisthus; his death to-day has paid in blood a bitter debt of blood.

Ch. Dear mistress, now with step as light as fawn

join in the dance; lift high the nimble foot and be glad. Victory crowns thy brother; he hath won a fairer wreath than ever victor gained beside the streams of Alpheus; so raise a fair hymn to victory, the while I dance.

El. O light of day! O bright careering sun! O earth! and night erewhile my only day! now may I open my eyes in freedom, for Ægisthus is dead, my father's murderer. Come friends, let me bring out whate'er my house contains to deck his head and wreath with crowns my conquering brother's brow.

Ch. Bring forth thy garlands for his head, and we will lead the dance the Muses love. Now shall the royal line, dear to us in days gone by, resume its sway o'er the realm, having laid low the usurper as he deserves. So let the shout go up, whose notes are those of joy.

Enter ORESTES *and* PYLADES, *with corpse of* ÆGISTHUS.

El. Hail! glorious victor, Orestes, son of a sire who won the day 'neath Ilium's walls, accept this wreath to bind about the tresses of thy hair. Not in vain hast thou run thy course unto the goal and reached thy home again; no! but thou hast slain thy foe, Ægisthus, the murderer of our father. Thou too, O Pylades, trusty squire, whose training shows thy father's sterling worth, receive a garland from my hand, for thou no less than he hast a share in this emprise; and so I pray, good luck be thine for ever!

Or. First recognize the gods, Electra, as being the authors of our fortune, and then praise me their minister and fate's. Yea, I come from having slain Ægisthus in very deed, no mere pretence; and to make thee the more certain of this, I am bringing thee his corpse, which, if thou wilt, expose for beasts to rend, or set it upon a stake for birds, the children of the air, to pray upon; for now is he thy slave, once called thy lord and master.

El. I am ashamed to utter my wishes.

Or. What is it? speak out, for thou art through the gates of fear.

El. I am ashamed to flout the dead, for fear some spite assail me.

Or. No one would blame thee for this.

El. Our folk are hard to please, and love scandal.

Or. Speak all thy mind, sister; for we entered on this feud with him on terms admitting not of truce.

El. Enough! (*Turning to the corpse of* ÆGISTHUS) With which of thy iniquities shall I begin my recital? With which shall I end it? To which allot a middle place? And yet I never ceased, as each day dawned, to rehearse the story I would tell thee to thy face, if ever I were freed from my old terrors; and now I am; so I will pay thee back with the abuse I fain had uttered to thee when alive. Thou wert my ruin, making me and my brother orphans, though we had never injured thee, and thou didst make a shameful marriage with my mother, having slain her lord who led the host of Hellas, though thyself didst never go to Troy. Such was thy folly, thou didst never dream that my mother would prove thy curse when thou didst marry her, though thou wert wronging my father's honour. Know this; whoso defiles his neighbour's wife, and afterward is forced to take her to himself, is a wretched wight, if he supposes she will be chaste as his wife, though she sinned against her former lord. Thine was a life most miserable, though thou didst pretend 'twas otherwise; well thou knewest how guilty thy marriage was, and my mother knew she had a villain for husband. Sinners both, ye took each other's lot, she thy fortune, thou her curse. While everywhere in Argos thou wouldst hear such phrases as, "that woman's husband," never, "that man's wife." Yet 'tis shameful for the wife and not the man to rule the house; wherefore I loathe those children, who are called in the city not the sons of the man, their father, but of their mother. For instance, if a man makes a great match above his rank, there is no talk of the husband but only of the wife. Herein lay thy grievous error, due to ignorance; thou thoughtest thyself some one, relying on thy wealth, but this is naught save to stay with us a space. 'Tis nature that stands fast, not wealth. For it, if it abide unchanged, exalts man's horn; but riches dishonestly acquired and in the hands of fools, soon take their flight, their blossom quickly shed. As for thy sins with women, I pass them by, 'tis not for maiden's lips to mention them, but I will shrewdly hint thereat. And then thy arrogance! because forsooth thou hadst a palace and some looks to boast. May I never have a husband with a girl's face, but one that bears him like a man! For the children of these latter cling to a life of arms, while those, who are so fair to see, do only serve to grace the dance. Away from me! (*Spurning the corpse with her foot*) Time has shown thy villainy, little as thou reckest of the forfeit thou hast paid for it. Let none suppose, though he have run the first stage of his course with joy, that he will get the better of Justice, till he have reached the goal and ended his career.

Ch. Terrible alike his crime and your revenge; for mighty is the power of justice.

Or. 'Tis well. Carry his body within the house and hide it, sirrahs, that, when my mother comes, she may not see his corpse before she is smitten herself.

El. Hold! let us strike out another scheme.

Or. How now? Are those allies from Mycenæ whom I see?

El. No, 'tis my mother, that bare me.

Or. Full into the net she is rushing, oh, bravely!

El. See how proudly she rides in her chariot and fine robes!

Or. What must we do to our mother? Slay her?

El. What! has pity seized thee at sight of her?

Or. O God! how can I slay her that bare and suckled me?

El. Slay her as she slew thy father and mine.

Or. O Phœbus, how foolish was thy oracle—

El. Where Apollo errs, who shall be wise?

Or. In bidding me commit this crime—my mother's murder!

El. How canst thou be hurt by avenging thy father?

Or. Though pure before, I now shall carry into exile the stain of a mother's blood.

El. Still, if thou avenge not thy father, thou wilt fail in thy duty.

Or. And if I slay my mother, I must pay the penalty to her.

El. And so must thou to him, if thou resign the avenging of our father.

Or. Surely it was a fiend in the likeness of the god that ordered this!

El. Seated on the holy tripod? I think not so.

Or. I cannot believe this oracle was meant.

El. Turn not coward! Cast not thy manliness away!

Or. Am I to devise the same crafty scheme for her?

El. The self-same death thou didst mete out to her lord Ægisthus.

Or. I will go in; 'tis an awful task I undertake; an awful deed I have to do; still if it is Heaven's will, be it so; I loathe and yet I love the enterprise.

ORESTES *withdraws into the house.*

Enter CLYTAEMNESTRA.

Ch. Hail! Queen of Argos, daughter of Tyndareus, sister of those two noble sons of Zeus, who dwell in the flame-lit firmament amid the stars, whose guerdon high it is to save the sailor tossing on the sea. All hail! because of thy wealth and high prosperity, I do thee homage as I do the blessed gods. Now is the time, great queen, for us to pay our court unto thy fortunes.

Clytaemnestra. Alight from the car, ye Trojan maids, and take my hand that I may step down from the chariot. With Trojan spoils the temples of the gods are decked, but I have obtained these maidens as a special gift from Troy, in return for my lost daughter, a trifling boon no doubt, but still an ornament to my house.

El. And may not I, mother, take that highly-favoured hand of thine? I am a slave like them, an exile from my father's halls in this miserable abode.

Cl. See, my servants are here; trouble not on my account.

El. Why, thou didst make me thy prisoner by robbing me of my home; like these I became a captive when my home was taken, an orphan all forlorn.

Cl. True; but thy father plotted so wickedly against those of his own kin whom least of all he should have treated so. Speak I must; albeit, when a woman gets an evil reputation, there is a feeling of bitterness against all she says; unfairly indeed in my case, for it were only fair to hate after learning the circumstances, and seeing if the object deserves it; otherwise, why hate at all? Now Tyndareus bestowed me on thy father not that I or any children I might bear should be slain. Yet he went and took my daughter from our house to the fleet at Aulis, persuading me that Achilles was to wed her; and there he held her o'er the pyre, and cut Iphigenia's snowy throat. Had he slain her to save his city from capture, or to benefit his house, or to preserve his other children, a sacrifice of one for many, I could have pardoned him. But, as it was, his reasons for murdering my child were these: the wantonness of Helen and her husband's folly in not punishing the traitress. Still, wronged as I was, my rage had not burst forth for this, nor would I have slain my lord, had he not returned to me with that frenzied maiden and made her his mistress, keeping at once two brides beneath the same roof. Women maybe are given to folly, I do not deny it; this granted, when a husband goes astray and sets aside his own true wife, she fain will follow his example and find another love; and then in our case hot abuse is heard, while the men, who are to blame for this, escape without a word. Again, suppose Menelaus had been secretly snatched from his home, should I have had to kill Orestes to save Menelaus, my sister's husband? How would thy father have endured this? Was he then to escape death for slaying what was mine, while I was to suffer at his hands? I slew him, turning, as my only course, to his enemies. For which of all thy father's friends would have joined me in his murder? Speak all that is in thy heart, and prove against me with all free speech, that thy father's death was not deserved.

El. Justly urged! but thy justice is not free from shame; for in all things should every woman of sense yield to her husband. Whoso thinketh otherwise comes not within the scope of what I say. Remember, mother, those last words of thine, allowing me free utterance before thee.

Cl. Daughter, far from refusing it, I grant it again.

El. Thou wilt not, when thou hearest, wreak thy vengeance on me?

Cl. No, indeed; I shall welcome thy opinion.

El. Then will I speak, and this shall be the prelude of my speech: Ah, mother mine! would thou hadst had a better heart; for though thy beauty and Helen's win you praises well deserved, yet are ye akin in nature, a pair of wantons, unworthy of Castor. She was carried off, 'tis true, but her fall was voluntary; and thou hast slain the bravest soul in Hellas, excusing thyself on the ground that thou didst kill a husband to avenge a daughter; the world does not know thee so well as I do, thou who before ever thy daughter's death was decided, yea, soon as thy lord had started from his home, wert combing thy golden tresses at thy mirror. That wife who, when her lord is gone from home, sets to beautifying herself, strike off from virtue's list; for she has no need to carry her beauty abroad, save she is seeking some mischief. Of all the wives in Hellas thou wert the only one I know who wert overjoyed when Troy's star was in the ascendant, while, if it set, thy brow was clouded, since thou hadst no wish that Agamemnon should return from Troy. And yet thou couldst have played a virtuous part to thy own glory. The husband thou hadst was no whit inferior to Ægisthus, for he it was whom Hellas chose to be her captain. And when thy sister Helen wrought that deed of shame, thou couldst have won thyself great glory, for vice is a warning and calls attention to virtue. If, as thou allegest, my father slew thy daughter, what is the wrong I and my brother have done thee? How was it thou didst not bestow on us our father's halls after thy husband's death, instead of bartering them to buy a paramour? Again, thy husband is not exiled for thy son's sake, nor is he slain to avenge my death, although by him this life is quenched twice as much as e'er my sister's was; so if murder is to succeed murder in requital, I and thy son Orestes must slay thee to avenge our father; if that was just, why so is this. Whoso fixes his gaze on wealth or noble birth and weds a wicked woman, is a fool; better is a humble partner in his home, if she be virtuous, than a proud one.

Ch. Chance rules the marriages of women; some I see turn out well, others ill, amongst mankind.

Cl. Daughter, 'twas ever thy nature to love thy father. This too one finds; some sons cling to their father, others have a deeper affection for their mother. I will forgive thee, for myself am not so exceeding glad at the deed that I have done, my child.

But thou—why thus unwashed and clad in foul attire, now that the days of thy lying-in are accomplished? Ah me, for my sorry schemes! I have goaded my husband into anger more than e'er I should have done.

El. Thy sorrow comes too late; the hour of remedy has gone from thee; my father is dead. Yet why not recall that exile, thy own wandering son?

Cl. I am afraid; 'tis my interest, not his that I regard. For they say he is wroth for his father's murder.

El. Why, then, dost thou encourage thy husband's bitterness against us?

Cl. 'Tis his way; thou too hast a stubborn nature.

El. Because I am grieved; yet will I check my spirit.

Cl. I promise then he shall no longer oppress thee.

El. From living in my home he grows too proud.

Cl. Now there! 'tis thou that art fanning the quarrel into new life.

El. I say no more; my dread of him is even what it is.

Cl. Peace! Enough of this. Why didst thou summon me, my child?

El. Thou hast heard, I suppose, of my confinement; for this I pray thee, since I know not how, offer the customary sacrifice on the tenth day after birth, for I am a novice herein, never having had a child before.

Cl. This is work for another, even for her who delivered thee.

El. I was all alone in my travail and at the babe's birth.

Cl. Dost live so far from neighbours?

El. No one cares to make the poor his friends.

Cl. Well, I will go to offer to the gods a sacrifice for the child's completion of the days; and when I have done thee this service, I will seek the field where my husband is sacrificing to the Nymphs. Take this chariot hence, my servants, and tie the horses to the stalls; and when ye think that I have finished my offering to the gods, attend me, for I must likewise pleasure my lord.

Going into the house.

El. Enter our humble cottage; but, prithee, take care that my smoke-grimed walls soil not thy robes; now wilt thou offer to the gods a fitting sacrifice. There stands the basket ready, and the knife is sharpened, the same that slew the bull, by whose side thou soon wilt lie a corpse; and thou shalt be his bride in Hades' halls whose wife thou wast on earth. This is the boon I will grant thee, while thou shalt pay me for my father's blood. *Exit* ELECTRA.

Ch. Misery is changing sides; the breeze veers round, and now blows fair upon my house. The day is past when my chief fell murdered in his bath, and the roof and the very stones of the walls rang with his cry: "O cruel wife, why art thou murdering me on my return to my dear country after ten long years?"

The tide is turning, and justice that pursues the faithless wife is drawing within its grasp the murderess, who slew her hapless lord, when he came home at last to these towering Cyclopean walls—aye, with her own hand she smote him with the sharpened steel, herself the axe uplifting. Unhappy husband! whate'er the curse that possessed that wretched woman. Like a lioness of the hills that rangeth through the woodland for her prey, she wrought the deed.

Cl. (*Within*) O my children, by Heaven I pray ye spare your mother!

Ch. Dost hear her cries within the house?

Cl. O God! ah me!

Ch. I too bewail thee, dying by thy children's hands. God deals out His justice in His good time. A cruel fate is thine, unhappy one; yet didst thou sin in murdering thy lord.

But lo! from the house they come, dabbled in their mother's fresh-spilt gore, their triumph proving the piteous butchery. There is not nor has ever been a race more wretched than the line of Tantalus.

The two corpses are shown.

Enter ORESTES *and* ELECTRA.

Or. O Earth, and Zeus whose eye is over all! behold this foul deed of blood, these two corpses lying here that I have slain in vengeance for my sufferings.

*[1] * *
* * *

El. Tears are all too weak for this, brother; and I am the guilty cause. Ah, woe is me! How hot my fury burned against the mother that bare me!

Or. Alas! for thy lot, O mother mine! A piteous, piteous doom, aye, worse than that, hast thou incurred at children's hands! Yet justly hast thou paid forfeit for our father's blood. Ah, Phœbus! thine was the voice that praised this vengeance; thou it is that hast brought these hideous scenes to light, and caused this deed of blood. To what city can I go henceforth? what friend, what man of any piety will bear the sight of a mother's murderer like me?

[1]Two verses have been lost here.

El. Ah me! alas! and whither can I go? What share have I henceforth in dance or marriage rite? What husband will accept me as his bride?

Or. Again thy fancy changes with the wind; for now thou thinkest aright, though not so formerly; an awful deed didst thou urge thy brother against his will to commit, dear sister. Oh! didst thou see how the poor victim threw open her robe and showed her bosom as I smote her, sinking on her knees, poor wretch? My heart melted within me.

El. Full well I know the agony through which thou didst pass at hearing thy own mother's bitter cry.

Or. Ah yes! she laid her hand upon my chin, and cried aloud, "My child, I entreat thee!" and she clung about my neck, so that I let fall the sword.

El. O my poor mother! How didst thou endure to see her breathe her last before thy eyes?

Or. I threw my mantle o'er them and began the sacrifice by plunging the sword into my mother's throat.

El. Yet 'twas I that urged thee on, yea, and likewise grasped the steel. Oh! I have done an awful deed.

Or. Oh! take and hide our mother's corpse beneath a pall, and close her gaping wound. (*Turning to the corpse*) Ah! thy murderers were thine own children.

El. (*Covering the corpse*) There! thou corpse both loved and loathed; still o'er thee I cast a robe, to end the grievous troubles of our house.

(THE DIOSCURI *are seen hovering above the house*)

Ch. See! where o'er the roof-top spirits are appearing, or gods maybe from heaven, for this is not a road that mortals tread. Why come they thus where mortal eyes can see them clearly?

The Dioscuri. Hearken, son of Agamemnon. We, the twin sons of Zeus, thy mother's sisters, call thee, even Castor and his brother Polydeuces. 'Tis but now we have reached Argos after stilling the fury of the sea for mariners, having seen the slaying of our sister, thy mother. She hath received her just reward, but thine is no righteous act, and Phœbus—but no! he is my king, my lips are sealed—is Phœbus still, albeit the oracle he gave thee was no great proof of his wisdom. But we must acquiesce herein. Henceforth must thou follow what Zeus and destiny ordain for thee. On Pylades bestow Electra for his wife to take unto his home; do thou leave Argos, for after thy mother's murder thou mayst not set foot in the city. And those grim goddesses of doom, that glare like savage hounds, will drive thee mad and chase thee to and fro; but go thou to Athens and make thy prayer to the holy image of Pallas, for she will close their fierce serpents' mouths, so that they touch thee not, holding o'er thy head her ægis with the Gorgon's head. A hill there is, to Ares sacred, where first the gods in conclave sat to decide the law of blood, in the day that savage Ares slew Halirrothius, son of the ocean-king, in anger for the violence he offered to his daughter's honour; from that time all decisions given there are most holy and have heaven's sanction. There must thou have this murder tried; and if equal votes are given, they shall save thee from death in the decision, for Loxias will take the blame upon himself, since it was his oracle that advised thy mother's murder. And this shall be the law for all posterity; in every trial the accused shall win his case if the votes are equal. Then shall those dread goddesses, stricken with grief at this, vanish into a cleft of the earth close to the hill, revered by men thenceforth as a place for holy oracles; whilst thou must settle in a city of Arcadia on the banks of the river Alpheus near the shrine of Lycæan Apollo, and the city shall be called after thy name. To thee I say this. As for the corpse of Ægisthus, the citizens of Argos must give it burial; but Menelaus, who has just arrived at Nauplia from the sack of Troy, shall bury thy mother, Helen helping him; for she hath come from her sojourn in Egypt in the halls of Proteus, and hath never been to Troy; but Zeus, to stir up strife and bloodshed in the world, sent forth a phantom of Helen to Ilium. Now let Pylades take his maiden wife and bear her to his home in Achæa; also he must conduct thy so-called kinsman to the land of Phocis, and there reward him well. But go thyself along the narrow Isthmus, and seek Cecropia's happy home. For once thou hast fulfilled the doom appointed for this murder, thou shalt be blest and free from all thy troubles.

Ch. Ye sons of Zeus, may we draw near to speak with you?

Di. Ye may, since ye are not polluted by this murder.

Or. May I too share your converse, sons of Tyndareus?

Di. Thou too; for to Phœbus will I ascribe this deed of blood.

Ch. How was it that ye, the brothers of the murdered woman, gods too, did not ward the doom-goddesses from her roof?

Di. 'Twas fate that brought resistless doom to her, and that thoughtless oracle that Phœbus gave.

El. But why did the god, and wherefore did his oracles make me my mother's murderer?

Di. A share in the deed, a share in its doom; one ancestral curse hath ruined both of you.

Or. Ah, sister mine! at last I see thee again only to be robbed in a moment of thy dear love; I must leave thee, and by thee be left.

Di. Hers are a husband and a home; her only suffering this, that she is quitting Argos.

Or. Yet what could call forth deeper grief than exile from one's fatherland? I must leave my father's house, and at a stranger's bar be sentenced for my mother's blood.

Di. Be of good cheer; go to the holy town of Pallas; keep a stout heart only.

El. O my brother, best and dearest! clasp me to thy breast; for now is the curse of our mother's blood cutting us off from the home of our fathers.

Or. Throw thy arms in close embrace about me. Oh! weep as o'er my grave when I am dead.

Di. Ah me! that bitter cry makes even gods shudder to hear. Yea, for in my breast and in every heavenly being's dwells pity for the sorrows of mankind.

Or. Never to see thee more!

El. Never again to stand within thy sight!

Or. This is my last good-bye to thee.

El. Farewell, farewell, my city! and ye my fellow-countrywomen, a long farewell to you!

Or. Art thou going already, truest of thy sex?

El. I go, the teardrop dimming my young eye.

Or. Go, Pylades, and be happy; take and wed Electra.

Di. Their only thoughts will be their marriage; but haste thee to Athens, seeking to escape these hounds of hell, for they are on thy track in fearful wise, swart monsters, with snakes for hands, who reap a harvest of man's agony. But we twain must haste away o'er the Sicilian main to save the seaman's ship. Yet as we fly through heaven's expanse we help not the wicked; but whoso in his life loves piety and justice, all such we free from troublous toils and save. Wherefore let no man be minded to act unjustly, or with men foresworn set sail; such the warning I, a god, to mortals give.

Ch. Farewell! truly that mortal's is a happy lot, who can thus fare, unafflicted by any calamity.

Exeunt OMNES.

THE BACCHANTES

DRAMATIS PERSONAE

DIONYSUS	CADMUS
PENTHEUS	SERVANT
CHORUS OF BACCHANTES	FIRST MESSENGER
TEIRESIAS	SECOND MESSENGER
AGAVE	

Before the Palace of Pentheus at Thebes. Enter DIONYSUS.

Dionysus. Lo! I am come to this land of Thebes, Dionysus, the son of Zeus, of whom on a day Semele, the daughter of Cadmus, was delivered by a flash of lightning. I have put off the god and taken human shape, and so present myself at Dirce's springs and the waters of Ismenus. Yonder I see my mother's monument where the bolt slew her nigh her house, and there are the ruins of her home smouldering with the heavenly flame that blazeth still—Hera's deathless outrage on my mother. To Cadmus all praise I offer, because he keeps this spot hallowed, his daughter's precinct, which my own hands have shaded round about with the vine's clustering foliage.

Lydia's glebes, where gold abounds, and Phrygia have I left behind; o'er Persia's sun-baked plains, by Bactria's walled towns and Media's wintry clime have I advanced through Arabia, land of promise; and Asia's length and breadth, outstretched along the brackish sea, with many a fair walled town, peopled with mingled race of Hellenes and barbarians; and this is the first city in Hellas I have reached. There too have I ordained dances and established my rites, that I might manifest my godhead to men; but Thebes is the first city in the land of Hellas that I have made ring with shouts of joy, girt in a fawn-skin, with a thyrsus, my ivy-bound spear, in my hand; since my mother's sisters, who least of all should have done it, denied that Dionysus was the son of Zeus, saying that Semele, when she became a mother by some mortal lover, tried to foist her sin on Zeus—a clever ruse of Cadmus, which, they boldly asserted, caused Zeus to slay her for the falsehood about the marriage. Wherefore these are they whom I have driven frenzied from their homes, and they are dwelling on the hills with mind distraught; and I have forced them to assume the dress worn in my orgies, and all the women-folk of Cadmus' stock have I driven raving from their homes, one and all alike; and there they sit upon the roofless rocks beneath the green pine-trees, mingling amongst the sons of Thebes. For this city must learn, however loth, seeing that it is not initiated in my Bacchic rites, and I must take up my mother's defence, by showing to mortals that the child she bore to Zeus is a deity. Now Cadmus gave his sceptre and its privileges to Pentheus, his daughter's child, who wages war 'gainst my divinity, thrusting me away from his drink-offerings, and making no mention of me in his prayers. Therefore will I prove to him and all the race of Cadmus that I am a god. And when I have set all in order here, I will pass hence to a fresh country, manifesting myself; but if the city of Thebes in fury takes up arms and seeks to drive my votaries from the mountain, I will meet them at the head of my frantic rout. This is why I have assumed a mortal form, and put off my godhead to take man's nature.

O ye who left Tmolus, the bulwark of Lydia, ye women, my revel rout! whom I brought from your foreign homes to be ever by my side and bear me company, uplift the cymbals native to your Phrygian home, that were by me and the great mother Rhea first devised, and march around the royal halls of Pentheus smiting them, that the city of Cadmus may see you; while I will seek Cithæron's glens, there with my Bacchanals to join the dance.

Exit DIONYSUS.

Enter CHORUS.

Chorus. From Asia o'er the holy ridge of Tmolus I hasten to a pleasant task, a toil that brings no weariness, for Bromius' sake, in honour of the Bacchic god. Who loiters in the road? who lingers 'neath the roof? Avaunt! I say, and let every lip be hushed in solemn silence; for I will raise a hymn to Dionysus, as custom aye ordains. O happy he! who to his joy is initiated in heavenly mysteries and leads a holy life, joining heart and soul in Bacchic revelry upon the hills, purified from every sin; observing the rites of Cybele, the mighty mother, and brandishing the thyrsus, with ivy-wreathèd head, he worships Dionysus. Go forth, go forth, ye Bacchanals, bring home the Bromian god Dionysus, child of a god, from the mountains of Phrygia to the spacious streets of Hellas, bring home the Bromian god! whom on a day his mother in her sore travail brought forth untimely, yielding up her life beneath the lightning stroke of Zeus' wingèd bolt; but forthwith Zeus, the son of Cronos, found for him another womb wherein to rest, for he hid him in his thigh and fastened it with golden pins to conceal him from Hera.

And when the Fates had fully formed the horned god, he brought him forth and crowned him with a coronal of snakes, whence it is the thyrsus-bearing Mænads hunt the snake to twine about their hair. O Thebes, nurse of Semele! crown thyself with ivy; burst forth, burst forth with blossoms fair of green convolvulus, and with the boughs of oak and pine join in the Bacchic revelry; don thy coat of dappled fawn-skin, decking it with tufts of silvered hair; with reverent hand the sportive wand now wield. Anon shall the whole land be dancing, when Bromius leads his revellers to the hills, to the hills away! where wait him groups of maidens from loom and shuttle roused in frantic haste by Dionysus. O hidden cave of the Curetes! O hallowed haunts in Crete, that saw Zeus born, where Corybantes with crested helms devised for me in their grotto the rounded timbrel of ox-hide, mingling Bacchic minstrelsy with the shrill sweet accents of the Phrygian flute, a gift bestowed by them on mother Rhea, to add its crash of music to the Bacchantes' shouts of joy; but frantic satyrs won it from the mother-goddess for their own, and added it to their dances in festivals, which gladden the heart of Dionysus, each third recurrent year. Oh! happy that votary, when from the hurrying revel-rout he sinks to earth, in his holy robe of fawnskin, chasing the goat to drink its blood, a banquet sweet of flesh uncooked, as he hastes to Phrygia's or to Libya's hills; while in the van the Bromian god exults with cries of Evoe. With milk and wine and streams of luscious honey flows the earth, and Syrian incense smokes. While the Bacchante holding in his hand a blazing torch of pine uplifted on his wand waves it, as he speeds along, rousing wandering votaries, and as he waves it cries aloud with wanton tresses tossing in the breeze; and thus to crown the revelry, he raises loud his voice, "On, on, ye Bacchanals, pride of Tmolus with its rills of gold! to the sound of the booming drum, chanting in joyous strains the praises of your joyous god with Phrygian accents lifted high, what time the holy lute with sweet complaining note invites you to your hallowed sport, according well with feet that hurry wildly to the hills; like a colt that gambols at its mother's side in the pasture, with gladsome heart each Bacchante bounds along."

Enter TEIRESIAS.

Teiresias. What loiterer at the gates will call Cadmus from the house, Agenor's son, who left the city of Sidon and founded here the town of Thebes? Go one of you, announce to him that Teiresias is seeking him; he knows himself the reason of my coming and the compact I and he have made in our old age to bind the thyrsus with leaves and don the fawnskin, crowning our heads the while with ivy-sprays.

Enter CADMUS.

Cadmus. Best of friends! I was in the house when I heard thy voice, wise as its owner. I come prepared, dressed in the livery of the god. For 'tis but right I should magnify with all my might my own daughter's son, Dionysus, who hath shown his godhead unto men. Where are we to join the dance? where plant the foot and shake the hoary head? Do thou, Teiresias, be my guide, age leading age, for thou art wise. Never shall I weary, night or day, of beating the earth with my thyrsus. What joy to forget our years?

Te. Why, then thou art as I am. For I too am young again, and will essay the dance.

Ca. We will drive then in our chariot to the hill.

Te. Nay, thus would the god not have an equal honour paid.

Ca. Well, I will lead thee, age leading age.

Te. The god will guide us both thither without toil.

Ca. Shall we alone of all the city dance in Bacchus' honour?

Te. Yea, for we alone are wise, the rest are mad.

Ca. We stay too long; come, take my hand.

Te. There! link thy hand in my firm grip.

Ca. Mortal that I am, I scorn not the gods.

Te. No subtleties do I indulge about the powers of heaven. The faith we inherited from our fathers, old as time itself, no reasoning shall cast down; no! though it were the subtlest invention of wits refined. Maybe some one will say, I have no respect for my grey hair in going to dance with ivy round my head; not so, for the god did not define whether old or young should dance, but from all alike he claims a universal homage, and scorns nice calculations in his worship.

Ca. Teiresias, since thou art blind, I must prompt thee what to say. Pentheus is coming hither to the house in haste, Echion's son, to whom I resign the government. How scared he looks! what strange tidings will he tell?

Enter PENTHEUS.

Pentheus. I had left my kingdom for awhile, when tidings of strange mischief in this city reached me; I hear that our women-folk have left their homes on pretence of Bacchic rites, and on the wooded hills rush wildly to and fro, honouring in the dance this new god Dionysus, whoe'er he is; and in the midst of each revel-rout the brimming wine-bowl stands, and one by one they steal away to lonely spots to gratify their lust, pretending forsooth that they are Mænads bent on sacrifice, though it is Aphrodite they are placing before the Bacchic god. As many as I caught, my gaolers are keeping safe in the public prison fast bound; and all who are gone forth, will I chase from the hills, Ino and Agave too who bore me to Echion, and Actæon's mother Autonoe. In fetters of iron will I bind them and soon put an end to these outrageous Bacchic rites. They say there came a stranger hither, a trickster and a sorcerer, from Lydia's land, with golden hair and perfumed locks, the flush of wine upon his face, and in his eyes each grace that Aphrodite gives; by day and night he lingers in our maidens' company on the plea of teaching Bacchic mysteries. Once let me catch him within these walls, and I will put an end to his thyrsus-beating and his waving of his tresses, for I will cut his head from his body. This is the fellow who says that Dionysus is a god, says that he was once stitched up in the thigh of Zeus—that child who with his mother was blasted by the lightning flash, because the woman falsely said her marriage was with Zeus. Is not this enough to deserve the awful penalty of hanging, this stranger's wanton insolence, whoe'er he be?

But lo! another marvel. I see Teiresias, our diviner, dressed in dappled fawn-skins, and my mother's father too, wildly waving the Bacchic wand; droll sight enough! Father, it grieves me to see you two old men so void of sense. Oh! shake that ivy from thee! Let fall the thyrsus from thy hand, my mother's sire! Was it thou, Teiresias, urged him on to this? Art bent on introducing this fellow as another new deity amongst men, that thou mayst then observe the fowls of the air and make a gain from fiery divination? Were it not that thy grey hairs protected thee, thou shouldst sit in chains amid the Bacchanals, for introducing knavish mysteries; for where the gladsome grape is found at women's feasts, I deny that their rites have any longer good results.

Ch. What impiety! Hast thou no reverence, sir stranger, for the gods or for Cadmus who sowed the crop of earth-born warriors? Son of Echion as thou art, thou dost shame thy birth.

Te. Whenso a man of wisdom finds a good topic for argument, it is no difficult matter to speak well; but thou, though possessing a glib tongue as if endowed with sense, art yet devoid thereof in all thou sayest. A headstrong man, if he have influence and a capacity for speaking, makes a bad citizen because he lacks sense. This new deity, whom thou deridest, will rise to power I cannot say how great, throughout Hellas. Two things there are, young prince, that hold first rank among men, the goddess Demeter, that is, the earth, call her which name thou please; she it is that feedeth men with solid food; and as her counterpart came this god, the son of Semele, who discovered the juice of the grape and introduced it to mankind, stilling thereby each grief that mortals suffer from, soon as e'er they are filled with the juice of the vine; and sleep also he giveth, sleep that brings forgetfulness of daily ills, the sovereign charm for all our woe. God though he is, he serves all other gods for libations, so that through him mankind is blest. He it is whom thou dost mock, because he was sewn up in the thigh of Zeus. But I will show thee this fair mystery. When Zeus had snatched him from the lightning's blaze, and to Olympus borne the tender babe, Hera would have cast him forth from heaven, but Zeus, as such a god well might, devised a counterplot. He broke off a fragment of the ether which surrounds the world, and made thereof a hostage against Hera's bitterness, while he gave out Dionysus into other hands; hence, in time, men said that he was reared in the thigh of Zeus, having changed the word and invented a legend, because the god was once a hostage to the goddess Hera. This god too hath prophetic power, for there is no small prophecy inspired by Bacchic frenzy; for whenever the god in his full might enters the human frame, he makes his frantic votaries foretell the future. Likewise he hath some share in Ares' rights; for oft, or ever a weapon is touched, a panic seizes an army when it is marshalled in array; and this too is a frenzy sent by Dionysus. Yet shalt thou behold him e'en on Delphi's rocks leaping o'er the cloven height, torch in hand, waving and brandishing the branch by Bacchus loved, yea, and through the length and breadth of Hellas. Hearken to me, Pentheus; never boast that might alone doth sway the world, nor if thou think so, unsound as thy opinion is, credit thyself with any wisdom; but receive the god into thy realm, pour out libations, join the revel rout, and crown thy head. It is not Dionysus that will force chastity on women in their love; but this is what we should consider, whether chastity is part of their nature for good and all; for if it is, no really modest maid will ever fall 'mid Bacchic mysteries. Mark this: thou thyself art glad when thousands throng thy gates, and citizens extol the name of Pentheus; he too, I trow, delights in being honoured. Wherefore I and Cadmus, whom thou jeerest so, will wreath our brows with ivy and join the dance; pair of greybeards though we be, still must we take part therein; never will I for any words of thine fight against heaven. Most grievous is thy madness, nor canst thou find a charm to cure thee, albeit charms have caused thy malady.

Ch. Old sir, thy words do not discredit Phœbus, and thou art wise in honouring Bromius, potent deity.

Ca. My son, Teiresias hath given thee sound advice; dwell with us, but o'erstep not the threshold of custom; for now thou art soaring aloft, and thy wisdom is no wisdom. E'en though he be no god, as thou assertest, still say he is; be guilty of a splendid fraud, declaring him the son of Semele, that she may be thought the mother of a god, and we and all our race gain honour. Dost thou mark the awful fate of Actæon? whom savage hounds of his own rearing rent in pieces in the meadows, because he boasted himself a better hunter than Artemis. Lest thy fate be the same, come let me crown thy head with ivy; join us in rendering homage to the god.

Pe. Touch me not! away to thy Bacchic rites thyself! never try to infect me with thy foolery! Vengeance will I have on the fellow who teaches thee such senselessness. Away one of you without delay! seek yonder seat where he observes his birds, wrench it from its base with levers, turn it upside down, o'erthrowing it in utter confusion, and toss his garlands to the tempest's blast. For by so doing shall I wound him most deeply. Others of you range the city and hunt down this girl-faced stranger, who is introducing a new complaint amongst our women, and doing outrage to the marriage tie. And if haply ye catch him, bring him hither to me in chains, to be stoned to death, a bitter ending to his revelry in Thebes.

Exit PENTHEUS.

Te. Unhappy wretch! thou little knowest what thou art saying. Now art thou become a raving madman, even before unsound in mind. Let us away, Cadmus, and pray earnestly for him, spite of his savage temper, and likewise for the city, that the god inflict not a signal vengeance. Come, follow me with thy ivy-wreathed staff; try to support my tottering frame as I do thine, for it is unseemly that two old men should fall; but let that pass. For we must serve the Bacchic god, the son of Zeus. Only, Cadmus, beware lest Pentheus[1] bring sorrow to thy house; it is not my prophetic art, but circumstances that lead me to say this; for the words of a fool are folly. *Exeunt* CADMUS *and* TEIRESIAS.

Ch. O holiness, queen amongst the gods, sweeping on golden pinion o'er the earth! dost hear the words of Pentheus, dost hear his proud blaspheming against Bromius, the son of Semele, first of all the blessed gods at every merry festival? His it is to rouse the revellers to dance, to laugh away dull care, and wake the flute, whene'er at banquets of the gods the luscious grape appears, or when the winecup in the feast sheds sleep on men who wear the ivy-spray. The end of all unbridled speech and lawless senselessness is misery; but the life of calm repose and the rule of reason abide unshaken and support the home; for far away in heaven though they dwell, the powers divine behold man's state. Sophistry is not wisdom, and to indulge in thoughts beyond man's ken is to shorten life; and if a man on such poor terms should aim too high, he may miss the pleasures in his reach. These, to my mind, are the ways of madmen and idiots. Oh! to make my way to Cyprus, isle of Aphrodite, where dwell the love-gods strong to soothe man's soul, or to Paphos, which that foreign river, never fed by rain, enriches with its hundred mouths! Oh! lead me, Bromian god, celestial guide of Bacchic pilgrims, to the hallowed slopes of Olympus, where Pierian Muses have their haunt most fair. There dwell the Graces; there is soft desire; there thy votaries may hold their revels freely. The joy of our god, the son of Zeus, is in banquets, his delight is in peace, that giver of riches and nurse divine of youth. Both to rich and poor alike hath he granted the delight of wine, that makes all pain to cease; hateful to him is every one who careth not to live the life of bliss, that lasts through days and nights of joy. True wisdom is to keep the heart and soul aloof from over-subtle wits. That which the less enlightened crowd approves and practises, will I accept.

Re-enter PENTHEUS. *Enter* SERVANT *bringing* DIONYSUS *bound.*

Servant. We are come, Pentheus, having hunted down this prey, for which thou didst send us forth; not in vain hath been our quest. We found our quarry tame; he did not fly from us, but yielded himself without a struggle; his cheek ne'er blanched, nor did his ruddy colour change, but with a smile he bade me bind and lead him away, and he waited, making my task an easy one. For very shame I said to him, "Against my will, sir stranger, do I lead thee hence, but Pentheus ordered it, who sent me hither."

[1] "The son of sorrow," one of the many plays on names in Euripides.

As for his votaries whom thou thyself didst check, seizing and binding them hand and foot in the public gaol, all these have loosed their bonds and fled into the meadows where they now are sporting, calling aloud on the Bromian god. Their chains fell off their feet of their own accord, and doors flew open without man's hand to help. Many a marvel hath this stranger brought with him to our city of Thebes; what yet remains must be thy care.

Pe. Loose his hands; for now that I have him in the net he is scarce swift enough to elude me. So, sir stranger, thou art not ill-favoured from a woman's point of view, which was thy real object in coming to Thebes; thy hair is long because thou hast never been a wrestler, flowing right down thy cheeks most wantonly; thy skin is white to help thee gain thy end, not tanned by ray of sun, but kept within the shade, as thou goest in quest of love with beauty's bait. Come, tell me first of thy race.

Di. That needs no braggart's tongue, 'tis easily told; maybe thou knowest Tmolus by hearsay.

Pe. I know it, the range that rings the city of Sardis round.

Di. Thence I come, Lydia is my native home.

Pe. What makes thee bring these mysteries to Hellas?

Di. Dionysus, the son of Zeus, initiated me.

Pe. Is there a Zeus in Lydia, who begets new gods?

Di. No, but Zeus who married Semele in Hellas.

Pe. Was it by night or in the face of day that he constrained thee?

Di. 'Twas face to face he intrusted his mysteries to me.

Pe. Pray, what special feature stamps thy rites?

Di. That is a secret to be hidden from the uninitiated.

Pe. What profit bring they to their votaries?

Di. Thou must not be told, though 'tis well worth knowing.

Pe. A pretty piece of trickery, to excite my curiosity!

Di. A man of godless life is an abomination to the rites of the god.

Pe. Thou sayest thou didst see the god clearly; what was he like?

Di. What his fancy chose; I was not there to order this.

Pe. Another clever twist and turn of thine, without a word of answer.

Di. He were a fool, methinks, who would utter wisdom to a fool.

Pe. Hast thou come hither first with this deity?

Di. All foreigners already celebrate these mysteries with dances.

Pe. The reason being, they are far behind Hellenes in wisdom.

Di. In this at least far in advance, though their customs differ.

Pe. Is it by night or day thou performest these devotions?

Di. By night mostly; darkness lends solemnity.

Pe. Calculated to entrap and corrupt women.

Di. Day too for that matter may discover shame.

Pe. This vile quibbling settles thy punishment.

Di. Brutish ignorance and godlessness will settle thine.

Pe. How bold our Bacchanal is growing! a very master in this wordy strife!

Di. Tell me what I am to suffer; what is the grievous doom thou wilt inflict upon me?

Pe. First will I shear off thy dainty tresses.

Di. My locks are sacred; for the god I let them grow.

Pe. Next surrender that thyrsus.

Di. Take it from me thyself; 'tis the wand of Dionysus I am bearing.

Pe. In dungeon deep thy body will I guard.

Di. The god himself will set me free, whene'er I list.

Pe. Perhaps he may, when thou standest amid thy Bacchanals and callest on his name.

Di. Even now he is near me and witnesses my treatment.

Pe. Why, where is he? To my eyes he is invisible.

Di. He is by my side; thou art a godless man and therefore dost not see him.

Pe. Seize him! the fellow scorns me and Thebes too.

Di. I bid you bind me not, reason addressing madness.

Pe. But I say "bind!" with better right than thou.

Di. Thou hast no knowledge of the life thou art leading; thy very existence is now a mystery to thee.

Pe. I am Pentheus, son of Agave and Echion.

Di. Well-named to be misfortune's mate!

Pe. Avaunt! Ho! shut him up within the horses' stalls hard by, that for light he may have pitchy gloom. Do thy dancing there, and these women whom thou bringest with thee to share thy villainies I will either sell as slaves or make their hands cease from this noisy beating of drums, and set them to work at the loom as servants of my own.

Di. I will go; for that which fate forbids, can never befall me. For this thy mockery be sure Dionysus will exact a recompense of thee—even the god whose existence thou deniest; for thou art injuring him by haling me to prison.

Exit DIONYSUS, *guarded, and* PENTHEUS.

Ch. Hail to thee, Dirce, happy maid, daughter revered of Achelous! within thy founts thou didst receive in days gone by the babe of Zeus, what time his father caught him up into his thigh from out the deathless flame, while thus he cried: "Go rest, my Dithyrambus, there within thy father's womb; by this name, O Bacchic god, I now proclaim thee to Thebes." But thou, blest Dirce, thrustest me aside, when in thy midst I strive to hold my revels graced with crowns. Why dost thou scorn me? Why avoid me? By the clustered charm that Dionysus sheds o'er the vintage I vow there yet shall come a time when thou wilt turn thy thoughts to Bromius. What furious rage the earth-born race displays, even Pentheus sprung of a dragon of old, himself the son of earth-born Echion, a savage monster in his very mien, not made in human mould, but like some murderous giant pitted against heaven; for he means to bind me, the handmaid of Bromius, in cords forthwith, and e'en now he keeps my fellow-reveller pent within his palace, plunged in a gloomy dungeon. Dost thou mark this, O Dionysus, son of Zeus, thy prophets struggling 'gainst resistless might? Come, O king, brandishing thy golden thyrsus along the slopes of Olympus; restrain the pride of this bloodthirsty wretch! Oh! where in Nysa, haunt of beasts, or on the peaks of Corycus art thou, Dionysus, marshalling with thy wand the revellers? or haply in the thick forest depths of Olympus, where erst Orpheus with his lute gathered trees to his minstrelsy, and beasts that range the fields. Ah, blest Pieria! Evius honours thee, to thee will he come with his Bacchic rites to lead the dance, and thither will he lead the circling Mænads, crossing the swift current of Axius and the Lydias, that giveth wealth and happiness to man, yea, and the father of rivers, which, as I have heard, enriches with his waters fair a land of steeds.

Di. (*Within*) What ho! my Bacchantes, ho! hear my call, oh! hear.

Ch. I. Who art thou? what Evian cry is this that calls me? whence comes it?

Di. What ho! once more I call, I the son of Semele, the child of Zeus.

Ch. II. My master, O my master, hail!

Ch. III. Come to our revel-band, O Bromian god.

Ch. IV. Thou solid earth!

Ch. V. Most awful shock!

Ch. VI. O horror! soon will the palace of Pentheus totter and fall.

Ch. VII. Dionysus is within this house.

Ch. VIII. Do homage to him.

Ch. IX. We do! we do!

Ch. X. Did ye mark yon architrave of stone upon the columns start asunder?

Ch. XI. Within these walls the triumph-shout of Bromius himself will rise.

Di. Kindle the blazing torch with lightning's fire, abandon to the flames the halls of Pentheus.

Ch. XII. Ha! dost not see the flame, dost not clearly mark it at the sacred tomb of Semele, the lightning flame which long ago the hurler of the bolt left there?

Ch. XIII. Your trembling limbs prostrate, ye Mænads, low upon the ground.

Ch. XIV. Yea, for our king, the son of Zeus, is assailing and utterly confounding this house.

Enter DIONYSUS.

Di. Are ye so stricken with terror that ye have fallen to the earth, O foreign dames? Ye saw then, it would seem, how the Bacchic god made Pentheus' halls to quake; but arise, be of good heart, compose your trembling limbs.

Ch. O chiefest splendour of our gladsome Bacchic sport, with what joy I see thee in my loneliness!

Di. Were ye cast down when I was led into the house, to be plunged into the gloomy dungeons of Pentheus?

Ch. Indeed I was. Who was to protect me, if thou shouldst meet with mishap? But how wert thou set free from the clutches of this godless wretch?

Di. My own hands worked out my own salvation, easily and without trouble.

Ch. But did he not lash fast thy hands with cords?

Di. There too I mocked him; he thinks he bound me, whereas he never touched or caught hold of me, but fed himself on fancy. For at the stall, to which he brought me for a gaol, he found a bull, whose legs and hoofs he straightly tied, breathing out fury the while, the sweat trickling from his body, and he biting his lips; but I from near at hand sat calmly looking on. Meantime came the Bacchic god and made the house quake, and at his mother's tomb relit the fire; but Pentheus, seeing this, thought his palace was ablaze, and hither and thither he rushed, bidding his servants bring water; but all in vain was every servant's busy toil. Thereon he let this labour be awhile, and, thinking maybe that I had escaped, rushed into the palace with his murderous sword unsheathed. Then did Bromius—so at least it seemed to me; I only tell you what I thought—made a phantom in the hall, and he rushed after it in headlong haste, and stabbed the lustrous air, thinking he wounded me. Further the Bacchic god did other outrage to him; he dashed the building to the ground, and there it lies a mass of ruin, a sight to make him rue most bitterly my bonds. At last from sheer fatigue he dropped his sword and fell fainting; for he a mortal frail, dared to wage war upon a god; but I meantime quietly left the house and am come to you, with never a thought of Pentheus. But methinks he will soon appear before the house; at least there is a sound of steps within. What will he say, I wonder, after this? Well, be his fury never so great, I will lightly bear it; for 'tis a wise man's way to school his temper into due control.

Enter PENTHEUS.

Pe. Shamefully have I been treated; that stranger, whom but now I made so fast in prison, hath escaped me. Ha! there is the man! What means this? How didst thou come forth, to appear thus in front of my palace?

Di. Stay where thou art; and moderate thy fury.

Pe. How is it thou hast escaped thy fetters and art at large?

Di. Did I not say, or didst thou not hear me, "There is one will loose me."

Pe. Who was it? there is always something strange in what thou sayest.

Di. He who makes the clustering vine to grow for man.

Pe. * * *

Di. A fine taunt indeed thou hurlest here at Dionysus!

Pe. (*To his servants*) Bar every tower that hems us in, I order you.

Di. What use? Cannot gods pass even over walls?

Pe. How wise thou art, except where thy wisdom is needed!

Di. Where most 'tis needed, there am I most wise. But first listen to yonder messenger and hear what he says; he comes from the hills with tidings for thee; and I will await thy pleasure, nor seek to fly.

Enter MESSENGER.

Messenger. Pentheus, ruler of this realm of Thebes! I am come from Cithæron, where the dazzling flakes of pure white snow ne'er cease to fall.

Pe. What urgent news dost bring me?

Me. I have seen, O king, those frantic Bacchanals, who darted in frenzy from this land with bare white feet, and I am come to tell thee and the city the wondrous deeds they do, deeds passing strange. But I fain would hear, whether I am freely to tell all I saw there, or shorten my story; for I fear thy hasty temper, sire, thy sudden bursts of wrath and more than princely rage.

Pe. Say on, for thou shalt go unpunished by me in all respects; for to be angered with the upright is wrong. The direr thy tale about the Bacchantes, the heavier punishment will I inflict on this fellow who brought his secret arts amongst our women.

Me. I was just driving the herds of kine to a ridge of the hill as I fed them, as the sun shot forth his rays and made the earth grow warm; when lo! I see three revel-bands of women; Autonoe was chief of one, thy mother Agave of the second, while Ino's was the third. There they lay asleep, all tired out; some were resting on branches of the pine, others had laid their heads in careless ease on oak-leaves piled upon the ground, observing all modesty; not, as thou sayest, seeking to gratify their lusts alone amid the woods, by wine and soft flute-music maddened.

Anon in their midst thy mother uprose and cried aloud to wake them from their sleep, when she heard the lowing of my hornèd kine. And up they started to their feet, brushing from their eyes sleep's quickening dew, a wondrous sight of grace and modesty, young and old and maidens yet unwed. First o'er their shoulders they let stream their hair; then all did gird their fawn-skins up, who hitherto had left the fastenings loose, girdling the dappled hides with snakes that licked their cheeks. Others fondled in their arms gazelles or savage whelps of wolves, and suckled them—young mothers these with babes at home, whose breasts were still full of milk; crowns they wore of ivy or of oak or blossoming convolvulus. And one took her thyrsus and struck it into the earth, and forth there gushed a limpid spring; and another plunged her wand into the lap of earth and there the god sent up a fount of wine; and all who wished for draughts of milk had but to scratch the soil with their finger-tips and there they had it in abundance, while from every ivy-wreathed staff sweet rills of honey trickled.

Hadst thou been there and seen this, thou wouldst have turned to pray to the god, whom now thou dost disparage. Anon we herdsmen and shepherds met to discuss their strange and wondrous doings; then one, who wandereth oft to town and hath a trick of speech, made harangue in the midst, "O ye who dwell upon the hallowed mountain-terraces!

shall we chase Agave, mother of Pentheus, from her Bacchic rites, and thereby do our prince a service?" We liked his speech, and placed ourselves in hidden ambush among the leafy thickets; they at the appointed time began to wave the thyrsus for their Bacchic rites, calling on Iacchus, the Bromian god, the son of Zeus, in united chorus, and the whole mount and the wild creatures re-echoed their cry; all nature stirred as they rushed on. Now Agave chanced to come springing near me, so up I leapt from out my ambush where I lay concealed, meaning to seize her. But she cried out, "What ho! my nimble hounds, here are men upon our track; but follow me, ay, follow, with the thyrsus in your hand for weapon." Thereat we fled, to escape being torn in pieces by the Bacchantes; but they, with hands that bore no weapon of steel, attacked our cattle as they browsed. Then wouldst thou have seen Agave mastering some sleek lowing calf, while others rent the heifers limb from limb. Before thy eyes there would have been hurling of ribs and hoofs this way and that; and strips of flesh, all blood-bedabbled, dripped as they hung from the pine-branches. Wild bulls, that glared but now with rage along their horns, found themselves tripped up, dragged down to earth by countless maidens' hands. The flesh upon their limbs was stripped therefrom quicker than thou couldst have closed thy royal eye-lids. Then off they sped, like birds that skim the air, to the plains beneath the hills, which bear a fruitful harvest for Thebes beside the waters of Asopus; to Hysiae and Erythrae, hamlets 'neath Cithæron's peak, with fell intent, swooping on everything and scattering all pellmell; and they would snatch children from their homes; but all that they placed upon their shoulders, abode there firmly without being tied, and fell not to the dusky earth, not even brass or iron; and on their hair they carried fire and it burnt them not; but the country-folk rushed to arms, furious at being pillaged by Bacchanals; whereon ensued, O king, this wondrous spectacle. For though the iron-shod dart would draw no blood from them, they with the thyrsus, which they hurled, caused many a wound and put their foes to utter rout, women chasing men, by some god's intervention. Then they returned to the place whence they had started, even to the springs the god had made to spout for them; and there washed off the blood, while serpents with their tongues were licking clean each gout from their cheeks. Wherefore, my lord and master, receive this deity, whoe'er he be, within the city; for, great as he is in all else, I have likewise heard men say, 'twas he that gave the vine to man, sorrow's antidote. Take wine away and Cypris flies, and every other human joy is dead.

Ch. Though I fear to speak my mind with freedom in the presence of my king, still must I utter this; Dionysus yields to no deity in might.

Pe. Already, look you! the presumption of these Bacchantes is upon us, swift as fire, a sad disgrace in the eyes of all Hellas. No time for hesitation now! away to the Electra gate! order a muster of all my men-at-arms, of those that mount fleet steeds, of all who brandish light bucklers, of archers too that make the bowstring twang; for I will march against the Bacchanals. By Heaven! this passes all, if we are to be thus treated by women.

Exit MESSENGER.

Di. Still obdurate, O Pentheus, after hearing my words! In spite of all the evil treatment I am enduring from thee, still I warn thee of the sin of bearing arms against a god, and bid thee cease; for Bromius will not endure thy driving his votaries from the mountains where they revel.

Pe. A truce to thy preaching to me! thou hast escaped thy bonds, preserve thy liberty; else will I renew thy punishment.

Di. I would rather do him sacrifice than in a fury kick against the pricks; thou a mortal, he a god.

Pe. Sacrifice! that will I, by setting afoot a wholesale slaughter of women 'mid Cithæron's glens, as they deserve.

Di. Ye will all be put to flight—a shameful thing that they with the Bacchic thyrsus should rout your mail-clad warriors.

Pe. I find this stranger a troublesome foe to encounter; doing or suffering he is alike irrepressible.

Di. Friend, there is still a way to compose this bitterness.

Pe. Say how; am I to serve my own servants?

Di. I will bring the women hither without weapons.

Pe. Ha! ha! this is some crafty scheme of thine against me.

Di. What kind of scheme, if by my craft I purpose to save thee?

Pe. You have combined with them to form this plot, that your revels may go on for ever.

Di. Nay, but this is the very compact I made with the god; be sure of that.

Pe. (*Preparing to start forth*) Bring forth my arms. Not another word from thee!

Di. Ha! wouldst thou see them seated on the hills?

Pe. Of all things, yes! I would give untold sums for that.

Di. Why this sudden, strong desire?

Pe. 'Twill be a bitter sight, if I find them drunk with wine.

Di. And would that be a pleasant sight which will prove bitter to thee?

Pe. Believe me, yes! beneath the fir-trees as I sit in silence.

Di. Nay, they will track thee, though thou come secretly.

Pe. Well, I will go openly; thou wert right to say so.

Di. Am I to be thy guide? wilt thou essay the road?

Pe. Lead on with all speed, I grudge thee all delay.

Di. Array thee then in robes of fine linen.

Pe. Why so? Am I to enlist among women after being a man?

Di. They may kill thee, if thou show thy manhood there.

Pe. Well said! Thou hast given me a taste of thy wit already.

Di. Dionysus schooled me in this lore.

Pe. How am I to carry out thy wholesome advice?

Di. Myself will enter thy palace and robe thee.

Pe. What is the robe to be? a woman's? Nay, I am ashamed.

Di. Thy eagerness to see the Mænads goes no further.

Pe. But what dress dost say thou wilt robe me in?

Di. Upon thy head will I make thy hair grow long.

Pe. Describe my costume further.

Di. Thou wilt wear a robe reaching to thy feet; and on thy head shall be a snood.

Pe. Wilt add aught else to my attire?

Di. A thyrsus in thy hand, and a dappled fawnskin.

Pe. I can never put on woman's dress.

Di. Then wilt thou cause bloodshed by coming to blows with the Bacchanals.

Pe. Thou art right. Best go spy upon them first.

Di. Well, e'en that is wiser than by evil means to follow evil ends.

Pe. But how shall I pass through the city of the Cadmeans unseen?

Di. We will go by unfrequented paths. I will lead the way.

Pe. Anything rather than that the Bacchantes should laugh at me.

Di. We will enter the palace and consider the proper steps.

Pe. Thou hast my leave. I am all readiness. I will enter, prepared to set out either sword in hand or following thy advice. *Exit* PENTHEUS.

Di. Women! our prize is nearly in the net. Soon shall he reach the Bacchanals, and there pay forfeit with his life. O Dionysus! now 'tis thine to act, for thou art not far away; let us take vengeance on him. First drive him mad by fixing in his soul a wayward frenzy; for never, whilst his senses are his own, will he consent to don a woman's dress; but when his mind is gone astray he will put it on. And fain would I make him a laughing-stock to Thebes as he is led in woman's dress through the city, after those threats with which he menaced me before. But I will go to array Pentheus in those robes which he shall wear when he sets out for Hades' halls, a victim to his own mother's fury; so shall he recognize Dionysus, the son of Zeus, who proves himself at last a god most terrible, for all his gentleness to man. *Exit* DIONYSUS.

Ch. Will this white foot e'er join the night-long dance? what time in Bacchic ecstasy I toss my neck to heaven's dewy breath, like a fawn, that gambols 'mid the meadow's green delights, when she hath escaped the fearful chase, clear of the watchers, o'er the woven nets; while the huntsman, with loud halloo, harks on his hounds' full cry, and she with laboured breath at lightning speed bounds o'er the level water-meadows, glad to be far from man amid the foliage of the bosky grove. What is true wisdom, or what fairer boon has heaven placed in mortals' reach, than to gain the mastery o'er a fallen foe? What is fair is dear for aye. Though slow be its advance, yet surely moves the power of the gods, correcting those mortal wights, that court a senseless pride, or, in the madness of their fancy, disregard the gods. Subtly they lie in wait, through the long march of time, and so hunt down the godless man. For it is never right in theory or in practice to o'erride the law of custom. This is a maxim cheaply bought: whatever comes of God, or in time's long annals, has grown into a law upon a natural basis, this is sovereign. What is true wisdom, or what fairer boon has heaven placed in mortals' reach, than to gain the mastery o'er a fallen foe? What is fair is dear for aye. Happy is he who hath escaped the wave from out the sea, and reached the haven; and happy he who hath triumphed o'er his troubles; though one surpasses another in wealth and power; yet there be myriad hopes for all the myriad minds; some end in happiness for man, and others come to naught; but him, whose life from day to day is blest, I deem a happy man.

Enter DIONYSUS.

Di. Ho! Pentheus, thou that art so eager to see what is forbidden, and to show thy zeal in an unworthy cause, come forth before the palace, let me see thee clad as a woman in frenzied Bacchante's dress, to spy upon thy own mother and her company.

Enter PENTHEUS.

Yes, thou resemblest closely a daughter of Cadmus.

Pe. Of a truth I seem to see two suns, and two towns of Thebes, our seven-gated city; and thou, methinks, art a bull going before to guide me, and on thy head a pair of horns have grown. Wert thou really once a brute beast? Thon hast at any rate the appearance of a bull.

Di. The god attends us, ungracious heretofore, but now our sworn friend; and now thine eyes behold the things they should.

Pe. Pray, what do I resemble? Is not mine the carriage of Ino, or Agave my own mother?

Di. In seeing thee, I seem to see them in person. But this tress is straying from its place, no longer as I bound it 'neath the snood.

Pe. I disarranged it from its place as I tossed it to and fro within my chamber, in Bacchic ecstasy.

Di. Well, I will rearrange it, since to tend thee is my care; hold up thy head.

Pe. Come, put it straight; for on thee do I depend.

Di. Thy girdle is loose, and the folds of thy dress do not hang evenly below thy ankles.

Pe. I agree to that as regards the right side, but on the other my dress hangs straight with my foot.

Di. Surely thou wilt rank me first among thy friends, when contrary to thy expectation thou findest the Bacchantes virtuous.

Pe. Shall I hold the thyrsus in the right or left hand to look most like a Bacchanal?

Di. Hold it in thy right hand, and step out with thy right foot; thy change of mind compels thy praise.

Pe. Shall I be able to carry on my shoulders Cithæron's glens, the Bacchanals and all?

Di. Yes, if so thou wilt; for though thy mind was erst diseased, 'tis now just as it should be.

Pe. Shall we take levers, or with my hands can I uproot it, thrusting arm or shoulder 'neath its peaks?

Di. No, no! destroy not the seats of the Nymphs and the haunts of Pan, the place of his piping.

Pe. Well said! Women must not be mastered by brute force; amid the pines will I conceal myself.

Di. Thou shalt hide thee in the place that fate appoints, coming by stealth to spy upon the Bacchanals.

Pe. Why, methinks they are already caught in the pleasant snares of dalliance, like birds amid the brakes.

Di. Set out with watchful heed then for this very purpose; maybe thou wilt catch them, if thou be not first caught thyself.

Pe. Conduct me through the very heart of Thebes, for I am the only man among them bold enough to do this deed.

Di. Thou alone bearest thy country's burden, thou and none other; wherefore there await thee such struggles as needs must. Follow me, for I will guide thee safely thither; another shall bring thee thence.

Pe. My mother maybe.

Di. For every eye to see.

Pe. My very purpose in going.

Di. Thou shalt be carried back,

Pe. What luxury!

Di. In thy mother's arms.

Pe. Thou wilt e'en force me into luxury.

Di. Yes, to luxury such as this.

Pe. Truly, the task I am undertaking deserves it.

Exit PENTHEUS.

Di. Strange, ah! strange is thy career, leading to scenes of woe so strange, that thou shalt achieve a fame that towers to heaven. Stretch forth thy hands, Agave, and ye her sisters, daughters of Cadmus; mighty is the strife to which I am bringing the youthful king, and the victory shall rest with me and Bromius; all else the event will show.

Exit DIONYSUS.

Ch. To the hills! to the hills! fleet hounds of madness, where the daughters of Cadmus hold their revels, goad them into wild fury against the man disguised in woman's dress, a frenzied spy upon the Mænads. First shall his mother mark him as he peers from some smooth rock or riven tree, and thus to the Mænads she will call, "Who is this of Cadmus' sons comes hasting to the mount, to the mountain away, to spy on us, my Bacchanals? Whose child can he be? For he was never born of woman's blood; but from some lioness maybe or Libyan Gorgon is he sprung." Let justice appear and show herself, sword in hand, to plunge it through and through the throat of the godless, lawless, impious son of Echion, earth's monstrous child! who with wicked heart and lawless rage, with mad intent and frantic purpose, sets out to meddle with thy holy rites, and with thy mother's, Bacchic god, thinking with his weak arm to master might as masterless as thine. This is the life that saves all pain, if a man confine his thoughts to human themes, as is his mortal nature, making no pretence where heaven is concerned. I envy not deep subtleties; far other joys have I, in tracking out great truths writ clear from all eternity, that a man should live his life by day and night in purity and holiness, striving toward a noble goal, and should honour the gods by casting from him each ordinance that lies outside the pale of right. Let justice show herself, advancing sword in hand to plunge it through and through the throat of Echion's son, that godless, lawless, and abandoned child of earth! Appear, O Bacchus, to our eyes as a bull or serpent with a hundred heads, or take the shape of a lion breathing flame! Oh! come, and with a mocking smile cast the deadly noose about the hunter of thy Bacchanals, e'en as he swoops upon the Mænads gathered yonder.

Enter 2ND MESSENGER.

2nd. Messenger. O house, so prosperous once through Hellas long ago, home of the old Sidonian prince, who sowed the serpent's crop of earth-born men, how do I mourn thee! slave though I be, yet still the sorrows of his master touch a good slave's heart.

Ch. How now? Hast thou fresh tidings of the Bacchantes?

2nd. Me. Pentheus, Echion's son is dead.

Ch. Bromius, my king! now art thou appearing in thy might divine.

2nd. Me. Ha! what is it thou sayest? art thou glad, woman, at my master's misfortunes?

Ch. A stranger I, and in foreign tongue I express my joy, for now no more do I cower in terror of the chain.

2nd. Me. Dost think Thebes so poor in men * * ?

* * *[1]

Ch. 'Tis Dionysus, Dionysus, not Thebes that lords it over me.

2nd. Me. All can I pardon thee save this; to exult o'er hopeless suffering is sorry conduct, dames.

Ch. Tell me, oh! tell me how he died, that villain scheming villainy!

2nd. Me. Soon as we had left the homesteads of this Theban land and had crossed the streams of Asopus, we began to breast Cithæron's heights, Pentheus and I, for I went with my master, and the stranger too, who was to guide us to the scene. First then we sat us down in a grassy glen, carefully silencing each footfall and whispered breath, to see without being seen. Now there was a dell walled in by rocks, with rills to water it, and shady pines o'erhead; there were the Mænads seated, busied with joyous toils. Some were wreathing afresh the drooping thyrsus with curling ivy-sprays; others, like colts let loose from the carved chariot-yoke, were answer-

[1]Probably the whole of one iambic line with part of another is here lost.

ing each other in hymns of Bacchic rapture. But Pentheus, son of sorrow, seeing not the women gathered there, exclaimed, "Sir stranger, from where I stand, I cannot clearly see the mock Bacchantes; but I will climb a hillock or a soaring pine whence to see clearly the shameful doings of the Bacchanals." Then and there I saw the stranger work a miracle; for catching a lofty fir-branch by the very end he drew it downward to the dusky earth, lower yet and ever lower; and like a bow it bent, or rounded wheel, whose curving circle grows complete, as chalk and line describe it; e'en so the stranger drew down the mountain-branch between his hands, bending it to earth, by more than human agency. And when he had seated Pentheus aloft on the pine branches, he let them slip through his hands gently, careful not to shake him from his seat. Up soared the branch straight into the air above, with my master perched thereon, seen by the Mænads better far than he saw them; for scarce was he beheld upon his lofty throne, when the stranger disappeared, while from the sky there came a voice, 'twould seem, by Dionysus uttered—

"Maidens, I bring the man who tried to mock you and me and my mystic rites; take vengeance on him." And as he spake, he raised 'twixt heaven and earth a dazzling column of awful flame. Hushed grew the sky, and still hung each leaf throughout the grassy glen, nor couldst thou have heard one creature cry. But they, not sure of the voice they heard, sprang up and peered all round; then once again his bidding came; and when the daughters of Cadmus knew it was the Bacchic god in very truth that called, swift as doves they darted off in eager haste, his mother Agave and her sisters dear and all the Bacchanals; through torrent glen, o'er boulders huge they bounded on, inspired with madness by the god. Soon as they saw my master perched upon the fir, they set to hurling stones at him with all their might, mounting a commanding eminence, and with pine-branches he was pelted as with darts; and others shot their wands through the air at Pentheus, their hapless target, but all to no purpose. For there he sat beyond the reach of their hot endeavours, a helpless, hopeless victim. At last they rent off limbs from oaks and were for prising up the roots with levers not of iron. But when they still could make no end to all their toil, Agave cried: "Come stand around, and grip the sapling trunk, my Bacchanals! that we may catch the beast that sits thereon, lest he divulge the secrets of our god's religion."

Then were a thousand hands laid on the fir, and from the ground they tore it up, while he from his seat aloft came tumbling to the ground with lamentations long and loud, e'en Pentheus; for well he knew his hour was come. His mother first, a priestess for the nonce, began the bloody deed and fell upon him; whereon he tore the snood from off his hair, that hapless Agave might recognize and spare him, crying as he touched her cheek, "O mother! it is I, thy own son Pentheus, the child thou didst bear in Echion's halls; have pity on me, mother dear! oh! do not for any sin of mine slay thy own son."

But she, the while, with foaming mouth and wildly rolling eyes, bereft of reason as she was, heeded him not; for the god possessed her. And she caught his left hand in her grip, and planting her foot upon her victim's trunk she tore the shoulder from its socket, not of her own strength, but the god made it an easy task to her hands; and Ino set to work upon the other side, rending the flesh with Autonoe and all the eager host of Bacchanals; and one united cry arose, the victim's groans while yet he breathed, and their triumphant shouts. One would make an arm her prey, another a foot with the sandal on it; and his ribs were stripped of flesh by their rending nails; and each one with blood-dabbled hands was tossing Pentheus' limbs about. Scattered lies his corpse, part beneath the rugged rocks, and part amid the deep dark woods, no easy task to find; but his poor head hath his mother made her own, and fixing it upon the point of a thyrsus, as it had been a mountain lion's, she bears it through the midst of Cithæron, having left her sisters with the Mænads at their rites. And she is entering these walls exulting in her hunting fraught with woe, calling on the Bacchic god her fellow-hunter who had helped her to triumph in a chase, where her only prize was tears.

But I will get me hence, away from this piteous scene, before Agave reach the palace. To my mind self-restraint and reverence for the things of God point alike the best and wisest course for all mortals who pursue them.

Exit 2ND MESSENGER.

Ch. Come, let us exalt our Bacchic god in choral strain, let us loudly chant the fall of Pentheus from the serpent sprung, who assumed a woman's dress and took the fair Bacchic wand, sure pledge of death, with a bull to guide him to his doom. O ye Bacchanals of Thebes! glorious is the triumph ye have achieved, ending in sorrow and tears. 'Tis a noble enterprise to dabble the hand in the blood of a son till it drips. But hist! I see Agave, the mother of Pentheus, with wild rolling eye hasting to the house; welcome the revellers of the Bacchic god.

Enter AGAVE.

Agave. Ye Bacchanals from Asia!

Ch. Why dost thou rouse me? why?

Ag. From the hills I am bringing to my home a tendril freshly-culled, glad guerdon of the chase.

Ch. I see it, and I will welcome thee unto our revels. All hail!

Ag. I caught him with never a snare, this lion's whelp, as ye may see.

Ch. From what desert lair?

Ag. Cithæron—

Ch. Yes, Cithæron?

Ag. Was his death.

Ch. Who was it gave the first blow?

Ag. Mine that privilege; "Happy Agave!" they call me 'mid our revellers.

Ch. Who did the rest?

Ag. Cadmus—

Ch. What of him?

Ag. His daughters struck the monster after me; yes, after me.

Ch. Fortune smiled upon thy hunting here.

Ag. Come, share the banquet.

Ch. Share? ah! what?

Ag. 'Tis but a tender whelp, the down just sprouting on its cheek beneath a crest of falling hair.

Ch. The hair is like some wild creature's.

Ag. The Bacchic god, a hunter skilled, roused his Mænads to pursue this quarry skilfully.

Ch. Yea, our king is a hunter indeed.

Ag. Dost approve?

Ch. Of course I do.

Ag. Soon shall the race of Cadmus—

Ch. And Pentheus, her own son, shall to his mother—

Ag. Offer praise for this her quarry of the lion's brood.

Ch. Quarry strange!

Ag. And strangely caught.

Ch. Dost thou exult?

Ag. Right glad am I to have achieved a great and glorious triumph for my land that all can see.

Ch. Alas for thee! show to the folk the booty thou hast won and art bringing hither.

Ag. All ye who dwell in fair fenced Thebes, draw near! that ye may see the fierce wild beast that we daughters of Cadmus made our prey, not with the thong-thrown darts of Thessaly, nor yet with snares, but with our fingers fair. Ought men idly to boast and get them armourers' weapons? when we with these our hands have caught this prey and torn the monster limb from limb? Where is my aged sire? let him approach. And where is Pentheus, my son? Let him bring a ladder and raise it against the house to nail up on the gables this lion's head, my booty from the chase.

Enter CADMUS.

Ca. Follow me, servants to the palace-front, with your sad burden in your arms, ay, follow, with the corpse of Pentheus, which after long weary search I found, as ye see it, torn to pieces amid Cithæron's glens, and am bringing hither; no two pieces did I find together, as they lay scattered through the trackless wood. For I heard what awful deeds one of my daughters had done, just as I entered the city-walls with old Teiresias returning from the Bacchanals; so I turned again unto the hill and bring from thence my son who was slain by Mænads. There I saw Autonoe, that bare Actæon on a day to Aristæus, and Ino with her, still ranging the oak-groves in their unhappy frenzy; but one told me that that other, Agave, was rushing wildly hither, nor was it idly said, for there I see her, sight of woe!

Ag. Father, loudly mayst thou boast, that the daughters thou hast begotten are far the best of mortal race; of one and all I speak, though chiefly of myself, who left my shuttle at the loom for nobler enterprise, even to hunt savage beasts with my hands; and in my arms I bring my prize, as thou seest, that it may be nailed up on thy palace-wall; take it, father, in thy hands, and proud of my hunting, call thy friends to a banquet; for blest art thou, ah! doubly blest in these our gallant exploits.

Ca. O grief that has no bounds, too cruel for mortal eye! 'tis murder ye have done with your hapless hands. Fair is the victim thou hast offered to the gods, inviting me and my Thebans to the feast! Ah, woe is me! first for thy sorrows, then for mine. What ruin the god, the Bromian king, hath brought on us, just maybe, but too severe, seeing he is our kinsman!

Ag. How peevish old age makes men! what sullen looks! Oh, may my son follow in his mother's footsteps and be as lucky in his hunting, when he goes in quest of game in company with Theban youths! But he can do naught but wage war with gods. Father, 'tis thy duty to warn him. Who will summon him hither to my sight to witness my happiness?

Ca. Alas for you! alas! Terrible will be your grief when ye are conscious of your deeds; could ye remain for ever till life's close in your present state, ye would not, spite of ruined bliss, appear so cursed with woe.

Ag. Why? what is faulty here? what here for sorrow?

Ca. First let thine eye look up to heaven.

Ag. See! I do so. Why dost thou suggest my looking thereupon?

Ca. Is it still the same, or dost think there's any change?

Ag. 'Tis brighter than it was, and clearer too.

Ca. Is there still that wild unrest within thy soul?

Ag. I know not what thou sayest now; yet methinks my brain is clearing, and my former frenzy passed away.

Ca. Canst understand, and give distinct replies?

Ag. Father, how completely I forget all we said before!

Ca. To what house wert thou brought with marriage-hymns?

Ag. Thou didst give me to earthborn Echion, as men call him.

Ca. What child was born thy husband in his halls?

Ag. Pentheus, of my union with his father.

Ca. What head is that thou barest in thy arms?

Ag. A lion's; at least they said so, who hunted it.

Ca. Consider it aright; 'tis no great task to look at it.

Ag. Ah! what do I see? what is this I am carrying in my hands?

Ca. Look closely at it; make thy knowledge more certain.

Ag. Ah, woe is me! O sight of awful sorrow!

Ca. Dost think it like a lion's head?

Ag. Ah no! 'tis Pentheus' head which I his unhappy mother hold.

Ca. Bemoaned by me, or ever thou didst recognize him.

Ag. Who slew him? How came he into my hands?

Ca. O piteous truth! how ill-timed thy presence here!

Ag. Speak; my bosom throbs at this suspense.

Ca. 'Twas thou didst slay him, thou and thy sisters.

Ag. Where died he? in the house or where?

Ca. On the very spot where hounds of yore rent Actæon in pieces.

Ag. Why went he, wretched youth! to Cithæron?

Ca. He would go and mock the god and thy Bacchic rites.

Ag. But how was it we had journeyed thither?

Ca. Ye were distraught; the whole city had the Bacchic frenzy.

Ag. 'Twas Dionysus proved our ruin; now I see it all.

Ca. Yes, for the slight he suffered; ye would not believe in his godhead.

Ag. Father, where is my dear child's corpse?

Ca. With toil I searched it out and am bringing it myself.

Ag. Is it all fitted limb to limb in seemly wise?

Ca.[1] * * *

Ag. But what had Pentheus to do with folly of mine?

Ca. He was like you in refusing homage to the god, who, therefore, hath involved you all in one common ruin, you and him alike, to destroy this house and me, forasmuch as I, that had no sons, behold this youth, the fruit of thy womb, unhappy mother! foully and most shamefully slain. To thee, my child, our house looked up, to thee my daughter's son, the stay of my palace, inspiring the city with awe; none caring to flout the old king when he saw thee by, for he would get his deserts. But now shall I be cast out dishonoured from my halls, Cadmus the great, who sowed the crop of Theban seed and reaped that goodly harvest. O beloved child! dead though thou art, thou still shalt be counted by me amongst my own dear children; no more wilt thou lay thy hand upon my chin in fond embrace, my child, and calling on thy mother's sire demand, "Who wrongs thee or dishonours thee, old sire? who vexes thy heart, a thorn within thy side? Speak, that I may punish thy oppressor, father mine!"

But now am I in sorrow plunged, and woe is thee, and woe thy mother and her suffering sisters too! Ah! if there be any man that scorns the gods, let him well mark this prince's death and then believe in them.

Ch. Cadmus, I am sorry for thy fate; for though thy daughter's child hath met but his deserts, 'tis bitter grief to thee.

Ag. O father, thou seest how sadly my fortune is changed.[2]

* * *

Di. * * *

Thou shalt be changed into a serpent; and thy wife Harmonia, Ares' child, whom thou in thy human life didst wed, shall change her nature for a snake's, and take its form. With her shalt thou, as leader of barbarian tribes, drive thy team of steers, so saith an oracle of Zeus; and many a city shalt thou sack with an army numberless; but in the day they plunder the oracle of Loxias, shall they rue their homeward march; but thee and Harmonia will Ares rescue, and set thee to live henceforth in the land of the blessed. This do I declare, I Dionysus, son of no mortal father but of Zeus. Had ye learnt wisdom when ye would not, ye would now be happy with the son of Zeus for your ally.

Ag. O Dionysus! we have sinned; thy pardon we implore.

Di. Too late have ye learnt to know me; ye knew me not at the proper time.

Ag. We recognize our error; but thou art too revengeful.

Di. Yea, for I, though a god, was slighted by you.

Ag. Gods should not let their passion sink to man's level.

Di. Long ago my father Zeus ordained it thus.

Ag. Alas! my aged sire, our doom is fixed; 'tis woful exile.

Di. Why then delay the inevitable? *Exit*.

Ca. Daughter, to what an awful pass are we now come, thou too, poor child, and thy sisters, while I alas! in my old age must seek barbarian shores, to sojourn there; but the oracle declares that I shall yet lead an army, half-barbarian, half-Hellene, to Hellas; and in serpent's shape shall I carry my wife Harmonia, the daughter of Ares, transformed like me to a savage snake, against the altars and tombs of Hellas at the head of my troops; nor shall I ever cease from my woes, ah me! nor ever cross the downward stream of Acheron and be at rest.

Ag. Father, I shall be parted from thee and exiled.

Ca. Alas! my child, why fling thy arms around me, as a snowy cygnet folds its wings about the frail old swan?

Ag. Whither can I turn, an exile from my country?

Ca. I know not, my daughter; small help is thy father now.

Ag. Farewell, my home! farewell, my native city! with sorrow I am leaving thee, an exile from my bridal bower.

Ca. Go, daughter, to the house of Aristæus,[3]

* * *

Ag. Father, I mourn for thee.

Ca. And I for thee, my child; for thy sisters too I shed a tear.

Ag. Ah! terribly was king Dionysus bringing this outrage on thy house.

Ca. Yea, for he suffered insults dire from you, his name receiving no meed of honour in Thebes.

Ag. Farewell, father mine!

Ca. Farewell, my hapless daughter! and yet thou scarce canst reach that bourn.

Ag. Oh! lead me, guide me to the place where I shall find my sisters, sharers in my exile to their

[1]One line, if not more, is wanting here.

[2]After this line a very large lacuna occurs in the MS.

[3]Another lacuna follows.

sorrow! Oh! to reach a spot where cursed Cithæron ne'er shall see me more nor I Cithæron with mine eyes; where no memorial of the thyrsus is set up! Be they to other Bacchantes dear!

Ch. Many are the forms the heavenly will assumes, and many a thing the gods fulfil contrary to all hope; that which was expected is not brought to pass, while for the unlooked-for Heaven finds out a way. E'en such hath been the issue here.

Exeunt OMNES.

HECUBA

DRAMATIS PERSONAE

The Ghost of Polydore
Hecuba
Chorus of Captive Trojan Women
Polyxena
Odysseus
Talthybius
Maid
Agamemnon
Polymestor, *and his children*

Scene: *Before Agamemnon's tent upon the shore of the Thracian Chersonese. Enter* ghost of polydore.

Ghost. Lo! I am come from out the charnel-house and gates of gloom, where Hades dwells apart from gods, I, Polydore, a son of Hecuba the daughter of Cisseus and of Priam. Now my father, when Phrygia's capital was threatened with destruction by the spear of Hellas, took alarm and conveyed me secretly from the land of Troy unto Polymestor's house, his friend in Thrace, who sows these fruitful plains of Chersonese, curbing by his might a nation delighting in horses. And with me my father sent great store of gold by stealth, that, if ever Ilium's walls should fall, his children that survived might not want for means to live. I was the youngest of Priam's sons; and this it was that caused my stealthy removal from the land; for my childish arm availed not to carry weapons or to wield the spear. So long then as the bulwarks of our land stood firm, and Troy's battlements abode unshaken, and my brother Hector prospered in his warring, I, poor child, grew up and flourished, like some vigorous shoot, at the court of the Thracian, my father's friend. But when Troy fell and Hector lost his life and my father's hearth was rooted up, and himself fell butchered at the god-built altar by the hands of Achilles' murderous son; then did my father's friend slay me his helpless guest for the sake of the gold, and thereafter cast me into the swell of the sea, to keep the gold for himself in his house. And there I lie one time upon the strand, another in the salt sea's surge, drifting ever up and down upon the billows, unwept, unburied; but now am I hovering o'er the head of my dear mother Hecuba, a disembodied spirit, keeping my airy station these three days, ever since my poor mother came from Troy to linger here in Chersonese. Meantime all the Achæans sit idly here in their ships at the shores of Thrace; for the son of Peleus, even Achilles, appeared above his tomb and stayed the whole host of Hellas, as they were making straight for home across the sea, demanding to have my sister Polyxena offered at his tomb, and to receive his guerdon.[1] And he will obtain this prize, nor will they that are his friends refuse the gift; and on this very day is fate leading my sister to her doom. So will my mother see two children dead at once, me and that ill-fated maid. For I, to win a grave, ah me! will appear amid the rippling waves before her bond-maid's feet. Yes! I have won this boon from the powers below, that I should find a tomb and fall into my mother's hands; so shall I get my heart's desire; wherefore I will go and waylay aged Hecuba, for yonder she passeth on her way from the shelter of Agamemnon's tent, terrified at my spectre. (*Enter* hecuba) Woe is thee! ah, mother mine! from a palace dragged to face a life of slavery! how sad thy lot, as sad as once 'twas blest! Some god is now destroying thee, setting this in the balance to outweigh thy former bliss. ghost *vanishes*.

Hecuba. Guide these aged steps, my servants, forth before the house; support your fellow-slave, your queen of yore, ye maids of Troy. Take hold upon my aged hand, support me, guide me, lift me up; and I will lean upon your bended arm as on a staff and quicken my halting footsteps onwards. O dazzling light of Zeus! O gloom of night! why am I thus scared by fearful visions of the night? O earth, dread queen, mother of dreams that flit on sable wings! I am seeking to avert the vision of the night, the sight of horror which I saw so clearly in my dreams touching my son, who is safe in Thrace, and Polyxena my daughter dear. Ye gods of this land! preserve my son, the last and only anchor of my house, now settled in Thrace, the land of snow, safe in the keeping of his father's friend. Some fresh disaster is in store, a new strain of sorrow will be added to our woe. Such ceaseless thrills of terror never wrung my heart before. Oh! where, ye Trojan maidens, can I find inspired Helenus or Cassandra, that they may read me my dream? For I saw a dappled hind mangled by a wolf's bloody fangs, torn from my knees by force in piteous wise. And this too filled me with affright; o'er the summit of his tomb appeared Achilles' phantom, and for his guerdon he would have one of the luckless maids of Troy. Wherefore, I implore you, powers divine, avert this horror from my daughter, from my child.

Enter chorus of captive trojan women.

Chorus. Hecuba, I have hastened away to thee, leaving my master's tent, where the lot assigned me

[1] Polyxena is said to have been betrothed to Achilles.

as his appointed slave, in the day that I was driven from the city of Ilium, hunted by Achæans thence at the point of the spear; no alleviation bring I for thy sufferings; nay, I have laden myself with heavy news, and am a herald of sorrow to thee, lady. 'Tis said the Achæans have determined in full assembly to offer thy daughter in sacrifice to Achilles; for thou knowest how one day he appeared standing on his tomb in golden harness, and stayed the sea-borne barques, though they had their sails already hoisted, with this pealing cry, "Whither away so fast, ye Danai, leaving my tomb without its prize?" Thereon arose a violent dispute with stormy altercation, and opinion was divided in the warrior host of Hellas, some being in favour of offering the sacrifice at the tomb, others dissenting. There was Agamemnon, all eagerness in thy interest, because of his love for the frenzied prophetess; but the two sons of Theseus, scions of Athens, though supporting different proposals, yet agreed on the same decision, which was to crown Achilles' tomb with fresh-spilt blood; for they said they never would set Cassandra's love before Achilles' valour. Now the zeal of the rival disputants was almost equal, until that shifty, smooth-mouthed varlet, the son of Laertes, whose tongue is ever at the service of the mob, persuaded the army not to put aside the best of all the Danai for want of a bond-maid's sacrifice, nor have it said by any of the dead that stand beside Persephone, "The Danai have left the plains of Troy without one thought of gratitude for their brethren who died for Hellas." Odysseus will be here in an instant, to drag the tender maiden from thy breast and tear her from thy aged arms. To the temples, to the altars with thee! at Agamemnon's knees throw thyself as a suppliant! Invoke alike the gods in heaven and those beneath the earth. For either shall thy prayers avail to spare thee the loss of thy unhappy child, or thou must live to see thy daughter fall before the tomb, her crimson blood spurting in deep dark jets from her neck with gold encircled.

He. Woe, woe is me! What words, or cries, or lamentations can I utter? Ah me! for the sorrows of my closing years! for slavery too cruel to brook or bear! Woe, woe is me! What champion have I? Sons, and city—where are they? Aged Priam is no more; no more my children now. Which way am I to go, or this or that? Whither shall I turn my steps? Where is any god or power divine to succour me? Ah, Trojan maids! bringers of evil tidings! messengers of woe! ye have made an end, an utter end of me; life on earth has no more charm for me. Ah! luckless steps, lead on, guide your aged mistress to yon tent. My child, come forth; come forth, thou daughter of the queen of sorrows; listen to thy mother's voice, my child, that thou mayst know the hideous rumour I now hear about thy life.

Enter POLYXENA.

Polyxena. O mother, mother mine! why dost thou call so loud? what news is it thou hast proclaimed, scaring me, like a cowering bird, from my chamber by this alarm?

He. Alas, my daughter!

Polyx. Why this ominous address? it bodeth sorrow for me.

He. Woe for thy life!

Polyx. Tell all, hide it no longer. Ah mother! how I dread, ay dread the import of thy loud laments.

He. Ah my daughter! a luckless mother's child!

Polyx. Why dost thou tell me this?

He. The Argives with one consent are eager for thy sacrifice to the son of Peleus at his tomb.

Polyx. Ah! mother mine! how canst thou speak of such a dire mischance? Yet tell me all, yes all, O mother dear!

He. 'Tis a rumour ill-boding I tell, my child; they bring me word that sentence is passed upon thy life by the Argives' vote.

Polyx. Alas, for thy cruel sufferings! my persecuted mother! woe for thy life of grief! What grievous outrage some fiend hath sent thee, hateful, horrible! No more shall I thy daughter share thy bondage, hapless youth on hapless age attending. For thou, alas! wilt see thy hapless child torn from thy arms, as a calf of the hills is torn from its mother, and sent beneath the darkness of the earth with severed throat for Hades, where with the dead shall I be laid, ah me! For thee I weep with plaintive wail, mother doomed to a life of sorrow! for my own life, its ruin and its outrage, never a tear I shed; nay, death is become to me a happier lot than life.

Ch. See where Odysseus comes in haste, to announce some fresh command to thee, Hecuba.

Enter ODYSSEUS.

Odysseus. Lady, methinks thou knowest already the intention of the host, and the vote that has been passed; still will I declare it. It is the Achæans' will to sacrifice thy daughter Polyxena at the mound heaped o'er Achilles' grave; and they appoint me to take the maid and bring her thither, while the son of Achilles is chosen to preside o'er the sacrifice and act as priest. Dost know then what to do? Be not forcibly torn from her, nor match thy might 'gainst mine; recognize the limits of thy strength, and the presence of thy troubles. Even in adversity 'tis wise to yield to reason's dictates.

He. Ah me! an awful trial is nigh, it seems, fraught with mourning, rich in tears. Yes, I too escaped death where death had been my due, and Zeus destroyed me not but is still preserving my life, that I may witness in my misery fresh sorrows surpassing all before. Still if the bond may ask the free of things that grieve them not nor wrench their heart-strings, 'tis well that thou shouldst make an end and hearken to my questioning.

Od. Granted; put thy questions; that short delay I grudge thee not.

He. Dost remember the day thou camest to spy on Ilium, disguised in rags and tatters, while down thy cheek ran drops of blood?

Od. Remember it! yes; 'twas no slight impression it made upon my heart.

He. Did Helen recognize thee and tell me only?

Od. I well remember the awful risk I ran.

He. Didst thou embrace my knees in all humility?

Od. Yea, so that my hand grew dead and cold upon thy robe.

He. What saidst thou then, when in my power?

Od. Doubtless I found plenty to say, to save my life.

He. Was it I that saved and sent thee forth again?

Od. Thou didst, and so I still behold the light of day.

He. Art not thou then playing a sorry part to plot against me thus, after the kind treatment thou didst by thy own confession receive from me, showing me no gratitude but all the ill thou canst? A thankless race! all ye who covet honour from the mob for your oratory. Oh that ye were unknown to me! ye who harm your friends and think no more of it, if ye can but say a word to win the mob. But tell me, what kind of cleverness did they think it, when against this child they passed their bloody vote? Was it duty led them to slay a human victim at the tomb, where sacrifice of oxen more befits? or does Achilles, if claiming the lives of those who slew him as his recompense, show his justice by marking her out for death? No! she at least ne'er injured him. He should have demanded Helen as a victim at his tomb, for she it was that proved his ruin, bringing him to Troy; or if some captive of surpassing beauty was to be singled out for doom, this pointed not to us; for the daughter of Tyndareus was fairer than all womankind, and her injury to him was proved no less than ours. Against the justice of his plea I pit this argument. Now hear the recompense due from thee to me at my request. On thy own confession, thou didst fall at my feet and embrace my hand and aged cheek; I in my turn now do the same to thee, and claim the favour then bestowed; and I implore thee, tear not my child from my arms, nor slay her. There be dead enough; she is my only joy, in her I forget my sorrows; my one comfort she in place of many a loss, my city and my nurse, my staff and journey's guide. 'Tis never right that those in power should use it out of season, or when prosperous suppose they will be always so. For I like them was prosperous once, but now my life is lived, and one day robbed me of all my bliss. Friend, by thy beard, have some regard and pity for me; go to Achæa's host, and talk them over, saying how hateful a thing it is to slay women whom at first ye spared out of pity, after dragging them from the altars. For amongst you the self-same law holds good for bond and free alike respecting bloodshed; such influence as thine will persuade them even though thy words are weak; for the same argument, when proceeding from those of no account, has not the same force as when it is uttered by men of mark.

Ch. Human nature is not so stony-hearted as to hear thy plaintive tale and catalogue of sorrows, without shedding a tear.

Od. O Hecuba! be schooled by me, nor in thy passion count him a foe who speaketh wisely. Thy life I am prepared to save, for the service I received; I say no otherwise. But what I said to all, I will not now deny, that after Troy's capture I would give thy daughter to the chiefest of our host because he asked a victim. For herein is a source of weakness to most states, whene'er a man of brave and generous soul receives no greater honour than his inferiors. Now Achilles, lady, deserves honour at our hands, since for Hellas he died as nobly as a mortal can. Is not this a foul reproach to treat a man as a friend in life, but, when he is gone from us, to treat him so no more? How now? what will they say, if once more there comes a gathering of the host and a contest with the foe? "Shall we fight or nurse our lives, seeing the dead have no honours?" For myself, indeed, though in life my daily store were scant, yet would it be all-sufficient, but as touching a tomb I should wish mine to be an object of respect, for this gratitude has long to run. Thou speakest of cruel sufferings; hear my answer. Amongst us are aged dames and grey old men no less miserable than thou, and brides of gallant husbands reft, o'er whom this Trojan dust has closed. Endure these sorrows; for us, if we are wrong in resolving to honour the brave, we shall bring upon ourselves a charge of ignorance; but as for you barbarians, regard not your friends as such and pay no homage to your gallant dead, that Hellas may prosper and ye may reap the fruits of such policy.

Ch. Alas! how cursed is slavery alway in its nature, forced by the might of the stronger to endure unseemly treatment.

He. Daughter, my pleading to avert thy bloody death was wasted idly on the air; do thou, if in aught endowed with greater power to move than thy mother, make haste to use it, uttering every pleading note like the tuneful nightingale, to save thy soul from death. Throw thyself at Odysseus' knees to move his pity, and try to move him. Here is thy plea: he too hath children, so that he can feel for thy sad fate.

Polyx. Odysseus, I see thee hiding thy right hand beneath thy robe and turning away thy face, that I may not touch thy beard. Take heart; thou art safe from the suppliant's god in my case, for I will follow thee, alike because I must and because it is my wish to die; for were I loth, a coward should I show myself, a woman faint of heart. Why should I prolong my days? I whose sire was king of all the Phrygians—my chiefest pride in life. Then was I nursed on fair fond hopes to be a bride for kings, the centre of keen jealousy amongst suitors, to see whose home I would make my own; and o'er each dame of Ida I was queen; ah me! a maiden marked amid her fellows, equal to a goddess, save for death alone, but now a slave! That name first makes me long for death, so strange it sounds; and then maybe my lot might give me to some savage master, one that would buy me for money—me the sister of Hector and many another chief—who would make me knead him bread within his halls, or sweep his house or set me working at the loom, leading a life of misery; while some slave, bought I know not whence, will taint my maiden charms, once deemed worthy of royalty. No, never! Here I close my eyes upon the light, free as yet, and dedicate myself to Hades. Lead me hence, Odysseus, and do thy worst, for I see naught within my reach to make me hope or expect with any confidence that I am ever again to be happy. Mother mine! seek not to hinder me by word or deed, but join in my wish for death ere I meet with shameful treatment undeserved. For whoso is not used to taste of sorrow's cup, though he bears it, yet it galls him when he puts his neck within the yoke; far happier would he be dead than alive, for life of honour reft is toil and trouble.

Ch. A wondrous mark, most clearly stamped, doth noble birth imprint on men, and the name goeth still further where it is deserved.

He. A noble speech, my daughter! but there is sorrow linked with its noble sentiments.

Odysseus, if ye must pleasure the son of Peleus, and avoid reproach, slay not this maid, but lead me to Achilles' pyre and torture me unsparingly; 'twas I that bore Paris, whose fatal shaft laid low the son of Thetis.

Od. 'Tis not thy death, old dame, Achilles' wraith hath demanded of the Achæans, but hers.

He. At least then slaughter me with my child; so shall there be a double draught of blood for the earth and the dead that claims this sacrifice.

Od. The maiden's death suffices; no need to add a second to the first; would we needed not e'en this!

He. Die with my daughter I must and will.

Od. How so? I did not know I had a master.

He. I will cling to her like ivy to an oak.

Od. Not if thou wilt hearken to those who are wiser than thyself.

He. Be sure I will never willingly relinquish my child.

Od. Well, be equally sure I will never go away and leave her here.

Polyx. Mother, hearken to me; and thou, son of Laertes, make allowance for a parent's natural wrath. My poor mother, fight not with our masters. Wilt thou be thrown down, be roughly thrust aside and wound thy aged skin, and in unseemly wise be torn from me by youthful arms? This wilt thou suffer; do not so, for 'tis not right for thee. Nay, dear mother mine! give me thy hand beloved, and let me press thy cheek to mine; for never, nevermore, but now for the last time shall I behold the dazzling sun-god's orb. My last farewells now take! O mother, mother mine! beneath the earth I pass.

He. O my daughter, I am still to live and be a slave.

Polyx. Unwedded I depart, never having tasted the married joys that were my due!

He. Thine, my daughter, is a piteous lot, and sad is mine also.

Polyx. There in Hades' courts shall I be laid apart from thee.

He. Ah me, what shall I do? where shall I end my life?

Polyx. Daughter of a free-born sire, a slave I am to die.

He. Not one of all my fifty children left!

Polyx. What message can I take for thee to Hector or thy aged lord?

He. Tell them that of all women I am the most miserable.

Polyx. Ah! breast and paps that fed me with sweet food!

He. Woe is thee, my child, for this untimely fate!

Polyx. Farewell, my mother! farewell, Cassandra!

He. "Fare well!" others do, but not thy mother, no!

Polyx. Thou too, my brother Polydore, who art in Thrace, the home of steeds!

He. Aye, if he lives, which much I doubt; so luckless am I every way.

Polyx. Oh yes, he lives; and, when thou diest, he will close thine eyes.

He. I *am* dead; sorrow has forestalled death here.

Polyx. Come veil my head, Odysseus, and take me hence; for now, ere falls the fatal blow, my heart is melted by my mother's wailing, and hers no less by mine. O light of day! for still may I call thee by thy name, though now my share in thee is but the time I take to go 'twixt this and the sword at Achilles' tomb. *Exeunt* ODYSSEUS *and* POLYXENA.

He. Woe is me! I faint; my limbs sink under me. O my daughter, embrace thy mother, stretch out thy hand, give it me again; leave me not childless! Ah, friends! 'tis my death-blow. Oh! to see that Spartan woman, Helen, sister of the sons of Zeus, in such a plight; for her bright eyes have caused the shameful fall of Troy's once prosperous town.

She swoons.

Ch. O breeze from out the deep arising, that waftest swift galleys, ocean's coursers, across the surging main whither wilt thou bear me the child of sorrow? To whose house shall I be brought, to be his slave and chattel? to some haven in the Dorian land,[1] or in Phthia, where men say Apidanus, father of fairest streams, makes fat and rich the tilth? or to an island home, sent on a voyage of misery by oars that sweep the brine, leading a wretched existence in halls where[2] the first-created palm and the bay-tree put forth their sacred shoots for dear Latona, memorial fair of her divine travail? and there with the maids of Delos shall I hymn the golden snood and bow of Artemis their goddess? or in the city of Pallas, the home of Athena of the beauteous chariot, shall I upon her saffron robe[3] yoke horses to the car, embroidering them on my web in brilliant varied shades, or the race of Titans, whom Zeus the son of Cronos lays to their unending sleep with bolt of flashing flame?

Woe is me for my children! woe for my ancestors, and my country which is falling in smouldering ruin 'mid the smoke, sacked by the Argive spear! while

[1]The Peloponnesus.

[2]Delos.

[3]The embroidered robe presented to this goddess at the Panathenaea.

I upon a foreign shore am called a slave forsooth, leaving Asia, Europe's handmaid, and receiving in its place a deadly marriage-bower.

Enter TALTHYBIUS.

Talthybius. Where can I find Hecuba, who once was queen of Ilium, ye Trojan maidens?

Ch. There she lies near thee, Talthybius, stretched full length upon the ground, wrapt in her robe.

Ta. Great Zeus! what can I say? that thine eye is over man? or that we hold this false opinion all to no purpose, thinking there is any race of gods, when it is chance that rules the mortal sphere? Was not this the queen of wealthy Phrygia, the wife of Priam highly blest? And now her city is utterly o'erthrown by the foe, and she, a slave in her old age, her children dead, lies stretched upon the ground, soiling her hair, poor lady! in the dust. Well, well; old as I am, may death be my lot before I am involved in any foul mischance. Arise, poor queen! lift up thyself and raise that hoary head.

He. Ah! who art thou that wilt not let my body rest? why disturb me in my anguish, whosoe'er thou art?

Ta. 'Tis I Talthybius, who am here, the minister of the Danai; Agamemnon has sent me for thee, lady.

He. Good friend, art come because the Achæans are resolved to slay me too at the grave? How welcome would thy tidings be! Let us hasten and lose no time; prithee, lead the way, old sir.

Ta. I am come to fetch thee to bury thy daughter's corpse, lady; and those that send me are the two sons of Atreus and the Achæan host.

He. Ah! what wilt thou say? Art thou not come, as I had thought, to fetch me to my doom, but to announce ill news? Lost, lost, my child! snatched from thy mother's arms! and I am childless now, at least as touches thee; ah, woe is me!

How did ye end her life? was any mercy shown? or did ye deal ruthlessly with her as though your victim were a foe, old man? Speak, though thy words must be pain to me.

Ta. Lady, thou art bent on making mine a double meed of tears in pity for thy child; for now too as I tell the sad tale a tear will wet my eye, as it did at the tomb when she was dying.

All Achæa's host was gathered there in full array before the tomb to see thy daughter offered; and the son of Achilles took Polyxena by the hand and set her on the top of the mound, while I stood near; and a chosen band of young Achæans followed to hold thy child and prevent her struggling. Then did Achilles' son take in his hands a brimming cup of gold and poured an offering to his dead sire, making a sign to me to proclaim silence throughout the Achæan host. So I stood at his side and in their midst proclaimed, "Silence, ye Achæans! hushed be the people all! peace! be still!" Therewith I hushed the host. Then spake he, "Son of Peleus, father mine, accept the offering I pour thee to appease thy spirit, strong to raise the dead; and come to drink the black blood of a virgin pure, which I and the host are offering thee; oh! be propitious to us; grant that we may loose our prows and the cables of our ships, and, meeting with a prosperous voyage from Ilium, all to our country come." So he; and all the army echoed his prayer. Then seizing his golden sword by the hilt he drew it from its scabbard, signing the while to the picked young Argive warriors to hold the maid. But she, when she was ware thereof, uttered her voice and said; "O Argives, who have sacked my city! of my free will I die; let none lay hand on me; for bravely will I yield my neck. Leave me free, I do beseech; so slay me, that death may find me free; for to be called a slave amongst the dead fills my royal heart with shame." Thereat the people shouted their applause, and king Agamemnon bade the young men loose the maid. So they set her free, as soon as they heard this last command from him whose might was over all. And she, hearing her captors' words took her robe and tore it open from the shoulder to the waist, displaying a breast and bosom fair as a statue's; then sinking on her knee, one word she spake more piteous than all the rest, "Young prince, if 'tis my breast thou'dst strike, lo! here it is, strike home! or if at my neck thy sword thou'lt aim, behold! that neck is bared."

Then he, half glad, half sorry in his pity for the maid, cleft with the steel the channels of her breath, and streams of blood gushed forth; but she, e'en in death's agony, took good heed to fall with maiden grace, hiding from gaze of man what modest maiden must. Soon as she had breathed her last through the fatal gash, each Argive set his hand to different tasks, some strewing leaves o'er the corpse in handfuls, others bringing pine-logs and heaping up a pyre; and he, who brought nothing, would hear from him who did such taunts as these, "Stand'st thou still, ignoble wretch, with never a robe or ornament to bring for the maiden? Wilt thou give naught to her that showed such peerless bravery and spirit?"

Such is the tale I tell about thy daughter's death, and I regard thee as blest beyond all mothers in thy noble child, yet crossed in fortune more than all.

Ch. Upon the race of Priam and my city some fearful curse hath burst; 'tis sent by God, and we must bear it.

He. O my daughter! 'mid this crowd of sorrows I know not where to turn my gaze; for if I set myself to one, another will not give me pause; while from this again a fresh grief summons me, finding a successor to sorrow's throne. No longer now can I efface from my mind the memory of thy sufferings sufficiently to stay my tears; yet hath the story of thy noble death taken from the keenness of my grief. Is it not then strange that poor land, when blessed by heaven with a lucky year, yields a good crop, while that which is good, if robbed of needful care, bears but little increase; yet 'mongst men the knave is never other than a knave, the good man aught but good, never changing for the worse because of misfortune, but ever the same? Is then the difference due to birth or bringing up? Good training doubtless gives lessons in good conduct, and if a man have mastered this, he knows what is base by the standard of good. Random shafts of my soul's shooting these, I know.

(*To* TALTHYBIUS) Go thou and proclaim to the Argives that they touch not my daughter's body but keep the crowd away. For when a countless host is gathered, the mob knows no restraint, and the unruliness of sailors exceeds that of fire, all abstinence from crime being counted criminal.

Exit TALTHYBIUS.

(*Addressing a servant*) My aged handmaid, take a pitcher and dip it in the salt sea and bring hither thereof, that I for the last time may wash my child, a virgin wife, a widowed maid, and lay her out—as she deserves, ah! whence can I? impossible! but as best I can; and what will that amount to? I will collect adornment from the captives, my companions in these tents, if haply any of them escaping her master's eye have some secret store from her old home. O towering halls, O home so happy once, O Priam, rich in store of fairest wealth, most blest of sires, and I no less, the grey-haired mother of thy race, how are we brought to naught, stripped of our former pride! And spite of all we vaunt ourselves, one on the riches of his house, another because he has an honoured name amongst his fellow-citizens! But these things are naught; in vain are all our thoughtful schemes, in vain our vaunting words. He is happiest who meets no sorrow in his daily walk. *Exit* HECUBA.

Ch. Woe and tribulation were made my lot in life, soon as ever Paris felled his beams of pine in Ida's woods, to sail across the heaving main in quest of Helen's hand, fairest bride on whom the sun-god turns his golden eye. For here beginneth trouble's cycle, and, worse than that, relentless fate; and from one man's folly came a universal curse, bringing death to the land of Simois, with trouble from an alien shore. The strife the shepherd decided on Ida 'twixt three daughters of the blessed gods, brought as its result war and bloodshed and the ruin of my home; and many a Spartan maiden too is weeping bitter tears in her halls on the banks of fair Eurotas, and many a mother whose sons are slain, is smiting her hoary head and tearing her cheeks, making her nails red in the furrowed gash.

Enter MAID.

Maid (*Attended by bearers bringing in a covered corpse*) Oh! where, ladies, is Hecuba, our queen of sorrow, who far surpasses all in tribulation, men and women both alike? None shall wrest the crown from her.

Ch. What now, thou wretched bird of boding note? Thy evil tidings never seem to rest.

Ma. 'Tis to Hecuba I bring my bitter news; no easy task is it for mortal lips to speak smooth words in sorrow's hour.

Ch. Lo! she is coming even now from the shelter of the tent, appearing just in time to hear thee speak.

Re-enter HECUBA.

Ma. Alas for thee! most hapless queen, ruined beyond all words of mine to tell; robbed of the light of life; of children, husband, city reft; hopelessly undone!

He. This is no news but insult; I have heard it all before. But why art thou come, bringing hither to me the corpse of Polyxena, on whose burial Achæa's host was reported to be busily engaged?

Ma. (*Aside*) She little knows what I have to tell, but mourns Polyxena, not grasping her new sorrows.

He. Ah! woe is me! thou art not surely bringing hither mad Cassandra, the prophetic maid?

Ma. She lives, of whom thou speakest; but the dead thou dost not weep is here. (*Uncovering the corpse*) Mark well the body now laid bare; is not this a sight to fill thee with wonder, and upset thy hopes?

He. Ah me! 'tis the corpse of my son Polydore I behold, whom he of Thrace was keeping safe for me in his halls. Alas! this is the end of all; my life is o'er. O my son, my son, alas for thee! a frantic strain I now begin; thy fate I learnt, a moment gone, from some foul fiend.[1]

Ma. What! so thou knewest thy son's fate, poor lady.

He. I cannot, cannot credit this fresh sight I see. Woe succeeds to woe; time will never cease henceforth to bring me groans and tears.

Ch. Alas! poor lady, our sufferings are cruel indeed.

He. O my son, child of a luckless mother, what was the manner of thy death? what lays thee dead at my feet? Who did the deed?

Ma. I know not. On the sea-shore I found him.

He. Cast up on the smooth sand, or thrown there after the murderous blow?

Ma. The waves had washed him ashore.

He. Alas! alas! I read aright the vision I saw in my sleep, nor did the phantom dusky-winged escape my ken, even the vision I saw concerning my son, who is now no more within the bright sunshine.

Ch. Who slew him then? Can thy dream-lore tell us that?

He. 'Twas my own familiar friend, the knight of Thrace, with whom his aged sire had placed the boy in hiding.

Ch. O horror! what wilt thou say? did he slay him to get the gold?

He. O awful crime! O deed without a name! beggaring wonder! impious! intolerable! Where are now the laws 'twixt guest and host? Accursed monster! how hast thou mangled his flesh, slashing the poor child's limbs with ruthless sword, lost to all sense of pity!

Ch. Alas for thee! how some deity, whose hand is heavy on thee, hath sent thee troubles beyond all other mortals! But yonder I see our lord and master Agamemnon coming; so let us be still henceforth, my friends.

Enter AGAMEMNON.

Agamemnon. Hecuba, why art thou delaying to come and bury thy daughter? for it was for this that Talthybius brought me thy message begging

[1] *i.e.*, in a dream.

that none of the Argives should touch thy child. And so I granted this, and none is touching her, but this long delay of thine fills me with wonder. Wherefore am I come to send thee hence; for our part there is well performed; if herein there be any place for "well."

Ha! what man is this I see near the tents, some Trojan's corpse? 'tis not an Argive's body; *that* the garments it is clad in tell me.

He. (*Aside*) Unhappy one! in naming thee I name myself; O Hecuba, what shall I do? throw myself here at Agamemnon's knees, or bear my sorrows in silence?

Ag. Why dost thou turn thy back towards me and weep, refusing to say what has happened, or who this is?

He. (*Aside*) But should he count me as a slave and foe and spurn me from his knees, I should but add to my anguish.

Ag. I am no prophet born; wherefore, if I be not told, I cannot learn the current of thy thoughts.

He. (*Aside*) Can it be that in estimating this man's feelings I make him out too ill-disposed, when he is not really so?

Ag. If thy wish really is that I should remain in ignorance, we are of one mind; for I have no wish myself to listen.

He. (*Aside*) Without his aid I shall not be able to avenge my children. Why do I still ponder the matter? I must do and dare whether I win or lose. (*Turning to* AGAMEMNON) O Agamemnon! by thy knees, by thy beard and conquering hand I implore thee.

Ag. What is thy desire? to be set free? that is easily done.

He. Not that; give me vengeance on the wicked, and evermore am I willing to lead a life of slavery.

Ag. Well, but why dost thou call me to thy aid?

He. 'Tis a matter thou little reckest of, O king. Dost see this corpse, for whom my tears now flow?

Ag. I do; but what is to follow, I cannot guess.

He. He was my child in days gone by; I bore him in my womb.

Ag. Which of thy sons is he, poor sufferer?

He. Not one of Priam's race who fell 'neath Ilium's walls.

Ag. Hadst thou any son besides those, lady?

He. Yes, him thou seest here, of whom, methinks, have small gain.

Ag. Where then was he, when his city was being destroyed?

He. His father, fearful of his death, conveyed him out of Troy.

Ag. Where did he place him apart from all the sons he then had?

He. Here in this very land, where his corpse was found.

Ag. With Polymestor, the king of this country?

He. Hither was he sent in charge of gold, most bitter trust!

Ag. By whom was he slain? what death o'ertook him?

He. By whom but by this man? His Thracian host slew him.

Ag. The wretch! could he have been so eager for the treasure?

He. Even so; soon as ever he heard of the Phrygians' disaster.

Ag. Where didst find him? or did some one bring his corpse?

He. This maid, who chanced upon it on the seashore.

Ag. Was she seeking it, or bent on other tasks?

He. She had gone to fetch water from the sea to wash Polyxena.

Ag. It seems then his host slew him and cast his body out to sea.

He. Aye, for the waves to toss, after mangling him thus.

Ag. Woe is thee for thy measureless troubles!

He. I am ruined; no evil now is left, O Agamemnon.

Ag. Look you! what woman was ever born to such misfortune?

He. There is none, unless thou wouldst name misfortune herself. But hear my reason for throwing myself at thy knees. If my treatment seems to thee deserved, I will be content; but, if otherwise, help me to punish this most godless host, that hath wrought a deed most damned, fearless alike of gods in heaven or hell; who, though full oft he had shared my board and been counted first of all my guest-friends and after meeting with every kindness he could claim and receiving my consideration, slew my son, and bent though he was on murder, deigned not to bury him but cast his body forth to sea.

I may be a slave and weak as well, but the gods are strong, and custom too which prevails o'er them, for by custom it is that we believe in them and set up bounds of right and wrong for our lives. Now if this principle, when referred to thee, is to be set at naught, and they are to escape punishment who murder guests or dare to plunder the temples of gods, then is all fairness in things human at an end. Deem this then a disgrace and show regard for me, have pity on me, and, like an artist standing back from his picture, look on me and closely scan my piteous state. I was once a queen, but now I am thy slave; a happy mother once, but now childless and old alike, reft of city, utterly forlorn, the most wretched woman living. Ah! woe is me! whither wouldst thou withdraw thy steps from me? (*As* AGAMEMNON *is turning away*) My efforts then will be in vain, ah me! ah me! Why, oh! why do we mortals toil, as needs we must, and seek out all other sciences, but persuasion, the only real mistress of mankind, we take no further pains to master completely by offering to pay for the knowledge, so that any man might upon occasion convince his fellows as he pleased and gain his point as well? How shall anyone hereafter hope for prosperity? All those my sons are gone from me, and I, their mother, am led away into captivity to suffer shame, while yonder I see the smoke leaping up o'er my city. Further, though perhaps this were idly urged, to plead thy love, still will I put the case: at thy side lies my daughter, Cassandra, the maid inspired, as the Phrygians call her. How then, O king, wilt thou acknowledge those nights of rapture, or what return shall she my daughter or I her mother have for all the love she has lavished on her lord? For from darkness and the endearments of the night mortals reap by far their keenest joys. Hearken then; dost see this corpse? By doing him a service thou wilt do it to a kinsman of thy bride's. One thing only have I yet to urge. Oh! would I had a voice in arms, in hands, in hair and feet, placed there by the arts of Dædalus or some god, that all together they might with tears embrace thy knees, bringing a thousand pleas to bear on thee! O my lord and master, most glorious light of Hellas, listen, stretch forth a helping hand to this aged woman, for all she is a thing of naught; still do so. For 'tis ever a good man's duty to succour the right, and to punish evil-doers wherever found.

Ch. 'Tis strange how each extreme doth meet in human life! Custom determines even our natural ties, making the most bitter foes friends, and regarding as foes those who formerly were friends.

Ag. Hecuba, I feel compassion for thee and thy son and thy ill-fortune, as well as for thy suppliant gesture, and I would gladly see yon impious host pay thee this forfeit for the sake of heaven and justice, could I but find some way to help thee without appearing to the army to have plotted the death of the Thracian king for Cassandra's sake. For on one point I am assailed by perplexity; the army count this man their friend, the dead their foe; that he is dear to thee is a matter apart, wherein the army has no share. Reflect on this; for though thou find'st me ready to share thy toil and quick to lend my aid, yet the risk of being reproached by the Achæans makes me hesitate.

He. Ah! there is not in the world a single man free; for he is either a slave to money or to fortune, or else the people in their thousands or the fear of public prosecution prevents him from following the dictates of his heart.

But since thou art afraid, deferring too much to the rabble, I will rid thee of that fear. Thus; be privy to my plot if I devise mischief against this murderer, but refrain from any share in it. And if there break out among the Achæans any uproar or attempt at rescue, when the Thracian is suffering his doom, check it, though without seeming to do so on my account. For what remains, take heart; I will arrange everything well.

Ag. How? what wilt thou do? wilt take a sword in thy old hand and slay the barbarian, or hast thou drugs or what to help thee? Who will take thy part? whence wilt thou procure friends?

He. Sheltered beneath these tents is a host of Trojan women.

Ag. Dost mean the captives, the booty of the Hellenes?

He. With their help will I punish my murderous foe.

Ag. How are women to master men?

He. Numbers are a fearful thing, and joined to craft a desperate foe.

Ag. True; still I have a mean opinion of the female race.

He. What? did not women slay the sons of Ægyptus, and utterly clear Lemnos of men? But let it be even thus; put an end to our conference, and send this woman for me safely through the host. And do thou (*to a servant*) draw near my Thracian friend and say, "Hecuba, once queen of Ilium, summons thee, on thy own business no less than hers, thy children too, for they also must hear what she has to say." Defer awhile, Agamemnon, the burial of Polyxena lately slain, that brother and sister may be laid on the same pyre and buried side by side, a double cause of sorrow to their mother.

Ag. So shall it be; yet had the host been able to sail, I could not have granted thee this boon; but, as it is, since the god sends forth no favouring breeze, we needs must abide, seeing, as we do, that sailing is at a standstill. Good luck to thee! for this is the interest alike of individual and state, that the wrongdoer be punished and the good man prosper.

Exit AGAMEMNON.

Ch. No more, my native Ilium, shalt thou be counted among the towns ne'er sacked; so thick a cloud of Hellene troops is settling all around, wasting thee with the spear; shorn art thou of thy coronal of towers, and fouled most piteously with filthy soot; no more, ah me! shall I tread thy streets.

'Twas in the middle of the night my ruin came, in the hour when sleep steals sweetly o'er the eyes after the feast is done. My husband, the music o'er, and the sacrifice that sets the dance afoot now ended, was lying in our bridal-chamber, his spear hung on a peg; with never a thought of the sailor-throng encamped upon the Trojan shores; and I was braiding up my tresses 'neath a tight-drawn snood before my golden mirror's countless rays, that I might lay me down to rest; when lo! through the city rose a din, and a cry went ringing down the streets of Troy, "Ye sons of Hellas, when, oh! when will ye sack the citadel of Ilium, and seek your homes?" Up sprang I from my bed, with only a mantle about me, like a Dorian maid, and sought in vain, ah me! to station myself at the holy hearth of Artemis; for, after seeing my husband slain, I was hurried away o'er the broad sea; with many a backward look at my city, when the ship began her homeward voyage and parted me from Ilium's strand; till alas! for very grief I fainted, cursing Helen the sister of the Dioscuri, and Paris the baleful shepherd of Ida; for 'twas their marriage, which was no marriage but a curse by some demon sent, that robbed me of my country and drove me from my home. Oh! may the sea's salt flood ne'er carry her home again; and may she never set foot in her father's halls!

Enter POLYMESTOR *and his sons.*

Polymestor. My dear friend Priam, and thou no less, Hecuba, I weep to see thee and thy city thus, and thy daughter lately slain. Alas! there is naught to be relied on; fair fame is insecure, nor is there any guarantee that weal will not be turned to woe. For the gods confound our fortunes, tossing them to and fro, and introduce confusion, that our perplexity may make us worship them. But what boots it to bemoan these things, when it brings one no nearer to heading the trouble? If thou art blaming me at all for my absence, stay a moment; I was away in the very heart of Thrace when thou wast brought hither; but on my return, just as I was starting from my home for the same purpose, thy maid fell in with me, and gave me thy message, which brought me here at once.

He. Polymestor, I am holden in such wretched plight that I blush to meet thine eye; for my present evil case makes me ashamed to face thee who didst see me in happier days, and I cannot look on thee with unfaltering gaze. Do not then think it ill-will on my part, Polymestor; there is another cause as well, I mean the custom which forbids women to meet men's gaze.

Polym. No wonder, surely. But what need hast thou of me? Why didst send for me to come hither from my house?

He. I wish to tell thee and thy children a private matter of my own; prithee, bid thy attendants withdraw from the tent.

Polym. (*To his Attendants*) Retire; this desert spot is safe enough. (*To* HECUBA) Thou art my friend, and this Achæan host is well-disposed to me. But thou must tell me how prosperity is to succour its unlucky friends; for ready am I to do so.

He. First tell me of the child Polydore, whom thou art keeping in thy halls, received from me and his father; is he yet alive? The rest will I ask thee after that.

Polym. Yes, thou still hast a share in fortune there.

He. Well said, dear friend! how worthy of thee!

Polym. What next wouldst learn of me?

He. Hath he any recollection of me his mother?

Polym. Aye, he was longing to steal away hither to thee.

He. Is the gold safe, which he brought with him from Troy?

Polym. Safe under lock and key in my halls.

He. There keep it, but covet not thy neighbour's goods.

Polym. Not I; God grant me luck of what I have, lady!

He. Dost know what I wish to say to thee and thy children?

Polym. Not yet; thy words maybe will declare it.

He. May it grow as dear to thee as thou now art to me!

Polym. What is it that I and my children are to learn?

He. There be ancient vaults filled full of gold by Priam's line.

Polym. Is it this thou wouldst tell thy son?

He. Yes, by thy lips, for thou art a righteous man.

Polym. What need then of these children's presence?

He. 'Tis better they should know it, in case of thy death.

Polym. True; 'tis also the wiser way.

He. Well, dost thou know where stands the shrine of Trojan Athena?

Polym. Is the gold there? what is there to mark it?

He. A black rock rising above the ground.

Polym. Is there aught else thou wouldst tell me about the place?

He. I wish to keep safe the treasure I brought from Troy.

Polym. Where can it be? inside thy dress, or hast thou it hidden?

He. 'Tis safe amid a heap of spoils within these tents.

Polym. Where? This is the station built by the Achæans to surround their fleet.

He. The captive women have huts of their own.

Polym. Is it safe to enter? are there no men about?

He. There are no Achæans within; we are alone. Enter then the tent, for the Argives are eager to set sail from Troy for home; and, when thou hast accomplished all that is appointed thee, thou shalt return with thy children to that bourn where thou hast lodged my son.

Exit HECUBA *with* POLYMESTOR *and his children.*

Ch. Not yet hast thou paid the penalty, but maybe thou yet wilt; like one who slips and falls into the surge with no haven near, so shalt thou lose thy own life for the life thou hast taken. For where liability to justice coincides with heaven's law, there is ruin fraught with death and doom. Thy hopes of this journey shall cheat thee, for it hath led thee, unhappy wretch! to the halls of death; and to no warrior's hand shalt thou resign thy life.

Polym. (*Within the tent*) O horror! I am blinded of the light of my eyes, ah me!

Ch. Heard ye, friends, that Thracian's cry of woe?

Polym. (*Within*) O horror! horror! my children! O the cruel blow.

Ch. Friends, there is strange mischief afoot in yon tent.

Polym. (*Within*) Nay, ye shall never escape for all your hurried flight; for with my fist will I burst open the inmost recesses of this building.

Ch. Hark! how he launches ponderous blows! Shall we force an entry? The crisis calls on us to aid Hecuba and the Trojan women.

Enter HECUBA.

He. Strike on, spare not, burst the doors! thou shalt ne'er replace bright vision in thy eyes nor ever see thy children, whom I have slain, alive again.

Ch. What! hast thou foiled the Thracian, and is the stranger in thy power, mistress mine? is all thy threat now brought to pass?

He. A moment, and thou shalt see him before the tent, his eyes put out, with random step advancing as a blind man must; yea, and the bodies of his two children whom I with my brave daughters of Troy did slay; he hath paid me his forfeit; look where he cometh from the tent. I will withdraw out of his path and stand aloof from the hot fury of this Thracian, my deadly foe.

Enter POLYMESTOR.

Polym. Woe is me! whither can I go, where halt, or whither turn? shall I crawl upon my hands like a wild four-footed beast on their track? Which path shall I take first, this or that, eager as I am to clutch those Trojan murderesses that have destroyed me? Out upon ye, cursed daughters of Phrygia! to what corner have ye fled cowering before me? O sun-god, would thou couldst heal my bleeding orbs, ridding me of my blindness!

Ha! hush! I catch their stealthy footsteps here. Where can I dart on them and gorge me on their flesh and bones, making for myself a wild beast's meal, exacting vengeance in requital of their outrage on me? Ah, woe is me! whither am I rushing, leaving my babes unguarded for hell-hounds to mangle, to be murdered and ruthlessly cast forth upon the hills, a feast of blood for dogs? Where shall I stay or turn my steps? where rest? like a ship that lies anchored at sea, so gathering close my linen robe I rush to that chamber of death, to guard my babes.

Ch. Woe is thee! what grievous outrage hath been wreaked on thee! a fearful penalty for thy foul deed hath the deity imposed, whoe'er he is whose hand is heavy upon thee.

Polym. Woe is me! Ho! my Thracian spearmen, clad in mail, a race of knights whom Ares doth inspire! Ho! Achæans! sons of Atreus ho! to you I loudly call; come hither, in God's name come! Doth any hearken, or will no man help me? Why do ye delay? Women, captive women have destroyed me. A fearful fate is mine; ah me! my hideous outrage! Whither can I turn or go? Shall I take wings and soar aloft to the mansions of the sky, where Orion and Sirius dart from their eyes a flash as of fire, or shall I, in my misery, plunge to Hades' murky flood?

Ch. 'Tis a venial sin, when a man, suffering from evils too heavy to bear, rids himself of a wretched existence.

Enter AGAMEMNON.

Ag. Hearing a cry I am come hither; for Echo, child of the mountain-rock, hath sent her voice loud-ringing through the host, causing a tumult. Had I not known that Troy's towers were levelled by the might of Hellas, this uproar had caused no slight panic.

Polym. Best of friends, for by thy voice I know thee, Agamemnon, dost see my piteous state?

Ag. What! hapless Polymestor, who hath stricken thee? who hath reft thine eyes of sight, staining the pupils with blood? who hath slain these children? whoe'er he was, fierce must have been his wrath against thee and thy children.

Polym. Hecuba, helped by the captive women, hath destroyed me; no! not destroyed, far worse than that.

Ag. (*Addressing* HECUBA) What hast thou to say? Was it thou that didst this deed, as he avers? thou, Hecuba, that hast ventured on this inconceivable daring?

Polym. Ha! what is that? is she somewhere near? show me, tell me where, that I may grip her in my hands and rend her limb from limb, bespattering her with gore.

Ag. Ho! madman, what wouldst thou?

Polym. By heaven I entreat thee, let me vent on her the fury of my arm.

Ag. Hold! banish that savage spirit from thy heart and plead thy cause, that after hearing thee and her in turn I may fairly decide what reason there is for thy present sufferings.

Polym. I will tell my tale. There was a son of Priam, Polydore, the youngest, a child by Hecuba, whom his father Priam sent to me from Troy to bring up in my halls, suspecting no doubt the fall of Troy. Him I slew; but hear my reason for so doing, to show how cleverly and wisely I had thought it out. My fear was that if that child were left to be thy enemy, he would re-people Troy and settle it afresh; and the Achæans, knowing that a son of Priam survived, might bring another expedition against the Phrygian land and harry and lay waste these plains of Thrace hereafter, for the neighbours of Troy to experience the very troubles we were lately suffering, O king. Now Hecuba, having discovered the death of her son, brought me hither on the following pretext, saying she would tell me of hidden treasure stored up in Ilium by the race of Priam; and she led me apart with my children into the tent, that none but I might hear her news. So I sat me down on a couch in their midst to rest; for there were many of the Trojan maidens seated there, some on my right hand, some on my left, as it had been beside a friend; and they were praising the weaving of our Thracian handiwork, looking at this robe as they held it up to the light; meantime others examined my Thracian spear and so stripped me of the protection of both. And those that were young mothers were dandling my children in their arms, with loud admiration, as they passed them on from hand to hand to remove them far from their father; and then after their smooth speeches, (wouldst thou believe it?) in an instant snatching daggers from some secret place in their dress they stab my children; whilst others, like foes, seized me hand and foot; and if I tried to raise my head, anxious to help my babes, they would clutch me by the hair; while if I stirred my hands, I could do nothing, poor wretch! for the numbers of the women. At last they wrought a fearful deed, worse than what had gone before; for they took their brooches and stabbed the pupils of my hapless eyes, making them gush with blood, and then fled through the chambers; up I sprang like a wild beast in pursuit of the shameless murderesses, searching along each wall with hunter's care, dealing buffets, spreading ruin. This then is what I have suffered because of my zeal for thee, O Agamemnon, for slaying an enemy of thine. But to spare thee a lengthy speech; if any of the men of former times have spoken ill of women, if any doth so now, or shall do so hereafter, all this in one short sentence will I say; for neither land or sea produces a race so pestilent, as whosoever hath had to do with them knows full well.

Ch. Curb thy bold tongue, and do not, because of thy own woes, thus embrace the whole race of women in one reproach; for though some of us, and those a numerous class, deserve to be disliked, there are others amongst us who rank naturally amongst the good.

He. Never ought words to have outweighed deeds in this world, Agamemnon. No! if a man's deeds had been good, so should his words have been; if, on the other hand, evil, his words should have betrayed their unsoundness, instead of its being possible at times to give a fair complexion to injustice. There are, 'tis true, clever persons, who have made a science of this, but their cleverness cannot last for ever; a miserable end awaits them; none ever yet escaped. This is a warning I give thee at the outset. Now will I turn to this fellow, and will give thee thy answer, thou who sayest it was to save Achæa double toil and for Agamemnon's sake that thou didst slay my son. Nay, villain, in the first place how could the barbarian race ever be friends with Hellas? Impossible, ever. Again, what interest hadst thou to further by thy zeal? was it to form some marriage, or on the score of kin, or, prithee, why? or was it likely that they would sail hither again and destroy thy country's crops? Whom dost thou expect to persuade into believing that? Wouldst thou but speak the truth, it was the gold that slew my son, and thy greedy spirit. Now tell me this; why, when Troy was victorious, when her ramparts still stood round her, when Priam was alive, and Hector's warring prospered, why didst thou not, if thou wert really minded to do Agamemnon a service, then slay the child, for thou hadst him in thy palace 'neath thy care, or bring him with thee alive to the Argives? Instead of this, when our sun was set and the smoke of our city showed it was in the enemy's power, thou didst murder the guest who had come to thy hearth. Furthermore, to prove thy villainy, hear this; if thou wert really a friend to those Achæans, thou shouldst have brought the gold, which thou sayest thou art keeping not for thyself but for Agamemnon, and given it to them, for they were in need and had endured a long exile from their native land. Whereas not even now canst thou bring thyself to part with it, but persistest in keeping it in thy palace. Again, hadst thou kept my son safe and sound, as thy duty was, a fair renown would have been thy reward, for it is in trouble's hour that the good most clearly show their friendship; though prosperity of itself in every case finds friends. Wert thou in need of money and he prosperous, that son of mine would have been as a mighty treasure for thee to draw upon; but now thou hast him no longer to be thy friend, and the benefit of the gold is gone from thee, thy children too are dead, and thyself art in this sorry plight.

To thee, Agamemnon, I say, if thou help this man, thou wilt show thy worthlessness; for thou wilt be serving one devoid of honour or piety, a stranger to the claims of good faith, a wicked host; while I shall say thou delightest in evil-doers, being such an one thyself; but I am not abusing my masters.

Ch. Look you! how good a cause ever affords men an opening for a good speech.

Ag. To be judge in a stranger's troubles goes much against my grain, but still I must; yea, for to take this matter in hand and then put it from me is a shameful course. My opinion, that thou mayst know it, is that it was not for the sake of the Achæans or me that thou didst slay thy guest, but to keep that gold in thy own house. In thy trouble thou makest a case in thy own interests. Maybe amongst you 'tis a light thing to murder guests, but with us in Hellas 'tis a disgrace. How can I escape reproach if I judge thee not guilty? I cannot do it. Nay, since thou didst dare thy horrid crime, endure as well its painful consequence.

Polym. Woe is me! worsted by a woman and a slave, I am, it seems, to suffer by unworthy hands.

He. Is it not just for thy atrocious crime?

Polym. Ah, my children! ah, my blinded eyes! woe is me!

He. Dost thou grieve? what of me? thinkst thou I grieve not for my son?

Polym. Thou wicked wretch! thy delight is in mocking me.

He. I am avenged on thee; have I not cause for joy?

Polym. The joy will soon cease, in the day when ocean's flood—

He. Shall convey me to the shores of Hellas?

Polym. Nay, but close o'er thee when thou fallest from the masthead.

He. Who will force me to take the leap?

Polym. Of thy own accord wilt thou climb the ship's mast.

He. With wings upon my back, or by what means?

Polym. Thou wilt become a dog with bloodshot eyes.

He. How knowest thou of my transformation?

Polym. Dionysus, our Thracian prophet, told me so.

He. And did he tell thee nothing of thy present trouble?

Polym. No; else hadst thou never caught me thus by guile.

He. Shall I die or live, and so complete my life on earth?

Polym. Die shalt thou; and to thy tomb shall be given a name—

He. Recalling my form, or what wilt thou tell me?

Polym. "The hapless hound's grave,"[1] a mark for mariners.

He. 'Tis naught to me, now that thou hast paid me forfeit.

Polym. Further, thy daughter Cassandra must die.

[1]Cynossema, a promontory in the Thracian Chersonese.

He. I scorn the prophecy! I give it to thee to keep for thyself.

Polym. Her shall the wife of Agamemnon, grim keeper of his palace, slay.

He. Never may the daughter of Tyndareus do such a frantic deed!

Polym. And she shall slay this king as well, lifting high the axe.

Ag. Ha! sirrah, art thou mad? art so eager to find sorrow?

Polym. Kill me, for in Argos there awaits thee a murderous bath.

Ag. Ho! servants, hale him from my sight!

Polym. Ha! my words gall thee.

Ag. Stop his mouth!

Polym. Close it now; for I have spoken.

Ag. Haste and cast him upon some desert island, since his mouth is full of such exceeding presumption. Go thou, unhappy Hecuba, and bury thy two corpses; and you, Trojan women, to your masters' tents repair, for lo! I perceive a breeze just rising to waft us home. God grant we reach our country and find all well at home, released from troubles here!

Ch. Away to the harbour and the tents, my friends, to prove the toils of slavery! for such is fate's relentless hest.

Exeunt OMNES.

HERACLES MAD

DRAMATIS PERSONAE

Amphitryon	Madness
Megara	Messenger
Lycus	Heracles
Iris	Theseus

Chorus of Old Men of Thebes

At the entrance of Heracles' house in Thebes, before the altar of Zeus. Enter AMPHITRYON, MEGARA, *and her three sons.*

Amphitryon. What mortal hath not heard of him who shared a wife with Zeus, Amphitryon of Argos, whom on a day Alcæus, son of Perseus, begat, Amphitryon the father of Heracles? He it was dwelt here in Thebes, where from the sowing of the dragon's teeth grew up a crop of earth-born giants; for of these Ares saved a scanty band, and their children's children people the city of Cadmus. Hence sprung Creon, son of Menœceus, king of this land; and Creon became the father of this lady Megara, whom once all Cadmus' race escorted with the glad music of lutes at her wedding, in the day that Heracles, illustrious chief, led her to my halls. Now he, my son, left Thebes where I was settled, left his wife Megara and her kin, eager to make his home in Argolis, in that walled town[1] which the Cyclopes built, whence I am exiled for the slaying of Electryon; so he, wishing to lighten my affliction and to find a home in his own land, did offer Eurystheus a mighty price for my recall, even to free the world of savage monsters, whether it was that Hera goaded him to submit to this or that fate was leagued against him. Divers are the toils he hath accomplished, and last of all hath he passed through the mouth of Tænarus into the halls of Hades to drag to the light that hound with bodies three, and thence is he never returned. Now there is an ancient legend amongst the race of Cadmus, that one Lycus in days gone by was husband to Dirce, being king of this city with its seven towers, before that Amphion and Zethus, sons of Zeus, lords of the milk-white steeds, became rulers in the land. His son, called by the same name as his father, albeit no Theban but a stranger from Eubœa, slew Creon, and after that seized the government, having fallen on this city when weakened by dissension. So this connection with Creon is likely to prove to us a serious evil; for now that my son is in the bowels of the earth, this illustrious monarch Lycus is bent on extirpating the children of Heracles, to quench one bloody feud with another, likewise his wife and me, if useless age like mine is to rank amongst men, that the boys may never grow up to exact a blood-penalty of their uncle's family. So I, left here by my son, whilst he is gone into the pitchy darkness of the earth, to tend and guard his children in his house, am taking my place with their mother, that the race of Heracles may not perish, here at the altar of Zeus the Saviour, which my own gallant child set up to commemorate his glorious victory over the Minyæ. And here we are careful to keep our station, though in need of everything, of food, of drink, and raiment, huddled together on the hard bare ground; for we are barred out from our house and sit here for want of any other safety. As for friends, some I see are insincere; while others, who are staunch, have no power to help us further. This is what misfortune means to man; God grant it may never fall to the lot of any who bears the least goodwill to me, to apply this never-failing test of friendship!

Megara. Old warrior, who erst did raze the citadel of the Taphians leading on the troops of Thebes to glory, how uncertain are God's dealings with man! I for instance, as far as concerned my sire[2] was never an outcast of fortune, for he was once accounted a man of might by reason of his wealth, possessed as he was of royal power, for which long spears are launched at the lives of the fortunate through love of it; children too he had; and me did he betroth to thy son, matching me in glorious marriage with Heracles. Whereas now all that is dead and gone from us; and I and thou, old friend, art doomed to die, and these children of Heracles, whom I am guarding 'neath my wing as a bird keepeth her tender chicks under her. And they the while in turn keep asking me, "Mother, whither is our father gone from the land? what is he about? when will he return?" Thus they inquire for their father, in childish perplexity; while I put them off with excuses, inventing stories; but still I wonder if 'tis he whenever a door creaks on its hinges, and up they all start, thinking to embrace their father's knees. What hope or way of salvation art thou now devising, old friend? for to thee I look. We can never steal beyond the boundaries of the land unseen, for there is too strict a watch set on us at every outlet, nor have

[1] Mycenæ.

[2] Creon.

we any longer hopes of safety in our friends. Whatever thy scheme is, declare it, lest our death be made ready, while we are only prolonging the time, powerless to escape.

Am. 'Tis by no means easy, my daughter, to give one's earnest advice on such matters offhand, without weary thought.

Meg Dost need a further taste of grief, or cling so fast to life?

Am. Yes, I love this life, and cling to its hopes.

Meg. So do I; but it boots not to expect the unexpected, old friend.

Am. In these delays is left the only cure for our evils.

Meg. 'Tis the pain of that interval I feel so.

Am. Daughter, there may yet be a happy escape from present troubles for me and thee; my son, thy husband, may yet arrive. So calm thyself, and wipe those tears from thy children's eyes, and sooth them with soft words, inventing a tale to delude them, piteous though such fraud be. Yea, for men's misfortunes ofttimes flag, and the stormy wind doth not always blow so strong, nor are the prosperous ever so; for all things change, making way for each other. The bravest man is he who relieth ever on his hopes, but despair is the mark of a coward.

Enter CHORUS OF OLD MEN OF THEBES.

Chorus. To the sheltering roof, to the old man's couch, leaning on my staff have I set forth, chanting a plaintive dirge like some bird grown grey, I that am but a voice and nothing more, a fancy bred of the visions of sleep by night, palsied with age, yet meaning kindly. All hail! ye orphaned babes! all hail, old friend! thou too, unhappy mother, wailing for thy husband in the halls of Hades! Faint not too soon upon your way, nor let your limbs grow weary, even as a colt beneath the yoke grows weary as he mounts some stony hill, dragging the weight of a wheeled car. Take hold of hand or robe, whoso feels his footsteps falter. Old friend, escort another like thyself, who erst amid his toiling peers in the days of our youth would take his place beside thee, no blot upon his country's glorious record.

See how like their father's sternly flash these children's eyes! Misfortune, God wot, hath not failed his children, nor yet hath his comeliness been denied them. O Hellas! if thou lose these, of what allies wilt thou rob thyself!

But hist! I see Lycus, the ruler of this land, drawing near the house.

Enter Lycus.

Lycus. One question, if I may, to this father of Heracles and his wife; and certainly as your lord and master I have a right to put what questions I choose. How long do ye seek to prolong your lives? What hope, what succour do ye see to save you from death? Do you trust that these children's father, who lies dead in the halls of Hades, will return? How unworthily ye show your sorrow at having to die, thou (*to* AMPHITRYON) after thy idle boasts, scattered broadcast through Hellas, that Zeus was partner in thy marriage-bed and there begat a new god; and thou (*to* MEGARA) after calling thyself the wife of so peerless a lord.

After all, what was the fine exploit thy husband achieved, if he *did* kill a water-snake in a marsh or that monster of Nemea? which he caught in a snare, for all he says he strangled it to death in his arms. Are these your weapons for the hard struggle? Is it for this then that Heracles' children should be spared? a man who has won a reputation for valour in his contests with beasts, in all else a weakling; who ne'er buckled shield to arm nor faced the spear, but with a bow, that coward's weapon, was ever ready to run away. Archery is no test of manly bravery; no! he *is* a man who keeps his post in the ranks and steadily faces the swift wound the spear may plough. My policy, again, old man, shows no reckless cruelty, but caution; for I am well aware I slew Creon, the father of Megara, and am in possession of his throne. So I have no wish that these children should grow up and be left to take vengeance on me in requital for what I have done.

Am. As for Zeus, let Zeus defend his son's case; but as for me, Heracles, I am only anxious on thy behalf to prove by what I say this tyrant's ignorance; for I cannot allow thee to be ill spoken of. First then for that which should never have been said—for to speak of thee Heracles as a coward is, methinks, outside the pale of speech—of that must I clear thee with heaven to witness. I appeal then to the thunder of Zeus, and the chariot wherein he rode, when he pierced the giants, earth's brood, to the heart with his winged shafts, and with gods uplifted the glorious triumph-song; or go to Pholoe and ask the insolent tribe of four-legged Centaurs, thou craven king, ask them who they would judge their bravest foe; will they not say my son, who according to thee is but a pretender? Wert thou to ask Eubœan Dirphys, thy native place, it would nowise sing thy praise, for thou hast never done a single gallant deed to which thy country can witness. Next thou dost disparage that clever invention, an archer's weapon; come, listen to me and learn wisdom. A man who fights in line is a slave to his weapons, and if his fellow-comrades want for courage he is slain himself through the cowardice of his neighbours, or, if he break his spear, he has not wherewithal to defend his body from death, having only one means of defence; whereas all who are armed with the trusty bow, though they have but one weapon, yet is it the best; for a man, after discharging countless arrows, still has others whereto defend himself from death, and standing at a distance keeps off the enemy, wounding them for all their watchfulness with shafts invisible, and never exposing himself to the foe, but keeping under cover; and this is far the wisest course in battle, to harm the enemy, if they are not stationed out of shot, and keep safe oneself. These arguments completely contradict thine with regard to the matter at issue. Next, why art thou desirous of slaying these children? What have they done to thee? One piece of wisdom I credit thee with, thy coward terror of a brave man's descendants. Still it is hard on us, if for thy cowardice we must die; a fate that ought to have overtaken thee at our braver hands, if Zeus had been fairly disposed towards us. But, if thou art so anxious to make thyself supreme in the land, let us at least go into exile; abstain from all violence, else thou wilt suffer by it whenso the deity causes fortune's breeze to veer round.

Ah! thou land of Cadmus—for to thee too will I turn, upbraiding thee with words of reproach—is this your succour of Heracles and his children? the man who faced alone the Minyan host in battle and allowed Thebes to see the light with freemen's eyes. I cannot praise Hellas, nor will I ever keep silence, finding her so craven as regards my son; she should have come with fire and sword and warrior's arms to help these tender babes, to requite him for all his labours in purging land and sea. Such help, my children, neither Hellas nor the city of Thebes affords you; to me a feeble friend ye look, that am but empty sound and nothing more. For the vigour which once I had, is gone from me; my limbs are palsied with age, and my strength is decayed. Were I but young and still a man of my hands, I would have seized my spear and dabbled those flaxen locks of his with blood, so that the coward would now be flying from my prowess beyond the bounds of Atlas.

Ch. Have not the brave amongst mankind a fair opening for speech, albeit slow to begin?

Ly. Say what thou wilt of me in thy exalted phrase, but I by deeds will make thee rue those words. (*Calling to his servants*) Ho! bid wood-cutters go, some to Helicon, others to the glens of Parnassus, and cut me logs of oak, and when they are brought to the town, pile up a stack of wood all round the altar on either side thereof, and set fire to it and burn them all alive, that they may learn that the dead no longer rules this land, but that for the present I am king. (*Angrily to the* CHORUS) As for you, old men, since ye thwart my views, not for the children of Heracles alone shall ye lament, but likewise for every blow that strikes his house, and ye shall ne'er forget ye are slaves and I your prince.

Ch. Ye sons of Earth, whom Ares on a day did sow, when from the dragon's ravening jaw he had torn the teeth, up with your staves, whereon ye lean your hands, and dash out this miscreant's brains! a fellow who, without even being a Theban, but a foreigner, lords it shamefully o'er the younger folk; but *my* master shalt thou never be to thy joy, nor shalt thou reap the harvest of all my toil; begone with my curse upon thee! carry thy insolence back to the place whence it came. For never whilst I live, shalt thou slay these sons of Heracles; not so deep beneath the earth hath their father disappeared from his children's ken. Thou art in possession of this land which thou hast ruined, while he its benefactor has missed his just reward; and yet do I take too much upon myself because I help those I love after their death, when most they need a friend? Ah! right hand, how fain wouldst thou wield the spear, but thy weakness is a death-blow to thy fond desire; for then had I stopped thee calling me slave, and I would have governed Thebes, wherein thou art now exulting, with credit; for a city sick with dissension and evil counsels thinketh not aright; otherwise it would never have accepted thee as its master.

Meg. Old sirs, I thank you; 'tis right that friends should feel virtuous indignation on behalf of those they love; but do not on our account vent your anger on the tyrant to your own undoing. Hear my advice, Amphitryon, if haply there appear to thee to be aught in what I say. I love my children; strange if I did not love those whom I laboured to bring forth! Death I count a dreadful fate; but the man, who wrestles with necessity, I esteem a fool. Since we must die, let us do so without being burnt alive, to furnish our foes with food for merriment, which to my mind is an evil worse than death; for many a fair guerdon do we owe our family. Thine has ever been a warrior's fair fame, so 'tis not to be endured that thou shouldst die a coward's death; and my husband's reputation needs no one to witness that he would ne'er consent to save these children's lives by letting them incur the stain of cowardice; for the noble are afflicted by disgrace on account of their children, nor must I shrink from following my lord's example. As to thy hopes consider how I weigh them. Thou thinkest thy son will return from beneath the earth: who ever has come back from the dead out of the halls of Hades? Thou hast a hope perhaps of softening this man by entreaty: no, no! better to fly from one's enemy when he is so brutish, but yield to men of breeding and culture; for thou wilt more easily obtain mercy there by friendly overtures. True, a thought has already occurred to me that we might by entreaty obtain a sentence of exile for the children; yet this too is misery, to compass their deliverance with dire penury as the result; for 'tis a saying that hosts look sweetly on banished friends for a day and no more. Steel thy heart to die with us, for that awaits thee after all. By thy brave soul I challenge thee, old friend; for whoso struggles hard to escape destiny shows zeal no doubt, but 'tis zeal with a taint of folly; for what must be, no one will ever avail to alter.

Ch. If a man had insulted thee, while yet my arms were lusty, there would have been an easy way to stop him; but now am I a thing of naught; and so thou henceforth, Amphitryon, must scheme how to avert misfortune.

Am. 'Tis not cowardice or any longing for life that hinders my dying, but my wish to save my son's children, though no doubt I am vainly wishing for impossibilities. Lo! here is my neck ready for thy sword to pierce, my body for thee to hack or hurl from the rock; only one boon I crave for both of us, O king; slay me and this hapless mother before thou slay the children, that we may not see the hideous sight, as they gasp out their lives, calling on their mother and their father's sire; for the rest work thy will, if so thou art inclined; for we have no defence against death.

Meg. I too implore thee add a second boon, that by thy single act thou mayst put us both under a double obligation; suffer me to deck my children in robes of death—first opening the palace gates, for now are we shut out—that this at least they may obtain from their father's halls.

Ly. I grant it, and bid my servants undo the bolts. Go in and deck yourselves; robes I grudge not. But soon as ye have clothed yourselves, I will return to you to consign you to the nether world.

Exit LYCUS.

Meg. Children, follow the footsteps of your hapless mother to your father's halls, where others possess his substance, though his name is still ours.

Exit MEGARA *with her children.*

Am. O Zeus, in vain, it seems, did I get thee to share my bride with me; in vain used we to call thee father of my son. After all thou art less our friend than thou didst pretend. Great god as thou art, I, a mere mortal, surpass thee in true worth. For I did not betray the children of Heracles; but thou by stealth didst find thy way to my couch, taking another's wife without leave given, while to save thy own friends thou hast no skill. Either thou art a god of little sense, or else naturally unjust.

Exit AMPHITRYON.

Ch. Phœbus is singing a plaintive dirge to drown his happier strains, striking with key of gold his sweet-tongued lyre; so too am I fain to sing a song of praise, a crown to all his toil, concerning him who is gone to the gloom beneath the nether world, whether I am to call him son of Zeus or of Amphitryon. For the praise of noble toils accomplished is a glory to the dead. First he cleared the grove of Zeus of a lion, and put its skin upon his back, hiding his auburn hair in its fearful gaping jaws; then on a day, with murderous bow he wounded the race of wild Centaurs, that range the hills, slaying them with winged shafts; Peneus, the river of fair eddies, knows him well, and those far fields unharvested, and the steadings on Pelion and they[1] who haunt the glens of Homole bordering thereupon, whence they rode forth to conquer Thessaly, arming themselves with pines for clubs; likewise he slew that dappled hind with horns of gold, that preyed upon the country-folk, glorifying Artemis, huntress queen of Œnoe; next he mounted on a car and tamed with the bit the steeds of Diomede, that greedily champed their bloody food at gory mangers with jaws unbridled, devouring with hideous joy the flesh of men; then crossing Hebrus' silver stream he still toiled on to perform the hests of the tyrant of Mycenæ, till he came to the strand of Malian gulf by the streams of Anaurus, where he slew with his arrows Cycnus, murderer of his guests, unsocial wretch who dwelt in Amphanæ; also he came to those minstrel maids, to their orchard in the west, to pluck from the leafy apple-tree its golden fruit, when he had slain the tawny dragon, whose awful coils were twined all round to guard it; and he made his way into ocean lairs, bringing calm to men that use the oar;[2] moreover he sought the home of Atlas, and stretched out his hands to uphold the firmament, and on his manly shoulders took the starry mansions of the gods; then he went through the waves of heaving Euxine against the mounted host of Amazons dwelling round Mæotis, the lake that is fed by many a stream, having gathered to his standard all his friends from Hellas, to fetch the gold-embroidered raiment of the warrior queen, a deadly quest for a girdle. And Hellas won those glorious spoils of the barbarian maid, and safe in Mycenæ are they now. On Lerna's murderous hound, the many-headed water-snake, he set his branding-iron, and smeared its venom on his darts, wherewith he slew the shepherd of Erytheia[3] a monster with three bodies; and many another glorious achievement he brought to a happy issue; to Hades' house of tears hath he now sailed, the goal of his labours, where he is ending his career of toil, nor cometh he thence again. Now is thy house left without a friend, and Charon's boat awaits thy children to bear them on that journey out of life, whence is no returning, contrary to God's law and man's justice; and it is to thy prowess that thy house is looking although thou art not here. Had I been strong and lusty, able to brandish the spear in battle's onset, my Theban compeers too, I would have stood by thy children to champion them; but now my happy youth is gone and I am left.

But lo! I see the children of Heracles who was erst so great, clad in the vesture of the grave, and his loving wife dragging her babes along at her side, and that hero's aged sire. Ah! woe is me! no longer can I stem the flood of tears that spring to my old eyes.

Enter AMPHITRYON, MEGARA, *and children.*

Meg. Come now, who is to sacrifice or butcher these poor children? or rob me of my wretched life? Behold! the victims are ready to be led to Hades' halls. O my children! an ill-matched company are we hurried off to die, old men and babes, and mothers, all together. Alas! for my sad fate and my children's, whom these eyes now for the last time behold. So I gave you birth and reared you only for our foes to mock, to flout, and slay. Ah me! how bitterly my hopes have disappointed me in the expectation I once formed from the words of your father. (*Addressing each of her three sons in turn*) To *thee* thy dead sire was for giving Argos; and thou wert to dwell in the halls of Eurystheus, lording it o'er the fair fruitful land of Argolis; and o'er thy head would he throw that lion's skin wherewith himself was girt. *Thou* wert to be king of Thebes, famed for its chariots, receiving as thy heritage my broad lands, for so thou didst coax thy father dear; and to thy hand used he to resign the carved club, his sure defence, pretending to give it thee. To *thee* he promised to give Œchalia, which once his archery had

[1]The Centaurs.

[2]*i.e.*, he cleared the sea of pirates.

[3]Geryon.

wasted. Thus with three principalities would your father exalt you his three sons, proud of your manliness; while I was choosing the best brides for you, scheming to link you by marriage to Athens, Thebes, and Sparta, that ye might live a happy life with a fast sheet-anchor to hold by. And now that is all vanished; fortune's breeze hath veered and given to you for brides the maidens of death in their stead, and tears to me to bathe them in; woe is me for my foolish thoughts! and your grandsire here is celebrating your marriage-feast, accepting Hades as the father of your brides, a grim relationship to make. Ah me! which of you shall I first press to my bosom, which last? on which bestow my kiss, or clasp close to me? Oh! would that like the bee with russet wing, I could collect from every source my sighs in one, and, blending them together, shed them in one copious flood! Heracles, dear husband mine, to thee I call, if haply mortal voice can make itself heard in Hades' halls; thy father and children are dying, and I am doomed, I who once because of thee was counted blest as men count bliss. Come to our rescue; appear, I pray, if but as a phantom, since thy mere coming would be enough, for they are cowards compared with thee, who are slaying thy children.

Am. Lady, do thou prepare the funeral rites; but I, O Zeus, stretching out my hand to heaven, call on thee to help these children, if such be thy intention; for soon will any aid of thine be unavailing; and yet thou hast been oft invoked; my toil is wasted; death seems inevitable. Ye aged friends, the joys of life are few; so take heed that ye pass through it as gladly as ye may, without a thought of sorrow from morn till night; for time recks little of preserving our hopes; and, when he has busied himself on his own business, away he flies. Look at me, a man who had made a mark amongst his fellows by deeds of note; yet hath fortune in a single day robbed me of it as of a feather that floats away toward the sky. I know not any whose plenteous wealth and high reputation is fixed and sure; fare ye well, for now have ye seen the last of your old friend, my comrades.

Meg. Ha! old friend, is it my own, my dearest I behold? or what am I to say?

Am. I know not, my daughter; I too am struck dumb.

Meg. Is this he who, they told us, was beneath the earth?

Am. 'Tis he, unless some day-dream mocks our sight.

Meg. What am I saying? What visions do these anxious eyes behold? Old man, this is none other than thy own son. Come hither, my children, cling to your father's robe, make haste to come, never loose your hold, for here is one to help you, nowise behind our saviour Zeus.

Enter HERACLES.

Heracles. All hail! my house, and portals of my home, how glad am I to emerge to the light and see thee. Ha! what is this? I see my children before the house in the garb of death, with chaplets on their heads, and my wife amid a throng of men, and my father weeping o'er some mischance. Let me draw near to them and inquire; lady, what strange stroke of fate hath fallen on the house?

Meg. Dearest of all mankind to me! O ray of light appearing to thy sire! art thou safe, and is thy coming just in time to help thy dear ones?

He. What meanest thou? what is this confusion I find on my arrival, father?

Meg. We are being ruined; forgive me, old friend, if I have anticipated that which thou hadst a right to tell him; for woman's nature is perhaps more prone than man's to grief, and they are my children that were being led to death, which was my own lot too.

He. Great Apollo! what a prelude to thy story!

Meg. Dead are my brethren, dead my hoary sire.

He. How so? what befell him? who dealt the fatal blow?

Meg. Lycus, our splendid monarch, slew him.

He. Did he meet him in fair fight, or was the land sick and weak?

Meg. Aye, from faction; now is he master of the city of Cadmus with its seven gates.

He. Why hath panic fallen on thee and my aged sire?

Meg. He meant to kill thy father, me, and my children.

He. Why, what had he to fear from my orphan babes?

Meg. He was afraid they might some day avenge Creon's death.

He. What means this dress they wear, suited to the dead?

Meg. 'Tis the garb of death we have already put on.

He. And were ye being haled to death? O woe is me!

Meg. Yes, deserted by every friend, and informed that thou wert dead.

He. What put such desperate thoughts into your heads?

Meg. That was what the heralds of Eurystheus kept proclaiming.

He. Why did ye leave my hearth and home?

Meg. He forced us; thy father was dragged from his bed.

He. Had he no mercy, to ill-use the old man so?

Meg. Mercy forsooth! that goddess and he dwell far enough apart.

He. Was I so poor in friends in my absence?

Meg. Who are the friends of a man in misfortune?

He. Do they make so light of my hard warring with the Minyæ?

Meg. Misfortune, to repeat it to thee, has no friends.

He. Cast from your heads these chaplets of death, look up to the light, for instead of the nether gloom your eyes behold the welcome sun. I, meantime, since here is work for my hand, will first go raze this upstart tyrant's halls, and when I have beheaded the miscreant, I will throw him to dogs to tear; and every Theban who I find has played the traitor after my kindness, will I destroy with this victorious club; the rest will I scatter with my feathered shafts and fill Ismenus full of bloody corpses, and Dirce's clear fount shall run red with gore. For whom ought I to help rather than wife and children and aged sire? Farewell my labours! for it was in vain I accomplished them rather than succoured these. And yet I ought to die in their defence, since they for their sire were doomed; else what shall we find so noble in having fought a hydra and a lion at the hests of Eurystheus, if I make no effort to save my own children from death? No longer I trow, as heretofore, shall I be called Heracles the victor.

Ch. 'Tis only right that parents should help their children, their aged sires, and the partners of their marriage.

Am. My son, 'tis like thee to show thy love for thy dear ones and thy hate for all that is hostile; only curb excessive hastiness.

He. Wherein, father, am I now showing more than fitting haste?

Am. The king hath a host of allies, needy villains though pretending to be rich, who sowed dissension and o'erthrew the state with a view to plundering their neighbours; for the wealth they had in their houses was all spent, dissipated by their sloth. Thou was seen entering the city; and, that being so, beware that thou bring not thy enemies together and be slain unawares.

He. Little I reck if the whole city saw me; but happening to see a bird perched in an unlucky position, from it I learnt that some trouble had befallen my house; so I purposely made my entry to the land by stealth.

Am. For thy lucky coming hither, go salute thy household altar, and let thy father's halls behold thy face. For soon will the king be here in person to drag away thy wife and children and murder them, and to add me to the bloody list. But if thou remain on the spot all will go well, and thou wilt profit by this security; but do not rouse thy city ere thou hast these matters well in train, my son.

He. I will do so; thy advice is good; I will enter my house. After my return at length from the sunless den of Hades and the maiden queen of hell, I will not neglect to greet first of all the gods beneath my roof.

Am. Why, didst thou in very deed go to the house of Hades, my son?

He. Aye, and brought to the light that three-headed monster.

Am. Didst worst him in fight, or receive him from the goddess?

He. In fair fight; for I had been lucky enough to witness the rites of the initiated.[1]

Am. Is the monster really lodged in the house of Eurystheus?

He. The grove of Demeter and the city of Hermione are his prison.

Am. Does not Eurystheus know that thou hast returned to the upper world?

He. He knows not; I came hither first to learn your news.

Am. How is it thou wert so long beneath the earth?

He. I stayed awhile attempting to bring back Theseus from Hades, father.

Am. Where is he? gone to his native land?

He. He set out for Athens right glad to have escaped from the lower world. Come, children, attend your father to the house. My entering in is fairer in your eyes, I trow, than my going out. Take heart, and no more let the tears stream from your eyes; thou too, dear wife, collect thy courage, cease from fear; leave go of my robe; for I cannot fly away, nor have I any wish to flee from those I love. Ah! they do not loose their hold, but cling to my garments all the more; were ye in such jeopardy? Well, I must lead them, taking them by the hand to draw them after me, like a ship when towing; for I too do not reject the care of my children; here all mankind are equal; all love their children, both those of high estate and those who are naught; 'tis wealth that makes distinctions among them; some have, others want; but all the human race loves its offspring.

Exeunt HERACLES, AMPHITRYON, *and* MEGARA, *with their children.*

Ch. Dear to me is youth, but old age is ever hanging o'er my head, a burden heavier than Ætna's crags, casting its pall of gloom upon my eyes. Oh! never may the wealth of Asia's kings tempt me to barter for houses stored with gold my happy youth, which is in wealth and poverty alike most fair! But old age is gloomy and deathly; I hate it; let it sink beneath the waves! Would it had never found its way to the homes and towns of mortal men, but were still drifting on for ever down the wind! Had the gods shown discernment and wisdom, as mortals count these things, men would have gotten youth twice over, a visible mark of worth amongst whomsoever found, and after death would these have retraced their steps once more to the sun-light, while the mean man would have had but a single portion of life; and thus would it have been possible to distinguish the good and the bad, just as sailors know the number of the stars amid the clouds. But, as it is, the gods have set no certain boundary 'twixt good and bad, but time's onward roll brings increase only to man's wealth.

Never will I cease to link in one the Graces and the Muses, fairest union. Never may my lines be cast among untutored boors, but ever may I find a place among the crownèd choir! Yes, still the aged bard lifts up his voice of bygone memories; still is my song of the triumphs of Heracles, whether Bromius the giver of wine is nigh, or the strains of the seven-stringed lyre and the Libyan flute are rising; not yet will I cease to sing the Muses' praise, my patrons in the dance. As the maids of Delos raise their song of joy, circling round the temple gates in honour of Leto's fair son, the graceful dancer; so I with my old lips will sing songs of victory

[1] *i.e.,* the Eleusinian mysteries.

at thy palace-doors, a song of my old age, such as sings the dying swan; for there is a goodly theme for minstrelsy; he is the son of Zeus; yet high above his noble birth tower his deeds of prowess, for his toil secured this life of calm for man, having destroyed all fearsome beasts.

Enter LYCUS *and* AMPHITRYON.

Ly. Ha! Amphitryon, 'tis high time thou camest forth from the palace; ye have been too long arraying yourselves in the robes and trappings of the dead. Come, bid the wife and children of Heracles show themselves outside the house, to die on the conditions you yourselves offered.

Am. O king, thou dost persecute me in my misery and heapest insult upon me over and above the loss of my son; thou shouldst have been more moderate in thy zeal, though thou art my lord and master. But since thou dost impose death's stern necessity on me, needs must I acquiesce and do thy will.

Ly. Pray, where is Megara? where are the children of Alcmena's son?

Am. She, I believe, so far as I can guess from outside—

Ly. What grounds hast thou to base thy fancy on?

Am. Is sitting as a suppliant on the altar's hallowed steps.

Ly. Imploring them quite uselessly to save her life.

Am. And calling on her dead husband, quite in vain.

Ly. He is nowhere near, and he certainly will never come.

Am. No, unless perhaps a god should raise him from the dead.

Ly. Go to her and bring her from the palace.

Am. By doing so I should become an accomplice in her murder.

Ly. Since thou hast this scruple, I, who have left fear behind, will myself bring out the mother and her children. Follow me, servants, that we may put an end to this delay of our work to our joy.

Exit LYCUS.

Am. Then go thy way along the path of fate; for what remains, maybe another will provide. Expect for thy evil deeds to find some trouble thyself. Ah! my aged friends, he is marching fairly to his doom; soon will he be entangled in the snare of the sword, thinking to slay his neighbours, the villain! I will hence, to see him fall dead; for the sight of a foe being slain and paying the penalty of his misdeeds affords pleasurable feelings. *Exit* AMPHITRYON.

Ch. (1) Evil has changed sides; he who was erst a mighty king is now turning his life backward into the road to Hades.

(2) Hail to thee! Justice and heavenly retribution.

(3) At last hast thou reached the goal where thy death will pay the forfeit,

(4) For thy insults against thy betters.

(5) Joy makes my tears burst forth.

(6) There is come a retribution, which the prince of the land never once thought in his heart would happen.

(7) Come, old friends, let us look within to see if one we know has met the fate I hope.

Ly. (*Within*) Ah me! ah me!

Ch. (8) Ha! how sweet to hear that opening note of his within the house; death is not far off him now.

(9) Hark! the prince cries out in his agony; that preludes death.

Ly. (*Within*) O kingdom of Cadmus, by treachery I am perishing!

Ch. (10) Thou wert thyself for making others perish; endure thy retribution; 'tis only the penalty of thy own deeds thou art paying.

(11) Who was he, weak son of man, that aimed his silly saying at the blessed gods of heaven with impious blasphemy, maintaining that they are weaklings after all?

(12) Old friends, our godless foe is now no more.

(13) The house is still; let us to our dancing.

(14) Yea, for fortune smiles upon my friends as I desire.

Dances and banquets now prevail throughout the holy town of Thebes. For release from tears and respite from sorrow give birth to song. The upstart king is dead and gone; our former monarch now is prince, having made his way even from the bourn of Acheron. Hope beyond all expectation is fulfilled. To heed the right and wrong is heaven's care. 'Tis their gold and their good luck that lead men's hearts astray, bringing in their train unholy tyranny. For no man ever had the courage to reflect what reverses time might bring; but, disregarding law to gratify lawlessness, he shatters in gloom the car of happiness. Deck thee with garlands, O Ismenus! break forth into dancing, ye paved streets of our seven-gated city! come Dirce, fount of waters fair; and joined with her ye daughters of Asopus, come from your father's waves to add your maiden voices to our hymn, the victor's prize that Heracles hath won. O Pythian rock, with forests crowned, and haunts of the Muses on Helicon! make my city and her walls re-echo with cries of joy; where sprang the earth-born crop to view, a warrior-host with shields of brass, who are handing on their realm to children's children, a light divine to Thebes. All hail the marriage! wherein two bridegrooms shared; the one, a mortal; the other, Zeus, who came to wed the maiden sprung from Perseus; for that marriage of thine, O Zeus, in days gone by has been proved to me a true story beyond all expectation; and time hath shown the lustre of Heracles' prowess, who emerged from caverns 'neath the earth after leaving Pluto's halls below. To me art thou a worthier lord than that base-born king, who now lets it be plainly seen in this struggle 'twixt armed warriors, whether justice still finds favour in heaven.

(*The forms of* MADNESS *and* IRIS *appear above the palace*) Ha! see there, my old comrades! is the same wild panic fallen on us all, what phantom is this I see hovering o'er the house? Fly, fly, bestir thy tardy steps! begone! away! O saviour prince, avert calamity from me!

Iris. Courage, old men! she, whom you see, is Madness, daughter of night, and I am Iris, the handmaid of the gods. We have not come to do your city any hurt, but against the house of one man only is our warfare, even against him whom they call the son of Zeus and Alcmena. For until he had finished all his grievous toils, Destiny was preserving him, nor would father Zeus ever suffer me or Hera to harm him. But now that he hath accomplished the labours of Eurystheus, Hera is minded to brand him with the guilt of shedding kindred blood by slaying his own children, and I am one with her. Come then, maid unwed, child of murky Night, harden thy heart relentlessly, send forth frenzy upon him, confound his mind even to the slaying of his children, drive him, goad him wildly on his mad career, shake out the sails of death, that when he has sent o'er Acheron's ferry that fair group of children by his own murderous hand, he may learn to know how fiercely against him the wrath of Hera burns and may also experience mine; otherwise, if he escape punishment, the gods will become as naught, while man's power will grow.

Madness. Of noble parents was I born, the daughter of Night, sprung from the blood of Uranus; and these prerogatives I hold, not to use them in anger against friends, nor have I any joy in visiting the homes of men; and fain would I counsel Hera, before I see her make a mistake, and thee too, if ye will hearken to my words. This man, against whose house thou art sending me, has made himself a name alike in heaven and earth; for, after taming pathless wilds and raging sea, he by his single might raised up again the honours of the gods when sinking before man's impiety; wherefore I counsel thee, do not wish him dire mishaps.

Ir. Spare us *thy* advice on Hera's and my schemes.

Ma. I seek to turn thy steps into the best path instead of into this bad one.

Ir. 'Twas not to practise self-control that the wife of Zeus sent thee hither.

Ma. I call the sun-god to witness that herein I am acting against my will; but if indeed I must forthwith serve thee and Hera and follow you in full cry as hounds follow the huntsman, why go I will; nor shall ocean with its moaning waves, nor the earthquake, nor the thunderbolt with blast of agony be half so furious as the headlong rush I will make into the breast of Heracles; through his roof will I burst my way and swoop upon his house, after first slaying his children; nor shall their murderer know that he is killing his own-begotten babes, till he is released from my madness. Behold him! see how even now he is wildly tossing his head at the outset, and rolling his eyes fiercely from side to side without a word; nor can he control his panting breath; but like a bull in act to charge, he bellows fearfully, calling on the goddesses of nether hell. Soon will I rouse thee to yet wilder dancing and sound a note of terror in thine ear. Soar away, O Iris, to Olympus on thy honoured course; while I unseen will steal into the halls of Heracles.

Exeunt IRIS *and* MADNESS.

Ch. Alas! alas! lament, O city; the son of Zeus, thy fairest bloom, is being cut down.

(1) Woe is thee, Hellas! that wilt cast from thee thy benefactor, and destroy him as he madly, wildly dances where no pipe is heard.

(2) She is mounted on her car, the queen of sorrow and sighing, and is goading on her steeds, as if for outrage, the Gorgon child of night, with hundred hissing serpent-heads, Madness of the flashing eyes.

(3) Soon hath the god changed his good fortune; soon will his children breathe their last, slain by a father's hand.

(4) Ah me! alas! soon will vengeance, mad, relentless, lay low by a cruel death thy unhappy son, O Zeus, exacting a full penalty.

(5) Alas, O house! the fiend begins her dance of death without the cymbal's crash, with no glad waving of the wine-god's staff.

(6) Woe to these halls! toward bloodshed she moves and not to pour libations of the juice of the grape.

(7) O children, haste to fly; that is the chant of death her piping plays.

(8) Ah, yes! he is chasing the children. Never, ah! never will Madness lead her revel rout in vain.

(9) Ah misery!

(10) Ah me! how I lament that aged sire, that mother too that bore his babes in vain.

(11) Look! look!

(12) A tempest rocks the house; the roof is falling with it.

(13) Oh! what art thou doing, son of Zeus?

(14) Thou art sending hell's confusion against thy house, as erst did Pallas on Enceladus.

Enter MESSENGER.

Messenger. Ye hoary men of eld!

Ch. Why, oh! why this loud address to me?

Mes. Awful is the sight within!

Ch. No need for me to call another to announce that.

Mes. Dead lie the children.

Ch. Alas!

Mes. Ah weep! for here is cause for weeping.

Ch. A cruel murder, wrought by parents' hands!

Mes. No words can utter more than we have suffered.

Ch. What, canst thou prove this piteous mischief was a father's outrage on his children? Tell me how these heavensent woes came rushing on the house; say how the children met their sad mischance.

Mes. Victims to purify the house were stationed before the altar of Zeus, for Heracles had slain and cast from his halls the king of the land. There stood his group of lovely children, with his sire and Megara; and already the basket was being passed round the altar, and we were keeping holy silence. But just as Alcmena's son was bringing the torch in his right hand to dip it in the holy water,[1] he stopped without a word. And as their father lingered, his children looked at him; and lo! he was changed; his eyes were rolling; he was quite distraught; his eyeballs were bloodshot and starting from their sockets, and foam was oozing down his bearded cheek. Anon he spoke, laughing the while a madman's laugh, "Father, why should I sacrifice before I have slain Eurystheus, why kindle the purifying flame and have the toil twice over, when I might at one stroke so fairly end it all? Soon as I have brought the head of Eurystheus hither, I will cleanse my hands for those already slain. Spill the water, cast the baskets from your hands. Ho! give me now my bow and club! To famed Mycenæ will I go; crow-bars and pick-axes must I take, for I will heave from their very base with iron levers those city-walls which the Cyclopes squared with red plumbline and mason's tools."

Then he set out, and though he had no chariot there, he thought he had, and was for mounting to its seat, and using a goad as though his fingers really held one. A twofold feeling filled his servants' breasts, half amusement, and half fear; and one looking to his neighbour said, "Is our master making sport for us, or is he mad?" But he the while was pacing to and fro in his house; and, rushing into the men's chamber, he thought he had reached the city of Nisus,[2] albeit he had gone into his own halls. So he threw himself upon the floor, as if he were there, and made ready to feast. But after waiting a brief space he began saying he was on his way to the plains amid the valleys of the Isthmus; and then stripping himself of his mantle, he fell to competing with an imaginary rival, o'er whom he proclaimed himself victor with his own voice, calling on imaginary spectators to listen. Next, fancy carrying him to Mycenæ, he was uttering fearful threats against Eurystheus. Meantime his father caught him by his stalwart arm, and thus addressed him, "My son, what meanest thou hereby? What strange doings are these? Can it be that the blood of thy late victims has driven thee frantic?" But he, supposing it was the father of Eurystheus striving in abject supplication to touch his hand, thrust him aside, and then against his own children aimed his bow and made ready his quiver, thinking to slay the sons of Eurystheus. And they in wild affright darted hither and thither, one to his hapless mother's skirts, another to the shadow of a pillar, while a third cowered 'neath the altar like a bird. Then cried their mother, "O father, what art thou doing? dost mean to slay thy children?" Likewise his aged sire and all the gathered servants cried aloud. But he, hunting the child round and round the column, in dreadful circles, and coming face to face with him shot him to the heart; and he fell upon his back, sprinkling the tone pillars with blood as he gasped out his life.

[1] A lighted brand from the altar was dipped in the holy vater, and those present were sprinkled with it.

[2] Megara.

Then did Heracles shout for joy and boasted loud, "Here lies one of Eurystheus' brood dead at my feet, atoning for his father's hate." Against a second did he aim his bow, who had crouched at the altar's foot thinking to escape unseen. But ere he fired, the poor child threw himself at his father's knees, and, flinging his hand to reach his beard or neck, cried, "Oh! slay me not, dear father mine! I am thy child, thine own; 'tis no son of Eurystheus thou wilt slay."

But that other, with savage Gorgon-scowl, as the child now stood in range of his baleful archery, smote him on the head, as smites a smith his molten iron, bringing down his club upon the fair-haired boy, and crushed the bones. The second caught, away he hies to add a third victim to the other twain. But ere he could, the poor mother caught up her babe and carried him within the house and shut the doors; forthwith the madman, as though he really were at the Cyclopean walls, prizes open the doors with levers, and, hurling down their posts, with one fell shaft laid low his wife and child. Then in wild career he starts to slay his aged sire; but lo! there came a phantom—so it seemed to us on-lookers—of Pallas, with plumed helm, brandishing a spear; and she hurled a rock against the breast of Heracles, which stayed him from his frenzied thirst for blood and plunged him into sleep; to the ground he fell, smiting his back against a column that had fallen on the floor in twain when the roof fell in. Thereon we rallied from our flight, and with the old man's aid bound him fast with knotted cords to the pillar, that on his awakening he might do no further mischief. So there he sleeps, poor wretch! a sleep that is not blest, having murdered wife and children; nay, for my part I know not any son of man more miserable than he. *Exit* MESSENGER.

Ch. That murder wrought by the daughters of Danaus, whereof my native Argos wots, was formerly the most famous and notorious in Hellas; but this hath surpassed and outdone those previous horrors. I could tell of the murder of that poor son of Zeus, whom Procne, mother of an only child, slew and offered to the Muses; but thou hadst three children, wretched parent, and all of them hast thou in thy frenzy slain. What groans or wails what funeral dirge, or chant of death am I to raise? Alas and woe! see, the bolted doors of the lofty palace are being rolled apart. Ah me! behold these children lying dead before their wretched father, who is sunk in awful slumber after shedding their blood. Round him are bonds and cords, made fast with many a knot about the body of Heracles, and lashed to the stone columns of his house. While he, the aged sire, like mother-bird wailing her unfledged brood, comes hasting hither with halting steps on his bitter journey.

The palace doors opening disclose HERACLES *lying asleep, bound to a shattered column.*

Am. Softly, softly! ye aged sons of Thebes, let him sleep on and forget his sorrows.

Ch. For thee, old friend, I weep and mourn, for the children too and that victorious chief.

Am. Stand further off, make no noise nor outcry, rouse him not from his calm deep slumber.

Ch. O horrible! all this blood—

Am. Hush, hush! ye will be my ruin.

Ch. That he has spilt is rising up against him.

Am. Gently raise your dirge of woe, old friends; lest he wake, and, bursting his bonds, destroy the city, rend his sire, and dash his house to pieces.

Ch. I cannot possibly speak lower.

Am. Hush! let me note his breathing; come, let me put my ear close.

Ch. Is he sleeping?

Am. Aye, that is he, a deathly sleep, having slain wife and children with the arrows of his twanging bow.

Ch. Ah! mourn—

Am. Indeed I do.

Ch. The children's death;

Am. Ah me!

Ch. And thy own son's doom.

Am. Ah misery!

Ch. Old friend—

Am. Hush! hush! he is turning over, he is waking! Oh! let me hide myself beneath the covert of yon roof.

Ch. Courage! darkness still broods o'er thy son's eye.

Am. Oh! beware; 'tis not that I shrink from leaving the light after my miseries, poor wretch! but should he slay me that am his father, then will he be devising mischief on mischief, and to the avenging curse will add a parent's blood.

Ch. Well for thee hadst thou died in that day, when, to win thy wife, thou didst go forth to exact vengeance for her slain brethren by sacking the Taphians' sea-beat town.

Am. Fly, fly, my aged friends, haste from before the palace, escape his waking fury! For soon will he heap up fresh carnage on the old, ranging wildly once more through the streets of Thebes.

Ch. O Zeus, why hast thou shown such savage hate against thine own son and plunged him in this sea of troubles?

He. (*Waking*) Aha! my breath returns; I am alive; and my eyes resume their function, opening on the sky and earth and yon sun's darting beam; but how my senses reel! in what strange turmoil am I plunged! my fevered breath in quick spasmodic gasps escapes my lungs. How now? why am I lying here, made fast with cables like a ship, my brawny chest and arms tied to a shattered piece of masonry, with corpses for my neighbours; while o'er the floor my bow and arrows are scattered, that erst like trusty squires to my arm both kept me safe and were kept safe of me? Surely I am not come a second time to Hades' halls, having just returned from thence for Eurystheus? No, I do not see Sisyphus with his stone, or Pluto, or his queen, Demeter's child. Surely I am distraught; I cannot remember where I am. Ho, there! which of my friends is near or far to help me in my perplexity? For I have no clear knowledge of things once familiar.

Am. My aged friends, shall I approach the scene of my sorrow?

Ch. Yes, and let me go with thee, nor desert thee in thy trouble.

He. Father, why dost thou weep and veil thy eyes, standing aloof from thy beloved son?

Am. My child! mine still, for all thy misery.

He. Why, what is there so sad in my case that thou dost weep?

Am. That which might make any of the gods weep, were he to suffer so.

He. A bold assertion that, but thou art not yet explaining what has happened.

Am. Thine own eyes see that, if by this time thou art restored to thy senses.

He. Fill in thy sketch if any change awaits my life.

Am. I will explain, if thou art no longer mad as a fiend of hell.

He. God help us! what suspicions these dark hints of thine again excite!

Am. I am still doubtful whether thou art in thy sober senses.

He. I never remember being mad.

Am. Am I to loose my son, old friends, or what?

He. Loose and say who bound me; for I feel shame at this.

Am. Rest content with what thou knowest of thy woes; the rest forego.

He. Enough! I have no wish to probe thy silence.

Am. O Zeus, dost thou behold these deeds proceeding from the throne of Hera?

He. What! have I suffered something from her enmity?

Am. A truce to the goddess! attend to thy own troubles.

He. I am undone; what mischance wilt thou unfold?

Am. See here the corpses of thy children.

He. O horror! what hideous sight is here? ah me!

Am. My son, against thy children hast thou waged unnatural war.

He. War! what meanst thou? who killed these?

Am. Thou and thy bow and some god, whoso he be that is to blame.

He. What sayst thou? what have I done? speak, father, thou messenger of evil.

Am. Thou wert distraught; 'tis a sad explanation thou art asking.

He. Was it I that slew my wife also?

Am. Thy own unaided arm hath done all this.

He. Ah, woe is me! a cloud of sorrow wraps me round.

Am. The reason this that I lament thy fate.

He. Did I dash my house to pieces or incite others thereto.

Am. Naught know I save this, that thou art utterly undone.

He. Where did my frenzy seize me? where did it destroy me?

Am. In the moment thou wert purifying thyself with fire at the altar.

He. Ah me! why do I spare my own life when I have taken that of my dear children? Shall I not hasten to leap from some sheer rock, or aim the sword against my heart and avenge my children's blood, or burn my body in the fire and so avert from my life the infamy which now awaits me?

But hither I see Theseus coming to check my deadly counsels, my kinsman and friend. Now shall I stand revealed, and the dearest of my friends will see the pollution I have incurred by my children's murder. Ah, woe is me! what am I to do? Where can I find release from my sorrows? shall I take wings or plunge beneath the earth? Come, let me veil my head in darkness; for I am ashamed of the evil I have done, and, since for these I have incurred fresh blood-guiltiness, I would fain not harm the innocent.

Enter THESEUS.

Theseus. I am come, and others with me, young warriors from the land of Athens, encamped at present by the streams of Asopus, to help thy son, old friend. For a rumour reached the city of the Erechthidæ, that Lycus had usurped the sceptre of this land and was become your enemy even to battle. Wherefore I came making recompense for the former kindness of Heracles in saving me from the world below, if haply ye have any need of such aid as I or my allies can give, old prince.

Ha! what means this heap of dead upon the floor? Surely I have not delayed too long and come too late to check a revolution? Who slew these children? whose wife is this I see? Boys do not go to battle; nay, it must be some other strange mischance I here discover.

Am. O king, whose home is that olive-clad hill!

Th. Why this piteous prelude in addressing me?

Am. Heaven has afflicted us with grievous suffering.

Th. Whose be these children, o'er whom thou weepest?

Am. My own son's children, woe is him! their father and butcher both was he, hardening his heart to the bloody deed.

Th. Hush! good words only!

Am. I would I could obey!

Th. What dreadful words!

Am. Fortune has spread her wings, and we are ruined, ruined.

Th. What meanest thou? what hath he done?

Am. Slain them in a wild fit of frenzy with arrows dipped in the venom of the hundred-headed hydra.

Th. This is Hera's work; but who lies there among the dead, old man?

Am. My son, my own enduring son, that marched with gods to Phlegra's plain, there to battle with giants and slay them, warrior that he was.

Th. Ah, woe for him! whose fortune was e'er so curst as his?

Am. Never wilt thou find another that hath borne a larger share of suffering or been more fatally deceived.

Th. Why doth he veil his head, poor wretch, in his robe?

Am. He is ashamed to meet thine eye; his kinsman's kind intent and his children's blood make him abashed.

Th. But I come to sympathize; uncover him.

Am. My son, remove that mantle from thine eyes, throw it from thee, show thy face unto the sun; a counterpoise to weeping is battling for the mastery. In suppliant wise I entreat thee, as I grasp thy beard, thy knees, thy hands, and let fall the tear from my old eyes. O my child! restrain thy savage lion-like temper, for thou art rushing forth on an unholy course of bloodshed, eager to join mischief to mischief.

Th. What ho! To thee I call who art huddled there in thy misery, show to thy friends thy face; for no darkness is black enough to hide thy sad mischance. Why dost thou wave thy hand at me, signifying murder? is it that I may not be polluted by speaking with thee? If I share thy misfortune, what is that to me? For if I too had luck in days gone by, I must refer it to the time when thou didst bring me safe from the dead to the light of life. I hate a friend whose gratitude grows old; one who is ready to enjoy his friends' prosperity but unwilling to sail in the same ship with them when their fortune lours. Arise, unveil thy head, poor wretch! and look on me. The gallant soul endures without a word such blows as heaven deals.

He. O Theseus, didst thou witness this struggle with my children?

Th. I heard of it, and now I see the horrors thou meanest.

He. Why then hast thou unveiled my head to the sun?

Th. Why have I? Thou, a man, canst not pollute what is of God.

He. Fly, luckless wretch, from my unholy taint.

Th. The avenging fiend goes not forth from friend to friend.

He. For this I thank thee; I do not regret the service I did thee.

Th. While I, for kindness then received, now show my pity for thee.

He. Ah yes! I am a piteous object, a murderer of my own sons.

Th. I weep for thee in thy changed fortunes.

He. Didst ever find another more afflicted?

Th. Thy misfortunes reach from earth to heaven.

He. Therefore am I resolved on death.

Th. Dost thou suppose the gods attend to these thy threats?

He. Remorseless hath heaven been to me; so I will prove the like to it.

Th. Hush! lest thy presumption add to thy sufferings.

He. My barque is freighted full with sorrow; there is no room to stow aught further.

Th. What wilt thou do? whither is thy fury drifting thee?

He. I will die and return to that world below whence I have just come.

Th. Such language is fit for any common fellow.

He. Ah! thine is the advice of one outside sorrow's pale.

Th. Are these indeed the words of Heracles, the much-enduring?

He. Never so much as this though. Endurance must have a limit.

Th. Is this man's benefactor, his chiefest friend?

He. Man brings no help to me; no! Hera has her way.

Th. Never will Hellas suffer thee to die through sheer perversity.

He. Hear me a moment, that I may enter the lists with arguments in answer to thy admonitions; and I will unfold to thee why life now as well as formerly has been unbearable to me. First I am the son of a man who incurred the guilt of blood, before he married my mother Alcmena, by slaying her aged sire. Now when the foundation is badly laid at birth, needs must the race be cursed with woe; and Zeus, whoever this Zeus may be, begot me as a butt for Hera's hate; yet be not thou vexed thereat, old man; for thee rather than Zeus do I regard as my father. Then whilst I was yet being suckled, that bride of Zeus did foist into my cradle fearsome snakes to compass my death. After I was grown to man's estate, of all the toils I then endured what need to tell? of all the lions, Typhons triple-bodied, and giants that I slew; or of the battle I won against the hosts of four-legged Centaurs? or how when I had killed the hydra, that monster with a ring of heads with power to grow again, I passed through countless other toils besides and came unto the dead to fetch to the light at the bidding of Eurystheus the three-headed hound, hell's porter. Last, ah, woe is me! have I perpetrated this bloody deed to crown the sorrows of my house with my children's murder. To this sore strait am I come; no longer may I dwell in Thebes, the city that I love; for suppose I stay, to what temple or gathering of friends shall I repair? For mine is no curse that invites address. Shall I go to Argos? how can I, when I am an exile from my country? Well, is there a single other city I can fly to? And if there were, am I to be looked at askance as a marked man, branded by cruel stabbing tongues, "Is not this the son of Zeus that once murdered wife and children? Plague take him from the land!"

Now to one who was erst called happy, such changes are a grievous thing; though he who is always unfortunate feels no such pain, for sorrow is his birthright. This, methinks, is the piteous pass I shall one day come to; earth, for instance, will cry out forbidding me to touch her, the sea and the river-springs will refuse me a crossing, and I shall become like Ixion who revolves in chains upon that wheel. Wherefore this is best, that henceforth I be seen by none of the Hellenes, amongst whom in happier days I lived in bliss. What right have I to live? what profit can I have in the possession of a useless, impious life? So let that noble wife of Zeus break forth in dancing, beating with buskined foot on heaven's bright floor; for now hath she worked her heart's desire in utterly confounding the chiefest of Hellas' sons. Who would pray to such a goddess? Her jealousy of Zeus for his love of a woman hath destroyed the benefactors of Hellas, guiltless though they were.

Ch. This is the work of none other of the gods than the wife of Zeus; thou art right in that surmise.

Th. . . . . .[1] rather than to go on suffering. There is not a man alive that hath wholly 'scaped misfortune's taint, nor any god either, if what poets sing is true. Have they not intermarried in ways that law forbids? Have they not thrown fathers into ignominious chains to gain the sovereign power? Still they inhabit Olympus and brave the issue of their crimes. And yet what shalt thou say in thy defence, if thou, a child of man, dost kick against the pricks of fate, while they do not? Nay, then, leave Thebes in compliance with the law, and come with me to the city of Pallas. There, when I have purified thee of thy pollution, will I give thee temples and the half of all I have. Yea, I will give thee all those presents I received from the citizens for saving their children, seven sons and daughters seven, in the day I slew the bull of Crete; for I have plots of land assigned me throughout the country; these shall henceforth be called after thee by men, whilst thou livest; and at thy death, when thou art gone to Hades' halls, the city of Athens shall unite in exalting thy honour with sacrifices and a monument of stone. For 'tis a noble crown for citizens to win from Hellas, even a reputation fair, by helping a man of worth. This is the return that I will make thee for saving me, for now art thou in need of friends. But when heaven delights to honour a man, he has no need of friends; for the god's aid, when he chooses to give it, is enough.

He. Tush! this is quite beside the question of my troubles. For my part, I do not believe that the gods indulge in unholy unions; and as for putting fetters on parents' hands, I have never thought that worthy of credit, nor will I now be so persuaded, nor again that one god is naturally lord and master of another. For the deity, if he be really such, has no wants; these are miserable fictions of the poets. But I, for all my piteous plight, reflected whether I should let myself be branded as a coward for giving up my life. For whoso schooleth not his frail mortal nature to bear fate's buffets as he ought, will never be able to withstand even a man's weapon. I will harden my heart against death and seek thy city, with grateful thanks for all thou offerest me.

Of countless troubles have I tasted, God knows, but never yet did I faint at any or shed a single tear; nay, nor ever dreamt that I should come to this, to let the tear-drop fall. But now, it seems, I must be fortune's slave. Well, let it pass; old father mine, thou seest me go forth to exile, and in me beholdest

[1]There is a lacuna before line 1313.

my own children's murderer. Give them burial, and lay them out in death with the tribute of a tear, for the law forbids my doing so. Rest their heads upon their mother's bosom and fold them in her arms, sad pledges of our union, whom I, alas! unwittingly did slay. And when thou hast buried these dead, live on here still, in bitterness maybe, but still constrain thy soul to share my sorrows. O children! he who begat you, your own father, hath been your destroyer, and ye have had no profit of my triumphs, all my restless toil to win you a fair name in life, a glorious guerdon from a sire. Thee too, unhappy wife, this hand hath slain, a poor return to make thee for preserving mine honour so safe, for all the weary watch thou long hast kept within my house. Alas for you, my wife, my sons! and woe for me, how sad my lot, cut off from wife and child! Ah! these kisses, bitter-sweet! these weapons which 'tis pain to own! I am not sure whether to keep or let them go; dangling at my side they thus will say, "With us didst thou destroy children and wife; we are thy children's slayers, and thou keepest us." Shall I carry them after that? what answer can I make? Yet, am I to strip me of these weapons, the comrades of my glorious career in Hellas, and put myself thereby in the power of my foes, to die a death of shame? No! I must not let them go, but keep them, though it grieve me. In one thing, Theseus, help my misery; come to Argos with me and aid in settling my reward for bringing Cerberus thither; lest, if I go all alone, my sorrow for my sons do me some hurt.

O land of Cadmus, and all ye folk of Thebes! cut off your hair, and mourn with me; go to my children's burial, and with united dirge lament alike the dead and me; for on all of us hath Hera inflicted the same cruel blow of destruction.

Th. Rise, unhappy man! thou hast had thy fill of tears.

He. I cannot rise; my limbs are rooted here.

Th. Yea, even the strong are o'erthrown by misfortunes.

He. Ah! would I could grow into a stone upon this spot, oblivious of trouble!

Th. Peace! give thy hand to a friend and helper.

He. Nay, let me not wipe off the blood upon thy robe.

Th. Wipe it off and spare not; I will not say thee nay.

He. Reft of my own sons, I find thee as a son to me.

Th. Throw thy arm about my neck; I will be thy guide.

He. A pair of friends in sooth are we, but one a man of sorrows. Ah! aged sire, this is the kind of man to make a friend.

Am. Blest in her sons, the country that gave him birth!

He. O Theseus, turn me back again to see my babes.

Th. What charm dost think to find in this to soothe thy soul?

He. I long to do so, and would fain embrace my sire.

Am. Here am I, my son; thy wish is no less dear to me.

Th. Hast thou so short a memory for thy troubles?

He. All that I endured of yore was easier to bear than this.

Th. If men see thee play the woman, they will scoff.

He. Have I by living grown so abject in *thy* sight? 'twas not so once, methinks.

Th. Aye, too much so; for how dost show thyself the glorious Heracles of yore?

He. What about thyself? what kind of hero wert thou when in trouble in the world below?

Th. I was worse than anyone as far as courage went.

He. How then canst thou say of me, that I am abased by my troubles?

Th. Forward!

He. Farewell, my aged sire!

Am. Farewell to thee, my son!

He. Bury my children as I said.

Am. But who will bury me, my son?

He. I will.

Am. When wilt thou come?

He. After thou hast buried my children.

Am. How?

He. I will fetch thee from Thebes to Athens. But carry my children within, a grievous burden to the earth. And I, after ruining my house by deeds of shame, will follow in the wake of Theseus, a total wreck. Whoso prefers wealth or might to the possession of good friends, thinketh amiss.

Ch. With grief and many a bitter tear we go our way, robbed of all we prized most dearly.

Exeunt OMNES.

THE PHŒNICIAN MAIDENS

DRAMATIS PERSONAE

JOCASTA	ETEOCLES
OLD RETAINER	CREON
ANTIGONE	TEIRESIAS
CHORUS OF PHŒNICIAN MAIDENS	MENŒCEUS
POLYNICES	FIRST MESSENGER
	SECOND MESSENGER

ŒDIPUS

Before the royal palace at Thebes. Enter JOCASTA.

Jocasta. O sun-god, who cleavest thy way along the starry sky, mounted on golden-studded car, rolling on thy path of flame behind fleet coursers, how curst the beam thou didst shed on Thebes, the day that Cadmus left Phœnicia's realm beside the sea and reached this land! He it was that in days long gone wedded Harmonia, the daughter of Cypris, and begat Polydore from whom they say sprung Labdacus, and Laius from him. I am known as the daughter of Menœceus, and Creon is my brother by the same mother. Men call me Jocasta, for so my father named me, and I am married to Laius. Now when he was still childless after being wedded to me a long time, he went and questioned Phœbus, craving moreover that our love might be crowned with sons born to his house. But the god said, "King of Thebes for horses famed! seek not to beget children against the will of heaven; for if thou beget a son, that child shall slay thee, and all thy house shall wade through blood." But he, yielding to his lust in a drunken fit, begat a son of me, and when his babe was born, conscious of his sin and of the god's warning, he gave the child to shepherds to expose in Hera's meadow on mount Cithæron, after piercing his ankles with iron spikes; whence it was that Hellas named him Œdipus. But the keepers of the horses of Polybus finding him took him home and laid him in the arms of their mistress. So she suckled the child that I had borne and persuaded her husband she was its mother. Soon as my son was grown to man's estate, the tawny beard upon his cheek, either because he had guessed the fraud or learnt if from another, he set out for the shrine of Phœbus, eager to know for certain who his parents were; and likewise Laius, my husband, was on his way thither, anxious to find out if the child he had exposed was dead. And they twain met where the branching roads to Phocis unite; and the charioteer of Laius called to him, "Out of the way, stranger, room for my lord!" But he, with never a word, strode on in his pride; and the horses with their hoofs drew blood from the tendons of his feet. Then—but why need I tell aught beyond the sad issue?—son slew father, and taking his chariot gave it to Polybus his foster-father. Now when the Sphinx was grievously harrying our city after my husband's death, my brother Creon proclaimed that he would wed me to any who should guess the riddle of that crafty maiden. By same strange chance, my own son, Œdipus guessed the Sphinx's riddle, and so he became king of this land and received its sceptre as his prize, and married his mother, all unwitting, luckless wretch! nor did I his mother know that I was wedded to my son; and I bore him two sons, Eteocles and the hero Polynices, and two daughters as well; the one her father called Ismene, the other, which was the elder, I named Antigone. Now when Œdipus, that awful sufferer, learnt that I, his wedded wife, was his mother too, he inflicted a ghastly outrage upon his eyes, tearing the bleeding orbs with a golden brooch. But since my sons have grown to bearded men, they have confined their father closely, that his misfortune, needing as it did full many a shift to hide it, might be forgotten. He is still living in the palace, but his misfortunes have so unhinged him that he imprecates the most unholy curses on his sons, praying that they may have to draw the sword before they share this house between them. So they, fearful that heaven may accomplish his prayer if they dwell together, have made an agreement, arranging that Polynices, the younger, should first leave the land in voluntary exile, while Eteocles should stay and hold the sceptre for a year and then change places. But as soon as Eteocles was seated high in power, he refused to give up the throne, and drove Polynices into exile from the kingdom; so Polynices went to Argos and married into the family of Adrastus, and having collected a numerous force of Argives is leading them hither; and he is come up against our seven-gated walls, demanding the sceptre of his father and his share in the kingdom. Wherefore I, to end their strife, have prevailed on one son to meet the other under truce, before appealing to arms; and the messenger I sent tells me that he will come. O Zeus, whose home is heaven's radiant vault, save us, and grant that my sons may be reconciled!

For thou, if thou art really wise, must not suffer the same poor mortal to be for ever wretched.

Exit JOCASTA.

Enter OLD RETAINER *and* ANTIGONE.

Old Retainer. (*From the roof*) Antigone, choice blossom in a father's house, although thy mother allowed thee at thy earnest entreaty to leave thy maiden chamber for the topmost story of the house, thence to behold the Argive host, yet stay a moment that I may first reconnoitre the path, whether there be any of the citizens visible on the road, lest reproach, little as it matters to a slave like me, fasten on thee, my royal mistress; and when I am quite sure I will tell thee everything that I saw and heard from the Argives, when I carried the terms of the truce to and fro between this city and Polynices. (*After a slight pause*) No, there is no citizen approaching the palace; so mount the ancient cedar steps, and view the plains that skirt Ismenus and the fount of Dirce to see the mighty host of foemen.

Antigone. Stretch out thy hand to me from the stairs, the hand of age to youth, helping me to mount.

O. R. There! clasp it, my young mistress; thou art come at a lucky moment, for Pelasgia's host is just upon the move, and their several contingents are separating.

An. O Hecate, dread child of Latona! the plain is one blaze of bronze.

O. R. Ah! this is no ordinary home-coming of Polynices; with many a knight and clash of countless arms he comes.

An. Are the gates fast barred, and the brazen bolts shot home into Amphion's walls of stone?

O. R. Never fear! all is safe within the town. But mark him who cometh first, if thou wouldst learn his name.

An. Who is that with the white crest, who marches in the van, lightly bearing on his arm a buckler all of bronze?

O. R. A chieftain, lady—

An. Who is he? whose son? his name? tell me, old man.

O. R. Mycenæ claims him for her son; in Lerna's glens he dwells, the prince Hippomedon.

An. Ah! how proud and terrible his mien! like to an earth-born giant he moves, with stars engraved upon his targe, resembling not a child of earth.

O. R. Dost see yon chieftain crossing Dirce's stream?

An. His harness is quite different. Who is that?

O. R. Tydeus, the son of Œneus; true Ætolian spirit fires his breast.

An. Is this he, old man, who wedded a sister of the wife of Polynices? What a foreign look his armour has! a half-barbarian he!

O. R. Yes, my child; all Ætolians carry shields, and are most unerring marksmen with their darts.

An. How art thou so sure of these descriptions, old man?

O. R. I carefully noted the blazons on their shields before when I went with the terms of the truce to thy brother; so when I see them now I know who carry them.

An. Who is that youth passing close to the tomb of Zethus, with long flowing hair, but a look of fury in his eye? is he a captain? for crowds of warriors follow at his heels.

O. R. That is Parthenopæus, Atalanta's son.

An. May Artemis, who hies o'er the hills with his mother, lay him low with an arrow, for coming against my city to sack it!

O. R. May it be so, my daughter; but with justice are they come hither, and my fear is that the gods will take the rightful view.

An. Where is he who was born of the same mother as I was by a cruel destiny? Oh! tell me, old friend, where Polynices is.

O. R. He is yonder, ranged next to Adrastus near the tomb of Niobe's seven unwed daughters. Dost see him?

An. I see him, yes! but not distinctly; 'tis but the outline of his form, the semblance of his stalwart limbs I see. Would I could speed through the sky, swift as a cloud before the wind, towards my own dear brother, and throw my arms about my darling's neck, so long, poor boy! an exile. How bright his golden weapons flash like the sun-god's morning rays!

O. R. He will soon be here, to fill thy heart with joy, according to the truce.

An. Who is that, old man, on yonder car driving snow-white steeds?

O. R. That, lady, is the prophet Amphiaraus; with him are the victims, whose streaming blood the thirsty earth will drink.

An. Daughter of Latona with the dazzling zone, O moon, thou orb of golden light! how quietly, with what restraint he drives, goading first one horse, then the other! But where is Capaneus who utters those dreadful threats against this city?

O. R. Yonder he is, calculating how he may scale the towers, taking the measure of our walls from base to summit.

An. O Nemesis, with booming thunder-peals of Zeus and blazing levin-light, thine it is to silence such presumptuous boasting. Is this the man, who says he will give the maids of Thebes as captives of his spear to Mycenæ's dames, to Lerna's Trident, and the waters of Amymone, dear to Poseidon, when he has thrown the toils of slavery round them? Never, never, Artemis, my queen revered, child of Zeus with locks of gold, may I endure the yoke of slavery!

O. R. My daughter, go within, and abide beneath the shelter of thy maiden chamber, now that thou hast had thy wish and seen all that thy heart desired; for I see a crowd of women moving toward the royal palace, confusion reigning in the city. Now the race of women by nature loves scandal; and if they get some slight handle for their gossip they exaggerate it, for they seem to take a pleasure in saying everything bad of one another.

Exeunt ANTIGONE *and* OLD RETAINER.

Enter CHORUS.

Chorus. From the Tyrian main I come, an offering choice for Loxias from a Phœnician isle, to minister to Phœbus in his halls, where his fane lies nestling 'neath the snow-swept peaks of Parnassus; over the Ionian sea I rowed my course, for above the plains unharvested, that fringe the coast of Sicily, the boisterous west-wind coursed, piping sweetest music in the sky.

Chosen from my city as beauty's gift for Loxias, to the land of Cadmus I came, sent thither to the towers of Laius, the home of my kin, the famous sons of Agenor; and there I became the handmaid of Phœbus, dedicated like his offerings of wrought gold. But as yet the water of Castaly is waiting for me to bedew the maiden glory of my tresses for the service of Phœbus.

Hail! thou rock that kindlest bright fire above the twin-peaked heights of Dionysus. Hail! thou vine, that, day by day, makest the lush bunches of thy grapes to drip. Hail! awful cavern of the serpent, and the god's outlook on the hills, and sacred mount by snow-storms lashed! would I were now circling in the dance of the deathless god, free from wild alarms, having left Dirce ere this for the vales of Phœbus at the centre of the world! But now I find the impetuous god of war is come to battle before these walls, and hath kindled murder's torch in this city. God grant he fail! for a friend's sorrows are also mine; and if this land with its seven towers suffer any mischance, Phœnicia's realm must share it. Ah me! our stock is one; all children we of Io, that hornèd maid, whose sorrows I partake. Around the city a dense array of serried shields is rousing the spectre of bloody strife, whose issue Ares shall soon learn to his cost, if he brings upon the sons of Œdipus the horrors of the curse. O Argos, city of Pelasgia! I dread thy prowess and the vengeance Heaven sends; for he who cometh against our home in full panoply is entering the lists with justice on his side.

Enter POLYNICES.

Polynices. Those who kept watch and ward at the gate admitted me so readily within the walls that my only fear is, that now they have caught me in their toils, they will not let me out unscathed; so I must turn my eye in every direction, hither and thither, to guard against all treachery. Armed with this sword, though, I shall inspire myself with the confidence born of boldness. (*Starting*) What ho! who goes there? or is it an idle sound I fear? Everything seems a danger to venturous spirits, when their feet begin to tread an enemy's country. Still I trust my mother, and at the same time mistrust her for persuading me to come hither under truce. Well, there is help at hand, for the altar's hearth is close and there are people in the palace. Come, let me sheath my sword in its dark scabbard and ask these maidens standing near the house, who they are.

Ladies of another land, tell me from what country ye come to the halls of Hellas.

Ch. Phœnicia is my native land where I was born and bred; and Agenor's children's children sent me hither as a first-fruits of the spoils of war for Phœbus; but when the noble son of Œdipus was about to escort me to the hallowed oracle and the altars of Loxias, came Argives meantime against his city. Now tell me in return who *thou* art that comest to this fortress of the Theban realm with its seven gates.

Po. My father was Œdipus, the son of Laius; my mother Jocasta, daughter of Menœceus; and I am called Polynices by the folk of Thebes.

Ch. O kinsman of Agenor's race, my royal masters who sent me hither, at thy feet, prince, I throw myself, according to the custom of my home. At last art thou come to thy native land; at last! Hail to thee! all hail! Come forth, my honoured mistress, open wide the doors. Dost hear, O mother of this chief? Why art thou delaying to leave the sheltering roof to fold thy son in thy embrace?

Enter JOCASTA.

Jo. Maidens, I hear you call in your Phœnician tongue, and my old feet drag their tottering steps to meet my son. O my son, my son, at last after many a long day I see thee face to face; throw thy arms about thy mother's bosom; reach hither thy cheek to me and thy dark locks of clustering hair, o'ershadowing my neck therewith. Hail to thee! all hail! scarce now restored to thy mother's arms, when hope and expectation both were dead. What can I say to thee? how recall in every way, by word, by deed, the bliss of days long past, expressing my joy in the mazy measures of the dance? Ah! my son, thou didst leave thy father's halls desolate, when thy brother's despite drove thee thence in exile. Truly thou wert missed alike by thy friends and Thebes. This was why I cut off my silvered locks and let them fall for grief with many a tear, not clad in robes of white, my son, but instead thereof taking for my wear these sorry sable tatters; while within the palace that aged one with sightless orbs, ever nursing the sorrow of a double regret for the pair of brethren estranged from their home, rushed to lay hands upon himself with the sword or by the noose suspended o'er his chamber-roof, moaning his curses on his sons; and now he buries himself in darkness, weeping ever and lamenting. And thou, my child—I hear thou hast taken an alien to wife and art begetting children to thy joy in thy home; they tell me thou art courting a foreign alliance, a ceaseless regret to me thy mother and to Laius thy ancestor, to have this woful marriage foisted on us. 'Twas no hand of mine that lit for thee the marriage-torch, as custom ordains and as a happy mother ought; no part had Ismenus at thy wedding in supplying the luxurious bath; and there was silence through the streets of Thebes, what time thy young bride entered her home. Curses on them! whether it be the sword or strife or thy sire that is to blame, or heaven's visitation that hath burst so riotously upon the house of Œdipus; for on me is come all the anguish of these troubles.

Ch. Wondrous dear to woman is the child of her travail, and all her race hath some affection for its babes.

Po. Mother, I have come amongst enemies wisely or foolishly; but all men needs must love their native land; whoso saith otherwise is pleased to say so but his thoughts are turned elsewhere. So fearful was I and in such terror, lest my brother might slay me by treachery that I made my way through the city sword in hand, casting my eyes all round me. My only hope is the truce and thy plighted word which induced me to enter my paternal walls; and many a tear I shed by the way, seeing after a weary while my home and the altars of the gods, the training ground, scene of my childhood, and Dirce's founts from which I was unjustly driven to sojourn in a strange city, with tears ever gushing from mine eyes. Yea, and to add to my grief I see thee with hair cut short and clad in sable robe; woe is me for my sorrows!

How terrible, dear mother, is hatred 'twixt those once near and dear; how hard it makes all reconciliation! What doth my aged sire within the house, his light all darkness now? what of my sisters twain? Ah! they, I know, bewail my bitter exile.

Jo. Some god with fell intent is plaguing the race of Œdipus. Thus it all began; I broke God's law and bore a son, and in an evil hour married thy father and thou wert born. But why repeat these horrors? what Heaven sends we have to bear. I am afraid to ask thee what I fain would, for fear of wounding thy feelings; yet I long to.

Po. Nay, question me, leave naught unsaid; for thy will, mother, is my pleasure too.

Jo. Well then, first I ask thee what I long to have answered. What means exile from one's country? is it a great evil?

Po. The greatest; harder to bear than tell.

Jo. What is it like? what is it galls the exile?

Po. One thing most of all; he cannot speak his mind.

Jo. This is a slave's lot thou describest, to refrain from uttering what one thinks.

Po. The follies of his rulers must he bear.

Jo. That too is bitter, to join in the folly of fools.

Po. Yet to gain our ends we must submit against our nature.

Jo. Hope, they say, is the exile's food.

Po. Aye, hope that looks so fair; but she is ever in the future.

Jo. But doth not time expose her futility?

Po. She hath a certain winsome charm in misfortune.

Jo. Whence hadst thou means to live, ere thy marriage found it for thee?

Po. One while I had enough for the day, and then maybe I had it not.

Jo. Did not thy father's friends and whilom guests assist thee?

Po. Seek to be prosperous; once let fortune lour, and the aid supplied by friends is naught.

Jo. Did not thy noble breeding exalt thy horn for thee?

Po. Poverty is a curse; breeding would not find me food.

Jo. Man's dearest treasure then, it seems, is his country.

Po. No words of thine could tell how dear.

Jo. How was it thou didst go to Argos? what was thy scheme?

Po. I know not; the deity summoned me thither in accordance with my destiny.

Jo. He doubtless had some wise design; but how didst thou win thy wife?

Po. Loxias had given Adrastus an oracle.

Jo. What was it? what meanest thou? I cannot guess.

Po. That he should wed his daughters to a boar and a lion.

Jo. What hadst thou, my son, to do with the name of beasts?

Po. It was night when I reached the porch of Adrastus.

Jo. In search of a resting-place, or wandering thither in thy exile?

Po. Yes, I wandered thither; and so did another like me.

Jo. Who was he? he too it seems was in evil plight.

Po. Tydeus, son of Œneus, was his name.

Jo. But why did Adrastus liken you to wild beasts?

Po. Because we came to blows about our bed.

Jo. Was it then that the son of Talaus understood the oracle?

Po. Yes, and he gave to us his daughters twain.

Jo. Art thou blest or curst in thy marriage?

Po. As yet I have no fault to find with it.

Jo. How didst thou persuade an army to follow thee hither?

Po. To me and to Tydeus who is my kinsman by marriage, Adrastus sware an oath, even to the husbands of his daughters twain, that he would restore us both to our country, me first. So many a chief from Argos and Mycenæ has joined me, doing me a bitter though needful service, for 'tis against my own city I am marching. Now I call heaven to witness, that it is not willingly I have raised my arm against parents whom I love full well. But to thee, mother, it belongs to dissolve this unhappy feud, and, by reconciling brothers in love, to end my troubles and thine and this whole city's. 'Tis an old-world maxim, but I will cite it for all that: "Men set most store by wealth, and of all things in this world it hath the greatest power." This am I come to secure at the head of my countless host; for good birth is naught if poverty go with it.

Ch. Lo! Eteocles comes hither to discuss the truce. Thine the task, O mother Jocasta, to speak such words as may reconcile thy sons.

Enter ETEOCLES.

Eteocles. Mother, I am here; but it was only to pleasure thee I came. What am I to do? Let some one begin the conference; for I stopped marshalling the citizens in double lines around the walls, that I might hear thy arbitration between us; for it is under this truce that thou hast persuaded me to admit this fellow within the walls.

Jo. Stay a moment; haste never carries justice with it; but slow deliberation oft attains a wise result. Restrain the fierceness of thy look, that panting rage; for this is not the Gorgon's severed head but thy own brother whom thou seest here. Thou too, Polynices, turn and face thy brother; for if thou and he stand face to face, thou wilt adopt a kindlier tone and lend a readier ear to him. I fain would give you both one piece of wholesome counsel; when a man that is angered with his friend confronts him face to face, he ought only to keep in view the object of his coming, forgetting all previous quarrels. Polynices my son, speak first, for thou art come at the head of a Danaid host, alleging wrongful treatment; and may some god judge betwixt us and reconcile the trouble.

Po. The words of truth are simple, and justice needs no subtle interpretations, for it hath a fitness in itself; but the words of injustice, being rotten in themselves, require clever treatment. I provided for his interests and mine in our father's palace, being anxious to avoid the curse which Œdipus once uttered against us of my own free-will I left the land, allowing him to rule our country for one full year, on condition that I should then take the sceptre in turn, instead of plunging into deadly enmity and thereby doing others hurt or suffering it myself, as is now the case. But he, after consenting to this and calling the gods to witness his oath, has performed none of his promises, but is still keeping the sovereignty in his own hands together with my share of our heritage. Even now am I ready to take my own and dismiss my army from this land, receiving my house in turn to dwell therein, and once more restore it to him for a like period instead of ravaging our country and planting scaling-ladders against the towers, as I shall attempt to do if I do not get my rights. Wherefore I call the gods to witness that spite of my just dealing in everything I am being unjustly robbed of my country by most godless fraud. Here, mother, have I stated the several points on their own merits, without collecting words to fence them in, but urging a fair case, I think, alike in the judgment of skilled or simple folk.

Ch. To me at least, albeit I was not born and bred in Hellas, thy words seem full of sense.

Et. If all were unanimous in their ideas of honour and wisdom, there would have been no strife to make men disagree; but, as it is, fairness and equality have no existence in this world beyond the name; there is really no such thing. For instance, mother, I will tell thee this without any concealment; I would ascend to the rising of the stars and the sun or dive beneath the earth, were I able so to do, to win a monarch's power, the chief of things divine. Therefore, mother, I will never yield this blessing to another, but keep it for myself; for it were a coward's act to lose the greater and to win the less. Besides, I blush to think that he should gain his object by coming with arms in his hand and ravaging the land; for this were foul disgrace to glorious Thebes, if I should yield my sceptre up to him for fear of Argive might. He ought not, mother, to have attempted reconcilement by armed force, for words compass everything that even the sword of an enemy might effect. Still, if on any other terms he cares to dwell here, he may; but the sceptre will I never willingly let go. Shall I become his slave, when I can be his master? Never! Wherefore come fire, come sword! harness your steeds, fill the plains with chariots, for I will not forego my throne for him. For if we must do wrong, to do so for a kingdom were the fairest cause, but in all else virtue should be our aim.

Ch. Fair words are only called for when the deeds they crown are fair; otherwise they lose their charm and offend justice.

Jo. Eteocles, my child, it is not all evil that attends old age; sometimes its experience can offer sager counsel than can youth. Oh! why, my son, art thou so set upon ambition, that worst of deities? Forbear; that goddess knows not justice; many are the homes and cities once prosperous that she hath entered and left after the ruin of her votaries; she it is thou madly followest. Better far, my son, prize equality that ever linketh friend to friend, city to city, and allies to each other; for equality is man's natural law; but the less is always in opposition to the greater, ushering in the dayspring of dislike. For it is equality that hath set up for man measures and divisions of weights and hath distinguished numbers; night's sightless orb, and radiant sun proceed upon their yearly course on equal terms, and neither of them is envious when it has to yield. Though sun and gloom then both are servants in man's interests, wilt not thou be content with thy fair share of thy heritage and give the same to him? if not, why where is justice? Why prize beyond its worth the monarch's power, injustice in prosperity? why think so much of the admiring glances turned on rank? Nay, 'tis vanity. Or wouldst thou by heaping riches in thy halls, heap up toil therewith? what advantage is it? 'tis but a name; for the wise find that enough which suffices for their wants. Man indeed hath no possessions of his own; we do but hold a stewardship of the gods' property; and when they will, they take it back again. Riches make no settled home, but are as transient as the day. Come, suppose I put before thee two alternatives, whether thou wilt rule or save thy city? Wilt thou say "Rule"?

Again, if Polynices win the day and his Argive warriors rout the ranks of Thebes, thou wilt see this city conquered and many a captive maid brutally dishonoured by the foe; so will that wealth thou art so bent on getting become a grievous bane to Thebes; but still ambition fills thee. This I say to thee; and this to thee, Polynices; Adrastus hath conferred a foolish favour on thee; and thou too hast shown little sense in coming to lay thy city waste. Suppose thou conquer this land, (which Heaven forefend!) tell me, I conjure thee, how wilt thou rear a trophy to Zeus? how wilt thou begin the sacrifice after thy country's conquest or inscribe the spoils at the streams of Inachus with—"Polynices gave Thebes to the flames and dedicated these shields to the gods"? Oh! never, my son, be it thine to win such fame from Hellas! If, on the other hand, thou art worsted and thy brother's cause prevail, how shalt thou return to Argos, leaving countless dead behind? Some one will be sure to say, "Out on thee! Adrastus, for the evil bridegroom thou hast brought unto thy house; thanks to one maid's marriage, ruin is come on us."

Towards two evils, my son, art thou hasting—loss of influence there and ruin in the midst of thy efforts here. Oh! my children, lay aside your violence; two men's follies, once they meet, result in very deadly mischief.

Ch. O heaven, avert these troubles and reconcile the sons of Œdipus in some way!

Et. Mother, the season for parley is past; the time we still delay is idle waste; thy good wishes are of no avail, for we shall never be reconciled except upon the terms already named, namely, that I should keep the sceptre and be king of this land: wherefore cease these tedious warnings and let me be. (*Turning to* POLYNICES) And as for thee, outside the walls, or die!

Po. Who will slay me? who is so invulnerable as to plunge his sword in my body without reaping the self-same fate?

Et. Thou art near him, aye, very near; dost see my arm?

Po. I see it; but wealth is cowardly, a craven too fond of life.

Et. Was it then to meet a dastard thou camest with all that host to war?

Po. In a general caution is better than foolhardiness.

Et. Relying on the truce, which saves thy life, thou turnest boaster.

Po. Once more I ask thee to restore my sceptre and share in the kingdom.

Et. I have naught to restore; 'tis my own house, and I will dwell therein.

Po. What! and keep more than thy share?

Et. Yes, I will. Begone!

Po. O altars of my fathers' gods!

Et. Which thou art here to raze.

Po. Hear me.

Et. Who would hear thee after thou hast marched against thy fatherland?

Po. O temples of those gods that ride on snow-white steeds![1]

Et. They hate thee.

Po. I am being driven from my country.

Et. Because thou camest to drive others thence.

Po. Unjustly, O ye gods!

Et. Call on the gods at Mycenæ, not here.

Po. Thou hast outraged right—

Et. But I have not like thee become my country's foe.

Po. By driving me forth without my portion.

Et. I will slay thee to boot.

Po. O father, dost thou hear what I am suffering?

Et. Yea, and he hears what thou art doing.

Po. Thou too, mother mine?

Et. Thou hast no right to mention thy mother.

Po. O my city!

Et. Get thee to Argos, and invoke the waters of Lerna.

Po. I will; trouble not thyself; all thanks to thee though, mother mine.

Et. Forth from the land!

Po. I go, yet grant me to behold my father.

Et. Thou shalt not have thy wish.

Po. At least then my tender sisters.

Et. No! them too thou shalt never see.

Po. Ah, sisters mine!

Et. Why dost thou, their bitterest foe, call on them?

Po. Mother dear, to thee at least farewell!

Jo. A joyous faring mine in sooth, my son!

Po. Thy son no more!

Jo. Born to sorrow, endless sorrow, I!

Po. 'Tis because my brother treats me despitefully.

Et. I am treated just the same.

Po. Where wilt thou be stationed before the towers?

Et. Why ask me this?

Po. I will array myself against thee for thy death.

Et. I too have the same desire.

Jo. Woe is me! what will ye do, my sons?

Po. The event will show.

Jo. Oh, fly your father's curse! *Exit* JOCASTA.

Et. Destruction seize our whole house!

Po. Soon shall my sword be busy, plunged in gore. But I call my native land and heaven too to witness, with what contumely and bitter treatment I am being driven forth, as though I were a slave, not a son of Œdipus as much as he. If aught happen to thee, my city, blame him, not me; for I came not willingly, and all unwillingly am I driven hence. Farewell, king Phœbus, lord of highways; farewell palace and comrades; farewell ye statues of the gods, at which men offer sheep; for I know not if I shall ever address you again, though hope is still awake, which makes me confident that with heaven's help I shall slay this fellow and rule my native Thebes.

Exit POLYNICES.

Et. Forth from the land! 'twas a true name our father gave thee, when, prompted by some god, he called thee Polynices, a name denoting strife.

Ch. To this land came Cadmus of Tyre, at whose feet an unyoked heifer threw itself down, giving effect to an oracle on the spot where the god's response bade him take up his abode in Aonia's rich corn-lands, where gushing Dirce's fair rivers of water pour o'er verdant fruitful fields; here was born the Bromian god by her whom Zeus made a mother, round whom the ivy twined its wreaths while he was yet a babe, swathing him amid the covert of its green foliage as a child of happy destiny, to be a theme for Bacchic revelry among the maids and wives inspired in Thebes.

There lay Ares' murderous dragon, a savage warder, watching with roving eye the watered glens

[1] Amphion and Zethus, the Theban Dioscuri.

and quickening streams; him did Cadmus slay with a jagged stone, when he came thither to draw him lustral water, smiting that fell head with a blow of his death-dealing arm; but by the counsel of Pallas, motherless goddess, he cast the teeth upon the earth into deep furrows, whence sprang to sight a mail-clad host above the surface of the soil; but grim slaughter once again united them to the earth they loved, bedewing with blood the ground that had disclosed them to the sunlit breath of heaven.

Thee too, Epaphus, child of Zeus, sprung from Io our ancestress, I call on in my foreign tongue; all hail to thee! hear my prayer uttered in accents strange, and visit this land; 'twas in thy honour thy descendants settled here, and those goddesses of two-fold name, Persephone and kindly Demeter or Earth the queen of all, that feedeth every mouth, won it for themselves; send to the help of this land those torch-bearing queens; for to gods all things are easy.

Et. (*To an attendant*) Go, fetch Creon son of Menœceus, the brother of Jocasta my mother; tell him I fain would confer with him on matters affecting our public and private weal, before we set out to battle and the arraying of our host. But lo! he comes and saves thee the trouble of going; I see him on his way to my palace.

Enter CREON.

Creon. To and fro have I been, king Eteocles, in my desire to see thee, and have gone all round the gates and sentinels of Thebes in quest of thee.

Et. Why, and I was anxious to see thee, Creon; for I found the terms of peace far from satisfactory, when I came to confer with Polynices.

Cr. I hear that he has wider aims than Thebes, relying on his alliance with the daughter of Adrastus and his army. Well, we must leave this dependent on the gods; meantime I am come to tell thee our chief obstacle.

Et. What is that? I do not understand what thou sayest.

Cr. There is come one that was captured by the Argives.

Et. What news does he bring from their camp?

Cr. He says the Argive army intend at once to draw a ring of troops round the city of Thebes, about its towers.

Et. In that case the city of Cadmus must lead out its troops.

Cr. Whither? art thou so young that thine eyes see not what they should?

Et. Across yon trenches for immediate action.

Cr. Our Theban forces are small, while theirs are numberless.

Et. I well know they are reputed brave.

Cr. No mean repute have those Argives among Hellenes.

Et. Never fear! I will soon fill the plain with their dead.

Cr. I could wish it so; but I see great difficulties in this.

Et. Trust me, I will not keep my host within the walls.

Cr. Still victory is entirely a matter of good counsel.

Et. Art anxious then that I should have recourse to any other scheme?

Cr. Aye to every scheme, before running the risk once for all.

Et. Suppose we fall on them by night from ambuscade?

Cr. Good! provided in the event of defeat thou canst secure thy return hither.

Et. Night equalizes risks, though it rather favours daring.

Cr. The darkness of night is a terrible time to suffer disaster.

Et. Well, shall I fall upon them as they sit at meat?

Cr. That might cause a scare, but victory is what we want.

Et. Dirce's ford is deep enough to prevent their retreat.

Cr. No plan so good as to keep well guarded.

Et. What if our cavalry make a sortie against the host of Argos?

Cr. Their troops too are fenced all round with chariots.

Et. What then can I do? am I to surrender the city to the foe?

Cr. Nay, nay! but of thy wisdom form some plan.

Et. Pray, what scheme is wiser than mine?

Cr. They have seven chiefs, I hear.

Et. What is their appointed task? their might can be but feeble.

Cr. To lead the several companies and storm our seven gates.

Et. What are we to do? I will not wait till every chance is gone.

Cr. Choose seven chiefs thyself to set against them at the gates.

Et. To lead our companies, or to fight single-handed?

Cr. Choose our very bravest men to lead the troops.

Et. I understand; to repel attempts at scaling our walls.

Cr. With others to share the command, for one man sees not everything.

Et. Selecting them for courage or thoughtful prudence?

Cr. For both; for one is naught without the other.

Et. It shall be done; I will away to our seven towers and post captains at the gates, as thou advisest, pitting them man for man against the foe. To tell thee each one's name were grievous waste of time, when the foe is camped beneath our very walls. But I will go, that my hands may no longer hang idle. May I meet my brother face to face, and encounter him hand to hand, e'en to the death, for coming to waste my country! But if I suffer any mischance, thou must see to the marriage 'twixt Antigone my sister and Hæmon, thy son; and now, as I go forth to battle, I ratify their previous espousal. Thou art my mother's brother, so why need I say more? take care of her, as she deserves, both for thy own sake and mine. As for my sire he hath been guilty of folly against himself in putting out his eyes; small praise have I for him; by his curses maybe he will slay us too. One thing only have we still to do, to ask Teiresias, the seer, if he has aught to tell of heaven's will. Thy son Menœceus, who bears thy father's name, will I send to fetch Teiresias hither, Creon; for with thee he will readily converse, though I have ere now so scorned his art prophetic to his face, that he has reasons to reproach me. This commandment, Creon, I lay upon the city and thee; should my cause prevail, never give Polynices' corpse a grave in Theban soil, and if so be some friend should bury him, let death reward the man. Thus far to thee; and to my servants thus, bring forth my arms and coat of mail, that I may start at once for the appointed combat, with right to lead to victory. To save our city we will pray to Caution, the best goddess to serve our end. *Exit* ETEOCLES.

Ch. O Ares, god of toil and trouble! why, why art thou possessed by a love of blood and death, out of harmony with the festivals of Bromius? 'Tis for no crowns of dancers fair that thou dost toss thy youthful curls to the breeze, singing the while to the lute's soft breath a strain to charm the dancers' feet; but with warriors clad in mail thou dost lead thy sombre revelry, breathing into Argive breasts a lust for Theban blood; with no wild waving of the thyrsus, clad in fawnskin thou dancest, but with chariots and bitted steeds wheelest thy charger strong of hoof. O'er the waters of Ismenus in wild career thou art urging thy horses, inspiring Argive breasts with hate of the earth-born race, arraying in brazen harness against these stone-built walls a host of warriors armed with shields.

Truly Strife is a goddess to fear, who devised these troubles for the princes of this land, for the much-enduring sons of Labdacus.

O Cithæron, apple of the eye of Artemis, holy vale of leaves, amid whose snows fully many a beast lies couched, would thou hadst never reared the child exposed to die, Œdipus the fruit of Jocasta's womb, when as a babe he was cast forth from his home, marked with a golden brooch; and would the Sphinx, that wingèd maid, fell monster from the hills, had never come to curse our land with inharmonious strains; she that erst drew nigh our walls and snatched the sons of Cadmus away in her taloned feet to the pathless fields of light, a fiend sent by Hades from hell to plague the men of Thebes; once more unhappy strife is bursting out between the sons of Œdipus in city and home. For never can wrong be right, ... nor children of unnatural parentage come as a glory to the mother that bears them, but as a stain on the marriage of him who is father and brother at once.

O earth, thou once didst bear—so long ago I heard the story told by foreigners in my own home —a race which sprang of the teeth of a snake with blood-red crest, that fed on beasts, to be the glory and reproach of Thebes.

In days gone by the sons of heaven came to the wedding of Harmonia, and the walls of Thebes arose to the sound of the lyre and her towers stood up as Amphion played, in the midst between the double streams of Dirce, that watereth the green meadows fronting the Ismenus; and Io, our hornèd ancestress, was mother of the kings of Thebes; thus our city through an endless succession of divers blessings has set herself upon the highest pinnacle of martial glory.

Enter TEIRESIAS *and* MENŒCEUS.

Teiresias. (*Led by his daughter*) Lead on, my daughter; for thou art as an eye to my blind feet, as certain as a star to mariners; lead my steps on to level ground; then go before, that we stumble not, for thy father has no strength; keep safe for me in thy maiden hand the auguries I took in the days I observed the flight and cries of birds seated in my holy prophet's chair. Tell me, young Menœceus, son of Creon, how much further toward the city is it ere I reach thy father? for my knees grow weary, and I can scarce keep up this hurried pace.

Cr. Take heart, Teiresias, for thou hast reached thy moorings and art near thy friends; take him by the hand, my child; for just as every carriage has to wait for outside help to steady it, so too hath the step of age.

Te. Enough; I have arrived; why, Creon, dost thou summon me so urgently?

Cr. I have not forgotten that; but first collect thyself and regain breath, shaking off the fatigue of thy journey.

Te. I am indeed worn out, having arrived here only yesterday from the court of the Erechthidæ; for they too were at war, fighting with Eumolpus, in which contest I insured the victory of Cecrops' sons; and I received the golden crown, which thou seest me wearing, as firstfruits of the enemy's spoil.

Cr. I take thy crown of victory as an omen. We, as thou knowest, are exposed to the billows of an Argive war, and great is the struggle for Thebes. Eteocles, our king, is already gone in full harness to meet Mycenæ's champions, and hath bidden me inquire of thee our best course to save the city.

Te. For Eteocles I would have closed my lips and refrained from all response, but to thee I will speak, since 'tis thy wish to learn. This country, Creon, has been long afflicted, ever since Laius became a father in heaven's despite, begetting hapless Œdipus to be his own mother's husband. That bloody outrage on his eyes was planned by heaven as an ensample to Hellas; and the sons of Œdipus made a gross mistake in wishing to throw over it the veil of time, as if forsooth they could outrun the gods' decree; for by robbing their father of his due honour and allowing him no freedom, they exasperated the poor sufferer; so he, stung by suffering and disgrace as well, vented awful curses against them; and I, because I left nothing undone or unsaid to prevent this, incurred the hatred of the sons of Œdipus. But death inflicted by each other's hands awaits them, Creon; and the many heaps of slain, some from Argive, some from Theban missiles, shall cause bitter lamentation in the land of Thebes. Alas! for thee, poor city, thou art being involved in their ruin, unless I can persuade one man. The best course was to prevent any child of Œdipus becoming either citizen or king in this land, on the ground that they were under a ban and would overthrow the city. But since evil has the mastery of good, there is still one other way of safety; but this it were unsafe for me to tell, and painful too for those whose high fortune it is to supply their city with the saving cure. Farewell! I will away; amongst the rest must I endure my doom, if need be; for what will become of me?

Cr. Stay here, old man.

Te. Hold me not.

Cr. Abide, why dost thou seek to fly?

Te. 'Tis thy fortune that flies thee, not I.

Cr. Tell me what can save Thebes and her citizens.

Te. Though this be now thy wish, it will soon cease to be.

Cr. Not wish to save my country? how can that be?

Te. Art thou still eager to be told?

Cr. Yea; for wherein should I show greater zeal?

Te. Then straightway shalt thou hear my words prophetic. But first I would fain know for certain, where Menœceus is who led me hither.

Cr. Here, not far away, but at thy side.

Te. Let him retire far from my prophetic voice.

Cr. He is my own son and will preserve due silence.

Te. Wilt thou then that I tell thee in his presence?

Cr. Yea, for he will rejoice to hear the means of safety.

Te. Then hear the purport of my oracle, the which if ye observe ye shall save the city of Cadmus.

Thou must sacrifice Menœceus thy son here for thy country, since thine own lips demand the voice of fate.

Cr. What mean'st thou? what is this thou hast said, old man?

Te. To that which is to be thou also must conform.

Cr. O the eternity of woe thy minute's tale proclaims!

Te. Yes to thee, but to thy country great salvation.

Cr. I shut my ears; I never listened; to city now farewell!

Te. Ha! the man is changed; he is drawing back.

Cr. Go in peace; it is not thy prophecy I need.

Te. Is truth dead, because thou art curst with woe?

Cr. By thy knees and honoured locks I implore thee!

Te. Why implore me? thou art craving a calamity hard to guard against.

Cr. Keep silence; tell not the city thy news.

Te. Thou biddest me act unjustly; I will not hold my peace.

Cr. What wilt thou then do to me? slay my child?

Te. That is for others to decide; I have but to speak.

Cr. Whence came this curse on me and my son?

Te. Thou dost right to ask me and to test what I have said. In yonder lair, where the earth-born dragon kept watch and ward o'er Dirce's springs, must this youth be offered and shed his life-blood on the ground by reason of Ares' ancient grudge against Cadmus, who thus avenges the slaughter of his earth-born snake. If ye do this, ye shall win Ares as an ally; and if the earth receive crop for crop and human blood for blood, ye shall find her kind again, that erst to your sorrow reared from that dragon's seed a crop of warriors with golden casques; for needs must one sprung from the dragon's teeth be slain. Now thou art our only survivor of the seed of that sown race, whose lineage is pure alike on mother's and on father's side, thou and these thy sons. Hæmon's marriage debars him from being the victim, for he is no longer single; for even if he have not consummated his marriage, yet is he betrothed; but this tender youth, consecrated to the city's service, might by dying rescue his country; and bitter will he make the return of Adrastus and his Argives, flinging o'er their eyes death's dark pall, and will glorify Thebes. Choose thee one of these alternatives; either save the city or thy son.

Now hast thou all I have to say. Daughter, lead me home. A fool, the man who practises the diviner's art; for if he should announce an adverse answer, he makes himself disliked by those who seek to him; while, if from pity he deceives those who are consulting him, he sins against Heaven. Phœbus should have been man's only prophet, for he fears no man.

Exit TEIRESIAS.

Ch. Why so silent, Creon, why are thy lips hushed and dumb? I too am no less stricken with dismay.

Cr. Why, what could one say? 'Tis clear what my words must be. For I will never plunge myself so deeply into misfortune as to devote my son to death for the city; for love of children binds all men to life, and none would resign his own son to die. Let no man praise me into slaying my children. I am ready to die myself—for I am ripe in years—to set my country free. But thou, my son, ere the whole city learn this, up and fly with all haste away from this land, regardless of these prophets' unbridled utterances; for he will go to the seven gates and the captains there and tell all this to our governors and leaders; now if we can forestal him, thou mayst be saved, but if thou art too late, 'tis all over with us and thou wilt die.

Menœceus. Whither can I fly? to what city? to which of our guest-friends?

Cr. Fly where thou wilt be furthest removed from this land.

Men. 'Tis for thee to name a place, for me to carry out thy bidding.

Cr. After passing Delphi—

Men. Whither must I go, father?

Cr. To Ætolia.

Men. Whither thence?

Cr. To the land of Thesprotia.

Men. To Dodona's hallowed threshold?

Cr. Thou followest me.

Men. What protection shall I find me there?

Cr. The god will send thee on thy way.

Men. How shall I find the means?

Cr. I will supply thee with money.

Men. A good plan of thine, father. So go; for I will to thy sister, Jocasta, at whose breast I was suckled as a babe when reft of my mother and left a lonely orphan, to give her kindly greeting and then will I seek my safety. Come, come! be going, that there be no hindrance on thy part.

Exit CREON.

How cleverly, ladies, I banished my father's fears by crafty words to gain my end; for he is trying to convey me hence, depriving the city of its chance and surrendering me to cowardice. Though an old man may be pardoned, yet in my case there is no excuse for betraying the country that gave me birth. So I will go and save the city, be assured thereof, and give my life up for this land. For this were shame, that they whom no oracles bind and who have not come under Fate's iron law, should stand there, shoulder to shoulder, with never a fear of death, and fight for their country before her towers, while I escape the kingdom like a coward, a traitor to my father and brother and city; and wheresoe'er I live, I shall appear a dastard. Nay, by Zeus and all his stars, by Ares, god of blood, who 'stablished the warrior-crop that sprung one day from earth as princes of this land, that shall not be! but go I will, and standing on the topmost battlements, will deal my own death-blow over the dragon's deep dark den, the spot the seer described, and will set my country free. I have spoken. Now I go to make the city a present of my life, no mean offering, to rid this kingdom of its affliction. For if each were to take and expend all the good within his power, contributing it to his country's weal, our states would experience fewer troubles and would for the future prosper.

Exit MENŒCEUS.

Ch. Thou cam'st, O winged fiend, spawn of earth and hellish viper-brood, to prey upon the sons of Cadmus, rife with death and fraught with sorrow, half a monster, half a maid, a murderous prodigy, with roving wings and ravening claws, that in days gone by didst catch up youthful victims from the haunts of Dirce, with discordant note, bringing a deadly curse, a woe of bloodshed to our native land. A murderous god he was who brought all this to pass. In every house was heard a cry of mothers wailing and of wailing maids, lamentation and the voice of weeping, as each took up the chant of death from street to street in turn. Loud rang the mourners' wail, and one great cry went up, whene'er that winged maiden bore some victim out of sight from the city. At last came Œdipus, the man of sorrow, on his mission from Delphi to this land of Thebes, a joy to them then but afterwards a cause of grief; for, when he had read the riddle triumphantly, he formed with his mother an unhallowed union, woe to him! polluting the city; and by his curses, luckless wight, he plunged his sons into a guilty strife, causing them to wade through seas of blood.

All reverence do we feel for him, who is gone to his death in his country's cause, bequeathing to Creon a legacy of tears, but destined to crown with victory our seven fenced towers. May our motherhood be blessed with such noble sons, O Pallas, kindly queen, who with well-aimed stone didst spill the serpent's blood, rousing Cadmus as thou didst to brood upon the task, whereof the issue was a demon's curse that swooped upon this land and harried it.

Enter MESSENGER.

1st. Messenger. Ho there! who is at the palace-gates? Open the door, summon Jocasta forth. Ho there! once again I call; spite of this long delay come forth; hearken, noble wife of Œdipus; cease thy lamentation and thy tears of woe.

Enter JOCASTA.

Jo. Surely thou art not come, my friend, with the sad news of Eteocles' death, beside whose shield thou hast ever marched, warding from him the foeman's darts? What tidings art thou here to bring me? Is my son alive or dead? Declare that to me.

1st. Mes. To rid thee of thy fear at once, he lives; that terror banish.

Jo. Next, how is it with the seven towers that wall us in?

1st. Mes. They stand unshattered still; the city is not yet a prey.

Jo. Have they been in jeopardy of the Argive spear?

1st. Mes. Aye, on the very brink; but our Theban warriors proved too strong for Mycenæ's might.

Jo. One thing tell me, I implore; knowest thou aught of Polynices, is he yet alive? for this too I long to learn.

1st. Mes. As yet thy sons are living, the pair of them.

Jo. God bless thee! How did you succeed in beating off from our gates the Argive hosts, when thus beleaguered? Tell me, that I may go within and cheer the old blind man, since our city is still safe.

1st. Mes. After Creon's son, who gave up life for country, had taken his stand on the turret's top and plunged a sword dark-hilted through his throat to save this land, thy son told off seven companies with their captains to the seven gates to keep watch on the Argive warriors, and stationed cavalry to cover cavalry, and infantry to support infantry, that assistance might be close at hand for any weak point in the walls. Then from our lofty towers we saw the Argive host with their white shields leaving Teumessus, and, when near the trench, they charged up to our Theban city at the double. In one loud burst from their ranks and from our battlements rang out the battle-cry and trumpet-call. First to the Neistian gate, Parthenopæus, son of the huntress maid, led a company bristling with serried shields, himself with his own peculiar badge in the centre of his targe, Atalanta slaying the Ætolian boar with an arrow shot from far. To the gates of Prœtus came the prophet Amphiaraus, bringing the victims on a chariot; no vaunting blazon he carried, but weapons chastely plain. Next prince Hippomedon came marching to the Ogygian port with this device upon his boss, Argus the all-seeing with his spangled eyes upon the watch whereof some open with the rising stars, while others he closes when they set, as one could see after he was slain. At the Homoloian gates Tydeus was posting himself, a lion's skin with shaggy mane upon his buckler, while in his right hand he bore a torch, like Titan Prometheus, to fire the town. Thy own son Polynices led the battle 'gainst the Fountain gate; upon his shield for blazon were the steeds of Potniæ galloping at frantic speed, revolving by some clever contrivance on pivots inside the buckler close to the handle, so as to appear distraught. At Electra's gate famed Capaneus brought up his company, bold as Ares for the fray; this device his buckler bore upon its iron back, an earth-born giant carrying on his shoulders a whole city which he had wrenched from its base, a hint to us of the fate in store for Thebes. Adrastus was stationed at the seventh gate; a hundred vipers filled his shield with graven work, as he bore on his left arm that proud Argive badge, the hydra, and serpents were carrying off in their jaws the sons of Thebes from within their very walls. Now I was enabled to see each of them, as I carried the watch-word along the line to the leaders of our companies. To begin with, we fought with bows and thonged javelins, with slings that shoot from far and showers of crashing stones; and as we were conquering, Tydeus and thy son on a sudden cried aloud, "Ye sons of Argos, before being riddled by their fire, why delay to fall upon the gates with might and main, the whole of you, light-armed and horse and charioteers?" No loitering then, soon as they heard that call; and many a warrior fell with bloody crown, and not a few of us thou couldst have seen thrown to the earth like tumblers before the walls, after they had given up the ghost, bedewing the thirsty ground with streams of gore. Then Atalanta's son, who was not an Argive but an Arcadian, hurling himself like a hurricane at the gates, called for fire and picks to raze the town; but Periclymenus, son of the ocean-god, stayed his wild career, heaving on his head a waggon-load of stone, even the coping torn from the battlements; and it shattered his head with the hair and crashed through the sutures of the skull, dabbling with blood his cheek just showing manhood's flush; and never shall he go back alive to his fair archer-mother, the maid of Mænalus.

Thy son then, seeing these gates secure, went on to the next, and I with him. There I saw Tydeus and his serried ranks of targeteers hurling their Ætolian spears into the opening at the top of the turrets, with such good aim that our men fled and left the beetling battlements; but thy son rallied them once more, as a huntsman cheers his hounds, and made them man the towers again. And then away we hastened to other gates, after stopping the panic there. As for the madness of Capaneus, how am I to describe it? There was he, carrying with him a long scaling-ladder and loudly boasting that even the awful lightning of Zeus would not stay him from giving the city to utter destruction; and even as he spoke, he crept up beneath the hail of stones, gathered under the shelter of his shield, mounting from rung to rung on the smooth ladder; but, just as he was scaling the parapet of the wall, Zeus smote him with a thunderbolt; loud the earth re-echoed, and fear seized every heart; for his limbs were hurled from the ladder far apart as from a sling, his head toward the sky, his blood toward earth, while his legs and arms went spinning round like Ixion's wheel, till his charred corpse fell to the ground. But when Adrastus saw that Zeus was leagued against his army, he drew the Argive troops outside the trench and halted them. Meantime our horse, marking the lucky omen of Zeus, began driving forth their chariots, and our men-at-arms charged into the thick of the Argives, and everything combined to their discomfiture; men were falling and hurled headlong from chariots, wheels flew off, axles crashed together, while ever higher grew the heaps of slain; so for today at least have we prevented the destruction of our country's bulwarks; but whether fortune will hereafter smile upon this land, that rests with Heaven; for, even as it is, it owes its safety to some deity.

Ch. Victory is fair; and if the gods are growing kinder, it would be well with me.

Jo. Heaven and fortune smile; for my sons are yet alive and my country hath escaped ruin. But Creon seems to have reaped the bitter fruit of my marriage with Œdipus, by losing his son to his sorrow, a piece of luck for Thebes, but bitter grief to him. Prithee to thy tale again and say what my two sons intend to do next.

1st. Mes. Forbear to question further; all is well with thee so far.

Jo. Thy words but rouse my suspicions; I cannot leave it thus.

1st. Mes. Hast thou any further wish than thy sons' safety?

Jo. Yea, I would learn whether in the sequel I am also blest.

1st. Mes. Let me go; thy son is left without his squire.

Jo. There is some evil thou art hiding, veiling it in darkness.

1st. Mes. Maybe; I would not add ill news to the good thou hast heard.

Jo. Thou must, unless thou take wings and fly away.

1st. Mes. Ah! why didst thou not let me go after announcing my good news, instead of forcing me to disclose evil? Those two sons of thine are resolved on deeds of shameful recklessness, a single combat apart from the host, addressing to Argives and Thebans alike words I would they had never uttered. Eteocles, taking his stand on a lofty tower, after ordering silence to be proclaimed to the army, began on this wise, "Ye captains of Hellas, chieftains of Argos here assembled, and ye folk of Cadmus, barter not your lives for Polynices or for me! For I myself excuse you from this risk, and will engage my brother in single combat; and if I slay him, I will possess my palace without rival, but if I am worsted I will bequeath the city to him. Ye men of Argos, give up the struggle and return to your land, nor lose your lives here; of the earth-sown folk as well there are dead enough in those already slain."

So he; then thy son Polynices rushed from the array and assented to his proposal; and all the Argives and the people of Cadmus shouted their approval, as though they deemed it just. On these terms the armies made a truce, and in the space betwixt them took an oath of each other for their leaders to abide by. Forthwith in brazen mail those two sons of aged Œdipus were casing themselves; and lords of Thebes with friendly care equipped the captain of this land, while Argive chieftains armed the other. There they stood in dazzling sheen, neither blenching, all eagerness to hurl their lances each at the other. Then came their friends to their side, first one, then another, with words of encouragement, to wit:

"Polynices, it rests with thee to set up an image of Zeus as a trophy, and crown Argos with fair renown."

Others hailed Eteocles: "Now art thou fighting for thy city; now, if victorious, thou hast the sceptre in thy power."

So spake they, cheering them to the fray.

Meantime the seers were sacrificing sheep and noting the tongues and forks of fire, the damp reek which is a bad omen, and the tapering flame, which gives decisions on two points, being both a sign of victory and defeat. But, if thou hast any power or subtle speech or charmèd spell, go, stay thy children from this fell affray, for great is the risk they run. The issue thereof will be grievous sorrow for thee, if to-day thou art reft of both thy sons.

Exit MESSENGER.

Jo. Antigone, my daughter, come forth before the palace; this heaven-sent crisis is no time for thee to be dancing or amusing thyself with girlish pursuits. But thou and thy mother must prevent two gallant youths, thy own brothers, from plunging into death and falling by each other's hand.

Enter ANTIGONE.

An. Mother mine, what new terror art thou proclaiming to thy dear ones before the palace?

Jo. Daughter, thy brothers are in danger of their life.

An. What mean'st thou?

Jo. They have resolved on single combat.

An. O horror! what hast thou to tell, mother?

Jo. No welcome news; follow me.

An. Whither away from my maiden-bower?

Jo. To the army.

An. I cannot face the crowd.

Jo. Coyness is not thy cue now.

An. But what can I do?

Jo. Thou shalt end thy brothers' strife.

An. By what means, mother mine?

Jo. By falling at their knees with me.

An. Lead on till we are 'twixt the armies; no time for lingering now.

Jo. Haste, my daughter, haste! For, if I can forestal the onset of my sons, I may yet live; but if they be dead, I will lay me down and die with them.

Exeunt JOCASTA *and* ANTIGONE.

Ch. Ah me! my bosom thrills with terror; and through my flesh there passed a throb of pity for the hapless mother. Which of her two sons will send the other to a bloody grave? ah, woe is me! O Zeus, O earth, alas! brother severing brother's throat and robbing him of life, cleaving through his shield to spill his blood? Ah me! ah me! which of them will claim my dirge of death? Woe unto thee, thou land of Thebes! two savage beasts, two murderous souls, with brandished spears will soon be draining each his fallen foeman's gore. Woe is them, that they ever thought of single combat! in foreign accent will I chant a dirge of tears and wailing in mourning for the dead. Close to murder stands their fortune; the coming day will decide it. Fatal, ah! fatal will this slaughter be, because of the avenging fiends.

But hist! I see Creon on his way hither to the palace with brow o'ercast; I will check my present lamentations.

Enter CREON *with body of* MENŒCEUS.

Cr. Ah me! what shall I do? Am I to mourn with bitter tears myself or my city, round which is settling a swarm thick enough to send us to Acheron? My own son hath died for his country, bringing glory to his name but grievous woe to me. His body I rescued but now from the dragon's rocky lair and sadly carried the self-slain victim hither in my arms; and my house is filled with weeping; but now I come to fetch my sister Jocasta, age seeking age, that she may bathe my child's corpse and lay it out. For the living must reverence the nether god by paying honour to the dead.

Ch. Thy sister, Creon, hath gone forth and her daughter Antigone went with her.

Cr. Whither went she? and wherefore? tell me.

Ch. She heard that her sons were about to engage in single combat for the royal house.

Cr. What is this? I was paying the last honours to my dead son, and so am behindhand in learning this fresh sorrow.

Ch. 'Tis some time, Creon, since thy sister's departure, and I expect the struggle for life and death is already decided by the sons of Œdipus.

Cr. Alas! I see an omen there, the gloomy look and clouded brow of yonder messenger coming to tell us the whole matter.

Enter 2ND MESSENGER.

2nd. Messenger. Ah, woe is me! what language can I find to tell my tale?

Cr. Our fate is sealed; thy opening words do naught to reassure us.

2nd. Mes. Ah, woe is me! I do repeat; for beside the scenes of woe already enacted I bring tidings of new horror.

Cr. What is thy tale?

2nd. Mes. Thy sister's sons are now no more, Creon.

Cr. Alas! thou hast a heavy tale of woe for me and Thebes!

Ch. O house of Œdipus, hast thou heard these tidings?

Cr. Of sons slain by the self-same fate.

Ch. A tale to make it weep, were it endowed with sense.

Cr. Oh! most grievous stroke of fate! woe is me for my sorrows! woe!

2nd. Mes. Woe indeed! didst thou but know the sorrows still to tell.

Cr. How can they be more hard to bear than these?

2nd. Mes. With her two sons thy sister has sought her death.

Ch. Loudly, loudly raise the wail, and with white hands smite upon your heads!

Cr. Ah! woe is thee, Jocasta! what an end to life and marriage hast thou found the riddling of the Sphinx! But tell me how her two sons wrought the bloody deed, the struggle caused by the curse of Œdipus.

2nd. Mes. Of our successes before the towers thou knowest, for the walls are not so far away as to prevent thy learning each event as it occurred. Now when they, the sons of aged Œdipus, had donned their brazen mail, they went and took their stand betwixt the hosts, chieftains both and generals too, to decide the day by single combat. Then Polynices, turning his eyes towards Argos, lifted up a prayer. "O Hera, awful queen—for thy servant I am, since I have wedded the daughter of Adrastus and dwell in his land—grant that I may slay my brother, and stain my lifted hand with the blood of my conquered foe. A shameful prize it is I ask, my own brother's blood." And to many an eye the tear would rise at their sad fate, and men looked at one another, casting their glances round.

But Eteocles, looking towards the temple of Pallas with the golden shield, prayed thus, "Daughter of Zeus, grant that this right arm may launch the spear of victory against my brother's breast and slay him who hath come to sack my country." Soon as the Tuscan trumpet blew, the signal for the bloody fray, like the torch that falls,[1] they darted wildly at one another and, like boars whetting their savage tusks, began the fray, their beards wet with foam; and they kept shooting out their spears, but each couched beneath his shield to let the steel glance idly off; but if either saw the other's face above the rim, he would aim his lance thereat, eager to outwit him.

But both kept such careful outlook through the spy-holes in their shields, that their weapons found naught to do; while from the on-lookers far more than the combatants trickled the sweat caused by terror for their friends. Suddenly Eteocles, in kicking aside a stone that rolled beneath his tread, exposed a limb outside his shield, and Polynices seeing a chance of dealing him a blow, aimed a dart at it, and the Argive shaft went through his leg; whereat the Danai, one and all, cried out for joy. But the wounded man, seeing a shoulder unguarded in this effort, plunged his spear with all his might into the breast of Polynices, restoring gladness to the citizens of Thebes, though he brake off the spear-head; and so, at a loss for a weapon, he retreated foot by foot, till catching up a splintered rock he let it fly and shivered the other's spear; and now was the com bat equal, for each had lost his lance. Then clutching their sword-hilts they closed, and round and round, with shields close-locked, they waged their wild warfare. Anon Eteocles introduced that crafty Thessalian trick, having some knowledge thereof from his intercourse with that country; disengaging himself from the immediate contest, he drew back his left foot but kept his eye closely on the pit of the other's stomach from a distance; then advancing his right foot he plunged his weapon through his navel and fixed it in his spine. Down falls Polynices, blood-bespattered, ribs and belly contracting in his agony. But that other, thinking his victory now complete, threw down his sword and set to spoiling him, wholly intent thereon, without a thought for himself. And this indeed was his ruin; for Polynices, who had fallen first, was still faintly breathing, and having in his grievous fall retained his sword, he made a last effort and drove it through the heart of Eteocles. There they lie, fallen side by side, biting the dust with their teeth, without having decided the mastery.

Ch. Ah, woe is thee! Œdipus, for thy sorrows! how I pity thee! Heaven, it seems, has fulfilled those curses of thine.

2nd. Mes. Now hear what further woes succeeded. Just as her two sons had fallen and lay dying, comes their wretched mother on the scene, her daughter with her, in hot haste; and when she saw their mortal wounds, "Too late," she moaned, "my sons, the help I bring"; and throwing herself on each in turn she wept and wailed, sorrowing o'er all her toil in suckling them; and so too their sister, who was with her, "Supporters of your mother's age! dear brothers, leaving me forlorn, unwed!" Then prince Eteocles with one deep dying gasp, hearing his mother's cry, laid on her his clammy hand, and though he could not say a word, his moistened eye was eloquent to prove his love. But Polynices was still alive, and seeing his sister and his aged mother he said, "Mother mine, our end is come; I pity thee and my sister Antigone and my dead brother. For I loved him though he turned my foe, I loved him, yes! in spite of all. Bury me, mother mine, and thou, my sister dear, in my native soil; pacify the city's wrath that I may get at least that much of my own fatherland, although I lost my home. With thy hand, mother, close mine eyes (therewith he himself places her fingers on the lids); and fare ye well; for already the darkness wraps me round."

So both at once breathed out their life of sorrow. But when their mother saw this sad mischance, in her o'ermastering grief she snatched from a corpse its sword and wrought an awful deed, driving the steel right through her throat; and there she lies,

[1] This was the signal for the start at the Lampadephoria, an Athenian ceremony at the festivals of the fire-gods Prometheus, Hephæstus and Athena.

dead with the dead she loved so well, her arms thrown round them both.

Thereon the host sprang to their feet and fell to wrangling, we maintaining that victory rested with my master, they with theirs; and amid our leaders the contention raged, some holding that Polynices gave the first wound with his spear, others that, as both were dead, victory rested with neither. Meantime Antigone crept away from the host; and those others rushed to their weapons, but by some lucky forethought the folk of Cadmus had sat down under arms; and by a sudden attack we surprised the Argive host before it was fully equipped. Not one withstood our onset, and they filled the plain with fugitives, while blood was streaming from the countless dead our spears had slain. Soon as victory crowned our warfare, some began to rear an image to Zeus for the foe's defeat, others were stripping the Argive dead of their shields and sending their spoils inside the battlements; and others with Antigone are bringing her dead brothers hither for their friends to mourn. So the result of this struggle to our city hovers between the two extremes of good and evil fortune.

Exit MESSENGER.

Ch. No longer do the misfortunes of this house extend to hearsay only; three corpses of the slain lie here at the palace for all to see, who by one common death have passed to their life of gloom.

Enter ANTIGONE.

An. No veil I draw o'er my tender cheek shaded with its clustering curls; no shame I feel from maiden modesty at the hot blood mantling 'neath my eyes, the blush upon my face, as I hurry wildly on in death's train, casting from my hair its tire and letting my delicate robe of saffron hue fly loose, a tearful escort to the dead. Ah me!

Woe to thee, Polynices! rightly named, I trow; woe to thee, Thebes! no mere strife to end in strife was thine; but murder completed by murder hath brought the house of Œdipus to ruin with bloodshed dire and grim. O my home, my home! what minstrel can I summon from the dead to chant a fitting dirge o'er my tearful fate, as I bear these three corpses of my kin, my mother and her sons, a welcome sight to the avenging fiend that destroyed the house of Œdipus, root and branch, in the hour that his shrewdness solved the Sphinx's riddling rhyme and slew that savage songstress. Woe is me! my father! what other Hellene or barbarian, what noble soul among the bygone tribes of man's poor mortal race ever endured the anguish of such visible afflictions?

Ah! poor maid, how piteous is thy plaint! What bird from its covert 'mid the leafy oak or soaring pine-tree's branch will come to mourn with me, the maid left motherless, with cries of woe, lamenting, ere it comes, the piteous lonely life, that henceforth must be always mine with tears that ever stream? On which of these corpses shall I throw my offerings first, plucking the hair from my head? on the breast of the mother that suckled me, or beside the ghastly death-wounds of my brothers' corpses? Woe to thee, Œdipus, my aged sire with sightless orbs, leave thy roof, disclose the misery of thy life, thou that draggest out a weary existence within the house, having cast a mist of darkness o'er thine eyes. Dost hear, thou whose aged step now gropes its way across the court, now seeks repose on wretched pallet couch?

Enter ŒDIPUS.

Œdipus. Why, daughter, hast thou dragged me to the light, supporting my blind footsteps from the gloom of my chamber, where I lie upon my bed and make piteous moan, a hoary sufferer, invisible as a phantom of the air, or as a spirit from the pit, or as a dream that flies?

An. Father, there are tidings of sorrow for thee to bear; no more thy sons behold the light, or thy wife who ever would toil to tend thy blind footsteps as with a staff. Alas for thee, my sire!

Œ. Ah me, the sorrows I endure! I may well say that. Tell me, child, what fate o'ertook those three, and how they left the light.

An. Not to reproach or mock thee say I this, but in all sadness; 'tis thy own avenging curse, with all its load of slaughter, fire, and ruthless war, that is fallen on thy sons. Alas for thee, my sire!

Œ. Ah me!

An. Why that groan?

Œ. 'Tis for my sons.

An. Couldst thou have looked towards yon sungod's four-horsed car and turned the light of thine eyes on these corpses, it would have been agony to thee.

Œ. 'Tis clear enough how their evil fate o'ertook my sons; but she, my poor wife—oh! tell me, daughter, how she came to die.

An. All saw her weep and heard her moan, as she rushed forth to carry to her sons her last appeal, a mother's breast. But the mother found her sons at the Electran gate, in a meadow where the lotus blooms, fighting out their duel like lions in their lair, eager to wound each other with spears, their blood already congealed, a murderous libation to the Death-god poured out by Ares. Then, snatching from a corpse a sword of hammered bronze, she plunged it in her flesh, and in sorrow for her sons fell with her arms around them. So to-day, father, the god, whosoe'er this issue is, has gathered to a head the sum of suffering for our house.

Ch. To-day is the beginning of many troubles to the house of Œdipus; may he live to be more fortunate!

Cr. Cease now your lamentations; 'tis time we bethought us of their burial. Hear what I have to say, Œdipus. Eteocles, thy son, left me to rule this land, by assigning it as a marriage portion to Hæmon with the hand of thy daughter Antigone. Wherefore I will no longer permit thee to dwell therein, for Teiresias plainly declared that the city would never prosper so long as thou wert in the land. So begone! And this I say not to flout thee, nor because I bear thee any grudge, but from fear that some calamity will come upon the realm by reason of those fiends that dog thy steps.

Œ. O destiny! to what a life of pain and sorrow didst thou bear me beyond all men that ever were, e'en from the very first; yea for when I was yet unborn, or ever I had left my mother's womb and seen the light, Apollo foretold to Laius that I should become my father's murderer; woe is me! So, as soon as I was born, my father tried to end again the hapless life he had given, deeming me his foe, for it was fated he should die at my hand; so he sent me still unweaned to make a pitiful meal for beasts, but I escaped from that. Ah! would that Cithæron had sunk into hell's yawning abyss, in that it slew me not! Instead thereof Fate made me a slave in the service of Polybus; and I, poor wretch, after slaying my own father came to wed my mother to her sorrow, and begat sons that were my brothers, whom also I have destroyed, by bequeathing unto them the legacy of curses I received from Laius. For nature did not make me so void of understanding, that I should have devised these horrors against my own eyes and my children's life without the intervention of some god. Let that pass. What am I, poor wretch, to do? Who now will be my guide and tend the blind man's step? Shall she, that is dead? Were she alive, I know right well she would. My pair of gallant sons, then? But they are gone from me. Am I still so young myself that I can find a livelihood? Whence could I? O Creon, why seek thus to slay me utterly? For so thou wilt, if thou banish me from the land. Yet will I never twine my arms about thy knees and betray cowardice, for I will not belie my former gallant soul, no! not for all my evil case.

Cr. Thy words are brave in refusing to touch my knees, and I am equally resolved not to let thee abide in the land. For these dead, bear one forthwith to the palace; but the other, who came with stranger folk to sack his native town, the dead Polynices, cast forth unburied beyond our frontiers. To all the race of Cadmus shall this be proclaimed, that whosoe'er is caught decking his corpse with wreaths or giving it burial, shall be requited with death; unwept, unburied let him lie, a prey to birds. As for thee, Antigone, leave thy mourning for these lifeless three and betake thyself indoors to abide there in maiden state until to-morrow, when Hæmon waits to wed thee.

An. O father, in what cruel misery are we plunged! For thee I mourn more than for the dead; for in thy woes there is no opposite to trouble, but universal sorrow is thy lot. As for thee, thou new-made king, why, I ask, dost thou mock my father thus with banishment? why start making laws over a helpless corpse?

Cr. This was what Eteocles, not I, resolved.

An. A foolish thought, and foolish art thou for entertaining it!

Cr. What! ought I not to carry out his behests?

An. No; not if they are wrong and ill-advised.

Cr. Why, is it not just for that other to be given to the dogs?

An. Nay, the vengeance ye are exacting is no lawful one.

Cr. It is; for he was his country's foe, though not a foeman born.

An. Well, to fate he rendered up his destinies.

Cr. Let him now pay forfeit in his burial too.

An. What crime did he commit in coming to claim his heritage?

Cr. Be very sure of this, yon man shall have no burial.

An. I will bury him, although the state forbids.

Cr. Do so, and thou wilt be making thy own grave by his.

An. A noble end, for two so near and dear to be laid side by side!

Cr. (*To his servants*) Ho! seize and bear her within the palace.

An. Never! for I will not loose my hold upon this corpse.

Cr. Heaven's decrees, girl, fit not thy fancies.

An. Decrees! here is another, "No insult to the dead."

Cr. Be sure that none shall sprinkle over this corpse the moistened dust.

An. O Creon, by my mother's corpse, by Jocasta, I implore thee!

Cr. 'Tis but lost labour; thou wilt not gain thy prayer.

An. Let me but bathe the dead body—

Cr. Nay, that would be part of what the city is forbidden.

An. At least let me bandage the gaping wounds.

Cr. No; thou shalt never pay honour to this corpse.

An. O my darling! one kiss at least will I print upon thy lips.

Cr. Do not let this mourning bring disaster on thy marriage.

An. Marriage! dost think I will live to wed thy son?

Cr. Most certainly thou must; how wilt thou escape the match?

An. Then if I must, our wedding-night will find another Danaid bride in me.

Cr. (*Turning to* ŒDIPUS) Dost witness how boldly she reproached me?

An. Witness this steel, the sword by which I swear!

Cr. Why art so bent on being released from this marriage?

An. I mean to share my hapless father's exile.

Cr. A noble spirit thine but somewhat touched with folly.

An. Likewise will I share his death, I tell thee further.

Cr. Go, leave the land; thou shalt not murder son of mine. *Exit* CREON.

Œ. Daughter, for this loyal spirit I thank thee.

An. Were I to wed, then thou, my father, wouldst be alone in thy exile.

Œ. Abide here and be happy; I will bear my own load of sorrow.

An. And who shall tend thee in thy blindness, father?

Œ. Where fate appoints, there will I lay me down upon the ground.

An. Where is now the famous Œdipus, where that famous riddle?

Œ. Lost for ever! one day made, and one day marred my fortune.

An. May not I too share thy sorrows?

Œ. To wander with her blinded sire were shame unto his child.

An. Not so, father, but glory rather, if she be a maid discreet.

Œ. Lead me nigh that I may touch thy mother's corpse.

An. So! embrace the aged form so dear to thee.

Œ. Woe is thee, thy motherhood, thy marriage most unblest!

An. A piteous corpse, a prey to every ill at once!

Œ. Where lies the corpse of Eteocles, and of Polynices, where?

An. Both lie stretched before thee, side by side.

Œ. Lay the blind man's hand upon his poor sons' brows.

An. There then! touch the dead, thy children.

Œ. Woe for you! dear fallen sons, sad offspring of a sire as sad!

An. O my brother Polynices, name most dear to me!

Œ. Now is the oracle of Loxias being fulfilled, my child.

An. What oracle was that? canst thou have further woes to tell?

Œ. That I should die in glorious Athens after a life of wandering.

An. Where? what fenced town in Attica will take thee in?

Œ. Hallowed Colonus, home of the god of steeds. Come then, attend on thy blind father, since thou art minded to share his exile.

An. To wretched exile go thy way; stretch forth thy hand, my aged sire, taking me to guide thee, like a breeze that speedeth barques.

Œ. See, daughter, I am advancing; be thou my guide, poor child.

An. Ah, poor indeed! the saddest maid of all in Thebes.

Œ. Where am I planting my aged step? Bring my staff, child.

An. This way, this way, father mine! plant thy footsteps here, like a dream for all the strength thou hast.

Œ. Woe unto thee that art driving my aged limbs in grievous exile from their land! Ah me! the sorrows endure!

An. "Endure"! why speak of enduring? Justice regardeth not the sinner and requiteth not men's follies.

Œ. I am he, whose name passed into high songs of victory because I guessed the maiden's baffling riddle.

An. Thou art bringing up again the reproach of the Sphinx. Talk no more of past success. This misery was in store for thee all the while, to become an exile from thy country and die thou knowest not where; while I, bequeathing to my girlish friends tears of sad regret, must go forth from my native land, roaming as no maiden ought.

Ah! this dutiful resolve will crown me with glory in respect of my father's sufferings. Woe is me for the insults heaped on thee and on my brother whose dead body is cast forth from the palace unburied; poor boy! I will yet bury him secretly, though I have to die for it, father.

Œ. To thy companions show thyself.

An. My own laments suffice.

Œ. Go pray then at the altars.

An. They are weary of my piteous tale.

Œ. At least go seek the Bromian god in his hallowed haunt amongst the Mænads' hills.

An. Offering homage that is no homage in Heaven's eyes to him in whose honour I once fringed my dress with the Theban fawn-skin and led the dance upon the hills for the holy choir of Semele?

Œ. My noble fellow-countrymen, behold me; I am Œdipus, who solved the famous riddle, and once was first of men, I who alone cut short the murderous Sphinx's tyranny am now myself expelled the land in shame and misery. Go to; why make this moan and bootless lamentation? Weak mortal as I am, I must endure the fate that God decrees.

Exeunt ŒDIPUS *and* ANTIGONE.

Ch. Hail! majestic Victory! keep thou my life nor ever cease to crown my song! *Exeunt* OMNES.

ORESTES

DRAMATIS PERSONAE

Electra	Pylades
Helen	Messenger
Chorus of Argive Maidens	Hermione
Orestes	A Phrygian Eunuch, *in Helen's retinue*
Menelaus	Apollo
Tyndareus	

Before the royal palace at Argos. ORESTES *lies sleeping on a couch in the background.* ELECTRA *is watching him.*

Electra. There is naught so terrible to describe, be it physical pain or heaven-sent affliction, that man's nature may not have to bear the burden of it. Tantalus, for instance, once so prosperous—and I am not now taunting him with his misfortunes—that Tantalus, the reputed son of Zeus, hangs suspended in mid air, quailing at the crag which looms above his head; paying this penalty, they say, for the shameful weakness he displayed in failing to keep a bridle on his lips, when admitted by gods, though he was but a mortal, to share the honours of their feasts like one of them.

He it was that begat Pelops, the father of Atreus, for whom the goddess, when she had carded her wool, spun a web of strife, even to the making of war with his own brother Thyestes. But why need I repeat that hideous tale?

Well, Atreus slew Thyestes' children and feasted him on them; but—passing over intermediate events—from Atreus and Ærope of Crete sprang Agamemnon, that famous chief—if his was really fame—and Menelaus. Now it was this Menelaus who married Helen, Heaven's abhorrence; while his brother, King Agamemnon, took Clytaemnestra to wife, name of note in Hellas, and we three daughters were his issue, Chrysothemis, Iphigenia, and myself Electra; also a son Orestes; all of that one accursed mother, who slew her lord, after snaring him in a robe that had no outlet. Her reason a maiden's lips may not declare, and so I leave that unexplained for the world to guess at. What need for me to charge Phœbus with wrong-doing, though he instigated Orestes to slay his own mother, a deed that few approved; still it was his obedience to the god that made him slay her; I, too, feebly as a woman would, shared in the deed of blood, as did Pylades who helped us to bring it about.

After this my poor Orestes fell sick of a cruel wasting disease; upon his couch he lies prostrated, and it is his mother's blood that goads him into frenzied fits; this I say, from dread of naming those goddesses, whose terrors are chasing him before them—even the Eumenides. 'Tis now the sixth day since the body of his murdered mother was committed to the cleansing fire; since then no food has passed his lips, nor hath he washed his skin; but wrapped in his cloak he weeps in his lucid moments, whenever the fever leaves him; otherwhiles he bounds headlong from his couch, as a colt when it is loosed from the yoke. Moreover this city of Argos has decreed, that no man give us shelter at his fireside or speak to matricides like us; yea, and this is the fateful day, on which Argos will decide our sentence, whether we are both to die by stoning, or to whet the steel and plunge it in our necks. There is, 'tis true, one hope of escape still left us; Menelaus has landed from Troy; his fleet now crowds the haven of Nauplia where he is come to anchor, returned at last from Troy after ceaseless wanderings; but Helen, that "lady of sorrows," as she styles herself, hath he sent on to our palace, carefully waiting for the night, lest any of those parents whose sons were slain beneath the walls of Troy, might see her if she went by day, and set to stoning her. Within she sits, weeping for her sister and the calamities of her family, and yet *she* hath still some solace in her woe; for Hermione, the child she left at home in the hour she sailed for Troy—the maid whom Menelaus brought from Sparta and entrusted to my mother's keeping—is still a cause of joy to her and a reason to forget her sorrows.

I, meantime, am watching each approach, against the moment I see Menelaus arriving; for unless we find some safety there, we have but a feeble anchor to ride on otherwise.

A helpless thing, an unlucky house!

Enter HELEN.

Helen. Daughter of Clytaemnestra and Agamemnon, hapless Electra, too long now left a maid unwed! how is it with thee and thy brother, this ill-starred Orestes who slew his mother! Speak; for referring the sin as I do to Phœbus, I incur no pollution by letting thee accost me; and yet I am truly sorry for the fate of my sister Clytæmnestra, on whom I ne'er set eyes after I was driven by heaven-sent frenzy to sail on my disastrous voyage to Ilium;

but now that I am parted from her I bewail our misfortunes.

El. Prithee, Helen, why should I speak of that which thine own eyes can see the son of Agamemnon in his misery?

Beside his wretched corpse I sit, a sleepless sentinel; for corpse he is, so faint his breath; not that I reproach him with his sufferings; but thou art highly blest and thy husband too, and ye are come upon us in the hour of adversity.

Hel. How long hath he been laid thus upon his couch?

El. Ever since he spilt his mother's blood.

Hel. Unhappy wretch! unhappy mother! what a death she died!

El. Unhappy enough to succumb to his misery.

Hel. Prithee, maiden, wilt hear me a moment?

El. Aye, with such small leisure as this watching o'er a brother leaves.

Hel. Wilt go for me to my sister's tomb?

El. Wouldst have me seek my mother's tomb? And why?

Hel. To carry an offering of hair and a libation from me.

El. Art forbidden then to go to the tombs of those thou lovest?

Hel. Nay, but I am ashamed to show myself in Argos.

El. A late repentance surely for one who left her home so shamefully then.

Hel. Thou hast told the truth, but thy telling is not kind to me.

El. What is this supposed modesty before the eyes of Mycenæ that possesses thee?

Hel. I am afraid of the fathers of those who lie dead beneath the walls of Ilium.

El. Good cause for fear; thy name is on every tongue in Argos.

Hel. Then free me of my fear and grant me this boon.

El. I could not bear to face my mother's grave.

Hel. And yet 'twere shame indeed to send these offerings by a servant's hand.

El. Then why not send thy daughter Hermione?

Hel. 'Tis not seemly for a tender maid to make her way amongst a crowd.

El. And yet she would thus be repaying her dead foster-mother's care.

Hel. True; thou hast convinced me, maiden. Yes, I *will* send my daughter; for thou art right. (*Calling*) Hermione, my child, come forth before the palace; (*enter* HERMIONE) take these libations and these tresses of mine in thy hands, and go pour round Clytaemnestra's tomb a mingled cup of honey, milk, and frothing wine; then stand upon the heaped-up grave, and proclaim therefrom, "Helen, thy sister, sends thee these libations as her gift, fearing herself to approach thy tomb from terror of the Argive mob"; and bid her harbour kindly thoughts towards me and thee and my husband; towards these two wretched sufferers, too, whom Heaven hath afflicted. Likewise promise that I will pay in full whatever funeral gifts are due from me to a sister. Now go, my child, and tarry not; and soon as thou hast made the offering at the tomb, bethink thee of thy return.

Exit HELEN *and* HERMIONE.

El. O human nature, what a grievous curse thou art in this world! and what salvation, too, to those who have a goodly heritage therein!

Did ye mark how she cut off her hair only at the ends, careful to preserve its beauty? 'Tis the same woman as of old. May Heaven's hate pursue thee! for thou hast proved the ruin of me and my poor brother and all Hellas.

Alack! here are my friends once more, coming to unite their plaintive dirge with mine; they will soon put an end to my brother's peaceful sleep and cause my tears to flow when I see his frenzied fit.

Enter CHORUS OF ARGIVE MAIDENS.

Good friends, step softly; not a sound! not a whisper! for though this kindness is well-meant, rouse him and I shall rue it.

Chorus. Hush! hush! let your footsteps fall lightly! not a sound! not a whisper!

El. Further, further from his couch! I beseech ye.

Ch. There! there! I obey.

El. Hush! hush! good friend, I pray. Soft as the breath of slender reedy pipe be thy every accent!

Ch. Hark, how soft and low I drop my voice!

El. Yes, lower thy voice e'en thus; approach now, softly, softly! Tell me what reason ye had for coming at all. 'Tis so long since he laid him down to sleep.

Ch. How is it with him? Impart thy news, dear lady. Is it weal or woe I am to tell?

El. He is still alive, but his moans grow feeble.

Ch. What sayest thou? (*Turning to* ORESTES) Poor wretch!

El. Awake him from the deep sweet slumber he is now enjoying and thou wilt cause his death.

Ch. Ah, poor sufferer! victim of Heaven's vengeful hate!

El. Ah, misery! It seems it was a wicked utterance by a wicked god delivered, the day that Loxias from his seat upon the tripod of Themis decreed my mother's most unnatural murder.

Ch. He stirs beneath his robe! Dost see?

El. Alas! I do; thy noisy chatter has roused him from his sleep.

Ch. Nay, methinks he slumbers still.

El. Begone! quit the house! retrace thy footsteps! a truce to this din!

Ch. He sleeps. Thou art right.

El. O Night, majestic queen, giver of sleep to toiling men, rise from the abyss of Erebus and wing thy way to the palace of Agamemnon! For beneath our load of misery and woe we sink, aye, sink oppressed.

There! (*to the* CHORUS) that noise again! Do be still and keep that high-pitched voice of thine away from his couch; suffer him to enjoy his sleep in peace!

Ch. Tell me, what end awaits his troubles?

El. Death, death; what else? for he does not even miss his food.

Ch. Why, then his doom is full in view.

El. Phœbus marked us out as his victims by imposing a foul unnatural task, even the shedding of the blood of our mother, who slew our sire.

Ch. 'Twas just, but 'twas not well.

El. Dead, dead, O mother mine! and thou hast slain a father and these children of thy womb; for we are dead or as the dead. Yes, thou art in thy grave, and more than half my life is spent in weeping and wailing and midnight lamentations; oh, look on me! a maid unwed, unblest with babes, I drag out a joyless existence as if for ever.

Ch. My daughter Electra, from thy near station there see whether thy brother hath not passed away without thy knowing it; for I like not his utter prostration.

Orestes. (*Awaking refreshed*) Sweet charm of sleep! saviour in sickness! how dear to me thy coming was! how needed! All hail, majestic power, oblivion of woe! How wise this goddess is, how earnestly invoked by every suffering soul! (*Addressing* ELECTRA) Whence came I hither? How is it I am here? for I have lost all previous recollection and remember nothing.

El. Dearest brother, how glad I was to see thee fall asleep! Wouldst have me take thee in my arms and lift thy body?

Or. Take, oh! take me in thy arms, and from this sufferer's mouth and eyes wipe off the flakes of foam.

El. Ah! 'tis a service I love; nor do I scorn with sister's hand to tend a brother's limbs.

Or. Prop me up, thy side to mine; brush the matted hair from off my face, for I see but dimly.

El. Ah, poor head! how squalid are thy locks become! How wild they look from remaining so long unwashed!

Or. Lay me once more upon the couch; when my fit leaves me, I am all unnerved, unstrung.

El. (*As she lays him down*) Welcome to the sick man is his couch, for painful though it be to take thereto, yet is it necessary.

Or. Set me upright once again, turn me round; it is their helplessness makes the sick so hard to please.

El. Wilt put thy feet upon the ground and take a step at last? Change is always pleasant.

Or. That will I; for that has a semblance of health; and that seeming, though it be far from the reality, is preferable to this.

El. Hear me then, O brother mine, while yet the avenging fiends permit thee to use thy senses.

Or. Hast news to tell? so it be good, thou dost me a kindness; but if it tend to my hurt, lo! I have sorrow enough.

El. Menelaus, thy father's brother, is arrived; in Nauplia his fleet lies at anchor.

Or. Ha! is he come to cast a ray of light upon our gloom, a man of our own kin who owes our sire a debt of gratitude?

El. Yes, he is come, and is bringing Helen with him from the walls of Troy; accept this as a sure proof of what I say.

Or. Had he returned alone in safety, he were more to be envied; for if he is bringing his wife with him, he is bringing a load of mischief.

El. Tyndareus begat a race of daughters notorious for the shame they earned, infamous throughout Hellas.

Or. Be thou then different from that evil brood, for well thou mayest, and that not only in profession, but also in heart.

El. Ah! brother, thine eye is growing wild, and in a moment art thou passing from thy recent saneness back to frenzy.

Or. (*Starting up wildly*) Mother, I implore thee! let not loose on me those maidens with their bloodshot eyes and snaky hair. Ha! see, see where they approach to leap upon me!

El. Lie still, poor sufferer, on thy couch; thine eye sees none of the things which thy fancy paints so clear.

Or. O Phœbus! they will kill me, yon hounds of hell, death's priestesses with glaring eyes, terrific goddesses.

El. I will not let thee go; but with arms twined round thee will prevent thy piteous tossing to and fro.

Or. Loose me! thou art one of those fiends that plague me, and art gripping me by the waist to hurl my body into Tartarus.

El. Woe is me! what succour can I find, seeing that we have Heaven's forces set against us?

Or. Give me my horn-tipped bow, Apollo's gift, wherewith that god declared that I should defend myself against these goddesses, if ever they sought to scare me with wild transports of madness.

A mortal hand will wound one of these goddesses, unless she vanish from my sight. Do ye not heed me, or mark the feathered shaft of my far-shooting bow ready to wing its flight? What! do ye linger still? Spread your pinions, skim the sky, and blame those oracles of Phœbus.

Ah! why am I raving, panting, gasping? Whither, oh! whither have I leapt from off my couch? Once more the storm is past; I see a calm.

Sister, why weepest thou, thy head wrapped in thy robe? I am ashamed that I should make thee a partner in my sufferings and distress a maid like thee through sickness of mine. Cease to fret for my troubles; for though thou didst consent to it, yet 'twas I that spilt our mother's blood. 'Tis Loxias I blame, for urging me on to do a deed most damned, encouraging me with words but no real help; for I am sure that, had I asked my father to his face whether I was to slay my mother, he would have implored me oft and earnestly by this beard never to plunge a murderer's sword into my mother's breast, since he would not thereby regain his life, whilst I, poor wretch, should be doomed to drain this cup of sorrow.

E'en as it is, dear sister, unveil thy face and cease to weep, despite our abject misery; and whensoe'er thou seest me give way to despair, be it thine to calm and soothe the terrors and distorted fancies of my brain; likewise when sorrow comes to thee, I must be at thy side and give thee words of comfort; for to help our friends like this is a gracious task.

Seek thy chamber now, poor sister; lie down and close awhile thy sleepless eyes; take food and bathe thy body; for if thou leave me or fall sick from nursing me, my doom is sealed; for thou art the only champion I now have, by all the rest deserted, as thou seest.

El. I leave thee! never! With thee I am resolved to live and die; for 'tis the same; if thou diest, what can I, a woman, do? How shall I escape alone, reft of brother, sire, and friends?

Still if it be thy pleasure, I must do thy bidding. But lay thee down upon thy couch, and pay not too great heed to the terrors and alarms that scare thee from thy rest; lie still upon thy pallet bed; for e'en though one be not sick but only fancy it, this is a source of weariness and perplexity to mortals.

Exit ELECTRA.

Ch. Ah! ye goddesses terrific, swiftly careering on outspread pinions, whose lot it is 'mid tears and groans to hold revel not with Bacchic rites; ye avenging spirits swarthy-hued, that dart along the spacious firmament, exacting a penalty for blood, a penalty for murder, to you I make my suppliant prayer: suffer the son of Agamemnon to forget his wild whirling frenzy!

Ah, woe for the troublous task! which thou, poor wretch, didst strive to compass to thy ruin, listening to the voice prophetic, proclaimed aloud by Phœbus from the tripod throughout his sanctuary, where is a secret spot they call "the navel of the earth."

O Zeus! What pity will be shown? what deadly struggle is here at hand, hurrying thee on o'er thy path of woe, victim on whom some fiend is heaping tribulation, by bringing on thy house thy mother's bloodshed which drives thee raving mad? I weep for thee, for thee I weep.

Great prosperity abideth not amongst mankind; but some power divine, shaking it to and fro like the sail of a swift galley, plunges it deep in the waves of grievous affliction, boisterous and deadly as the waves of the sea. For what new family am I henceforth to honour by preference other than that which sprung from a marriage divine, even from Tantalus?

Behold a king draws near, prince Menelaus! From his magnificence 'tis plain to see that he is a scion of the race of Tantalus.

All hail! thou that didst sail with a thousand ships to Asia's strand, and by Heaven's help accomplish all thy heart's desire, making good-fortune a friend to thyself.

Enter MENELAUS.

Menelaus. All hail, my home! Some joy I feel on seeing thee again on my return from Troy, some sorrow too the sight recalls; for never yet have I beheld a house more closely encircled by the net of dire affliction.

Concerning Agamemnon's fate and the awful death he died at his wife's hands I learnt as I was trying to put in at Malea, when the sailors' seer from out the waves, unerring Glaucus, Nereus' spokesman, brought the news to me; for he stationed himself in full view by our ship and thus addressed me, "Yonder, Menelaus, lies thy brother slain, plunged in a fatal bath, the last his wife will ever give him"; filling high the cup of tears for me and my brave crew. Arrived at Nauplia, my wife already on the point of starting hither, I was dreaming of folding Orestes, Agamemnon's son, and his mother in a fond embrace, as if 'twere well with them, when I heard a mariner relate the murder of the daughter of Tyndareus. Tell me then, good girls, where to find the son of Agamemnon, the daring author of that fearful crime; for he was but a babe in Clytaemnestra's arms that day I left my home to go to Troy, so that I should not recognize him, e'en were I to see him.

Or. (*Staggering towards him from the couch*) Behold the object of thy inquiry, Menelaus; this is Orestes. To thee will I of mine own accord relate my sufferings. But as the prelude to my speech I clasp thy knees in suppliant wise, seeking thus to tie[1] to thee the prayer of lips that lack the suppliant's bough; save me, for thou art arrived at the very crisis of my trouble.

Men. Ye gods! what do I see? what death's-head greets my sight?

Or. Thou art right; I *am* dead through misery, though I still gaze upon the sun.

Men. How wild the look thy unkempt hair gives thee, poor wretch!

Or. 'Tis not my looks, but my deeds that torture me.

Men. How terribly thy tearless eyeballs glare!

Or. My body is vanished and gone, though my name hath not yet deserted me.

Men. Unsightly apparition, so different from what I expected!

Or. In me behold a man that hath slain his hapless mother.

Men. I have heard all; be chary of thy tale of woe.

Or. I will; but the deity is lavish of woe in my case.

Men. What ails thee? what is thy deadly sickness?

Or. My conscience; I know that I am guilty of an awful crime.

Men. Explain thyself; wisdom is shown in clearness, not in obscurity.

Or. 'Tis grief that is my chief complaint.

Men. True; she is a goddess dire; yet are there cures for her.

[1]The allusion is to the sacred wreaths worn by suppliants, one end of which they retained, while the other was fastened to the altar, thus identifying them with its sanctity.

Or. Mad transports too, and the vengeance due to a mother's blood.

Men. When did thy fit begin? which day was it?

Or. On the day I was heaping the mound o'er my poor mother's grave.

Men. When thou wast in the house, or watching by the pyre?

Or. As I was waiting by night to gather up her bones.

Men. Was any one else there to help thee rise?

Or. Yes, Pylades who shared with me the bloody deed, my mother's murder.

Men. What phantom forms afflict thee thus?

Or. Three maidens black as night I seem to see.

Men. I know of whom thou speakest, but I will ıot name them.

Or. Do not; they are too dread; thou wert wise to void naming them.

Men. Are these the fiends that persecute thee with the curse of kindred blood?

Or. Oh! the torment I endure from their hot pursuit!

Men. That they who have done an awful deed should be so done by is not strange.

Or. Ah, well! I must have recourse in these troubles—

Men. Speak not of dying; that were folly.

Or. To Phœbus, by whose command I shed my mother's blood.

Men. Showing a strange ignorance of what is fair and right.

Or. We must obey the gods, whatever those gods are.

Men. Spite of all this doth not Loxias help thy affliction?

Or. He will in time; to wait like this is the way with gods.

Men. How long is it since thy mother breathed her last?

Or. This is now the sixth day; her funeral pyre is still warm.

Men. How soon the goddesses arrived to require thy mother's blood of thee!

Or. To cleverness I lay no claim, but I was a true friend to friends.

Men. Does thy father afford thee any help at all?

Or. Not as yet; and delaying to do so is, methinks, equivalent to not doing it.

Men. How dost thou stand towards the city after that deed of thine?

Or. So hated am I that I cannot speak to any man.

Men. Have not thy hands been even cleansed of their blood-guiltiness, as the law requires?

Or. No; for where'er I go, the door is shut against me.

Men. Which of the citizens drive thee from the land?

Or. Œax, who refers to my father his reason for hating Troy.

Men. I understand; he is visiting on thee the blood of Palamedes.

Or. I at least had naught to do with that; yet am I utterly o'erthrown.

Men. Who else? some of the friends of Ægisthus perhaps?

Or. Yes, they insult me, and the city listens to them now.

Men. Will it not suffer thee to keep the sceptre of Agamemnon?

Or. How should it? seeing that they will not suffer me to remain alive.

Men. What is their method? canst thou tell me plainly?

Or. To-day is sentence to be passed upon me.

Men. Exile, or death, or something else?

Or. Death by stoning at the hands of the citizens.

Men. Then why not cross the frontier and fly?

Or. Why not? because I am hemmed in by a ring of armed men.

Men. Private foes or Argive troops?

Or. By all the citizens, to the end that I may die; 'tis shortly told.

Men. Poor wretch! thou hast arrived at the extremity of woe.

Or. In thee I still have hopes of escape from my troubles. Yea, since fortune smiles upon thy coming, impart to thy less favoured friends some of thy prosperity, not reserving that luck exclusively for thyself; no! take thy turn too at suffering, and so pay back my father's kindness to those who have a claim on thee. For such friends as desert us in the hour of adversity, are friends in name but not in reality.

Ch. Lo! Tyndareus, the Spartan, is making his way hither with the step of age, clad in black raiment, with his hair shorn short in mourning for his daughter.

Or. Menelaus, I am ruined. See! Tyndareus approaches, the man of all others I most shrink from facing, because of the deed I have done; for he it was that nursed me when a babe, and lavished on me many a fond caress, carrying me about in his arms as the son of Agamemnon, and so did Leda; for they both regarded me as much as the Dioscuri.

Ah me! my wretched heart and soul! 'twas a sorry return I made them. What darkness can I find to veil my head? what cloud can I spread before me in my efforts to escape the old man's eye?

Enter TYNDAREUS.

Tyndareus. Where, where may I find Menelaus, my daughter's husband? for as I was pouring libations on Clytaemnestra's grave I heard that he was come to Nauplia with his wife, safe home again after many a long year. Lead me to him; for I would fain stand at his right hand and give him greeting as a friend whom at last I see again.

Men. Hail, reverend father! rival of Zeus for a bride!

Ty. All hail to thee! Menelaus, kinsman mine! Ha! (*Catching sight of* ORESTES) What an evil it is to be ignorant of the future! There lies that matricide before the house, a viper darting venom from his eyes, whom my soul abhors. What! Menelaus, speaking to a godless wretch like him?

Men. And why not? He is the son of one whom I loved well.

Ty. *This* his son? this creature here?

Men. Yes, his son; and therefore worthy of respect, albeit in distress.

Ty. Thou hast been so long amongst barbarians that thou art one of them.

Men. Always to respect one's kith and kin is a custom in Hellas.

Ty. Aye, another custom is to yield a willing deference to the laws.

Men. The wise hold that everything which depends on necessity, is its slave.

Ty. Keep that wisdom for thyself; I will not admit it.

Men. No, for thou art angry, and old age is not wise.

Ty. What could a dispute about wisdom have to do with him? If right and wrong are clear to all, who was ever more senseless than this man, seeing that he never weighed the justice of the case, nor yet appealed to the universal law of Hellas? For instance, when Agamemnon breathed his last beneath the blow my daughter dealt upon his head—a deed most foul, which I will never defend—he should have brought a charge against his mother and inflicted the penalty allowed by law for bloodshed, banishing her from his house; thus would he have gained the credit of forbearance from the calamity, keeping strictly to the law and showing his piety as well. As it is, he is come into the same misfortune as his mother; for though he had just cause for thinking her a wicked woman, he has surpassed her himself by murdering her. I will ask thee, Menelaus, just one question. Take this case: the wife of his bosom has slain him; *his* son follows suit and kills his mother in revenge; next the avenger's son to expiate this murder commits another; where, pray, will the chain of horrors end?

Our forefathers settled these matters the right way. They forbade any one with blood upon his hands to appear in their sight or cross their path; "purify him by exile," said they, "but no retaliation!" Otherwise there must always have been one who, by taking the pollution last upon his hands, would be liable to have his own blood shed.

For my part I abhor wicked women, especially my daughter who slew her husband; Helen, too, thy own wife, will I ne'er commend; no! I would not even speak to her, and little I envy thee a voyage to Troy for so worthless a woman. But the law will I defend with all my might, seeking to check this brutal spirit of murder, which is always the ruin of countries and cities alike. Wretch! (*Turning to* ORESTES) Hadst thou no heart when thy mother was baring her breast in her appeal to thee? True; I did not witness that awful deed, yet do my poor old eyes run down with tears. One thing at least attests the truth of what I say: thou art abhorred by Heaven, and this aimless wandering, these transports of madness and terror are thy atonement for a mother's blood. What need have I of others to testify where I can see for myself? Take warning therefore, Menelaus; seek not to oppose the gods from any wish to help this wretch, but leave him to be stoned to death by his fellow-citizens; else set not foot on Sparta's soil. My daughter is dead, and she deserved her fate; but it should not have been his hand that slew her. In all except my daughters have I been a happy man; there my fortune stopped.

Ch. His is an enviable lot, who is blest in his children, and does not find himself brought into evil notoriety.

Or. I am afraid to speak before thee, aged prince, in a matter where I am sure to grieve thee to the heart. Only let thy years, which frighten me from speaking, set no barrier in the path of my words, and I will go forward; but, as it is, I fear thy grey hairs. My crime is, I slew my mother; yet on another count this is no crime, being vengeance for my father. What ought I to have done? Set one thing against another. My father begat me; thy daughter gave me birth, being the field that received the seed from another; for without a sire no child would ever be born. So I reasoned thus: I ought to stand by the author of my being rather than the woman who undertook to rear me. Now thy daughter—*mother* I blush to call her—was engaged in secret intrigues with a lover (reviling her I shall revile myself; yet speak I will); Ægisthus was that stealthy paramour who lived with her; him I slew, and after him I sacrificed my mother—a crime, no doubt, but done to avenge my father. Now, as regards the matters for which I deserve to be stoned as thou threatenest, hear the service I am conferring on all Hellas. If women become so bold as to murder their husbands, taking refuge in their children, with the mother's breast to catch their pity, they would think nothing of destroying their husbands on any plea whatsoever. But I, by a horrible crime—such is thy exaggerated phrase—have put an end to this custom. I hated my mother and had good cause to slay her. She was false to her husband when he was gone from his home to fight for all Hellas at the head of its armies, neither did she keep his honour undefiled; and when her sin had found her out, she wreaked no punishment upon herself, but, to avoid the vengeance of her lord, visited her sins on my father and slew him. By Heaven! ill time as it is for me to mention Heaven, when defending the cause of murder; still, suppose I had by my silence consented to my mother's conduct, what would the murdered man have done to me? Would he not now for very hate be tormenting me with avenging fiends? or are there goddesses to help my mother, and are there none to aid him in his deeper wrong? Thou, yes! thou, old man, hast been my ruin by begetting a daughter so abandoned; for it was owing to her audacious deed that I lost my father and became my mother's murderer.

Attend, I say. Telemachus did not kill the wife of Odysseus; why? because she wedded not a second husband, but the marriage-bed remained untainted in her halls. Once more; Apollo, who makes the navel of the earth his home, vouchsafing unerring prophecies to man, the god whom we obey in all he saith—'twas he to whom I hearkened when I slew my mother. Find him guilty of the crime, slay him; his was the sin, not mine. What ought I to have done? or is not the god competent to expiate the pollution when I refer it to him? Whither should one fly henceforth, if he will not rescue me from death after giving his commands? Say not then that the deed was badly done, but unfortunately for me who did it.

A blessed life those mortals lead who make wise marriages; but those who wed unhappily are alike unfortunate in their public and private concerns.

Ch. 'Tis ever woman's way to thwart men's fortunes to the increase of their sorrow.

Ty. Since thou adoptest so bold a tone, suppressing naught, but answering me back in such wise that my heart is vexed within me, thou wilt incense me to go to greater lengths in procuring thy execution; and I shall regard this as a fine addition to my purpose in coming hither to deck my daughter's grave. Yes; I will go to the chosen council of Argos and set the citizens, whether they will or not, on thee and thy sister, that ye may suffer stoning. She deserves to die even more than thou, for it was she who embittered thee against thy mother by carrying tales to thine ear from time to time to whet thy hate the more announcing dreams from Agamemnon, and speaking of the amour with Ægisthus as an abomination to the gods in Hades, for even here on earth it was hateful, till she set the house ablaze with fires never kindled by Hephæstus. This I tell thee, Menelaus; and more—I will perform it. If then thou makest my hatred or our connexion of any account, seek not to avert this miscreant's doom in direct defiance of the gods, but leave him to be stoned to death by the citizens; else never set foot on Spartan soil. Remember thou hast been told all this, and choose not for friends the ungodly, excluding more righteous folk.

Ho! servants, lead me hence. *Exit* TYNDAREUS.

Or. Get thee gone! that the remainder of my speech may be addressed to Menelaus without interruption, free from the restrictions thy old age exerts.

Wherefore, Menelaus, art thou pacing round and round to think the matter over, up and down in thought perplexed?

Men. Let me alone! I am somewhat at a loss, as I turn it over in my mind, towards which side I am to lean.

Or. Do not then decide finally, but after first hearing what I have to say, then make up thy mind.

Men. Good advice! say on. There are occasions when silence would be better than speech; there are others when the reverse holds good.

Or. I will begin forthwith. A long statement has advantages over a short one and is more intelligible to listen to. Give me nothing of thine own, Menelaus, but repay what thou didst thyself receive from my father. (*As* MENELAUS *makes a deprecating gesture*) 'Tis not goods I mean; save my life, and that is goods, the dearest I possess.

Say I am doing wrong. Well, I have a right to a little wrong-doing at thy hands to requite that wrong; for my father Agamemnon also did wrong in gathering the host of Hellas and going up against Ilium, not that he had sinned himself, but he was trying to find a cure for the sin and wrong-doing of thy wife. So this is one thing thou art bound to pay me back. For he had really sold his life to thee, a duty owed by friend to friend, toiling hard in the press of battle that so thou mightest win thy wife again. This is what thou didst receive at Troy; make me the same return. For one brief day exert thyself, not ten full years, on my behalf, standing up in my defence.

As for the loan paid to Aulis in the blood of my sister, I leave that to thy credit, not saying "Slay Hermione"; for in my present plight thou must needs have an advantage over me and I must let that pass. But grant my hapless sire this boon, my life and the life of her who has pined so long in maidenhood, my sister; for by my death I shall leave my father's house without an heir.

"Impossible!" thou'lt say. Why, there's the point of that old adage, "Friends are bound to succour friends in trouble." But when fortune giveth of her best, what need of friends? for God's help is enough of itself when he chooses to give it.

All Hellas credits thee with deep affection for thy wife—and I am not saying this with any subtle attempt at wheedling thee—by her I implore thee. (*As* MENELAUS *turns away*) Ah me, my misery! at what a pass have I arrived! what avails my wretched effort? Still, (*preparing to make a final appeal*) 'tis my whole family on whose behalf I am making this appeal! O my uncle, my father's own brother! imagine that the dead man in his grave is listening, that his spirit is hovering o'er thy head and speaking through my lips. I have said my say with reference to tears and groans and misfortunes, and I have begged my life—the aim of every man's endeavour, not of mine alone.

Ch. I, too, weak woman though I am, beseech thee, as thou hast the power, succour those in need.

Men. Orestes, thou art a man for whom I have a deep regard, and I would fain help thee bear thy load of woe; yea, for it is a duty, too, to lend a kinsman such assistance by dying or slaying his enemies, provided Heaven grants the means. I only wish I had that power granted me by the gods; as it is, I have arrived quite destitute of allies, after my long weary wanderings, with such feeble succour as my surviving friends afford. As then we should never get the better of Pelasgian Argos by fighting, our hopes now rest on this, the chance of prevailing by persuasion; and we must try that,. for how can you win a great cause by small efforts? it were senseless even to wish it. For when the people fall into a fury and their rage is still fresh, they are as hard to appease as a fierce fire is to quench; but if you gently slacken your hold. and yield a little to their tension, cautiously watching your opportunity, they may possibly exhaust their fit; and then as soon as they have spent their rage, thou mayest obtain whatever thou wilt from them without any trouble; for they have a natural sense of pity, and a hot temper too, an invaluable quality if you watch it closely. So I will go and try to persuade Tyndareus and the citizens to moderate their excessive anger against thee; for it is with them as with a ship; she dips if her sheet is hauled too taut, but rights herself again if it is let go.

Attempts to do too much are as keenly resented by the citizens as they are by the gods; and so it must be by cleverness, not by the force of superior numbers, I frankly tell thee, that I must try to save thee. No prowess of mine as perhaps thou fanciest, could do it; for, had it been so easy to triumph single-handed over the troubles that beset thee, I should never have tried to bring Argives over to the side of mercy; but, as it is, the wise find themselves forced to bow to fortune. *Exit* MENELAUS.

Or. O thou that hast no use, save to head a host in a woman's cause! thou traitor in thy friends' defence! dost turn thy back on me? What Agamemnon did is all forgotten.

Ah, my father! thy friends, it seems, desert thee in adversity. Alas! I am betrayed; no longer have I any hope of finding a refuge where I may escape the death-sentence of Argos; for this man was my haven of safety.

Ha! a welcome sight, there comes Pylades, my best of friends, running hither from Phocis. A trusty comrade is a more cheering sight in trouble than a calm is to sailors.

Enter PYLADES.

Pylades. On my way hither I traversed the town with more haste than I need have used, to find thee and thy sister, having heard or rather myself seen the citizens assembling, under the belief that they intend your immediate execution. What is happening here? how is it with thee? how farest thou, my best of comrades, friends, and kin? for thou art all these to me.

Or. Let one brief word declare to thee my evil case—it is "Ruin."

Py. Include me then in it; for friends have all in common.

Or. Menelaus is a traitor to me and my sister.

Py. 'Tis only natural that the husband of a traitress should prove a traitor.

Or. He no more repaid me when he came than if he had never come.

Py. Has he really arrived then in this land?

Or. He was a long time coming, but very soon detected for all that in treachery to his friends.

Py. And did he bring his wife, that queen of traitresses, with him on his ship?

Or. It was not he who brought her, but she him.

Py. Where is she who proved the ruin of so many Achæans, though she was only a woman?

Or. In my house; if, that is, I ought to call it mine.

Py. And thou—what didst thou say to thy father's brother?

Or. I besought him not to look on, while I and my sister were slain by the citizens.

Py. By heaven! what said he to this? I fain would know.

Or. Caution was the line he took—the usual policy of traitorous friends.

Py. What excuse does he allege? when I have heard that, I know all.

Or. The worthy sire arrived, who begat those peerless daughters.

Py. Thou meanest Tyndareus; he was angry with thee, perhaps, for his daughter's sake.

Or. Thou hast it; and Menelaus preferred his relationship to my father's.

Py. Had he not courage enough to share thy troubles, when he *did* come?

Or. Not he; he never was a warrior, though a doughty knight amongst women.

Py. Thy case is desperate, it seems, and thou must die.

Or. The citizens are to give their vote about us on the question of the murder.

Py. And what is that to decide? tell me, for I am alarmed.

Or. Our life or death; so short the words that tell of things so long!

Py. Leave the palace, then, with thy sister and fly.

Or. Look! we are being watched by guards on every side.

Py. I saw that the streets of the city were secured with armed men.

Or. We are as closely beleaguered as a city by its foes.

Py. Ask me also of my state; for I too am ruined.

Or. By whom? this would be a further sorrow to add to mine.

Py. Strophius, my father, in a fit of anger, hath banished me his halls.

Or. On some private charge, or one in which the citizens share?

Py. He says it is a crime to have helped thee slay thy mother.

Or. Woe is me! it seems my troubles will cause thee grief as well.

Py. I am not like Menelaus; this must be endured.

Or. Art thou not afraid that Argos will desire thy death as well as mine?

Py. I am not theirs to punish; I belong to Phocis.

Or. A terrible thing is the mob, when it has villains to lead it.

Py. Aye, but with honest leaders its counsels are honest.

Or. Go to; we must consult together.

Py. What is it we must consider?

Or. Suppose I go and tell the citizens—

Py. That thy action was just—

Or. In avenging my father?

Py. I am afraid they will be glad enough to catch thee.

Or. Well, am I to crouch in fear and die without a word?

Py. That were cowardly.

Or. How then shall I act?

Py. Suppose thou stay here, what means of safety hast thou?

Or. None.

Py. And if thou go away, is there any hope of escaping thy troubles?

Or. There might be possibly.

Py. Well, is not that better than staying?

Or. Am I to go, then?

Py. Yes; if thou *art* slain, there will be some honour in dying thus.

Or. True; thus I escape cowardice.

Py. Better than by staying.

Or. After all, I can justify my action.

Py. Pray that this may be the only view they take.

Or. Some one or two maybe will pity me—

Py. Yes, thy noble birth is a great point.

Or. Resenting my father's death.

Py. That is all quite clear.

Or. I must go, for to die ignobly is a coward's part.

Py. Well said!

Or. Shall we tell my sister?

Py. God forbid!

Or. True, there might be tears.

Py. Would not that be a grave omen?

Or. Yes, silence is manifestly the better course.

Py. Thou wilt thus gain time.

Or. There is only one obstacle in my way,—

Py. What fresh objection now?

Or. I am afraid the goddesses will prevent me by madness.

Py. Nay, but I will take care of thee.

Or. A wretched task, to come in contact with a sick man.

Py. That is not my view in thy case.

Or. Beware of becoming a partner in my madness.

Py. Let that pass!

Or. Thou wilt not hesitate?

Py. Not I; hesitation is a grave mischief amongst friends.

Or. On then, pilot of my course!

Py. A service I am glad to render.

Or. And guide me to my father's tomb.

Py. For what purpose?

Or. That I may appeal to him to save me.

Py. No doubt that is the proper way.

Or. May I not even see my mother's grave!

Py. No; she was an enemy. But hasten, supporting those limbs, so slow from sickness, on mine, that the decision of Argos may not catch thee first; for I will carry thee through the town, careless of the mob and unabashed. For how shall I prove my friendship if not by helping thee in sore distress?

Or. Ah! the old saying again, "Get friends, not relations only." For a man whose soul is knit with thine, though he is not of thy kin, is better worth owning as a friend than a whole host of relations.

Exeunt ORESTES *and* PYLADES.

Ch. Long, long ago, by reason of an old misfortune to their house, the sons of Atreus saw the tide roll back from weal to woe, carrying with it their great prosperity and that prowess proudly vaunted through the length of Hellas and by the streams of Simois, on the day that strife found its way to the sons of Tantalus—that strife for a golden ram, to end in bitter banqueting and the slaughter of high-born babes; and this is why a succession of murders committed by kinsmen never fails the twin Atridæ.

What seemed so right became so wrong, to cut a mother's skin with ruthless hand and show the blood-stained sword to the sun's bright beams; and yet her guilty deed was a piece of frantic wickedness and the folly of beings demented. Hapless daughter of Tyndareus! in terror of death she screamed to him, "My son, this is a crime, thy bold attempt upon thy mother's life; do not, whilst honouring thy father, fasten on thyself an eternity of shame."

To stain the hand in a mother's blood! What affliction on earth surpasseth this? what calls for keener grief or pity? Oh! what an awful crime Agamemnon's son committed, ending in his raving madness, so that he is become a prey to the avenging fiends for the murder, darting distracted glances round him! O the wretch! to have seen a mother's bosom o'er her robe of golden woof, and yet make her his victim, in recompense for his father's sufferings!

Enter ELECTRA.

El. Surely, friends, my poor Orestes hath never left the house, mastered by the heaven-sent madness?

Ch. No; but he is gone to stand the trial appointed concerning his life before the Argive populace, in which it will be decided whether he and thou are to live or die.

El. Oh! why did he do it? who persuaded him?

Ch. Pylades; but this messenger, now close at hand, will no doubt tell us thy brother's fate at the trial.

Enter MESSENGER.

Messenger. Woe is thee, unhappy daughter of our captain Agamemnon, my lady Electra! hearken to the sad tidings I bring thee.

El. Alas! our fate is sealed; thy words show it; thou art clearly come with tidings of woe.

Mes. To-day have the folk decided by vote that thou and thy brother are to die, poor lady.

El. Alas! my expectations are realized; I have long feared this, and been wasting away in mourning for what was sure to happen. But come, old friend, describe the trial, and tell me what was said in the Argive assembly to condemn us and confirm our doom; is it stoning or the sword that is to cut short my existence? for I share my brother's misfortunes.

Mes. I had just come from the country and was entering the gates, anxious to learn what was decided about thee and Orestes—for I was ever well-disposed to thy father, and it was thy house that fed and reared me, poor, 'tis true, yet loyal in the service of friends—when lo! I saw a crowd streaming to their seats on yonder height, where 'tis said Danaus first gathered his people and settled them in new homes, when he was paying the penalty to Ægyptus. So, when I saw them thronging together, I asked a citizen, "What news in Argos? Have tidings of hostilities ruffled the city of Danaus?" But he replied, "Dost thou not see the man Orestes on his way to be tried for his life?" Then I beheld an unexpected sight, which I would I ne'er had seen—Pylades and thy brother approaching together; the one with his head sunken on his breast, weakened by sickness; the other like a brother in the way he shared his friend's sorrow, tending his complaint with constant care.

Now when the Argives were fully gathered, a herald rose and asked, "Who wishes to give his opinion whether Orestes is to be slain or not for the murder of his mother?" Then up stood Talthybius, who helped thy father sack the Phrygians' city. He adopted a trimming tone, a mere tool of those in power as he always is, expressing high admiration for thy father, but saying not a word for thy brother, urging his crooked sentiments in specious words, to this effect: "it is not a good precedent he is establishing as regards parents," and all the while he had a pleasant look for the friends of Ægisthus. That is like the tribe of heralds; they always trip across to the lucky side; whoso hath influence in the city or a post in the government, he is the friend for them. After him prince Diomedes made harangue; not death but exile was the punishment he would have had them inflict on thee and thy brother, and so keep clear of guilt. Some murmured their assent, saying his words were good, but others disapproved.

Next stood up a fellow, who cannot close his lips; one whose impudence is his strength; an Argive, but not of Argos;[1] an alien forced on us; confident in bluster and licensed ignorance, and plausible enough to involve his hearers in some mischief sooner or later; for when a man with a pleasing trick of speech, but of unsound principles, persuades the mob, it is a serious evil to the state; whereas all who give sound and sensible advice on all occasions, if not immediately useful to the state, yet prove so afterwards. And this is the light in which to regard a party leader; for the position is much the same in the case of an orator and a man in office. This fellow was for stoning thee and Orestes to death, but it was Tyndareus who kept suggesting arguments of this kind to him as he urged the death of both of you.

Another then stood up, not fair to outward view perhaps but a brave man, rarely coming in contact with the town or the gatherings in the market-place; a yeoman, one of a class who form the only real support of our country; shrewd enough, and eager to grapple with the arguments; his character without a blemish, his walk in life beyond reproach. He moved that they should crown Orestes, the son of Agamemnon, for showing his willingness to avenge a father in the blood of a wicked profligate who was preventing men from taking up arms and going on foreign service; "since," said he, "those, who remain behind, corrupt and seduce our wives left at home to keep house." To the better sort his words carried conviction; and no one rose to speak after him. So thy brother advanced and spoke. "Ye dwellers in the land of Inachus! Pelasgians in ancient times, and later Danai, I helped you no less than my father when I slew my mother; for if the murder of men by women is to be sanctioned, then the sooner you die, the better for you; otherwise you must needs become the slaves of women; and that will be doing the very reverse of what ye should. As it is, she who betrayed my father's honour has met her death, but if ye take my life, as is proposed, the strictness of the law becomes relaxed, and the sooner every one of you is dead, the better; for it will never be daring at any rate that they will lack." Yet, for all he seemed to speak so fair, he could not persuade the assembly; but that villain who spoke in favour of slaying thee and thy brother, gained his point by appealing to the mob.

Orestes, poor wretch, scarce prevailed on them to spare him death by stoning, promising to die by his own hand, and thou by thine, within the space of to-day; and Pylades is now bringing him from the conclave, weeping the while, and his friends bear him company, with tears and lamentation; so he cometh, a sad and piteous sight for thee to see. Make ready the sword, prepare the noose for thy neck, for thou must die; thy noble birth availed thee naught, nor Phœbus either from his seat on the tripod at Delphi; no! he was thy undoing.

Exit MESSENGER.

Ch. Ah, hapless maid! How dumb thou art, thy face veiled and bent upon the ground, as if ere long to start on a course of lamentation and wailing!

El. Land of Argos! I take up the dirge, doing bloody outrage on my cheek with pearly nail, and beating on my head, the meed of Persephone that fair young goddess of the nether world. Let the land of the Cyclopes break forth into wailing for the sorrows of our house, laying the steel upon the head to crop it close. This is the piteous strain that goeth up for those who are doomed to perish, the chieftains once of Hellas.

Gone, gone and brought to naught is all the race of Pelop's sons! and with them the blessedness that crowned their happy home of yore; the wrath of God gat hold on them and that cruel murdering vote which prevails among the citizens.

Woe to you! ye tribes of short-lived men, full of tears and born to suffering, see how fate runs counter to your hopes! All in time's long march receive in turn their several troubles; and man throughout his life can never rest.

[1]Said to be Cleophon, the demogogue of Athens; he was of Thracian extraction.

Oh! to reach that rock which hangs suspended midway 'twixt earth and heaven, that fragment from Olympus torn, which swings on chains of gold in ceaseless revolution, that I may utter my lament to Tantalus my forefather, who begat the ancestors of my house; these were witnesses of infatuate deeds when Pelops in four-horsed car drove winged steeds in hot pursuit along the sea, hurling the corpse of murdered Myrtilus into the heaving deep, after his race near the foam-flecked strand of Geræstus. From this came a woful curse upon my house, in the day that there appeared among the flocks of Atreus, breeder of horses, that baleful portent of a lamb with golden fleece, the creation of the son of Maia; for from it sprang a quarrel, which made the sun's winged steeds swerve from their course, turning them by a westward track along the sky towards the single horse of Dawn; and Zeus diverted the career of the seven Pleiads into a new path; yea, and it is that banquet to which Thyestes gave his name, and the guilty love of Cretan Ærope, the treacherous wife, that is requiting those murders with others; but the crowning woe is come on me and on my sire by reason of the bitter destinies of our house.

Ch. See where thy brother comes, condemned to die, and with him Pylades, most loyal of friends, true as a brother, guiding the feeble steps of Orestes, as he paces carefully at his side.

Enter ORESTES *and* PYLADES.

El. Ah! brother mine, I weep to see thee stand before the tomb, face to face with the funeral pyre. Again that sigh escapes me; my senses leave me as I take my last fond look at thee.

Or. Peace! an end to womanish lamenting! resign thyself to thy fate. True, 'tis a piteous end, but yet we needs must bear the present.

El. How can I hold my peace, when we poor sufferers are no more to gaze upon the sun-god's light?

Or. Oh! spare me *that* death! Enough that this unhappy wretch is already slain by Argives; forego our present sufferings.

El. Alas for thy young life, Orestes! alas for the untimely death o'ertaking it! Thou shouldst have begun to live just as thou art dying.

Or. Unman me not, I do adjure thee! bringing me to tears by the recollection of my sorrows.

El. We are to die, and I cannot but bemoan our fate; for all men grieve to lose dear life.

Or. This is the day appointed us; and we must fit the dangling noose about our necks or whet the sword for use.

El. Be thou my executioner, brother, that no Argive may insult the child of Agamemnon and slay her.

Or. Enough that I have a mother's blood upon me; thee I will not slay; but die by any self-inflicted death thou wilt.

El. Agreed; I will not be behind thee in using the sword; only I long to throw my arms about thy neck.

Or. Enjoy that idle satisfaction, if embraces have any joy for those who are come so nigh to death.

El. Dear brother mine! bearer of a name that sounds most sweet in thy sister's ear, partner in one soul with her!

Or. Oh! thou wilt melt my heart. I long to give thee back a fond embrace; and why should such a wretch as I feel any shame henceforth? (*Embracing* ELECTRA) Heart to heart, O sister mine! how sweet to me this close embrace! In place of wedded joys, in place of babes, this greeting is all that is possible to us poor sufferers.

El. Ah, would the self-same sword, if only it might be, could slay us both, and one coffin of cedar-wood receive us!

Or. That would be an end most sweet; but surely thou seest we are too destitute of friends to be allowed one tomb between us.

El. Did not that coward Menelaus, that traitor to my father's memory, even speak for thee, making an effort to save thy life?

Or. He did not so much as show himself, but having his hopes centred on the throne he was more cautious than to attempt the rescue of relatives.

Ah! well, let us take care to quit ourselves gallantly and die as most befits the children of Agamemnon. I, for my part, will let this city see my noble spirit when I plunge the sword to my heart, and thou, for thine, must imitate my brave example. Do thou, Pylades, stand umpire to our bloody feat, and, when we both are dead, lay out our bodies decently; then carry them to our father's grave and bury us there with him. Farewell now; I go to do the deed, as thou seest.

Py. Stay a moment; there is first one point I have to blame thee for, if thou thinkest I care to live when thou art dead.

Or. But why art thou called on to die with me?

Py. Canst ask? What is life to me with thee my comrade gone?

Or. Thou didst not slay thy mother, as I did to my sorrow.

Py. At least I helped thee; and so I ought to suffer alike.

Or. Surrender to thy father; and seek not to die with me. Thou hast still a city, while I no longer have; thou hast still thy father's home, and mighty stores of wealth; and though thou art disappointed in thy marriage with my poor sister, whom I betrothed to thee from a deep regard for thy fellowship, yet choose thee another bride and rear a family; for the tie which bound us binds no more. Fare thee well, my comrade fondly called; for us such faring cannot be, for thee perhaps; for we that are as dead are robbed of joy henceforth.

Py. How far thou art from grasping what I mean! Oh! may the fruitful earth, the radiant sky refuse to hold my blood, if ever I turn traitor and desert thee when I have cleared myself; for I not only shared in the murder, which I will not disown, but also schemed the whole plot for which thou art now paying the penalty; wherefore I ought also to die as much as thou or she; for I consider her, whose hand thou didst promise me, as my wife. What specious tale shall I ever tell, when I reach Delphi, the citadel of Phocis? I who, before your misfortunes came, was so close a friend, but ceased to be, when thou wert unlucky. That must not be; no! this is my business too. But since we are to die, let us take counsel together that Menelaus may share our misfortune.

Or. Best of friends! if only I could see this ere I die!

Py. Hearken then, and defer awhile the fatal stroke.

Or. I will wait in the hope of avenging me on my foe.

Py. Hush! I have small confidence in women.

Or. Have no fear of these; for they are our friends who are here.

Py. Let us kill Helen, a bitter grief to Menelaus.

Or. How? I am ready enough, if there is any chance of success.

Py. With our swords; she is hiding in thy house.

Or. Aye, that she is, and already she is putting her seal on everything.

Py. She shall do so no more, after she is wedded to Hades.

Or. Impossible! she has her barbarian attendants.

Py. Barbarians indeed! I am not the man to fear any Phrygian.

Or. Creatures only fit to look after mirrors and unguents!

Py. What! has she brought Trojan effeminacy with her here?

Or. So much so that Hellas is become too small for her to live in.

Py. The race of slaves is no match for free-born men.

Or. Well, if I can do this deed, I fear not death twice over.

Py. No, nor I either, if it is thee I am avenging.

Or. Declare the matter and tell me what thou proposest.

Py. We will enter the house on the pretence of going to our death.

Or. So far I follow thee, but not beyond.

Py. We will begin bewailing our sufferings to her.

Or. Aye, so that she will shed tears, although her heart is glad.

Py. And we shall then be in the same predicament as she.

Or. How shall we proceed next in the enterprise?

Py. We shall have swords concealed in our cloaks.

Or. But, before attacking her, how are we to kill her attendants?

Py. We will shut them up in different parts of the house.

Or. And whoever refuses to be quiet, we must kill.

Py. That done, our very deed shows us to what we must direct our efforts.

Or. To Helen's slaughter; I understand that watchword.

Py. Thou hast it; now hear how sound my scheme is; if we had drawn the sword upon a woman of better morals, it would have been foul murder; but, as it is, she will be punished for the sake of all Hellas, whose sires she slew; while those whose children she destroyed, whose wives she widowed, will shout aloud for joy and kindle the altars of the gods, invoking on our heads a thousand blessings, because we shed this wicked woman's blood; for after killing her, thy name shall no more be "the matricide," but, resigning that title, thou shalt succeed to a better and be called "the slayer of Helen the murderess." It can never, never be right that Menelaus should prosper, and thy father, thy sister and thou be put to death, and thy mother too—(but I pass that by, for it is not seemly to mention it)—while he possesses thy home, though it was by Agamemnon's prowess that he recovered his wife. May I perish then, if I draw not my sword upon her! But if after all we fail to compass Helen's death, we will fire the palace and die; for we will not fail to achieve one distinction, be it an honourable death or an honourable escape therefrom.

Ch. The daughter of Tyndareus, who has brought shame on her sex, has justly earned the hate of every woman.

Or. Ah! there is nothing better than a trusty friend, neither wealth nor princely power; mere number is a senseless thing to set off against a noble friend. Such art thou, for thou didst not only devise the vengeance we took on Ægisthus, but didst stand by me at the gates of danger, and now again thou art offering me a means to punish my foes and dost not stand aloof thyself; but I will cease praising thee, for there is something wearisome even in being praised to excess. Now since in any case I must breathe my last, I would fain my death should do my foes some hurt, that I may requite with ruin those who betrayed me, and that they too who made me suffer may taste of sorrow. Lo! I am the son of that Agamemnon, who was counted worthy to rule Hellas, exerting no tyrant's power but yet possessed of almost god-like might; him will I not disgrace by submitting to die like a slave; no! my last breath shall be free and I will avenge me on Menelaus. For could we but secure one object we should be lucky, if from some unexpected quarter a means of safety should arise and we be the slayers, not the slain; this is what I pray for; for this wish of mine is a pleasant dream to cheer the heart, without cost, by means of the tongue's winged utterances.

El. Why, brother, I have it! a means of safety, first for thee, then for him, and thirdly for myself.

Or. Divine providence, I suppose. But what use in suggesting that? seeing that I know the natural shrewdness of thy heart.

El. Hearken a moment; do thou (*to* PYLADES) likewise attend.

Or. Say on; the prospect of hearing good news affords a certain pleasure.

El. Thou knowest Helen's daughter? of course thou must.

Or. Hermione, whom my own mother reared—know her? yes.

El. She hath gone to Clytæmnestra's grave.

Or. With what intent? What hope art thou hinting at?

El. Her purpose was to pour a libation over the tomb of our mother.

Or. Well, granting that, how does this which thou hast mentioned conduce to our safety?

El. Seize her as a hostage on her way back.

Or. What good can thy suggested remedy do us three friends?

El. If, after Helen's slaughter, Menelaus does anything to thee or to Pylades and me—for we three friends are wholly one—say thou wilt slay Hermione; then draw thy sword and keep it at the maiden's throat. If Menelaus, when he sees Helen weltering in her blood, tries to save thee to insure his daughter's life, allow him to take his child to his father's arms; but if he makes no effort to curb the angry outburst and leaves thee to die, then do thou plunge thy sword in his daughter's throat. Methinks, though he show himself violent at first, he will gradually grow milder; for he is not naturally bold or brave. That is the tower of defence I have for us, and now my tale is told.

Or. O thou that hast the spirit of a man, though thy body clearly shows thee a tender woman, how far more worthy thou to live than die! This, Pylades, is the peerless woman thou wilt lose to thy sorrow, or, shouldst thou live, wilt marry to thy joy!

Py. Then may I live and may she be brought to the capital of Phocis with all the honours of a happy marriage!

Or. How soon will Hermione return to the palace? All else thou saidst was well, if only we are lucky in catching the villain's child.

El. I expect she is near the house already, for the time agrees exactly.

Or. 'Tis well. Plant thyself before the palace, Electra my sister, and await the maid's approach; keep watch in case any one, an ally maybe or my father's brother, forestal us by his entry, ere the bloody deed is completed; and then make a signal to be heard inside the house, either by beating on a panel of the door or calling to us within.

Let us enter now, Pylades, and arm ourselves for the final struggle, for thou art the comrade that sharest the enterprise with me. Hearken! father, in thy home of darkest gloom! it is thy son Orestes who is calling thee to come to the rescue of the destitute; it is on thy account I am unjustly suffering woe, and it is by thy brother that I have been betrayed for practising justice; wherefore I would fain take and slay his wife; and do thou help us compass this.

El. Oh! come, my father, come! if within the ground thou hearest the cry of thy children, who for thy sake are dying.

Py. Hear my prayer too, Agamemnon, kinsman of my father, and save thy children.

Or. I slew my mother—

Py. I held the sword—

El. 'Twas I that urged them on and set them free from fear—

Or. All to succour thee, my sire.

El. I proved no traitress either.

Py. Wilt thou not hearken then to these reproaches and save thy children?

Or. With tears I pour thee a libation.

El. And I with notes of woe.

Py. Cease, and let us about our business. If prayers do really penetrate the ground, he hears. O Zeus, god of my fathers, O Justice, queen revered, vouchsafe us three success; three friends are we, but one the struggle, one the forfeit all must pay, to live or die.

Exeunt ORESTES *and* PYLADES.

El. My own townswomen, of foremost rank in Argos, the home of the Pelasgi!

Ch. Mistress, why dost thou address us? for still this honoured name is left thee in the Danaid town.

El. Station yourselves, some here along the high road, others yonder on some other path, to watch the house.

Ch. But why dost thou summon me to this service? tell me, dear mistress.

El. I am afraid that some one, who is stationed at the house for a bloody purpose, may cause troubles, only to find them himself.

Semi-Chorus I. Lead on; let us hasten; I will keep careful watch upon this track towards the east.

Semi-Ch. II. And I on this, that leadeth westward. Throw a glance sideways, letting the eye range from point to point; then look back again.

Semi Ch. I. We are directing them as thou biddest.

El. Cast your eyes around, let them peer in every direction through your tresses.

Semi-Ch. II. Who is that on the road? Who is yonder countryman I see wandering round thy house?

El. Ah! friends, we are undone; he will at once reveal to our enemies the armed ambush of that lion-like pair.

Semi-Ch. I. (*Reconnoitring*) Calm thy fears; the road is not occupied, as thou thinkest, dear mistress.

El. (*Turning to the other watchers*) And can I count thy side safe still? reassure me; is yonder space before the court-yard still deserted?

Semi-Ch. II. All goes well here; look to thy own watch, for no Argive is approaching us.

Semi-Ch. I. Thy report agrees with mine; there is no noise here either.

El. Well then, let me make myself heard in the gateway. (*Calling through the door*) Why are ye within the house delaying to spill your victim's blood, now that all is quiet? They do not hear; ah, woe is me! Can it be that their swords have lost their edge at the sight of her beauty? Soon will some mail-clad Argive, hurrying to her rescue, attack the palace. Keep a better look-out; 'tis no time for sitting still; bestir yourselves, some here, some there.

Ch. My eye is ranging to and fro all along the road.

Hel. (*Within*) Help, Pelasgian Argos! I am being foully murdered.

Semi-Ch. I. Heard ye that? Those men are now about the bloody deed.

Semi-Ch. II. 'Tis Helen screaming, to hazard a guess.

El. Come, eternal might of Zeus, oh, come to help my friends!

Hel. (*Within*) Menelaus, I am being murdered, but thou, though near, affordest me no aid.

El. Cut, stab, and kill; all eager for the fray dart out your swords, double-handed, double-edged, against the woman who left her father's home and husband's side, and did to death so many of the men of Hellas, slain beside the river-bank, where tears rained down beneath the iron darts all round Scamander's eddying tides.

Ch. Hush! hush! I caught the sound of a foot-fall on the road near the house.

El. Ladies, my dearest friends, it is Hermione advancing into the midst of the bloodshed. Let our clamour cease; on she comes headlong into the meshes of the net. Fair will the quarry prove if caught. Resume your station, looks composed and faces not betraying what has happened; and I too will wear a look of melancholy, as if forsooth I knew nothing of that desperate deed. (HERMIONE *enters*) Ah! maiden, hast thou come from wreathing Clytemnestra's grave and from pouring libations to the dead?

Her. Yes, I have returned after securing a gracious recognition; but I was filled with some alarm as to the import of a cry I heard in the palace as I was still at a distance.

El. But why? Our present lot gives cause for groans.

Her. Hush! What is thy news?

El. Argos has sentenced Orestes and myself to death.

Her. Kinsfolk of my own! God forbid!

El. It is decreed; the yoke of necessity is on our necks.

Her. Was this the reason then of the cry within?

El. Yes, 'twas the cry of the suppliant as he fell at Helen's knees.

Her. Who is he? I am none the wiser, if thou tell me not.

El. Orestes the hapless, entreating mercy for himself and me.

Her. Good reason then has the house to cry out.

El. What else would make a man entreat more earnestly? Come, throw thyself before thy mother in her proud prosperity, and join thy friends in beseeching Menelaus not to look on and see us die. O thou that wert nursed in the same mother's arms as I, have pity on us and relieve our pain. Come hither to the struggle, and I myself will be thy guide; for thou and thou alone, hast the issue of our safety in thy hands.

Her. Behold me hastening to the house; as far as rests with me, regard yourselves as safe.

Exit HERMIONE.

El. Now, friends, secure the prey in your armed ambush in the house.

Her. (*Calling from within*) Ah! who are these I see?

Or. (*Within*) Silence! 'tis our safety, not thine, thou art here to insure.

El. Hold her hard and fast; point a sword at her throat; then wait in silence, that Menelaus may learn that they are men, not Phrygian cowards, whom he has found and treated as only cowards deserve.

Ch. What ho! my comrades, raise a din, a din and shouting before the house, that the murder done may not inspire the Argives with wild alarm, to make them bring aid to the royal palace, before I see for certain whether Helen's corpse lies weltering in the house or hear the news from one of her attendants; for I know but a part of the tragedy, of the rest I am not sure. Thanks to Justice the wrath of God has come on Helen; for she filled all Hellas with tears because of her accursed paramour, Paris of Ida, who took our countrymen to Troy.

But hist! the bolts of the palace-doors rattle; be silent; for one of her Phrygians is coming out, from whom we will inquire of the state of matters within.

Enter PHRYGIAN EUNUCH.

Phrygian Eunuch. (*Expressing the most abject terror*) From death escaped, in my barbaric slippers have I fled away, away from the Argive sword, escaping as best a barbarian might by clambering over the cedar beams that roof the porch and through the Doric triglyphs. (O my country, my country!) Alack, alack! oh! whither can I fly, ye foreign dames, winging my way through the clear bright sky or over the sea, whose circle hornèd Ocean draws, as he girdles the world in his embrace?

Ch. What news, slave of Helen, creature from Ida?

P.E. Ah me for Ilium, for Ilium, the city of Phrygia, and for Ida's holy hill with fruitful soil! in foreign accents hear me raise a plaintive strain over thee, whose ruin luckless Helen caused—that lovely child whom Leda bore to a feathered swan, to be a curse to Apollo's towers of polished stone. Ah! well-a-day! woe to Dardania for the wailings wrung from it by the steeds that bought his minion Ganymede for Zeus.

Ch. Tell us plainly exactly what happened in the house, for till now I have been guessing at what I do not clearly understand.

P.E. "Ah, for Linus! woe is him!" that is what barbarians say in their eastern tongue as a prelude to the dirge of death, whene'er royal blood is spilt upon the ground by deadly iron blades.

To tell thee exactly what happened; there came into the palace two lion-like men of Hellas, twins in nature; your famous chief was sire of one, 'twas said; the other was the son of Strophius; a crafty knave was he, like to Odysseus, subtle, silent, but staunch to his friends, daring enough for any valiant deed, versed in war and bloodthirsty as a serpent. Ruin seize him for his quiet plotting, the villain!

In they came, their eyes bedimmed with tears, and took their seats in all humility near the chair of the lady whom Paris the archer once wedded, one on this side, one on that, to right and left, with weapons on them; and both threw their suppliant arms round the knees of Helen; whereon her Phrygian servants started to their feet in wild alarm, each in his terror calling to his fellow, "Beware of treachery!" To some there seemed no cause, but others thought that the viper, who had slain his mother, was entangling the daughter of Tyndareus in the toils of his snare.

Ch. And where wert thou the while? fled long before in terror?

P.E. It happened that I, in Phrygian style, was wafting the breeze past Helen's curls with a round feather-fan, stationed before her face; and she the while, as eastern ladies use, was twisting flax on her distaff with her fingers but letting her yarn fall on the floor, for she was minded to embroider purple raiment as an offering from the Trojan spoils, a gift for Clytaemnestra at her tomb.

Then to the Spartan maid Orestes spake, "Daughter of Zeus, quit thy chair and cross the floor to a seat at the old altar of Pelops, our ancestor, to hear something I have to say." Therewith he led the way and she followed, little guessing his designs. Meantime his accomplice, the Phocian miscreant, was off on other business. "Out of my way! Well, Phrygians always were cowards." So he shut them up in different parts of the house, some in the stables, others in private chambers, one here, one there, disposing of them severally at a distance from their mistress.

Ch. What happened next?

P.E. Mother of Ida, mighty parent! Oh! the murderous scenes and lawless wickedness that I witnessed in the royal palace! They drew forth swords from under their purple cloaks, each darting his eye all round him in either direction to see that none was near, and then, like boars that range the hills, they stood at bay before her, crying, "Thou must die; it is thy craven husband that will slay thee, because he betrayed his brother's son to death in Argos." But she with piercing screams brought down her snow-white arm upon her bosom and loudly smote on her poor head; then turned her steps in flight, shod in her golden shoon; but Orestes, outstripping her slippered feet, clutched his fingers in her hair and bending back her neck on to her left shoulder was on the point of driving the grim steel into her throat.

Ch. Where were those Phrygians in the house to help her then?

P.E. With a loud cry we battered down the doors and doorposts of the rooms we had been penned in, by means of bars, and ran to her assistance from every direction, one arming himself with stones, another with javelins, a third having a drawn sword; but Pylades came to meet us, all undaunted, like Hector of Troy or Aias triple-plumed, as I saw him on the threshold of Priam's palace; and we met point to point. But then it became most manifest how inferior we Phrygians were to the warriors of Hellas in martial prowess. There was one man flying, another slain, a third wounded, yet another craving mercy to stave off death; but we escaped under cover of the darkness; while some were falling, others staggering, and some laid low in death. And just as her unhappy mother sunk to the ground to die, came luckless Hermione to the palace; whereon those twain, like Bacchanals when they drop their wands and seize a mountain-cub, rushed and seized her; then turned again to the daughter of Zeus to slay her; but lo! she had vanished from the room, passing right through the house by magic spells or wizards' arts or heavenly fraud; O Zeus and earth, O day and night!

What happened afterwards I know not, for I stole out of the palace and ran away. So Menelaus went through all his toil and trouble to recover his wife Helen from Troy to no purpose.

Ch. Behold another strange sight succeeding its predecessors; I see Orestes sword in hand before the palace, advancing with excited steps.

Enter ORESTES.

Or. Where is he who fled from the palace to escape my sword?

P.E. (*Falling at the feet of* ORESTES) Before thee I prostrate myself, O prince, and do obeisance in my foreign way.

Or. 'Tis not Ilium that is now the scene, but the land of Argos.

P.E. No matter where, the wise love life more than death.

Or. I suppose that shouting of thine was not for Menelaus to come to the rescue?

P.E. Oh no! it was to help thee I called out, for thou art more deserving.

Or. Was it a just fate that overtook the daughter of Tyndareus?

P.E. Most just, though she had had three throats to die with.

Or. Thy cowardice makes thee glib; these are not thy real sentiments.

P.E. Why, surely she deserved it for the havoc she made of Hellas as well as Troy?

Or. Swear thou art not saying this to humour me, or I will slay thee.

P.E. By my life I swear—an oath likely to be true in my case.

Or. Did every Phrygian in Troy show the same terror of steel as thou dost?

P.E. Oh, take thy sword away! held so near it throws a horrid gleam of blood.

Or. Art thou afraid of being turned to stone, as if it were a Gorgon thou seest?

P.E. To a stone, no! but to a corpse; that Gorgon's head is not within my ken.

Or. A slave, and so fearful of death, which will release thee from trouble!

P.E. Bond or free, every one is glad to gaze upon the light.

Or. Well said! thy shrewdness saves thee; go within.

P.E. Thou wilt not kill me after all?

Or. Thou art spared!

P.E. O gracious words!

Or. Come, I shall change my mind—

P.E. Ill-omened utterance!

Or. Thou fool! dost think I could endure to plunge my sword in throat of thine, thou that neither art woman nor amongst men hast any place? The reason I left the palace was to gag thy noisy tongue; for Argos is quickly roused, once it hears a cry to the rescue. As for Menelaus, we are not afraid of measuring swords with him; no! he may go upon his way proud of the golden ringlets on his shoulders; for if, to avenge the slaying of Helen, he gathers the Argives and leads them against the palace, refusing to attempt the rescue of me, my sister, and Pylades my fellow-conspirator, he shall have two corpses to behold, his daughter's as well as his wife's. *Exeunt* ORESTES *and the* PHRYGIAN EUNUCH.

Ch. Ah! fortune, fortune! again and yet again the house is entering on a fearful contest for the race of Atreus.

Semi-Ch. I. What are we to do? carry tidings to the town, or hold our peace?

Semi-Ch. II. It is safer to keep silence, friends.

Semi-Ch. I. Look, look at that sudden rush of smoke to the sky in front of the palace, telling its tale in advance!

Semi-Ch. II. They are kindling torches to fire the halls of Tantalus; they do not shrink even from murder.

Ch. God holds the issue in his hand, to give to mortal men what end he will. Some mighty power is his; it was through a vengeful fiend that this family started on its career of murder, by reason of the hurling of Myrtilus from the chariot.

But lo! I see Menelaus approaching the palace in hot haste; no doubt he has heard what is happening here. (*Calling inside*) What ho! within, descendants of Atreus, make haste and secure the doors with bars. A man in luck is a dangerous adversary for luckless wretches like thyself, Orestes. ORESTES *and* PYLADES *appear on the roof, holding* HERMIONE.

Enter MENELAUS.

Men. Strange news of violent deeds perpetrated by a pair of savages—men I do not call them—has brought me hither. What I heard was that my wife was not killed after all, but had vanished out of sight—an idle rumour doubtless, brought to me by some dupe of his own terror; a ruse perhaps of the matricide to turn the laugh against me.

Throw wide the palace doors! My orders to my servants are that they force the doors, that I may rescue my child at any rate from the hands of the murderers and recover my poor wife's corpse, that dear partner whose slayers must die with her by my arm.

Or. (*From the roof*) Ho, fellow! Keep thy fingers off those bolts, thou Menelaus, who vauntest thyself so high; else I will tear off the ancient parapet, the work of masons, and shatter thy skull with this coping-stone. The doors are bolted and barred, which will prevent thy entrance to the palace and thy eagerness to bring aid.

Men. Ha! what now? I see a blaze of torches and men standing at bay on the house-top yonder, with a sword held at my daughter's throat.

Or. Wouldst question me or hear me speak?

Men. Neither; but I suppose I *must* hear thee.

Or. Well, if thou art anxious to know, I intend to slay thy daughter.

Men. After slaying Helen, art thou bent on adding another murder?

Or. I would I had compassed that, instead of being duped by the gods!

Men. Dost thou deny having slain her, saying this out of wanton insult?

Or. Yes, I do deny it to my sorrow. Would God—

Men. Would God—what? Thou provokest my fears.

Or. I had hurled to Hades the pollution of Hellas!

Men. Surrender my wife's dead body, that I may bury her.

Or. Ask the gods for her; but thy daughter I will slay.

Men. This matricide is bent on adding murder to murder.

Or. This champion of his sire, betrayed by thee to death.

Men. Art thou not content with the stain of the mother's blood which is on thee?

Or. I should not grow tired if I had these wicked women to slay for ever.

Men. Art thou too, Pylades, a partner in this bloody work?

Or. His silence says he is; so my saying it will suffice.

Men. Not without thy ruing it, unless thou take wings and fly.

Or. Fly we never will, but will fire the palace.

Men. What! wilt thou destroy the home of thy ancestors?

Or. To prevent thee getting it I will, offering this maid in sacrifice upon its flames.

Men. Kill her, for thou wilt be punished by me for such a murder.

Or. Agreed.

Men. No, no! refrain!

Or. Silence! thy sufferings are just; endure them.

Men. Pray, is it just that thou shouldst live?

Or. And rule a kingdom, yes.

Men. A kingdom—where?

Or. Here in Pelasgian Argos.

Men. Thou art so well qualified to handle sacred water!

Or. And, pray, why not?

Men. And to slay victims before battle!

Or. Well, art thou?

Men. Yes, my hands are clean.

Or. But not thy heart.

Men. Who would speak to thee?

Or. Every man that loves his father.

Men. And the man who honours his mother?

Or. He's a happy man.

Men. Thou didst not honour thine, at any rate.

Or. No, for I delight not in your wicked women.

Men. Remove that sword from my daughter's throat.

Or. Thou art wrong.

Men. What! wilt slay her?

Or. Right once more.

Men. Ah me! what can I do?

Or. Go to the Argives and persuade them—

Men. To what?

Or. Entreat the city that we may not die.

Men. Otherwise, will ye slay my child?

Or. That is the alternative.

Men. Alas for thee, Helen!

Or. And is it not "alas!" for me?

Men. I brought her back from Troy only for thee to butcher.

Or. Would I had!

Men. After troubles innumerable.

Or. Except where I was concerned.

Men. Dreadful treatment mine!

Or. The reason being thy refusal to help me then?

Men. Thou hast me there.

Or. Thy own cowardice has. (*Calling from the roof to* ELECTRA) Ho there! fire the palace from beneath, Electra; and, Pylades, my trusty friend, kindle the parapet of yonder walls. (*The palace is seen to be ablaze.*)

Men. Help, help, ye Danai! gird on your harness and come, ye dwellers in knightly Argos! for here is a fellow trying to wrest his life from your whole city, though he has caused pollution by shedding his mother's blood.

APOLLO *appears in the clouds with* HELEN.

Apollo. Menelaus, calm thy excited mood; I am Phœbus, the son of Latona, who draw nigh to call thee by name, and thou no less, Orestes, who, sword in hand, art keeping guard on yonder maid, that thou mayst hear what I have come to say. Helen, whom all thy eagerness failed to destroy, when thou wert seeking to anger Menelaus, is here as ye see in the enfolding air, rescued from death instead of slain by thee. 'Twas I that saved her and snatched her from beneath thy sword at the bidding of her father Zeus; for she his child must put on immortality, and take her place with Castor and Polydeuces in the bosom of the sky, a saviour to mariners. Choose thee then another bride and take her to thy home, for the gods by means of Helen's loveliness embroiled Troy and Hellas, causing death thereby, that they might lighten mother Earth of the outrage done her by man's excessive population. Such is Helen's end.

But as for thee, Orestes, thou must cross the frontier of this land and dwell for one whole year on Parrhasian soil, which from thy flight thither shall be called the land of Orestes by Azanians and Arcadians; and when thou returnest thence to the city of Athens, submit to be brought to trial by "the Avenging Three" for thy mother's murder, for the gods will be umpires between you and will pass a most righteous sentence on thee upon the hill of Ares, where thou art to win thy case. Likewise, it is ordained, Orestes, that thou shalt wed Hermione, at whose neck thou art pointing thy sword; Neoptolemus shall never marry her, though he thinks he will; for his death is fated to o'ertake him by a Delphian sword, when he claims satisfaction of me for the death of his father Achilles.[1] Bestow thy sister's hand on Pylades, to whom thou didst formerly promise her; the life awaiting him henceforth is one of bliss.

Menelaus, leave Orestes to rule Argos; go thou and reign o'er Sparta, keeping it as the dowry of a wife, who till this day ne'er ceased exposing thee to toils innumerable. Between Orestes and the citizens, I, who forced his mother's murder on him, will bring about a reconciliation.

Or. Hail to thee, prophetic Loxias, for these thy utterances! Thou art not a lying prophet after all, but a true seer; and yet there came a dreadful thought into my heart that it was some fiend I had listened to, when I seemed to hear thy voice; but all is ending well, and I obey thy word. There! I release Hermione from a violent death and agree to make her my wife whenever her father gives consent.

Men. All hail, Helen, daughter of Zeus! I wish thee joy of thy home in heaven's happy courts.

To thee, Orestes, I betroth my daughter according to the word of Phœbus, and good luck attend thee, a noble wooer nobly wived, and me the parent of thy bride!

Ap. Repair each one of you to the place appointed by me; reconcile all strife.

Men. Obedience is a duty.

Or. I think so too, Menelaus; so here I make a truce with sorrow and with thy oracles, O Loxias.

Ap. Go your ways, and honour Peace, most fair of goddesses; I, meantime, will escort Helen to the mansions of Zeus, soon as I reach the star-lit firmament. There, seated side by side with Hera and Hebe, the bride of Heracles, she shall be honoured by men with drink-offerings as a goddess for ever, sharing with those Zeus-born sons of Tyndareus their empire o'er the sea, for the good of mariners.

Ch. Hail! majestic Victory, still in thy keeping hold my life and ne'er withhold the crown!

Exeunt OMNES.

[1] Cf. *Andromache* ll. 1085, *seq.*

IPHIGENIA AMONG THE TAURI

DRAMATIS PERSONAE

IPHIGENIA
ORESTES
PYLADES
CHORUS OF CAPTIVE WOMEN, *from Hellas*
HERDSMAN
THOAS, *King of the Tauri*
MESSENGER
ATHENA

On the sea-shore, in the Tauric Chersonese, near a temple of Artemis. Enter IPHIGENIA.

Iphigenia. Pelops, the son of Tantalus, came to Pisa with swift steeds and won his bride, the daughter of Œnomaus, who bare Atreus to him; Atreus had issue Menelaus and Agamemnon; and I am Agamemnon's child, Iphigenia, by the daughter of Tyndareus, the maid whom 'tis thought my father offered to Artemis for the sake of Helen in the famous bay of Aulis, hard by the eddies which Euripus turneth ever to and fro before the changing breeze, as he rolls along his deep dark wave; for there it was that king Agamemnon gathered a fleet of a thousand ships from Hellas, wishing his Achæans to win the fair crown of victory over Ilium and avenge the outrage offered to Helen's marriage-vow, all for the sake of Menelaus. But when, owing to foul weather, he could not get a favouring wind, he had recourse to the diviner's flame, and this was what Calchas told him: "O Agamemnon, captain of this host of Hellas, no chance hast thou of unmooring thy ships, till Artemis has received thy daughter Iphigenia in sacrifice; for thou didst vow to offer to the goddess of light the fairest thing the year produced. Now thy wife Clytaemnestra has given birth to a daughter in thy house, whom thou must sacrifice," ascribing to me the title of "fairest"; and by the arts of Odysseus they took me from my mother's side, on the pretext of wedding me to Achilles; but, when I reached Aulis, I was seized, poor maid, and lifted high above the pyre; I saw the sword in act to strike, when Artemis stole me out of the Achæans' hands, leaving a hind in my place; and she carried me through the radiant air and set me to dwell here in the land of the Tauri, where a barbarian is king over barbarians, e'en Thoas, whose name is due to his fleetness, for swift as a bird on the wing he speeds his course. He made me priestess in the temple here; and this is why, in accordance with the observances of a festival in which the goddess Artemis delights, a festival fair only in name—but I say no more from fear of that deity; for I sacrifice each son of Hellas who touches at these shores, this being the custom in the city even before I came; I begin the rite, but the awful act of slaughter belongs to others inside the shrine of the goddess.

Strange visions the past night brought me, which I will tell to the air, if there is really any help in that. As I slept, methought I had escaped this land and was once more in Argos, sleeping in the midst of my maidens, when lo! the surface of the ground was shaken by an earthquake; whereat I fled, and, standing outside the house, I saw its coping falling and the whole building dashed in ruin from roof to base. Only one column, methought, of my father's halls was left standing, and from its capital it let stream the auburn hair and took a human tongue; and I, observant of the murderous craft I practise against strangers, began sprinkling it, as it had been a victim, weeping the while.

Now this is my interpretation of the dream: Orestes is dead; 'twas for him I began the rites; for son are the pillars of a house, and death is the lot of all whom once my lustral waters sprinkle. Again, I cannot fix the dream upon my friends, for Strophius had no son at the time I was called to die. Now therefore I mean to pour a drink-offering to my brother who is far from me here, for this I can do, with the help of the maidens from Hellas whom the king has given me as attendants. But wherefore are they not yet here? I will enter the courts of the goddess's temple, where I dwell. *Exit* IPHIGENIA.

Enter ORESTES *and* PYLADES.

Orestes. (*Entering cautiously*) Take care and see whether there is any one in the road.

Pylades. I am doing so, keeping a careful look-out in every direction.

Or. Thinkest thou, Pylades, this is the abode of the goddess towards which we steered our sea-borne barque from Argos?

Py. I think it is, Orestes; and thou must share my opinion.

Or. And is that the altar, o'er which the blood of Hellenes trickles?

Py. Its edges at any rate are discoloured with blood-stains.

Or. Dost see a string of spoils just beneath the coping?

Py. Aye, trophies of strangers who have been murdered.

Or. Well, we must cast our eyes all round and keep a good look-out.

Ah, Phœbus! why have thy oracles brought me

once more into this strait, after I had avenged the blood of my sire by slaying my mother? An exile from hearth and home, I was persecuted by relays of avenging fiends, completing many a lengthy course. So I went and questioned thee how to find an end to the whirling madness and distress I was enduring in ranging up and down through Hellas; and thy answer was that I should seek the confines of the Taurian land, where Artemis thy sister has her altars, and take from thence an image of the goddess, which fell from heaven, so men say, into her temple there; then when I had secured it by craft or luck maybe, when every risk was run, I was to present it to the land of Athens. Beyond this naught was said; that done, I was to have relief from trouble. So in obedience to thy bidding I have come hither to a strange and cheerless shore.

Now, Pylades, as my partner in this hard emprise, I ask thee, what are we to do? for thou seest the height of these encircling walls. Shall we mount the steps leading to the building? how then escape detection? or can we force the brazen bolts with levers, when we know nothing about them? If we are caught trying to open the doors or plotting an entrance, we shall be slain; ere that let us escape upon our ship, wherein we sailed hither.

Py. Flight is intolerable; we are not used to it; and the god's oracle must not be slighted; but let us quit the temple and hide ourselves in some cavern, washed by the sea's black tide, apart from our ship, lest some one see it and tell the rulers, and we be then seized by force. But when the eye of darksome night appears, we must e'en dare to take the polished image from the shrine, bringing all our craft to bear on it. Look there between the rafters, where an empty space is left by which to lower oneself. 'Tis well; the brave can face hardship, but cowards are never of any account. What! shall we, after toiling at the oar so long and far, turn back again and leave the goal?

Or. Well said! obedience is my cue. We must find some spot where we can both hide ourselves out of sight; for assuredly the god will not be the cause of his own oracle falling fruitless to the ground; courage is all that is required, for the young have no excuse for shirking toil.

Exeunt ORESTES *and* PYLADES.

Enter IPHIGENIA *and* CHORUS.

Chorus. Hush! a solemn silence! ye dwellers on the double clashing rocks that guard the Euxine sea!

All hail, Latona's child, Dictynna, goddess of the hills! to thy court I guide my steps in maiden saintliness, to thy gilded dome with beauteous colonnades, to wait on her that keeps thy keys in holy trust, bidding farewell for this to the embattled walls of Hellas, the land of horses, to Eurotas with its meadows 'mid the trees, where stood my father's house.

I am here; what news? why so thoughtful? wherefore hast thou summoned me to the temple? O daughter of him who sought the towers of Troy with the famous fleet of a thousand ships and their crews of countless warriors, gathered by the noble sons of Atreus!

Ip. My handmaids, ye find me busied with most woful dirges, dismal strains ne'er uttered by the Muse, as I mourn a kinsman dead, ah me! for this is the trouble that has befallen me; I am weeping for my brother reft of life, so sure the vision I beheld in the darkness of the night just past.

Undone! undone! Ah me! my father's house is now no more; our race is dead and gone. Woe! woe for the troubles in Argos! Out on thee, destiny! that robbest me of my only brother, sending him to Hades; for him I am about to pour this offering on the lap of earth, a cup for the departed dead—milk of mountain-roving kine, a draught of Bacchus' own drink, and what the russet bees have garnered by their toil—the soothing gift which custom gives the dead.

(*To a servant*) Hand me the solid urn of gold, the death-god's drink-offering.

Scion of Agamemnon's line beneath the earth! to thee as dead I send these gifts; accept them thus, for I shall never bring thee at thy tomb my golden locks or tears; for very far I dwell from the land of our fathers, where men thought this luckless maiden died beneath the knife.

Ch. Lady, to thee will I now pour out an answering strain, an eastern dirge that wails in foreign key, a litany of woe, chanted o'er the dead in mourning, a song of Hades' singing, wherein the pæan plays no part.

Woe for the royal house of the Atridæ! its light is quenched. Woe for their ancestral home! Who of all the prosperous kings in Argos shall rule o'er it? Trouble born of trouble darteth on it; and the sun-god with winged careering steeds turned from his place and changed his light divine. Woe on woe, and death on death, with anguish unto anguish added, has come upon this house, all for a golden lamb; from this source vengeance made its way into the family for those who were slain before of the race of Tantalus; while against thee Fate is eager in the pursuit of mischief.

Ip. Bitter to me from the very first the fate of my mother's marriage; from the first on that night I was conceived, the goddesses, who rule men's destiny, strove to make my childhood hard. I was the first fair babe she bore in her marriage-bower, that hapless daughter of Leda whom all Hellas wooed, born and reared by her to be the victim of my father's despite, a joyless offering, when, to pay his vow, they brought me in a chariot drawn by steeds and set me on the strand of Aulis to be the bride—ah! bride of sorrow—to the Nereid's son. But now beside the ruthless sea I make my cheerless home, an alien, torn from home and friends, with none to call me wife or mother; never singing Hera's praise, my queen in Argos, nor 'mid the merry whirr of looms broidering with the shuttle a picture of Athenian Pallas and the Titans, but staining altars instead with the streaming blood of doomed strangers, whose moans and tears are piteous, no theme for minstrel's lyre. Of them I am not thinking now, but I weep for my brother, dead in Argos, even for Orestes the heir to the Argive throne, whom I left a babe unweaned, an infant in his mother's arms, still hanging at her breast.

Ch. Behold, a herdsman is come from the beach to bring thee tidings.

Enter HERDSMAN.

Herdsman. Daughter of Agamemnon and Clytaemnestra hearken to the news I have to tell.

Ip. Why, what is here to interrupt our present conversation?

He. Two youths, escaping on a ship, have reached the misty coast of the Symplegades, a grateful sacrifice for thee to offer to the goddess Artemis. Haste then to make all ready, the lustral water and the opening rites.

Ip. Whence come they? what is the name of these strangers' country?

He. They are from Hellas; that is all I know, nothing further.

Ip. Didst thou not even catch the strangers' names, so that thou canst tell me?

He. Pylades one called the other.

Ip. And the stranger's comrade, what was his name?

He. That no one knows; for we never heard it.

Ip. Where were ye, when ye saw and captured them?

He. Upon the extreme edge of the cheerless sea.

Ip. Pray, what were herdsmen doing by the sea?

He. We had gone to wash our cattle in its briny spray.

Ip. Return to that other point; where did ye take them, and how? for this is what I wish to know. 'Tis long since strangers came, and our goddess' altar has not been crimsoned all that while with streams of Hellene blood.

He. We were just driving our cattle from their woodland pastures to yonder sea which flows between "the Clashing Rocks," where is a certain hollow cleft, scooped by the rush of the tide, a shelter used by purple-fishers, when a herdsman of our company saw two young men, and, coming back to us on tiptoe, he said, "Do ye not see them? there are deities seated yonder." Then one of us, a god-fearing man, lifted up his hands and, looking towards them, prayed thus: "Lord Palæmon, son of the nymph Leucothea, in whose keeping are all ships, have mercy on us! whether ye twain now seated on the beach are 'the Twin Brethren' or darlings of father Nereus, who begot that lovely choir of fifty Nereids."

But another, with a reckless disregard of what is right, scoffed at his prayers, and would have it that they were shipwrecked mariners sheltering in the gully for fear of our custom, having heard how we sacrifice strangers in this land.

Now most of us, thinking he was right, determined to hunt them for the goddess, victims such as our country offers. Meantime one of the two strangers, leaving the rocky cave, suddenly stood still and fell to shaking his head wildly up and down and groaning loudly, trembling to his very fingertips in a frenzied fit, and shouting like a hunter, "There! Pylades, dost see her? there! dost see her now, the hellish snake, how eager she is for my blood, with her fearsome vipers all agape to bite me? and yet a third, who belches fire and death, wings her way to a rocky height with my mother in her arms, to hurl her thence upon me. Oh, horror! she will kill me; where am I to fly?"

We could not see these weird shapes, but he mistook the lowing of cows and the barking of dogs for the sounds which he said the fiends were uttering in imitation of them. Now we were sitting huddled together in silence, as doomed men, when lo! he drew his sword, and, rushing like a lion into the midst of the heifers, fell to slashing at their flanks and plunging his sword in their sides, thinking he was thus warding off the vengeful goddesses, so that the surface of the sea broke out in clots of gore. We meantime, seeing our cattle harried and slain, began to arm us, one and all, blowing the while on curved shells and calling the people of the place together, and very soon we were gathered in full force; but then the stranger left his sudden fit, and, foaming at the mouth, he falls; we, seeing him fallen so opportunely, set-to, each man of us, to hurl and smite at him, but the other of that pair wiped the foam from his lips and was careful of his body, holding out his finely-woven robe to cover him, watching anxiously for threatened wounds and ministering to his friend most tenderly. Suddenly the mad-man recovering his senses sprang up from where he fell and was ware of the surging press of foes and of the nearness of that calamity which is upon them now, and he gave one groan, but we the while ne'er ceased pelting them from every side with right goodwill; whereon we heard this fearful order given, "Pylades, we have to die; see that it be with honour; draw thy sword and follow me."

But when we saw the brandished blades of our two enemies, we took to flight and were filling the rocky glens; still, if one or two did fly, the rest kept up a vigorous fire at them, and if perchance they drove these off, the party, which was giving way at first, set-to stoning them again. This sounds incredible, but not a man of all the crowd that threw succeeded in hitting the goddess's victims. At last however we mastered them—not by bravery, 'tis true—but, surrounding them completely, we contrived to knock the swords from their hands with stones, and they sank to the ground through fatigue; at once we bring them to our monarch, who no sooner sees them than he despatches them to thee to purify and sacrifice. Be thy prayer, maiden, that such strangers may be forthcoming for thy offering; go on slaying men like these, and Hellas will make atonement for thy own blood, expiating that sacrifice in Aulis.

Ch. A strange story thou tellest about this waif, whoever he is, that is come from the land of Hellas to the cheerless sea.

Ip. Enough! go, bring the strangers hither; while I will see to what is needed here. *Exit* HERDSMAN.

Alas, my suffering heart! in days gone by thou wert always kind and compassionate towards strangers, paying their kindred race the tribute of a tear, whenever thou hadst Hellenes in thy power; but now, by reason of dreams which have made me cruel from thinking that Orestes is no longer alive, ye will find my heart hardened, whoe'er ye are that have arrived. So then this also is a true saying, friends, and I experience it; "The unfortunate, having once known prosperity themselves, bear no kind feelings towards their luckier neighbours."

No breeze from Zeus hath ever blown, nor vessel sailed, which might have carried Helen hither from her course between "the clashing rocks"—Helen, my bane, and Menelaus with her—that so I might have taken vengeance on them, putting Aulis here to balance Aulis there, where Danaid chiefs with brutal violence were for slaughtering me like a heifer, my own father being the priest.

Oh! I can never forget that hideous scene, the many times I strained my hands to touch his beard, and how I clung to my father's knees and cried, "'Tis to a sorry wedding I am brought by thee, my sire; e'en now while thou art slaying me, my mother and the Argive maids are singing my marriage-hymn, and our house is filled with music; but I am dying all the time, slain by thee. Hades, it seems, and not the son of Peleus was the Achilles thou didst offer me as lord, having brought me in thy chariot to a bloody wedding by a trick." A fine-spun veil was o'er my eyes, so I never took my brother in my arms—that brother now no more—nor kissed my sister on the lips from modesty, as if it were for Peleus' halls that I was bound; but many a fond caress I kept in store for the future, believing I should yet return to Argos.

Ah! Orestes, woe is thee! if thou art dead; from what a glorious lot and envied heritage art thou cut off! I blame these subtle quibbles of our goddess; say a man has spilt another's blood or even come in contact with a labouring woman or a corpse, she bars him from her altars, counting him unclean, and yet herself delights in human sacrifice. It cannot be that Leto, bride of Zeus, ever bore so senseless a daughter. No! for my part I put no credit in that banquet served by Tantalus to the gods, to believe that they felt pleasure in devouring a child; rather I suspect that the natives of this land, being cannibals themselves, impute this failing to their deity; for I cannot believe that any god is such a sinner.

Exit.

Ch. Ye dim dark rocks where meet the seas, o'er whose forbidding billows Io crossed, driven from Argos by the winged gad-fly, passing from Europe to the strand of Asia! who can these be that left the fair waters of Eurotas, with green beds of reeds, or Dirce's holy streams, to tread this savage soil, where the daughter of Zeus bedews her altars and columned fanes with blood of men? Can they have sped a chariot of the deep across the waves with oars of pine, dashed in on either side, before the breeze that fills the sail, heaping up riches for their homes in eager rivalry? for hope, fond hope, appears to man's undoing, insatiate in the hearts of those who carry home a load of wealth, wanderers they across the main, visitors to foreign towns in idle expectation. Some there are whose thoughts of wealth are not timed right, and some who find it come to them.

How did they pass those clashing rocks or the restless beach of Phineus, racing along the sea-beat strand o'er the breakers of Ocean's queen, before the breeze that filled their sails, to the land where choirs of fifty Nereid maids circle in the dance and sing—the rudder steady at the stern and whistling to the breath of south-west wind or zephyr, on to that gleaming strand, where fowls in plenty roost, to the fair race-course of Achilles along the cheerless sea?

Oh! that chance would bring Helen, the darling child of Leda, hither on her way from Troy-town, as my lady prayed, that she might have the fatal water sprinkled round her hair and die by my mistress' knife, paying to her a proper recompense!

What joy to hear the welcome news that some mariner from Hellas had landed here, to end the sufferings of my bitter bondage! Oh! to set foot, if only in a dream, in my father's home and city, a luxury sweet sleep affords, a pleasure shared by us with wealth!

Enter ORESTES *and* PYLADES, *guarded.*

But see where the prisoners twain approach, their hands fast bound with chains, new victims for our goddess. Silence now, my friends! for those choice offerings from Hellas are now close to the temple, and it was no false news the herdsman announced.

Thou awful queen! if by such acts this city wins thy favour, accept its sacrifice, not sanctioned by Hellenes, though openly offered by our custom.

Enter IPHIGENIA.

Ip. Ah, well! my first thought must be the due performance of the goddess's service.

Loose the hands of the strangers; they are now devoted and must not be chained; then enter the temple and make ready, whatever present need requires or custom ordains. (*Exit guards.*)

(*Turning to the prisoners*) Ah! who was the mother that bare you? your father, who was he? or your sister, if haply ye had one? of what a gallant pair of brothers will she be bereft! Who knows on whom such strokes of fate will fall? for all that Heaven decrees, proceeds unseen, and no man knoweth of the ills in store; for Fate misleads us into doubtful paths.

Whence come ye, hapless strangers? for long as ye have been in sailing hither, so shall ye be long absent from your homes, aye for ever in that world below.

Or. Woman, whoe'er thou art, why weep'st thou thus, or why distress us at the thought of our impending doom? No wise man I count him, who, when death looms near, attempts to quell its terrors by piteous laments, nor yet the man who bewails the Death-god's arrival, when he has no hope of rescue; for he makes two evils out of one; he lets himself be called a fool and all the same he dies; he should let his fortune be. Weep not thou for us, for well we know what rites are offered here.

Ip. Which of you bears the name of Pylades, as they called it here? This is what I wish to learn first.

Or. This is he, if the knowledge really gives thee any pleasure.

Ip. What state in Hellas calls him son?

Or. What canst thou gain by learning this, lady?

Ip. Are ye brothers, the sons of one mother?

Or. Brothers in friendship, not in blood.

Ip. What name did the author of thy being give thee?

Or. I might with justice be called "Misfortune."

Ip. That is not what I ask; refer that to chance.

Or. If I die nameless, I shall not be mocked.

Ip. Why grudge me this? Art so exceeding proud?

Or. 'Tis my body, not my name, that thou wilt sacrifice.

Ip. Wilt thou not even tell me the name of thy city?

Or. No, for thy inquiry boots me not, seeing I am doomed to die.

Ip. What hinders thee from granting me this boon?

Or. Glorious Argos is my home; I own it with pride.

Ip. What! Argos? wert thou really born there, sir stranger?

Or. Aye, in Mycenæ, so prosperous of yore.

Ip. Was it as an exile or from what mischance that thou didst quit thy country?

Or. An exile I am in a certain sense, not of my own free will, nor yet against it.

Ip. And yet thy coming from Argos was welcome to me.

Or. Not so to myself, but if thou art pleased, see to that thyself.

Ip. Wilt tell me something that I wish to learn myself?

Or. To serve as an appendix to my misery!

Ip. Maybe thou hast some knowledge of Troy, which is spoken of everywhere.

Or. Would God I knew it not so much as in a dream!

Ip. They say that it is now no more, a city sacked.

Or. Why, so it is; ye heard aright.

Ip. Did Helen return to the house of Menelaus?

Or. Aye, that she did, to the sorrow of one I loved.

Ip. Where is she now? I too owe her a grudge.

Or. She is living in Sparta with her first husband.

Ip. O creature hateful in the eyes of Hellenes, not in mine alone!

Or. I too have reaped some fruit of that woman's marriages.

Ip. Did the Achæans make good their return, as 'tis rumoured?

Or. Thy question embraces everything at once.

Ip. I would fain get an answer to it before thy death.

Or. Put thy questions, since thou art bent on it; I will answer.

Ip. There was a seer Calchas—did he return from Troy?

Or. He was reported dead in Mycenæ.

Ip. Great queen! how well deserved! What of Laertes' son?

Or. He has not yet returned, but 'tis said he is still alive.

Ip. Perdition seize him! ne'er may he reach home again!

Or. Spare thy curses; dire affliction is his lot.

Ip. Is the son of Thetis the Nereid still living?

Or. No, dead; his marriage at Aulis came to naught.

Ip. Aye, 'twas all a trick; at least they, who suffered by it, say so.

Or. Why, who art thou? thy questions touching Hellas are so apt.

Ip. I am from Hellas; but, when a child, I lost that home.

Or. Then art thou right, lady, to long for news of it.

Ip. What of that general, whom men style "the blest"?

Or. Who is that? The man of whom *I* wot is not among the blest.

Ip. A prince called Agamemnon, said to be the son of Atreus.

Or. I knew him not; leave this theme, lady.

Ip. I do entreat thee, no! but speak, fair sir, to gladden me.

Or. He is dead, poor king! and has caused another's death as well.

Ip. Dead? why, what befell him? woe is me!

Or. Why that heavy sigh? Was he related to thee?

Ip. 'Tis for his former prosperity I grieve.

Or. And rightly too, for he came to a fearful end at a woman's hands.

Ip. O the piteous fate of that murderess and her victim!

Or. Prithee, cease and ask no more.

Ip. Only this; is the wretched victim's wife alive?

Or. No, dead; her son—the child she bore—he slew her.

Ip. O house sore troubled! What could be his object?

Or. Vengeance on her for his father's death.

Ip. Alas for him! how well he exacted his evil justice.

Or. Spite of his justice, he has no luck at Heaven's hand.

Ip. Did Agamemnon leave any other issue in his halls?

Or. Yes, one maiden child, Electra.

Ip. What! is no mention made of a daughter who was sacrificed?

Or. No, none, except that she has closed her eyes upon the light.

Ip. Ah, woe is her and him that slew her, her own sire!

Or. In a thankless cause she died—the cause of a wicked woman.

Ip. Is the son of the murdered man still alive at Argos?

Or. Alive he is, unhappy wretch, and wandering without a home.

Ip. Begone, ye lying dreams, proved worthless after all!

Or. Even the gods, who at least bear the title of wise, prove no less false than flitting dreams; in things divine as well as human, confusion reigns; and 'tis only one cause of grief, when a man, through no folly of his own but from obeying the dictates of prophets, is ruined, as ruined he is in the judgment of those who know.

Ch. Ah, well-a-day! and what is the fate of our dear fathers? are they still alive, or dead? who can tell?

Ip. Listen, sirs, for I have hit upon a plan, I think, to further your interests and my own at the same time; and this is the best guarantee of success, if all approve the same object. Wouldst thou, were I to spare thee, return to Argos for me with a message to my friends there, and carry them a letter, written by a captive out of pity for me; for he regarded not mine as the hand that slew him, but held our custom answerable for his death, such being the view our goddess takes of justice? For I had no one to return to Argos with my message and convey my letter to some friend of mine, if spared; but as thou seemest to be a man of no mean breeding and knowest Mycenæ and the persons I mean, accept thyself the means of rescue, earning a noble wage—thy safety for a scrap of writing; but thy friend must be parted from thee and offered to the goddess, for this is our city's stern decree.

Or. A fair proposal, lady stranger, save in one respect. That he should have to bleed is a heavy weight upon my heart; for 'tis I who steer this troubled craft; he but sails with me to save my toil. Wherefore it is not right that I should pleasure thee on terms that seal his doom, while I escape myself from trouble. No! be this the way; give him the letter; for he will convey it to Argos, and so thy end is served; but let who will slay me. Foul shame were it for a man to plunge his friends into trouble and escape himself; and this man is a friend, whose life I prize as highly as my own.

Ip. Heroic spirit! what a noble stock was thine! how true thou art to friends! Oh, may the last survivor of my race prove such another! for I, too, sirs, am not left brotherless; only I see him not.

This being thy wish, I will send him to carry the letter, and thou shalt die; but thy goodwill towards him must be something great!

Or. But who will offer me and dare that awful deed?

Ip. Myself; for this is the office I hold of the goddess.

Or. A sad unenviable task, fair maid.

Ip. But I am the slave of necessity, whose law I must observe.

Or. Is this the hand—this woman's hand—that draws the knife on men?

Ip. Not that, but round thy brow I shall sprinkle lustral water.

Or. Who gives the fatal blow? if I may ask thee this.

Ip. Inside this building are men, whose office this is.

Or. What kind of tomb will await me, when I am dead?

Ip. The sacred fire within and a gaping chasm in the rock.

Or. Ah! would that a sister's hand could lay me out!

Ip. An idle prayer, poor wretch! whoever thou art, for her home lies far from this savage shore. Still, as thou art an Argive, I will not let thee want for aught that is in my power; I will place in thy grave good store of ornament and quench thy charred remains with yellow olive oil and will pour upon thy pyre the nectar sucked from many a flower by russet mountain bees.

I go now to fetch my letter from the goddess's temple; yet regard not this ill-will as mine.

Watch them, guards, without binding them. It may be I shall send unlooked-for tidings to a friend in Argos, even to him whom most I love, and the letter announcing that they live, whom he thinks dead, will confirm the message of joy.

Exit IPHIGENIA.

Ch. (*To* ORESTES) I weep for thee, the victim of her fatal sprinkling.

Or. Nay, there is nothing here for tears; rather rejoice, ye lady strangers.

Ch. (*To* PYLADES) I give thee joy, young sir, on thy happy fortune, in that thou wilt tread thy native soil.

Py. No cause surely to envy a man, when his friends are dying!

Ch. Alas, cruel mission!

Woe is thee! thy doom is sealed. Ah! which of the pair is the more undone? My mind is still distraught with two-fold doubt whether to mourn for thee or thee the more.

Or. Prithee, Pylades, art thou in like case with myself?

Py. I know not; thy question finds me with no answer ready.

Or. Who is this maid? How like a daughter of Hellas she questioned us of the toils at Troy and the Achæans' return, of Calchas the clever augur and famous Achilles! what pity she expressed for Agamemnon's fate, and how she pressed me about his wife and children! This stranger maid is haply an Argive by descent; else would she never have been sending a letter and inquiring so straitly about these matters, as if she shared herself in the welfare of Argos.

Py. Thou hast forestalled me slightly, but for all that thy conclusions are the same, except on one point; all of course who have ever had dealings with others hear about the misfortunes of kings. But there was quite another theme she discussed.

Or. What was that? divulge it to me and thou mayest understand it better.

Py. It is shameful that I should live and thou be slain; as I shared thy voyage, so ought I to share thy death; else shall I get a name for cowardice and knavery through Argos and in all the vales of Phocis; and the mob, being a host of knaves, will think that I betrayed thee and secured a return to my home only for myself, or haply that I murdered thee, while thy house was weak, devising destruction for thee with a view to thy throne, as the husband of thy sister who would succeed. This then is what I fear; of this I am ashamed; and it needs must be my bounden duty to breathe my last with thee, slain by the same knife and burnt on the same pyre, as one who was thy friend and fears reproach.

Or. Hush! my own sorrows I am bound to bear, and I will not double my burden of grief, when I may carry it single; for that grief and foul reproach of which thou speakest is mine, if I slay thee my fellow-toiler; for me, afflicted as I am by Heaven, 'tis not amiss to leave this life; but thou art prosperous and thy home is pure of taint and sound, while mine is cursed alike by Heaven and destiny. So save thyself and get children of my sister, whom I gave thee to wife; thus will my name live on and my father's house will never be blotted out through having no heir. Go hence and live; make my father's house thy home; but when thou art come to Hellas and to chivalrous Argos, I charge thee by this right hand, heap up my grave and lay thereon memorials of me, and let my sister shed a tear and strew her tresses on my tomb; and tell her how I perished by an Argive maiden's hand, consecrated at the altar by bloodshed. Forsake not my sister when thou seest thy new kin and my father's house forlorn; and fare thee well, my best of friends, for so have I ever found thee, fellow hunter, foster-brother, that oft hast borne the burden of my sorrows! 'Twas Phœbus who deceived us by his prophecies; and so he has devised a trick to drive me as far as might be from Hellas, for very shame of his bygone oracles; for, after yielding up my all to him and obeying his word, even to the slaying of my mother, I find myself undone in return.

Py. A tomb shalt thou have, my luckless friend, nor will I ever prove false to thy sister; for Orestes dead will be e'en dearer to me than Orestes living. Still the god's oracle hath not destroyed thee yet, albeit thou standest now at the gates of death; nay, but misfortune at her worst sometimes admits a thorough change.

Or. Cease; the words of Phœbus are no help to me, for yonder comes the maiden from the temple.

Enter IPHIGENIA.

Ip. (*To the guard*) Hence! go help the ministers of death to make their preparations within.

Here is my letter, sirs, with its many folded leaves; but listen to my further wishes. As no man is the same under affliction as when he has suddenly passed from fear to confidence, I am much afraid that when he, who is to carry the letter to Argos, is safely on his way from this land, he will make my message of no account.

Or. What then wouldst thou? what is troubling thee?

Ip. Let him give me an oath that he will convey this writing to Argos to the friends I wish it to reach.

Or. Wilt thou give him a similar oath in return?

Ip. What to do? from what refrain? tell me that.

Or. To let him go forth alive from this savage land.

Ip. Justly urged; for how else could he carry my message?

Or. But will the king agree to this?

Ip. Yes, I will persuade him, and will myself put thy friend aboard.

Or. Swear then (*to* PYLADES); and do thou dictate some solemn oath.

Ip. (*To* PYLADES) Thou must promise to give this letter to my friends.

Py. I will give this letter to thy friends.

Ip. And I will send thee safe beyond those sombre rocks.

Py. By which of the gods dost swear to this?

Ip. By Artemis, in whose temple I hold my honoured office.

Py. And I by Heaven's king, majestic Zeus.

Ip. Suppose thou fail to keep this oath to my injury?

Py. May I ne'er return! and thou—what if thou save me not?

Ip. May I never live to set foot in Argos!

Py. Pray, hear me on a subject we have overlooked.

Ip. Well, 'tis not too late, provided it be opportune.

Py. Grant me one exemption; if aught happens to the ship and the letter goes down with the cargo in the waves and I save only myself, let this oath be no longer binding.

Ip. Dost know what I will do? "Much adventure, much achieve." I will tell thee all that is written in the leaves of this letter, so that thou mayst repeat it to my friends; yes, that insures its safety; on the one hand, suppose thou save the writing, the silent lines will of themselves tell its contents; whereas, if what is written here is lost at sea, thy safety will involve the safety of my message.

Py. A good provision for thy own interests and me; but signify to whom I am to carry this letter to Argos and likewise the message I must repeat from thy lips.

Ip. Go tell Orestes, the son of Agamemnon, "Thy sister Iphigenia, the victim of Aulis, sends thee this message, being still alive, though dead to all in Argos."

Or. Iphigenia still alive! where? is she risen from the dead?

Ip. I, whom thine eyes behold, am she; distract me not by speaking. "Bear me to Argos, brother, ere I die, remove me from this savage land and from the goddess's sacrifices at which I am appointed to slay strangers."

Or. Pylades, what am I to say? where can we be?

Ip. "Else will I become a curse to thy house, Orestes"; (*stopping to address* PYLADES) thou hast heard the name twice to impress it on thee.

Or. Ye gods!

Ip. Why invoke the gods in matters which only concern me?

Or. 'Tis nothing; read on; my thoughts had strayed elsewhere. Perhaps if I question thee, I shall arrive at the truth.

Ip. Tell him, the goddess Artemis saved my life by substituting a hind in my stead, which my father sacrificed, when he thought he plunged the sharp knife in me; and she put me to dwell in this land.

There is my message, and that is what is written in the letter.

Py. How easy for me to observe the oath by which thou hast bound me! how fair thine own! I will make no long delay, but ratify what I have sworn.

There! Orestes, I bring this letter and deliver it to thee from this lady, thy sister.

Or. I accept it, but letting its folded pages wait awhile I will first indulge my joy, not in mere words. (*Approaching to embrace* IPHIGENIA) My own dear sister! struck with wonder though I am, I yet will fold thee to my doubting heart and rejoice in my wondrous news.

Ch. Thou hast no right, sir stranger, to pollute the handmaid of our goddess by throwing thy arms about her holy robes.

Or. Oh! turn not from me, sister mine, sprung from Agamemnon like myself, now that thou hast found thy brother beyond all expectation.

Ip. Found my brother in thee! A truce to this idle talk! Why, Argos and Nauplia are filled with his presence now.

Or. That is not where he dwells, poor maid.

Ip. Can thy mother have been a daughter of Spartan Tyndareus?

Or. Yes, and my father a grandson of Pelops.

Ip. What dost thou say? hast any proof to give me of this?

Or. I have; ask me something about our father's home.

Ip. Nay, 'tis surely for thee to speak, for me to answer.

Or. Well, I will tell thee first a story I heard Electra tell; knowest thou ought of a quarrel 'twixt Atreus and Thyestes?

Ip. I have heard that they fell out about a golden lamb.

Or. Canst thou remember broidering this on the fine texture of thy web?

Ip. Dearest brother! thou comest very near my heart.

Or. Hast thou forgotten the picture on thy loom, the changing of the sun-god's course?

Ip. That was the very pattern I embroidered with fine-woven thread!

Or. Next, didst thou receive the bridal bath sent by thy mother to Aulis?

Ip. I have not forgotten; that marriage was not so happy as to take away the memory of it.

Or. Once more, dost remember giving a lock of hair to be carried to thy mother?

Ip. Aye, as a memorial of myself for my tomb in place of my body.

Or. Next will I name as proofs what I have seen myself; the ancient spear of Pelops in our father's house, hidden away in thy maiden-bower, that spear he brandished in his hand to slay Œnomaus and win Hippodamia, Pisa's prize.

Ip. Orestes, O my brother dear, dearer than aught else to me, I hold thee in my arms, my best-beloved, far from Argos, the home of our fathers.

Or. And I hold thee, whom all thought dead; while tears, that are not tears of sorrow, with grief and joy commingling, bedew alike thy eyes and mine.

Ip. I left thee in our halls a new-born babe, still in thy nurse's arms, that fatal day. O blest in fortune past all words to tell! What can I say? These things have come upon us transcending wonder or description.

Or. May we be happy together for the future!

Ip. Good friends, I feel a strange unwonted joy; my only fear is that he will fly from my arms and soar away into the air.

All hail, Cyclopean hearths and homes! my country, dear Mycenæ, hail! I thank thee, yea, I thank thee both for life and bringing up, for that thou hast reared my brother from his youth to be a light unto our house.

Or. Lucky in our birth, sister, were we, but our life has not proved so lucky in its haps.

Ip. Ah me! how well I recollect the day when my wretched father held the sword-blade at my throat!

Or. Horrible! I seem to see thee there, though I was not present.

Ip. I remember, brother, being taken away by trickery, as if to wed Achilles; no marriage-hymn was sung; but instead were tears and wailing at the altar. Woe for the water sprinkled on me there!

Or. And I repeat, woe for our father's reckless deed!

Ip. 'Twas no true father meted out that fate to me, and now one trouble is following on another—

Or. Yes, if thou hadst slain thy brother, hapless maid.

Ip. By some god's intervention. Oh! that I should have dared so dire a crime! Alas! brother, I ventured on a fearful deed; thou didst but just escape an unholy doom, death at my hands. How will the matter end? what will be my fate? what means can I discover to convey thee hence from this murderous land to thy home in Argos, before the sword requires thy blood? Ah, suffering soul! 'tis thy business to devise a means for this. Wilt thou fly by land, not on shipboard, relying on thy speed of foot? Why, then thou wilt have death ever at thy elbow, as thou farest through savage tribes and over pathless ways; it must be the narrow passage 'twixt "the misty rocks" after all, a tedious course for ships to run.

Ah me! a hapless lot is mine. What god or man or unforeseen event could bring about a happy release, a deliverance from trouble for the two survivors of the house of Atreus?

Ch. This that I have seen with mine eyes, not merely heard men tell may rank with miracles; 'tis stranger than fiction.

Py. Orestes, it is natural for friends to embrace each other when they meet, but thou must leave lamenting and face that other question as well, how we are to escape from this savage land, with our safety honourably secured. For the wise man's way, when once he gets a chance, is not to indulge in pleasures foreign to it, abandoning his fortune.

Or. Thou art right; and fortune, I feel sure, is bent on helping our efforts here; for if a man exerts himself, the gods naturally have greater power.

Ip. (*To* PYLADES) Thou shalt not stop me or prevent me from first inquiring how Electra fares; for any news of her will be welcome to me.

Or. Here is her husband (*pointing to* PYLADES), with whom she leads a happy life.

Ip. What is his country? who his sire?

Or. His father's name is Strophius, a Phocian.

Ip. Why then, he is the son of Atreus' daughter and my kinsman?

Or. Thy cousin, yes; my one loyal friend.

Ip. He was not born, when my father sought my life.

Or. No, for Strophius had no son for some time.

Ip. My sister's husband, hail!

Or. My saviour too and no mere kinsman.

Ip. How didst thou bring thyself to that awful deed regarding our mother?

Or. Let us say nothing of the deed; 'twas my vengeance for my sire.

Ip. What was her reason for slaying her husband?

Or. Forego our mother's story; 'tis no tale for thy ears.

Ip. I say no more; but does Argos now look up to thee?

Or. Menelaus is king, and I an exile from my country.

Ip. Surely our uncle never so insulted our afflicted house?

Or. No, but the fear of the avenging fiends drives me from the land.

Ip. Then that explains the story of thy madness even here upon the beach.

Or. This is not the first time I have been seen in my misery.

Ip. I understand; the goddesses were chasing thee on account of thy mother's murder.

Or. To put a bloody bridle in my mouth.

Ip. But why was it to this land thou didst guide thy steps?

Or. I came obedient to an oracle of Phœbus.

Ip. With what intent? Is it a secret or may it be told?

Or. I will tell thee. All my sorrows date from this; after my mother's punishment—of which I say nothing—had devolved on me, I was chased into exile by vengeful fiends in hot pursuit, till Loxias at last guided my footsteps to Athens to make atonement to the unnamed goddesses; for there is there a holy tribunal, which Zeus set up one day to try Ares for some pollution, it is said. Now, on my arrival at Athens, not one of my friends was ready to receive me at first, as a man abhorred by Heaven; afterwards they, who had pity on me, supplied me with stranger's cheer at a table apart, being in the same room with me, but by their silence they contrived to exclude me from conversation, that I might keep aloof from their eating and drinking; and, filling each man's cup with the same measure of wine for all, they were enjoying themselves. I meantime did not presume to question my hosts, but was sorrowing in silence and pretending not to notice it, though grieving bitterly that I was my mother's murderer. Moreover, I hear that amongst the Athenians my misfortunes have become the occasion for a festival, and the custom yet survives of the people of Pallas honouring the pitcher. But when I came to Ares' hill and stood my trial, I on one platform, the eldest of the vengeful fiends upon the other, Phœbus, having made his speech and heard the evidence about my mother's murder, saved me by his testimony, and Pallas, counting out the votes in her hand, made them equal for me; so I came off triumphant in the murder-trial. Thereon as many of the avenging fiends as agreed with the verdict and were for settling there, resolved to have a temple close to the tribunal; but such of them as concurred not with the precedent, continued to persecute me in restless pursuit, till once again I sought the hallowed soil of Phœbus, and stretching myself starving before his shrine, I swore to end my life then and there, unless he who had ruined me would find me salvation; whereupon the voice of Phœbus pealed from his golden tripod, and he sent me hither to fetch the image, which fell from heaven, and set it up in Attica. Help me then to compass the means of safety he has appointed me; for if I can secure the image of the goddess, I shall not only cease from my mad fits, but setting out on well-rowed ship restore thee to Mycenæ once again. Ah! my sister, well-beloved! preserve thy father's house and send me hence in safety; for I and the fortunes of Pelops' race are utterly undone, unless we secure the image of the goddess, that fell from heaven.

Ch. Some god's dire anger once burst forth against the seed of Tantalus, and it is leading them through trouble.

Ip. It was long my eager wish, brother, even before thy coming, to be at Argos and see thee face to face; and my desire is thine, to set thee free from suffering and restore my father's stricken house, harbouring no angry thoughts towards him who would have slain me; for so should I be spared thy blood and save my house; but how am I to elude the goddess, and the king, when he finds the stone pedestal robbed of its image? That is my fear. How shall I escape death? what account can I give? If thou canst combine the acts of carrying off the image and placing me upon thy gallant ship, the risk becomes worth running; but, once I am separated from it, I am lost, although thou mayest succeed in thy enterprise and find a safe return; not that I shrink from death—if die I must—when I have saved thee; no, indeed! for a man's loss from his family is felt, while a woman's is of little moment.

Or. I will never be thy murderer as well as my mother's; enough that I have shed her blood! With thee I fain would live one life or dying share the self-same fate. For if I fall not here myself, I will take thee home, or else remain and die with thee. Hear my reasoning; were this opposed to the will of Artemis, how could Loxias have bidden me carry the image of the goddess to the citadel of Pallas? . . . . and see thy face; wherefore, putting all these facts together, I am hopeful of securing our return.

Ip. How can we possibly escape death and likewise achieve our object? That is the weak point in our homeward route; that is what we must devise.

Or. Could we contrive to kill the king?

Ip. That is a fearful risk, for new-comers to slay their hosts.

Or. But we must run the risk, if it will save us.

Ip. I commend your zeal, but you could not succeed.

Or. Well, suppose thou wert to hide me stealthily in yonder fane?

Ip. That we might avail ourselves of the darkness, I suppose, and escape?

Or. Yes, for darkness is the robber's day; the light was made for truth.

Ip. There are guards inside the temple, whom we cannot elude.

Or. Alas! we are utterly undone; how are we to escape?

Ip. I have hit upon a novel scheme, methinks.

Or. Of what kind? Impart thy thoughts to me, that I may know it too.

Ip. I will make a cunning use of thy troubles.

Or. No doubt thou wilt; women are clever at inventing tricks.

Ip. I shall say thou art a matricide fresh from Argos.

Or. Make use of my misfortunes, if it will serve thy turn.

Ip. And I shall tell them thou art no proper sacrifice for the goddess—

Or. What reason canst thou give? I half suspect.

Ip. Because thou art unclean; whereas I must have what is pure to offer.

Or. And how does this bring the goddess's image any nearer capture.

Ip. It will be my wish to purify thee in fresh seawater.

Or. Still is the image left in the temple, and that was our object in sailing hither.

Ip. I will say I must wash it also, as if thou hadst touched it.

Or. But where? Is it a sea-filled creek thou meanest?

Ip. There where thy ship is riding at anchor, moored with ropes.

Or. Will the image be in thy hands or some other's?

Ip. In mine, for I alone may touch it.

Or. What part will Pylades have assigned him in the murder?

Ip. He will be described as having the same stain on his hands as thou hast.

Or. Wilt thou do this unknown to the king or with his knowledge?

Ip. After persuading him, for I could never elude his vigilance.

Or. Well, at any rate the ship is there with its oars ready to smite the waves. Thy business must it be to see that all else is well arranged. One thing alone is wanting, these ladies' secrecy; implore them and find persuasive arguments; woman is gifted with a power of moving sympathy; and for the rest, all perhaps may turn out well.

Ip. Dearest friends, I look to you; on you my fortunes are hanging, whether for weal or woe, and loss of fatherland and brother and sister dear.

Be this the text of what I have to say—our womanhood, with its kindly feeling towards members of our sex, and our intense loyalty in preserving secrets, that affect us all. For my sake hold your peace and help us might and main to escape; an honour to its owner is a trusty tongue. Now ye see how a single chance is left these three fast friends, either to return to their fatherland or die here. If once my safety is secured, I will bring thee safe to Hellas, that thou mayst also share my fortune. To thee, and thee (*addressing different members of the* CHORUS) I make my prayer by thy right hand; to thee by thy dear cheek, thy knees, and all thou prizest most at home, by father, mother, aye, and babes, if there be any mothers here. What say ye? which of you assents to this and which refuses? Speak; for if ye agree not to my proposal, both I and my luckless brother are lost.

Ch. Take heart, dear lady mine; only save thyself; for thou shalt find me dumb, wherever thou enjoinest silence; so help me mighty Zeus!

Ip. A blessing on you for those words! may happiness be yours! 'Tis now thy part and thine (*to* ORESTES *and* PYLADES) to enter the temple, for our monarch will soon be here, inquiring if the sacrifice of the strangers is over.

Dread queen! that once didst save my life from my father's hand and murder dire, save me now again, and these as well; else will the words of Loxias cease to be believed by men because of thee. Oh! be gracious and quit this savage shore for glorious Athens; for 'tis not right that thou shouldst live on here, when a city so blest may be thine.

Exeunt IPHIGENIA, ORESTES, *and* PYLADES.

Ch. O bird by ocean's rocky reefs! thou halcyon, that singest thy hard fate in doleful song, whose note the well-trained ear can catch, and know that thou art ever moaning for thy mate; with thee I match my tearful plaint, an unwinged songstress, longing for the gatherings of Hellas, for Artemis our help in childbirth, whose home is by the Cynthian hill with its luxuriant palm and sprouting bay and sacred shoots of olive pale, welcome to Latona in her travail, beside the rounded eddying mere, where tuneful swans do service to the Muse. Woe! for the streams of tears that coursed adown my cheeks, what time our turrets fell, and I, the prey of oar and spear, was set aboard a foeman's ship; then, purchased at a costly price, was carried to this foreign port, where I minister to the daughter of Agamemnon, priestess of the huntress queen, serving at altars on which sheep are never sacrificed, and envying her that hath been always unhappy; for if a man is born and bred in hardships, he fainteth not under them; but happiness is subject to change, and to be afflicted after prosperous days is a grievous lot for mortals.

Home the Argive ship will bear thee, lady, and piercing notes from mountain Pan's wax-fastened reed, will cheer the rowers to their task, and prophetic Phœbus will bring his deep-toned lyre with seven strings and escort thee with singing to fair bright Attica. Thee will dashing oar-blades speed away, leaving me still here; and over the bows of thy speeding bark the sheets will make her canvas swell against the forestays in the breeze.

Oh! to tread yon dazzling track where the fiery sun goes gladly forth, and, when above my chamber-roof, to rest the rapid pinions on my back! Oh! to take my station in the dance, where once at noble marriages I circled round in friendly strife of charms with my compeers, and roused them to vie with the rich splendour of my dress, as I drew my broidered veil about me and shaded my cheek with clustering curls.

Enter THOAS.

Thoas. Where is the warder of these temple-gates, the maid of Hellas? Has she yet begun the rites on the strangers? are their bodies ablaze in the holy shrine?

Ch. Here she is, O king, to explain everything to thee.

Enter IPHIGENIA.

Th. Ha! daughter of Agamemnon, why art thou bearing yon image of the goddess in thine arms from the sacred pedestal?

Ip. Stay there, O king, at the entrance.

Th. What news now in the temple, Iphigenia?

Ip. Avaunt! I say; (*turning to* THOAS *to explain*) 'tis in purity's cause I utter this word.

Th. What is thy news, requiring such a preface? Explain.

Ip. The victims, sire, which ye had captured for me are unclean.

Th. What proof of this hast thou? or is it mere conjecture?

Ip. The statue of the goddess turned away from its position.

Th. Of its own accord, or did an earthquake turn it?

Ip. Of its own accord, and it closed its eyes.

Th. What is the cause? the strangers' pollution?

Ip. Yes, that and nothing else; they have committed a crime.

Th. Can they have slain one of my subjects on the beach?

Ip. They brought the guilt of murder with them, —the guilt of kindred slain.

Th. Who was their victim? I am desirous of learning.

Ip. 'Twas a mother's blood they spilt, having conspired to stab her.

Th. O Apollo! even amongst barbarians none would have had the heart to do it.

Ip. They were hunted from every corner of Hellas.

Th. Is this the reason thou art carrying the image from the shrine?

Ip. Yes, to remove it from the taint of bloodshed by placing it beneath the holy firmament.

Th. In what way didst thou discover the impurity of these strangers?

Ip. When the image of the goddess turned away, I questioned them.

Th. Thou art a shrewd daughter of Hellas to have guessed this so cleverly.

Ip. Yea, and only now they dangled before me a tempting bait to catch my fancy.

Th. By bringing news of those in Argos to lure thee?

Ip. Good news of Orestes, my only brother.

Th. No doubt to induce thee to spare them for their glad tidings.

Ip. They said too that my father was alive and well.

Th. Naturally thy escape was a reference to the claims of the goddess.

Ip. Yes, for I hate all Hellas, that betrayed me.

Th. What, pray, are we to do with the strangers?

Ip. We must piously observe the established custom.

Th. Is not the lustral water ready, and thy knife?

Ip. My purpose is to cleanse them first by purification.

Th. In fresh spring water or salt sea-spray?

Ip. The sea washes away from man all that is ill.

Th. True, they would then be holier victims for the goddess.

Ip. Yes, and this would suit my own views better.

Th. Well, do not the waves dash full upon the temple-walls?

Ip. Solitude is necessary; for we have other duties to perform.

Th. Take them where thou wilt; I have no wish to witness what may not be told.

Ip. I must also purify the image of the goddess.

Th. Yes, if any taint has come upon it from the matricides.

Ip. Had there been none, I should never have removed it from its pedestal.

Th. Thy piety and forethought are right.

Ip. Let me have the things thou knowest I require.

Th. 'Tis for thee to name those wants.

Ip. Load the strangers with fetters.

Th. Whither could they escape from thee?

Ip. Good faith is quite unknown among Hellenes.

Th. (*To his servants*) Away, and bind them, sirrahs!

Ip. Next let them bring the strangers forth.

Th. It shall be done.

Ip. After drawing a veil over their heads—

Th. In presence of the radiant sun.

Ip. Send some of thy attendants with me.

Th. Here are those who will form thy escort.

Ip. Also dispatch a messenger to warn the citizens.

Th. What will happen?

Ip. To remain indoors, all of them.

Th. Lest they meet with murderers?

Ip. Aye, for such things bring pollution.

Th. (*to a servant*) Hence and proclaim this!

Ip. Above all must my friends—

Th. Thou meanest me.

Ip. Keep wholly out of sight.

Th. Thou takest good heed for the city's weal.

Ip. No wonder.

Th. No wonder the whole city looks up to thee.

Ip. Do thou stay here before the shrine to help the goddess.

Th. With what object?

Ip. Purify the building with torches.

Th. That thou mayst find it pure on thy return?

Ip. As soon as the strangers pass out—

Th. What must I do?

Ip. Hold thy robe before thine eyes.

Th. To avoid the murderer's taint?

Ip. But if I appear to be tarrying over long—

Th. Is there to be any limit to my waiting?

Ip. Feel no surprise.

Th. Take thine own time and serve the goddess well.

Ip. Oh may this purification have the end I wish!

Th. I add my prayers to that. *Exit* THOAS.

Ip. Behold, I see the strangers just leaving the temple with ornaments for the goddess and young lambs for me to purge the taint of blood by shedding more; with blazing torches too, and all else that I myself prescribed for the cleansing of the strangers and the goddess.

Away from this pollution, citizens! each warden of the temple-gates keeping pure his hands in Heaven's service; whoso is eager to marry a wife; all women labouring with child; hence! hence! away! that this pollution cross not your path.

(*Aside*) Virgin Queen, daughter of Zeus and Latona! if I wash the murderers of their guilt and sacrifice where 'tis right I should, thy temple will be pure for thy habitation, and we shall be blest; more I say not, but still my meaning is plain to thee, goddess, and to those like thee who know the rest.

Exit IPHIGENIA.

Ch. Fair was the child Latona bore one day in the fruitful vales of Delos, a babe with golden hair, well skilled in harping and his darling archery, and, leaving the scene of her glorious travail, she brought him from that sea-beat ridge to the peak of Parnassus, parent of gushing streams, where Dionysus holds his revels. There 'neath the shade of leafy bays a speckled snake with blood-red eyes, armoured in gleaming scales, an earth-born monster, huge, terrific, kept guard o'er the oracle beneath the ground; but thou, whilst yet a babe still struggling in thy mother's arms, didst slay him, Phœbus, and enter on most holy prophecy, and thou sittest on the golden tripod, thy throne of truth, dispensing Heaven's oracles to men from beneath the sanctuary, in thy home at earth's centre, hard by the founts of Castaly.

But when Apollo's coming had dispossessed Earth's daughter, Themis, of the holy oracles, her mother raised a brood of nightly phantoms seen in dreams, telling to many a mortal wight, as he lay asleep in the darkness, what has been and yet shall be; and Earth, jealous for her daughter's sake, robbed Phœbus of the honour of his oracles; but he, the prince, went hurrying off to Olympus and twined his childish arms round Zeus's throne, beseeching him to take from his Pythian home the visions nightly sent by angry Earth; and Zeus smiled to see his son come straight to him, because he would keep his worship, rich in precious gifts; and he nodded his locks, promising to stop the voices heard at night, and took from mortals the divination of darkness, restoring his honours to Loxias, and to mortals their confidence in the oracles he chanted on his throne amid the throng of pilgrims.

Enter MESSENGER.

Messenger. Guardians of the temple and ministers of the altar, where is Thoas the king of this land? throw wide those bolted doors and call the monarch outside the building.

Ch. What is wrong? if I may speak unbidden.

Me. The pair of youths have disappeared, seeking to fly the land, by the tricks of Agamemnon's child, and they have taken the sacred statue in the hold of their ship.

Ch. Incredible! But the king of the land, whom thou wishest to see, has already left the shrine in hot haste.

Me. Whither away? for he must be told what is happening.

Ch. We know not; but set off in pursuit, and, when thou hast found him, tell thy news.

Me. See how treacherous women are! *Ye* have had some share in these doings.

Ch. Art mad? What have we to do with the strangers' escape? Away and lose no time in reaching thy master's gates!

Me. Not until some one makes this point quite clear, whether the ruler of the land is in the shrine or not

What ho! unbar the doors! to those inside I call; tell my master I am here at the gate with heavy news for him.

Th. (*appearing at the temple door*) Who is raising this uproar at the temple, battering the doors and spreading panic within?

Me. These women tried to get me away, asserting falsely that thou wert gone forth, though in the temple all the time.

Th. What did they expect to gain? What was their object?

Me. I will tell thee about them later; listen now to the matter in hand. The maid Iphigenia, who used to be the priestess here, has fled the land with the strangers, taking the goddess's holy image with her; that cleansing was all a sham.

Th. How now? what evil influence possessed her?

Me. In her efforts to save Orestes. Yes, that will astonish thee.

Th. Which Orestes? him whom the daughter of Tyndareus bare?

Me. Him whom our goddess consecrated to herself at her altar.

Th. Miraculous event! How can I find too strong a name for thee?

Me. Turn not thy attention thither, but listen to me; and, when thou hast heard all and weighed the matter, devise a means of pursuit to hunt the strangers down.

Th. Say on, for thy words are good; 'tis no short voyage they have before them, that so they can escape my ships.

Me. As soon as we reached the beach where the ship of Orestes was moored in hiding, the daughter of Agamemnon signed to us, whom thou sentest with her to carry fetters for the strangers, to stand aloof, as if she were about to light the mystic flame and offer the cleansing rites, which she had come to perform. Holding in her hands the cord that bound the strangers, she went on behind them. This seemed suspicious, sire, but thy attendants were satisfied. After a while, to make us think she was really doing something unusual, she lifted up her voice and began chanting magic spells in a strange tongue, as if forsooth she were cleansing them of their blood-guiltiness. Now after we had continued sitting a long time, it occurred to us that the strangers might have broken loose and slain her and taken to flight; still as we were afraid of witnessing what we ought not to have seen, we remained seated in silence, until at last the same proposal was made by all of us, to go to them, although no leave was given. And there we see the hull of a vessel of Hellas with winged broadside of oar-blades fitted to it, and fifty sailors, oar in hand, at the tholes, and the youths, now free, standing astern the ship; while some were steadying the prow with poles, others hanging the anchor to the cat-heads, and the rest hauling in cables, getting ladders ready the while and letting them down into the sea for the strangers' use. Now when we saw their crafty tricks, we laid hold of the stranger maid and the hawsers recklessly, trying at the same time to unship the helm from the gallant craft through its rudderport; and words passed between us: "What pretext have ye for this stealthy raid on images and priestesses from our land? who, and whose son art thou that seekest to smuggle this maiden hence?" And answer came, "I am Orestes, the son of Agamemnon, this maiden's own brother, that thou mayst learn the truth; for she whom I am taking hence with me is the sister I once lost from my home." None the less we held the stranger maid and were for forcing her to follow us to thee, and that was how my cheeks came by these fearful blows; for they had no weapons in their hands, nor yet had we; but there was sturdy buffeting of fists, and likewise feet were aimed at side and heart by both those youths, so we closed with them and were at once exhausted. Then we fled to the cliff, most terribly marked, covered with bloody weals, some on their heads and others on their eyes; but once stationed on the rocks, we fought more cautiously and began by pelting them with stones; but archers, posted on the stern, kept us off with arrows, compelling us to retire to a distance. Meantime a monster wave had driven the vessel shoreward, and as the maiden feared to wet her feet, Orestes took his sister on his left shoulder, and, stepping into the sea, he leapt upon the ladder and set her down inside the gallant ship, with the image of the daughter of Zeus, which fell from heaven. Anon a voice was heard speaking from the vessel's midst, "Ye mariners of Hellas! grip your oars and dash the billows into foam, for now the prize is ours, which we sailed to the Euxine Sea to win, through the jaws of the clashing rocks."

With deep-drawn sighs of joy they smote the brine, and the ship made way, so long as she was inside the haven, but, meeting a furious surge, as she was crossing the harbour-bar, she began to labour; for on a sudden a tempestuous wind arose and forced her shoreward stern foremost; and the rowers tugged and strained to fight the wave, but still its backward wash would drive their ship to land again. Then Agamemnon's daughter rose and prayed, "O daughter of Latona, save me, bring thy priestess unto Hellas out of this savage land, and pardon my theft. As thou, O goddess, lovest thy brother, so believe that I too love my kith and kin." Therewith the sailors sung their pæan to second the maiden's prayer, and, baring their arms from the shoulder down, gripped their oars tightly at the boatswain's cry. But ever nearer to the rocks the ship drew on, and some sprang into the sea, others began fastening twisted nooses to the shore; while I was straightway sent hither to thee, my liege, to announce what had befallen there. So haste thee hence with gyves and cords; for, unless the waves grow calm, those strangers have no hope of safety.

It is Poseidon, majestic ruler of the main, who is regarding Ilium with favour but frowning on the race of Pelops; and now, it seems, he will deliver up into thy hands and the hands of thy subjects the son of Agamemnon with his sister, for she stands convicted of faithlessness to the goddess in forgetting the sacrifice at Aulis. *Exit* MESSENGER.

Ch. Alas for thee, Iphigenia! once more within the tyrant's clutch thou wilt be slain with thy brother.

Th. Ho! every dweller in this foreign land, up and bridle your steeds and gallop to the beach! there await the stranding of the Hellenes' ship, and then hunt the godless wretches eagerly with the help of the goddess. Go, you others, and launch my swiftest galleys, that we may either overhaul them by sea or ride them down by land and hurl them headlong from a precipice or impale their limbs on stakes.

(*Turning to the* CHORUS) As for you women, their accomplices herein, I will punish you hereafter, when

I have leisure, but now with the present business before me, I will not remain idle.

ATHENA *appears above the stage.*

Athena. Whither, King Thoas, whither art thou carrying this pursuit? Hearken to the words of Athena who is here. Cease pursuing or sending soldiers streaming after them; for Orestes was destined by Apollo's oracle to come hither, first to escape the fury of the avenging fiends, and then to convey his sister home to Argos and the sacred image to my land, a respite from his present afflictions. This I say to thee; and for Orestes, whom they thinkest to catch at sea and slay, e'en now is Poseidon guiding him hence on his ship for my sake, smoothing the surface of the deep.

Orestes—thou hearest the voice, for it is a goddess speaking, although thou art not here—mark well my hests, take the image and thy sister, and go hence; and when thou art come to Athens, that god-built town, thou wilt find a spot upon the utmost bounds of Attica, bordering on Carystus' ridge, a holy place called Halae by my people. There build a temple and set up the image, named after the Taurian land and the labours long endured by thee in ranging Hellas to and fro through the goading of avenging fiends. Henceforth shall mortal men chant her praises as Artemis the Taurian goddess. Ordain this law also; when the people celebrate her festival, the priest, to compensate her for thy sacrifice, must hold his knife to a human throat and blood must flow to satisfy the sacred claims of the goddess, that she may have her honours.

As for thee, Iphigenia, thou must keep her temple-keys at Brauron's hallowed path of steps;[1] there shalt thou die and there shall they bury thee, honouring thee with offerings of robes, e'en all the finely-woven vestments left in their homes by such as die in child-birth. (*To* THOAS) And I charge thee send these daughters of Hellas on their way hence because of their righteous decision . . . . . I saved thee once before, Orestes, when I allotted the votes equally on the hill of Ares; and this shall be an ordinance; whoever secures an equal division of votes wins his case. So bear thy sister from the land, son of Agamemnon, and thou, Thoas, be no longer angry.

[1]Said to refer to steps cut in the rock leading to the temple of Artemis at Brauron.

Th. Whoso hears the voice of God and disobeys is no sane man, O queen Athena. For my part, I am not wroth with Orestes or his sister, though he *has* taken the image hence; for what credit is there in struggling with the mighty gods? Let them go with the goddess's image to thy land and there erect it to their joy. Moreover I will send these women to Hellas, their happy home, as thou commandest me, and will check my spear which I am lifting against the strangers, and stop the sailing of my ships, since this is thy good pleasure, goddess.

At. Well said; for necessity is stronger than thee, aye, and than the gods.

Go, ye breezes, waft the son of Agamemnon on his way to Athens; and I myself will share his voyage, keeping the image of my sister safe.

Ch. Go and luck go with you, happy in your preservation!

Hail to thee! Pallas Athena, name revered by deathless gods as well as mortal men! we will perform all thy bidding; for very welcome and unlooked for are the words I have heard.

Most holy Victory! possess my life and never grudge thy crown! *Exeunt* OMNES.

• • •

IPHIGENIA AT AULIS

DRAMATIS PERSONAE

Agamemnon	Clytaemnestra
Attendant, *an old man*	Iphigenia
Chorus of Women of Chalcis	Achilles
Menelaus	Messenger

The sea-coast at Aulis. Enter agamemnon *and* attendant.

Agamemnon. Old man, come hither and stand before my dwelling.

Attendant. I come; what new schemes now, king Agamemnon?

Ag. Thou shalt hear.

At. I am all eagerness. 'Tis little enough sleep old age allows me and keenly it watches o'er my eyes.

Ag. What can that star be, steering his course yonder?

At. Sirius, still shooting o'er the zenith on his way near the Pleiads' sevenfold track.

Ag. The birds are still at any rate and the sea is calm; hushed are the winds, and silence broods o'er this narrow firth.

At. Then why art thou outside thy tent, why so restless, my lord Agamemnon? All is yet quiet here in Aulis, the watch on the walls is not yet astir. Let us go in.

Ag. I envy thee, old man, aye, and every man who leads a life secure, unknown and unrenowned; but little I envy those in office.

At. And yet 'tis there we place the be-all and end-all of existence.

Ag. Aye, but that is where the danger comes; and ambition, sweet though it seems, brings sorrow with its near approach. At one time the unsatisfied claims of Heaven upset our life, at another the numerous peevish fancies of our subjects shatter it.

At. I like not these sentiments in one who is a chief. It was not to enjoy all blessings that Atreus begot thee, O Agamemnon; but thou must needs experience joy and sorrow alike, mortal as thou art. E'en though thou like it not, this is what the gods decree; but thou, after letting thy taper spread its light abroad, writest the letter which is still in thy hands and then erasest the same words again, sealing and re-opening the scroll, then flinging the tablet to the ground with floods of tears and leaving nothing undone in thy aimless behaviour to stamp thee mad. What is it troubles thee? what news is there affecting thee, my liege? Come, share with me thy story; to a loyal and trusty heart wilt thou be telling it; for Tyndareus sent me that day to form part of thy wife's dowry and to wait upon the bride with loyalty.

Ag. Leda, the daughter of Thestius, had three children, maidens, Phœbe, Clytaemnestra my wife, and Helen; this last it was who had for wooers the foremost of the favoured sons of Hellas; but terrible threats of spilling his rival's blood were uttered by each of them, should he fail to win the maid. Now the matter filled Tyndareus, her father, with perplexity; at length this thought occurred to him; the suitors should swear unto each other and join right hands thereon and pour libations with burnt-sacrifice, binding themselves by this curse, "Whoever wins the child of Tyndareus for wife, him will we assist, in case a rival takes her from his house and goes his way, robbing her husband of his rights; and we will march against that man in armed array and raze his city to the ground, Hellene no less than barbarian."

Now when they had once pledged their word and old Tyndareus with no small cleverness had beguiled them by his shrewd device, he allowed his daughter to choose from among her suitors the one towards whom the breath of love might fondly waft her. Her choice fell on Menelaus; would she had never taken him! Anon there came to Lacedæmon from Phrygia's folk the man who, legend says, adjudged the goddesses' dispute; in robes of gorgeous hue, ablaze with gold, in true barbaric pomp; and he, finding Menelaus gone from home, carried Helen off with him to his steading on Ida, a willing paramour. Goaded to frenzy Menelaus flew through Hellas, invoking the ancient oath exacted by Tyndareus and declaring the duty of helping the injured husband. Whereat the chivalry of Hellas, brandishing their spears and donning their harness, came hither to the narrow straits of Aulis with armaments of ships and troops, with many a steed and many a car, and they chose me to captain them all for the sake of Menelaus, since I was his brother. Would that some other had gained that distinction instead of me! But after the army was gathered and come together, we still remained at Aulis weather-bound; and Calchas, the seer, bade us in our perplexity sacrifice my own begotten child Iphigenia to Artemis, whose home is in this land, declaring that if we offered her, we should sail and sack the Phrygians' capital, but if we forbore, this was not for us. When I heard this, I commanded Talthybius with loud proclamation to disband the whole host, as I could never bear to slay daughter of mine. Whereupon my brother, bringing every argument to bear, persuaded me at last to face the crime; so I wrote in a folded scroll and sent to my wife, bidding her despatch our daughter to me on the pretence of wedding Achilles, at the same time magnifying his exalted rank and saying that he refused to sail with the Achæans, unless a bride of our lineage should go to Phthia. Yes, this was the inducement I offered my wife, inventing, as I did, a sham marriage for the maiden. Of all the Achæans we alone know the real truth, Calchas, Odysseus, Menelaus and myself; but that which I then decided wrongly, I now rightly countermand again in this scroll, which thou, old man, hast found me opening and resealing beneath the shade of night. Up now and away with this missive to Argos, and I will tell thee by word of mouth all that is written herein, the contents of the folded scroll, for thou art loyal to my wife and house.

At. Say on and make it plain, that what my tongue utters may accord with what thou hast written.

Ag. "Daughter of Leda, in addition to my first letter, I now send thee word not to despatch thy daughter to Eubœa's embosomed wing, to the waveless bay of Aulis; for after all we will celebrate our child's wedding at another time."

At. And how will Achilles, cheated of his bride, curb the fury of his indignation against thee and thy wife?

Ag. Here also is a danger.[1]

At. Tell me what thou meanest.

Ag. It is but his name, not himself, that Achilles is lending, knowing nothing of the marriage or of my scheming or my professed readiness to betroth my daughter to him for a husband's embrace.

At. A dreadful venture thine, king Agamemnon! thou that, by promise of thy daughter's hand to the son of the goddess, wert for bringing the maid hither to be sacrificed for the Danaï.

Ag. Woe is me! ah woe! I am utterly distraught; bewilderment comes o'er me.

Away! hurry thy steps, yielding nothing to old age.

At. In haste I go, my liege.

Ag. Sit not down by woodland founts; scorn the witcheries of sleep.

At. Hush!

Ag. And when thou passest any place where roads diverge, cast thine eyes all round, taking heed that no mule-wain pass by on rolling wheels, bearing my daughter hither to the ships of the Danaï, and thou see it not.

At. It shall be so.

Ag. Start then from the bolted gates, and if thou meet the escort, start them back again, and drive at full speed to the abodes of the Cyclopes.

At. But tell me, how shall my message find credit with thy wife or child?

[1] Paley follows Musgrave in assigning these words to Agamemnon, assuming that the king passes over the servant's last remark and adds a new cause of alarm, viz., the fraud that is being practised on Achilles.

Ag. Preserve the seal which thou bearest on this scroll. Away! already the dawn is growing grey, lighting the lamp of day yonder and the fire of the sun's four steeds; help me in my trouble.

Exit ATTENDANT.

None of mortals is prosperous or happy to the last, for none was ever born to a painless life.

Exit AGAMEMNON.

Enter CHORUS OF WOMEN OF CHALCIS.

Chorus. To the sandy beach of sea-coast Aulis I came after a voyage through the tides of Euripus, leaving Chalcis on its narrow firth, my city which feedeth the waters of far-famed Arethusa near the sea, that I might behold the army of the Achæans and the ships rowed by those god-like heroes; for our husbands tell us that fair-haired Menelaus and high-born Agamemnon are leading them to Troy on a thousand ships in quest of the lady Helen, whom herdsman Paris carried off from the banks of reedy Eurotas—his guerdon from Aphrodite, when that queen of Cyprus entered beauty's lists with Hera and Pallas at the gushing fount.

Through the grove of Artemis, rich with sacrifice, I sped my course, the red blush mantling on my cheeks from maiden modesty, in my eagerness to see the soldiers' camp, the tents of the mail-clad Danai, and their gathered steeds. Two chieftains there I saw met together in council; one was Aias, son of Oileus; the other Aias, son of Telamon, crown of glory to the men of Salamis; and I saw Protesilaus and Palamedes, sprung from the son of Poseidon, sitting there amusing themselves with intricate figures at draughts; Diomedes too at his favourite sport of hurling quoits; and Meriones, the War-god's son, a marvel to mankind, stood at his side; likewise I beheld the offspring of Laertes, who came from his island hills, and with him Nireus, handsomest of all Achæans; Achilles next, that nimble runner, swift on his feet as the wind, whom Thetis bore and Chiron trained; him I saw upon the beach, racing in full armour along the shingle, and straining every nerve to beat a team of four horses, as he sped round the track on foot; and Eumelus, the grandson of Pheres, their driver, was shouting when I saw him, goading on his goodly steeds, with their bits of chased goldwork; whereof the centre pair, that bore the yoke, had dappled coats picked out with white, while the trace-horses, on the outside, facing the turning-post in the course, were bays with spotted fetlocks. Close beside them Peleus' son leapt on his way, in all his harness, keeping abreast the rail by the axle-box.

Next I sought the countless fleet, a wonder to behold, that I might fill my girlish eyes with gazing, a sweet delight. The warlike Myrmidons from Phthia held the right wing with fifty swift cruisers, upon whose sterns, right at the ends, stood Nereid goddesses in golden effigy, the ensign of Achilles' armament. Near these were moored the Argive ships in equal numbers, o'er which Mecisteus' son, whom Taulaus his grandsire reared, and Sthenelus, son of Capaneus, were in command; next in order, Theseus' son was stationed at the head of sixty ships from

Attica, having the goddess Pallas set in a winged car drawn by steeds with solid hoof, a lucky sight for mariners. Then I saw Bœotia's fleet of fifty sails decked with ensigns; these had Cadmus at the stern holding a golden dragon at the beaks of the vessels, and earth-born Leitus was their admiral. Likewise there were ships from Phocis; and from Locris came the son of Oileus with an equal contingent, leaving famed Thronium's citadel; and from Mycenæ, the Cyclopes' town, Atreus' son sent a hundred well-manned galleys, his brother being with him in command, as friend with friend, that Hellas might exact vengeance on her, who had fled her home to wed a foreigner. Also I saw upon Gerenian Nestor's prows from Pylos the sign of his neighbour Alpheus, four-footed like a bull. Moreover there was a squadron of twelve Ænianian sail under King Gouneus; and next the lords of Elis, stationed near them, whom all the people named Epeians; and Eurytus was lord of these; likewise he led the Taphian warriors with the white oar-blades, the subjects of Meges, son of Phyleus, who had left the isles of the Echinades, where sailors cannot land. Lastly, Aias, reared in Salamis, was joining his right wing to the left of those near whom he was posted, closing the line with his outermost ships—twelve barques obedient to the helm—as I heard and then saw the crews; no safe return shall he obtain, who bringeth his barbaric boats to grapple Aias. There I saw the naval armament, but some things I heard at home about the gathered host, whereof I still have a recollection.

Enter MENELAUS *and* ATTENDANT.

At. (*As* MENELAUS *wrests a letter from him*) Strange daring thine, Menelaus, where thou hast no right.

Menelaus. Stand back! thou carriest loyalty to thy master too far.

At. The very reproach thou hast for me is to my credit.

Men. Thou shalt rue it, if thou meddle in matters that concern thee not.

At. Thou hadst no right to open a letter, which I was carrying.

Men. No, nor thou to be carrying sorrow to all Hellas.

At. Argue that point with others, but surrender that letter to me.

Men. I shall not let go.

At. Nor yet will I let loose my hold.

Men. Why then, this staff of mine will be dabbling thy head with blood ere long.

At. To die in my master's cause were a noble death.

Men. Let go! thou art too wordy for a slave.

At. (*Seeing* AGAMEMNON *approaching*) Master, he is wronging me; he snatched thy letter violently from my grasp, Agamemnon, and will not heed the claims of right.

Enter AGAMEMNON.

Ag. How now? what means this uproar at the gates, this indecent brawling?

Men. My tale, not his, has the better right to be spoken.

Ag. Thou, Menelaus! what quarrel hast thou with this man, why art thou haling him hence?

Exit ATTENDANT.

Men. Look me in the face! Be that the prelude to my story.

Ag. Shall I, the son of Atreus, close my eyes from fear?[1]

Men. Seest thou this scroll, the bearer of a shameful message?

Ag. I see it, yes; and first of all surrender it.

Men. No, not till I have shewn its contents to all the Danai.

Ag. What! hast thou broken the seal and dost know already what thou shouldst never have known?

Men. Yes, I opened it and know to thy sorrow the secret machinations of thy heart.

Ag. Where didst thou catch my servant? Ye gods! what a shameless heart thou hast!

Men. I was awaiting thy daughter's arrival at the camp from Argos.

Ag. What right hast thou to watch my doings? Is not this a proof of shamelessness?

Men. My wish to do it gave the spur, for I am no slave to thee.

Ag. Infamous! Am I not to be allowed the management of my own house?

Men. No, for thou thinkest crooked thoughts, one thing now, another formerly, and something different presently.

Ag. Most exquisite refining on evil themes! A hateful thing the tongue of cleverness!

Men. Aye, but a mind unstable is an unjust possession, disloyal to friends. Now I am anxious to test thee, and seek not thou from rage to turn aside from the truth, nor will I on my part overstrain the case. Thou rememberest when thou wert all eagerness to captain the Danai against Troy, making a pretence of declining, though eager for it in thy heart; how humble thou wert then! taking each man by the hand and keeping open doors for every fellow-townsman who cared to enter, affording each in turn a chance to speak with thee, even though some desired it not, seeking by these methods to purchase popularity from all bidders; then when thou hadst secured the command, there came a change over thy manners; thou wert no longer so cordial as before to whilom friends, but hard of access, seldom to be found at home. But the man of real worth ought not to change his manners in the hour of prosperity, but should then show himself most staunch to friends, when his own good fortune can help them most effectually. This was the first cause I had to reprove thee, for it was here I first discovered thy villainy; but afterwards, when thou camest to Aulis with all the gathered hosts of Hellas, thou wert of no account; no! the want of a favourable breeze filled thee with consternation at the chance dealt out by Heaven. Anon the Danai began demanding that thou shouldst send the fleet away instead of vainly

[1]The point lies in the play on the name 'Ατρεύς, *i. e.*, "the fearless," "shall I the son of fearlessness fear, etc.?"

toiling on at Aulis; what dismay and confusion was then depicted in thy looks, to think that thou, with a thousand ships at thy command, hadst not occupied the plains of Priam with thy armies! And thou wouldst ask my counsel, "What am I to do? what scheme can I devise, where find one?" to save thyself being stripped of thy command and losing thy fair fame. Next when Calchas bade thee offer thy daughter in sacrifice to Artemis, declaring that the Danai should then sail, thou wert overjoyed, and didst gladly undertake to offer the maid, and of thine own accord—never allege compulsion!—thou art sending word to thy wife to despatch thy daughter hither on pretence of wedding Achilles. This is the same air that heard thee say it; and after all thou turnest round and hast been caught recasting thy letter to this effect, "I will no longer be my daughter's murderer." Exactly so! Countless others have gone through this phase in their conduct of public affairs; they make an effort while in power, and then retire dishonourably, sometimes owing to the senselessness of the citizens, sometimes deservedly, because they are too feeble of themselves to maintain their watch upon the state. For my part, I am more sorry for our unhappy Hellas, whose purpose was to read these worthless foreigners a lesson, while now she will let them escape and mock her, thanks to thee and thy daughter. May I never then appoint a man to rule my country or lead its warriors because of his kinship! Ability is what the general must have; since any man, with ordinary intelligence, can govern a state.

Ch. For brethren to come to words and blows, whene'er they disagree, is terrible.

Ag. I wish to rebuke thee in turn, briefly, not lifting mine eyes too high in shameless wise, but in more sober fashion, as a brother; for it is a good man's way to be considerate. Prithee, why this burst of fury, these bloodshot eyes? who wrongs thee? what is it thou wantest? Thou art fain to win a virtuous bride. Well, I cannot supply thee; for she, whom thou once hadst, was ill controlled by thee. Am I then, a man who never went astray, to suffer for thy sins? or is it my popularity that galls thee? No! it is the longing thou hast to keep a fair wife in thy embrace, casting reason and honour to the winds. A bad man's pleasures are like himself. Am I mad, if I change to wiser counsels, after previously deciding amiss? Thine is the madness rather in wishing to recover a wicked wife, once thou hadst lost her—a stroke of Heaven-sent luck. Those foolish suitors swore that oath to Tyndareus in their longing to wed; but Hope was the goddess that led them on, I trow, and she it was that brought it about rather then thou and thy mightiness. So take the field with them; they are ready for it in the folly of their hearts; for the deity is not without insight, but is able to discern where oaths have been wrongly pledged or forcibly extorted. I will not slay my children, nor shall thy interests be prospered by justice in thy vengeance for a worthless wife, while I am left wasting, night and day, in sorrow for what I did to one of my own flesh and blood, contrary to all law and justice. There is thy answer shortly given, clear and easy to understand; and if thou wilt not come to thy senses, I shall do the best for myself.

Ch. This differs from thy previous declaration, but there is good in it—thy child's reprieve.

Men. Ah me, how sad my lot! I have no friends then after all.

Ag. Friends thou hast, if thou seek not their destruction.

Men. Where wilt thou find any proof that thou art sprung from the same sire as I?

Ag. Thy moderation, not thy madness do I share by nature.

Men. Friends should sympathize with friends in sorrow.

Ag. Claim my help by kindly service, not by paining me.

Men. So thou hast no mind to share this trouble with Hellas?

Ag. No, Hellas is diseased like thee according to some god's design.

Men. Go vaunt thee then on thy sceptre, after betraying thine own brother! while I will seek some different means and other friends.

Enter MESSENGER.

Messenger. Agamemnon, lord of all Hellenes! I am come and bring thee thy daughter, whom thou didst call Iphigenia in thy home; and her mother, thy wife Clytemnestra, is with her, and the child Orestes, a sight to gladden thee after thy long absence from thy palace; but, as they had been travelling long and far, they are now refreshing their tender feet at the waters of a fair spring, they and their horses, for we turned these loose in the grassy meadow to browse their fill; but I am come as their forerunner to prepare thee for their reception; for the army knows already of thy daughter's arrival, so quickly did the rumour spread; and all the folk are running together to the sight, that they may see thy child; for Fortune's favourites enjoy a world-wide fame and have all eyes fixed on them. "Is it a wedding?" some ask, "or what is happening? or has king Agamemnon from fond yearning summoned his daughter hither?" From others thou wouldst have heard: "They are presenting the maiden to Artemis, queen of Aulis, previous to marriage; who can the bridegroom be, that is to lead her home?"

Come, then, begin the rites—that is the next step—by getting the baskets ready; crown your heads; prepare the wedding-hymn, thou and prince Menelaus with thee; let flutes resound throughout the tents with noise of dancer's feet; for this is a happy day, that is come for the maid.

Ag. Thou hast my thanks; now go within; for the rest it will be well, as Fate proceeds.

Exit MESSENGER.

Ah, woe is me! unhappy wretch, what can I say? where shall I begin? Into what cruel straits have I been plunged! Fortune has outwitted me, proving far cleverer than any cunning of mine. What an advantage humble birth possesses! for it is easy for her sons to weep and tell out all their sorrows; while to the high-born man come these same sorrows, but we have dignity throned o'er our life and are the people's slaves. I, for instance, am ashamed to weep, nor less, poor wretch, to check my tears at the awful pass to which I am brought. Oh! what am I to tell my wife? how shall I welcome her? with what face meet her? for she too has undone me by coming uninvited in this my hour of sorrow; yet it was but natural she should come with her daughter to prepare the bride and perform the fondest duties, where she will discover my villainy. And for this poor maid—why maid? Death, methinks, will soon make her his bride—how I pity her! Thus will she plead to me, I trow: "My father will thou slay me? Be such the wedding thou thyself mayst find, and whosoever is a friend to thee!" while Orestes, from his station near us, will cry in childish accents, inarticulate, yet fraught with meaning. Alas! to what utter ruin Paris, the son of Priam, the cause of these troubles, has brought me by his union with Helen!

Ch. I pity her myself, in such wise as a woman, and she a stranger, may bemoan the misfortunes of royalty.

Men. (*Offering his hand*) Thy hand, brother! let me grasp it.

Ag. I give it; thine is the victory, mine the sorrow.

Men. By Pelops our reputed grandsire and Atreus our father I swear to tell thee the truth from my heart, without any covert purpose, but only what I think. The sight of thee in tears made me pity thee, and in return I shed a tear for thee myself; I withdraw from my former proposals, ceasing to be a cause of fear to thee; yea, and I will put myself in thy present position; and I counsel thee, slay not thy child nor prefer my interests to thine; for it is not just that thou shouldst grieve, while I am glad, or that thy children should die, while mine still see the light of day. What is it, after all, I seek? If I am set on marriage, could I not find a bride as choice elsewhere? Was I to lose a brother—the last I should have lost—to win a Helen, getting bad for good? I was mad, impetuous as a youth, till I perceived, on closer view, what slaying children really meant. Moreover I am filled with compassion for the hapless maiden, doomed to bleed that I may wed, when I reflect that we are kin. What has thy daughter to do with Helen? Let the army be disbanded and leave Aulis; dry those streaming eyes, brother, and provoke me not to tears. Whatever concern *thou* hast in oracles that affect thy child, let it be none of mine; into thy hands I resign my share therein. A sudden change, thou'lt say, from my fell proposals! A natural course for me; affection for my brother caused the change. These are the ways of a man not void of virtue, to pursue on each occasion what is best.

Ch. A generous speech, worthy of Tantalus, the son of Zeus! Thou dost not shame thy ancestry.

Ag. I thank thee, Menelaus, for this unexpected suggestion; 'tis an honourable proposal, worthy of thee.

Men. Sometimes love, sometimes the selfishness of their families causes a quarrel between brothers; I loathe a relationship of this kind which is bitterness to both.

Ag. 'Tis useless, for circumstances compel me to carry out the murderous sacrifice of my daughter.

Men. How so? who will compel thee to slay thine own child?

Ag. The whole Achæan army here assembled.

Men. Not if thou send her back to Argos.

Ag. I might do that unnoticed, but there will be another thing I cannot.

Men. What is that? Thou must not fear the mob too much.

Ag. Calchas will tell the Argive host his oracles.

Men. Not if he be killed ere that—an easy matter.

Ag. The whole tribe of seers is a curse with its ambition.

Men. Yes, and good for nothing and useless, when amongst us.

Ag. Has the thought, which is rising in my mind, no terrors for thee?

Men. How can I understand thy meaning, unless thou declare it?

Ag. The son of Sisyphus knows all.

Men. Odysseus cannot possibly hurt us.

Ag. He was ever shifty by nature, siding with the mob.

Men. True, he is enslaved by the love of popularity, a fearful evil.

Ag. Bethink thee then, will he not arise among the Argives and tell them the oracles that Calchas delivered, saying of me that I undertook to offer Artemis a victim, and after all am proving false? Then, when he has carried the army away with him, he will bid the Argives slay us and sacrifice the maiden; and if I escape to Argos, they will come and destroy the place, razing it to the ground, Cyclopean walls and all. That is my trouble. Woe is me! to what straits Heaven has brought me at this pass! Take one precaution for me, Menelaus, as thou goest through the host, that Clytemnestra learn this not, till I have taken my child and devoted her to death, that my affliction may be attended with the fewest tears. (*Turning to the* CHORUS) And you, ye stranger dames, keep silence.

Exeunt AGAMEMNON *and* MENELAUS.

Ch. Happy they who find the goddess come in moderate might, sharing with self-restraint in Aphrodite's gift of marriage and enjoying calm and rest from frenzied passions, wherein the Love-god, golden-haired, stretches his charmèd bow with arrows twain, and one is aimed at happiness, the other at life's confusion. O lady Cypris, queen of beauty! far from my bridal bower I ban the last. Be mine delight in moderation and pure desires, and may I have a share in love, but shun excess therein!

Men's natures vary, and their habits differ, but true virtue is always manifest. Likewise the training that comes of education conduces greatly to virtue; for not only is modesty wisdom, but it has also the rare grace of seeing by its better judgment what is right; whereby a glory, ever young, is shed o'er life by reputation. A great thing it is to follow virtue's footsteps—for women in their secret loves; while in men again an inborn sense of order, shown in countless ways, adds to a city's greatness.

Thou camest, O Paris, to the place where thou wert reared to herd the kine amid the white heifers of Ida, piping in foreign strain and breathing on thy reeds an echo of the Phrygian airs Olympus played. Full-uddered cows were browsing at the spot where that verdict 'twixt goddesses was awaiting thee—the cause of thy going to Hellas to stand before the ivory palace, kindling love in Helen's trancèd eyes and feeling its flutter in thine own breast; whence the fiend of strife brought Hellas with her chivalry and ships to the towers of Troy.

Oh! great is the bliss the great enjoy. Behold Iphigenia, the king's royal child, and Clytaemnestra, the daughter of Tyndareus; how proud their lineage! how high their pinnacle of fortune! These mighty ones, whom wealth attends, are very gods in the eyes of less favoured folk.

Halt we here, maidens of Chalcis, and lift the queen from her chariot to the ground without stumbling, supporting her gently in our arms, with kind intent, that the renowned daughter of Agamemnon but just arrived may feel no fear; strangers ourselves, avoid we aught that may disturb or frighten the strangers from Argos.

Enter CLYTAEMNESTRA *and* IPHIGENIA.

Clytaemnestra. I take this as a lucky omen, thy kindness and auspicious greeting, and have good hope that it is to a happy marriage I conduct the bride. (*To Attendants*) Take from the chariot the dowry I am bringing for my daughter and convey it within with careful heed.

My daughter, leave the horse-drawn car, planting thy faltering footstep delicately. (*To the* CHORUS) Maidens, take her in your arms and lift her from the chariot, and let one of you give me the support of her hand, that I may quit my seat in the carriage with fitting grace.

Some of you stand at the horses' heads; for the horse has a timid eye, easily frightened; here take this child Orestes, son of Agamemnon, babe as he still is.

What! sleeping, little one, tired out by thy ride in the chariot? Awake to bless thy sister's wedding; for thou, my gallant boy, shalt get by this marriage a kinsman gallant as thyself, the Nereid's godlike offspring. Come hither to thy mother, my daughter, Iphigenia, and seat thyself beside me, and stationed near show my happiness to these strangers; yes, come hither and welcome the sire thou lovest so dearly.

Hail! my honoured lord, king Agamemnon! we have obeyed thy commands and are come.

Enter AGAMEMNON.

Iphigenia. (*Throwing herself into* AGAMEMNON'S *arms*) Be not wroth with me, mother, if I run from thy side and throw myself on my father's breast.

O my father! I long to outrun others and embrace thee after this long while; for I yearn to see thy face; be not wroth with me.

Cl. Thou mayst do so, daughter; for of all the children I have born, thou hast ever loved thy father best.

Ip. I see thee, father, joyfully after a long season.

Ag. And I thy father thee; thy words do equal duty for both of us.

Ip. All hail, father! thou didst well in bringing me hither to thee.

Ag. I know not how I am to say yes or no to that, my child.

Ip. Ha! how wildly thou art looking, spite of thy joy at seeing me.

Ag. A man has many cares when he is king and general too.

Ip. Be mine, all mine to-day; turn not unto moody thoughts.

Ag. Why so I am, all thine to-day; I have no other thought.

Ip. Then smooth thy knitted brow, unbend and smile.

Ag. Lo! my child, my joy at seeing thee is even as it is.

Ip. And hast thou then the tear-drop streaming from thy eyes?

Ag. Aye, for long is the absence from each other, that awaits us.

Ip. I know not, dear father mine, I know not of what thou art speaking.

Ag. Thou art moving my pity all the more by speaking so sensibly.

Ip. My words shall turn to senselessness, if that will cheer thee more.

Ag. (*Aside*) Ah, woe is me! this silence is too much. (*To* IPHIGENIA) Thou hast my thanks.

Ip. Stay with thy children at home, father.

Ag. My own wish! but to my sorrow I may not humour it.

Ip. Ruin seize their warring and the woes of Menelaus!

Ag. First will that, which has been my life-long ruin, bring ruin unto others.

Ip. How long thou wert absent in the bays of Aulis!

Ag. Aye, and there is still a hindrance to my sending the army forward.

Ip. Where do men say the Phrygians live, father?

Ag. In a land where I would Paris, the son of Priam, ne'er had dwelt.

Ip. 'Tis a long voyage thou art bound on, father, after thou leavest me.

Ag. Thou wilt meet thy father again, my daughter.

Ip. Ah! would it were seemly that thou shouldst take me as a fellow-voyager!

Ag. Thou too hast a voyage to make to a haven where thou wilt remember thy father.

Ip. Shall I sail thither with my mother or alone?

Ag. All alone, without father or mother.

Ip. What! hast thou found me a new home, father!

Ag. Enough of this! 'tis not for girls to know such things.

Ip. Speed home from Troy, I pray thee, father, as soon as thou hast triumphed there.

Ag. There is a sacrifice I have first to offer here.

Ip. Yea, 'tis thy duty to heed religion with aid of holy rites.

Ag. Thou wilt witness it, for thou wilt be standing near the laver.

Ip. Am I to lead the dance then round the altar, father?

Ag. (*Aside*) I count thee happier than myself because thou knowest nothing. (*To* IPHIGENIA) Go within into the presence of maidens, after thou hast given me thy hand and one sad kiss, on the eve of thy lengthy sojourn far from thy father's side.

Bosom, cheek, and golden hair! ah, how grievous ye have found Helen and the Phrygians' city! I can no more; the tears come welling to my eyes, the moment I touch thee. *Exit* IPHIGENIA.

(*Turning to* CLYTAEMNESTRA) Herein I crave thy pardon, daughter of Leda, if I showed excessive grief at the thought of resigning my daughter to Achilles; for though we are sending her to taste of bliss, still it wrings a parent's heart, when he, the father who has toiled so hard for them, commits his children to the homes of strangers.

Cl. I am not so void of sense; bethink thee, I shall go through this as well, when I lead the maiden from the chamber to the sound of the marriage-hymn; wherefore I chide thee not; but custom will combine with time to make the smart grow less.

As touching him, to whom thou hast betrothed our daughter, I know his name, 'tis true, but would fain learn his lineage and the land of his birth.

Ag. There was one Ægina, the daughter of Asopus.

Cl. Who wedded her? some mortal or a god?

Ag. Zeus, and she bare Æacus, the prince of Œnone.[1]

Cl. What son of Æacus secured his father's halls?

Ag. Peleus, who wedded the daughter of Nereus.

Cl. With the god's consent, or when he had taken her in spite of gods?

Ag. Zeus betrothed her, and her guardian gave consent.

Cl. Where did he marry her? amid the billows of the sea?

Ag. In Chiron's home, at sacred Pelion's foot.

Cl. What! the abode ascribed to the race of Centaurs?

Ag. It was there the gods celebrated the marriage-feast of Peleus.

Cl. Did Thetis or his father train Achilles?

Ag. Chiron brought him up, to prevent his learning the ways of the wicked.

Cl. Ah! wise the teacher, still wiser the father, who intrusted his son to such hands.

Ag. Such is the future husband of thy daughter.

Cl. A blameless lord; but what city in Hellas is his?

Ag. He dwells on the banks of the river Apidanus, in the borders of Phthia.

Cl. Wilt thou convey our daughter thither?

Ag. He who takes her to himself will see to that.

[1]The old name of Ægina.

Cl. Happiness attend the pair! Which day will he marry her?

Ag. As soon as the full moon comes to give its blessing.

Cl. Hast thou already offered the goddess a sacrifice to usher in the maiden's marriage?

Ag. I am about to do so; that is the very thing I was engaged in.

Cl. Wilt thou celebrate the marriage-feast thereafter?

Ag. Yes, when I have offered a sacrifice required by Heaven of me.

Cl. But where am I to make ready the feast for the women?

Ag. Here beside our gallant Argive ships.

Cl. Finely here! but still I must; good come of it for all that!

Ag. I will tell thee, lady, what to do; so obey me now.

Cl. Wherein? for I was ever wont to yield thee obedience.

Ag. Here, where the bridegroom is, will I—

Cl. Which of my duties will ye perform in the mother's absence?

Ag. Give thy child away with help of Danai.

Cl. And where am I to be the while?

Ag. Get thee to Argos, and take care of thy unwedded daughters.

Cl. And leave my child? Then who will raise her bridal torch?

Ag. I will provide the proper wedding torch.

Cl. That is not the custom; but thou thinkest lightly of these things.

Ag. It is not good thou shouldst be alone among a soldier-crowd.

Cl. It is good that a mother should give her own child away.

Ag. Aye, and that those maidens at home should not be left alone.

Cl. They are in safe keeping, pent in their maiden-bowers.

Ag. Obey.

Cl. Nay, by the goddess-queen of Argos! go, manage matters out of doors; but in the house it is my place to decide what is proper for maidens at their wedding. *Exit.*

Ag. Woe is me! my efforts are baffled; I am disappointed in my hope, anxious as I was to get my wife out of sight; foiled at every point, I form my plots and subtle schemes against my best-beloved. But I will go, in spite of all, with Calchas the priest, to inquire the goddess's good pleasure, fraught with ill-luck as it is to me, and with trouble to Hellas. He who is wise should keep in his house a good and useful wife or none at all. *Exit.*

Ch. They say the Hellenes' gathered host will come in arms aboard their ships to Simois with its silver eddies, even to Ilium, the plain of Troy beloved by Phœbus; where famed Cassandra, I am told, whene'er the god's resistless prophecies inspire her, wildly tosses her golden tresses, wreathed with crown of verdant bay. And on the towers of Troy and round her walls shall Trojans stand, when sea-borne troops with brazen shields row in on shapely ships to the channels of the Simois, eager to take Helen, the sister of that heavenly pair whom Zeus begat, from Priam, and bear her back to Hellas by toil of Achæa's shields and spears; encircling Pergamus, the Phrygians' town, with murderous war around her stone-built towers, dragging men's heads backward to cut their throats, and sacking the citadel of Troy from roof to base, a cause of many tears to maids and Priam's wife; and Helen, the daughter of Zeus, shall weep in bitter grief, because she left her lord.

Oh! ne'er may there appear to me or to my children's children the prospect which the wealthy Lydian dames and Phrygia's brides will have, as at their looms they hold converse: "Say who will pluck this fair blossom from her ruined country, tightening his grasp on lovely tresses till the tears flow? 'Tis all through thee, the offspring of the long-necked swan; if indeed it be a true report that Leda bare thee to a winged bird, when Zeus transformed himself thereto, or whether, in the pages of the poets, fables have carried these tales to men's ears idly, out of season."

Enter ACHILLES.

Achilles. Where in these tents is Achæa's general? Which of his servants will announce to him that Achilles, the son of Peleus, is at his gates seeking him? For this delay at the Euripus is not the same for all of us; there be some, for instance, who, though still unwed, have left their houses desolate and are idling here upon the beach, while others are married and have children; so strange the longing for this expedition that has fallen on their hearts by Heaven's will. My own just plea must I declare, and whoso else hath any wish will speak for himself. Though I have left Pharsalia and Peleus, still I linger here by reason of these light breezes at the Euripus, restraining my Myrmidons, while they are ever instant with me saying, "Why do we tarry, Achilles? how much longer must we count the days to the start for Ilium? do something, if thou art so minded; else lead home thy men, and wait not for the tardy action of these Atridæ."

Enter CLYTAEMNESTRA.

Cl. Hail to thee, son of the Nereid goddess! I heard thy voice from within the tent and therefore came forth.

Ac. O modesty revered! who can this lady be whom I behold, so richly dowered with beauty's gifts?

Cl. No wonder thou knowest me not, seeing I am one thou hast never before set eyes on; I praise thy reverent address to modesty.

Ac. Who art thou, and wherefore art thou come to the mustering of the Danai—thou, a woman, to a fencèd camp of men?

Cl. The daughter of Leda I; my name Clytaemnestra; and my husband king Agamemnon.

Ac. Well and shortly answered on all important points! but it ill befits that I should stand talking to women.

Cl. Stay; why seek to fly? Give me thy hand, a prelude to a happy marriage.

Ac. What is it thou sayest? I give thee my hand? Were I to lay a finger where I have no right, I could ne'er meet Agamemnon's eye.

Cl. The best of rights hast thou, seeing it is my child thou wilt wed, O son of the sea-goddess, whom Nereus begat.

Ac. What wedding dost thou speak of? words fail me, lady; can thy wits have gone astray and art thou inventing this?

Cl. All men are naturally shy in the presence of new relations, when these remind them of their wedding.

Ac. Lady, I have never wooed daughter of thine, nor have the sons of Atreus ever mentioned marriage to me.

Cl. What can it mean? thy turn now to marvel at my words, for thine are passing strange to me.

Ac. Hazard a guess; that we can both do in this matter; for it may be we are both correct in our statements.

Cl. What! have I suffered such indignity? The marriage I am courting has no reality, it seems; I am ashamed of it.

Ac. Some one perhaps has made a mock of thee and me; pay no heed thereto; make light of it.

Cl. Farewell; I can no longer face thee with unfaltering eyes, after being made a liar and suffering this indignity.

Ac. 'Tis "farewell" too I bid thee, lady; and now I go within the tent to seek thy husband.

At. (*Calling through the tent-door*) Stranger of the race of Æacus, stay awhile! Ho there! thee I mean, O goddess-born, and thee, daughter of Leda.

Ac. Who is it calling through the half-opened door? what fear his voice betrays!

At. A slave am I; of that I am not proud, for fortune permits it not.

Ac. Whose slave art thou? not mine; for mine and Agamemnon's goods are separate.

At. I belong to this lady who stands before the tent, a gift to her from Tyndareus her father.

Ac. I am waiting; tell me, if thou art desirous, why thou hast stayed me.

At. Are ye really all alone here at the door?

Cl. To us alone wilt thou address thyself; come forth from the king's tent.

At. (*Coming out*) O Fortune and my own foresight, preserve whom I desire!

Ac. That speech will save them—in the future; it has a certain pompous air.

Cl. Delay not for the sake of touching my right hand, if there is aught that thou wouldst say to me.

At. Well, thou knowest my character and my devotion to thee and thy children.

Cl. I know thou hast grown old in the service of my house.

At. Likewise thou knowest it was in thy dowry king Agamemnon received me.

Cl. Yes, thou camest to Argos with me, and hast

been mine this long time past.

At. True; and though I bear thee all goodwill, I like not thy lord so well.

Cl. Come, come, unfold whate'er thou hast to say.

At. Her father, he that begat her, is on the point of slaying thy daughter with his own hand—

Cl. How? Out upon thy story, old dotard! thou art mad.

At. Severing with a sword the hapless maid's white throat.

Cl. Ah, woe is me! Is my husband haply mad?

At. Nay; sane, except where thou and thy daughter are concerned; there he is mad.

Cl. What is his reason? what vengeful fiend impels him?

At. Oracles—at least so Calchas says, in order that the host may start—

Cl. Whither? Woe is me, and woe is thee, thy father's destined victim!

At. To the halls of Dardanus, that Menelaus may recover Helen.

Cl. So Helen's return then was fated to affect Iphigenia?

At. Thou knowest all; her father is about to offer thy child to Artemis.

Cl. But that marriage—what pretext had it for bringing me from home?

At. An inducement to thee to bring thy daughter cheerfully, to wed her to Achilles.

Cl. On a deadly errand art thou come, my daughter, both thou, and I, thy mother.

At. Piteous the lot of both of you—and fearful Agamemnon's venture.

Cl. Alas! I am undone; my eyes can no longer stem their tears.

At. What more natural than to weep the loss of thy children?

Cl. Whence, old man, dost say thou hadst this news?

At. I had started to carry thee a letter referring to the former writing.

Cl. Forbidding or combining to urge my bringing the child to her death?

At. Nay, forbidding it, for thy lord was then in his sober senses.

Cl. How comes it then, if thou wert really bringing me a letter, that thou dost not now deliver it into my hands?

At. Menelaus snatched it from me—he who caused this trouble.

Cl. Dost thou hear that, son of Peleus, the Nereid's child?

Ac. I have been listening to the tale of thy sufferings, and I am indignant to think I was used as a tool.

Cl. They will slay my child; they have tricked her with thy marriage.

Ac. Like thee I blame thy lord, nor do I view it with mere indifference.

Cl. No longer will I let shame prevent my kneeling to thee, a mortal to one goddess-born; why do I affect reserve? whose interests should I consult before my child's? (*Throwing herself before* ACHILLES) Oh! help me, goddess-born, in my sore distress, and her that was called thy bride—in vain, 'tis true, yet called she was. For thee it was I wreathed her head and led her forth as if to marriage, but now it is to slaughter I am bringing her. On thee will come reproach because thou didst not help her; for though not wedded to her, yet wert thou the loving husband of my hapless maid in name at any rate. By thy beard, right hand, and mother too I do implore thee; for thy name it was that worked my ruin, and thou art bound to stand by that. Except thy knees I have no altar whereunto to fly; and not a friend stands at my side. Thou hast heard the cruel abandoned scheme of Agamemnon; and I, a woman, am come, as thou seest, to a camp of lawless sailor-folk, bold in evil's cause, though useful when they list; wherefore if thou boldly stretch forth thine arm in my behalf, our safety is assured; but if thou withhold it, we are lost.

Ch. A wondrous thing is motherhood, carrying with it a potent spell, wherein all share, so that for their children's sake they will endure affliction.

Ac. My proud spirit is stirred to range aloft, but it has learnt to grieve in misfortune and rejoice in high prosperity with equal moderation. For these are the men who can count on ordering all their life aright by wisdom's rules. True, there are cases where 'tis pleasant not to be too wise, but there are others, where some store of wisdom helps. Brought up in godly Chiron's halls myself, I learnt to keep a single heart; and provided the Atridæ lead aright, I will obey them; but when they cease therefrom, no more will I obey. Nay, but here and in Troy I will show the freedom of my nature, and, as far as in me lies, do honour to Ares with my spear. Thee, lady, who hast suffered so cruelly from thy nearest and dearest, will I, by every effort in a young man's power, set right, investing thee with that amount of pity, and never shall thy daughter, after being once called my bride, die by her father's hand; for I will not lend myself to thy husband's subtle tricks; no! for it will be my name that kills thy child, although it wieldeth not the steel. Thy own husband is the actual cause, but I shall no longer be guiltless, if, because of me and my marriage, this maiden perishes, she that hath suffered past endurance and been the victim of affronts most strangely undeserved. So am I made the poorest wretch in Argos; I a thing of naught, and Menelaus counting for a man! No son of Peleus I, but the issue of a vengeful fiend, if my name shall serve thy husband for the murder. Nay! by Nereus, who begat my mother Thetis, in his home amid the flowing waves, never shall king Agamemnon touch thy daughter, no! not even to the laying of a finger-tip upon her robe; else will Sipylus, that frontier town of barbarism, the cradle of those chieftains' line, be henceforth a city indeed, while Phthia's name will nowhere find mention. Calchas, the seer, shall rue beginning the sacrifice with his barley-meal and lustral water. Why, what is a seer? A man who with luck tells the truth sometimes, with frequent falsehoods, but when his luck deserts him, collapses then and there. It is not to secure a bride that I have spoken thus—there be maids unnumbered eager to have my love—no! but king Agamemnon has put an insult on me; he should have asked my leave to use my name as a means to catch the child, for it was I chiefly who induced Clytaemnestra to betroth her daughter to me; verily I had yielded this to Hellas, if that was where our going to Ilium broke down; I would never have refused to further my fellow-soldiers' common interest. But, as it is, I am as naught in the eyes of those chieftains, and little they reck of treating me well or ill. My sword shall soon know if any one is to snatch thy daughter from me, for then will I make it reek with the bloody stains of slaughter, ere it reach Phrygia. Calm thyself then; as a god in his might I appeared to thee, without being so, but such will I show myself for all that.

Ch. Son of Peleus, thy words are alike worthy of thee and that sea-born deity, the holy goddess.

Cl. Ah! would I could find words to utter thy praise without excess, and yet not lose the graciousness thereof by stinting it; for when the good are praised, they have a feeling, as it were, of hatred for those who in their praise exceed the mean. But I am ashamed of intruding a tale of woe, since my affliction touches myself alone and thou art not affected by troubles of mine; but still it looks well for the man of worth to assist the unfortunate, even when he is not connected with them. Wherefore pity us, for our sufferings cry for pity; in the first place, I have harboured an idle hope in thinking to have thee wed my daughter; and next, perhaps, the slaying of my child will be to thee an evil omen in thy wooing hereafter, against which thou must guard thyself. Thy words were good, both first and last; for if thou will it so, my daughter will be saved. Wilt have her clasp thy knees in suppliant wise? 'Tis no maid's part; yet if it seem good to thee, why come she shall with the modest look of free-born maid; but if I shall obtain the self-same end from thee without her coming, then let her abide within, for there is dignity in her reserve; still reserve must only go as far as the case allows.

Ac. Bring not thou thy daughter out for me to see, lady, nor let us incur the reproach of the ignorant; for an army, when gathered together without domestic duties to employ it, loves the evil gossip of malicious tongues. After all, should ye supplicate me, ye will attain a like result as if I had ne'er been supplicated; for I am myself engaged in a mighty struggle to rid you of your troubles. One thing be sure thou hast heard; I will not tell a lie; if I do that or idly mock thee, may I die, but live if I preserve the maid.

Cl. Bless thee for ever succouring the distressed!

Ac. Hearken then to me, that the matter may succeed.

Cl. What is thy proposal? for hear thee I must.

Ac. Let us once more urge her father to a better frame of mind.

Cl. He is something of a coward, and fears the army too much.

Ac. Still argument o'erthroweth argument.

Cl. Cold hope indeed; but tell me what I must do.

Ac. Entreat him first not to slay his children, and if he is stubborn, come to me. For if he consents to thy request, my intervention need go no further, since this consent insures thy safety. I too shall show myself in a better light to my friend, and the army will not blame me, if I arrange the matter by reason rather than force; while, should things turn out well, the result will prove satisfactory both to thee and thy friends, even without my interference.

Cl. How sensibly thou speakest! I must act as seemeth best to thee; but should I fail of my object, where am I to see thee again? whither must I turn my wretched steps and find thee ready to champion my distress?

Ac. I am keeping watch to guard thee, where occasion calls, that none see thee passing through the host of Danai with that scared look. Shame not thy father's house; for Tyndareus deserveth not to be ill spoken of, being a mighty man in Hellas.

Cl. 'Tis even so. Command me; I must play the slave to thee. If there are gods, thou for thy righteous dealing wilt find them favourable; if there are none, what need to toil?

Exeunt ACHILLES *and* CLYTAEMNESTRA.

Ch. What wedding-hymn was that which raised its strains to the sound of Libyan flutes, to the music of the dancer's lyre, and the note of the pipe of reeds?

'Twas in the day Pieria's fair-tressed choir came o'er the slopes of Pelion to the marriage-feast of Peleus, beating the ground with print of golden sandals at the banquet of the gods, and hymning in dulcet strains the praise of Thetis and the son of Æacus, o'er the Centaurs' hill, down through the woods of Pelion.

There was the Dardanian boy, Phrygian Ganymede, whom Zeus delights to honour, drawing off the wine he mixed in the depths of golden bowls; while, along the gleaming sand, the fifty daughters of Nereus graced the marriage with their dancing, circling in a mazy ring.

Came too the revel-rout of Centaurs, mounted on horses, to the feast of the gods and the mixing-bowl of Bacchus, leaning on fir-trees, with wreaths of green foliage round their heads; and loudly cried the prophet Chiron, skilled in arts inspired by Phœbus; "Daughter of Nereus, thou shalt bear a son"—whose name he gave—"a dazzling light to Thessaly; for he shall come with an army of Myrmidon spearmen to the far-famed land of Priam, to set it in a blaze, his body cased in a suit of golden mail forged by Hephæstus, a gift from his goddess-mother, even from Thetis who bore him."

Then shed the gods a blessing on the marriage of the high-born bride, who was first of Nereus' daughters, and on the wedding of Peleus. But thee[1] will Argives crown, wreathing the lovely tresses of thy hair, like a dappled mountain hind brought from

[1] *i.e.*, Iphigenia.

some rocky cave or a heifer undefiled, and staining with blood thy human throat; though thou wert never reared like these amid the piping and whistling of herdsmen, but at thy mother's side, to be decked one day by her as the bride of a son of Inachus. Where now does the face of modesty or virtue avail aught? seeing that godlessness holds sway, and virtue is neglected by men and thrust behind them, lawlessness o'er law prevailing, and mortals no longer making common cause to keep the jealousy of gods from reaching them.

Cl. (*Reappearing from the tent*) I have come from the tent to look out for my husband, who went away and left its shelter long ago; while that poor child, my daughter, hearing of the death her father designs for her, is in tears, uttering in many keys her piteous lamentation. (*Catching sight of* AGAMEMNON) It seems I was speaking of one not far away; for there is Agamemnon, who will soon be detected in the commission of a crime against his own child.

Enter AGAMEMNON.

Ag. Daughter of Leda, 'tis lucky I have found thee outside the tent, to discuss with thee in our daughter's absence subjects not suited for the ears of maidens on the eve of marriage.

Cl. What, pray, is dependent on the present crisis?

Ag. Send the maiden out to join her father, for the lustral water stands there ready, and barley-meal to scatter with the hand on the cleansing flame, and heifers to be slain in honour of the goddess Artemis, to usher in the marriage, their black blood spouting from them.

Cl. Though fair the words thou usest, I know not how I am to name thy deeds in terms of praise.

Come forth, my daughter; full well thou knowest what is in thy father's mind; take the child Orestes, thy brother, and bring him with thee in the folds of thy robe.

Enter IPHIGENIA.

Behold! she comes, in obedience to thy summons. Myself will speak the rest alike for her and me.

Ag. My child, why weepest thou and no longer lookest cheerfully? why art thou fixing thine eyes upon the ground and holding thy robe before them?

Cl. Alas! with which of my woes shall I begin? for I may treat them all as first, or put them last or midway anywhere.

Ag. How now? I find you all alike, confusion and alarm in every eye.

Cl. My husband, answer frankly the questions I ask thee.

Ag. There is no necessity to order me; I am willing to be questioned.

Cl. Dost thou mean to slay thy child and mine?

Ag. (*Starting*) Ha! these are heartless words, unwarranted suspicions!

Cl. Peace! answer me that question first.

Ag. Put a fair question and thou shalt have a fair answer.

Cl. I have no other questions to put; give me no other answers.

Ag. O fate revered, O destiny, and fortune mine!

Cl. Aye, and mine and this maid's too; the three share one bad fortune.

Ag. Whom have I injured?

Cl. Dost thou ask *me* this question? A thought like that itself amounts to thoughtlessness.

Ag. Ruined! my secret out!

Cl. I know all; I have heard what thou art bent on doing to me. Thy very silence and those frequent groans are a confession; tire not thyself by telling it.

Ag. Lo! I am silent; for, if I tell thee a falsehood, needs must I add effrontery to misfortune.

Cl. Well, listen; for I will now unfold my meaning and no longer employ dark riddles. In the first place—to reproach thee first with this—it was not of my own free will but by force that thou didst take and wed me, after slaying Tantalus, my former husband, and dashing my babe on the ground alive, when thou hadst torn him from my breast with brutal violence. Then, when those two sons of Zeus, who were likewise my brothers, came flashing on horseback to war with thee, Tyndareus, my aged sire, rescued thee because of thy suppliant prayers, and thou in turn hadst me to wife. Once reconciled to thee upon this footing, thou wilt bear me witness I have been a blameless wife to thee and thy family, chaste in love, an honour to thy house, that so thy coming in might be with joy and thy going out with gladness. And 'tis seldom a man secures a wife like this, though the getting of a worthless woman is no rarity.

Besides three daughters, of one of whom thou art heartlessly depriving me, I am the mother of this son of thine. If anyone asks thee thy reason for slaying her, tell me, what wilt thou say? or must I say it for thee? "It is that Menelaus may recover Helen." An honourable exchange, indeed, to pay a wicked woman's price in children's lives! 'Tis buying what we most detest with what we hold most dear. Again, if thou go forth with the host, leaving me in thy halls, and art long absent at Troy, what will my feelings be at home, dost think? when I behold each vacant chair and her chamber now deserted, and then sit down alone in tears, making ceaseless lamentation for her, "Ah! my child, he that begat thee hath slain thee himself, he and no one else, nor was it by another's hand." . . . . . [1]to thy home, after leaving such a price to be paid; for it needs now but a trifling pretext for me and the daughters remaining to give thee the reception it is right thou shouldst receive. I adjure thee by the gods, compel me not to sin against thee, nor sin thyself. Go to; suppose thou sacrifice the child; what prayer wilt thou utter, when 'tis done? what will the blessing be that thou wilt invoke upon thyself as thou art slaying our daughter? an ill returning maybe, seeing the disgrace that speeds thy going forth. Is it right that I should pray for any luck to attend thee? Surely we should deem the gods devoid of sense, if we harboured a kindly feeling towards murderers. Shalt thou embrace thy

[1]A line here fallen out to effect, "How wilt thou dare to return to thy wife and . . ."

children on thy coming back to Argos? Nay, thou hast no right. Will any child of thine e'er face thee, if thou have surrendered one of them to death? Has this ever entered into thy calculations, or does thy one duty consist in carrying a sceptre about and marching at the head of an army? when thou mightest have made this fair proposal among the Argives; "Is it your wish, Achæans, to sail for Phrygia's shores? Why then, cast lots whose daughter has to die." For that would have been a fair course for thee to pursue, instead of picking out thy own child for the victim and presenting her to the Danaï; or Menelaus, inasmuch as it was his concern, should have slain Hermione for her mother. As it is, I, who still am true to thee, must lose my child; while she, who went astray, will return with her daughter, and live in happiness at Sparta. If I am wrong in aught herein, answer me; but if my words have been fairly urged, do not still slay thy child, who is mine too, and thou wilt be wise.

Ch. Hearken to her, Agamemnon, for to join in saving thy children's lives is surely a noble deed; none would gainsay this.

Ip. Had I the eloquence of Orpheus, my father, to move the rocks by chanted spells to follow me, or to charm by speaking whom I would, I had resorted to it. But as it is, I'll bring my tears—the only art I know; for that I might attempt. And about thy knees, in suppliant wise, I twine my limbs—these limbs thy wife here bore. Destroy me not before my time, for sweet it is to look upon the light, and force me not to visit scenes below. I was the first to call thee father, thou the first to call me child; the first was I to sit upon thy knee and give and take the fond caress. And this was what thou then wouldst say, "Shall I see thee, my child, living a happy prosperous life in a husband's home one day, in a manner worthy of myself?" And I in my turn would ask, as I hung about thy beard, whereto I now am clinging, "How shall I see thee? Shall I be giving thee a glad reception in my halls, father, in thy old age, repaying all thy anxious care in rearing me?"

I remember all we said, 'tis thou who hast forgotten and now wouldst take my life. By Pelops, I entreat thee spare me, by thy father Atreus and my mother here, who suffers now a second time the pangs she felt before when bearing me! What have I to do with the marriage of Paris and Helen? why is his coming to prove my ruin, father? Look upon me; one glance, one kiss bestow, that this at least I may carry to my death as a memorial of thee, though thou heed not my pleading.

(*Holding up the babe* ORESTES) Feeble ally though thou art, brother, to thy loved ones, yet add thy tears to mine and entreat our father for thy sister's life; even in babes there is a natural sense of ill. O father, see this speechless supplication made to thee; pity me; have mercy on my tender years! Yea, by thy beard we two fond hearts implore thy pity, the one a babe, a full-grown maid the other. By summing all my pleas in one, I will prevail in what I say. To gaze upon yon light is man's most cherished gift; that life below is nothingness, and whoso longs for death is mad. Better live a life of woe than die a death of glory!

Ch. Ah, wretched Helen! Awful the struggle that has come to the sons of Atreus and their children, thanks to thee and those marriages of thine.

Ag. While loving my own children, I yet understand what should move my pity and what should not; I were a madman else. 'Tis terrible for me to bring myself to this, nor less terrible is it to refuse, daughter; for I must fare the same. Ye see the vastness of yon naval host, and the numbers of bronzeclad warriors from Hellas, who can neither make their way to Ilium's towers nor raze the far-famed citadel of Troy, unless I offer thee according to the word of Calchas the seer. Some mad desire possesses the host of Hellas to sail forthwith to the land of the barbarians, and put a stop to the rape of wives from Hellas, and they will slay my daughters in Argos as well as you and me, if I disregard the goddess's behests. It is not Menelaus who hath enslaved me to him, child, nor have I followed wish of his; nay, 'tis Hellas, for whom I must sacrifice thee whether I will or no; to this necessity I bow my head; for her freedom must be preserved, as far as any help of thine, daughter, or mine can go; nor must they, who are the sons of Hellas, be pillaged of their wives by barbarian robbery. AGAMEMNON *rushes from the stage.*

Cl. My child! Ye stranger ladies!

Woe is me for this thy death! Thy father flies, surrendering thee to Hades.

Ip. Woe is me, O mother mine! for the same strain hath fallen to both of us in our fortune. No more for me the light of day! no more the beams of yonder sun! Woe for that snow-beat glen in Phrygia and the hills of Ida, where Priam once exposed a tender babe, torn from his mother's arms to meet a deadly doom, e'en Paris, called the child of Ida in the Phrygians' town. Would Priam ne'er had settled him, the herdsman reared amid the herds, beside that water crystal-clear, where are fountains of the Nymphs and their meadow rich with blooming flowers, where hyacinths and rose-buds blow for goddesses to gather! Hither one day came Pallas and Cypris of the subtle heart, Hera too and Hermes messenger of Zeus—Cypris, proud of the longing she causes; Pallas of her prowess; and Hera of her royal marriage with king Zeus—to decide a hateful strife about their beauty; but it is my death, maidens—fraught, 'tis true, with glory to the Danaï—that Artemis has received as an offering, before they begin the voyage to Ilium.

O mother, mother! he that begat me to this life of sorrow has gone and left me all alone. Ah! woe is me! a bitter, bitter sight for me was Helen, evil Helen! to me now doomed to bleed and die, slaughtered by an impious sire.

I would this Aulis had never received in its havens here the sterns of their bronze-beaked ships, the fleet which was speeding them to Troy; and would that Zeus had never breathed on the Euripus a wind to stop the expedition, tempering, as he doth, a different breeze to different men, so that some have joy in setting sail, and sorrow some, and others hard constraint, to make some start and others stay and others furl their sails!

Full of trouble then, it seems, is the race of mortals, full of trouble verily; and 'tis ever Fate's decree that man should find distress.

Woe! woe to thee, thou child of Tyndareus, for the suffering and anguish sore, which thou art causing the Danai!

Ch. I pity thee for thy cruel fate—a fate I would thou ne'er hadst met!

Ip. O mother that bare me! I see a throng of men approaching.

Cl. It is the goddess-born thou seest, child, for whom thou camest hither.

Ip. (*Calling into the tent*) Open the tent-door to me, servants, that I may hide myself.

Cl. Why seek to fly, my child?

Ip. I am ashamed to face Achilles.

Cl. Wherefore?

Ip. The luckless ending to our marriage causes me to feel abashed.

Cl. No time for affectation now in face of what has chanced. Stay then; reserve will do no good, if only we can——

Enter ACHILLES.

Ac. Daughter of Leda, lady of sorrows!

Cl. No misnomer that.

Ac. A fearful cry is heard among the Argives.

Cl. What is it? tell me.

Ac. It concerns thy child.

Cl. An evil omen for thy words.

Ac. They say her sacrifice is necessary.

Cl. And is there no one to say a word against them?

Ac. Indeed I was in some danger myself from the tumult.

Cl. In danger of what? kind sir.

Ac. Of being stoned.

Cl. Surely not for trying to save my daughter?

Ac. The very reason.

Cl. Who would have dared to lay a finger on thee?

Ac. The men of Hellas, one and all.

Cl. Were not thy Myrmidon warriors at thy side?

Ac. They were the first who turned against me.

Cl. My child! we are lost, undone, it seems.

Ac. They taunted me as the man whom marriage had enslaved.

Cl. And what didst thou answer them?

Ac. I craved the life of her I meant to wed——

Cl. Justly so.

Ac. The wife her father promised me.

Cl. Aye, and sent to fetch from Argos.

Ac. But I was overcome by clamorous cries.

Cl. Truly the mob is a dire mischief.

Ac. But I will help thee for all that.

Cl. Wilt thou really fight them single-handed?

Ac. Dost see these warriors here, carrying my arms?

Cl. Bless thee for thy kind intent!

Ac. Well, I shall be blessed.

Cl. Then my child will not be slaughtered now?

Ac. No, not with my consent at any rate.

Cl. But will any of them come to lay hands on the maid?

Ac. Thousands of them, with Odysseus at their head.

Cl. The son of Sisyphus?

Ac. The very same.

Cl. Acting for himself or by the army's order?

Ac. By their choice—and his own.

Cl. An evil choice indeed, to stain his hands in blood!

Ac. But I will hold him back.

Cl. Will he seize and bear her hence against her will?

Ac. Aye, by her golden hair no doubt.

Cl. What must I do, when it comes to that?

Ac. Keep hold of thy daughter.

Cl. Be sure that she shall not be slain, as far as that can help her.

Ac. Believe me, it will come to this.

Ip. Mother, hear me while I speak, for I see that thou art wroth with thy husband to no purpose; 'tis hard for us to persist in impossibilities. Our thanks are due to this stranger for his ready help; but thou must also see to it that he is not reproached by the army, leaving us no better off and himself involved in trouble. Listen, mother; hear what thoughts have passed across my mind. I am resolved to die; and this I fain would do with honour, dismissing from me what is mean. Towards this now, mother, turn thy thoughts, and with me weigh how well I speak; to me the whole of mighty Hellas looks; on me the passage o'er the sea depends; on me the sack of Troy; and in my power it lies to check henceforth barbarian raids on happy Hellas, if ever in the days to come they seek to seize her daughters, when once they have atoned by death for the violation of Helen's marriage by Paris. All this deliverance will my death insure, and my fame for setting Hellas free will be a happy one. Besides, I have no right at all to cling too fondly to my life; for thou didst not bear me for myself alone, but as a public blessing to all Hellas. What! shall countless warriors, armed with shields, those myriads sitting at the oar, find courage to attack the foe and die for Hellas, because their fatherland is wronged, and my one life prevent all this? What kind of justice is that? could I find a word in answer? Now turn we to that other point. It is not right that this man should enter the lists with all Argos or be slain for a woman's sake. Better a single man should see the light than ten thousand women. If Artemis is minded to take this body, am I, a weak mortal, to thwart the goddess? Nay, that were impossible. To Hellas I resign it; offer this sacrifice and make an utter end of Troy. This is my enduring monument; marriage, motherhood, and fame—all these is it to me. And it is but right, mother, that Hellenes should rule barbarians, but not barbarians Hellenes, those being slaves, while these are free.

Ch. Thou playest a noble part, maiden; but sickly are the whims of Fate and the goddess.

Ac. Daughter of Agamemnon! some god was bent on blessing me, could I but have won thee for my wife. In thee I reckon Hellas happy, and thee in Hellas; for this that thou hast said is good and worthy of thy fatherland; since thou, abandoning a strife with heavenly powers, which are too strong for thee, has fairly weighed advantages and needs. But now that I have looked into thy noble nature, I feel still more a fond desire to win thee for my bride. Look to it; for I would fain serve thee and receive thee in my halls; and witness Thetis, how I grieve to think I shall not save thy life by doing battle with the Danai. Reflect, I say; a dreadful ill is death.

Ip. This I say, without regard to anyone. Enough that the daughter of Tyndareus is causing wars and bloodshed by her beauty; then be not slain thyself, sir stranger, nor seek to slay another on my account; but let me, if I can, save Hellas.

Ac. Heroic spirit! I can say no more to this, since thou art so minded; for thine is a noble resolve; why should not one avow the truth? Yet will I speak, for thou wilt haply change thy mind; that thou mayst know then what my offer is, I will go and place these arms of mine near the altar, resolved not to permit thy death but to prevent it; for brave as thou art, at sight of the knife held at thy throat, thou wilt soon avail thyself of what I said. So I will not let thee perish through any thoughtlessness of thine, but will go to the temple of the goddess with these arms and await thy arrival there.

Exit ACHILLES.

Ip. Mother, why so silent, thine eyes wet with tears?

Cl. I have reason, woe is me! to be sad at heart.

Ip. Forbear; make me not a coward; here in one thing obey me.

Cl. Say what it is, my child, for at my hands thou shalt ne'er suffer injury.

Ip. Cut not off the tresses of thy hair for me, nor clothe thyself in sable garb.

Cl. Why, my child, what is it thou hast said? Shall I, when I lose thee——

Ip. "Lose" me, thou dost not; I am saved and thou renowned, as far as I can make thee.

Cl. How so? Must I not mourn thy death?

Ip. By no means, for I shall have no tomb heaped o'er me.

Cl. What, is not the act of dying held to imply burial?

Ip. The altar of the goddess, Zeus's daughter, will be my tomb.

Cl. Well, my child, I will let thee persuade me, for thou sayest well.

Ip. Aye, as one who prospereth and doeth Hellas service.

Cl. What message shall I carry to thy sisters?

Ip. Put not mourning raiment on them either.

Cl. But is there no fond message I can give the maidens from thee?

Ip. Yes, my farewell words; and promise me to rear this babe Orestes to manhood.

Cl. Press him to thy bosom; 'tis thy last look.

Ip. O thou that art most dear to me! thou hast helped thy friends as thou hadst means.

Cl. Is there anything I can do to pleasure thee in Argos?

Ip. Yes, hate not my father, thy own husband.

Cl. Fearful are the trials through which he has to go because of thee.

Ip. It was against his will he ruined me for the sake of Hellas.

Cl. Ah! but he employed base treachery, unworthy of Atreus.

Ip. Who will escort me hence, before my hair is torn?

Cl. I will go with thee.

Ip. No, not thou; thou say'st not well.

Cl. I will, clinging to thy robes.

Ip. Be persuaded by me, mother, stay here; for this is the better way alike for me and thee; but let one of these attendants of my father conduct me to the meadow of Artemis, where I shall be sacrificed.

Cl. Art gone from me, my child?

Ip. Aye, and with no chance of ever returning.

Cl. Leaving thy mother?

Ip. Yes, as thou seest, undeservedly.

Cl. Hold! leave me not!

Ip. I cannot let thee shed a tear. (*Exit* CLYTAEMNESTRA. *To the* CHORUS) Be it yours, maidens, to hymn in joyous strains Artemis, the child of Zeus, for my hard lot; and let the order for a solemn hush go forth to the Danai. Begin the sacrifice with the baskets, let the fire blaze for the purifying meal of sprinkling, and my father pace from left to right about the altar; for I come to bestow on Hellas safety crowned with victory. Lead me hence, me the destroyer of Ilium's town and the Phrygians; give me wreaths to cast about me; bring them hither; here are my tresses to crown; bring lustral water too. Dance to Artemis, queen Artemis the blest, around her fane and altar; for by the blood of my sacrifice I will blot out the oracle, if it needs must be.

O mother, lady revered! for thee shall my tears be shed, and now; for at the holy rites I may not weep.

Sing with me, maidens, sing the praises of Artemis, whose temple faces Chalcis, where angry spearmen madly chafe, here in the narrow havens of Aulis, because of me.

O Pelasgia, land of my birth, and Mycenæ, my home!

Ch. Is it on Perseus' citadel thou callest, that town Cyclopean workmen builded?

Ip. To be a light to Hellas didst thou rear me, and so I say not No to death.

Ch. Thou art right; no fear that fame will e'er desert thee!

Ip. Hail to thee, bright lamp of day and light of Zeus! A different life, a different lot is henceforth mine. Farewell I bid thee, light beloved!

Exit IPHIGENIA.

Ch. Behold the maiden on her way, the destroyer of Ilium's town and its Phrygians, with garlands twined about her head, and drops of lustral water on her, soon to besprinkle with her gushing blood the altar of a murderous goddess, what time her shapely neck is severed.

For thee fair streams of a father's pouring and lustral waters are in store, for thee Achæa's host is waiting, eager to reach the citadel of Ilium. But let us celebrate Artemis, the daughter of Zeus, queen among the gods, as if upon some happy chance.

O lady revered, delighting in human sacrifice, send on its way to Phrygia's land the host of the Hellenes, to Troy's abodes of guile, and grant that Agamemnon may wreathe his head with deathless fame, a crown of fairest glory for the spearmen of Hellas.

Enter MESSENGER.

Me. Come forth, O Clytaemnestra, daughter of Tyndareus, from the tent, to hear my news.

Enter CLYTAEMNESTRA.

Cl. I heard thy voice and am come in sad dismay and fearful dread, not sure but what thou hast arrived with tidings of some fresh trouble for me besides the present woe.

Me. Nay, rather would I unfold to thee a story strange and marvellous about thy child.

Cl. Delay not, then, but speak at once.

Me. Dear mistress, thou shalt learn all clearly; from the outset will I tell it, unless my memory fail me somewhat and confuse my tongue in its account. As soon as we reached the grove of Artemis, the child of Zeus, and the meadows gay with flowers, where the Achæan troops were gathered, bringing thy daughter with us, forthwith the Argive host began assembling; but when king Agamemnon saw the maiden on her way to the grove to be sacrificed, he gave one groan, and, turning away his face, let the tears burst from his eyes, as he held his robe before them. But the maid, standing close by him that begot her, spake on this wise, "O my father, here am I to do thy bidding; freely I offer this body of mine for my country and all Hellas, that ye may lead me to the altar of the goddess and sacrifice me, since this is Heaven's ordinance. Good luck be yours for any help that I afford! and may ye obtain the victor's gift and come again to the land of your fathers. So then let none of the Argives lay hands on me, for I will bravely yield my neck without a word."

She spake; and each man marvelled, as he heard the maiden's brave, unflinching speech. But in the midst up stood Talthybius—for his this duty was—and bade the host refrain from word or deed; and Calchas, the seer, drawing a sharp sword from out its scabbard laid it in a basket of beaten gold, crowning the maiden's head the while. Then the son of Peleus, taking the basket and with it lustral water in his hand, ran round the altar of the goddess uttering these words, "O Artemis, thou child of Zeus, slayer of wild beasts, that wheelest thy dazzling light amid the gloom, accept this sacrifice, which we, the host of the Achæans and king Agamemnon with us, offer to thee, even pure blood from a beauteous maiden's neck; and grant us safe sailing for our ships and the sack of Troy's towers by our spears."

Meantime the sons of Atreus and all the host stood looking on the ground, while the priest, seizing his knife, offered up a prayer and was closely scanning the maiden's throat to see where he should strike. 'Twas no slight sorrow filled my heart, as I stood by with bowed head; when lo! a sudden miracle! Each one of us distinctly heard the sound of a blow, but none saw the spot where the maiden vanished. Loudly the priest cried out, and all the host took up the cry at the sight of a marvel all unlooked for, due to some god's agency, and passing all belief, although 'twas seen; for there upon the ground lay a hind of size immense and passing fair to see, gasping out her life, with whose blood the altar of the goddess was thoroughly bedewed. Whereon spake Calchas thus —his joy thou canst imagine—"Ye captains of this leagued Achæan host, do ye see this victim, which the goddess has set before her altar, a mountain-roaming hind? This is more welcome to her by far than the maid, that she may not defile her altar by shedding noble blood. Gladly has she accepted it and is granting us a prosperous voyage for our attack on Ilium. Wherefore take heart, sailors, each man of you, and away to your ships, for to-day must we leave the hollow bays of Aulis and cross the Ægean main."

Then, when the sacrifice was wholly burnt to ashes in the blazing flame, he offered such prayers as were meet, that the army might win return; but me Agamemnon sends to tell thee this, and say what Heaven-sent luck is his, and how he hath secured undying fame throughout the length of Hellas. Now I was there myself and speak as an eye-witness; without a doubt thy child flew away to the gods. A truce then to thy sorrowing, and cease to be wroth with thy husband; for God's ways with man are not what we expect, and those whom he loves, he keepeth safe; yea, for this day hath seen thy daughter dead and brought to life again. *Exit* MESSENGER.

Ch. What joy to hear these tidings from the messenger! He tells thee thy child is living still, among the gods.

Cl. Which of the gods, my child, hath stolen thee? How am I to address thee? How can I be sure that this is not an idle tale told to cheer me, to make me cease my piteous lamentation for thee?

Ch. Lo! king Agamemnon approaches, to confirm this story for thee.

Enter AGAMEMNON.

Ag. Happy may we be counted, lady, as far as concerns our daughter; for she hath fellowship with gods in very sooth. But thou must take this tender babe and start for home, for the host is looking now to sail. Fare thee well! 'tis long ere I shall greet thee on my return from Troy; may it be well with thee!

Ch. Son of Atreus, start for Phrygia's land with joy and so return, I pray, after taking from Troy her fairest spoils. *Exeunt* OMNES.

THE CYCLOPS

DRAMATIS PERSONAE

SILENUS — ODYSSEUS
CHORUS OF SATYRS — THE CYCLOPS
MUTE: *Companions of Odysseus*

Mount Ætna in Sicily, before the cave of the Cyclops. Enter SILENUS.

Silenus. O Bromius, unnumbered are the toils I bear because of thee, no less now than when I was young and hale; first, when thou wert driven mad by Hera and didst leave the mountain nymphs, thy nurses; next, when in battle with earth-born spearmen I stood beside thee on the right as squire, and slew Enceladus, smiting him full in the middle of his targe with my spear. Come, though, let me see; must I confess 'twas all a dream? No, by Zeus! since I really showed his spoils to the Bacchic god. And now am I enduring to the full a toil still worse than those. For when Hera sent forth a race of Tyrrhene pirates against thee, that thou mightest be smuggled far away, I, as soon as the news reached me, sailed in quest of thee with my children; and, taking the helm myself, I stood on the end of the stern and steered our trim craft; and my sons, sitting at the oars, made the grey billows froth and foam as they sought thee, my liege. But just as we had come nigh Malea in our course, an east-wind blew upon the ship and drove us hither to the rock of Ætna, where in lonely caverns dwell the one-eyed children of ocean's god, the murdering Cyclopes. Captured by one of them we are slaves in his house; Polyphemus they call him whom we serve; and instead of Bacchic revelry we are herding a godless Cyclops' flocks; and so it is my children, striplings as they are, tend the young thereof on the edge of the downs; while my appointed task is to stay here and fill the troughs and sweep out the cave, or wait upon the ungodly Cyclops at his impious feasts. His orders now compel obedience; I have to scrape out his house with the rake you see, so as to receive the Cyclops, my absent master, and his sheep in clean caverns.

But already I see my children driving their browsing flocks towards me.

What means this? is the beat of feet in the Sicinnis dance the same to you now as when ye attended the Bacchic god in his revelries and made your way with dainty steps to the music of lyres to the halls of Althæa?

Enter CHORUS OF SATYRS.

Chorus. Offspring of well-bred sires and dams, pray whither wilt thou be gone from me to the rocks? Hast thou not here a gentle breeze, and grass to browse, and water from the eddying stream set near the cave in troughs? and are not thy young ones bleating for thee?

Pst! pst! wilt thou not browse here, here on the dewy slope? Ho! ho! ere long will I cast a stone at thee. Away, away! O horned one, to the fold-keeper of the Cyclops, the country-ranging shepherd. Loosen thy bursting udder; welcome to thy teats the kids, whom thou leavest in the lambkins' pens. Those little bleating kids, asleep the livelong day, miss thee; wilt then leave at last the rich grass pastures on the peaks of Ætna and enter the fold? . . .

Here we have no Bromian god; no dances here, or Bacchantes thyrsus-bearing; no roll of drums, or drops of sparkling wine by gurgling founts; nor is it now with Nymphs in Nysa I sing a song of Bacchus, Bacchus! to the queen of love, in quest of whom I once sped on with Bacchantes, white of foot.

Dear friend, dear Bacchic god, whither art roaming alone, waving thy auburn locks, while I, thy minister, do service to the one-eyed Cyclops, a slave and wanderer I, clad in this wretched goat-skin dress, severed from thy love?

Si. Hush, children! and bid our servants fold the flocks in the rock-roofed cavern.

Ch. (*To* SERVANTS) Away! (*To* SILENUS) But prithee, why such haste, father?

Si. I see the hull of a ship from Hellas at the shore, and men, that wield the oar, on their way to this cave with some chieftain. About their necks they carry empty vessels and pitchers for water; they are in want of food. Luckless strangers! who can they be? They know not what manner of man our master Polyphemus is, to have set foot here in his cheerless abode and come to the jaws of the cannibal Cyclops in an evil hour. But hold ye your peace, that we may inquire whence they come to the peak of Sicilian Ætna.

Enter ODYSSEUS *and crew.*

Odysseus. Pray tell us, sirs, of some river-spring whence we might draw a draught to slake our thirst, or of someone willing to sell victuals to mariners in need.

Why, what is this? We seem to have chanced upon a city of the Bromian god; here by the caves I see a group of Satyrs. To the eldest first I bid "All hail!"

Si. All hail, sir! tell me who thou art, and name thy country.

Od. Odysseus of Ithaca, king of the Cephallenians' land.

Si. I know him for a prating knave, one of Sisyphus' shrewd offspring.

Od. I am the man; abuse me not.

Si. Whence hast thou sailed hither to Sicily?

Od. From Ilium and the toils of Troy.

Si. How was that? didst thou not know the passage to thy native land?

Od. Tempestuous winds drove me hither against my will.

Si. God wot! thou art in the same plight as I am.

Od. Why, wert thou too drifted hither against thy will?

Si. I was, as I pursued the pirates who carried Bromius off.

Od. What land is this and who are its inhabitants?

Si. This is mount Ætna, the highest point in Sicily.

Od. But where are the city-walls and ramparts?

Si. There are none; the headlands, sir, are void of men.

Od. Who then possess the land? the race of wild creatures?

Si. The Cyclopes, who have caves, not roofed houses.

Od. Obedient unto whom? or is the power in the people's hands?

Si. They are rovers; no man obeys another in anything.

Od. Do they sow Demeter's grain, or on what do they live?

Si. On milk and cheese and flesh of sheep.

Od. Have they the drink of Bromius, the juice of the vine?

Si. No indeed! and thus it is a joyless land they dwell in.

Od. Are they hospitable and reverent towards strangers?

Si. Strangers, they say, supply the daintiest meat.

Od. What, do they delight in killing men and eating them?

Si. No one has ever arrived here without being butchered.

Od. Where is the Cyclops himself? inside his dwelling?

Si. He is gone hunting wild beasts with hounds on Ætna.

Od. Dost know then what to do, that we may be gone from the land?

Si. Not I, Odysseus; but I would do anything for thee.

Od. Sell us food, of which we are in need.

Si. There is nothing but flesh, as I said.

Od. Well, even that is a pleasant preventive of hunger.

Si. And there is cheese curdled with fig-juice, and the milk of kine.

Od. Bring them out; a man should see his purchases.

Si. But tell me, how much gold wilt thou give me in exchange?

Od. No gold bring I, but Dionysus' drink.

Si. Most welcome words! I have long been wanting that.

Od. Yes, it was Maron, the god's son, who gave me a draught.

Si. What! Maron whom once I dandled in these arms?

Od. The son of the Bacchic god, that thou mayst learn more certainly.

Si. Is it inside the ship, or hast thou it with thee?

Od. This, as thou seest, is the skin that holds it, old sir.

Si. Why, that would not give me so much as a mouthful.

Od. This, and twice as much again as will run from the skin.

Si. Fair the rill thou speakest of, delicious to me.

Od. Shall I let thee taste the wine unmixed, to start with?

Si. A reasonable offer; for of a truth a taste invites the purchase.

Od. Well, I haul about a cup as well as the skin.

Si. Come, let it gurgle in, that I may revive my memory by a pull at it.

Od. There then!

Si. Ye gods! what a delicious scent it has!

Od. What! didst thou see it?

Si. No, i' faith, but I smell it.

Od. Taste it then, that thy approval may not stop at words.

Si. Zounds! Bacchus is inviting me to dance; ha! ha!

Od. Did it not gurgle finely down thy throttle?

Si. Aye that it did, to the ends of my fingers.

Od. Well, we will give thee money besides.

Si. Only undo the skin, and never mind the money.

Od. Bring out the cheeses then and lambs.

Si. I will do so, with small thought of any master. For let me have a single cup of that and I would turn madman, giving in exchange for it the flocks of every Cyclops and then throwing myself into the sea from the Leucadian rock, once I have been well drunk and smoothed out my wrinkled brow. For if a man rejoice not in his drinking, he is mad; for in drinking there is love with all its frolic, and dancing withal, and oblivion of woe. Shall not I then purchase so rare a drink, bidding the senseless Cyclops and his central eye go hang? *Exit* SILENUS.

Ch. Hearken, Odysseus, let us hold some converse with thee.

Od. Well, do so; ours is a meeting of friends.

Ch. Did you take Troy and capture the famous Helen?

Od. Aye, and we destroyed the whole family of Priam.

Ch. After capturing your blooming prize, were all of you in turn her lovers? for she likes variety in husbands; the traitress! the sight of a man with embroidered breeches on his legs and a golden chain about his neck so fluttered her, that she left Menelaus, her excellent little husband. Would there had never been a race of women born into the world at all, unless it were for me alone!

Re-enter SILENUS.

Si. (*With food*) Lo! I bring you fat food from the flocks, king Odysseus, the young of bleating sheep and cheeses of curdled milk without stint. Carry them away with you and be gone from the cave at once, after giving me a drink of merry grape-juice in exchange.

Ch. Alack! yonder comes the Cyclops; what shall we do?

Od. Then truly are we lost, old sir! whither must we fly?

Si. Inside this rock, for there ye may conceal yourselves.

Od. Dangerous advice of thine, to run into the net!

Si. No danger; there are ways of escape in plenty in the rock.

Od. No, never that; for surely Troy will groan and loudly too, if we flee from a single man, when I have oft withstood with my shield a countless host of Phrygians. Nay, if die we must, we will die a noble death; or, if we live, we will maintain our old renown at least with credit.

Enter CYCLOPS.

Cyclops. A light here! hold it up! what is this? what means this idleness, your Bacchic revelry? Here have we no Dionysus, nor clash of brass, nor roll of drums. Pray, how is it with my newly-born lambs in the caves? are they at the teat, running close to the side of their dams? Is the full amount of milk for cheeses milked out in baskets of rushes? How now? what say you? One of ye will soon be shedding tears from the weight of my club; look up, not down.

Ch. There! my head is bent back till I see Zeus himself; I behold both the stars and Orion.

Cy. Is my breakfast quite ready?

Ch. 'Tis laid; be thy throat only ready.

Cy. Are the bowls too full of milk?

Ch. Aye, so that thou canst swill off a whole hogshead, so it please thee.

Cy. Sheeps' milk or cows' milk or a mixture of both?

Ch. Whichever thou wilt; don't swallow me, that's all.

Cy. Not I; for you would start kicking in the pit of my stomach and kill me by your antics. (*Catching sight of* ODYSSEUS *and his followers*) Ha! what is this crowd I see near the folds? Some pirates or robbers have put in here. Yes, I really see the lambs from my caves tied up there with twisted osiers, cheese-presses scattered about, and old Silenus with his bald pate all swollen with blows.

Si. Oh! oh! poor wretch that I am, pounded to a fever.

Cy. By whom? who has been pounding thy head, old sirrah?

Si. These are the culprits, Cyclops, all because I refused to let them plunder thee.

Cy. Did they not know I was a god and sprung from gods?

Si. That was what I told them, but they persisted in plundering thy goods, and, in spite of my efforts, they actually began to eat the cheese and carry off the lambs; and they said they would tie thee in a three-cubit pillory and tear out thy bowels by force at thy navel, and flay thy back thoroughly with the scourge; and then, after binding thee, fling thy carcase down among the benches of their ship to sell to some one for heaving up stones, or else throw thee into a mill.

Cy. Oh, indeed! Be off then and sharpen my cleavers at once; heap high the faggots and light them; for they shall be slain forthwith and fill this maw of mine, what time I pick my feast hot from the coals, waiting not for carvers, and fish up the rest from the cauldron boiled and sodden; for I have had my fill of mountain-fare and sated myself with banquets of lions and stags, but 'tis long I have been without human flesh.

Si. Truly, master, a change like this is all the sweeter after everyday fare; for just of late there have been no fresh arrivals of strangers at these caves.

Od. Hear the strangers too in turn, Cyclops. We had come near the cave from our ship, wishing to procure provisions by purchase, when this fellow sold us the lambs and handed them over for a stoup of wine to drink himself—a voluntary act on both sides—there was no violence employed at all. No, there is not a particle of truth in the story he tells, now that he has been caught selling thy property behind thy back.

Si. I? Perdition catch thee!

Od. If I am lying, yes.

Si. O Cyclops, by thy sire Poseidon, by mighty Triton and Nereus, by Calypso and the daughters of Nereus, by the sacred billows and all the race of fishes! I swear to thee, most noble sir, dear little Cyclops, master mine, it is not I who sell thy goods to strangers, else may these children, dearly as I love them, come to an evil end.

Ch. Keep that for thyself; with my own eyes I saw thee sell the goods to the strangers; and if I lie, perdition catch my sire! but injure not the strangers.

Cy. Ye lie; for my part I put more faith in him than Rhadamanthus, declaring him more just. But I have some questions to ask. Whence sailed ye, strangers? of what country are you? what city was it nursed your childhood?

Od. We are Ithacans by birth, and have been driven from our course by the winds of the sea on our way from Ilium, after sacking its citadel.

Cy. Are ye the men who visited on Ilium, that bordereth on Scamander's wave, the rape of Helen, worst of women?

Od. We are; that was the fearful labour we endured.

Cy. A sorry expedition yours, to have sailed to the land of Phrygia for the sake of one woman!

Od. It was a god's doing; blame not any son of man. But thee do we implore, most noble son of Ocean's god, speaking as free-born men; be not so cruel as to slay thy friends on their coming to thy cave, nor regard us as food for thy jaws, an impious meal; for we preserved thy sire, O king, in possession of his temple-seats deep in the nooks of Hellas; and the sacred port of Tænarus and Malea's furthest coves remain unharmed; and Sunium's rock, the silver-veined, sacred to Zeus-born Athena, still is safe, and Geræstus, the harbour of refuge; and we did not permit Phrygians to put such an intolerable reproach on Hellas. Now in these things thou too hast a share, for thou dwellest in a corner of the land of Hellas beneath Ætna's fire-streaming rock; and although thou turn from arguments, still it is a custom amongst mortal men to receive shipwrecked sailors as their suppliants and show them hospitality and help them with raiment; not that these should fill thy jaws and belly, their limbs transfixed with spits for piercing ox-flesh. The land of Priam hath emptied Hellas quite enough, drinking the blood of many whom the spear laid low, with the ruin it has brought on widowed wives, on aged childless dames, and hoary-headed sires; and if thou roast and consume the remnant—a meal thou wilt rue—why, where shall one turn? Nay, be persuaded by me, Cyclops; forego thy ravenous greed and choose piety rather than wickedness; for on many a man ere now unrighteous gains have brought down retribution.

Si. . . . . . I will give thee a word of advice! as for his flesh, leave not a morsel of it, and if thou eat his tongue, Cyclops, thou wilt become a monstrous clever talker.

Cy. Wealth, manikin, is the god for the wise; all else is mere vaunting and fine words. Plague take the headlands by the sea, on which my father seats himself! Why hast thou put forward these arguments? I shudder not at Zeus' thunder, nor know I wherein Zeus is a mightier god than I, sir stranger; what is more, I reck not of him; my reasons hear. When he pours down the rain from above, here in this rock in quarters snug, feasting on roast calf's flesh or some wild game and moistening well my upturned paunch with deep draughts from a tub of milk, I rival the thunderclaps of Zeus with my artillery; and when the north-wind blows from Thrace and sheddeth snow, I wrap my carcase in the hides of beasts and light a fire, and what care I for snow? The earth perforce, whether she like it or not, produces grass and fattens my flocks, which I sacrifice to no one save myself and this belly, the greatest of deities; but to the gods, not I! For surely to eat and drink one's fill from day to day and give oneself no grief at all, this is the king of gods for your wise man, but lawgivers go hang, chequering, as they do, the life of man! And so I will not cease from indulging myself by devouring thee; and thou shalt receive this stranger's gift, that I may be free of blame—fire and my father's element yonder, and a cauldron to hold thy flesh and boil it nicely in collops. So in with you, that ye may feast me well, standing round the altar to honour the cavern's god. *Enters his cave.*

Od. Alas! escaped from the troubles of Troy and the sea, my barque now strands upon the whim and forbidding heart of this savage.

O Pallas, mistress mine, goddess-daughter of Zeus, help me, help me now; for I am come to toils and depths of peril worse than all at Ilium; and thou, O Zeus, the stranger's god, who hast thy dwelling 'mid the radiant stars, behold these things; for, if thou regard them not, in vain art thou esteemed the great god Zeus, though but a thing of naught.

Follows the CYCLOPS *reluctantly.*

Ch. Ope wide the portal of thy gaping throat, Cyclops; for strangers' limbs, both boiled and grilled, are ready from off the coals for thee to gnaw and tear and mince up small, reclining in thy shaggy goatskin coat.

Relinquish not thy meal for me; keep that boat for thyself alone. Avaunt this cave! avaunt the burnt-offerings, which the godless Cyclops offers on Ætna's altars, exulting in meals on strangers' flesh!

Oh! the ruthless monster! to sacrifice his guests at his own hearth, the suppliants of his halls, cleaving and tearing and serving up to his loathsome teeth a feast of human flesh, hot from the coals.

Od. (*Reappearing with a look of horror*) O Zeus! what can I say after the hideous sights I have seen inside the cave, things past belief, resembling more the tales men tell than aught they do?

Ch. What news, Odysseus? has the Cyclops, most godless monster, been feasting on thy dear comrades?

Od. Aye, he singled out a pair, on whom the flesh was fattest and in best condition, and took them up in his hand to weigh.

Ch. How went it with you then, poor wretch?

Od. When we had entered yonder rocky abode, he lighted first a fire, throwing logs of towering oak upon his spacious hearth, enough for three waggons to carry as their load; next, close by the blazing flame, he placed his couch of pine-boughs laid upon the floor, and filled a bowl of some ten firkins, pouring white milk thereinto, after he had milked his kine; and by his side he put a can of ivy-wood, whose breadth was three cubits and its depth four maybe; next he set his brazen pot a-boiling on the fire, spits too he set beside him, fashioned of the branches of thorn, their points hardened in the fire and the rest of them trimmed with the hatchet, and the blood-bowls of Ætna for the axe's edge.[1] Now when that hell-cook, god-detested, had everything quite ready, he caught up a pair of my companions and proceeded deliberately to cut the throat of one of them over the yawning brazen pot; but the other he clutched by the tendon of his heel, and, striking him against a sharp point of rocky stone, dashed out his brains; then, after hacking the fleshy parts with glutton cleaver, he set to grilling them, but the limbs he threw into his cauldron to seethe. And I, poor wretch, drew near with streaming eyes and waited on the Cyclops; but the others kept cower-

[1] *i.e.*, to catch the blood as the axe strikes.

ing like frightened birds in crannies of the rock, and the blood forsook their skin. Anon, when he had gorged himself upon my comrades' flesh and had fallen on his back, breathing heavily, there came a sudden inspiration to me. I filled a cup of this Maronian wine and offered him a draught, saying, "Cyclops, son of Ocean's god, see here what heavenly drink the grapes of Hellas yield, glad gift of Dionysus." He, glutted with his shameless meal, took and drained it at one draught, and, lifting up his hand, he thanked me thus, "Dearest to me of all my guests! fair the drink thou givest me to crown so fair a feast." Now when I saw his delight, I gave him another cup, knowing the wine would make him rue it, and he would soon be paying the penalty. Then he set to singing; but I kept filling bumper after bumper and heating him with drink. So there he is singing discordantly amid the weeping of my fellow-sailors, and the cave re-echoes; but I have made my way out quietly and would fain save thee and myself, if thou wilt. Tell me then, is it your wish, or is it not, to fly from this unsocial wretch and take up your abode with Naiad nymphs in the halls of the Bacchic god? Thy father within approves this scheme; but there! he is powerless, getting all he can out of his liquor; his wings are snared by the cup as if he had flown against bird-lime, and he is fuddled; but thou art young and lusty; so save thyself with my help and regain thy old friend Dionysus, so little like the Cyclops.

Ch. Best of friends, would we might see that day, escaping the godless Cyclops! for 'tis long we have been without the joys of men, unable to escape him.

Od. Hear then how I will requite this vile monster and rescue you from thraldom.

Ch. Tell me how; no note of Asiatic lyre would sound more sweetly in our ears then news of the Cyclops' death.

Od. Delighted with this liquor of the Bacchic god, he fain would go a-revelling with his brethren.

Ch. I understand; thy purpose is to seize and slay him in the thickets when alone, or push him down a precipice.

Od. Not at all; my plan is fraught with subtlety.

Ch. What then? Truly we have long heard of thy cleverness.

Od. I mean to keep him from this revel, saying he must not give this drink to his brethren but keep it for himself alone and lead a happy life. Then when he falls asleep, o'ermastered by the Bacchic god, I will put a point with this sword of mine to an olive-branch I saw lying in the cave, and will set it on fire; and when I see it well alight, I will lift the heated brand, and, thrusting it full in the Cyclops' eye, melt out his sight with its blaze; and, as when a man in fitting the timbers of a ship makes his auger spin to and fro with a double strap, so will I make the brand revolve in the eye that gives the Cyclops light and will scorch up the pupil thereof.

Ch. Ho! ho! how glad I feel! wild with joy at the contrivance!

Od. That done, I will embark thee and those thou lovest with old Silenus in the deep hold of my black ship, my ship with double banks of oars, and carry you away from this land.

Ch. Well, can I too lay hold of the blinding brand, as though the god's libation had been poured? for I would fain have a share in this offering of blood.

Od. Indeed thou *must*, for the brand is large, and thou must help hold it.

Ch. How lightly would I lift the load of e'en a hundred wains, if that will help us to grub out the eye of the doomed Cyclops, like a wasp's nest.

Od. Hush! for now thou knowest my plot in full, and when I bid you, obey the author of it; for I am not the man to desert my friends inside the cave and save myself alone. And yet I might escape; I am clear of the cavern's depths already; but no! to desert the friends with whom I journeyed hither and only save myself is not a righteous course.

Re-enters the cave.

Semi-Chorus I. Come, who will be the first and who the next to him upon the list to grip the handle of the brand, and, thrusting it into the Cyclops' eye, gouge out the light thereof?

Semi-Ch. II. Hush! hush! Behold the drunkard leaves his rocky home, trolling loud some hideous lay, a clumsy tuneless clown, whom tears await. Come, let us give this boor a lesson in revelry. Ere long will he be blind at any rate.

Semi-Ch. I. Happy he who plays the Bacchanal amid the precious streams distilled from grapes, stretched at full length for a revel, his arm around the friend he loves, and some fair dainty damsel on his couch, his hair perfumed with nard and glossy, the while he calls, "Oh! who will ope the door for me?"

Enter CYCLOPS *with* ODYSSEUS *and* SILENUS.

Cy. Ha! ha! full of wine and merry with the feast's good cheer am I, my hold freighted like a merchant-ship up to my belly's very top. This turf graciously invites me to seek my brother Cyclopes for a revel in the spring-tide.

Come, stranger, bring the wine-skin hither and hand it over to me.

Semi-Ch. II. Forth from the house its fair lord comes, casting his fair glance round him. We have some one to befriend us. A hostile brand is awaiting thee, no tender bride in dewy grot. No single colour will those garlands have, that soon shall cling so close about thy brow.

Od. (*Returning with the wine-skin*) Hearken, Cyclops; for I am well versed in the ways of Bacchus, whom I have given thee to drink.

Cy. And who is Bacchus? some reputed god?

Od. The greatest god men know to cheer their life.

Cy. I like his after-taste at any rate.

Od. This is the kind of god he is; he harmeth no man.

Cy. But how does a god like being housed in a wine-skin?

Od. Put him where one may, he is content there.

Cy. It is not right that gods should be clad in leather.

Od. What of that, provided he please thee? does the leather hurt thee?

Cy. I hate the wine-skin, but the liquor we have here I love.

Od. Stay, then, Cyclops; drink and be merry.

Cy. Must I not give my brethren a share in this liquor?

Od. No, keep it thyself and thou wilt appear of more honour.

Cy. Give it my friends and I shall appear of more use.

Od. Revelling is apt to end in blows, abuse, and strife.

Cy. I may be drunk, but no man will lay hands on me for all that.

Od. Better stay at home, my friend, after a carouse.

Cy. Who loves not revelling then is but a simpleton.

Od. But whoso stays at home, when drunk, is wise.

Cy. What shall we do, Silenus? art minded to stay?

Si. That I am; for what need have we of others to share our drink, Cyclops?

Cy. Well, truly the turf is soft as down with its fresh flowering plants.

Si. (*Seating himself*) Aye, and 'tis pleasant drinking in the warm sunshine.

Cy. . . . . .[1]

Si. Come, let me see thee stretch thy carcase on the ground.

Cy. (*Sitting down*) There then! Why art thou putting the mixing-bowl behind me?

Si. That no one passing by may come upon it.

Cy. Nay, but thy purpose is to drink upon the sly; set it between us. (*To* ODYSSEUS) Now tell me, stranger, by what name to call thee.

Od. Noman. What boon shall I receive of thee to earn my thanks?

Cy. I will feast on thee last, after all thy comrades.

Od. Fair indeed the honour thou bestowest on thy guest, sir Cyclops!

Cy. (*Turning suddenly to* SILENUS) Ho, sirrah! what art thou about? taking a stealthy pull at the wine?

Si. No, but it kissed me for my good looks.

Cy. Thou shalt smart, if thou kiss the wine when it kisses not thee.

Si. Oh! but it did, for it says it is in love with my handsome face.

Cy. (*Holding out his cup*) Pour in; only give me my cup full.

Si. H'm! how is it mixed? just let me make sure. (*Takes another pull*)

Cy. Perdition! give it me at once.

Si. Oh, no! I really cannot, till I see thee with a crown on, and have another taste myself.

[1]A line has been lost here.

Cy. My cup-bearer is a cheat.

Si. No really, but the wine is so luscious. Thou must wipe thy lips, though, to get a draught.

Cy. There! my lips and beard are clean now.

Si. Bend thine elbow gracefully, and then quaff thy cup, as thou seest me do, and as now thou seest me not. (*Burying his face in his cup*)

Cy. Aha! what next?

Si. I drunk it off at a draught with much pleasure.

Cy. Stranger, take the skin thyself and be my cup-bearer.

Od. Well, at any rate the grape is no stranger to my hand.

Cy. Come, pour it in.

Od. In it goes! keep silence, that is all.

Cy. A difficult task when a man is deep in his cups.

Od. Here, take and drink it off; leave none.

Cy. . . . .[2]

Od. Thou must be silent and only give in when the liquor does.

Cy. God wot! it is a clever stock that bears the grape.

Od. Aye, and if thou but swallow plenty of it after a plentiful meal, moistening thy belly till its thirst is gone, it will throw thee into slumber; but if thou leave aught behind, the Bacchic god will parch thee for it.

Cy. Ha! ha! what a trouble it was getting out! This is pleasure unalloyed; earth and sky seem whirling round together; I see the throne of Zeus and all the godhead's majesty. Kiss *thee!* no! There are the Graces trying to tempt me. I shall rest well enough with my Ganymede here; yea, by the Graces, right fairly.

Si. What! Cyclops, am I Ganymede, Zeus' minion?

Cy. (*Attempting to carry him into the cave*) To be sure, Ganymede whom I am carrying off from the halls of Dardanus.

Si. I am undone, my children; outrageous treatment waits me.

Ch. Dost find fault with thy lover? dost scorn him in his cups?

Si. Woe is me! most bitter shall I find the wine ere long. *Exit* SILENUS, *dragged away by* CYCLOPS.

Od. Up now, children of Dionysus, sons of a noble sire, soon will yon creature in the cave, relaxed in slumber as ye see him, spew from his shameless maw the meat. Already the brand inside his lair is vomiting a cloud of smoke; and the only reason we prepared it was to burn the Cyclops' eye; so mind thou quit thee like a man.

Ch. I will have a spirit as of rock or adamant; but go inside, before my father suffers any shameful treatment; for here thou hast things ready.

Od. O Hephæstus, lord of Ætna, rid thyself for once and all of a troublesome neighbour by burning his bright eye out. Come, Sleep, as well, offspring of sable Night, come with all thy power on the

[2]A line has been lost here in which the Cyclops asked "And how must I drink this?"

monster god-detested; and never after Troy's most glorious toils destroy Odysseus and his crew by the hands of one who recketh naught of God or man; else must we reckon Chance a goddess, and Heaven's will inferior to hers. ODYSSEUS *re-enters the cave.*

Ch. Tightly the pincers shall grip the neck of him who feasts upon his guest; for soon will he lose the light of his eye by fire; already the brand, a tree's huge limb, lurks amid the embers charred.

Oh! come ye then and work his doom, pluck out the maddened Cyclops' eye, that he may rue his drinking. And I too fain would leave the Cyclops' lonely land and see king Bromius, ivy-crowned, the god I sorely miss. Ah! shall I ever come to that?

Od. (*Leaving the cave cautiously*) Silence, ye cattle! I adjure you; close your lips; make not a sound! I'll not let a man of you so much as breathe or wink or clear his throat, that yon pest awake not, until the sight in the Cyclops' eye has passed through the fiery ordeal.

Ch. Silent we stand with 'bated breath.

Od. In then, and mind your fingers grip the brand, for it is splendidly red-hot.

Ch. Thyself ordain who first must seize the blazing bar and burn the Cyclops' eye out, that we may share alike whate'er betides.

Semi-Ch. I. Standing where I am before the door, I am too far off to thrust the fire into his eye.

Semi-Ch. II. I have just gone lame.

Semi-Ch. I. Why, then, thou art in the same plight as I; for somehow or other I sprained my ankle, standing still.

Od. Sprained thy ankle, standing still?

Semi-Ch. II. Yes, and my eyes are full of dust or ashes from somewhere or other.

Od. These are sorry fellows, worthless as allies.

Ch. Because I feel for my back and spine, and express no wish to have my teeth knocked out, I am a coward, am I? Well, but I know a spell of Orpheus, a most excellent one, to make the brand enter his skull of its own accord, and set alight the one-eyed son of Earth.

Od. Long since I knew thou wert by nature such an one, and now I know it better; I must employ my own friends; but, though thou bring no active aid, cheer us on at any rate, that I may find my friends emboldened by thy encouragement.

Exit ODYSSEUS.

Ch. That will I do; the Carian[1] shall run the risk for us; and as far as encouragement goes, let the Cyclops smoulder.

What ho! my gallants, thrust away, make haste and burn his eye-brow off, the monster's guest-devouring. Oh! singe and scorch the shepherd of Ætna; twirl the brand and drag it round and be careful lest in his agony he treat thee to some wantonness.

[1]*i.e.*, to let some one, whose life is less valuable, run the risk instead of doing so oneself. The Carians, being the earliest mercenaries, were commonly selected for any very dangerous enterprise, and so this proverb arose.

Cy. (*Bellowing in the cave*) Oh! oh! my once bright eye is burnt to cinders now.

Ch. Sweet indeed the triumph-song; pray sing it to us, Cyclops.

Cy. (*From within*) Oh! oh! once more; what outrage on me and what ruin! But never shall ye escape this rocky cave unpunished, ye worthless creatures; for I will stand in the entrance of the cleft and fit my hands into it thus.

Staggering to the entrance.

Ch. Why dost thou cry out, Cyclops?

Cy. I am undone.

Ch. Thou art indeed a sorry sight.

Cy. Aye, and a sad one, too.

Ch. Didst fall among the coals in a drunken fit?

Cy. Noman has undone me.

Ch. Then there is no one hurting thee after all.

Cy. Noman is blinding me.

Ch. Then art thou not blind.

Cy. As blind as thou, forsooth.

Ch. How, pray, could no man have made thee blind?

Cy. Thou mockest me; but where is this Noman.

Ch. Nowhere, Cyclops.

Cy. It was the stranger, vile wretch! who proved my ruin, that thou mayst understand rightly, by swilling me with the liquor he gave me.

Ch. Ah! wine is a terrible foe, hard to wrestle with.

Cy. Tell me, I adjure thee, have they escaped or are they still within?

Ch. Here they are ranged in silence, taking the rock to screen them.

Cy. On which side?

Ch. On thy right.

Cy. Where?

Ch. Close against the rock. Hast caught them?

Cy. Trouble on trouble! I have run my skull against the rock and cracked it.

Ch. Aye, and they are escaping thee.

Cy. This way, was it not? 'Twas this way thou saidst.

Ch. No, not this way.

Cy. Which then?

Ch. They are getting round thee on the left.

Cy. Alas! I am being mocked; ye jeer me in my evil plight.

Ch. They are no longer there; but facing thee that stranger stands.

Cy. Master of villainy, where, oh! where art thou?

Od. Some way from thee I am keeping careful guard over the person of Odysseus.

Cy. What, a new name! hast changed thine?

Od. Yes, Odysseus the name my father gave me. But thou wert doomed to pay for thy unholy feast; for I should have seen Troy burned to but sorry purpose, unless I had avenged on thee the slaughter of my comrades.

Cy. Woe is me! 'tis an old oracle coming true; yes, it said I should have my eye put out by thee on thy way home from Troy; but it likewise foretold that thou wouldst surely pay for this, tossing on the sea for many a day.

Od. Go hang! E'en as I say, so have I done. And now will I get me to the beach and start my hollow ship across the sea of Sicily to the land of my fathers.

Cy. Thou shalt not; I will break a boulder off this rock and crush thee, crew and all, beneath my throw. Blind though I be, I will climb the hill, mounting through yonder tunnel.

Ch. As for us, henceforth will we be the servants of Bacchus, sharing the voyage of this hero Odysseus.

Exeunt OMNES.

THE PLAYS OF
ARISTOPHANES

BIOGRAPHICAL NOTE

Aristophanes, *c.* 445–*c.* 380 B.C.

Aristophanes, the son of Philippus of the tribe Pandionis in the deme Cydathene, was almost certainly a full Athenian citizen by birth. The exact year of his birth is not known. However, his first play, the *Banqueters*, won the second prize in 427 B.C., and he must then have been less than eighteen years of age, since, as he notes in the *Clouds*, he was too young to produce it in his own name.

It is inferred from his comedies that Aristophanes passed much of his boyhood in the country. His family owned land on Aegina, which may have been acquired when that island was expropriated by Athens in 431. His political sympathies, as revealed in the plays, seem to be conservative and to favor the "ancestral democracy" of the landowning class.

The character of the "Old Comedy," to which most of Aristophanes' plays belong, made it almost inevitable for him to enter into political disputes. Comedy then served something of the function of a satirical censorship and was expected to deal with the issues and personalities before the public. Aristophanes' first play was concerned with the contrast between the old and the new systems of education. His second, the *Babylonians*, although like the first no longer extant, is known to have involved Aristophanes in his conflict with Cleon, which lasted until the demagogue's death in 422. In this play Aristophanes attacked the policy towards the allies of Athens in the Peloponnesian War as one that made slaves, or "Babylonians," of them. Cleon responded by subjecting Aristophanes to prosecution, and accused him among other things of falsely claiming the privileges of citizenship. The poet was acquitted, but only after, as he charged in the *Acharnians*, Cleon had "slanged, and lied, and slandered, and betongued me . . . till I well nigh was done to death." The treatment failed to silence Aristophanes. Two years later in the *Knights* (424) he made his sharpest attack upon Cleon, who then enjoyed his greatest popularity, and the play won the first prize in the contest of that year.

The dramatic career of Aristophanes lasted for forty years or more, extending from the time when Athens was at the height of its power in the first years of the Peloponnesian War, through its fall in 404, and into the period when the city had begun to recover its fortunes after the Athenian league of 395. The various attempts made during that time to restrict the freedom of comedy are reflected to some extent in the character of Aristophanes' work. He wrote somewhere between forty and sixty plays, eleven of which have survived. The oldest surviving play is the *Acharnians*, which won first place in 425. The *Knights* was victorious the following year; the *Clouds*, produced in 423, although much admired by its author, failed to win a prize. With the *Wasps*, Aristophanes again took first place in 422. The *Peace* (421) and the *Birds*, produced seven years later, were awarded second prize. The *Lysistrata* and the *Thesmophoriazusae* belong to 411. The *Frogs* (405) was produced when Athens was making her last effort in the Peloponnesian War. The *Ecclesiazusae* was presented around 392, and the *Plutus* (388), which is the last of the extant plays, already belongs to the so-called "Middle Comedy."

Despite his frequent and bitter attacks upon such idols of the Athenian populace as Cleon and Euripides, Aristophanes appears to have been widely appreciated throughout his long career. Plato is known to have been particularly fond of his plays. He included the comic poet in his *Symposium*, and a copy of Aristophanes is said to have been found on his death bed. The story is also told that when asked by Dionysius of Syracuse for an analysis of the Athenian constitution, Plato sent an edition of Aristophanes' plays.

Aristophanes produced a play for the last time in 388. The following year, his son, Araros, won the first prize with one of his father's plays. Since Araros was producing his own plays by 375, it has been inferred that Aristophanes died somewhere between 385 and 375 B.C.

CONTENTS

THE ACHARNIANS

DRAMATIS PERSONAE

DICAEOPOLIS
CRIER
AMPHITHEUS
AMBASSADORS
PSEUDO-ARTABAS
THEORUS
WIFE OF DICAEOPOLIS
DAUGHTER OF DICAEOPOLIS
CEPHISOPHON, *servant of Euripides*
EURIPIDES
LAMACHUS
A MEGARIAN
TWO YOUNG GIRLS, *daughters of the Megarian*
AN INFORMER
A BOEOTIAN
NICARCHUS
SERVANT OF LAMACHUS
A FARMER
A GROOMSMAN
MESSENGER
CHORUS OF ACHARNIAN CHARCOAL BURNERS

In the background are three houses: the central one that of DICAEOPOLIS, *the other two those of* EURIPIDES *and* LAMACHUS. *In the foreground is a rough representation of the Pnyx where* DICAEOPOLIS *is awaiting the opening of the Assembly.*

Dicaeopolis. What heaps of things have bitten me to the heart!
A small few pleased me, very few, just four;
But those that vexed were sand-dune-hundredfold.
Let's see: what pleased me, worth my gladfulness?
I know a thing it cheered my heart to see;
'Twas those five talents vomited up by Cleon.
At that I brightened; and I love the Knights
For that performance; 'twas of price to Hellas.
Then I'd a tragic sorrow, when I looked
With open mouth for Aeschylus, and lo,
The Crier called, "Bring on your play, Theognis."
Judge what an icy shock that gave my heart!
Next; pleased I was when Moschus left, and in
Dexitheus came with his Boeotian song.
But oh this year I nearly cracked my neck,
When in slipped Chaeris for the Orthian nome.
But never yet since first I washed my face
Was I so bitten—in my brows with soap,
As now, when here's the fixed Assembly Day,
And morning come, and no one in the Pnyx.
They're in the Agora chattering, up and down
Scurrying to dodge the vermeil-tinctured cord.[1]
Why even the Prytanes are not here! They'll come
Long after time, elbowing each other, jostling
For the front bench, streaming down all together
You can't think how. But as for making Peace
They do not care one jot. O City! City!
But I am always first of all to come,
And here I take my seat; then, all alone,
I pass the time complaining, yawning, stretching,
I fidget, write, twitch hairs out, do my sums,
Gaze fondly country-wards, longing for Peace,
Loathing the town, sick for my village-home,
Which never cried, "Come, buy my charcoal," or
"My vinegar, my oil," my anything;
But freely gave us all; no *buy*-word there.
So here I'm waiting, thoroughly prepared
To riot, wrangle, interrupt the speakers
Whene'er they speak of anything but Peace.
—But here they come, our noon-day Prytanes!
Aye, there they go! I told you how 'twould be;
Every one jostling for the foremost place.
Crier. Move forward all,
Move up, within the consecrated line.
Amphitheus (*entering in a violent hurry*). Speaking begun?
Cr. Who will address the meeting?
Am. I.
Cr. Who are *you*?
Am. Amphitheus.
Cr. Not a man?
Am. No, an immortal. For the first Amphitheus
Was of Demeter and Triptolemus
The son: his son was Celeus; Celeus married
Phaenarete, who bare my sire Lycinus.
Hence I'm immortal; and the gods committed
To me alone the making peace with Sparta.
But, though immortal, I've no journey-money;
The Prytanes won't provide it.
Cr. Archers, there!
Am. (*as the archers seize him*) O help me, Celeus! help, Triptolemus!
Di. Ye wrong the Assembly, Prytanes, ye do wrong it,
Haling away a man who only wants
To give us Peace, and hanging up of shields.
The archers release AMPHITHEUS.
Cr. St! Take your seat.
Di. By Apollo, no, not I,
Unless ye prytanize about the Peace.
Cr. O yes! The Ambassadors from the Great King!

[1]A rope used to sweep in loiterers from the Agora.

Enter, clad in gorgeous Oriental apparel, the envoys sent to the Persian court eleven years previously in the archonship of Euthymenes 437–6 B.C.

Di. What King! I'm sick to death of embassies,
And all their peacocks and their impositions.

Cr. Keep silence!

Di. Hey! Ecbatana, here's a show.

Ambassador. Ye sent us, envoys to the Great King's Court,
Receiving each two drachmas daily, when
Euthymenes was Archon.

Di. (*aside*) O me, the drachmas!

Amb. And weary work we found it, sauntering on,
Supinely stretched in our luxurious litters
With awnings o'er us, through Caÿstrian plains.
'Twas a bad time.

Di. (*aside*) Aye, the good time was mine,
Stretched in the litter on the ramparts here!

Amb. And oft they fêted us, and we perforce
Out of their gold and crystal cups must drink
The pure sweet wine.

Di. (*aside*) O Cranaan city, mark you
The insolent airs of these ambassadors?

Amb. For only those are *there* accounted *men*
Who drink the hardest, and who eat the most.

Di. (*aside*) As *here* the most debauched and dissolute.

Amb. In the fourth year we reached the Great King's Court.
But he, with all his troops, had gone to sit
An eight-months' session on the Golden Hills!

Di. (*aside*) Pray, at what time did he conclude his session?

Amb. At the full moon; and so came home again.
Then he too fêted us, and set before us
Whole pot-baked oxen—

Di. (*aside*) And who ever heard
Of pot-baked oxen? Out upon your lies!

Amb. And an enormous bird, three times the size
Of our Cleonymus: its name was—Gull.

Di. (*aside*) That's why you gulled us out of all those drachmas!

Amb. And now we bring you Pseudo-Artabas[1]
The Great King's Eye.

Di. O how I wish some raven
Would come and strike out yours, the Ambassador's.

Cr. O yes! the Great King's Eye!

Enter PSEUDO-ARTABAS.

Di. O Heracles!
By Heaven, my man, you wear a war-ship look!
What! Do you round the point, and spy the docks?
Is that an oar-pad underneath your eye?

Amb. Now tell the Athenians, Psuedo-Artabas,
What the Great King commissioned you to say.

Pseudo-Artabas. Ijisti boutti furbiss upde rotti.[2]

[1]*Artaba*: a Persian measure. Thus, Pseudo-Artabas signifies one who gives false measure.

[2]This jumble is supposed to mean: "I have just begun to repair what is rotten."

Amb. Do you understand?

Di. By Apollo, no not I.

Amb. He says the King is going to send you gold.
(*to* PSEUDO-ARTABAS) Be more distinct and clear about the gold.

P.-A. No getti goldi, nincompoop Iawny.

Di. Wow, but that's clear enough!

Amb. What does he say?

Di. He says the Ionians must be nincompoops
If they're expecting any gold from Persia.

Amb. No, no: he spoke of golden income-coupons.

Di. What income-coupons? You're a great big liar!
You, get away; I'll test the man myself.
(*to* PSUEDO-ARTABAS)
Now look at this (*showing his fist*): and answer Yes, or No!
Or else I'll dye you with a Sardian dye.
Does the Great King intend to send us gold?
(PSEUDO-ARTABAS *nods dissent.*)
Then are our envoys here bamboozling us?
(*He nods assent.*)
These fellows nod in pure Hellenic style;
I do believe they come from hereabouts.
Aye, to be sure; why, one of these two eunuchs
Is Cleisthenes, Sibyrtius's son!
O thou young shaver of the hot-souled rump,
With such a beard, thou monkey, dost thou come
Tricked out amongst us in a eunuch's guise?
And who's this other chap? Not Straton, surely?

Cr. St! Take your seat! O yes!
The Council ask the Great King's Eye to dinner
At the Town Hall.

Exit Ambassadors and PSEUDO-ARTABAS.

Di. Now is not that a throttler?
Here must I drudge at soldiering; while these rogues,
The Town-Hall door is never closed to *them.*
Now then, I'll do a great and startling deed.
Amphitheus! Where's Amphitheus?

Am. Here am I.

Di. Here be eight drachmas; take them; and with all
The Lacedaemonians make a private peace
For me, my wife and children: none besides.
(*to the* PRYTANES *and citizens*)
Stick to your embassies and befoolings, you.

Exit AMPHITHEUS.

Cr. O yes! Theorus from Sitalces!

Theorus (*rising*) Here!

Di. O here's another humbug introduced.

Th. We should not, sirs, have tarried long in Thrace—

Di. But for the salary you kept on drawing.

Th. But for the storms, which covered Thrace with snow
And froze the rivers. 'Twas about the season
At which Theognis was performing here.
I all that time was drinking with Sitalces;
A most prodigious Athens-lover he,
Yea such a true admirer, he would scribble
On every wall "My beautiful Athenians"!

His son, our newly-made Athenian, longed
To taste his Apaturian sausages,
And bade his father help his fatherland.
And *he*, with deep libations, vowed to help us
With such an host that every one would say,
"Heavens! what a swarm of locusts comes this way!"

Di. Hang me, if I believe a single word
Of all that speech, except about the locusts.

Th. And here he sends you the most warlike tribe
Of all in Thrace.

Di. Come, here's proof positive.

Cr. The Thracians whom Theorus brought, come forward!

Di. What the plague's this?

Th. The Odomantian host.

Di. The Odomantians, pho! Hallo, look here.
Are Odomantians all equipped like this?

Th. Give them two drachmas each a day, and these
Will targeteer Boeotia all to bits.

Di. Two drachmas for *these* scarecrows! Oh, our tars,
Our noble tars, the safeguard of our state,
Well may they groan at this. O! Murder! O!
These Odomantian thieves have sacked my garlic.
Put down the garlic! drop it!

Th. You rapscallion,
How dare you touch them, when they're garlic-primed.

Di. O will you let them, Prytanes, use me thus,
Barbarians too, in this my fatherland?
But stop! I warn you not to hold the Assembly
About the Thracians' pay. I tell you there's
A portent come; I felt a drop of rain!

Cr. The Thracians are to go, and two days hence
Come here again. The Assembly is dissolved.

Exeunt all but DICAEOPOLIS.

Di. O me, the salad I have lost this day!
But here's Amphitheus, back from Lacedaemon.
Well met, Amphitheus!

Enter AMPHITHEUS.

Am. Not till I've done running.
I needs must flee the Acharnians, clean away.

Di. What mean you?

Am. I was bringing back in haste
The treaties, when some veterans smelt them out,
Acharnians, men of Marathon, hard in grain
As their own oak and maple, rough and tough;
And all at once they cried, "O villain, dare you
Bring treaties when our vineyards are cut down?"
Then in their lappets up they gathered stones;
I fled away: they followed roaring after.

Di. So let them roar. But have you got the treaties?

Am. O yes, I have. Three samples; here they are.
These are the *five-year* treaties; take and taste them.

Di. Pheugh!

Am. What's the matter?

Di. I don't like the things,
They smell of tar and naval preparations.

Am. Then taste the *ten-year* samples; here they are

Di. These smell of embassies to all the states,
Urgent, as if the Allies are hanging back.

Am. Then here are treaties both by land and sea
For *thirty* years.

Di. O Feast of Dionysus!
These have a smell of nectar and ambrosia,
And never mind about the three days' rations,
And in your mouth they say, "Go where you please."
These do I welcome, these I pour, and drain,
Nor care a hang about your old Acharnians.
But I, released from War and War's alarms,
Will hold, within, the Rural Dionysia.

Am. And I will flee those peppery old Acharnians.

Exeunt DICAEOPOLIS *and* AMPHITHEUS.

Enter, running in pursuit of AMPHITHEUS, *twenty-four old Acharnians who constitute the* CHORUS.

Chorus. Here's the trail; pursue, pursue him;
follow, follow, every man;
Question whosoever meets you
whitherwards the fellow ran.
Much it boots the state to catch him!
(*to the audience*) O inform me, if ye know,
Where the man who bears the treaties
managed from my sight to go.
Fled and gone! Disappears!
O this weary weight of years!
O were I Now as spry
As in youthful days gone by,
When I stuck Like a man
To Phaÿllus as he ran,
And achieved Second place In the race,
Though a great Charcoal freight
I was bearing on my head,—
Not so light From my sight
Had this treaty-bearer fled,
Nor escaped With such ease From the chase.
Now because my joints have stiffened,
and my shins are young no more,
And the legs of Lacrateides
by old age are burdened sore,
He's escaped us! But we'll follow:
but he shall not boast that he
Got away from us Acharnians,
howsoever old we be.
Who has dared Father Zeus!
Gods of heaven! to make a truce,
Who has pledged Faith with those
Who are evermore my foes;
Upon whom War I make
For my ruined vineyard's sake;
And I ne'er From the strife Will give o'er,
No, I ne'er Will forbear,
Till I pierce them in return,
Like a reed, Sharply barbed
Dagger-pointed, and they learn
Not to tread Down my vines Any more.
Now 'tis ours to seek the fellow,
and Pelténe-wards to look,

And from land to land to chase him,
till we bring the rogue to book.
Never shall I tire of pelting,
pelting him to death with stones.
Di. (*within*) Keep ye all the holy silence!
Ch. Hush! we've got him. Heard ye, comrades,
"silence" called in solemn tones?
This is he, the man we're seeking.
Stand aside, and in a trice
He, methinks, will stand before us,
coming out to sacrifice!
Di. (*coming out followed by his* WIFE *and* DAUGHTER) Keep ye all the holy silence!
Now, basket-bearer, go you on in front,
You Xanthias, hold the phallus-pole erect.
Wife. Set down the basket, girl: and we'll begin.
Daughter. O mother, hand me here the gravy-spoon,
To ladle out the gravy o'er the cake.
Di. 'Tis well. Lord Dionysus, grant me now
To show the show and make the sacrifice
As thou would'st have me, I and all my house;
Then keep with joy the Rural Dionysia;
No more of soldiering now. And may this Peace
Of thirty summers answer to my hopes.
Wi. O daughter, bear the basket sweetly, sweet,
With savory-eating look. Happy the man,
Whoe'er he is, who weds thee and begets
Kittens as fair and saucy as thyself.
Move on! but heed lest any in the crowd
Should nibble off, unseen, thy bits of gold.
Di. O Xanthias, walk behind the basket-bearer,
Holding, you two, the phallus-pole erect.
And I'll bring up the rear, and sing the hymn:
Wife, watch me from the roof. Now then, proceed.

(*singing*) O Phales, comrade revel-roaming
Of Bacchus, wanderer of the gloaming,
Of wives and boys the naughty lover,
Here in my home I gladly greet ye,
Six weary years of absence over;
For I have made a private treaty
And said good-bye to toils and fusses,
And fights, and fighting Lamachuses.

Far happier 'tis to me and sweeter,
O Phales, Phales, some soft glade in,
To woo the saucy, arch, deceiving,
Young Thratta (Strymodore his maiden),
As from my woodland fells I meet her
Descending with my fagots laden,
And catch her up, and ill entreat her,
And make her pay the fine for thieving.

O Phales, Phales, come and sup,
And in the morn, to brace you up,
Of Peace you'll quaff a jovial cup;
And mid the chimney sparks our useless shield we'll hang.

Ch. That's the man who made the treaty;
There he stands Full in view;
Pelt him, pelt him, pelt him, pelt him,
Pelt him you! Pelt him you!
Di. Heracles! what ails the fellows?
Hang it all, ye'll smash the pot!
Ch. It is *you* we will smash with our
stones, you detestable head.
Di. O most worshipful Acharnians,
why? what reason have ye got?
Ch. Dare you ask? Traitor base!
Dare you look me in the face?
You who make, You alone,
Private treaties of your own!
Shameless heart! Shameless hand!
Traitor to your fatherland!
Di. But ye know not why I did it:
hear me now the facts declare.
Ch. Hear you? No! You're to die;
'Neath a stony cairn to lie!
Di. Not, O not until ye've heard me;
worthy sirs, forbear, forbear!
Ch. No delay! Thee to slay
We'll immediately begin.
No debate! Thee we hate
Worse than Cleon's self, whose skin
I'll ere long Cut to shoes
For the worthy Knights to use.
But from *you*, who made a treaty
with the false Laconian crew,
I will hear no long orations,
I will surely punish you.
Di. Worthy fellows, for the moment
those Laconians pretermit;
'Tis a question of my treaty,
was I right in making it.
Ch. Right to make it! when with Sparta
no engagement sacred stands,
Not the altar, not the oath-pledge,
not the faith of clasped right hands!
Di. Yet I know that these our foemen,
who our bitter wrath excite,
Were not always wrong entirely,
nor ourselves entirely right.
Ch. Not entirely, shameless rascal?
Do you such opinions dare
Openly to flaunt before me?
Shall I then a traitor spare?
Di. Not entirely, not entirely!
I can prove by reasons strong
That in many points the Spartans
at our hands have suffered wrong.
Ch. This is quite a heart-perplexing,
terrible affair indeed,
If you mean that you will venture
for our enemies to plead.
Di. Aye, and if I plead not truly,
or the people doubt display,
On a chopping-block I'm willing,
whilst I speak, my head to lay.
Ch. Why so slack, my fellow-burghers?
Let us stone the naughty varlet,
Let us scarify and shred him
to an uniform of scarlet.

Di. What a red and dangerous ember
sparkled up within you then!
Won't you hear me, won't you hear me,
good Acharnians, worthy men?
Ch. Never, never, will we hear you.
Di. That will cause me bitter woe.
Ch. If I do, perdition seize me!
Di. O Acharnians, say not so.
Ch. Know that you must die this instant.
Di. Then I'll make you suffer too.
For my safety I've a hostage,
one that's very dear to you.
Now I'll bring him out and slay him;
you shall see your darling's end.

DICAEOPOLIS *goes into the house and returns three lines later carrying in one hand a hamper full of charcoal and in the other a drawn sword.*

Ch. O Acharnian fellow-burghers,
what can words like these portend
To our noble band of brethren?
Think you that the man can hold
Any child of ours in durance?
What can make him wax so bold?
Di. Now then pelt me; here's the hostage!
I will slay and will not spare.
I shall speedily discover
which of you for charcoal care.
Ch. Heaven preserve us! 'tis a scuttle,
'tis my fellow-burgher true!
Never do the thing you mention:
never do, O never do!
Di. Cry aloud! I'm going to slay him;
I shall neither hear nor heed.
Ch. You will slay then this charcoal-adorer,
its equal in years!
Di. Aye, for when I craved a hearing
you refused to hear me plead.
Ch. Ah! but now! Now you may!
Whatsoever suits you say.
Say you love, Say you prize,
Our detested enemies.
Ne'er will I Faithless prove
To the scuttle which I love.
Di. Well then first, the stones you gathered,
throw them out upon the ground.
Ch. Out they go! All my hoard!
Prithee, lay aside the sword.
Di. But I fear that in your lappets
other missiles may be found.
Ch. All are gone! Every one!
See my garment shaken wide!
Don't evade Promise made.
Lay, O lay the sword aside.
Here's my robe Shaken out,
As I twist and twirl about.
Di. You would then, would you, shake your cries aloft,
And this Parnesian charcoal all but died,
Slain by the madness of its fellow-burghers.
And in its fright this scuttle, cuttle-wise,
Voided its inky blackness on my clothes.
Alas that men should carry hearts as sour
As unripe grapes, to pelt and roar, nor hear
A tempered statement mingled half and half;
Not though I'm willing o'er a chopping-block
To say my say for Lacedaemon's folk.
And yet I love, be sure, my own dear life.

DICAEOPOLIS *exits to house.*

Ch. O why not bring the block
out of doors without delay,
And speak the mighty speech
which you think will win the day?
For really I've a longing
to hear what you will say!
So in the fashion you yourself prescribed,
Place here the chopping-block and start your speech.
Di. (*re-entering, with a block*) Well look and see, the chopping-block is here,
And I'm to speak, poor little friendless I.
Still never mind; I won't enshield myself,
I'll speak my mind for Lacedaemon's folk.
And yet I fear; for well I know the moods
Of our good country people, how they love
To hear the City and themselves bepraised
By some intriguing humbug, right or wrong.
Nor ever dream they are being bought and sold.
And well I know the minds of those old men
Looking for nothing but a verdict-bite.
Aye and I know what I myself endured
At Cleon's hands for last year's Comedy.
How to the Council-house he haled me off,
And slanged, and lied, and slandered, and betongued me,
Roaring Cycloborus-wise; till I well nigh
Was done to death, bemiryslushified.
Now therefore suffer me, before I start,
To dress me up the loathliest way I can.
Ch. O why keep putting off with that shilly-shally air?
Hieronymus may lend you, for anything I care,
The shaggy "Cap of Darkness" from his tangle-matted hair.
Then open all the wiles of Sisyphus,
Since this encounter will not brook delay.
Di. Now must my heart be strong, and I depart
To find Euripides. Boy! Ho there, boy!
Cephisophon. Who calls me?
Di. Is Euripides within?
Ce. Within and not within, if you conceive me.
Di. Within and not within?
Ce. 'Tis even so.
His mind, without, is culling flowers of song,
But he, within, is sitting up aloft
Writing a play.
Di. O lucky, lucky poet,
Whose very servant says such clever things!
But call him.
Ce. But it can't be done.
Di. But still . . . !
For go I won't. I'll hammer at the door.
Euripides, my sweet one!
O if you ever hearkened, hearken now.

'Tis I, Cholleidian Dicaeopolis.

Euripides. But I've no time.

Di. But pivot.[1]

Eu. But it can't be done.

Di But still . . . !

Eu. Well then, I'll pivot, but I can't come down.

Di. Euripides!

The eccyclema turns.

Eu. Aye.

Di. Why do you write up there, And not down here? That's why you make lame heroes. And wherefore sit you robed in tragic rags, A pitiful garb? That's why you make them beggars. But by your knees, Euripides, I pray, Lend me some rags from that old play of yours; For to the Chorus I to-day must speak A lengthy speech; and if I fail, 'tis *death.*

Eu. Rags! Rags! what rags? Mean you the rags wherein This poor old Oeneus came upon the stage?

Di. Not Oeneus, no; a wretcheder man than he.

Eu. Those that blind Phoenix wore?

Di. Not Phoenix, no; Some other man still wretcheder than Phoenix.

Eu. What shreds of raiment can the fellow mean? Can it be those of beggarly Philoctetes?

Di. One far, far, far, more beggarly than he.

Eu. Can it be then the loathly gaberdine Wherein the lame Bellerophon was clad?

Di. Bellerophon? no; yet mine too limped and begged, A terrible chap to talk.

Eu. I know the man. The Mysian Telephus.

Di. Telephus it is! Lend me, I pray, that hero's swaddling-clothes.

Eu. Boy, fetch him out the rags of Telephus. They lie above the Thyestean rags, 'Twixt those and Ino's.

Ce. (*to* DICAEOPOLIS) Take them; here they are.

Di. (*holding up the tattered garment against the light*) Lord Zeus, whose eyes can pierce through everywhere, Let me be dressed the loathliest way I can. Euripides, you have freely given the rags, Now give, I pray you, what pertains to these, The Mysian cap to set upon my head. For I've to-day to act a beggar's part, To be myself, yet not to seem myself; The audience there will know me, who I am, Whilst all the Chorus stand like idiots by, The while I fillip them with cunning words.

Eu. Take it; you subtly plan ingenious schemes.

Di. To thee, good luck; to Telephus—what I wish him! Yah! why I'm full of cunning words already. But now, methinks, I need a beggar's staff.

Eu. Take this, and get thee from the marble halls.

Di. O Soul, thou seest me from the mansion thrust, Still wanting many a boon. Now in thy prayer Be close and instant. Give, Euripides, A little basket with a hole burnt through it.

Eu. What need you, hapless one, of this poor wicker?

Di. No need perchance; but O I want it so.

Eu. Know that you're wearisome, and get you gone.

Di. Alas! Heaven bless you, as it blessed your mother.

Eu. Leave me in peace.

Di. Just one thing more, but one, A little tankard with a broken rim.

Eu. Here. Now be off. You trouble us; begone.

Di. You know not yet what ill you do yourself. Sweet, dear Euripides, but one thing more, Give me a little pitcher, plugged with sponge.

Eu. Fellow, you're taking the whole tragedy. Here, take it and begone.

Di. I'm going now. And yet! there's one thing more, which if I get not I'm ruined. Sweetest, best Euripides, With this I'll go, and never come again; Give me some withered leaves to fill my basket.

Eu. You'll slay me! Here! My plays are disappearing.

Di. Enough! I go. Too troublesome by far Am I, not witting that the chieftains hate me! Good Heavens! I'm ruined. I had clean forgotten The thing whereon my whole success depends. My own Euripides, my best and sweetest, Perdition seize me if I ask aught else Save this one thing, this only, only this, Give me some chervil, borrowing from your mother.

Eu. The man insults us. Shut the palace up.

Here EURIPIDES *is wheeled in again, and* DICAEOPOLIS *advances to the block to make his speech.*

Di. O Soul, without our chervil we must go. Knowest thou the perilous strife thou hast to strive, Speaking in favour of Laconian men? On, on, my Soul! Here is the line. How? What? Swallow Euripides, and yet not budge? Oh, good! Advance, O long-enduring heart, Go thither, lay thine head upon the block, And say whatever to thyself seems good. Take courage! Forward! March! O well done, heart!

Ch. What will you say? What will you do? Man, is it true
You are made up of iron and of shamelessness too?
You who will, one against us all, debate,
Offering your neck a hostage to the State!
Nought does he fear.
Since you will have it so, speak, we will hear.

Di. Bear me no grudge, spectators, if, a beggar,

[1] *I.e.*, "show yourself by means of the eccyclema," a piece of machinery by which the wall of the house is turned as if on a pivot, disclosing the interior.

I dare to speak before the Athenian people
About the city in a comic play.
For what is true even comedy can tell.
And I shall utter startling things but true.
Nor now can Cleon slander me because,
With strangers present, I defame the State.
'Tis the Lenaea, and we're all alone;
No strangers yet have come; nor from the states
Have yet arrived the tribute and allies.
We're quite alone clean-winnowed; for I count
Our alien residents the civic bran.
The Lacedaemonians I detest entirely;
And may Poseidon, Lord of Taenarum,
Shake all their houses down about their ears;
For I, like you, have had my vines cut down.
But after all—for none but friends are here—
Why the Laconians do we blame for this?
For men of ours, I do not say the State,
Remember this, I do not say the State,
But worthless fellows of a worthless stamp,
Ill-coined, ill-minted, spurious little chaps,
Kept on denouncing Megara's little coats.
And if a cucumber or hare they saw,
Or sucking-pig, or garlic, or lump-salt,
All were Megarian, and were sold off-hand.
Still these were trifles, and our country's way.
But some young tipsy cottabus-players went
And stole from Megara-town the fair Simaetha.
Then the Megarians, garlicked with the smart,
Stole, in return, two of Aspasia's hussies.
From these three Wantons o'er the Hellenic race
Burst forth the first beginnings of the War.
For then, in wrath, the Olympian Pericles
Thundered and lightened, and confounded Hellas,
Enacting laws which ran like drinking-songs.
"That the Megarians presently depart
From earth and sea, the mainland, and the mart."
Then the Megarians, slowly famishing,
Besought their Spartan friends to get the Law
Of the three Wantons cancelled and withdrawn.
And oft they asked us, but we yielded not.
Then followed instantly the clash of shields.
Ye'll say "They should not"; but what should they, then?
Come now, had some Laconian, sailing out,
Denounced and sold a small Seriphian dog,
Would you have sat unmoved? Far, far from that!
Ye would have launched three hundred ships of war,
And all the City had at once been full
Of shouting troops, of fuss with trierarchs,
Of paying wages, gilding Pallases,
Of rations measured, roaring colonnades,
Of wineskins, oarloops, bargaining for casks,
Of nets of onions, olives, garlic-heads,
Of chaplets, pilchards, flute-girls, and black eyes.
And all the arsenal had rung with noise
Of oar-spars planed, pegs hammered, oarloops fitted,
Of boatswains' calls, and flutes, and trills, and whistles.
This had ye done; and shall not Telephus,
Think we, do this? we've got no brains at all.

Semi-Chorus I. Aye, say you so, you rascally villain you?
And this from you, a beggar? Dare you blame us.
Because perchance, we've got informers here?

Semi-Chorus II. Aye, by Poseidon, every word he says
Is true and right; he tells no lies at all.

S.C. I. True or untrue, is he the man to say it?
I'll pay him out, though, for his insolent speech.

S.C. II. Whither away? I pray you stay. If him you hurt,
You'll find your own self hoisted up directly.

A scuffle takes place in the orchestra, in which the LEADER OF THE FIRST SEMICHORUS *is worsted.*

S.C. I. Lamachus! Help! with thy glances of lightning;
Terrible-crested, appear in thy pride,
Come, O Lamachus, tribesman and friend to us;
Is there a stormer of cities beside?
Is there a captain? O come ye in haste,
Help me, O help! I am caught by the waist.

Enter LAMACHUS.

Lamachus. Whence came the cry of battle to my ears?
Where shall I charge? where cast the battle-din?
Who roused the sleeping Gorgon from its case?

Di. O Lamachus hero, O those crests and cohorts!

S.C. I. O Lamachus, here has this fellow been
With frothy words abusing all the State.

La. You dare, you beggar, say such things as those?

Di. O Lamachus hero, grant me pardon true
If I, a beggar, spake or chattered aught.

La. What said you? Hey?

Di. I can't remember yet.
I get so dizzy at the sight of arms.
I pray you lay that terrible shield aside.

La. There then.

Di. Now set it upside down before me.

La. 'Tis done.

Di. Now give me from your crest that plume.

La. Here; take the feather.

Di. Now then, hold my head,
And let me vomit. I so loathe those crests.

La. What! use my feather, rogue, to make you vomit?

Di. A feather is it, Lamachus? Pray what bird
Produced it? Is it a Great Boastard's plume?

La. Death and Destruction!

Di. No, no, Lamachus.
That's not for strength like yours. If strong you are
Why don't you circumcise me? You're well armed.

La. What! you, a beggar, beard the general so?

Di. A beggar am I, Lamachus?

La. What else?

Di. An honest townsman, not an office-seekrian,
Since war began, an active-service-seekrian,
But you're, since war began, a full-pay-seekrian.

La. The people chose me—

Di. Aye, three cuckoo-birds.
That's what I loathe; that's why I made my treaty.
When grey-haired veterans in the ranks I saw,
And boys like you, paltry malingering boys,
Off, some to Thrace—their daily pay three drachmas—
Phaenippuses, Hipparchidreprobatians,
And some with Chares, to Chaonia some,
Geretotheodores, Diomirogues, and some
To Camarina, Gela, and Grineela.
La. The people chose them—
Di. And how comes it, pray,
That you are always in receipt of pay,
And these are *never*? Come, Marilades,
You are old and grey; when have you served as envoy?
Never! Yet he's a steady, active man.
Well then, Euphorides, Prinides, Dracyllus,
Have *you* Ecbatana or Chaonia seen?
Never! But Coesyra's son and Lamachus,
They have; to whom, for debts and calls unpaid,
Their friends but now, like people throwing out
Their slops at eve, were crying "Stand away!"
La. O me! Democracy! can this be borne?
Di. No, not if Lamachus receive no pay.
La. But I with all the Peloponnesian folk
Will always fight, and vex them everyway,
By land, by sea, with all my might and main.
Exit.
Di. And I to all the Peloponnesian folk,
Megarians and Boeotians, give full leave
To trade with me; but not to Lamachus.
Exit.

Chorus

The man has the best of the wordy debate, and the hearts of the people is winning
To his plea for the truce. Now doff we our robes, our own anapaestics beginning.

Since first to exhibit his plays he began, our chorus-instructor has never
Come forth to confess in this public address how tactful he is and how clever.
But now that he knows he is slandered by foes before Athens so quick to assent,
Pretending he jeers our City and sneers at the people with evil intent,
He is ready and fain his cause to maintain before Athens so quick to repent.
Let honour and praise be the guerdon, he says, of the poet whose satire has stayed you
From believing the orators' novel conceits wherewith they cajoled and betrayed you·
Who bids you despise adulation and lies nor be citizens Vacant and Vain.
For before, when an embassy came from the states intriguing your favour to gain,
And called you the town of the *violet crown*, so grand and exalted ye grew,
That at once on your tiptails erect ye would sit, those *crowns* were so pleasant to you.
And then, if they added the *shiny*, they got whatever they asked for their praises,
Though apter, I ween, for an oily sardine than for you and your City the phrase is.
By this he's a true benefactor to you, and by showing with humour dramatic
The way that our wise democratic allies are ruled by our State democratic.
And therefore their people will come oversea, their tribute to bring to the City,
Consumed with desire to behold and admire the poet so fearless and witty,
Who dared in the presence of Athens to speak the thing that is rightful and true.
And truly the fame of his prowess, by this, has been bruited the universe through,
When the Sovereign of Persia, desiring to test what the end of our warfare will be,
Inquired of the Spartan ambassadors, first, which nation is queen of the sea,
And next, which the wonderful Poet has got, as its stern and unsparing adviser;
For those who are lashed by his satire, he said, must surely be better and wiser,
And they'll in the war be the stronger by far, enjoying his counsel and skill.
And therefore the Spartans approach you to-day with proffers of Peace and Goodwill,
Just asking indeed that Aegina ye cede; and nought do they care for the isle,
But you of the Poet who serves you so well they fain would despoil and beguile.
But be *you* on your guard nor surrender the bard; for his Art shall be righteous and true.
Rare blessings and great will he work for the State, rare happiness shower upon you;
Not fawning, or bribing, or striving to cheat with an empty unprincipled jest;
Not seeking your favour to curry or nurse, but teaching the things that are best.

And therefore I say to the people to-day,
Let Cleon the worst of his villainies try,
His anger I fear not, his threats I defy!
For Honour and Right beside me will fight,
And never shall I
In ought that relates to the city be found
Such a craven as he, such a profligate hound.

O Muse, fiery-flashing, with temper of flame, energetic, Acharnian, come to my gaze,
Like the wild spark that leaps from the evergreen oak,
when its red-glowing charcoal is fanned to a blaze,
And the small fish are lying all in order for the frying;
And some are mixing Thasian, richly dight, shiny-bright,
And some dip the small fish therein;
Come, fiery-flashing Maid, to thy fellow-burgher's aid,
With exactly such a song, so glowing and so strong,

To our old rustic melodies akin.

We the veterans blame the City.
Is it meet and right that we,
Who of old, in manhood's vigour,
fought your battles on the sea,
Should in age be left untended,
yea exposed to shame and ill?
Is it right to let the youngsters
air their pert forensic skill,
Grappling us with writs and warrants,
holding up our age to scorn?
We who now have lost our music,
feeble nothings, dull, forlorn,
We whose only "Safe Poseidon"
is the staff we lean upon,
There we stand, decayed and muttering,
hard beside the Court-house Stone,
Nought discerning all around us
save the darkness of our case.
Comes the youngster, who has compassed
for himself the accuser's place,
Slings his tight and nipping phrases,
tackling us with legal scraps,
Pulls us up and cross-examines,
setting little verbal traps,
Rends and rattles old Tithonus
till the man is dazed and blind;
Till with toothless gums he mumbles,
then departs condemned and fined;
Sobbing, weeping, as he passes,
to his friends he murmurs low,
"All I've saved to buy a coffin
now to pay the fine must go."

How can it be seemly a grey-headed man by the water-clock's stream to decoy and to slay,
Who of old, young and bold, laboured hard for the State, who would wipe off his sweat and return to the fray?
At Marathon arrayed, to the battle-shock we ran,
And our mettle we displayed, foot to foot, man to man,
and our name and our fame shall not die.
Aye in youth we were Pursuers on the Marathonian plain,
But in age Pursuers vex us, and our best defence is vain.
To this what can Marpsias reply?

Oh, Thucydides to witness,
bowed with age, in sore distress,
Feebly struggling in the clutches
of that Scythian wilderness
Fluent glib Cephisodemus—
Oh the sorrowful display!
I myself was moved with pity,
yea and wiped a tear away,
Grieved at heart the gallant veteran
by an archer mauled to view;
Him who, were he, by Demeter,
that Thucydides we knew,
Would have stood no airs or nonsense
from the Goddess Travel-sore,[1]
Would have thrown, the mighty wrestler,
ten Evathluses or more,
Shouted down three thousand archers
with his accents of command,
Shot his own accuser's kinsmen
in their Scythian fatherland.
Nay, but if ye will not leave us
to our hardly earned repose,
Sort the writs, divide the actions,
separating these from those;
Who assails the old and toothless
should be old and toothless too;
For a youngster, wantons, gabblers,
Cleinias' son[2] the trick may do.
So for future fines and exiles,
fair and square the balance hold,
Let the youngster sue the youngster,
and the old man sue the old.

Enter DICAEOPOLIS.

Di. These are the boundaries of my market-place;
In this new scene what was the Pnyx somehow becomes the market-place of DICAEOPOLIS.
And here may all the Peloponnesian folk,
Megarians and Boeotians, freely trade
Selling to me, but Lamachus may not.
And these three thongs, of Leprous make, I set
As market-clerks, elected by the lot.
Within these bounds may no informer come,
Or any other syco-Phasian man.
But I'll go fetch the Treaty-Pillar here,
And set it up in some conspicuous place.
Exit DICAEOPOLIS, *and a half-starved* MEGARIAN *enters, followed by two little girls whom he bids "mount" the stage from the side-scenes.*

Megarian. Guid day, Athanian market, Megara's luve!
By Frien'ly Zeus, I've miss't ye like my mither.
But ye, puir bairnies o' a waefu' father,
Speel up, ye'll aiblins fin' a barley-bannock.
Now listen, bairns; atten' wi' a' yere—painch;
Whilk wad ye liefer, to be sellt or clemmed?

Girls. Liefer be sellt! Liefer be sellt!

Meg. An' sae say I mysel'! But wha sae doited
As to gie aught for *you*, a sicker skaith?
Aweel, I ken a pawkie Megara-trick,
I'se busk ye up, an' say I'm bringin' piggies.
Here, slip these wee bit clooties on yere nieves,
An' shaw yeresells a decent grumphie's weans.
For gin' I tak' ye hame unsellt, by Hairmes
Ye'll thole the warst extremities o' clemmin'.
Ne'est, pit thir lang pig-snowties owre yere nebs,
An' stech yere bodies in this sackie. Sae.
An' min' ye grunt an' grane an' g-r-r awa',
An' mak' the skirls o' little Mystery piggies.
Mysel' will ca' for Dicaeopolis.
Hae! Dicaeopolis!

[1]Demeter.
[2]Alcibiades.

Are ye for buyin' onie pigs the day?
Enter DICAEOPOLIS.
Di. How now, Megarian?
Meg. Come to niffer, guidman.
Di. How fare ye all?
Meg. A' greetin' by the fire.
Di. And very jolly too if there's a piper.
What do your people do besides?
Meg. Sae sae.
For when I cam' frae Megara toun the morn,
Our Lairds o' Council were in gran' debate
How we might quickliest perish, but an' ben.
Di. So ye'll lose all your troubles.
Meg. What for no?
Di. What else at Megara? What's the price of wheat?
Meg. Och! high eneugh: high as the Gudes, an' higher.
Di. Got any salt?
Meg. Ye're maisters o' our saut.
Di. Or garlic?
Meg. Garlic, quotha! when yeresells,
Makin' yere raids like onie swarm o' mice,
Howkit up a' the rooties wi' a stak'.
Di. What *have* you got then?
Meg. Mystery piggies, I.
Di. That's good; let's see them.
Meg. Hae! They're bonnie piggies.
Lift it, an't please you; 'tis sae sleek an' bonnie.
Di. What on earth's this?
Meg. A piggie that, by Zeus.
Di. A pig! What sort of pig?
Meg. A Megara piggie.
What! no a piggie that?
Di. It doesn't seem so.
Meg. 'Tis awfu'! Och the disbelievin' carle!
Uphaudin' she's na piggie! Will ye wad,
My cantie frien', a pinch o' thymy saut
She's no a piggie in the Hellanian use?
Di. A human being's—
Meg. Weel, by Diocles,
She's mine; wha's piggie did ye think she was?
Mon? wad ye hear them skirlin'?
Di. By the Powers,
I would indeed.
Meg. Now piggies, skirl awa'.
Ye winna? winna skirl, ye graceless hizzies?
By Hairmes then I'se tak' ye hame again.
Girls. Wee! wee! wee!
Meg. This no a piggie?
Di. Faith, it seems so now,
But 'twont remain so for five years I'm thinking.
Meg. Trowth, tak' my word for't, she'll be like her mither.
Di. But she's no good for offerings.
Meg. What for no?
What for nae guid for offerins?
Di. She's no tail.
Meg. Aweel, the puir wee thing, she's owre young yet.
But when she's auld, she'll have a gawcie tail.
But wad ye rear them, here's a bonnie piggie!
Di. Why she's the staring image of the other.
Meg. They're o' ane father an' ane mither, baith.
But bide a wee, an' when she's fat an' curlie
She'll be an offerin' gran' for Aphrodite.
Di. A pig's no sacrifice for Aphrodite.
Meg. What, no for Her! Mon, for hirsel' the lane.
Why there's nae flesh sae tastie as the flesh
O' thae sma piggies, roastit on a spit.
Di. But can they feed without their mother yet?
Meg. Poteidan, yes! withouten father too.
Di. What will they eat most freely?
Meg. Aught ye gie them.
But spier yoursel'.
Di. Hey, piggy, piggy!
1st. Girl. Wee!
Di. Do you like pease, you piggy?
1st. Girl. Wee, wee, wee!
Di. What, and Phibalean figs as well?
1st. Girl. Wee, wee!
Di. What, and you other piggy?
2nd. Girl. Wee, wee, wee!
Di. Eh, but ye're squealing bravely for the figs.
Bring out some figs here, one of you within,
For these small piggies. Will they eat them? Yah!
Worshipful Heracles! how they are gobbling now.
Whence come the pigs? They seem to me Aetallian.
Meg. Na, na; they haena eaten a' thae figs.
See here; here's ane I pickit up mysel'.
Di. Upon my word, they are jolly little beasts.
What shall I give you for the pair? let's hear.
Meg. Gie me for ane a tie o' garlic, will ye,
An' for the tither half a peck o' saut.
Di. I'll buy them: stay you here awhile. *Exit.*
Meg. Aye, aye.
Traffickin' Hairmes, wad that I could swap
Baith wife an' mither on sic terms as thae.
Enter INFORMER.
Informer. Man! who are *you*?
Meg. Ane Megara piggie-seller.
In. Then I'll denounce your goods and you yourself
As enemies!
Meg. Hech, here it comes again,
The vera primal source of a' our wae.
In. You'll Megarize to your cost. Let go the sack.
Meg. Dicaeopolis! Dicaeopolis! Here's a chiel
Denouncin' me.
Di. (*re-entering*) Where is he? Market-clerks,
Why don't you keep these sycophants away?
What! show him up without a lantern-wick?
In. Not show our enemies up?
Di. You had better not.
Get out, and do your showing other-where.
Exit INFORMER.
Meg. The pest thae birkies are in Athans toun!
Di. Well never mind, Megarian, take the things,
Garlic and salt, for which you sold the pigs.
Fare well!
Meg. That's na our way in Megara toun.
Di. Then on my head the officious wish return!
Meg. O piggies, try withouten father now

To eat wi' saut yere bannock, an' ye git ane.

Exeunt DICAEOPOLIS *and* MEGARIAN.

Chorus

A happy lot the man has got:
his scheme devised with wondrous art
Proceeds and prospers as you see;
and now he'll sit in his private Mart
The fruit of his bold design to reap.
And O if a Ctesias come this way,
Or other informers vex us, they
Will soon for their trespass weep.

No sneak shall grieve you buying first
the fish you wanted to possess,
No Prepis on your dainty robes
wipe off his utter loathsomeness.
You'll no Cleonymus jostle there;
But all unsoiled through the Mart you'll go,
And no Hyperbolus work you woe
With writs enough and to spare.

Never within these bounds shall walk
the little fop we all despise,
The young Cratinus neatly shorn
with single razor wanton-wise,
That Artemon-engineer of ill,
Whose father sprang from an old he-goat,
And father and son, as ye all may note,
Are rank with its fragrance still.

No Pauson, scurvy knave, shall here
insult you in the market-place,
No vile Lysistratus, to all
Cholargian folk a dire disgrace,
That deep-dyed sinner, that low buffoon,
Who always shivers and hungers sore
Full thirty days, or it may be more,
In every course of the moon.

Enter BOEOTIAN, *with slave and musicians.*

Boeotian. Hech sirs, my shouther's sair, wat Heracles!
Ismeny lad, pit doon thae pennyroyal
Wi' tentie care. Pipers wha cam' frae Thaibes
Blaw oop the auld tyke's hurdies wi' the banes.

Di. Hang you! shut up! Off from my doors, you wasps!
Whence flew these curst Chaeridian bumble-drones
Here, to my door? Get to the ravens! Hence!

Exeunt musicians.

Bo. An' recht ye are, by Iolaus, stranger.
They've blawn behint me a' the wa' frae Thaibes,
An' danged the blossom aff my pennyroyal.
But buy, an't please you, onie thing I've got,
Some o' thae cleckin' or thae four-winged gear.

Di. O welcome, dear Boeotian muffin-eater,
What have you there?

Bo. A' that Boeoty gies us
Mats, dittany, pennyroyal, lantern-wicks,
An' dooks, an' kaes, an' francolins, an' coots,
Plivers an' divers.

Di. Eh? Why then, methinks,
You've brought fowl weather to my market-place.

Bo. Aye, an' I'm bringin' maukins, geese, an' tods.
Easels an' weasels, urchins, moles, an' cats,
An' otters too, an' eels frae Loch Copaïs.

Di. O man, to men their daintiest morsel bringing,
Let me salute the eels, if eels you bring.

Bo. Primest o' Loch Copaïs' fifty dochters
Come oot o' that; an' mak' the stranger welcome.

Di. O loved, and lost, and longed for, thou art come,
A presence grateful to the Comic choirs,
And dear to Morychus. Bring me out at once,
O kitchen-knaves, the brasier and the fan.
Behold, my lads, this best of all the eels,
Six years a truant, scarce returning now.
O children, welcome her; to you I'll give
A charcoal fire for this sweet stranger's sake.
Out with her! Never may I lose again,
Not even in death, my darling dressed in—beet.

Bo. Whaur sall I get the siller for the feesh?

Di. This you shall give me as a market-toll.
But tell me, are these other things for sale?

Bo. Aye are they, a' thae goods.

Di. And at what price?
Or would you swap for something else?

Bo. I'se swap
For gear we haena, but ye Attics hae.

Di. Well then, what say you to Phaleric sprats,
Or earthenware?

Bo. Sprats! ware! we've thae at hame.
Gie us some gear we lack, an' ye've a rowth o'.

Di. I'll tell you what; pack an informer up,
Like ware for exportation.

Bo. Mon! that's guid.
By the Twa Gudes,[1] an' unco gain I'se mak'.
Takin' a monkey fu' o' plaguy tricks.

Enter NICARCHUS.

Di. And here's Nicarchus coming to denounce you!

Bo. He's sma' in bouk.

Di. But every inch is bad.

Nicarchus. Whose is this merchandise?

Bo. 'Tis a' mine here.
Frae Thaibes, wat Zeus, I bure it.

Ni. Then I here
Denounce it all as enemies!

Bo. Hout awa!
Do ye mak' war an' enmity wi' the burdies?

Ni. Them and you too.

Bo. What hae I dune ye wrang?

Ni. That will I say for the bystanders' sake.
A lantern-wick you are bringing from the foe.

Di. Show him up, would you, for a lantern-wick?

Ni. Aye, for that lantern-wick will fire the docks.

Di. A lantern-wick the docks! O dear, and how?

Ni. If a Boeotian stuck it in a beetle,
And sent it, lighted, down a watercourse
Straight to the docks, watching when Boreas blew

[1]The two gods of a Boeotian are Zethus and Amphion.

His stiffest breeze, then if the ships caught fire,
They'd blaze up in an instant.

Di. Blaze, you rascal!
What, with a beetle and a lantern-wick?

Ni. Bear witness!

Di. Stop his mouth, and bring me litter.
I'll pack him up, like earthenware, for carriage,
So they mayn't crack him on their journey home.

Ch. Tie up, O best of men, with care
The honest stranger's piece of ware,
For fear they break it,
As homeward on their backs they take it.

Di. To that, be sure, I'll have regard;
Indeed it creaks as though 'twere charred,
By cracks molested,
And altogether God-detested.

Ch. How shall he deal with it?

Di. For every use 'tis fit,
A cup of ills, a lawsuit can,
For audits an informing pan,
A poisoned chalice
Full filled with every kind of malice.

Ch. But who can safely use, I pray,
A thing like this from day to day
In household matters,
A thing that always creaks and clatters?

Di. He's strong, my worthy friend, and tough:
He will not break for usage rough,
Not though you shove him
Head foremost down, his heels above him.

Ch. (*to* BOEOTIAN) You've got a lovely pack.

Bo. A bonnie hairst I'se mak'.

Ch. Aye, best of friends, your harvest make,
And whereso'er it please you take
This artful, knowing
And best equipped informer going.

Di. 'Twas a tough business, but I've packed the scamp.
Lift up and take your piece of ware, Boeotian.

Bo. Gae, pit your shouther underneath, Ismeny.

Di. And pray be careful as you take him home.
You've got a rotten bale of goods, but still!
And if you make a harvest out of *him*,
You'll be in luck's way, as regards informers.

Exeunt DICAEOPOLIS, BOEOTIAN *and his slave.*

Enter SERVANT OF LAMACHUS.

Servant. Dicaeopolis!

Di. Well? why are you shouting?

Se. Why?
Lamachus bids you, towards the Pitcher-feast,
Give him some thrushes for this drachma here,
And for three drachmas one Copaïc eel.

Enter DICAEOPOLIS.

Di. Who is this Lamachus that wants the eel?

Se. The dread, the tough, the terrible, who wields
The Gorgon targe, and shakes three shadowy plumes.

Di. An eel for *him*? Not though his targe he gave me!
Let him go shake his plumes at his salt fish.
If he demur, I'll call the Market clerks.
Now for myself I'll carry all these things
Indoors, to the tune *o' merles an' mavises wings. Exit.*

Chorus

Have ye seen him, all ye people,
seen the man of matchless art,
Seen him, by his private treaty,
traffic gain from every mart.
Goods from every neighbour;
Some required for household uses;
some 'twere pleasant warm to eat;
All the wealth of all the cities
lavished here before his feet,
Free from toil and labour.

War I'll never welcome in
to share my hospitality,
Never shall the fellow sing
Harmodius in my company,
Always in his cups he acts
so rudely and offensively.
Tipsily he burst upon
our happy quiet family,
Breaking this, upsetting that,
and brawling most pugnaciously.
Yea when we entreated him
with hospitable courtesy,
"Sit you down, and drink a cup,
a Cup of Love and Harmony,"
All the more he burnt the poles
we wanted for our husbandry,
Aye and spilt perforce the liquor
treasured up within our vines.
Proudly he prepares to banquet.
Did ye mark him, all elate,
As a sample of his living
cast these plumes before his gate?
Grand his ostentation!
O of Cypris foster-sister,
and of every heavenly Grace,
Never knew I till this moment
all the glory of thy face,
Reconciliation!

O that Love would you and me
unite in endless harmony,
Love as he is pictured with
the wreath of roses smilingly.
Maybe you regard me as
a fragment of antiquity:
Ah, but if I get you, dear,
I'll show my triple husbandry.
First a row of vinelets will I
plant prolonged and orderly,
Next the little fig-tree shoots
beside them, growing lustily,
Thirdly the domestic vine;
although I am so elderly.
Round them all shall olives grow,
to form a pleasant boundary.
Thence will you and I anoint us,
darling, when the New Moon shines.

Enter CRIER, *while the eccyclema exposes to view the interior of* DICAEOPOLIS's *house.*

Cr. O yes! O yes!
Come, drain your pitchers to the trumpet's sound,
In our old fashion. Whoso drains *his* first,
Shall have, for prize, a skin of—Ctesiphon.

Di. Lads! Lassies! heard ye not the words he said?
What are ye at? Do ye not hear the Crier?
Quick! stew and roast, and turn the roasting flesh,
Unspit the haremeat, weave the coronals,
Bring the spits here, and I'll impale the thrushes.

Ch. I envy much your happy plan,
I envy more, you lucky man,
The joys you're now possessing.

Di. What, when around the spits you see
the thrushes roasting gloriously?

Ch. And that's a saying I admire.

Di. Boy, poke me up the charcoal fire.

Ch. O listen with what cookly art
And gracious care, so trim and smart,
His own repast he's dressing.

Enter DERCETES, *an Athenian farmer.*

Farmer. Alas! Alas!

Di. O Heracles, who's there?

Fa. An ill-starred man.

Di. Then keep it to yourself.

Fa. O—for you only hold the truces, dear—
Measure me out though but five years of Peace.

Di. What ails you?

Fa. Ruined! Lost my oxen twain.

Di. Where from?

Fa. From Phyle. The Boeotians stole them.

Di. And yet you are clad in white, you ill-starred loon!

Fa. They twain maintained me in the very lap
Of affluent muckery.

Di. Well, what want you now?

Fa. Lost my two eyes, weeping my oxen twain.
Come, if you care for Dercetes of Phyle,
Rub some Peace-ointment, do, on my two eyes.

Di. Why, bless the fool, I'm not a public surgeon.

Fa. *Do* now; I'll maybe find my oxen twain.

Di. No, go and weep at Pittalus's door.

Fa. Do, just one single drop. Just drop me here
Into this quill one little drop of Peace.

Di. No, not one twitterlet; take your tears elsewhere.

Fa. Alas! Alas! my darling yoke of oxen. *Exit.*

Ch. He loves the Treaty's pleasant taste;
He will not be, methinks, in haste
To let another share it.

Di. Pour on the tripe the honey, you!
And you, the cuttle richly stew!

Ch. How trumpet-like his orders sound.

Di. Be sure the bits of eel are browned.

Ch. The words you speak, your savoury rites,
Keep sharpening so our appetites
That we can hardly bear it.

Di. Now roast these other things and brown them nicely.

Enter GROOMSMAN.

Groomsman. O Dicaeopolis!

Di. Who's there? who's there?

Gr. A bridegroom sends you from his wedding-banquet
These bits of meat.

Di. Well done, whoe'er he is.

Gr. And in return he bids you pour him out,
To keep him safely with his bride at home,
Into this ointment-pot one dram of Peace.

Di. Take, take your meat away; I can't abide it.
Not for ten thousand drachmas would I give him
One drop of Peace. (*Enter* BRIDESMAID.) Hey, who comes here?

Gr. The bridesmaid
Bringing a private message from the bride.

Di. Well, what have *you* to say? What wants the bride?
(*Affects to listen.*)
O heaven, the laughable request she makes
To keep her bridegroom safely by her side.
I'll do it; bring the truces; she's a woman,
Unfit to bear the burdens of the war.
Now, hold the myrrh-box underneath, my girl.
Know you the way to use it? Tell the bride,
When they're enrolling soldiers for the war,
To rub the bridegroom every night with this.

Exeunt GROOMSMAN *and* BRIDESMAID.

Now take the truces back, and bring the ladle.
I'll fill the winecups for the Pitcher-feast.

Ch. But here runs one with eyebrows puckered up.
Methinks he comes a messenger of woe.

Enter CRIER.

Cr. O toils, and fights, and fighting Lamachuses!

La. (*within*) Who clangs around my bronze-accoutred halls? *Enter* LAMACHUS.

Cr. The generals bid you take your crests and cohorts,
And hurry off this instant; to keep watch
Amongst the mountain passes in the snow.
For news has come that at this Pitcher-feast
Boeotian bandits mean to raid our lands.

La. O generals, great in numbers, small in worth!
Shame that I may not even enjoy the feast.

Di. O expedition battle-Lamachaean!

La. O dear, what *you!* Do *you* insult me too?

Di. What would you fight with Geryon, the four-winged?

La. O woe!
O what a message has this Crier brought me!

Di. Oho! what message will this runner bring me?

Enter MESSENGER.

Messenger. Dicaeopolis!

Di. Well?

Mes. Come at once to supper,
And bring your pitcher, and your supper-chest.
The priest of Bacchus sends to fetch you thither.
And do be quick: you keep the supper waiting.
For all things else are ready and prepared,
The couches, tables, sofa-cushions, rugs,
Wreaths, sweetmeats, myrrh, the harlotry are there,
Whole-meal cakes, cheese-cakes, sesame-, honey-cakes,

And dancing-girls, "Harmodius' dearest ones."
So pray make haste.

La. O wretched, wretched me!

Di. Aye the great Gorgon 'twas you chose for patron.
Now close the house, and pack the supper up.

La. Boy, bring me out my soldier's knapsack here.

Di. Boy, bring me out my supper-basket here.

La. Boy, bring me onions, with some thymy salt.

Di. For me, fish-fillets: onions I detest.

La. Boy, bring me here a leaf of rotten fish.

Di. A tit-bit leaf for me; I'll toast it there.

La. Now bring me here my helmet's double plume.

Di. And bring me here my thrushes and ring-doves.

La. How nice and white this ostrich-plume to view.

Di. How nice and brown this pigeon's flesh to eat.

La. Man, don't keep jeering at my armour so.

Di. Man, don't keep peering at my thrushes so.

La. Bring me the casket with the three crests in it.

Di. Bring me the basket with the hare's flesh in it.

La. Surely the moths my crest have eaten up.

Di. Sure this hare-soup I'll eat before I sup.

La. Fellow, I'll thank you not to talk to *me*.

Di. Nay, but the boy and I, we can't agree.
Come will you bet, and Lamachus decide,
Locusts or thrushes, which the daintier are?

La. Insolent knave!

Di. (*to the boy*) Locusts, he says, by far.

La. Boy, boy, take down the spear, and bring it here.

Di. Boy, take the sweetbread off and bring it here.

La. Hold firmly to the spear whilst I pull off
The case.

Di. And you, hold firmly to the spit.

La. Boy, bring the framework to support my shield.

Di. Boy, bring the bakemeats to support my frame.

La. Bring here the grim-backed circle of the shield.

Di. And here the cheese-backed circle of the cake.

La. Is not this—mockery, plain for men to see?

Di. Is not this—cheese-cake, sweet for men to eat?

La. Pour on the oil, boy. Gazing on my shield,
I see an old man tried for cowardliness.

Di. Pour on the honey. Gazing on my cake,
I see an old man mocking Lamachus.

La. Bring me a casque, to arm the outer man.

Di. Bring me a cask to warm the inner man.

La. With this I'll arm myself against the foe.

Di. With this I'll warm myself against the feast.

La. Boy, lash the blankets up against the shield.

Di. Boy, lash the supper up against the chest.

La. Myself will bear my knapsack for myself.

Di. Myself will wear my wraps, and haste away.

La. Take up the shield, my boy, and bring it on.
Snowing! good lack, a wintry prospect mine.

Di. Take up the chest; a suppery prospect mine.

Exeunt DICAEOPOLIS *and* LAMACHUS.

Ch. Off to your duties, my heroes bold.
Different truly the paths ye tread;
One to drink with wreaths on his head;
One to watch, and shiver with cold,
Lonely, the while his antagonist passes
The sweetest of hours with the sweetest of lasses.

Pray we that Zeus calmly reduce
to destruction emphatic and utter
That meanest of poets and meanest of men,
Antimachus, offspring of Sputter;
The Choregus who sent me away
without any supper at all
At the feast of Lenaea; I pray,
two Woes that Choregus befall.
May he hanker for a dish
of the subtle cuttle-fish;
May he see the cuttle sailing
through its brine and through its oil,
On its little table lying,
hot and hissing from the frying,
Till it anchor close beside him,
when alas! and woe betide him!
As he reaches forth his hand
for the meal the Gods provide him,
May a dog snatch and carry off the spoil, off the spoil,
May a dog snatch and carry off the spoil.

Duly the first Woe is rehearsed;
attend whilst the other I'm telling.
It is night, and our gentleman, after a ride,
is returning on foot to his dwelling;
With ague he's sorely bested,
and he's feeling uncommonly ill,
When suddenly down on his head
comes Orestes's club with a will.
'Tis Orestes, hero mad,
'tis the drunkard and the pad.
Then stooping in the darkness
let him grope about the place,
If his hand can find a brickbat
at Orestes to be flung;
But instead of any brickbat
may he grasp a podge of dung,
And rushing on with this, Orestes may he miss,
And hit young Cratinus in the face, in the face,
And hit young Cratinus in the face.

Enter ATTENDANT.

Attendant. Varlets who dwell in Lamachus's halls,
Heat water, knaves, heat water in a pot.
Make ready lint, and salves, and greasy wool,
And ankle-bandages. Your lord is hurt,
Pierced by a stake whilst leaping o'er a trench.
Then, twisting round, he wrenched his ankle out,
And, falling, cracked his skull upon a stone;
And shocked the sleeping Gorgon from his shield.

Then the Great Boastard's plume being cast away
Prone on the rocks, a dolorous cry he raised,
"O glorious Eye, with this my last fond look
The heavenly light I leave; my day is done."
He spake, and straightway falls into a ditch:
Jumps up again: confronts the runaways,
And prods the fleeing bandits with his spear.
But here he enters. Open wide the door.

Re-enter LAMACHUS *wounded, supported by attendants, and* DICAEOPOLIS *jovial between two courtesans.*

La. O lack-a-day! O lack-a-day!
I'm hacked, I'm killed, by hostile lances!
But worse than wound or lance 'twill grieve me
If Dicaeopolis perceive me
And mock, and mock at my mischances.

Di. O lucky day! O lucky day!
What mortal ever can be richer,
Than he who feels, my golden misses,
Your softest, closest, loveliest kisses.
'Twas I, 'twas I, first drained the pitcher.

La. O me, my woful dolorous lot!
O me, the gruesome wounds I've got!

Di. My darling Lamachippus, is it not?

La. O doleful chance!

Di. O cursed spite!

La. Why give me a kiss?

Di. Why give me a bite?

La. O me the heavy, heavy charge they tried.

Di. Who makes a charge this happy Pitcher-tide?

La. O Paean, Healer! heal me, Paean, pray.

Di. 'Tis not the Healer's festival to-day.

La. O lift me gently round the hips,
My comrades true!

Di. O kiss me warmly on the lips,
My darlings, do!

La. My brain is dizzy with the blow
Of hostile stone.

Di. Mine's dizzy too: to bed I'll go,
And not alone.

La. O take me in your healing hands, and bring
To Pittalus this battered frame of mine.

Di. O take me to the judges. Where's the King
That rules the feast? hand me my skin of wine.

La. A lance has struck me through the bone
So piteously! so piteously!

He is helped off the stage.

Di. I've drained the pitcher all alone;
Sing ho! Sing ho! for Victory.

Ch. Sing ho! Sing ho! for Victory then,
If so you bid, if so you bid.

Di. I filled it with neat wine, my men,
And quaffed it at a gulp, I did.

Ch. Sing ho! brave heart, the wineskin take,
And onward go, and onward go.

Di. And ye must follow in my wake,
And sing for Victory ho! sing ho!

Ch. O yes, we'll follow for your sake
Your wineskin and yourself, I trow.
Sing ho! for Victory won, sing ho!

THE KNIGHTS

DRAMATIS PERSONAE

Demosthenes	Paphlagon
Nicias	Demus
Sausage-Seller	Chorus of Knights

In the foreground is a loose arrangement of stones, which will, later on, be taken to represent the Pnyx. Behind are three houses; the central one, with a harvest-wreath over the door, is the abode of DEMUS; *whilst the others serve for* PAPHLAGON, *who is* CLEON *and the* SAUSAGE-SELLER. *Out of the house of* DEMUS *run two slaves, howling; their masks represent the two famous Athenian generals,* NICIAS *and* DEMOSTHENES.

Demosthenes. O! O! This Paphlagon, with all his wiles,
This newly-purchased pest, I wish the Gods
Would "utterly abolish and destroy"!
For since he entered, by ill-luck, our house,
He's always getting all the household flogged.
Nicias. I wish they would, this chief of Paphlagons,
Him and his lies!
De. Ha! how feel *you*, poor fellow?
Ni. Bad, like yourself.
De. Then come, and let us wail
A stave of old Olympus, both together.
Both. (*sobbing*) Mumu! Mumu! Mumu! Mumu! Mumu!
De. Pah! What's the good of whimpering? Better far
To dry our tears, and seek some way of safety.
Ni. Which way? You, tell me.
De. Rather, tell me you,
Or else we'll fight.
Ni. By Apollo, no not I.
You say it first, and then I'll say it after.
De. O that thou said'st the thing that I would say.
Ni. I've not the pluck. I wish I could suggest
Some plan in smart Euripidean style.
De. Don't do it! Don't! Pray don't be-chervil me
But find some caper-cutting trick from master.
Ni. Will you say "sert," like that, speaking it crisply?
De. Of course I'll say it, "sert."
Ni. Now, after "sert"
Say "de."
De. "De."
Ni. Yes, that's very nicely said.
Now, first say "sert," and then say "de," beginning
Slowly at first, but quickening as you go.
De. Aye; "sert-de, sert-de, sert, de-sert."
Ni. There 'tis!
Do you not like it?
De. Like it, yes; but—
Ni. What?
De. There's an uncanny sound about "desert."
Ni. Uncanny? How?
De. They flog deserters so.
Ni. O then 'twere better that we both should go,
And fall before the statues of the Gods.
De. Stat-at-ues is it? What, do you really think
That there are Gods?
Ni. I know it.
De. Know it! How?
Ni. I'm such a wretched God-detested chap.
De. Well urged indeed; but seek some other way.
Would you I told the story to the audience?
Ni. Not a bad plan; but let us ask them first
To show us plainly by their looks and cheer
If they take pleasure in our words and acts.
De. I'll tell them now. We two have got a master,
Demus of Pnyx-borough, such a sour old man,
Quick-tempered, country-minded, bean-consuming,
A trifle hard of hearing. Last new moon
He bought a slave, a tanner, Paphlagon,
The greatest rogue and liar in the world.
This tanning-Paphlagon, he soon finds out
Master's weak points; and cringing down before him
Flatters, and fawns, and wheedles, and cajoles,
With little apish leather-snippings, thus;
"O Demus, try one case, get the three-obol,
Then take your bath, gorge, guzzle, eat your fill.
Would you I set your supper?" Then he'll seize
A dish some other servant has prepared,
And serve it up for master; and quite lately
I'd baked a rich Laconian cake at Pylus,
When in runs Paphlagon, and bags my cake,
And serves it up to Demus as his own.
But us he drives away, and none but he
Must wait on master; there he stands through dinner
With leathern flap, and flicks away the speakers.
And he chants oracles, till the dazed old man
Goes Sibyl-mad; then, when he sees him mooning,
He plies his trade. He slanders those within
With downright lies; so then we're flogged, poor wretches,
And Paphlagon runs round, extorting, begging,
Upsetting everyone; and "Mark," says he,
"There's Hylas flogged; that's all my doing; better
Make friends with me, or *you*'ll be trounced to-day."
So then we bribe him off; or if we don't,

We're sure to catch it thrice as bad from master.
Now let's excogitate at once, good fellow,
Which way to turn our footsteps, and to whom.
Ni. There's nothing better than my *sert*, good fellow.
De. But nought we do is hid from Paphlagon.
His eyes are everywhere; he straddles out,
One foot in Pylus, in the Assembly one.
So vast his stride, that at the self-same moment
His seat is in Chaonia, and his hands
Are set on Begging, and his mind on Theft.
Ni. Well then, we had better die; but just consider
How we can die the manliest sort of death.
De. The manliest sort of death? Let's see; which is it?
Ni. Had we not better drink the blood of bulls?
'Twere fine to die Themistocles' death.
De. Blood? no: pure wine, to the toast of Happy Fortune!
From that we'll maybe get some happy thought.
Ni. Pure wine indeed! Is this a tippling matter?
How can one get, when drunk, a happy thought?
De Aye, say you so, you water-fountain-twaddler?
And dare you rail at wine's inventiveness?
I tell you nothing has such go as wine.
Why, look you now; 'tis when men drink, they thrive,
Grow wealthy, speed their business, win their suits,
Make themselves happy, benefit their friends.
Go, fetch me out a stoup of wine, and let me
Moisten my wits, and utter something bright.
Ni. O me, what good will all your tippling do?
De. Much; bring it out; I'll lay me down awhile;
For when I'm drunk, I'll everything bespatter
With little scraps of schemes, and plots, and plans.

NICIAS *enters the house and returns with a bottle.*

Ni. I've got the wine; nobody saw me take it.
Wasn't that luck?
De. What's Paphlagon about?
Ni. Drunk! Snoring on his back amidst his hides,
The juggler; gorged with confiscation pasties.
De. Come, tinkle out a bumper of pure wine,
To pour.
Ni. Here, take; and pour to Happy Fortune.
Quaff, quaff the loving-cup of *Pramnian* Fortune.
De. O Happy Fortune, thine's the thought, not mine!
Ni. Pray you, what is it?
De. Steal from Paphlagon,
While yet he sleeps, those oracles of his,
And bring them out.
Ni. I will; and yet I'm fearful
That I may meet with most *un*happy Fortune.

Enters house.

De. Come now, I'll draw the pitcher to myself,
Moisten my wits, and utter something bright.
Ni. (*returning*) Paphlagon's snoring so! He never saw me.
I've got the sacred oracle which he keeps
So snugly.
De. O you clever fellow you,
I'll read it; hand it over; you the while
Fill me the cup. Let's see: what have we here?
O! Prophecies! Give me the cup directly.
Ni. Here! What do they say?
De. Fill me another cup.
Ni. "Fill me another?" Is that really there?
De. O Bakis!
Ni. Well?
De. Give me the cup directly.
Ni. Bakis seems mighty partial to the cup.
De. O villainous Paphlagon, this it was you feared,
This oracle about yourself!
Ni. What is it?
De. Herein is written how himself shall perish.
Ni. How shall he?
De. How? The oracle says straight out,
That first of all there comes an oakum-seller
Who first shall manage all the State's affairs.
Ni. One something-seller; well, what follows, pray?
De. Next after him there comes a sheep-seller.
Ni. Two something-sellers; what's this seller's fortune?
De. He'll hold the reins, till some more villainous rogue
Arise than he; and thereupon he'll perish.
Then follows Paphlagon, our leather-seller,
Thief, brawler, roaring as Cycloborus roars.
Ni. The leather-seller, then, shall overthrow
The sheep-seller?
De. He shall.
Ni. O wretched me,
Is there no other something-seller left?
De. There is yet one; a wondrous trade *he* has.
Ni. What, I beseech you?
De. Shall I tell you?
Ni. Aye.
De. A sausage-seller ousts the leather-seller.
Ni. A sausage-seller! Goodness, what a trade!
Wherever shall we find one?
De. That's the question.
Ni. Why here comes one, 'tis providential surely,
Bound for the agora.
De. Hi, come hither! here!
You dearest man, you blessed sausage-seller!
Arise, a Saviour to the State and us.

Enter SAUSAGE-SELLER.

Sausage-Seller. Eh! What are you shouting at?
De. Come here this instant,
And hear your wonderful amazing luck.
Ni. Make him put down his dresser; tell him all
The news about that oracle we've got.
I'll keep an eye on Paphlagon the while.

Exit NICIAS.

De. Come, put you down those cookery implements,
Then make your reverence to the Gods and earth—
S.-S. There! what's the row?
De. O happy man, and rich,
Nothing to-day, to-morrow everything!
O mighty ruler of Imperial Athens!
S.-S. Good fellow, let me wash the guts, and sell

My sausages. What need to flout me so?
De. You fool! the guts indeed! Now look you here.
You see those people on the tiers?
S.-S. I do.
De. You shall be over-lord of all those people,
The Agora, and the Harbours, and the Pnyx.
You'll trim the Generals, trample down the Council,
Fetter, imprison, make the Hall your brothel.
S.-S. What, I?
De. Yes, you yourself! And that's not all.
For mount you up upon the dresser here
And view the islands all around.
S.-S. I see.
De. And all the marts and merchant-ships?
S.-S. I see.
De. And aren't you then a lucky man?
And *that's* not all. Just cast your eyes askew,
The right to Caria, and the left to Carthage.
S.-S. A marvellous lucky man, to twist my neck!
De. Nay, but all these shall be your—perquisites.
You shall become, this oracle declares,
A Man most mighty!
S.-S. Humbug! How can I,
A sausage-selling chap, become a Man?
De. Why, that's the very thing will make you great,
Your roguery, impudence, and agora-training.
S.-S. I am not worthy of great power, methinks.
De. O me, not worthy! what's the matter now?
You've got, I fear, some good upon your conscience.
Spring you from gentlemen?
S.-S. By the powers, not I.
From downright blackguards.
De. Lucky, lucky man,
O what a start you've got for public life.
S.-S. But I know nothing, friend, beyond my letters,
And even of them but little, and that badly.
De. The mischief is that you know *anything*.
To be a Demus-leader is not now
For lettered men, nor yet for honest men,
But for the base and ignorant. Don't let slip
The bright occasion which the Gods provide you.
S.-S. How goes the oracle?
De. Full of promise good,
Wrapped up in cunning enigmatic words:
"Nay, but if once the Eagle, the black-tanned mandible-curver,
Seize with his beak the Serpent, the dullard, the drinker of life-blood,
Then shall the sharp sour brine of the Paphlagon tribe be extinguished,
Then to the entrail-sellers shall God great glory and honour
Render, unless they elect to continue the sale of the sausage."
S.-S. But what in the world has this to do with me?
De. The black-tanned Eagle, that means Paphlagon.
S.-S. And what the mandibles?
De. That's self-evident.
His fingers, crooked to carry off their prey.
S.-S. What does the Serpent mean?
De. That's plainer still.
A serpent's long; a sausage too is long.
Serpents drink blood, and sausages drink blood.
The Serpent then, it says, shall overcome
The black-tanned Eagle, if it's not talked over.
S.-S. I like the lines: but how can I, I wonder,
Contrive to manage Demus' affairs.
De. Why nothing's easier. Do what now you do:
Mince, hash, and mash up everything together.
Win over Demus with the savoury sauce
Of little cookery phrases. You've already
Whatever else a Demagogue requires.
A brutal voice, low birth, an agora training;
Why you've got all one wants for public life.
The Pythian shrine and oracles concur.
Crown, crown your head; pour wine to mighty—Dulness;
Prepare to fight the man.
S.-S. But what ally
Will stand beside me, for the wealthy men
Tremble before him, and the poor folk blench.
De. A thousand Knights, all honest men and true,
Detest the scoundrel, and will help the cause;
And whosoe'er is noblest in the State,
And whosoe'er is brightest in the tiers,
And I myself. And God will lend his aid.
And fear him not; he is not pictured really;
For all the mask-providers feared to mould
His actual likeness; but our audience here
Are shrewd and bright; they'll recognize the man.
Enter NICIAS.
Ni. Mercy upon us! here comes Paphlagon.
Enter PAPHLAGON.
Paphlagon. By the Twelve Gods, you two shall pay for this,
Always conspiring, plotting ill to Demus!
What's this Chalcidian goblet doing here?
Hah! ye're inciting Chalcis to revolt.
Villains and traitors! ye shall die the death.
De. (*to* SAUSAGE-SELLER) Hi! where are you off to? Stop! For goodness' sake,
Don't fail us now, most doughty Sausage-seller!
The CHORUS OF KNIGHTS *enter the orchestra.*
Hasten up, my gallant horsemen, now's the time your foe to fight.
Now then Simon, now Panaetius, charge with fury on the right.
Here they're coming! Worthy fellow, wheel about, commence the fray;
Lo, the dust of many horsemen rushing on in close array!
Turn upon him, fight him, smite him, scout him, rout him, every way.
Chorus. Smite the rascal, smite him, smite him, troubler of our Knightly train,
Foul extortioner, Charybdis, bottomless abyss of gain.
Smite the rascal; smite the rascal; many times the word I'll say,

For he proved himself a rascal
many, many times a day.
Therefore smite him, chase him, pound him,
rend and rattle and confound him!
Show your loathing, show as *we* do;
press with angry shouts around him.
Take you heed, or he'll evade you;
watch him closely, for the man
Knows how Eucrates escaped us,
fleeing to his stores of bran.
Pa. O my Heliastic veterans,
of the great Triobol clan,
Whom through right and wrong I nourish,
bawling, shouting all I can,
Help me, by conspiring traitors
shamefully abused and beaten.
Ch. Rightly, for the public commons
you before your turn have eaten,
And you squeeze the audit-passers,
pinching them like figs, to try
Which is ripe, and which is ripening,
which is very crude and dry.
Find you one of easy temper,
mouth agape, and vacant look,
Back from Chersonese you bring him,
grasp him firmly, fix your hook,
Twist his shoulder back and, glibly,
gulp the victim down at once.
And you search amongst the townsmen
for some lambkin-witted dunce,
Wealthy, void of tricks and malice,
shuddering at disputes and fuss.
Pa. *You* assail me too, my masters?
'tis for you they beat me thus;
'Tis because I thought of moving
that 'twere proper here to make
Some memorial of your worships
for your noble valour's sake.
Ch. Hear him trying to cajole us!
O the supple-bending sneak,
Playing off his tricks upon us,
as on dotards old and weak.
Nay, but there my arm shall smite him
if to pass you there he seek;
If he dodge in this direction,
here against my leg he butts.
Pa. Athens! Demus! see the monsters,
see them punch me in the guts.
Ch. Shouting, are you? you who always
by your shouts subvert the town.
S.-S. But in this I'll first surpass him;
thus I shout the fellow down.
Ch. If in bawling you defeat him,
sing we ho! for Victory's sake.
If in shamelessness you beat him,
then indeed we take the cake.
Pa. I denounce this smuggling fellow;
contraband of war he takes
For the Peloponnesian galleys,
frapping them with—girdle-cakes.
S.-S. I denounce this juggling fellow;
at the Hall, from day to day,
In he runs with empty belly,
with a full one hies away.
Ch. Fish, and flesh, and bread exporting,
and a hundred things like these,
Contraband of peace, which never
were allowed to Pericles.
Pa. Death awaits you at once, you two.
S.-S. Thrice as loud can I squall as you.
Pa. Now will I bawl you down by bawling.
S.-S. Now will I squall you down by squalling.
Pa. Lead our armies, and I'll backbite you.
S.-S. I'll with dog-whips slash you and smite you.
Pa. I'll outwit you by fraud and lying.
S.-S. I'll your pettitoes chop for frying.
Pa. Now unblinking regard me, you.
S.-S. I was bred in the agora too.
Pa. Say but g-r-r, and to strips I'll tear you.
S.-S. Speak one word, and as dung I'll bear you.
Pa. I confess that I steal. Do you?
S.-S. Agora Hermes! yes, I do.
If I'm seen, I'm a perjurer too.
Pa. Somebody else's tricks you're vaunting;
Now to the Prytanes off I'll run,
Tell them you've got some holy pig-guts.
Tell them you've paid no tithe thereon.
Ch. O villain, O shameless of heart,
O Bawler and Brawler self-seeking,
The land, the Assembly, the Tolls,
are all with thine impudence reeking,
And the Courts, and the actions at law;
they are full unto loathing and hate!
Thou stirrest the mud to its depths,
perturbing the whole of the State.
Ruffian, who hast deafened Athens
with thine everlasting din,
Watching from the rocks the tribute,
tunny-fashion, shoaling in.
Pa. Well I know the very quarter
where they cobbled up the plot.
S.-S. You're a knowing hand at cobbling,
else in mincing meat I'm not;
You who cheated all the rustics
with a flabby bullock-hide,
Cutting it aslant to make it
look like leather firm and dried;
In a day, the shoes you sold them
wobbled half a foot too wide.
Ni. That's the very trick the rascal
played the other day on me,
And my friends and fellow burghers
laughed with undissembled glee,
I was swimming in my slippers
ere I got to Pergasae.
Ch. So then thou hast e'en from the first
that shameless bravado displayed
Which alone is the Orators' Patron.
And foremost of all by its aid
Thou the wealthy strangers milkest,
draining off their rich supplies;
And the son of Hippodamus
watches thee with streaming eyes.
Ah, but another has dawned on us now,

Viler and fouler and coarser than thou,
Viler and fouler and coarser by far,
One who'll beat thee and defeat thee
(therefore jubilant we are),
Beat thee in jackanapes tricks and rascality,
Beat thee in impudence, cheek, and brutality.
O trained where Men are trained who best
deserve that appellation,
Now show us of how little worth
is liberal education.

S.-S. The sort of citizen he is, I'll first expose to view.

Pa. Give *me* precedence.

S.-S. No, by Zeus, for I'm a blackguard too.

Ch. And if to that he yield not, add "as all my fathers were."

Pa. Give *me* precedence.

S.-S. No, by Zeus.

Pa. O yes, by Zeus.

S.-S. I swear
I'll fight you on that very point; you never *shall* be first.

Pa. O, I shall burst.

S.-S. You never shall.

Ch. O let him, let him burst.

Pa. How dare you try in speech to vie
with *me*? On what rely you?

S.-S. Why I can speak first-rate, and eke
with piquant sauce supply you.

Pa. O speak you can! and you're the man,
I warrant, who is able
A mangled mess full well to dress,
and serve it up to table.
I know your case, the common case;
against some alien folk
You had some petty suit to plead,
and fairly well you spoke.
For oft you'd conned the speech by night,
and in the streets discussed it,
And, quaffing water, shown it off,
and all your friends disgusted.
Now you're an orator, you think.
O fool, the senseless thought!

S.-S. Pray what's the draught which you have quaffed
that Athens you have brought
Tongue-wheedled by yourself alone
to sit so mute and still?

Pa. Who to compare with *me* will dare?
I'll eat my tunny grill,
And quaff thereon a stoup of wine
which water shall not touch,
And then with scurrilous abuse
the Pylian generals smutch.

S.-S. I'll eat the paunch of cow and swine,
and quaff thereon their stew,
And rising from the board with hands
which water never knew
I'll throttle all the orators, and flutter Nicias too.

Ch. With all beside I'm satisfied,
but one thing likes me not,
You speak as if you ate alone
whatever stew you've got.

Pa. You'll not consume your basse and then
Miletus bring to grief.

S.-S. But mines I'll purchase when I've first
devoured my ribs of beef.

Pa. I'll leap the Council-chamber in,
and put them all to rout.

S.-S. I'll treat you like a sausage-skin,
and twirl your breech about.

Pa. I'll hoist you by your crupper up,
and thrust you through the gate, sir.

Ch. If him you thrust, me too you must;
you must as sure as fate, sir.

Pa. Your feet in the stocks I'll fix full tight.

S.-S. And you for your cowardice I'll indict.

Pa. Outstretched on my board your hide I'll pin.

S.-S. "Pickpocket's purse" I'll make your skin.

Pa. Your limbs on the tanhouse floor I'll stake.

S.-S. Your flesh into force-meat balls I'll bake.

Pa. I'll twitch the lashes off both your eyes.

S.-S. I'll cut your gizzard out, poulterer-wise.

De. Prop open his mouth with all your strength;
Insert the extender from jaw to jaw;
Pull out his tongue to its utmost length,
And, butcher-fashion, inspect his maw,
And whilst his gape is so broad and fine,
See if he's not. The symptoms got
Which show that he's nought but a measly swine.

Ch. There are things, then, hotter than fire;
there are speeches more shameless still
Than the shameless speeches of those
who rule the City at will.
No trifling task is before you;
upon him and twist and garotte him.
Do nought that is little or mean;
for round the waist you have got him.
If in this assault you knead him
limp and supple to your hand,
You will find the man a craven;
I his habits understand.

S.-S. Truly for an arrant coward
he has all his life been known;
Yet a Man he seemed but lately,
reaping where he had not sown.
Now the ears of corn he brought us,
he aspires to parch and dry,
Shuts them up in wood and fetters,
hopes to sell them by and by.

Pa. You and your allies I fear not,
while the Council lives, and while
Demus moons upon the benches
with his own unmeaning smile.

Ch. O see how he brazens it out!
The colour remains as before
In his shameless impudent face.
And O, if I hate you not sore,
Let me be a filthy sheepskin,
that whereon Cratinus lay,
Or let Morsimus instruct me
as the Chorus to his Play.
Thou in all places, and thou at all hours,
Flitting and sitting in bri-berry flowers,

Sucking and sipping the gold they contain,
Mayest thou lightly, as 'twas swallowed,
cast thy mouthful up again.
Then will I ever the roundelay sing
"Drink for the luck which the Destinies bring,"
And old Iulius' son, the pantler Prytanean,
For joy will "Bacche-Bacchus" shout,
and chant his Io-Paean.
Pa. Think you in shamelessness to win?
No, by Poseidon, no!
Or may I evermore the feasts
of Agora Zeus forgo.
S.-S. Now by the knuckles which in youth
would discipline my head,
And those hard-handled butchers' knives
they often used instead,
I think in shamelessness I'll win;
else vainly in the slums
Have I to such a bulk been reared
on finger-cleaning crumbs.
Pa. On finger-pellets like a dog?
And reared on these, you seek
To fight a dog-faced fierce baboon!
I marvel at your cheek.
S.-S. And lots of other monkey-tricks
I practised as a boy.
O how I used to chouse the cooks
by shrieking out "Ahoy!
Look lads, a swallow! spring is here.
Look up, look up, I pray."
So up they looked whilst I purloined
a piece of meat away.
Ch. Shrewd body, you were provident,
and stole away your meat
Before the vernal swallow came,
as folk their nettles eat.
S.-S. And no one caught me out, or else,
if any saw me pot it,
I clapped the meat between my thighs
and vowed I hadn't got it;
Whereat an orator observed,
who watched me at my tricks,
"Some day this boy will make his mark
as leader in the Pnyx."
Ch. His inference was just; but still
'tis plain from whence he drew it;
He saw you filch the meat away,
and swear you didn't do it.
Pa. I'll stop your insolence, my man;
your friend's and yours together.
I'll swoop upon you like a gale
of fresh and stormy weather,
And all the land and all the sea
in wild confusion throw.
S.-S. But I will furl my sausages,
and down the tide will go
With prosperous seas, and favouring breeze,
at you my fingers snapping.
De. And if your bark a leak should spring,
the water I'll be tapping.
Pa. Full many a talent have you filched,
and dearly shall you pay,
You public-treasury thief!
Ch. Look out, and slack the sheet away,
I hear a loud Nor'-Easter there
or Sycophanter blow.
Pa. From Potidaea you received
ten talents, that I know.
S.-S. Will you take one, and hold your tongue?
Ch. He'd take it like a shot.
Let out the yard-arm ropes a bit.
S.-S. The gale has milder got.
The stormy blast is falling fast.
Pa. You'll have, for bribery and deceit,
Four hundred-talent writs to meet.
S.-S. And you, for cowardliness a score,
For theft a thousand writs and more.
Pa. From that old sacrilegious race
I'll say that your descent you trace.
S.-S. Your father's father marched, I'll swear,
As body-guard to—
Pa. Whom? Declare!
S.-S. To Hippias' Byrsine.
Pa. You jackanapes!
S.-S. You gallows-tree!
Ch. Strike like a man!
Pa. O help me! Oh!
These plotting traitors hurt me so.
Ch. Strike, strike him, well and manfully,
And with those entrails beat him,
And strings of sausage-meat, and try
Meet punishment to mete him.
O noblest flesh in all the world,
O spirit best and dearest,
To City and to citizens
a Saviour thou appearest.
How well and with what varied skill
thou foil'st him in debate!
O would that I could praise you so,
as our delight is great.
Pa. Now, by Demeter, it escaped me not
That these same plots were framing; well I knew
How they were pegged, and fixed, and glued together.
Ch. O, me!
(*to* SAUSAGE-SELLER) Can't *you* say something from the cartwright's trade?
S.-S. These Argos doings have escaped me not.
He goes, he says, to make a friend of Argos,
But 'tis with Sparta he's colloguing there.
Aye and I know the anvil whereupon
His plan is forged: 'tis welded on the captives.
Ch. Good! good! return him welding for his glue.
S.-S. And men from thence are hammering at it too.
And not by bribes of silver or of gold
Or sending friends, will you persuade me not
To tell the Athenians how you are going on.
Pa. I'll go this instant to the Council-board,
And all your vile conspiracies denounce,
And all your nightly gatherings in the town,
And how you plotted with the Medes and King,
And all your cheese-pressed doings in Boeotia.
S.-S. Pray, how's cheese selling in Boeotia now?

Pa. I'll stretch you flat, by Heracles I will. *Exit.*
Ch. Now then, what mean you? what are you going to do?
Now shall you show us if in very truth
You stole the meat and hid it as you said.
So to the Council-house you'll run, for he
Will burst in thither, and against us all
Utter his lies and bawl a mighty bawl.
S.-S. Well, I will go; but first I'll lay me down
Here, as I am, these guts and butchers'-knives.
De. Here take this ointment and anoint your neck,
So can you slip more easily through his lies.
S.-S. Well now, that's good and trainer-like advice.
De. And next, take this and swallow it.
S.-S. What for?
De. Why, if you are garlic-primed, you'll fight much better.
And now begone.
S.-S. I'm off. *Exit.*
De. And don't forget
To peck, to lie, to gobble down his combs,
And bite his wattles off. That done, return. *Exit.*

Chorus

Good-bye and good speed: may your daring succeed,
And Zeus of the Agora help you in need.
May you conquer in fight, and return to our sight
A Victor triumphant with garlands bedight.
But *ye* to our anapaests listen the while,
And give us the heed that is due,
Ye wits, who the Muse of each pattern and style
Yourselves have attempted to woo.

If one of the old-fashioned Comedy-bards
had our services sought to impress,
And make us before the spectators appear,
to deliver the public address,
He would not have easily gained us; but now,
with pleasure we grant the request
Of a poet who ventures the truth to declare,
and detests what we also detest,
And against the Tornado and Whirlwind, alone,
with noble devotion advances.
But as for the question that puzzles you most,
so that many inquire how it chances
That he never a Chorus had asked for himself,
or attempted in person to vie,
On this we're commissioned his views to explain,
and this is the Poet's reply;
That 'twas not from folly he lingered so long,
but discerning by shrewd observation
That Comedy-Chorus-instruction is quite
the most difficult thing in creation.
For out of the many who courted the Muse
she has granted her favours to few,
While e'en as the plants that abide but a year,
so shifting and changeful are *you*;
And the Poets who flourished before him, he saw,
ye were wont in their age to betray.
Observing the treatment which Magnes received
when his hair was besprinkled with grey,
Than whom there was none more trophies had won
in the fields of dramatic display.
All voices he uttered, all forms he assumed,
the Lydian, the fig-piercing Fly,
The Harp with its strings, the Bird with its wings,
the Frog with its yellow-green dye.
Yet all was too little; he failed in the end,
when the freshness of youth was gone by,
And at last in his age he was hissed from the stage
when lost was his talent for jeering.
Then he thought of Cratinus who flowed through the plains
'mid a tumult of plaudits and cheering;
And sweeping on all that obstructed his course,
with a swirl from their stations he tore them,
Oaks, rivals, and planes; and away on his flood
uprooted and prostrate he bore them.
And never a song at a banquet was sung
but "Doro fig-sandaled and true,"
Or "Framers of terse and artistical verse,"
such a popular poet he grew.
Yet now that he drivels and dotes in the streets,
and Time of his ambers has reft him,
And his framework is gaping asunder with age,
and his strings and his music have left him,
No pity ye show; no assistance bestow;
but allow him to wander about
Like Connas, with coronal withered and sere,
and ready to perish with drought;
Who ought for his former achievements to *drink*
in the Hall, nor be laid on the shelf,
But to sit in the Theatre shining and bright,
beside Dionysus himself.
And then he remembered the stormy rebuffs
which Crates endured in his day,
Who a little repast at a little expense
would provide you, then send you away;
Who the daintiest little devices would cook
from the driest of mouths for you all;
Yet he, and he only held out to the end,
now standing, now getting a fall.
So in fear of these dangers he lingered; besides,
a sailor, he thought, should abide
And tug at the oar for a season, before
he attempted the vessel to guide;
And next should be stationed awhile at the prow,
the winds and the weather to scan;
And then be the Pilot, himself for himself.
So seeing our Poet began
In a mood so discreet, nor with vulgar conceit
rushed headlong before you at first,
Loud surges of praise to his honour upraise;
salute him, all hands, with a burst

Of hearty triumphant Lenaean applause,
That the bard may depart, all radiant and bright
To the top of his forehead with joy and delight,
Having gained, by your favour, his cause.
Dread Poseidon, the Horseman's King,
Thou who lovest the brazen clash,

Clash and neighing of warlike steeds;
Pleased to watch where the trireme speeds
Purple-beaked, to the oar's long swing,
Winning glory (and pay); but chief
Where bright youths in their chariots flash
Racing (coming perchance to grief);
Cronus' son,
Throned on Geraestus and Sunium bold,
Swaying thy dolphins with trident of gold,
Come, O come, at the call of us;
Dearest to Phormio thou,
Yea and dearest to all of us,
Dearest to all of us now.

Let us praise our mighty fathers,
men who ne'er would quake or quail,
Worthy of their native country,
worthy of Athene's veil;
Men who with our fleets and armies
everywhere the victory won,
And adorned our ancient city
by achievements nobly done.
Never stayed they then to reckon
what the numbers of the foe,
At the instant that they saw him,
all their thought was "At him go!"
If they e'er in desperate struggling
on their shoulder chanced to fall,
Quick they wiped away the dust-mark,
swore they ne'er were thrown at all,
Closed again in deadly grapple.
None of all our generals brave
Then had stooped a public banquet
from Cleaenetus to crave.
Now unless ye grant them banquets,
grant precedence as their right,
They will fight no more, they tell you.
Our ambition is to fight
Freely for our Gods and country,
as our fathers fought before,
No reward or pay receiving;
asking this and nothing more,
When returning Peace shall set us
free from all our warlike toil,
Grudge us not our flowing ringlets,
grudge us not our baths and oil.

Holy Pallas, our guardian Queen,
Ruling over the holiest land,
Land poetic, renowned, and strong,
First in battle and first in song,
Land whose equal never was seen,
Come to prosper our Choral band!
Bring thou with thee the Maiden bright,
Her who greets us in every fight,
Victory!
She in the choir-competition abides with us,
Always against our antagonists sides with us.
Come, great Goddess, appear to us,
Now, if ever, we pray,
Bring thou victory dear to us,
Crown thine Horsemen to-day.

What we witnessed with our horses
we desire to eulogize.
Worthy they of praise and honour!
many a deed of high emprize,
Many a raid and battle-onset
they with us have jointly shared.
Yet their feats ashore surprise not,
with their feats afloat compared,
When they bought them cans and garlic,
bought them strings of onions too,
Leapt at once aboard the transports,
all with manful hearts and true,
Took their seats upon the benches,
dipped their oar-blades in the sea,
Pulled like any human beings,
neighing out their Hippapae!
"Pull my hearties, pull your strongest,
don't be shirking, Sigma-brand!"
Then they leapt ashore at Corinth,
and the youngest of the band
Hollowed with their hoofs their couches
or for bedding searched about.
And they fed on crabs, for clover,
if they met one crawling out,
Or detected any lurking
in the Ocean's deepest bed,
Till at length a crab of Corinth,
so Theorus tells us, said:
"Hard it is, my Lord Poseidon,
if the Knights we cannot flee
Even in the depths of Ocean, anywhere by land or sea."

Enter the SAUSAGE-SELLER.

Ch. Dearest of men, my lustiest, trustiest friend,
Good lack! how anxious has your absence made us!
But now that safe and sound you are come again,
Say what has happened, and how went the fight.

S.-S. How else but thus? The Council-victor I.

Ch. Now may we, joyous, raise the song of sacred praise.
Fair the words you speak, but fairer
Are the deeds you do.
Far I'd go, This I know,
But to hear them through.
Now then tell us all the story,
All that, where you went, befell;
Fearless be, Sure that we
All delight in all you tell.

S.-S. Aye and 'tis worth the hearing. When behind him
I reached the Council-chamber, there was he
Crashing and dashing, hurling at the Knights
Strange wonder-working thunder-driving words,
Calling them all, with all-persuading force,
Conspirators! And all the Council, hearing,
Grew full of lying orach at his talk,
Wore mustard looks, and puckered up their brows.
So when I saw them taking in his words,
Gulled by his knavish tricks, "Ye Gods," said I,
"Ye Gods of knavery, Skitals, and Phenaces,
And ye Beresceths, Cobals, Mothon, and

Thou Agora, whence my youthful training came,
Now give me boldness and a ready tongue
And shamless voice!" And as I pondered thus,
I heard a loud explosion on my right,
And made my reverence; then I dashed apart
The railing-wicket, opened wide my mouth,
And cried aloud, "O Council, I have got
Some lovely news which first I bring to you.
For never, never, since the War broke out,
Have I seen pilchards cheaper than to-day."
They calmed their brows and grew serene at once,
And crowned me for my news; and I suggested,
Bidding them keep it secret, that forthwith,
To buy these pilchards, many for a penny,
'Twere best to seize the cups in all the shops.
They clapped their hands, and turned agape to me.
But Paphlagon perceived, and well aware
What kind of measures please the Council best,
Proposed a resolution; "Sirs," quoth he,
"I move that for these happy tidings brought,
One hundred beeves be offered to Athene."
The Council instantly inclined to him.
So, overpowered with cow-dung, in a trice
I overshot him with "two hundred beeves."
And "vow," said I, "to slay to-morrow morn,
If pilchards sell one hundred for an obol,
A thousand she-goats to our huntress Queen."
Back came their heads, expectantly, to me.
He, dazed at this, went babbling idly on;
So then the Prytanes and the Archers seized him.
And *they* stood up, and raved about the pilchards;
And *he* kept begging them to wait awhile
And hear the tale the Spartan envoy brings;
"He has just arrived about a peace," shrieked he.
But all the Council with one voice exclaimed,
"What! Now about a peace? No doubt, my man,
Now they've heard pilchards are so cheap at Athens!
We want no truces; let the War go on!"
With that, "Dismiss us, Prytanes!" shouted they;
An overleaped the railings everywhere.
And I slipped out, and purchased all the leeks
And all the coriander in the market;
And as they stood perplexed, I gave them all
Of my free bounty garnish for their fish.
And they so praised and purred about me, that
With just one obol's worth of coriander
I've all the Council won, and here I am.

Ch. What rising men should do
Has all been done by you.
He, the rascal, now has met a
Bigger rascal still,
Full of guile Plot and wile,
Full of knavish skill.
Mind you carry through the conflict
In the same undaunted guise.
Well you know Long ago
We're your faithful true allies.

S.-S. See here comes Paphlagon, driving on before him
A long ground-swell, all fuss and fury, thinking
To drink me up. Boh! for your impudent bluster.

Enter PAPHLAGON.

Pa. O if I've any of my old lies left,
And don't destroy you, may I fall to bits!

S.-S. I like your threats; I'm wonderfully tickled
To hear you fume; I skip and cuckoo around you.

Pa. O by Demeter, if I eat you not
Out of the land, I'll never live at all.

S.-S. You won't? Nor I, unless I drink you up,
And swill you up, and burst myself withal.

Pa. I'll crush you, by my Pylus-won precedence.

S.-S. Precedence, is it? I'm in hopes to see you
In the last tier, instead of here in front.

Pa. By Heaven, I'll clap you in the public stocks.

S.-S. How fierce it's growing! what would it like to eat?
What is its favourite dainty? Money-bags?

Pa. I'll tear your guts out with my nails, I will.

S.-S. I'll scratch your Town Hall dinners out, I will.

Pa. I'll hale you off to Demus; then you'll catch it.

S.-S. Nay, I'll hale *you*, and then out-slander you.

Pa. Alack, poor chap, he pays no heed to you,
But I can fool him to my heart's content.

S.-S. How sure you seem that Demus is your own!

Pa. Because I know the titbits he prefers.

S.-S. And feed him badly as the nurses do.
You chew, and pop a morsel in his mouth,
But thrice as much you swallow down yourself.

Pa. And I'm so dexterous-handed, I can make
Demus expand, and then contract again.

S.-S. I can do that with many things, I trow.

Pa. 'Twon't be like bearding me in the Council now!
No, come along to Demus.

S.-S. Aye, why not?
I'm ready; march; let nothing stop us now.

Pa. O Demus, come out here.

S.-S. O yes, by Zeus,
Come out, my father.

Pa. Dearest darling Demus,
Come out, and hear how they're ill-treating me!

Enter DEMUS *and* DEMOSTHENES.

Demus. What's all this shouting? go away, you fellows.
You've smashed my harvest-garland all to bits!
Who wrongs you, Paphlagon?

Pa. He, and these young men,
Keep beating me because of you.

Dem. Why so?

Pa. Because I love you and adore you, Demus.

Dem. (*To* SAUSAGE-SELLER) And who are you?

S.-S. A rival for your love.
Long have I loved, and sought to do you good,
With many another honest gentleman,
But Paphlagon won't let us. You yourself,
Excuse me sir, are like the boys with lovers.
The honest gentlemen you won't accept,
Yet give yourself to lantern-selling chaps,
To sinew-stitchers, cobblers, aye and tanners.

Pa. Because I am good to Demus.

S.-S. Tell me how.

Pa. 'Twas I slipped in before the general there
And sailed to Pylus, and brought back the Spartans.

S.-S. And I walked round, and from the workshop stole
A mess of pottage, cooked by someone else.
Pa. Come, make a full Assembly out of hand,
O Demus, do; then find which loves you best,
And so decide, and give that man your love.
S.-S. O Demus, do. Not in the Pnyx however.
Dem. Aye, in the Pnyx, not elsewhere will I sit.
So forward all, move forward to the Pnyx.
S.-S. O luckless me, I'm ruined! The old fellow
Is, when at home, the brightest man alive;
But once he sits upon his rock, he moons
With open mouth, as one who gapes for figs.

DEMUS *now takes his seat as the audience in the mimic Pnyx, and the orators take their places.*

Ch. Now loosen every hawser,
now speed your bark along,
And mind your soul is eager,
and mind your words are strong,
No subterfuge admitting;
the man has many a trick
From hopeless things, in hopeless times,
a hopeful course to pick.
Upon him with a whirlwind's force,
impetuous, fresh and quick.
But keep on his movements a watch; and be sure
that before he can deal you a blow,
You hoist to the mast your dolphins, and cast
your vessel alongside the foe.

Pa. To the Lady who over the city presides,
to our mistress Athene, I pray
If beyond all the rest I am stoutest and best,
in the service of Demus to-day,
Except Salabaccho, and Cynna the bold,
and Lysicles—then in the Hall
May I dine as of late at the cost of the State
for doing just nothing at all.
But O if I hate you, nor stride to the van
to protect you from woes and mishaps,
Then slay me, and flay me, and saw me to bits,
to be cut into martingale straps.

S.-S. And I, if I love you not, Demus, am game
to be slaughtered by chopping and mincing,
And boiled in a sausage-meat pie; and if *that*
is, you think, not entirely convincing,
Let me here, if you please, with a morsel of cheese,
upon this to a salad be grated,
Or to far Cerameicus be dragged through the streets
with my flesh-hook, and there be cremated.

Pa. O Demus, how can there be ever a man
who loves you as dearly as I?
When on *me* you relied your finances to guide,
your Treasury never was dry,
I was begging of these, whilst those I would squeeze
and rack to extort what was due,
And nought did I care how a townsman might fare,
so long as I satisfied you.

S.-S. Why, Demus, there's nothing to boast of in that;
to do it I'm perfectly able.
I've only to steal from my comrade a meal,
and serve it up hot on your table.
And as for his loving and wishing you well,
it isn't for you that he cares,
Excepting indeed for the gain that he gets,
and the snug little fire that he shares.
Why you, who at Marathon fought with the Medes,
for Athens and Hellas contending,
And won the great battle, and left us a theme
for our songs and our speeches unending,
He cares not a bit that so roughly you sit
on the rocks, nor has dreamed of providing
Those seats with the thing I have stitched you and bring.
Just lift yourself up and subside in
This ease-giving cushion for fear you should gall
what at Salamis sat by the oar.

Dem. Who are *you*? I opine you are sprung from the line
of Harmodius famous of yore;
So noble and Demus-relieving an act
I never have witnessed before!

Pa. O me, by what paltry attentions and gifts
you contrive to attract and delude him!

S.-S. 'Twas by baits that are smaller and poorer than mine,
you rascal, you hooked and subdued him.

Pa. Was there ever a man since the City began
who for Demus has done such a lot,
Or fought for his welfare so stoutly as I?
I will wager my head there is not.

S.-S. You love him right well who permit him to dwell
eight years in the clefts of the City,
In the nests of the vulture, in turrets and casks,
nor ever assist him or pity,
But keep him in durance to rifle his hive;
and that is the reason, no doubt,
Why the peace which, unsought, Archeptolemus brought,
you were quick from the city to scout
And as for the embassies coming to treat,
you spanked them and chivied them out.

Pa. That over all Hellas our Demus may rule;
for do not the oracles say,
He will surely his verdicts in Arcady give,
receiving five obols a day,
If he grow not aweary of fighting? Meanwhile,
it is I who will nourish and pet him,
And always the daily triobol he earns,
unjustly or justly I'll get him.

S.-S No not that o'er Arcady Demus may rule,
but rather that *you* might essay
To harry and plunder the cities at will,
while Demus is looking away,
And the war with the haze and the dust that you raise
is obscuring your actions from view,
And Demus, constrained by his wants and his pay,
is a gaping dependent on you.
But if once to the country in peace he returns,
away from all fighting and fusses,
And strengthens his system with furmety there,
and a confect of olive discusses,

He will know to your cost what a deal he has lost,
while the pay you allowed him he drew,
And then, like a hunter, irate he will come
on the trail of a vote against you.
You *know* it; and Demus you swindle with dreams,
crammed full of yourself and your praises.
Pa. It is really distressing to hear you presume
to arraign with such scurrilous phrases
Before the Athenians and Demus a man
who more for the city has done
Than e'er by Demeter Themistocles did
who glory undying has won.
S.-S. O city of Argos! yourself would you match
with mighty Themistocles, him
Who made of our city a bumper indeed,
though he found her scarce filled to the brim,
Who, while she was lunching, Peiraeus threw in,
as a dainty additional dish,
Who secured her the old, while providing untold
and novel assortments of fish;
Whilst you, with your walls of partition forsooth,
and the oracle-chants which you hatch,
Would dwarf and belittle the city again,
who yourself with Themistocles match!
And *he* was an exile, but *you* upon crumbs
Achilléan your fingers are cleaning.
Pa. Now is it not monstrous that I must endure
accusations so coarse and unmeaning,
And all for the love that I bear you?
Dem. Forbear! no more of your wrangle and row!
Too long have your light-fingered tricks with my bread
my notice escaped until now.
S.-S. He's the vilest of miscreants, Demus, and works
more mischief than any, I vow.
While you're gaping about, he is picking from out
Of the juiciest audit the juiciest sprout,
And devours it with zest; while deep in the chest
Of the public exchequer both hands are addressed
To ladling out cash for himself, I protest.
Pa. All this you'll deplore when it comes to the fore
That of drachmas you stole thirty thousand or more.
S.-S. Why make such a dash with your oar-blades, and thrash
The waves into foam with your impotent splash?
'Tis but fury and sound; and you'll shortly be found
The worst of the toadies who Demus surround.
And proof I will give, or I ask not to live,
That a bribe by the Mitylenaeans was sent,
Forty minas and more; to your pockets it went.
Ch. O sent to all the nation
a blessing and a boon!
O wondrous flow of language!
Fight thus, and you'll be soon
The greatest man in Hellas,
and all the State command,
And rule our faithful true allies,
a trident in your hand,
Wherewith you'll gather stores of wealth,
by shaking all the land.
And if he lend you once a hold,
then never let him go;
With ribs like these you ought with ease
to subjugate the foe.
Pa. O matters have not come to that,
my very worthy friends!
I've done a deed, a noble deed,
a deed which so transcends
All other deeds, that all my foes
of speech are quite bereft,
While any shred of any shield,
from Pylus brought, is left.
S.-S. Halt at those Pylian shields of yours!
a lovely hold you're lending.
For if you really Demus love,
what meant you by suspending
Those shields with all their handles on,
for action ready strapped?
O Demus, there's a dark design
within those handles wrapped,
And if to punish him you seek,
those shields will bar the way.
You see the throng of tanner-lads
he always keeps in pay,
And round them dwell the folk who sell
their honey and their cheeses;
And these are all combined in one,
to do whate'er he pleases.
And if the oyster-shelling game
you seem inclined to play,
They'll come by night with all their might
and snatch those shields away,
And then with ease will run and seize
the passes of—your wheat.
Dem. Oh, are the handles really there?
You rascal, what deceit
Have you so long been practising
that Demus you may cheat?
Pa. Pray don't be every speaker's gull,
nor dream you'll ever get
A better friend than I, who all
conspiracies upset.
Alone I crushed them all, and now,
if any plots are brewing
Within the town, I scent them down,
and raise a grand hallooing.
S.-S. O ay, you're like the fisher-folk,
the men who hunt for eels,
Who when the mere is still and clear
catch nothing for their creels,
But when they rout the mud about
and stir it up and down,
'Tis then they do; and so do you,
when you perturb the town.
But answer me this single thing:
you sell a lot of leather,
You say you're passionately fond
of Demus—tell me whether
You've given a clout to patch his shoes.
Dem. No never, I declare.

S.-S. You see the sort of man he is!
but I, I've bought a pair
Of good stout shoes, and here they are,
I give them you to wear.
Dem. O worthy, patriotic gift!
I really don't suppose
There ever lived a man so kind
to Demus and his toes.
Pa. 'Tis shameful that a pair of shoes
should have the power and might
To put the favours I've conferred
entirely out of sight,
I who struck Gryttus from the lists,
and stopped the boy-loves quite.
S.-S. 'Tis shameful, I with truth retort,
that you should love to pry
Into such vile degrading crimes
as that you name. And why?
Because you fear 'twill make the boys
for public speaking fit.
But Demus, at his age, you see
without a tunic sit,
In winter too; and nought from you
his poverty relieves,
But here's a tunic I have brought,
well-lined, with double sleeves.
Dem. O, why Themistocles himself
ne'er thought of such a vest!
Peiraeus was a clever thing,
but yet, I do protest,
That on the whole, between the two,
I like the tunic best.
Pa. (*to* SAUSAGE-SELLER) Pah! would you circumvent me thus,
with such an apish jest?
S.-S. Nay as one guest, at supper-time,
will take another's shoes,
When dire occasion calls him out,
so I your methods use.
Pa. Fawn on: you won't outdo me there.
I'll wrap him round about
With this of mine. Now go and whine, you rascal.
Dem. Pheugh! get out!
(*to* PAPHLAGON'S *wrapper*) Go to the crows, you brute, with that
disgusting smell of leather.
S.-S. He did it for the purpose, Sir;
to choke you altogether.
He tried to do it once before:
don't you remember when
A stalk of silphium sold so cheap?
Dem. Remember? yes: what then?
S.-S. Why that was his contrivance too:
he managed there should be a
Supply for all to buy and eat;
and in the Heliaea
The dicasts one and all were seized
with violent diarrhoea.
Dem. O ay, a Coprolitish man
described the sad affair.
S.-S. And worse and worse and worse you grew,
till yellow-tailed you were.
Dem. It must have been Pyrrhander's trick,
the fool with yellow hair.
Pa. (*to* SAUSAGE-SELLER) With what tomfooleries,
you rogue, you harass and torment me.
S.-S. Yes, 'tis with humbug I'm to win;
for that the Goddess sent me.
Pa. You shall not win! O Demus dear,
be idle all the day,
And I'll provide you free, to swill,
a foaming bowl of—pay.
S.-S. And I'll this gallipot provide,
and healing cream within it;
Whereby the sores upon your shins
you'll doctor in a minute.
Pa. I'll pick these grey hairs neatly out,
and make you young and fair.
S.-S. See here; this hare-scut take to wipe
your darling eyes with care.
Pa. Vouchsafe to blow your nose, and clean
your fingers on my hair.
S.-S. No, no; on mine, on mine, on mine!
Pa. A trierarch's office you shall fill,
And by my influence I'll prevail
That you shall get, to test your skill,
A battered hull with tattered sail.
Your outlay and your building too
On such a ship will never end;
No end of work you'll have to do,
No end of cash you'll have to spend.
Ch. O see how foamy-full he gets.
Good Heavens, he's boiling over; stay!
Some sticks beneath him draw away,
Bale out a ladleful of threats.
Pa. Rare punishment for this you'll taste;
I'll make the taxes weigh you down;
Amongst the wealthiest of the town
I'll manage that your name is placed.
S.-S. I will not use a single threat;
I only most devoutly wish
That on your brazier may be set
A hissing pan of cuttle-fish;
And you the Assembly must address
About Miletus,—'tis a job
Which, if it meets entire success,
Will put a talent in your fob—
And O that ere your feast begin,
"The Assembly waits," your friend may cry,
And you, afire the fee to win
And very loth to lose the fry,
May strive in greedy haste to swallow
The cuttles and be *choked* thereby.
Ch. Good! Good! by Zeus, Demeter, and Apollo.[1]
Dem. Aye, and in all respects he seems to me
A worthy citizen. When lived a man
So good to the Many (the Many for a penny)?
You, Paphlagon, pretending that you loved me,
Primed me with garlic. Give me back my ring;
You shall no more be steward.

[1]This line is in prose; it is the solemn formula used in the heliastic oath.

Pa. Take the ring;
And be you sure, if I'm no more your guardian,
You'll get, instead, a greater rogue than I.
Dem. Bless me, this can't be mine, this signet-ring.
It's not the same device, it seems to me;
Or can't I see?
S.-S. What's the device on yours?
Dem. A leaf of beef-fat stuffing, roasted well.
S.-S. No, that's not here.
Dem. What then?
S.-S. A cormorant
With open mouth haranguing on a rock.
Dem. Pheugh!
S.-S. What's the matter?
Dem. Throw the thing away.
He's got Cleonymus's ring, not mine.
Take this from me, and you be steward now.
Pa. O not yet, master, I beseech, not yet;
Wait till you've heard my oracles, I pray.
S.-S. And mine as well.
Pa. And if to *his* you listen,
You'll be a liquor-skin.
S.-S. And if to *his*,
You'll find yourself severely circumcised.
Pa. Nay mine foretell that over all the land
Thyself shalt rule, with roses garlanded.
S.-S. And mine that crowned, in spangled purple robe,
Thou in thy golden chariot shalt pursue
And sue the lady Smicythe and her lord.
Pa. Well, go and fetch them hither, so that *he*
May hear them.
S.-S. Certainly; and you fetch yours.
Pa. Here goes. *Exit to house of* DEMUS.
S.-S. Here goes, by Zeus. There's nought to stop us. *Exit.*

Chorus

O bright and joyous day,
O day most sweet to all
Both near and far away,
The day of Cleon's fall.
Yet in our Action-mart
I overheard by chance
Some ancient sires and tart
This counter-plea advance,
That but for him the State
Two things had ne'er possessed:—
A *stirrer*-up of hate,
A *pestle* of unrest.

His swine-bred music we
With wondering hearts admire;
At school, his mates agree,
He always tuned his lyre
In Dorian style to play.
His master wrathful grew;
He sent the boy away,
And this conclusion drew,
"This boy from all his friends
Donations seeks to wile,
His art begins and ends
In Dono-do-rian style."

Pa. (*re-entering*) Look at them, see! and there are more behind.
S.-S. (*re-entering*) O what a weight! and there are more behind.
Dem. What *are* they?
Pa. Oracles!
Dem. All?
Pa. You seem surprised;
By Zeus, I've got a chestful more at home.
S.-S. And I a garret and two cellars full.
Dem. Come, let me see. Whose oracles are these?
Pa. Mine are by Bakis.
Dem. (*To* SAUSAGE-SELLER) And by whom are yours?
S.-S. Mine are by Glanis, Bakis' elder brother.
Dem. What do they treat of?
Pa. Mine? Of Athens, Pylus,
Of you, of me, of every blessed thing.
Dem. (*To* SAUSAGE-SELLER) And you; of what treat yours?
S.-S. Of Athens, pottage,
Of Lacedaemon, mackerel freshly caught,
Of swindling barley-measurers in the mart,
Of you, of me. That nincompoop be hanged.
Dem. Well read them out; and prithee don't forget
The one I love to hear about myself,
That I'm to soar, an Eagle, in the clouds.
Pa. Now then give ear, and hearken to my words:
"Heed thou well, Erechtheides,
the oracle's drift, which Apollo
Out of his secret shrine
through priceless tripods delivered.
Keep thou safely the dog,
thy jag-toothed holy protector.
Yapping before thy feet,
and terribly roaring to guard thee,
He thy pay will provide:
if he fail to provide it, he'll perish;
Yea, for many the daws
that are hating and cawing against him."
Dem. This, by Demeter, beats me altogether.
What does Erechtheus want with daws and dog?
Pa. I am the dog: I bark aloud for you.
And Phoebus bids you guard the dog; that's me.
S.-S. It says not that; but this confounded dog
Has gnawn the oracle, as he gnaws the door.
I've the right reading here about the dog.
Dem. Let's hear; but first I'll pick me up a stone
Lest this dog-oracle take to gnawing *me*.
S.-S. "Heed thou well, Erechtheides,
the kidnapping Cerberus ban-dog;
Wagging his tail he stands,
and fawning upon thee at dinner,
Waiting thy slice to devour
when aught distract thine attention.
Soon as the night comes round
he steals unseen to the kitchen
Dog-wise; then will his tongue
clean out the plates and the—islands."
Dem. Aye, by Poseidon, Glanis, that's far better.
Pa. Nay, listen first, my friend, and then decide:
"Woman she is, but a lion
she'll bear us in Athens the holy;

One who for Demus will fight
with an army of stinging mosquitoes,
Fight, as if shielding his whelps;
whom see thou guard with devotion
Building a wooden wall
and an iron fort to secure him."
Do you understand?

Dem. By Apollo, no, not I.

Pa. The God, 'tis plain, would have you keep me safely,
For I'm a valiant lion, for your sake.

Dem. What, you Antileon and I never knew it!

S.-S. One thing he purposely informs you not,
What that oracular wall of wood and iron,
Where Loxias bids you keep him safely, is.

Dem. What means the God?

S.-S. He means that you're to clap
Paphlagon in the five-holed pillory-stocks.

Dem. I shouldn't be surprised if that came true.

Pa. Heed not the words; for jealous
the crows that are croaking against me.
Cherish the lordly falcon,
nor ever forget that he brought thee,
Brought thee in fetters and chains
the young Laconian minnows.

S.-S. This did Paphlagon dare
in a moment of drunken bravado.
Why think much of the deed,
Cecropides foolish in counsel?
Weight a Woman will bear,
if a Man impose it upon her,
Fight she won't and she can't:
in fighting she's always a fright in.

Pa. Nay, but remember the word,
"How Pylus," he said, "before Pylus";
Pylus there is before Pylus.

Dem. What mean you by that "before Pylus"?

S.-S. Truly your pile of baths
will he capture before you can take them.

Dem. O dear, then bathless must I go to-day

S.-S. Because he has carried off our pile of baths.
But here's an oracle about the fleet;
Your best attention is required to this.

Dem. I'll give it too; but prithee, first of all,
Read how my sailors are to get their pay.

S.-S. "O Aegeides, beware
of the hound-fox, lest he deceive thee,
Stealthily snapping, the crafty,
the swift, the tricky marauder."
Know you the meaning of this?

Dem. Philostratus, plainly, the hound-fox.

S.-S. Not so; but Paphlagon is evermore
Asking swift triremes to collect the silver,
So Loxias bids you not to give him these.

Dem. Why is a trireme called a hound-fox?

S.-S. Why?
A trireme's fleet; a hound is also fleet.

Dem. But for what reason adds he "fox" to "hound"?

S.-S. The troops, he means, resemble little foxes,
Because they scour the farms and eat the grapes.

Dem. Good.
But where's the cash to pay these little foxes?

S.-S. That I'll provide: within three days I'll do it.
List thou further the rede
by the son of Leto delivered;
"Keep thou aloof," said he,
"from the wiles of hollow Cyllene."

Dem. Hollow Cyllene! what's that?

S.-S. 'Tis Paphlagon's hand he's describing.
Paphlagon's outstretched hand,
with his "Drop me a coin in the hollow."

Pa. There this fellow is wrong.
When he spake of the hollow Cyllene,
Phoebus was hinting, I ween,
at the hand of the maimed Diopeithes.
Nay, but I've got me, for you,
a wingèd oracular message,
"Thou shalt an Eagle become,
and rule all lands as a Monarch."

S.-S. Nay, but I've got me the same:
"and the Red Sea too thou shalt govern,
Yea in Ecbatana judge,
rich cakes as thou judgest devouring."

Pa. Nay, but I dreamed me a dream,
and methought the Goddess Athene
Health and wealth was ladling
in plentiful streams upon Demus.

S.-S. Nay, but I dreamed one myself;
and methought of the Goddess Athene
Down from the Citadel stepped,
and an owl sat perched on her shoulder;
Then from a bucket she poured
ambrosia down upon Demus,
Sweetest of scents upon *you*,
upon Paphlagon sourest of pickles.

Dem. Good! Good!
There never *was* a cleverer chap than Glanis.
So now, my friend, I yield myself to you;
Be you the tutor of my thoughtless—Age.

Pa. Not yet! pray wait awhile, and I'll provide
Your barley-grain, and daily sustenance.

Dem. I can't abide your barley-talk; too often
Have I been duped by you and Thuphanes.

Pa. I'll give you barley-meal, all ready-made.

S.-S. I'll give you barley-cakes, all ready-baked,
And well-broiled fish. Do nothing else but eat.

Dem. Make haste and do it then, remembering this,
Whichever brings me most titbits to-day,
To him alone I'll give the Pnyx's reins.

Pa. O then I'll run in first. *Exit.*

S.-S. Not you, but I. *Exit.*

Ch. Proud, O Demus, thy sway.
Thee, as Tyrant and King,
All men fear and obey,
Yet, O yet, 'tis a thing
Easy, to lead thee astray.
Empty fawning and praise
Pleased thou art to receive;
All each orator says
Sure at once to believe;
Wit thou hast, but 'tis roaming;
Ne'er we find it its home in.

Dem. Wit there's none in your hair.
What, you think me a fool!
What, you know not I wear,
Wear my motley by rule!
Well all day do I fare,
Nursed and cockered by all;
Pleased to fatten and train
One prime thief in my stall.
When full gorged with his gain,
Up that instant I snatch him,
Strike one blow and dispatch him.

Ch. Art thou really so deep?
Is such artfulness thine?
Well for all if thou keep
Firm to this thy design.
Well for all if, as sheep
Marked for victims, thou feed
These thy knaves in the Pnyx,
Then, if dainties thou need,
Haste on a victim to fix;
Slay the fattest and finest;
There's thy meal when thou dinest.

Dem. Ah! they know not that I
Watch them plunder and thieve.
Ah! " 'tis easy," they cry,
"Him to gull and deceive."
Comes *my* turn by and by!
Down their gullet, full quick,
Lo, my verdict-tube coils,
Turns them giddy and sick,
Up they vomit their spoils:
Such, with rogues, is my dealing,
'Tis for *myself* they are stealing.

Enter PAPHLAGON *and* SAUSAGE-SELLER.

Pa. Go and be blest!
S.-S. Be blest yourself, you filth.
Pa. O Demus, I've been sitting here prepared
Three ages past, longing to do you good.
S.-S. And I ten ages, aye twelve ages, aye
A thousand ages, ages, ages, ages.
Dem. And I've been waiting, till I loathe you both,
For thirty thousand ages, ages, ages.
S.-S. Do—know you what?
Dem. And if I don't ,you'll tell me.
S.-S. Do start us from the signal-post, us two,
All fair, no favour.
Dem. Right you are; move off.
Pa. and S.-S. Ready!
Dem. Away!
S.-S. No "cutting in" allowed.
Dem. Zeus! if I don't, with these two lovers, have
A rare good time, 'tis dainty I must be.
Pa. See, I'm the first to bring you out a chair.
S.-S. But not a table; I'm the firstlier there.
Pa. Look, here's a jolly little cake I bring,
Cooked from the barley-grain I brought from Pylus.
S.-S. And here I'm bringing splendid scoops of bread,
Scooped by the Goddess with her ivory hand.
Dem. A mighty finger you must have, dread lady!
Pa. And here's pease-porridge, beautiful and brown.
Pallas Pylaemachus it was that stirred it.
S.-S. O Demus, plain it is the Goddess guards you,
Holding above your head this—soup-tureen.
Dem. Why, think you Athens had survived, unless
She plainly o'er us held her soup-tureen?
Pa. This slice of fish the Army-frightener sends you.
S.-S. This boiled broth-meat the Nobly-fathered gives you,
And this good cut of tripe and guts and paunch.
Dem. And well done she, to recollect the peplus.
Pa. The Terror-crested bids you taste this cake
With roe of fish, that we may row the better.
S.-S. And now take these.
Dem. Whatever shall I do
With these insides?
S.-S. The Goddess sends you these
To serve as planks inside your ships of war.
Plainly she looks with favour on our fleet.
Here, drink this also, mingled three and two.
Dem. Zeus! but it's sweet and bears the three parts well.
S.-S. Tritogeneia 'twas that three'd and two'd it.
Pa. Accept from me this slice of luscious cake.
S.-S. And this whole luscious cake accept from me.
Pa. Ah, you've no hare to give him; that give I.
S.-S. O me, wherever can I get some hare?
Now for some mountebank device, my soul.
Pa. Yah, see you this, poor Witless?
S.-S. What care I?
For there they are! Yes, there they are coming!
Pa. Who?
S.-S. Envoys with bags of silver, all for me.
Pa. Where? Where?
S.-S. What's that to you? Let be the strangers.
My darling Demus, take the hare I bring.
Pa. You thief, you've given what wasn't yours to give!
S.-S. Poseidon, yes; you did the same at Pylus.
Dem. Ha! Ha! what made you think of filching that?
S.-S. The thought's Athene's, but the theft was mine.
De. 'Twas I that ran the risk!
Pa. 'Twas I that cooked it!
Dem. Be off: the credit's his that served it up.
Pa. Unhappy me! I'm over-impudenced.
S.-S. Why not give judgement, Demus, of us two
Which is the better towards your paunch and you?
Dem. Well, what's the test will make the audience think
I give my judgement cleverly and well?
S.-S. I'll tell you what; steal softly up, and search
My hamper first, then Paphlagon's, and note
What's in them; then you'll surely judge aright.
Dem. Well, what does *yours* contain?
S.-S. See here, it's empty.
Dear Father mine, I served up all for you.
Dem. A Demus-loving hamper, sure enough.

S.-S. Now come along, and look at Paphlagon's.
Hey! only see!
Dem. Why here's a store of dainties!
Why, here's a splendid cheesecake he put by!
And me he gave the tiniest slice, *so* big.
S.-S. And, Demus, that is what he always does;
Gives you the pettiest morsel of his gains,
And keeps by far the largest share himself.
Dem. O miscreant, did you steal and gull me so,
The while I crowned thy pow and gied thee gifties.
Pa. And if I stole 'twas for the public good.
Dem. Off with your crown this instant, and I'll place it
On *him* instead.
S.-S. Off with it, filth, this instant.
Pa. Not so; a Pythian oracle I've got
Describing him who only can defeat me.
S.-S. Describing *me*, without the slightest doubt.
Pa. Well then I'll test and prove you, to discern
How far you tally with the God's predictions.
And first I ask this question,—when a boy
Tell me the teacher to whose school you went.
S.-S. Hard knuckles drilled me in the singeing pits.
Pa. How say you? Heavens, the oracle's word strikes home!
Well!
What at the trainer's did you learn to do?
S.-S. Forswear my thefts, and stare the accuser down.
Pa. Phoebus Apollo! Lycius! what means this?
Tell me what trade you practised when a man.
S.-S. I sold sausages—
Pa. Well?
S.-S. And sold myself.
Pa. Unhappy me! I'm done for. There remains
One slender hope whereon to anchor yet.
Where did you sell your sausages? Did you stand
Within the Agora, or beside the Gates?
S.-S. Beside the Gates, where the salt-fish is sold.
Pa. O me, the oracle has all come true!
Roll in, roll in, this most unhappy man.
O crown, farewell. Unwillingly I leave thee.
Begone, but thee some other will obtain,
A luckier man perchance, but not more—thievish.
S.-S. Hellanian Zeus, the victory-prize is thine!
De. Hail, mighty Victor, nor forget 'twas I
Made you a Man; and grant this small request,
Make *me* your Phanus, signer of your writs.
Dem. Your name, what is it?
S.-S. Agoracritus.
An Agora-life I lived, and thrived by wrangling.
Dem. To Agoracritus I commit myself,
And to *his* charge consign this Paphlagon.
S.-S. And, Demus, I will always tend you well,
And you shall own there never lived a man
Kinder than I to the Evergaping City.

Exeunt all but CHORUS *to house of* DEMUS.

Chorus

O what is a nobler thing,
Beginning or ending a song,
For horsemen who joy in driving
Their fleet-foot coursers along,
Than—Never to launch a lampoon at Lysistratus, scurvy buffoon;
Or at heartless Thumantis to gird, poor starveling, in lightness of heart;
Who is weeping hot tears at thy shrine, Apollo, in Pytho divine,
And, clutching thy quiver, implores to be healed of his poverty's smart!

For lampooning worthless wretches, none should bear the bard a grudge;
'Tis a sound and wholesome practice, if the case you rightly judge.
Now if he whose evil-doings I must needs expose to blame
Were himself a noted person, never had I named the name
Of a man I love and honour. Is there one who knows not well
Arignotus, prince of harpers? None, believe me, who can tell
How the whitest colour differs from the stirring tune he plays.
Arignotus has a brother (not a brother in his ways)
Named Ariphrades, a rascal— nay, but that's the fellow's whim—
Not an ordinary rascal, or I had not noticed him.
Not a thorough rascal merely; he's invented something more,
Novel forms of self-pollution, bestial tricks unknown before.
Yea, to nameless filth and horrors does the loathsome wretch descend,
Works the work of Polymnestus, calls Oeonichus his friend.
Whoso loathes not such a monster never shall be a friend of mine,
Never from the selfsame goblet quaff, with us, the rosy wine.

And oft in the watches of night
My spirit within me is thrilled,
To think of Cleonymus eating
As though he would never be filled.
O whence could the fellow acquire that appetite deadly and dire?
They say when he grazes with those whose table with plenty is stored
That they never can get him away from the trencher, though humbly they pray,
"Have mercy, O King, and depart! O spare, we beseech thee, the board!"

Recently, 'tis said, our galleys met their prospects to discuss,
And an old experienced trireme introduced the subject thus;
"Have ye heard the news, my sisters? 'tis the talk in every street,

That Hyperbolus the worthless,
vapid townsman, would a fleet
Of a hundred lovely galleys
lead to Carthage far away."
Over every prow there mantled
deep resentment and dismay.
Up and spoke a little galley,
yet from man's pollution free,
"Save us! such a scurvy fellow
never shall be lord of me.
Here I'd liefer rot and moulder,
and be eaten up of worms."
"Nor Nauphante, Nauson's daughter,
shall he board on any terms;
I, like you, can feel the insult;
I'm of pine and timber knit.
Wherefore, if the measure passes,
I propose we sail and sit
Suppliant at the shrine of Theseus,
or the Dread Avenging Powers.
He shall ne'er, as our commander,
fool it o'er this land of ours.
If he wants a little voyage,
let him launch his sale-trays, those
Whereupon he sold his lanterns,
steering to the kites and crows."

Enter SAUSAGE-SELLER.

S.-S. O let not a word of ill omen be heard;
away with all proof and citation,
And close for to-day the Law Courts, though they
are the joy and delight of our nation.
At the news which I bring let the theatre ring
with Paeans of loud acclamation.
Ch. O Light of the City, O Helper and friend
of the islands we guard with our fleets,
What news have you got? O tell me for what
shall the sacrifice blaze in our streets?
S.-S. Old Demus I've stewed till his youth is renewed,
and his aspect most charming and nice is.
Ch. O where have you left him, and where is he now,
you inventor of wondrous devices?
S.-S. He dwells in the City of ancient renown,
which the violet chaplet is wearing.
Ch. O would I could see him! O what is his garb,
and what his demeanour and bearing?
S.-S. As when, for his mess-mates, Miltiades bold
and just Aristeides he chose.
But now ye shall see him, for, listen, the bars
of the great Propylaea unclose.
Shout, shout to behold, as the portals unfold,
fair Athens in splendour excelling,
The wondrous, the ancient, the famous in song,
where the noble Demus is dwelling!
Ch. O shining old town of the violet crown,
O Athens the envied, display
The Sovereign of Hellas himself to our gaze,
the monarch of all we survey.

Enter DEMUS.

S.-S. See, see where he stands, no vote in his hands,
but the golden cicala his hair in,
All splendid and fragrant with peace and with myrrh,
and the grand old apparel he's wearing!
Ch. Hail, Sovereign of Hellas! with thee we rejoice,
right glad to behold thee again
Enjoying a fate that is worthy the State
and the trophy on Marathon's plain.
Dem. O Agoracritus, my dearest friend,
What good your stewing did me!
S.-S. Say you so?
Why, if you knew the sort of man you were,
And what you did, you'd reckon me a god.
Dem. What was I like? What did I do? Inform me.
S.-S. First, if a speaker in the Assembly said
"O Demus, I'm your lover, I alone
Care for you, scheme for you, tend and love you well,"
I say if anyone began like that
You clapped your wings and tossed your horns.
Dem. What, I?
S.-S. Then in return he cheated you and left.
Dem. O did they treat me so, and I not know it!
S.-S. Because, by Zeus, your ears would open wide
And close again, like any parasol.
Dem. Had I so old and witless grown as that?
S.-S. And if, by Zeus, two orators proposed,
One to build ships of war, one to increase
Official salaries, the salary man
Would beat the ships-of-war man in a canter.
Hallo! why hang your head and shift your ground?
Dem. I am ashamed of all my former faults.
S.-S. You're not to blame; pray don't imagine that.
'Twas they who tricked you so. But answer this;
If any scurvy advocate should say,
"Now please remember, justices, ye'll have
No barley, if the prisoner gets off free,"
How would you treat that scurvy advocate?
Dem. I'd tie Hyperbolus about his neck,
And hurl him down into the Deadman's Pit.
S.-S. Why now you are speaking sensibly and well.
How else, in public business, will you act?
Dem. First, when the sailors from my ships of war
Come home, I'll pay them all arrears in full.
S.-S. For that, full many a well-worn rump will bless you.
Dem. Next, when a hoplite's placed in any list,
There shall he stay, and not for love or money
Shall he be shifted to some other list.
S.-S. That bit the shield-strap of Cleonymus.
Dem. No beardless boy shall haunt the agora now.
S.-S. That's rough on Straton and on Cleisthenes.
Dem. I mean those striplings in the perfume-mart,
Who sit them down and chatter stuff like this,
"Sharp fellow, Phaeax; wonderful defence;
Coercive speaker; most conclusive speaker;
Effective; argumentative; incisive;
Superlative against the combative."

S.-S. You're quite derisive of these talkatives.
Dem. I'll make them all give up their politics,
And go a-hunting with their hounds instead.
S.-S. Then on these terms accept this folding-stool;
And here's a boy to carry it behind you.
No eunuch he!
Dem. O, I shall be once more
A happy Demus as in days gone by.
S.-S. I think you'll think so when you get the sweet
Thirty-year treaties. Treaties dear, come here.
Dem. Worshipful Zeus! how beautiful they are.
Wouldn't I like to solemnize them all.
Whence got you these?
S.-S. Why, had not Paphlagon
Bottled them up that you might never see them?
Now then I freely give you them to take
Back to your farms, with you.
Dem. But Paphlagon
Who wrought all this, how will you punish *him*?
S.-S. Not much: this only: he shall ply my trade,
Sole sausage-seller at the City gates.
There let him dogs'-meat mix with asses' flesh,
There let him, tipsy, with the harlots wrangle,
And drink the filthy scouring of the bath.
Dem. A happy thought; and very fit he is
To brawl with harlots and with bathmen there.
But you I ask to dinner in the Hall,
To take the place that scullion held before.
Put on this frog-green robe and follow me.
Whilst him they carry out to ply his trade,
That so the strangers, whom he wronged, may see him.

THE CLOUDS

DRAMATIS PERSONAE

STREPSIADES
PHEIDIPPIDES
SERVANT OF STREPSIADES
STUDENT OF SOCRATES
SOCRATES
RIGHT LOGIC
WRONG LOGIC
PASIAS
AMYNIAS
A WITNESS
CHAEREPHON
CHORUS OF CLOUDS

At the back of the stage are two buildings—the house of STREPSIADES *and the* PHRONTISTERION. *The interior of the first is exposed to view by means of the eccyclema.*

STREPSIADES *and* PHEIDIPPIDES *discovered in bed.*

Strepsiades. O dear! O dear!
O Lord! O Zeus! these nights, how long they are.
Will they ne'er pass? will the day never come?
Surely I heard the cock crow, hours ago.
Yet still my servants snore. These are new customs.
O 'ware of war for many various reasons;
One fears in war even to flog one's servants.
And here's this hopeful son of mine wrapped up
Snoring and sweating under five thick blankets.
Come, we'll wrap up and snore in opposition.
Tries to sleep.
But I can't sleep a wink, devoured and bitten
By ticks, and bugbears, duns, and race-horses,
All through this son of mine. *He* curls his hair,
And sports his thoroughbreds, and drives his tandem;
Even in dreams he rides: while I—I'm ruined,
Now that the Moon has reached her twentieths,
And paying-time comes on. Boy! light a lamp,
And fetch my ledger: now I'll reckon up
Who are my creditors, and what I owe them.
Come, let me see then. *Fifty pounds to Pasias!*
Why fifty pounds to Pasias? what were they for?
O, for the hack from Corinth. O dear! O dear!
I wish my eye had been hacked out before—
Pheidippides. (*in his sleep*) You are cheating, Philon; keep to your own side.
St. Ah! there it is! that's what has ruined me!
Even in his very sleep he thinks of horses.
Ph. (*in his sleep*) How many heats do the war-chariots run?
St. A pretty many heats you have run your father.
Now then, what debt assails me after Pasias?
A curricle and wheels. Twelve pounds. Amynias.
Ph. (*in his sleep*) Here, give the horse a roll, and take him home.
St. You have rolled me *out* of house and home, my boy,
Cast in some suits already, while some swear
They'll seize my goods for payment.
Ph. Good, my father,
What makes you toss so restless all night long?
St. There's a bumbailiff from the mattress bites me.
Ph. Come now, I prithee, let me sleep in peace.
St. Well then, you sleep; only be sure of this,
These debts will fall on your own head at last.
Alas, alas!
Forever cursed be that same match-maker,
Who stirred me up to marry your poor mother.
Mine in the country was the pleasantest life,
Untidy, easy-going, unrestrained,
Brimming with olives, sheepfolds, honey-bees.
Ah! then I married—I a rustic—her
A fine town-lady, niece of Megacles.
A regular, proud, luxurious, Coesyra.
This wife I married, and we came together,
I rank with wine-lees, fig-boards, greasy woolpacks;
She all with scents, and saffron, and tongue-kissings,
Feasting, expense, and lordly modes of loving.
She was not idle though, she was too fast.
I used to tell her, holding out my cloak,
Threadbare and worn; "Wife, you're too fast by half."
Enter SERVANT-BOY.
Servant-Boy. Here's no more oil remaining in the lamp.
St. O me! what made you light the tippling lamp?
Come and be whipp'd.
S.-B. Why, what would you whip me for?
St. Why did you put one of those thick wicks in?
Well, when at last to me and my good woman
This hopeful son was born, our son and heir,
Why then we took to wrangle on the name.
She was for giving him some knightly name,
"Callippides," "Xanthippus," or "Charippus":
I wished "Pheidonides," his grandsire's name.
Thus for some time we argued: till at last
We compromised it in Pheidippides.
This boy she took, and used to spoil him, saying,
"Oh! when you are driving to the Acropolis, clad
Like Megacles, in your purple"; whilst I said,
"Oh! when the goats you are driving from the fells,
Clad like your father, in your sheepskin coat."
Well, he cared nought for my advice, but soon

A galloping consumption caught my fortunes.
Now cogitating all night long, I've found
One way, one marvellous transcendent way,
Which if he'll follow, we may yet be saved.
So—but, however, I must rouse him first;
But how to rouse him kindliest? that's the rub.
Pheidippides, my sweet one.

Ph. Well, my father.

St. Shake hands, Pheidippides, shake hands and kiss me.

Ph. There; what's the matter?

St. Dost thou love me, boy?

Ph. Ay, by Poseidon there, the God of horses.

St. No, no, not that: miss out the God of horses,
That God's the origin of all my evils.
But if you love me from your heart and soul,
My son, obey me.

Ph. Very well: what in?

St. Strip with all speed, strip off your present habits,
And go and learn what I'll advise you to.

Ph. Name your commands.

St. Will you obey?

Ph. I will,
By Dionysus!

St. Well then, look this way.
See you that wicket and the lodge beyond?

Ph. I see: and prithee what is that, my father?

St. That is the thinking-house of sapient souls.
There dwell the men who teach—aye, who persuade us,
That Heaven is one vast fire-extinguisher
Placed round about us, and that we're the cinders.
Aye, and they'll teach (only they'll want some money),
How one may speak and conquer, right or wrong.

Ph. Come, tell their names.

St. Well, I can't quite remember,
But they're deep thinkers, and true gentlemen.

Ph. Out on the rogues! I know them. Those rank pedants,
Those palefaced, barefoot vagabonds you mean:
That Socrates, poor wretch, and Chaerephon.

St. Oh! Oh! hush! hush! don't use those foolish words;
But if the sorrows of my barley touch you,
Enter their Schools and cut the Turf for ever.

Ph. I wouldn't go, so help me Dionysus,
For all Leogoras' breed of Phasians!

St. Go, I beseech you, dearest, dearest son,
Go and be taught.

Ph. And what would you have me learn?

St. 'Tis known that in their Schools they keep two Logics,
The Worse, Zeus save the mark, the Worse and Better.
This second Logic then, I mean the Worse one,
They teach to talk unjustly and—prevail.
Think then, you only learn that Unjust Logic,
And all the debts, which I have incurred through you,
I'll never pay, no, not one farthing of them.

Ph. I will not go. How could I face the knights
With all my colour worn and torn away!

St. O! then, by Earth, you have eat your last of mine,
You, and your coach-horse, and your sigma-brand:
Out with you! Go to the crows, for all I care.

Ph. But uncle Megacles won't leave me long
Without a horse: I'll go to him: good-bye. *Exit.*

STREPSIADES *crosses to the Phrontisterion.*

St. I'm thrown, by Zeus, but I won't long lie prostrate.
I'll pray the Gods and send myself to school:
I'll go at once and try their thinking-house.
Stay: how can I, forgetful, slow, old fool,
Learn the nice hair-splittings of subtle Logic?
Well, go I must. 'Twont do to linger here.
Come on, I'll knock the door. Boy! Ho there, boy!

Student. (*within*) O, hang it all! who's knocking at the door?

St. Me! Pheidon's son: Strepsiades of Cicynna.

Stu. Why, what a clown you are! to kick our door,
In such a thoughtless, inconsiderate way!
You've made my cogitation to miscarry.

St. Forgive me: I'm an awkward country fool.
But tell me, what was that I made miscarry?

Stu. 'Tis not allowed: Students alone may hear.

St. O that's all right: you may tell *me*: I'm come
To be a student in your thinking-house.

Stu. Come then. But they're high mysteries, remember.
'Twas Socrates was asking Chaerephon,
How many feet of its own a flea could jump.
For one first bit the brow of Chaerephon,
Then bounded off to Socrates' head.

St. How did he measure this?

Stu. Most cleverly.
He warmed some wax, and then he caught the flea,
And dipped its feet into the wax he'd melted:
Then let it cool, and there were Persian slippers!
These he took off, and so he found the distance.

St. O Zeus and king, what subtle intellects!

Stu. What would you say then if you heard another,
Our Master's own?

St. O come, do tell me that.

Stu. Why, Chaerephon was asking him in turn,
Which theory did he sanction; that the gnats
Hummed through their mouth, or backwards, through the tail?

St. Aye, and what said your Master of the gnat?

Stu. He answered thus: the entrail of the gnat
Is small: and through this narrow pipe the wind
Rushes with violence straight towards the tail;
There, close against the pipe, the hollow rump
Receives the wind, and whistles to the blast.

St. So then the rump is trumpet to the gnats!
O happy, happy in your entrail-learning!
Full surely need he fear nor debts nor duns,
Who knows about the entrails of the gnats.

Stu. And yet last night a mighty thought we lost
Through a green lizard.

St. Tell me, how was that?

Stu. Why, as Himself, with eyes and mouth wide open,
Mused on the moon, her paths and revolutions,
A lizard from the roof squirted full on him.
St. He, he, he, he. I like the lizard's spattering Socrates.
Stu. Then yesterday, poor we, we'd got no dinner.
St. Hah! what did he devise to do for barley?
Stu. He sprinkled on the table—some fine ash—
He bent a spit—he grasped it compass-wise—
And—filched a mantle from the Wrestling School.
St. Good heavens! Why Thales was a fool to this!
O open, open, wide the study door,
And show me, show me, show me Socrates.
I die to be a student. Open, open![1]
O Heracles, what kind of beasts are these!
Stu. Why, what's the matter? what do you think they're like?
St. Like? why those Spartans whom we brought from Pylus:
What makes them fix their eyes so on the ground?
Stu. They seek things underground.
St. O! to be sure,
Truffles! You there, don't trouble about that!
I'll tell you where the best and finest grow.
Look! why do those stoop down so very much?
Stu. They're diving deep into the deepest secrets.
St. Then why's their rump turned up towards the sky?
Stu. It's taking private lessons on the stars.
(*to the other Students*)
Come, come: get in: HE'll catch us presently.
St. Not yet! not yet! just let them stop one moment,
While I impart a little matter to them.
Stu. No, no: they must go in: 'twould never do
To expose themselves too long to the open air.
St. O! by the Gods, now, what are these? do tell me.
Stu. This is Astronomy.
St. And what is this?
Stu. Geometry.
St. Well, what's the use of that?
Stu. To mete out lands.
St. What, for allotment grounds?
Stu. No, but all lands.
St. A choice idea, truly.
Then every man may take his choice, you mean.
Stu. Look; here's a chart of the whole world. Do you see?
This city's Athens.
St. Athens? I like that.
I see no dicasts sitting. That's not Athens.
Stu. In very truth, this is the Attic ground.
St. And where then are my townsmen of Cicynna?
Stu. Why, thereabouts; and here, you see, Euboea:
Here, reaching out a long way by the shore.

[1] "The entire front of the house is wheeled round . . . exposing the inner court of the Phrontisterion": Rogers.

St. Yes, overreached by us and Pericles.
But now, where's Sparta?
Stu. Let me see: O, here.
St. Heavens! how near us. O do please manage this,
To shove her off from us, a long way further.
Stu. We can't do that, by Zeus.
St. The worse for you.
Hallo! who's that? that fellow in the basket?
Stu. That's *he*.
St. Who's *he*?
Stu. Socrates.
St. Socrates!
You sir, call out to him as loud as you can.
Stu. Call him yourself: I have not leisure now.
The machine swings SOCRATES *in.*
St. Socrates! Socrates!
Sweet Socrates!
Socrates. Mortal! why call'st thou me?
St. O, first of all, please tell me what you are doing.
So. I walk on air, and contem-plate the Sun.
St. O then from a basket you contemn the Gods,
And not from the earth, at any rate?
So. Most true.
I could not have searched out celestial matters
Without suspending judgement, and infusing
My subtle spirit with the kindred air.
If from the ground I were to seek these things,
I could not find: so surely doth the earth
Draw to herself the essence of our thought.
The same too is the case with water-cress.
St. Hillo! what's that?
Thought draws the essence into water-cress?
Come down, sweet Socrates, more near my level,
And teach the lessons which I come to learn.
So. (*descending*) And wherefore art thou come?
St. To learn to speak.
For owing to my horrid debts and duns,
My goods are seized, I'm robbed, and mobbed, and plundered.
So. How did you get involved with your eyes open?
St. A galloping consumption seized my money.
Come now: do let me learn the unjust Logic
That can shirk debts: now do just let me learn it.
Name your own price, by all the Gods I'll pay it.
So. The Gods! why you must know the Gods with us
Don't pass for current coin.
St. Eh? what do you use then?
Have you got iron, as the Byzantines have?
So. Come, would you like to learn celestial matters,
How their truth stands?
St. Yes, if there's any truth.
So. And to hold intercourse with yon bright Clouds,
Our virgin Goddesses?
St. Yes, that I should.
So. Then sit you down upon that sacred bed.
St. Well, I am sitting.

So. Here then, take this chaplet.
St. Chaplet? why? why? now, never, Socrates:
Don't sacrifice poor me, like Athamas.
So. Fear not: our entrance-services require
All to do this.
St. But what am I to gain?
So. You'll be the flower of talkers, prattlers, gossips:
Only keep quiet.
St. Zeus! your words come true!
I shall be flour indeed with all this peppering.
So. Old man sit you still, and attend to my will,
and hearken in peace to my prayer,
O Master and King, holding earth in your swing,
O measureless infinite Air;
And thou glowing Ether, and Clouds who enwreathe her
with thunder, and lightning, and storms,
Arise ye and shine, bright Ladies Divine,
to your student in bodily forms.
St. No, but stay, no, but stay, just one moment I pray,
while my cloak round my temples I wrap.
To think that I've come, stupid fool, from my home,
with never a waterproof cap!
So. Come forth, come forth, dread Clouds, and to earth
your glorious majesty show;
Whether lightly ye rest on the time-honoured crest
of Olympus environed in snow,
Or tread the soft dance 'mid the stately expanse
of Ocean, the nymphs to beguile,
Or stoop to enfold with your pitchers of gold,
the mystical waves of the Nile,
Or around the white foam of Maeotis ye roam,
or Mimas all wintry and bare,
O hear while we pray, and turn not away
from the rites which your servants prepare.
CHORUS OF CLOUDS *appears.*
Chorus. Clouds of all hue,
Rise we aloft with our garments of dew.
Come from old Ocean's unchangeable bed,
Come, till the mountain's green summits we tread,
Come to the peaks with their landscapes untold,
Gaze on the Earth with her harvests of gold,
Gaze on the rivers in majesty streaming,
Gaze on the lordly, invincible Sea,
Come, for the Eye of the Ether is beaming,
Come, for all Nature is flashing and free.
Let us shake off this close-clinging dew
From our members eternally new,
And sail upwards the wide world to view.
Come away! Come away!
So. O Goddesses mine, great Clouds and divine,
ye have heeded and answered my prayer.
Heard ye their sound, and the thunder around,
as it thrilled through the tremulous air?
St. Yes, by Zeus, and I shake, and I'm all of a quake,
and I fear I must sound a reply,
Their thunders have made my soul so afraid,
and those terrible voices so nigh:
So if lawful or not, I must run to a pot,
by Zeus, if I stop I shall die.
So. Don't act in our schools like those Comedy-fools
with their scurrilous scandalous ways.
Deep silence be thine: while this Cluster divine
their soul-stirring melody raise.
Ch. Come then with me,
Daughters of Mist, to the land of the free.
Come to the people whom Pallas hath blest,
Come to the soil where the Mysteries rest;
Come, where the glorified Temple invites
The pure to partake of its mystical rites:
Holy the gifts that are brought to the Gods,
Shrines with festoons and with garlands are crowned,
Pilgrims resort to the sacred abodes,
Gorgeous the festivals all the year round.
And the Bromian rejoicings in Spring,
When the flutes with their deep music ring,
And the sweetly-toned Choruses sing
Come away! Come away!
St. O Socrates pray, by all the Gods, say,
for I earnestly long to be told,
Who are these that recite with such grandeur and might?
are they glorified mortals of old?
So. No mortals are there, but Clouds of the air,
great Gods who the indolent fill:
These grant us discourse, and logical force,
and the art of persuasion instil,
And periphrasis strange, and a power to arrange,
and a marvellous judgement and skill.
St. So then when I heard their omnipotent word,
my spirit felt all of a flutter,
And it yearns to begin subtle cobwebs to spin
and about metaphysics to stutter,
And together to glue an idea or two,
and battle away in replies:
So if it's not wrong, I earnestly long
to behold them myself with my eyes.
So. Look up in the air, towards Parnes out there,
for I see they will pitch before long
These regions about.
St. Where? point me them out.
So. They are drifting, an infinite throng,
And their long shadows quake over valley and brake.
St. Why, whatever's the matter to-day?
I can't see, I declare.
So. By the Entrance; look there!
St. Ah, I just got a glimpse, by the way.
So. There, now you must see how resplendent they be,
or your eyes must be pumpkins, I vow.
St. Ah! I see them proceed; I should think so indeed:
great powers! they fill everything now.
So. So then till this day that celestials were they,
you never imagined or knew?

St. Why, no, on my word, for I always had heard
they were nothing but vapour and dew.
So. O, then I declare, you can't be aware
that 'tis these who the sophists protect,
Prophets sent beyond sea, quacks of every degree,
fops signet-and-jewel-bedecked,
Astrological knaves, and fools who their staves
of dithyrambs proudly rehearse—
'Tis the Clouds who all these support at their ease,
because they exalt them in verse.
St. 'Tis for this then they write of "the on-rushin' might
o' the light-stappin' rain-drappin' Cloud,"
And the "thousand black curls whilk the Tempest-lord whirls,"
and the "thunder-blast stormy an' loud,"
And "birds o' the sky floatin' upwards on high,"
and "air-water leddies" which "droon
Wi' their saft falling dew the gran' Ether sae blue,"
and then in return they gulp doon
Huge gobbets o' fishes an' bountifu' dishes
o' mavises prime in their season.
So. And is it not right such praise to requite?
St. Ah, but tell me then what is the reason
That if, as you say, they are Clouds, they to-day
as women appear to our view?
For the ones in the air are not women, I swear.
So. Why, what do they seem then to you?
St. I can't say very well, but they straggle and swell
like fleeces spread out in the air;
Not like women they flit, no, by Zeus, not a bit,
but these have got noses to wear.
So. Well, now then, attend to this question, my friend.
St. Look sharp, and propound it to me.
So. Didst thou never espy a Cloud in the sky,
which a centaur or leopard might be,
Or a wolf, or a cow?
St. Very often, I vow:
and show me the cause, I entreat.
So. Why, I tell you that these become just what they please,
and whenever they happen to meet
One shaggy and wild, like the tangle-haired child
of old Xenophantes, their rule
Is at once to appear like Centaurs, to jeer
the ridiculous look of the fool.
St. What then do they do if Simon they view,
that fraudulent harpy to shame?
So. Why, his nature to show to us mortals below,
a wolfish appearance they frame.
St. O, they then I ween having yesterday seen
Cleonymus quaking with fear,
(Him who threw off his shield as he fled from the field),
metamorphosed themselves into deer.
So. Yes, and now they espy soft Cleisthenes nigh,
and therefore as women appear.
St. O then without fail, All hail! and All hail!
my welcome receive; and reply
With your voices so fine, so grand and divine,
majestical Queens of the Sky!
Ch. Our welcome to thee, old man, who wouldst see
the marvels that science can show:
And thou, the high-priest of this subtlety feast,
say what would you have us bestow?
Since there is not a sage for whom we'd engage
our wonders more freely to do,
Except, it may be, for Prodicus; he
for his knowledge may claim them, but you,
For that sideways you throw your eyes as you go,
and are all affectation and fuss;
No shoes will you wear, but assume the grand air
on the strength of your dealings with us.
St. O Earth! what a sound, how august and profound!
it fills me with wonder and awe.
So. These, these then alone, for true Deities own,
the rest are all Godships of straw.
St. Let Zeus be left out: He's a God beyond doubt:
come, that you can scarcely deny.
So. Zeus, indeed! there's no Zeus: don't you be so obtuse.
St. No Zeus up aloft in the sky!
Then, you first must explain, who it is sends the rain;
or I really must think you are wrong.
So. Well then, be it known, these send it alone:
I can prove it by arguments strong.
Was there ever a shower seen to fall in an hour
when the sky was all cloudless and blue?
Yet on a fine day, when the Clouds are away,
he might send one, according to you.
St. Well, it must be confessed, that chimes in with the rest:
your words I am forced to believe.
Yet before, I had dreamed that the rain-water streamed
from Zeus and his chamber-pot sieve.
But whence then, my friend, does the thunder descend?
that does make me quake with affright!
So. Why 'tis they, I declare, as they roll through the air.
St. What the Clouds? did I hear you aright?
So. Ay: for when to the brim filled with water they swim,
by Necessity carried along,
They are hung up on high in the vault of the sky,
and so by Necessity strong
In the midst of their course, they clash with great force,
and thunder away without end.
St. But is it not He who compels this to be?
does not Zeus this Necessity send?
So. No Zeus have we there, but a Vortex of air.
St. What! Vortex? that's something, I own.
I knew not before, that Zeus was no more,
but Vortex was placed on his throne!
But I have not yet heard to what cause you referred
the thunder's majestical roar.

So. Yes, 'tis they, when on high full of water they fly,
and then, as I told you before,
By Compression impelled, as they clash, are compelled
a terrible clatter to make.
St. Come, how can that be? I really don't see.
So Yourself as my proof I will take.
Have you never then eat the broth-puddings you get
when the Panathenaea comes round,
And felt with what might your bowels all night
in turbulent tumult resound?
St. By Apollo, 'tis true, there's a mighty to-do,
and my belly keeps rumbling about;
And the puddings begin to clatter within
and kick up a wonderful rout:
Quite gently at first, papapax, papapax,
but soon pappapappax away,
Till at last, I'll be bound, I can thunder as loud,
papapappappapappax, as They.
So. Shalt thou then a sound so loud and profound
from thy belly diminutive send,
And shall not the high and the infinite Sky
go thundering on without end?
For both, you will find, on an impulse of wind
and similar causes depend.
St. Well, but tell me from Whom comes the bolt
through the gloom,
with its awful and terrible flashes;
And wherever it turns, some it singes and burns,
and some it reduces to ashes!
For this 'tis quite plain, let who will send the rain,
that Zeus against perjurers dashes.
So. And how, you old fool of a dark-ages school,
and an antediluvian wit,
If the perjured they strike, and not all men alike,
have they never Cleonymus hit?
Then of Simon again, and Theorus explain:
known perjurers, yet they escape.
But he smites his own shrine with his arrows divine,
and "Sunium, Attica's cape,"
And the ancient gnarled oaks: now what prompted those strokes? *They* never forswore I should say.
St. Can't say that they do: your words appear true.
Whence comes then the thunderbolt, pray?
So. When a wind that is dry, being lifted on high,
is suddenly pent into these,
It swells up their skin, like a bladder, within,
by Necessity's changeless decrees:
Till, compressed very tight, it bursts them outright,
and away with an impulse so strong,
That at last by the force and the swing of its course,
it takes fire as it whizzes along.
St. That's exactly the thing that I suffered one Spring,
at the great feast of Zeus, I admit:
I'd a paunch in the pot, but I wholly forgot
about making the safety-valve slit.
So it spluttered and swelled, while the saucepan I held,
till at last with a vengeance it flew:
Took me quite by surprise, dung-bespattered my eyes,
and scalded my face black and blue!
Ch. O thou who wouldst fain great wisdom attain,
and comest to us in thy need,
All Hellas around shall thy glory resound,
such a prosperous life thou shalt lead:
So thou art but endued with a memory good,
and accustomed profoundly to think,
And thy soul wilt inure all wants to endure,
and from no undertaking to shrink,
And art hardy and bold, to bear up against cold,
and with patience a supper thou losest:
Nor too much dost incline to gymnastics and wine,
but all lusts of the body refusest:
And esteemest it best, what is always the test
of a truly intelligent brain,
To prevail and succeed whensoever you plead,
and hosts of tongue-conquests to gain.
St. But as far as a sturdy soul is concerned
and a horrible restless care,
And a belly that pines and wears away
on the wretchedest, frugalest fare,
You may hammer and strike as long as you like;
I am quite invincible there.
So. Now then you agree in rejecting with me
the Gods you believed in when young,
And *my* creed you'll embrace "I believe in wide space,
in the Clouds, in the eloquent Tongue."
St. If I happened to meet other Gods in the street,
I'd show the cold shoulder, I vow.
No libation I'll pour: not one victim more
on their altars I'll sacrifice now.
Ch. Now be honest and true, and say what we shall do:
since you never shall fail of our aid,
If you hold us most dear in devotion and fear,
and will ply the philosopher's trade.
St. O Ladies Divine, small ambition is mine:
I only most modestly seek,
Out and out for the rest of my life to be best
of the children of Hellas to speak.
Ch. Say no more of your care, we have granted your prayer:
and know from this moment, that none
More acts shall pass through in the People than you:
such favour from us you have won.
St. Not acts, if you please: I want nothing of these:
this gift you may quickly withdraw;
But I wish to succeed, just enough for my need,
and to slip through the clutches of law.
Ch. This then you shall do, for your wishes are few:
not many nor great your demands,
So away with all care from henceforth, and prepare
to be placed in our votaries' hands.

St. This then will I do, confiding in you,
for Necessity presses me sore,
And so sad is my life, 'twixt my cobs and my wife,
that I cannot put up with it more.
So now, at your word, I give and afford
My body to these, to treat as they please,
To have and to hold, in squalor, in cold,
In hunger and thirst, yea by Zeus, at the worst,
To be flayed out of shape from my heels to my nape
So along with my hide from my duns I escape,
And to men may appear without conscience or fear,
Bold, hasty, and wise, a concocter of lies,
A rattler to speak, a dodger, a sneak,
A regular claw of the tables of law,
A shuffler complete, well worn in deceit,
A supple, unprincipled, troublesome cheat;
A hang-dog accurst, a bore with the worst,
In the tricks of the jury-courts thoroughly versed.
If all that I meet this praise shall repeat,
Work away as you choose, I will nothing refuse,
Without any reserve, from my head to my shoes.
You shan't see me wince though my gutlets you mince,
And these entrails of mine for a sausage combine,
Served up for the gentlemen students to dine.

Ch. Here's a spirit bold and high
Ready-armed for any strife.
(*to* STREPSIADES)
If you learn what I can teach
Of the mysteries of speech,
Your glory soon shall reach To the summit of the sky.

St. And what am I to gain?

Ch. With the Clouds you will obtain
The most happy, the most enviable life.

St. Is it possible for me Such felicity to see?

Ch. Yes, and men shall come and wait
In their thousands at your gate,
Desiring consultations and advice
On an action or a pleading
From the man of light and leading,
And you'll pocket many talents in a trice.
(*to* SOCRATES)
Here, take the old man, and do all that you can,
your new-fashioned thoughts to instil,
And stir up his mind with your notions refined,
and test him with judgement and skill.

So. Come now, you tell me something of your habits:
For if I don't know them, I can't determine
What engines I must bring to bear upon you.

St. Eh! what? Not going to storm me, by the Gods?

So. No, no: I want to ask you a few questions.
First: is your memory good?

St. Two ways, by Zeus:
If I'm owed anything, I'm mindful, very:
But if I owe, (Oh dear!) forgetful, very.

So. Well then: have you the gift of speaking in you?

St. The gift of speaking, no: of cheating, yes.

So. No? how then can you learn?

St. Oh, well enough.

So. Then when I throw you out some clever notion
About the laws of nature, you must catch it.

St. What! must I snap up sapience, in dog-fashion?

So. Oh! why the man's an ignorant old savage:
I fear, my friend, that you'll require the whip.
Come, if one strikes you, what do you do?

St. I'm struck:
Then in a little while I call my witness:
Then in another little while I summon him.

So. Put off your cloak.

St. Why, what have I done wrong?

So. O, nothing, nothing: all go in here naked.

St. Well, but I have not come with a search-warrant.

So. Fool! throw it off.

St. Well, tell me this one thing;
If I'm extremely careful and attentive,
Which of your students shall I most resemble?

So. Why, Chaerephon. You'll be his very image.

St. What! I shall be half-dead! O luckless me!

So. Don't chatter there, but come and follow me;
Make haste now, quicker, here.

St. Oh, but do first
Give me a honied cake: Zeus! how I tremble,
To go down there, as if to see Trophonius.

So. Go on! why keep you pottering round the door?

SOCRATES *and* STREPSIADES *enter the Phrontisterion.*

Chorus

Yes! go, and farewell; as your courage is great,
So bright be your fate.
May all good fortune his steps pursue,
Who now, in his life's dim twilight haze,
Is game such venturesome things to do,
To steep his mind in discoveries new,
To walk, a novice, in wisdom's ways.

O Spectators, I will utter
honest truths with accents free,
Yea! by mighty Dionysus,
Him who bred and nurtured me.
So may I be deemed a poet,
and this day obtain the prize,
As till that unhappy blunder
I had always held you wise,
And of all my plays esteeming
this the wisest and the best,
Served it up for your enjoyment,
which had, more than all the rest,
Cost me thought, and time, and labour:
then most scandalously treated,
I retired in mighty dudgeon,
by unworthy foes defeated.
This is why I blame your critics,
for whose sake I framed the play:

Yet the clever ones amongst you
even now I won't betray.
No! for ever since from judges
unto whom 'tis joy to speak,
Brothers Profligate and Modest
gained the praise we fondly seek,
When, for I was yet a Virgin,
and it was not right to bear,
I exposed it, and Another
did the foundling nurse with care,
But 'twas ye who nobly nurtured,
ye who brought it up with skill;
From that hour I proudly cherish
pledges of your sure good will.
Now then comes its sister hither,
like Electra in the Play,
Comes in earnest expectation
kindred minds to meet to-day;
She will recognize full surely,
if she find, her brother's tress.
And observe how pure her morals:
who, to notice her first dress,
Enters not with filthy symbols
on her modest garments hung,
Jeering bald-heads, dancing ballets,
for the laughter of the young.
In this play no wretched greybeard
with a staff his fellow pokes,
So obscuring from the audience
all the poorness of his jokes.
No one rushes in with torches,
no one groans, "Oh, dear! Oh, dear!"
Trusting in its genuine merits
comes this play before you here
Yet, though such a hero-poet,
I, the bald-head, do not grow
Curling ringlets: neither do I
twice or thrice my pieces show.
Always fresh ideas sparkle,
always novel jests delight,
Nothing like each other, save that
all are most exceeding bright.
I am he who floored the giant,
Cleon, in his hour of pride,
Yet when down I scorned to strike him,
and I left him when he died!
But the others, when a handle
once Hyperbolus did lend,
Trample down the wretched caitiff,
and his mother, without end.
In his Maricas the Drunkard,
Eupolis the charge began,
Shamefully my "Knights" distorting,
as he is a shameful man,
Tacking on the tipsy beldame,
just the ballet-dance to keep,
Phrynichus' prime invention,
eat by monsters of the deep.
Then Hermippus on the caitiff
opened all his little skill,
And the rest upon the caitiff
are their wit exhausting still;
And my simile to pilfer
"of the Eels" they all combine.
Whoso laughs at their productions,
let him not delight in mine.
But for you who praise my genius,
you who think my writings clever,
Ye shall gain a name for wisdom,
yea! forever and forever.

O mighty God, O heavenly King,
First unto Thee my prayer I bring,
O come, Lord Zeus, to my choral song;—
And Thou, dread Power, whose resistless hand
Heaves up the sea and the trembling land,
Lord of the trident, stern and strong;—
And Thou who sustainest the life of us all
Come, Ether, our parent, O come to my call;—
And Thou who floodest the world with light,
Guiding thy steeds through the glittering sky,
To men below and to Gods on high
A Potentate heavenly-bright!

O most sapient wise spectators,
hither turn attention due,
We complain of sad ill-treatment,
we've a bone to pick with you:
We have ever helped your city,
helped with all our might and main;
Yet you pay us no devotion,
that is why we now complain.
We who always watch around you.
For if any project seems
Ill-concocted, then we thunder,
then the rain comes down in streams.
And, remember, very lately,
how we knit our brows together,
"Thunders crashing, lightnings flashing,"
never was such awful weather;
And the Moon in haste eclipsed her,
and the Sun in anger swore
He would curl his wick within him
and give light to you no more,
Should you choose that mischief-worker,
Cleon, whom the Gods abhor,
Tanner, Slave, and Paphlagonian,
to lead out your hosts to war.
Yet you chose him! yet you chose him!
For they say that Folly grows
Best and finest in this city,
but the gracious Gods dispose
Always all things for the better,
causing errors to succeed:
And how this sad job may profit,
surely he who runs may read.
Let the Cormorant be convicted,
in command, of bribes and theft,
Let us have him gagged and muzzled,
in the pillory chained and left,
Then again, in ancient fashion,
all that ye have erred of late,
Will turn out your own advantage,
and a blessing to the State.

"Phoebus, my king, come to me still."
Thou who holdest the Cynthian hill,
The lofty peak of the Delian isle;—
And Thou, his sister, to whom each day
Lydian maidens devoutly pray
In Thy stately gilded Ephesian pile;—
And Athene, our Lady, the queen of us all,
With the Aegis of God, O come to my call;—
And Thou whose dancing torches of pine
Flicker, Parnassian glades along,
Dionysus, Star of Thy Maenad throng,
Come, Reveller most divine!

We, when we had finished packing,
and prepared our journey down,
Met the Lady Moon, who charged us
with a message for your town.
First, All hail to noble Athens,
and her faithful true Allies;
Then, she said, your shameful conduct
made her angry passions rise,
Treating her so ill who always
aids you, not in words, but clearly;
Saves you, first of all, in torchlight
every month a drachma nearly,
So that each one says, if business
calls him out from home by night,
"Buy no link, my boy, this evening,
for the Moon will lend her light."
Other blessings too she sends you,
yet you will not mark your days
As she bids you, but confuse them,
jumbling them all sorts of ways,
And, she says, the Gods in chorus
shower reproaches on her head,
When in bitter disappointment
they go supperless to bed,
Not obtaining festal banquets
duly on the festal day;
Ye are badgering in the law-courts
when ye should arise and slay!
And full oft when we celestials
some strict fast are duly keeping,
For the fate of mighty Memnon,
or divine Sarpedon weeping,
Then you feast and pour libations:
and Hyperbolus of late
Lost the crown he wore so proudly
as Recorder of the Gate,
Through the wrath of us immortals:
so perchance he'll rather know
Always all his days in future
by the Lady Moon to go.

SOCRATES *here comes out of the Phrontisterion where he has been endeavouring to teach* STREPSIADES.

So. Never by Chaos, Air, and Respiration,
Never, no never have I seen a clown
So helpless, and forgetful, and absurd!
Why if he learns a quirk or two he clean
Forgets them ere he has learnt them: all the same,
I'll call him out of doors here to the light.
Take up your bed, Strepsiades, and come!

St. By Zeus, I can't: the bugs make such resistance.

So. Make haste. There, throw it down, and listen.

St. (*entering, with bed*) Well!

So. Attend to me. what shall I teach you first
That you've not learnt before? Which will you have,
Measures or rhythms or the right use of words?

St. Oh! measures to be sure: for very lately
A grocer swindled me of full three pints.

So. I don't mean that: but which do you like the best
Of all the measures; six feet, or eight feet?

St. Well, I like nothing better than the yard.

So. Fool! don't talk nonsense.

St. What will you bet me now
That two yards don't exactly make six feet?

So. Consume you! what an ignorant clown you are!
Still, perhaps you can learn tunes more easily.

St. But will tunes help me to repair my fortunes?

So. They'll help you to behave in company:
If you can tell which kind of tune is best
For the sword-dance, and which for finger music.

St. For fingers! aye, but I know that.

So. Say on, then.

St. What is it but this finger? though before,
Ere this was grown, I used to play with that.

So. Insufferable dolt!

St. Well but, you goose,
I don't want to learn this.

So. What *do* you want then?

St. Teach me the Logic! teach me the unjust Logic!

So. But you must learn some other matters first:
As, what are males among the quadrupeds.

St. I should be mad indeed not to know that.
The Ram, the Bull, the Goat, the Dog, the Fowl.

So. Ah! there you are! there's a mistake at once!
You call the male and female fowl the same.

St How! tell me how.

So. Why fowl and fowl of course.

St. That's true though! what then shall I say in future?

So. Call one a fowless and the other a fowl.

St. A fowless? Good! Bravo! Bravo! by Air.
Now for that one bright piece of information
I'll give you a barley bumper in your trough.

So. Look there, a fresh mistake; you called it trough,
Masculine, when it's feminine.

St. How, pray?
How did I make it masculine?

So. Why "trough,"
Just like "Cleonymus."

St. I don't quite catch it.

So. Why "trough," "Cleonymus," both masculine.

St. Ah, but Cleonymus has got no trough,
His bread is kneaded in a rounded mortar:
Still, what must I say in future?
So. What! why call it
A "troughess," female, just as one says "an actress."
St. A "troughess," female?
So. That's the way to call it.
St. O "troughess" then and Miss Cleonymus.
So. Still you must learn some more about these names;
Which are the names of men and which of women.
St. Oh, I know which are women.
So. Well, repeat some.
St. Demetria, Cleitagora, Philinna.
So. Now tell me some men's names.
St. O yes, ten thousand.
Philon, Melesias, Amynias.
So. Hold! I said men's names: these are women's names.
St. No, no, they're men's.
So. They are *not* men's, for how
Would you address Amynias if you met him?
St. How? somehow thus. "Here, here, Amynia!"
So. Amynia! a woman's name, you see.
St. And rightly too; a sneak who shirks all service!
But all know this: let's pass to something else.
So. Well, then, you get into the bed.
St. And then?
So. Excogitate about your own affairs.
St. Not there: I do beseech, not there: at least
Let me excogitate on the bare ground.
So. There is no way but this.
St. O luckless me!
How I shall suffer from the bugs to-day.
So. Now then survey in every way,
with airy judgement sharp and quick:
Wrapping thoughts around you thick:
And if so be in one you stick,
Never stop to toil and bother,
Lightly, lightly, lightly leap,
To another, to another;
Far away be balmy sleep.
St. Ugh! Ugh! Ugh! Ugh! Ugh!
Ch. What's the matter? where's the pain?
St. Friends! I'm dying. From the bed
Out creep bugbears scantly fed.
And my ribs they bite in twain,
And my life-blood out they suck,
And my manhood off they pluck,
And my loins they dig and drain,
And I'm dying, once again.
Ch. O take not the smart so deeply to heart.
St. Why, what can I do?
Vanished my skin so ruddy of hue,
Vanished my life-blood, vanished my shoe,
Vanished my purse, and what is still worse
As I hummed an old tune till my watch should be past,
I had very near vanished myself at the last.
So. Hallo there, are you pondering?
St. Eh! what? I?
Yes to be sure.
So. And what have your ponderings come to?
St. Whether these bugs will leave a bit of me.
So. Consume you, wretch!
St. Faith, I'm consumed already.
So. Come, come, don't flinch: pull up the clothes again:
Search out and catch some very subtle dodge
To fleece your creditors.
St. O me, how can I
Fleece any one with all these fleeces on me?
(*Puts his head under the clothes.*)
So. Come, let me peep a moment what he's doing.
Hey! he's asleep!
St. No, no! no fear of that!
So. Caught anything?
St. No, nothing.
So. Surely, something.
St. Well, I had something in my hand, I'll own.
So. Pull up the clothes again, and go on pondering.
St. On what? now do please tell me, Socrates.
So. What is it that you want? first tell me that.
St. You have heard a million times what 'tis I want:
My debts! my debts! I want to shirk my debts.
So. Come, come, pull up the clothes: refine your thoughts
With subtle wit: look at the case on all sides:
Mind you divide correctly.
St. Ugh! O me.
So. Hush: if you meet with any difficulty
Leave it a moment: then return again
To the same thought: then lift and weigh it well.
St. Oh, here, dear Socrates!
So. Well, my old friend.
St. I've found a notion how to shirk my debts.
So. Well then, propound it.
St. What do you think of this?
Suppose I hire some grand Thessalian witch
To conjure down the Moon, and then I take it
And clap it into some round helmet-box,
And keep it fast there, like a looking-glass,—
So. But what's the use of that?
St. The use, quotha:
Why if the Moon should never rise again.
I'd never pay one farthing.
So. No! why not?
St. Why, don't we pay our interest by the month?
So. Good! now I'll proffer you another problem.
Suppose an action: damages, five talents:
Now tell me how you can evade that same.
St. How! how! can't say at all: but I'll go seek.
So. Don't wrap your mind for ever round yourself,
But let your thoughts range freely through the air,
Like chafers with a thread about their feet.
St. I've found a bright evasion of the action:
Confess yourself, 'tis glorious.
So. But what is it?

St. I say, haven't you seen in druggists' shops
That stone, that splendidly transparent stone,
By which they kindle fire?
So. The burning-glass?
St. That's it: well then, I'd get me one of these,
And as the clerk was entering down my case,
I'd stand, like this, some distance towards the sun,
And burn out every line.
So. By the Three Graces,
A clever dodge!
St. O me, how pleased I am
To have a debt like that clean blotted out.
So. Come, then, make haste and snap up this.
St. Well, what?
So. How to prevent an adversary's suit
Supposing you were sure to lose it; tell me.
St. O, nothing easier.
So. How, pray?
St. Why thus,
While there was yet one trial intervening,
Ere mine was cited, I'd go hang myself.
So. Absurd!
St. No, by the Gods, it isn't though:
They could not prosecute me were I dead.
So. Nonsense! Be off: I'll try no more to teach you.
St. Why not? do, please: now, please do, Socrates.
So. Why you forget all that you learn, directly.
Come, say what you learnt first: there's a chance for you.
St. Ah! what was first?—Dear me: whatever was it?—
Whatever's that we knead the barley in?—
Bless us, what was it?
So. Be off, and feed the crows,
You most forgetful, most absurd old dolt!
St. O me! what will become of me, poor wretch!
I'm clean undone: I haven't learnt to speak.—
O gracious Clouds, now do advise me something.
Ch. Our counsel, ancient friend, is simply this,
To send your son, if you have one at home,
And let him learn this wisdom in your stead.
St. Yes! I've a son, quite a fine gentleman:
But he won't learn, so what am I to do?
Ch. What! is he master?
St. Well: he's strong and vigorous,
And he's got some of the Coesyra blood within him:
Still I'll go for him, and if he won't come
By all the Gods I'll turn him out of doors.
Go in one moment, I'll be back directly.

SOCRATES *exits to Phrontisterion, and* STREPSIADES *to his house.*

Ch. Dost thou not see how bounteous we our favours free
Will shower on you,
Since whatsoe'er your will prepare
This dupe will do.
But now that you have dazzled and elated so your man,
Make haste and seize whate'er you please as quickly as you can,
For cases such as these, my friend, are very prone to change and bend.

Enter STREPSIADES *and* PHEIDIPPIDES.

St. Get out! you shan't stop here: so help me Mist!
Be off, and eat up Megacles' columns.
Ph. How now, my father? what's i' the wind to-day?
You're wandering; by Olympian Zeus, you are.
St. Look there! Olympian Zeus! you blockhead you,
Come to *your* age, and yet believe in Zeus!
Ph. Why prithee, what's the joke?
St. 'Tis so preposterous
When babes like you hold antiquated notions.
But come and I'll impart a thing or two,
A wrinkle, making you a man indeed.
But, mind: don't whisper this to any one.
Ph. Well, what's the matter?
St. Didn't you swear by Zeus?
Ph. I did.
St. See now, how good a thing is learning.
There is no Zeus, Pheidippides.
Ph. Who then?
St. Why Vortex reigns, and he has turned out Zeus.
Ph. Oh me, what stuff.
St. Be sure that this is so.
Ph. Who says so, pray?
St. The Melian—Socrates,
And Chaerephon, who knows about the flea-tracks.
Ph. And are you come to such a pitch of madness
As to put faith in brain-struck men?
St. O hush!
And don't blaspheme such very dexterous men
And sapient too: men of such frugal habits
They never shave, nor use your precious ointment,
Nor go to baths to clean themselves: but you
Have taken *me* for a corpse and cleaned me out.
Come, come, make haste, do go and learn for me.
Ph. What can one learn from them that is worth knowing?
St. Learn! why, whatever's clever in the world:
And you shall learn how gross and dense you are.
But stop one moment: I'll be back directly. *Exit.*
Ph. O me! what must I do with my mad father?
Shall I indict him for his lunacy,
Or tell the undertakers of his symptoms?
St. (*re-entering*) Now then! you see this, don't you? what do you call it?
Ph. That? why a fowl.
St. Good! now then, what is this?
Ph. That's a fowl too.
St. What both! Ridiculous!
Never say that again, but mind you always
Call this a fowless and the other a fowl.
Ph. A fowless! These then are the mighty secrets
You have picked up amongst those earth-born fellows.

St. And lots besides: but everything I learn
I straight forget: I am so old and stupid.
Ph. And this is what you have lost your mantle for?
St. It's very absent sometimes: 'tisn't lost.
Ph. And what have you done with your shoes, you dotard you?
St. Like Pericles, all for the best, I've lost them.
Come, come; go with me: humour me in this,
And then do what you like. Ah! I remember
How I to humour you, a coaxing baby,
With the first obol which my judgeship fetched me
Bought you a go-cart at the great Diasia.
Ph. The time will come when you'll repent of this.
St. Good boy to obey me. Hallo! Socrates.

Enter SOCRATES.

Come here; come here; I've brought this son of mine,
Trouble enough, I'll warrant you.
So. Poor infant,
Not yet aware of my suspension-wonders.
Ph. You'd make a wondrous piece of ware, suspended.
St. Hey! Hang the lad! Do you abuse the Master?
So. And look, "suthspended!" In what foolish fashion
He mouthed the word with pouting lips agape.
How can *he* learn evasion of a suit,
Timely citation, damaging replies?
Hyperbolus, though, learnt them for a talent.
St. O never fear! he's very sharp, by nature.
For when he was a little chap, *so* high,
He used to build small baby-houses, boats,
Go-carts of leather, darling little frogs
Carved from pomegranates, you can't think how nicely!
So now, I prithee, teach him both your Logics,
The Better, as you call it, and the Worse
Which with the worse cause can defeat the Better;
Or if not both, at all events the Worse.
So. Aye, with his own ears he shall hear them argue.
I shan't be there.
St. But please remember this,
Give him the knack of reasoning down all Justice.

Exit SOCRATES.

Enter RIGHT LOGIC *and* WRONG LOGIC.

Right Logic. Come show yourself now
with your confident brow.
—To the stage, if you dare!
Wrong Logic. "Lead on where you please":
I shall smash you with ease,
If an audience be there.
R.L. You'll smash me, you say! And who are *you*, pray?
W.L. A Logic, like you.
R.L. But the Worst of the two.
W.L. Yet you I can drub whom my Better they dub.
R.L. By what artifice taught?
W.L. By original thought.
R.L. Aye, truly your trade so successful is made.
By means of these noodles of ours, I'm afraid.
W.L. Not noodles, but wise.
R.L. I'll smash you and your lies!
W.L. By what method, forsooth?
R.L. By speaking the Truth.
W.L. Your words I will meet, and entirely defeat:
There never *was* Justice or Truth, I repeat.
R.L. No Justice! you say?
W.L. Well, where does it stay?
R.L. With the Gods in the air.
W.L. If Justice be there,
How comes it that Zeus could his father reduce,
Yet live with their Godships unpunished and loose?
R.L. Ugh! Ugh! These evils come thick,
I feel awfully sick,
A basin, quick, quick!
W.L. You're a useless old drone with one foot in the grave!
R.L. You're a shameless, unprincipled, dissolute knave!
W.L. Hey! a rosy festoon.
R.L. And a vulgar buffoon!
W.L. What! Lilies from *you*?
R.L. And a parricide too!
W.L. 'Tis with gold (you don't know it) you sprinkle my head.
R.L. O gold is it now? but it used to be lead!
W.L. But now it's a grace and a glory instead.
R.L. You're a little too bold.
W.L. You're a good deal too old.
R.L. 'Tis through you I well know not a stripling will go
To attend to the rules which are taught in the Schools;
But Athens one day shall be up to the fools.
W.L. How squalid your dress!
R.L. Yours is fine, I confess.
Yet of old, I declare, but a pauper you were;
And passed yourself off, our compassion to draw
As a Telephus, (Euripidéan)
Well pleased from a beggarly wallet to gnaw
At inanities Pandeletéan.
W.L. O me! for the wisdom you've mentioned in jest!
R.L. O me! for the folly of you, and the rest
Who you to destroy their children employ!
W.L. Him you never shall teach: you are quite out of date.
R.L. If not, he'll be lost, as he'll find to his cost:
Taught nothing by you but to chatter and prate.
W.L. He raves, as you see: let him be, let him be.
R.L. Touch him if you dare! I bid you beware.
Ch. Forbear, forbear to wrangle and scold!
Each of you show
You what you taught their fathers of old,
You let us know
Your system untried, that hearing each side
From the lips of the Rivals the youth may decide
To which of your schools he will go.

R.L. This then will I do.
W.L. And so will I too.
Ch. And who will put in his claim to begin?
W.L. If *he* wishes, he may: I kindly give way:
And out of his argument quickly will I
Draw facts and devices to fledge the reply
Wherewith I will shoot him and smite and refute him.
And at last if a word from his mouth shall be heard
My sayings like fierce savage hornets shall pierce
His forehead and eyes,
Till in fear and distraction he yields and he—dies!
Ch. With thoughts and words and maxims pondered well
Now then in confidence let both begin:
Try which his rival can in speech excel:
Try which this perilous wordy war can win,
Which all my votaries' hopes are fondly centred in.
O Thou who wert born our sires to adorn
with characters blameless and fair,
Say on what you please, say on and to these
your glorious Nature declare.
R.L. To hear then prepare of the Discipline rare
which flourished in Athens of yore
When Honour and Truth were in fashion with youth
and Sobriety bloomed on our shore;
First of all the old rule was preserved in our school
that "boys should be seen and not heard":
And then to the home of the Harpist would come
decorous in action and word
All the lads of one town, though the snow peppered down,
in spite of all wind and all weather:
And they sang an old song as they paced it along,
not shambling with thighs glued together:
"O the dread shout of War how it peals from afar,"
or "Pallas the Stormer adore,"
To some manly old air all simple and bare
which their fathers had chanted before.
And should anyone dare the tune to impair
and with intricate twistings to fill,
Such as Phrynis is fain, and his long-winded train,
perversely to quaver and trill,
Many stripes would he feel in return for his zeal,
as to genuine Music a foe.
And every one's thigh was forward and high
as they sat to be drilled in a row,
So that nothing the while indecent or vile
the eye of a stranger might meet;
And then with their hand they would smooth down the sand
whenever they rose from their seat,
To leave not a trace of themselves in the place
for a vigilant lover to view.
They never would soil their persons with oil
but were inartificial and true.
Nor tempered their throat to a soft mincing note
and sighs to their lovers addressed:
Nor laid themselves out, as they strutted about,
to the wanton desires of the rest:
Nor would anyone dare such stimulant fare
as the head of the radish to wish:
Nor to make over bold with the food of the old,
the anise, and parsley, and fish:
Nor dainties to quaff, nor giggle and laugh,
nor foot within foot to enfold.
W.L. Faugh! this smells very strong of some musty old song,
and Chirrupers mounted in gold;
And Slaughter of beasts, and old-fashioned feasts.
R.L. Yet these are the precepts which taught
The heroes of old to be hardy and bold,
and the Men who at Marathon fought!
But now must the lad from his boyhood be clad
in a Man's all-enveloping cloak:
So that, oft as the Panathenaea returns,
I feel myself ready to choke
When the dancers go by with their shields to their thigh,
not caring for Pallas a jot.
You therefore, young man, choose me while you can;
cast in with my Method your lot;
And then you shall learn the forum to spurn,
and from dissolute baths to abstain,
And fashions impure and shameful abjure,
and scorners repel with disdain:
And rise from your chair if an elder be there,
and respectfully give him your place,
And with love and with fear your parents revere,
and shrink from the brand of Disgrace,
And deep in your breast be the Image impressed
of Modesty, simple and true,
Nor resort any more to a dancing-girl's door,
nor glance at the harlotry crew,
Lest at length by the blow of the Apple they throw
from the hopes of your Manhood you fall.
Nor dare to reply when your Father is nigh,
nor "musty old Japhet" to call
In your malice and rage that Sacred Old Age
which lovingly cherished your youth.
W.L. Yes, yes, my young friend, if to him you attend,
by Bacchus I swear of a truth
You will scarce with the sty of Hippocrates vie,
as a mammy-suck known even there!
R.L. But then you'll excel in the games you love well,
all blooming, athletic and fair:
Not learning to prate as your idlers debate
with marvellous prickly dispute,
Nor dragged into Court day by day to make sport
in some small disagreeable suit:
But you will below to the Academe go,
and under the olives contend
With your chaplet of reed, in a contest of speed
with some excellent rival and friend:
All fragrant with woodbine and peaceful content,
and the leaf which the lime blossoms fling,
When the plane whispers love to the elm in the grove
in the beautiful season of Spring.
If then you'll obey and do what I say,
And follow with me the more excellent way,
Your chest shall be white, your skin shall be bright,

Your arms shall be tight, your tongue shall be slight,
And everything else shall be proper and right.
But if you pursue what men nowadays do,
You will have, to begin, a cold pallid skin,
Arms small and chest weak, tongue practised to speak,
Special laws very long, and the symptoms all strong
Which show that your life is licentious and wrong.
And your mind he'll prepare so that foul to be fair
And fair to be foul you shall always declare;
And you'll find yourself soon, if you listen to him,
With the filth of Antimachus filled to the brim!

Ch. O glorious Sage! with loveliest Wisdom teeming!
Sweet on thy words does ancient Virtue rest!
Thrice happy they who watched thy Youth's bright beaming!
Thou of the vaunted genius, do thy best;
This man has gained applause: His Wisdom stands confessed.
And you with clever words and thoughts must needs your case adorn
Else he will surely win the day, and you retreat with scorn.

W.L. Aye, say you so? why I have been half-burst; I do so long
To overthrow his arguments with arguments more strong.
I am the Lesser Logic? True: these Schoolmen call me so,
Simply because I was the first of all mankind to show
How old established rules and laws might contradicted be:
And this, as you may guess, is worth a thousand pounds to me,
To take the feebler cause, and yet to win the disputation.
And mark me now, how I'll confute his boasted Education!
You said that always from warm baths the stripling must abstain:
Why must he? on what grounds do you of these warm baths complain?

R.L. Why, it's the worst thing possible, it quite unstrings a man.

W.L. Hold there: I've got you round the waist: escape me if you can.
And first: of all the sons of Zeus which think you was the best?
Which was the manliest? which endured more toils than all the rest?

R.L. Well, I suppose that Heracles was bravest and most bold.

W.L. And are the baths of Heracles so wonderfully cold?
Aha! you blame warm baths, I think.

R.L. This, this is what they say:
This is the stuff our precious youths are chattering all the day!
This is what makes them haunt the baths, and shun the manlier Games!

W.L. Well then, we'll take the Forum next: I praise it, and he blames.
But if it *was* so bad, do you think old Homer would have made
Nestor and all his worthies ply a real forensic trade?
Well: then he says a stripling's tongue should always idle be:
I say it should be used of course: so there we disagree.
And next he says you must be chaste. A most preposterous plan!
Come, tell me did you ever know one single blessed man
Gain the least good by chastity? come, prove I'm wrong: make haste.

R.L. Yes, many, many! Peleus gained a sword by being chaste.

W.L. A sword indeed! a wondrous meed the unlucky fool obtained.
Hyperbolus the Lamp-maker hath many a talent gained
By knavish tricks which I have taught: but not a sword, no, no!

R.L. Then Peleus did to his chaste life the bed of Thetis owe.

W.L. And then she cut and ran away! for nothing so engages
A woman's heart as forward warmth, old shred of those dark Ages!
For take this chastity, young man: sift it inside and out:
Count all the pleasures, all the joys, it bids you live without:
No kind of dames, no kind of games, no laughing, feasting, drinking—
Why, life itself is little worth without these joys, I'm thinking.
Well, I must notice now the wants by Nature's self implanted;
You love, seduce, you can't help that, you're caught, convicted. Granted.
You're done for; you can't say one word: while if you follow me
Indulge your genius, laugh and quaff, hold nothing base to be.
Why if you're in adultery caught, your pleas will still be ample:
You've done no wrong, you'll say, and then bring Zeus as your example.
He fell before the wondrous powers by Love and Beauty wielded:
And how can you, the Mortal, stand, where He, the Immortal, yielded?

R.L. Aye, but suppose in spite of all, he must be wedged and sanded.[1]
Won't he be probed, or else can you prevent it? now be candid.

W.L. And what's the damage if it should be so?

[1]Punishments of those taken in adultery.

R.L. What greater damage can the young man know?
W.L. What will you do, if this dispute I win?
R.L. I'll be for ever silent.
W.L. Good, begin.
The Counsellor: from whence comes he?
R.L. From probed adulterers.
W.L. I agree.
The Tragic Poets: whence are they?
R.L. From probed adulterers.
W.L. So I say.
The Orators: what class of men?
R.L. All probed adulterers.
W.L. Right again.
You feel your error, I'll engage,
But look once more around the stage,
Survey the audience, which they be,
Probed or not Probed.
R.L. I see, I see.
W.L. Well, give your verdict.
R.L. It must go
For probed adulterers: him I know,
And him, and him: the Probed are most.
W.L. How stand we then?
R.L. I own, I've lost.
O Cinaeds, Cinaeds, take my robe!
Your words have won, to you I run
To live and die with glorious Probe!

The two LOGICS *go out, and enter* SOCRATES *from the Phrontisterion and* STREPSIADES *from his own house to see how his son's education has been progressing. During the interval of the* CHORUS (1114-1130) *that education is supposed to be completed.*

So. Well, what do you want? to take away your son
At once, or shall I teach him how to speak?
St. Teach him, and flog him, and be sure you well
Sharpen his mother wit, grind the one edge
Fit for my little law-suits, and the other,
Why, make that serve for more important matters.
So. Oh, never fear! He'll make a splendid sophist.
St. Well, well, I hope he'll be a poor pale rascal.
Ch. Go: but in us the thought is strong,
you will repent of this ere long.
Now we wish to tell the Judges
all the blessings they shall gain
If, as Justice plainly warrants,
we the worthy prize obtain.
First, whenever in the Season
ye would fain your fields renew,
All the world shall wait expectant
till we've poured our rain on you:
Then of all your crops and vineyards
we will take the utmost care
So that neither drought oppress them,
nor the heavy rain impair.
But if anyone amongst you
dare to treat our claims with scorn,
Mortal he, the Clouds immortal,
better had he ne'er been born!
He from his estates shall gather
neither corn, nor oil, nor wine,
For whenever blossoms sparkle
on the olive or the vine
They shall all at once be blighted:
we will ply our slings so true.
And if ever we behold him
building up his mansions new,
With our tight and nipping hailstones
we will all his tiles destroy.
But if he, his friends or kinsfolk,
would a marriage-feast enjoy,
All night long we'll pour in torrents:
so perchance he'll rather pray
To endure the drought of Egypt,
than decide amiss to-day!
St. The fifth, the fourth, the third, and then the second,
And then that day which more than all the rest
I loathe and shrink from and abominate,
Then comes at once that hateful Old-and-New day.
And every single blessed dun has sworn
He'll stake his gage, and ruin and destroy me.
And when I make a modest small request,
"O my good friend, part don't exact at present,
And part defer, and part remit," they swear
So they shall never touch it, and abuse me
As a rank swindler, threatening me with actions.
Now let them bring their actions! Who's afraid?
Not I: if these have taught my son to speak.
But here's the door: I'll knock and soon find out.
Boy! Ho there, boy!
So. I clasp Strepsiades.
St. And I clasp you: but take this meal-bag first.
'Tis meet and right to glorify one's Tutors.
But tell me, tell me, has my son yet learnt
That Second Logic which he saw just now?
So. He hath.
St. Hurrah! great Sovereign Knavery!
So. You may escape whatever suit you please.
St. What, if I borrowed before witnesses?
So. Before a thousand, and the more the merrier.
St. "Then shall my song be loud and deep."
Weep, obol-weighers, weep, weep, weep,
Ye, and your principals, and compound interests,
For ye shall never pester me again.
Such a son have I bred,
(He is within this door),
Born to inspire my foemen with dread,
Born his old father's house to restore:
Keen and polished of tongue is he,
He my Champion and Guard shall be,
He will set his old father free,
Run you, and call him forth to me.
"O my child! O my sweet! come out, I entreat;
'Tis the voice" of your sire.
So. Here's the man you require.
St. Joy, joy of my heart!
So. Take your son and depart.
St. O come, O come, my son, my son,
O dear! O dear!
O joy, to see your beautiful complexion!

Aye now you have an aspect Negative
And Disputative, and our native query
Shines forth there "What d'ye say?" You've the true face
Which rogues put on, of injured innocence.
You have the regular Attic look about you.
So now, you save me, for 'twas you undid me.
Ph. What is it ails you?
St. Why the Old-and-New day.
Ph. And is there such a day as Old-and-New?
St. Yes: that's the day they mean to stake their gages.
Ph. They'll lose them if they stake them. What! do you think
That one day can be two days, both together?
St. Why, can't it be so?
Ph. Surely not; or else
A woman might at once be old and young.
St. Still, the law says so.
Ph. True: but I believe
They don't quite understand it.
St. You explain it.
Ph. Old Solon had a democratic turn.
St. Well, but that's nothing to the Old-and-New.
Ph. Hence then he fixed that summonses be issued
For these two days, the old one and the new one,
So that the gage be staked on the New-month.
St. What made him add "the old" then?
Ph. I will tell you.
He wished the litigants to meet on *that* day
And compromise their quarrels: if they could not,
Then let them fight it out on the New-month.
St. Why then do Magistrates receive the stakes
On the Old-and-New instead of the New-month?
Ph. Well, I believe they act like the Foretasters.
They wish to bag the gage as soon as possible,
And thus they gain a whole day's foretaste of it.
St. Aha! poor dupes, why sit ye mooning there,
Game for us Artful Dodgers, you dull stones,
You ciphers, lambkins, butts piled up together!
Oh! my success inspires me, and I'll sing
Glad eulogies on me and thee, my son.
"Man, most blessed, most divine,
What a wondrous wit is thine,
What a son to grace thy line,"
Friends and neighbours day by day
Thus will say,
When with envious eyes my suits they see you win:
But first I'll feast you, so come in, my son, come in.
Enter PASIAS[1] *and his* WITNESS.
Pasias. What! must a man lose his own property!
No: never, never. Better have refused
With a bold face, than be so plagued as this.
See! to get paid my own just debts, I'm forced
To drag you to bear witness, and what's worse
I needs must quarrel with my townsman here.
Well, I won't shame my country, while I live,
I'll go to law, I'll summon him.
St. (*entering*) Hallo!
Pa. To the next Old-and-New.
St. Bear witness, all!
He named two days. You'll summon me; what for?
Pa. The fifty pounds I lent you when you bought
That iron-grey.
St. Just listen to the fellow!
The whole world knows that I detest all horses.
Pa. I swear you swore by all the Gods to pay me.
St. Well, now I swear I won't: Pheidippides
Has learnt since then the unanswerable Logic.
Pa. And will you therefore shirk my just demand?
St. Of course I will: else why should he have learnt it?
Pa. And will you dare forswear it by the Gods?
St. The Gods indeed! What Gods?
Pa. Poseidon, Hermes, Zeus.
St. By Zeus I would,
Though I gave twopence halfpenny for the privilege.
Pa. O then confound you for a shameless rogue!
St. Hallo! this butt should be rubbed down with salt.
Pa. Zounds! you deride me!
St. Why 'twill hold four gallons.
Pa. You 'scape me not, by Mighty Zeus, and all
The Gods!
St. I wonderfully like the Gods;
An oath by Zeus is sport to knowing ones.
Pa. Sooner or later you'll repent of this.
Come do you mean to pay your debts or don't you?
Tell me, and I'll be off.
St. Now do have patience;
I'll give you a clear answer in one moment.
Pa. What do you think he'll do?
Witness. I think he'll pay you.
St. Where is that horrid dun? O here: now tell me
What you call this.
Pa. What I call that? a trough.
St. Heavens! what a fool: and do *you* want your money?
I'd never pay one penny to a fellow
Who calls my troughless, trough. So there's your answer.
Pa. Then you won't pay me?
St. No, not if I know it.
Come put your best foot forward, and be off:
March off, I say, this instant!
Pa. May I die
If I don't go at once and stake my gage!
Exit.
St. No don't: the fifty pounds are loss enough:
And really on my word I would not wish you
To lose this too just for one silly blunder.
Enter AMYNIAS.[2]
Amynias. Ah me! Oh! Oh! Oh!
St. Hallo! who's that making that horrible noise?
Not one of Carcinus' snivelling Gods?
Am. Who cares to know what I am? what imports it?
An ill-starred man.
St. Then keep it to yourself.

[1]The creditor mentioned in l. 22.

[2]The creditor mentioned in l. 31.

Am. "O heavy fate!" "O Fortune, thou hast broken
My chariot wheels!" "Thou hast undone me, Pallas!"
St. How! has Tlepolemus been at you, man?
Am. Jeer me not, friend, but tell your worthy son
To pay me back the money which I lent him:
I'm in a bad way and the times are pressing.
St. What money do you mean?
Am. Why what he borrowed.
St. You *are* in a bad way, I really think.
Am. Driving my four-wheel out I fell, by Zeus.
St. You rave as if you'd fall'n times out-of-mind.
Am. I rave? how so? I only claim my own.
St. You can't be quite right, surely.
Am. Why, what mean you?
St. I shrewdly guess your brain's received a shake.
Am. I shrewdly guess that you'll receive a summons
If you don't pay my money.
St. Well, then, tell me,
Which theory do you side with, that the rain
Falls fresh each time, or that the Sun draws back
The same old rain, and sends it down again?
Am. I'm very sure I neither know nor care.
St. Not care! good heavens! and do *you* claim your money,
So unenlightened in the Laws of Nature?
Am. If you're hard up then, pay me back the Interest
At least.
St. Int-er-est? what kind of a beast is that?
Am. What else than day by day and month by month
Larger and larger still the silver grows
As time sweeps by?
St. Finely and nobly said.
What then! think you the Sea is larger now
Than 'twas last year?
Am. No surely, 'tis no larger:
It is not right it should be.
St. And do you then,
Insatiable grasper! when the Sea,
Receiving all these Rivers, grows no larger,
Do you desire your silver to grow larger?
Come now, you prosecute your journey off!
Here, fetch the whip.
Am. Bear witness, I appeal.
St. Be off! what, won't you? Gee up, sigmabrand!
Am. I say! a clear assault!
St. You won't be off?
I'll stimulate you; Zeus! I'll goad your haunches.
Exit AMYNIAS.
Aha! you run: I thought I'd stir you up
You and your phaetons, and wheels, and all! *Exit.*

Chorus

What a thing it is to long for matters which are wrong!
For you see how this old man
Is seeking, if he can
His creditors trepan:
And I confidently say
That he will this very day
Such a blow
Amid his prosperous cheats receive,
that he will deeply deeply grieve.

For I think that he has won what he wanted for his son,
And the lad has learned the way
All justice to gainsay,
Be it what or where it may:
That he'll trump up any tale,
Right or wrong, and so prevail.
This I know.
Yea! and perchance the time will come
when he shall wish his son were dumb.

Enter STREPSIADES *and* PHEIDIPPIDES.

St. Oh! Oh!
Help! Murder! Help! O neighbours, kinsfolk, townsmen,
Help, one and all, against this base assault,
Ah! Ah! my cheek! my head! O luckless me!
Wretch! do you strike your father?
Ph. Yes, Papa.
St. See! See! he owns he struck me.
Ph. To be sure.
St. Scoundrel! and parricide! and house-breaker!
Ph. Thank you: go on, go on: do please go on.
I am quite delighted to be called such names!
St. O probed Adulterer.
Ph. Roses from your lips.
St. Strike you your father?
Ph. O dear yes: what's more,
I'll prove I struck you justly.
St. Struck me justly!
Villain! how can you strike a father justly?
Ph. Yes, and I'll demonstrate it, if you please.
St. Demonstrate this?
Ph. O yes, quite easily.
Come, take your choice, which Logic do you choose?
St. Which what?
Ph. Logic: the Better or the Worse?
St. Ah, then, in very truth I've had you taught
To reason down all Justice, if you think
You can prove this, that it is just and right
That fathers should be beaten by their sons!
Ph. Well, well, I think I'll prove it, if you'll listen,
So that even you won't have one word to answer.
St. Come, I should like to hear what you've to say.
Ch. 'Tis yours, old man, some method to contrive
This fight to win:
He would not without arms wherewith to strive
So bold have been.
He knows, be sure, whereon to trust.
His eager bearing proves he must.
So come and tell us from what cause
this sad dispute began;
Come, tell us how it first arose:
do tell us if you can.
St. Well from the very first I will
the whole contention show:
'Twas when I went into the house
to feast him, as you know,

I bade him bring his lyre and sing,
the supper to adorn,
Some lay of old Simonides,
as, how the Ram was shorn:
But he replied, to sing at meals
was coarse and obsolete;
Like some old beldame humming airs
the while she grinds her wheat.
Ph. And should you not be thrashed who told
your son, from food abstaining
To SING! as though you were, forsooth
cicalas entertaining.
St. You hear him! so he said just now
or e'er high words began:
And next he called Simonides
a very sorry man.
And when I heard him, I could scarce
my rising wrath command;
Yet so I did, and him I bid
take myrtle in his hand
And chant some lines from Aeschylus,
but he replied with ire,
"Believe me, I'm not one of those
who Aeschylus admire,
That rough, unpolished, turgid bard,
that mouther of bombast!"
When he said this, my heart began
to heave extremely fast;
Yet still I kept my passion down,
and said, "Then prithee you,
Sing one of those new-fangled songs
which modern striplings do."
And he began the shameful tale
Euripides has told
How a brother and a sister lived
incestuous lives of old.
Then, then I could no more restrain,
but first I must confess
With strong abuse I loaded him,
and so, as you may guess,
We stormed and bandied threat for threat:
till out at last he flew,
And smashed and thrashed and thumped and bumped
and bruised me black and blue.
Ph. And rightly too, who coolly dared
Euripides to blame,
Most sapient bard.
St. Most sapient bard!
you, what's your fitting name?
Ah! but he'll pummel me again.
Ph. He will: and justly too.
St. What! justly, heartless villain! when
'twas I who nurtured you.
I knew your little lisping ways,
how soon, you'd hardly think,
If you cried "bree!" I guessed your wants,
and used to give you drink:
If you said "mamm!" I fetched you bread
with fond discernment true,
And you could hardly say "Cacca!"
when through the door I flew
And held you out a full arm's length
your little needs to do:
But now when I was crying
That I with pain was dying,
You brute! you would not tarry
Me out of doors to carry,
But choking with despair
I've been and done it there.
Ch. Sure all young hearts are palpitating now
To hear him plead,
Since if those lips with artful words avow
The daring deed,
And once a favouring verdict win,
A fig for every old man's skin.
O thou! who rakest up new thoughts
with daring hands profane.
Try all you can, ingenious man,
that verdict to obtain.
Ph. How sweet it is these novel arts,
these clever words to know,
And have the power established rules
and laws to overthrow.
Why in old times when horses were
my sole delight, 'twas wonder
If I could say a dozen words
without some awful blunder!
But now that he has made me quit
that reckless mode of living,
And I have been to subtle thoughts
my whole attention giving,
I hope to prove by logic strict
'tis right to beat my father.
St. O! buy your horses back, by Zeus,
since I would ten times rather
Have to support a four-in-hand,
so I be struck no more.
Ph. Peace. I will now resume the thread
where I broke off before.
And first I ask: when I was young,
did you not strike me then?
St. Yea: for I loved and cherished you.
Ph. Well, solve me this again,
Is it not just that I your son
should cherish you alike,
And strike you, since, as you observe,
to cherish means to strike?
What! must my body needs be scourged
and pounded black and blue
And yours be scathless? was not I
as much freeborn as you?
"Children are whipped, and shall not sires be
whipped?"
Perhaps you'll urge that children's minds
alone are taught by blows:—
Well: Age is Second Childhood then:
that everybody knows.
And as by old experience Age
should guide its steps more clearly,
So when they err, they surely should
be punished more severely.
St. But Law goes everywhere for me:
deny it, if you can.
Ph. Well was not he who made the law,
a man, a mortal man,
As you or I, who in old times

talked over all the crowd?
And think you that to you or me
the same is not allowed,
To change it, so that sons by blows
should keep their fathers steady?
Still, we'll be liberal, and blows
which we've received already
We will forget, we'll have no ex-
post-facto legislation.
—Look at the game-cocks, look at all
the animal creation,
Do not *they* beat their parents? Aye:
I say then, that in fact
They are as we, except that they
no special laws enact.

St. Why don't you then, if always where
the game-cock leads you follow,
Ascend your perch to roost at night,
and dirt and ordure swallow?

Ph. The case is different there, old man,
as Socrates would see.

St. Well then you'll blame yourself at last,
if you keep striking me.

Ph. How so?

St. Why, if it's right for me to punish you my son,
You can, if you have got one, yours.

Ph. Aye, but suppose I've none.
Then having gulled me you will die,
while I've been flogged in vain.

St. Good friends! I really think he has
some reason to complain.
I must concede he has put the case
in quite a novel light:
I really think we should be flogged
unless we act aright!

Ph. Look to a fresh idea then.

St. He'll be my death I vow.

Ph. Yet then perhaps you will not grudge
ev'n what you suffer now.

St. How! will you make me like the blows
which I've received to-day?

Ph. Yes, for I'll beat my mother too.

St. What! What is that you say!
Why, this is worse than all.

Ph. But what, if as I proved the other,
By the same Logic I can prove
'tis right to beat my mother?

St. Aye! what indeed! if this you plead,
If this you think to win,
Why then, for all I care, you may
To the Accursed Pit convey
Yourself with all your learning new,
Your master, and your Logic too,
And tumble headlong in.
O Clouds! O Clouds! I owe all this to you!
Why did I let you manage my affairs!

Ch. Nay, nay, old man, you owe it to yourself.
Why didst thou turn to wicked practices?

St. Ah, but ye should have asked me that before,
And not have spurred a poor old fool to evil.

Ch. Such is our plan. We find a man
On evil thoughts intent,
Guide him along to shame and wrong,
Then leave him to repent.

St. Hard words, alas! yet not more hard than just.
It was not right unfairly to keep back
The money that I borrowed. Come, my darling,
Come and destroy that filthy Chaerephon
And Socrates; for they've deceived us both!

Ph. No. I will lift no hand against my Tutors.

St. Yes do, come, reverence Paternal Zeus.

Ph. Look there! Paternal Zeus! what an old fool.
Is there a Zeus?

St. There is.

Ph. There is *no* Zeus.
Young Vortex reigns, and he has turned out Zeus.

St. No Vortex reigns: that was my foolish thought
All through this vortex here. Fool that I was,
To think a piece of earthenware a God.

Ph. Well, rave away, talk nonsense to yourself. *Exit.*

St. Oh! fool, fool, fool, how mad I must have been
To cast away the Gods, for Socrates.
Yet Hermes, gracious Hermes, be not angry
Nor crush me utterly, but look with mercy
On faults to which his idle talk hath led me.
And lend thy counsel; tell me, had I better
Plague them with lawsuits, or how else annoy them.
(*Affects to listen.*)
Good: your advice is good: I'll have no lawsuits,
I'll go at once and set their house on fire,
The prating rascals. Here, here, Xanthias,
Quick, quick here, bring your ladder and your pitchfork,
Climb to the roof of their vile thinking-house,
Dig at their tiles, dig stoutly, an' thou lovest me.
Tumble the very house about their ears.
And someone fetch me here a lighted torch,
And I'll soon see if, boasters as they are,
They won't repent of what they've done to me.

1st Student (*within*). O dear! O dear!

St. Now, now, my torch, send out a lusty flame.

1st Stu. (*within*) Man! what are you at there?

St. What am I at? I'll tell you.
I'm splitting straws with your house-rafters here.

2nd Stu. (*within*) Oh me! who's been and set our house on fire?

St. Who was it, think you, that you stole the cloak from?

3rd Stu. (*within*) O Murder! Murder!

St. That's the very thing,
Unless this pick prove traitor to my hopes,
Or I fall down, and break my blessed neck.

So. (*at the window*) Hallo! what are you at, up on our roof?

St. I walk on air, and contemplate the Sun.

So. O! I shall suffocate. O dear! O dear!

Chaerephon. And I, poor devil, shall be burnt to death.

St. For with what aim did ye insult the Gods,
And pry around the dwellings of the Moon?
Strike, smite them, spare them not, for many reasons,
But most because they have blasphemed the Gods!

Ch. Lead out of the way: for I think we may say
We have acted our part very fairly to-day.

THE WASPS

DRAMATIS PERSONAE

Sosias, *servant of Philocleon*	Curs
Xanthias, *servant of Philocleon*	A Guest
Philocleon	A Baking-Girl
Bdelycleon, *son of Philocleon*	A Complainant
Boys	Chorus of Wasps

The play opens with a dialogue between two drowsy slaves who have been keeping guard all night before an Athenian house. It is still dark, but the day is at hand.

Sosias. You ill-starred Xanthias, what's the matter now?
Xanthias. The nightly watch I'm studying to relieve.
So. Why then, your ribs will have a score against you.
Do you forget what sort of beast we're guarding?
Xa. No, but I'd fain just drowse dull care away.
So. Well, try your luck: for I too feel a sort
Of drowsy sweetness settling o'er my eyes.
Xa. Sure you're a maniac or a Corybant.
So. (*producing a wine flask*) Nay 'tis a sleep from great Sabazius holds me.
Xa. (*producing another*) Aha! and I'm your fellow-votary there.
My lids too felt just now the fierce assault
Of a strong Median nod-compelling sleep.
And then I dreamed a dream; such a strange dream!
So. And so did I: the strangest e'er I heard of.
But tell yours first.
Xa. Methought a monstrous eagle
Came flying towards the market-place, and there
Seized in its claws a wriggling brassy shield,
And bore it up in triumph to the sky,
And then—Cleonymus fled off and dropped it.
So. Why then, Cleonymus is quite a riddle.
Xa. How so?
So. A man will ask his boon companions,
"What is that brute which throws away its shield
Alike in air, in ocean, in the field?"
Xa. O what mishap awaits me, that have seen
So strange a vision?
So. Take it not to heart,
'Twill be no harm, I swear it by the Gods.
Xa. No harm to see a man throw off his shield!
But now tell yours.
So. Ah, mine's a big one, mine is;
About the whole great vessel of the state.
Xa. Tell us at once the keel of the affair.
So. 'Twas in my earliest sleep methought I saw
A flock of sheep assembled in the Pnyx,
Sitting close-packed, with little cloaks and staves;
Then to these sheep I heard, or seemed to hear
An all-receptive grampus holding forth
In tone and accents like a scalded pig.
Xa. Pheugh!
So. Eh?
Xa. Stop, stop, don't tell us any more.
Your dream smells horribly of putrid hides.
So. Then the vile grampus, scales in hand, weighed out
Bits of fat beef, cut up.
Xa. Woe worth the day!
He means to cut our city up in bits.
So. Methought beside him, on the ground, I saw
Theorus seated, with a raven's head.
Then Alcibiades lisped out to me,
"Cwemark! Theocwus has a cwaven's head."
Xa. Well lisped! and rightly, Alcibiades!
So. But is this not ill-omened, that a man
Turn to a crow?
Xa. Nay, excellent.
So. How?
Xa. How!
Being a man he straight becomes a crow:
Is it not obvious to conjecture that
He's going to leave us, going to the crows?
So. Shall I not pay two obols then, and hire
One who so cleverly interprets dreams?
Xa. Come, let me tell the story to the audience
With just these few remarks, by way of preface.
Expect not from us something mighty grand,
Nor yet some mirth purloined from Megara.
We have no brace of servants here, to scatter
Nuts from their basket out among the audience,
No Heracles defrauded of his supper,
Nor yet Euripides besmirched again;
No, nor though Cleon shine, by fortune's favour,
Will we to mincemeat chop the man again.
Ours is a little tale, with meaning in it,
Not too refined and exquisite for you,
Yet wittier far than vulgar comedy.
You see that great big man, the man asleep
Up on the roof, aloft: well, that's our master.
He keeps his father here, shut up within,
And bids us guard him that he stir not out.
For he, the father, has a strange disease,
Which none of you will know, or yet conjecture,
Unless we tell: else, if you think so, guess.

Amynias there, the son of Pronapes,
Says he's a dice-lover: but he's quite out.
So. Ah, he conjectures from his own disease.
Xa. Nay, but the word does really end with -lover.
Then Sosias here observes to Dercylus,
That 'tis a *drink*-lover.
So. Confound it, no:
That's the disease of honest gentlemen.
Xa. Then next, Nicostratus of Scambon says,
It is a sacrifice- or stranger-lover.
So. What, like Philoxenus? No, by the dog,
Not quite so lewd, Nicostratus, as that.
Xa. Come, you waste words: you'll never find it out,
So all keep silence if you want to know.
I'll tell you the disease old master has.
He is a *lawcourt*-lover, no man like him.
Judging is what he dotes on, and he weeps
Unless he sit on the front bench of all.
At night he gets no sleep, no, not one grain,
Or if he doze the tiniest speck, his soul
Flutters in dreams around the water-clock.
So used he is to holding votes, he wakes
With thumb and first two fingers closed, as one
That offers incense on a new moon's day.
If on a gate is written "Lovely Demus,"
Meaning the son of Pyrilamp, he goes
And writes beside it "Lovely Verdict-box."
The cock which crew from eventide, he said,
Was tampered with, he knew, to call him late,
Bribed by officials whose accounts were due.
Supper scarce done, he clamours for his shoes,
Hurries ere daybreak to the Court, and sleeps
Stuck like a limpet to the doorpost there.
So sour he is, the long condemning line
He marks for all, then homeward like a bee
Laden with wax beneath his finger-nails.
Lest he lack votes, he keeps, to judge withal,
A private pebble-beach secure within.
Such is his frenzy, and the more you chide him
The more he judges: so with bolts and bars
We guard him straitly that he stir not out.
For ill the young man brooks his sire's disease.
And first he tried by soft emollient words
To win him over, not to don the cloak
Or walk abroad: but never a jot he yielded.
He washed and purged him then: but never a jot.
A Corybant next he made him, but old master,
Timbrel and all, into the New Court bursts
And there sits judging. So when these rites failed,
We cross the Strait, and, in Aegina, place him,
To sleep the night inside Asclepius' temple:
Lo! with the dawn he stands at the Court rails!
Then, after that, we let him out no more.
But he! he dodged along the pipes and gutters,
And so made off: we block up every cranny,
Stopping and stuffing them with clouts of rag:
Quick he drove pegs into the wall, and clambered
Up like an old jackdaw, and so hopped out.
Now then, we compass all the house with nets,
Spreading them round, and mew him safe within.
Well, sirs, Philocleon is the old man's name;
Ay truly; and the son's, Bdelycleon;
A wondrous high-and-mighty mannered man.
Bdelycleon. (*from the roof*) Xanthias and Sosias! are ye fast asleep?
Xa. O dear!
So. What now?
Xa. Bdelycleon is up.
Bd. One of you two run hither instantly,
For now my father's got into the kitchen,
Scurrying, mouselike, somewhere. Mind he don't
Slip through the hole for turning off the water.
And you, keep pressing at the door.
So. Ay, ay, sir.
Bd. O heavens! what's that? what makes the chimney rumble?
Hallo, sir! who are you?
Philocleon. (*in the chimney*) I'm smoke escaping.
Bd. Smoke? of what wood?
Ph. I'm of the fig-tree panel.
Bd. Ay, and there's no more stinging smoke than that.
Come, trundle back: what, won't you? where's the board?
In with you! nay, I'll clap this log on too.
There now, invent some other stratagem.
But I'm the wretchedest man that ever was;
They'll call me now the son of Chimney-smoked.
So. He's at the door now, pushing.
Bd. Press it back then
With all your force: I'm coming there directly.
And O be careful of the bolt and bar,
And mind he does not nibble off the door-pin.
Ph. (*within*) Let me out, villains! let me out to judge.
What, shall Dracontides escape unpunished!
Bd. What if he should?
Ph. Why once, when I consulted
The Delphian oracle, the God replied,
That I should wither if a man escaped me.
Bd. Apollo shield us, what a prophecy!
Ph. O let me out, or I shall burst, I shall.
Bd. No, by Poseidon! no, Philocleon, never!
Ph. O then by Zeus I'll nibble through the net.
Bd. You've got no teeth, my beauty.
Ph. Fire and fury!
How shall I slay thee, how? Give me a sword,
Quick, quick, or else a damage-cessing tablet.
Bd. Hang it, he meditates some dreadful deed.
Ph. O no, I don't: I only want to take
And sell the donkey and his panniers too.
'Tis the new moon to-day.
Bd. And if it is,
Cannot I sell them?
Ph. Not so well as I.
Bd. No, but much better: drive the donkey out.
Xa. How well and craftily he dropped the bait
To make you let him through.
Bd. But he caught nothing
That haul at least, for I perceived the trick.
But I will in, and fetch the donkey out.
No, no; he shan't come slipping through again.
(*Gets donkey.*)

Donkey, why grieve? at being sold to-day?
Gee up! why grunt and groan, unless you carry
Some new Odysseus there?
Xa. And, in good truth,
Here *is* a fellow clinging on beneath.
Bd. Who? where?
Xa. Why, here.
Bd. Why, what in the world is this?
Who are you, sirrah?
Ph. Noman I, by Zeus.
Bd. Where from?
Ph. From Ithaca, son of Runaway.
Bd. Noman I promise to no good you'll be.
Drag him out there from under. O the villain,
The place he had crept to! Now he seems to me
The very image of a sompnour's foal.
Ph. Come now, hands off: or you and I shall fight.
Bd. Fight! what about?
Ph. About a donkey's shadow.
Bd. You're a born bad one, with your tricks and fetches.
Ph. Bad! O my gracious! then you don't know yet
How good I am: but wait until you taste
The seasoned paunchlet of a prime old judge.
Bd. Get along in, you and your donkey too.
Ph. O help me, fellow-dicasts: help me, Cleon!
Bd. Bellow within there when the door is shut.
Now pile a heap of stones against the door,
And shoot the door-pin home into the bar,
And heave the beam athwart it, and roll up,
Quick, the great mortar-block.
So. (*starting*) Save us! what's that?
Whence fell that clod of dirt upon my head?
Xa. Belike some mouse dislodged it from above.
So. A mouse? O, no, a rafter-haunting dicast,
Wriggling about behind the tiling there.
Bd. Good lack! the man is changing to a sparrow
Sure he'll fly off: where, where's the casting-net?
Shoo! shoo there! shoo! 'Fore Zeus, 'twere easier work
To guard Scione than a sire like this.
So. Well but at last we have fairly scared him in,
He can't slip out, he can't elude us now,
So why not slumber just a—just a—drop?
Bd. Slumber, you rogue! when in a little while
His fellow-justices will come this way
Calling him up.
So. Why sir, 'tis twilight yet.
Bd. Why then, by Zeus, they are very late to-day.
Soon after midnight is their usual time
To come here, carrying lights, and warbling tunes
Sweet-charming-old-Sidono-Phrynichéan
Wherewith they call him out.
So. And if they come.
Had we not better pelt them with some stones?
Bd. Pelt them, you rogue! you might as well provoke
A nest of wasps as anger these old men.
Each wears beside his loins a deadly sting,
Wherewith they smite, and on with yells and cries
They leap, and strike at you, like sparks of fire.
So. Tut, never trouble, give me but some stones,
I'll chase the biggest wasps-nest of them all.

Enter CHORUS OF WASPS.

Chorus. Step out, step out, my comrades stout:
no loitering, Comias, pound along,
You're shirking now, you used, I vow,
to pull as tough as leathern thong,
Yet now, with ease, Charinades
can walk a brisker pace than you.
Ho! Strymodore of Conthylè,
the best of all our dicast crew,
Has old Euergides appeared,
and Chabes too from Phlya, pray?
Ah! here it strains, the poor remains,
alas! alas! alack the day,
Of that mad set, I mind it yet,
when once we paced our nightly round,
In years gone by, both you and I,
along Byzantium's wall, and found
And stole away the baker's tray,
and sliced it up, and chopped it well,
A merry blaze therewith to raise,
and so we cooked our pimpernel.
On, on again, with might and main:
for Laches' turn is come to-day:
Quick, look alive, a splendid hive
of wealth the fellow's got, they say.
And Cleon too, our patron true,
enjoined us each betimes to bring
Of anger sore an ample store,
a good three days' provisioning:
On all the man's unrighteous plans
a vengeance well-deserved to take.
Come, every dear and tried compeer,
come, quickly come, ere morning break,
And as you go, be sure you throw
the light around on every side;
Lest somewhere nigh a stone may lie,
and we therefrom be damnified.
Boy. O father, father, here's some mud!
look sharp or in you'll go.
Ch. Pick up a stick, and trim the wick,
a better light to show.
Boy. Nay, father, with my finger, thus,
I choose to trim the lamp.
Ch. How dare you rout the wick about,
you little wasteful scamp,
And that with oil so scarce? but no,
it don't disturb *your* quiet,
However dear the oil may be,
when I have got to buy it.
Boy. If with your knuckles once again
you 'monish us, I swear
We'll douse the light, and take to flight,
and leave you floundering there.
Then wading on without the lamp
in darkness, I'll be bound
You'll stir and splash the mud about,
like snipes in marshy ground.

Chorus

Ah, greater men than you, my boy,
'tis often mine to beat.
But, bless me, this is filth indeed
I feel beneath my feet:

Ay, and within four days from this,
or sooner, it is plain,
God will send down upon our town
a fresh supply of rain:
So dense and thick around the wick
these thieves collect and gather,
And that's, as everybody knows,
a sign of heavy weather.
Well, well, 'tis useful for the fruits,
and all the backward trees,
To have a timely fall of rain,
and eke a good North breeze.
But how is this? Our friend not here!
how comes it he's so slack?
By Zeus, he never used to be
at all a hanger-back.
He always marched before us all,
on legal cares intent,
And some old tune of Phrynichus
he warbled as he went.
O he's a wonder for the songs!
Come, comrades, one and all,
Come stand around the house, and sing,
its master forth to call.
If once he hears me tuning up,
I know it won't be long
Before he comes creep, creeping out,
from pleasure at the song.

How is it our friend is not here to receive us?
Why comes he not forth from his dwelling?
Can it be that he's had the misfortune to lose
His one pair of shoes;
Or striking his toe in the dark, by the grievous
Contusion is lamed, and his ankle inflamed?
Or his groin has, it may be, a swelling.
He of us all, I ween,
Was evermore the austerest, and most keen.
Alone no prayers he heeded:
Whene'er for grace they pleaded,
He bent (like this) his head,
"You cook a stone," he said.

Is it all of that yesterday's man who cajoled us,
And slipped through our hands, the deceiver
Pretending a lover of Athens to be,
Pretending that he
Was the first, of the Samian rebellion that told us?
Our friend may be sick with disgust at the trick,
And be now lying ill of a fever.
That would be like him quite.
But now up, up, nor gnaw your soul with spite
There comes a traitor base,
A wealthy rogue from Thrace.
Safe in our toils we've got him,
Up, up, old friend, and pot him!

On with you, boy, on with you.

Boy. Father, if a boon I pray,
Will you grant it, father, eh?
Ch. Certainly I will, my son.
Tell me what you'd have me buy
Dibs, my son? Hey, my son?
Dibs it is, undoubtedly.
Boy. Dibs, my father! No, my father!
Figs! for they are sweeter far.
Ch. You be hanged first: yet you shall not
Have them, monkey, when you are.
Boy. Then, my father, woe betide you!
Not another step I'll guide you.
Ch. Is it not enough that I
With this paltry pay must buy
Fuel, bread, and sauce for three?
Must I needs buy figs for thee!
Boy. Father, if the Archon say
That the Court won't sit to-day.
Tell me truly, father mine,
Have we wherewithal to dine?
O my father, should not we
Then in "Straits of Helle" be?
Ch. Out upon it! out upon it!
Then, indeed, I should not know
For a little bit of supper
Whither in this world to go.
Boy. Why, my mother, didst thou breed me,
giving nothing else to feed me,
But a store of legal woe?
Ch. Empty scrip! O empty show,
Bootless, fruitless ornament!
Boy. O! O! woe! woe!
Ours to sorrow and lament.
Ph. (*appearing above*) Long my reins have been stirred,
Long through chinks have I heard,
Heard your voices below.
Vain my efforts to sing,
These forbid me to go.
Vainly my sad heart yearns,
Yearns to be marching with you,
On to the judgement urns,
There some mischief to do.
O change to smoke by a lightning stroke,
Dread-thundering Zeus! this body of mine,
Till I'm like Proxenides, like the son
Of Sellus, that false tree-vine.
O Sovereign, pity my woeful lot,
Vouchsafe to grant me my heart's desire,
Fry me in dust with a glittering, hot,
Red bolt of celestial fire,
Then take me up with thy hand divine,
And puff me, and plunge me in scalding brine.
Or turn me into the stone, whereon
They count the votes when the trial is done.
Ch. Who is he that thus detains you?
Who with bolted door restrains you?
Tell us, you will speak to friends.
Ph. 'Tis my son, but don't be bawling:
for he's slumbering now at ease
There, upon the roof before you:
drop your tone a little, please.
Ch. What's his object, idle trifler,
that he does such things as these?
What's the motive he pretends?

Ph. He will let me do no mischief,
and no more a lawsuit try.
True it is he'll feast and pet me,
but with that I won't comply.
Ch. This the Demagogcleon blared
Out against you, since you dared
Truth about the fleet to show.
He must be involved, I see,
In some dark *conspiracy*,
Else he durst not use you so.
It is time some means of escape to find,
some novel, ingenious plan, that so,
Unseen of your son, you may get you down,
alighting in safety here below.
Ph. O what shall it be? consider it ye!
I'm ready to do whatever is planned:
So sorely I'm longing a circuit to go,
through the lists of the Court, with a vote in my hand.
Ch. Can you find no cranny or secret run,
through which, from within, your path to urge,
And then like wily Odysseus, here,
disguised in tatters and rags, emerge?
Ph. Each cranny is barred: there's never a run,
thro' which though it were but a midge could squeeze.
You must think, if you can, of a likelier plan:
I can't run out like a runnet cheese.
Ch. O don't you remember the old campaign,
when you stole the spit, and let yourself down,
And away by the side of the wall you hied?
'Twas when we had captured Naxos town.
Ph. Ah, well I remember! but what of that?
it is quite another affair to-day.
For then I was young, and then I could steal,
and over myself I possessed full sway.
And then none guarded my steps, but I
Was free, wherever I chose, to fly;
Whilst now, in every alley and street,
Armed men with arms are stationed about,
Watching with care that I steal not out.
And there at the gate you may see those two
Waiting with spits to spit me through,
Like a cat that is running away with the meat.
Ch. Well but now be quickly shaping
Some contrivance for escaping;
Morning breaks, my honey-bee.
Ph. Then the best that I can think of,
is to gnaw these meshes through.
May Dictynna, queen of hunters,
pardon me the deed I do.
Ch. Spoken like a man whose efforts
will salvation's goal ensue.
Ply your jaw then lustily.
Ph. There, I've gnawn them through completely
—Ah! but do not raise a shout,
We must use the greatest caution,
lest Bdelycleon find us out.
Ch. Fear not: fear not: if he speak,
He shall gnaw his heart, and seek
For his life to run amain.
We will quickly make him learn
Nevermore again to spurn
Th' holy statutes of the Twain.
So now to the window lash the cord,
and twine it securely your limbs around.
With all Diopeithes fill your soul,
then let yourself cleverly down to the ground.
Ph. But suppose they catch me suspended here,
and hoist me up by the line again,
And angle me into the house once more,
say what ye will do to deliver me then.
Ch. Our hearts of oak we'll summon to aid,
and all give battle at once for you.
'Twere vain to attempt to detain you more:
such wonderful feats we are going to do.
Ph. This then will I do, confiding in you:
and if anything happens to me, I implore
That you take me up and bewail my fate,
and bury me under the court-house floor.
Ch. O nothing, nothing will happen to you:
keep up, old comrade, your heart and hope;
First breathe a prayer to your father's gods:
then let yourself down by the trusty rope.
Ph. O Lycus, neighbour and hero and lord!
thou lovest the selfsame pleasures as I;
Day after day we both enjoy
the suppliant's tears and his wailing cry.
Thou camest here thine abode to fix,
on purpose to listen to sounds so sweet,
The only hero of all that deigns
by the mourner's side to assume his seat:
O pity thine old familiar friend:
O save me and succour me, Power Divine!
And never again will I do my needs
by the osier matting that guards thy shrine.
Bd. Get up, get up.
BDELYCLEON *suddenly reappears and wakes up the slumbering slaves.*
So. Why, what's in the wind?
Bd. Some voice seems circling me round and round.
So. Is the old man slipping away thro' a hole?
Bd. No, by Zeus, but he lets himself down to the ground
Tied on to the rope.
So. You infamous wretch!
what, won't you be quiet and not come down?
Bd. Climb up by the other window-sill,
and wallop him well with the harvest crown.
I warrant he'll speedily back stern first,
when he's thrashed with the branch of autumnal fruits.
Ph. Help! help! all those whoever propose
this year to busy themselves with suits.
Smicythion, help! Tisiades, help!
Pheredeipnus, Chremon, the fray begin:
O now or never assist your friend,
before I'm carried away within.
Ch. Wherefore slumbers, wherefore slumbers,
that resentment in our breast,
Such as when a rash assailant
dares provoke our hornets-nest?

Now protruding, now protruding,
Comes the fierce and dreadful sting,
Which we wield for punishing.
Children, hold these garments for us:
then away with all your speed,
Shout and run and bawl to Cleon,
tell him of this direful deed;
Bid him quickly hither fly
As against a city-hater,
And a traitor doomed to die,
One who actually proposes
That we should no lawsuits try. *Exit* BOYS.

Bd. (*entering*) Listen, worthy sirs, to reason:
goodness! don't keep screaming so.

Ch. Scream! we'll scream as high as heaven.

Bd. I don't intend to let him go.

Ch. These be frightful things to see!
This is open *tyranny*!
Rouse the State! Rouse the great
God-abhorred Sneak Theorus!
And whoe'er Else is there,
Fawning lord Ruling o'er us.

Xa. Heracles! they've stings beside them!
Master, master, don't you see?

Bd. Ay, which slew the son of Gorgias,
Philip, with their sharp decree.

Ch. You we'll also slay directly!
Wheel about him, everyone,
Draw your stings, and, all together,
in upon the fellow run.
Close your ranks, collect your forces,
brimming full of rage and hate,
He shall know the sort of wasps-nest
he has dared to irritate.

Xa. Now with such as these to combat
is, by Zeus, a serious thing:
Verily I quake and tremble,
but to look upon their sting.

Ch. Let him go! Loose your hold!
If you don't I declare
You shall bless Tortoise-backs
For the shells Which they wear.

Ph. On then, on, my fellow-dicasts,
brother wasps of heart severe,
Some fly in with angry buzzings,
and attack them in the rear,
Some surround them in a ring, and
both their eyes and fingers sting.

Bd. Ho there! Midas! Phryx! Masyntias!
hither! hither! haste to me!
Take my father, guard him safely:
suffer none to set him free;
Else you both shall lunch off nothing,
clapped in fetters strong and stout.
There's a sound of many fig-leaves
(well I know it) buzzed about.

Ch. This shall stand infixed within you
if you will not let him go.

Ph. Mighty Cecrops! King and hero!
Dragon-born and -shaped below,
Wilt thou let these rude barbarians
vex and maul me at their pleasure,
Me who heretofore have made them
weep in full imperial measure?

Ch. Truly, of abundant evils,
age is evermore the source:
Only see how these two scoundrels
hold their ancient lord perforce,
Clean forgetting how, aforetime,
he their daily wants supplied,
Bought them little sleeveless jackets,
bought them caps and coats of hide,
Clean forgetting all the kindness
shown their feet in wintry weather,
How from chill and cold he kept them:
ah! but these have altogether
Banished from their eyes the reverence
owing to those dear old brogues.

Ph. Won't you even now unhand me,
shameless villain, worst of rogues?
When the grapes I caught you stealing,
O remember, if you can,
How I tied you to the olive,
and I flogged you like a man,
So that all beheld with envy:
but a grateful soul you lack!
Oh, unhand me, you, and you,
at once, before my son come back.

Ch. But a famous retribution
ye for this shall undergo,
One that will not lag nor linger;
so that ye betimes shall know,
Know the mood of angry-tempered,
righteous, mustard-glancing men.

Here BDELYCLEON *suddenly issues from the house, followed by* XANTHIAS *and* SOSIAS, *the former armed with a stick, the latter carrying an apparatus for smoking-out wasps.*

Bd. Beat them, Xanthias, from the door-way;
beat the wasps away again.

Xa. That I will, sir.

Bd. Fume them, Sosias,
drive the smoke in dense and thick.
Shoo there, shoo! be off, confound you.
At them, Xanthias, with the stick!
Smoke them, Sosias, smoke, infusing
Aeschines, Selartius' son.

So. So then we at last were going,
as it seems, to make you run.

Bd. But you never would have managed
thus to beat them off with ease,
Had it chanced that they had eaten
of the songs of Philocles.

Ch. Creeping o'er us, creeping o'er us,
Here at least the poor can see,
Stealthy-creeping *tyranny*!
If you from the laws debar us,
which the city has ordained,
You, a curly-haired Amynias,
you, a rascal double-grained,
Not by words of wit persuading,
Not for weighty reasons shown,
But because, forsooth, you *will* it,
Like an autocrat, alone.

Bd. Can't we now, without this outcry,
and this fierce denunciation,
Come to peaceful terms together,
terms of reconciliation?
Ch. Terms with *thee*, thou people-hater,
and with Brasidas, thou traitor,
Hand and glove! You who dare
Woolly-fringed Clothes to wear,
Yes, and show Beard and hair
Left to grow Everywhere.
Bd. O, by Zeus, I'd really liefer
drop my father altogether
Than endure these daily conflicts,
buffeting with waves and weather.
Ch. Why, as yet you've hardly entered
on the parsley and the rue:
(That we'll just throw in, a sample
of our three-quart words for you.)
Now you care not, wait a little,
till the prosecutor trounce you,
Sluicing out these selfsame charges,
and *conspirator* denounce you.
Bd. O by all the gods I ask you,
will ye never go away?
Are ye quite resolved to linger,
thwacked and thwacking all the day?
Ch. Never more Will I while
There's a grain Left of me
Leave your door, Traitor vile
Bent to gain *Tyranny.*
Bd. Ay "Conspiracy" and "Tyrant,"
These with you are all in all,
Whatsoe'er is brought before you,
be the matter great or small.
Everywhere the name of Tyrant,
now for fifty years unknown,
Is than cheap salt-fish at Athens
commoner and cheaper grown.
Everywhere about the market
it is bandied to and fro:
If you wish a basse to purchase,
and without a pilchard go,
Straight the man who sells the pilchards
grumbles from his stall hard by,
"Here is plainly one that caters
with a view to Tyranny."
If a leek, besides, you order,
relish for your sprats perchance,
Says the potherb-girl directly,
eyeing you with looks askance,
"Leeks indeed! and leeks I prithee!
what, with Tyranny in view?
Athens must be taxed, you fancy,
relish to supply for *you!*"
Xa. Even so a naughty damsel
yesternoon observed to me,
Just because I said her manners
were a little bit too free,
She supposed that I was wishing
Hippias's Tyranny.
Bd. Ay, by charges such as these
our litigious friends they please.
Now because I'd have my father
(quitting all this toil and strife,
This up-early-false-informing-
troublesome-litigious life)
Live a life of ease and splendour,
live like Morychus, you see
Straight I'm charged with Tyrant leanings,
charged with foul conspiracy.
Ph. Yes, by Zeus, and very justly.
Not for pigeon's milk in store
I the pleasant life would barter
which you let me lead no more.
Nought I care for eels and rayfish:
daintier food to me would seem
Just a little, tiny lawsuit,
dished and stifled in its steam.
Bd. Yes, for that's the sort of dainty
you, by Zeus, have loved so long.
Yet I think I'll soon convince you
that your mode of life is wrong,
If you can but once be silent,
and to what I say give heed.
Ph. I am wrong to be a dicast!
Bd. Laughed to utter scorn indeed,
Mocked by men you all but worship,
for you can't their treachery see,
You're a slave, and yet don't know it.
Ph. Name not slavery to me:
I am lord of all, I tell you.
Bd. You're the veriest drudge, I vow,
Thinking that you're lord of all. For
come, my father, teach us now,
If you reap the fruits of Hellas,
what's the benefit to you?
Ph. Willingly. Let these be umpires.
Bd. I'll accept their judgement too.
Now then all at once release him.
Ph. And besides a sword supply,
If in this dispute I'm worsted,
here upon this sword I'll die.
Bd. But suppose you won't their final
(what's the phrase) award obey?
Ph. May I never drink thereafter,
pure and neat, good fortune's—pay.
Ch. Now must the champion, going
Out of our school, be showing
Keen wit and genius new,
Bd. Bring forth my memorandum-book:
bring forth my desk to write in.
I'll quickly show you what you're like,
if that's your style of fighting.
Ch. In quite another fashion
To aught this youth can do.
Stern is the strife and anxious
For all our earthly good,
If he intends to conquer,
Which Heaven forfend he should.
Bd. Now I'll observe his arguments,
and take a note of each.
Ph. What would you say, if he to-day
should make the conquering speech?
Ch. Ah! should that mischance befall us,

Our old troop were nothing worth:
In the streets with ribald mirth
Idle boys would dotards call us,
Fit for nought but olive-bearing,
Shrivelled husks of counter swearing.
O friend upon whom it devolves to plead
the cause of our Sovereign Power to-day,
Now show us your best; now bring to the test
each trick that an eloquent tongue can play.

Ph. Away, away, like a racer gay,
I start at once from the head of the lists,
To prove that no kinglier power than ours
in any part of the world exists.
Is there any creature on earth more blest,
more feared and petted from day to day,
Or that leads a happier, pleasanter life,
than a Justice of Athens, though old and grey?
For first when rising from bed in the morn,
to the criminal Court betimes I trudge,
Great six-foot fellows are there at the rails,
in anxious haste to salute their Judge.
And the delicate hand, which has dipped so deep
in the public purse, he claps into mine,
And he bows before me, and makes his prayer,
and softens his voice to a pitiful whine:
"O pity me, pity me, Sire," he cries,
"if you ever indulged your longing for pelf,
When you managed the mess on a far campaign,
or served some office of state yourself."
The man would never have heard my name,
if he had not been tried and acquitted before.

Bd. (*writing*) I'll take a note of the point you make,
that "suppliant fellows your grace implore."

Ph. So when they have begged and implored me enough,
and my angry temper is wiped away,
I enter in and I take my seat,
and then I do none of the things I say.
I hear them utter all sorts of cries
design'd expressly to win my grace,
What won't they utter, what don't they urge,
to coax a Justice who tries their case?
Some vow they are needy and friendless men,
and over their poverty wail and whine,
And reckon up hardships, false and true,
till he makes them out to be equal to mine.
Some tell us a legend of days gone by,
or a joke from Aesop witty and sage,
Or jest and banter, to make me laugh,
that so I may doff my terrible rage.
And if all this fails, and I stand unmoved,
he leads by the hand his little ones near,
He brings his girls and he brings his boys;
and I, the Judge, am composed to hear.
They huddle together with piteous bleats:
while trembling above them he prays to me,
Prays as to a God his accounts to pass,
to give him a quittance, and leave him free.
"If thou lovest a bleating male of the flock,
O lend thine ear to this boy of mine:
Or pity this sweet little delicate girl,
if thy soul delights in the squeaking of swine."
So then we relax the pitch of our wrath,
and screw it down to a peg more low.
Is *this* not a fine dominion of mine,
a derision of wealth with its pride and show?

Bd. (*Writing*) A second point for my note-book that,
"A derision of wealth with its show and its pride."
Go on to mention the good you get
by your empire of Hellas so vast and wide.

Ph. 'Tis ours to inspect the Athenian youths,
when we enter their names on the rolls of men.
And if ever Oeagrus gets into a suit,
be sure that he'll never get out again
Till he give us a speech from his Niobe part,
selecting the best and the liveliest one.
And then if a piper gain his cause,
he pays us our price for the kindness done,
By piping a tune with his mouth-band on,
quick march as out of the Court we go.
And what if a father by will to a friend
his daughter and heiress bequeath and bestow,
We care not a rap for the Will, or the cap
which is there on the seal so grand and sedate,
We bid them begone, and be hanged, and ourselves
take charge of the girl and her worthy estate;
And we give her away to whoever we choose,
to whoever may chance to persuade us: yet we,
Whilst other officials must pass an account,
alone from control and accounting are free.

Bd. Ay that, and that only, of all you have said,
I own is a privilege lucky and rare,
But uncapping the seal of the heiress's will
seems rather a shabby and doubtful affair.

Ph. And if ever the Council or People have got
a knotty and difficult case to decide,
They pass a decree for the culprits to go
to the able and popular Courts to be tried:
Evathlus, and He! the loser of shields,
the fawning, the great Cowardonymus say
"They'll always be fighting away for the mob,"
"the people of Athens they'll never betray."
And none in the People a measure can pass,
unless he propose that the Courts shall be free,
Dismissed and discharged for the rest of the day
when once we have settled a single decree.
Yea, Cleon the Bawler and Brawler himself,
at us, and us only, to nibble forbears,
And sweeps off the flies that annoy us, and still
with a vigilant hand for our dignity cares.
You never have shown such attention as this,
or displayed such a zeal in your father's affairs.
Yet Theorus, a statesman as noble and grand
as lordly Euphemius, runs at our call
And whips out a sponge from his bottle, and stoops,
to black and to polish the shoes of us all.
Such, such is the glory, the joy, the renown,
from which you desire to retain and withhold me,
And *this* you will show, this Empire of mine,
to be bondage and slavery merely, you told me.

Bd. Ay, chatter your fill, you will cease before long:
and then I will show that your boasted success

Is just the success of a tail that is washed,
going back to its filth and its slovenliness.
Ph. But the nicest and pleasantest part of it all
is this, which I'd wholly forgotten to say,
'Tis when with my fee in my wallet I come,
returning home at the close of the day,
O then what a welcome I get for its sake;
my daughter, the darling, is foremost of all,
And she washes my feet and anoints them with care,
and above them she stoops, and a kiss lets fall,
Till at last by the pretty Papas of her tongue
she angles withal my three-obol away.
Then my dear little wife, she sets on the board
nice manchets of bread in a tempting array,
And cosily taking a seat by my side,
with loving entreaty constrains me to feed:
"I beseech you taste this, I implore you try that."
This, this I delight in, and ne'er may I need
To look to yourself and your pantler, a scrub
who, whenever I ask him my breakfast to set,
Keeps grumbling and murmuring under his breath.
No! no! if he haste not a manchet to get,
Lo here my defence from the evils of life,
my armour of proof, my impregnable shield.
And what if you pour me no liquor to drink,
yet here's an old Ass, full of wine, that I wield,
And I tilt him, and pour for myself, and imbibe;
whilst sturdy old Jack, as a bumper I drain,
Lets fly at your goblet a bray of contempt,
a mighty and masterful snort of disdain.
Is this not a fine dominion of mine?
Is it less than the empire of Zeus?
Why the very same phrases, so grand and divine,
For me, as for Him, are in use.
For when we are raging loud and high
In stormy, tumultuous din,
"O Lord! O Zeus!" say the passers-by,
"How thunders the Court within!"
The wealthy and great, when my lightnings glare,
Turn pale and sick, and mutter a prayer.
You fear me too: I protest you do:
Yes, yes, by Demeter I vow 'tis true.
But hang me if I am afraid of you.
Ch. I never, no, I never
Have heard so clear and clever
And eloquent a speech—
Ph. Ay, ay, he thought he'd steal my grapes,
and pluck them undefended,
For well he knew that I'm in this
particularly splendid.
Ch. No topic he omitted,
But he duly went through each.
I waxed in size to hear him
Till with ecstasy possessed
Methought I sat a-judging
In the Islands of the Blest.
Ph. See how uneasily he stands,
and gapes, and shifts his ground.
I warrant, sir, before I've done,
you'll look like a beaten hound.
Ch. You must now, young man, be seeking
Every turn and every twist
Which can your defence assist.
To a youth against me speaking
Mine's a heart 'tis hard to render
(So you'll find it) soft and tender.
And therefore unless you can speak to the point,
you must look for a millstone handy and good,
Fresh hewn from the rock, to shiver and shock
the unyielding grit of my resolute mood.
Bd. Hard were the task, and shrewd the intent,
for a Comedy-poet all too great
To attempt to heal an inveterate, old
disease engrained in the heart of the state.
Yet, O dread Cronides, Father and Lord,
Ph. Stop, stop, don't talk in that father-me way,
Convince me at once that I'm only a slave,
or else I protest you shall die this day
Albeit I then must ever abstain
from the holy flesh of the victims slain.
Bd. Then listen my own little pet Papa,
and smooth your brow from its frowns again.
And not with pebbles precisely ranged,
but roughly thus on your fingers count
The tribute paid by the subject States,
and just consider its whole amount;
And then, in addition to this, compute
the many taxes and one-per-cents,
The fees and the fines, and the silver mines,
the markets and harbours and sales and rents.
If you take the total result of the lot,
'twill reach two thousand talents or near.
And next put down the Justices' pay,
and reckon the sums they receive a year:
Six thousand Justices, count them through,
there dwell no more in the land as yet,
One hundred and fifty talents a year
I think you will find is all they get.
Ph. Then not one tithe of our income goes
to furnish forth the Justices' pay.
Bd. No, certainly not.
Ph. And what becomes
of all the rest of the revenue, pray?
Bd. Why, bless you, it goes to the pockets of those,
"To the rabble of Athens I'll ever be true,
I'll always battle away for the mob."
O father, my father, 'tis owing to you:
By such small phrases as these cajoled,
you lift them over yourselves to reign.
And then, believe me, they soon contrive
some fifty talents in bribes to gain,
Extorting them out of the subject states,
by hostile menace and angry frown:
"Hand over," they say, "the tribute-pay,
or else my thunders shall crush your town."
You joy the while at the remnants vile,
the trotters and tips of your power to gnaw.
So when our knowing, acute allies
the rest, the scum of the Populace, saw
On a vote-box pine, and on nothingness dine,
and marked how lanky and lean ye grow,

They count you all as a Connas's vote,
and ever and ever on these bestow
Wines, cheeses, necklaces, sesamè fruit,
and jars of pickle and pots of honey,
Rugs, cushions, and mantles, and cups, and crowns,
and health, and vigour, and lots of money.
Whilst *you!* from out of the broad domain
for which on the land and the wave you toiled,
None gives you so much as a garlic head,
to flavour the dish when your sprats are boiled.
Ph. That's true no doubt, for I just sent out,
and bought, myself, from Eucharides three:
But you wear me away by your long delay
in proving my bondage and slavery.
Bd. Why *is* it not slavery pure and neat,
when these (themselves and their parasites too)
Are all in receipt of their pay, God wots,
as high officials of state: whilst you
Must thankful be for your obols three,
those obols which ye yourselves have won
In the battle's roar, by sea and by shore,
'mid sieges and miseries many a one.
But O what throttles me most of all,
is this, that under constraint you go,
When some young dissolute spark comes in,
some son of a Chaereas, straddling—so,
With his legs apart, and his body poised,
and a mincing, soft, effeminate air,
And bids you Justices, one and all,
betimes in the morn to the Court repair,
For that any who after the signal come
shall lose and forfeit their obols three.
Yet come as late as he choose himself,
he pockets his drachma, "Counsel's fee."
And then if a culprit give him a bribe,
he gets his fellow the job to share,
And into each other's hands they play,
and manage together the suit to square.
Just like two men at a saw they work,
and one keeps pulling, and one gives way.
While you at the Treasurer stare and gape,
and never observe the tricks they play.
Ph. Is *that* what they do! O can it be true!
Ah me, the depths of my being are stirred,
Your statements shake my soul, and I feel
I know not how, at the things I've heard.
Bd. And just consider when you and all
might revel in affluence, free as air,
How these same demagogues wheel you round,
and cabin and coop you I know not where.
And you, the lord of such countless towns,
from Pontus to Sardo, nought obtain
Save this poor pittance you earn, and this
they dole you in driblets, grain by grain,
As though they were dropping oil from wool,
as much forsooth as will life sustain.
They *mean* you all to be poor and gaunt,
and I'll tell you, father, the reason why.
They want you to know your keeper's hand;
and then if he hiss you on to fly
At some helpless foe, away you go,
with eager vehemence ready and rough.
Since if they wished to maintain you well,
the way to do it were plain enough.
A thousand cities our rule obey,
a thousand cities their tribute pay,
Allot them twenty Athenians each,
to feed and nourish from day to day,
And twice ten thousand citizens there,
are living immersed in dishes of hare,
With creams and beestings and sumptuous fare,
and garlands and coronals everywhere,
Enjoying a fate that is worthy the state,
and worthy the trophy on Marathon plain.
Whilst now like gleaners ye all are fain
to follow along in the paymaster's train.
Ph. O what can this strange sensation mean,
this numbness that over my hand is stealing?
My arm no longer can hold the sword:
I yield, unmanned, to a womanish feeling.
Bd. Let a panic possess them, they're ready to give
Euboea at once for the State to divide,
And engage to supply for every man
full fifty bushels of wheat beside.
But five poor bushels of barley each
is all that you ever obtained in fact,
And that doled out by the quart, while first
they worry you under the Alien Act.
And therefore it was that I locked you away
To keep you in ease; unwilling that these
With empty mouthings your age should bilk.
And now I offer you here to-day
Without any reserve whatever you please,
Save only a draught of—Treasurer's milk.
Ch. 'Twas a very acute and intelligent man,
whoever it was, that happened to say,
"Don't make up your mind till you've heard both sides,"
for now I protest you have gained the fray.
Our staves of justice, our angry mood,
for ever and ever aside we lay.
And we turn to talk to our old compeer,
our choir-companion of many a day.
Don't be a fool: give in, give in,
Nor too perverse and stubborn be;
I would to Heaven my kith and kin
Would show the like regard for me.
Some deity, 'tis plain, befriends
Your happy lot, believe, believe it;
With open arms his aid he sends,
Do you with open arms receive it.
Bd. I'll give him whatever his years require,
A basin of gruel, and soft attire,
And a good warm rug, and a handmaid fair,
To chafe and cherish his limbs with care.
—But I can't like this, that he stands so mute,
And speaks not a word nor regards my suit.
Ch. 'Tis that his soberer thoughts review
The frenzy he indulged so long,
And (what he would not yield to you)
He feels his former life was wrong.
Perchance he'll now amend his plan,
Unbend his age to mirth and laughter,

A better and a wiser man
By your advice he'll live hereafter.
Ph. O misery! O misery!
Bd. O father, why that dolorous cry?
Ph. Talk not of things like these to me!
Those are my pleasures, *there* would I be
Where the Usher cries
"Who has not voted? let him arise."
And O that the last of the voting band
By the verdict-box I could take my stand.
On, on, my soul! why, where is she gone?
Hah! by your leave, my shadowy one!
Zounds, if I catch when in Court I'm sitting
Cleon again a theft committing!
Bd. O father, father, by the Gods comply.
Ph. Comply with what? name any wish, save one.
Bd. Save what, I prithee?
Ph. Not to judge; but that
Hades shall settle ere my soul comply.
Bd. Well but if these are really your delights,
Yet why go *There*? why not remain at home
And sit and judge among your household here?
Ph. Folly! judge what?
Bd. The same as There you do.
Suppose you catch your housemaid on the sly
Opening the door: fine her for that, one drachma.
That's what you did at every sitting There.
And very aptly, if the morning's fine,
You'll fine your culprits, sitting in the sun.
In snow, enter your judgements by the fire
While it rains on: and—though you sleep till midday,
No archon here will close the door against you.
Ph. Hah! I like that.
Bd. And then, however long
An orator proses on, no need to fast,
Worrying yourself (ay, and the prisoner too).
Ph. But do you really think that I can judge
As well as now, whilst eating and digesting?
Bd. As well? much better. When there's reckless swearing,
Don't people say, what time and thought and trouble
It took the judges to digest the case?
Ph. I'm giving in. But you've not told me yet
How I'm to get my pay.
Bd. I'll pay you.
Ph. Good,
Then I shall have mine to myself, alone;
For once Lysistratus, the funny fool,
Played me the scurviest trick. We'd got one drachma
Betwixt us two: he changed it at the fish-stall;
Then laid me down three mullet scales: and I,
I thought them obols, popped them in my mouth;
O the vile smell! O la! I spat them out
And collared him.
Bd. And what said he?
Ph. The rascal!
He said I'd got the stomach of a cock.
"You'll soon digest hard coin," he says, says he.
Bd. Then there again you'll get a great advantage.
Ph. Ay, ay, that's something: let's begin at once.
Bd. Then stop a moment whilst I fetch the traps. *Exit.*
Ph. See here now, how the oracles come true.
Oft have I heard it said that the Athenians
One day would try their lawsuits in their homes,
That each would have a little Courtlet built
For his own use, in his own porch, before
His entrance, like a shrine of Hecate.
Bd. (*bustling in with a quantity of judicial properties*)
Now then I hope you're satisfied: I've brought
All that I promised, and a lot besides.
See here I'll hang this vessel on a peg,
In case you want it as the suit proceeds.
Ph. Now that I call extremely kind and thoughtful,
And wondrous handy for an old man's needs.
Bd. And here's a fire, and gruel set beside it,
All ready when you want it.
Ph. Good again.
Now if I'm feverish I shan't lose my pay,
For here I'll sit, and sip my gruel too.
But why in the world have ye brought me out the cock?
Bd. To wake you, father, crowing over head
In case you're dozing whilst a prisoner pleads.
Ph. One thing I miss, and only one.
Bd. What's that?
Ph. If you could somehow fetch the shrine of Lycus!
Bd. Here then it is, and here's the king in person.
Ph. O hero lord, how stern you are to see!
Bd. Almost, methinks, like our—Cleonymus.
Xa. Ay, and 'tis true the hero has no shield!
Bd. If you got seated sooner, I should sooner
Call a suit on.
Ph. Call on, I've sat for ages.
Bd. Let's see: what matter shall I bring on first?
Who's been at mischief of the household here?
That careless Thratta now, she charred the pitcher.
Ph. O stop, for goodness' sake! you've all but killed me.
What! call a suit on with no railing here,
Always the first of all our sacred things?
Bd. No more there is, by Zeus.
Ph. I'll run myself
And forage out whatever comes to hand. *Exit.*
Bd. Heyday! where now? The strange infatuation!
Enter XANTHIAS.
Xa. Psha! rot the dog! To keep a cur like this!
Bd. What's happened now?
Xa. Why, has not Labes here
Got to the kitchen safe, and grabbed a cheese,
A rich Sicilian cheese, and bolted it?
Bd. Then that's the first indictment we'll bring on
Before my father: you shall prosecute.
Xa. Thank you, not I. This other Cur declares
If there's a charge, he'll prosecute with pleasure.
Bd. Bring them both here.
Xa. Yes, yes, sir, so I will. *Exit.*
Enter PHILOCLEON.

Bd. (*to* PHILOCLEON) Hallo, what's this?
Ph. Pig-railings from the hearth.
Bd. Sacrilege, eh?
Ph. No, but I'd trounce some fellow
(As the phrase goes) even from the very hearth.
So call away: I'm keen for passing sentence.
Bd. Then now I'll fetch the cause-lists and the pleadings. *Exit.*
Ph. O these delays! You weary and wear me out.
I've long been dying to commence my furrows.
Bd. (*re-entering*) Now then!
Ph. Call on.
Bd. Yes, certainly.
Ph. And who
Is first in order?
Bd. Dash it, what a bother!
I quite forgot to bring the voting-urns.
Ph. Goodness! where now?
Bd. After the urns.
Ph. Don't trouble,
I'd thought of that. I've got these ladling-bowls.
Bd. That's capital: then now methinks we have
All that we want. No, there's no water-piece.
Ph. Water-piece, quotha! pray what call you this?
Bd. Well thought on, father: and with shrewd home wit.
Ho, there within! some person bring me out
A pan of coals, and frankincense, and myrtle,
That so our business may commence with prayer.
Ch. We too, as ye offer the prayer and wine,
We too will call on the Powers Divine
To prosper the work begun;
For the battle is over and done,
And out of the fray and the strife to-day
Fair peace ye have nobly won.
Bd. Now hush all idle words and sounds profane.
Ch. O Pythian Phoebus, bright Apollo, deign
To speed this youth's design
Wrought here, these gates before,
And give us from our wanderings rest
And peace for evermore.
The shout of "Io Paean" is raised.
Bd. Aguieus! my neighbour and hero and lord! who dwellest in front of my vestibule gate,
I pray thee be graciously pleased to accept the rite that we new for my father create.
O bend to a pliant and flexible mood the stubborn and resolute oak of his will.
And into his heart, so crusty and tart, a trifle of honey for syrup instil.
Endue him with sympathies wide,
A sweet and humane disposition,
Which leans to the side of the wretch that is tried,
And weeps at a culprit's petition.
From harshness and anger to turn,
May it now be his constant endeavour,
And out of his temper the stern
Sharp sting of the nettle to sever.
Ch. We in thy prayers combine, and quite give in
To the new rule, for the aforesaid reasons.
Our heart has stood our friend
And loved you, since we knew
That you affect the people more
Than other young men do.
Enter XANTHIAS *with two persons as dogs.*
Bd. Is any Justice out there? let him enter.
We shan't admit him when they've once begun.
Ph. Where is the prisoner fellow? won't he catch it!
Bd. O yes! attention! (*Reads the indictment*) "Cur of Cydathon
Hereby accuses Labes of Aexone,
For that, embezzling a Sicilian cheese,
Alone he ate it. Fine, one fig-tree collar."
Ph. Nay, but a dog's death, an' he's once convicted.
Bd. Here stands, to meet the charge, the prisoner Labes.
Ph. O the vile wretch! O what a thievish look!
See how he grins, and thinks to take me in.
Where's the Accuser, Cur of Cydathon?
Cur. Bow!
Bd. Here he stands.
Xa. Another Labes this,
Good dog to yelp and lick the platters clean.
Bd. St! take your seat. (*to* CUR) Go up and prosecute.
Ph. Meanwhile I'll ladle out and sip my gruel.
Xa. Ye have heard the charge, most honourable judges,
I bring against him. Scandalous the trick
He played us all, me and the Sailor-laddies.
Alone, in a corner, in the dark, he gorged,
And munched, and crunched, and Siciliced the cheese!
Ph. Pheugh! the thing's evident: the brute this instant
Breathed in my face the filthiest whiff of cheese.
O the foul skunk!
Xa. And would not give me any,
Not though I asked. Yet can *he* be your friend
Who won't throw anything to Me, the dog?
Ph. Not give you any! No, nor Me, the state.
The man's a regular scorcher (*burns his mouth*), like this gruel.
Bd. Come don't decide against us, pray don't, father,
Before you've heard both sides.
Ph. But, my dear boy,
The thing's self-evident, speaks for itself.
Xa. Don't let him off; upon my life he is
The most lone-eatingest dog that ever was.
The brute went coasting round and round the mortar,
And snapped up all the rind off all the cities.
Ph. And I've no mortar even to mend my pitcher!
Xa. So then be sure you punish him. For why?
One bush, they say, can never keep two thieves.
Lest I should bark, and bark, and yet get nothing.
And if I do I'll never bark again.
Ph. Soh! soh!
Here's a nice string of accusations truly!
A rare thief of a man! You think so too,

Old gamecock? Ay, he winks his eye, he thinks so.
Archon! Hi, fellow, hand me down the vessel.
Bd. Reach it yourself; I'll call my witnesses.
The witnesses for Labes, please stand forward!
Pot, pestle, grater, brazier, water-jug,
And all the other scarred and charred utensils.
(*To* PHILOCLEON)
Good heavens, sir, finish there, and take your seat!
Ph. I guess I'll finish *him* before I've done.
Bd. What! always hard and pitiless, and that
To the prisoners, always keen to bite!
(*To* LABES)
Up, plead your cause: what, quite dumbfounded? speak.
Ph. Seems he's got nothing in the world to say.
Bd. Nay, 'tis a sudden seizure, such as once
Attacked Thucydides when brought to trial.
'Tis tongue-paralysis that stops his jaws.
(*To* LABES)
Out of the way! I'll plead your cause myself.
O sirs, 'tis hard to argue for a dog
Assailed by slander: nevertheless, I'll try.
'Tis a good dog, and drives away the wolves.
Ph. A thief I call him, and *conspirator*.
Bd. Nay, he's the best and worthiest dog alive,
Fit to take charge of any number o' sheep.
Ph. What use in that, if he eat up the cheese?
Bd. Use! why, he fights your battles, guards your door;
The best dog altogether. If he filched,
Yet O forgive: he never learnt the lyre.
Ph. I would to heaven he had never learned his letters,
Then he'd not given us all this tiresome speech.
Bd. Nay, nay, sir, hear my witnesses, I beg.
Grater, get in the box, and speak well out.
You kept the mess; I ask you, answer plainly,
Did you not grate the spoil between the soldiers?
He says he did.
Ph. Ay, but I vow he's lying.
Bd. O sir, have pity upon poor toiling souls.
Our Labes here, he lives on odds and ends,
Bones, gristle: and is always on the go.
That other Cur is a mere stay-at-home,
Sits by the hearth, and when one brings aught in
Asks for a share: if he gets none, he bites.
Ph. O me, what ails me that I grow so soft!
Some ill's afoot: I'm nearly giving in.
Bd. O, I beseech you, father, show some pity,
Don't crush him quite. Where are his little cubs?
Enter a group of children dressed as puppies.
Up, little wretches, up; and whimpering there
Plead for your father: weep, implore, beseech.
Ph. (*deeply affected*) Get down, get down, get down, get down.
Bd. I will.
Yet that "get down," I know, has taken in
A many men. However I'll get down.
Ph. Dash it! this guzzling ain't the thing at all.
Here was I shedding tears, and seems to me
Only because I have gorged myself with gruel.
Bd. Then will he not get off?
Ph. 'Tis hard to know.
Bd. O take, dear father, take the kindlier turn.
Here, hold this vote: then with shut eyes dash by
To the Far Urn. O father, do acquit him.
Ph. No, no, my boy. I never learnt the lyre.
Bd Here, let me lead you round the handiest way.
Ph. Is this the Nearer?
Bd. This is.
Ph. In she goes.
Bd. (*aside*) Duped, as I live! acquits him by mistake!
(*aloud*) I'll do the counting.
Ph. Well, how went the battle?
Bd. We shall soon see. O Labes, you're acquitted!
Why, how now, father?
Ph. (*faintly*) Water, give me water!
Bd. Hold up, sir, do.
Ph. Just tell me only this,
Is he *indeed* acquitted?
Bd. Yes.
Ph. I'm done for.
Bd. Don't take it so to heart: stand up, sir, pray.
Ph. How shall I bear this sin upon my soul?
A man acquitted! What awaits me now?
Yet, O great gods! I pray you pardon me,
Unwilled I did it, not from natural bent.
Bd. And don't begrudge it; for I'll tend you well,
And take you, father, everywhere with me,
To feasts, to suppers, to the public games.
Henceforth in pleasure you shall spend your days,
And no Hyperbolus delude and mock you.
But go we in.
Ph. Yes, if you wish it, now.
Exeunt all but CHORUS.

Chorus

Yea, go rejoicing your own good way,
Wherever your path may be;
But you, ye numberless myriads, stay
And listen the while to me.
Beware lest the truths I am going to say
Unheeded to earth should fall;
For that were the part of a fool to play,
And not your part at all.

Now *all* ye people attend and hear,
if ye love a simple and genuine strain.
For now our poet, with right good will,
of you, spectators, must needs complain.
Ye have wronged him much, he protests, a bard
who had served you often and well before;
Partly, indeed, himself unseen,
assisting others to please you more;
With the art of a Eurycles, weird and wild,
he loved to dive in a stranger's breast,
And pour from thence through a stranger's lips
full many a sparkling comical jest;
And partly at length in his own true form,
as he challenged his fate by himself alone,
And the Muses whose bridled mouths he drave,
were never another's, were all his own.

And thus he came to a height of fame
which none had ever achieved before,
Yet waxed not high in his own conceit,
nor ever an arrogant mind he bore.
He never was found in the exercise-ground,
corrupting the boys: he never complied
With the suit of some dissolute knave, who loathed
that the vigilant lash of the bard should chide
His vile effeminate boylove. No!
he kept to his purpose pure and high,
That never the Muse, whom he loved to use,
the villainous trade of a bawd should ply.
When first he began to exhibit plays,
no paltry *men* for his mark he chose,
He came in the mood of a Heracles forth
to grapple at once with the mightiest foes.
In the very front of his bold career
with the jag-toothed Monster he closed in fight,
Though out of its fierce eyes flashed and flamed
the glare of Cynna's detestable light,
And a hundred horrible sycophants' tongues
were twining and flickering over its head,
And a voice it had like the roar of a stream
which has just brought forth destruction and dread,
And a Lamia's groin, and a camel's loin,
and foul as the smell of a seal it smelt.
But He, when the monstrous form he saw,
no bribe he took and no fear he felt,
For you he fought, and for you he fights:
and then last year with adventurous hand
He grappled besides with the Spectral Shapes,
the Agues and Fevers that plagued our land;
That loved in the darksome hours of night
to throttle fathers, and grandsires choke,
That laid them down on their restless beds,
and against your quiet and peaceable folk
Kept welding together proofs and writs
and oath against oath, till many a man
Sprang up, distracted with wild affright,
and off in haste to the Polemarch ran.
Yet although such a champion as this ye had found,
to purge your land from sorrow and shame,
Ye played him false when to reap, last year,
the fruit of his novel designs he came,
Which, failing to see in their own true light,
ye caused to fade and wither away.
And yet with many a deep libation,
invoking Bacchus, he swears this day
That never a man, since the world began,
has witnessed a cleverer comedy.
Yours is the shame that ye lacked the wit
its infinite merit at first to see.
But none the less with the wise and skilled
the bard his accustomed praise will get,
Though when he had distanced all his foes,
his noble Play was at last upset.

But O for the future, my Masters, pray
Show more regard for a genuine Bard
Who is ever inventing amusements new
And fresh discoveries, all for you.
Make much of his play, and store it away,
And into your wardrobe throw it
With the citrons sweet: and if this you do,
Your clothes will be fragrant, the whole year through,
With the volatile wit of the Poet.

O of old renowned and strong,
in the choral dance and song,
In the deadly battle throng,
And in this, our one distinction,
manliest we, mankind among!
Ah, but that was long ago:
Those are days forever past:
Now my hairs are whitening fast,
Whiter than the swan they grow.
Yet in these our embers low
still some youthful fires must glow.
Better far our old-world fashion,
Better far our ancient truth,
Than the curls and dissipation
Of your modern youth.

Do *you* wonder, O spectators,
thus to see me spliced and braced,
Like a wasp in form and figure,
tapering inwards at the waist?
Why I am so, what's the meaning
of this sharp and pointed sting,
Easily I now will teach you,
though you "knew not anything."
We on whom this stern-appendage,
this portentous tail is found,
Are the genuine old Autochthons,
native children of the ground;
We the only true-born Attics,
of the staunch heroic breed,
Many a time have fought for Athens,
guarding her in hours of need;
When with smoke and fire and rapine
forth the fierce Barbarian came,
Eager to destroy our wasps-nests,
smothering all the town in flame,
Out at once we rushed to meet him:
on with shield and spear we went,
Fought the memorable battle,
primed with fiery hardiment;
Man to man we stood, and, grimly,
gnawed for rage our under lips.
Hah! their arrows hail so densely,
all the sun is in eclipse!
Yet we drove their ranks before us,
ere the fall of eventide:
As we closed, an owl flew o'er us,
and the Gods were on our side!
Stung in jaw, and cheek, and eyebrow,
fearfully they took to flight,
We behind them, we harpooning
at their slops with all our might:
So that in barbarian countries,
even now the people call
Attic wasps the best, and bravest,
yea, the manliest tribe of all!

Mine was then a life of glory,
never craven fear came o'er me
Every foeman quailed before me
As across the merry waters,
fast the eager galleys bore me.
'Twas not then our manhood's test,
Who can make a fine oration?
Who is shrewd in litigation?
It was, "*Who can row the best?*"
Therefore did we batter down
many a hostile Median town.
And 'twas we who for the nation
Gathered in the tribute pay,
Which the younger generation
Merely steal away.

You will find us very wasplike,
if you scan us through and through,
In our general mode of living,
and in all our habits too.
First, if any rash assailant dare provoke us, can
there be
Any creature more vindictive,
more irascible than we?
Then we manage all our business
in a waspish sort of way,
Swarming in the Courts of Justice,
gathering in from day to day,
Many where the Eleven invite us,
many where the Archon calls,
Many to the great Odeum, many to the city walls.
There we lay our heads together,
densely packed, and stooping low,
Like the grubs within their cells, with
movement tremulous and slow.
And for ways and means in general
we're superlatively good,
Stinging every man about us,
culling thence a livelihood
Yet we've stingless drones amongst us,
idle knaves who sit them still,
Shrink from work, and toil, and labour,
stop at home, and eat their fill,
Eat the golden tribute-honey
our industrious care has wrought.
This is what extremely grieves us,
that a man who never fought
Should contrive our fees to pilfer,
one who for his native land
Never to this day had oar, or
lance, or blister in his hand.
Therefore let us for the future
pass a little short decree,
"Whoso wears no sting shall never carry off the
obols three."

Enter PHILOCLEON *and* BDELYCLEON.

Ph. No! No! I'll never put this off alive.
With this I was arrayed, and found my safety,
In the invasion of the great north wind.
Bd. You seem unwilling to accept a good.
Ph. 'Tis not expedient: no by Zeus it is not.
'Twas but the other day I gorged on sprats
And had to pay three obols to the fuller.
Bd. Try it at all events: since once for all
Into my hands you have placed yourself for good.
Ph. What would you have me do?
Bd. Put off that cloak.
And wear this mantle in a cloak-like way.
Ph. Should we beget and bring up children then,
When here my son is bent on smothering me?
Bd. Come, take and put it on, and don't keep chattering.
Ph. Good heavens! and what's this misery of a thing?
Bd. Some call it Persian, others Caunacès.
Ph. There! and I thought it a Thymaetian rug.
Bd. No wonder: for you've never been to Sardis,
Else you'd have known it: now you don't.
Ph. Who? I?
No more I do by Zeus: it seemed to me
Most like an overwrap of Morychus.
Bd. Nay, in Ecbatana they weave this stuff.
Ph. What! have they wool-guts in Ecbatana?
Bd. Tut, man: they weave it in their foreign looms
At wondrous cost: this very article
Absorbed with ease a talent's weight of wool.
Ph. Why, then, *wool-gatherer* were its proper name
Instead of Caunacès.
Bd. Come, take it, take it,
Stand still and put it on.
Ph. O dear, O dear,
O what a sultry puff the brute breathed o'er me!
Bd. Quick, wrap it round you.
Ph. No, I won't, that's flat.
You had better wrap me in a stove at once.
Bd. Come then, I'll throw it round you.
(*to the cloak*) You, begone.
Ph. Do keep a flesh-hook near.
Bd. A flesh-hook! why?
Ph. To pull me out before I melt away.
Bd. Now off at once with those confounded shoes,
And on with these Laconians, instantly.
Ph. What I, my boy! I bring myself to wear
The hated foe's insufferable—cloutings!
Bd. Come, sir, insert your foot, and step out firmly
In this Laconian.
Ph. 'Tis too bad, it is,
To make a man set foot on hostile—leather.
Bd. Now for the other.
Ph. O no, pray not that,
I've a toe there, a regular Lacon-hater.
Bd. There is no way but this.
Ph. O luckless I,
Why I shan't have, to bless my age, one—chilblain.
Bd. Quick, father, get them on: and then move forward
Thus; in an opulent swaggering sort of way.
Ph. Look then! observe my attitudes: think which
Of all your opulent friends I walk most like.
Bd. Most like a pimple bandaged round with garlic.

Ph. Ay, ay, I warrant I've a mind for wriggling.
Bd. Come, if you get with clever well-read men
Could you tell tales, good gentlemanly tales?
Ph. Ay, that I could.
Bd. What sort of tales?
Ph. Why, lots,
As, first, how Lamia spluttered when they caught her,
And, next, Cardopion, how he swinged his mother.
Bd. Pooh, pooh, no legends: give us something human,
Some what we call domestic incident.
Ph. O, ay, I know a rare domestic tale,
"How once upon a time a cat and mouse—"
Bd. "O fool and clown," Theogenes replied
Rating the scavenger, what! would you tell
Tales of a cat and mouse, in company!
Ph. What, then?
Bd. Some stylish thing, as how you went
With Androcles and Cleisthenes, surveying.
Ph. Why, bless the boy, I never went surveying,
Save once to Paros, at two obols a day.
Bd. Still you must tell how splendidly, for instance,
Ephudion fought the pancratiastic fight
With young Ascondas: how the game old man
Though grey, had ample sides, strong hands, firm flanks,
An iron chest.
Ph. What humbug! could a man
Fight the pancratium with an iron chest!
Bd. This is the way our clever fellows talk.
But try another tack: suppose you sat
Drinking with strangers, what's the pluckiest feat,
Of all your young adventures, you could tell them?
Ph. My pluckiest feat? O much my pluckiest, much,
Was when I stole away Ergasion's vine-poles.
Bd. Tcha! poles indeed! Tell how you slew the boar,
Or coursed the hare, or ran the torch-race, tell
Your gayest, youthfullest act.
Ph. My youthfullest action?
'Twas that I had, when quite a hobbledehoy,
With fleet Phaÿllus: and I caught him too:
Won by two—votes. 'Twas for abuse, that action.
Bd. No more of that: but lie down there, and learn
To be convivial and companionable.
Ph. Yes; how lie down?
Bd. In an elegant graceful way.
Ph. Like this, do you mean?
Bd. No, not in the least like that.
Ph. How then?
Bd. Extend your knees, and let yourself
With practised ease subside along the cushions;
Then praise some piece of plate: inspect the ceiling;
Admire the woven hangings of the hall.
Ho! water for our hands! bring in the tables!
Dinner! the after-wash! now the libation.
Ph. Good heavens! then is it in a dream we are feasting?
Bd. The flute-girl has performed! our fellow-guests
Are Phanus, Aeschines, Theorus, Cleon,
Another stranger at Acestor's head.
Could you with these cap verses properly?
Ph. Could I? Ay, truly; no Diacrian better.
Bd. I'll put you to the proof. Suppose I'm Cleon.
I'll start the catch Harmodius. You're to cap it.
(*singing*) "Truly Athens never knew"
Ph. (*singing*) "Such a rascally thief as you."
Bd. Will you do that? You'll perish in your noise.
He'll swear he'll fell you, quell you, and expel you
Out of this realm.
Ph. Ay, truly, will he so?
And if he threaten, I've another strain.
"Mon, lustin' for power supreme, ye'll mak'
The city capseeze; she's noo on the shak'."
Bd. What if Theorus, lying at his feet,
Should grasp the hand of Cleon, and begin,
"From the story of Admetus learn, my friend, to love the good."
How will you take that on?
Ph. I, very neatly,
"It is not good the fox to play,
Nor to side with both in a false friend's way."
Bd. Next comes that son of Sellus, Aeschines,
Clever, accomplished fellow, and he'll sing
"O the money, O the might,
How Cleitagora and I,
With the men of Thessaly"—
Ph. "How we boasted, you and I."
Bd. Well, that will do: you're fairly up to that:
So come along: we'll dine at Philoctemon's.
Boy! Chrysus! pack our dinner up; and now
For a rare drinking-bout at last.
Ph. No, no,
Drinking ain't good: I know what comes of drinking,
Breaking of doors, assault, and battery,
And then, a headache and a fine to pay.
Bd. Not if you drink with gentlemen, you know.
They'll go to the injured man, and beg you off,
Or you yourself will tell some merry tale,
A jest from Sybaris, or one of Aesop's,
Learned at the feast. And so the matter turns
Into a joke, and off he goes contented.
Ph. O I'll learn plenty of those tales, if so
I can get off, whatever wrong I do.
Come, go we in: let nothing stop us now. *Exeunt.*

Chorus

Often have I deemed myself
exceeding bright, acute, and clever,
Dull, obtuse, and awkward never.
That is what Amynias is,
of Curling-borough, Sellus' son;
Him who now upon an apple
and pomegranate dines, I saw
At Leogoras's table
Eat as hard as he was able,
Goodness, what a hungry maw!
Pinched and keen as Antiphon.

Once he travelled to Pharsalus, our ambassador
to be,
There a solitary guest, he
Stayed with only the Penestae,
Coming from the tribe himself,
the kindred tribe, of Penury.

Fortunate Automenes, we envy your felicity;
Every son of yours is of an infinite dexterity:
First the Harper, known to all, and loved of all
excessively,
Grace and wit attend his steps, and elegant festivity,
Next the Actor, shrewd of wit beyond all
credibility:
Last of all Ariphrades, that soul of ingenuity,
He who of his native wit, with rare originality,
Hit upon an undiscovered trick of bestiality:
All alone, the father tells us, striking out a novel line.

Some there are who said that I
was reconciled in amity,
When upon me Cleon pressed,
and made me smart with injury,
Currying and tanning me:
then as the stripes fell heavily
Th' outsiders laughed to see the sport,
and hear me squalling lustily,
Caring not a whit for me, but only looking merrily,
To know if squeezed and pressed I chanced
to drop some small buffoonery.
Seeing this, I played the ape a little bit undoubtedly.
So then, after all, the Vine-pole
proved unfaithful to the Vine.

Enter XANTHIAS.

Xa. O lucky tortoises, to have such skins,
Thrice lucky for the case upon your ribs:
How well and cunningly your backs are roofed
With tiling strong enough to keep out blows:
Whilst I, I'm cudgelled and tattooed to death.
Ch. How now, my boy? for though a man be old,
Still, if he's beaten, we may call him boy.
Xa. Was not the old man the most outrageous
nuisance,
Much the most drunk and riotous of all?
And yet we'd Lycon, Antiphon, Hippyllus,
Lysistratus, Theophrastus, Phrynichus;
But he was far the noisiest of the lot.
Soon as he'd gorged his fill of the good cheer,
He skipped, he leapt, and laughed, and frisked, and
whinnied,
Just like a donkey on a feed of corn:
And slapped me youthfully, calling "Boy! Boy!"
So then Lysistratus compared him thus:
"Old man," says he, "you're like new wine fermenting,
Or like a sompnour, scampering to its bran."
But he shrieked back, "And you, you're like a locust
That has just shed the lappets of its cloak,
Or Sthenelus, shorn of his goods and chattels."
At this all clapped, save Theophrast; but he
Made a wry face, being forsooth a wit.
"And pray," the old man asked him, "what makes
you
"Give yourself airs, and think yourself so grand,
You grinning flatterer of the well-to-do?"
Thus he kept bantering every guest in turn,
Making rude jokes, and telling idle tales,
In clownish fashion, relevant to nothing.
At last, well drunk, homeward he turns once more,
Aiming a blow at everyone he meets.
Ah! here he's coming; stumbling, staggering on.
Methinks I'll vanish ere I'm slapped again.

Enter PHILOCLEON *with a girl, and* GUEST.

Ph. Up ahoy! out ahoy!
Some of you that follow me
Shall ere long be crying.
If they don't shog off, I swear
I'll frizzle 'em all with the torch I bear,
I'll set the rogues a-frying
Guest. Zounds! we'll all make you pay for this
to-morrow,
You vile old rake, however young you are!
We'll come and cite and summon you all together.
Ph. Yah! hah! summon and cite!
The obsolete notion! don't you know
I'm sick of the names of your suits and
claims.
Faugh! Faugh! Pheugh!
Here's my delight!
Away with the verdict-box! Won't he go?
Where's the Heliast? out of my sight!
My little golden chafer, come up here,
Hold by this rope, a rotten one perchance,
But strong enough for you. Mount up, my dear.
See now, how cleverly I filched you off,
A wanton hussy, flirting with the guests.
You owe me, child, some gratitude for that.
But you're not one to pay your debts, I know.
O no! you'll laugh and chaff and slip away,
That's what you always do. But listen now,
Be a good girl, and don't be disobliging,
And when my son is dead, I'll ransom you,
And make you an honest woman. For indeed
I'm not yet master of my own affairs.
I am so young, and kept so very strict.
My son's my guardian, such a cross-grained man,
A cummin-splitting, mustard-scraping fellow.
He's so afraid that I should turn out badly,
For I'm in truth his only father now.
But here he runs. Belike he's after us.
Quick, little lady, hold these links an instant;
And won't I quiz him boyishly and well,
As he did me before the initiation.
Bd. You there! you there! you old lascivious
dotard!
Enamoured, eh? ay of a fine ripe coffin.
Oh, by Apollo, you shall smart for this!
Ph. Dear, dear, how keen to taste a suit in pickle!
Bd. No quizzing, sir, when you have filched away
The flute-girl from our party.
Ph. Eh? what? flute-girl?
You're out of your mind, or out of your grave, or
something.

Bd. Why, bless the fool, here's Dardanis beside you!
Ph. What, this? why, *this* is a torch in the market-place!
Bd. A torch, man?
Ph. Clearly; pray observe the punctures.
Bd. Then what's this black here, on the top of her head?
Ph. Oh, that's the rosin, oozing while it burns.
Bd. Then this of course is not a woman's arm?
Ph. Of course not; that's a sprouting of the pine.
Bd. Sprouting be hanged.
(*to* DARDANIS) You come along with me.
Ph. Hi! hi! what are you at?
Bd. Marching her off
Out of your reach; a rotten, as I think,
And impotent old man. (*He leads girl into house.*)
Ph. Now look ye here:
Once, when surveying at the Olympian games,
I saw how splendidly Ephudion fought
With young Ascondas: saw the game old man
Up with his fist, and knock the youngster down.
So mind your eye, or you'll be pummelled too.
Bd. (*re-entering*) Troth, you have learned Olympia to some purpose.

Enter BAKING-GIRL *with* CHAEREPHON.

Baking-Girl. Oh, there he is! Oh, pray stand by me now!
There's the old rascal who misused me so,
Banged with his torch, and toppled down from here
Bread worth ten obols, and four loaves to boot.
Bd. There now, you see; troubles and suits once more
Your wine will bring us.
Ph. Troubles? Not at all.
A merry tale or two sets these things right.
I'll soon set matters right with this young woman.
B.-G. No, by the Twain! you shan't escape scot-free,
Doing such damage to the goods of Myrtia,
Sostrata's daughter, and Anchylion's, sir!
Ph. Listen, good woman: I am going to tell you
A pleasant tale.
B.-G. Not me, by Zeus, sir, no!
Ph. At Aesop, as he walked one eve from supper,
There yapped an impudent and drunken bitch.
Then Aesop answered, "O you bitch! you bitch!
If in the stead of that ungodly tongue
You'd buy some wheat, methinks you'd have more sense."
B.-G. Insult me too? I summon you before
The Market Court for damage done my goods,
And for my sompnour have this Chaerephon.
Ph. Nay, nay, but listen if I speak not fair.
Simonides and Lasus once were rivals.
Then Lasus says, "Pish, I don't care," says he.
B.-G. You will, sir, will you?
Ph. And you, Chaerephon,
Are you her sompnour, you, like fear-blanched Ino
Pendent before Euripides's feet?

Exeunt BAKING-GIRL *and* CHAEREPHON.

Bd. See, here's another coming, as I live,
To summon you: at least he has got his sompnour.

Enter COMPLAINANT.

Complainant. O dear! O dear! Old man, I summon you
For outrage.
Bd. Outrage? no, by the Gods, pray don't.
I'll make amends for everything he has done
(Ask what you will), and thank you kindly too.
Ph. Nay, I'll make friends myself without compulsion.
I quite admit the assault and battery.
So tell me which you'll do; leave it to me
To name the compensation I must pay
To make us friends, or will you fix the sum?
Co. Name it yourself: I want no suits nor troubles.
Ph. There was a man of Sybaris, do you know,
Thrown from his carriage, and he cracked his skull,
Quite badly too. Fact was, he could not drive.
There was a friend of his stood by, and said,
"Let each man exercise the art he knows."
So you, run off to Doctor Pittalus.
Bd. Ay, this is like the rest of your behaviour.
Co. (*to* BDELYCLEON) You, sir, yourself, remember what he says.
Ph. Stop, listen. Once in Sybaris a girl
Fractured a jug.
Co. I call you, friend, to witness.
Ph. Just so the jug: *it* called a friend to witness.
Then said the girl of Sybaris, "By'r Lady,[1]
If you would leave off calling friends to witness,
And buy a rivet, you would show more brains."
Co. Jeer, till the Magistrate call on my case.

Exit.

Bd. No, by Demeter, but you shan't stop here,
I'll take and carry you—
Ph. What now!
Bd. What now?
Carry you in: or soon there won't be sompnours
Enough for all your summoning complainants.
Ph. The Delphians once charged Aesop—
Bd. I don't care.
Ph. With having filched a vessel of their God.
But Aesop up and told them that a beetle—
Bd. Zounds! but I'll finish you, beetles and all.

Exeunt PHILOCLEON *and* BDELYCLEON.

Chorus

I envy much his fortune
As he changes from his dry
Ungenial life and manners,
Another path to try.
Now all to soft indulgence
His eager soul will take,
And yet perchance it will not,
For, ah! 'tis hard to break
From all your lifelong habits;
Yet some the change have made,
With other minds consorting,
By other counsels swayed.

[1]Persephone.

With us and all good people
  Great praise Philocleon's son
For filial love and genius
  In this affair has won.
Such sweet and gracious manners
  I never saw before,
Nor ever with such fondness
  My doting heart gushed o'er.
Where proved he not the victor
  In all this wordy strife,
Seeking to raise his father
  To higher paths of life?

Enter XANTHIAS.

Xa. O Dionysus! here's a pretty mess
Into our house some power has whirligigged.
Soon as the old man heard the pipe, and drank
The long untasted wine, he grew so merry
He won't stop dancing all the whole night through
Those strange old dances such as Thespis taught;
And your new bards he'll prove old fools, he says,
Dancing against them in the lists directly.

Re-enter PHILOCLEON *and* BDELYCLEON.

Ph. Who sits, who waits at the entrance gates?
Xa. More and more is this evil advancing!
Ph. Be the bolts undone, we have just begun;
  This, this is the first evolution of dancing.
Xa. First evolution of madness, I think.
Ph. With the strong contortion the ribs twist round,
  And the nostril snorts, and the joints resound,
  And the tendons crack.
Xa. O, hellebore drink!
Ph. Cocklike, Phrynichus crouches and cowers,
Xa. You'll strike by and by.
Ph. Then he kicks his leg to the wondering sky,
Xa. O look to yourself, look out, look out.
Ph. For now in these sinewy joints of ours
  The cup-like socket is twirled about.
Bd. 'Twon't do, by Zeus: 'twon't do: 'tis downright madness.
Ph. Come on, I challenge all the world to dance.
Now what tragedian thinks he dances well,
Let him come in and dance a match with me.
Well, is there one, or none?
Bd. Here's only one.

Enter Dancer as a crab.

Ph. Who's he, poor devil?
Bd. 'Tis the midmost son
Of poet Carcinus, the Crabbe.
Ph. I'll eat him.
'Sdeath! I'll destroy him with a knuckle-dance.
He's a born fool at rhythm.
Bd. Nay, but look here!
Here comes a brother crab, another son
Of Carcinus.

Enter another Dancer.

Ph. 'Faith, I've got crab enough.
Bd. Nothing but crabs! 'fore Zeus, nothing but crabs!
Here creeps a third of Carcinus's brood.
Ph. Heyday! what's this? a vinaigrette, or spider?

Enter a third Dancer.

Bd. This is the Pinnoteer, of all the tribe
The tiniest crab: a tragic poet too!
Ph. O Carcinus! O proud and happy father!
Here's a fine troop of wrynecks settling down.
Well, I must gird me to the fight: and you,
Mix pickles for these crabs, in case I beat them.
Ch. Come draw we aside, and leave them a wide,
  a roomy and peaceable exercise-ground,
That before us therein like tops they may spin,
  revolving and whirling and twirling around.
O lofty-titled sons of the ocean-roving sire,
Ye brethren of the shrimps, come and leap
On the sand and on the strand
  of the salt and barren deep.
Whisk nimble feet around you;
  kick out, till all admire,
The Phrynichean kick to the sky;
That the audience may applaud,
  as they view your leg on high.
On, on, in mazy circles; hit your stomach with your heel
Fling legs aloft to heaven,
  as like spinning-tops you wheel.
Your Sire is creeping onward, the Ruler of the Sea,
He gazes with delight at his hobby-dancers three.
Come, dancing as you are, if you like it, lead away,
For never yet, I warrant, has an actor till to-day
Led out a chorus, dancing, at the ending of the Play.

THE PEACE

DRAMATIS PERSONAE

TWO SERVANTS OF TRYGAEUS	A CREST-MAKER
TRYGAEUS	A BREASTPLATE-SELLER
DAUGHTERS OF TRYGAEUS	A TRUMPETER
HERMES	A HELMET-SELLER
WAR	A SPEAR-BURNISHER
RIOT	SON OF LAMACHUS
HIEROCLES	SON OF CLEONYMUS
A SICKLE-MAKER	CHORUS OF FARMERS

The scene represents the exterior of the house of TRYGAEUS, *two of whose* SERVANTS *are visible in the foreground, ministering to the wants of an enormous dung-beetle, which is confined in one of the outer courts, the walls of the court being sufficiently high to conceal its inmate from the audience.*

1st Servant. Bring, bring the beetle cake;
quick there, quick! quick.
2nd Servant. Here!
1st S. Give it him, the abominable brute.
2nd S. O may he never taste a daintier morsel!
1st S. Now bring another, shaped from asses' dung.
2nd S. Here, here again.
1st S. Where's that you brought just now?
He can't have eaten it.
2nd S. No; he trundled it
With his two feet, and bolted it entire.
1st S. Quick, quick, and beat up several, firm and tight.
2nd S. O help me, scavengers, by all the Gods!
Or I shall choke and die before your eyes.
1st S. Another cake, a boy-companion's bring him:
He wants one finelier moulded.
2nd S. Here it is.
There's one advantage in this work, my masters:
No man will say I pick my dishes now.
1st S. Pah! more, bring more, another and another;
Keep kneading more.
2nd S. By Apollo, no, not I!
I can't endure this muck a moment longer;
I'll take and pitch the muck-tub in and all.
1st S. Aye to the crows, and follow it yourself.
2nd S. Can any one of you, I wonder, tell me
Where I can buy a nose not perforated?
There's no more loathly miserable task
Than to be mashing dung to feed a beetle.
A pig or dog will take its bit of muck
Just as it falls: but this conceited brute
Gives himself airs, and, bless you, he won't touch it
Unless I mash it all day long, and serve it
As for a lady, in a rich round cake.
Now I'll peep in and see if he has done,
Holding the door, thus, that he mayn't observe me.
Aye, tuck away; go gobbling on, don't stop;
I hope you'll burst yourself before you know it.
Wretch! how he throws himself upon his food,
Squared like a wrestler, grappling with his jaws,
Twisting his head and hands, now here, now there,
For all the world like men who plait and weave
Those great thick ropes to tow the barges with.
'Tis a most stinking, foul, voracious brute.
Nor can I tell whose appanage he is:
I really think he can't be Aphrodite's,
Nor yet the Graces'.
1st S. No? then whose?
2nd S. I take it
This is the sign of sulphur-bolting Zeus.
Now I suspect some pert young witling there
Is asking, "Well, but what's it all about?
What can the beetle mean?" And then I think
That some Ionian, sitting by, will answer,
"Now, I've nae doubt but this is aimed at Cleon,
It eats the muck sae unco shamelessly."
But I will in, and give the beetle drink.
1st S. And I will tell the story to the boys,
And to the lads, and also to the men,
And to the great and mighty men among you,
And to the greatest mightiest men of all.
My master's mad; a novel kind of madness,
Not your old style, but quite a new invention.
For all day long he gazes at the sky,
His mouth wide open, thus; and rails at Zeus:
"O Zeus," says he, "what seekest thou to do?
Lay down thy besom, sweep not Hellas bare!"
Trygaeus. (*behind the scenes*) Ah me! Ah me!
2nd S. Hush! for methinks I hear him speaking now.
Tr. (*behind the scenes*) O Zeus,
What wouldest thou with our people? Thou wilt drain
The lifeblood from our cities ere thou knowest!
2nd S. Aye, there it is; that's just what I was saying:
Ye hear yourselves a sample of his ravings.
But what he did when first the frenzy seized him
I'll tell you; he kept muttering to himself,
"Oh if I could but somehow get to Zeus!"
With that he got thin scaling ladders made,

And tried by them to scramble up to heaven,
Till he came tumbling down, and cracked his skull.
Then yesterday he stole I know not whither,
And brought a huge Aetnaean beetle home,
And made me groom it, while he coaxed it down
Like a young favourite colt, and kept on saying,
"Wee Pegasus, my flying thoroughbred,
Your wings must waft me straight away to Zeus!"
Now I'll peep in and see what he's about.
Oh, mercy on us! neighbours! neighbours! help!
My master's got astride upon the beetle,
And up they go ascending in the air.

Enter TRYGAEUS *on a great dung-beetle with wings spread.*

Tr. Fair and softly, my beastlet, at first.
Start not at once with a violent burst,
In the proud delight of your eager might,
Ere your joints with sweat are relaxed and wet
From the powerful swing of your stalwart wing.
And breathe not strong as we soar along;
If you can't refrain, you had best remain
Down here in the stalls of your master's halls.

2nd S. O master of me! why how mad you must be!

Tr. Keep silence! keep silence!

2nd S. Why, where do you try so inanely to fly?

Tr. My flight for the sake of all Hellas I take,
A novel and daring adventure preparing.

2nd S. Why can't you remain at home, and be sane?

Tr. O let not a word of ill omen be heard,
But greet me with blessings and cheers as I go,
And order mankind to be silent below;
And please to be sure with bricks to secure
All places receptive of dung and manure.

2nd S. No, no; I won't keep still, unless you tell me
Whither you're flying off.

Tr. Whither, except
To visit Zeus in heaven?

1st S. Whatever for?

Tr. I'm going to ask him what he is going to do
About the Hellenic peoples, one and all.

1st S. And if he won't inform you?

Tr. I'll indict him
As giving Hellas over to the Medes.

2nd S. (*struggling with* TRYGAEUS)
Not while I live, so help me Dionysus!

Tr. There is no way but this.

2nd S. Here! children! here!
Quick! quick! your father's stealing off to heaven,
Leaving you here deserted and forlorn.
Speak to him, plead with him, you ill-starred maidens.

Enter the DAUGHTERS OF TRYGAEUS.

Girl. O father, O father, and can it be true
The tale that is come to our ears about you,
That along with the birds you are going to go,
And to leave us alone and be off to the crow?
Is it a fact, O my father?
O tell me the truth if you love me.

Tr. Yes, it appears so, my children:
in truth, I am sorry to see you
Calling me dearest papa,
and asking me bread for your dinner,
When I have got in the house
not an atom of silver to buy it;
But if I ever return with success
ye shall soon be enjoying
Buns of enormous size,
with strong fist-sauce to improve them.

Gi And what's to be the method of your passage?
Ships will not do: they cannot go this journey.

Tr. I ride a steed with wings: no ships for me.

Gi. But what's the wit of harnessing a beetle
To ride on it to heaven, papa, papa?

Tr. It is the only living thing with wings,
So Aesop says, that ever reached the Gods.

Gi. O father, father, that's too good a story
That such a stinking brute should enter heaven!

Tr. It went to take revenge upon the eagle,
And break her eggs, a many years ago.

Gi. But should you not have harnessed Pegasus,
And so, in tragic style, approach the Gods?

Tr. Nay, then I must have had supplies for two;
But now the very food I eat myself,
All this will presently be food for him.

Gi. What if he fall in wintry watery waves,
How will his wings help extricate him then?

Tr. Oh, I've a rudder all prepared for that:
My ship's a beetle-sloop, of Naxian make.

Gi. What bay will land you drifting drifting on?

Tr. Why, in Peiraeus, there's the Beetle Bay.

Gi. Yet, O be careful lest you tumble off,
And (lame for life) afford Euripides
A subject, and become a tragic hero.

Tr. I'll see to that: goodbye, goodbye, my dears!
But you, for whom I toil and labour so,
Do for three days resist the calls of nature;
Since, if my beetle in the air should smell it,
He'll toss me headlong off, and turn to graze.
Up, up, my Pegasus, merrily, cheerily,
With ears complacent, while blithe and bold
Your curbs shake out their clatter of gold.
(I wonder what in the world he means
By pointing his nose at those foul latrines.)
Rise, gallantly rise, from the earth to the skies,
And on with the beat of your pinion fleet
Till you come to Zeus in his heavenly seat.
From all your earthly supplies of dirt,
From ordure and muck your nostril avert.
Man! man in Peiraeus! you'll kill me I swear,
Committing a nuisance! good fellow, forbear;
Dig it down in the ground, scatter perfumes around,
Heap, heap up the earth on the top,
Plant sweet-smelling thyme to encircle the mound,
Bring myrrh on its summit to drop;
For if I through your folly shall tumble to-day,
And my enterprise fail to succeed in,
Five talents the city of Chios shall pay
On account of your breach—of good-breeding.

The scene suddenly changes.[1]

[1]Trygaeus has been in the air supported by some sort of crane, but now some sort of platform is pushed forward, with the Palace of Zeus for its background, and on this Trygaeus dismounts.

Zounds! how you scared me: I'm not joking now.
I say, scene-shifter, have a care of me.
You gave me quite a turn; and if you don't
Take care, I'm certain I shall feed my beetle.
But now, methinks, we must be near the Gods;
And sure enough there stand the halls of Zeus.
Oh, open! open! who's in waiting here?

Hermes. (*within*) A breath of man steals o'er me: whence, whence comes it? (*Opens door.*)
O Heracles, what's this?
Tr. A beetle-horse.
He. O shameless miscreant, vagabond, and rogue,
O miscreant, utter miscreant, worst of miscreants,
How came you here, you worst of all the miscreants?
Your name? what is it? speak!
Tr. The worst of miscreants.
He. Your race? your country? answer!
Tr. Worst of miscreants.
He. And who's your father?
Tr. Mine? the worst of miscreants.
He. O by the Earth but you shall die the death
Unless you tell me who and what you are.
Tr. Trygaeus, an Athmonian, skilled in vines;
No sycophant, no lover of disputes.
He. Why are you come?
Tr. To offer you this meat.
He. How did you get here, Wheedling?
Tr. Oho, Greedling!
Then I'm not quite the worst of miscreants now.
So just step in and summon Zeus.
He. O! O!
When you're not likely to come *near* the Gods!
They're gone: they left these quarters yesterday.
Tr. Where on Earth are they?
He. Earth, indeed!
Tr. But where?
He. Far, far away, close to Heaven's highest dome,
Tr. How came they then to leave you here alone?
He. I have to watch the little things they left,
Pipkins and pannikins and trencherlets.
Tr. And what's the reason that they went away?
He. They were so vexed with Hellas: therefore here
Where they were dwelling, they've established War,
And given you up entirely to his will.
But they themselves have settled up aloft,
As high as they can go; that they no more
May see your fightings or receive your prayers.
Tr. Why have they treated us like that? do tell me.
He. Because, though They were oftentimes for Peace,
You always would have War. If the Laconians
Achieved some slight advantage, they would say,
"Noo by the Twa[1] sall master Attic catch it";
Or if the Attics had their turn of luck,
And the Laconians came to treat for peace,
At once ye cried, "We're being taken in,
Athene! Zeus! we can't consent to this;
They're sure to come again if we keep Pylus."
Tr. Yes; that's exactly how we talked: exactly.
He. So that I know not if ye e'er again
Will see the face of Peace.
Tr. Why, where's she gone to?
He. War has immured her in a deep deep pit.
Tr. Where?
He. Here, beneath our feet. And you may see
The heavy stones he piled about its mouth,
That none should take her out.
Tr. I wish you'd tell me
How he proposes now to deal with us.
He. I only know that yester eve he brought
Into this house a most gigantic mortar.
Tr. What is he going to do with that, I wonder!
He. He means to put the cities in and pound them.
But I shall go. He's making such a din
I think he's coming out. *Exit.*
Tr. Shoo! let me run
Out of his way: methought that I myself
Heard a great mortar's war-inspiring blast.

Enter WAR, *bearing a gigantic mortar, in which he is about to mix a salad.*

War. O mortals! mortals! wondrous-woeful mortals!
How ye will suffer in your jaws directly!
Tr. O King Apollo, what a great big mortar!
Oh the mere look of War how bad it is!
Is this the actual War from whom we flee,
The dread tough War, the War upon the legs?
War. (*throwing in leeks*)
O Prasiae! O thrice wretched, five times wretched,
And tens of times, how you'll be crushed to-day!
Tr. Friends, this as yet is no concern of ours,
This is a blow for the Laconian side.
War. (*throwing in garlic*)
O Megara! Megara! in another moment,
How you'll be worn, and torn, and ground to salad!
Tr. Good gracious! O what heavy, bitter tears
He has thrown in to mix for Megara.
War. (*throwing in cheese*)
O Sicily! and you'll be ruined too.
Tr. Ah, how that hapless state will soon be grated!
War. And now I'll pour some Attic honey in.
Tr. Hey, there, I warn you, use some other honey:
Be sparing of the Attic; that costs sixpence.
War. Ho, boy! boy! Riot!
Riot. (*entering*) What's your will?
War. You'll catch it,
You rascal, standing idle there! take that!
Ri. Ugh, how it stings. O me! O me! why, master,
Sure you've not primed your knuckles with the garlic?
War. Run in and get a pestle.
Ri. We've not got one;
We only moved in yesterday, you know.
War. Then run at once and borrow one from Athens.
Ri. I'll run by Zeus; or else I'm sure to catch it. *Exit.*

[1]The Dioscuri.

Tr. What's to be done, my poor dear mortals, now?
Just see how terrible our danger is:
For if that varlet bring a pestle back,
War will sit down and pulverize our cities.
Heavens! may he perish, and not bring one back.
Ri. You there!
War. What! Don't you bring it?
Ri. Just look here, sir:
The pestle the Athenians had is lost,
The tanner fellow that disturbed all Hellas.
Tr. O well done he, Athene, mighty mistress;
Well is he lost, and for the state's advantage,
Before they've mixed us up this bitter salad.
War. Then run away and fetch from Lacedaemon
Another pestle.
Ri. Yes, sir.
War. Don't be long.
Tr. Now is the crisis of our fate, my friends.
And if there's here a man initiate
In Samothrace, 'tis now the hour to pray
For the averting of—the varlet's feet.
Ri. Alas! alas! and yet again, alas!
War. What ails you? don't you bring one now?
Ri. O Sir,
The Spartans too have lost their pestle now.
War. How so, you rascal?
Ri. Why, they lent it out
To friends up Thraceward, and they lost it there.
Tr. And well done they! well done! Twin sons of Zeus!
Take courage, mortals: all may yet be well.
War. Pick up the things, and carry them away;
I'll go within and make myself a pestle.
Exeunt WAR *and* RIOT.
Tr. Now may I sing the ode that Datis[1] made,
The ode he sang in ecstasy at noon,
"Eh, sirs, I'm pleased, and joyed, and comforted."
Now, men of Hellas, now the hour has come
To throw away our troubles and our wars,
And, ere another pestle rise to stop us,
To pull out Peace, the joy of all mankind.
O all ye farmers, merchants, artisans,
O all ye craftsmen, aliens, sojourners,
O all ye islanders, O all ye peoples,
Come with ropes, and spades, and crowbars,
come in eager hurrying haste,
Now the cup of happy fortune,
brothers, it is ours to taste.
Enter CHORUS OF LABORERS.
Chorus. Come then, heart and soul, my comrades,
haste to win this great salvation,
Now or never, now if ever,
come, the whole Hellenic nation!
Throw away your ranks and squadrons,
throw your scarlet plagues away,
Lo, at length the day is dawning,
Lamachus-detesting day!
O be thou our guide and leader,
managing, presiding o'er us,
For I think I shan't give over
in this noble task before us,
Till with levers, cranes, and pulleys
once again to light we haul
Peace, the Goddess best and greatest,
vineyard-lovingest of all.
Tr. O be quiet! O be quiet! by your noisy loud delight
You will waken War, the demon,
who is crouching out of sight.
Ch. O we joy, we joy, we joy, to
hear your glorious proclamations,
So unlike that odious "Wanted
at the camp with three days' rations."
Tr. Yet beware, beware, remember!
Cerberus is down below:
He may come with fuss and fury
(as when he was here you know),
Every obstacle and hindrance
in the way of Peace to throw.
Ch. Who shall bear her, who shall tear her,
from these loving arms away,
If I once can clasp and grasp her?
O hurrah! hurrah! hurrah!
Tr. Zounds! you'll surely be our ruin:
stop your clamour, I entreat:
War will by and bye come trampling
everything beneath his feet.
Ch. Let him stamp, and tramp, and trample,
let him do whate'er he will,
I am so immensely happy that I really can't be still.
Tr. What the mischief! what's the matter?
do not, by the Gods, I pray,
With your dancings and your prancings
spoil our noble work to-day.
Ch. Really now I didn't mean to: no I didn't, I declare:
Quite without my will my ankles
will perform this joyous air.
Tr. Well, but don't go on at present;
cease your dancing or you'll rue it.
Ch. Look, observe, I've really ceased it.
Tr. So you say, but still you do it.
Ch. Only once, I do beseech you; only just a single hop.
Tr. Well then, one: make haste about it;
only one, and then you stop.
Ch. Stop? of course we stop with pleasure
if 'twill your designs assist.
Tr. Well, but look: you're still proceeding.
Ch. Just, by Zeus, one other twist
Let me fling my right leg upwards,
and I'll really then refrain.
Tr. This indulgence too I'll grant you,
so you don't offend again.
Ch. Hah! but here's my left leg also:
it must have its turn, 'tis plain.
(*dancing vigorously with both legs*)
I'm so happy, glad, delighted,
getting rid of arms at last,
More than if, my youth renewing,
I the slough of Age had cast.

[1]Persian commander at Marathon and noted for his blunders in Greek. Thus, the verb endings of l. 291.

Tr. Well, but don't exult at present,
for we're all uncertain still,
But, when once we come to hold her,
then be merry if you will;
Then will be the time for laughing,
Shouting out in jovial glee,
Sailing, sleeping, feasting, quaffing,
All the public sights to see.
Then the Cottabus be playing,
Then be hip-hip-hip-hurrahing,
Pass the day and pass the night
Like a regular Sybarite.
Ch. O that it were yet my fortune
those delightful days to see!
Woes enough I've had to bear,
Sorry pallets, trouble, care,
Such as fell to Phormio's share,
I would never more thereafter so morose and bitter be,
Nor a judge so stubborn-hearted,
unrelenting, and severe;
You shall find me yielding then,
Quite a tender youth again,
When these weary times depart.
Long enough we've undergone
Toils and sorrows many a one,
Worn and spent and sick at heart,
From Lyceum, to Lyceum,
trudging on with shield and spear.
Now then tell us what you would
Have us do, and we'll obey,
Since by fortune fair and good
You're our sovereign Lord to-day.
Tr. Come let me see which way to move the stones.

Re-enter HERMES.

He. Rogue! miscreant! what are you up to now?
Tr. No harm;
Everything's right, as Cillicon observed.
He. Wretch! you shall die!
Tr. When it's my lot, of course,
For being Hermes you'll use lots, I know.
He. O you are doomed! doomed! doomed!
Tr. Yes? for what day?
He. This very instant.
Tr. But I'm not prepared:
I've bought no bread and cheese, as if to die.
He. Ah, well, you're absolutely gone!
Tr. That's odd,
To get such famous luck and yet not know it.
He. Then don't you know that death's denounced by Zeus
On all found digging here?
Tr. And is it so?
And must I die indeed?
He. You must indeed.
Tr. O then, I prithee, lend me half a crown.
I'll buy a pig, and get initiate first.
He. Ho! Zeus! Zeus! thunder-crasher!
Tr. O pray don't.
O by the heavenly powers don't peach upon us.
He. No, no, I won't keep silence.
Tr. O pray do.
O by the heavenly meat I brought you, master.
He. Why, bless you, Zeus will quite demolish me
If I don't shout and tell him all about it.
Tr. O pray don't shout, my darling dearest Hermes.
Don't stand gaping there, my comrades;
are ye quite deprived of speech?
What's the matter? speak, ye rascals!
if you don't, he's safe to peach.
Ch. Do not, do not, mighty Hermes,
do not, do not shout, I pray,
If you e'er have tasted swine,
Tasted sucking-pigs of mine,
Which have soothed your throat divine,
Think upon it, think upon it,
nor despise the deed to-day.
Tr. King and master, won't you listen
to the coaxing words they say?
Ch. View us not with wrathful eye,
Nor our humble prayers deny,
From this dungeon let us hand her.
O if you indeed detest,
And abhor the sweeping crest
And the eyebrows of Peisander,
Let us now, O God most gracious!
let us carry Peace away.
Then we'll glad processions bring,
Then with sacrifices due,
We will always, lord and king,
We will always honour you.
Tr. O sir, be pitiful, and heed their cry:
They never showed you such respect as now.
He. Why, no; they never were such thieves as now.
Tr. And then I'll tell you a tremendous secret,
A horrid dreadful plot against the Gods.
He. Well, tell away: I'm open to conviction.
Tr. 'Tis that the Moon and vile immoral Sun
Have long been plotting to your hurt: and now
They're giving Hellas up to the Barbarians.
He. Why are they doing that?
Tr. Because, by Zeus!
We sacrifice to *you*, but those Barbarians
Only to *them*. So naturally they
Are very anxious that we all should perish,
And they get all the rites of all the Gods.
He. Then that's the reason why they clipped the days,
And nibbled off their rounds, misguiding sinners.
Tr. It is, it is: come, Hermes, lend a hand,
Help us to pull her out. And then for you
We'll celebrate the great Panathenaea,
And all the other rites of all the Gods,
Demeter, Zeus, Adonis, all for you;
And everywhere the cities saved from woe
Will sacrifice to you, the Saviour Hermes.
Much, much besides you'll gain: and first of all
I give you this (*producing a gold cup*),
a vessel for libations.
He. Fie! how I soften at the sight of gold!
There, my men, the work's before you!
I've got nothing more to say.

Quick, take up your spades, and enter,
shovelling all the stones away.
Ch. Gladly, gladly will we do it,
wisest of the Gods; and you,
Like a skilled superior craftsman,
teach us what we ought to do.
I warrant, when the way we know,
you'll find us anything but slow.
Tr. Hold out the vessel, and we'll launch the work
With free libations and with holy prayers.
He. Pour libations.
Silence! silence! pour libations.
Tr. And as we pour we'll pray. O happy morn,
Be thou the source of every joy to Hellas!
And O may he who labours well to-day
Be never forced to bear a shield again!
Ch. No; may he spend his happy days in peace,
Stirring the fire, his mistress at his side.
Tr. If there be any that delights in war,
King Dionysus, may he never cease
Picking out spearheads from his funny-bones.
Ch. If any, seeking to be made a Captain,
Hates to see Peace return, O may he ever
Fare in his battles like Cleonymus.
Tr. If any merchant, selling spears or shields,
Would fain have battles, to improve his trade,
May he be seized by thieves and eat raw barley.
Ch. If any would-be General won't assist us,
Or any slave preparing to desert,
May he be flogged, and broken on the wheel.
But on ourselves all joy: hip, hip, hurrah!
Tr. Don't talk of being hipped: Hurrah's the word.
Ch. Hurrah! hurrah! hurrah's the word to-day.
Tr. (*pouring libations*)
To Hermes, Love, Desire, the Hours, and Graces.
Ch. Not Ares?
Tr. (*with disgust*) No!
Ch. Nor Enyalius?
Tr. No.
Ch. Now all set to, and labour at the ropes.
He. Yo ho! pull away.
Ch. Pull away a little stronger.
He. Yo ho! pull away.
Ch. Keep it up a little longer.
He. Pull, pull, pull, pull.
Tr. Ah they don't pull all alike.
Cease your craning: 'tis but feigning:
Pull, Boeotians! or I'll strike.
He. Yo ho! pull away.
Tr. Pull away, away, away.
Ch. (*to* TRYGAEUS *and* HERMES)
Verily you should be helping us too.
Tr. (*indignantly*) Don't I strain, might and main,
Cling and swing tug and haul?
Ch. Yet we don't advance at all.
Tr. Now don't sit there and thwart us, Lamachus.
We don't require your Bugaboo,[1] my man.

[1]The Gorgon shield of Lamachus, one of the Athenian generals in the Sicilian expedition.

He. These Argives, too, they give no help at all.
They only laugh at us, our toils and troubles,
And all the while take pay from either side.
Tr. But the Laconians, comrade, pull like men.
He. Ah, mark, 'tis only such as work in wood
That fain would help us: but the smith impedes.
Tr. And the Megarians do no good: they pull, though,
Scrabbling away like ravenous puppy dogs.
Good lack! they're regularly starved and ruined.
Ch. We make no way, my comrades: we must try
A strong pull, and a long pull, all together.
He. Yo ho! pull away.
Tr. Keep it up a little longer.
He. Yo ho! pull away.
Tr. Yes, by Zeus! a little stronger.
Ch. Very slow, now we go.
Tr. What a shameful dirty trick!
Some are working, others shirking,
Argives, ye shall feel the stick.
He. Yo ho! pull away.
Tr. Pull away, away, away.
Ch. Some of you still are designing us ill.
Tr. Ye who fain Peace would gain,
Pull and strain, might and main.
Ch. Some one's hindering us again.
He. Plague take you, men of Megara; get out!
The Goddess hates you: she remembers well
'Twas you that primed her up at first with garlic.
Stop, stop, Athenians: shift your hold a little;
It's no use pulling as you're now disposed.
You don't do anything but go to law.
No, if you really want to pull her out,
Stand back a trifle further towards the sea.
Ch. Come, let us farmers pull alone,
and set our shoulders to it.
He. Upon my word you're gaining ground:
I think you're going to do it.
Ch. He says we're really gaining ground:
cheer up, cheer up, my hearty.
Tr. The farmers have it all themselves,
and not another party.
Ch. Pull again, pull, my men,
Now we're gaining fast.
Never slacken, put your back in,
Here she comes at last.
Pull, pull, pull, pull, every man, all he can;
Pull, pull, pull, pull, pull,
Pull, pull, pull, pull, all together.

PEACE *is lifted out with her two attendants,* HARVESTHOME *and* MAYFAIR.

Tr. Giver of grapes, O how shall I address you?
O for a word ten thousand buckets big
Wherewith to accost you: for I've none at hand.
Good morning, Harvesthome: good morn, Mayfair.
O what a lovely charming face, Mayfair!
(*Kisses her*)
O what a breath! how fragrant to my heart,
How sweet, how soft, with perfume and inaction.
He. Not quite the odour of a knapsack, eh?
Tr. Faugh! that odious pouch of odious men, I hate it.

It has a smell of rancid-onion-whiffs;
But *she* of harvests, banquets, festivals,
Flutes, thrushes, plays, the odes of Sophocles,
Euripidean wordlets,
He. O how dare you
Slander her so: I'm sure she does not like
That logic-monger's wordy disputations.
Tr. (*continuing*) The bleating lambs, the ivy-leaf, the vat,
Full-bosomed matrons hurrying to the farm,
The tipsy maid, the drained and emptied flask,
And many another blessing.
He. And look there,
See how the reconciled cities greet and blend
In peaceful intercourse, and laugh for joy;
And that, too, though their eyes are swoln and blackened,
And all cling fast to cupping instruments.
Tr. Yes, and survey the audience: by their looks
You can discern their trades.
He. O dear! O dear!
Don't you observe the man that makes the crests
Tearing his hair? and yon's a pitchfork-seller;
Fie! how he fillips the sword-cutler there.
Tr. And see how pleased that sickle-maker looks,
Joking and poking the spear-burnisher.
He. Now then give notice: let the farmers go.
Tr. O yes! O yes! the farmers all may go
Back to their homes, farm-implements and all.
You can leave your darts behind you:
yea, for sword and spear shall cease.
All things all around are teeming
with the mellow gifts of Peace;
Shout your Paeans, march away
to labour in your fields to-day.
Ch. Day most welcome to the farmers
and to all the just and true,
Now I see you I am eager
once again my vines to view,
And the fig-trees which I planted
in my boyhood's early prime,
I would fain salute and visit
after such a weary time.
Tr. First, then, comrades, to the Goddess
be our grateful prayers addressed,
Who has freed us from the Gorgons
and the fear-inspiring crest.
Next a little salt provision fit for country uses buy,
Then with merry expedition
homeward to the fields we'll hie.
He. O Poseidon! fair their order,
sweet their serried ranks to see:
Right and tight, like rounded biscuits,
or a thronged festivity.
Tr. Yes, by Zeus! the well-armed mattock
seems to sparkle as we gaze,
And the burnished pitchforks glitter
in the sun's delighted rays.
Very famously with those
will they clear the vineyard rows.
So that I myself am eager
homeward to my farm to go,
Breaking up the little furrows
(long-neglected) with the hoe.
Think of all the thousand pleasures,
Comrades, which to Peace we owe,
All the life of ease and comfort
Which she gave us long ago:
Figs and olives, wine and myrtles,
Luscious fruits preserved and dried,
Banks of fragrant violets, blowing
By the crystal fountain's side;
Scenes for which our hearts are yearning,
Joys that we have missed so long——
—Comrades, here is Peace returning,
Greet her back with dance and song!
Ch. Welcome, welcome, best and dearest,
welcome, welcome, welcome, home.
We have looked and longed for thee,
Looking, longing, wondrously,
Once again our farms to see.
O the joy, the bliss, the rapture,
really to behold thee come.
Thou wast aye our chief enjoyment,
thou wast aye our greatest gain.
We who ply the farmer's trade
Used, through thy benignant aid,
All the joys of life to hold.
Ah! the unbought pleasures free
Which we erst received of thee
In the merry days of old,
When thou wast our one salvation
and our roasted barley grain.
Now will all the tiny shoots,
Sunny vine and fig-tree sweet,
All the happy flowers and fruits,
Laugh for joy thy steps to greet.
Ah, but where has Peace been hiding
all these long and weary hours?
Hermes, teach us all the story,
kindest of the heavenly Powers.
He. O most sapient worthy farmers,
listen now and understand,
If you fain would learn the reason,
why it was she left the land.
Pheidias began the mischief,
having come to grief and shame,
Pericles was next in order,
fearing he might share the blame,
Dreading much your hasty temper,
and your savage bulldog ways,
So before misfortune reached him,
he contrived a flame to raise,
By his Megara-enactment[1]
setting all the world ablaze.
Such a bitter smoke ascended
while the flames of war he blew,
That from every eye in Hellas
everywhere the tears it drew.
Wailed the vine, and rent its branches,
when the evil news it heard;

[1]The interdict prohibiting the Megarians from all intercourse with the Athenian empire.

Butt on butt was dashed and shivered,
by revenge and anger stirred;
There was none to stay the tumult;
Peace in silence disappeared.
Tr. By Apollo I had never
heard these simple facts narrated,
No, nor knew she was so closely
to our Pheidias related.
Ch. No, nor I, till just this moment:
that is why she looks so fair.
Goodness me! how many things
escape our notice I declare.
He. Then when once the subject cities,
over whom ye bare the sway,
Saw you at each other snarling,
growling angrier day by day,
To escape the contributions,
every willing nerve they strained,
And the chief Laconian leaders
by enormous bribes they gained.
These at once for filthy lucre,
guest-deluders as they are,
Hustling out this gracious lady,
greedily embraced the War.
But from this their own advantage
ruin to their farmers came;
For from hence the eager galleys
sailing forth with vengeful aim,
Swallowed up the figs of people
who were not, perchance, to blame.
Tr. Very justly, very justly!
richly had they earned the blow,
Lopping down the dusky fig-tree
I had loved and nurtured so.
Ch. Very justly, very justly!
since my great capacious bin,
Ugh! the rascals came across it,
took a stone, and stove it in.
He. Then your labouring population,
flocking in from vale and plain,
Never dreamed that, like the others,
they themselves were sold for gain,
But as having lost their grape-stones,
and desiring figs to get,
Every one his rapt attention
on the public speakers set;
These beheld you poor and famished,
lacking all your home supplies,
Straight they pitchforked out the Goddess,
scouting her with yells and cries,
Whensoe'er (for much she loved you)
back she turned with wistful eyes.
Then with suits they vexed and harassed
your substantial rich allies,
Whispering in your ear, "The fellow
leans to Brasidas," and you
Like a pack of hounds in chorus
on the quivering victim flew.
Yea, the City, sick and pallid,
shivering with disease and fright,
Any calumny they cast her,
ate with ravenous appetite.
Till at last your friends perceiving
whence their heavy wounds arose,
Stopped with gold the mouths of speakers
who were such disastrous foes.
Thus the scoundrels throve and prospered:
whilst distracted Hellas came
Unobserved to wrack and ruin:
but the fellow most to blame
Was a tanner.[1]
Tr. Softly, softly, Hermes master, say not so;
Let the man remain in silence,
wheresoe'er he is, below;
For the man is ours no longer:
he is all your own, you know;
Therefore whatsoe'er you call him,
Knave and slave while yet amongst us,
Wrangler, jangler, false accuser,
Troubler, muddler, all-confuser,
You will all these names be calling
One who now is yours alone.
(*to* PEACE)
But tell me, lady, why you stand so mute.
He. Oh, she won't speak one word before this audience:
No, no; they've wronged her far too much for that.
Tr. Then won't she whisper, all alone, to you?
He. Will you, my dearest, speak your thoughts to me?
Come, of all ladies most shield-handle-hating.
(*affects to listen.*)
Yes, good; that's their offence: I understand.
Listen, spectators, why she blames you so.
She says that after that affair in Pylus
She came, unbidden, with a chest of treaties,
And thrice you blackballed her in full assembly.
Tr. We erred in that; but, lady, pardon us,
For then our wits were swaddled up in skins.
He. Well then, attend to what she asks me now.
Who in your city loves her least? and who
Loves her the best and shrinks from fighting most?
Tr. Cleonymus, I think, by far the most.
He. What sort of man is this Cleonymus
In military matters?
Tr. Excellent:
Only he's not his so-called father's son;
For if he goes to battle, in a trice
He proves himself a castaway—of shields.
He. Still further listen what she asks me now.
Who is it now that sways the Assembly-stone?
Tr. Hyperbolus at present holds the place.
But how now, Mistress? Why avert your eyes?
He. She turns away in anger from the people,
For taking to itself so vile a leader.
Tr. He's a mere makeshift: we'll not use him now.
'Twas that the people, bare and stripped of leaders,
Just caught him up to gird itself withal.
He. She asks how this can benefit the state.
Tr. 'Twill make our counsels brighter.
He. Will it? how?

[1] Cleon.

Tr. Because he deals in lamps: before he came
We all were groping in the dark, but now
His lamps may give our council-board some light.
He. Oh! oh!
What things she wants to know!
Tr. What sort of things?
He. All the old things existing when she left.
And first, she asks if Sophocles be well.
Tr. He's well, but strangely metamorphosed.
He. How?
Tr. He's now Simonides, not Sophocles.
He. What do you mean?
Tr. He's grown so old and sordid,
He'd put to sea upon a sieve for money.
He. Lives the old wit Cratinus?
Tr. No; he perished
When the Laconians made their raid.
He. How so?
Tr. Swooned dead away: he could not bear to see
A jolly butt of wine all smashed and wasted.
Much, much beside we've suffered; wherefore, lady,
We'll never never let you go again.
He. Then on these terms I'll give you Harvest-home
To be your bride and partner in your fields.
Take her to wife, and propagate young vines.
Tr. O Harvesthome! come here and let me kiss you.
But, Hermes, won't it hurt me if I make
Too free with fruits of Harvesthome at first?
He. Not if you add a dose of pennyroyal.
But, since you're going, please to take Mayfair
Back to the Council, whose of old she was.
Tr. O happy Council to possess Mayfair!
O what a three-days' carnival you'll have!
What soup! what tripe! what delicate tender meat!
But fare thee well, dear Hermes.
He. And do you
Farewell, dear mortal, and remember me.
Tr. Home, home, my beetle! let us now fly home.
He. Your beetle's gone, my friend.
Tr. Why, where's he gone to?
He. Yoked to the car of Zeus, he bears the thunder.
Tr. What will he get to eat, poor creature, there?
He. Why, Ganymede's ambrosia, to be sure.
Tr. And how shall I get down?
He. O well enough.
There, by the side of Peace.
Tr. Now girls, now girls,
Keep close to me: our youngsters I well know
Are sore all over for the love of you.

Exeunt TRYGAEUS *with* HARVESTHOME *and* MAYFAIR.

Chorus

Yes, go, and good fortune escort you, my friend;
meanwhile the machines and the wraps,
We'll give to our faithful attendants to guard,
for a number of dissolute chaps
Are sure to be lurking about on the stage,
to pilfer and plunder and steal;
Here, take them and watch them and keep them with care,
while we to the audience reveal
The mind of our Play, and whatever we may
By our native acumen be prompted to say.

'*Twere* proper and right for the Ushers to smite,
if ever a bard, we confess,
Were to fill with the praise of himself and his plays
our own anapaestic address.
But if ever, O daughter of Zeus, it were fit
with honour and praise to adorn
A Chorus-Instructor, the ablest of men,
the noblest that ever was born,
Our Poet is free to acknowledge that he
is deserving of high commendation:
It was he that advancing, unaided, alone,
compelled the immediate cessation
Of the jokes which his rivals were cutting at rags,
and the battles they waged with the lice.
It was he that indignantly swept from the stage
the paltry ignoble device
Of a Heracles needy and seedy and greedy,
a vagabond sturdy and stout,
Now baking his bread, now swindling instead,
now beaten and battered about.
And freedom he gave to the lachrymose slave
who was wont with a howl to rush in,
And all for the sake of a joke which they make
on the wounds that disfigure his skin:
"Why, how now, my poor knave?" so they bawl to the slave,
"has the whipcord invaded your back,
Spreading havoc around, hacking trees to the ground,
with a savage resistless attack?"
Such vulgar contemptible lumber at once
he bade from the drama depart,
And then, like an edifice stately and grand,
he raised and ennobled the Art.
High thoughts and high language he brought on the stage,
a humour exalted and rare,
Nor stooped with a scurrilous jest to assail
some small-man-and-woman affair.
No, he at the mightiest quarry of all
with the soul of a Heracles flew,
And he braved the vile scent of the tan-pit, and went
through foul-mouthed revilings for you.
And I at the outset came down in the lists
with the jaggèd-fanged monster to fight,
Whose eyeballs were lurid and glaring with flames
of Cynna's detestable light;
And around his forehead the thin forked tongues
of a hundred sycophants quiver,
And his smell was the smell of a seal, and his voice
was a brawling tempestuous River,
And his hinder parts like a furnace appeared,
and a goblin's uncleansable liver.
But I recked not the least for the look of the beast;
I never desponded or quailed,

And I fought for the safety of you and the Isles;
I gallantly fought and prevailed.
You therefore should heed and remember the deed,
and afford me my guerdon to-day,
For I never went off to make love to the boys
in the schools of athletic display
Heretofore when I gained the theatrical prize:
but I packed up my traps and departed,
Having caused you great joy and but little annoy,
and mightily pleased the true-hearted.

It is right then for all, young and old, great and small,
Henceforth of my side and my party to be,
And each bald-headed man should do all that he can
That the prize be awarded to me.
For be sure if this play be triumphant to-day,
That whene'er you recline at the feast or the wine,
Your neighbour will say,
"Give this to the bald-head, give that to the bald-head,
And take not away
That sweetmeat, that cake, but present and bestow it
On the man with the brow of our wonderful Poet!"

Muse having driven afar this terrible business of war,
Join with Me the chorus.
Come singing of Nuptials divine and earthly banquets,
Singing the joys of the blessed: this of old to Thee belongs.
But and if Carcinus coming
Ask thee to join with his sons in choral dances,
Hearken not, come not, stand not
As an ally beside them,
Think of them all as merely
Little domestical quails, ballet-dancers with wallet necks,
Nipped from the droppings of goats, small, stunted, machinery-hunters.
Yea, for their father declared that the drama which
Passed all his hopes, in the evening
By the cat was strangled.

These are the songs of the fair
sweet Graces with beautiful hair,
Which it well beseemeth
This poet of wisdom to chant, while softly resting
Warbles the swallow of spring; and Morsimus no chorus gains,
No, nor Melanthius either.
Well I remember his shrill discordant chatter,
When the tragedians' chorus
He and his brother tutored,
Both of them being merely
Gorgons, devourers of sweets, skate-worshippers, and harpies,
Pests of old maids, rank fetid as goats, destroyers of fishes.

Thou having spit on them largely and heavily,
Join in the festival dances,
Heavenly Muse, beside me.

Enter TRYGAEUS, HARVESTHOME, *and* MAYFAIR.

Tr. O what a job it was to reach the Gods!
I know I'm right fatigued in both my legs.
How small ye seemed down here! why from above
Methought ye looked as bad as bad could be,
But here ye look considerably worse.

Enter FIRST SERVANT.

1st S. What, master, *you* returned!
Tr. So I'm informed.
1st S. What have you got?
Tr. Got? pains in both my legs.
Faith! it's a rare long way.
1st S. Nay, tell me,
Tr. What?
1st S. Did you see any wandering in the air
Besides yourself?
Tr. No; nothing much to speak of,
Two or three souls of dithyrambic poets.
1st S. What were they after?
Tr. Flitting round for odes,
Those floating-on-high-in-the-airy-sky affairs.
1st S. Then 'tisn't true what people say about it,
That when we die, we straightway turn to stars?
Tr. O yes it is.
1st S. And who's the star there now?
Tr. Ion of Chios, who on earth composed
"Star o' the Morn," and when he came there, all
At once saluted him as "Star o' the Morn."
1st S. And did you learn about those falling stars
Which sparkle as they run?
Tr. Yes, those are some
Of the rich stars returning home from supper,
Lanterns in hand, and in the lanterns fire.
But take this girl at once, and lead her in;
Deluge the bath, and make the water warm;
Then spread the nuptial couch for her and me:
And when you've finished, hither come again.
Meanwhile I'll give this other to the Council.
1st S. Whence have you brought these maidens?
Tr. Whence? from heaven.
1st S. I wouldn't give three halfpence for the Gods
If they keep brothels as we mortals do.
Tr. No, no; yet even there some live by these.
1st S. Come on then, mistress: tell me, must I give her
Nothing to eat?
Tr. O no, she will not touch
Our wheat and barley bread: her wont has been
To lap ambrosia with the Gods in heaven.
1st S. Lap! we'll prepare her lap then here on earth.

Exeunt SERVANT *and* HARVESTHOME.

Ch. O what a lucky old man!
Truly the whole of your plan
Prospers as well as it can.
Tr. I really wonder what you'll say
when I'm a bridegroom spruce and gay.
Ch. All men will gaze with delight.
Old as you are you'll be quite
Youthful and perfumed and bright.

Tr. What, when you see her tender waist
by these encircling arms embraced?
Ch. Why then we'll think you happier far
than Carcinus's twistlings are.
Tr. And justly too, methinks, for I
On beetleback essayed to fly,
And rescued Hellas, worn with strife,
And stored your life
With pleasant joys of home and wife,
With country mirth and leisure.

Re-enter SERVANT.

1st S. Well, sir, the girl has bathed and looks divinely:
They mix the puddings, and they've made the cakes;
Everything's done: we only want the husband.
Tr. Come then and let us give Mayfair at once
Up to the Council.
1st S. What do you say? Mayfair!
Is this May Fair? the Fair we kept at Brauron,
When we were fresh and mellow, years ago?
Tr. Aye, and 'twas work enough to catch her.
1st S. O!
How neat her pasterns, quite a five-year-old.
Tr. (*looking round upon the audience*)
Now, have you any there that I can trust?
One who will lead her safely to the Council?
(*to the* SERVANT)
What are you scribbling?
1st S. Marking out a place
To pitch my tent in, at the Isthmian games.
Tr. Well, is there none can take her? come to me then;
I'll go myself, and set you down amongst them.
1st S. Here's some one making signs.
Tr. Who is it?
1st S. Who!
Ariphrades: he wants her brought *his* way.
Tr. No: I can't bear his dirty, sloppy way;
So come to me, and lay those parcels down.
(*Leads her forward.*)
Councillors! Magistrates! behold Mayfair!
And O remember what a deal of fun
That word implies: what pastimes and what feasts.
See here's a famous kitchen-range she brings;
'Tis blacked a little: for in times of Peace
The jovial Council kept its saucepans there.
Take her and welcome her with joy; and then
To-morrow morning let the sports begin:
Then we'll enjoy the Fair in every fashion,
With boxing-matches and with wrestling-bouts,
And tricks and games, while striplings soused in oil
Try the pancratium, fist and leg combined.
Then the third day from this, we'll hold the races;
The eager jockeys riding: the great cars
Puffing and blowing through the lists, till dashed
Full on some turning-post, they reel and fall
Over and over: everywhere you see
The hapless coachmen wallowing on the plain.
You lucky Magistrate, receive Mayfair!
Just look, how pleased he seems to introduce her;
You would not though, if you got nothing by it,
No, you'd be holding a Reception day:

Ch. Truly we envy your fate:
All must allow you're a great
Blessing and boon to the state.
Tr. Ah, when your grapes you gather in,
you'll know what sort of friend I've been.
Ch. Nay, but already 'tis known;
Yea, for already we own
You have preserved us alone.
Tr. I think you'll think so when you drain
a bowl of new-made wine again.
Ch. We'll always hold you first and best,
except the Gods the ever blest.
Tr. In truth you owe a deal to me,
Trygaeus, sprung from Athmone,
For I've released the burgher crew
And farmers too
From toils and troubles not a few;
Hyperbolus I've done for.
1st S. Now what's the next thing that we have to do?
Tr. What but to dedicate her shrine with pipkins?
1st S. With pipkins! like a wretched little Hermes!
Tr. Well then, what think you of a stall-fed bull?
1st S. A bull? O no! no need of bull-works now.
Tr. Well then, a great fat pig?
1st S. No, no.
Tr. Why not?
1st S. Lest, like Theagenes, we grow quite piggish.
Tr. What other victim shall we have?
1st S. A baa-lamb.
Tr. A baa-lamb!
1st S. Yes, by Zeus!
Tr. But that's Ionic,
That word is.
1st S. All the better: then, you see,
If any speak for war, the whole assembly
Will talk Ionic and cry out Bah! Bah!
Tr. Good, very good.
1st S. And they'll be milder so,
And we shall live like lambs among ourselves,
And be much gentler towards our dear allies.
Tr. There, get the sheep as quickly as you can,
I'll find an altar for the sacrifice.

Exeunt TRYGAEUS *and* SERVANT.

Ch. Sure each design, when God and fortune speed it,
Succeeds to our mind, what is wanted we find
Just at the moment we need it.
Tr. (*returning*) The truths you mention none can doubt,
for see I've brought the altar out.
Ch. Then hasten the task to perform:
War, with its vehement storm,
Seems for the instant to cease;
Its soughings decrease,
Shifting and veering to Peace.
Tr. Well, here's the basket ready stored
with barley grain, and wreath, and sword.
And here's the pan of sacred fire:
the sheep alone we now require.
Ch. Make haste, make haste: if Chaeris see,
He'll come here uninvited,

And pipe and blow to that degree,
His windy labours needs must be
By some small gift requited.
Enter SERVANT.
Tr. Here, take the basket and the lustral water,
And pace the altar round from left to right.
1st S. See, I've been round: now tell me something else.
Tr. Then next I'll take this torch and dip it in.
(*to the victim, as he sprinkles it*)
Shake your head, sirrah,
(*to the* SERVANT) bring the barley, you;
I'll hold the bason while you wash your hands.
Now throw the corn amongst the audience.
1st S. There.
Tr. What! thrown it out already?
1st S. Yes, by Hermes!
There's not a single man amongst them all
But has at least one corn, I'll warrant you.
Tr. Aye, but the women?
1st S. If they haven't got one,
They'll get it by and by.
Tr. Now, then to prayers:
Who's here? where are our honest simple folk?
1st S. Here: these are simple folk; I'll give to them.
Tr. What, these good simple folk?
1st S. I'faith I think so;
Who, though we've poured such lots of water on them
Yet stand stock still, and never budge a step.
Tr. Come, let us pray, no dallying; let us pray.

O Peace most holy, august, serene,
O heavenborn queen
Of the dance and song and the bridal throng,
These offerings take which thy votaries make.
1st S. O mistress dear, we beseech you hear,
And act not you as the wantons do:
They love to spy at the passers by
Through the half-closed door,
And then if you heed, they are gone with speed;
If you turn away, in an instant they
Peep out once more as they did before.
But deal not thus unkindly with us.
Tr. No, by Zeus! but display in a true honest way
Your perfect entire full form to our view,
Who with constant desire
These thirteen long years have been pining for you.
When our fightings are stayed, and our tumults allayed,
We will hail thee a Lady forever:
And O put an end to the whispers of doubt,
These wonderful clever
Ingenious suspicions we bandy about;
And solder and glue the Hellenes anew
With the old-fashioned true
Elixir of love, and attemper our mind
With thoughts of each other more genial and kind.
Moreover we pray that our market-place may
Be furnished each day with a goodly display,
And for garlic, and cucumbers early and rare,
Pomegranates, and apples in heaps to be there,
And wee little coats for our servants to wear.
And Boeotia to send us her pigeons and widgeons,
And her geese and her plovers: and plentiful creels
Once more from Copaïs to journey with eels,
And for us to be hustling, and tussling, and bustling,
With Morychus, Teleas, Glaucetes, all
The gluttons together besieging the stall,
To purchase the fish: and then I could wish
For Melanthius to come too late for the fair,
And for *them* to be sold, and for *him* to despair,
And out of his own Medea a groan
Of anguish to borrow,
"I perish! I perish! bereaved of my sweet,
My treasure, my darling, embowered in her beet";
And for all men to laugh at his sorrow.
These things we pray; O mistress, grant us these.

1st S. Here, take the cleaver: now with clever skill
Slaughter the sheep.
Tr. No, no, I must not.
1st S. Why?
Tr. Peace loves not, friend, the sight of victims slain:
Hers is a bloodless altar. Take it in,
And when you have slain it, bring the thighs out here.
There: now the sheep is—saved for the Choregus.
Exit SERVANT.
Ch. But you the while, outside with us remaining,
Lay, handy and quick, these fagots of stick,
Whatever is needful ordaining.
Tr. Now don't you think I have laid the wood
as well as most diviners could?
Ch. (*admiringly*) Yes! just what I looked for from you.
All that is wise you can do.
All things that daring and skill
Suffice to fulfil
You can perform if you will.
Tr. (*coughing*) Dear! how this lighted brand is smoking,
your Stilbides is nearly choking;
I'll bring the table out with speed;
a servant's help we shall not need. *Exit.*
Ch. Sure all with admiration true
Will praise a man so clever,
Who passed such toils and dangers through,
And saved the holy city too;
An envied name forever.
Enter SERVANT *and* TRYGAEUS.
1st S. I've done the job; here take and cook the thighs
While I go fetch the inwards and the cates.
Tr. I'll see to this: you should have come before.
1st S. Well, here I am: I'm sure I've not been long.
Tr. Take these, and roast them nicely: here's a fellow
Coming this way, with laurel round his head.
Who can he be?
1st S. He looks an arrant humbug.
Some seer, I think.
Tr. No, no; 'tis Hierocles,
The oracle-mongering chap from Oreus town.

1st S. What brings him here?
Tr. 'Tis evident he comes
To raise some opposition to our truces.
1st S. No, 'tis the savour of the roast attracts him.
Tr. Don't let us seem to notice him.
1st S. All right.
Enter HIEROCLES.
Hierocles. What is this sacrifice, and made to whom?
Tr. Roast on: don't speak: hands off the haunch remember.
Hi. Will ye not say to whom ye sacrifice?
This tail looks right.
1st S. Sweet Peace! it does indeed.
Hi. Now then begin and hand the firstlings here.
Tr. It must be roasted first.
Hi. It's roasted now.
Tr. You're over-busy, man, whoe'er you are.
Cut on: why, where's the table? bring the wine.
Exit SERVANT.
Hi. The tongue requires a separate cut.
Tr. We know.
Now will you please?
Hi. Yes, tell me.
Tr. Mind your business.
Don't talk to us: we sacrifice to Peace.
Hi. O ye pitiful fools!
Tr. Pray speak for yourself, my good fellow.
Hi. Ye who, blindly perverse,
with the will of the Gods unacquainted,
Dare to traffic for Peace,
true men with truculent monkeys.
1st S. (*re-entering*) O! O! O!
Tr. What's the matter?
1st S. I like his truculent monkeys.
Hi. Silly and timorous gulls,
ye have trusted the children of foxes
Crafty of mind and crafty of soul.
Tr. You utter impostor,
O that your lungs were as hot
as a piece of the meat I am roasting!
Hi. If the prophetic nymphs
have not been imposing on Bakis,
No, nor Bakis on men,
nor the nymphs, I repeat, upon Bakis,
Tr. O perdition be yours
if you don't have done with your Bakis!
Hi. Then is the hour not come
for the fetters of Peace to be loosened.
No; for before that hour—
Tr. This piece is with salt to be sprinkled.
Hi. Yea, it is far from the mind
of the Ever-blessed Immortals
That we should cease from the strife,
till the wolf and the lamb be united.
Tr. How, you scoundrel accurst,
can the wolf and the lamb be united?
Hi. Doth not the beetle, alarmed,
emit a most horrible odour?
Doth not the wagtail yapper
produce blind young in its hurry?
So is the hour not come
for Peace to be sanctioned between us.
Tr. What then, what is to come?
Are we never to cease from the battle,
Always to chance it out,
which most can enfeeble the other,
When we might both join hands,
and share the dominion of Hellas?
Hi. Canst thou tutor the crab
to advance straight forward? thou canst not.
Tr. Wilt thou dine any more
in the Hall of Assembly? thou wilt not;
No, nor ever again
shall thy cheating knavery prosper.
Hi. Thou wilt never be able
to smooth the spines of the hedgehog.
Tr. Wilt thou never desist
bamboozling the people of Athens?
Hi. Say, what oracle taught you
to burn the thighs of the victim?
Tr. This, the wisest and best,
delivered by Homer the poet:
"When they had driven afar
the detestable cloud of the battle,
Then they established Peace,
and welcomed her back with oblations,
Duly the thighs they burned,
and ate the tripe and the inwards,
Then poured out the libations;
and I was the guide and the leader;
None to the soothsayer gave
the shining beautiful goblet."
Hi. Nothing I know of these:
these did not come from the Sibyl.
Tr. Nay, but wisely and well
spake Homer the excellent poet:
"Tribeless, lawless, and hearthless
is he that delighteth in bloodshed,
Bloodshed of kith and kin,
heart-sickening, horrible, hateful!"
Hi. Take thou heed, or a kite,
by a trick thy attention beguiling,
Down with a swoop may pounce.
Tr. (*to the* SERVANT) Ah! take heed really and truly.
That's an alarming hint:
it bodes no good to the inwards.
Pour the libation in,
and hand me a piece of the inwards.
Hi. Nay, but if such is the plan,
I too for myself will be caterer.
Tr. Pour libation! pour libation!
Hi. Pour it in also for me,
and reach me a share of the inwards.
Tr. That is far from the mind
of the Ever-blessed Immortals.
Yea, for before that hour—
—*you* go, *we'll* pour the libation.
Holy and reverend Peace,
abide with thy servants forever.
Hi. Now, fetch hither the tongue.
Tr. You, take yours off I'd advise you.
Hi. Pour the libation in.
Tr. Take that to assist the libation.
Hi. What! will none of you give me some meat?

Tr. 'Tis strictly forbidden.
You no inwards can have
till the wolf and the lamb be united.
Hi. Do, by your knees I beseech.
Tr. But fruitless are all your beseechings.
Thou wilt never be able
to smooth the spines of the hedgehog.
Come now, spectators, won't you share the mess
Along with us?
Hi. And I?
Tr. You? eat your Sibyl.
Hi. No, by the Earth, you two shan't feast alone!
I'll snatch a piece away: 'tis all in common.
Tr. Strike Bakis, strike!
Hi. I call them all to witness—
Tr. And so do I, that you're a rogue and glutton.
Lay on him with the stick: strike, strike the rascal!
1st S. You manage that, while I peel off the skins
Which he has gathered by his cozening tricks.
Now, sacrificer, off with all your skins.
What, won't you? here's a crow from Oreus town!
Back to Elymnium! flutter off: shoo! shoo!

Exeunt HIEROCLES, TRYGAEUS, *and* SERVANT.

Chorus

What a pleasure, what a treasure,
What a great delight to me,
From the cheese and from the onions
And the helmet to be free.
For I can't enjoy a battle,
But I love to pass my days
With my wine and boon companions
Round the merry, merry blaze,
When the logs are dry and seasoned,
And the fire is burning bright,
And I roast the pease and chestnuts
In the embers all alight,
—Flirting too with Thratta
When my wife is out of sight.

Ah, there's nothing half so sweet as
when the seed is in the ground,
God a gracious rain is sending,
and a neighbour saunters round.
"O Comarchides!" he hails me:
"how shall we enjoy the hours?"
"Drinking seems to suit my fancy,
what with these benignant showers.
Therefore let three quarts, my mistress,
of your kidney-beans be fried,
Mix them nicely up with barley,
and your choicest figs provide;
Syra run and shout to Manes,
call him in without delay,
'Tis no time to stand and dawdle
pruning out the vines to-day,
Nor to break the clods about them,
now the ground is soaking through.
Bring me out from home the fieldfare,
bring me out the siskins two,
Then there ought to be some beestings,
four good plates of hare beside
(Hah! unless the cat purloined them
yesterday at eventide;
Something scuffled in the pantry,
something made a noise and fuss);
If you find them, one's for father,
bring the other three to us.
Ask Aeschinades to send us
myrtle branches green and strong;
Bid Charinades attend us,
shouting as you pass along.
Then we'll sit and drink together,
God the while refreshing, blessing
All the labour of our hands."

O to watch the grape of Lemnos
Swelling out its purple skin,
When the merry little warblings
Of the Chirruper begin;
For the Lemnian ripens early.
And I watch the juicy fig
Till at last I pick and eat it
When it hangeth soft and big;
And I bless the friendly seasons
Which have made a fruit so prime,
And I mix a pleasant mixture,
Grating in a lot of thyme,
—Growing fat and hearty
In the genial summer clime.

This is better than a Captain
hated of the Gods to see,
Triple-crested, scarlet-vested,
scarlet bright as bright can be.
'Tis, he says, true Sardian tincture,
which they warrant not to run;
But if e'er it gets to fighting,
though his scarlet coat be on,
He himself becomes as pallid
as the palest Cyzicene,
Running like a tawny cockhorse,
he's the first to quit the scene;
Shake and quake his crests above him:
I stood gaping while he flew.
Ah, but when at home they're stationed,
things that can't be borne they do,
Making up the lists unfairly,
striking out and putting down
Names at random. 'Tis to-morrow
that the soldiers leave the town;
One poor wretch has bought no victuals,
for he knew not he must go
Till he on Pandion's statue
spied the list and found 'twas so,
Reading there his name inserted;
off he scuds with aspect wry.
This is how they treat the farmers,
but the burghers certainly
Somewhat better: godless wretches,
rogues with neither shame nor—shield,
Who one day, if God be willing,
strict accounts to me shall yield.
For they've wronged me much and sorely:

Very lions in the city,
Very foxes in the fight.

Re-enter TRYGAEUS *and* SERVANT.

Tr. Hillo! Hillo!
What lots are coming to the wedding supper!
Here, take this crest and wipe the tables down,
I've no more use for that, at all events.
And now serve up the thrushes and the cates,
And the hot rolls, and quantities of hare.

Enter SICKLE-MAKER.

Sickle-Maker. Where, where's Trygaeus?
Tr. Stewing thrushes here.
S.-M. O, my best friend, Trygaeus! O what blessings
Your gift of Peace has brought us. Till to-day
No man would give one farthing for a sickle;
And now! I'm selling them two pounds apiece.
And my friend here sells casks for country use
Half a crown each. Trygaeus, freely take
As many casks and sickles as you please.
And take this too (*giving money*); out of our sales and gains
We bring you these, we two, as wedding presents.
Tr. Well, lay your presents down, and hie you in
To join the marriage feast: here comes a man
Who trades in arms: he seems put out at something.

Enter CREST-MAKER, BREASTPLATE-SELLER, TRUMPETER, HELMET-SELLER, *and* SPEAR-BURNISHER.

Crest-Maker. O you've destroyed me root and branch, Trygaeus.
Tr. How now, poor wretch! what ails you? got a crestache?
C.-M. You have destroyed my living and my trade,
And this man's too, and yon spear-burnisher's.
Tr. What shall I give you, then, for these two crests?
C.-M. What *will* you give?
Tr. Faith, I'm ashamed to say:
Come, there's a deal of work about this juncture;
I'll give three quarts of raisins for the pair.
'Twill do to wipe my table down withal.
C.-M. Go in, then, go, and fetch the raisins out.
Better have that than nothing, O my friend.
Tr. Consume the things! here, take them, take them off.
The hairs are dropping out; they're not worth having.
Zounds! I'll not give one raisin for the pair.
Breastplate-Seller. O what's the use of this habergeon now?
So splendidly got up: cost forty pounds.
Tr. Well, well, you shan't lose anything by that:
I'll buy it of you at its full cost price.
'Twill do superbly for my chamber-pan,
B.-S. Come, don't be mocking at my wares and me.
Tr. Placing three stones anent it: ain't that clever?
B.-S. And how, you blockhead, can you cleanse yourself?
Tr. How? slip my hands in through the portholes, here,
And here.
B.-S. What, both at once!
Tr. Yes; I'll not cheat.
I'll have fair play: an arm for every hole.
B.-S. Sure, you won't use a forty-pounder so.
Tr. Why not, you rascal? Marry, I suppose
My seat of honour's worth eight hundred shillings.
B.-S. Well, fetch the silver out.
Tr. Plague take the thing;
It galls my stern: off with you: I won't buy it.
Trumpeter. See, here's a trumpet, cost me two pounds ten:
How in the world am I to use it now?
Tr. I'll tell you how. Fill up this mouth with lead,
Then fix a longish rod, here at the top,
And there you'll have a dropping cottabus.
Tru. O me! he mocks me.
Tr. Here's another plan:
Pour in the lead as I advised before,
Then at the top suspend a pair of scales
With little cords, and there's a famous balance
To weigh out figs for labourers on the farm.
Helmet-Seller. Thou hast destroyed me, dread unpitying Fate!
These helmets stood me in a good four pounds.
What am I now to do? who'll buy them now?
Tr. Take them to Egypt: you can sell them there.
They're just the things they measure physic in.
Tru. O, helmet-seller, we are both undone.
Tr. Why, *he's* received no hurt.
H.-S. Received no hurt!
Pray what's the use of all these helmets now?
Tr. Just clap on each a pair of ears, like these,
They'll sell much better then than now they will.
H.-S. O come away, spear-burnisher.
Tr. No, no.
I'm going to buy his spears: I really am.
Spear-Burnisher. What are you going to give?
Tr. Saw them in two,
I'll buy them all for vine-poles, ten a penny.
S.-B. The man insults us: come away, my friend.
Tr. Aye, go your way, for here come out the boys,
Those whom the guests have brought us; I suppose
They're going to practise what they're going to sing.
Come and stand here by me, my boy, and then
Let's hear you practise what you mean to sing.

Enter a group of young BOYS.

1st Boy. "Sing of the younger blood, whose deeds"—
Tr. Plague take you, be quiet
Singing of deeds of blood:
and that, you unfortunate ill-starred
Wretch, in the time of Peace;
you're a shameful and ignorant blockhead.
1st B. "Slowly the hosts approached,
till at length with a shock of encounter[1]
Shield was dashed upon shield,
and round-bossed buckler on buckler."
Tr. Buckler? you'd better be still:
how dare you be talking of bucklers?

[1]Quoting a line that occurs eleven times in the *Iliad*. The other lines quoted by the Boy are from Homer or in the Homeric language.

1st B. "Rose the rattle of war
commingled with groans of the dying."
Tr. Groans of the dying?
by great Dionysus, I'll make you repent it,
Singing of groans of the dying,
especially such as are round-bossed.
1st B. What, then, what shall I sing?
you, tell me the songs you delight in.
Tr. "Then on the flesh of beeves
they feasted"; something of *that* sort.
"Then a repast they served,
and whatever is best for a banquet."
1st B. "Then on the flesh of beeves
they feasted, aweary of fighting;
Then from the yoke they loosed
the reeking necks of the horses."
Tr. Good: they were tired of war, and so they feasted:
Sing on, O sing, how they were tired and feasted.
1st B. "Quickly, refreshed, they called for the casques."
Tr. Casks? gladly, I warrant.
1st B. "Out from the towers they poured,
and the roar of battle ascended."
Tr. Perdition seize you, boy, your wars and all!
You sing of nought but battles: who's your father?
1st B. Whose? mine?
Tr. Yes, yours, by Zeus!
1st B. Why, Lamachus.
Tr. Ugh, out upon it!
Truly I marvelled, and thought
to myself as I heard your performance,
This is the son of some hacker,
and thwacker, and sacker of cities.
Get to the spearmen, sing to *them*: begone.
Here, here, I want Cleonymus's son.
You, sing before we enter: sure I am
You won't sing wars: you've too discreet a father.
2nd Boy "Ah! some Saean is vaunting
the targe, which I in the bushes
Sadly, a blameless shield,
left as I fled from the field."
Tr. Tell me, you pretty baboon,
are you making a mock of your father?
2nd B. "Nay, but my *life* I preserved,"
Tr. But you shamed the parents who gave it.
Well go we in, for sure I am that you,
Being your father's son, will nevermore
Forget the song you sang about the shield.
Now then 'tis right, my jolly rogues,
that you should, here remaining,
Munch, crunch, and bite with all your might,
no empty vessels draining;
With manly zeal attack the meal,
And saw and gnaw with either jaw,
there's no advantage really
In having white and polished teeth
unless you use them freely.
Ch. O aye, we know: we won't be slow;
but thanks for thus reminding.
Tr. Set to, set to: you starving crew:
you won't be always finding
Such dishes rare of cake and hare
An easy prey in open day
thus wandering unprotected.
Set to, set to: or soon you'll rue
a splendid chance neglected.
Ch. O let not a word of ill-omen be heard,
but some of you run for the bride;
Some, torches to bring while the multitudes sing
and dance and rejoice by her side.
We'll carry the husbandry implements back
our own little homesteads about,
When we've had our ovation, and poured our libation, and hunted Hyperbolus out.
But first we'll pray to the Gods that they
May with rich success the Hellenes bless,
And that every field may its harvest yield,
And our garners shine with the corn and wine,
While our figs in plenty and peace we eat,
And our wives are blest with an increase sweet;
And we gather back in abundant store
The many blessings we lost before;
And the fiery steel—be it known no more.
Tr. Come then, come, my bride,
Midst the free green fields with me
Sweetly, sweet, abide.
Hymen, Hymenaeus O!
Hymen, Hymenaeus O!
Ch. Happy, happy, happy you,
And you well deserve it too.
Hymen, Hymenaeus O!
Hymen, Hymenaeus O!
Semi-Chorus. What shall with the bride be done,
What be done with Harvesthome?
Semi-Ch. She shall yield him, one by one,
All the joys of Harvest-home.
Semi-Ch. Ye to whom the task belongs
Raise the happy bridegroom, raise,
Bear him on with goodly songs,
Bear him on with nuptial lays.
Hymen, Hymenaeus O!
Hymen, Hymenaeus O!
Semi-Ch. Go and dwell in peace:
Not a care your lives impair,
Watch your figs increase.
Hymen, Hymenaeus O!
Hymen, Hymenaeus O!
Semi-Ch. He is stout and big.
Semi-Ch. She a sweeter fig.
Tr. So you all will think
When you feast and drink.
Ch. Hymen, Hymenaeus O!
Hymen, Hymenaeus O!
Tr. Away, away, good day, good day;
Follow me, sirs, if ye will,
And of bridecakes eat your fill.

THE BIRDS

DRAMATIS PERSONAE

EUELPIDES
PEISTHETAERUS
TROCHILUS, *servant of Epops*
EPOPS, THE HOOPOE
A PRIEST
A POET
AN ORACLE-MONGER
METON, A GEOMETRICIAN
A COMMISSIONER
A STATUTE-SELLER
A MESSENGER
A GUARD
IRIS
A HERALD
A SIRE-STRIKER
CINESIAS, *a Dithyrambic Poet*
A SYCOPHANT
PROMETHEUS
POSEIDON
TRIBALLIAN
HERACLES
A SERVANT OF PEISTHETAERUS
CHORUS OF BIRDS

A desolate scene, with a tree and a rock. Enter PEISTHETAERUS, *carrying a crow, and* EUELPIDES, *carrying a jackdaw.*

Euelpides. Straight on do you bid me go, where the tree stands?
Peisthetaerus. O hang it all! mine's croaking back again.
Eu. Why are we wandering up and down, you rogue?
This endless spin will make an end of *us*.
Pe. To think that I, poor fool, at a crow's bidding,
Should trudge about, an hundred miles and more!
Eu. To think that I, poor wretch, at a daw's bidding,
Should wear the very nails from off my feet!
Pe. Why, where we are, I've not the least idea.
Eu. Could you from hence find out your fatherland?
Pe. No, that would pose even—Execestides!
Eu. O, here's a nuisance!
Pe. Go *you* there, then, friend.
Eu. I call Philocrates a regular cheat,
The fool that sells the bird-trays in the market.
He swore these two would lead us straight to Tereus,
The hoopoe, made a bird in that same market.[1]
So then this daw, this son of Tharreleides,
We bought for an obol, and that crow for three.
But what knew they? Nothing, but how to—bite!
Where are you gaping now? Do you want to lead us
Against the rocks? There's no road here, I tell you.
Pe. No, nor yet here; not even the tiniest path.
Eu. Well, but what says your crow about the road?
Pe. By Zeus, she croaks quite differently now.
Eu. (*shouting*) *What does she say about the road?*
Pe. She says
She'll gnaw my fingers off: that's all she says.
Eu. Now isn't it a shame that when we are here
Ready and willing as two men can be
To go to the ravens, we can't find the way.
For we are sick, spectators, with a sickness
Just the reverse of that which Sacas has.
He, no true townsman, would perforce press in;
Whilst we, with rights of tribe and race unchallenged,
Townsmen mid townsmen, no man scaring us,
Spread both our—feet, and flew away from home.
Not that we hate our city, as not being
A prosperous mighty city, free for all
To spend their wealth in, paying fines and fees.
Aye, the cicalas chirp upon the boughs
One month, or two; but our Athenians chirp
Over their lawsuits all their whole life long.
That's why we are journeying on this journey now,
Trudging along with basket, pot, and myrtles,
To find some quiet easy-going spot,
Where we may settle down, and dwell in peace.
Tereus, the hoopoe, is our journey's aim,
To learn if he, in any place he has flown to,
Has seen the sort of city that we want.
Pe. You there!
Eu. What now?
Pe. My crow keeps croaking upwards
Ever so long.
Eu. And here's my jackdaw gaping
Up in the air, as if to show me something.
There must be birds about, I am sure of that.
Let's make a noise and we shall soon find out.
Pe. Then harkye; bang your leg against the rock.

[1]The hoopoe is really an actor who has obtained his plumage in the bird-market, where these birds were also bought; they might therefore be expected to find him. Pandion of Athens had two daughters, Procne and Philomela; Tereus of Thrace married the one and outraged the other; the sisters killed his son Itys, and served him up for his father's dinner; he pursued them, and they were changed, Tereus into a hoopoe, Procne into a nightingale, and Philomela into a swallow.

Eu. And you, your head; and there'll be twice the noise.
Pe. Well, take a stone and knock.
Eu. Yes, I'll do that.
Boy! Boy!
Pe. Eh! What! do you call the hoopoe "Boy"?
You should call "Whoop-ho there," not "Boy" of course.
Eu. O, Whoop-ho there! What, must I knock again? Whoop-ho!

A door opens in the rock, and an actor emerges, with a headdress representing the head of a Dunlin or PLOVER-PAGE *with a long and wide gaping beak.* PEISTHETAERUS *and* EUELPIDES *stumble back, and* PEISTHETAERUS *falls; their birds escape.*

Plover-Page. Whoever are these? Who calls my master?
Eu. Apollo shield us, what a terrible gape!
P.-P. These be two bird-catchers. O dear, O dear!
Eu. (*aside*) As nasty-speaking, as unpleasant-looking!
P.-P. Ye shall both die!
Eu. O, we're not men.
P.-P. What then?
Eu. Well, I'm the Panic-struck, a Libyan bird.
P.-P. Nonsense!
Eu. No nonsense: look for yourself and see.
P.-P. And *he*—what bird is he? come, won't you answer?
Pe. I? I'm a pheasant, and a yellow-tailed one.
Eu. But O by all the Gods, whatever are you?
P.-P. A serving-bird.
Eu. What, vanquished by some gamecock
In fight?
P.-P. No, but my master, when he first
Became a hoopoe, prayed that I might turn
Into a bird, to be his servant still.
Eu. What, does a bird require a serving-bird?
P.-P. He does, as having been a man, I fancy.
So when he wants to taste Phaleric sardines,
I run for the sardines, catching up a dish.
Does he want soup? then where's the pot and ladle?
I run for the ladle.
Eu. A regular running-page.
Now harkye, Plover-page, run in and call
Your master out.
P.-P. Great Zeus! he has just been eating
Myrtles and midges, and is gone to roost.
Eu. But still, do wake him.
P.-P. Well, I know he won't
Like to be waked, still for your sake I'll do it.

Exit the PLOVER-PAGE.

Pe. Confound the bird! he frightened me to death.
Eu. O dear! O dear! my heart went pit-a-pat,
My daw's gone too.
Pe. (*severely*) Gone! O you coward you,
You *let* him go!
Eu. Well, didn't you fall down,
And let your crow go?
Pe. No, I didn't. No!
Eu. Where is she then?
Pe. She flew away herself.
Eu. You didn't let her go. You're a brave boy!

Enter HOOPOE *upon the platform, which bears a small coppice in which his wife the Nightingale lies asleep. The* HOOPOE *has no feathers except on head and wings.*

Hoopoe. Throw wide the wood, that I may issue forth!
Eu. O Heracles, why what in the world is this?
What feathering's here? What style of triple-cresting?
Ho. Who be the folk that seek me?
Eu. The Twelve Gods
Would seem to have wrought your ruin.
Ho. What, do you jeer me,
Seeing the way I'm feathered? Strangers, I
Was once a man.
Eu. It's not at you we're laughing.
Ho. What is it then?
Eu. Your beak looks rather funny.
Ho. This is the way that Sophocles disfigures
The manly form of Tereus in his play.
Eu. What, are you Tereus? Are you bird or peacock?
Ho. I am a bird.
Eu. Then, where are all your feathers?
Ho. They've fallen off!
Eu. What! from disease, or why?
Ho. No, but in winter-time all birds are wont
To moult their feathers, and then fresh ones grow.
But tell me what *ye* are.
Eu. We? mortal men.
Ho. And of what race?
Eu. Whence the brave galleys come.
Ho. Not dicasts, are ye?
Eu. No, the other sort.
We're anti-dicasts.
Ho. Grows that seedling there?
Eu. Aye in the country you can find a few,
If you search closely.
Ho. But what brings you hither?
Eu. To talk with you a little.
Ho. What about?
Eu. You were a man at first, as we are now,
And had your creditors, as we have now,
And loved to shirk your debts, as we do now;
And then you changed your nature, and became
A bird, and flew round land and sea, and know
All that men feel, and all that birds feel too.
That's why we are come as suppliants here, to ask
If you can tell us of some city, soft
As a thick rug, to lay us down within.
Ho. Seek ye a mightier than the Cranaan town?
Eu. A mightier, no; a more commodious, yes.
Ho. Aristocratic?
Eu. Anything but that!
I loathe the very name of Scellias' son.[1]
Ho. What sort of city would ye like?
Eu. Why, one

[1]Aristocrates, chosen because of his name. He took part in the oligarchical revolution of the Four Hundred.

Where my worst trouble would be such as this;
A friend at daybreak coming to my door
And calling out, "O by Olympian Zeus,
Take your bath early: then come round to me,
You and your children, to the wedding banquet
I'm going to give. Now pray don't disappoint me,
Else, keep your distance, when my money's—
gone."

Ho. Upon my word, you are quite in love with troubles!
And *you*?

Pe. I love the like.

Ho. But tell me what.

Pe. To have the father of some handsome lad
Come up and chide me with complaints like these,
"Fine things I hear of you, Stilbonides,
You met my son returning from the baths,
And never kissed, or hugged, or fondled him,
You, his paternal friend! You're a nice fellow."

Ho. Poor Poppet, you are in love with ills indeed.
Well, there's the sort of city that ye want
By the Red Sea.

Eu. Not by the sea! Not where
The Salaminian, with a process-server
On board, may heave in sight some early morn.
But can't you mention some Hellenic town?

Ho. Why don't ye go and settle down in Elis,
At Lepreus?

Eu. Leprous! I was never there,
But for Melanthius' sake I loathe the name.

Ho. Well then, the Opuntians up in Locris, there's
The place to dwell in!

Eu. I become Opuntius!
No thank you, no, not for a talent of gold.
But this, this bird-life here, you know it well,
What is this like?

Ho. A pleasant life enough.
Foremost and first you don't require a purse.

Eu. There goes a grand corrupter of our life!

Ho. Then in the gardens we enjoy the myrtles,
The cress, the poppy, the white sesame.

Eu. Why, then, ye live a bridegroom's jolly life.

Pe. Oh! Oh!
O the grand scheme I see in the birds' reach,
And power to grasp it, if ye'd trust to me!

Ho. Trust you in what?

Pe. What? First don't fly about
In all directions, with your mouths wide open.
That makes you quite despised. With *us*, for instance,
If you should ask the flighty people there,
"Who is that fellow?" Teleas would reply,
"The man's a bird, a flighty feckless bird,
Inconsequential, always on the move."

Ho. Well blamed, i'faith; but what we ought to do,
Tell us.

Pe. Live all together: found one State.

Ho. What sort of State are birds to found, I wonder.

Pe. Aye, say you so? You who have made the most
Idiotic speech, look down.

Ho. I do.

Pe. Look up.

Ho. I do.

Pe. Twirl round your head.

Ho. Zeus! I shall be
A marvellous gainer, if I twist my neck!

Pe. What did you see?

Ho. I saw the clouds and sky.

Pe. And is not that the Station of the Birds?

Ho. Station?

Pe. As one should say, their habitation.
Here while the heavens revolve, and yon great dome
Is moving round, ye keep your Station still.
Make this your city, fence it round with walls,
And from your Station is evolved your State.
So ye'll be lords of men, as now of locusts,
And Melian famine shall destroy the Gods.

Ho. Eh! how?

Pe. The Air's betwixt the Earth and Sky.
And just as we, if we would go to Pytho,
Must crave a grant of passage from Boeotia,
Even so, when men slay victims to the Gods,
Unless the Gods pay tribute, ye in turn
Will grant no passage for the savoury steam
To rise through Chaos, and a realm not theirs.

Ho. Hurrah!
O Earth! ods traps, and nets, and gins, and snares,
This is the nattiest scheme that e'er I heard of!
So with your aid I'm quite resolved to found
The city, if the other birds concur.

Pe. And who shall tell them of our plan?

Ho. Yourself.
O they're not mere barbarians, as they were
Before I came. I've taught them language now.

Pe. But how to call them hither?

Ho. That's soon done.
I've but to step within the coppice here,
And wake my sleeping nightingale, and then
We'll call them, both together. Bless the birds,
When once they hear our voices, they'll come
running.

Pe. You darling bird, now don't delay one instant.
O I beseech you get at once within
Your little copse, and wake the nightingale!

Ho. Awake, my mate!
Shake off thy slumbers, and clear and strong
Let loose the floods of thy glorious song,
The sacred dirge of thy mouth divine
For sore-wept Itys, thy child and mine;
Thy tender trillings his name prolong
With the liquid note of thy tawny throat;
Through the leafy curls of the woodbine sweet
The pure sound mounts to the heavenly seat,
And Phoebus, lord of the golden hair,
As he lists to thy wild plaint echoing there,
Draws answering strains from his ivoried lyre,
Till he stirs the dance of the heavenly choir,
And calls from the blessed lips on high
Of immortal Gods, a divine reply
To the tones of thy witching melody.

The sound of a flute is heard within, imitating the nightingale's song.

Eu. O Zeus and King, the little birdie's voice!
O how its sweetness honied all the copse!

Pe. Hi!
Eu. Well?
Pe. Keep quiet.
Eu. Why?
Pe. The Hoopoe here
Is going to favour us with another song.

The Bird-call by the HOOPOE *and Nightingale conjointly; the Nightingale's song being imitated, as before, by the flute.*

Ho. Whoop-ho! Whoop-ho!
Whoop-hoop-hoop-hoop-hoop-ho!
Hoi! Hoi! Hoi! Come, come, come, come, come!
(*The land-birds*)
Come hither any bird with plumage like my own;
Come hither ye that batten on the acres newly sown,
On the acres by the farmer neatly sown;
And the myriad tribes that feed on the barley and the seed,
The tribes that lightly fly, giving out a gentle cry;
And ye who round the clod, in the furrow-riven sod,
With voices sweet and low, twitter flitter to and fro,
Singing, "Tío, tio, tío, tiotinx";
And ye who in the gardens a pleasant harvest glean,
Lurking in the branches of the ivy ever green;
And ye who top the mountains with gay and airy flight;
And ye who in the olive and the arbutus delight;
Come hither one and all, come flying to our call,
"Triotó, triotó, totobrinx."
(*The marsh-birds*)
Ye that snap up the gnats, shrilly voiced,
Mid the deep water-glens of the fens,
Or on Marathon's expanse haunt the lea, fair to see,
Or career o'er the swamps, dewy-moist,
And the bird with the gay mottled plumes, come away,
Francolín! Francolín! come away!
(*The sea-birds*)
Ye with the halcyons flitting delightedly
Over the surge of the infinite Sea,
Come to the great Revolution awaiting us,
Hither, come hither, come hither to me.
Hither, to listen to wonderful words,
Hither we summon the taper-necked birds.
For hither has come a shrewd old file,
Such a deep old file, such a sharp old file,
His thoughts are new, new deeds he'll do,
Come here, and confer with this shrewd old file.
Come hither! Come hither! Come hither!
Toro-toro-toro-torotinx!
Kikkabau, kikkabau!
Toro-toro-toro-toro-lililinx!

Pe. See any bird?
Eu. By Apollo no, not I,
Though up I gaze with mouth and eyes wide open.
Pe. Methinks the Hoopoe played the lapwing's trick,
Went in the copse, and whooped, and whooped for nothing.
Ho. Torotinx! Torotinx.
Pe. Comrade, here's a bird approaching,
coming to receive our visit.

Four birds pass before the audience, and disappear on the other side.

Eu. Aye by Zeus, what bird do you call it?
Surely not a peacock, is it?
Pe. That the Hoopoe here will teach us.
Prithee, friend, what bird is he?
Ho. That is not a common object,
such as you can always see;
That's a marsh-bird.
Eu. Lovely creature! nice and red like flaming flame.
Ho. So he should be, for Flamingo
is the lovely creature's name.
Eu. Hi there!
Pe. What? The row you're making!
Eu. Here's another, full in view.
Pe. Aye by Zeus, another truly,
with a foreign aspect too.
Who is he, the summit-ascending,
Muse-prophetical, wondrous bird?
Ho. He's a Median.
Pe. He a Median! Heracles, the thing's absurd.
How on earth without a camel
could a Median hither fly?
Eu. Here they're coming; here's another,
with his crest erected high.
Pe. Goodness gracious, that's a hoopoe;
yes, by Zeus, another one!
Are not *you* the only Hoopoe?
Ho. I'm his grandsire; he's the son
Of the Philocléan hoopoe:
as with you a name will pass,
Callias siring Hipponicus, Hipponicus Callias.
Pe. O then that is Callias is it?
How his feathers moult away!
Ho. Aye, the simple generous creature,
he's to parasites a prey.
And the females flock around him,
plucking out his feathers too.
Pe. O Poseidon, here's another;
here's a bird of brilliant hue!
What's the name of this, I wonder.
Ho. That's a Glutton styled by us.
Pe. Is there then another Glutton
than our own Cleonymus?
Eu. Our Cleonymus, I fancy,
would have thrown his crest away.
Pe. But what means the crest-equipment
of so many birds, I pray?
Are they going to race in armour?
Ho. No, my worthy friend, they make
Each his dwelling, like the Carians,
on the crests for safety's sake.

Enter CHORUS *of twenty-four birds, all crowding together.*

Pe. O Poseidon, what the mischief!
see the birds are everywhere
Fluttering onward.
Eu. King Apollo, what a cloud! O! O! look there,
Now we cannot see the entrance
for the numbers crowding in.

Pe. Here you see a partridge coming,
there by Zeus a francolin,
Here a widgeon onward hurries,
there's a halcyon, sure as fate.
Eu. Who's behind her?
Pe. That's a clipper; he's the lady halcyon's mate.
Eu. Can a clipper be a bird then?
Pe. Sporgilus is surely so.
Here's an owl.
Eu. And who to Athens brought an owl, I'd like to know.
Pe. Jay and turtle, lark and sedgebird,
thyme-finch, ring-dove first, and then
Rock-dove, stock-dove, cuckoo, falcon,
fiery-crest, and willow wren,
Lammergeyer, porphyrion, kestrel,
waxwing, nuthatch, water-hen.
Eu. (*singing*) Ohó for the birds, Ohó! Ohó!
Ohó for the blackbirds, ho!
How they twitter, how they go,
shrieking and screaming to and fro.
Goodness! are they going to charge us?
They are gazing here, and see
All their beaks they open widely.
Pe. That is what occurs to me.
Chorus. Wh-wh-wh-wh-wh-wh-wh-wh-where may he be
that was calling for me? In what locality pastureth he?
Ho. I am ready, waiting here;
never from my friends I stir.
Ch. Te-te-te-te-te-te-te-te-teach me, I pray, in an amicable way,
what is the news you have gotten to say.
Ho. News amazing! News auspicious!
News delightful, safe, and free!
Birds! Two men of subtlest genius
hither have arrived to me.
Ch. Who! What! When! say that again.
Ho. Here, I say, have come two elders,
travelling to the birds from man,
And the stem they are bringing with them
of a most stupendous plan.
Ch. You who have made the greatest error
since my callow life began,
What do you say?
Ho. Now don't be nervous.
Ch. What is the thing you have done to me?
Ho. I've received two men, enamoured
of your sweet society.
Ch. You have really dared to do it?
Ho. Gladly I the deed avow.
Ch. And the pair are now amongst us?
Ho. Aye, if I'm amongst you now.
Ch. O! O! Out upon you!
We are cheated and betrayed,
we have suffered shame and wrong!
For our comrade and our friend
who has fed with us so long,
He has broken every oath, and his holy plighted troth,
And the old social customs of our clan.
He has led us unawares into wiles, and into snares,
He has given us a prey, all helpless and forlorn,
To those who were our foes
from the time that they were born,
To vile and abominable Man!
But for him, our bird-companion,
comes a reckoning by and by;
As for these two old deceivers,
they shall suffer instantly,
Bit by bit we'll tear and rend them.
Pe. Here's a very horrid mess.
Eu. Wretched man, 'twas you that caused it,
you and all your cleverness!
Why you brought me I can't see.
Pe. Just that you might follow me.
Eu. Just that I might die of weeping.
Pe. What a foolish thing to say!
Weeping will be quite beyond you,
when your eyes are pecked away.
Ch. On! On! In upon them!
Make a very bloody onset,
spread your wings about your foes,
Assail them and attack them,
and surround them and enclose.
Both, both of them shall die,
and their bodies shall supply
A rare dainty pasture for my beak.
For never shall be found any distant spot of ground,
Or shadowy mountain covert, or foamy Ocean wave,
Or cloud in Ether floating,
which these reprobates shall save
From the doom that upon them I will wreak.
On then, on, my flying squadrons,
now's the time to tear and bite,
Tarry ye not an instant longer.
Brigadier, advance our right.
Eu. Here it comes! I'm off, confound them.
Pe. Fool, why can't you remain with me?
Eu. What! that these may tear and rend me?
Pe. How can you hope from birds to flee?
Eu. Truly, I haven't the least idea.
Pe. Then it is I the affair must guide.
Seize we a pot and, the charge awaiting,
here we will combat side by side.
Eu. Pot! and how can a pot avail us?
Pe. Never an owl will then come near.
Eu. What of these birds of prey with talons?
Pe. Snatch up a spit, like a hoplite's spear,
Planting it firmly there before you.
Eu. What shall I do about my eyes?
Pe. Take a platter, or take a saucer,
holding it over them buckler-wise.
Eu. What a skilful neat contrivance!
O you clever fellow you,
In your military science Nicias you far outdo!
Ch. Eleleleu! advance! no loitering;
level your beaks and charge away.
Shatter the pot at once to pieces;
worry, and scratch, and tear, and flay!
Ho. O, whatever is your purpose? is your villainy so great,

You would slay two worthy persons,
kinsmen, clansmen, of my mate?
Men who never sought to harm you,
would you tear and lacerate?
Ch. Why, I wonder, should we spare them,
more than ravening beasts of prey?
Shall we ever find, for vengeance,
enemies more rank than they?
Ho. Enemies, I grant, by nature,
very friends in heart and will;
Here they come with kindly purpose,
useful lessons to instil.
Ch. What, they come with words of friendship?
What, you really then suppose
They will teach us useful lessons,
they our fathers' fathers' foes?
Ho. Yet to clever folk a foeman
very useful hints may show;
Thus, that foresight brings us safety,
from a friend we ne'er should know,
But the truth is forced upon us, very quickly, by a foe.
Hence it is that all the Cities,
taught by foe, and not by friend,
Learn to build them ships of battle,
and their lofty walls extend;
So by this, a foeman's, teaching
children, home, and wealth defend.
Ch. Well, I really think 'tis better
that their errand we should know;
I admit that something useful
may be taught us by a foe.
Pe. (*to* EUELPIDES) Now their anger grows more slack;
now we had better just draw back.
Ho. (*to* CHORUS) This is right and friendly conduct,
such as I deserve from you.
Ch. Well, I am sure that we have never
gone against you hitherto.
Pe. Now they are growing a deal more peaceful,
now is the time the pot to ground,
Now we may lower the platters twain.
Nay, but the spit we had best retain,
Walking within the encampment's bound,
Letting our watchful glances skim
Over the edge of the pot's top rim;
Never a thought of flight must strike us.
Eu. Well, but tell me, suppose we die,
Where in the world will our bodies lie?
Pe. They shall be buried in Cerameicus,
That will be done at the public cost,
For we will say that our lives we lost
Gallantly fighting the public foe
(Yea, we will tell the commanders so),
Gallantly fighting at Orneae.
Ch. Fall back, fall back to your ranks once more,
And stand at ease as ye stood before,
And lay your wrath on the ground, in line
With your angry mood, as a warrior should;
We'll ask the while who the men may be,
And whence they come, and with what design.
Hey, Hoopoe, hey! to you I speak.
Ho. What is it that to learn you seek?
Ch. Whence are these visitors and who?
Ho. From clever Hellas strangers two.
Ch. What's their aim? Canst thou tell
Why they came Here to dwell?
Ho. Love of you, Love of your
Life and ways Was the lure.
Here they fain Would remain
Comrades true All their days.
Ch. Hey, hey, what do you say?
What is the tale they tell?
Ho. In brief,
'Tis something more than past belief.
Ch. But wherefore is he come? What is it
He seeks to compass by his visit?
Think you he's got some cunning plan
Whereby, allied with us, he can
Assist a friend, or harm a foe?
What brings him here, I'd like to know.
Ho. Too great, too great, for thought or words,
The bliss he promises the birds.
All things are yours, he says, whate'er
Exists in space, both here and there,
And to and fro, and everywhere.
Ch. Mad a little, eh?
Ho. More sane than words can say.
Ch. Wide awake?
Ho. Wide as day.
The subtlest cunningest fox,
All scheme, invention, craft; wit, wisdom, paradox.
Ch. His speech, his speech, bid him begin it.
The things you show excite me, so,
I'm fit to fly this very minute.
Ho. Now you and you, take back this panoply,
And hang it up, God bless it, out of sight
Within the kitchen there, beside the Jack.
But you (*to* PEISTHETAERUS) the things we summoned them to hear
Expound, declare.
Pe. By Apollo no, not I,
Unless they pledge me such a treaty-pledge
As that small jackanapes who makes the swords
Pledged with his wife, to wit that they'll not bite me
Nor pull me about, nor scratch my—
Ch. Fie, for shame!
Not *this*? no, no!
Pe. *My eyes*, I was going to say.
Ch. I pledge it.
Pe. Swear!
Ch. I swear on these conditions;
So may I win by every judge's vote,
And the whole Theatre's.
Pe. *And so you shall.*
Ch. But if I'm false, then by one vote alone.
Ho. O yes! O yes! Hoplites, take up your arms
And march back homewards; there await the orders
We're going to publish on the notice-boards.
Ch. Full of wiles, full of guiles, at all times, in all ways,
Are the children of Men; still we'll hear what he says.
Thou hast haply detected

Something good for the Birds which we never suspected;
Some power of achievement, too high
For my own shallow wit by itself to descry.
But if aught you espy,
Tell it out; for whate'er of advantage shall fall
To ourselves by your aid, shall be common to all.
So expound us the plan you have brought us, my man,
not doubting, it seems, of success.
And don't be afraid, for the treaty we made
we won't be the first to transgress.
Pe. I am hot to begin, and my spirit within
is fermenting the tale to declare.
And my dough I will knead, for there's nought to impede. Boy, bring me a wreath for my hair,
And a wash for my hands.
Eu. Why, what mean these commands?
Is a dinner in near contemplation?
Pe. No dinner, I ween; 'tis a *speech* that I mean,
a stalwart and brawny oration,
Their spirit to batter, and shiver and shatter.
(*To the* BIRDS) So sorely I grieve for your lot
Who once in the prime and beginning of time
were Sovereigns—
Ch. We Sovereigns! of what?
Pe. Of all that you see; of him and of me;
of Zeus up above on his throne;
A lineage older and nobler by far
than the Titans and Cronos ye own,
And than Earth.
Ch. And than Earth!
Pe. By Apollo 'tis true.
Ch. And I never had heard it before!
Pe. Because you've a blind uninquisitive mind,
unaccustomed on Aesop to pore.
The lark had her birth, so he says, before Earth;
then her father fell sick and he died.
She laid out his body with dutiful care,
but a grave she could nowhere provide;
For the Earth was not yet in existence; at last,
by urgent necessity led,
When the fifth day arrived, the poor creature contrived
to bury her sire in her head.
Eu. So the sire of the lark, give me leave to remark,
on the crest of a headland lies dead.
Pe. If therefore, by birth, ye are older than Earth,
if before all the Gods ye existed,
By the right of the firstborn the sceptre is yours;
your claim cannot well be resisted.
Eu. I advise you to nourish and strengthen your beak,
and to keep it in trim for a stroke.
Zeus won't in a hurry the sceptre restore
to the woodpecker tapping the oak.
Pe. In times prehistoric 'tis easily proved,
by evidence weighty and ample,
That Birds, and not Gods, were the Rulers of men,
and the Lords of the world; for example,
Time was that the Persians were ruled by the Cock,
a King autocratic, alone;
The sceptre he wielded or ever the names
"Megabazus," "Darius" were known;
And the "Persian" he still by the people is called
from the Empire that once was his own.
Eu. And thus, to this hour, the symbol of power
on his head you can always detect:
Like the Sovereign of Persia, alone of the Birds,
he stalks with tiara erect.
Pe. So mighty and great was his former estate,
so ample he waxed and so strong,
That still the tradition is potent, and still,
when he sings in the morning his song,
At once from their sleep all mortals upleap,
the cobblers, the tanners, the bakers,
The potters, the bathmen, the smiths, and the
shield-and-the-musical-instrument-makers;
And some will at eve take their sandals and leave.
Eu. I can answer for that, to my cost.
'Twas all through his crowing at eve that my cloak,
the softest of Phrygians, I lost.
I was asked to the Tenth-day feast of a child;
and I drank ere the feast was begun;
Then I take my repose; and anon the cock crows;
so thinking it daybreak I run
To return from the City to Halimus town;
but scarce I emerge from the wall,
When I get such a whack with a stick on my back
from a rascally thief, that I fall,
And he skims off my cloak from my shoulders or
e'er for assistance I'm able to bawl.
Pe. Then a Kite was the Sovereign of Hellas of old,
and ruled with an absolute sway.
Ch. The Sovereign of Hellas!
Pe. And, taught by his rule,
we wallow on earth to this day
When a Kite we espy.
Eu. By Bacchus, 'twas I
saw a Kite in the air; so I wallow
Then raising my eyne from my posture supine,
I give such a gulp that I swallow
O what but an obol I've got in my mouth,
and am forced to return empty-handed.
Pe. And the whole of Phoenice and Egypt was erst
by a masterful Cuckoo commanded.
When his loud cuckoo-cry was resounding on high,
at once the Phoenicians would leap
All hands to the plain, rich-waving with grain,
their wheat and their barley to reap.
Eu. So that's why we cry to the circumcised "Hi!"
"Cuckoo! To the plain! Cuckoo!"
Pe. And whene'er in the cities of Hellas a chief
to honour and dignity grew,
Menelaus or King Agamemnon perchance,
your rule was so firm and decided
That a bird on his sceptre would perch, to partake
of the gifts for his Lordship provided.
Eu. Now of that I declare I was never aware;
and I oft have been filled with amaze,
When Priam so noble and stately appeared,
with a bird, in the Tragedy-plays.
But the bird was no doubt for the gifts looking out,
to Lysicrates brought on the sly.

Pe. But the strongest and clearest of proofs is that Zeus
who at present is Lord of the sky
Stands wearing, as Royalty's emblem and badge,
an Eagle erect on his head,
Our Lady an owl, and Apollo forsooth,
as a lackey, a falcon instead.
Eu. By Demeter, 'tis true; that is just what they do;
but tell me the reason, I pray.
Pe. That the bird may be ready and able, whene'er
the sacrificed inwards we lay,
As custom demands, in the deity's hands,
to seize before Zeus on the fare.
And none by the Gods, but all by the Birds,
were accustomed aforetime to swear:
And Lampon will vow by the Goose even now,
whenever he's going to cheat you:
So holy and mighty they deemed you of old,
with so deep a respect did they treat you!
Now they treat you as knaves,
and as fools, and as slaves;
Yea they pelt you as though ye were mad.
No safety for you can the Temples ensure,
For the bird-catcher sets his nooses and nets,
And his traps, and his toils, and his bait, and his lure,
And his lime-covered rods in the shrine of the Gods!
Then he takes you, and sets you for sale in the lump;
And the customers, buying, come poking and prying
And twitching and trying,
To feel if your bodies are tender and plump.
And if they decide on your flesh to sup
They don't just roast you and serve you up,
But over your bodies, as prone ye lie,
They grate their cheese and their silphium too,
And oil and vinegar add,
Then a gravy, luscious and rich, they brew,
And pour it in soft warm streams o'er you,
As though ye were carrion noisome and dry.
Ch. O man, 'tis indeed a most pitiful tale
Thou hast brought to our ears; and I can but bewail
Our fathers' demerit,
Who born such an Empire as this to inherit
Have lost it, have lost it, for me!
But now thou art come, by good Fortune's decree,
Our Saviour to be,
And under thy charge, whatsoever befall,
I will place my own self, and my nestlings, and all.
Now therefore do you tell us what we must do;
since life is not worth our retaining,
Unless we be Lords of the world as before,
our ancient dominion regaining.
Pe. Then first I propose that the Air ye enclose,
and the space 'twixt the Earth and the sky,
Encircling it all with a brick-builded wall,
like Babylon's, solid and high;
And there you must place the abode of your race,
and make them one State, and one nation.
Eu. O Porphyrion! O Cebriones!
how stupendous the fortification!
Pe. When the wall is complete, send a messenger fleet,
the empire from Zeus to reclaim.
And if he deny, or be slow to comply,
nor retreat in confusion and shame,
Proclaim ye against him a Holy War,
and announce that no longer below,
On their lawless amours through these regions of yours,
will the Gods be permitted to go.
No more through the air (to their Alopes fair,
their Alcmenas, their Semeles wending)
May they post in hot love, as of old, from above,
for if ever you catch them descending,
You will clap on their dissolute persons a seal,
their evil designs to prevent!
And then let another ambassador-bird
to men with this message be sent,
That the Birds being Sovereigns, to them must be paid
all honour and worship divine,
And the Gods for the future to them be postponed.
Now therefore assort and combine
Each God with a bird, whichever will best
with his nature and attributes suit;
If to Queen Aphrodite a victim ye slay,
first sacrifice grain to the coot;
If a sheep to Poseidon ye slay, to the duck
let wheat as a victim be brought;
And a big honey-cake for the cormorant make,
if ye offer to Heracles aught.
Bring a ram for King Zeus! But ye first must produce
for our Kinglet, the gold-crested wren,
A masculine midge, full formed and entire,
to be sacrificed duly by men.
Eu. I am tickled and pleased with the sacrificed midge.
Now thunder away, great Zan![1]
Ch. But men, will they take us for Gods, and not daws,—
do ye really believe that they can—
If they see us on wings flying idly about?
Pe. Don't say such ridiculous things!
Why, Hermes, and lots of the deities too,
go flying about upon wings.
There is Victory, bold on her pinions of gold;
and then, by the Powers, there is Love;
And Iris, says Homer, shoots straight through the skies,
with the ease of a terrified dove.
Eu. And the thunderbolt flies upon wings, I surmise:
what if Zeus upon *us* let it fall?
Pe. But suppose that mankind, being stupid and blind,
should account you as nothing at all,
And still in the Gods of Olympus believe—
why then, like a cloud, shall a swarm
Of sparrows and rooks settle down on their stooks,
and devour all the seed in the farm.

[1]Doric for Zeus.

Demeter may fill them with grain, if she will,
when hungry and pinched they entreat her.
Eu. O no, for by Zeus, she will make some excuse;
that is always the way with Demeter.
Pe. And truly the ravens shall pluck out the eyes
of the oxen that work in the plough,
Of the flocks and the herds, as a proof that the Birds
are the Masters and Potentates now.
Apollo the leech, if his aid they beseech,
may cure them; but then they must pay!
Eu. Nay but hold, nay but hold, nor begin till I've sold
my two little oxen I pray.
Pe. But when once to esteem you as God, and as Life,
and as Cronos and Earth they've begun,
And as noble Poseidon, what joys shall be theirs!
Ch. Will you kindly inform me of one?
Pe. The delicate tendrils and bloom of the vine
no more shall the locusts molest,
One gallant brigade of the kestrels and owls
shall rid them at once of the pest.
No more shall the mite and the gall-making blight
the fruit of the fig-tree devour;
Of thrushes one troop on their armies shall swoop,
and clear them all off in an hour.
Ch. But how shall we furnish the people with wealth?
It is wealth that they mostly desire.
Pe. Choice blessings and rare ye shall give them whene'er
they come to your shrine to inquire.
To the seer ye shall tell when 'tis lucky and well
for a merchant to sail o'er the seas,
So that never a skipper again shall be lost.
Ch. What, "never"? Explain if you please.
Pe. Are they seeking to know when a voyage to go?
The Birds shall give answers to guide them.
"Now stick to the land, there's a tempest at hand!
Now sail!" and good luck shall betide them.
Eu. A galley for me; I am off to the sea!
No longer with you will I stay.
Pe. The treasures of silver long since in the earth
by their forefathers hidden away
To men ye shall show, for the secret ye know.
How often a man will declare,
"There is no one who knows where my treasures repose,
if it be not a bird of the air."
Eu. My galley may go; I will buy me a hoe,
and dig for the crock and the casket.
Ch. But Health, I opine, is a blessing divine;
can we give it to men if they ask it?
Pe. If they've plenty of wealth, they'll have plenty of health;
ye may rest quite assured that they will.
Did you ever hear tell of a man that was well,
when faring remarkably ill?
Ch. Long life 'tis Olympus alone can bestow;
so can men live as long as before?
Must they die in their youth?
Pe. Die? No! why in truth
their lives by three hundred or more
New years ye will lengthen.
Ch. Why, whence will they come?
Pe. From your own inexhaustible store.
What! dost thou not know that the noisy-tongued crow
lives five generations of men?
Eu. O fie! it is plain they are fitter to reign
than the Gods; let us have them again.
Pe. Ay fitter by far!
No need for their sakes to erect and adorn
Great temples of marble with portals of gold.
Enough for the birds on the brake and the thorn
And the evergreen oak their receptions to hold.
Or if any are noble, and courtly, and fine,
The tree of the olive will serve for their shrine.
No need, when a blessing we seek, to repair
To Delphi or Ammon, and sacrifice there;
We will under an olive or arbutus stand
With a present of barley and wheat,
And piously lifting our heart and our hand
The birds for a boon we'll entreat,
And the boon shall be ours, and our suit we shall gain
At the cost of a few little handfuls of grain.
Ch. I thought thee at first of my foemen the worst;
and lo, I have found thee the wisest
And best of my friends, and our nation intends
to do whatsoe'er thou advisest.
A spirit so lofty and rare
Thy words have within me excited,
That I lift up my soul, and I swear
That if Thou wilt with Me be united
In bonds that are holy and true
And honest and just and sincere,
If our hearts are attuned to one song,
We will march on the Gods without fear;
The sceptre—*my* sceptre, *my* due—
They shall not be handling it long!
So all that by muscle and strength can be done,
we Birds will assuredly do;
But whatever by prudence and skill must be won,
we leave altogether to you.
Ho. Aye and, by Zeus, the time is over now
For drowsy nods and Nicias-hesitations.
We must be up and doing! And do you,
Or e'er we start, visit this nest of mine,
My bits of things, my little sticks and straws;
And tell me what your names are.
Pe. That's soon done.
My name is Peisthetaerus.
Ho. And your friend's?
Pe. Euelpides of Crio.
Ho. Well, ye are both
Heartily welcome.
Pe. Thank you.
Ho. Come ye in.
Pe. Aye, come we in; you, please, precede us.
Ho. Come.
Pe. But—dear! what was it? step you back a moment.

O yes—but tell us, how can he and I
Consort with you, we wingless and you winged?
Ho. Why, very well.
Pe. Nay, but in Aesop's fables
There's something, mind you, told about the fox
How ill it fared, consorting with an eagle.
Ho. O never fear; for there's a little root
Which when ye have eaten, ye will both be winged.
Pe. That being so, we'll enter. Xanthias there,
And Manodorus, bring along the traps.
Ch. O stay, and O stay!
Ho. Why what ails you to-day?
Ch. Take the gentlemen in, and regale them, we say
But O for the nightingale peerless in song,
who chants in the choir of the Muses her lay;
Our sweetest and best, fetch her out of the nest,
and leave her awhile with the Chorus to play.
Pe. O do, by Zeus, grant them this one request;
Fetch out the little warbler from the reeds.
Eu. Yes, fetch her out by all the Gods, that so
We too may gaze upon the nightingale.
Ho. Well, if you wish it, so we'll have it. Procne,
Come hither, dear, and let the strangers see you.

Enter PROCNE, *with nightingale's head and wings, otherwise clad as a girl, in a rich costume.*

Pe. Zeus, what a darling lovely little bird!
How fair, and tender!
Eu. O the little love,
Wouldn't I like to be her mate this instant!
Pe. And O the gold she is wearing, like a girl.
Eu. Upon my word, I've half a mind to kiss her!
Pe. Kiss her, you fool! Her beak's a pair of spits.
Eu. But I would treat her like an egg, and strip
The egg-shell from her poll, and kiss her so.
Ho. Come, go we in.
Pe. Lead on, and luck go with us.

Exeunt HOOPOE, EUELPIDES, *and* PEISTHETAERUS.

Chorus

O darling! O tawny-throat!
Love, whom I love the best,
Dearer than all the rest,
Playmate and partner in
All my soft lays,
Thou art come! Thou art come!
Thou hast dawned on my gaze,
I have heard thy sweet note,
Nightingále! Nightingále!
Thou from thy flute Softly-sounding canst bring
Music to suit With our songs of the Spring:
Begin then I pray
Our own anapaestic address to essay.

Ye men who are dimly existing below,
who perish and fade as the leaf,
Pale, woebegone, shadowlike, spiritless folk,
life feeble and wingless and brief,
Frail castings in clay, who are gone in a day,
like a dream full of sorrow and sighing,
Come listen with care to the Birds of the air,
the ageless, the deathless, who flying
In the joy and the freshness of Ether, are wont
to muse upon wisdom undying.
We will tell you of things transcendental; of Springs
and of Rivers the mighty upheaval;
The nature of Birds; and the birth of the Gods:
and of Chaos and Darkness primeval.
When this ye shall know, let old Prodicus go,
and be hanged without hope of reprieval.
There was Chaos at first, and Darkness, and Night,
and Tartarus vasty and dismal;
But the Earth was not there, nor the Sky, nor the Air,
till at length in the bosom abysmal
Of Darkness an egg, from the whirlwind conceived,
was laid by the sable-plumed Night.
And out of that egg, as the Seasons revolved,
sprang Love, the entrancing, the bright,
Love brilliant and bold with his pinions of gold,
like a whirlwind, refulgent and sparkling!
Love hatched us, commingling in Tartarus wide,
with Chaos, the murky, the darkling,
And brought us above, as the firstlings of love,
and first to the light we ascended.
There was never a race of Immortals at all
till Love had the universe blended;
Then all things commingling together in love,
there arose the fair Earth, and the Sky,
And the limitless Sea; and the race of the Gods,
the Blessed, who never shall die.
So we than the Blessed are older by far;
and abundance of proof is existing
That we are the children of Love, for we fly,
unfortunate lovers assisting.
And many a man who has found, to his cost,
that his powers of persuasion have failed,
And his loves have abjured him forever, again
by the power of the Birds has prevailed;
For the gift of a quail, or a Porphyry rail,
or a Persian, or goose, will regain them.
And the chiefest of blessings ye mortals enjoy,
by the help of the Birds ye obtain them.
'Tis from us that the signs of the Seasons in turn,
Spring, Winter, and Autumn are known.
When to Libya the crane flies clanging again,
it is time for the seed to be sown,
And the skipper may hang up his rudder awhile,
and sleep after all his exertions,
And Orestes may weave him a wrap to be warm
when he's out on his thievish excursions.
Then cometh the kite, with its hovering flight,
of the advent of Spring to tell,
And the Spring sheep-shearing begins; and next,
your woollen attire you sell,
And buy you a lighter and daintier garb,
when you note the return of the swallow.
Thus your Ammon, Dodona, and Delphi are we;
we are also your Phoebus Apollo.
For whatever you do, if a trade you pursue,
or goods in the market are buying,
Or the wedding attend of a neighbour and friend,
first you look to the Birds and their flying.

And whene'er you of omen or augury speak,
'*tis a bird* you are always repeating;
A Rumour's a bird, and a sneeze is a bird,
and so is a word or a meeting,
A servant's a bird, and an ass is a bird.
It must therefore assuredly follow
That the Birds are to you (I protest it is true)
your prophetic divining Apollo.

Then take us for Gods, as is proper and fit,
And Muses Prophetic ye'll have at your call
Spring, winter, and summer, and autumn and all.
And we won't run away from your worship, and sit
Up above in the clouds, very stately and grand,
Like Zeus in his tempers: but always at hand
Health and wealth we'll bestow, as the formula runs,
"On yourselves, and your sons, and the sons of your sons";
And happiness, plenty, and peace shall belong
To you all; and the revel, the dance, and the song,
And laughter, and youth, and the milk of the birds
We'll supply, and we'll never forsake you.
Ye'll be quite overburdened with pleasures and joys,
So happy and blest we will make you.

O woodland Muse.
"tío, tio, tío, tiotinx,"
Of varied plume, with whose dear aid
On the mountain top, and the sylvan glade,
"tío, tio, tío, tiotinx,"
I, sitting up aloft on a leafy ash, full oft,
"tío, tio, tío, tiotinx,"
Pour forth a warbling note from my little tawny throat,
Pour festive choral dances to the mountain mother's praise,
And to Pan the holy music of his own immortal lays:
"totótototótototótotinx,"
Whence Phrynichus of old,
Sipping the fruit of our ambrosial lay,
Bore, like a bee, the honied store away,
His own sweet songs to mould,
"Tio, tío, tio, tío, tiotinx."

Is there any one amongst you,
O spectators, who would lead
With the birds a life of pleasure,
let him come to us with speed
All that here is reckoned shameful,
all that here the laws condemn,
With the birds is right and proper,
you may do it all with them.
Is it here by law forbidden
for a son to beat his sire?
That a chick should strike his father,
strutting up with youthful ire,
Crowing, "Raise your spur and fight me,"
that is what the birds admire.
Come you runaway deserter,
spotted o'er with marks of shame,
Spotted Francolin we'll call you,
that, with us, shall be your name.
You who style yourself a tribesman,
Phrygian pure as Spintharus,
Come and be a Phrygian linnet,
of Philemon's breed, with us.
Come along, you slave and Carian,
Execestides to wit,
Breed with us your Cuckoo-rearers,
they'll be guildsmen apt and fit.
Son of Peisias, who to outlaws
would the city gates betray,
Come to us, and be a partridge
(*cockerel like the cock*, they say),
We esteem it no dishonour
knavish partridge-tricks to play.
Even thus the Swans,
"tío, tio, tío, tiotinx,"
Their clamorous cry were erst up-raising,
With clatter of wings Apollo praising,
"tio, tio, tio, tiotinx,"
As they sat in serried ranks on the river Hebrus' banks.
"tío, tio, tío, tiotinx,"
Right upward went the cry
through the cloud and through the sky.
Quailed the wild-beast in his covert,
and the bird within her nest,
And the still and windless Ether
lulled the ocean-waves to rest.
"Totótotótotótotótotinx."
Loudly Olympus rang!
Amazement seized the kings; and every Grace
And every Muse within that heavenly place
Took up the strain, and sang.
"Tio, tío, tio, tío, tiotinx."

Truly to be clad in feather
is the very best of things.
Only fancy, dear spectators,
had you each a brace of wings,
Never need you, tired and hungry,
at a Tragic Chorus stay,
You would lightly, when it bored you,
spread your wings and fly away,
Back returning, after luncheon,
to enjoy our Comic Play.
Never need a Patrocleides,
sitting here, his garment stain;
When the dire occasion seized him,
he would off with might and main
Flying home, then flying hither,
lightened and relieved, again.
If a gallant should the husband
on the Council-bench behold
Of a gay and charming lady,
one whom he had loved of old,
Off at once he'd fly to greet her,
have a little converse sweet,
Then be back, or e'er ye missed him,
calm and smiling in his seat.
Is not then a suit of feathers
quite the very best of things?
Why, Diitrephes was chosen,
though he had but wicker wings,

First a Captain, then a Colonel,
till from nothing he of late
Has become a tawny cock-horse,
yea a pillar of the State!

Enter PEISTHETAERUS *and* EUELPIDES, *equipped with wings.*

Pe. Well, here we are. By Zeus, I never saw
In all my life a sight more laughable.
Eu. What are you laughing at?
Pe. At your flight-feathers.
I'll tell you what you're like, your wings and you,
Just like a gander, sketched by some cheap-Jack.
Eu. And you, a blackbird, with a bowl-cropped noddle.
Pe. These shafts of ridicule are winged by nought
But our own plumes, as Aeschylus would say.
Ch. What's the next step?
Pe. First we must give the city
Some grand big name: and then we'll sacrifice
To the high Gods.
Eu. That's my opinion also.
Ch. Then let's consider what the name shall be.
Pe. What think you of that grand Laconian name,
Sparta?
Eu. What! Sparta for my city? No.
I wouldn't use esparto for my pallet,
Not if I'd cords; by Heracles, not I.
Pe. How shall we name it then?
Ch. Invent some fine
Magniloquent name, drawn from these upper spaces
And clouds.
Pe. What think you of Cloudcuckoobury?
Ch. Good! Good!
You have found a good big name, and no mistake.
Eu. Is this the great Cloudcuckoobury town
Where all the wealth of Aeschines lies hid,
And all Theagenes's?
Pe. Best of all,
This is the plain of Phlegra, where the Gods
Outshot the giants at the game of Brag.
Eu. A glistering sort of a city! Who shall be
Its guardian God? For whom shall we weave the Peplus?
Pe. Why not retain Athene, City-keeper?
Eu. And how can that be a well-ordered State,
Where she, a woman born, a Goddess, stands
Full-armed, and Cleisthenes assumes a spindle?
Pe. And who shall hold the citadel's Storkade?
Ch. A bird of ours, one of the Persian breed,
Everywhere noted as the War-god's own
Armipotent cockerel.
Eu. O, Prince Cockerel? Yes,
He's just the God to perch upon the rocks.
Pe. Now, comrade, get you up into the air,
And lend a hand to those that build the wall.
Bring up the rubble; strip, and mix the mortar;
Run up the ladder with the hod; fall off;
Station the sentinels; conceal the fire;
Round with the alarum bell; go fast asleep;
And send two heralds, one to heaven above,
And one to earth below; and let them come
From thence, for me.
Eu. And you, remaining here,
Be hanged—for me!
Pe. Go where I send you, comrade,

Exit EUELPIDES, *who does not appear again.*

Without your help there, nothing will be done.
But I, to sacrifice to these new Gods,
Must call the priest to regulate the show.
Boy! Boy! take up the basket and the laver.
Ch. I'm with you, you'll find me quite willing:
I highly approve of your killing
A lambkin, to win us the favour divine,
Mid holy processionals, stately and fine,
Up high, up high, let the Pythian cry,
The Pythian cry to the God be sent;
Let Chaeris play the accompaniment.
Pe. O stop that puffing! Heracles, what's this?
Faith, I've seen many a sight, but never yet
A mouth-band-wearing raven! Now then, priest,
To the new Gods commence the sacrifice.

Enter PRIEST.

Priest. I'll do your bidding. Where's the basket-bearer?
Let us pray
To the Hestia-bird of the household shrine,
And the Kite that watches her feasts divine,
And to all the Olympian birds and birdesses,
Pe. O Sunium-hawking, King of the Sea—mew, hail!
Pr. And to the holy Swan, the Pythian and Delian one,
And to thee too, Quail-guide Leto,
And to Artemis the Thistle-finch,
Pe. Aye, Thistle-finch; no more Colaenis now!
Pr. And to Sabazius the Phrygian linnet; and then
To Rhea the Great Mother of Gods and men;
Pe. Aye, Ostrich-queen, Cleocritus's Mother!
Pr. That they may grant health and salvation
To the whole Cloudcuckooburian nation,
For themselves and the Chians.
Pe. I like the Chians everywhere tacked on.
Pr. And to the hero-birds and sons of heroes,
And to the Porphyrion rail;
And to the pelican white, and pelican grey;
And to the eagle, and to the capercaillie;
And to the peacock, and to the sedgewarbler;
And to the teal, and to the skua;
And to the heron, and to the gannet;
And to the blackcap, and to the titmouse—
Pe. Stop, stop your calling, hang you. O, look here.
To what a victim, idiot, are you calling
Ospreys and vultures? Don't you see that one
One single kite could carry off the whole?
Get away hence, you and your garlands too!
Myself alone will sacrifice this victim.

Exit PRIEST.

Ch. Once more as the laver they're bringing,
Once more I my hymns must be singing,
Hymns holy and pious, the Gods to invite—
One alone, only one,—to our festival rite.

Your feast for two, I am sure won't do.
For what you are going to offer there.
Is nothing at all but horns and hair.

Pe. Let us pray,
Offering our victim to the feathery gods.

Enter a POET, *to celebrate the founding of the new colony.*

Poet. (*singing*) Cloudcuckoobury
With praise and glory crown,
Singing, O Muse,
Of the new and happy town!

Pe. Whatever's this? Why, who in the world are you?

Po. O I'm a warbler, carolling sweet lays,
An eager meagre servant of the Muses,
As Homer says.

Pe. What! you a slave and wear your hair so long?

Po. No, but all we who teach sweet choral lays
Are eager meagre servants of the Muses,
As Homer says.

Pe. That's why your cloak so meagre seems, no doubt.
But, poet, what ill wind has blown you hither?

Po. Oh I've been making, making lovely songs,
Simonideans, virgin songs, and sweet
Dithyrambic songs, on your Cloudcuckooburies.

Pe. When did you first begin these lovely songs?

Po. Long, long ago, O yes! Long, long ago!

Pe. Why, is not this the City's Tenth-day feast?
I've just this instant given the child its name.

Po. But fleet, as the merry many-twinkling horses' feet,
The airy fairy Rumour of the Muses.
Aetna's Founder, father mine,
Whose name is the same as the holy altar flame,
Give to me what thy bounty chooses
To give me willingly of thine.

Pe. He'll cause us trouble now, unless we give him
Something, and so get off. Hallo, you priest,
Why, you've a jerkin and a tunic too;
Strip, give the jerkin to this clever poet.
Take it; upon my word you *do* seem cold.

Po. This little kindly gift the Muse
Accepts with willing condescension;
But let me to an apt remark
Of Pindar call my lord's attention.

Pe. The fellow does not seem inclined to leave us.

Po. Out among the Scythians yonder
See poor Straton wander, wander,
Poor poor Straton, not possessed
of a whirly-woven vest.
All inglorious comes, I trow, leather jerkin, if below
No soft tunic it can show.
Conceive my drift, I pray.

Pe. Aye, I conceive you want the tunic too.
Off with it, you. Needs must assist a Poet.
There, take it, and depart.

Po. Yes, I'll depart,
And make to the city pretty songs like this;
O Thou of the golden throne,
Sing Her, the quivering, shivering;
I came to the plains many-sown,
I came to the snowy, the blowy.
Alalae! *Exit* POET.

Pe. Well, well, but now you surely have escaped
From all those shiverings, with that nice warm vest.
This is, by Zeus, a plague I never dreamed of
That he should find our city out so soon.
Boy, take the laver and walk round once more.
Now hush! *Enter* ORACLE-MONGER.

Oracle-Monger. Forbear! touch not the goat awhile.

Pe. Eh? Who are you?

O.-M. A soothsayer.

Pe. You be hanged!

O.-M. O think not lightly, friend, of things divine;
Know I've an oracle of Bakis, bearing
On your Cloudcuckooburies.

Pe. Eh? then why
Did you not soothsay that before I founded
My city here?

O.-M. The Power within forbade me.

Pe. Well, well, there's nought like hearing what it says.

O.-M. "Nay but if once grey crows
and wolves shall be banding together,
Out in the midway space,
'twixt Corinth and Sicyon, dwelling—"

Pe. But what in the world have I to do with Corinth?

O.-M. Bakis is riddling: Bakis means the Air.
"First to Pandora offer
a white-fleeced ram for a victim.
Next, who first shall arrive
my verses prophetic expounding,
Give him a brand-new cloak
and a pair of excellent sandals."

Pe. Are sandals in it?

O.-M. Take the book and see.
"Give him moreover a cup,
and fill his hands with the inwards."

Pe. Are inwards in it?

O.-M. Take the book and see.
"Youth, divinely inspired,
if thou dost as I bid, thou shalt surely
Soar in the clouds as an Eagle;
refuse, and thou ne'er shalt become an
Eagle, or even a dove,
or a woodpecker tapping the oak-tree."

Pe. Is all that in it?

O.-M. Take the book and see.

Pe. O how unlike your oracle to mine,
Which from Apollo's words I copied out;
"But if a cheat, an impostor,
presume to appear uninvited,
Troubling the sacred rites,
and lusting to taste of the inwards,
Hit him betwixt the ribs
with all your force and your fury."

O.-M. You're jesting surely.

Pe. Take the book and see.
"See that ye spare not the rogue,
though he soar in the clouds as an Eagle,
Yea, be he Lampon himself
or even the great Diopeithes."

O.-M. Is all that in it?
Pe. Take the book and see.
Get out! be off, confound you! (*striking him*)
O.-M. O! O! O!
Pe. There, run away and soothsay somewhere else.
Exit ORACLE-MONGER; *enter* METON, *with the instruments of a land-surveyor.*
Meton. I come amongst you—
Pe. Some new misery this!
Come to do what? What's your scheme's form and outline?
What's your design? What buskin's on your foot?
Me. I come to land-survey this Air of yours,
And mete it out by acres.
Pe. Heaven and Earth!
Whoever are you?
Me. (*scandalized*) Whoever am I! I'm *Meton*,
Known throughout Hellas and Colonus.
Pe. Aye,
And what are *these*?
Me. They're rods for Air-surveying.
I'll just explain. The Air's, in outline, like
One vast extinguisher; so then, observe,
Applying here my flexible rod, and fixing
My compass there—you understand?
Pe. I don't.
Me. With the straight rod I measure out, that so
The circle may be squared; and in the centre
A market-place; and streets be leading to it
Straight to the very centre; just as from
A star, though circular, straight rays flash out
In all directions.
Pe. Why, the man's a Thales! Meton!
Me. Yes, what?
Pe. You know I love you, Meton,
Take my advice, and slip away unnoticed.
Me. Why, what's the matter?
Pe. As in Lacedaemon
There's stranger-hunting; and a great disturbance;
And blows in plenty.
Me. What, a Revolution?
Pe. No, no, not that.
Me. What then?
Pe. They've all resolved
With one consent to wallop every quack.
Me. I'd best be going.
Pe. Faith, I'm not quite certain
If you're in time; see, see the blows are coming!
(*striking him*)
Me. O, murder! help!
Pe. I told you how 'twould be.
Come, measure off your steps some other way.
Exit METON. *Enter a* COMMISSIONER, *to inspect the new colony.*
Commissioner. Ho! consuls, ho!
Pe. Sardanapalus, surely!
Co. Lo, I to your Cloudcuckooburies come,
By lot Commissioner.
Pe. Commissioner?
Who sent you hither?
Co. Lo, a paltry scroll
Of Teleas.
Pe. Come now, will you take your pay
And get you gone in peace?
Co. By Heaven I will.
I ought to be at home on public business,
Some little jobs I've had with Pharnaces.
Pe. Then take your pay, and go: your pay's just —this. (*Striking him.*)
Co. What's that?
Pe. A motion about Pharnaces.
Co. Witness! he's striking a Commissioner.
Pe. Shoo! Shoo! begone; you and your verdict-urns.
Enter STATUTE-SELLER.
The shame it is! They send Commissioners
Before we've finished our inaugural rites.
Statute-Seller. (*reading*) "But if the Cloudcuckooburian wrong the Athenian—"
Pe. Here's some more writing. What new misery's this?
S.-S. I am a Statute-seller, and I'm come
Bringing new laws to sell you.
Pe. Such as what?
S.-S. "Item, the Cloudcuckooburians are to use the selfsame weights and measures, and the selfsame coinage as the Olophyxians."
Pe. And you the selfsame as the Oh! Oh! -tyxians.
(*striking him*)
S.-S. Hi! what are you at?
Pe. Take off those laws, you rascal.
Laws you won't like I'll give you in a minute.
Exit STATUTE-SELLER; *but he and the* COMMISSIONER *each make two brief reappearances, and vanish.*
Co. (*reappearing*) I summon Peisthetaerus for next Munychion on a charge of outrage.
Pe. O that's it, is it? What, are you there still?
S.-S. (*reappearing*) "Item, if any man drive away the magistrates, and do not receive them according to the pillar—"
Pe. O mercy upon us, and are *you* there still?
Co. (*reappearing*) I'll ruin you! I claim ten thousand drachmas!
Pe. I'll overturn your verdict-urn, I will.
S.-S. (*reappearing*) Think of that evening when you fouled the pillar.
Pe. Ugh! seize him, somebody! Ha, you're off there, are you?
Let's get away from this, and go within,
And there we'll sacrifice the goat in peace.
Exeunt OMNES, *and the goat is supposed to be sacrificed within.*

Chorus

Unto me, the All-controlling,
All-surveying,
Now will men, at every altar,
Prayers be praying;
Me who watch the land, protecting
Fruit and flower,
Slay the myriad-swarming insects
Who the tender buds devour
In the earth and on the branches
with a never-satiate malice,

Nipping off the blossom as it widens from the chalice.
And I slay the noisome creatures
Which consume
And pollute the garden's freshly scented bloom;
And every little biter, and every creeping thing
Perish in destruction at the onset of my wing.
Listen to the City's notice,
specially proclaimed to-day:
"Sirs, Diagoras[1] the Melian
whosoever of you slay,
Shall receive, reward, one talent;
and another we'll bestow
If you slay some ancient tyrant,
dead and buried long ago."
We, the Birds, will give a notice,
we proclaim with right good will,
"Sirs, Philocrates, Sparrovian,
whosoever of you kill,
Shall receive, reward, one talent,
if alive you bring him, four;
Him who strings and sells the finches,
seven an obol, at his store,
Blows the thrushes out and, rudely,
to the public gaze exposes,
Shamefully entreats the blackbirds,
thrusting feathers up their noses.
Pigeons too the rascal catches,
keeps and mews them up with care,
Makes them labour as decoy-birds,
tethered underneath a snare."
Such the notice we would give you.
And we wish you all to know,
Who are keeping birds in cages,
you had better let them go.
Else the Birds will surely catch you,
and yourselves in turn employ,
Tied and tethered up securely,
other rascals to decoy.

O the happy clan of birds
Clad in feather;
Needing not a woollen vest in
Wintry weather;
Heeding not the warm far-flashing
Summer ray,
For within the leafy bosoms
Of the flowery meads I stay,
When the Chirruper in ecstasy
is shrilling forth his tune,
Maddened with the sunshine,
and the rapture of the noon.
And I winter in the caverns'
Hollow spaces,
With the happy Oreads playing; and in Spring
I crop the virgin flowers of the myrtles white and tender,
Dainties that are fashioned in the gardens of the Graces.

[1]Diagoras, an atheist, had divulged and reviled the Mysteries.

Now we wish to tell the Judges,
in a friendly sort of way,
All the blessings we shall give them
if we gain the prize to-day.
Ne'er were made to Alexander
lovelier promises or grander.
First, what every Judge amongst you
most of all desires to win,
Little Lauriotic owlets
shall be always flocking in.
Ye shall find them all about you,
as the dainty brood increases.
Building nests within your purses,
hatching little silver pieces.
Then as if in stately Temples
shall your happy lives be spent,
For the birds will top your mansions
with the Eagle pediment.
If you hold some petty office,
if you wish to steal and pick,
In your hands we'll place a falcon,
very keen and small and quick.
If a dinner is in question,
crops we'll send you for digestion.
But should you the prize deny us,
you had better all prepare,
Like the statues in the open,
little copper disks to wear;
Else whene'er abroad ye're walking,
clad in raiment white and new,
Angry birds will wreak their vengeance,
spattering over it and you.

Enter PEISTHETAERUS.

Pe. Dear Birds, our sacrifice is most auspicious.
But strange it is, no messenger has come
From the great wall we are building, with the news.
Hah! here runs one with true Alpheian pantings.

Enter MESSENGER, *panting like an Olympian runner.*

Messenger. Where, where,—O where, where, where—
O where, where, where,
Where, where's our leader Peisthetaerus?
Pe. Here.
Mes. Your building's built! The wall's complete!
Pe. Well done.
Mes. And a most grand, magnificent work it is.
So broad, that on its top the Braggadocian
Proxenides could pass Theagenes
Each driving in his chariot, drawn by horses
As bulky as the Trojan.
Pe. Heracles!
Mes. And then its height, I measured that, is just
Six hundred feet.
Pe. Poseidon, what a height!
Who built it up to that enormous size?
Mes. The birds, none other; no Egyptian, bearing
The bricks, no mason, carpenter was there;
Their own hands wrought it, marvellous to see.
From Libya came some thirty thousand cranes

With great foundation-stones they had swallowed down;
And these the corn-crakes fashioned with their beaks.
Ten thousand storks were carrying up the bricks;
And lapwings helped, and the other water-birds,
To bring the water up into the air.

Pe. Who bare aloft the mortar for them?

Mes. Herons
In hods.

Pe. But how did they get the mortar in?

Mes. O that was most ingeniously contrived.
The geese struck down their feet, and slid them under,
Like shovels, and so heaved it on the hods.

Pe. Then is there anything that *feet* can't do?

Mes. And then the ducks, with girdles round their waists,
Carried the bricks: and up the swallows flew,
Like serving-lads, carrying behind them each
His trowel, and the mortar in their mouths.

Pe. Then why should men hire hirelings any more!
Well, well, go on; who was it finished off
The great wall's woodwork?

Mes. Canny Pelicans,
Excellent workmen, hewing with huge beaks
Gate-timber; and the uproar as they hewed
Was like an arsenal when ships are building.
Now every gateway has its gate, fast-barred,
And watched the whole way round; and birds are pacing
Their beats, and carrying bells, and everywhere
The guards are stationed, and the beacons blaze
On every tower. But I must hurry off
And wash myself. You, manage what remains.

Exit.

Ch. O man, what ails you? Do you feel surprised
To hear the building has been built so soon?

Pe. By all the Gods I do; and well I may.
In very truth it seems to me like—lies.
But see! a guard, a messenger from thence
Is running towards us with a war-dance look!

Enter a GUARD.

Guard. Hallo! Hallo! Hallo! Hallo! Hallo!

Pe. Why, what's up now?

Gu. A terrible thing has happened.
One of the Gods, of Zeus's Gods, has just,
Giving our jackdaw sentinels the slip,
Shot through the gates and flown into the air.

Pe. A dreadful deed! A wicked scandalous deed!
Which of the Gods?

Gu. We know not. Wings he had,
So much we know.

Pe. Ye should have sent at once
The civic guard in hot pursuit.

Gu. We sent
The mounted archers, thirty thousand falcons,
All with their talons curved, in fighting trim,
Hawk, buzzard, vulture, eagle, eagle-owl.
Yea, Ether vibrates with the whizz and whirr
Of beating pinions, as they seek the God.
Ay, and he's near methinks; he's very near;
He's somewhere here.

Pe. A sling, a sling, I say!
Arrows and bows! Fall in, my merrymen all!
Shoot, smite, be resolute. A sling! a sling!

Ch. War is begun, inexpressive war,
War is begun twixt the Gods and me!
Look out, look out, through the cloud-wrapt air
Which erst the Darkness of Erebus bare,
Lest a God slip by, and we fail to see.
Glance eager-eyed on every side,
For close at hand the wingèd sound I hear
Of some Immortal hurtling through the Sky.

Enter IRIS.

Pe. Hoi! whither away there? whither away? Stop! stop!
Stop where you are! keep quiet! stay! remain!
Who, what, whence are you? where do you come from? Quick!

Iris. Whence do I come? From the Olympian Gods.

Pe. Your name! What is it? Sloop or Head-dress?

Ir. Iris
The fleet.

Pe. The Paralus, or the Salaminian?

Ir. Why, what's all this?

Pe. Fly up, some buzzard there,
Fly up, and seize her.

Ir. Me! Seize *me*, do you say?
What the plague's this?

Pe. You'll find to your cost, directly

Ir. Well now, this passes!

Pe. Answer! By what gates
Got you within the city wall, Miss Minx?

Ir. I' faith, I know not, fellow, by what gates.

Pe. You hear the jade, how she prevaricates!
Saw you the daw-commanders? What, no answer?
Where's your stork-pass?

Ir. My patience, what do you mean?

Pe. You never got one?

Ir. Have you lost your wits?

Pe. Did no bird-captain stick a label on you?

Ir. On *me*? None stuck a label, wretch, on *me*.

Pe. So then you thought in this sly stealthy way
To fly through Chaos and a realm not yours?

Ir. And by what route, then, ought the Gods to fly?

Pe. I' faith, I know not. Only not by this.
This is a trespass! If you got your rights,
Of all the Irises that ever were
You'd be most justly seized and put to death.

Ir. But I am deathless.

Pe. All the same for that
You should have died. A pretty thing, forsooth,
If, whilst all else obey us, you the Gods
Run riot, and forget that you in turn
Must learn to yield obedience to your betters.
But tell me, where do you navigate your wings?

Ir. I? From the Father to mankind I'm flying,
To bid them on their bullock-slaughtering hearths
Slay sheep to the Olympian Gods, and steam
The streets with savour.

Pe. What do you say? What Gods?
Ir. What Gods? To us, the Gods in Heaven, of course.
Pe. (*with supreme contempt*) What, are *you* Gods?
Ir. What other Gods exist?
Pe. Birds are now Gods to men; and men must slay
Victims to them; and not, by Zeus, to Zeus.
Ir. O fool, fool, fool! Stir not the mighty wrath
Of angry Gods, lest Justice, with the spade
Of vengeful Zeus, demolish all thy race,
And fiery vapour, with Licymnian strokes,
Incinerate thy palace and thyself!
Pe. Now listen, girl; have done with that bombast.
(Don't move.) A Lydian or a Phrygian is it,
You think to terrify with words like those?
Look here. If Zeus keep troubling me, I'll soon
Incinerate his great Amphion's domes
And halls of state with eagles carrying fire.
And up against him, to high heaven, I'll send
More than six hundred stout Porphyrion rails
All clad in leopard-skins. Yet I remember
When one Porphyrion gave him toil enough.
And as for you, his waiting-maid, if you
Keep troubling me with your outrageous ways,
I'll outrage *you*, and you'll be quite surprised
To find the strength of an old man like me.
Ir. O shame upon you, wretch, your words and you.
Pe. Now then begone; shoo, shoo! Eurax patax!
Ir. My father won't stand this; I vow he won't.
Pe. Now Zeus-a-mercy, maiden; fly you off.
Incinerate some younger man than I. *Exit* IRIS.
Ch. Never again shall the Zeus-born Gods,
Never again shall they pass this way!
Never again through this realm of ours
Shall men send up to the heavenly Powers
The savour of beasts which on earth they slay!

Pe. Well but that herald whom we sent to men,
'Tis strange if he should nevermore return.
Enter HERALD.
Herald. O Peisthetaerus, O thou wisest, best,
Thou wisest, deepest, happiest of mankind,
Most glorious, most—O give the word!
Pe. What news?
He. Accept this golden crown, wherewith all peoples
Crown and revere thee for thy wisdom's sake!
Pe. I do. What makes them all revere me so?
He. O thou who hast built the ethereal glorious city,
Dost thou not know how men revere thy name,
And burn with ardour for this realm of thine?
Why, till ye built this city in the air,
All men had gone Laconian-mad; they went
Long-haired, half-starved, unwashed, Socratified,
With scytales in their hands; but O the change!
They are all bird-mad now, and imitate
The birds, and joy to do whate'er birds do.
Soon as they rise from bed at early dawn,
They settle down on laws, as we on lawns,
And then they brood upon their leaves and leaflets,
And feed their fill upon a crop of statutes.
So undisguised their madness, that full oft
The names of birds are fastened on to men.
One limping tradesman now is known as "Partridge";
They dub Menippus "Swallow"; and Opuntius
"Blind Raven"; Philocles is "Crested Lark,"
Theagenes is nicknamed "Sheldrake" now;
Lycurgus "Ibis"; Chaerephon the "Vampire";
And Syracosius "Jay"; whilst Meidias there
Is called the "Quail"; aye and he's like a quail
Flipped on the head by some quail-filliper.
So fond they are of birds that all are singing
Songs where a swallow figures in the verse,
Or goose, or may-be widgeon, or ring-dove,
Or wings, or even the scantiest shred of feather.
So much from earth. And let me tell you this;
More than ten thousand men will soon be here,
All wanting wings and taloned modes of life.
Somehow or other you must find them wings.
Pe. O then, by Zeus, no time for dallying now;
Quick, run you in; collect the crates and baskets,
And fill them all with wings; that done, let Manes
Bring me them out; whilst I, remaining here,
Receive the wingless travellers as they come.
Ch. Very soon "fully-manned" will this City be called,
If men in such numbers invade us.
Pe. So fortune continue to aid us.
Ch. O, the love of my City the world has enthralled!
Pe. (*to* MANES) Bring quicker the baskets they're packing.
Ch. For in what is it lacking
That a man for his home can require?
Here is Wisdom, and Wit, and each exquisite Grace,
And here the unruffled, benevolent face
Of Quiet, and loving Desire.
Pe. Why, what a lazy loon are you!
Come, move a little faster, do.
Ch. O see that he brings me a basket of wings.
Rush out in a whirlwind of passion,
And wallop him, after this fashion.
For the rogue is as slow as a donkey to go.
Pe. No pluck has your Manes, 'tis true.
Ch. But now 'tis for *you*
The wings in due order to set;
Both the musical wings, and the wings of the seers,
And the wings of the sea, that as each one appears,
The wings that he wants you can get.
Pe. O, by the kestrels, I can't keep my hands
From banging you, you lazy, crazy oaf.
Enter a SIRE-STRIKER.
Sire-Striker. (*singing*) O that I might as an eagle be,
Flying, flying, flying, flying
Over the surge of the untilled sea!
Pe. Not false, methinks, the tale our envoy told us.
For here comes one whose song is all of eagles.

S.-St. Fie on it!
There's nothing in this world so sweet as flying;
I've quite a passion for these same bird-laws.
In fact I'm gone bird-mad, and fly, and long
To dwell with you, and hunger for your laws.
Pe. Which of our laws? for birds have many laws.
S.-St. All! All! but most of all that jolly law
Which lets a youngster throttle and beat his father.
Pe. Aye, if a cockerel beat his father here,
We do indeed account him quite a—Man.
S.-St. That's why I moved up hither and would fain
Throttle my father and get all he has.
Pe. But there's an ancient law among the birds,
You'll find it in the tablets of the storks:
"When the old stork has brought his storklings up,
And all are fully fledged for flight, then they
Must in their turn maintain the stork their father."
S.-St. A jollylot of good I've gained by coming,
If now I've got to feed my father too!
Pe. Nay, my poor boy, you came here well-disposed,
And so I'll rig you like an orphan bird.
And here's a new suggestion, not a bad one,
But what I learnt myself when I was young.
Don't beat your father, lad; but take this wing,
And grasp this spur of battle in your hand,
And think this crest a game-cock's martial comb.
Now march, keep guard, live on your soldier's pay,
And let your father be. If you want fighting,
Fly off to Thraceward regions, and fight there.
S.-St. By Dionysus, I believe you're right.
I'll do it too.
Pe. You'll show your sense, by Zeus!
Exit SIRE-STRIKER; *enter* CINESIAS.
Cinesias. (*singing*) On the lightest of wings I am soaring on high,
Lightly from measure to measure I fly;
Pe. Bless me, this creature wants a pack of wings!
Ci. (*singing*) And ever the new I am flitting to find,
With timorless body, and timorless mind.
Pe. We clasp Cinesias, man of linden-wyth.
Why in the world have you whirled your splay foot hither?
Ci. (*singing*) To be a bird, a bird, I long,
A nightingale of thrilling song.
Pe. O stop that singing; prithee speak in prose.
Ci. O give me wings, that I may soar on high,
And pluck poetic fancies from the clouds,
Wild as the whirling winds, and driving snows.
Pe. What, do you pluck your fancies from the clouds?
Ci. Why our whole trade depends upon the clouds;
What are our noblest dithyrambs but things
Of air, and mist, and purple-gleaming depths,
And feathery whirlwings? You shall hear, and judge.
Pe. No, no, I won't.
Ci. By Heracles you shall.
I'll go through all the air, dear friend, for you.
(*Singing*) Shadowy visions of
Wing-spreading, air-treading,
Taper-necked birds.
Pe. Steady, there!
Ci. (*singing*) Bounding along on the path to the seas,
Fain would I float on the stream of the breeze.
Pe. O by the Powers, I'll stop your streams and breezes.
Ci. (*singing*) First do I stray on a southerly way;
Then to the northward my body I bear,
Cutting a harbourless furrow of air.
PEISTHETAERUS *begins to flap him round the stage.*
A nice trick that, a pleasant trick, old man.
Pe. O you don't like being feathery-whirl-winged, do you?
Ci. That's how you treat the Cyclian-chorus-trainer
For whose possession all the tribes compete!
Pe. Well, will you stop and train a chorus here
For Leotrophides, all flying birds,
Crake-oppidans?
Ci. You're jeering me, that's plain.
But I won't stop, be sure of that, until
I get me wings, and peragrate the air. *Exit.*
Enter SYCOPHANT.
Sycophant. (*singing*) Who be these on varied wing, birds who have not anything?
O tell me, swallow, tell me, tell me true,
O long-winged bird, O bird of varied hue!
Pe. Come, it's no joke, this plague that's broken out;
Here comes another, warbling like the rest.
Sy. (*singing*) Again I ask thee, tell me, tell me true,
O long-winged bird, O bird of varied hue!
Pe. At his own cloak his catch appears to point;
More than one swallow *that* requires, I'm thinking.
Sy. Which is the man that wings the visitors?
Pe. He stands before you. What do you please to want?
Sy. Wings, wings I want. You need not ask me twice.
Pe. Is it Pellene that you're going to fly to?
Sy. No, no: but I'm a sompnour for the Isles,
Informer—
Pe. O the jolly trade you've got!
Sy. And law-suit-hatcher; so I want the wings
To scare the cities, serving writs all round.
Pe. You'll summon them more cleverly, I suppose,
To the tune of wings?
Sy. No, but to dodge the pirates,
I'll then come flying homeward with the cranes,
First swallowing down a lot of suits for ballast.
Pe. Is this your business? you, a sturdy youngster,
Live by informing on the stranger-folk?
Sy. What can I do? I never learnt to dig.
Pe. O, but by Zeus, there's many an honest calling
Whence men like you can earn a livelihood,
By means more suitable than hatching suits.

Sy. Come, come, no preaching; wing me, wing me, please.
Pe. I wing you now by talking.
Sy. What, by talk
Can you wing men?
Pe. Undoubtedly. By talk
All men are winged.
Sy. All!
Pe. Have you never heard
The way the fathers in the barbers' shops
Talk to the children, saying things like these,
"Diitrephes has winged my youngster so
By specious talk, he's all for chariot-driving."
"Aye," says another, "and that boy of mine
Flutters his wings at every Tragic Play."
Sy. So then by talk they are winged.
Pe. Exactly so.
Through talk the mind flutters and soars aloft,
And all the man takes wing. And so even now
I wish to turn you, winging you by talk,
To some more honest trade.
Sy. But I *don't* wish.
Pe. How then?
Sy. I'll not disgrace my bringing up.
I'll ply the trade my father's fathers plied.
So wing me, please, with light quick-darting wings
Falcon's or kestrel's, so I'll serve my writs
Abroad on strangers; then accuse them here;
Then dart back there again.
Pe. I understand.
So when they come, they'll find the suit decided,
And payment ordered.
Sy. Right! you understand.
Pe. And while they're sailing hither you'll fly there,
And seize their goods for payment.
Sy. That's the trick!
Round like a top I'll whizz.
Pe. I understand.
A whipping-top; and here by Zeus I've got
Fine Corcyraean wings to set you whizzing.
Sy. O, it's a whip!
Pe. Nay, friend, a pair of wings,
To set you spinning round and round to-day.
(*Striking him.*)
Sy. O! O! O! O!
Pe. Come, wing yourself from hence.
Wobble away, you most confounded rascal!
I'll make you spin! I'll law-perverting-trick you!
Now let us gather up the wings and go.
Exit PEISTHETAERUS *with* SYCOPHANT.

Chorus

We've been flying, we've been flying
Over sea and land, espying
Many a wonder strange and new.
First, a tree of monstrous girth,
Tall and stout, yet nothing worth,
For 'tis rotten through and through:
It has got no heart, and we
Heard it called "Cleonymus-tree."
In the spring it blooms gigantic,
Fig-traducing, sycophantic,
Yet in falling leaf-time yields
Nothing but a fall of shields.

Next a spot by darkness skirted,
Spot, by every light deserted,
Lone and gloomy, we descried.
There the human and divine,
Men with heroes, mix and dine
Freely, save at even-tide.
'Tis not safe for mortal men
To encounter heroes then.
Then the great Orestes, looming
Vast and awful through the glooming,
On their right a stroke delivering,
Leaves them palsied, stript, and shivering.

Enter PROMETHEUS, *concealing his face, probably recalling some scene in the* Prometheus Fire-bringer *of Aeschylus.*

Prometheus. O dear! O dear! Pray Heaven that Zeus won't see me!
Where's Peisthetaerus?
Enter PEISTHETAERUS.
Pe. Why, whatever is here?
What's this enwrapment?
Pro. See you any God
Following behind me there?
Pe. Not I, by Zeus.
But who are you?
Pro. And what's the time of day?
Pe. The time of day? A little after noon.
(*Shouting*) But who are you?
Pro. Ox-loosing time, or later?
Pe. Disgusting idiot!
Pro. What's Zeus doing now?
The clouds collecting or the clouds dispersing?
Pe. Out on you, stupid!
Pro. Now then, I'll unwrap.
Pe. My dear Prometheus!
Pro. Hush! don't shout like that.
Pe. Why, what's up now?
Pro. Don't speak my name so loudly.
'Twould be my ruin, if Zeus see me here.
But now I'll tell you all that's going on
Up in the sky, if you'll just take the umbrella,
And hold it over, that no God may see me.
Pe. Ha! Ha!
The crafty thought! Prometheus-like all over.
Get under then; make haste: and speak out freely.
Pro. Then listen.
Pe. Speak: I'm listening, never fear.
Pro. All's up with Zeus!
Pe. Good gracious me! since when?
Pro. Since first you built your city in the air.
For never from that hour does mortal bring
Burnt-offerings to the Gods, or savoury steam
Ascend to heaven from flesh of victims slain.
So now we fast a Thesmophorian fast,
No altars burning; and the Barbarous Gods
Half-starved, and gibbering like Illyrians, vow
That they'll come marching down on Zeus, unless

He gets the marts reopened, and the bits
Of savory inwards introduced once more.
Pe. What, are there really other Gods, Barbarians,
Up above you?
Pro. Barbarians? Yes; thence comes
The ancestral God of Execestides.
Pe. And what's the name of these Barbarian Gods?
Pro. The name? Triballians.
Pe. Aye, I understand.
'Tis from that quarter Tribulation comes.
Pro. Exactly so. And now I tell you this;
Envoys will soon be here to treat for peace,
Sent down by Zeus and those Triballians there.
But make no peace, mind that, unless king Zeus
Restores the sceptre to the Birds again,
And gives yourself Miss Sovereignty to wife.
Pe. And who's Miss Sovereignty?
Pro. The loveliest girl.
'Tis she who keeps the thunderbolts of Zeus,
And all his stores—good counsels, happy laws,
Sound common sense, dockyards, abusive speech,
All his three-obols, and the man who pays them.
Pe. Then she keeps *everything!*
Pro. Of course she does.
Win her from Zeus, and *you'll* have *everything.*
I hastened here that I might tell you this,
You know I am always well-disposed to men.
Pe. Aye, but for you we could not fry our fish.
Pro. And I hate every God, you know that, don't you?
Pe. Yes, hatred of the Gods; you always felt it.
Pro. A regular Timon! but 'tis time to go;
Let's have the umbrella; then, if Zeus perceives me,
He'll think I'm following the Basket-bearer.
Pe. Here, take the chair, and act the Chair-girl too.

Exeunt PROMETHEUS *and* PEISTHETAERUS.

Chorus

Next we saw a sight appalling,
Socrates, unwashed, was calling
Spirits from the lake below,
('Twas on that enchanted ground
Where the Shadow-feet are found).
There Peisander came to know
If the spirit cowards lack
Socrates could conjure back;
Then a camel-lamb he slew,
Like Odysseus, but withdrew,
Whilst the camel's blood upon
Pounced the Vampire, Chaerephon.

Enter POSEIDON, HERACLES, *and* TRIBALLIAN.

Poseidon. There, fellow envoys, full in sight, the town
Whereto we are bound, Cloudcuckoobury, stands!
(*To the* TRIBALLIAN)
You, what are you at, wearing your cloak left-sided?
Shift it round rightly; so. My goodness, you're
A born Laispodias! O Democracy,
What will you bring us to at last, I wonder,
If voting Gods elect a clown like this!
Triballian. Hands off there, will yer?
Pos. Hang you, you're by far
The uncouthest God I ever came across.
Now, Heracles, what's to be done?
Heracles. You have heard
What I propose; I'd throttle the man off-hand,
Whoever he is, that dares blockade the Gods.
Pos. My dear good fellow, you forget we are sent
To treat for peace.
Her. I'd throttle him all the more.

Re-enter PEISTHETAERUS.

Pe. (*to servants*) Hand me the grater; bring the silphium, you;
Now then, the cheese; blow up the fire a little.
Pos. We three, immortal Gods, with words of greeting
Salute the Man!
Pe. I'm grating silphium now.
Her. What's this the flesh of?
Pe. Birds! Birds tried and sentenced
For rising up against the popular party
Amongst the birds.
Her. Then you grate silphium, do you,
Over them first?
Pe. O welcome, Heracles!
What brings you hither?
Pos. We are envoys, sent
Down by the Gods to settle terms of peace.
Servant. There's no more oil remaining in the flask.
Her. O dear! and bird's-flesh should be rich and glistering.
Pos. We Gods gain nothing by the war; and you,
Think what ye'll get by being friends with us;
Rain-water in the pools, and halcyon days
Shall be your perquisites the whole year through.
We've ample powers to settle on these terms.
Pe. It was not we who ever wished for war,
And now, if even now ye come prepared
With fair proposals, ye will find us ready
To treat for peace. What I call fair is this;
Let Zeus restore the sceptre to the birds,
And all make friends. If ye accept this offer,
I ask the envoys in to share our banquet.
Her. I'm altogether satisfied, and vote—
Pos. (*interrupting*)
What, wretch? A fool and glutton, that's what *you* are!
What! would you rob your father of his kingdom?
Pe. Aye, say you so? Why, ye'll be mightier far,
Ye Gods above, if Birds bear rule below.
Now men go skulking underneath the clouds,
And swear false oaths, and call the Gods to witness.
But when ye've got the Birds for your allies,
If a man swear by the Raven and by Zeus,
The Raven will come by, and unawares
Fly up, and swoop, and peck the perjurer's eye out.
Pos. Now by Poseidon there's some sense in that.
Her. And so say I.
Pe. (*to* TRIBALLIAN) And you?

Tr. Persuasitree.
Pe. You see? he quite assents. And now I'll give you
Another instance of the good ye'll gain.
If a man vow a victim to a God,
And then would shuffle off with cunning words,
Saying, in greedy lust, "The Gods wait long,"
This too we'll make him pay you.
Pos. Tell me how?
Pe. Why, when that man is counting out his money,
Or sitting in his bath, a kite shall pounce
Down unawares, and carry off the price
Of two fat lambs, and bear it to the God.
Her. I say again, I vote we give the sceptre
Back to the Birds.
Pos. Ask the Triballian next.
Her. You there, do you want a drubbing?
Tr. Hideythine
I'se stickybeatums.
Her. There! he's all for me.
Pos. Well then, if so you wish it, so we'll have it.
Her. (*to* PEISTHETAERUS) Hi! we accept your terms about the sceptre.
Pe. By Zeus, there's one thing more I've just remembered.
Zeus may retain his Hera, if he will,
But the young girl, Miss Sovereignty, he must
Give me to wife.
Pos. This looks not like a treaty.
Let us be journeying homewards.
Pe. As you will.
Now, cook, be sure you make the gravy rich.
Her. Why, man alive, Poseidon, where are you off to?
What, are we going to fight about one woman?
Pos. What shall we do?
Her. Do? Come to terms at once.
Pos. You oaf, he's gulling you, and you can't see it.
Well, it's yourself you are ruining. If Zeus
Restore the kingdom to the Birds, and die,
You'll be a pauper. You are the one to get
Whatever money Zeus may leave behind him.
Pe. O! O! the way he's trying to cozen you!
Hist, step aside, I want to whisper something.
Your uncle's fooling you, poor dupe. By law
No shred of all your father's money falls
To you. Why, you're a bastard, you're not heir.
Her. Eh! What? A bastard? I?
Pe. Of course you are.
Your mother was an alien. Bless the fool,
How did you think Athene could be "Heiress,"
(Being a girl), if she had lawful brethren?
Her. Well, but suppose my father leaves me all
As bastard's heritage?
Pe. The law won't let him.
Poseidon here, who now excites you on,
Will be the first to claim the money then,
As lawful brother, and your father's heir.
Why here, I'll read you Solon's law about it.
"A bastard is to have no right of inheritance, if there be lawful children. And if there be no lawful children, the goods are to fall to the next of kin."
Her. What! none of all my father's goods to fall
To me?
Pe. No, not one farthing! tell me this,
Has he enrolled you ever in the guild?
Her. He never has. I've often wondered why.
Pe. Come, don't look up assault-and-battery-wise.
Join *us*, my boy; I'll make you autocrat,
And feed you all your days on pigeon's milk.
Her. I'm quite convinced you're right about the girl:
I said Restore her; and I say so now.
Pe. (*to* POSEIDON) And what say you?
Pos. I vote the other way.
Pe. All rests with this Triballian. What say you?
Tr. Me gulna charmi grati Sovranau
Birdito stori.
Her. There! he said Restore her.
Pos. O no by Zeus, he never said Restore her;
He said to migrate as the swallows do.
Her. O then he said Restore her to the swallows.
Pos. You two conclude, and settle terms of peace,
Since you both vote it, I will say no more.
Her. (*to* PEISTHETAERUS) We're quite prepared to give you all you ask.
So come along, come up to heaven yourself,
And take Miss Sovereignty and all that's there.
Pe. So then these birds were slaughtered just in time
To grace our wedding banquet.
Her. Would you like me
To stay, and roast the meat, while you three go?
Pos. To *roast* the meat! To *taste* the meat, you mean.
Come along, do.
Her. I'd have enjoyed it though.
Pe. Ho there within! bring out a wedding robe.
Exeunt PEISTHETAERUS, POSEIDON, TRIBALLIAN, *and* HERACLES.
Ch. In the fields of Litigation,
Near the Water-clock, a nation
With its tongue its belly fills;
With its tongue it sows and reaps,
Gathers grapes and figs in heaps,
With its tongue the soil it tills.
For a Barbarous tribe it passes,
Philips all and Gorgiases.
And from this tongue-bellying band
Everywhere on Attic land,
People who a victim slay
Always cut the tongue away.
Enter MESSENGER.
Messenger. O all-successful, more than tongue can tell!
O ye, thrice blessèd wingèd race of birds,
Welcome your King returning to his halls!
He comes; no Star has ever gleamed so fair,
Sparkling refulgent in its gold-rayed home.
The full far-flashing splendour of the Sun
Ne'er shone so gloriously as he, who comes
Bringing a bride too beautiful for words,
Wielding the wingèd thunderbolt of Zeus.
Up to Heaven's highest vault, sweet sight, ascends
Fragrance ineffable; while gentlest airs

The fume of incense scatter far and wide.
He comes; he is here! Now let the heavenly Muse
Open her lips with pure auspicious strains.

Enter PEISTHETAERUS *and* MISS SOVEREIGNTY.

Chorus

Back with you! out with you!
off with you! up with you!
Flying around
Welcome the Blessèd with blessedness crowned.
O! O! for the youth and the beauty, O!
Well hast thou wed for the town of the Birds.

Great are the blessings, and mighty, and wonderful,
Which through his favour our nation possesses.
Welcome them back, both himself and Miss Sovereignty,
Welcome with nuptial and bridal addresses.

Mid just such a song hymenaean
Aforetime the Destinies led
The King of the thrones empyréan,
The Ruler of Gods, to the bed
Of Hera his beautiful bride.
Hymen, O Hymenaeus!

And Love, with his pinions of gold,
Came driving, all blooming and spruce,
As groomsman and squire to behold
The wedding of Hera and Zeus,
Of Zeus and his beautiful bride.
Hymen, O Hymenaeus!
Hymen, O Hymenaeus!

Pe. I delight in your hymns, I delight in your songs;
Your words I admire.

Ch. Now sing of the trophies he brings us from Heaven,
The earth-crashing thunders, deadly and dire,
And the lightning's angry flashes of fire,
And the dread white bolt of the levin.
Blaze of the lightning, so terribly beautiful,
Golden and grand!
Fire-flashing javelin, glittering ever in
Zeus's right hand!
Earth-crashing thunder, the hoarsely resounding, the
Bringer of showers!
He is your Master, 'tis he that is shaking the
Earth with your powers!

All that was Zeus's of old
Now is our hero's alone;
Sovereignty, fair to behold,
Partner of Zeus on his throne,
Now is forever his own.
Hymen, O Hymenaeus!

Pe. Now follow on, dear feathered tribes,
To see us wed, to see us wed;
Mount up to Zeus's golden floor,
And nuptial bed, and nuptial bed.
And O, my darling, reach thine hand,
And take my wing and dance with me,
And I will lightly bear thee up,
And carry thee, and carry thee.

Ch. Raise the joyous Paean-cry,
Raise the song of Victory.
Io Paean, alalalae,
Mightiest of the Powers, to thee!

THE FROGS

DRAMATIS PERSONAE

XANTHIAS, *servant of Dionysus*
DIONYSUS
HERACLES
A CORPSE
CHARON
AEACUS
A MAID-SERVANT OF PERSEPHONE
HOSTESS, *keeper of cook-shop*
PLATHANE, *her partner*
EURIPIDES
AESCHYLUS
PLUTO
CHORUS OF FROGS
CHORUS OF BLESSED MYSTICS

The scene shows the house of HERACLES *in the background. There enter two travellers:* DIONYSUS *on foot, in his customary yellow robe and buskins but also with the club and lion's skin of Heracles, and his servant* XANTHIAS *on a donkey, carrying the luggage on a pole over his shoulder.*

Xanthias. Shall I crack any of those old jokes, master,
At which the audience never fail to laugh?
Dionysus. Aye, what you will, except "I'm getting crushed":
Fight shy of that: I'm sick of that already.
Xa. Nothing else smart?
Di. Aye, save "my shoulder's aching."
Xa. Come now, that comical joke?
Di. With all my heart.
Only be careful not to shift your pole,
And—
Xa. What?
Di. And vow that you've a belly-ache.
Xa. May I not say I'm overburdened so
That if none ease me, I must ease myself?
Di. For mercy's sake, not till I'm going to vomit.
Xa. What! must I bear these burdens, and not make
One of the jokes Ameipsias and Lycis
And Phrynichus, in every play they write,
Put in the mouths of all their burden-bearers?
Di. Don't make them; no! I tell you when I see
Their plays, and hear those jokes, I come away
More than a twelvemonth older than I went.
Xa. O thrice unlucky neck of mine, which now
Is *getting crushed*, yet must not crack its joke!
Di. Now is not this fine pampered insolence
When I myself, Dionysus, son of—Pipkin,
Toil on afoot, and let this fellow ride,
Taking no trouble, and no burden bearing?
Xa. What, don't I bear?
Di. How can you when you're riding?
Xa. Why, I bear these.
Di. How?
Xa. Most unwillingly.
Di. Does not the donkey bear the load you're bearing?
Xa. Not what I bear myself: by Zeus, not he.
Di. How can you bear, when you are borne yourself?
Xa. Don't know: but anyhow *my shoulder's aching*.
Di. Then since you say the donkey helps you not,
You lift him up and carry him in turn.
Xa. O hang it all! why didn't I fight at sea?
You should have smarted bitterly for this.
Di. Get down, you rascal; I've been trudging on
Till now I've reached the portal, where I'm going
First to turn in. Boy! Boy! I say there, Boy!
Enter HERACLES *from house.*
Heracles. Who banged the door? How like a prancing Centaur
He drove against it! Mercy o' me, what's this?
Di. Boy.
Xa. Yes.
Di. Did you observe?
Xa. What?
Di. How alarmed
He is.
Xa. Aye truly, lest you've lost your wits.
He. O by Demeter, I can't choose but laugh.
Biting my lips won't stop me. Ha! ha! ha!
Di. Pray you, come hither, I have need of you.
He. I vow I can't help laughing, I can't help it.
A lion's hide upon a yellow silk,
A club and buskin! What's it all about?
Where were you going?
Di. I was serving lately
Aboard the—Cleisthenes.
He. And fought?
Di. And sank
More than a dozen of the enemy's ships.
He. You two?
Di. We two.
He. And then I awoke, and lo!
Di. There as, on deck, I'm reading to myself
The *Andromeda*, a sudden pang of longing
Shoots through my heart, you can't conceive how keenly.
He. How big a pang?
Di. A small one, Molon's size.
He. Caused by a woman?
Di. No.

He. A boy?
Di. No, no.
He. A man?
Di. Ah! ah!
He. Was it for Cleisthenes?
Di. Don't mock me, brother: on my life I am
In a bad way: such fierce desire consumes me.
He. Aye, little brother? how?
Di. I can't describe it.
But yet I'll tell you in a riddling way.
Have you e'er felt a sudden lust for soup?
He. Soup! Zeus-a-mercy, yes, ten thousand times.
Di. Is the thing clear, or must I speak again?
He. Not of the soup: I'm clear about the soup.
Di. Well, just that sort of pang devours my heart
For lost Euripides.
He. A dead man too.
Di. And no one shall persuade me not to go
After the man.
He. Do you mean below, to Hades?
Di. And lower still, if there's a lower still.
He. What on earth for?
Di. I want a genuine poet,
"For some are not, and those that are, are bad."
He. What! does not Iophon live?
Di. Well, he's the sole
Good thing remaining, if even he is good.
For even of that I'm not exactly certain.
He. If go you must, there's Sophocles—he comes
Before Euripides—why not take *him*?
Di. Not till I've tried if Iophon's coin rings true
When he's alone, apart from Sophocles.
Besides, Euripides, the crafty rogue,
Will find a thousand shifts to get away,
But *he* was easy here, is easy there.
He. But Agathon, where is he?
Di. He has gone and left us.
A genial poet, by his friends much missed.
He. Gone where?
Di. To join the blessed in their banquets.
He. But what of Xenocles?
Di. O he be hanged!
He. Pythangelus?
Xa. But never a word of me,
Not though my shoulder's chafed so terribly.
He. But have you not a shoal of little songsters,
Tragedians by the myriad, who can chatter
A furlong faster than Euripides?
Di. Those be mere vintage-leavings, jabberers, choirs
Of swallow-broods, degraders of their art,
Who get one chorus, and are seen no more,
The Muses' love once gained. But O, my friend,
Search where you will, you'll never find a true
Creative genius, uttering startling things.
He. Creative? how do you mean?
Di. I mean a man
Who'll dare some novel venturesome conceit,
"Air, Zeus's chamber," or "Time's foot," or this,
"'Twas not my mind that swore: my tongue committed
A little perjury on its own account."
He. You like that style?
Di. Like it? I dote upon it.
He. I vow its ribald nonsense, and you know it.
Di. "Rule not my mind": you've got a house to mind.
He. Really and truly though 'tis paltry stuff.
Di. Teach me to dine!
Xa. But never a word of me.
Di. But tell me truly—'twas for this I came
Dressed up to mimic you—what friends received
And entertained you when you went below
To bring back Cerberus, in case I need them.
And tell me too the havens, fountains, shops,
Roads, resting-places, stews, refreshment-rooms,
Towns, lodgings, hostesses, with whom were found
The fewest bugs.
Xa. But never a word of me.
He. You are really game to go?
Di. O drop that, can't you?
And tell me this: of all the roads you know
Which is the quickest way to get to Hades?
I want one not too warm, nor yet too cold.
He. Which shall I tell you first? which shall it be?
There's one by rope and bench: you launch away
And—hang yourself.
Di. No thank you: that's too stifling.
He. Then there's a track, a short and beaten cut,
By pestle and mortar.
Di. Hemlock, do you mean?
He. Just so.
Di. No, that's too deathly cold a way;
You have hardly started ere your shins get numbed.
He. Well, would you like a steep and swift descent?
Di. Aye, that's the style: my walking powers are small.
He. Go down to the Cerameicus.
Di. And do what?
He. Climb to the tower's top pinnacle—
Di. And then?
He. Observe the torch-race started, and when all
The multitude is shouting "Let them go,"
Let yourself go.
Di. Go! whither?
He. To the ground.
Di. And lose, forsooth, two envelopes of brain.
I'll not try that.
He. Which *will* you try?
Di. The way
You went yourself.
He. A parlous voyage that,
For first you'll come to an enormous lake
Of fathomless depth.
Di. And how am I to cross?
He. An ancient mariner will row you over
In a wee boat, *so* big. The fare's two obols.
Di. Fie! The power two obols have, the whole world through!
How came they thither!
He. Theseus took them down.
And next you'll see great snakes and savage monsters
In tens of thousands.

Di. You needn't try to scare me,
I'm going to go.
He. Then weltering seas of filth
And ever-rippling dung: and plunged therein,
Whoso has wronged the stranger here on earth,
Or robbed his boylove of the promised pay,
Or swinged his mother, or profanely smitten
His father's cheek, or sworn an oath forsworn,
Or copied out a speech of Morsimus.
Di. There too, perdie, should *he* be plunged, whoe'er
Has danced the sword-dance of Cinesias.
He. And next the breath of flutes will float around you,
And glorious sunshine, such as ours, you'll see,
And myrtle groves, and happy bands who clap
Their hands in triumph, men and women too.
Di. And who are they?
He. The happy mystic bands,
Xa. And I'm the donkey in the mystery show.
But I'll not stand it, not one instant longer.
He. Who'll tell you everything you want to know.
You'll find them dwelling close beside the road
You are going to travel, just at Pluto's gate.
And fare thee well, my brother.
Di. And to you
Good cheer. (*Exit* HERACLES.) Now sirrah, pick you up the traps.
Xa. Before I've put them down?
Di. And quickly too.
Xa. No, prithee, no: but hire a body, one
They're carrying out, on purpose for the trip.
Di. If I can't find one?
Xa. Then I'll take them.
Di. Good.
And see! they are carrying out a body now.

Here a CORPSE, *wrapped in its grave-clothes, and lying on a bier, is carried across the stage.*

Hallo! you there, you deadman, are you willing
To carry down our little traps to Hades?
Corpse. What are they?
Di. These.
Co. Two drachmas for the job?
Di. Nay, that's too much.
Co. Out of the pathway, you!
Di. Beshrew thee, stop: may-be we'll strike a bargain.
Co. Pay me two drachmas, or it's no use talking.
Di. One and a half.
Co. I'd liefer live again!
Xa. How absolute the knave is! He be hanged!
I'll go myself.
Di. You're the right sort, my man.
Now to the ferry.

Enter CHARON.

Charon. Yoh, up! lay her to.
Xa. Whatever's that?
Di. Why, that's the lake, by Zeus,
Whereof he spake, and yon's the ferry-boat.
Xa. Poseidon, yes, and that old fellow's Charon.
Di. Charon! O welcome, Charon! welcome, Charon!

Ch. Who's for the Rest from every pain and ill?
Who's for the Lethe's plain? the Donkey-shearings?
Who's for Cerberia? Taenarum? or the Ravens?
Di. I.
Ch. Hurry in.
Di. But where are you going really?
In truth to the Ravens?
Ch. Aye, for your behoof.
Step in.
Di. (*to* XANTHIAS) Now, lad.
Ch. A slave? I take no slave,
Unless he has fought for his bodyrights at sea.
Xa. I couldn't go. I'd got the eye-disease.
Ch. Then fetch a circuit round about the lake.
Xa. Where must I wait?
Ch. Beside the Withering stone,
Hard by the Rest.
Di. You understand?
Xa. Too well.
O, what ill omen crossed me as I started! *Exit.*
Ch. (*to* DIONYSUS) Sit to the oar. (*calling*) Who else for the boat? Be quick.
(*to* DIONYSUS) Hi! what are you doing?
Di. What am I doing? Sitting
On to the oar. You told me to, yourself.
Ch. Now sit you there, you little Potgut.
Di. So?
Ch. Now stretch your arms full length before you.
Di. So?
Ch. Come, don't keep fooling; plant your feet, and now
Pull with a will.
Di. Why, how am *I* to pull?
I'm not an oarsman, seaman, Salaminian.
I can't.
Ch. You can. Just dip your oar in once,
You'll hear the loveliest timing songs.
Di. What from?
Ch. Frog-swans, most wonderful.
Di. Then give the word.
Ch. Heave ahoy! heave ahoy!
Frogs. (*off stage*) Brekekekex, ko-ax, ko-ax,
Brekekekex, ko-ax, ko-ax!
We children of the fountain and the lake
Let us wake
Our full choir-shout, as the flutes are ringing out,
Our symphony of clear-voiced song.
The song we used to love in the Marshland up above,
In praise of Dionysus to produce,
Of Nysaean Dionysus, son of Zeus,
When the revel-tipsy throng, all crapulous and gay,
To our precinct reeled along on the holy Pitcher day,
Brekekekex, ko-ax, ko-ax.
Di. O, dear! O, dear! now I declare
I've got a bump upon my rump,
Fr. Brekekekex, ko-ax, ko-ax.
Di. But you, perchance, don't care.
Fr. Brekekekex, ko-ax, ko-ax.

Di. Hang you, and your ko-axing too!
There's nothing but ko-ax with you.
Fr. That is right, Mr. Busybody, right!
For the Muses of the lyre love us well;
And hornfoot Pan who plays
on the pipe his jocund lays;
And Apollo, Harper bright,
in our Chorus takes delight;
For the strong reed's sake
which I grow within my lake
To be girdled in his lyre's deep shell.
Brekekekex, ko-ax, ko-ax.
Di. My hands are blistered very sore;
My stern below is sweltering so,
'Twill soon, I know, upturn and roar
Brekekekex, ko-ax, ko-ax.
O tuneful race, O pray give o'er,
O sing no more.
Fr. Ah, no! ah, no!
Loud and louder our chant must flow.
Sing if ever ye sang of yore,
When in sunny and glorious days
Through the rushes and marsh-flags springing
On we swept, in the joy of singing
Myriad-diving roundelays.
Or when fleeing the storm, we went
Down to the depths, and our choral song
Wildly raised to a loud and long
Bubble-bursting accompaniment.
Fr. and Di. Brekekekex, ko-ax, ko-ax.
Di. This timing song I take from you.
Fr. That's a dreadful thing to do.
Di. Much more dreadful, if I row
Till I burst myself, I trow.
Fr. and Di. Brekekekex, ko-ax, ko-ax.
Di. Go, hang yourselves; for what care I?
Fr. All the same we'll shout and cry,
Stretching all our throats with song,
Shouting, crying, all day long,
Fr. and Di. Brekekekex, ko-ax, ko-ax.
Di. In this you'll never, never win.
Fr. This you shall not beat us in.
Di. No, nor ye prevail o'er me.
Never! never! I'll my song
Shout, if need be, all day long,
Until I've learned to master your ko-ax.
Brekekekex, ko-ax, ko-ax.
I thought I'd put a stop to your ko-ax.
Ch. Stop! Easy! Take the oar and push her to.
Now pay your fare and go.
Di. Here 'tis: two obols.
Xanthias! where's Xanthias? Is it Xanthias there?
Xa. (*off stage*) Hoi, hoi!
Di. Come hither.
Xa. (*entering*) Glad to meet you, master.
Di. What have you there?
Xa. Nothing but filth and darkness.
Di. But tell me, did you see the parricides
And perjured folk he mentioned?
Xa. Didn't you?
Di. Poseidon, yes. Why look! (*pointing to the audience*) I see them now.
What's the next step?
Xa. We'd best be moving on.
This is the spot where Heracles declared
Those savage monsters dwell.
Di. O hang the fellow.
That's all his bluff: he thought to scare me off,
The jealous dog, knowing my plucky ways.
There's no such swaggerer lives as Heracles.
Why, I'd like nothing better than to achieve
Some bold adventure, worthy of our trip.
Xa. I know you would. Hallo! I hear a noise.
Di. Where? what?
Xa. Behind us, there.
Di. Get you behind.
Xa. No, it's in front.
Di. Get you in front directly.
Xa. And now I see the most ferocious monster.
Di. O, what's it like?
Xa. Like everything by turns.
Now it's a bull: now it's a mule: and now
The loveliest girl.
Di. O, where? I'll go and meet her.
Xa. It's ceased to be a girl: it's a dog now.
Di. It is Empusa!
Xa. Well, its face is all
Ablaze with fire.
Di. Has it a copper leg?
Xa. A copper leg? yes, one; and one of cow dung.
Di. O, whither shall I flee?
Xa. O, whither I?
Di. My priest, protect me, and we'll sup together.
Xa. King Heracles, we're done for.
Di. O, forbear,
Good fellow, call me anything but that.
Xa. Well then, Dionysus.
Di. O, that's worse again,
Xa. (*to the* SPECTRE) Aye, go thy way. O master, here, come here.
Di. O, what's up now?
Xa. Take courage; all's serene.
And, like Hegelochus, we now may say
"Out of the storm there comes a new fine wether."
Empusa's gone.
Di. Swear it.
Xa. By Zeus she is.
Di. Swear it again.
Xa. By Zeus.
Di. Again.
Xa. By Zeus.
O dear, O dear, how pale I grew to see her,
But *he*, from fright has yellowed me all over.
Di. Ah me, whence fall these evils on my head?
Who is the god to blame for my destruction?
Air, Zeus's chamber, or the Foot of Time?
(*A flute is played behind the scenes.*)
Hist!
Xa. What's the matter?
Di. Didn't you hear it?
Xa. What?
Di. The breath of flutes.
Xa. Aye, and a whiff of torches
Breathed o'er me too; a very mystic whiff.

Di. Then crouch we down, and mark what's going on.

Chorus. (*in the distance*)

O Iacchus! O Iacchus! O Iacchus!

Xa. I have it, master: 'tis those blessed Mystics,
Of whom he told us, sporting hereabouts.
They sing the Iacchus which Diagoras made.

Di. I think so too: we had better both keep quiet
And so find out exactly what it is.

Enter CHORUS, *who had chanted the songs of the* FROGS, *as initiates.*

Chorus

O Iacchus! power excelling,
here in stately temples dwelling.
O Iacchus! O Iacchus!
Come to tread this verdant level,
Come to dance in mystic revel,
Come whilst round thy forehead hurtles
Many a wreath of fruitful myrtles,
Come with wild and saucy paces
Mingling in our joyous dance,
Pure and holy, which embraces
all the charms of all the Graces,
When the mystic choirs advance.

Xa. Holy and sacred queen, Demeter's daughter,
O, what a jolly whiff of pork breathed o'er me!

Di. Hist! and perchance you'll get some tripe yourself.

Chorus

Come, arise, from sleep awaking,
come the fiery torches shaking,
O Iacchus! O Iacchus!
Morning Star that shinest nightly.
Lo, the mead is blazing brightly,
Age forgets its years and sadness,
Agèd knees curvet for gladness,
Lift thy flashing torches o'er us,
Marshal all thy blameless train,
Lead, O lead the way before us;
lead the lovely youthful Chorus
To the marshy flowery plain.

All evil thoughts and profane be still:
far hence, far hence from our choirs depart,
Who knows not well what the Mystics tell,
or is not holy and pure of heart;
Who ne'er has the noble revelry learned,
or danced the dance of the Muses high;
Or shared in the Bacchic rites which old
bull-eating Cratinus's words supply;
Who vulgar coarse buffoonery loves,
though all untimely the jests they make;
Or lives not easy and kind with all,
or kindling faction forbears to slake,
But fans the fire, from a base desire
some pitiful gain for himself to reap;
Or takes, in office, his gifts and bribes,
while the city is tossed on the stormy deep;
Who fort or fleet to the foe betrays;
or, a vile Thorycion, ships away
Forbidden stores from Aegina's shores,
to Epidaurus across the Bay
Transmitting oar-pads and sails and tar,
that curst collector of five per cents;
The knave who tries to procure supplies
for the use of the enemy's armaments;
The Cyclian singer who dares befoul
the Lady Hecate's wayside shrine;
The public speaker who once lampooned
in our Bacchic feasts would, with heart malign,
Keep nibbling away the Comedians' pay;—
to these I utter my warning cry,
I charge them once, I charge them twice,
I charge them thrice, that they draw not nigh
To the sacred dance of the Mystic choir.
But *ye*, my comrades, awake the song,
The night-long revels of joy and mirth
which ever of right to our feast belong.

Advance, true hearts, advance!
On to the gladsome bowers,
On to the sward, with flowers
Embosomed bright!
March on with jest, and jeer, and dance,
Full well ye've supped to-night.

March, chanting loud your lays,
Your hearts and voices raising,
The Saviour goddess praising
Who vows she'll still
Our city save to endless days,
Whate'er Thorycion's will.

Break off the measure, and change the time;
and now with chanting and hymns adorn
Demeter, goddess mighty and high,
the harvest-queen, the giver of corn.

O Lady, over our rites presiding,
Preserve and succour thy choral throng,
And grant us all, in thy help confiding,
To dance and revel the whole day long;
AND MUCH in earnest, and much in jest,
Worthy thy feast, may we speak therein.
And when we have bantered and laughed our best,
The victor's wreath be it ours to win.

Call we now the youthful god,
call him hither without delay,
Him who travels amongst his chorus,
dancing along on the Sacred Way.

O, come with the joy of thy festival song,
O, come to the goddess, O, mix with our throng
Untired, though the journey be never so long.
O Lord of the frolic and dance,
Iacchus, beside me advance!
For fun, and for cheapness, our dress thou hast rent,
Through thee we may dance to the top of our bent,

Reviling, and jeering, and none will resent.
O Lord of the frolic and dance,
Iacchus, beside me advance!
A sweet pretty girl I observed in the show,
Her robe had been torn in the scuffle, and lo,
There peeped through the tatters a bosom of snow.
O Lord of the frolic and dance,
Iacchus, beside me advance!

Di. Wouldn't I like to follow on, and try
A little sport and dancing?
Xa. Wouldn't I?
Cho. Shall we all a merry joke
At Archedemus poke,
Who has not cut his guildsmen yet, though seven years old;
Yet up among the dead
He is demagogue and head,
And contrives the topmost place of the rascaldom to hold?
And Cleisthenes, they say,
Is among the tombs all day,
Bewailing for his lover with a lamentable whine.
And Callias, I'm told,
Has become a sailor bold,
And casts a lion's hide o'er his members feminine.
Di. Can any of you tell
Where Pluto here may dwell,
For we, sirs, are two strangers who were never here before?
Cho. O, then no further stray,
Nor again inquire the way,
For know that ye have journeyed to his very entrance-door.
Di. Take up the wraps, my lad.
Xa. Now is not this too bad?
Like "Zeus's Corinth," he "the wraps" keeps saying o'er and o'er.

Chorus

Now wheel your sacred dances through the glade with flowers bedight,
All ye who are partakers of the holy festal rite;
And I will with the women and the holy maidens go
Where they keep the nightly vigil, an auspicious light to show.

Now haste we to the roses,
And the meadows full of posies,
Now haste we to the meadows
In our own old way,
In choral dances blending,
In dances never ending,
Which only for the holy
The Destinies array.

O, happy mystic chorus,
The blessed sunshine o'er us
On us alone is smiling,
In its soft sweet light:
On us who strove forever
With holy, pure endeavour,
Alike by friend and stranger
To guide our steps aright.

Di. What's the right way to knock? I wonder how
The natives here are wont to knock at doors.
Xa. No dawdling: taste the door. You've got, remember,
The lion-hide and pride of Heracles.
Di. (*knocking*) Boy! boy!

The door opens. AEACUS *appears.*

Aeacus. Who's there?
Di. I, Heracles the strong!
Ae. O, you most shameless desperate ruffian, you!
O, villain, villain, arrant vilest villain!
Who seized our Cerberus by the throat, and fled,
And ran, and rushed, and bolted, haling off
The dog, my charge! But now I've got thee fast.
So close the Styx's inky-hearted rock,
The blood-bedabbled peak of Acheron
Shall hem thee in: the hell-hounds of Cocytus
Prowl round thee; whilst the hundred-headed Asp
Shall rive thy heart-strings: the Tartesian Lamprey
Prey on thy lungs: and those Tithrasian Gorgons
Mangle and tear thy kidneys, mauling them,
Entrails and all, into one bloody mash.
I'll speed a running foot to fetch them hither.

Exit AEACUS.

Xa. Hallo! what now?
Di. I've done it: call the god.
Xa. Get up, you laughing-stock; get up directly,
Before you're seen.
Di. What, *I* get up? I'm fainting.
Please dab a sponge of water on my heart.
Xa. Here! Dab it on.
Di. Where is it?
Xa. Ye golden gods,
Lies your heart *there*?
Di. It got so terrified
It fluttered down into my stomach's pit.
Xa. Cowardliest of gods and men!
Di. The cowardliest? I?
What I, who asked you for a sponge, a thing
A coward never would have done!
Xa. What then?
Di. A coward would have lain there wallowing;
But I stood up, and wiped myself withal.
Xa. Poseidon! quite heroic.
Di. 'Deed I think so.
But weren't *you* frightened at those dreadful threats
And shoutings?
Xa. Frightened? Not a bit. I cared not.
Di. Come then, if you're so *very* brave a man,
Will you be I, and take the hero's club
And lion's skin, since you're so monstrous plucky?
And I'll be now the slave, and bear the luggage.
Xa. Hand them across. I cannot choose but take them.
And now observe the Xanthio-heracles
If I'm a coward and a sneak like you.
Di. Nay, you're the rogue from Melite's own self.
And I'll pick up and carry on the traps.

Enter a MAID-SERVANT *of Persephone, from door.*

Maid. O welcome, Heracles! come in, sweetheart.
My Lady, when they told her, set to work,
Baked mighty loaves, boiled two or three tureens
Of lentil soup, roasted a prime ox whole,
Made rolls and honey-cakes. So come along.

Xa. (*declining*) You are too kind.

Ma. I will not let you go.
I will not *let* you! Why, she's stewing slices
Of juicy bird's-flesh, and she's making comfits,
And tempering down her richest wine. Come, dear,
Come along in.

Xa. (*still declining*) Pray thank her.

Ma. O you're jesting,
I shall not let you off: there's such a lovely
Flute-girl all ready, and we've two or three
Dancing-girls also.

Xa. Eh! what! Dancing-girls?

Ma. Young budding virgins, freshly tired and trimmed.
Come, dear, come in. The cook was dishing up
The cutlets, and they are bringing in the tables.

Xa. Then go you in, and tell those dancing-girls
Of whom you spake, I'm coming in Myself.

Exit MAID.

Pick up the traps, my lad, and follow me.

Di. Hi! stop! you're not in earnest, just because
I dressed you up, in fun, as Heracles?
Come, don't keep fooling, Xanthias, but lift
And carry in the traps yourself.

Xa. Why! what!
You are never going to strip me of these togs
You gave me!

Di. Going to? No, I'm doing it now.
Off with that lion-skin.

Xa. Bear witness all,
The gods shall judge between us.

Di. Gods, indeed!
Why, how could *you* (the vain and foolish thought!)
A slave, a mortal, act Alcmena's son?

Xa. All right then, take them; maybe, if God will,
You'll soon require my services again.

Cho. This is the part of a dexterous clever
Man with his wits about him ever,
One who has travelled the world to see;
Always to shift, and to keep through all
Close to the sunny side of the wall;
Not like a pictured block to be,
Standing always in one position;
Nay but to veer, with expedition,
And ever to catch the favouring breeze,
This is the part of a shrewd tactician,
This is to be a—*Theramenes*!

Di. Truly an exquisite joke 'twould be,
Him with a dancing-girl to see,
Lolling at ease on Milesian rugs;
Me, like a slave, beside him standing,
Aught that he wants to his lordship handing;
Then as the damsel fair he hugs,
Seeing me all on fire to embrace her,
He would perchance (for there's no man baser),
Turning him round like a lazy lout,
Straight on my mouth deliver a facer,
Knocking my ivory choirmen out.

Enter HOSTESS *and* PLATHANE.

Hostess. O Plathane! Plathane! Here's that naughty man,
That's he who got into our tavern once,
And ate up sixteen loaves.

Plathane. O, so he is!
The very man.

Xa. Bad luck for somebody!

Ho. O and, besides, those twenty bits of stew,
Half-obol pieces.

Xa. Somebody's going to catch it!

Ho. That garlic too.

Di. Woman, you're talking nonsense.
You don't know what you're saying.

Ho. O, you thought
I shouldn't know you with your buskins on!
Ah, and I've not yet mentioned all that fish,
No, nor the new-made cheese: he gulped it down,
Baskets and all, unlucky that we were.
And when I just alluded to the price,
He looked so fierce, and bellowed like a bull.

Xa. Yes, that's his way: that's what he always does.

Ho. O, and he drew his sword, and seemed quite mad.

Pla. O, that he did.

Ho. And terrified us so
We sprang up to the cockloft, she and I.
Then out he hurled, decamping with the rugs.

Xa. That's his way too; but something must be done.

Ho. Quick, run and call my patron Cleon here!

Pla. O, if you meet him, call Hyperbolus!
We'll pay you out to-day.

Ho. O filthy throat,
O how I'd like to take a stone, and hack
Those grinders out with which you chawed my wares.

Pla. I'd like to pitch you in the deadman's pit.

Ho. I'd like to get a reaping-hook and scoop
That gullet out with which you gorged my tripe.
But I'll to Cleon: he'll soon serve his writs;
He'll twist it out of you to-day, he will.

Exeunt HOSTESS *and* PLATHANE.

Di. Perdition seize me, if I don't love Xanthias.

Xa. Aye, aye, I know your drift: stop, stop that talking
I won't be Heracles.

Di. O, don't say so,
Dear, darling Xanthias.

Xa. Why, how can I,
A slave, a mortal, act Alcmena's son!

Di. Aye, aye, I know you are vexed, and I deserve it,
And if you pummel me, I won't complain.
But if I strip you of these togs again,
Perdition seize myself, my wife, my children,
And, most of all, that blear-eyed Archedemus.

Xa. That oath contents me: on those terms I take them.

Cho. Now that at last you appear once more,
Wearing the garb that at first you wore,
Wielding the club and the tawny skin,
Now it is yours to be up and doing,
Glaring like mad, and your youth renewing,
Mindful of him whose guise you are in.
If, when caught in a bit of a scrape, you
Suffer a word of alarm to escape you,
Showing yourself but a feckless knave,
Then will your master at once undrape you,
Then you'll again be the toiling slave.

Xa. There, I admit, you have given to me a
Capital hint, and the like idea,
Friends, had occurred to myself before.
Truly if anything good befell
He would be wanting, I know full well,
Wanting to take to the togs once more.
Nevertheless, while in these I'm vested,
Ne'er shall you find me craven-crested,
No, for a dittany look I'll wear,
Aye and methinks it will soon be tested,
Hark! how the portals are rustling there.

Re-enter AEACUS *with assistants.*

Ae. Seize the dog-stealer, bind him, pinion him,
Drag him to justice!

Di. Somebody's going to catch it.

Xa. (*striking out*) Hands off! get away! stand back!

Ae. Eh? You're for fighting.
Ho! Ditylas, Sceblyas, and Pardocas,
Come hither, quick; fight me this sturdy knave.

Di. Now isn't it a shame the man should strike
And he a thief besides?

Ae. A monstrous shame!

Di. A regular burning shame!

Xa. By the Lord Zeus,
If ever I was here before, if ever
I stole one hair's-worth from you, let me die!
And now I'll make you a right noble offer,
Arrest my lad: torture him as you will,
And if you find I'm guilty, take and kill me.

Ae. Torture him, how?

Xa. In any mode you please.
Pile bricks upon him: stuff his nose with acid:
Flay, rack him, hoist him; flog him with a scourge
Of prickly bristles: only not with this,
A soft-leaved onion, or a tender leek.

Ae. A fair proposal. If I strike too hard
And maim the boy, I'll make you compensation.

Xa. I shan't require it. Take him out and flog him.

Ae. Nay, but I'll do it here before your eyes.
Now then, put down the traps, and mind you speak
The truth, young fellow.

Di. (*in agony*) Man! don't torture *me*!
I am a god. You'll blame yourself hereafter
If you touch *me*.

Ae. Hillo! What's that you are saying?

Di. I say I'm Bacchus, son of Zeus, a god,
And *he's* the slave.

Ae. You hear him?

Xa. Hear him? Yes.
All the more reason you should flog him well.
For if he is a god, he won't perceive it.

Di. Well, but you say that you're a god yourself.
So why not *you* be flogged as well as I?

Xa. A fair proposal. And be this the test,
Whichever of us two you first behold
Flinching or crying out—he's not the god.

Ae. Upon my word you're quite the gentleman,
You're all for right and justice. Strip then, both.

Xa. How can you test us fairly?

Ae. Easily,
I'll give you blow for blow.

Xa. A good idea.
We're ready! Now! (AEACUS *strikes him*) see if you catch me flinching.

Ae. I struck you.

Xa. (*incredulously*) No!

Ae. Well, it seems "no" indeed.
Now then I'll strike the other. (*Strikes* DIONYSUS.)

Di. Tell me when?

Ae. I struck you.

Di. Struck me? Then why didn't I sneeze?

Ae. Don't know, I'm sure. I'll try the other again.

Xa. And quickly too. Good gracious!

Ae. Why "good gracious"?
Not hurt you, did I?

Xa. No, I merely thought of
The Diomeian feast of Heracles.

Ae. A holy man! 'Tis now the other's turn.

Di. Hi! Hi!

Ae. Hallo!

Di. Look at those horsemen, look!

Ae. But why these tears?

Di. There's such a smell of onions.

Ae. Then you don't mind it?

Di. (*cheerfully*) Mind it? Not a bit.

Ae. Well, I must go to the other one again.

Xa. O! O!

Ae. Hallo!

Xa. Do pray pull out this thorn.

Ae. What does it mean? 'Tis this one's turn again.

Di. (*shrieking*) Apollo! Lord! (*calmly*) of Delos and of Pytho.

Xa. He flinched! You heard him?

Di. Not at all; a jolly
Verse of Hipponax flashed across my mind.

Xa. You don't half do it: cut his flanks to pieces.

Ae. By Zeus, well thought on. Turn your belly here.

Di. (*screaming*) Poseidon!

Xa. There! he's flinching.

Di. (*singing*) who dost reign
Amongst the Aegean peaks and creeks
And o'er the deep blue main.

Ae. No, by Demeter, still I can't find out
Which is the god, but come ye both indoors;
My lord himself and Persephassa there,
Being gods themselves, will soon find out the truth.

Di. Right! right! I only wish you had thought of that
Before you gave me those tremendous whacks.

Exeunt DIONYSUS, XANTHIAS, AEACUS, *and attendants.*

Chorus

Come, Muse, to our Mystical Chorus,
O come to the joy of my song,
O see on the benches before us
that countless and wonderful throng,
Where wits by the thousand abide,
with more than a Cleophon's pride—
On the lips of that foreigner base,
of Athens the bane and disgrace,
There is shrieking, his kinsman by race,
The garrulous swallow of Thrace;
From that perch of exotic descent,
Rejoicing her sorrow to vent,
She pours to her spirit's content,
a nightingale's woful lament,
That e'en though the voting be equal,
his ruin will soon be the sequel.

Well it suits the holy Chorus
evermore with counsel wise
To exhort and teach the city;
this we therefore now advise—
End the townsmen's apprehensions;
equalize the rights of all;
If by Phrynichus's wrestlings
some perchance sustained a fall,
Yet to these 'tis surely open,
having put away their sin,
For their slips and vacillations
pardon at your hands to win.
Give your brethren back their franchise.
Sin and shame it were that slaves,
Who have once with stern devotion
fought your battle on the waves,
Should be straightway lords and masters,
yea Plataeans fully blown—
Not that this deserves our censure;
there I praise you; there alone
Has the city, in her anguish,
policy and wisdom shown—
Nay but these, of old accustomed
on our ships to fight and win,
(They, their fathers too before them),
these our very kith and kin,
You should likewise, when they ask you,
pardon for their single sin.
O by nature best and wisest,
O relax your jealous ire,
Let us all the world as kinsfolk
and as citizens acquire,
All who on our ships will battle
well and bravely by our side.
If we cocker up our city,
narrowing her with senseless pride,
Now when she is rocked and reeling
in the cradles of the sea,
Here again will after ages deem we acted brainlessly.

And O if I'm able to scan
the habits and life of a man
Who shall rue his iniquities soon!
not long shall that little baboon,
That Cleigenes shifty and small,
the wickedest bathman of all
Who are lords of the earth—which is brought
from the isle of Cimolus, and wrought
With nitre and lye into soap—
Not long shall he vex us, I hope.
And this the unlucky one knows,
Yet ventures a peace to oppose,
And being addicted to blows
he carries a stick as he goes,
Lest while he is tipsy and reeling,
some robber his cloak should be stealing.

Often has it crossed my fancy,
that the city loves to deal
With the very best and noblest
members of her commonweal,
Just as with our ancient coinage,
and the newly-minted gold.
Yea for these, our sterling pieces,
all of pure Athenian mould,
All of perfect die and metal,
all the fairest of the fair,
All of workmanship unequalled,
proved and valued everywhere
Both amongst our own Hellenes
and Barbarians far away,
These we use not: but the worthless
pinchbeck coins of yesterday,
Vilest die and basest metal,
now we always use instead.
Even so, our sterling townsmen,
nobly born and nobly bred,
Men of worth and rank and mettle,
men of honourable fame,
Trained in every liberal science,
choral dance and manly game,
These we treat with scorn and insult,
but the strangers newliest come,
Worthless sons of worthless fathers,
pinchbeck townsmen, yellowy scum,
Whom in earlier days the city
hardly would have stooped to use
Even for her scapegoat victims,
these for every task we choose.
O unwise and foolish people,
yet to mend your ways begin;
Use again the good and useful:
so hereafter, if ye win
'Twill be due to this your wisdom:
if ye fall, at least 'twill be
Not a fall that brings dishonour,
falling from a worthy tree.

Enter AEACUS, XANTHIAS *and two attendants.*

Ae. By Zeus the Saviour, quite the gentleman
Your master is.
Xa. Gentleman? I believe you.
He's all for wine and women, is my master.
Ae. But not to have flogged you, when the truth came out
That you, the slave, were passing off as master!
Xa. He'd get the worst of that.

Ae. Bravo! that's spoken
Like a true slave: that's what I love myself.
Xa. You love it, do you?
Ae. Love it? I'm entranced
When I can curse my lord behind his back.
Xa. How about grumbling, when you have felt the stick,
And scurry out of doors?
Ae. That's jolly too.
Xa. How about prying?
Ae. That beats everything!
Xa. Great Kin-god Zeus! And what of overhearing
Your master's secrets?
Ae. What? I'm mad with joy.
Xa. And blabbing them abroad?
Ae. O heaven and earth!
When I do that, I can't contain myself.
Xa. Phoebus Apollo! clap your hand in mine,
Kiss and be kissed: and prithee tell me this,
Tell me by Zeus, our rascaldom's own god,
What's all that noise within? What means this hubbub
And row?
Ae. That's Aeschylus and Euripides.
Xa. Eh?
Ae. Wonderful, wonderful things are going on.
The dead are rioting, taking different sides.
Xa. Why, what's the matter?
Ae. There's a custom here
With all the crafts, the good and noble crafts,
That the chief master of his art in each
Shall have his dinner in the assembly hall,
And sit by Pluto's side.
Xa. I understand.
Ae. Until another comes, more wise than he
In the same art: then must the first give way.
Xa. And how has this disturbed our Aeschylus?
Ae. 'Twas he that occupied the tragic chair,
As, in his craft, the noblest.
Xa. Who does now?
Ae. But when Euripides came down, he kept
Flourishing off before the highwaymen,
Thieves, burglars, parricides—these form our mob
In Hades—till with listening to his twists
And turns, and pleas and counterpleas, they went
Mad on the man, and hailed him first and wisest:
Elate with this, he claimed the tragic chair
Where Aeschylus was seated.
Xa. Wasn't he pelted?
Ae. Not he: the populace clamoured out to try
Which of the twain was wiser in his art.
Xa. You mean the rascals?
Ae. Aye, as high as heaven!
Xa. But were there none to side with Aeschylus?
Ae. Scanty and sparse the good, (*regards the audience*) the same as here.
Xa. And what does Pluto now propose to do?
Ae. He means to hold a tournament, and bring
Their tragedies to the proof.
Xa. But Sophocles,
How came not he to claim the tragic chair?
Ae. Claim it? Not he! When *he* came down, he kissed
With reverence Aeschylus, and clasped his hand,
And yielded willingly the chair to him.
But now he's going, says Cleidemides,
To sit third-man: and then if Aeschylus win,
He'll stay content: if not, for his art's sake,
He'll fight to the death against Euripides.
Xa. Will it come off?
Ae. O yes, by Zeus, directly.
And then, I hear, will wonderful things be done,
The art poetic will be weighed in scales.
Xa. What! weigh out tragedy, like butcher's meat?
Ae. Levels they'll bring, and measuring-tapes for words,
And moulded oblongs,
Xa. Is it bricks they are making?
Ae. Wedges and compasses: for Euripides
Vows that he'll test the dramas, word by word.
Xa. Aeschylus chafes at this, I fancy.
Ae. Well,
He lowered his brows, upglaring like a bull.
Xa. And who's to be the judge?
Ae. There came the rub.
Skilled men were hard to find: for with the Athenians
Aeschylus, somehow, did not hit it off,
Xa. Too many burglars, I expect, he thought.
Ae. And all the rest, he said, were trash and nonsense
To judge poetic wits. So then at last
They chose your lord, an expert in the art.
But we go in: for when our lords are bent
On urgent business, that means blows for us.
Cho. O surely with terrible wrath
will the thunder-voiced monarch be filled,
When he sees his opponent beside him,
the tonguester, the artifice-skilled,
Stand, whetting his tusks for the fight!
O surely, his eyes rolling-fell
Will with terrible madness be fraught!
O then will be charging of plume-waving words
with their wild-floating mane,
And then will be whirling of splinters,
and phrases smoothed down with the plane,
When the man would the grand-stepping maxims,
the language gigantic, repel
Of the hero-creator of thought.
There will his shaggy-born crest
upbristle for anger and woe,
Horribly frowning and growling,
his fury will launch at the foe
Huge-clamped masses of words,
with exertion Titanic up-tearing
Great ship-timber planks for the fray.
But here will the tongue be at work,
uncoiling, word-testing, refining,
Sophist-creator of phrases,
dissecting, detracting, maligning,

Shaking the envious bits,
and with subtle analysis paring
The lung's large labour away.

Here apparently there is a complete change of scene, to the Hall of Pluto, with PLUTO *himself sitting on his throne, and* DIONYSUS, AESCHYLUS, *and* EURIPIDES *in the foreground.*

Euripides. Don't talk to me; I won't give up the chair,
I say I am better in the art than he.

Di. You hear him, Aeschylus: why don't you speak?

Eu. He'll do the grand at first, the juggling trick
He used to play in all his tragedies.

Di. Come, my fine fellow, pray don't talk too big.

Eu. I know the man, I've scanned him through and through,
A savage-creating stubborn-pulling fellow,
Uncurbed, unfettered, uncontrolled of speech,
Unperiphrastic, bombastiloquent.

Aeschylus. Hah! sayest thou so, child of the garden quean!
And this to *me*, thou chattery-babble-collector,
Thou pauper-creating rags-and-patches-stitcher?
Thou shalt abye it dearly!

Di. Pray, be still;
Nor heat thy soul to fury, Aeschylus.

Aes. Not till I've made you see the sort of man
This cripple-maker is who crows so loudly.

Di. Bring out a ewe, a black-fleeced ewe, my boys:
Here's a typhoon about to burst upon us.

Aes. Thou picker-up of Cretan monodies,
Foisting thy tales of incest on the stage—

Di. Forbear, forbear, most honoured Aeschylus;
And you, my poor Euripides, begone
If you are wise, out of this pitiless hail,
Lest with some heady word he crack your scull
And batter out your brain—less Telephus.
And not with passion, Aeschylus, but calmly
Test and be tested. 'Tis not meet for poets
To scold each other, like two baking-girls.
But you go roaring like an oak on fire.

Eu. I'm ready, I! I don't draw back one bit.
I'll lash or, if he will, let him lash first
The talk, the lays, the sinews of a play:
Aye and my Peleus, aye and Aeolus.
And Meleager, aye and Telephus.

Di. And what do *you* propose? Speak, Aeschylus.

Aes. I could have wished to meet him otherwhere.
We fight not here on equal terms.

Di. Why not?

Aes. My poetry survived me: his died with him:
He's got it here, all handy to recite.
Howbeit, if so you wish it, so we'll have it.

Di. O bring me fire, and bring me frankincense.
I'll pray, or e'er the clash of wits begin,
To judge the strife with high poetic skill.
Meanwhile (*to the* CHORUS) invoke the Muses with a song.

Chorus

O Muses, the daughters divine
of Zeus, the immaculate Nine,
Who gaze from your mansions serene
on intellects subtle and keen,
When down to the tournament lists,
in bright-polished wit they descend,
With wrestling and turnings and twists
in the battle of words to contend,
O come and behold what the two
antagonist poets can do,
Whose mouths are the swiftest to teach
grand language and filings of speech:
For now of their wits is the sternest
encounter commencing in earnest.

Di. Ye two, put up your prayers before ye start.

Aes. Demeter, mistress, nourisher of my soul,
O make me worthy of thy mystic rites!

Di. (*to* EURIPIDES) Now put on incense, you.

Eu. Excuse me, no;
My vows are paid to other gods than these.

Di. What, a new coinage of your own?

Eu. Precisely.

Di. Pray then to them, those private gods of yours.

Eu. Ether, my pasture, volubly-rolling tongue,
Intelligent wit and critic nostrils keen,
O well and neatly may I trounce his plays!

Cho. We also are yearning from these to be learning
Some stately measure, some majestic grand
Movement telling of conflicts nigh.
Now for battle arrayed they stand,
Tongues embittered, and anger high.
Each has got a venturesome will,
Each an eager and nimble mind;
One will wield, with artistic skill,
Clearcut phrases, and wit refined;
Then the other, with words defiant,
Stern and strong, like an angry giant
Laying on with uprooted trees,
Soon will scatter a world of these
Superscholastic subtleties.

Di. Now then, commence your arguments,
and mind you both display
True wit, not metaphors, nor things
which any fool could say.

Eu. As for myself, good people all,
I'll tell you by-and-by
My own poetic worth and claims;
but first of all I'll try
To show how this portentous quack
beguiled the silly fools
Whose tastes were nurtured, ere he came,
in Phrynichus's schools.
He'd bring some single mourner on,
seated and veiled, 'twould be
Achilles, say, or Niobe
—the face you could not see—
An empty show of tragic woe,
who uttered not one thing.

Di. 'Tis true.

Eu. Then in the Chorus came,
and rattled off a string

Of four continuous lyric odes:
the mourner never stirred.
Di. I liked it too. I sometimes think
that I those mutes preferred
To all your chatterers now-a-days.
Eu. Because, if you must know,
You were an ass.
Di. An ass, no doubt;
what made him do it though?
Eu. That was his quackery, don't you see,
to set the audience guessing
When Niobe would speak; meanwhile,
the drama was progressing.
Di. The rascal, how he took me in!
'Twas shameful, was it not?
(*To* AESCHYLUS) What makes you stamp and fidget so?
Eu. He's catching it so hot.
So when he had humbugged thus awhile,
and now his wretched play
Was halfway through, a dozen words,
great wild-bull words, he'd say,
Fierce Bugaboos, with bristling crests,
and shaggy eyebrows too,
Which not a soul could understand.
Aes. O heavens!
Di. Be quiet, do.
Eu. But not one single word was clear.
Di. St! don't your teeth be gnashing.
Eu. 'Twas all Scamanders, moated camps,
and griffin-eagles flashing
In burnished copper on the shields,
chivalric-precipice-high
Expressions, hard to comprehend.
Di. Aye, by the Powers, and I
Full many a sleepless night have spent
in anxious thought, because
I'd find the tawny cock-horse out,
what sort of bird it was!
Aes. It was a sign, you stupid dolt,
engraved the ships upon.
Di. Eryxis I supposed it was,
Philoxenus's son.
Eu. Now really should a cock be brought
into a tragic play?
Aes. You enemy of gods and men,
what was *your* practice, pray?
Eu. No cock-horse in *my* plays, by Zeus,
no goat-stag there you'll see,
Such figures as are blazoned forth
in Median tapestry.
When first I took the art from you,
bloated and swoln, poor thing,
With turgid gasconading words
and heavy dieting,
First I reduced and toned her down,
and made her slim and neat
With wordlets and with exercise
and poultices of beet,
And next a dose of chatterjuice,
distilled from books, I gave her,
And monodies she took, with sharp
Cephisophon for flavour.
I never used haphazard words,
or plunged abruptly in;
Who entered first explained at large
the drama's origin
And source.
Aes. Its source, I really trust,
was better than your own.
Eu. Then from the very opening lines
no idleness was shown;
The mistress talked with all her might,
the servant talked as much,
The master talked, the maiden talked,
the beldame talked.
Aes. For such
An outrage was not death your due?
Eu. No, by Apollo, no:
That was my democratic way.
Di. Ah, let that topic go.
Your record is not there, my friend,
particularly good.
Eu. Then next I taught all these to speak.
Aes. You did so, and I would
That ere such mischief you had wrought,
your very lungs had split.
Eu. Canons of verse I introduced,
and neatly chiselled wit;
To look, to scan: to plot, to plan:
to twist, to turn, to woo:
On all to spy; in all to pry.
Aes. You did: I say so too.
Eu. I showed them scenes of common life,
the things we know and see,
Where any blunder would at once
by all detected be.
I never blustered on, or took
their breath and wits away
By Cycnuses or Memnons clad
in terrible array,
With bells upon their horses' heads,
the audience to dismay.
Look at *his* pupils, look at mine:
and there the contrast view.
Uncouth Megaenetus is his,
and rough Phormisius too;
Great long-beard-lance-and-trumpet-men,
flesh-tearers with the pine:
But natty smart Theramenes,
and Cleitophon are mine.
Di. Theramenes? a clever man
and wonderfully sly:
Immerse him in a flood of ills,
he'll soon be high and dry,
"A Kian with a kappa, sir,
not Chian with a chi."
Eu. I taught them all these knowing ways
By chopping logic in my plays,
And making all my speakers try
To reason out the How and Why.
So now the people trace the springs,
The sources and the roots of things,
And manage all their households too
Far better than they used to do,

Scanning and searching "What's amiss?"
And, "Why was that?" And, "How is this?"
Di. Ay, truly, never now a man
Comes home, but he begins to scan;
And to his household loudly cries,
"Why, where's my pitcher? What's the matter?
'Tis dead and gone my last year's platter.
Who gnawed these olives? Bless the sprat,
Who nibbled off the head of that?
And where's the garlic vanished, pray,
I purchased only yesterday?"
—Whereas, of old, our stupid youths
Would sit, with open mouths and eyes,
Like any dull-brained Mammacouths.
Cho. *All this thou beholdest, Achilles our boldest."
And what wilt thou reply? Draw tight the rein
Lest that fiery soul of thine
Whirl thee out of the listed plain,
Past the olives, and o'er the line.
Dire and grievous the charge he brings.
See thou answer him, noble heart,
Not with passionate bickerings.
Shape thy course with a sailor's art,
Reef the canvas, shorten the sails,
Shift them edgewise to shun the gales.
When the breezes are soft and low,
Then, well under control, you'll go
Quick and quicker to strike the foe.
O first of all the Hellenic bards
high loftily-towering verse to rear,
And tragic phrase from the dust to raise,
pour forth thy fountain with right good cheer.

Aes. My wrath is hot at this vile mischance,
and my spirit revolts at the thought that I
Must bandy words with a fellow like *him*:
but lest he should vaunt that I can't reply—
Come, tell me what are the points for which
a noble poet our praise obtains.
Eu. For his ready wit, and his counsels sage,
and because the citizen folk he trains
To be better townsmen and worthier men.
Aes. If then you have done the very reverse,
Found noble-hearted and virtuous men,
and altered them, each and all, for the worse,
Pray what is the meed you deserve to get?
Di. Nay, ask not *him*. He deserves to die.
Aes. For just consider what style of men
he received from me, great six-foot-high
Heroical souls, who never would blench
from a townsman's duties in peace or war;
Not idle loafers, or low buffoons,
or rascally scamps such as now they are.
But men who were breathing spears and helms,
and the snow-white plume in its crested pride,
The greave, and the dart, and the warrior's heart
in its sevenfold casing of tough bull-hide.
Di. He'll stun me, I know, with his armoury-work;
this business is going from bad to worse.
Eu. And how did you manage to make them so grand,
exalted, and brave with your wonderful verse?
Di. Come, Aeschylus, answer, and don't stand mute
in your self-willed pride and arrogant spleen.
Aes. A drama I wrote with the War-god filled.
Di. Its name?
Aes. 'Tis the *Seven against Thebes* that I mean.
Which whoso beheld, with eagerness swelled
to rush to the battlefield there and then.
Di. O that was a scandalous thing you did!
You have made the Thebans mightier men,
More eager by far for the business of war.
Now, therefore, receive this punch on the head.
Aes. Ah, *ye* might have practised the same yourselves,
but ye turned to other pursuits instead.
Then next the *Persians* I wrote, in praise
of the noblest deed that the world can show,
And each man longed for the victor's wreath,
to fight and to vanquish his country's foe.
Di. I was pleased, I own, when I heard their moan
for old Darius, their great king, dead;
When they smote together their hands, like this,
and "Evir alake" the Chorus said.
Aes. Aye, such are the poet's appropriate works:
and just consider how all along
From the very first they have wrought you good,
the noble bards, the masters of song.
First, Orpheus taught you religious rites,
and from bloody murder to stay your hands:
Musaeus healing and oracle lore;
and Hesiod all the culture of lands,
The time to gather, the time to plough.
And gat not Homer his glory divine
By singing of valour, and honour, and right,
and the sheen of the battle-extended line,
The ranging of troops and the arming of men?
Di. O ay, but he didn't teach *that*, I opine,
To Pantacles; when he was leading the show
I couldn't imagine what he was at,
He had fastened his helm on the top of his head,
he was trying to fasten his plume upon that.
Aes. But others, many and brave, he taught,
of whom was Lamachus, hero true;
And thence my spirit the impress took,
and many a lion-heart chief I drew,
Patrocluses, Teucers, illustrious names;
for I fain the citizen-folk would spur
To stretch themselves to *their* measure and height,
whenever the trumpet of war they hear.
But Phaedras and Stheneboeas? No!
no harlotry business deformed my plays.
And none can say that ever I drew
a love-sick woman in all my days.
Eu. For *you* no lot or portion had got
in Queen Aphrodite.
Aes. Thank Heaven for that.
But ever on you and yours, my friend,
the mighty goddess mightily sat;
Yourself she cast to the ground at last.
Di. O ay, that uncommonly pat.
You showed how cuckolds are made, and lo,
you were struck yourself by the very same fate.

Eu. But say, you cross-grained censor of mine,
how *my* Stheneboeas could harm the state.
Aes. Full many a noble dame, the wife
of a noble citizen, hemlock took,
And died, unable the shame and sin
of your Bellerophon-scenes to brook.
Eu. Was then, I wonder, the tale I told
of Phaedra's passionate love untrue?
Aes. Not so: but tales of incestuous vice
the sacred poet should hide from view,
Nor ever exhibit and blazon forth
on the public stage to the public ken.
For boys a teacher at school is found,
but we, the poets, are teachers of men.
We are *bound* things honest and pure to speak.
Eu. And to speak great Lycabettuses, pray,
And massive blocks of Parnassian rocks,
is *that* things honest and pure to say?
In human fashion we ought to speak.
Aes. Alas, poor witling, and can't you see
That for mighty thoughts and heroic aims,
the words themselves must appropriate be?
And grander belike on the ear should strike
the speech of heroes and godlike powers,
Since even the robes that invest their limbs
are statelier, grander robes than ours.
Such was *my* plan: but when *you* began,
you spoilt and degraded it all.
Eu. How so?
Aes. Your kings in tatters and rags you dressed,
and brought them on, a beggarly show,
To move, forsooth, our pity and ruth.
Eu. And what was the harm, I should like to know.
Aes. No more will a wealthy citizen now
equip for the state a galley of war.
He wraps his limbs in tatters and rags,
and whines he is "poor, too poor by far."
Di. But under his rags he is wearing a vest,
as woolly and soft as a man could wish.
Let him gull the state, and he's off to the mart;
an eager, extravagant buyer of fish.
Aes. Moreover to prate, to harangue, to debate,
is now the ambition of all in the state.
Each exercise-ground is in consequence found
deserted and empty: to evil repute
Your lessons have brought our youngsters, and taught
our sailors to challenge, discuss, and refute
The orders they get from their captains and yet,
when *I* was alive, I protest that the knaves
Knew nothing at all, save for rations to call,
and to sing "Rhyppapae" as they pulled
through the waves.
Di. And bedad to let fly from their sterns in the eye
of the fellow who tugged at the undermost oar,
And a jolly young messmate with filth to besmirch,
and to land for a filching adventure ashore;
But now they harangue, and dispute, and won't row
And idly and aimlessly float to and fro.
Aes. Of what ills is he *not* the creator and cause?
Consider the scandalous scenes that he draws,
His bawds, and his panders, his women who give
Give birth in the sacredest shrine,
Whilst others with brothers are wedded and bedded,
And others opine
That "not to be living" is truly "to live."
And therefore our city is swarming to-day
With clerks and with demagogue-monkeys, who play
Their jackanape tricks at all times, in all places,
Deluding the people of Athens; but none
Has training enough in athletics to run
With the torch in his hand at the races.
Di. By the Powers, you are right! At the Panathenaea
I laughed till I felt like a potsherd to see a
Pale, paunchy young gentleman pounding along,
With his head butting forward, the last of the throng,
In the direst of straits; and behold at the gates,
The Ceramites flapped him, and smacked him, and slapped him,
In the ribs, and the loin, and the flank, and the groin,
And still, as they spanked him, he puffed and he panted,
Till at one mighty cuff, he discharged such a puff
That he blew out his torch and levanted.

Chorus

Dread the battle, and stout the combat,
mighty and manifold looms the war.
Hard to decide is the fight they're waging,
One like a stormy tempest raging,
One alert in the rally and skirmish,
clever to parry and foin and spar.
Nay but don't be content to sit
Always in one position only:
many the fields for your keen-edged wit.
On then, wrangle in every way,
Argue, battle, be flayed and flay,
Old and new from your stores display,
Yea, and strive with venturesome daring
something subtle and neat to say.

Fear ye this, that to-day's spectators
lack the grace of artistic lore,
Lack the knowledge they need for taking
All the points ye will soon be making?
Fear it not: the alarm is groundless:
that, be sure, is the case no more.
All have fought the campaign ere this:
Each a book of the words is holding;
never a single point they'll miss.
Bright their natures, and now, I ween,
Newly whetted, and sharp, and keen.
Dread not any defect of wit,
Battle away without misgiving,
sure that the audience, at least, are fit.

Eu. Well then I'll turn me to your prologues now,
Beginning first to test the first beginning

Of this fine poet's plays. Why he's obscure
Even in the enunciation of the facts.

Di. Which of them will you test?

Eu. Many: but first
Give us that famous one from the Oresteia.

Di. St! Silence all! Now, Aeschylus, begin.

Aes. "Grave Hermes, witnessing a father's power,
Be thou my saviour and mine aid to-day,
For here I come and hither I return."

Di. Any fault there?

Eu. A dozen faults and more.

Di. Eh! why the lines are only three in all.

Eu. But every one contains a score of faults.

Di. Now Aeschylus, keep silent; if you don't
You won't get off with three iambic lines.

Aes. Silent for *him*!

Di. If *my* advice you'll take.

Eu. Why, at first starting here's a fault skyhigh.

Aes. (*to* DIONYSUS) You see your folly?

Di. Have your way; I care not.

Aes. (*to* EURIPIDES) What is my fault?

Eu. Begin the lines again.

Aes. "Grave Hermes, witnessing a father's power—"

Eu. And this beside his murdered father's grave
Orestes speaks?

Aes. I say not otherwise.

Eu. Then does he mean that when his father fell
By craft and violence at a woman's hand,
The god of craft was witnessing the deed?

Aes. It was not he: it was the Helper Hermes
He called the grave: and this he showed by adding
It was his sire's prerogative he held.

Eu. Why this is worse than all. If from his father
He held this office grave, why then—

Di. He was
A graveyard rifler on his father's side.

Aes. Bacchus, the wine you drink is stale and fusty.

Di. Give him another: (*to* EURIPIDES) you, look out for faults.

Aes. "Be thou my saviour and mine aid to-day,
For here I come, and hither I return."

Eu. The same thing twice says clever Aeschylus.

Di. How twice?

Eu. Why, just consider: I'll explain.
"I come," says he; and "I return," says he:
It's the same thing, to "come" and to "return."

Di. Aye, just as if you said, "Good fellow, lend me
A kneading trough: likewise, a trough to knead in."

Aes. It is not so, you everlasting talker,
They're not the same, the words are right enough.

Di. How so? inform me how you use the words.

Aes. A man, not banished from his home, may "come"
To any land, with no especial chance.
A home-bound exile both "returns" and "comes."

Di. O good, by Apollo!
What do you say, Euripides, to that?

Eu. I say Orestes never did "return."
He came in secret: nobody recalled him.

Di. O good, by Hermes!
(*Aside*) I've not the least suspicion what he means.

Eu. Repeat another line.

Di. Ay, Aeschylus,
Repeat one instantly: *you*, mark what's wrong.

Aes. "Now on this funeral mound I call my father
To hear, to hearken."

Eu. There he is again.
To "hear," to "hearken"; the same thing, exactly.

Di. Aye, but he's speaking to the dead, you knave,
Who cannot hear us though we call them thrice.

Aes. And how do you make *your* prologues?

Eu. You shall hear;
And if you find one single thing said twice,
Or any useless padding, spit upon me.

Di. Well, fire away: I'm all agog to hear
Your very accurate and faultless prologues.

Eu. "A happy man was Oedipus at first—"

Aes. Not so, by Zeus; a most unhappy man.
Who, not yet born nor yet conceived, Apollo
Foretold would be his father's murderer.
How could *he* be a happy man at first?

Eu. "Then he became the wretchedest of men."

Aes. Not so, by Zeus; he never ceased to be.
No sooner born, than they exposed the babe,
(And that in winter), in an earthen crock,
Lest he should grow a man, and slay his father.
Then with both ankles pierced and swoln, he limped
Away to Polybus: still young, he married
An ancient crone, and her his mother too.
Then scratched out both his eyes.

Di. Happy indeed
Had he been Erasinides's colleague!

Eu. Nonsense; I say my prologues are firstrate.

Aes. Nay then, by Zeus, no longer line by line
I'll maul your phrases: but with heaven to aid
I'll smash your prologues with a bottle of oil.

Eu. You mine with a bottle of oil?

Aes. With only one.
You frame your prologues so that each and all
Fit in with a "bottle of oil," or "coverlet-skin,"
Or "reticule-bag." I'll prove it here, and now.

Eu. You'll prove it? You?

Aes. I will.

Di. Well then, begin.

Eu. "Aegyptus, sailing with his fifty sons,
As ancient legends mostly tell the tale,
Touching at Argos"

Aes. Lost his bottle of oil.

Eu. Hang it, what's that? Confound that bottle of oil!

Di. Give him another: let him try again.

Eu. "Bacchus, who, clad in fawnskins, leaps and bounds
With torch and thyrsus in the choral dance
Along Parnassus"

Aes. Lost his bottle of oil.

Di. Ah me, we are stricken—with that bottle again!

Eu. Pooh, pooh, that's nothing. I've a prologue here,

He'll never tack his bottle of oil to this:
"No man is blest in every single thing.
One is of noble birth, but lacking means.
Another, baseborn,"

Aes. Lost his bottle of oil.

Di. Euripides!

Eu. Well?

Di. Lower your sails, my boy;
This bottle of oil is going to blow a gale.

Eu. O, by Demeter, I don't care one bit;
Now from his hands I'll strike that bottle of oil.

Di. Go on then, go: but ware the bottle of oil.

Eu. "Once Cadmus, quitting the Sidonian town,
Agenor's offspring"

Aes. Lost his bottle of oil.

Di. O pray, my man, buy off that bottle of oil,
Or else he'll smash our prologues all to bits.

Eu. I buy of *him*?

Di. If *my* advice you'll take.

Eu. No, no, I've many a prologue yet to say,
To which he can't tack on his bottle of oil.
"Pelops, the son of Tantalus, while driving
His mares to Pisa"

Aes. Lost his bottle of oil.

Di. There! he tacked on the bottle of oil again.
O for heaven's sake, pay him its price, dear boy;
You'll get it for an obol, spick and span.

Eu. Not yet, by Zeus; I've plenty of prologues left.
"Oeneus once reaping"

Aes. Lost his bottle of oil.

Eu. Pray let me finish one entire line first.
"Oeneus once reaping an abundant harvest,
Offering the firstfruits"

Aes. Lost his bottle of oil.

Di. What, in the act of offering? Fie! Who stole it?

Eu. O don't keep bothering! Let him try with this!
"Zeus, as by Truth's own voice the tale is told,"

Di. No, he'll cut in with "Lost his bottle of oil!"
Those bottles of oil on all your prologues seem
To gather and grow, like styes upon the eye.
Turn to his melodies now for goodness' sake.

Eu. O I can easily show that he's a poor
Melody-maker; makes tham all alike.

Cho. What, O what will be done!
Strange to think that he dare
Blame the bard who has won,
More than all in our days,
Fame and praise for his lays,
Lays so many and fair.
Much I marvel to hear
What the charge he will bring
'Gainst our tragedy king;
Yea for himself do I fear.

Eu. Wonderful lays! O yes, you'll see directly.
I'll cut down all his metrical strains to one.

Di. And I, I'll take some pebbles, and keep count.

A slight pause, during which the music of a flute is heard. The music continues to the end of line 1277 as an accompaniment to the recitative.

Eu. "Lord of Phthia, Achilles, why hearing the voice of the hero-dividing
Hah! smiting! approachest thou not to the rescue?
We, by the lake who abide, are adoring our ancestor Hermes.
Hah! smiting! approachest thou not to the rescue?"

Di. O Aeschylus, twice art thou smitten!

Eu. "Hearken to me, great king; yea, hearken Atreides, thou noblest of all the Achaeans.
Hah! smiting! approachest thou not to the rescue?"

Di. Thrice, Aeschylus, thrice art thou smitten!

Eu. "Hush! the bee-wardens are here: they will quickly the Temple of Artemis open.
Hah! smiting! approachest thou not to the rescue?
I will expound (for I know it) the omen the chieftains encountered.
Hah! smiting! approachest thou not to the rescue?"

Di. O Zeus and King, the terrible lot of smitings!
I'll to the bath: I'm very sure my kidneys
Are quite inflamed and swoln with all these smitings.

Eu. Wait till you've heard another batch of lays
Culled from his lyre-accompanied melodies.

Di. Go on then, go: but no more smitings, please.

Eu. "How the twin-throned powers of Achaea, the lords of the mighty Hellenes.
O phlattothrattophlattothrat!
Sendeth the Sphinx, the unchancy, the chieftainness bloodhound.
O phlattothrattophlattothrat!
Launcheth fierce with brand and hand the avengers the terrible eagle.
O phlattothrattophlattothrat!
So for the swift-winged hounds of the air he provided a booty.
O phlattothrattophlattothrat!
The throng down-bearing on Aias.
O phlattothrattophlattothrat!"

Di. Whence comes that phlattothrat? From Marathon, or
Where picked you up these cable-twister's strains?

Aes. From noblest source for noblest ends I brought them,
Unwilling in the Muses' holy field
The self-same flowers as Phrynichus to cull.
But *he* from all things rotten draws his lays,
From Carian flutings, catches of Meletus,
Dance-music, dirges. You shall hear directly.
Bring me the lyre. Yet wherefore need a lyre
For songs like these? Where's she that bangs and jangles
Her castanets? Euripides's Muse,
Present yourself: fit goddess for fit verse.

Di. The Muse herself can't be a wanton? No!

Aes. Halycons, who by the ever-rippling
Waves of the sea are babbling,
Dewing your plumes with the drops that fall
From wings in the salt spray dabbling.

Spiders, ever with twir-r-r-r-rling fingers
Weaving the warp and the woof,
Little, brittle, network, fretwork,
Under the coigns of the roof.

The minstrel shuttle's care.

Where in the front of the dark-prowed ships
Yarely the flute-loving dolphin skips.

Races here and oracles there.

And the joy of the young vines smiling,
And the tendril of grapes, care-beguiling.
O embrace me, my child, O embrace me.
(*To* DIONYSUS) You see this foot?
Di. I do.
Aes. And this?
Di. And that one too.
Aes. (*to* EURIPIDES) You, such stuff who compile,
Dare my songs to upbraid;
You, whose songs in the style
Of Cyrene's embraces are made.
So much for them: but still I'd like to show
The way in which your monodies are framed
"O darkly-light mysterious Night,
What may this Vision mean,
Sent from the world unseen
With baleful omens rife;
A thing of lifeless life,
A child of sable night,
A ghastly curdling sight,
In black funereal veils,
With murder, murder in its eyes,
And great enormous nails?
Light ye the lanterns, my maidens,
and dipping your jugs in the stream,
Draw me the dew of the water,
and heat it to boiling and steam;
So will I wash me away the ill effects of my dream.
God of the sea!
My dream's come true.
Ho, lodgers, ho,
This portent view.
Glyce has vanished, carrying off my cock,
My cock that crew!
O Mania, help! O Oreads of the rock
Pursue! pursue!
For I, poor girl, was working within,
Holding my distaff heavy and full,
Twir-r-r-r-rling my hand as the threads I spin,
Weaving an excellent bobbin of wool;
Thinking 'To-morrow I'll go to the fair,
In the dusk of the morn, and be selling it there.'
But he to the blue upflew, upflew,
On the lightliest tips of his wings outspread;
To me he bequeathed but woe, but woe,
And tears, sad tears, from my eyes o'erflow,
Which I, the bereaved, must shed, must shed.
O children of Ida, sons of Crete,
Grasping your bows to the rescue come;
Twinkle about on your restless feet,
Stand in a circle around her home.
O Artemis, thou maid divine,
Dictynna, huntress, fair to see,
O bring that keen-nosed pack of thine,
And hunt through all the house with me.
O Hecate, with flameful brands,
O Zeus's daughter, arm thine hands,
Those swiftliest hands, both right and left;
Thy rays on Glyce's cottage throw
That I serenely there may go,
And search by moonlight for the theft."
Di. Enough of both your odes.
Aes. Enough for me.
Now would I bring the fellow to the scales.
That, that alone, shall test our poetry now,
And prove whose words are weightiest, his or mine.
Di. Then both come hither, since I needs must weigh
The art poetic like a pound of cheese.

Here a large balance is brought out and placed upon the stage.

Cho. O the labour these wits go through!
O the wild, extravagant, new,
Wonderful things they are going to do!
Who but they would ever have thought of it?
Why, if a man had happened to meet me
Out in the street, and intelligence brought of it,
I should have thought he was trying to cheat me;
Thought that his story was false and deceiving.
That were a tale I could never believe in.
Di. Each of you stand beside his scale.
Aes. and Eu. We're here.
Di. And grasp it firmly whilst ye speak your lines,

Each holds his own scale steady while he speaks his line into it.

And don't let go until I cry "Cuckoo."
Aes. and Eu. Ready!
Di. Now speak your lines into the scale.
Eu. "O that the Argo had not winged her way—"
Aes. "River Spercheius, cattle-grazing haunts—"
Di. Cuckoo! let go. O look, by far the lowest
His scale sinks down.
Eu. Why, how came that about?
Di. He threw a river in, like some wool-seller
Wetting his wool, to make it weigh the more.
But *you* threw in a light and wingèd word.
Eu. Come, let him match another verse with mine.
Di. Each to his scale.
Aes. and Eu. We're ready.
Di. Speak your lines.
Eu. "Persuasion's only shrine is eloquent speech."
Aes. "Death loves not gifts, alone amongst the gods."
Di. Let go, let go. Down goes his scale again.
He threw in Death, the heaviest ill of all.
Eu. And I Persuasion, the most lovely word.
Di. A vain and empty sound, devoid of sense.
Think of some heavier-weighted line of yours,
To drag your scale down: something strong and big.
Eu. Where have I got one? Where? Let's see.

Di. I'll tell you.
"Achilles threw two singles and a four."
Come, speak your lines: this is your last set-to.
Eu. "In his right hand he grasped an iron-clamped mace."
Aes. "Chariot on chariot, corpse on corpse was hurled."
Di. There now! again he has done you.
Eu. Done me? How?
Di. He threw two chariots and two corpses in;
Five-score Egyptians could not lift that weight.
Aes. No more of "line for line"; let him—himself,
His children, wife, Cephisophon—get in,
With all his books collected in his arms,
Two lines of mine shall overweigh the lot.
Di. Both are my friends; I can't decide between them:
I don't desire to be at odds with either:
One is so clever, one delights me so.
Pluto. (*coming forward*) Then you'll effect nothing for which you came?
Di. And how, if I decide?
Pl. Then take the winner;
So will your journey not be made in vain.
Di. Heaven bless your Highness! Listen, I came down
After a poet.
Eu. To what end?
Di. That so
The city, saved, may keep her choral games.
Now then, whichever of you two shall best
Advise the city, *he* shall come with me.
And first of Alcibiades, let each
Say what he thinks; the city travails sore.
Eu. What does she think herself about him?
Di. What?
She loves, and hates, and longs to have him back.
But give me *your* advice about the man.
Eu. I loathe a townsman who is slow to aid,
And swift to hurt, his town: who ways and means
Finds for himself, but finds not for the state.
Di. Poseidon, but that's smart! (*to* AESCHYLUS) And what say *you*?
Aes. 'Twere best to rear no lion in the state:
But having reared, 'tis best to humour him.
Di. By Zeus the Saviour, still I can't decide.
One is so clever, and so clear the other.
But once again. Let each in turn declare
What plan of safety for the state ye've got.
Eu. [First with Cinesias wing Cleocritus,
Then zephyrs waft them o'er the watery plain.
Di. A funny sight, I own: but where's the sense?
Eu. If, when the fleets engage, they holding cruets
Should rain down vinegar in the foemen's eyes,]
I know, and I can tell you.
Di. Tell away.
Eu. When things, mistrusted now, shall trusted be,
And trusted things, mistrusted.
Di. How! I don't
Quite comprehend. Be clear, and not so clever.
Eu. If we mistrust those citizens of ours
Whom now we trust, and those employ whom now
We don't employ, the city will be saved.
If on our present tack we fail, we surely
Shall find salvation in the opposite course.
Di. Good, O Palamedes! Good, you genius you.
Is this *your* cleverness or Cephisophon's?
Eu. This is my own: the cruet-plan was his.
Di. (*to* AESCHYLUS) Now, you.
Aes. But tell me whom the city uses.
The good and useful?
Di. What are you dreaming of?
She hates and loathes them.
Aes. Does she love the bad?
Di. Not love them, no: she uses them perforce.
Aes. How can one save a city such as this,
Whom neither frieze nor woollen tunic suits?
Di. O, if to earth you rise, find out some way.
Aes. There will I speak: I cannot answer here.
Di. Nay, nay; send up your guerdon from below.
Aes. When they shall count the enemy's soil their own,
And theirs the enemy's: when they know that ships
Are their true wealth, their so-called wealth delusion.
Di. Aye, but the justices suck that down, you know.
Pl. Now then, decide.
Di. I will; and thus I'll do it.
I'll choose the man in whom my soul delights.
Eu. O, recollect the gods by whom you swore
You'd take me home again; and choose your friends.
Di. 'Twas my tongue swore; my choice is—Aeschylus.
Eu. Hah! what have you done?
Di. Done? Given the victor's prize
To Aeschylus; why not?
Eu. And do you dare
Look in my face, after that shameful deed?
Di. What's shameful, if the audience think not so?
Eu. Have you no heart? Wretch, would you leave me dead?
Di. Who knows if death be life, and life be death,
And breath be mutton broth, and sleep a sheepskin?
Pl. Now, Dionysus, come ye in,
Di. What for?
Pl. And sup before ye go.
Di. A bright idea.
I'faith, I'm nowise indisposed for that.

Exeunt AESCHYLUS, EURIPIDES, PLUTO, *and* DIONYSUS.

Chorus

Blest the man who possesses a
Keen intelligent mind.
This full often we find.
He, the bard of renown,
Now to earth reascends,
Goes, a joy to his town,
Goes, a joy to his friends,

Just because he possesses a
Keen intelligent mind.
Right it is and befitting,
Not, by Socrates sitting,
Idle talk to pursue,
Stripping tragedy-art of
All things noble and true.
Surely the mind to school
Fine-drawn quibbles to seek,
Fine-set phrases to speak,
Is but the part of a fool!

Re-enter PLUTO *and* AESCHYLUS.

Pl. Farewell then Aeschylus, great and wise,
Go, save our state by the maxims rare
Of thy noble thought; and the fools chastise,
For many a fool dwells there.
And *this* (*handing him a rope*) to Cleophon give, my friend,
And *this* to the revenue-raising crew,
Nichomachus, Myrmex, next I send,
And *this* to Archenomus too.
And bid them all that without delay,
To my realm of the dead they hasten away.
For if they loiter above, I swear
I'll come myself and arrest them there.
And branded and fettered the slaves shall go
With the vilest rascal in all the town,
Adeimantus, son of Leucolophus, down,
Down, down to the darkness below.

Aes. I take the mission. This chair of mine
Meanwhile to Sophocles here commit,
(For I count him next in our craft divine,)
Till I come once more by thy side to sit.
But as for that rascally scoundrel there,
That low buffoon, that worker of ill,
O let him not sit in my vacant chair,
Not even against his will.

Pl. (*to the* CHORUS) Escort him up with your mystic throngs,
While the holy torches quiver and blaze.
Escort him up with his own sweet songs,
And his noble festival lays.

Cho. First, as the poet triumphant is passing away to the light,
Grant him success on his journey, ye powers that are ruling below.
Grant that he find for the city good counsels to guide her aright;
So we at last shall be freed from the anguish, the fear, and the woe,
Freed from the onsets of war. Let Cleophon now and his band
Battle, if battle they must, far away in their own fatherland.

THE LYSISTRATA

DRAMATIS PERSONAE

LYSISTRATA
CALONICE
MYRRHINA
LAMPITO
MAGISTRATES
STRATYLLIS
CINESIAS
A CHILD OF CINESIAS
A HERALD OF THE LACONIANS
LACONIAN AMBASSADORS
ATHENIAN AMBASSADORS
IDLERS
A PORTER
CHORUS OF MEN
CHORUS OF WOMEN

It is daybreak at Athens; and LYSISTRATA, *a young and beautiful woman, is standing alone, with marks of evident anxiety in her countenance and demeanour. The scene represents the sloping hill which rises from the Lower to the Upper City. In the background are the Propylaea, the splendid portals of the Athenian Acropolis.* LYSISTRATA *is on the look-out for persons who do not come, and after exhibiting various symptoms of impatience, she suddenly begins to speak with abrupt and indignant emphasis.*

Lysistrata. Now were they summoned to some shrine of Bacchus,
Pan, Colias, Genetyllis,[1] there had been
No room to stir, so thick the crowd of timbrels.
And *now*!—there's not one woman to be seen.
Stay, here comes one, my neighbour Calonice.
Good morning, friend.

Enter CALONICE.

Calonice. Good morn, Lysistrata.
Why, what's the matter? don't look gloomy, child.
It don't become you to knit-knot your eyebrows.
Ly. My heart is hot within me, Calonice,
And sore I grieve for sake of womankind,
Because the men account us all to be
Sly, shifty rogues,
Ca. And so, by Zeus, we are.
Ly. Yet though I told them to be here betimes,
To talk on weighty business, they don't come,
They're fast asleep.
Ca. They'll come, dear heart, they'll come.
'Tis hard, you know, for women to get out.
One has to mind her husband: one, to rouse
Her servant: one, to put the child to sleep:
One, has to wash him: one, to give him pap.
Ly. Ah! but they've other duties still more pressing
Than such as these.
Ca. Well but, Lysistrata,
Why have you, dear, convoked us? Is the matter
A weighty subject?
Ly. Weighty? yes.
Ca. And pregnant?
Ly. Pregnant, by Zeus.
Ca. Why ever don't we come, then?
Ly. No, it's not that: we'd have come fast enough
For such-like nonsense. 'Tis a scheme I've hit on,
Tossing it over many a sleepless night.
Ca. Tossing it over? then 'tis light, I fancy.
Ly. Light? ay, so light, my dear, that all the hopes
Of all the States are anchored on us women.
Ca. Anchored on us! a slender stay to lean on.
Ly. Ay, all depends on us: whether as well the
Peloponnesians all shall cease to be—
Ca. Sure and 'tis better they should cease to be.
Ly. And all the dwellers in Boeotia perish—
Ca. Except the eels; do pray except the eels.
Ly. But about Athens, mark you, I won't utter
Such words as these: you must supply my meaning.
But if the women will but meet here now,
Boeotian girls, Peloponnesian girls,
And we ourselves, we'll save the States between us.
Ca. What can we women do? What brilliant scheme
Can we, poor souls, accomplish? we who sit
Trimmed and bedizened in our saffron silks,
Our cambric robes, and little finical shoes.
Ly. Why, they're the very things I hope will save us,
Your saffron dresses, and your finical shoes,
Your paints, and perfumes, and your robes of gauze.
Ca. How mean you, save us?
Ly. So that nevermore
Men in our day shall lift the hostile spear
Ca. O, by the Twain,[2] I'll use the saffron dye.
Ly. Or grasp the shield—
Ca. I'll don the cambric robe.
Ly. Or draw the sword.
Ca. I'll wear the finical shoes.
Ly. Should not the women, then, have come betimes?
Ca. Come? no, by Zeus; they should have flown with wings.

[1] "Gods of Wine and Love, chief pleasures, according to Aristophanes, of the Athenian women": Rogers.

[2] Demeter and Persephone.

Ly. Ah, friend, you'll find them Attic to the core:
Always too late in everything they do.
Not even one woman from the coast has come,
Not one from Salamis.
Ca. O they, no doubt,
Will cross this morning, early, in their boats.
Ly. And those I counted sure to come the first,
My staunch Acharnian damsels, they're not here—
Not they.
Ca. And yet Theagenes's wife
Consulted Hecate, as if to come.

Several women enter, headed by MYRRHINA, *from the village of Anagyrus.*

Hi! but they're coming now: here they all are:
First one, and then another. Hoity toity!
Whence come all these?
Ly. From Anagyre.
Ca. Aha!
We've stirred up Anagyre at all events.

Other women enter.

Myrrhina. Are we too late, Lysistrata? Well? What?
Why don't you speak?
Ly. I'm sorry, Myrrhina,
That you should come so late on such a business.
My. I scarce could find my girdle in the dark.
But if the thing's so pressing, tell us now.
Ly. No, no, let's wait a little, till the women
Of Peloponnesus and Boeotia come
To join our congress.
My. O yes, better so.
And here, good chance, is Lampito approaching.

LAMPITO, *a Spartan woman, enters, accompanied by her friends.*

Ly. O welcome, welcome, Lampito, my love.
O the sweet girl! how hale and bright she looks!
Here's nerve! here's muscle! here's an arm could fairly
Throttle a bull!
Lampito. Weel, by the Twa,[1] I think sae.
An' I can loup an' fling an' kick my hurdies.
Ly. See here's a neck and breast; how firm and lusty!
La. Wow, but ye pradd me like a fatted calf.
Ly. And who's this other damsel? whence comes she?
La. Ane deputation frae Boeoty, comin'
To sit amang you.
Ly. Ah, from fair Boeotia,
The land of plains!
Ca. A very lovely land,
Well cropped, and trimmed, and spruce with penny royal.
Ly. And who's the next?
La. A bonnie burdie she,
She's a Corinthian lassie.
Ly. Ay, by Zeus,
And so she is. A bonnie lass, indeed.
La. But wha ha' ca'ed thegither a' thae thrangs
O' wenches?

[1]Castor and Pollux, the Dioscuri.

Ly. I did.
La. Did ye noo? then tell us
What 'tis a' for.
Ly. O yes, my dear, I will.
My. Ay, surely: tell us all this urgent business.
Ly. O yes, I'll tell you now; but first I'd ask you
One simple question.
My. Ask it, dear, and welcome.
Ly. Do ye not miss the fathers of your babes,
Always on service? well I wot ye all
Have got a husband absent at the wars.
Ca. Ay, mine, worse luck, has been five months away
In Thracian quarters, watching Eucrates.
My. And mine's been stationed seven whole months at Pylus.
La. An' my gude mon nae suner comes frae war
Than he straps targe an' gangs awa' again.
Ly. No husbands now, no sparks, no anything.
For ever since Miletus played us false,
We've had no joy, no solace, none at all.
So will you, will you, if I find a way,
Help me to end the war?
My. Ay, that we will.
I will, be sure, though I'd to fling me down
This mantling shawl, and have a bout of—drinking.
Ca. And I would cleave my very self in twain
Like a cleft turbot, and give half for Peace.
La. An' I, to glint at Peace again, wad speel
Up to the tap rig o' Taygety.
Ly. I'll tell you now: 'tis meet ye all should know.
O ladies! sisters! if we really mean
To make the men make Peace, there's but one way,
We must abstain—
My. Well! tell us.
Ly. Will ye do it?
My. Do it? ay, surely, though it cost our lives.
Ly. We must abstain—each—from the joys of Love.
How! what! why turn away? where are ye going?
What makes you pout your lips, and shake your heads?
What brings this falling tear, that changing colour?
Will ye, or will ye not? What mean ye, eh?
My. I'll never do it. Let the war go on.
Ca. Zeus! nor I either. Let the war go on.
Ly. You, too, Miss Turbot? you who said just now
You'd cleave, for Peace, your very self in twain?
Ca. Ask anything but this. Why, if needs be,
I'd walk through fire: only, not give up Love.
There's nothing like it, dear Lysistrata.
Ly. And what say you?
My. I'd liefer walk through fire.
Ly. O women! women! O our frail, frail sex!
No wonder tragedies are made from us.
Always the same: nothing but loves and cradles.
O friend! O Lampito! if you and I
Are of one mind, we yet may pull things through;
Won't *you* vote with me, dear?
La. Haith, by the Twa',
'Tis sair to bide your lane, withouten men.
Still it maun be: we maun hae Peace, at a' risks.

Ly. O dearest friend; my one true friend of all.
Ca. Well, but suppose we do the things you say,
Pray Heaven avert it, but put case we do,
Shall we be nearer Peace?
Ly. Much, much, much nearer.
For if we women will but sit at home,
Powdered and trimmed, clad in our daintiest lawn,
Employing all our charms, and all our arts
To win men's love, and when we've won it, then
Repel them, firmly, till they end the war,
We'll soon get Peace again, be sure of that.
La. Sae Menelaus, when he glowered, I ween,
At Helen's breastie, coost his glaive awa'.
Ca. Eh, but suppose they leave us altogether?
Ly. O, faddle! then we'll find some substitute.
Ca. If they try force?
Ly. They'll soon get tired of that
If we keep firm. Scant joy a husband gets
Who finds himself at discord with his wife.
Ca. Well, then, if so you wish it, so we'll have it.
La. An' our gude folk we'se easily persuade
To keep the Peace wi' never a thocht o' guile:
But your Athanian hairumscairum callants
Wha sall persuade *them* no to play the fule?
Ly. O we'll persuade our people, never fear.
La. Not while ye've gat thae gallies rigged sae trim,
An' a' that rowth o' siller nigh the Goddess.[1]
Ly. O but, my dear, we've taken thought for that:
This very morn we seize the Acropolis.
Now, whilst we're planning and conspiring here,
The elder women have the task assigned them,
Under pretence of sacrifice, to seize it.
La. A' will gae finely, an' ye talk like that.
Ly. Then why not, Lampito, at once combine
All in one oath, and clench the plot securely?
La. Weel, you propound the aith, an' we'se a' tak' it.
Ly. Good; now then, Scythianess,[2] don't stand there gaping.
Quick, set a great black shield here, hollow upwards,
And bring the sacrificial bits.
Ca. And how
Are we to swear, Lysistrata?
Ly. We'll slay
(Like those Seven Chiefs in Aeschylus) a lamb
Over a shield.
Ca. Nay, when our object's Peace,
Don't use a shield, Lysistrata, my dear.
Ly. Then what shall be the oath?
Ca. Could we not somehow
Get a grey mare, and cut her up to bits?
Ly. Grey mare, indeed!
Ca. Well, what's the oath will suit
Us women best?

[1]A reserve of a thousand talents set aside for pressing emergency (Thucydides, ii. 24). It was now proposed (Thucydides, viii. 15) to use this in building a fleet to replace the ships lost at Syracuse.

[2]Scythian archers were employed in Athens as police; the women have therefore a Scythianess.

My. I'll tell you what I think.
Let's set a great black *cup* here, hollow upwards:
Then for a lamb we'll slay a Thasian wine-jar,
And firmly swear to—pour no water in.
La. Hech, the braw aith! my certie, hoo I like it.
Ly. O yes, bring out the wine-jar and the cup.

A maiden brings out a jar of wine and an immense cup.

Ca. La! here's a splendid piece of ware, my dears.
Now that's a cup 'twill cheer one's heart to take.
Ly. (*to the servant*) Set down the cup, and take the victim boar.
O Queen Persuasion, and O Loving Cup,
Accept our offerings, and maintain our cause!
Ca. 'Tis jolly coloured blood, and spirts out bravely
La. Ay, an' by Castor, vera fragrant too!
My. Let *me* swear first, my sisters?
Ca. Yes, if *you*
Draw the first lot; not else, by Aphrodite.
Ly. All place your hands upon the wine-cup: so.
One, speak the words, repeating after me.
Then all the rest confirm it. Now begin.
I will abstain from Love and Love's delights.
Ca. *I will abstain from Love and Love's delights.*
Ly. And take no pleasure though my lord invites.
Ca. *And take no pleasure though my lord invites.*
Ly. And sleep a vestal all alone at nights.
Ca. *And sleep a vestal all alone at nights.*
Ly. And live a stranger to all nuptial rites.
Ca. *And live a stranger to all nuptial rites.*
I don't half like it though, Lysistrata.
Ly. I will abjure the very name of Love.
Ca. *I will abjure the very name of Love.*
Ly. So help me Zeus, and all the Powers above.
Ca. *So help me Zeus, and all the Powers above.*
Ly. If I do this, my cup be filled with wine.
Ca. *If I do this, my cup be filled with wine.*
Ly. But if I fail, a water draught be mine.
Ca. *But if I fail, a water draught be mine.*
Ly. You all swear this?
My. O yes, my dear, we do.
Ly. I'll now consume these fragments.

LYSISTRATA *takes the wine-cup in her hand.*

Ca. Shares, my friend,
Now at first starting let us show we're friends.
La. Hark! what's yon skirlin'?

A sound of persons cheering is heard in the distance.

Ly. That's the thing I said.
They've seized the Acropolis, Athene's castle,
Our comrades have. Now, Lampito, be off:
You, go to Sparta, and arrange things there,
Leaving us here these girls as hostages.
And We will pass inside the castle walls,
And help the women there to close the bars.
Ca. But don't you think that very soon the Men
Will come, in arms, against us?
Ly. Let them come!
They will not bring or threats or fire enough
To awe our woman hearts, and make us open
These gates again, save on the terms we mentioned.

Ca. By Aphrodite, no! else 'twere for nought
That people call us bold, resistless jades.

The crowd now disperses: LAMPITO *leaving for her homeward journey, and the others disappearing through the gates of the Propylaea. After a pause the* CHORUS OF MEN *are seen slowly approaching from the Lower City. They are carrying heavy logs of firewood, and a jar of lighted cinders; and as they move, they sing their entrance song.*

Chorus of Men

On, sure and slow, my Draces, go:
though that great log you're bringing
of olive green, is sore, I ween,
your poor old shoulder wringing.
O dear, how many things in life
belie one's expectations!
Since who'd have thought, my Strymodore,
that these abominations,
Who would have thought that sluts like these,
Our household pests, would have waxed so bold,
As the Holy Image by fraud to seize,
As the City Castle by force to hold,
With block and bolt and barrier vast,
Making the Propylaea fast.
Press on, Philurgus, towards the heights;
we'll pile a great amazing
Array of logs around the walls,
and set them all a-blazing:
And as for these conspirators,
a bonfire huge we'll make them,
One vote shall doom the whole to death,
one funeral pyre shall take them,
And thus we'll burn the brood accurst,
but Lycon's wife we'll burn the first.
No, never, never, whilst I live,
shall woman-folk deride me:
Not scatheless went Cleomenes,
when he like this defied me,
And dared my castle to seize: yet He,
A Spartan breathing contempt and pride,
Full soon surrendered his arms to me,
And a scanty coat round his loins he tied,
And with unwashed limbs, and with unkempt head,
And with six years' dirt, the intruder fled;
So strict and stern a watch around
my mates and I were keeping,
In seventeen rows of serried shields
before the fortress sleeping.
And *these*, whom both Euripides
and all the Powers on high
Alike detest, shall these, shall these,
my manly rage defy?
Then never be my Trophy shown,
on those red plains of Marathon!
But over this snubby protruding steep
Ere we reach our goal at the Castle keep,
We've still, with our burdensome load, to creep.
And how to manage that blunt incline
Without a donkey, I can't divine.
Dear, how these two great firelogs make
my wearied shoulders toil and ache.
But still right onward we needs must go,
And still the cinders we needs must blow,
Else we'll find the fire extinguished,
ere we reach our journey's end.
Puff! Puff! Puff!
O the smoke! the smoke!

O royal Heracles! what a lot
Of fire came raging out of the pot,
And flew, like a dog, at my eyes, red hot.
'Twas a jet from the Lemnian mines, I ween,
It came so fierce, and it bit so keen,
And worried, with persistence sore,
my two poor eyes, inflamed before.
On, Laches, on! to the castle press,
And aid the God in her dire distress;
Surely, if we e'er would help her,
now's the very time, my friend.
Puff! Puff! Puff!
O the smoke! the smoke!
Thank heaven the fire is still alight,
and burning beautifully bright.
So here we'll lay our burdens down,
with eager hearts delighted,
And dip the vine-torch in the pot,
and get it there ignited.
Then all together at the gates
like battering rams we'll butt.
And if our summons they reject,
and keep the barriers shut,
We'll burn the very doors with fire,
and them with smoke we'll smother.
So lay the burdens down. Pheugh! Pheugh!
O how this smoke does bother!
What general from the Samian lines
an active hand will lend us?
Well, well, I'm glad my back is freed
from all that weight tremendous.
O pot, 'tis now your turn to help:
O send a livelier jet
Of flame this way, that I to-day
the earliest light may get.
O Victory, immortal Queen,
assist us Thou in rearing
A trophy o'er these woman-hosts,
so bold and domineering.

During the last few lines the MEN *have been completing their preparations, and the air above them is now growing lurid with the smoke and flame of their torches. As the* MEN *relapse into silence, the voices of the* CHORUS OF WOMEN *are heard in the distance. They come sweeping round from the north side of the Acropolis, carrying their pitchers of water, and singing, in turn, their entrance song. The two* CHORUSES *are for the present concealed from each other by the north-western angle of the Acropolis.*

Chorus of Women

Redly up in the sky
the flames are beginning to flicker,
Smoke and vapour of fire!
come quicker, my friends, come quicker.
Fly, Nicodice, fly,
Else will Calyce burn,
Else Critylla will die,
Slain by the laws so stern,
Slain by the old men's hate.
Ah, but I fear! I fear!
can it chance that I come too late?
Trouble it was, forsooth, before my jug I could fill,
All in the dusk of the morn,
at the spring by the side of the hill,
What with the clatter of pitchers,
The noise and press of the throng,
Jostling with knaves and slaves,
Till at last I snatched it along,
Abundance of water supplying
To friends who are burning and dying.

Yea, for hither, they state,
Dotards are dragging, to burn us,
Logs of enormous weight,
Fit for a bath-room furnace,
Vowing to roast and to slay
Sternly the reprobate women.
O Lady, O Goddess, I pray,
Ne'er may I see them in flames!
I hope to behold them with gladness,
Hellas and Athens redeeming
from battle and murder and madness.
This is the cause why they venture,
Lady, thy mansions to hold,
Tritogeneia,[1] Eternal
Champion with helmet of gold!
And O, if with fire men invade them,
O help us with water to aid them.

At this juncture CHORUS OF WOMEN *wheel round the corner of the Acropolis, and the two* CHORUSES *suddenly meet face to face.*

Stop! easy all! what have we here?
(*To the* MEN) You vile, abandoned crew,
No good and virtuous men, I'm sure,
would act in the way you do.
M. Ch. Hey, here's an unexpected sight!
hey, here's a demonstration!
A swarm of women issuing out
with warlike preparation!
W. Ch. Hallo, you seem a little moved!
does this one troop affright you?
You see not yet the myriadth part
of those prepared to fight you.
M. Ch. Now, really, Phaedrias, shall we stop
to hear such odious treason?
Let's break our sticks about their backs,
let's beat the jades to reason.

W. Ch. Hi, sisters, set the pitchers down,
and then they won't embarrass
Our nimble fingers, if the rogues
attempt our ranks to harass.
M. Ch. I warrant, now, if twice or thrice
we slap their faces neatly,
That they will learn, like Bupalus,
to hold their tongues discreetly.
W. Ch. Well, here's my face: I won't draw back:
now slap it if you dare,
And I won't leave one ounce of you
for other dogs to tear.
M. Ch. Keep still, or else your musty Age
to very shreds I'll batter.
W. Ch. Now only touch Stratyllis, sir;
just lift one finger at her!
M. Ch. And what if with these fists, my love,
I pound the wench to shivers?
W. Ch. By Heaven, we'll gnaw your entrails out,
and rip away your livers.
M. Ch. There is not than Euripides
a bard more wise and knowing,
For women *are* a shameless set,
the vilest creatures going.
W. Ch. Pick up again, Rhodippe dear,
your jug with water brimming.
M. Ch. What made you bring that water here,
you God-detested women?
W. Ch. What made you bring that light, old Tomb?
to set *yourselves* afire?
M. Ch. No, but to kindle for your friends
a mighty funeral pyre.
W. Ch. Well, then, we brought this water here
to put your bonfire out, sirs.
M. Ch. *You* put our bonfire out, indeed!
W. Ch. You'll see, beyond a doubt, sirs.
M. Ch. I swear that with this torch, offhand,
I've half a mind to fry you.
W. Ch. Got any soap, my lad? if so,
a bath I'll soon supply you.
M. Ch. A bath for *me*, you mouldy hag!
W. Ch. And that a bride-bath, too.
M. Ch. Zounds, did you hear her impudence?
W. Ch. Ain't I freeborn as you?
M. Ch. I'll quickly put a stop to this.
W. Ch. You'll judge no more, I vow!
M. Ch. Hi! set the vixen's hair on fire.
W. Ch. Now, Achelous,[2] now!
M. Ch. Good gracious!
W. Ch. What! you find it hot?
M. Ch. Hot? murder! stop! be quiet!
W. Ch. I'm watering you, to make you grow.
M. Ch. I wither up from shivering so.
W. Ch. I tell you what: a fire you've got,
So warm your members by it.

At this crisis the tumult is stayed for an instant by the appearance on the stage of a venerable official personage, one of the MAGISTRATES *who, after the Sicilian catastrophe, were appointed, under the name of Probuli, to form a Directory*

[1]Athena.

[2]Denotes water.

or Committee of Public Safety. He is attended by four Scythian archers, part of the ordinary police of the Athenian Republic. The WOMEN *retire into the background.*

Magistrate. Has then the women's wantonness blazed out,
Their constant timbrels and Sabaziuses,
And that Adonis-dirge upon the roof
Which once I heard in full Assembly-time.
'Twas when Demostratus (beshrew him) moved
To sail to Sicily: and from the roof
A woman, dancing, shrieked "Woe, woe, Adonis!"
And *he* proposed to enrol Zacynthian hoplites;
And *she* upon the roof, the maudlin woman,
Cried "Wail Adonis!" yet he forced it through,
That God-detested, vile Ill-temprian.
Such are the wanton follies of the sex.

M. Ch. What if you heard their insolence to-day,
Their vile, outrageous goings on? And look,
See how they've drenched and soused us from their pitchers,
Till we can wring out water from our clothes.

Ma. Ay, by Poseidon, and it serves us right.
'Tis all our fault: they'll never know their place,
These pampered women, whilst we spoil them so.
Hear how we talk in every workman's shop.
"Goldsmith," says one, "this necklace that you made,
My gay young wife was dancing yester-eve,
And lost, sweet soul, the fastening of the clasp;
Do please reset it, Goldsmith." Or, again:
"O Shoemaker, my wife's new sandal pinches
Her little toe, the tender, delicate child,
Make it fit easier, please." Hence all this nonsense!
Yea, things have reached a pretty pass, indeed,
When I, the State's Director, wanting money
To purchase oar-blades, find the Treasury gates
Shut in my face by these preposterous women.
Nay, but no dallying now: bring up the crowbars,
And I'll soon stop *your* insolence, my dears.

He turns to the Scythians, who, instead of setting to work, are poking idly around them.

What! gaping, fool? and *you*, can *you* do nothing
But stare about with tavern-squinting eye?
Push in the crowbars underneath the gates,
You, stand that side and heave them: I'll stop here
And heave them here.

The gates are thrown open, and LYSISTRATA *comes out.*

Ly. O let your crowbars be.
Lo, I come out unfetched! What need of crowbars?
'Tis wits, not crowbars, that ye need to-day.

Ma. Ay, truly, traitress, say you so? Here, Archer!
Arrest her, tie her hands behind her back.

Ly. And if he touch me with his finger-tip,
The public scum! 'fore Artemis, he'll rue it.

Ma. What, man, afeared? why, catch her round the waist.
And *you* go with him, quick, and bind her fast.

Ca. (*coming out*) And if you do but lay one hand upon her,
'Fore Pandrosus, I'll stamp your vitals out.

Ma. Vitals, ye hag? Another Archer, ho!
Seize this one first, because she chatters so.

My. (*coming out*) And if you touch her with your finger-tip,
'Fore Phosphorus, you'll need a cupping shortly.

Ma. Tcha! what's all this? lay hold of this one, Archer!
I'll stop this sallying out, depend upon it.

Stratyllis. And if he touch her, 'fore the Queen of Tauris,
I'll pull his squealing hairs out, one by one.

Ma. O dear! all's up! I've never an archer left.
Nay, but I swear we won't be done by women.
Come, Scythians, close your ranks, and all together
Charge!

Ly. Charge away, my hearties, and you'll soon
Know that we've here, impatient for the fight,
Four woman-squadrons, armed from top to toe.

Ma. Attack them, Scythians, twist their hands behind them.

Ly. Forth to the fray, dear sisters, bold allies!
O egg-and-seed-and-potherb-market-girls,
O garlic-selling-barmaid-baking-girls,
Charge to the rescue, smack and whack, and thwack them,
Slang them, I say: show them what jades ye be.

The WOMEN *come forward. After a short struggle the archers are routed.*

Fall back! retire! forbear to strip the slain.

Ma. Hillo! my archers got the worst of that.

Ly. What did the fool expect? Was it to fight
With *slaves* you came? Think you we Women feel
No thirst for glory?

Ma. Thirst enough, I trow;
No doubt of that, when there's a tavern handy.

M. Ch. O thou who wastest many words,
Director of this nation,
Why wilt thou with such brutes as these
thus hold negotiation?
Dost thou not see the bath wherewith
the sluts have dared to lave me,
Whilst all my clothes were on, and ne'er
a bit of soap they gave me?

W. Ch. For 'tis not right, nor yet polite,
to strike a harmless neighbour,
And if you do, 'tis needful too
that she your eyes belabour.
Full fain would I, a maiden shy,
in maiden peace be resting,
Not making here the slightest stir,
nor any soul molesting,
Unless indeed some rogue should strive
to rifle and despoil my hive.

M. Ch. O how shall we treat, Lord Zeus, such creatures as these?
Let us ask the cause for which they have dared to seize,
To seize this fortress of ancient and high renown,
This shrine where never a foot profane hath trod,
The lofty-rocked, inaccessible Cranaan town,
The holy Temple of God.

Now to examine them closely and narrowly,
probing them here and sounding them there,
Shame if we fail to completely unravel the
intricate web of this tangled affair.
Ma. Foremost and first I would wish to inquire of
them, what is this silly disturbance about?
Why have ye ventured to seize the Acropolis,
locking the gates and barring us out?

The field is now open for a suspension of hostilities, and a parley takes place between the leaders of the two contending factions.

Ly. Keeping the silver securely in custody,
lest for its sake ye continue the war.
Ma. What, is the war for the sake of the silver,
then?
Ly. Yes; and all other disputes that there are.
Why is Peisander forever embroiling us,
why do the rest of our officers feel
Always a pleasure in strife and disturbances?
Simply to gain an occasion to steal.
Act as they please for the future, the treasury
never a penny shall yield them, I vow.
Ma. How, may I ask, will you hinder their getting
it?
Ly. We will ourselves be the Treasurers now.
Ma. You, woman, you be the treasurers?
Ly. Certainly.
Ah, you esteem us unable, perchance!
Are we not skilled in domestic economy,
do we not manage the household finance?
Ma. O, that is different.
Ly. Why is it different?
Ma. This is required for the fighting, my dear.
Ly. Well, but the fighting itself isn't requisite.
Ma. Only, without it, we're ruined, I fear.
Ly. We will deliver you.
Ma. You will deliver us!
Ly. Truly we will.
Ma. What a capital notion!
Ly. Whether you like it or not, we'll deliver you.
Ma. Impudent hussy!
Ly. You seem in commotion.
Nevertheless we will do as we promise you.
Ma. That were a terrible shame, by Demeter.
Ly. Friend, we must save you.
Ma. But how if I wish it not?
Ly. That will but make our resolve the completer.
Ma. Fools! what on earth can possess you to
meddle with
matters of war, and matters of peace?
Ly. Well, I will tell you the reason.
Ma. And speedily,
else you will rue it.
Ly. Then listen, and cease
Clutching and clenching your fingers so angrily;
keep yourself peaceable.
Ma. Hanged if I can;
Such is the rage that I feel at your impudence.
St. Then it is *you* that will rue it, my man.
Ma. Croak your own fate, you ill-omened antiquity.
(*To* LYSISTRATA) *You* be the spokeswoman, lady.
Ly. I will.
Think of our old moderation and gentleness,
think how we bore with your pranks, and were still,
All through the days of your former pugnacity,
all through the war that is over and spent:
Not that (be sure) we approved of your policy;
never our griefs you allowed us to vent.
Well we perceived your mistakes and mismanagement.
Often at home on our housekeeping cares,
Often we heard of some foolish proposal you
made for conducting the public affairs.
Then would we question you mildly and pleasantly,
inwardly grieving, but outwardly gay;
"Husband, how goes it abroad?" we would ask of
him;
"what have ye done in Assembly to-day?"
"What would ye write on the side of the Treaty
stone?"
Husband says angrily, "What's that to you?
You, hold your tongue!" And I held it accordingly.
St. That is a thing which I *never* would do!
Ma. Ma'am, if you hadn't, you'd soon have
repented it.
Ly. Therefore I held it, and spake not a word.
Soon of another tremendous absurdity,
wilder and worse than the former we heard.
"Husband," I say, with a tender solicitude,
"Why have ye passed such a foolish decree?"
Vicious, moodily, glaring askance at me,
"Stick to your spinning, my mistress," says he,
"Else you will speedily find it the worse for you,
War is the care and the business of men!"
Ma. Zeus! 'twas a worthy reply, and an excellent!
Ly. What! you unfortunate, shall we not then,
Then, when we see you perplexed and incompetent,
shall we not tender advice to the State?
So when aloud in the streets and the thoroughfares
sadly we heard you bewailing of late,
"Is there a Man to defend and deliver us?"
"No," says another, "there's none in the land";
Then by the Women assembled in conference
jointly a great Revolution was planned,
Hellas to save from her grief and perplexity.
Where is the use of a longer delay?
Shift for the future our parts and our characters;
you, as the women, in silence obey;
We, as the men, will harangue and provide for you;
then shall the State be triumphant again,
Then shall we do what is best for the citizens.
Ma. Women to do what is best for the men!
That were a shameful reproach and unbearable!
Ly. Silence, old gentleman.
Ma. Silence for *you*?
Stop for a wench with a wimple enfolding her?
No, by the Powers, may I *die* if I do!
Ly. Do not, my pretty one, do not, I pray,
Suffer my wimple to stand in the way.
Here, take it, and wear it, and gracefully tie it,
Enfolding it over your head, and be quiet.
Now to your task.

Ca. Here is an excellent spindle to pull.
My. Here is a basket for carding the wool.
Ly. Now to your task.
Haricots chawing up, petticoats drawing up,
Off to your carding, your combing, your trimming,
War is the care and the business of women.

During the foregoing lines the WOMEN *have been arraying the* MAGISTRATE *in the garb and with the apparatus of a spinning-woman: just as in the corresponding system, below, they bedeck him in the habiliments of a corpse.*

W. Ch. Up, up, and leave the pitchers there,
and on, resolved and eager,
Our own allotted part to bear
in this illustrious leaguer.

I will dance with resolute, tireless feet all day;
My limbs shall never grow faint, my strength give way;
I will march all lengths with the noble hearts and the true,
For theirs is the ready wit and the patriot hand,
And womanly grace, and courage to dare and do,
And Love of our own bright land.

Children of stiff and intractable grandmothers,
heirs of the stinging viragoes that bore you,
On, with an eager, unyielding tenacity, wind in your sails, and the haven before you.

Ly. Only let Love, the entrancing, the fanciful,
only let Queen Aphrodite to-day
Breathe on our persons a charm and a tenderness,
lend us their own irresistible sway,
Drawing the men to admire us and long for us;
then shall the war everlastingly cease,
Then shall the people revere us and honour us,
givers of Joy, and givers of Peace.
Ma. Tell us the mode and the means of your doing it.
Ly. First we will stop the disorderly crew,
Soldiers in arms promenading and marketing.
St. Yea, by divine Aphrodite, 'tis true.
Ly. Now in the market you see them like Corybants,
jangling about with their armour of mail.
Fiercely they stalk in the midst of the crockery,
sternly parade by the cabbage and kail.
Ma. Right, for a soldier should always be soldierly!
Ly. Troth, 'tis a mighty ridiculous jest,
Watching them haggle for shrimps in the market-place,
grimly accoutred with shield and with crest.
St. Lately I witnessed a captain of cavalry,
proudly the while on his charger he sat,
Witnessed him, soldierly, buying an omelet,
stowing it all in his cavalry hat.
Comes, like a Tereus, a Thracian irregular,
shaking his dart and his target to boot;
Off runs a shop-girl, appalled at the sight of him,
down he sits soldierly, gobbles her fruit.
Ma. You, I presume, could adroitly and gingerly
settle this intricate, tangled concern:
You in a trice could relieve our perplexities.
Ly. Certainly.
Ma. How? permit me to learn.
Ly. Just as a woman, with nimble dexterity,
thus with her hands disentangles a skein,
Hither and thither her spindles unravel it,
drawing it out, and pulling it plain.
So would this weary Hellenic entanglement
soon be resolved by our womanly care,
So would our embassies neatly unravel it,
drawing it here and pulling it there.
Ma. Wonderful, marvellous feats, not a doubt of it,
you with your skeins and your spindles can show;
Fools! do you really expect to unravel a
terrible war like a bundle of tow?
Ly. Ah, if you only could manage your politics
just in the way that we deal with a fleece!
Ma. Tell us the recipe.
Ly. First, in the washing-tub
plunge it, and scour it, and cleanse it from grease,
Purging away all the filth and the nastiness;
then on the table expand it and lay,
Beating out all that is worthless and mischievous,
picking the burrs and the thistles away.
Next, for the clubs, the cabals, and the coteries,
banding unrighteously, office to win,
Treat them as clots in the wool, and dissever them,
lopping the heads that are forming therein.
Then you should card it, and comb it, and mingle it,
all in one Basket of love and of unity,
Citizens, visitors, strangers, and sojourners,
all the entire, undivided community.
Know you a fellow in debt to the Treasury?
Mingle him merrily in with the rest.
Also remember the cities, our colonies,
outlying states in the east and the west,
Scattered about to a distance surrounding us,
these are our shreds and our fragments of wool;
These to one mighty political aggregate
tenderly, carefully, gather and pull,
Twining them all in one thread of good fellowship;
thence a magnificent bobbin to spin,
Weaving a garment of comfort and dignity,
worthily wrapping the People therein.
Ma. Heard any ever the like of their impudence,
these who have nothing to do with the war,
Preaching of bobbins, and beatings, and washing-tubs?
Ly. Nothing to do with it, wretch that you are!
We are the people who feel it the keenliest,
doubly on us the affliction is cast;
Where are the sons that we sent to your battle-fields?
Ma. Silence! a truce to the ills that are past.
Ly. Then in the glory and grace of our womanhood,
all in the May and the morning of life,
Lo, we are sitting forlorn and disconsolate,
what has a soldier to do with a wife?
We might endure it, but ah! for the younger ones,
still in their maiden apartments they stay,
Waiting the husband that never approaches them,
watching the years that are gliding away.

Ma. Men, I suppose, have their youth everlastingly.
Ly. Nay, but it isn't the same with a man:
Grey though he be when he comes from the battle-field, still if he wishes to marry, he can.
Brief is the spring and the flower of our womanhood, once let it slip, and it comes not again;
Sit as we may with our spells and our auguries, never a husband will marry us then.
Ma. Truly whoever is able to wed—
Ly. Truly, old fellow, 'tis time you were dead.
So a pig shall be sought, and an urn shall be bought,
And I'll bake you and make you a funeral cake.
Take it and go.
Ca. Here are the fillets all ready to wear.
My. Here is the chaplet to bind in your hair.
Ly. Take it and go.
What are you prating for?
What are you waiting for?
Charon is staying, delaying his crew,
Charon is calling and bawling for you.
Ma. See, here's an outrage! here's a scandalous shame!
I'll run and show my fellow magistrates
The woeful, horrid, dismal plight I'm in.
Ly. Grumbling because we have not laid you out?
Wait for three days, and then with dawn will come,
All in good time, the third-day funeral rites.

The MAGISTRATE *runs off in his grave-clothes to complain of and exhibit the treatment he has received.* LYSISTRATA *and her friends withdraw into the Acropolis. The two* CHORUSES *remain without, and relieve the tedium of the siege with a little banter.*

M. Ch. This is not a time for slumber; now let all the bold and free,
Strip to meet the great occasion, vindicate our rights with me.
I can smell a deep, surprising
Tide of Revolution rising,
Odour as of folk devising
Hippias's tyranny.
And I feel a dire misgiving,
Lest some false Laconians, meeting in the house of Cleisthenes,
Have inspired these wretched women all our wealth and pay to seize,
Pay from whence I get my living.
Gods! to hear these shallow wenches taking citizens to task,
Prattling of a brassy buckler, jabbering of a martial casque!
Gods! to think that they have ventured with Laconian men to deal,
Men of just the faith and honour that a ravening wolf might feel!
Plots they're hatching, plots contriving, plots of rampant Tyranny;
But o'er *us* they shan't be Tyrants, no, for on my guard I'll be,
And I'll dress my sword in myrtle, and with firm and dauntless hand,
Here beside Aristogeiton resolutely take my stand,
Marketing in arms beside him.
This the time and this the place
When my patriot arm must deal a —blow upon that woman's face.
W. Ch. Ah, your mother shall not know you, impudent! when home you go.
Strip, my sisters, strip for action, on the ground your garments throw.
Right it is that I my slender
Tribute to the state should render,
I, who to her thoughtful tender care my happiest memories owe:[1]
Bore, at seven, the mystic casket;
Was, at ten, our Lady's miller; then the yellow Brauron bear;
Next (a maiden tall and stately with a string of figs to wear)
Bore in pomp the holy Basket.
Well may such a gracious City all my filial duty claim.
What though I was born a woman, comrades, count it not for blame
If I bring the wiser counsels; I an equal share confer
Towards the common stock of Athens, I contribute men to her.
But the noble contribution, but the olden tribute-pay,
Which your fathers' fathers left you, relic of the Median fray,
Dotards, ye have lost and wasted! nothing in its stead ye bring,
Nay ourselves ye're like to ruin, spend and waste by blundering.
Murmuring are ye? Let me hear you, only let me hear you speak,
And from this unpolished slipper comes a—slap upon your cheek!
M. Ch. Is not this an outrage sore?
And methinks it blows not o'er,
But increases more and more.
Come, my comrades, hale and hearty, on the ground your mantles throw,
In the odour of their manhood men to meet the fight should go,
Not in these ungodly wrappers swaddled up from top to toe.
On, then on, my white-foot veterans, ye who thronged Leipsydrium's height
In the days when we were Men!
Shake this chill old Age from off you,
Spread the wings of youth again.
O these women! give them once a handle howsoever small,
And they'll soon be nought behind us in the manliest feats of all.

[1]They recite the duties of the four girls, between the ages of seven and eleven, chosen yearly to serve Athena.

Yea, they'll build them fleets and navies
and they'll come across the sea,
Come like Carian Artemisia,
fighting in their ships with me.
Or they'll turn their first attention,
haply, to equestrian fights,
If they do, I know the issue,
there's an end of all the knights!
Well a woman sticks on horseback:
look around you, see, behold,
Where on Micon's living frescoes
fight the Amazons of old!
Shall we let these wilful women,
O my brothers, do the same?
Rather first their necks we'll rivet
tightly in the pillory frame.

He seizes the neck of STRATYLLIS.

W. Ch. If our smouldering fires ye wake,
Soon our wildbeast wrath will break
Out against you, and we'll make,
Make you howl to all your neighbours,
currycombed, poor soul, and tanned.
Throw aside your mantles, sisters,
come, a firm determined band,
In the odour of your wrathful
snappish womanhood to stand.
Who'll come forth and fight me? garlic,
nevermore, nor beans for him.
Nay, if one sour word ye say,
I'll be like the midwife beetle,
Following till the eagle lay.
Yea, for you and yours I reck not
whilst my Lampito survives,
And my noble, dear Ismenia,
lovliest of the Theban wives.
Keep decreeing seven times over,
not a bit of good you'll do,
Wretch abhorred of all the people
and of all our neighbours too.
So that when in Hecate's honour
yesterday I sent to get
From our neighbours in Boeotia
such a dainty darling pet,
Just a lovely, graceful, slender,
white-fleshed eel divinely tender,
Thanks to your decrees, confound them,
one and all refused to send her.
And you'll never stop from making
these absurd decrees I know,
Till I catch your leg and toss you
—Zeus-ha'-mercy, there you go!

An interval of several days must here be supposed to elapse. The separation of the sexes has now become unsupportable to both parties, and the only question is which side will hold out the longest. The CHORUS OF WOMEN *are alarmed at seeing* LYSISTRATA *come on the stage, and walk up and down with an anxious and troubled air. The first twelve lines of the dialogue which ensues are borrowed and burlesqued from Euripides.*

W. Ch. Illustrious leader of this bold emprize,
What brings thee forth, with trouble in thine eyes?

Ly. Vile women's works: the feminine hearts they show:
These make me pace, dejected, to and fro.

W. Ch. O what! and O what!

Ly. 'Tis true! 'tis true!

W. Ch. O to your friends, great queen, the tale unfold.

Ly. 'Tis sad to tell, and sore to leave untold.

W. Ch. What, what has happened? tell us, tell us quick.

Ly. Aye, in one word. The girls are—husband-sick.

W. Ch. O Zeus! Zeus! O!

Ly. Why call on Zeus? the fact is surely so.
I can no longer keep the minxes in.
They slip out everywhere. One I discovered
Down by Pan's grotto, burrowing through the loophole:
Another, wriggling down by crane and pulley:
A third deserts outright: a fourth I dragged
Back by the hair, yestreen, just as she started
On sparrow's back, straight for Orsilochus's:
They make all sorts of shifts to get away.

A WOMAN *is seen attempting to cross the stage.*

Ha! here comes one, deserting. Hi there, Hi!
Where are you off to?

1st Woman. (*hurriedly*) I must just run home.
I left some fine Milesian wools about,
I'm sure the moths are at them.

Ly. Moths indeed!
Get back.

1st W. But really I'll return directly,
I only want to spread them on the couch.

Ly. No spreadings out, no running home to-day.

1st W. What! leave my wools to perish?

Ly. If need be.

A SECOND WOMAN *now attempts to cross the stage.*

2nd W. O goodness gracious! O that lovely flax
I left at home unhackled!

Ly. Here's another!
She's stealing off to hackle flax forsooth.
(*to the* SECOND WOMAN)
Come, come, get back.

2nd W. O yes, and so I will,
I'll comb it out and come again directly.

Ly. Nay, nay, no combing: once begin with that
And other girls are sure to want the same.

Several women enter one after the other.

3rd W. O holy Eileithyia, stay my labour
Till I can reach some lawful travail-place.

Ly. How now!

3rd W. My pains are come.

Ly. Why, yesterday
You were not pregnant.

3rd W. But to-day I am
Quick, let me pass, Lysistrata, at once
To find a midwife.

Ly. What's it all about?
What's this hard lump?

3rd W. That's a male child.

Ly. Not it.

It's something made of brass, and hollow too.
Come, come, out with it. O you silly woman,
What! cuddling up the sacred helmet there
And say you're pregnant?

3rd W. Well, and so I am.

Ly. What's this for then?

3rd W. Why, if my pains o'ertake me
In the Acropolis, I'd creep inside
And sit and hatch there as the pigeons do.

Ly. Nonsense and stuff: the thing's as plain as can be
Stay and keep here the name-day of your—helmet.

4th W. But I can't sleep a single wink up here,
So scared I was to see the holy serpent.

5th W. And I shall die for lack of rest, I know,
With this perpetual hooting of the owls.

Ly. O ladies, ladies, cease these tricks, I pray.
Ye want your husbands. And do you suppose
They don't want *us*? Full wearisome, I know,
Their nights without us. O bear up, dear friends,
Be firm, be patient, yet one little while,
For I've an oracle (here 'tis) which says
We're sure to conquer if we hold together.

5 Women. O read us what it says.

Ly. Then all keep silence.
"Soon as the swallows are seen
collecting and crouching together,
Shunning the hoopoes' flight
and keeping aloof from the Love-birds,
Cometh a rest from ill,
and Zeus the Lord of the Thunder
Changeth the upper to under."

5 W. Preserve us, shall *we* be the upper?

Ly. "Nay, but if once they wrangle,
and flutter away in dissension
Out of the Temple of God,
then all shall see and acknowledge,
Never a bird of the air
so perjured and frail as the swallow."

5 W. Wow, but that's plain enough! O all ye Gods,
Let us not falter in our efforts now.
Come along in. O friends, O dearest friends,
'Twere sin and shame to fail the oracle.

The WOMEN, *with* LYSISTRATA, *re-enter the Acropolis. The two* CHORUSES *again indulge in an interchange of banter. The* MEN *begin.*

M. Ch. Now to tell a little story
Fain, fain I grow,
One I heard when quite an urchin
Long, long ago.
How that once
All to shun the nuptial bed
From his home Melanion fled,
To the hills and deserts sped,
Kept his dog,
Wove his snares,
Set his nets,
Trapped his hares;
Home he nevermore would go,
He detested women so.
We are of Melanion's mind,
We detest the womankind.

Man. May I, mother, kiss your cheek?

Woman. Then you won't require a leek.

M. Hoist my leg, and kick you, so?

W. Fie! what stalwart legs you show!

M. Just such stalwart legs and strong,
Just such stalwart legs as these,
To the noble chiefs belong,
Phormio and Myronides.

It is now the WOMEN'S *turn. The two systems are of course antistrophical.*

W. Ch. Now to tell a little story
Fain, fain am I,
To your tale about Melanion
Take this reply.
How that once
Savage Timon, all forlorn,
Dwelt amongst the prickly thorn
Visage-shrouded, Fury-born.
Dwelt alone,
Far away,
Cursing men
Day by day;
Never saw his home again,
Kept aloof from haunts of men:
Hating men of evil mind,
Dear to all the womankind.

W. Shall I give your cheek a blow?

M. No, I thank you, no, no, no!

W. Hoist my foot and kick you too?

M. Fie! what vulgar feet I view.

W. Vulgar feet! absurd, absurd,
Don't such foolish things repeat;
Never were, upon my word,
Tinier, tidier little feet.

The two CHORUSES *now retire into the background; and there is again a short pause. Suddenly the voice of* LYSISTRATA *is heard calling eagerly to her friends.*

Ly. Ho, ladies! ladies! quick, this way, this way!

1st W. O what's the matter and what means that cry?

Ly. A man! a man! I see a man approaching
Wild with desire, beside himself with love.

1st W. O lady of Cyprus, Paphos, and Cythera,
Keep on, straight on, the way you are going now!
But where's the man?

Ly. (*pointing*) Down there, by Chloe's chapel.[1]

1st W. O so he is: whoever can he be!

Ly. Know you him, anyone?

My. O yes, my dear,
I know him. That's Cinesias, my husband.

Ly. O then 'tis yours to roast and bother him well;
Coaxing, yet coy: enticing, fooling him,
Going all lengths, save what our Oath forbids.

My. Ay, ay, trust *me*.

Ly. And I'll assist you, dear;
I'll take my station here, and help befool
And roast our victim. All the rest, retire.

The others withdraw, leaving LYSISTRATA *alone upon the wall.* CINESIAS *approaches underneath.*

[1]Demeter.

Cinesias. O me! these pangs and paroxysms of love,
Riving my heart, keen as a torturer's wheel!
Ly. Who's this within the line of sentries?
Ci. I.
Ly. A man?
Ci. A man, no doubt.
Ly. Then get you gone.
Ci. Who bids me go?
Ly. I, guard on outpost duty.
Ci. O call me out, I pray you, Myrrhina.
Ly. Call you out Myrrhina! And who are you?
Ci. Why, I'm her husband, I'm Cinesias.
Ly. O welcome, welcome, dearest man; your name
Is not unknown nor yet unhonoured here.
Your wife for ever has it on her lips.
She eats no egg, no apple, but she says
"This to Cinesias!"
Ci. O, good heaven! good heaven!
Ly. She does, indeed: and if we ever chance
To talk of men, she vows that all the rest
Are veriest trash beside Cinesias.
Ci. Ah! call her out.
Ly. And will you give me aught?
Ci. O yes, I'll give you anything I've got.
Gives money.
Ly. Then I'll go down and call her.
Descends from the wall into the Acropolis.
Ci. Pray be quick.
I have no joy, no happiness in life,
Since she, my darling, left me. When I enter
My vacant home I weep; and all the world
Seems desolate and bare: my very meals
Give me no joy, now Myrrhina is gone.
My. (*within*) Ay, ay, I love, I love him, but he won't
Be loved by me: call me not out to him.
As she speaks, she appears on the wall.
Ci. What mean you, Myrrhina, my sweet, sweet love?
Do, do come down.
My. No, no, sir, not to you.
Ci. What, won't you when I call you, Myrrhina?
My. Why, though you call me, yet you want me not.
Ci. Not want you, Myrrhina! I'm dying for you.
My. Good-bye.
Ci. Nay, nay, but listen to the child
At all events: speak to Mama, my child.
Child. Mama! Mama! Mama!
Ci. Have you no feeling, mother, for your child,
Six days unwashed, unsuckled?
My. Ay, 'tis I
That feel for baby, 'tis Papa neglects him.
Ci. Come down and take him, then?
My. O what it is
To be a mother! I must needs go down.
She descends from the wall, and four lines below reappears through the gate. While she is gone CINESIAS *speaks.*
Ci. She looks, methinks, more youthful than she did,
More gentle-loving, and more sweet by far.
Her very airs, her petulant, saucy ways,
They do but make me love her, love her more.
My. O my sweet child, a naughty father's child,
Mama's own darling, let me kiss you, pet.
Ci. Why treat me thus, you baggage, letting others
Lead you astray: making me miserable
And yourself too?
My. Hands off! don't touch me, sir.
Ci. And all our household treasures, yours and mine,
Are gone to wrack and ruin.
My. I don't care.
Ci. Not care, although the fowls are in the house
Pulling your threads to pieces?
My. Not a bit.
Ci. Nor though the sacred rites of wedded love
Have been so long neglected? won't you come?
My. No, no, I won't, unless you stop the war,
And all make friends.
Ci. Well, then, if such your will,
We'll e'en do this.
My. Well, then, if such your will,
I'll e'en come home: but now I've sworn I won't.
Ci. Come to my arms, do, after all this time!
My. No, no—and yet I won't say I don't love you.
Ci. You love me? then come to my arms, my dearie!
My. You silly fellow, and the baby here?
Ci. O, not at all—(*to slave*) here, take the baby home.
There now: the baby's gone out of the way;
Come to my arms!
My. Good heavens, where, I ask you!
Ci. Pan's grotto will do nicely.
My. Oh, indeed!
How shall I make me pure to ascend the Mount?
Ci. Easy enough: bathe in the Clepsydra.
My. I've sworn an oath, and shall I break it, man?
Ci. On my head be it: never mind the oath.
My. Well, let me bring a pallet.
Ci. Not at all;
The ground will do.
My. What—one so much to me?
I swear I'll never let you lie o' the ground.
Exit MYRRHINA.
Ci. The woman loves me, plain enough, you see.
Enter MYRRHINA *with pallet.*
My. There, lie down, do make haste; I'll take my things off
But wait a minute, I must find a mattress.
Ci. Bother the mattress, not for me.
My. Why yes,
It's nasty on the cords.
Ci. Give me a kiss.
My. There then.
Ci. Smack, smack. Come back, look sharp about it.
Exit MYRRHINA *and returns with mattress.*
My. There now, lie down, see, I take off my things—
But wait a minute—what about a pillow?

Ci. But I don't want a pillow.
My. I do, though.
Exit MYRRHINA.
Ci. A veritable feast of Barmecides!
My. (*returning with pillow*) Up with your head, hop up!
Ci. I've all I want.
My. What, *all*?
Ci. Yes, all but you; come here, my precious!
My. There goes the girdle. But remember now,
You must not play me false about the peace.
Ci. God damn me if I do!
My. You have no rug.
Ci. I want no rug, I want you in my arms.
My. Oh, all right, you shall have me, I'll be quick.
Exit MYRRHINA.
Ci. She'll be the death of me with all these bed-clothes!
My. (*returning with rug*) Up now!
Ci. I'm up enough be sure of that.
My. Some nice sweet ointment?
Ci. By Apollo, no!
My. By Aphrodite, yes! say what you like.
Exit MYRRHINA.
Ci. Lord Zeus, I pray the ointment may be spilt!
My. (*returning with ointment*) Put out your hand, take some, anoint yourself.
Ci. I swear this stuff is anything but sweet,
The brand is Wait-and-see, no marriage smell!
My. How stupid! here I've brought the Rhodian kind.
Ci. It's good enough, my dear.
My. Rubbish, good man!
Exit MYRRHINA.
Ci. Perdition take the man that first made ointment!
My. (*returning with flask*) Here, take this flask.
Ci. I've all the flask I want.
Come to my arms, you wretched creature you!
No more things, please!
My. I will, by Artemis.
There go my shoes, at least. Now don't forget,
You'll vote for peace, my dearest.
Exit MYRRHINA.
Ci. Oh, I'll see.
The creature's done for me, bamboozled me,
Gone off and left me in this wretched state.
What will become of me? whom shall I fondle
Robbed of the fairest fair?
Who will be ready this orphan to dandle?
Where's Cynalopex? where?
Find me a nurse!
M. Ch. She's left you a curse.
Oh I'm so sorry, O I grieve for ye,
Tis more than a man can bear:
Not a soul, not a loin, not a heart, not a groin,
Can endure such pangs of despair.
Ci. O Zeus, what pangs and throes I bear!
M. Ch. All this woe she has wrought you, she only, the
Utterly hateful, the utterly vile.
W. Ch. Not so; but the darling, the utterly sweet.
Exit.
M. Ch. Sweet, sweet, do you call her? Vile, vile, I repeat.
Zeus, send me a storm and a whirlwind, I pray,
To whisk her away, like a bundle of hay,
Up, up, to the infinite spaces,
And toss her and swirl her, and twist her, and twirl her,
Till, tattered and torn, to the earth she is borne,
To be crushed—in my ardent embraces.
Enter HERALD.
Herald. Whaur sall a body fin' the Athanian senate,
Or the gran' lairds? Ha' gotten news to tell.
Enter MAGISTRATE.
Ma. News have you, friend?
And what in the world are you?
He. A heralt, billie! jist a Spartian heralt,
Come, by the Twa', anent a Peace, ye ken.
Ma. And so you come with a spear beneath your armpit!
He. Na, na, not I.
Ma. Why do you turn away?
Why cast your cloak before you? Is your groin
A trifle swollen from the march?
He. by Castor
This loon's a rogue.
Ma. Look at yourself, you brute!
He. There's naught amiss wi' me, don't play the fule.
Ma. Why then, what's this?
He. A Spartan letter-staff.
Ma. (*pointing to himself*)
Yes, if *this* is a Spartan letter-staff!
Well, and how fare the Spartans? tell me that:
And tell me truly, for I know the fact.
He. They're bad eneugh, they canna weel be waur;
They're sair bested, Spartans, allies, an' a'.
Ma. And how and whence arose this trouble first?
From Pan?
He. Na, na, 'twer' Lampito, I ween,
First set it gangin': then our hizzies, a'
Risin' like rinners at ane signal word,
Loupit, an' jibbed, an' dang the men awa'.
Ma. How like ye that?
He. Och, we're in waefu' case.
They stan' abeigh, the lassies do, an' vow
They'll no be couthie wi' the laddies mair
Till a' mak' Peace, and throughly en' the War.
Ma. This is a plot they have everywhere been hatching,
These villainous women: now I see it all.
Run home, my man, and bid your people send
Envoys with absolute powers to treat for peace,
And I will off with all the speed I can,
And get our Council here to do the same.
He. Nebbut, I'se fly, ye rede me weel, I'm thinkin'.

The HERALD *leaves for Spartae; the* MAGISTRATE *returns to the Senate; and the two* CHORUSES *now advance for a final skirmish.*

M. Ch. There is nothing so resistless
as a woman in her ire,

She is wilder than a leopard,
she is fiercer than a fire.
W. Ch. And yet you're so daft
as with women to contend,
When 'tis in your power to win me
and have me as a friend.
M. Ch. I'll never, never cease
all women to detest.
W. Ch. That's as you please hereafter:
meanwhile you're all undressed.
I really can't allow it,
you are getting quite a joke;
Permit me to approach you
and to put you on this cloak.
M. Ch. Now that's not so bad
or unfriendly I declare;
It was only from bad temper
that I stripped myself so bare.
W. Ch. There, now you look a man:
and none will joke and jeer you:
And if you weren't so spiteful
that no one can come near you,
I'd have pulled out the insect
that is sticking in your eye.
M. Ch. Ay, that is what's consuming me,
that little biter-fly.
Yes, scoop it out and show me,
when you've got him safe away:
The plaguy little brute,
he's been biting me all day.
W. Ch. I'll do it, sir, I'll do it:
but you're a cross one, you.
O Zeus! here's a monster
I am pulling forth to view.
Just look! don't you think
'tis a Tricorysian gnat?
M. Ch. And he's been dig, dig, digging
(so I thank you much for that)
Till the water, now he's gone,
keeps running from my eye.
W. Ch. But although you've been so naughty,
I'll come and wipe it dry,
And I'll kiss you.
M. Ch. No, not kiss me!
W. Ch. Will you, nill you, it must be.
M. Ch. Get along, a murrain on you.
Tcha! what coaxing rogues are ye!
That was quite a true opinion
which a wise man gave about you,
We can't live with such tormentors,
no, by Zeus, nor yet without you.
Now we'll make a faithful treaty,
and for evermore agree,
I will do no harm to women,
they shall do no harm to me.
Join our forces, come along:
one and all commence the song.

Joint Chorus

Not to objurgate and scold you,
Not unpleasant truths to say,
But with words and deeds of bounty
Come we here to-day.
Ah, enough of idle quarrels,
Now attend, I pray.
Now whoever wants some money,
Minas two or minas three,
Let them say so, man and woman,
Let them come with me.
Many purses, large and—empty,
In my house they'll see.
Only you must strictly promise,
Only you indeed must say
That whenever Peace re-greet us,
You will—not repay.

Some Carystian friends are coming,
Pleasant gentlemen, to dine;
And I've made some soup, and slaughtered
Such a lovely swine;
Luscious meat ye'll have and tender
At this feast of mine.
Come along, yourselves and children,
Come to grace my board to-day;
Take an early bath, and deck you
In your best array;
Then walk in and ask no questions,
Take the readiest way.
Come along, like men of mettle;
Come as though 'twere all for you:
Come, you'll find my only entrance
Locked and bolted too.

The LACONIAN AMBASSADORS *are seen approaching.*

Lo here from Sparta the envoys come:
in a pitiful plight they are hobbling in.
Heavily hangs each reverend beard;
heavily droops and trails from the chin.
Laconian envoys! first I bid you welcome,
And next I ask how goes the world with *you*?

Enter LACONIAN AMBASSADORS.

Laconian. I needna mony words to answer that!
'Tis unco plain hoo the warld gangs wi' us.
Ch. Dear, dear, this trouble grows from bad to worse.
Lac. 'Tis awfu' bad: 'tis nae gude talkin', cummer.
We maun hae peace whatever gaet we gang till't.
Ch. And here, good faith, I see our own Autochthons
Bustling along. They seem in trouble too.

The ATHENIAN AMBASSADORS *enter.*

Athenian. Can some good soul inform me where to find
Lysistrata? our men are (*shrugging his shoulders*) as you see.

He perceives the LACONIAN AMBASSADORS.

Ch. Sure, we are smitten with the same complaint.
Say, don't you get a fit i' the early morning?
At. Why, we are all worn out with doing this:
So Cleisthenes will have to serve our turn
Unless we can procure a speedy peace.
Ch. If you are wise, wrap up, unless you wish
One of those Hermes-choppers to catch sight o' you.
At. Prudent advice, by Zeus.

Lac. Aye, by the Twa:
Gie us the clout to cover up oorsels.
At. Aha, Laconians! a bad business this.
Lac. 'Deed is it, lovey; though it grow nae waur,
Gin they see us too all agog like this.
At. Well, well, Laconians, come to facts at once.
What brings you here?
Lac. We're envoys sent to claver
Anent a Peace.
At. Ah, just the same as we.
Then let's call out Lysistrata at once,
There's none but she can make us friends again.
Lac. Ay, by the Twa, ca' oot Lysistrata.
At. Nay, here she is! no need, it seems, to call.
She heard your voices, and she comes uncalled.

LYSISTRATA *comes forward attended by her handmaid* RECONCILIATION.

Ch. O Lady, noblest and best of all!
arise, arise, and thyself reveal,
Gentle, severe, attractive, harsh,
well skilled with all our complaints to deal,
The first and foremost of Hellas come,
they are caught by the charm of thy spell-drawn wheel,
They come to Thee to adjust their claims,
disputes to settle, and strifes to heal.
Ly. And no such mighty matter, if you take them
In Love's first passion, still unsatisfied.
I'll try them now. Go, *Reconciliation*,
Bring those Laconians hither, not with rude
Ungenial harshness hurrying them along,
Not in the awkward style our husbands used,
But with all tact, as only women can.
So; so: now bring me those Athenians too.
Now then, Laconians, stand beside me here,
And you stand there, and listen to my words.
I am a woman, but I don't lack sense;
I'm of myself not badly off for brains,
And often listening to my father's words
And old men's talk, I've not been badly schooled.
And now, dear friends, I wish to chide you both,
That ye, all of one blood, all brethren sprinkling
The selfsame altars from the selfsame laver,
At Pylae, Pytho, and Olympia, ay
And many others which 'twere long to name,
That ye, Hellenes—with barbarian foes
Armed, looking on—fight and destroy Hellenes!
So far one reprimand includes you both.
At. And I, I'm dying all for love, sweetheart.
Ly. And ye, Laconians, for I'll turn to you,
Do ye not mind how Pericleidas came,
(His coat was scarlet but his cheeks were white),
And sat a suppliant at Athenian altars
And begged for help? 'Twas when Messene pressed
Weighing you down, and God's great earthquake too.
And Cimon went, Athenian Cimon went
With his four thousand men, and saved your State.
And ye, whom Athens aided, now in turn
Ravage the land which erst befriended you.
At. 'Fore Zeus they're wrong, they're wrong,
Lysistrata.
Lac. O ay, we're wrang, but she's a braw ane, she.
Ly. And you, Athenians, think ye that I mean
To let You off? Do *ye* not mind, when ye
Wore skirts of hide, how these Laconians came
And stood beside you in the fight alone,
And slew full many a stout Thessalian trooper,
Full many of Hippias's friends and helpers,
And freed the State, and gave your people back
The civic mantle for the servile skirt?
Lac. Danged, an' there ever waur a bonnier lassie!
At. Hanged if I ever saw so sweet a creature!
Ly. Such friends aforetime, helping each the other,
What is it makes you fight and bicker now?
Why can't ye come to terms? Why can't ye, hey?
Lac. Troth an' we're willin', gin they gie us back
Yon girdled neuk.
At. What's that?
Lac. Pylus, ye ninny,
Whilk we've been aye langin' an' graipin' for.
At. No, by Poseidon, but you won't get that.
Ly. O let them have it, man.
At. How can we stir
Without it?
Ly. Ask for something else instead.
At. Hum! haw! let's see; suppose they give us back
Echinus first, then the full-bosomed gulf
Of Melis, then the straight Megaric limbs.
Lac. Eh, mon, ye're daft; ye'll no hae everything.
Ly. O let it be: don't wrangle about the limbs.
At. I'fecks, I'd like to strip, and plough my field.
Lac. An' I to bring the midden, by the Twa.
Ly. All this ye'll do, when once ye come to terms.
So if ye would, go and consult together
And talk it over, each with your allies.
At. Allies, says she! Now my good soul consider:
What *do* they want, what *can* they want, but this,
Their wives again?
Lac. The fient anither wiss
Ha' mine, I ween.
At. Nor my Carystians either.
Ly. O that is well: so purify yourselves;
And in the Acropolis we'll feast you all
On what our cupboards still retain in store.
There, each to other, plight your oath and troth,
Then every man receive his wife again,
And hie off homeward.
At. That we will, and quickly.
Lac. Gae on: we'se follow.
At. Ay, as quick as quick.

LYSISTRATA *and the* AMBASSADORS *go in.*

Chorus

Gorgeous robes and golden trinkets,
Shawls and mantles rich and rare,
I will lend to all who need them,
Lend for youths to wear,
Or if any comrade's daughter
Would the Basket bear.
One and all I here invite you,
Freely of my goods partake,
Nought is sealed so well, but boldly
Ye the seals may break,
And of all that lurks behind them,

Quick partition make.
Only, if you find the treasures,
Only, if the stores you spy,
You must have, I tell you plainly,
Keener sight than I.

Is *there* any man among you,
With a lot of children small,
With a crowd of hungry servants,
Starving in his hall?
I have wheat to spare in plenty,
I will feed them all.
Loaves, a quart apiece, I'll give them,
Come along, whoever will,
Bring your bags, and bring your wallets
For my slave to fill;
Manes, he's the boy to pack them
Tight and tighter still.
Only you must keep your distance,
Only you must needs take care,
Only—don't approach my doorway,
Ware the watch-dog, ware!

Some IDLERS *come in from the market-place, and attempt to enter the house in which the* AMBASSADORS *are feasting.*

1st Idler. Open the door there, ho!
Porter. Be off, you rascal!
1st Id. What, won't you stir? I've half a mind to roast you
All with this torch. No, that's a vulgar trick.
I won't do that. Still if the audience wish it,
To please their tastes we'll undertake the task.
2nd Id. And we, with you, will undertake the task.
Po. Hang you, be off! what are you at? you'll catch it.
Come, come, begone; that these Laconians here,
The banquet ended, may depart in peace.

The banqueters begin to come out.

1st At. Well, if I ever saw a feast like this!
What cheery fellows those Laconians were,
And we were wondrous witty in our cups.
2nd At. Ay, ay, 'tis when we're sober, we're so daft.
Now if the State would take a friend's advice,
'Twould make its envoys always all get drunk.
When we go dry to Sparta, all our aim
Is just to see what mischief we can do.
We don't hear aught they say; and we infer
A heap of things they never said at all.
Then we bring home all sorts of differing tales.
Now everything gives pleasure: if a man,
When he should sing Cleitagora, strike up
With Telamon's song, we'd clap him on the back,
And say 'twas excellent; ay, and swear it too.

The IDLERS *again approach.*

Po. Why, bless the fellows, here they come again,
Crowding along. Be off, you scoundrels, will you?
1st Id. By Zeus, we must: the guests are coming out.

The AMBASSADORS *come out from the banquet.*

Lac. O lovey mine, tak' up the pipes an' blaw.
An' I'se jist dance an' sing a canty sang
Anent the Athanians an' our ainsells too.
At. Ay, by the Powers, take up the pipes and blow.
Eh, but I dearly love to see you dance.

Lac. Stir, Memory, stir the chiels
Wi' that auld sang o' thine,
Whilk kens what we an' Attics did
In the gran' fechts lang syne.

At Artemisium They
A' resolute an' strang
Rushed daurly to the fray,
Hurtlin' like Gudes amang
The timmered ships, an' put the Medes to rout.
An' Us Leonidas led out
Like gruesome boars, I ween,
Whettin' our tuskies keen.
Muckle around the chaps was the white freath gleamin',
Muckle adoon the legs was the white freath streamin',
For a' unnumbered as the sands
Were they, thae Persian bands.

O Artemis, the pure, the chaste,
The virgin Queller o' the beasties,
O come wi' power an' come wi' haste,
An' come to join our friendly feasties.
Come wi' thy stoutest tether,
To knit our sauls thegither,
An' gie us Peace in store,
An' Luve for evermore.
Far hence, far hence depart
The tod's deceitfu' heart!
O virgin huntress, pure an' chaste,
O come wi' power, an' come wi' haste.

Ly. There, all is settled, all arranged at last.
Now, take your ladies; you, Laconians, those,
And you, take these; then standing side by side,
Each by his partner, lead your dances out
In grateful honour to the Gods, and O
Be sure you nevermore offend again.

Ch. Now for the Chorus, the Graces, the minstrelsy.
Call upon Artemis, queen of the glade;
Call on her brother, the Lord of festivity,
Holy and gentle one, mighty to aid.
Call upon Bacchus, afire with his Maenades;
Call upon Zeus, in the lightning arrayed;
Call on his queen, ever blessed, adorable;
Call on the holy, infallible Witnesses,
Call them to witness the peace and the harmony,
This which divine Aphrodite has made.
Allala! Lallala! Lallala, Lallala!
Whoop for victory, Lallalalae!
Evoi! Evoi! Lallala, Lallala!
Evae! Evae! Lallalalae.

Our excellent new song is done;
Do you, Laconian, give us one.

Lac. Leave Taygety, an' quickly
Hither, Muse Laconian, come.
Hymn the Gude o' braw Amyclae,
Hymn Athana, Brassin-dome.
Hymn the Tyndarids, forever
Sportin' by Eurotas river.
Noo then, noo the step begin,
Twirlin' licht the fleecy skin;
Sae we'se join our blithesome voices,
Praisin' Sparta, loud an' lang,
Sparta wha of auld rejoices
In the Choral dance an' sang.
O to watch her bonnie dochters
Sport alang Eurotas' waters!
Winsome feet forever plyin',
Fleet as fillies, wild an' gay,
Winsome tresses tossin', flyin',
As o' Bacchanals at play.
Leda's dochter, on before us,
Pure an' sprety, guides the Chorus.
Onward go,
Whilst your eager hand represses
A' the glory o' your tresses;
Whilst your eager foot is springin'
Like the roe;
Whilst your eager voice is singin'
Praise to Her in might excellin'
Goddess o' the Brassin Dwellin'.

THE THESMOPHORIAZUSAE

DRAMATIS PERSONAE

MNESILOCHUS	CLEISTHENES
EURIPIDES	CRITYLLA
A SERVANT OF AGATHON	A POLICEMAN
AGATHON	A SCYTHIAN
CRIERESS	ECHO
WOMEN	CHORUS OF THESMOPHORIAZUSAE

Two elderly men are discovered, when the Play opens, pacing along an Athenian street. In one, both by his gait and by his language, we at once recognize a Philosopher and a Genius. His companion is a garrulous and cheery old man, evidently tired out by a long promenade. They prove to be the poet EURIPIDES, *and* MNESILOCHUS, *his connexion by marriage, in the translation inaccurately styled his cousin. The latter is the first to speak.*

Mnesilochus. Zeus! is the swallow *never* going to come?
Tramped up and down since daybreak! I can't stand it.
Might I, before my wind's *entirely* gone,
Ask where you're taking me, Euripides?
Euripides. You're not to hear the things which face to face
You're going to see.
Mn. What! Please say that again.
I'm not to hear?
Eu. The things which you shall see.
Mn. And not to see?
Eu. The things which you shall hear.
Mn. A pleasant jest! a mighty pleasant jest!
I'm not to hear or see at all, I see.
Eu. (*in high philosophic rhapsody*)
To hear! to see! full different things, I ween;
Yea verily, generically diverse.
Mn. What's "diverse"?
Eu. I will explicate my meaning.
When Ether first was mapped and parcelled out,
And living creatures breathed and moved in her,
She, to give sight, implanted in their heads
The Eye, a mimic circlet of the Sun,
And bored the funnel of the Ear, to hear with.
Mn. Did *she*! That's why I'm not to hear or see!
I'm very glad to get that information!
O, what a thing it is to talk with Poets!
Eu. Much of such knowledge I shall give you.
Mn. (*involuntarily*) O!
Then p'raps (excuse me) you will tell me how
Not to be lame to-morrow, after this.
Eu. (*loftily disregarding the innuendo*)
Come here and listen.
Mn. (*courteously*) Certainly I will.
Eu. See you that wicket?
Mn. Why, by Heracles,
Of course I do.
Eu. Be still.
Mn. Be still the wicket?
Eu. And most attentive.
Mn. Still attentive wicket?
Eu. There dwells, observe, the famous Agathon,
The Tragic Poet.
Mn. (*considering*) Agathon. Don't know him.
Eu. He is that Agathon—
Mn. (*interrupting*) Dark, brawny fellow?
Eu. O no, quite different; don't you know him really?
Mn. Big-whiskered fellow?
Eu. Don't you know him really?
Mn. No. (*Thinks again*) No, I don't; at least I don't remember.
Eu. (*severely*) I fear there's much you don't remember, sir.
But step aside: I see his servant coming.
See, he has myrtles and a pan of coals
To pray, methinks, for favourable rhymes.
The two retire into the background. Agathon's SERVANT *enters from the house.*
Servant. All people be still!
Allow not a word from your lips to be heard,
For the Muses are here, and are making their odes
In my Master's abodes.
Let Ether be lulled, and forgetful to blow,
And the blue sea-waves, let them cease to flow,
And be noiseless.
Mn. Fudge!
Eu. Hush, hush, if you please.
Se. Sleep, birds of the air, with your pinions at ease;
Sleep, beasts of the field, with entranquillized feet;
Sleep, sleep, and be still.
Mn. Fudge, fudge, I repeat.
Se. For the soft and the terse professor of verse,
Our Agathon now is about to—
Mn. (*scandalized*) No, no!
Se. What's that?
Mn. 'Twas the *ether, forgetting to blow!*
Se. (*beginning pettishly, but soon falling back into his former tone*)

I was going to say he is going to lay
The stocks and the scaffolds for building a play.
And neatly he hews them, and sweetly he glues them,
And a proverb he takes, and an epithet makes,
And he moulds a most waxen and delicate song,
And he tunnels, and funnels, and—

Mn. Does what is wrong.

Se. What clown have we here, so close to our eaves?

Mn. Why, one who will take you and him, by your leaves,
Both you and your terse professor of verse,
And with blows and with knocks set you both on the stocks,
And tunnel and funnel, and pummel, and worse.

Se. Old man, you must have been a rare pert youngster.

Eu. O, heed not *him*; but quickly call me out
Your master Agathon; do pray make haste.

Se. No need of prayer: he's coming forth directly.
He's moulding odes; and in the cold hard winter
He cannot turn, and twist, and shape his strophes
Until they are warmed and softened in the sun.

The SERVANT *goes back into the house.*

Mn. And what am I to do?

Eu. You're to keep quiet.
O Zeus! the Hour is come, and so's the Man!

Mn. O, what's the matter? what disturbs you so?
O, tell me what: I really want to know.
Come, I'm your cousin; won't you tell your cousin?

Eu. There's a great danger brewing for my life.

Mn. O, tell your cousin what.

Eu. This hour decides
Whether Euripides shall live or die.

Mn. Why, how is that? There's no tribunal sitting,
No Court, no Council, will be held to-day.
'Tis the Mid-Fast, the third Home-Festival.

Eu. It is! it is! I wish enough it wasn't.
For on this day the womankind have sworn
To hold a great assembly, to discuss
How best to serve me out.

Mn. Good gracious! Why?

Eu. (*with the mild surprise of injured innocence*)
Because, they say, I write lampoons upon them.

Mn. Zeus and Poseidon! they may well say that.
But tell your cousin what you mean to do.

Eu. I want to get the poet Agathon
To go among them.

Mn. Tell your cousin why.

Eu. To mingle in the Assembly, perhaps to speak
On my behalf.

Mn. What, openly, do you mean?

Eu. O no, disguised: dressed up in women's clothes.

Mn. A bright idea that, and worthy you:
For in all craftiness we take the cake.

By a contrivance very common in ancient theatres, a portion of AGATHON'*s house is here wheeled forward, turning on a pivot, so as to disclose the interior of an apartment. The poet is discovered, surrounded by the most effeminate luxuries, and in the act of writing a tragic play. He has just composed, and is now about to recite, a little lyrical dialogue between his Chorus and one of his actors.*

Eu. O, hush!

Mn. What now?

Eu. Here's Agathon himself.

Mn. Where? Which?

Eu. Why there: the man in the machine.

Mn. O dear, what ails me? Am I growing blind?
I see Cyrene; but I see no man.

Eu. Do, pray, be silent; he's just going to sing.

AGATHON *now gives a fantastic little trill.*

Mn. Is it 'the Pathway of the Ants," or what?

AGATHON *now sings his little dialogue in a soft womanly voice and with pretty, effeminate gestures.*

Agathon. (*As actor*) Move ye slowly, with the holy
Torchlight dear to Awful Shades,
Singing sweetly, dancing featly,
Yes, and neatly, freeborn maids.

(*As Chorus*) Whose the song of festal praise?
Only tell us, we are zealous
Evermore our hymns to raise.

(*As actor*) Sing of Leto, sing of Thee too,
Archer of the golden bow,
Bright Apollo, in the hollow
Glades where Ilian rivers flow,
Building buildings, long ago.

(*As Chorus*) Raise the music, softly swelling
To the fame of Leto's name,
To the God in song excelling,
Brightest he, of all there be,
Giving gifts of minstrelsy.

(*As actor*) Sing the maiden, quiver-laden,
From the woodland oaks emerging,
Haunted shades of mountain glades,
Artemis, the ever Virgin.

(*As Chorus*) We rejoice, heart and voice,
Hymning, praising, gently phrasing,
Her, the maiden quiver-laden.

(*As actor*) Soft pulsation of the Asian
Lyre, to which the dancers go,
When the high and holy Graces
Weave their swiftly whirling paces,
Phrygian measure, to and fro.

(*As Chorus*) Lyre Elysian, heavenly vision,
When thy witching tones arise,
Comes the light of joy and gladness
Flashing from immortal eyes.
Eyes will glisten, ears will listen,
When our manful numbers ring.
Mighty master, Son of Leto,
Thine the glory, Thou the King.

MNESILOCHUS *utters a cry of delight.*

Mn. Wonderful! Wonderful!
How sweet, how soft, how ravishing the strain!
What melting words! and as I heard them sung,
Ye amorous Powers, there crept upon my soul
A pleasant, dreamy, rapturous titillation.
And now, dear youth, for I would question thee

And sift thee with the words of Aeschylus,
Whence art thou, what thy country, what thy garb?
Why all this wondrous medley? Lyre and silks,
A minstrel's lute, a maiden's netted hair,
Girdle and wrestler's oil! a strange conjunction.
How comes a sword beside a looking-glass?
What art thou, man or woman? If a man,
Where are his clothes? his red Laconian shoes?
If woman, 'tis not like a woman's shape.
What art thou, speak; or if thou tell me not,
Myself must guess thy gender from thy song.
Ag. Old man, old man, my ears receive the words
Of your tongue's utterance, yet I heed them not.
I choose my dress to suit my poesy.
A poet, sir, must needs adapt his ways
To the high thoughts which animate his soul.
And when he sings of women, he assumes
A woman's garb, and dons a woman's habits.
Mn. (*aside to* EURIPIDES) When you wrote Phaedra, did you take her habits?
Ag. But when he sings of men, his whole appearance
Conforms to man. What nature gives us not,
The human soul aspires to imitate.
Mn. (*as before*) Zounds, if I'd seen you when you wrote the Satyrs!
Ag. Besides, a poet never should be rough,
Or harsh, or rugged. Witness to my words
Anacreon, Alcaeus, Ibycus,
Who when they filtered and diluted song,
Wore soft Ionian manners and attire.
And Phrynichus, perhaps you have seen him, sir,
How fair he was, and beautifully dressed;
Therefore his plays were beautifully fair.
For as the Worker, so the Work will be.
Mn. Then that is why harsh Philocles writes harshly,
And that is why vile Xenocles writes vilely,
And cold Theognis writes such frigid plays.
Ag. Yes, that is why. And I perceiving this
Made myself womanlike.
Mn. My goodness, how?
Eu. O, stop that yapping: in my youthful days
I too was such another one as he.
Mn. Good gracious! I don't envy you your schooling.
Eu. (*sharply*) Pray, let us come to business, sir.
Mn. Say on.
Eu. A wise man, Agathon, compacts his words,
And many thoughts compresses into few.
So, I in my extremity am come
To ask a favour of you.
Ag. Tell me what.
Eu. The womankind at their Home-feast to-day
Are going to pay me out for my lampoons.
Ag. That's bad indeed, but how can I assist you?
Eu. Why, every way. If you'll disguise yourself,
And sit among them like a woman born,
And plead my cause, you'll surely get me off.
There's none but you to whom I dare entrust it.
Ag. Why don't you go yourself, and plead your cause?
Eu. I'll tell you why. They know me well by sight;
And I am grey, you see, and bearded too,
But you've a baby face, a treble voice,
A fair complexion, pretty, smooth, and soft.
Ag. Euripides!
Eu. Yes.
Ag. Wasn't it you who wrote
"You value life; do you think your father doesn't?"
Eu. It was: what then?
Ag. Expect not me to bear
Your burdens; that were foolishness indeed.
Each man must bear his sorrows for himself.
And troubles, when they come, must needs be met
By manful acts, and not by shifty tricks.
Mn. Aye, true for you, your wicked ways are shown
By sinful acts, and not by words alone.
Eu. But tell me really why you fear to go.
Ag. They'd serve me worse than you.
Eu. How so?
Ag. How so?
I'm too much like a woman, and they'd think
That I was come to poach on their preserves.
Mn. Well, I must say that's not a bad excuse.
Eu. Then won't you really help?
Ag. I really won't.
Eu. Thrice luckless I! Euripides is done for!
Mn. O friend! O cousin! don't lose heart like this.
Eu. Whatever can I do?
Mn. Bid *him* go hang!
See here am I; deal with me as you please.
Eu. (*striking while the iron is hot*)
Well, if you'll really give yourself to me,
First throw aside this overcloak.
Mn. 'Tis done.
But how are you going to treat me?
Eu. Shave you here,
And singe you down below.
Mn. (*magnanimously*) Well, do your worst;
I've said you may, and I'll go through with it.
Eu. You've always, Agathon, got a razor handy;
Lend us one, will you?
Ag. Take one for yourself
Out of the razor-case.
Eu. Obliging youth!
(*To* MNESILOCHUS) Now sit you down (MNESILOCHUS *seats himself in a chair*), and puff your right cheek out.
Mn. Oh!
Eu. What's the matter? Shut your mouth, or else
I'll clap a gag in.
Mn. Lackalackaday!
He jumps up, and runs away.
Eu. Where are you fleeing?
Mn. To sanctuary I.
Shall I sit quiet to be hacked like that?
Demeter, no!
Eu. Think how absurd you'll look,
With one cheek shaven, and the other not.
Mn. (*doggedly*) Well, I don't care.

Eu. O, by the Gods, come back.
Pray don't forsake me.
Mn. Miserable me!

He resumes his seat. EURIPIDES *goes on with the shaving.*

Eu. Sit steady; raise your chin; don't wriggle so.
Mn. (*wincing*) O tchi, tchi, tchi!
Eu. There, there, it's over now.
Mn. And I'm, worse luck, a Rifled Volunteer.
Eu. Well, never mind; you're looking beautiful.
Glance in this mirror.
Mn. Well then, hand it here.
Eu. What see you there?
Mn. (*in disgust*) Not me, but Cleisthenes.
Eu. Get up: bend forward. I've to singe you now.
Mn. O me, you'll scald me like a sucking-pig.
Eu. Someone within there, bring me out a torch.
Now then, stoop forward: gently; mind yourself.
Mn. I'll see to that. Hey! I've caught fire there.
Hey!
O, water! water! neighbours, bring your buckets.
Fire! Fire! I tell you; I'm on fire, I am!
Eu. There, it's all right.
Mn. All right, when I'm a cinder?
Eu. Well, well, the worst is over; 'tis indeed.
It won't pain now.
Mn. Faugh, here's a smell of burning!
Drat it, I'm roasted all about the stern.
Eu. Nay, heed it not. I'll have it sponged directly.
Mn. I'd like to catch a fellow sponging *me*.
Eu. Though you begrudge your active personal aid,
Yet, Agathon, you won't refuse to lend us
A dress and sash: you can't deny you've got them.
Ag. Take them, and welcome. I begrudge them not.
Mn. What's first to do?
Eu. Put on this yellow silk.
Mn. By Aphrodite, but 'tis wondrous nice.
Eu. Gird it up tighter.
Mn. Where's the girdle?
Eu. Here.
Mn. Make it sit neatly there about the legs.
Eu. Now for a snood and hair-net.
Ag. Will this do?
It's quite a natty hairdress; it's my nightcap.
Eu. The very thing: i'faith, the very thing.
Mn. Does it look well?
Eu. Zeus! I should think it did!
Now for a mantle.
Ag. Take one from the couch.
Eu. A pair of woman's shoes.
Ag. Well, here are mine.
Mn. Do they look well?
Eu. They are loose enough, I trow.
Ag. You see to that; I've lent you all you need.
Will someone kindly wheel me in again?

Agathon's apartment, with AGATHON *in it, is wheeled back into the house;* EURIPIDES *and* MNESILOCHUS *are left standing on the stage.* EURIPIDES *turns* MNESILOCHUS *round, and surveys him with complacency.*

Eu. There then, the man's a regular woman now,
At least to look at; and if you've to speak,
Put on a feminine mincing voice.
Mn. (*in a shrill treble*) I'll try.
Eu. And now begone, and prosper.
Mn. Wait a bit.
Not till you've sworn—
Eu. Sworn what?
Mn. That if I get
In any scrape, you'll surely see me through.
Eu. I swear by Ether, Zeus's dwelling-place.
Mn. As well by vile Hippocrates's cabin.
Eu. Well, then, I swear by every blessèd God.
Mn. And please remember 'twas your *mind* that swore,
Not your tongue only; please remember that.

The background of the scene opens and a large building is pushed forward upon the stage, representing the Thesmophorium or Temple of the Home-givers. The Athenian ladies, who form the CHORUS *of the Play, are seen, a few lines later, thronging into the orchestra, to assist in the solemnities of the festival, and to take part in the Assembly they are about to hold. The air above them is thick with the smoke of the torches they are bearing in their hands.* EURIPIDES *thinks it time to make himself scarce.* MNESILOCHUS *assumes the fussy airs and treble voice of an Athenian matron, talking to an imaginary maid-servant.*

Eu. O, get you gone: for there's the signal hoisted
Over the Temple; they are assembling now.
I think I'll leave you.
Mn. Thratta, come along.
O Thratta, Thratta, here's a lot of women
Coming up here! O, what a flare of torches!
O sweet Twain-goddesses, vouchsafe me now
A pleasant day, and eke a safe return.
Set down the basket, Thratta; give me out
The sacred cake to offer to the Twain.
O dread Demeter, high unearthly one,
O Persephassa, grant your votaress grace
To join in many festivals like this,
Or if not so, at least escape this once.
And may my daughter, by your leaves, pick up
A wealthy husband, and a fool to boot;
And little Bull-calf have his share of brains.
Now, then, I wonder which is the best place
To hear the speeches? Thratta, you may go.

The officials now take their places, and the Assembly at once begins.

These are not things for servant-girls to hear.
Crieress. Worldly clamour
Pass away!
Silence, Silence,
While we pray;
To the Twain, the Home-bestowers,
Holy Parent, holy Daughter,
And to Wealth, and Heavenly Beauty,
And to Earth the foster-mother,
And to Hermes and the Graces,
That they to this important high debate
Grant favour and success,

Making it useful to the Athenian State,
And to ourselves no less.
And O, that she who counsels best to-day
About the Athenian nation,
And our own commonwealth of women, may
Succeed by acclamation.
These things we pray, and blessings on our cause.
Sing Paean, Paean, ho! with merry loud applause.

Chorus. We in thy prayers combine,
And we trust the Powers Divine
Will on these their suppliants smile,
Both Zeus the high and awful,
And the golden-lyred Apollo
From the holy Delian isle.
And thou, our Mighty Maiden,
Lance of gold, and eye of blue,
Of the God-contested city,
Help us too:
And the many-named, the Huntress,
Gold-fronted Leto's daughter;
And the dread Poseidon ruling
Over Ocean's stormy water;
Come from the deep where fishes
Swarm, and the whirlwinds rave;
And the Oreads of the mountain,
And the Nereids of the wave.
Let the Golden Harp sound o'er us
And the Gods with favour crown
This Parliament of Women,
The free and noble matrons
Of the old Athenian town.

Cr. O yes! O yes!
Pray ye the Olympian Gods—and Goddesses,
And all the Pythian Gods—and Goddesses,
And all the Delian Gods—and Goddesses,
And all the other Gods—and Goddesses,
Whoso is disaffected, ill-disposed
Towards this commonwealth of womankind,
Or with Euripides, or with the Medes
Deals to the common hurt of womankind,
Or aims at tyranny, or fain would bring
The Tyrant back; or dares betray a wife
For palming off a baby as her own;
Or tells her master tales against her mistress;
Or does not bear a message faithfully;
Or, being a suitor, makes a vow, and then
Fails to perform; or, being a rich old woman,
Hires for herself a lover with her wealth;
Or, being a girl, takes gifts and cheats the giver;
Or, being a trading man or trading woman,
Gives us short measure in our drinking-cups;
Perish that man, himself and all his house;
But pray the Gods—and Goddesses—to order
To all the women always all things well.

Ch. We also pray,
And trust it may
Be done as thou premisest,
And hope that they
Will win the day
Whose words are best and wisest.
But they who fain
Would cheat for gain,
Their solemn oaths forgetting,
Our ancient laws
And noble cause
And mystic rites upsetting;
Who plot for greed,
Who call the Mede
With secret invitation,
I say that these
The Gods displease,
And wrong the Athenian nation.
O Zeus most high
In earth and sky,
All-powerful, all-commanding,
We pray to Thee,
Weak women we,
But help us notwithstanding.

Cr. O yes! O yes! The Women's Council-Board
Hath thus enacted (moved by Sostrata,
President Timocleia, clerk Lysilla),
To hold a morning Parliament to-day
When women most have leisure; to discuss
What shall be done about Euripides,
How best to serve him out; for that he's guilty
We all admit. Who will address the meeting?

1st. Woman. I wish to, I.

Cr. Put on this chaplet first.
Order! Order! Silence, ladies, if you please.
She's learnt the trick; she hems and haws;
she coughs in preparation;
I know the signs; my soul divines
a mighty long oration.

1st. W. 'Tis not from any feeling of ambition
I rise to address you, ladies, but because
I long have seen, and inly burned to see
The way Euripides insults us all,
The really quite interminable scoffs
This market-gardener's son pours out against us.
I don't believe that there's a single fault
He's not accused us of; I don't believe
That there's a single theatre or stage,
But there is he. calling us double-dealers,
False, faithless, tippling, mischief-making gossips,
A rotten set, a misery to men.
Well, what's the consequence?
The men come home
Looking so sour—O, *we* can see them peeping
In every closet, thinking friends are there.
Upon my word we can't do *anything*
We used to do; he has made the men so silly
Suppose I'm hard at work upon a chaplet,
"Hey, she's in love with somebody"; suppose
I chance to drop a pitcher on the floor,
And straightway 'tis, "For whom was that intended?
I warrant now, for our Corinthian friend."
Is a girl ill? Her brother shakes his head;
"The girl's complexion is not to my taste."
Why, if you merely want to hire a baby,
And palm it off as yours, you've got no chance,
They sit beside our very beds, they do.
Then there's another thing; the rich old men
Who used to marry us, are grown so shy
We never catch them now; and all because

Euripides declares, the scandal-monger,
"An old man weds a tyrant, not a wife."
You know, my sisters, how they mew us up,
Guarding our women's rooms with bolts and seals
And fierce Molossian dogs. That's all his doing.
We might put up with that; but, O my friends,
Our little special perquisites, the corn,
The wine, the oil, gone, gone, all gone forever.
They've got such keys, our husbands have, such brutes,
Laconian-made, with triple rows of teeth.
Then in old times we only had to buy
A farthing ring, and pantry-doors flew open.
But now this wretch Euripides has made them
Wear such worm-eaten perforated seals,
'Tis hopeless now to try it. Therefore, ladies,
What I propose is that we slay the man,
Either by poison or some other way;
Somehow or other he must die the death.
That's all I'll say in public: I'll write out
A formal motion with the clerkess there.

Ch. Good heavens! what force and tact combined!
O, what a many-woven mind!
A better speech, upon my word,
I don't believe I ever heard.
Her thoughts so clean dissected,
Her words so well selected,
Such keen discrimination,
Such power and elevation,
'Twas really quite a grand, superb, magnificent oration.
So that if, in opposition,
Xenocles came forth to speak,
Compared with her
You'd all aver
All his grandest, happiest efforts are immeasurably weak!

2nd. Woman. Ladies, I've only a few words to add.
I quite agree with the honourable lady
Who has just sat down: she has spoken well and ably.
But I can tell you what I've borne myself.
My husband died in Cyprus, leaving me
Five little chicks to work and labour for.
I've done my best, and bad's the best, but still
I've fed them, weaving chaplets for the Gods.
But now this fellow writes his plays, and says
There are no Gods; and so, you may depend,
My trade is fallen to half; men won't buy chaplets.
So then for many reasons he must die;
The man is bitterer than his mother's potherbs.
I leave my cause with you, my sisters: I
Am called away on urgent private business,
An order, just received, for twenty chaplets.

Ch. Better and better still.
A subtler intellect, a daintier skill.
Wise are her words, and few;
Well timed and spoken too.
A many-woven mind she too has got, I find.
And he must clearly,
This rascal man, be punished most severely.

The motion for putting EURIPIDES *to death having, so to say, been proposed and seconded,* MNESILOCHUS *rises to speak in opposition.*

Mn. Mrs. Speaker and ladies,
I'm not surprised, of course I'm not surprised,
To find you all so angry and aggrieved
At what Euripides has said against us.
For I myself—or slay my babies else—
Hate him like poison, to be sure I do,
He's most provoking, I admit he is.
But now we're all alone, there's no reporter,
All among friends, why not be fair and candid?
Grant that the man has really found us out,
And told a thing or two, sure they're all *true*,
And there's a many thousand still behind.
For I myself, to mention no one else,
Could tell a thousand plaguy tricks I've played
On my poor husband; I'll just mention one.
We'd been but three days married; I'm abed,
Husband asleep beside me; when my lover
(I'd been familiar with him from a child)
Came softly scratching at the outer door.
I hear; I know "the little clinking sound,"
And rise up stealthily, to creep downstairs.
"Where go you, pray?" says husband. "Where!" say I,
"I've such a dreadful pain in my inside
I must go down this instant." "Go," says he.
He pounds his anise, juniper, and sage,
To still my pains: *I* seize the water-jug,
And wet the hinge, to still its creaking noise,
Then open, and go out: and I and lover
Meet by Aguieus and his laurel-shade,
Billing and cooing to our hearts' content.
(*With vivacity*) Euripides has never found out that.
Nor how a wife contrived to smuggle out
Her frightened lover, holding up her shawl
To the sun's rays for husband to admire.
Nor how we grant our favours to bargees
And muleteers, if no one else we've got.
Nor how, arising from a night's debauch,
We chew our garlic, that our husbands, coming
Back from the walls at daybreak, may suspect
Nothing amiss at home. Then what's the odds
If he does rail at Phaedra? Let him rail.
What's that to us? Let him rail on, say I.
Phaedra indeed! He might come nearer home.
I knew a woman, I won't mention names,
Remained ten days in childbirth. Why, do you think?
Because she couldn't buy a baby sooner.
Her husband runs to every medicine-man
In dreadful agitation; while he's out,
They bring a little baby in a basket,
Bunging its mouth up that it mayn't cry out,
And stow it safe away till he comes home.
Then at a given sigh she feebly says,
"My time is come: please, husband, go away."
He goes; they open basket; baby cries.
O, what delight, surprise, congratulations!
The man runs in; the nurse comes running out,
(The same that brought the baby in the basket),

"A prodigy! a Lion! such a boy!
Your form, your features: just the same expression:
Your very image: lucky, lucky man!"
Don't we do this? By Artemis, we do.
Then wherefore rail we at Euripides?
We're not one bit more sinned against than sinning.
Ch. What a monstrous, strange proceeding!
Whence, I wonder, comes her breeding?
From what country shall we seek her,
Such a bold, audacious speaker?
That a woman so should wrong us,
Here among us, here among us,
I could never have believed it;
such a thing was never known.
But what *may* be, no man knoweth,
And the wise old proverb showeth,
That perchance a poisonous sophist
lurketh under every stone.
O, nothing, nothing in the world
so hateful you will find
As shameless women, save of course
the rest of womankind.
1st. W. What can possess us, sisters mine?
I vow by old Agraulus,
We're all bewitched, or else have had
some strange mischance befall us,
To let this shameless hussy tell
her shameful, bold, improper
Unpleasant tales, and we not make
the least attempt to stop her.
If anyone assist me, good; if not, alone we'll try,
We'll strip and whip her well, we will,
my serving-maids and I.
Mn. Not strip me, gentle ladies; sure
I heard the proclamation,
That every freeborn woman now
might make a free oration;
And if I spoke unpleasant truths
on this your invitation,
Is that a reason why I now
should suffer castigation?
1st. W. It is, indeed: how dare you plead
for him who always chooses
Such odious subjects for his plays,
on purpose to abuse us?
Phaedras and Melanippes too:
but ne'er a drama made he
About the good Penelope,
or such-like virtuous lady.
Mn. The cause I know; the cause I'll show:
you won't discover any
Penelope alive to-day, but Phaedras very many.
1st. W. You will? you dare? how *can* we bear
to hear such things repeated,
Such horrid, dreadful, odious things?
Mn. O, I've not near completed
The things I know; I'll give the whole:
I'm not disposed to grudge it.
1st. W. You can't, I vow; you've emptied now
your whole disgusting budget.
Mn. No, not one thousandth part I've told:
not even how we take
The scraper from the bathing-room,
and down the corn we rake,
And push it in, and tap the bin.
1st. W. Confound you and your slanders!
Mn. Nor how the Apaturian meat
we steal to give our panders,
And then declare the cat was there.
1st. W. You nasty telltale you!
Mn. Nor how with deadly axe a wife
her lord and master slew,
Another drove her husband mad
with poisonous drugs fallacious,
Nor how beneath the reservoir
the Acharnian girl—
1st. W. Good gracious!
Mn. Buried her father out of sight.
1st. W. Now really this won't do.
Mn. Nor how when late your servant bare
a child as well as you,
You took her boy, and in his stead
your puling girl you gave her.
1st. W. O, by the Two,[1] this jade shall rue
her insolent behaviour.
I'll comb your fleece, you saucy minx.
Mn. By Zeus, you had best begin it.
1st. W. Come on!
Mn. Come on!
1st. W. You will? you will?
(*Flinging her upper mantle to* PHILISTA)
Hold this, my dear, a minute.
Mn. Stand off, or else, by Artemis,
I'll give you such a strumming—
Ch. For pity's sake, be silent there:
I see a woman coming.
Who looks as if she'd news to tell.
Now prithee both be quiet
And let us hear the tale she brings,
without this awful riot.

Enter CLEISTHENES, *dressed as a woman.*

Cleisthenes. Dear ladies, I am one with you in heart;
My cheeks, unfledged, bear witness to my love,
I am your patron, aye, and devotee.
And now, for lately in the market-place
I heard a rumour touching you and yours,
I come to warn and put you on your guard,
Lest this great danger take you unawares.
Ch. What now, my child? for we may call thee child,
So soft, and smooth, and downy are thy cheeks.
Cl. Euripides, they say, has sent a cousin,
A bad old man, amongst you here to-day.
Ch. O, why and wherefore, and with what design?
Cl. To be a spy, a horrid, treacherous spy,
A spy on all your purposes and plans.
Ch. O, how should he be here, and we not know it?
Cl. Euripides has tweezered him, and singed him,
And dressed him up, disguised in women's clothes.

[1]Demeter and Persephone.

Mn. (*stamping about with a lively recollection of his recent sufferings*)
I don't believe it; not one word of it;
No man would let himself be tweezered so.
Ye Goddesses, I don't believe there's one.
Cl. Nonsense: I never should have come here else,
I had it on the best authority.
Ch. This is a most important piece of news.
We'll take immediate steps to clear this up.
We'll search him out: we'll find his lurking-place.
Zounds, if we catch him! r-r-r! the rascal man.
Will you, kind gentleman, assist the search?
Give us fresh cause to thank you, patron mine.
Cl. (*to* FIRST WOMAN) Well, who are you?
Mn. (*aside*) Wherever can I flee?
Cl. I'll find him, trust me.
Mn. (*aside*) Here's a precious scrape!
1st. W. Who? I?
Cl. Yes, you.
1st. W. Cleonymus's wife.
Cl. Do you know her, ladies? Is she speaking truth?
Ch. O yes, we know her: pass to someone else.
Cl. Who's this young person with the baby here?
1st. W. O, she's my nursemaid.
Mn. (*aside*) Here he comes; I'm done for.
Cl. Hey! where's she off to? Stop! Why, what the mischief!
Ch. (*aside to* CLEISTHENES) Yes, sift her well; discover who she is.
We know the others, but we don't know her.
Cl. Come, come, no shuffling, madam, turn this way.
Mn. (*fretfully*) Don't pull me, sir, I'm poorly.
Cl. Please to tell me
Your husband's name.
Mn. My husband's name? my husband's?
Why What-d'ye-call-him from Cothocidae.
Cl. Eh, what? (*Considers*)
There was a What-d'ye-call-him once—
Mn. He's Who-d'ye-call-it's son.
Cl. You're trifling with me.
Have you been here before?
Mn. O, bless you, yes.
Why, every year.
Cl. And with what tent-companion?
Mn. With What's-her-name.
Cl. This is sheer idling, woman.
1st. W. (*to* CLEISTHENES) Step back, sir, please, and let me question her
On last year's rites; a little further, please;
No *man* must listen now.
(*To* MNESILOCHUS) Now, stranger, tell me
What first we practised on that holy day.
Mn. Bless me, what was it? first? why, first we—drank.
1st. W. Right; what was second?
Mn. Second? Drank again.
1st. W. Somebody's told you this. But what was third?
Mn. Well, third, Xenylla had a drop too much.
1st. W. Ah, that won't do. Here, Cleisthenes, approach.
This is the *man* for certain.
Cl. Bring him up.

MNESILOCHUS *is seized, carried before a jury of matrons, and pronounced a man! A general uproar ensues.*

1st. W. Strip off his clothes! for there's no truth in him.
Mn. What! strip the mother of nine little ones?
Cl. Loosen that belt, look sharp, you shameless thing.
1st. W. She does appear a stout and sturdy one:
Upon my word, she has no breasts like ours.
Mn. Because I'm barren, never had a child.
1st. W. Yes, *now*; but *then* you had nine little ones!
Cl. Stand up and show yourself. See! he's a man!
1st. W. O, this is why you mocked and jeered us so!
And dared defend Euripides like that!
O, villain, villain. . . .
Mn. Miserable me!
I've put my foot in it, and no mistake.
1st. W. What shall we do with him?
Cl. Surround him here,
And watch him shrewdly that he 'scape you not.
I'll go at once and summon the police.

CLEISTHENES *goes out.*

Chorus

Light we our torches, my sisters,
and manfully girding our robes,
Gather them sternly about us,
and casting our mantles aside
On through the tents and the gangways,
and up by the tiers and the rows,
Eyeing, and probing, and trying,
where men would be likely to hide.

Now 'tis time, 'tis time, my sisters,
round and round and round to go,
Soft, with light and airy footfall,
creeping, peeping, high and low.
Look about in each direction,
make a rigid, close inspection,
Lest in any hole or corner,
other rogues escape detection.
Hunt with care, here and there,
Searching, spying, poking, prying,
up and down, and everywhere.

For if once the evil-doer we can see,
He shall soon be a prey to our vengeance to-day,
And to all men a warning he shall be
Of the terrible fate that is sure to await
The guilty sin-schemer and lawless blasphemer.
And then he shall find that the Gods are not blind
To what passes below;
Yea, and all men shall know
It is best to live purely, uprightly, securely,
It is best to do well,
And to practise day and night
what is orderly and right,
And in virtue and in honesty to dwell.

But if anyone there be who a wicked deed shall do
In his raving, and his raging,
and his madness, and his pride,
Every mortal soon shall see,
aye, and every woman too,
What a doom shall the guilty one betide.
For the wicked evil deed
shall be recompensed with speed,
The Avenger doth not tarry to begin,
Nor delayeth for a time,
but He searcheth out the crime,
And He punisheth the sinner in his sin.

Now we've gone through every corner,
every nook surveyed with care,
And there's not another culprit
skulking, lurking anywhere.

Just as the CHORUS *are concluding their search,* MNESILOCHUS *snatches the* FIRST WOMAN'S *baby from her arms, and takes refuge at the altar.*

1*st. W.* Hoy! Hoy there! Hoy!
He's got my child, he's got my darling, O!
He's snatched my little baby from my breast.
O, stop him, stop him! O, he's gone. O! O!
Mn. Aye, weep! you ne'er shall dandle him again,
Unless you loose me. Soon shall these small limbs,
Smit with cold edge of sacrificial knife,
Incarnadine this altar.
1*st. W.* O! O! O!
Help, women, help me. Sisters, help, I pray.
Charge to the rescue, shout, and rout, and scout
him.
Don't see me lose my baby, my one pet.
Ch. Alas! Alas!
Mercy o' me! what do I see?
What can it be?
What, will deeds of shameless violence
never, never, never, end?
What's the matter, what's he up to,
what's he doing now, my friend?
Mn. Doing what I hope will crush you
out of all your bold assurance.
Ch. Zounds, his words are very dreadful;
more than dreadful, past endurance.
1*st. W.* Yes, indeed, they're very dreadful,
and he's got my baby too.
Ch. Impudence rare! Look at him there,
Doing such deeds, and I vow and declare
Never minding or caring—
Mn. Or likely to care.
1*st. W.* Here you are come: here you shall stay,
Never again shall you wander away;
Wander away, glad to display
All the misdeeds you have done us to-day,
But dear you shall pay.
Mn. There at least I'm hoping, ladies,
I shall find your words untrue.
Ch. What God do you think his assistance will
lend,
You wicked old man, to escort you away?

Mn. Aha, but I've captured your baby, my friend,
And I shan't let her go, for the best you can say.
Ch. But no, by the Goddesses Twain,
Not long shall our threats be in vain,
Not long shall you flout at our pain.
Unholy your deeds, and you'll find
That *we* shall repay you in kind,
And perchance you will alter your mind
When Fate, veering round like the blast,
In its clutches has seized you at last,
Very fast.
Comrades, haste, collect the brushwood:
pile it up without delay:
Pile it, heap it, stow it, throw it,
burn and fire and roast and slay.
1*st. W.* Come, Mania, come; let's run and fetch
the fagots.
(*To* MNESILOCHUS) Ah, wretch, you'll be a cinder
before night.
Mn. (*Busily engaged in unpacking the baby*)
With all my heart. Now I'll undo these wrappers,
These Cretan long clothes; and remember, darling,
It's all your mother that has served you thus.
What have we here? a flask, and not a baby!
A flask of wine, for all its Persian slippers.
O ever thirsty, ever tippling women,
O ever ready with fresh schemes for drink,
To vintners what a blessing: but to us
And all our goods and chattels what a curse!
1*st. W.* Drag in the fagots, Mania; pile them up.
Mn. Aye, pile away; but tell me, is this baby
Really your own?
1*st. W.* My very flesh and blood.
Mn. Your flesh and blood?
1*st. W.* By Artemis it is.
Mn. Is it a pint?
1*st. W.* O, what have you been doing?
O, you have stripped my baby of its clothes.
Poor tiny morsel!
Mn. (*holding up a large bottle*) Tiny?
1*st. W.* Yes, indeed.
Mn. What is its age? Three Pitcher-feasts or four?
1*st. W.* Well, thereabouts, a little over now.
Please give it back.
Mn. No thank you, not exactly.
1*st. W.* We'll burn you then.
Mn. O, burn me by all means;
But anyhow I'll sacrifice this victim.
1*st. W.* O! O! O!
Make *me* your victim, anything you like;
But spare the child.
Mn. A loving mother truly.
But this dear child must needs be sacrificed.
1*st. W.* My child! my child! give me the bason,
Mania,
I'll catch my darling's blood at any rate.
Mn. And so you shall; I'll not deny you that.

Puts the bottle to his lips and drains every drop, taking care that none shall fall into the bason which the FIRST WOMAN *is holding underneath.*

1*st. W.* You spiteful man! you most ungenerous
man!

Mn. This skin, fair priestess, is your perquisite.
1st. W. What is my perquisite?
Mn. This skin, fair priestess.
Another woman, CRITYLLA, *now enters.*
Critylla. O Mica, who has robbed thee of thy flower,
And snatched thy babe, thine only one, away?
1st. W. This villain here: but I'm so glad you're come.
You see he doesn't run away, while I
Call the police, with Cleisthenes, to help us. *Exit.*
Mn. (*soliloquizes*) O me, what hope of safety still remains?
What plan? what stratagem? My worthy cousin,
Who first involved me in this dreadful scrape,
"He cometh not." Suppose I send him word.
But how to send it? Hah, I know a trick
Out of his *Palamede.*[1] I'll send a message
Written on oar-blades. Tush! I've got no oar-blades.
What shall I do for oar-blades? Why not send
These votive slabs instead? The very thing.
Oar-blades are wood, and slabs are wood. I'll try.
(*Writes, singing as he does so.*)
Now for the trick; fingers be quick;
Do what you can for my notable plan.
Slab, have the grace to permit me to trace
Grooves with my knife on your beautiful face.
The tale of my woe it is yours for to show.
O, o, what a furrow! I never did see
Such a horrible "R" as I've made it to be.
Well, that must do; so fly away you,
Hither and thither, off, off, and away.
Do not delay for a moment, I pray.
All the actors leave the stage; but MNESILOCHUS *is unable to leave, and* CRITYLLA *remains to keep watch.*

Chorus

Now let us turn to the people,
our own panegyric to render.
Men never speak a good word,
never one, for the feminine gender,
Every one says we're a Plague,
the source of all evils to man,
War, dissension, and strife.
Come, answer me this, if you can;
Why, if we're *really* a Plague,
you're so anxious to have us for wives;
And charge us not to be peeping,
nor to stir out of doors for our lives.
Isn't it silly to guard
a Plague with such scrupulous care?
Zounds! how you rave, coming home,
if your poor little wife isn't there.
Should you not rather be glad,
and rejoice all the days of your life,
Rid of a *Plague*, you know,
the source of dissension and strife?
If on a visit we sport,
and sleep when the sporting is over,
O, how you rummage about;
what a fuss, your lost Plague to discover.
Every one stares at your Plague
if she happens to look on the street:
Stares all the more if your Plague
thinks proper to blush and retreat.
Is it not plain then, I ask,
that Women are really the best?
What, can you doubt that we are?
I will bring it at once to the test.
We say Women are best;
you men (just like you) deny it,
Nothing on earth is so easy
as to come to the test, and to try it.
I'll take the name of a Man,
and the name of a Woman, and show it.
Did not Charminus give way
to Miss-Fortune? Do you not know it?
Is not Cleophon viler
than vile Salabaccho by far?
Is there a Man who can equal,
in matters of glory and war,
Lady Victoria, Mistress
of Marathon, queen of the Sea?
Is not Prudence a Woman,
and who is so clever as she?
Certainly none of your statesmen,
who only a twelvemonth ago
Gave up their place and their duty.
Would women demean themselves so?
Women don't ride in their coaches,
as Men have been doing of late,
Pockets and purses distended
with cash they have filched from the State.
We, at the very outside,
steal a wee little jorum of corn,
Putting it back in the even,
whatever we took in the morn.
But this is a true description of you.
Are ye not gluttonous, vulgar, perverse,
Kidnappers, housebreakers, footpads, and worse?
And we in domestic economy too
Are thriftier, shiftier, wiser than you.
For the loom which our mothers
employed with such skill,
With its Shafts and its Thongs,
we are working it still.
And the ancient umbrella by no means is done,
We are wielding it yet,
as our Shield from the Sun.
But O for the Shafts,
and the Thong of the Shield,
Which your Fathers in fight
were accustomed to wield.
Where are they to-day?
Ye have cast them away

[1]Palamede was put to death before Troy; and his brother Oeax, wishing to send the news to his father in Euboea, wrote it upon oar-blades which he cast into the sea. The "votive slabs" are tablets with votive inscriptions.

As ye raced, in hot haste,
and disgraced, from the fray!

Many things we have against you,
many rules we justly blame;
But the one we now will mention
is the most enormous shame.
What, my masters! ought a lady,
who has borne a noble son,
One who in your fleets and armies
great heroic deeds has done,
Ought she to remain unhonoured?
ought she not, I ask you, I,
In our Stenia and our Scira[1]
still to take precedence high?
Whoso breeds a cowardly soldier,
or a seaman cold and tame.
Crop her hair, and seat her lowly;
brand her with the marks of shame;
Set the nobler dame above her.
Can it, all ye Powers, be right
That Hyperbolus's mother,
flowing-haired, and robed in white,
Should in public places sit by
Lamachus's mother's side,
Hoarding wealth, and lending monies,
gathering profits far and wide?
Sure 'twere better every debtor,
calm, resolving not to pay,
When she comes exacting money,
with a mild surprise should say,
Keeping principal and income, "You to claim percentage due!
Sure a son so capital is *capital* enough for you."

The close of the Parabasis finds the position of MNESILOCHUS *unaltered. The dispatch of the tablets has, so far, produced no result.*

Mn. I've strained my eyes with watching; but my poet,
"He cometh not." Why not? Belike he feels
Ashamed of his old frigid *Palamede.*
Which is the play to fetch him? O, I know;
Which but his brand-new *Helen*? I'll be Helen.
I've got the woman's clothes, at all events.

Cr. What are you plotting? What is that you're muttering?
I'll Helen you, my master, if you don't
Keep quiet there till the policeman comes.

Mn. (*as Helen*) "These are the fair-nymphed waters of the Nile,
Whose floods bedew, in place of heavenly showers,
Egypt's white plains and black-dosed citizens."

Cr. Sweet-shining Hecate, what a rogue it is.

Mn. "Ah, not unknown my Spartan fatherland,
Nor yet my father Tyndareus."

Cr. My gracious!
Was *he* your father? Sure, Phrynondas was.

Mn. "And I was Helen."

Cr. What, again a woman?
You've not been punished for your first freak yet.

Mn. "Full many a soul, by bright Scamander's stream,
Died for my sake."

Cr. Would yours had died among them!

Mn. "And now I linger here; but Menelaus,
My dear, dear lord, ah wherefore comes he not?
O sluggish crows, to spare my hapless life!
But soft! some hope is busy at my heart,
A laughing hope—O Zeus, deceive me not."

EURIPIDES *enters disguised as Menelaus.*

Eu. Who is the lord of this stupendous pile?
Will he extend his hospitable care
To some poor storm-tossed, shipwrecked mariners?

Mn. "These are the halls of Proteus."

Eu. Proteus, are they?

Cr. O, by the Twain, he lies like anything.
I knew old Protteas; he's been dead these ten years.

Eu. "Then whither, whither have we steered our bark?"

Mn. "To Egypt."

Eu. "O, the weary, weary way!"

Cr. Pray don't believe one single word he says.
This is the holy temple of the Twain.

Eu. "Know you if Proteus be at home or not?"

Cr. Why, don't I tell you, he's been dead these ten years!
You can't have quite got over your sea-sickness,
Asking if Protteas be at home or not.

Eu. "Woe's me! is Proteus dead? and where's he buried?"

Mn. "This is his tomb whereon I'm sitting now."

Cr. O, hang the rascal; and he *shall* be hanged!
How dare he say this altar is a tomb?

Eu. "And wherefore sitt'st thou on this monument,
Veiled in thy mantle, lady?"

Mn. "They compel me,
A weeping bride, to marry Proteus' son."

Cr. Why do you tell the gentleman such fibs?
Good gentleman, he's a bad man; he came
Among the women here, to steal their trinkets.

Mn. "Aye, aye, rail on: revile me as you list."

Eu. "Who is the old woman who reviles you, lady?"

Mn. "Theonoë, Proteus' daughter."

Cr. What a story!
Why, I'm Critylla, of Gargettus, sir,
A very honest woman.

Mn. "Aye, speak on.
But never will I wed thy brother, no,
I won't be false to absent Menelaus."

Eu. "What, lady, what? O, raise those orbs to mine."

Mn. "O sir, I blush to raise them, with these cheeks."

Eu. "O dear, O dear, I cannot speak for trembling.
Ye Gods, is't possible? Who art thou, lady?"

Mn. "O, who art thou? I feel the same myself."

Eu. "Art thou Hellenic, or a born Egyptian?"

Mn. "Hellenic I: O, tell me what art thou."

[1]Women's feasts.

Eu. "O surely, surely, thou art Helen's self."
Mn. "O, from the greens thou must be Menelaus."
Eu. "Yes, yes, you see that miserable man."
Mn. "O, long in coming to these longing arms,
O, carry me, carry me, from this place,
O, wrap me in thy close embrace,
O, carry me, carry me, carry me home,
by this fond and loving kiss,
O, take me, take me, take me hence."
Cr. I say now, none of this.
Let go there, or I'll strike you with this link!
Eu. "Let go my wife, the child of Tyndareus,
Not take her home to Sparta? O, what mean you?"
Cr. O, that's it, is it? You're a bad one too!
Both of one gang. That's what your gipsying
meant!
But he at any rate shall meet his due.
Here's the policeman, and the Scythian coming.
Eu. Ah, this won't do: I must slip off awhile,
Mn. And what am I to do?
Eu. Keep quiet here,
Be sure I'll never fail you while I live;
I have ten thousand tricks to save you yet.
Mn. Well, you caught nothing by *that* haul, I think.

The high official, who is here inadequately called "A POLICEMAN," *now enters upon the stage, attended by one of the Scythian archers.*

Policeman. O archer, here's the vagabond, of
whom Cleisthenes told us.
(*to* MNESILOCHUS) Why do you hang your head?
(*to* SCYTHIAN) Take him within; there tie him on
the plank;
Then bring him here and watch him. Let not any
Approach too near him: should they try to, take
The whip, and smite them.
Cr. Aye, one came but now
Spinning his yarns, and all but got him off.
Mn. O sir! policeman! grant me one request,
O, by that hand I pray you, which you love
To hold out empty, and to draw back full.
Po. What should I grant you?
Mn. Don't expose me thus;
Do tell the Scythian he may strip me first;
Don't let a poor old man, in silks and snoods,
Provoke the laughter of the crows that eat him.
Po. Thus hath the Council ordered it, that so
The passers-by may see the rogue you are.
Mn. Alas! alas! O yellow silk, I hate ye!
O, I've no hope, no hope of getting free.

All the actors leave the stage. And the CHORUS *commence their great ceremonial worship of dance and song*

Chorus.

Now for the revels, my sisters,
which we to the great Twain Powers
Prayerfully, carefully raise,
in the holy festival hours.
And Pauson will join in our worship to-day,
And Pauson will join in the fasting,
And, keen for the fast, to the Twain he will pray
For the rite to be made everlasting, I ween,
For the rite to be made everlasting.

Now advance
In the whirling, twirling dance,
With hand linked in hand, as we deftly trip along,
Keeping time to the cadence
of the swiftly-flowing song;
And be sure as we go
That we dart careful glances,
up and down, and to and fro.

Now 'tis ours
To entwine our choicest flowers,
Flowers of song and adoration
to the great Olympian Powers.

Nor expect
That the garland will be flecked
With abuse of mortal men;
such a thought is incorrect.

For with prayer
And with sacred loving care,
A new and holy measure we will heedfully prepare.

To the high and holy Minstrel[1]
Let the dancers onward go,
And to Artemis, the maiden
Of the quiver and the bow;
O, hear us, Far-controller, and the victory bestow.
And we trust our merry music
Will the matron Hera please,
For she loves the pleasant Chorus
And the dances such as these,
—Wearing at her girdle
The holy nuptial keys.

To Pan and pastoral Hermes
And the friendly Nymphs we pray,
That they smile with gracious favour
On our festival to-day,
With their laughter-loving glances
beaming brightly on our Play,
As we dance the Double chorus
To the old familiar strain,
As we weave our ancient pastime
On our holy day again,
—Keeping fast and vigil
In the Temple of the Twain.

Turn the step, and change the measure,
Raise a loftier music now;
Come, the Lord of wine and pleasure,
Evoi, Bacchus, lead us thou!

Yea, for Thee we adore!
Child of Semele, thee
With thy glittering ivy-wreaths,
Thee with music and song
Ever and ever we praise.

[1]Apollo.

Thee with thy wood-nymphs delightedly singing,
Evoi! Evoi! Evoi!

Over the joyous hills
the sweet strange melody ringing
Hark! Cithaeron resounds,
Pleased the notes to prolong;
Hark! the bosky ravines
And the wild slopes thunder and roar,
Volleying back the song.
Round thee the ivy fair
With delicate tendril twines.

The SCYTHIAN *brings* MNESILOCHUS *in, fastened to his plank, and sets it up on the stage.*

Scythian. Dere now bemoany to de ouder air.
Mn. O, I entreat you.
Sc. Nod endread me zu.
Mn. Slack it a little.
Sc. Dat is vat I does.
Mn. O mercy! mercy! O, you drive it tighter.
Sc. Dighder zu wiss him?
Mn. Miserable me!
Out on you, villain.
Sc. Zilence, bad ole man.
I'se fetch de mad, an' vatch zu comfibly.
Mn. These are the joys Euripides has brought me!

EURIPIDES *makes a momentary appearance in the character of Perseus.*

O Gods! O Saviour Zeus! there's yet a hope.
Then he won't fail me! Out he flashed as Perseus.
I understand the signals, I'm to act
The fair Andromeda in chains. Ah, well,
Here are the chains, worse luck, wherewith to act her.
He'll come and succour me; he's in the wings.

(*Euripides enters singing airily.*)

Eu. Now to peep, now to creep
Soft and slily through.
Maidens, pretty maidens,
Tell me what I am to do.
Tell me how to glide
By the Scythian Argus-eyed,
And to steal away my bride.
Tell me, tell me, tell me, tell me,
tell me, tell me, tell,
Echo, always lurking in the cavern and the dell.

EURIPIDES *retires, and* MNESILOCHUS *commences a Euripidean monody, mostly composed of quotations from the* Andromeda *adapted to his own position.*

Mn. "A cold unpitying heart had he
Who bound me here in misery.
Hardly escaped from mouldy dame,
I'm caught and done for, just the same
Lo, the Scythian guard beside me,
Friendless, helpless, here he tied me;
Soon upon these limbs of mine
Shall the greedy ravens dine.
Seest thou? not to me belong
Youthful pleasures, dance and song,
Never, never more shall I
With my friends sweet law-suits try,
But woven chains with many a link surround me,
Till Glaucetes, that ravening whale, has found me.
Home I nevermore shall see;
Bridal songs are none for me,
Nought but potent incantations;
Sisters, raise your lamentations,
Woe, woe, woeful me,
Sorrow, and trouble, and misery,
Weeping, weeping, endless weeping,
Far from home and all I know,
Praying him who wronged me so.
O! O! Woe! woe!
First with razor keen he hacks me,
Next in yellow silk he packs me,
Sends me then to dangerous dome,
Where the women prowl and roam.
O heavy Fate! O fatal blow!
O woeful lot! and lots of woe!
O, how they will chide me,
and gibe, and deride me!
And O that the flashing, and roaring, and dashing
Red bolt of the thunder
might smite me in sunder—
The Scythian who lingers beside me!
For where is the joy of the sunshine and glow
To one who is lying, distracted and dying,
With throat-cutting agonies
riving him, driving him
Down, down to the darkness below."

A voice is heard from behind the scenes. It is the voice of ECHO.

Echo. O welcome, daughter; but the Gods destroy
Thy father Cepheus, who exposed thee thus.
Mn. O, who art thou that mournest for my woes?
Ec. Echo, the vocal mocking-bird of song,
I who, last year, in these same lists contended,
A faithful friend, beside Euripides.
And now, my child, for thou must play thy part,
Make dolorous wails.
Mn. And you wail afterwards?
Ec. I'll see to that; only begin at once.
Mn. "O Night most holy,
O'er dread Olympus, vast and far,
In thy dark car
Thou journeyest slowly
Through Ether ridged with many a star."
Ec. "With many a star."
Mn. "Why on Andromeda ever must flow
Sorrow and woe?"
Ec. Sorrow and woe?
Mn. "Heavy of fate."
Ec. Heavy of fate.
Mn. Old woman, you'll kill me, I know, with your prate.
Ec. Know with your prate.
Mn. Why, how tiresome you are: you are going too far.
Ec. You are going too far.
Mn. Good friend, if you kindly will leave me in peace,
You'll do me a favour, O prithee, cease.
Ec. Cease.

Mn. O, go to the crows!
Ec. O, go to the crows!
Mn. Why can't you be still?
Ec. Why can't you be still?
Mn. (*spitefully*) Old gossip!
Ec. (*spitefully*) Old gossip!
Mn. Lackaday!
Ec. Lackaday!
Mn. And alas!
Ec. And alas!

The SCYTHIAN *suddenly awakes to the fact that his prisoner is taking part in a conversation.*

Sc. O, vat does zu say?
Ec. O, vat does zu say?
Sc. I'se calls de police.
Ec. I'se calls de police.
Sc. Vat nosense is dis?
Ec. Vat nosense is dis?
Sc. Vy, vere is de voice?
Ec. Vy, vere is de voice?
Sc. (*to* MNESILOCHUS) Vos id zu?
Ec. Vos id zu?
Sc. Zu'll catch id.
Ec. Zu'll catch id.
Sc. Does zu mocksh?
Ec. Does zu mocksh?
Mn. 'Tisn't I, I declare: it is that woman there.
Ec. It is that woman there.
Sc. Vy, vere is de wretch?
Me mush catch, me mush catch.
Her's a gone, her's a fled.
Ec. Her's a gone, her's a fled.
Sc. Zu'll a suffer for dis.
Ec. Zu'll a suffer for dis.
Sc. Vat again?
Ec. Vat again?
Sc. Zeege ole o' de mix.
Ec. Zeege ole o' de mix.
Sc. Vat a babbled an' talketing ooman.

EURIPIDES *enters in the guise of Perseus.*

Eu. "Ah me, what wild and terrible coast is this?
Plying the pathless air with winged feet,
Steering for Argos, bearing in my hand
The Gorgon's head—"
Sc. Vat dat zu say o' Gorgo?
Dat zu has gots de writer Gorgo's head?
Eu. "Gorgon," I say.
Sc. An' me says "Gorgo" too.
Eu. "Alas, what crag is this, and lashed upon it
What maiden, beautiful as shapes divine,
A lovely craft too rudely moored?"
Mn. "O stranger,
Pity the sorrows of a poor young woman,
And loose my bonds."
Sc. Vat, vill zu no be quiet?
Vat, talkee, talkee, ven zu're goin' to die?
Eu. "Fair girl, I weep to see thee hanging there."
Sc. Disn't von gal: dis von ole vilain man,
Von vare bad rascal fellow.
Eu. Scythian, peace!
This is Andromeda, King Cepheus' daughter.
Sc. Von dawder! Dis? Vare obvious man, metinks.
Eu. O, reach thy hand, and let me clasp my love;
O Scythian, reach. Ah me, what passionate storms
Toss in men's souls; and as for mine, O lady,
Thou art my love!
Sc. Me nod admire zure dasde.
Sdill zu may tiss her, if zu wiss id, dere.
Eu. "Hard-hearted Scythian, give me up my love,
And I will take her—take her aye to wife."
Sc. Tiss her, me says; me nod objex to dat.
Eu. Ah me, I'll loose her bonds.
Sc. Zu bedder nod.
Eu. Ah me, I will.
Sc. Den, me'se cut off zure head.
Me draw de cudless, and zu die, zu dead.
Eu. "Ah, what avails me? Shall I make a speech?
His savage nature could not take it in.
True wit and wisdom were but labour lost
On such a rude barbarian. I must try
Some more appropriate, fitter stratagem."
He goes out
Sc. O, de vile vox! He jocket me vare near.
Mn. O, Perseus, Perseus, wilt thou leave me so?
Sc. Vat, does zu askin' for de vip again?

Chorus

Pallas we call upon,
Chastest and purest one,
Maiden and Virgin, our
Revels to see:
Guarding our portals
Alone of Immortals,
Mightily, potently,
Keeping the key.
Hater of Tyranny,
Come, for we call thee, we
Women in Chorus.
Bring Peace again with thee,
Jocundly, merrily,
Long to reign o'er us.

Sacred, unearthly ones,
Awfullest Shades,
Graciously, peacefully,
Come to your glades.
Man must not gaze on the
Rites at your shrine,
Torch-glimmer flashing o'er
Features divine.
Come, for we're pouring
Imploring, adoring,
Intense veneration;
Dawn on your worshippers,
Givers of Home and our
Civilization.

EURIPIDES *comes in, dressed as an old music-woman.*

Eu. Ladies, I offer terms. If well and truly
Your honourable sex befriend me now,
I won't abuse your honourable sex
From this time forth forever. This I offer.

Ch. (*suspiciously*) But what's your object in proposing this?

Eu. That poor old man there, he's my poor old cousin.
Let him go free, and nevermore will I
Traduce your worthy sex; but if you won't,
I'll meet your husbands coming from the Wars,
And put them up to all your goings-on.

Ch. We take your terms, so far as we're concerned,
But you yourself must manage with the Scythian.

Eu. I'll manage *him*. Now, Hop-o'-my-thumb, come forward,

A dancing-girl enters.

And mind the things I taught you on the way.
Hold up your frock: skip lightly through the dance.
The Persian air, Teredon, if you please.

Sc. Vy, vat dis buzbuz? revels come dis vay?

Eu. She's going to practise, Scythian, that is all.
She's got to dance in public by-and-by.

Sc. Yesh, practish, yesh. Hoick! how se bobs about!
Now here, now dere: von vlea upon de planket.

Eu. Just stop a moment; throw your mantle off;
Come, sit you down beside the Scythian here,
And I'll unloose your slippers. That will do.
We must be moving homeward.

Sc. May I tiss her?

Eu. Once, only once.

Sc. (*kissing her*) O, O, vat vare sweet tiss!
Dat's vare moche sweeter dan zure Attish honies.
Dooze let me tiss her tecon time, ole lady.

Eu. No, Scythian, no; we really can't allow it.

Sc. O doozy, doozy, dear ole lady, doozy.

Eu. Will you give silver for one kiss?

Sc. Yesh! yesh!

Eu. Well, p'raps on that consideration, Scythian,
We won't object; but give the silver first.

Sc. Silver? Vy, vere? I'se got none, Take dis bow-cus.
Zu, vat I call zu?

Eu. Artemisia.

Sc. Yesh. Hartomixer.

Eu. Hillo, what's that? She's off.

Sc. I'se fetch her pack; zu, look to bad ole man.

HOP-O'-MY-THUMB *runs out. The* SCYTHIAN *flings his bow-case to* EURIPIDES *and runs after her.*

Eu. O tricky Hermes, you befriend me still.
Good-bye, old Scythian; catch her if you can.
Meanwhile I'll free your prisoner: and do you
(*to* MNESILOCHUS) Run like a hero, when I've loosed your bonds,
Straight to the bosom of your family.

Mn. Trust me for that, so soon as these are off.

Eu. There then, they are off: now run away, before
The Scythian come and catch you.

Mn. Won't I just!

EURIPIDES *and* MNESILOCHUS *leave the stage. They are hardly out of sight when the* SCYTHIAN *returns.*

Sc. Ole lady, here's—vy, vere's ole lady fannish?
Vere's dat ole man? O bah, I smells de trick.
Ole lady, dis vare bad o' zu, ole lady!
Me nod expex dis of zu. Bad ole lady.
Hartomixer!
Bow-cusses? Yesh, zu von big howcus-bowcus.
Vat sall I does? vere can ole lady was?
Hartomixer!

Ch. Mean you the ancient dame who bore the lute?

Sc. Yesh, does zu saw her?

Ch. Yes, indeed I did.
She went *that* way: there was an old man with her.

Sc. Von yellow-shilk ole man?

Ch. Exactly so.
I think you'll catch them if you take *that* road.

Sc. Vare bad ole lady, did se vich vay run?
Hartomixer!

Ch. Straight up the hill; no, no, not that direction.

They are of course misdirecting him; notwithstanding which, he seems likely, in his flurry, to stumble on the right road.

You're going wrong: see, that's the way she went.

Sc. O dear, O dear, but Hartomixer runnish.

He runs out the wrong way.

Ch. Merrily, merrily, merrily on
to your own confusion go.
But we've ended our say,
and we're going away,
Like good honest women,
straight home from the Play.
And we trust that the twain-
Home-givers will deign
To bless with success our performance to-day.

THE ECCLESIAZUSAE

DRAMATIS PERSONAE

PRAXAGORA	A CRIER
TWO WOMEN	THREE HAGS
BLEPYRUS, *husband of Praxagora*	A GIRL
A CITIZEN	A YOUTH
CHREMES	A SERVANT-MAID OF PRAXAGORA
	CHORUS OF WOMEN

The stage represents an Athenian street, with three houses in the background, the houses of BLEPYRUS, CHREMES, *and the husband of the* SECOND WOMAN. *The hour is 3* A. M. *and the stars are still visible in the sky. A young and delicate woman, clad in masculine attire, is standing in the street, hanging up a lighted lamp in some conspicuous place. The woman is* PRAXAGORA, *the wife of Blepyrus, who has just left her husband asleep within, and has come out wearing his garments, with his sturdy walking-stick in her hand, and his red Laconian shoes upon her feet. And the lamp is to serve as a signal to other Athenian women who have agreed to meet her here before the break of day. No one is yet in sight: and while she is expecting their arrival, she apostrophizes the lamp in mock-heroic style, using such language as in tragedy might be addressed to the sun or moon or to some divine or heroic personage.*

Praxagora. O glowing visage of the earthen lamp,
On this conspicuous eminence well-hung—
(For through thy fates and lineage will we go,
Thou, who, by whirling wheel of potter moulded,
Dost with thy nozzle do the sun's bright duty)—
Awake the appointed signal of the flame!
Thou only knowest it, and rightly thou,
For thou alone, within our chambers standing,
Watchest unblamed the mysteries of love.
Thine eye, inspector of our amorous sports,
Beholdeth all, and no one saith "Begone!"
Thou comest, singeing, purifying all
The dim recesses which none else may see;
And when the garners, stored with corn and wine,
By stealth we open, thou dost stand beside us.
And though thou knowest all this, thou dost not peach.
Therefore our plans will we confide to thee,
What at the Scira we resolved to do.
Ah, but there's no one here who should be here.
Yet doth it draw towards daybreak; and the Assembly
Full soon will meet; and we frail womankind
Must take the seats Phyromachus assigned us
(You don't forget?) and not attract attention.
What can the matter be? Perchance their beards
Are not stitched on, as our decree commanded,
Perchance they found it difficult to steal
Their husband's garments. Stay! I see a lamp
Moving this way. I will retire and watch,
Lest it should haply be some *man* approaching!

She conceals herself: enter FIRST WOMAN, *with lamp.*

1st Woman. It is the hour to start. As I was coming
I heard the herald give his second—crow.

PRAXAGORA *reappears.*

Pr. I have been waiting, watching for you all
The whole night long; and now I'll summon forth
My neighbour here, scratching her door so gently
As not to rouse her husband.

Enter SECOND WOMAN.

2nd Woman. Yea, I heard
(For I was up and putting on my shoes)
The stealthy creeping of thy finger-nail.
My husband, dear—a Salaminian he—
Has all night long been tossing in his bed;
Wherefore I could not steal his garb till now.

1st W. O now they are coming! Here's Cleinarete,
Here's Sostrata, and here's Philaenete.

Enter seven women.

Semi-Chorus. Come, hurry up: for Glyce vowed a vow
That whosoever comes the last shall pay
One quart of chickpeas and nine quarts of wine.

1st W. And look! Melistiche, Smicythion's wife,
Wearing her husband's shoes. She, only she,
Has come away, methinks, at ease, unflurried.

2nd W. And look! Geusistrata, the tapster's wife,
In her right hand the torch.

Pr. And now the wives
Of Philodoretus and Chaeretades,
And many another, hurrying on I see,
All that is best and worthiest in the town.

S.Ch. O honey, I'd tremendous work to come.
My husband gorged his fill of sprats at supper,
And he's been cough, cough, coughing all night long.

Pr. Well, sit ye down, that I may ask you this,
Now that ye're all assembled: have ye done
What at the Scira 'twas resolved to do?

1st W. I have, for one. See, underneath my arms
The hair is growing thicker than a copse,
As 'twas agreed: and when my husband started

Off to the market-place, I'd oil my body
And stand all day decocting in the sun.
2nd W. I too have done it: flinging, first of all,
The razor out of doors, that so my skin
Might grow quite hairy, and unlike a woman.
Pr. But have ye got the beards, which, 'twas determined,
Ye all should bring, assembling here to-day?
1st W. I have, by Hecate! Look! a lovely one.
2nd W. And I, much lovelier than Epicrates's.
Pr. And what say *ye*?
1st W. They nod assent: they've got them.
Pr. The other matters, I perceive, are done.
Laconian shoes ye've got, and walking-sticks,
And the men's overcloaks, as we desired you.
1st W. O I've a splendid club I stole away
(See, here it is) from Lamias as he slept.
Pr. O yes, I know: "the clubs he sweltered with."
1st W. By Zeus the Saviour, he's the very man
To don the skins the All-eyed herdsman wore,
And, no man better, tend the—public hangman.
Pr. But now to finish what remains to do
While yet the stars are lingering in the sky;
For this Assembly, as you know, whereto
We all are bound, commences with the dawn.
1st W. And so it does: and we're to seat ourselves
Facing the prytanes, just below the speakers.
2nd W. See what I've brought, dear heart: I mean to do
A little spinning while the Assembly fills.
Pr. Fills? miserable woman!
2nd W. Yes, why not?
O I can spin and listen just as well.
Besides, my little chicks have got no clothes.
Pr. Fancy you *spinning*! when you must not have
The tiniest morsel of your person seen.
'Twere a fine scrape, if when the Assembly's full,
Some woman clambering o'er the seats, and throwing
Her cloak awry, should show that she's a woman.
No, if we sit in front and gather round us
Our husbands' garments, none will find us out.
Why, when we've got our flowing beards on there,
Who that beholds us will suppose we're women?
Was not Agyrrhius erst a woman? Yet
Now that he wears the beard of Pronomus,
He passes for a man, a statesman too.
O by yon dawning day, 'tis just for that,
We women dare this daring deed to do,
If we can seize upon the helm of state
And trim the ship to weather through the storm;
For neither sails nor oars avail it now.
1st W. How can the female soul of womankind
Address the Assembly?
Pr. Admirably well.
Youths that are most effeminate, they say,
Are always strongest in the speaking line;
And we've got that by nature.
1st W. Maybe so.
Still inexperience is a serious matter.
Pr. And is not that the very reason why
We've met together to rehearse the scene?
Now do make haste and fasten on your beards,
And all you others who have practised talking.
1st W. Practised, indeed! can't every woman talk?
Pr. Come, fasten on your beard, and be a man.
I'll lay these chaplets down, and do the same.
Maybe I'll make a little speech myself.
2nd W. O, here, sweet love, Praxagora: look, child!
O what a merry joke this seems to me!
Pr. Joke! where's the joke?
2nd W. 'Tis just as if we tied
A shaggy beard to toasting cuttlefish.
Pr. Now, Purifier carry round the—cat.
Come in! Ariphrades, don't chatter so.
Come in, sit down. Who will address the meeting?
1st W. I.
Pr. Wear this chaplet then, and luck be with you.
1st W. There.
Pr. Speak away.
1st W. What, speak before I drink?
Pr. Just listen. *Drink*!
1st W. Then what's this chaplet for?
Pr. O get away. Is this what you'd have done
Amongst the men?
1st W. What, don't men drink at meetings?
Pr. Drink, fool?
1st W. By Artemis, I know they do,
And strong drink too. Look at the acts they pass.
Do you mean to tell me that they'd pass such nonsense
If they weren't drunk? Besides, they pour libations.
Or what's the meaning of those tedious prayers
Unless they'd got some wine, I'd like to know.
Besides, they quarrel just like drunken men,
And when one drinks too much, and gets too noisy,
In come the Archer-boys, and run him out.
Pr. Begone and sit you down, for you're no good.
1st W. Good lack, I wish I'd never worn a beard;
I'm parched to death with thirst, I really am.
Pr. Would any other like to speak?
2nd W. Yes, I.
Pr. Put on this chaplet and be quick. Time presses.
Now lean your weight upon your walking-stick,
And speak your words out manfully and well.
2nd W. I could have wished some more experienced man
Had risen to speak, while I sat still and listened.
But now I say I'll not permit, for one,
That in their taverns men should make them tanks
Of water. 'Tis not proper, by the Twain.[1]
Pr. How! by the Twain? Girl, have you lost your wits?
2nd W. Why, what's amiss? *I* never asked for drink.
Pr. You are a man, and yet invoked the Twain.
All else you said was excellently right.
2nd W. O yes, by Apollo!
Pr. Mind then, I won't move
Another step in this Assembly business,
Unless you are strict and accurate in this.

[1]Demeter and Persephone.

2nd W. Give me the chaplet, and I'll try again.
I've thought of something very good to say.
In my opinion, O assembled women,
Pr. O monstrous! *women*, idiot, when they're *men*?
2nd W. 'Twas all Epigonus: he caught my eye
And so, methought 'twas women I harangued.
Pr. You, too, retire and sit you down again,
For I myself will wear the chaplet now
Your cause to further: and I pray the gods
That I may haply prosper our design.
I have, my friends, an equal stake with you
In this our country, and I grieve to note
The sad condition of the State's affairs.
I see the State employing evermore
Unworthy ministers; if one do well
A single day, he'll act amiss for ten.
You trust another: he'll be ten times worse.
Hard, hard it is to counsel wayward men,
Always mistrusting those who love you best,
And paying court to those who love you not.
There was a time, my friends, we never came
To these Assemblies; then we knew full well
Agyrrhius was a rogue: we come here now,
And he who gets the cash applauds the man,
And he who gets it not, protests that they
Who come for payment ought to die the death.
1st W. By Aphrodite now, but that's well said!
Pr. Heavens! Aphrodite! 'Twere a pleasant jest,
If in the Assembly you should praise me so!
1st W. Ah, but I won't.
Pr. Then don't acquire the habit.
This League[1] again, when first we talked it over,
It seemed the only thing to save the State.
Yet when they'd got it, they disliked it. He
Who pushed it through was forced to cut and run.
Ships must be launched; the poor men all approve,
The wealthy men and farmers disapprove.
You used to hate Corinthians, and they you;
They are friendly now: do you be friendly too.
Argeius was a fool: now Jerome's wise.
Safety just showed her face: but Thrasybulus,
No more called in, is quite excluded now.
1st W. Here's a shrewd man!
Pr. Ah, now you praise me rightly
Ye are to blame for this, Athenian people,
Ye draw your wages from the public purse,
Yet each man seeks his private gain alone.
So the State reels, like any Aesimus.
Still, if ye trust me, ye shall yet be saved.
I move that now the womankind be asked
To rule the State. In our own homes, ye know,
They are the managers and rule the house.
1st W. O good, good, good! speak on, speak on, dear man
Pr. That they are better in their ways than we
I'll soon convince you. First, they dye their wools
With boiling tinctures, in the ancient style.
You won't find *them*, I warrant, in a hurry
Trying new plans. And would it not have saved
The Athenian city had she let alone
Things that worked well, nor idly sought things new?
They roast their barley, sitting, as of old:
They on their heads bear burdens, as of old:
They keep their Thesmophoria, as of old:
They bake their honied cheesecakes, as of old:
They victimize their husbands, as of old:
They still secrete their lovers, as of old:
They buy themselves sly dainties, as of old:
They love their wine unwatered, as of old:
They like a woman's pleasures, as of old:
Then let us, gentlemen, give up to them
The helm of State, and not concern ourselves,
Nor pry, nor question what they mean to do;
But let them really govern, knowing this,
The statesman-mothers never will neglect
Their soldier-sons. And then a soldier's rations,
Who will supply as well as she who bare him?
For ways and means none can excel a woman.
And there's no fear at all that they'll be cheated
When they're in power, for they're the cheats themselves.
Much I omit. But if you pass my motion,
You'll lead the happiest lives that e'er you dreamed of.
1st W. O, good! Praxagora. Well done, sweet wench.
However did you learn to speak so finely?
Pr. I and my husband in the general flight
Lodged in the Pnyx, and there I heard the speakers.
1st W. Ah, you were clever to some purpose, dear.
And if you now succeed in your designs
We'll then and there proclaim you chieftainess.
But what if Cephalus, ill fare, insult you,
How will you answer *him* in full Assembly?
Pr. I'll say he's frenzied.
1st W. True enough; but all
The world know that.
Pr. I'll say he's moody-mad.
1st W. They know that too.
Pr. That he's more fit to tinker
The constitution than his pots and pans.
1st W. If Neocleides, blear-eyed oaf, insult you?
Pr. "Peep at a puppy's tail, my lad," quoth I.
1st W. What if they interrupt?
Pr. I'll meet them there,
I'm quite accustomed to that sort of thing.
1st W. O but suppose the archers hale you off,
What will you do?
Pr. Stick out my elbows, so.
They shan't seize *me*, the varlets, round my waist.
Semi-Ch. Aye, and we'll help: we'll bid the men let go.
1st W. Then that we've settled, wonderfully well.
But this we've not considered, how to mind
We lift our hands, and not our feet, in voting.
We're more for lifting feet than lifting hands.
Pr. A knotty point. However, we must each
Hold up one arm, bare from the shoulder, so.
Now then, my dears, tuck up your tunics neatly,
And slip your feet in those Laconian shoes,
Just as ye've seen your husbands do, whene'er

[1] The anti-Spartan League of 395 B.C.

They're going out, mayhap to attend the
Assembly.
And next, so soon as everything is right
With shoes and tunics, fasten on your beards,
And when ye've got them neatly fitted on,
Then throw your husbands' mantles over all,
Those which ye stole; and leaning on your sticks
Off to the Meeting, piping as ye go
Some old man's song, and mimicking the ways
Of country fellows.

1st W. Good! but let ourselves
Get on before them: other women soon
Will come I know from all the countryside
Straight for the Pnyx.

Pr. Be quick, for 'tis the rule
That whoso comes not with the early dawn
Must slink abashed, with never a doit, away.

PRAXAGORA *and* FIRST *and* SECOND WOMEN *depart; the rest remain and form the* CHORUS.

Semi-Ch. Time to be moving, gentlemen! 'tis best we keep repeating
This name of ours, lest we forget to use it at the Meeting.
For terrible the risk would be, if any man detected
The great and daring scheme which we in darkness have projected.

Semi-Ch. *On* to the Meeting, worthy sirs: for now the magistrate avers
That whoever shall fail to
Arrive while the dusk of the
Morning is grey,
All dusty and smacking of
Pickle and acid, that
Man shall assuredly
Forfeit his pay.
Now Charitimides,
Draces, and Smicythus,
Hasten along:
See that there fall from you
Never a word or a
Note that is wrong.
Get we our tickets, and
Sit we together, and
Choose the front rows.
Vote we whatever our
Sisters propose.
Our *sisters*! My wits are gone gleaning!
Our "brothers," of course, was my meaning.

Enter band of twelve COUNTRYWOMEN.

Semi-Ch. We'll thrust aside this bothering throng which from the city crowds along,
These men, who aforetime
When only an obol they
Got for their pay
Would sit in the wreath-market,
Chatting away.
Ah well, in the days of our
Noble Myronides
None would have stooped
Money to take for
Attending the meetings, but
Hither they trooped,
Each with his own little
Goatskin of wine,
Each with three olives, two
Onions, one loaf, in his
Wallet, to dine.
But now they are set
The three-obol to get,
And whene'er the State business engages,
They clamour, like hodmen, for wages.

The CHORUS *leave the orchestra for a time. Enter* BLEPYRUS *in his wife's dress.*

Blepyrus. What's up? Where's my wife gone? Why, bless the woman,
It's almost daybreak and she can't be found.
Here am I, taken with the gripes abed,
Groping about to find my overcloak
And shoes i' the dark; but hang it, they're gone too:
I could not find them anywhere. Meanwhile
Easums kept knocking hard at my back-door;
So on I put this kirtle of my wife's,
And shove my feet into her Persian slippers.
Where's a convenient place? or shall I say
All are alike convenient in the dark?
No man can see me here, I am sure of that.
Fool that I was, worse luck, to take a wife
In my old age. Ought to be thrashed, I ought!
'Tis for no good, I warrant, that she's out
This time of night. However, I can't wait.

Enter CITIZEN, *another husband.*

Citizen. Hey-day! who's this? Not neighbour Blepyrus?
Sure and it's he himself. Why, tell me, man,
What's all that yellow? Do you mean to say
You've had Cinesias at his tricks again?

Bl. No, no; I wanted to come out, and took
This little yellow kirtle of my wife's.

Ci. But where's your cloak?

Bl. I've not the least idea.
I searched amongst the clothes, and 'twasn't there.

Ci. Did you not ask your wife to find the thing?

Bl. I didn't. No. For why? *She* wasn't there.
She's wormed herself away out of the house;
Some revolution in the wind, I fear.

Ci. O by Poseidon, but your case is just
The same as mine. *My* wife has stolen away,
And carried off my cloak. And that's not all,
Hang her, she's carried off my shoes as well:
At least I could not find them anywhere.

Bl. No more can I: I could not anywhere
Find my Laconians: so, my case being urgent,
I shove her slippers on, and out I bolt
For fear I soil my blanket; 'twas a clean one.

Ci. What can it be? can any of her gossips
Have asked her out to breakfast?

Bl. I expect so
She's not a bad one: I don't *think* she is.

Ci. Why, man, you are paying out a cable: I
Must to the Assembly, when I've found my cloak,
My missing cloak: the only one I've got.

Bl. I too, when eased; but now an acrid pear
Is blocking up the passage of my food.

Ci. As Thrasybulus told the Spartans, eh? *Exit.*

Bl. By Dionysus, but it grips me tight,
And that's not all: whatever shall I do?
For how the food I am going to eat hereafter
Will find a passage out, I can't imagine;
So firm and close this Acridusian chap
Has fastened up its pathway to the door.
Who'll fetch a doctor, and what doctor, here?
Which of the pathicks knows this business best?
Amynon knows: but perhaps he won't admit it.
Fetch, fetch Antisthenes, by all means fetch him.
He's just the man (to judge from his complaints)
To know the pangs from which I'm suffering now.
Great Eileithyia, let me not remain
Thus plugged and barricaded, nor become
A public nightstool for the comic stage.

Enter CHREMES, *the other neighbour.*

Chremes. Taking your ease, good neighbour?
Bl. No, I'm not.
'Tis true I have been, but I've finished now.
Chr. O, and you've got your lady's kirtle on!
Bl. 'Twas dark indoors: I caught it up by chance
But whence come *you*?
Chr. I'm coming from the Assembly.
Bl. What, is it over?
Chr. Aye, betimes to-day.
And O, dear Zeus, the fun it was to see
The way they spattered the vermilion round.
Bl. Got your three-obol?
Chr. No, not I, worse luck.
I was too late: I'm carrying home, ashamed,
This empty wallet: nothing else at all.
Bl. Why, how was that?
Chr. There gathered such a crowd
About the Pnyx, you never saw the like;
Such pale-faced fellows; just like shoemakers
We all declared; and strange it was to see
How pallid-packed the whole Assembly looked.
So I and lots of us could get no pay.
Bl. Shall I get any if I run?
Chr. Not you!
Not had you been there when the cock was giving
Its second crow.
Bl. O weep, Antilochus,
Rather for me, the living, than for him,
The loved and lost—three-obol. All is gone!
Whatever was it though that brought together
So vast a crowd so early?
Chr. 'Twas determined
To put this question to the assembled people,
"How best to save the State." So first and foremost
Came Neocleides, groping up to speak.
And all the people shouted out aloud,
"What scandal that this blear-eyed oaf, who cannot
Save his own eyesight for himself, should dare
To come and teach us how to save the State."
But he cried out, and leered around, and said,
"What's to be done?"
Bl. "Pound garlic up with verjuice,
Throw in some spurge of the Laconian sort,
And rub it on your eyelids every night."
That's what, had I been present, I'd have said.
Chr. Next came Evaeon, smart accomplished chap,
With nothing on, as most of us supposed,
But he himself insisted he was clothed.
He made a popular democratic speech.
"Behold," says he, "I am myself in want
Of cash to save me; yet I know the way
To save the citizens, and save the State.
Let every clothier give to all that ask
Warm woolen robes, when first the sun turns back.
No more will pleurisy attack us then.
Let such as own no bedclothes and no bed,
After they've dined, seek out the furriers, there
To sleep; and whoso shuts the door against them
In wintry weather, shall be fined three blankets."
Bl. Well said indeed; and never a man would dare
To vote against him, had he added this:
"That all who deal in grain shall freely give
Three quarts to every pauper, or be hanged."
That good, at least, they'd gain from Nausicydes.
Chr. Then, after him, there bounded up to speak
A spruce and pale-faced youth, like Nicias.
And *he* declared we ought to place the State
Into the hands of (whom do you think?) the women!
Then the whole mob of shoemakers began
To cheer like mad; whilst all the country folk
Hooted and hissed.
Bl. They showed their sense, by Zeus.
Chr. But less their numbers; so the lad went on,
Speaking all good of women, but of you
Everything bad.
Bl. What?
Chr. First of all he called you
An arrant rogue.
Bl. And you?
Chr. Let be, awhile.
Also a thief.
Bl. Me only?
Chr. And by Zeus,
A sycophant.
Bl. Me only?
Chr. And by Zeus,
All our friends here.
Bl. Well, who says nay to that?
Chr. And then the woman is, he said, a thing
Stuffed full of wit and moneymaking ways.
They don't betray their Thesmophorian secrets,
But you and I blab all State secrets out.
Bl. By Hermes, there at least he told no lie.
Chr. And women lend each other, said the lad,
Their dresses, trinkets, money, drinking-cups,
Though quite alone, with never a witness there.
And all restore the loan, and none withhold it.
But men, he said, are always doing this.
Bl. Aye to be sure: though witnesses were there.
Chr. *They* don't inform, or prosecute, or put
The people down: but everything that's right.
And much, besides, he praised the womankind.
Bl. What was determined?
Chr. You're to put the State
Into their hands. This was the one reform
Not yet attempted.
Bl. 'Twas decreed?
Chr. It was.

Bl. So then the women now must undertake
All manly duties?
Chr. So I understand.
Bl. Then I shan't be a dicast, but my wife?
Chr. Nor you support your household, but your wife.
Bl. Nor I get grumbling up in early morn?
Chr. No: for the future that's your wife's affair.
You'll lie abed: no grumbling any more.
Bl. But hark ye, 'twould be rough on us old men
If, when the women hold the reins of State,
They should perforce compel us to—
Chr. Do what?
Bl. Make love to them.
Chr. But if we're not prepared?
Bl. They'll dock our breakfasts.
Chr. Therefore learn the way
How to make love, and eat your breakfast too.
Bl. Upon compulsion! Faugh!
Chr. If that is for
The public good, we needs must all obey.
There is a legend of the olden time,
That all our foolish plans and vain conceits
Are overruled to work the public good.
So be it now, high Pallas and ye gods!
But I must go. Farewell.
Bl. And farewell, Chremes.
Exeunt.
Enter CHORUS.
Chorus. Step strong! March along!
But search and scan if any man
be somewhere following in our rear.
Look out! Wheel about!
And O be sure that all's secure;
for many are the rogues, I fear.
Lest someone, coming up behind us,
in this ungodly guise should find us.
Be *sure* you make a clattering sound
with both your feet against the ground.
For dismal shame and scandal great
Will everywhere upon us wait,
if our disguise they penetrate.
So wrap your garments round you tight,
And peep about with all your might,
Both here and there and on your right,
Or this our plot to save the State
will in disaster terminate.
Move on, dear friends, move on apace,
for now we're very near the place
From whence we started, when we went
to join the men in Parliament.
And there's the mansion, full in view,
where dwells our lady chieftain, who
The wise and noble scheme invented
to which the State has just assented.
So *now* no longer must we stay,
no longer while the time away,
False-bearded with this bristly hair,
Lest someone see us and declare
our hidden secret everywhere.
So draw ye closer, at my call,
Beneath the shadow of the wall,
And glancing sideways, one and all,
Adjust and change your dresses there,
and bear the form which erst ye bare.
For *see* the noble lady fair,
our chieftainess, approaching there.
She's coming home with eager speed
from yon Assembly; take ye heed,
And loathe upon your chins to wear
that monstrous equipage of hair;
For 'neath its tickling mass, I know,
they've all been smarting long ago.

PRAXAGORA *is seen returning from the Assembly. She is still wearing her husband's garments, and enters the stage alone. We hear no more of the* TWO WOMEN *who had been her companions there before. And nobody else comes on the stage until* BLEPYRUS *and* CHREMES *emerge from their respective houses, twenty lines below.*

Pr. So far, dear sisters, these our bold designs
Have all gone off successfully and well.
But now at once, or e'er some wight perceive us,
Off with your woollens; cast your shoes; unloose
The jointed clasp of thy Laconian reins:
Discard your staves. Nay, but do *you*, my dear,
Get these in order: I myself will steal
Into the house, and ere my husband see me,
Put back his overcloak, unnoticed, where
I found it, and whatever else I took.

PRAXAGORA *retires into her house* (*the house of* BLEPYRUS) *to change her dress, whilst the* CHORUS *change theirs in the orchestra. She almost immediately returns, and henceforth all the women are clothed in their proper habiliments.*

Ch. We have done your behest, and as touching the rest,
We will do whatsoever you tell us is best.
For truly I ween that a woman so keen,
Resourceful and subtle we never have seen.

Pr. Then all by my side, as the councillors tried
Of the office I hold, be content to abide;
For *there*, in the fuss and hullabaloo,
Ye proved yourself women most manly and true.

Enter BLEPYRUS *and* CHREMES *from their respective houses.*

Bl. Hallo, Praxagora, whence come *you*?
Pr. What's that
To you, my man?
Bl. What's that to me? That's cool.
Pr. Not from a lover; *that* you know.
Bl. Perchance
From more than one.
Pr. That you can test, directly.
Bl. Marry and how?
Pr. Smell if my hair is perfumed.
Bl. Does not a woman sin unless she's perfumed?
Pr. *I* don't, at all events.
Bl. What made you steal
Away so early with my overcloak?
Pr. I was called out ere daybreak, to a friend
In pangs of childbirth.
Bl. Why not tell me first,
Before you went?

Pr. Not haste to help her in
Such straits, my husband?
Bl. After telling me.
Something's wrong there.
Pr. Nay, by the Twain, I went
Just as I was; the wench who came besought me
To lose no time.
Bl. Is that the reason why
You did not put your mantle on? You threw it
Over my bed and took my overcloak,
And left me lying like a corpse laid out;
Only I'd never a wreath, or bottle of oil.
Pr. The night was cold, and I'm so slight and fragile,
I took your overcloak to keep me warm.
And you I left well snuggled up in warmth
And rugs, my husband.
Bl. How came my staff to form
One of your party, and my red Laconians?
Pr. I took your shoes to save your overcloak;
Aping your walk, stumping with both my feet,
And striking down your staff against the stones.
Bl. You've lost eight quarts of wheat, I'd have you know,
Which the Assembly would have brought me in.
Pr. Well, never mind; she's got a bonny boy.
Bl. Who? the Assembly has?
Pr. No, fool, the woman.
But has it met?
Bl. I told you yesterday
'Twas going to meet.
Pr. O yes, I now remember.
Bl. Have you not heard then what's decreed?
Pr. No, dear.
Bl. Then sit you down and chew your cuttlefish.
The State, they say, is handed over to *you!*
Pr. What for? To weave?
Bl. No, govern.
Pr. Govern what?
Bl. All the whole work and business of the State.
Pr. O here's a lucky State, by Aphrodite,
We're going to have!
Bl. How so?
Pr. For many reasons.
For now no longer shall bold men be free
To shame the city: no more witnessing,
No false informing—
Bl. Hang it, don't do that.
Don't take away my only means of living!
Chr. Pray, sir, be still, and let the lady speak.
Pr. No thefts of overcloaks, no envyings now,
None to be poor and naked any more.
No wranglings, no distraining on your goods.
Chr. Now, by Poseidon, wondrous news if true.
Pr. Aye and I'll prove it, so that you'll support me,
And he himself have nought to say against it.
Ch. Now waken your intellect bright,
Your soul philosophic, that knows
So well for your comrades to fight.
For all to our happiness goes
The project your tongue will disclose,
As with thousands of joys you propose
The citizen life to endow.
Now show us what things you can do!
It is time; for the populace now
Requires an original new
Experiment; only do you
Some novelty bring from your store
Never spoken or done heretofore.
The audience don't like to be cheated
With humours too often repeated.
So come to the point, and at once; for delay
Is a thing the spectators detest in a play.
Pr. I've an excellent scheme, if you will but believe it;
But I cannot be sure how our friends will receive it;
Or what they will do, if the old I eschew,
And propound them a system erratic and new.
This makes me a trifle alarmed and faint-hearted.
Bl. As to that, you may safely be fearless and bold:
We adore what is new, and abhor what is old.
This rule we retain when all else has departed.
Pr. Then all to the speaker in silence attend,
And don't interrupt till I come to the end,
And weigh and perpend, till you quite comprehend,
The drift and intent of the scheme I present.
The rule which I dare to enact and declare,
Is that all shall be equal, and equally share
All wealth and enjoyments, nor longer endure
That one should be rich, and another be poor,
That one should have acres, far-stretching and wide,
And another not even enough to provide
Himself with a grave: that this at his call
Should have hundreds of servants, and that none at all.
All this I intend to correct and amend:
Now all of all blessings shall freely partake,
One life and one system for all men I make.
Bl. And how will you manage it?
Pr. First, I'll provide
That the silver, and land, and whatever beside
Each man shall possess, shall be common and free,
One fund for the public; then out of it we
Will feed and maintain you, like housekeepers true,
Dispensing, and sparing, and caring for you.
Bl. With regard to the land, I can quite understand,
But how, if a man have his money in hand,
Not farms, which you see, and he cannot withhold,
But talents of silver and Darics of gold?
Pr. All this to the stores he must bring.
Bl. But suppose
He choose to retain it, and nobody knows;
Rank perjury doubtless; but what if it be?
'Twas by that he acquired it at first.
Pr. I agree.
But now 'twill be useless; he'll need it no more.
Bl. How mean you?
Pr. All pressure from want will be o'er.
Now each will have all that a man can desire,
Cakes, barley-loaves, chestnuts, abundant attire,
Wine, garlands and fish: then why should he wish
The wealth he has gotten by fraud to retain?
If you know any reason, I hope you'll explain.

Bl. 'Tis those that have most of these goods, I believe,
That are always the worst and the keenest to thieve.
Pr. I grant you, my friend, in the days that are past,
In your old-fashioned system, abolished at last;
But what he's to gain, though his wealth he retain,
When all things are common, I'd have you explain.
Bl. If a youth to a girl his devotion would show,
He surely must woo her with presents.
Pr. O no.
All women and men will be common and free,
No marriage or other restraint there will be.
Bl. But if all should aspire to the favours of one,
To the girl that is fairest, what then will be done?
Pr. By the side of the beauty, so stately and grand,
The dwarf, the deformed, and the ugly will stand;
And before you're entitled the beauty to woo,
Your court you must pay to the hag and the shrew.
Bl. For the ladies you've nicely provided no doubt;
No woman will now be a lover without.
But what of the men? For the girls, I suspect,
The handsome will choose, and the ugly reject.
Pr. No girl will of course be permitted to mate
Except in accord with the rules of the State.
By the side of her lover, so handsome and tall,
Will be stationed the squat, the ungainly and small.
And before she's entitled the beau to obtain,
Her love she must grant to the awkward and plain.
Bl. O then such a nose as Lysicrates shows
Will vie with the fairest and best, I suppose.
Pr. O yes, 'tis a nice democratic device,
A popular system as ever was tried,
A jape on the swells with their rings and their pride.
"Now, fopling, away," Gaffer Hobnail will say,
"Stand aside: it is I have precedence to-day."
Bl. But how, may I ask, will the children be known?
And how can a father distinguish his own?
Pr. They will never be known: it can never be told;
All youths will in common be sons of the old.
Bl. If in vain to distinguish our children we seek,
Pray what will become of the agèd and weak?
At present I own, though a father be known,
Sons throttle and choke him with hearty goodwill;
But will they not do it more cheerily still,
When the sonship is doubtful?
Pr. No, certainly not.
For now if a boy should a parent annoy,
The lads who are near will of course interfere;
For they may themselves be his children, I wot.
Bl. In much that you say there is much to admire;
But what if Leucolophus claim me for sire,
Or vile Epicurus? I think you'll agree
That a great and unbearable nuisance 'twould be.
Chr. A nuisance much greater than this might befall you.
Bl. How so?
Chr. If the skunk Aristyllus should call you
His father, and seize you, a kiss to imprint.
Bl. O hang him! Confound him! O how I would pound him!
Chr. I fancy you soon would be smelling of mint.
Pr. But this, sir, is nonsense: it never could be.
That whelp was begotten before the Decree.
His kiss, it is plain, you can never obtain.
Bl. The prospect I view with disgust and alarm.
But who will attend to the work of the farm?
Pr. All labour and toil to your slaves you will leave;
Your business 'twill be, when the shadows of eve
Ten feet on the face of the dial are cast,
To scurry away to your evening repast.
Bl. Our clothes, what of them?
Pr. You have plenty in store,
When these are worn out, we will weave you some more.
Bl. Just one other thing. If an action they bring,
What funds will be mine for discharging the fine?
You won't pay it out of the stores, I opine.
Pr. A fine to be paid when an action they bring!
Why bless you, our people won't know such a thing
As an action.
Bl. No actions! I feel a misgiving.
Pray what are "our people" to do for a living?
Chr. You are right: there are many will rue it.
Pr. No doubt.
But what can one then bring an action about?
Bl. There are reasons in plenty; I'll just mention one.
If a debtor won't pay you, pray what's to be done?
Pr. If a debtor won't pay! Nay, but tell me, my friend,
How the creditor came by the money to lend?
All money, I thought, to the stores had been brought.
I've got a suspicion, I say it with grief,
Your creditor's surely a bit of a thief.
Chr. Now that is an answer acute and befitting.
Bl. But what if a man should be fined for committing
Some common assault, when elated with wine;
Pray what are his means for discharging that fine?
I have posed you, I think.
Pr. Why, his victuals and drink
Will be stopped by command for awhile; and I guess
That he will not again in a hurry transgress,
When he pays with his stomach.
Bl. Will thieves be unknown?
Pr. Why, how should they steal what is partly their own?
Bl. No chance then to meet at night in the street
Some highwayman coming our cloaks to abstract?
Pr. No, not if you're sleeping at home; nor, in fact,
Though you choose to go out. That trade, why pursue it?
There's plenty for all: but suppose him to do it,
Don't fight and resist him; what need of a pother?
You can go to the stores, and they'll give you another.
Bl. Shall we gambling forsake?

Pr. Why, what could you stake?
Bl. But what is the style of our living to be?
Pr. One common to all, independent and free,
All bars and partitions for ever undone,
All private establishments fused into one.
Bl. Then where, may I ask, will our dinners be laid?
Pr. Each court and arcade of the law shall be made
A banqueting-hall for the citizens.
Bl. Right.
But what will you do with the desk for the speakers?
Pr. I'll make it a stand for the cups and the beakers;
And there shall the striplings be ranged to recite
The deeds of the brave, and the joys of the fight,
And the cowards' disgrace; till out of the place
Each coward shall slink with a very red face,
Not stopping to dine.
Bl. O but that will be fine.
And what of the balloting-booths?
Pr. They shall go
To the head of the market-place, all in a row,
And there by Harmodius taking my station,
I'll tickets dispense to the whole of the nation,
Till each one has got his particular lot,
And manfully bustles along to the sign
Of the letter whereat he's empanelled to dine.
The man who has A shall be ushered away
To the Royal Arcade; to the next will go B;
And C to the Cornmarket.
Bl. Merely to *see*?
Pr. No, fool, but to dine.
Bl. 'Tis an excellent plan.
Then he who gets never a letter, poor man,
Gets never a dinner.
Pr. But 'twill not be so.
There'll be plenty for all, and to spare.
No stint and no grudging our system will know,
But each will away from the revelry go,
Elated and grand, with a torch in his hand
And a garland of flowers in his hair.
And then through the streets as they wander, a lot
Of women will round them be creeping,
"O come to my lodging," says one, "I have got
Such a beautiful girl in my keeping."
"But here is the sweetest and fairest, my boy,"
From a window another will say,
"But ere you're entitled her love to enjoy
Your toll to myself you must pay."
Then a sorry companion, flat-visaged and old,
Will shout to the youngster "Avast!
And where are *you* going, so gallant and bold,
And where are *you* hieing so fast?
'Tis in vain; you must yield to the laws of the State,
And I shall be courting the fair,
Whilst you must without in the vestibule wait,
And strive to amuse yourself there, dear boy,
And strive to amuse yourself there."
There now, what think ye of my scheme?
Bl. First-rate.
Pr. Then now I'll go to the market-place, and there,
Taking some clear-voiced girl as crieress,
Receive the goods as people bring them in.
This must I do, elected chieftainess
To rule the State and start the public feasts;
That so your banquets may commence to-day.
Bl. What, shall we banquet now at once?
Pr. You shall.
And next I'll make a thorough sweep of all
The flaunting harlots.
Bl. Why?
Pr. That these free ladies
May have the firstling manhood of our youths.
Those servile hussies shall no longer poach
Upon the true-love manors of the free.
No, let them herd with slaves, and lie with slaves,
In servile fashion, snipped and trimmed to match.
Bl. Lead on, my lass. I'll follow close behind;
That men may point and whisper as I pass,
There goes the husband of our chieftainess.
Chr. And I will muster and review my goods,
And bring them all, as ordered, to the stores.

Exeunt PRAXAGORA, BLEPYRUS, *and* CHREMES.

(*Here was a choral song, now lost, during which* CHREMES *is preparing to bring out his chattels from the house.*)

Chr. My sweet bran-winnower, come you sweetly here.
March out the first of all my household goods,
Powdered and trim, like some young basket-bearer.
Aye, many a sack of mine you have bolted down.
Now where's the chair-girl? Come along, dear pot,
(Wow! but you're black: scarce blacker had you chanced
To boil the dye Lysicrates employs),
And stand by *her*. Come hither, tiring-maid;
And pitcher-bearer, bear your pitcher here.
You, fair musician, take your station there,
You whose untimely trumpet-call has oft
Roused me, ere daybreak, to attend the Assembly.
Who's got the dish, go forward; take the combs
Of honey; set the olive branches nigh;
Bring out the tripods and the bottles of oil;
The pannikins and rubbish you can leave.

Now another door opens, the door upon which PRAXAGORA *had stealthily scratched,* 34 *above, and the* HUSBAND OF THE SECOND WOMAN *again comes out, as he did* 327 *above.*

Ci. I bring my goods to the stores! That were to be
A hapless greenhorn, ill endowed with brains.
I'll never do it; by Poseidon, never!
I'll test the thing and scan its bearings first.
I'm not the man to fling my sweat and thrift
So idly and so brainlessly away,
Before I've fathomed how the matter stands.
—You there! what means this long array of chattels?
Are they brought out because you're changing house,
Or are you going to pawn them?
Chr. No.
Ci. Then why
All in a row? Are they, in grand procession,
Marching to Hiero the auctioneer?

Chr. O no, I am going to bring them to the stores
For the State's use: so run the new-made laws.
Ci. (*in shrill surprise*) You are going to bring them!
Chr. Yes.
Ci. By Zeus the Saviour,
You're an ill-starred one!
Chr. How?
Ci. How? Plain enough.
Chr. What, must I not, forsooth, obey the laws?
Ci. The laws, poor wretch! What laws?
Chr. The new-made laws.
Ci. The new-made laws? O what a fool you are!
Chr. A fool?
Ci. Well, aren't you? Just the veriest dolt
In all the town!
Chr. Because I do what's ordered?
Ci. Is it a wise man's part to do what's ordered?
Chr. Of course it is.
Ci. Of course it is a fool's.
Chr. Then won't you bring yours in?
Ci. I'll wait awhile,
And watch the people what they're going to do.
Chr. What *should* they do but bring their chattels in
For the State's use?
Ci. *I saw it and believed.*
Chr. Why, in the streets they talk—
Ci. Ay, talk they will.
Chr. Saying they'll bring their goods—
Ci. Ay, say they will.
Chr. Zounds! you doubt everything.
Ci. Ay, doubt they will.
Chr. O, Heaven confound you.
Ci. Ay, confound they will.
What! think you men of sense will bring their goods?
Not they! That's not our custom: we're disposed
Rather to take than give, like the dear gods.
Look at their statues, stretching out their hands!
We pray the powers to give us all things good;
Still they hold forth their hands with hollowed palms,
Showing their notion is to take, not give.
Chr. Pray now, good fellow, let me do my work.
Hi! where's the strap? These must be tied together.
Ci. You are really going?
Chr. Don't you see I'm tying
These tripods up this instant?
Ci. O what folly!
Not to delay a little, and observe
What other people do, and then—
Chr. And then?
Ci. Why then put off, and then delay again.
Chr. Why so?
Ci. Why, if perchance an earthquake came,
Or lightning fell, or a cat cross the street,
They'll soon cease bringing in, you blockhead you!
Chr. A pleasant jest, if I should find no room
To bring my chattels!
Ci. To *receive*, you mean.
'Twere time to bring them, two days hence.
Chr. How mean you?
Ci. I know these fellows; voting in hot haste,
And straight ignoring the decree they've passed.
Chr. They'll bring them, friend.
Ci. But if they don't, what then?
Chr. No fear; they'll bring them.
Ci. If they don't, what then?
Chr. We'll fight them.
Ci. If they prove too strong, what then?
Chr. I'll leave them.
Ci. If they won't be left, what then?
Chr. Go, hang yourself.
Ci. And if I do, what then?
Chr. 'Twere a good deed.
Ci. You are really going to bring them?
Chr. Yes, that's exactly what I'm going to do.
I see my neighbours bringing theirs.
Ci. O ay,
Antisthenes for instance. Heavens, he'd liefer
Sit on the stool for thirty days and more.
Chr. Be hanged!
Ci. Well, but Callimachus the poet,
What, will *he* bring them?
Chr. More than Callias can.
Ci. Well, here's a man will throw away his substance.
Chr. That's a hard saying.
Ci. Hard? when every day
We see abortive resolutions passed!
That vote about the salt, you mind *that*, don't you?
Chr. I do.
Ci. And how we voted, don't you mind,
Those copper coins.
Chr. And a bad job for me
That coinage proved. I sold my grapes, and stuffed
My cheek with coppers; then I steered away
And went to purchase barley in the market;
When just as I was holding out my sack,
The herald cried, "No copper coins allowed!
Nothing but silver must be paid or taken!"
Ci. Then that late tax, the two-and-a-half per cent,
Euripides devised, weren't we all vowing
'Twould yield five hundred talents to the State?
Then every man would gild Euripides.
But when we reckoned up, and found the thing
A Zeus's Corinth, and no good at all,
Then every man would tar Euripides.
Chr. But times have altered; then the men bare sway,
'Tis now the women.
Ci. Who, I'll take good care,
Shan't try on *me* their little piddling ways.
Chr. You're talking nonsense. Boy, take up the yoke.

Enter a CRIER *to summon all citizens to the banquet.*

Crier. O all ye citizens (for now 'tis thus),
Come all, come quick, straight to your chieftainess.
There cast your lots; there fortune shall assign
To every man his destined feasting-place.
Come, for the tables now are all prepared
And laden heavily with all good things:
The couches all with rugs and cushions piled!
They're mixing wine: the perfume-selling girls

Are ranged in order: collops on the fire:
Hares on the spit; and in the oven, cakes;
Chaplets are woven: comfits parched and dried.
The youngest girls are boiling pots of broth;
And there amongst them, in his riding-suit,
The gallant Smoius licks their platters clean.
There Geron too, in dainty robe and pumps,
His threadbare cloak and shoon discarded now,
Struts on, guffawing with another lad.
Come, therefore, come, and quickly: bread in hand
The pantler stands; and open wide your mouths. *Exit.*

Ci. I'll go, for one. Why stand I idly here,
When thus the city has declared her will?
Chr. Where will *you* go? You haven't brought your goods.
Ci. To supper.
Chr. Not if they've their wits about them
Until you've brought your goods.
Ci. I'll bring them.
Chr. When?
Ci. My doings won't delay the job.
Chr. Why not?
Ci. Others will bring them later still than I.
Chr. You are going to supper?
Ci. What am I to do?
Good citizens must needs support the State
As best they can.
Chr. If they say no, what then?
Ci. At them, head foremost.
Chr. If they strike, what then?
Ci. Summon the minxes.
Chr. If they jeer, what then?
Ci. Why, then I'll stand beside the door, and—
Chr. What?
Ci. Seize on the viands as they bear them in.
Chr. Come later then. Now Parmeno and Sicon
Take up my goods and carry them along.
Ci. I'll help you bring them.
Chr. Heaven forbid! I fear
That when I'm there, depositing the goods
Beside the chieftainess, you'll claim them yours. *Exit.*

Ci. Now must I hatch some crafty shrewd device
To keep my goods, and yet secure a part
In all these public banquets, like the rest.
Hah! Excellent! 'Twill work. Away! Away!
On to the banquet-hall without delay. *Exit.*

(Here again was a choral song, now lost.)

The scenery seems to have remained unchanged throughout the play; and BLEPYRUS *comes out of the central house at 1128 below, just as he has already done at 311 and 520 above. But the houses on either side, hitherto the residences of Chremes and the Second Woman respectively, have changed their occupants; and one of them has become the abode of an ancient* HAG *and a young* GIRL.

Hag. Why don't the fellows come? The hour's long past:
And here I'm standing, ready, with my skin
Plastered with paint, wearing my yellow gown,
Humming an amorous ditty to myself,
Trying, by wanton sportiveness, to catch
Some passer-by. Come, Muses, to my lips,
With some sweet soft Ionian roundelay.
Girl. This once then, Mother Mouldy, you've forestalled me,
And peeped out first; thinking to steal my grapes,
I absent; aye, and singing to attract
A lover; sing then, and I'll sing against you.
For this, even though 'tis irksome to the audience,
Has yet a pleasant and a comic flavour.
Hag. Here, talk to this, and vanish: but do you,
Dear honey piper, take the pipes and play
A strain that's worthy you, and worthy me,
(*singing*) Whoever is fain love's bliss to attain,
Let him hasten to me, and be blest;
For knowledge is sure with the ripe and mature,
And not with the novice, to rest.
Would *she* be as faithful and true to the end,
And constant and loving as I?
No: she would be flitting away from her friend,
And off to another would fly,
Would fly, would fly, would fly,
And off to another would fly.
Gi. (*affettuosamente*) O grudge not the young their enjoyment.
For beauty the softest and best
Is breathed o'er the limbs of a maiden,
And blooms on the maidenly breast.
You have tweezered your brows, and bedizened your face,
And you look like a darling for—death to embrace.
Hag. (*con fuoco*) I hope that the cords of your bedstead will rot,
I hope that your tester will break,
And O when you think that a lover you've got,
I hope you will find him a snake,
A snake, a snake, a snake,
I hope you will find him a snake!
Gi. (*teneramente*) O dear, what will become of me?
Where can my lover be flown?
Mother is out; she has gone and deserted me,
Mother has left me alone.
Nurse, nurse, pity and comfort me,
Fetch me my lover, I pray;
So may it always be happy and well with thee,
O, I beseech thee, obey.
Hag (*fortissimo*) These, these, are the tricks of the harlotry
This, the Ionian itch!
Gi. (*con spirito*) No! no! you shall never prevail with me,
Mine are the charms that bewitch.
Hag. Aye, aye, sing on: keep peeping, peering out
Like a young cat. They'll all come first to me.
Gi. What, to your funeral? A new joke, hey?
Hag. No, very old.
Gi. Old jokes to an old crone.
Hag. My age won't trouble *you*.
Gi. No? Then what will?
Your artificial red and white, perchance.
Hag. Why talk to me?
Gi. Why peeping?

Hag. I? I'm singing
With bated breath to dear Epigenes.
Gi. I thought old Geres was your only dear.
Hag. You'll soon think otherwise: he'll come to *me.*
O here he is, himself.
Enter YOUTH, *bearing a torch.*
Gi. Not wanting aught
Of you, Old Plague.
Hag. O yes, Miss Pineaway.
Gi. His acts will show. I'll slip away unseen.
Exit.
Hag. And so will I. You'll find I'm right, my beauty.
Youth. O that I now might my darling woo!
Nor first be doomed to the foul embrace
Of an ancient hag with a loathsome face;
To a free-born stripling a dire disgrace!
Hag. That you never, my boy, can do!
'Tis not Charixena's style to-day;
Now the laws you must needs obey
Under our democratical sway.
I'll run and watch what next you are going to do.
Yo. O might I catch, dear gods, my fair alone,
To whom I hasten, flushed with love and wine.
Gi. (*re-appearing above*) That vile old Hag, I nicely cozened her.
She deems I'm safe within, and off she's gone.
But here's the very lad of whom we spake.
(*Singing*) This way, this way.
Hither, my soul's delight!
O come to my arms, my love, my own,
O come to my arms this night.
Dearly I long for my love;
My bosom is shaken and whirls,
My heart is afire with a wild desire
For my boy with the sunbright curls.
Ah me, what means this strange unrest,
This love which lacerates my breast?
O God of Love, I cry to thee;
Be pitiful, be merciful,
And send my love to me.
Yo. (*singing*). Hither, O hither, my love,
This way, this way.
Run, run down from above,
Open the wicket I pray:
Else I shall swoon, I shall die!
Dearly I long for thy charms,
Longing and craving and yearning to lie
In the bliss of thy snow-soft arms.
O Cypris, why my bosom stir,
Making me rage and rave for her?
O God of Love, I cry to thee,
Be pitiful, be merciful,
And send my love to me.
Enough, I trow, is said to show
the straits I'm in, my lonely grieving.
Too long I've made my serenade:
descend, sweet heart, thy chamber leaving,
Open, true welcome show,
Sore pangs for thee I undergo.
O Love, bedight with golden light,
presentment fair of soft embraces,
The Muses' bee, of Love's sweet tree
the flower, the nursling of the Graces,
Open, true welcome show,
Sore pangs for thee I undergo.
Exit GIRL.
Hag. (*re-appearing*) Hi! knocking? seeking *me*?
Yo. A likely joke.
Hag. You banged against my door.
Yo. Hanged if I did
Hag. Then why that lighted torch? What seek you here?
Yo. Some Anaphlystian burgher.
Hag. What's his name?
Yo. No, not Sebinus; whom *you* want belike.
Hag. By Aphrodite, will you, nill you, sir.
The HAG *tries to drag him into her house.*
Yo. Ah, but we're not now taking cases over
Sixty years old: they've been adjourned till later;
We're taking now those under twenty years.
Hag. Aha, but that was under, darling boy,
The old régime: now you must take us first.
Yo. Aye, if I will: so runs the Paetian law.
Hag. You didn't, did you, dine by Paetian law.
Yo. Don't understand you: there's the girl I want.
Hag. Aye, but *me* first: you must, you rogue, you must.
Yo. O we don't want a musty pack-cloth now,
Hag. I know I'm loved: but O you wonder, don't you,
To see me out of doors: come, buss me, do.
Yo. No, no, I dread your lover.
Hag. Whom do you mean?
Yo. That prince of painters.
Hag. Who is he, I wonder.
Yo. Who paints from life the bottles for the dead.
Away! begone! he'll see you at the door.
Hag. I know, I know your wishes.
Yo. And I yours.
Hag. I vow by Aphrodite, whose I am,
I'll never let you go.
Yo. You're mad, old lady.
Hag. Nonsense! I'll drag you recreant to my couch.
Yo. Why buy we hooks to raise our buckets then,
When an old hag like this, let deftly down,
Could claw up all the buckets from our wells?
Hag. No scoffing, honey: come along with me.
Yo. You've got no rights, unless you've paid the tax,
One-fifth per cent on all your wealth—of years.
Hag. O yes, you must; O yes, by Aphrodite,
Because I love to cuddle lads like you.
Yo. But I don't love to cuddle hags like you,
Nor will I: never! never!
Hag. O yes, you will,
This will compel you.
Yo. What in the world is *this*?
Hag. *This* is a law which bids you follow me.
Yo. Read what it says.
Hag. O yes, my dear, I will.
"Be it enacted," please to listen, you,
"By us the ladies: if a youth would woo

A maiden, he must first his duty do
By some old beldame; if the youth refuse,
Then may the beldames lawful violence use
And drag him in, in any way they choose."

Yo. A crusty law! a Procrustéan law!

Hag. Well, never mind; you must obey the law.

Yo. What if some Man, a friend or fellow-burgher,
Should come and bail me out?

Hag. A Man, forsooth?
No Man avails beyond a bushel now.

Yo. Essoign I'll challenge.

Hag. Nay, no quillets now.

Yo. I'll sham a merchant.

Hag. You'll repent it then.

Yo. And must I come?

Hag. You must.

Yo. Is it a stern
Necessity?

Hag. Yes, quite Diomedéan.

Yo. Then strew the couch with dittany, and set
Four well-crushed branches of the vine beneath;
Bind on the fillets; set the oil beside;
And at the entrance set the water-crock.

Hag. Now, by my troth, you'll buy me a garland yet.

Yo. A waxen garland. So, by Zeus, I will.
You'll fall to pieces, I expect, in there.

Enter GIRL.

Gi. Where drag you him?

Hag. I'm taking home my husband.

Gi. Not wisely then: the lad is far too young
To serve your turn. You're of an age, methinks
To be his mother rather than his wife.
If thus ye carry out the law, erelong
Ye'll have an Oedipus in every house.

Hag. You nasty spiteful girl, you made that speech
Out of sheer envy, but I'll pay you out. *Exit.*

Yo. Now by the Saviour Zeus, my sweetest sweet,
A rare good turn you have done me, scaring off
That vulturous Hag; for which, at eventide,
I'll make you, darling, what return I can.

Enter SECOND HAG.

2nd H. Hallo, Miss Break-the-law, where are you dragging
That gay young stripling, when the writing says
I'm first to wed him?

Yo. Miserable me!
Whence did *you* spring, you evil-destined Hag?
She's worse than the other: I protest she is.

2nd H. Come hither.

Yo. (*to the* GIRL) O my darling, don't stand by,
And see this creature drag me!

2nd H. 'Tis not I,
'Tis the *law* drags you.

Yo. 'Tis a hellish vampire,
Clothed all about with blood, and boils, and blisters.

2nd H. Come, chickling, follow me: and don't keep chattering.

Yo. O let me first, for pity's sake, retire
Into some draught-house. I'm in such a fright
That I shall yellow all about me else.

2nd H. Come, never mind; you can do that within.

Yo. More than I wish, I fear me. Come, pray do,
I'll give you bail with two sufficient sureties.

2nd H. No bail for me!

Enter THIRD HAG. *A struggle ensues.*

3rd H. (*to* YOUTH) Hallo, where are you gadding
Away with her?

Yo. Not "gadding": being dragged.
But blessings on you, whosoe'er you are,
Sweet sympathizer. Ah! Oh! Heracles!
Ye Pans! ye Corybants! Twin sons of Zeus!
She's worse than the other! Miserable me!
What shall I term this monstrous apparition?
A monkey smothered up in paint, or else
A witch ascending from the Greater Number?

3rd H. No scoffing: come *this* way.

2nd H. *This* way, I tell you.

3rd H. I'll never let you go.

2nd H. No more will I.

Yo. Detested kites, ye'll rend me limb from limb.

2nd H. Obey the law, which bids you follow me.

3rd H. Not if a fouler, filthier, hag appears.

Yo. Now if betwixt you two I am done to death,
How shall I ever reach the girl I love?

3rd H. That's *your* look-out; but this you needs must do.

Yo. Which shall I tackle first, and so get free?

2nd H. You know; come hither.

Yo. Make *her* let me go.

3rd H. No, no, come hither.

Yo. If *she*'ll let me go.

2nd H. Zeus! I'll not let you go.

3rd H. No more will I.

Yo. Rough hands ye'd prove as ferrymen.

2nd H. Why so?

Yo. Ye'd tear your passengers to bits by pulling.

2nd H. Don't talk, come hither.

3rd H. No, *this* way, I tell you.

Yo. O this is like Cannonus's decree,[1]
To play the lover, fettered right and left.
How can one oarsman navigate a pair?

2nd H. Tush, eat a pot of truffles, foolish boy.

Yo. O me, I'm dragged along till now I've reached
The very door.

3rd H. That won't avail you aught;
I'll tumble in beside you.

Yo. Heaven forbid!
Better to struggle with one ill than two.

3rd H. O yes, by Hecate, will you, nill you, sir.

Yo. Thrice hapless me, who first must play the man
With this old rotten carcase, and when freed
From her, shall find another Phryne there,
A bottle of oil beside her grinning chaps.
Ain't I ill-fated? Yea, most heavy-fated!
O Zeus the Saviour, what a wretch am I
Yoked with this pair of savage-hearted beasts!
And O should aught befall me, sailing in
To harbour, towed by these detested drabs,

[1]It set the death penalty for anyone who wronged the people of Athens.

Bury my body by the harbour's mouth;
And take the upper hag, who still survives,
And tar her well, and round her ankles twain
Pour molten lead, and plant her on my grave,
The staring likeness of a bottle of oil. *Exeunt.*

Enter Praxagora's MAID.

Maid. O lucky People, and O happy me,
And O my mistress, luckiest of us all,
And ye who now are standing at our door,
And all our neighbours, aye and all our town,
And I'm a lucky waiting-maid, who now
Have had my head with unguents rich and rare
Perfumed and bathed; but far surpassing all
Are those sweet flagons full of Thasian wine.
Their fragrance long keeps lingering in the head,
Whilst all the rest evaporate and fade.
There's nothing half so good; great gods, not half!
Choose the most fragrant, mix it neat and raw,
'Twill make us merry all the whole night through.
But tell me, ladies, where my master is;
I mean, the husband of my honoured mistress.

Ch. If you stay here, methinks you'll find him soon.

Ma. Aye, here he comes. (*Enter* BLEPYRUS *and the children.*) He's off to join the dinner.
O master, O you lucky, lucky man!

Bl. What I?

Ma. Yes you, by Zeus, you luckiest man.
What greater bliss than yours, who, out of more
Than thrice ten thousand citizens, alone,
Have managed, you alone, to get no dinner?

Ch. You tell of a happy man, and no mistake.

Ma. Hi! Hi! where now?

Bl. I'm off to join the dinner.

Ma. And much the last of all, by Aphrodite.
Well, well, my mistress bade me take you, sir,
You and these little girls and bring you thither.
Aye, and there's store of Chian wine remaining,
And other dainties too; so don't delay.
And all the audience who are well disposed,
And every judge who looks not otherwards,
Come on with us; we'll freely give you all.

Bl. Nay, no exceptions; open wide your mouth,
Invite them all in free and generous style,
Boy, stripling, grandsire; yea, announce that all
Shall find a table all prepared and spread
For their enjoyment, in—their own sweet homes.
But I! I'll hurry off to join the feast,
And here at least I've got a torch all handy.

Ch. Then why so long keep lingering here, nor take
These little ladies down? And as you go,
I'll sing a song, a Lay of Lay-the-dinner.
But first, a slight suggestion to the judges.
Let the wise and philosophic
choose me for my wisdom's sake,
Those who joy in mirth and laughter
choose me for the jests I make;
Then with hardly an exception
every vote I'm bound to win.
Let it nothing tell against me,
that my play must first begin;
See that, through the afterpieces,
back to me your memory strays;
Keep your oaths, and well and truly
judge between the rival plays.
Be not like the wanton women,
never mindful of the past,
Always for the new admirer,
always fondest of the last.
Now 'tis time, 'tis time, 'tis time,
Sisters dear, 'tis time for certain,
if we mean the thing to do,
To the public feast to hasten.
Therefore foot it neatly, you,
First throw up your right leg, so,
Then the left, and away to go,
Cretan measure.

Bl. Aye, with pleasure.

Ch. Now must the spindleshanks, lanky and lean,
Trip to the banquet, for soon will, I ween,
High on the table be smoking a dish
Brimming with game and with fowl and with fish,
All sorts of good things.
Plattero-filleto-mulleto-turboto-
-Cranio-morselo-pickleo-acido-
-Silphio-honeyo-pouredonthe-topothe-
-Ouzelo-throstleo-cushato-culvero-
-Cutleto-roastingo-marrowo-dippero-
-Leveret-syrupo-gibleto-wings.
So now ye have heard these tidings true,
Lay hold of a plate and an omelette too,
And scurry away at your topmost speed,
And so you will have whereon to feed.

Bl. They're guzzling already, I know, I know.

Ch. Then up with your feet and away to go.
Off, off to the supper we'll run.
With a whoop for the prize, hurrah, hurrah,
With a whoop for the prize, hurrah, hurrah,
Whoop, whoop, for the victory won!

THE PLUTUS

DRAMATIS PERSONAE

CARIO, *servant of Chremylus*	A GOOD MAN
CHREMYLUS	AN INFORMER
PLUTUS, *God of Wealth*	AN OLD LADY
BLEPSIDEMUS	A YOUTH
POVERTY	HERMES
WIFE OF CHREMYLUS	A PRIEST OF ZEUS

CHORUS OF NEEDY AGRICULTURISTS

Scene: a street in Athens with the house of CHREMYLUS *in the background. Groping along in front is a* BLIND MAN *of sordid appearance, followed by* CHREMYLUS, *an elderly citizen, and a slave,* CARIO, *wearing wreaths of bay.*

Cario. How hard it is, O Zeus and all ye Gods,
To be the slave of a demented master!
For though the servant give the best advice,
Yet if his owner otherwise decide,
The servant needs must share the ill results.
For a man's body, such is fate, belongs
Not to himself, but to whoe'er has bought it.
So much for that. But now with Loxias,
Who from his golden tripod chants his high
Oracular strains, I've got a bone to pick.
A wise Physician-seer they call him, yet
He has sent my master off so moody-mad,
That now he's following a poor blind old man,
Just the reverse of what he ought to do.
For we who see should go *before* the blind,
But he goes *after* (and constrains me too)
One who won't answer even with a gr-r-r.
I won't keep silence, master, no I won't,
Unless you tell me why you're following *him.*
I'll plague you, Sir; I know you won't chastise me
So long as I've this sacred chaplet on.
Chremylus. I'll pluck it off, that you may smart the more,
If you keep bothering.
Ca. Humbug! I won't stop
Until you have told me who the fellow is.
You know I ask it out of love for you.
Chr. I'll tell you, for of all my servants you
I count the truest and most constant—thief.
—I've been a virtuous and religious man
Yet always poor and luckless.
Ca. So you have.
Chr. While Temple-breakers, orators, informers,
And knaves grow rich and prosper.
Ca. So they do.
Chr. So then I went to question of the God—
Not for myself, the quiver of my life
Is well-nigh emptied of its arrows now—
But for my son, my only son, to ask
If, changing all his habits, he should turn
A rogue, dishonest, rotten to the core.
For such as they, methinks, succeed the best.
Ca. And what droned Phoebus from his wreaths of bay?
Chr. He told me plainly that with whomsoe'er
I first forgathered as I left the shrine,
Of him I never should leave go again,
But win him back, in friendship, to my home.
Ca. With whom then did you first forgather?
Chr. Him.
Ca. And can't you see the meaning of the God,
You ignoramus, who so plainly tells you
Your son should follow the prevailing fashion?
Chr. Why think you that?
Ca. He means that even the blind
Can see 'tis better for our present life
To be a rascal, rotten to the core.
Chr. 'Tis not that way the oracle inclines,
It cannot be. 'Tis something more than that.
Now if this fellow told us who he is,
And why and wherefore he has come here now,
We'd soon discover what the God intended.
Ca. (*to* WEALTH) Hallo, you sirrah, tell me who you are,
Or take the consequence! Out with it, quick!
Wealth. Go and be hanged!
Ca. O master, did you hear
The name he gave?
Chr. 'Twas menat for you, not me.
You ask in such a rude and vulgar way.
(*To* WEALTH) Friend, if you love an honest gentleman,
Tell *me* your name.
We. Get out, you vagabond!
Ca. O! O! Accept the omen, and the man.
Chr. O, by Demeter, you shall smart for this.
Answer this instant or you die the death.
We. Men, men, depart and leave me.
Chr. Wouldn't you like it?
Ca. O master, what I say is far the best:
I'll make him die a miserable death.
I'll set him on some precipice, and leave him,
So then he'll topple down and break his neck.
Chr. Up with him!

We. O pray don't.
Chr. Do you mean to answer?
We. And if I do, I'm absolutely sure
You'll treat me ill: you'll never let me go.
Chr. I vow we will, at least if you desire it.
We. Then first unhand me.
Chr. There, we both unhand you.
We. Then listen, both: for I, it seems, must needs
Reveal the secret I proposed to keep.
Know then, I'm Wealth!
Chr. You most abominable
Of all mankind, you, Wealth, and keep it snug!
Ca. You, Wealth, in such a miserable plight!
Chr. O King Apollo! O ye Gods and daemons!
O Zeus! what mean you? are you really HE?
We. I am.
Chr. Himself?
We. His own self's self.
Chr. Whence come you
So grimed with dirt?
We. From Patrocles's house,
A man who never washed in all his life.
Chr. And this, your sad affliction, how came this?
We. 'Twas Zeus that caused it, jealous of mankind.
For, when a little chap, I used to brag
I'd visit none except the wise and good
And orderly; he therefore made me blind,
That I might ne'er distinguish which was which,
So jealous is he always of the good!
Chr. And yet 'tis only from the just and good
His worship comes.
We. I grant you that.
Chr. Then tell me,
If you could see again as once you could,
Would you avoid the wicked?
We. Yes, I would.
Chr. And visit all the good?
We. Yes; more by token
I have not seen the good for many a day.
Chr. No more have I, although I've got my eyes.
We. Come, let me go; you know my story now.
Chr. And therefore, truly, hold we on the more.
We. I told you so: you vowed you'd let me go.
I knew you wouldn't.
Chr. O be guided, pray,
And don't desert me. Search where'er you will
You'll never find a better man than I.
Ca. No more there is, by Zeus—except myself.
We. They all say that; but when in sober earnest
They find they've got me, and are wealthy men,
They place no limit on their evil ways.
Chr. Too true! And yet not every one is bad.
We. Yes, every single one.
Ca. (*aside*) You'll smart for that.
Chr. Nay, nay, but hear what benefits you'll get
If you're presuaded to abide with us.
For well I trust,—I trust, with God to aid,
That I shall rid you of this eye-disease,
And make you see.
We. For mercy's sake, forbear.
I do not wish to see again.
Chr. Eh? what?
Ca. O why, the man's a born unfortunate!
We. Let Zeus but hear their follies, and I know
He'll pay me out.
Chr. And doesn't he do that now;
Letting you wander stumbling through the world?
We. Eh, but I'm horribly afraid of Zeus!
Chr. Aye, say you so, you cowardliest God alive?
What! do you think the imperial power of Zeus
And all his thunderbolts were worth one farthing,
Could you but see, for ever so short a time?
We. Ah, don't say that, you wretches!
Chr. Don't be frightened!
I'll prove that you're far stronger, mightier far
Than Zeus.
We. You'll prove that *I* am?
Chr. Easily.
Come, what makes Zeus the Ruler of the Gods?
Ca. His silver. He's the wealthiest of them.
Chr. Well,
Who gives him all his riches?
Ca. Our friend here.
Chr. And for whose sake do mortals sacrifice
To Zeus?
Ca. For *his*: and pray straight out for wealth.
Chr. 'Tis all his doing: and 'tis he can quickly
Undo it if he will.
We. How mean you that?
Chr. I mean that nevermore will mortal man
Bring ox, or cake, or any sacrifice,
If such thy will.
We. How so?
Chr. How can he buy
A gift to offer, if thy power deny
The needful silver? Single-handed, thou,
If Zeus prove troublesome, canst crush his power.
We. Men sacrifice to Zeus for *me*?
Chr. They do.
And whatsoever in the world is bright,
And fair, and graceful, all is done for thee.
For every mortal thing subserves to Wealth.
Ca. Hence for a little filthy lucre I'm
A slave, forsooth, because I've got no wealth.
Chr. And those Corinthian huzzies, so they say,
If he who sues them for their love is poor,
Turn up their noses at the man; but grant
A wealthy suitor more than he desires.
Ca. So too the boy-loves; just to get some money,
And not at all because they love their lovers.
Chr. Those are the baser, not the nobler sort,
These never ask for money.
Ca. No? what then?
Chr. O one a hunter, one a pack of hounds.
Ca. Ah, they're ashamed, I warrant, of their vice,
And seek to crust it over with a name.
Chr. And every art existing in the world,
And every craft, was for thy sake invented.
For thee one sits and cobbles all the day,
One works in bronze, another works in wood,
One fuses gold—the gold derived from thee—
Ca. One plies the footpad's, one the burglar's trade,
Chr. One is a fuller, one a sheepskin-washer,

One is a tanner, one an onion-seller,
Through thee the nabbed adulterer gets off
plucked.
We. O, and all this I never knew before!
Chr. Aye, 'tis on him the Great King plumes
himself;
And our Assemblies all are held for him;
Dost thou not man our triremes? Answer that.
Does he not feed the foreign troop at Corinth?
Won't Pamphilus be brought to grief for him?
Ca. Won't Pamphilus and the needle-seller too?
Does not Agyrrhius flout us all for him?
Chr. Does not Philepsius tell his tales for thee?
Dost thou not make the Egyptians our allies?
And Laïs love the uncouth Philonides?
Ca. Timotheus' tower—
Chr. Pray Heaven it fall and crush you!
Aye, everything that's done is done for thee.
Thou art alone, thyself alone, the source
Of all our fortunes, good and bad alike.
'Tis so in war; wherever *he* alights,
That side is safe the victory to win.
We. Can I, unaided, do such feats as these?
Chr. O yes, by Zeus, and many more than these.
So that none ever has enough of thee.
Of all things else a man may have too much,
Of love,
Ca. Of loaves,
Chr. Of literature,
Ca. Of sweets,
Chr. Of honour,
Ca. Cheesecakes,
Chr. Manliness,
Ca. Dried figs,
Chr. Ambition,
Ca. Barley-meal,
Chr. Command,
Ca. Pea soup.
Chr. But no man ever has enough of thee.
For give a man a sum of thirteen talents,
And all the more he hungers for sixteen;
Give him sixteen, and he must needs have forty
Or life's not worth his living, so he says.
We. Ye seem to me to speak extremely well,
Yet on one point I'm fearful.
Chr. What is that?
We. This mighty power which ye ascribe to me,
I can't imagine how I'm going to wield it.
Chr. O this it is that all the people say,
"Wealth is the cowardliest thing."
We. It is not true.
That is some burglar's slander; breaking into
A wealthy house, he found that everything
Was under lock and key, and so got nothing:
Wherefore he called my forethought, cowardliness.
Chr. Well, never mind; assist us in the work
And play the man; and very soon I'll make you
Of keener sight than ever Lynceus was.
We. Why, how can you, a mortal man, do that?
Chr. Good hope have I from that which Phoebus
told me,
Shaking the Pythian laurel as he spoke.

We. Is Phoebus privy to your plan?
Chr. He is.
We. Take heed!
Chr. Don't fret yourself, my worthy friend.
I am the man: I'll work the matter through,
Though I should die for it.
Ca. And so will I.
Chr. And many other bold allies will come,
Good virtuous men without a grain of—barley.
We. Bless me! a set of rather poor allies.
Chr. Not when you've made them wealthy men
once more.
Hi, Cario, run your fastest, and
Ca. Do what?
Chr. Summon my farm-companions from the
fields
(You'll find them there, poor fellows, hard at
work),
And fetch them hither; so that each and all
May have, with me, an equal share in Wealth.
Ca. Here goes! I'm off. Come out there, somebody,
And carry in my little piece of meat. *Exit* CARIO.
Chr. I'll see to that: you, run away directly.
But thou, dear Wealth, the mightiest Power of all,
Come underneath my roof. Here stands the house,
Which thou art going evermore to fill
With wealth and plenty, by fair means or foul.
We. And yet it irks me, I protest it does,
To enter in beneath a stranger's roof.
I never got the slightest good from that.
Was it a miser's house; the miser straight
Would dig a hole and pop me underground;
And if some worthy neighbour came to beg
A little silver for his urgent needs,
Would vow he'd never seen me in his life.
Or was it some young madcap's: in a jiffey
Squandered and lost amongst his drabs and dice
I'm bundled, naked, out of house and home.
Chr. You never chanced upon a moderate man,
But now you have; for such a man am I.
For much I joy in saving, no man more,
And much in spending when 'tis right to spend.
So go we in; I long to introduce
My wife and only son whom most I love—
After yourself of course.
We. That I believe.
Chr. Why should one say what is not true to you?
Exeunt.

Enter CARIO *with the* CHORUS OF NEEDY AGRICULTURISTS.

Ca. O ye who many a day have chewed
a root of thyme with master,
My labour-loving village-friends,
be pleased to step out faster;
Be staunch and strong, and stride along,
let nothing now delay you,
Your fortunes lie upon the die,
come save them quick, I pray you.
Chorus. Now don't you see we're bustling, we,
as fast as we can go, sir?
We're not so young as once we were,
and Age is somewhat slow, sir.

You'd think it fun to see us run,
and that before you've told us
The reason why your master seems
so anxious to behold us.
Ca. Why, I've been telling long ago;
'tis you are not attending!
He bade me call and fetch you all
that you, forever ending
This chill ungenial life of yours,
might lead a life luxurious.
Ch. Explain to me how that can be;
i' faith I'm rather curious.
Ca. He's got a man, an ancient man,
of sorriest form and feature,
Bald, toothless, squalid, wrinkled, bent,
a very loathsome creature.
I really should not be surprised
to hear the wretch is circumcised.
Ch. O Messenger of golden news,
you thrill my heart with pleasure.
I do believe the man has come
with quite a heap of treasure!
Ca. O aye, he's got a heap, I guess,
a heap of woes and wretchedness.
Ch. You think, I see, you think you're free
to gull me with impunity.
No, no; my stick I've got and quick
I'll get my opportunity.
Ca. What, think you I'm the sort of man
such things as that to do, sirs?
Am I the man a tale to tell
wherein there's nothing true, sirs?
Ch. How absolute the knave has grown!
your shins, my boy, are bawling
"Ah! Ah!" with all their might and main,
for gyves and fetters calling.
Ca. You've drawn your lot; the grave you've got
to judge in; why delay now?
Old Charon gives the ticket there;
why don't you pass away now?
Ch. Go hang yourself, you peevish elf,
you born buffoon and scoffer.
You love to tantalize and tease,
nor condescend to offer
A word of explanation why
we're summoned here so hurriedly.
I had to shirk some urgent work,
and here so quickly hasted,
That many a tempting root of thyme
I passed, and left untasted.
Ca. I'll hide it not: 'tis Wealth we've got;
the God of wealth we've captured,
You'll all be rich and wealthy now.
Ha, don't you look enraptured?
Ch. He says we'll all be wealthy now;
upon my word this passes, sirs.
Ca. O yes, you'll all be Midases,
if only you've the asses' ears.
Ch. O I'm so happy, I'm so glad,
I needs must dance for jollity,
If what you say is really true,
and not your own frivolity.

Ca. And I before your ranks will go,
"Threttanelo! Threttanelo!"
And I, the Cyclops, heel and toe,
will dance the sailor's hornpipe,—so!
Come up, come up, my little ones all,
come raise your multitudinous squall,
Come bleating loudly the tuneful notes
Of sheep and of rankly-odorous goats.
Come follow along on your loves intent;
come goats, 'tis time to your meal ye went.
Ch. And you we'll seek where'er you go,
"Threttanelo! Threttanelo!"
And you, the Cyclops, will we find
in dirty, drunken sleep reclined,
Your well-stuffed wallet beside you too,
with many a potherb bathed in dew.
And then from out of the fire we'll take
A sharply-pointed and burning stake,
And whirling it round till our shoulders ache,
its flame in your hissing eyeball slake.
Ca. And now I'll change to Circe's part,
who mixed her drugs with baleful art;
Who late in Corinth, as I've learned,
Philonides's comrades turned
To loathsome swine in a loathsome sty,
And fed them all on kneaded dung
which, kneading, she amongst them flung.
And turn you all into swine will I.
And then ye'll grunt in your bestial glee
Wee! wee! wee!
"Follow your mother, pigs," quoth she.
Ch. We'll catch you, Circe dear, we will;
who mix your drugs with baleful skill;
Who with enchantments strange and vile
ensnare our comrades and defile;
We'll hang you up as you erst were hung
By bold Odysseus, lady fair;
and then as if a goat you were
We'll rub your nose in the kneaded dung.
Like Aristyllus you'll gape with glee
Wee! wee! wee!
"Follow your mother, pigs," quoth he.
Ca. But now, old mates, break off, break off;
no longer may we jest and scoff;
No longer play the fool to-day.
And ye must sail on another tack,
Whilst I, behind my master's back,
Rummage for meat and bread to eat,
And then, whilst yet the food I chew,
I'll join the work we are going to do.

Exit CARIO *to get his bread and meat; enter* CHREMYLUS.

Chr. To bid you "welcome," fellow-burghers, now
Is old and musty; so I—"clasp" you all.
Ye who have come in this stout-hearted way,
This strenuous way, this unrelaxing way,
Stand by me now, and prove yourselves to-day
In very truth the Saviours of the God.
Ch. Fear not: I'll bear me like the God of War.
What, shall we push and hustle in the Assembly
To gain our three poor obols, and to-day
Let Wealth himself be wrested from our grasp?

Chr. And here, I see, comes Blepsidemus too.
Look! by his speed and bearing you can tell
He has heard a rumour of what's happening here.

Enter BLEPSIDEMUS.

Blepsidemus. What can it mean? Old Chremylus grown wealthy!
Then whence and how? I don't believe that story.
And yet by Heracles 'twas bruited wide
Amongst the loungers in the barbers' shops
That Chremylus had all at once grown rich.
And if he has, 'tis passing wonderful
That he should call his neighbours in to share.
That's not our country's fashion, anyhow.

Chr. I'll tell him everything. O Blepsidemus,
We're better off to-day then yesterday.
You are my friend, and you shall share in all.

Bl. What, are you really wealthy, as men say?

Chr. Well, if God will, I shall be presently.
But there's some risk, some risk, about it yet.

Bl. What sort of risk?

Chr. Such as—

Bl. Pray, pray go on.

Chr. If we succeed, we're prosperous all our lives:
But if we fail, we perish utterly.

Bl. I like not this; there's something wrong behind,
Some evil venture. To become, off-hand,
So over-wealthy, and to fear such risks,
Smacks of a man who has done some rotten thing.

Chr. Rotten! what mean you?

Bl. If you've stolen aught,
Or gold or silver, from the God out there,
And now perchance repent you of your sin—

Chr. Apollo shield us! no, I've not done that.

Bl. O don't tell *me*. I see it plainly now.

Chr. Pray don't suspect me of such crimes.

Bl. Alas!
There's nothing sound or honest in the world,
The love of money overcomes us all.

Chr. Now by Demeter, friend, you have lost your wits.

Bl. O how unlike the man he used to be!

Chr. Poor chap, you're moody-mad: I vow you are.

Bl. His very eye's grown shifty: he can't look you
Straight in the face: I warrant he's turned rogue.

Chr. I understand. You think I've stolen something,
And want a share.

Bl. I want a share? in what?

Chr. But 'tis not so: the thing's quite otherwise.

Bl. Not stol'n, but robbed outright?

Chr. The man's possessed.

Bl. Have you embezzled someone else's cash?

Chr. I haven't: no.

Bl. O Heracles, where now
Can a man turn! you won't confess the truth.

Chr. You bring your charge before you have heard the facts.

Bl. Now prithee let me hush the matter up
For a mere trifle, ere it all leaks out.
A few small coins will stop the speakers' mouths.

Chr. You'd like, I warrant, in your friendly way,
To spend three minas, and to charge me twelve.

Bl. I see an old man pleading for his life
With olive-branch in hand, and at his side
His weeping wife and children, shrewdly like
The suppliant Heracleids of Pamphilus.

Chr. Nay, luckless idiot, 'tis the good alone
And right- and sober-minded that I'm going
At once to make so wealthy.

Bl. Heaven and earth!
What, have you stol'n so largely?

Chr. O confound it,
You'll be my death.

Bl. You'll be your own, I fancy.

Chr. Not so, you reprobate; 'tis *Wealth* I've got.

Bl. You, Wealth! What sort of wealth?

Chr. The God himself.

Bl. Where? where?

Chr. Within.

Bl. Where?

Chr. In my house.

Bl. In yours?

Chr. Yes.

Bl. You be hanged! Wealth in your house?

Chr. I swear it.

Bl. Is this the truth?

Chr. It is.

Bl. By Hestia?

Chr. Aye; by Poseidon.

Bl. Him that rules the sea?

Chr. If there's another, by that other too.

Bl. Then don't you send him round for friends to share?

Chr. Not yet; things haven't reached that stage.

Bl. What stage?
The stage of sharing?

Chr. Aye, we've first to—

Bl. What?

Chr. Restore the sight—

Bl. Restore the sight of whom?

Chr. The sight of Wealth, by any means we can.

Bl. What, is he really blind?

Chr. He really is.

Bl. O that is why he never came to me.

Chr. But now he'll come, if such the will of Heaven.

Bl. Had we not better call a doctor in?

Chr. Is there a doctor now in all the town?
There are no fees, and therefore there's no skill.

Bl. Let's think awhile.

Chr. There's none.

Bl. No more there is.

Chr. Why then, 'tis best to do what I intended,
To let him lie inside Asclepius' temple
A whole night long.

Bl. That's far the best, I swear it.
So don't be dawdling: quick; get something done.

Chr. I'm going.

Bl. Make you haste.

Chr. I'm doing that.

Enter POVERTY, *a wild-looking woman.*

Poverty. You pair of luckless manikins who dare
A rash, unholy, lawless deed to do—
Where! What! Why flee ye? Tarry?

Bl. Heracles!

Po. I'll make you die a miserable death.
For ye have dared a deed intolerable
Which no one else has ever dared to do,
Or God or man! Now therefore ye must die.
Chr. But who are you that look so pale and wan?
Bl. Belike some Fury from a tragic play.
She has a wild and tragic sort of look.
Chr. No, for she bears no torch.
Bl. The worse for her.
Po. What do you take me for?
Chr. Some pot-house girl
Or omelette-seller: else you would not bawl
At us so loudly ere you're harmed at all.
Po. Not harmed! Why, is it not a shameful thing
That you should seek to drive me from the land?
Chr. At all events you've got the Deadman's Pit.
But tell us quickly who and what you are.
Po. One who is going to pay you out to-day
Because ye seek to banish me from hence.
Bl. Is it the barmaid from the neighbouring tap
Who always cheats me with her swindling pint-pots?
Po. It's *Poverty*, your mate for many a year!
Bl. O King Apollo and ye Gods, I'm off.
Chr. Hi! What are you at? Stop, stop, you coward you,
Stop, can't you?
Bl. Anything but that.
Chr. Pray stop.
What! shall one woman scare away two men?
Bl. But this is Poverty herself, you rogue,
The most destructive pest in all the world.
Chr. Stay, I implore you, stay.
Bl. Not I, by Zeus.
Chr. Why, this, I tell you, were the cowardliest deed
That ere was heard of, did we leave the God
Deserted here, and flee away ourselves
Too scared to strike one blow in his defence.
Bl. O, on what arms, what force, can we rely?
Is there a shield, a corslet, anywhere
Which this vile creature has not put in pawn?
Chr. Courage! the God will, single-handed, rear
A trophy o'er this atrophied assailant.
Po. What! dare you mutter, you two outcasts you,
Caught in the act, doing such dreadful deeds?
Chr. O, you accursed jade, why come you here
Abusing us? We never did you wrong.
Po. No wrong, forsooth! O by the heavenly Powers
No wrong to *me*, your trying to restore
Wealth's sight again?
Chr. How can it injure *you*,
If we are trying to confer a blessing
On all mankind?
Po. Blessing! what blessing?
Chr. What?
Expelling *you* from Hellas, first of all.
Po. Expelling *me* from Hellas! Could you do
A greater injury to mankind than that?
Chr. A greater? Yes; by not expelling you.
Po. Now that's a question I am quite prepared
To argue out at once; and if I prove
That I'm the source of every good to men,
And that by me ye live: but if I fail,
Then do thereafter whatsoe'er ye list.
Chr. You dare to offer this, you vixen you?
Po. And you, accept it: easily enough
Methinks I'll show you altogether wrong
Making the good men rich, as you propose.
Bl. O clubs and pillories! To the rescue! Help!
Po. Don't shout and storm before you have heard the facts.
Bl. Who can help shouting, when he hears such wild
Extravagant notions?
Po. Any man of sense.
Chr. And what's the penalty you'll bear, in case
You lose the day?
Po. Whate'er you please.
Chr. 'Tis well.
Po. But, if ye are worsted, ye must bear the same.
Bl. (*to* CHREMYLUS) Think you that twenty deaths are fine enough?
Chr. Enough for *her*; but two will do for us.
Po. Well then, be quick about it; for, indeed,
How can my statements be with truth gainsaid?
Ch. Find something, I pray, philosophic to say, whereby you may vanquish and rout her.
No thought of retreat; but her arguments meet with arguments stronger and stouter.
Chr. All people with me, I am sure, will agree, for to all men alike it is clear,
That the honest and true should enjoy, as their due, a successful and happy career,
Whilst the lot of the godless and wicked should fall in exactly the opposite sphere.
'Twas to compass this end that myself and my friend have been thinking as hard as we can,
And have hit on a nice beneficial device, a truly magnificent plan.
For if Wealth should attain to his eyesight again, nor amongst us so aimlessly roam,
To the dwellings I know of the good he would go, nor ever depart from their home.
The unjust and profane with disgust and disdain he is certain thereafter to shun,
Till all shall be honest and wealthy at last, to virtue and opulence won.
Is there any design more effective than mine a blessing on men to confer?
Bl. No, nothing, that's flat; I will answer for that; so don't be inquiring of *her*.
Chr. For our life of to-day were a man to survey and consider its chances aright,
He might fancy, I ween, it were madness or e'en the sport of some mischievous sprite.
So often the best of the world is possessed by the most undeserving of men,
Who have gotten their pile of money by vile injustice; so often again
The righteous are seen to be famished and lean, yea, with *thee* as their comrade to dwell.
Now if Wealth were to-night to recover his sight, and her from amongst us expel,

Can you tell me, I pray, a more excellent way
of bestowing a boon on mankind?
Po. O men on the least provocation prepared
to be crazy and out of your mind,
Men bearded and old, yet companions enrolled
in the Order of zanies and fools,
O what is the gain that the world would obtain
were it governed by you and your rules?
Why, if Wealth should allot himself equally out
(assume that his sight ye restore),
Then none would to science his talents devote
or practise a craft any more.
Yet if science and art from the world should depart,
pray whom would ye get for the future
To build you a ship, or your leather to snip,
or to make you a wheel or a suture?
Do ye think that a man will be likely to tan,
or a smithy or laundry to keep,
Or to break up the soil with his ploughshare, and toil
the fruits of Demeter to reap,
If regardless of these he can dwell at his ease,
a life without labour enjoying?
Chr. Absurd! why the troubles and tasks you describe
we of course shall our servants employ in.
Po. Your servants! But how will ye get any now?
I pray you the secret to tell.
Chr. With the silver we've got we can purchase a lot.
Po. But who is the man that will sell?
Chr. Some merchant from Thessaly coming, belike,
where most of the kidnappers dwell.
Who still, for the sake of the gain he will make,
with the slaves that we want will provide us.
Po. But first let me say, if we walk in the way
wherein ye are seeking to guide us,
There'll be never a kidnapper left in the world.
No merchant of course (can ye doubt it?)
His life would expose to such perils as those
had he plenty of money without it.
No, no; I'm afraid you must handle the spade
and follow the plough-tail in person,
Your life will have double the toil and the trouble
it used to.
Chr. Thyself be thy curse on!
Po. No more on a bed will you pillow your head,
for there won't be a bed in the land,
Nor carpets; for whom will you find at the loom,
when he's plenty of money in hand?
Rich perfumes no more will ye sprinkle and pour
as home ye are bringing the bride,
Or apparel the fair in habiliments rare
so cunningly fashioned and dyed.
Yet of little avail is your wealth if it fail
such enjoyments as these to procure you.
Ye fools, it is I who alone a supply
of the goods which ye covet ensure you.
I sit like a Mistress, by Poverty's lash
constraining the needy mechanic;
When I raise it, to earn his living he'll turn,
and work in a terrible panic.

Chr. Why, what have *you* got to bestow but a lot
of burns from the bathing-room station
And a hollow-cheeked rabble of destitute hags,
and brats on the verge of starvation?
And the lice, if you please, and the gnats and the fleas
whom I can't even count for their numbers,
Who around you all night will buzz and will bite,
and arouse you betimes from your slumbers.
"Up! up!" they will shrill, "'tis to hunger, but still
up! up! to your pain and privation."
For a robe but a rag, for a bed but a bag
of rushes which harbour a nation
Of bugs whose envenomed and tireless attacks
would the soundest of sleepers awaken.
And then for a carpet a sodden old mat,
which is falling to bits, must be taken.
And a jolly hard stone for a pillow you'll own;
and, for girdle-cakes barley and wheaten,
Must leaves dry and lean of the radish or e'en
sour stalks of the mallow be eaten.
And the head of a barrel, stove in, for a chair;
and, instead of a trough, for your kneading
A stave of a vat you must borrow, and that
all broken. So great and exceeding
Are the blessings which Poverty brings in her train
on the children of men to bestow!
Po. The life you define with such skill is not mine:
'tis the life of a beggar, I trow.
Chr. Well, Poverty, Beggary, truly the twain
to be sisters we always declare.
Po. Aye *you!* who to good Thrasybulus forsooth
Dionysius the Tyrant compare!
But the life I allot to my people is not,
nor shall be, so full of distresses.
'Tis a beggar alone who has nought of his own,
nor even an obol possesses.
My *poor* man, 'tis true, has to scrape and to screw
and his work he must never be slack in;
There'll be no superfluity found in his cot;
but then there will nothing be lacking.
Chr. Damater! a life of the Blessed you give:
forever to toil and to slave
At Poverty's call, and to leave after all
not even enough for a grave.
Po. You are all for your jeers and your comedy-sneers,
and you can't be in earnest a minute
Nor observe that alike in their bodily frame
and the spirit residing within it.
My people are better than Wealth's; for by *him*,
men bloated and gross are presented,
Fat rogues with big bellies and dropsical legs,
whose toes by the gout are tormented;
But mine are the lean and the wasplike and keen,
who strike at their foemen and sting them.
Chr. Ah, yes; to a wasplike condition, no doubt,
by the pinch of starvation you bring them.
Po. I can show you besides that Decorum abides
with those whom I visit; that mine
Are the modest and orderly folk, and that Wealth's
are "with insolence flushed and with wine."

Chr. 'Tis an orderly job, then, to thieve and to rob
and to break into houses by night.
Bl. Such modesty too! In whatever they do
they are careful to keep out of sight.
Po. Behold in the cities the Orator tribe;
when poor in their early career
How faithful and just to the popular trust,
how true to the State they appear.
When wealth at the City's expense they have gained,
they are worsened at once by the pelf,
Intriguing the popular cause to defeat,
attacking the People itself.
Chr. That is perfectly true though 'tis spoken by you,
you spiteful malevolent witch!
But still you shall squall for contending that all
had better be poor than be rich.
So don't be elate; for a terrible fate
shall your steps overtake before long.
Po. Why, I haven't yet heard the ghost of a word
to prove my contention is wrong.
You splutter and try to flutter and fly:
but of argument never a letter.
Chr. Pray why do all people abhor you and shun?
Po. Because I'm for making them better.
So children, we see, from their parents will flee
who would teach them the way they should go.
So hardly we learn what is right to discern;
so few what is best for them know.
Chr. Then Zeus, I suppose, is mistaken, nor knows
what most for his comfort and bliss is,
Since money and pelf he acquires for himself.
Bl. And *her* to the earth he dismisses.
Po. O dullards and blind! full of styles is your mind;
there are tumours titanic within it.
Zeus wealthy! Not he: he's as poor as can be:
and this I can prove in a minute.
If Zeus be so wealthy, how came it of yore
that out of his riches abounding
He could find but a wreath of wild olive for those
who should win at the games he was founding,
By all the Hellenes in each fourth year
on Olympia's plains to be holden?
If Zeus were as wealthy and rich as you say,
the wreath should at least have been golden.
Chr. It is plain, I should think, 'tis from love of the chink
that the conduct you mention arises;
The God is unwilling to lavish a doit
of the money he loves upon prizes.
The rubbish may go to the victors below;
the gold he retains in his coffers.
Po. How dare you produce such a libel on Zeus,
you couple of ignorant scoffers?
'Twere better, I'm sure, to be honest and poor,
than rich and so stingy and screwing.
Chr. Zeus crown you, I pray, with the wild olive spray,
and send you away to your ruin!
Po. To think that you dare to persist and declare
that Poverty does not present you
With all that is noblest and best in your lives!
Chr. Will Hecate's judgement content you?
If you question her which are the better, the rich
or the poor, she will say, I opine,
"Each month do the wealthy a supper provide,
to be used in my service divine,
But the poor lie in wait for a snatch at the plate,
or e'er it is placed on my shrine."
So away, nor retort with a g-r-r, you degraded
Importunate scold!
Persuade me you may, but I won't be persuaded.
Po. O Argos, behold!
Chr. Nay Pauson, your messmate, to aid you invite.
Po. O woe upon woe!
Chr. Be off to the ravens; get out of my sight.
Po. O where shall I go?
Chr. Go? Go to the pillory; don't be so slack,
Nor longer delay.
Po. Ah me, but ye'll speedily send for me back,
Who scout me to-day!
Exit.
Chr. When we send for you, come; not before. So farewell!
With Wealth as my comrade 'tis better to dwell.
Get you gone, and bemoan your misfortunes alone.
Bl. I too have a mind for an opulent life
Of revel and mirth with my children and wife,
Untroubled by Poverty's panics.
And then as I'm passing, all shiny and bright,
From my bath to my supper, what joy and delight
My fingers to snap in disdain at the sight
Of herself and her frowsy mechanics.
Chr. That cursed witch, thank Heaven, has gone and left us.
But you and I will take the God at once
To spend the night inside Asclepius' Temple.
Bl. And don't delay one instant, lest there come
Some other hindrance to the work in hand.
Chr. Hi! boy there, Cario, fetch me out the blankets,
And bring the God himself, with due observance,
And whatsoever is prepared within.

After 626 they all quit the stage. A whole night is supposed to pass, and next day CARIO *suddenly runs in with joyful news. He addresses the* CHORUS *in the orchestra.*

Ca. Here's joy, here's happiness, old friends, for you
Who, at the feast of Theseus, many a time
Have ladled up small sops of barley-broth!
Here's joy for you and all good folk besides.
Ch. How now, you best of all your fellow-knaves?
You seem to come a messenger of good.
Ca. With happiest fortune has my master sped,
Or rather Wealth himself; no longer blind,
"He hath relumed the brightness of his eyes,
So kind a Healer hath Asclepius proved."
Ch. (*singing*) Joy for the news you bring.
Joy! Joy! with shouts I sing.
Ca. Aye, will you, nill you, it is joy indeed.

Ch. (*singing*) Sing we with all our might Asclepius first and best,
To men a glorious light, Sire in his offspring blest.

Enter WIFE OF CHREMYLUS.

Wife. What means this shouting? Has good news arrived?
For I've been sitting till I'm tired within
Waiting for *him*, and longing for good news.

Ca. Bring wine, bring wine, my mistress; quaff yourself
The flowing bowl; (you like it passing well).
I bring you here all blessings in a lump.

Wi. Where?

Ca. That you'll learn from what I am going to say.

Wi. Be pleased to tell me with what speed you can.

Ca. Listen. I'll tell you all this striking business
Up from the foot on to the very head.

Wi. Not on *my* head, I pray you.

Ca. Not the blessings
We have all got?

Wi. Not all that striking business.

Ca. Soon as we reached the Temple of the God
Bringing the man, most miserable then,
But who so happy, who so prosperous now?
Without delay we took him to the sea
And bathed him there.

Wi. O what a happy man,
The poor old fellow bathed in the cold sea!

Ca. Then to the precincts of the God we went.
There on the altar honey-cakes and bakemeats
Were offered, food for the Hephaestian flame.
There laid we Wealth as custom bids; and we
Each for himself stitched up a pallet near.

Wi. Were there no others waiting to be healed?

Ca. Neocleides was, for one; the purblind man,
Who in his thefts out-shoots the keenest-eyed.
And many others, sick with every form
Of ailment. Soon the Temple servitor
Put out the lights, and bade us fall asleep,
Nor stir, nor speak, whatever noise we heard.
So down we lay in orderly repose.
And I could catch no slumber, not one wink,
Struck by a nice tureen of broth which stood
A little distance from an old wife's head,
Whereto I marvellously longed to creep.
Then, glancing upwards, I behold the priest
Whipping the cheese-cakes and the figs from off
The holy table; thence he coasted round
To every altar, spying what was left.
And everything he found he consecrated
Into a sort of sack; so I, concluding
This was the right and proper thing to do,
Arose at once to tackle that tureen.

Wi. Unhappy man! Did you not fear the God?

Ca. Indeed I did, lest he should cut in first,
Garlands and all, and capture my tureen.
For so the priest forewarned me he might do.
Then the old lady when my steps she heard
Reached out a stealthy hand; I gave a hiss,
And mouthed it gently like a sacred snake.
Back flies her hand; she draws her coverlets
More tightly round her, and, beneath them, lies
In deadly terror like a frightened cat.
Then of the broth I gobbled down a lot
Till I could eat no more, and then I stopped.

Wi. Did not the God approach you?

Ca. Not till later.
And then I did a thing will make you laugh.
For as he neared me, by some dire mishap
My wind exploded like a thunder-clap.

Wi. I guess the God was awfully disgusted.

Ca. No, but Iaso blushed a rosy red
And Panacea turned away her head
Holding her nose: my wind's not frankincense.

Wi. But he himself?

Ca. Observed it not, nor cared.

Wi. O why, you're making out the God a clown!

Ca. No, no; an ordure-taster.

Wi. Oh! you wretch.

Ca. So then, alarmed, I muffled up my head,
Whilst *he* went round, with calm and quiet tread,
To every patient, scanning each disease.
Then by his side a servant placed a stone
Pestle and mortar; and a medicine chest.

Wi. A stone one?

Ca. Hang it, not the medicine chest.

Wi. How saw you this, you villain, when your head,
You said just now, was muffled?

Ca. Through my cloak.
Full many a peep-hole has that cloak, I trow.
Well, first he set himself to mix a plaster
For Neocleides, throwing in three cloves
Of Tenian garlic; and with these he mingled
Verjuice and squills; and brayed them up together
Then drenched the mass with Sphettian vinegar,
And turning up the eyelids of the man
Plastered their inner sides, to make the smart
More painful. Up he springs with yells and roars
In act to flee; then laughed the God, and said,
"Nay, sit thou there, beplastered; I'll restrain thee,
Thou reckless swearer, from the Assembly now."

Wi. O what a clever, patriotic God!

Ca. Then, after this, he sat him down by Wealth,
And first he felt the patient's head, and next
Taking a linen napkin, clean and white,
Wiped both his lids, and all around them, dry.
Then Panacea with a scarlet cloth
Covered his face and head; then the God clucked,
And out there issued from the holy shrine
Two great enormous serpents.

Wi. O good heavens!

Ca. And underneath the scarlet cloth they crept
And licked his eyelids, as it seemed to me;
And, mistress dear, before you could have drunk
Of wine ten goblets, Wealth arose and saw.
O then for joy I clapped my hands together
And woke my master, and, hey presto! both
The God and serpents vanished in the shrine.
And those who lay by Wealth, imagine how
They blessed and greeted him, nor closed their eyes
The whole night long till daylight did appear.
And I could never praise the God enough
For both his deeds, enabling Wealth to see,
And making Neocleides still more blind.

Wi. O Lord and King, what mighty power is thine!
But prithee where is Wealth?
Ca. He's coming here,
With such a crowd collected at his heels.
For all the honest fellows, who before
Had scanty means of living, flocking round,
Welcomed the God and clasped his hand for joy.
—Though others, wealthy rascals, who had gained
Their pile of money by unrighteous means,
Wore scowling faces, knitted up in frowns,—
But those went following on, begarlanded,
With smiles and blessings; and the old men's shoes
Rang out in rhythmic progress as they marched.
Now therefore all, arise with one accord,
And skip, and bound, and dance the choral dance,
For nevermore, returning home, ye'll hear
Those fatal words: "No barley in the bin!"
Wi. By Hecate, for this good news you bring
I've half a mind to crown you with a wreath
Of barley loaves.
Ca. Well, don't be loitering now.
The men, by this, are nearly at your gates.
Wi. Then I will in, and fetch the welcoming-gifts
Wherewith to greet these newly-purchased—eyes.
Exit WIFE.
Ca. And I will out, and meet them as they come.
Exit CARIO. *Enter* WEALTH, *alone; to him later* CHREMYLUS, *with a crowd at his heels.*
We. And first I make obeisance to yon sun;
Then to august Athene's famous plain,
And all this hospitable land of Cecrops.
Shame on my past career! I blush to think
With whom I long consorted, unawares,
Whilst those who my companionship deserved
I shunned, not knowing. O unhappy me!
In neither this nor that I acted rightly.
But now, reversing all my former ways,
I'll show mankind 'twas through no wish of mine
I used to give myself to rogues and knaves.
Chr. Hang you, be off! the nuisance these friends are,
Emerging suddenly when fortune smiles.
Tcha! How they nudge your ribs, and punch your shins,
Displaying each some token of goodwill.
What man addressed me not? What aged group
Failed to enwreathe me in the market-place?
Enter WIFE.
Wi. Dearest of men, O welcome you and you.
Come now, I'll take these welcoming-gifts and pour them
O'er *you*, as custom bids.
We. Excuse me, no.
When first I'm entering with my sight restored
Into a house, 'twere meeter far that I
Confer a largess rather than receive.
Wi. Then won't you take the welcoming-gifts I bring?
We. Aye, by the hearth within, as custom bids.
So too we 'scape the vulgar tricks of farce.
It is not meet, with such a Bard as ours,
To fling a shower of figs and comfits out
Amongst the audience, just to make them laugh.
Wi. Well said indeed: for Dexinicus there
Is rising up, to scramble for the figs.
They all enter the house: henceforth CARIO *and* CHREMYLUS *come out by turns; they are never on the stage together. Some interval elapses before* CARIO'*s first entrance.*
Ca. How pleasant 'tis to lead a prosperous life,
And that, expending nothing of one's own.
Into this house a heap of golden joys
Has hurled itself though nothing wrong we've done.
Truly a sweet and pleasant thing is wealth.
With good white barley is our garner filled
And all our casks with red and fragrant wine.
And every vessel in the house is crammed
With gold and silver, wonderful to see.
The tank o'erflows with oil; the oil-flasks teem
With precious unguents; and the loft with figs.
And every cruet, pitcher, pannikin,
Is turned to bronze; the mouldy trencherlets
That held the fish are all of silver now.
Our lantern, all at once, is ivory-framed.
And we the servants, play at odd-or-even
With golden staters; and to cleanse us, use
Not stones, but garlic-leaves, so nice we are.
And master now, with garlands round his brow,
Is offering up hog, goat, and ram within.
But me the smoke drove out. I could not bear
To stay within; it bit my eyelids so.
Enter a prosperous and well-dressed citizen with an attendant carrying a tattered gaberdine and a disreputable pair of shoes.
Good Man. Now then, young fellow, come along with me
To find the God.
Ca. Eh? Who comes here, I wonder.
G. M. A man once wretched, but so happy now.
Ca. One of the honest sort, I dare aver.
G. M. Aye, aye.
Ca. What want you now?
G. M. I am come to thank
The God: great blessings hath he wrought for me.
For I, inheriting a fair estate,
Used it to help my comrades in their need,
Esteeming that the wisest thing to do.
Ca. I guess your money soon began to fail.
G. M. Aye, that it did!
Ca. And then you came to grief.
G. M. Aye, that I did! And I supposed that they
Whom I had succoured in their need, would now
Be glad to help me when in need myself.
But all slipped off as though they saw me not.
Ca. And jeered you, I'll be bound.
G. M. Aye, that they did!
The drought in all my vessels proved my ruin.
Ca. But not so now.
G. M. Therefore with right good cause
I come with thankfulness to praise the God.
Ca. But what's the meaning, by the Powers, of that,
That ancient gaberdine your boy is bearing?

G. M. This too I bring, an offering to the God.
Ca. That's not the robe you were initiate in?
G. M. No, but I shivered thirteen years therein.
Ca. Those shoes?
G. M. Have weathered many a storm with me.
Ca. And them you bring as votive offerings?
G. M. Yes.
Ca. What charming presents to the God you bring!

Enter INFORMER *with* WITNESS.

Informer. O me unlucky! O my hard, hard fate!
O thrice unlucky, four times, five times, yea
Twelve times, ten thousand times! O woe is me,
So strong the spirit of ill-luck that swamps me.
Ca. Apollo shield us and ye gracious Gods,
What dreadful misery has this poor wretch suffered?
In. What misery quoth'a? Shameful, scandalous wrong.
Why, all my goods are spirited away
Through this same God, who shall be blind again
If any justice can be found in Hellas.
G. M. Methinks I've got a glimmering of the truth.
This is some wretched fellow, come to grief;
Belike he is metal of the baser sort.
Ca. Then well done he to come to wrack and ruin.
In. Where, where is he who promised he would make
All of us wealthy in a trice, if only
He could regain his sight? Some of us truly
He has brought to ruin rather than to wealth.
Ca. Whom has he brought to ruin?
In. Me, this chap.
Ca. One of the rogues and housebreakers perchance?
In. O aye, by Zeus, and you're quite rotten too.
'Tis you have got my goods, I do believe.
Ca. How bold, Damater, has the Informing rogue
Come blustering in! 'Tis plain he's hunger-mad.
In. You, sirrah, come to the market-place at once,
There to be broken on the wheel, and forced
To tell your misdemeanours.
Ca. You be hanged!
G. M. O, if the God would extirpate the whole
Informer-brood, right well would he deserve,
O Saviour Zeus, of all the Hellenic race!
In. *You* jeer me too? Alack, you shared the spoil,
Or whence that brand new cloak? I'll take my oath
I saw you yesterday in a gaberdine.
G. M. I fear you not. I wear an antidote,
A ring Eudemus sold me for a drachma.
Ca. 'Tis not inscribed "For an Informer's bite."
In. Is not this insolence? Ye jest and jeer,
And have not told me what you are doing here.
'Tis for no good you two are here, I'm thinking.
Ca. Not for *your* good, you may be sure of that.
In. For off my goods ye are going to dine, I trow.
Ca. O that in very truth ye'd burst asunder,
You and your witness, crammed with nothingness.
In. Dare ye deny it? In your house they are cooking
A jolly lot of flesh and fish, you miscreants.
The INFORMER *gives five double sniffs.*

Ca. Smell you aught, lackpurse?
G. M. Maybe 'tis the cold,
Look what a wretched gaberdine he's wearing.
In. O Zeus and Gods, can such affronts be borne
From rogues like these? O me, how vexed I am
That I, a virtuous patriot, get such treatment.
Ca. What *you* a virtuous patriot?
In. No man more so.
Ca. Come then, I'll ask you—Answer me.
In. Well.
Ca. Are you
A farmer?
In. Do you take me for a fool?
Ca. A merchant?
In. Aye, I feign so, on occasion.
Ca. Have you learned *any* trade?
In. No, none by Zeus.
Ca. Then how and whence do you earn your livelihood?
In. All public matters and all private too
Are in my charge.
Ca. How so?
In. 'Tis *I who will.*
Ca. You virtuous, housebreaker? When all men hate you
Meddling with matters which concern you not.
In. What, think you, booby, it concerns me not
To aid the State with all my might and main?
Ca. To aid the State! Does that mean mischief-making?
In. It means upholding the established laws
And punishing the rogues who break the same.
Ca. I thought the State appointed Justices
For this one task.
In. And who's to prosecute?
Ca. Whoever will.
In. I am that *man who will.*
Therefore, at last, the State depends on me.
Ca. 'Fore Zeus, a worthless leader it has got.
Come, *will* you this, to lead a quiet life
And peaceful?
In. That's a sheep's life you're describing,
Living with nothing in the world to do.
Ca. Then you won't change?
In. Not if you gave me all
Battus's silphium, aye and Wealth to boot.
Ca. Put off your cloak!
G. M. Fellow, to *you* he's speaking.
Ca. And then your shoes.
G. M. All this to *you* he's speaking.
In. I dare you all. Come on and tackle me
Whoever will.
Ca. I am that *man who will.*

Exit WITNESS.

In. O me, they are stripping me in open day.
Ca. You choose to live by mischief-making, do you?
In. What are you at? I call you, friend, to witness.
Ca. Methinks the witness that you brought has cut it.
In. O me! I am trapped alone.
Ca. Aye, now you are roaring.

In. O me! once more.
Ca. (*to* GOOD MAN) Hand me your gaberdine,
I'll wrap this rogue of an Informer in it.
G. M. Nay, that long since is dedicate to Wealth.
Ca. Where can it then more aptly be suspended
Than on a rogue and housebreaker like this?
Wealth we will decorate with nobler robes.
G. M. How shall we manage with my cast-off shoes?
Ca. Those on his forehead, as upon the stock
Of a wild olive, will I nail at once.
In. I'll stay no longer; for, alone, I am weaker,
I know, than you; but give me once a comrade,
A *willing* one, and ere the day is spent
I'll bring this lusty God of yours to justice,
For that, being only one, he is overthrowing
Our great democracy; nor seeks to gain
The Council's sanction, or the Assembly's either.
Exit INFORMER.
G. M. Aye run you off, accoutred as you are
In all my panoply, and take the station
I held erewhile beside the bath-room fire,
The Coryphaeus of the starvelings there.
Ca. Nay, but the keeper of the baths will drag him
Out by the ears; for he'll at once perceive
The man is metal of the baser sort.
But go we in that you may pray the God.
The GOOD MAN *and* CARIO *enter the house. Enter* OLD LADY *with attendant, carrying cakes and sweetmeats on a tray.*
Old Lady. Pray, have we really reached, you dear old men,
The very dwelling where this new God dwells?
Or have we altogether missed the way?
Ch. No, you have really reached his very door,
You dear young girl; for girl-like is your speech.
O. L. O, then, I'll summon one of those within.
Enter CHREMYLUS.
Chr. Nay, for, unsummoned, I have just come out.
So tell me freely what has brought you here.
O. L. O, sad, my dear, and anguished is my lot,
For ever since this God began to see
My life's been not worth living; all through him.
Chr. What, were you too a she-informer then
Amongst the women?
O. L. No indeed, not I.
Chr. Or, not elected, sat you judging—wine?
O. L. You jest; but I, poor soul, am misery-stung.
Chr. What kind of misery stings you? tell me quick.
O. L. Then listen. I'd a lad that loved me well,
Poor, but so handsome, and so fair to see,
Quite virtuous too; whate'er I wished, he did
In such a nice and gentlemanly way;
And what he wanted, I in turn supplied.
Chr. What were the things he asked you to supply?
O. L. Not many: so prodigious the respect
In which he held me. 'Twould be twenty drachmas
To buy a cloak and, maybe, eight for shoes;
Then for his sisters he would want a gown,
And just one mantle for his mother's use,
And twice twelve bushels of good wheat perchance.
Chr. Not many truly were the gifts he asked!
'Tis plain he held you in immense respect.
O. L. And these he wanted not for greed, he swore,
But for love's sake, that when my robe he wore,
He might, by that, remember me the more.
Chr. A man prodigiously in love indeed!
O. L. Aye, but the scamp's quite other-minded now.
He's altogether changed from what he was.
So when I sent him this delicious cake,
And all these bon-bons here upon the tray,
Adding a whispered message that I hoped
To come at even—
Chr. Tell me what he did?
O.L. He sent them back, and sent this cream-cake too,
Upon condition that I come no more;
And said withal, "Long since, in war's alarms
Were the Milesians lusty men-at-arms."
Chr. O, then the lad's not vicious; now he's rich
He cares for broth no longer, though before,
When he was poor, he snapped up anything.
O.L. O, by the Twain, and every day before,
He used to come, a suppliant, to my door.
Chr. What, for your funeral?
O.L. No, he was but fain
My voice to hear.
Chr. Your bounty to obtain.
O.L. When in the dumps, he'd smother me with love,
Calling me "little duck" and "little dove."
Chr. And then begged something for a pair of shoes.
O.L. And if perchance, when riding in my coach
At the Great Mysteries, some gallant threw
A glance my way, he'd beat me black and blue,
So very jealous had the young man grown.
Chr. Aye, aye, he liked to eat his cake alone.
O.L. He vowed my hands were passing fair and white.
Chr. With twenty drachmas in them—well he might.
O.L. And much he praised the fragrance of my skin.
Chr. No doubt, no doubt, If Thasian you poured in.
O.L. And then he swore my glance was soft and sweet.
Chr. He was no fool: he knew the way to eat
The goodly substance of a fond old dame.
O.L. O then, my dear, the God is much to blame.
He said he'd right the injured, every one.
Chr. What shall he do? speak, and the thing is done.
O.L. He should, by Zeus, this graceless youth compel
To recompense the love that loved him well;
Or no good fortune on the lad should light.
Chr. Did he not then repay you every night?
O.L. He'd never leave me all my life, he said.
Chr. And rightly too; but now he counts you dead.
O.L. My dear, with love's fierce pangs I've pined away.

Chr. Nay rather, grown quite rotten, I should say.
O.L. O, you could draw me through a ring, I know.
Chr. A ring? A hoop that round a sieve could go.
O.L. O, here comes he of whom I've been complaining
All this long while; this is that very lad!
Bound to some revel surely.
Chr. So it seems.
At least, he has got the chaplets and the torch.

Enter YOUTH.

Youth. Friends, I salute you.
O.L. Eh?
Yo. Mine ancient flame,
How very suddenly you've got grey hair.
O.L. O me, the insults I am forced to bear.
Chr. 'Tis years since last he saw you, I dare say.
O.L. What years, you wretch? He saw me yesterday!
Chr. Why then, his case is different from the rest;
When in his cups, methinks, he sees the best.
O.L. No, this is just his naughty, saucy way.
Yo. O Gods of eld! Poseidon of the Main!
What countless wrinkles does her face contain!
O.L. O! O!
Keep your torch off me, do.
Chr. In that she's right.
For if one spark upon her skin should light,
'Twould set her blazing, like a shrivelled wreath.
Yo. Come, shall we play together?
O.L. Where? for shame!
Yo. Here with some nuts.
O.L. And what's your little game?
Yo. How many teeth you've got.
Chr. How many teeth?
I'll make a guess at that. She's three, no, four.
Yo. Pay up; you've lost: one grinder, and no more.
O.L. Wretch, are you crazy that you make your friend
A washing-pot before so many men?
Yo. Were you well washed, 'twould do you good belike.
Chr. No, no, she's got up for the market now.
But if her white-lead paint were washed away,
Too plain you'd see the tatters of her face.
O.L. So old and saucy! Are you crazy too?
Yo. What, is he trying to corrupt you, love,
Toying and fondling you when I'm not looking?
O.L. By Aphrodite, no, you villain you!
Chr. No, no, by Hecate, I'm not so daft.
But come, my boy, I really can't allow you
To hate the girl.
Yo. Hate her? I love her dearly.
Chr. Yet she complains of—
Yo. What?
Chr. Your flouts and jeers,
Sending her word, "Long since, in war's alarms
Were the Milesians lusty men-at-arms."
Yo. Well, I won't fight you for her sake.
Chr. How mean you?
Yo. For I respect your age, since be you sure
It is not everybody I'd permit
To take my girl. You, take her and begone.
Chr. I know, I know your drift; no longer now
You'd keep her company.
O.L. Who'll permit *that*?
Yo. I won't have anything to do with one
Who has been the sport of thirteen thousand—suns.
Chr. But, howsoever, as you drank the wine,
You should, in justice, also drink the dregs.
Yo. Pheugh! they're such very old and fusty dregs!
Chr. Won't a dreg-strainer remedy all that?
Yo. Well, go ye in. I want to dedicate
The wreaths I am wearing to this gracious God.
O.L. Aye then, I want to tell him something too.
Yo. Aye then, I'll not go in.
Chr. Come, don't be frightened.
Why, she won't ravish you.
Yo. I'm glad to hear it.
I've had enough of her in days gone by.
O.L. Come, go you on; I'll follow close behind.
Chr. O Zeus and King, the ancient woman sticks
Tight as a limpet to her poor young man.

They all enter the house, and the door is shut. HERMES *enters, knocks, and hides himself.* CARIO *opens, and sees no one: coming out he bears a pot containing tripe, and dirty water.*

Ca. Who's knocking at the door? Hallo, what's this!
'Twas nobody it seems. The door shall smart,
Making that row for nothing.
Hermes. Hoi, you sir,
Stop, Cario! don't go in.
Ca. Hallo, you fellow,
Was that you banging at the door so loudly?
He. No, I was going to when you flung it open.
But run you in and call your master out,
And then his wife, and then his little ones,
And then the serving-men, and then the dog,
And then yourself, and then the sow.
Ca. (*severely*) Now tell me
What all this means.
He. It means that Zeus is going
To mix you up, you rascal, in one dish,
And hurl you all into the Deadman's Pit!
Ca. Now for this herald must the tongue be cut.
But what's the reason that he is going to do us
Such a bad turn?
He. Because ye have done the basest
And worst of deeds. Since Wealth began to see,
No laurel, meal-cake, victim, frankincense,
Has any man on any altar laid
Or aught beside.
Ca. Or ever will; for scant
Your care for us in the evil days gone by.
He. And for the other Gods I'm less concerned,
But I myself am smashed and ruined.
Ca. Good.
He. For until now the tavern-wives would bring
From early dawn figs, honey, tipsy-cake,
Titbits for Hermes, such as Hermes loved;
But now I idly cross my legs and starve.

Ca. And rightly too who, though such gifts you got,
Would wrong the givers.
He. O, my hapless lot!
O me, the Fourth-day cake in days gone by!
Ca. You want the absent; nought avails your cry.
He. O me, the gammon which was erst my fare!
Ca. Here play your game on bladders, in the air.
He. O me, the inwards which I ate so hot!
Ca. In your own inwards now a pain you've got.
He. O me, the tankard, brimmed with half and half!
Ca. Begone your quickest, taking this to quaff.
He. Will you not help a fellow-knave to live?
Ca. If anything you want is mine to give.
He. O, could you get me but one toothsome loaf,
Or from the sacrifice you make within
One slice of lusty meat?
Ca. No exports here.
He. O, whenso'er your master's goods you stole,
'Twas I that caused you to escape detection.
Ca. Upon condition, ruffian, that you shared
The spoils. A toothsome cake would go to you.
He. And then you ate it every bit yourself.
Ca. But you, remember, never shared the kicks
Were I perchance detected at my tricks.
He. Well, don't bear malice, if you've Phyle got,
But take me in to share your happy lot.
Ca. What, leave the Gods, and settle here below?
He. For things look better here than there, I trow.
Ca. Think you Desertion is a name so grand?
He. Where most I prosper, there's my father-land.
Ca. How could we use you if we took you in?
He. Install me here, the Turn-god by the door.
Ca. The Turn-god? Turns and twists we want no more.
He. The God of Commerce?
Ca. Wealth we've got, nor need
A petty-huckstering Hermes now to feed.
He. The God of Craft?
Ca. Craft? quite the other way.
Not craft, but Honesty, we need to-day.
He. The God of guidance?
Ca. Wealth can see, my boy!
A guide no more 'tis needful to employ.
He. The God of games? Aha, I've caught you there.
For Wealth is always highly sympathetic
With literary games, and games athletic.
Ca. How lucky 'tis to have a lot of names!
He has gained a living by that "God of games."
Not without cause our Justices contrive
Their names to enter in more lists than one.
He. Then on these terms I enter?
Ca. Aye, come in.
And take these guts, and wash them at the well.
And so, at once, be Hermes Ministrant.

Exeunt CARIO *and* HERMES.

Enter the PRIEST OF ZEUS SOTER, *to find* CHREMYLUS.

Priest. O tell me, where may Chremylus be found?
Chr. (*entering*) What cheer, my worthy fellow?
Pr. What but ill?
For ever since this Wealth began to see,
I'm downright famished, I've got nought to eat,
And that, although I'm Zeus the Saviour's priest.
Chr. O, by the Powers, and what's the cause of that?
Pr. No man will slay a victim now.
Chr. Why not?
Pr. Because they all are wealthy; yet before,
When men had nothing, one, a merchant saved
From voyage-perils, one, escaped from law,
Would come and sacrifice; or else at home
Perform his vows, and summon me, the priest.
But not a soul comes now, or body either,
Except a lot of chaps to do their needs.
Chr. Then don't you take your wonted toll of that?
Pr. So I've myself a mind to cut the service
Of Zeus the Saviour now, and settle here.
Chr. Courage! God willing, all will yet be well.
For Zeus the Saviour is himself within,
Coming unasked.
Pr. O, excellent good news!
Chr. So we'll at once install—but bide awhile—
Wealth in the place where he was erst installed,
Guarding the Treasury in Athene's Temple.
Hi! bring me lighted candles. Take them, you,
And march before the God.
Pr. With all my heart.
Chr. Call Wealth out, somebody.

Enter OLD LADY *from the house.*

O.L. And I?
Chr. O, you.
Here, balance me these installation pots
Upon your head, and march along in state.
You've got your festive robes at all events.
O.L. But what I came for?
Chr. Everything is right.
The lad you love shall visit you to-night.
O.L. O, if you pledge your honour that my boy
Will come to-night, I'll bear the pots with joy.
Chr. These pots are not like other pots at all.
In other pots the mother is atop,
But here the mother's underneath the pot.
Ch. 'Tis the end of the Play, and we too must delay
our departure no longer, but hasten away,
And follow along at the rear of the throng,
rejoicing and singing our festival song.

GLOSSARY

A, Acharnians; K, Knights; C, Clouds; W, Wasps; P, Peace; B, Birds; F, Frogs; L, Lysistrata; T, Thesmophoriazusae; E, Ecclesiazusae; Pl, Plutus.

Acestor, an alien poet; also called Sacas, *W.* 1221
Achaia, a name of Demeter, *A.* 710
Acharnae, a deme of Athens, *A.* 180
Achelous, a river of Epirus, *L.* 381
Acheron, the river of sorrow, in the lower regions, *F.* 471
Adeimantus, an Athenian general, *F.* 1513
Adonia, a yearly feast in honour of Adonis, *P.* 420
Adonis, a youth beloved by Aphrodite, *L.* 389
Aegina, an island opposite the Peiraeus, *A.* 653, *W.* 122, *F.* 363
Aegyptus, a legendary King of Egypt, *F.* 1206
Aeolus, a play by Euripides, *F.* 864
Aeschinades, *P.* 1154
Aeschines, a needy blusterer and braggart, *W.* 325, 459, 1220, 1243, *B.* 823
Aeschylus, *C.* 1366, *L.* 188, *T.* 134
Aesimus, a cripple, *E.* 208
Aesop, *W.* 566, 1259
Aesop's fables, *P.* 129, *B.* 471, 651
Aetna, a city in Sicily, *B.* 926
Aetolia, a region in western Greece, *K.* 79
Agamemnon, *B.* 509
Agamemnon, by Aeschylus, quoted, *F.* 1285, 1289
Agathon, a tragic poet, born about 447 B.C., *F.* 83
Agoracritus, "market-place judge," *K.* 1335
Agraulus, daughter of Cecrops, king of Athens, *T.* 533
Agyieus, a title of Apollo, *W.* 875
Agyrrhius, a demagogue, and in his youth effeminate, had become great in the state by first proposing, a fee of one obol for attending the Assembly; then, after Heracleides had raised it to two, by fixing it at three, *E.* 102, 176, 184, *Pl.* 176
Alcaeus of Lesbos, an erotic poet, *T.* 161
Alcibiades, *F.* 1423
Alcmena, bore Heracles to Zeus, *B.* 558
Alexicacus, Averter of Ill, an epithet of Hermes (also of other gods), *P.* 422
Alope, bore Hippothoon to Poseidon, *B.* 559
Amazons, *L.* 679
Ameipsias, a comic poet, rival of Aristophanes, *F.* 14
Ammon, Zeus, had an oracle in Libya, *B.* 619, 716
Amphitheus, *A.* 46
Amyclae, a town near Sparta, *L.* 1299
Amynias, Aeschines' cowardly brother, *C.* 31, 694, *W.* 74, 1266
Amynon, a depraved politician, *E.* 365
Anacreon of Teos, an erotic poet, *T.* 161
Anagyrus, an Attic deme, *L.* 67
Anaphlystus, an Attic deme, *E.* 979
Androcles, a rogue, *W.* 1187
Andromeda, a play by Euripides, *F.* 53
Antigone, by Euripides, quoted, *F.* 1182, 1187, 1391
Antimachus, an effeminate, *A.* 1150, *C.* 1022
Antiphon, a needy glutton, *W.* 1270
Antisthenes, a depraved physician, *E.* 366, 806
Apaturia, a clan festival, *A.* 146, *T.* 558
Apollo, physician, *B.* 584
Arcadia, a mountainous region in the Peloponnesus, *K.* 798
Archedemus, *F.* 417; the blear-eyed, *F.* 588
Archegetis—Artemis or Athene, *L.* 644
Archelaus, by Euripides, quoted *F.* 1206
Archenomus, *F.* 1507
Archeptolemus, a conservative Athenian politician, *K.* 327, 794
Archilochus quoted, *A.* 1228
Argeius, politician, *E.* 201
Arginusae, scene of Athenian naval victory over the Spartans, *F.* 33, 191
Argives, *i.e.*, Greeks, *P.* 475
Argos, *K.* 465
Arignotus, son of Automenes, a harper, *K.* 1278, *W.* 1278
Ariphrades, son of Automenes, an evil man *K.* 1281, *W.* 1280, *E.* 128
Aristeides, son of Lysimachus "the Just," a statesman opposed to Themistocles, fought at Marathon, ostracized 483 B.C., but returned and took a great part in the political developments of Athens; died about 463, *K.* 1325
Aristogeiton, the slayer of the tyrant Hipparchus, *L.* 633
Aristyllus, a homosexual, *E.* 647, *Pl.* 314
Artemisia, a queen allied to Xerxes, *L.* 675
Artemisium, scene of a Greek naval victory over the Persians, *L.* 1251
Artemon, an effeminate, A. 85
Asclepius, god of healing, *W.* 123, *Pl.* 640
Ascondas, an athlete, *W.* 1383
Aspasia, mistress of Pericles, *A.* 527
Athamas, king of Orchomenus in Boeotia, married Nephele, and was father of Phrixus and Helle; he was stricken with madness, and fled into Thessaly, *C.* 257
Athmone, a deme of Athens, *P.* 190
Automenes, father of Arignotus and Ariphrades, *W.* 1275

Babylon, *B.* 552
Bacchus, shrine of, *L.* 2
Bakis, a Boeotian seer of Helicon; there was a collection current of his oracles, *K.* 123, 1003, *P.* 1071

Battus, king of Cyrene, *Pl.* 925
Bellerophon, *F.* 1051; represented as lame in the play of Euripides, *A.* 427, *P.* 148
Bereschethus, a goblin, *K.* 635
Boeotians, *P.* 466
Brasidas, a great Spartan leader in the Peloponnesian War, killed at Amphipolis 422 B.C., *W.* 475, *P.* 640
Brauron, an Attic deme, scene of a famous festival, *P.* 874
Brauronia, a feast of Artemis, *L.* 645
Bupalus, a sculptor, had caricatured Hipponax, who lampooned him and threatened to strike him, *L.* 361
Byzantium, the earlier city on the site of Constantinople, *C.* 249, *W.* 236

Cadmus, founder of Thebes, *F.* 1225
Caecias, the *N.E.* wind, *K.* 437
Callias, son of Hipponicus, a spendthrift, *B.* 283, *E.* 810
Callimachus, a poor poet, *E.* 809
Camarina, a town in Sicily, *A.* 605
Cannonus, a lawgiver, *E.* 1089
Cantharus, a harbour of the Peiraeus, *P.* 145
Carcinus, a comic poet, father of three dwarfish sons, *C.* 1261, *W.* 1508, *P.* 781, 866
Cardopion, a scandalous fellow, *W.* 1178
Caria, a country in southwestern Asia Minor, *K.* 173
Carthage, *K.* 174, 1303
Carystian (Euboean) allies in Athens, *L.* 1058, 1182
Caystrian (Lydian) plains, *A.* 68
Cebrione, a giant, *B.* 553
Cecrops, king of Attica, *C.* 301, *W.* 438
Celeus, son of Triptolemus, *A.* 49
Centaurs, *C.* 349
Cephale, an Attic deme, *B.* 476
Cephalus, a potter and demagogue, *E.* 248
Cephisodemus, an advocate, *A.* 705
Cephisophon, a slave of Euripides; he was credited with helping the dramatist in his tragedies, *F.* 939
Cerameicus, the potter's quarter at Athens, where public funerals took place, *K.* 772, *B.* 395, *F.* 127, 1093
Cerberus, the dog of Hades, *P.* 313, *F.* 111
Chaereas, *W.* 687
Chaerephon, a pupil of Socrates, *C.* 104, etc., *W.* 1408, *B.* 1296, 1564
Chaeretades, *E.* 51
Chaeris, a wretched Theban piper, *A.* 16, *P.* 950
Chalcis, Chalcidice in Thrace, *K.* 238
Chaonia, in Epirus, *A.* 613, *K.* 78
Chaos, *B.* 691
Charinades, *P.* 1154
Charites, the Graces, *B.* 781
Charixene, a poetess, *E.* 943
Charminius, a general, an Athenian officer, *T.* 804
Charon, ferryman of the Styx, *F.* 184
Chersonesus, the peninsula of Gallipoli, *K.* 262
Chios, a proverb relating to, *P.* 171
Chloe—Demeter, *L.* 835
Choae, the Pitcher feast, *A.* 961
Chytri, the Pitcher feast, *F.* 218
Cicynna, an Attic deme, *C.* 134
Cillicon, a traitor, *P.* 363
Cimolian earth, fuller's earth, *F.* 712
Cimon, an Athenian statesman, *L.* 1144
Cinesias, a dithyrambic poet, constantly ridiculed for his thinness, musical perversities, and profane and dissolute conduct, *B.* 1372, *F.* 153, 364, 1437, *E.* 330
Cithaeron, mt., *T.* 996
Cleaenetus, father of Cleon, *K.* 574
Cleidemides, *F.* 791
Cleigenes, F. 709
Cleinarete, *E.* 41
Cleinias, father of Alcibiades, *A.* 716
Cleisthenes, "son of Sibyrtius," a coward and effeminate, *A.* 118, *K.* 1374, *C.* 355, *W.* 1187, *B.* 831, *F.* 48, 422, *L.* 1092, *T.* 235
Cleocritus, an ungainly man, *B.* 873, *F.* 1437
Cleomenes, king of Sparta, *L.* 274
Cleon, son of Cleaenetus, a tanner, demagogue and popular leader after the death of Pericles in 429 B.C., He opposed peace. In 424 took part in the surrender of the Spartans at Sphacteria, which he laid to his own credit. Killed by Brasidas at Amphipolis, 422, *A.* 6, 300, 378, 502, 659, *K.* 137, 976, *C.* 549, 586, 591, *W.* 35, 62, 197, 241, 596, 841, 895, 1220, 1224, 1237, 1285, *P.* 47, 648, *F.* 569
Cleonymus, the butt of Athens for his bulk and his appetite, who cast away his shield at Delium, *A.* 88, 844, *K.* 958, 1293, 1372, *C.* 353, 450, 674, *W.* 20, 592, 822, *P.* 446, 672, 1295, *B.* 289, 1475, *T.* 605
Cleophon, a demagogue, *F.* 677, 1532
Cobalus, *K.* 635
Cocytus, the River of Wailing, in the lower regions, *F.* 471
Coesyra, a name in the great Alcmaeonid family, *A.* 614, *C.* 48, 800
Colaenis, a name of Artemis, *B.* 872
Colias, a title of Aphrodite, or of her attendant love-deities, *C.* 52, *L.* 2
Colonus, an eminence in the Agora, *B.* 998
Conisalus, a local Attic Priapus, *L.* 982
Connas, a drunken flute-player, *K.* 534, *W.* 675
Copaic eels, from Lake Copais (*A.* 880) in Boeotia, *P.* 1005
Corinth, *K.* 603, *B.* 968
Corinthians and the League, *E.* 199
Corybants, priests of Cybele, *L.* 558
Cothocidae, an Attic deme, *T.* 622
Cranaae—Athens, *B*, 123
Cranaan town—Athens, *L.* 481
Crates, a comic poet, flourished about 450 B.C. *K.* 536
Cratinus, a dandy, *A.* 849, 1173; a comic poet, 519-422 B.C., *K.* 400, 526, *P.* 700, *F.* 337
Cretan monodies, *F.* 849
Crioa, a deme of Athens, *B.* 645
Cronos, father of Zeus, *C.* 929, *B.* 469, 586

Ctesias, an informer, *A.* 839
Cybele—Rhea, mother of the gods, *B.* 876
Cycloborus, a hill-torrent in Attica, *K.* 137
Cyclops, *Pl.* 290
Cycnus, a robber slain by Heracles, *F.* 963
Cyllene, a port in Elis, *K.* 1081
Cynalopex, nickname of Philostratus, a pander, *L.* 957
Cynna, a courtesan, *K.* 765, *W.* 1032, *P.* 755
Cyprus, *L.* 833
Cyrene, a courtesan, *F.* 1328
Cythera, an island south of Greece, where Aphrodite had a temple, *L.* 833
Cyzicene dye, yellow: suggested by the alleged cowardice of the people of Cyzicus, *P.* 1176

Darius, king of Persia, *B.* 484
Datis, the Persian general defeated at Marathon, *P.* 289
Deigma, the Exchange at the Peiraeus, *K.* 979
Delphi, seat of an oracle, *B.* 618, 716
Demostratus, an Athenian who proposed the Sicilian expedition, *L.* 391
Dexinicus, *Pl.* 800
Dexitheus, a good harpist, *A.* 14
Diasia, a feast in honour of Zeus Meilichius, *C.* 408, 864
Dictynna, a name of Artemis, *W.* 368
Diocles, an Athenian who in some ancient battle had fought for Megara and given his life for a youth; a festival was held at his tomb, *A.* 774
Diomea, feast of Heracles, *F.* 651
Dionysia, a feast held every year in honour of Dionysus, god of wine; the Greater in the town, the Lesser in the country, *A.* 195, *P.* 530
Dionysius, tyrant of Syracuse, *Pl.* 550
Diopeithes, a crazy oracle-monger, *K.* 1085, *W.* 380, *B.* 988
Dipolia, a feast held yearly at Athens in honour of Zeus Polieus, also called Buphonia, from the sacrifice of a bull, *P.* 420
Ditrephes, having made his fortune by the manufacture of wicker flasks, was elected *phylarchus*, then *hipparchus*, and seems to have perished at Mycalessus, *B.* 798, 1442
Dodona, in Epirus, seat of oracle of Zeus, *B.* 716
Dracyllus, *A.* 612

Ecbatana, the old capital of the Medes, *A.* 64, *W.* 1143
Echinus, a town on the Melian Gulf, *L.* 1169
Egypt, *C.* 1130, *P.* 1253
Eileithyia, goddess of childbirth, *L.* 742, *E.* 369
Electra, a play by Aeschylus, *C.* 534
Elymnium, a place near Oreus, *P.* 1126
Empusa, a bogey, *F.* 293
Ephudion, an athlete, *W.* 1383
Epicrates, a demagogue who took part with Thrasybulus in the overthrow of the Thirty. He afterwards was ambassador to the king of Persia, and accepted bribes from him, *E.* 71
Epicurus, unknown, *E.* 645
Epidaurus, a city on the south side of the Saronic gulf, *F.* 364
Epigonus, an effeminate, *E.* 167
Erasinides, one of the generals executed after the battle of Arginusae, 406 B.C., *F.* 1196
Erebos, the underworld, *B.* 691
Erechtheus, a legendary king of Athens, *K.* 1022
Ergasion, *W.* 1201
Erinys—Fury, avenger of blood, *Pl.* 423
Eros, winged, *B.* 574, 700
Eryxis, son of Philoxenus, *F.* 934
Euaeon, a pauper, *E.* 408
Euathlus, a scoundrelly orator, *A.* 711, *W.* 592
Euboea, an island off Boeotia, *C.* 211, *W.* 715
Eubule, "good counsellor," *T.* 808
Eucharides, *W.* 680
Eucrates, no doubt the brother of Nicias, put to death under the Thirty, *L.* 103
Eucrates, an oakum-seller, *K.* 129, 253
Eudamus or Eudemus, a vendor of amulets, *Pl.* 884
Euphemius, a politician, *W.* 599
Euphorides, a carrier of charcoal, *A.* 612
Eupolis, an early comic poet born about 446 B.C., died probably in 411, *C.* 553
Euripides, the tragic poet, son of an herb-seller, 480–406 B.C., *A.* 394, 452, *K.* 18, *C.* 1371, 1376, *W.* 61, 1414, *P.* 148, *F.* 67, 80, *L.* 283, 368
Euripides, a politician, *E.* 825
Eurotas, the river of Sparta, *L.* 1308
Eurycles, a ventriloquist, *W.* 1019
Euthymenes, archon, *A.* 67
Execestides, a Carian slave, who managed to get enrolled as an Athenian citizen, *B.* 11, 762, 1527

Ganymede, cup-bearer of Zeus, *P.* 726
Gargettus, an Attic deme, *T.* 898
Gela, a town in Sicily, *A.* 606
Genetyllis, a title of Aphrodite, or of her attendant love-deities, *L.* 2, *T.* 130, C. 52
Geres, a dandy, *E.* 932
Geron, a dandy, *E.* 848
Geryones, a triple-bodied monster, giant, *A.* 1082
Geusistrate, *E.* 48
Glaucetes, a glutton, *T.* 1035
Glyce, a slave name, *F.* 1343, *E.* 430
Gorgias of Leontini, a rhetorician and sophist, *B.* 1701
Gorgon, a serpent-haired monster, *P.* 810
Gryttus, a homosexual, *K.* 877

Hades, cap of, *A.* 390
Halimus, a village near Peiraeus, *B.* 496
Harmodius, lover of Aristogeiton; they are the traditional liberators of Athens from the tyrants, *A.* 980, 1093, *K.* 786, *W.* 1225,; statue of, *E.* 682
Hebrus, river in Thrace, *B.* 774
Hecate, a dread goddess identified with the Moon, Artemis, and Persephone, *F.* 1362
Hecatea, shrines of Hecate erected at doors and cross-ways, *F.* 366
Hegelochus, an actor, *F.* 303

Helen, a play by Euripides, *L.* 155, *T.* 850
Heliaea, the supreme court of Athens, *K.* 897
Heracleids, children of Heracles, *P.* 385
Heracles, *B.* 1574, *L.* 927
Heracles, baths of, *C.* 1051
Hermes, Winged, *B.* 572
Hiero, an auctioneer, *E.* 757
Hieronymus, a wild and hairy man, *A.* 389, *C.* 349, *E.* 201
Hippias, the Tyrant, *K.* 448, *W.* 502, *L.* 617, 1153
Hippocrates and his sons, a dirty crew, *C.* 1001
Hippocrates, an Athenian general, nephew of Pericles, slain at Delium, *T.* 273
Hippodamus, father of Archeptolemus, *K.* 327
Hippolytus, by Euripides, alluded to, *F.* 1043
Hipponax, a writer of satires, *F.* 661
Hipponicus, son of Callias, *B.* 283
Homer, *P.* 1089, 1096, *B.* 575, 910 C. 1056
Hymen, god of marriage, *P.* 1334
Hyperbolus, a demagogue who succeeded Cleon, of servile origin, ostracized, finally killed by the oligarchs at Samos, 411 B.C., *A.* 846, *K.* 1304, 1363, *C.* 551, 876, *W.* 1007, *P.* 680, 921, 1319, *F.* 570, *T.* 840
Hysipyle, by Euripides, quoted, *F.* 1211, 1327

Iacchus, a personage in the Eleusinian mysteries, *F.* 316
Iapetus, one of the Titans, proverbial for antiquity, *C.* 998
Iaso, daughter of Asclepius, *Pl.* 701
Ibycus of Rhegium, an erotic poet, *T.* 161
Ida, a mountain in Crete, *F.* 1355
Ino, daughter of Cadmus, wife of Athamas, *A.* 434, *W.* 1414
Ion of Chios, a tragic poet, *P.* 835
Iophon, son of Sophocles, *F.* 73
Iphigenia in Tauris quoted, *F.* 1232
Iris, winged, *B.* 575
Ismenichus, *A.* 861

Lacedaemon, *B.* 1012
Laches, an Athenian commander in the Peloponnesian War, accused by Cleon of peculation; slain at Mantinea, *W.* 240, 836, 895
Laconians, Spartans, *P.* 212, 282, 478, 622
Lacrateides, an Athenian leader, possibly one of the accusers of Pericles, *A.* 220
Lais, a courtesan, *Pl.* 178
Laispodias, an Athenian general, *B.* 1569
Lamachus, son of Xenophanes, colleague of Alcibiades and Nicias in the Sicilian expedition 415 B.C., a brave and honorable soldier. He was killed in the siege, *A.* 270, 567, 963, *P.* 473, *T.* 841
Lamia, a goblin, *W.* 1035, 1177, *P.* 758
Lamias, keeper of the public prison, *E.* 77
Lampon, a soothsayer, one of the leaders of the colony sent to Thurii, *B.* 521, 998
Lasus of Hermione, a lyric poet, contemporary with Simonides, *W.* 1410
Leipsydrium, a fortress where the Alcmaeonidae fortified themselves after the death of Hipparchus; probably on Mt. Parnes, *L.* 665
Lenaea, a feast, at which the comedies were exhibited, *A.* 504
Leogoras, an epicure, *C.* 109, *W.* 1269
Leonidas, king of Sparta, who fell at Thermopylae, *L.* 1254
Leotrophides, a slim poet, *B.* 1406
Lepreus, in Elis, *B.* 149
Leucolophus, unknown, *F.* 1512, *E.* 645
Libya, *B.* 710
Limnae, a port of Athens near the Acropolis, *F.* 217
Loxias, a name of Apollo, *K.* 1072, *Pl.* 8
Lycabettus, a rocky hill which overshadows Athens, *F.* 1056
Lycis, an Athenian comic poet, *F.* 14
Lycon, husband of Rhodia, *L.* 270
Lycurgia, by Aeschylus, the tetralogy containing the *Edonians*, the *Bassarides*, the *Young Men*, and *Lycurgus* (satyric drama), *T.* 135
Lycus, patron hero of the Athenian dicasteries, *W.* 389, 819
Lynceus, a keen-sighted hero, *Pl.* 210
Lysicles, a sheep-seller, *K.* 132, 765
Lysicrates, an ugly snub-nosed man, *E.* 630, 736
Lysicrates, a corrupt Athenian officer, *P.* 992, *B.* 513
Lysistratus, a vicious man, *K.* 1267, *W.* 787

Magnes, an early comedian, *K.* 520
Mammacuthus, "blockhead," *F.* 990
Manes, a slave-name, *P.* 1146, *B.* 523
Mania, a slave-name, *F.* 1346
Marathon, scene of the famous victory, 490 B.C., *A.* 697, *K.* 781, 1334, *T.* 806
Marathon, songs from, *F.* 1296
Marilades, *A.* 609
Marpsias, a contentious orator, *A.* 701
Medea, by Euripides, quoted, *F.* 1382
Megabazus, *B.* 484
Megacles, a name in one of the great Athenian families, the Alcmaeonidae, *C.* 46, 815
Megaenetus, *F.* 965
Megara, a town near Athens, *A.* 519, 533, 738, *W.* 57, *P.* 246, 481, 500, 609
Megarian Walls, *L.* 1169
Melanion, the hero who won the race with Atalanta, *L.* 785
Melanippe, seduced by Aeolus, *T.* 547
Melanthius, a tragic poet, *P.* 804, 1009, *B.* 151
Meleager, a play by Euripides, *F.* 864, 1238, 1402
Meletus, a tragic poet, *F.* 1302
Melian famine, *B.* 186
Melian Gulf, *L.* 1169
Melistiche, *E.* 46
Melite, an Attic deme, *F.* 501
Melitides, a stupid man, *F.* 991
Memnon, son of Eos, slain by Achilles, *C.* 622, *F.* 963
Menelaus, husband of Helen, *B.* 509, *L.* 155
Messene (Messenia), a district in the southwestern Peloponnesus, whence Sparta recruited its helots, *L.* 1142

Meton, an astronomer and man of science, *B.* 992
Micon, a painter, *L.* 679
Midas, the wealthy king of Phrygia, who had the ears of an ass, *Pl.* 287
Milesian rugs, *F.* 543; *see* Miletus
Milesian wool, *L.* 729; *see* Miletus
Miletus, a great Greek city on the western coast of Asia Minor, *K.* 361, 932, *L.* 108
Miltiades, the victor of Marathon, son of Cimon, and tyrant of the Chersonesus, *K.* 1325
Mitylene, in Lesbos, *K.* 834
Molon, a tragic actor of large stature, *F.* 55
Morsimus, a poor tragic poet, *K.* 401, *P.* 803, *F.* 151
Morychus, an epicure, *A.* 887, *W.* 506, 1142, *P.* 1008
Moschus, a bad harpist, *A.* 13
Mothon, a crude dance, *K.* 635
Muses, *B.* 782
Myrmex, *F.* 1506
Myrmidons, by Aeschylus, quoted, *F.* 992, 1265
Myronides, about 457 B.C., led out an army of old men and boys, and defeated the Corinthians near Megara; and in 456 defeated the Boeotians at Oenophyta, *L.* 802, *E.* 304
Myrsine, wife of Hippias, *K.* 449
Mysteria, secret ceremonies held in honour of various deities, in which there was initiation of various degrees, *P.* 420

Nausicydes, a grain profiteer, *E.* 426
Neocleides, an orator, informer, and thief, *E.* 254, 398, *Pl.* 665
Nicarchus, an informer, *A.* 908
Nicias, son of Niceratus, a distinguished general, of the aristocratic party, and an opponent of Cleon; he perished in the Sicilian expedition, 413 B.C., *K.* 358, *B.* 363, 640
Nicias, probably a grandson of the famous general, *E.* 428
Nicomachus, a corrupt public official, *F.* 1506
Nicostratus, a personage fond of sacrifices and foreigners, *W.* 81
Nike, winged victory, *B.* 574
Niobe, a play by Aeschylus, *F.* 912, 1392

Odeum, a court in Athens, *W.* 1009
Odomantes, a Thracian tribe, *A.* 156
Odysseus, *W.* 181, 1351
Oeagrus, an actor, *W.* 579
Oeneus, king of Calydon, deposed and cast out by his nephews; name of a play by Euripides, *A.* 418
Oeonichus, a worthless man, *K.* 1287
Olympia, in Elis, scene of the great games, *W.* 1382, *L.* 1131
Olympus, a legendary flute-player, *K.* 8
Olympus, home of the gods, *B.* 781
Opuntius, an informer, *B.* 152
Orestea, a trilogy by Aeschylus, *F.* 1123
Orestes, a footpad, *A.* 1167, *B.* 712, 1491
Oreus, a town in northern Euboea, *P.* 1047, 1125
Orneae, in Argolis, *B.* 399
Orpheus, a character of legend, and a reputed poet, had his name attached later to certain secret societies, *F.* 1032
Orthian nome, *A.* 16

Palamede, a master of craft and inventor, *F.* 1451
Palamede, a play by Euripides, *T.* 848
Pamphilus, a dishonest demagogue, a painter, *Pl.* 173, 385
Pan, and panic, *L.* 998
Panaceia, daughter of Asclepius, *Pl.* 702
Panaetius, *K.* 243
Panathenaea, the great feast held every four years at Athens in honour of Athene, *C.* 386, 988, *P.* 418, *F.* 1090
Pandeletus, an informer, *C.* 924
Pandion, one of the ten eponymous heroes, whose statues were in the Agora at Athens, *P.* 1183
Panoptes—Argus, guardian of Io, *E.* 80
Pan's grotto in the Acropolis, *L.* 2, 721, 912
Paphlagon, a servile name describing the slave's country, *K.* 1, etc.
Paphos, in Cyprus, where Aphrodite had a temple, *L.* 833
Paralia, a district of Attica, *L.* 58
Parnassus, the mountain above Delphi, *F.* 1057
Parnes, a hill near Athens, *A.* 348, *C.* 323
Paros, an island in the Cyclades, *W.* 1189
Pasias, *C.* 21
Patrocleides, a politician of unpleasant habits. After the battle of Aegospotami, he brought in a bill to enfranchise the disfranchised citizens, *B.* 790
Patrocles, a sordid person, *Pl.* 84
Patroclus, the friend of Achilles, *F.* 1041
Pauson, a painter of animals and scurrilous caricatures, vicious and poor, *A.* 854, *T.* 949, *Pl.* 602
Pegasus, the winged horse, *P.* 76, 135, 154
Peiraeus, the harbour of Athens, *K.* 815, *P.* 145, 165
Peisander, a blustering coward, who took a large part in the revolution of the Four Hundred, *P.* 395, *B.* 1555, *L.* 490
Peisias, son of, *B.* 766
Pelargicon, prehistoric wall of the Acropolis, *B.* 832
Peleus, a play by Euripides, *F.* 863
Peleus, father of Achilles, *C.* 1063
Pellene, a courtesan, *B.* 1421, *L.* 996
Pelops, ancestor of Agamemnon and Menelaus, *F.* 1232
Penelope, *T.* 547
Pergasae, an Attic deme, *K.* 321
Pericleidae, the clan of Pericles, *L.* 1138
Pericles, the great Athenian statesman, died 429 B. C., *A.* 530, *K.* 283, *C.* 213, 859, *P.* 606
Persae, a play by Aeschylus, *F.* 1026
Persians, *B.* 484
Phaeax, a politician, *K.* 1377
Phaedra, wife of Theseus, fell in love with her step-son Hippolytus, *F.* 1042, *T.* 547
Phales, an imaginary name, *A.* 263
Phanus, a hanger-on of Cleon's *K.* 1256, *W.* 1220
Pharsalus, a town in Thessaly, *W.* 1271
Phayllus, a famous Olympian victor, *A.* 215, *W.* 1206

Pheidias, date of birth unknown, died just before 432 B.C., the famous sculptor, maker of the statues of Athene in the Parthenon and Zeus at Elis, *P.* 605, 616
Pherecrates, a comic poet, *L.* 158
Phersephatta—Persephone, daughter of Demeter, *F.* 671
Philablus, a district of Megara, *A.* 802
Philaenete, *E.* 42
Philemon, a Phrygian, *B.* 763
Philepsius, a composer of tales, *Pl.* 177
Philip, son or disciple of Gorgias, *W.* 421, *B.* 1701
Philocles, a bitter tragic poet, *W.* 462, *T.* 168
Philocrates, a bird-seller, *B.* 14
Philocrates, by Aeschylus, quoted, *F.* 1383
Philoctetes, a famous archer in the Trojan war, bitten by a snake and left in Lemnos; name of a play by Euripides, exhibited 431 B.C., *A.* 424
Philodoretus, *E.* 51
Philonides of Melite, a bulky and clumsy blockhead, but rich, *Pl.* 178, 303
Philostratus, a pander, *K.* 1069
Philoxenus, father of Eryxis, *F.* 934
Phoenix, accused by his father's wife of attempting her honour, was blinded by his father; name of a play by Euripides, *A.* 421
Phormio, a naval officer who distinguished himself in the Peloponnesian War, *K.* 562, *P.* 346, *L.* 804
Phormisius, a politician, *F.* 965, *E.* 97
Phrixus, by Euripides, quoted, *F.* 1225
Phrygians, a play by Aeschylus, alluded to, *F.* 912
Phrynichus, an Athenian comic poet, rival of Aristophanes, *W.* 220, 269, 1490, *F.* 13; a politician who helped to establish the Four Hundred, *F.* 689; an early tragedian, predecessor of Aeschylus, *B.* 750, *F.* 910, *T.* 164
Phrynondas, a rogue, *T.* 861
Phyle, a hill-fort in Attica which Thrasybulus made his headquarters, *A.* 1023, *Pl.* 1146
Phyromachus, a prude, *E.* 22
Pindar, the poet, *B.* 939; quoted, *K.* 1329
Pittalus, probably a doctor, *A.* 1032, 1221, *W.* 1432
Plataean franchise, *F.* 694
Pluto, *F*, 163
Pluto, for Plutus, *Pl.* 726
Pnyx, the place where the Athenian assembly held session, *K.* 749, *T.* 658
Polias, "guardian of cities," a title of Athene, *B.* 828
Polybus, a personage in the story of Oedipus, *F.* 1192
Polyeides, by Euripides, quoted, *F.* 1477
Polymnestus, a worthless man, also the name of a musician, *K.* 1287
Pontus, a district in northeastern Asia Minor, *W.* 700
Porphyrion, a giant, *B.* 553
Poseidon, *B.* 1565; as synonym for an intrigue, *L.* 139
Potidaia, on the peninsula of Pallene, revolted from Athens in 432 B.C., retaken 429, *K.* 438
Pramnian wine (from Icaria, west of Samos), *K.* 106
Prasiae, a town in Laconia, *P.* 242
Prepis, a dissolute man, *A.* 843
Priam, *B.* 512
Prinides, *A.* 612
Procne, slew her son Itys, and was changed into a nightingale, *B.* 665
Prodicus of Ceos, a famous sophist, *C.* 361, *B.* 692
Prometheus, *B.* 1494
Pronomus, a flute-player, *E.* 102
Propylaea, the entrance to the Athenian Acropolis, *K.* 1326
Proteus, a mythical king of Egypt, *T.* 883
Proxenides, a blusterer, *W.* 325
Prytaneum, the town hall of Athens, *K.* 167, *F.* 764
Pylae—Thermopylae, scene of Greek games, *L.* 1131
Pylus, a fort S. W. of Messenia taken by Demosthenes in 425 B.C., and held for Athens, *K.* 55, 76, 355, 703, 846, 1058, 1167, *C.* 185, *P.* 219, 665, *L.* 104, 1163
Pyrilampes, *W.* 98
Pyrrhandrus, "yellow man," *K.* 901
Pythangelus, *F.* 87
Pytho—Delphi, *K.* 1272, *B.* 188, *L.* 1131

Red Sea, *B.* 145

Sabazius, the Phrygian Bacchus, *W.* 9, *B.* 873, *L.* 388
Sacas, an alien poet, *B.* 31
Salabaccho, a courtesan, *K.* 765, *T.* 805
Salaminia, Athenian dispatch-boat *B.* 147
Salamis, scene of the naval victory over Xerxes in 480 B.C., *K.* 785
Samos, an island off the west coast of Asia Minor, *W.* 282, *L.* 313
Samothrace, an island in the northern Aegean Sea, headquarters of the secret rites of the Cabiri, *P.* 277
Sardanapalus, king of Assyria, *B.* 1021
Sardian dye (from Sardis), *P.* 1174
Sardis, capital of Lydia, *W.* 1139
Sardo—Sardinia, *W.* 700
Sarpedon, son of Zeus, slain by Patroclus, *C.* 622
Scamander, a river near Troy, *F.* 923
Scataebates, title of Zeus, comically formed after Cataebates, "Zeus who descends in thunder," *P.* 42
Scione, on the peninsula of Pallene, *W.* 210
Scira, the Parasol festival, *T.* 833, *E.* 18
Scitalus, a goblin, *K.* 634
Scythian wilderness, *A.* 704
Sebinus, an amorous Athenian, *F.* 427
Sellus, father of Aeschines, *W.* 325
Semele, bore Dionysus to Zeus, *B.* 559
Semnae, the Erinyes or Furies, *K.* 1312, *T.* 224
Seriphus, a small island of the Cyclades, *A.* 542
Seven against Thebes, a play by Aeschylus, *F.* 1021
Sibylla, title of several prophetic women in different countries, *P.* 1095, 1116
Sicily, *P.* 250
Sicyon, a gulf town west of Corinth, *B.* 968
Simaetha, a courtesan, *A.* 524
Simois, a river of Troy, *T.* 110
Simon, a dishonest politician, *K.* 242, *C.* 351

Simonides of Ceos, a lyric poet, 556-467 B.C., *K.* 406, *C.* 1356, *W.* 1410
Sisyphus, craftiest of mankind, *A.* 391
Sitalces, king of the Odrysians in Thrace, allied with Athens, *A.* 134
Smicythes (or Smicthion), an effeminate, *K.* 969, *E.* 46
Smoius, a disreputable man, *E.* 846
Socrates, the philosopher, *C.* 104, etc., *B.* 1558, *F.* 1491
Solon, the great lawgiver of Athens, born about 638 B.C., died about 558, *C.* 1187
Sophocles, the tragic poet, born B.C. 495, died about 406, *P.* 531, 695, *B.* 100
Sostrate, *E.* 41
Spintharus, a Phrygian who tried to get on the register of Athenian citizens, *B.* 762
Sporgilus, a barber, *B.* 300
Stenia, a feast, celebrated on the 9th of Pyanepsia just before the Thesmophoria, *T.* 833
Stheneboea, a play by Euripides; Stheneboea fell in love with Bellerophon, *F.* 1043
Stilbides, a diviner, *P.* 1032
Straton, an effeminate, *A.* 122, *K.* 1374, B. 942
Strymodorous, *A.* 274
Styx, a river in the lower regions, *F.* 470
Sunium, a cape of Attica, *C.* 401
Sybaris, a luxurious city in southern Italy, *W.* 1435
Syra, a slave name, *P.* 1146

Taenarum, a promontory of Laconia, where stood a temple of Poseidon, *A.* 510, *F.* 187
Tartarus, the underworld, *B.* 693
Tartesian lampreys, from Tartessus in Spain, *F.* 475
Taygetus, a mountain range between Sparta and Messenia, *L.* 117, 1296
Teleas, a flatterer, *B.* 168, 1025; a glutton, *P.* 1008
Telephus, a play by Euripides, acted 438 B.C. Telephus was son of Heracles and Auge, exposed as an infant, and brought up by a herdsman in poverty; he helped in the taking of Troy, *A.* 415, 432, 555, *C.* 922, *F.* 855, 1400
Teredon, a musician, *T.* 1175
Tereus, husband of Procne, *B.* 15, 201, *L.* 562
Teucer, a noted archer in the Trojan War, *F.* 1041
Thales of Miletus, one of the Seven Wise Men, *C.* 180, *B.* 1009
Theagenes, of Acharnae, who never left home without consulting the shrine of Hecate at his house-door, *L.* 64
Theagenes, a needy braggart, *B.* 822, 1127
Themistocles, the victor of Salamis, an Athenian statesman, *K.* 84, 813, 883
Theognis, a dull frigid poet, nicknamed Snow, *A.* 11, 140, *W.* 1183, *T.* 170
Theorus, a politician, *A.* 134, *C.* 400, *W.* 42, 599, 1220
Theramenes, the Trimmer, a prominent statesman and general, became notorious for his changes of opinion, and in particular, for his treachery to his fellow generals after the battle of Arginusae, 406 B.C., *F.* 541, 967
Theseum, the temple of Theseus, a sanctuary, *K.* 1312
Theseus, legendary king of Attica, *F.* 142
Thetis, mother of Achilles, *C.* 1067
Thorycion, *F.* 362, 382
Thouphanes, a secretary under Cleon, *K.* 1103
Thrace, a country northeast of Greece, *P.* 283
Thrasybulus, son of Lycus, who delivered Athens from the Thirty Tyrants, 404-3 B.C., killed at Aspendus 390, *E.* 203, 356, *Pl.* 550
Thratta, a slave name, *P.* 1138
Thucydides, son of Melesias, leader of the aristocratic party in opposition to Pericles, ostracized 444 B.C., *A.* 703, *W.* 947
Thyestes, brother of Atreus, son of Pelops; name of a play by Euripides, *A.* 433
Timon, the misanthrope, *B.* 1549, *L.* 808
Timotheus, son of Conon, a distinguished officer, *Pl.* 180
Titans, *B.* 469
Tithonus, husband of Aurora, made immortal, *A.* 688
Tlepolemus, *C.* 1266
Triballus, a rude personage from Thrace, *B.* 1572
Tricorythus, a town of the Tetrapolis, *L.* 1032
Triptolemus, a legendary pioneer of civilization, *A.* 48
Trophonius, a hero, who had an oracle in Lebadeia, in Boeotia, *C.* 508
Tyndaridae, descendents of Tyndareus, king of Sparta, *L.* 1301

Xanthias, a slave name, *A.* 243
Xenocles, a poor tragic poet, *F.* 86, *T.* 189, 441
Xenophantes, father of Hieronymus, *C.* 349

PRINTED IN THE U. S. A.

THE GREAT IDEAS, Volumes 2 and 3

ANGEL
ANIMAL
ARISTOCRACY
ART
ASTRONOMY
BEAUTY
BEING
CAUSE
CHANCE
CHANGE
CITIZEN
CONSTITUTION
COURAGE
CUSTOM AND CONVENTION
DEFINITION
DEMOCRACY
DESIRE
DIALECTIC
DUTY
EDUCATION
ELEMENT
EMOTION
ETERNITY
EVOLUTION
EXPERIENCE
FAMILY
FATE
FORM
GOD
GOOD AND EVIL
GOVERNMENT
HABIT
HAPPINESS
HISTORY
HONOR
HYPOTHESIS
IDEA
IMMORTALITY
INDUCTION
INFINITY
JUDGMENT
JUSTICE
KNOWLEDGE
LABOR
LANGUAGE
LAW
LIBERTY
LIFE AND DEATH
LOGIC
LOVE
MAN
MATHEMATICS